THE LAYMAN'S BIBLE COMMENTARY

OLD TESTAMENT

Dr. Tremper Longman
Consulting Editor

YOU are the reason we do what we do here at Barbour Publishing. We promise that we will always use our God-given talents to produce content with you in mind—and that we will remain biblically faithful, no matter what.

Thank you for being the heart of our business.

ISBN 979-8-89151-261-0

Produced with the assistance of Christopher D. Hudson & Associates. Contributing writers include Elizabeth Arlene, Stan Campbell, Laura Coggin, Gordon Lawrence, Beth Clayton Luthye, Anita Palmer, Heather Rippetoe, Carol Smith, Jane Vogel, and Jeff Walter.

Maps that appear in this volume are taken from *The Barbour Bible Atlas* (978-1-63609-771-8), published by Barbour Publishing, Inc.

Published by Barbour Publishing, Inc., 1810 Barbour Drive, Uhrichsville, Ohio 44683, www.barbourbooks.com

Our mission is to inspire the world with the life-changing message of the Bible.

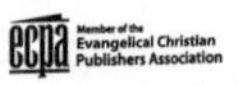

Printed in China.

CONTENTS

GENESIS

INTRODUCTION TO GENESIS

The first eleven chapters of Genesis trace events such as Creation, the Fall, the flood, and the establishing of the nations. The accounts of four great people complete the book in chapters 12–50: Abraham, Isaac, Jacob, and Joseph.

Genesis comes from the Greek word *geneseos*, meaning "origin, source, generation, or beginning." *Geneseos* is a translation of the Hebrew word *toledot* ("generations").

AUTHOR

Although Genesis does not directly name its author, Jesus and the writers of scripture clearly believed that Moses was the author of the Pentateuch (the first five books of the Bible, often referred to in the New Testament as "the Law," Mark 10:5; Luke 24:44).

OCCASION

Genesis spans more time than any other book in the Bible. In fact, it covers more than all the other sixty-five books of the Bible put together (approximately 2,400 years). The total duration is from the time of creation to the time when the Israelites arrive in Egypt and grow into a nation (about 1800 BC). The date of Genesis is sometime after the Exodus, during the fifteenth century BC.

THEMES

God's choice of a nation through which He would bless all nations is a theme throughout Genesis. It is the passing on of blessings from one generation to another.

HISTORICAL CONTEXT

The setting of Genesis divides neatly into three geographical areas:

1) The Fertile Crescent (1–11)
2) Canaan (12–36)
3) Egypt (37–50)

The setting of the first eleven chapters changes rapidly and spans more than 2,000 years and 1,500 miles. The middle section of Genesis spans about 200 years and moves from the Fertile Crescent to the land of Canaan. The final setting in Genesis is found in Egypt, where God transports the seventy souls.

CONTRIBUTION TO THE BIBLE

The story of Genesis is built around eleven accounts:

1) Introduction to the Generations, 1:1–2:3
2) Heaven and Earth, 2:4–4:26
3) Adam, 5:1–6:8
4) Noah, 6:9–9:29
5) Sons of Noah, 10:1–11:9
6) Shem, 11:10–26
7) Terah, 11:27–25:11
8) Ishmael, 25:12–18
9) Isaac, 25:19–35:29
10) Esau, 36:1–37:1
11) Jacob and Sons, 37:2–50:26

OUTLINE

CREATION	**1:1–2:25**
The Days of Creation	1:1–2:3
Man and Woman	2:4–25
THE FALL OF HUMANITY	**3:1–5:32**
The Serpent's Temptations	3:1–7
God's Judgments	3:8–24
Building the Family	4:1–24
Seth	4:25–26
Genealogy: Adam to Noah	5:1–32
THE FLOOD	**6:1–9:29**
Precursors to the Flood	6:1–13
The Flood	6:14–8:19
Results of the Flood	8:20–9:29
NOAH'S DESCENDANTS	**10:1–11:32**
Japheth	10:1–5
Ham	10:6–20
Shem	10:21–32
Babel	11:1–9
Shem's Descendants	11:10–26
Terah	11:27–32
ABRAHAM	**12:1–20:18**
Abram's Call	12:1–20
Abram and Lot	13:1–14:24
Abram's Covenant	15:1–21
Ishmael	16:1–16
Abraham's Circumcision	17:1–27
Sodom and Gomorrah	18:1–19:38
Abimelech	20:1–18
ISAAC	**21:1–25:18**
Isaac's Birth	21:1–34
An Offering	22:1–24
Sarah's Death	23:1–20
Isaac's Marriage	24:1–67
Abraham's Death	25:1–18

GENESIS 1:1–2:25

CREATION

Setting Up the Section

The initial recipients of this story are the Israelites of Moses' day. Because it is written to the people of God, not as an apologetic to convince those who do not believe, Genesis is much more of a declaration than a defense. These chapters are not intended to give an account of the Creation that would answer all of the scientific problems and phenomenon. Rather, there is an air of mystery that permeates these two chapters, and within that mystery is the fact that God created this world and it exists within His control.

The Summary of Creation:

God Formed the Earth	God Filled the Earth
Day 1: Light (1:3–5)	Day 4: Lights (1:14–19)
Day 2: Air (1:6–8)	Day 5: Birds (1:20–23)
Day 2: Water (1:6–8)	Day 5: Fish (1:20–23)
Day 3: Land (1:9–13)	Day 6: Animals (1:24–31)
Day 3: Plants (1:9–13)	Day 6: Man (1:24–31)

1:1–2:3

THE DAYS OF CREATION

There are two purposes in the opening of Genesis (1:1):

1) To identify God as the Creator
2) To explain the origin of the world

The Genesis account does not imply that absolutely nothing existed or had happened before this. The separate creation of angels and other heavenly beings is already assumed (1:26).

The first three words ("In the beginning") translate a single Hebrew word, *bereshit*. This word does not necessarily connote a brief period of time, though the creation event is described in terms of days in later verses.

The next keyword is *God*, a rendering from the Hebrew word *Elohim*, a plural noun. This implies that God is plural, even as God is singular.

The Hebrew word translated *created* is used throughout the Bible, only with God as its subject. This word stresses the newness and perfection of that being made.

The last four words in verse 1 describe the entire universe. The Hebrew language had no word for universe, so instead the author uses the phrase "heavens and earth." This figure of speech refers to everything in creation (sun, moon, stars, plants, rocks, rivers, mountains, and so on).

Some understand a gap of an indeterminate period of time between Genesis 1:1 and 1:2. The construction of the verses in the original languages, though, does not support a consecutive statement (this happened, then that happened) but rather something included in verse 1.

In the Old Testament, the word often translated *deep* refers to the ocean, which the ancient world regarded as a symbol of chaos and evil. In the Pentateuch (Genesis through Deuteronomy) it has the connotation of a wasteland.

The word *earth* can be translated "land" as well. In this context, *land* is preferred. To the original readers of Genesis, the term *earth* did not connote a planet. The development of science did not yet support an understanding of the universe as we know it today. Earth typically refers to a specific section of land, such as the land of Egypt (45:8), the dry ground (1:10), or the land promised to Abraham (15:18).

Verse 2 describes the earth as yet unfashioned and uninhabited. When read from a New Testament perspective, it also provides the first reference to the Holy Spirit in the Bible. Many believe it gives us an idea of the constant action of the Spirit.

On day one, light appears through the darkness (1:3). The word *light* can be interpreted several ways, and the sun is not listed as a creation until the fourth day. Nevertheless, like the sun, this light distinguishes day from night (1:4–5).

Regarding the word *day*, several interpretations have been suggested:

1) The extended geological ages prior to human presence on earth
2) Twenty-four-hour periods in which God reveals (but not necessarily initiates) His creative acts
3) A simple literary device to present the creation in a framework understandable to readers
4) Literal twenty-four-hour days of divine activity

When this same word is used elsewhere in the Old Testament, it refers to twenty-four-hour periods of time. However, those that disagree with this view hold that these are days of God's activity, not human work, and it is therefore unlikely that they are supposed to be literal twenty-four-hour periods of time. Indeed, the Hebrew word for *day* covers a variety of periods: the hours of daylight (29:7), a twenty-four-hour day (7:4), or an indefinite period (35:3). All these differences indicate that verses 1:1–2:3 serve as an overture to the rest of the book, and that it may not be intended to be taken as literally as what follows.

The expanse, or space, that God speaks into being on day two is a reference to the sky (1:6, 8; see also 1:8; 7:11–12). The water above is a reference to clouds, and the water below is a reference to the water of the earth (1:7).

On the third day, God carries out two distinct acts: He separates land from seas, just as He earlier separates light from darkness (1:3) and waters from waters (1:6), and He creates plant life. The distinct varieties of plants (1:11–12) bear witness to God's organizing power.

In contrast with day two, God's acts of creation on day three are called good. They are good because both are accomplished for humanity's benefit. The third day shows the provision of dry land, on which humanity can live, and plants to sustain life (1:29–30).

On the fourth day, the lights that God had created are given a purpose, namely, to separate day from night and serve as signs for seasons and days and years (1:14).

Critical Observation

The moon is called (only here) the lesser light, and the sun is called (also only here) the greater light for a reason. Among Israel's neighbors, their pagan contemporaries, the sun and moon were designations for deities. Even today in astrology people use stars and planets for guidance, but here they are simply referred to as lights. They were appointed to regulate the fundamental rhythms of human life by defining day and night and the seasons of the year.

On the fifth day God populates the land with many kinds of living creatures (birds and fish). This is the first time God blesses something in the Bible. The word is used more than eighty times in Genesis, where it usually speaks of fertility.

Living creatures created on the sixth day are categorized in three groups. In today's language, these three groups would probably best be described as domesticated animals, small creatures, and what we would consider game or wild animals. The idea of creeping animals has more to do with their style of movement than modern scientific categories like that of reptiles.

There are parallels in the six days of creation which provide a flow to the account:

Preparation Phrase	Day 1	Day 2	Day 3	Day 4	Day 5	Day 6
"God said, 'Let there be' "	1:3	1:6	1:9	1:14	1:20	1:24
"And it was so"	1:3	1:7	1:9	1:15	---	1:24
"God saw that it was good"	1:4	---	1:12	1:18	1:21	1:25
"God called"	1:5	1:8	1:10	---	---	---
"There was evening and there was morning, the ___ day"	1:5	1:8	1:13	1:19	1:23	1:31

The plural pronouns in verse 26 are seen by many as a hint of the Trinity, but also as a reference to the complete fullness of God. The idea that humanity is created in God's image has far-reaching implications: A relationship can exist between God and humanity, and men and women can reflect God's nature. As part of that reflection, people rule over nature. The idea of ruling carries with it the connotation of responsible management rather than dictatorial control or exploitation.

Verse 27 is in the form of poetry. While some translations use the word *man*, this is a reference to all of humanity, not simply to Adam. God created humanity, both male and female.

Critical Observation

Understanding the importance of God's blessing in verse 28 is essential. Throughout the remainder of the book of Genesis, the blessing remains a central theme. Blessing denotes all that fosters human fertility and assists in achieving dominion. Interpreters have generally recognized "be fruitful and multiply" as commands to Adam and Eve (and later to Noah; see 9:1) as the heads of the human race, not simply as individuals. That is, God has not charged every human being with begetting children.

Humanity is supposed to subdue the earth. While the word translated *subdue* means "bring under bondage," it doesn't mean to destroy or ruin. As with the idea of ruling in verse 26, this is a requirement to act as manager with God-given authority.

Many interpret verses 29–30 to mean that both people and animals were vegetarian prior to the flood, and that it is not until after the fall of humanity, and perhaps after the flood, that meat is given as food (9:3–4). Keep in mind, however, that this writing in

Genesis is not primarily concerned with whether people were originally vegetarian but with the fact that God provided them with food.

According to verse 31, God evaluates only this day's work as very good.

It is likely that, in 2:1–3, the author intends for the reader to understand the account of the seventh day in light of the "image of God" theme of the sixth day. We are expected to copy our Creator.

Verses 2–3 make it clear that the seventh day is set apart from the first six by not only stating specifically that God sanctified it as holy, but that God did not work. This theme is repeated three times in these three verses.

2:4–25

MAN AND WOMAN

Genesis 2:4–25 begins a descriptive account, with humanity as the central theme. This section is not meant to be chronological. Genesis 2:7 is simply an elaboration of 1:27. The two accounts look at a similar series of events from two distinct points of view. Genesis 1 simply notes that God created male and female, adding a few remarks about their relationship to the rest of creation. The first chapter emphasizes man as one *created with* authority; Genesis 2 emphasizes man as one *under* authority.

The phrase "the heavens and the earth" (2:4) is a figure of speech that refers to the entire universe. In the second part of the verse, though, the phrase is reversed. When this happens, the phrase takes on a more literal meaning: the land and sky.

Verses 5–6 are a flashback to conditions before Genesis 1:26. This is the setting of the stage. The land is set up and poised for humanity to enter the scene.

The word translated *formed* in verse 7 describes the activity of a potter, forming vessels out of clay—ground and water. The fact that God forms man out of dust reflects man's lowly origin (see also 3:19). The Hebrew word for *man* (Adam) sounds like, and may be related to, the Hebrew word for *ground.*

It's significant to note that God creates humanity with hands, not just words. He does not simply speak people into existence as He does with the lights of the universe; God breathes life into man. Since Adam's life came from God's breath, he is a combination of dust and divinity.

The description of Adam as living is the same term that is used of animal life in Genesis 1:24. In this phrase, we see how humans and animals are similar, but this breath of life makes humans distinct from all other creatures.

Critical Observation

In 2:8–9, God's care is made evident by His provision of a garden paradise with two trees—the Tree of Life and the Tree of the Knowledge of Good and Evil. Verses 10–14 describe the boundaries of this garden. Of the four rivers mentioned, the Pishon and Gihon are unknown in the modern world (though the land of Havilah is probably an area of southwestern Arabia). The Tigris and Euphrates are now in Babylonia. The name Eden means "delight, pleasure." This rather extensive description sets the stage for Adam and Eve's expulsion from the garden in 3:24. It also probably signifies to the Israelites an anticipation of the promised land. Two of these rivers are exactly the ones that God uses to explain to Abraham where the promised land will be (15:18).

The Hebrew word translated *put* (2:15) connotes more than simple placement, but rather rest and safety, as well as dedication in God's presence. The man's caring for the garden is actually the idea of serving. It's a word that is translated *worship* elsewhere in the Old Testament.

It is interesting that God seems to tell Adam, alone, that the fruit of the Tree of the Knowledge of Good and Evil must not be eaten. It is important to note that there is a positive aspect to this command: God gives man the enjoyment of all of the luscious trees in the garden, and all of God's creation is pronounced "good." The tree is not a sinister tree in and of itself. The temptation to eat from the Tree of the Knowledge of Good and Evil is the temptation to seek wisdom without reference to the Word of God.

Verses 18–25 are considered the apex of the first two chapters. Everything up until this point is called good, but now the Lord says it is not good.

Adam naming the animals means that he is studying their nature (2:19–20). Names in the ancient world were descriptions. The text does not necessarily mean that Adam named every individual animal; he apparently gives names to the different kinds God brings before him. This exercise demonstrates Adam's authority over the animals.

Demystifying Genesis

The word translated helper (and sometimes companion) does not mean a servant (2:20). In fact, following His ascension, Jesus Christ uses the Greek equivalent of this word to describe the Holy Spirit, who would help believers following the Lord's ascension (John 14:16, 26; 15:26; 16:7). It signifies the woman's essential contribution, not inadequacy. The description of this companion as suitable, or corresponding, suggests something that completes a polarity, as the North Pole corresponds to the South Pole.

The Lord meets Adam's need for companionship (2:21–22). God builds woman from one of man's ribs, which could also be simply translated *side*.

How does Adam respond? He rejoices. When Adam says the woman is bone of his bones and flesh of his flesh, he is giving the ancient equivalent of the modern marriage vow "in weakness and in strength" (2:23).

One of the meanings of the verb behind the noun *bone* is "to be strong." "Flesh," on the other hand, represents weakness in a person.

Chapter 2 closes with a description of the marriage partnership. Notice that the man is responsible for leaving his family of origin. This implies faithfulness, permanence, and loyalty as the responsibility on the part of the man. Elsewhere in the Old Testament these are covenant terms.

Take It Home

Some say that the naked condition of the man and woman, as described at the close of chapter 2, goes beyond a physical description; it also has application regarding the psychological oneness and transparency required for a marriage relationship. Physically they are naked and share their bodies with each other openly, and psychologically they are not ashamed and hide nothing from each other. They are at ease without any fear of exploitation for evil.

GENESIS 3:1–5:32

THE FALL OF HUMANITY

Setting Up the Section

This passage reveals how sin enters the world and how sin can be overcome. At the end of Genesis 2, life seems ideal—paradise. Then the events described in this section forever change the world. Fear and shame enter and judgment begins. But the seeds of redemption can be found as well.

3:1–7

THE SERPENT'S TEMPTATIONS

The word translated *serpent* is the same root as another Hebrew word that means "bronze" (3:1). The word translated *crafty,* or *shrewd,* often suggests wisdom, though here it has a clearly negative connotation.

The question asked by the serpent is the first question recorded in scripture (3:1). In this case, the question casts immediate doubt on God's command.

Instead of shunning the serpent, the woman obliges him by carrying on a conversation (3:2–3). In her reply to the serpent, she does not quote the commands exactly as they are listed in Genesis 2, but instead she lists them with subtle changes.

Original Command (2:16–17 NASB)	Eve's Reply (3:2–3 NASB)
"From any tree of the garden you may eat freely."	"From the fruit of the trees of the garden we may eat."
"But from the tree of the knowledge of good and evil you shall not eat, for in the day that you eat from it you will surely die."	"But from the fruit of the tree which is in the middle of the garden, God has said, 'You shall not eat from it or touch it, or you will die.'"

As verse 4 reveals, the first thing Satan does is deny God's judgment. To make this direct contradiction of God's Word seem reasonable, Satan invents a false motive for God (3:5). Thus, the serpent stands in direct conflict with God as He has revealed Himself.

Having set the trap, the serpent lets the woman's natural desire for food carry her into the trap (3:6). The fruit looks good to her. She will (seemingly) better herself in the taking of it. Not only does she sin, but in her distorted thinking and false sense of accomplishment, she also gives the fruit to her husband.

While Adam's companion is deceived, the scriptures have already revealed that Adam has been directly warned by God about eating this fruit. It would seem that he ate willingly, aware of the consequences.

Critical Observation

The effects described in verse 7 raise the question, why did Adam and Eve not die immediately? Genesis 5:5 reveals that Adam lived to be 930 years old.

Although God's warning may have referred to physical death, primarily in view was spiritual death, which entails the loss of fellowship with God and with one another. When the man and woman eat from the tree, they immediately change their relationship with God and with each other. From their lack of shame (at the end of chapter 2) to the moment of suddenly covering themselves (3:7), an eternal shift has occurred.

3:8–24

GOD'S JUDGMENTS

The cool time of the day (3:8) can be translated the *wind* or *spirit* of the day. Often, in the Bible, the wind is a symbol of God's presence (see 1:2). A more complete transformation could not be imagined than the one described here, as Adam and his wife attempt to hide from God. The trust of innocence is replaced by the fear of guilt.

God's question (3:9) carries the implied question of why Adam and Eve are there. It is a demand that Adam take personal responsibility for his actions. Adam's response (3:10) does not express personal responsibility, but it does acknowledge something important: Life has changed. Shame, fear, and guilt have entered paradise. (Verse 10 is the first time fear is mentioned in the Bible.) Fig leaves aren't enough to cover Adam up; spiritual vulnerability is the real issue. The only solution he can devise is denial and avoidance.

Adam answers God by making excuses for himself and playing the blame game. God then addresses the woman, and she blames the serpent (3:13). God addresses the serpent with a curse. In the Bible, to *curse* means to invoke God's judgment. Some commentators take this literally and conclude that the snake had legs before God cursed it. Others take it figuratively, as a reference to the resultant despised condition of the snake. This is confirmed by the word picture of the snake eating dust.

Critical Observation

Genesis 3:15 is one of the foundational verses of the Bible. Many see this verse as the first glimpse of the gospel of Jesus. The hostility described here certainly exists between snakes and people, but God's intention in this verse seems to include the person behind the snake (Satan) even more than the snake itself. The snake's offspring would remain in opposition to the woman's offspring. In this case, Eve's offspring points to one individual—the Messiah, Jesus, who would come forth from the Jewish people.

Verses 16–19 include God's judgments on all involved. The woman will experience suffering in having children and in her desire for her husband. Adam will suffer in his attempts to control his domain. The very dust he came from will force him to struggle to survive. Man's natural or original relationship to the ground—to rule over it—is reversed; instead of submitting to him, it now resists and eventually swallows him.

Adam expresses confidence in God's promise about his wife's offspring by finally giving her the name *Eve*, which means "living," "the mother of all living," or "she who gives life." Some see this as a kind of play on words: Not only will the human race descend from Eve, but spiritual life will come from her as well.

God provides special clothing for Adam and Eve. Instead of fig leaves, He clothes them in skins. God does for the couple what they cannot do for themselves. While some see the skins as a foreshadow of redemption, it is more likely simply the practical meeting of a need.

In verses 22–24, God says that humanity has become "like one of us." This is a reference to the newfound knowledge of good and evil. This is critical because the Tree of Life perpetuates physical life in the perfect environment of the garden. When people acquire a sin nature in the physical body, they begin the process of physical deterioration, which ultimately leads to physical death. If Adam were to eat of the Tree of Life at this time, it would perpetuate his physical life forever with the presence of the sin nature.

This passage contains a certain amount of irony, in that the human race, which has been created in God's image (1:26), seeks to be like God by eating the fruit (3:5–7) but afterward finds themselves no longer in union with God.

Demystifying Genesis

Angels called *cherubim* surround and symbolize God's presence in the Old Testament (Exodus 27:7–9; Ezekiel 10:15). They are similar to bodyguards. Genesis 3:24 pictures them defending the Tree of Life with a flaming sword to keep humanity away. This is an apt picture of the separation established between God and His creation. Humanity is completely excluded in this picture, with no resources of their own that would allow them to cross into God's paradise.

4:1–24

BUILDING THE FAMILY

Chapter 4 opens with the birth of Cain and Abel (4:1–2). The name *Cain* means "to acquire" or "possess." The literal rendering of Eve's reply is, "I have gotten [or have acquired] a son, the Lord." Some suppose that she understood enough of the prophecy in 3:16–19 that she believed her son would be the one to conquer the serpent. Certainly her response expresses enthusiasm and gratitude.

Unlike Cain's name, Abel's name is not explained. However, the Hebrew word *Abel* means "vanity," or "breath." Traditionally understood, Abel's name reflects on the temporary nature of his existence.

Critical Observation

Genesis 4:3–5 describes the vocations of the brothers. Both vocations are noble; one is not better than the other. And there does not appear to be anything wrong with offering fruit as opposed to animal sacrifice. Certainly grain offerings were a legitimate part of Israel's worship practices.

There may be clues in the description of the offerings themselves as to what was the problem with Cain's offering. Abel offers the *first* of his flock (4:4; see Exodus 34:19; Deuteronomy 12:6; 14:23) and the fattest (4:4; see Numbers 18:17). Abel gives what cost him most—the firstborn and the most choice selections. On the other hand, Cain's offering is not described as his first or his best, merely as *the fruit*. This difference in quality and attitude may be the key to God's differing reactions to the offerings.

When Cain learns that God is displeased with his offering, he becomes angry (Genesis 4:5). In response to Cain's anger, God asks him questions. His questions demonstrate that He is more displeased with Cain's response than with the actual offering. It is not the style of the offering, but the substance of Cain's heart that is called into question (4:6–7).

Not all of the earliest manuscripts of Genesis include Cain's request to Abel to go out to the field, but the detail is significant. According to Jewish law, the fact that Cain leads his brother to a private place would have indicated premeditation, and thus would have incurred an even harsher punishment (4:8).

God's question to Cain in verse 9 mirrors His question to Adam in 3:9. And like his father, Cain responds with a lie and defensiveness. The fact that Cain dispassionately denies what he has done shows a lack of care and concern that parallels Adam's lack of regard for his wife (3:12).

Verses 10–16 reveal God's judgment on Cain—that Cain would be an outcast wanderer. This is the first instance in scripture where a human is cursed. When God pronounced judgment on Adam, it was the ground that actually was cursed. While in modern culture, the death penalty is considered the ultimate punishment, in this ancient world, disenfranchisement was possibly worse than death. It was a loss of roots and a loss of all that defined someone.

Cain's character is revealed in his negotiation. His concern is not his dead brother or displeasing God; his concern is self-preservation. Cain settles in the land of Nod, which means, "wandering." We do not know what ultimately happens to him.

Demystifying Genesis

We do not know what sign God gave to Cain before He expelled him. Some have supposed it was a mark of some kind on Cain himself, while others suggest a special hairstyle. One of the ancient rabbis argued that the sign was a dog that accompanied Cain on his wanderings. Others think it was some sign in the external world, such as an intensified fear of killing another human being. Whatever form it took, the mark God gave Cain was not a stigma, but rather a guarantee of safe passage (4:15)—an act of mercy on God's part.

Of course, the other mystery concerning Cain is whom he married (4:17). He had probably married a sister or possibly a niece. Marriages between close relatives would have been at first unavoidable if the whole human race came from a single pair. Marriage between siblings and close relatives was not prohibited until the Mosaic Law, instituted thousands of years later (Leviticus 18:6–18). There would have been no genetic imperfections at the beginning of the human race. Genetic defects resulted from the fall and only occurred gradually, over long periods of time.

Verses 17–18 begin a history of Cain's descendants. Verse 19 introduces Lamech as a man with two wives. Bigamy was common in the ancient Near East. It is not unheard of even among the fathers of the faith. Jacob had two wives and two concubines. Solomon, famously, had thousands of wives. These men are notable as exceptions, though, among the Israelite nation.

In verses 20–22, we see that Cain prospers even though he rebelled against God. Cain's descendants take the lead in building cities, developing music, advancing agriculture, creating weapons, and spreading civilization.

One can easily see that the lines that make up verses 23–24 are parallel and poetical. Lamech is singing a song about polygamy, murder, and revenge. Lamech wears violence as a badge of honor.

4:25–26

SETH

Verses 25–26 are not events that fall chronologically after verses 17–24. Instead, at verse 25, Genesis picks up an alternate branch of Adam's family tree. Seth's birth is strategic. After God's promise that Eve's offspring would defeat the serpent, her oldest son takes the life of her youngest. That doesn't leave many offspring to champion the cause. But here is another birth, which can continue the hope of God's promise through the line of Seth, a name that means "to set," or "place."

Verse 26 reveals the beginning of the worship of the God of creation, who is the focal point of the Old Testament and the Israelite nation.

5:1–32

GENEALOGY: ADAM TO NOAH

Genesis 5 begins a second genealogy (the first is Genesis 4:17–34). This fifth chapter is a list of the ten descendants of Adam to Noah. The technique of mixing narrative and genealogy is found throughout the book of Genesis. A primary purpose seems to be to show the development of the human race from Adam to Noah, and to bridge the gap in time between these two major individuals.

Verse 2 returns to the theme of God blessing man (see 1:27). Throughout the remainder of the book of Genesis, there is a recurring theme of fathers blessing their children (9:26–27; 27:27; 48:15; 49:1–28). In keeping with such a theme, the author shows, at each crucial turning point in the narrative, that God Himself renews His blessing to the next generation of sons (1:28; 5:2; 9:1; 12:3; 24:11). Seen as a whole, the picture that emerges is that of a loving parent insuring the future well-being of His children through the provision of an inherited blessing.

In the description of each generation, the same literary structure is followed:

1) The age of the father at the birth of the firstborn
2) The name of the firstborn
3) How many years the father lives after the birth of this son
4) A reference to the fathering of other children
5) The father's total life span

This genealogy covers at least 1,600 years. Within the timeline of the Bible, this chapter covers the longest period in world history. The average age of the ten people listed in this genealogy is about 900.

One of the most important elements of this genealogy is the phrase that closes the account of each person: "and then he died" (NIV). This phrase (the translation of only one Hebrew word, *muth*) occurs eight times (5:5, 8, 11, 14, 17, 20, 27, and 31) and serves as a reminder of the consequences of Adam and Eve's fall. One of the most powerful functions of this phrase is the effect the one time it does not appear—Enoch does not die.

The phrase "walked with God" (NET) is only used of two men: Enoch and Noah (5:22; 6:9). *Walk* is a biblical figure for fellowship and obedience that results in divine blessing. It describes the closest communion with God—as if walking at His side.

Rather than dying, verse 24 tells us that Enoch disappears (5:24). There are no other details. In a similar situation, the prophet Elijah is picked up by a chariot (2 Kings 2:11–12), but no such details are given here.

Even though the death motif is strong in this chapter, there is even more emphasis on God's grace. We see this in the references to life, fertility (sons and daughters), Enoch's translation from this life, and other blessings.

GENESIS 6:1–9:29

THE FLOOD

Precursors to the Flood	6:1–13
The Flood	6:14–8:19
Results of the Flood	8:20–9:29

Setting Up the Section

Genesis 6–8 covers a lot of ground. These chapters document the degradation of society, Noah's great flood, and the beginnings of life beyond the flood with Noah's three sons, Shem, Ham, and Japheth.

6:1–13

PRECURSORS TO THE FLOOD

Genesis 6 begins by naming two groups: the sons of God and the daughters of men. Many view this as a way of describing the descendants of Cain and the descendants of Seth (4:1–25). The assumption, then, is that the descendants of Seth are God-following people, while the descendants of Cain are not. If this is the case, then the events described in verses 1–2 represent a mingling of the godly with the ungodly, and thus a watering down of righteousness on the earth.

Other interpretations of this passage include the idea that these are marriages between angels and humans, or between aristocrats and commoners.

The verb translated in some versions of the Bible as *strive* occurs only here in the Hebrew Old Testament (6:3). Other English translations use the words *contend* (NIV), *abide* (NRSV), *remain* (NET), or *put up with* (NLT).

There are two interpretations of the 120-year time limit cited in verse 3. One possibility is that the 120 years may signify the new age limit for people. Another view is that the 120 years refer to the time remaining between this announcement of judgment and the coming of the flood.

Demystifying Genesis

The word *Nephilim* occurs only in verse 4 and in Numbers 13:33, where it refers to the sons of Anak, who were people of great stature. There is another Hebrew word that simply designates a huge man—*rapha*. This word is used for men like Og and Goliath (see Deuteronomy 3:11; 1 Chronicles 20:6). The Nephilim were a more distinct group.

Genesis 6:4 is a parenthetical piece of information. Rather than relating the Nephilim to the marrying couples in verse 2, the Nephilim are simply contemporaries of that time.

Verses 5–8 describe the wickedness of the pre-flood civilization and God's offense at the state of His creation.

The keyword in verse 5 is *intent* (NKJV), or *inclination* (NIV). This word comes from the verb that describes a potter in the act of forming and molding his vessel (Isaiah 29:16). It is the description of something that is done not by happenstance but by design. Humanity's evil is far more than a surface foolishness. This passage describes an all-consuming depravity.

God's grief as described here is a mixture of rage and bitter anguish. His regret reflects the idea of breathing or sighing deeply.

Out of that regret comes a destructive plan. God's judgment will involve an almost complete erasure of man and all accompanying creatures from existence. God's pain over sin prompts Him to blot out the wicked (Genesis 6:5–7).

Noah stands as the first good news in this chapter (6:8). The *favor* that he finds is the translation of a Hebrew word that can also be translated *grace*. It comes from a root meaning "to bend or stoop."

Verses 9–13 offer us the back story. In the midst of an evil world stands a faithful man and his three sons: Noah, Shem, Ham, and Japheth.

Noah's description is noteworthy:

- Righteousness connotes conformity. In the case of Noah, he conforms to the standard set by God.
- Blameless involves the idea of completeness. Noah conforms to the standard set by God with no essential quality missing.
- Noah's character and lifestyle stand out among the culture around him. He is not only righteous in the sight of God, but he also has a credible reputation among the people of his day.

Three times in verses 11–12, the earth is described as *corrupt*. The Hebrew word translated here is rich in meaning. It was used to describe a shirt that was stained too badly to be used or a clay pot that was marred in the production process, making it unusable. The word translated *violence* (6:11) was used of acts of robbery, taking wives by force, and murder. These two words paint a vivid portrait of the deterioration of the creation that had been described in Genesis 1, by God Himself, as very good.

Verse 13 describes God's judgment. The word translated *destroy* is the same word that is rendered by *corrupt* in verse 12. God will permanently corrupt this wicked civilization.

6:14–8:19

THE FLOOD

In 6:14–16, Noah receives detailed instructions that he is to follow in building the ark. The ingredients are cypress wood and pitch. The dimensions are as follows:

Dimensions	Noah's Ark	Approximate Equivalent
Length	450 feet	1½ American football fields
Width	75 feet	7 parking spaces
Height	45 feet	3 stories
Cubic Feet	1.5 million	550 railroad boxcars
Capacity	14,000 gross tons	*Princess of the Orient*

While the Bible doesn't give enough detail to know exactly what the ark looked like, it probably was shaped like a shallow rectangular box topped with a roof, with an 18-inch space under the roof, interrupted only by roof supports, so that light could get into the vessel from every side. This design would use space efficiently and would have been stable in the water.

Along with God's proclamation of the terrible flood that He will send is a hopeful promise of a covenant (6:17–18). This is the first use of the word *covenant*, which refers to a binding promise. This covenant will mean safety for Noah and his family, even in the midst of tragic judgment.

Demystifying Genesis

How could Noah's ark potentially hold over a billion species of animals (6:19–21)? Keep in mind that the modern concept of species is not the same as a "kind" in the Bible. There were probably only several hundred different kinds of land animals that would have to be taken into the ark. The sea animals stayed in the sea, and many species could have survived in egg form. Also, Noah could have taken younger varieties of some larger animals. And finally, the ark was a huge structure—the size of a modern ocean liner three stories high.

Verse 22 presents a theme that is repeated three more times in chapter 7—Noah's obedience to God's command (7:5, 9, 16).

Take It Home

Noah's story reminds us that it is possible to be right with God, even when surrounded by wickedness. We can stand as Noah did, righteous and blameless among our contemporaries. It just requires that we listen to God's voice and do what He says.

While chapter 6 describes two of each kind of animal entering the ark (6:19–21), the instructions in the opening verses of chapter 7 become more specific (7:1–3). Noah is to take two of every unclean animal and seven of every clean animal. The purpose of this is to become clear after the flood. Birds will be needed to scout out the earth (8:7–12), and the clean animals and birds will be offered in sacrifice to the Lord (8:20). If Noah had taken only one pair of each and then offered each of these pairs in sacrifice, these species would have become completely extinct.

Critical Observation

God does not reveal the basis for His distinction between clean and unclean animals here (7:2). Noah predated Moses, who wrote down the dietary laws regarding which animals were ceremonially clean to eat, but the understanding of clean and unclean animals was already common. Even Israel's pagan neighbors observed distinctions between clean and unclean animals, though they varied from country to country.

The account of the floodwater inundating the earth (7:6–16) is both majestic and terrible, and is reminiscent of creation. Like Genesis 1, the account of the flood is structured by a careful counting of the days (371 total days):

- 7 days of waiting for the waters to come (7:4, 10)
- 40 days of water rising (7:12, 17)
- 150 days of waters prevailing (7:24; 8:3)
- 40 days of water receding (8:6)
- 7 days of waiting for the waters to recede (8:10)
- 7 more days of waiting for the waters to recede completely (8:12)

The description of the flood in verses 17–24 is a reminder of the reality of final judgment. But even with the severity of this event, there is debate on whether the flood was global or local. For those who favor the global flood perspective, the supporting factors include these:

1) The language used in the Bible text presents a global experience, though at this time in history, human perspective was not as broad as it is today.
2) The depth of water seems to support a global flood. Mount Ararat, on which the ark came to rest, is over 17,000 feet in altitude, and the waters were over 20 feet higher than all the mountains (notice the language of 7:19).
3) God's promise of never allowing another such flood seems to indicate a worldwide event (8:21; 9:11, 15). There have been devastating local floods since then.
4) When the New Testament authors speak of the flood, they speak of it as a worldwide flood (2 Peter 3:6).

The word *remember* in the opening verses of chapter 8 is a high point of this story. God remembers both His people and the promises He made to them.

Critical Observation

During the eleventh to twelfth centuries AD, Mount Ararat became the site traditionally associated with Noah's landing. Genesis 8:4, however, does not indicate a specific peak, and refers generally to its location as the "mountains of Ararat." The search for the ark's artifacts has been both a medieval and a modern occupation, but to the skeptic, such evidence is not convincing, and to the believer, while not irrelevant, it is not necessary to faith. Modern Mount Ararat lies on the border between Turkey and Armenia and encompasses parts of Turkey, Russia, and Iran—the frontier of the ancient world. From this region Noah's descendants spread out over the earth.

The picture painted by verses 6–12—the sending of the raven and the dove—reveals the hopeful waiting of those who had, at this point, been in the ark around a year (compare 7:11–13; 8:13–15). When the land is at last dry, God calls for a procession out of the ark and commands Noah and his children to replenish the earth (8:13–17). Verses 18–19 document the disembarking.

8:20–9:29

RESULTS OF THE FLOOD

Chapter 8 closes with Noah's sacrifice at the altar, a demonstration of his dedication and gratitude (8:20–22). This altar is the first mentioned in the Bible. As the head of the new repopulation, Noah's sacrifice represented all humanity.

Chapter 9 opens with a renewal of God's first blessing and commission to Adam (1:28; 9:1). Like Adam, Noah and his sons are blessed and are commanded to reproduce and fill the earth. The word *blessed* is a keyword in Genesis—"to confer benefit." It occurs approximately eighty times in this book.

Additional blessings are found in 9:2–4. Why does God put the fear of humanity in all creatures? Probably for the protection of both, since they are no longer at peace with one another. Humans could now use animals for food, with the restriction that they drain the animal's blood first.

Demystifying Genesis

What is the purpose of God's restriction that Noah and his sons drain the blood of the animals they use for food (9:4–5)? One reason is probably respect for life and the giver of life. In the centuries to come, as the Jewish laws were developed and documented, God's people were again forbidden to consume the blood, which was considered the life of the creature.

The last phrase of verse 5 can seem a bit confusing. The literal translation is "from the hand of a man, his brother." The point is that God would require the blood of a killer, since the person killed was a relative ("brother") of the killer. The language reflects Noah's situation (after the flood, everyone would be part of Noah's extended family), but also supports the concept of the brotherhood of humanity.

Verse 6, seen as a support for capital punishment by some, remains a controversial verse. However one makes its application in the modern world, this verse upholds the sanctity of human life and human responsibility before God to protect that life. And in the terms of this verse, the reason is more than simply preservation of the race. It is the acknowledgment of God's image borne by every person.

Verse 7 reiterates 9:1, which is itself a restatement of God's direction to Adam in Genesis 1:28.

In verses 8–17, God promises not to flood the earth again. He clearly makes this an eternal promise and marks it with the sign of the rainbow (9:12–16).

Critical Observation

God attaches significance to the rainbow as a sign of His covenant, though there may have been rainbows before this pronouncement. The Hebrew word for rainbow is also the word for a battle bow. The point seems to be that the bow is now put away, hung in place by the clouds, suggesting that the storm is over. As a result, whenever clouds appear over the earth and a rainbow appears, God will remember His covenant, while the rainbow reminds His people of the same thing.

In verses 18–29, the history of Noah and his family moves from rainbows (9:12–17) to shadows. The explanation in verse 18 that Ham is the father of Canaan has great relevance, because it anticipates the rest of the story. It is under Moses' leadership that the Israelites set out for the land of Canaan to reinhabit the area, so Moses' original audience would have found great significance in the identification of Ham's bloodline.

After leaving the ark, Noah takes up farming like his father, Lamech. Specifically, he plants a vineyard (5:28–29; 9:20). Eventually he gets drunk and careless. The word translated *uncovered*, the description of Noah in his tent (9:21), means "to be disgracefully exposed."

As the account explains, Ham sees his exposed father. The verb used to describe Ham's seeing Noah has such force that some say it means "he gazed with satisfaction." And when he tells his two brothers about Noah, the words used mean that he "boldly announced with delight." Ham seems to have gloated over his father's shame and to have done nothing to preserve his father's dignity.

In contrast to Ham, Shem and Japheth walk in backward and cover Noah. They honor their father and win the approval and blessing of God (9:23).

Verses 24–29 describe the aftermath of both Noah's and Ham's indiscretions. When Noah learns what has happened, he pronounces a curse on Ham's son, Canaan. It seems that Noah is prophesying that Canaan is already cursed simply because he is Ham's son. Prior to this in the Bible, only God had issued a curse against anyone or against anything (the serpent in 3:14; the ground in 3:17; 5:29; 8:21; and Cain in 4:11).

After cursing Canaan, Noah proclaims a blessing in store for Japheth—extended territory and a large number of descendants (9:26–27). The son who had protected Noah would find protection himself—in the tents of his brother, Shem, served by the family of his brother Ham.

Genesis 9 ends with a summary of Noah's subsequent life. Like his forebears, Noah lives to an advanced age (950).

GENESIS 10:1–11:32

NOAH'S DESCENDANTS

Setting Up the Section

Chapters 10–11 track the repopulation of the earth from Noah's sons and the separation of the nations into individual cultures.

The genealogies in Genesis 10 include reference to the separation of nations (10:5, 20, 31) that occurs at the Tower of Babel, which is described in chapter 11. This interspersed narrative (11:1–9) separates the two genealogies of Shem (10:21–31; 11:10–26), paving the way for the link between the Terah (father of Abraham) clan and Shem's lineage (11:27).

10:1–5

JAPHETH

This first section is the shortest and highlights fourteen of Japheth's descendants. The Japhethites split into two groups: One group settled in India and the other group in Europe. They became the coastline peoples, the Gentiles to whom the apostle Paul spread the gospel in the New Testament.

Japheth's bloodline plays a lesser role in the theme being developed in this book, which deals more with the conflict between Ham's descendants, the Canaanites, and Shem's descendants, the Semitic people.

The occupation of the lands described in verse 5 actually takes place after the account of the tower at Babel.

Demystifying Genesis

This is a modified genealogy, and it uses the words *son* and *father* even more flexibly than do the other genealogies of Genesis 4, 5, and 11. *Son* in Genesis 10 may mean "descendant," "successor," or "nation." *Father* may mean "ancestor," "predecessor," or "founder." This section has been called a "table of nations" because it traces the connected origins of various people groups. At this time, the nations of the world were being repopulated from the same family: the three sons of Noah.

10:6–20

HAM

Ham's descendants, the Canaanites, are significant because of the part they play in the future history of Israel, particularly the events at Babel (Babylon), Mizraim (Egypt), and Canaan (10:10, 13–15). The nations connected to Ham's bloodline inhabit an area from Egypt to Mesopotamia and the west coast of Arabia. The original readers of this writing were still in conflict with Ham's descendants, and would consider this history quite relevant.

10:21–32

SHEM

The descendants of Shem are the Semitic peoples who inhabit the eastern lands: modern-day Iraq, Iran, and eastern Saudi Arabia. This bloodline is mentioned last (though Shem is older) because it is the principle bloodline of the history covered in Genesis. The genealogy of Shem splits at the sons of Eber (10:25). It is from the name *Eber* that the word *Hebrew* originated. The Hebrews, of course, are later referred to as the Israelites (the bloodline descending from Abraham's grandson, Jacob) and the Jews (the people who descended from Jacob's son, Judah).

11:1–9

BABEL

The story of Genesis 11 occurs before the nations scatter around the world (as described in Genesis 10).

After the flood, all people spoke the same language. Noah's descendants, rather than spreading out, settle together in Shinar, a place that eventually becomes associated with evil.

Verses 3–4 describe the first idea of what becomes the famed tower at Babel. The motivation for building a city is to make a name for themselves and to keep from scattering out. This is not an act of worship, but rather an act of pride and self-preservation.

Verses 5–6, God's response to the people's efforts, is anthropomorphic; it describes God in human terms. It simply means that God wants a good look at what people are doing on earth. God, of course, doesn't need to leave heaven to see what is happening on earth.

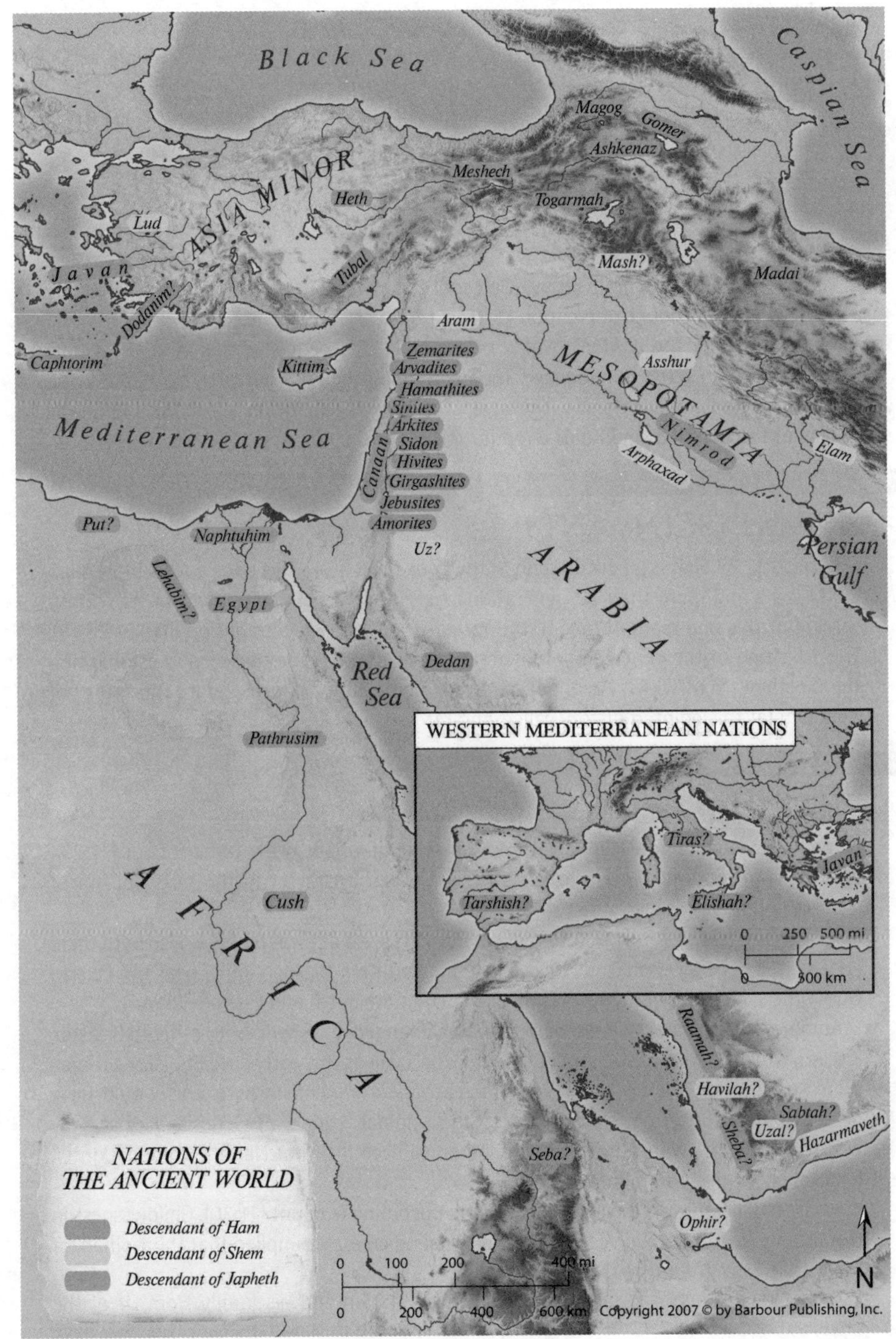
Black Sea
Caspian Sea
Magog
Gomer
Ashkenaz
Meshech
ASIA MINOR
Heth
Togarmah
Lud
Javan
Tubal
Mash?
Madai
Dodanim?
Aram
Caphtorim
Kittim
Zemarites
Arvadites
Hamathites
Sinites
Arkites
Sidon
Hivites
Girgashites
Jebusites
Amorites
Canaan
MESOPOTAMIA
Asshur
Nimrod
Arphaxad
Elam
Mediterranean Sea
Put?
Naphtuhim
Uz?
ARABIA
Persian Gulf
Lehabim?
Egypt
Red Sea
Dedan
Pathrusim
AFRICA
Cush
WESTERN MEDITERRANEAN NATIONS
Tiras?
Javan
Tarshish?
Elishah?
0 250 500 mi
0 500 km
Raamah?
Havilah?
Sabtah?
Uzal?
Hazarmaveth
Sheba?
Seba?
Ophir?
NATIONS OF THE ANCIENT WORLD
Descendant of Ham
Descendant of Shem
Descendant of Japheth
0 100 200 400 mi
0 200 400 600 km
N

Critical Observation

The language of Genesis 11:6 may sound as if God is worried. This verse, however, is not speaking of technology but of morality. God initiates a judgment to counter the rebellion of people who were putting their trust in their own efforts rather than His care. God is not threatened by what man might do. On the contrary, God is protecting man from himself.

Verse 7 employs the plural, "let us." God spoke of Himself in this same plural form early in Genesis in the account of creation (1:26).

As the result of the confusion of the languages, the people scatter over the whole earth rather than settle in one place. The name *Babel* means "confusion" in Hebrew and "the gate of gods" in Babylonian. This area, later known as Babylon, stands as a longtime enemy of the Israelites and holds a reputation for evil.

11:10–26

SHEM'S DESCENDANTS

Genesis 11:27 begins a new division in the book of Genesis. This book covers more than 2,000 years and more than 20 generations; yet, it spends almost a third of its text on the life of this one man: Abraham, the forefather of the Israelite nation (11:27–25:18). This revisiting of the genealogy of Shem in verses 10–26 is the first step in establishing the bloodline from which Abraham descends. Verse 26 introduces Terah, the father of Abraham (at this point in history called Abram).

11:27–32

TERAH

Terah, like Noah before him, has three sons, one of whom is the father of Lot (11:27–28). Lot is introduced quickly because he is a major character in the next portion of Genesis and serves as a contrast to Abram.

Though the text says only that Haran was born in Ur, Abram was probably also born there (11:28). It is generally held that Ur is located in southern Mesopotamia, near the Persian Gulf. Others, however, contend that Ur is located to the north and east of Haran.

Abram married Sarai, whose name is later changed to *Sarah*. She is his half-sister, (20:12), which is not unusual or contrary to God's will at this early date in history. It may seem strange that the details of Nahor's marriage are included here. This would have been significant information, though, to the original readers of Genesis, in that they would already be aware (since this is a historical account) that Nahor's granddaughter, Rebekah, becomes Abram's daughter-in-law.

Sarai's childlessness is a major factor in the upcoming account (11:30). Childlessness in the ancient Near East involved shame and social ridicule, and implied that the woman, or the couple, was not in the favor of the gods.

Verses 31–32 then inform us that Terah takes Abram and his family from Ur of the Chaldeans in order to settle in Canaan, but they settle in Haran instead. This may have been a matter of religion. Joshua 24:2 and 24:14–15 make it clear that Terah (and quite possibly his family) worshiped many gods. In fact, many of the names in Genesis 11:29 come right out of the cult of moon worship. Ur and Haran are both centers for this false religion, which may have been the motivation to settle there rather than moving on.

GENESIS 12:1–20:18

ABRAHAM

Abram's Call	12:1–20
Abram and Lot	13:1–14:24
Abram's Covenant	15:1–21
Ishmael	16:1–16
Abraham's Circumcision	17:1–27
Sodom and Gomorrah	18:1–19:38
Abimelech	20:1–18

Setting Up the Section

Chapter 11 describes the third time in Genesis that humanity strikes out—first in Eden, then with the flood, and finally at Babel. Beginning with chapter 12, we at last see the foundation God is laying for a solution. Through Abram, God promises a descendant who will eventually bring salvation. This is an act of grace. God is certainly a God of justice and judgment, but in His economy, grace always prevails.

12:1–20

ABRAM'S CALL

In the opening verse of chapter 12, the NIV, NKJV, and KJV include the word "had," which clarifies the timeline. These translations are suggesting that 12:1 flashes back to something that happened in Ur even though 11:31 ends with Abram in Haran.

God's command to go is the translation of a term that can emphasize loneliness and isolation; ideas of parting and seclusion are often implied.

The first three verses of chapter 12 as a whole convey the inauguration of God's covenant with Abram:

1) "I will make you a great nation."
2) "I will bless you."
3) "I will make your name great."
4) "You shall be a blessing." The original Hebrew wording actually says, "Be a blessing."
5) "I will bless those who bless you."
6) "The one who curses you I will curse."
7) "And in you all the families of the earth will be blessed."

Since Lot voluntarily chooses to accompany Abram, he probably believes the promises as well (12:4). While the acquired people could be a reference to slaves or servants, it could also refer to converts who Abram won during his sojourn in Haran.

Abram stops at Shechem (12:6–7), a place that becomes sacred to the Israelites because, while this is God's second revelation of Himself to Abram, it is the first revelation in the promised land. Shechem is near the geographic center of Canaan (Joshua 20:7).

The Hebrew term *Moreh* means "teacher," and may indicate that the oak tree mentioned in verse 6 is an ancient shrine, or a place where Canaanite priests declare oracles.

The fact that Abram pitches his tent between Bethel and Ai probably indicates that he stays there for some time (Genesis 12:8). During his time on the mountain, Abram continues to worship by building an altar. The word translated *worship* (NET) carries the idea of not only acknowledging but also proclaiming the name of the Lord.

Verses 10–20 give us a peek into Abram's humanity as he, out of fear, asks Sarai to pretend to be his sister rather than his wife. While Sarai is indeed Abram's half-sister, this is a ruse intended to deceive, and he is trusting in his deception to protect him instead of trusting in the Lord. While he has proven himself to be a man of faith, in this case he is more afraid of the Egyptians than of God.

Medieval commentators suggest that what Abram hopes to get out of being Sarai's brother is the right to receive and deny all suitors' requests to be Sarai's husband, in this way protecting her from adultery or bigamy.

Sure enough, the Pharaoh does notice Sarai and takes her into his household, and Abram seems to benefit from the arrangement (12:15–16). The gifts he receives are provisions of wealth in Abram's day. The last two gifts, the female donkeys and the camels, tell all. Female donkeys were far more controllable and dependable for riding and, therefore, the ride of choice for the rich.

The subsequent curse on Pharaoh's household is the first example of the cursing and blessing that God promises to Abram in Genesis 12:2–3. Any misfortune in the ancient world is looked upon as an indication of divine displeasure. So when God sends great plagues, Pharaoh and his advisers may have tried to pinpoint when the troubles started. When they trace the troubles back to the time of Sarai's arrival, this leads them to Abram. The word interpreted *plagues* (12:17) in some translations is probably better translated *diseases*.

Critical Observation

Everything that Abram receives in Egypt later causes him trouble. Because of the great wealth he acquires from Pharaoh, Abram and Lot choose to separate (13:5–6). Hagar, the Egyptian maidservant who Pharaoh gives to Abram, brings division and sorrow with far-reaching consequences (16:1–16).

ABRAM AND LOT

We have no clue as to how long Abram remains in Egypt. He builds no altars in Egypt, to our knowledge, nor does he ever call on the name of the Lord. But upon leaving Egypt, he returns to his altar (13:1–4).

Verses 5–18 chronicle the downfall of Abram and Lot. Their possessions became so large that they could no longer live together (13:6–7). This point is repeated twice for emphasis. As nomadic tribesmen, they had to travel about, looking continually for pasture for their sheep and cattle. Since the land was already inhabited, there wasn't a lot of land to choose from, and the men became competitors for the best pasture. The result was a range war.

According to verse 7, the conflict between Abram and Lot is on full display before the unbelieving Canaanites and Perizzites.

Abram's approach to Lot in verses 8–9 is tender and compromising. He appeals to their kinship and offers Lot a choice. The result of Lot's choice in verses 10–13 reveals a contrast between Lot and Abram and introduces the wicked city of Sodom. Lot chooses his own benefit over Abram's, his vocation over his family, and his immediate gratification over his long-term benefit.

Lot surveys the land before him with the eyes of one weighing financial promise (13:10), while Abram surveys the land before him while receiving God's third revelation (13:14). That revelation contains three specifics:

1) God will give the land to Abram and his descendants forever (13:15).
2) Abram's heir will be his own child (13:15–16).
3) Abram's descendants will be innumerable (13:16).

These blessings are good news for Abram but far from the reality he could see. Nevertheless, God tells him to walk the land. The practice of walking through land appears to have been a symbolic, legal practice related to the idea of staking a claim on a piece of real estate. In the ancient Near East, victorious armies claimed defeated territory simply by marching through it.

Chapter 13 closes with Abram building another altar, this time in *Hebron*, a name that means "communion." It is in the region of Hebron that Abram makes his home base (18:1) and is eventually buried (25:9).

The first twelve verses of chapter 14 serve as an introduction. They describe the first war ever recorded in scripture—a war between four eastern kings and five southern kings. Shinar (Babylon, modern-day Iraq) initiates this war (14:1–2). (It is Shinar in which the first families after the flood settle, and then unfortunately attempt to build a tower at Babel.)

The Bible includes very little information about the actual battles involved, but the account is laden with geographical and political details. The territory mentioned here is quite extensive, stretching from the north and west of the Sea of Galilee, down the Jordan Valley, all the way south to the Red Sea. This war is an international power struggle to control a strategic commercial land bridge between Mesopotamia and Egypt. Whoever controls this land bridge maintains a monopoly on international trade.

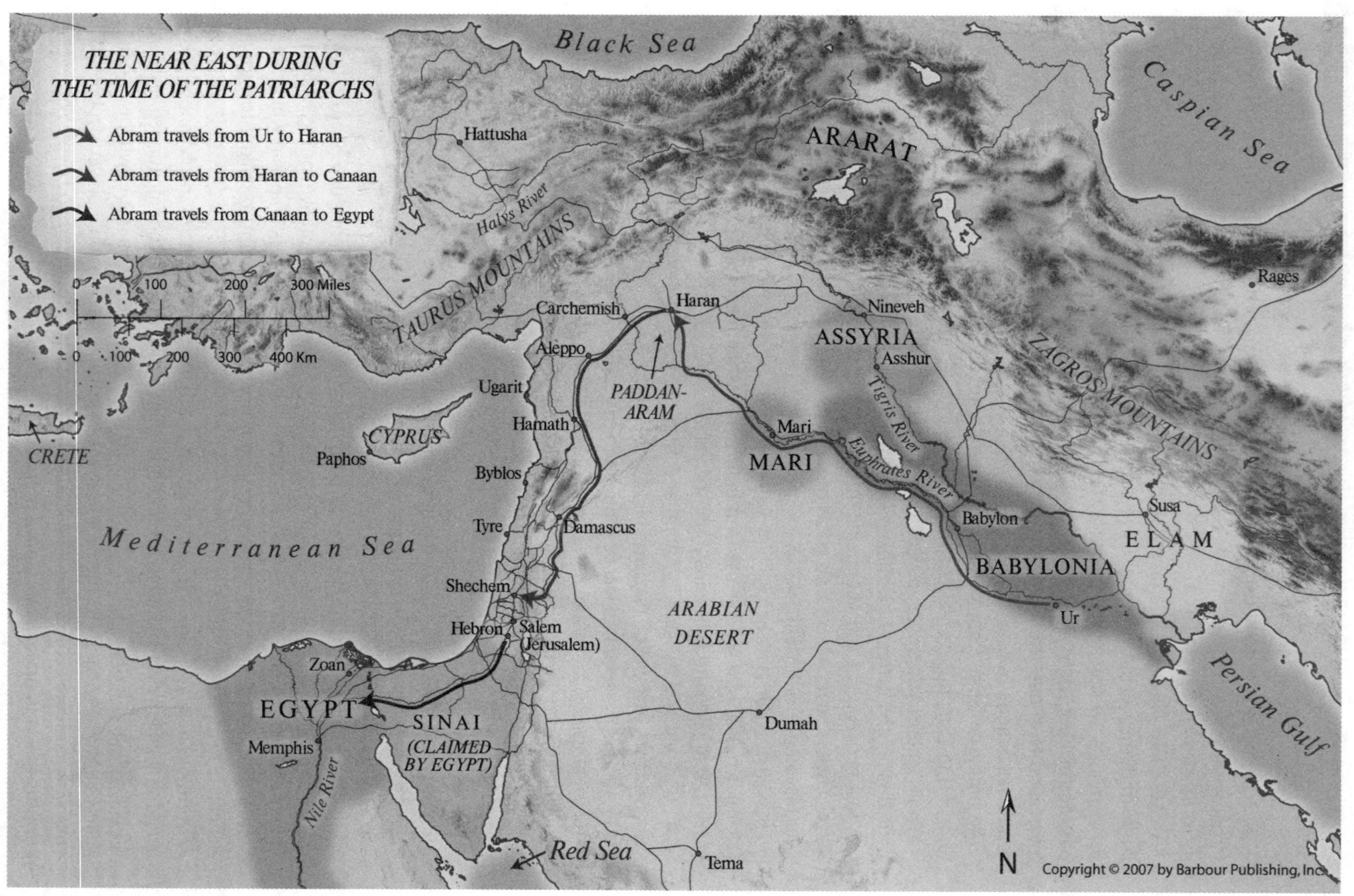
THE NEAR EAST DURING
THE TIME OF THE PATRIARCHS
Abram travels from Ur to Haran
Abram travels from Haran to Canaan
Abram travels from Canaan to Egypt
0 100 200 300 Miles
0 100 200 300 400 Km
Black Sea
Caspian Sea
Persian Gulf
Mediterranean Sea
Red Sea
ARARAT
ASSYRIA
MARI
BABYLONIA
ELAM
ZAGROS MOUNTAINS
TAURUS MOUNTAINS
PADDAN-ARAM
ARABIAN DESERT
EGYPT
SINAI
(CLAIMED BY EGYPT)
CYPRUS
CRETE
Hattusha
Halys River
Rages
Nineveh
Asshur
Tigris River
Euphrates River
Babylon
Susa
Ur
Mari
Haran
Carchemish
Aleppo
Hamath
Ugarit
Byblos
Tyre
Damascus
Shechem
Salem
(Jerusalem)
Hebron
Dumah
Tema
Paphos
Zoan
Memphis
Nile River
N
Copyright © 2007 by Barbour Publishing, Inc.

The southern kings had been subjugated for twelve years. In the thirteenth year, they attempt to throw off their shackles (14:3–4). In response, the eastern kings launch a punishing assault to end the rebellion (14:5–7). The kings of Sodom and Gomorrah, with their allies, prepare for all-out battle in the valley of Siddim, which is full of tar pits. The five southern kings think that these pits will be a natural defense, but they only meet defeat.

The events recounted are global in scope and end in the disgraceful defeat of the kings of Sodom and Gomorrah (14:10–11).

Critical Observation

Verse 13 marks the first time in the Bible that the term *Hebrew* is used—in this case of Abram, the foreigner living in Canaan.

Since Lot has separated from his uncle and moved into Sodom, he and his family are taken captive by the four eastern kings (14:12). Though Abram could have chosen to do nothing, he leads a pursuit to rescue Lot and his possessions. Abram divides his men and attacks at night. The march of Abram and his band of 318 men is one of the most remarkable forced marches in history. They travel the whole length of the Jordan River and launch a counter attack as the enemy indulges in a time of carousing and reveling in celebration of their victory (14:14–16).

This pursuit would have begun in the hill country south of Jerusalem and continued as far as Dan, the northernmost point of what came to be known as Israel. Abram traveled over 240 miles, one-way, to rescue Lot (14:16).

The king of Sodom comes to meet Abram (14:17). Abram fought his great battle for the sake of Lot and his family, but his victory also benefits the cities of Sodom and Gomorrah. A special welcoming committee had evidently been appointed, headed by the king himself, to confer upon Abram the usual reward for a conquering hero.

Melchizedek, mentioned in verse 18, is probably a title rather than a proper name. It means "King of Righteousness." Salem, of which Melchizedek is king, may be the shortened name for Jerusalem (Psalm 76:2), which at that time was occupied by the Canaanites. Melchizedek was a Canaanite, but he is called a priest of God Most High (14:18). The biblical record does not mention Melchizedek's parents, his ancestry, his birth, or his death. In that sense he is different from any other individual found in this narrative.

Melchizedek's blessing on Abram acknowledges God's work in Abram's victory. This would have been an unexpected turn of events. Though Melchizedek is certainly a Canaanite, Abram acknowledges his priestly dignity by giving him a tithe (4:19–20). (The tithe of the Mosaic Law has not been established yet.)

The story concludes with a conversation between Abram and the king of Sodom, and Abram's acknowledgement of his God and Creator. By all rights, the spoils Abram captured should belong to him, but Abram accepts none for himself. The men who fought with him, however, are rewarded their share (14:23).

This passage concludes with Abram's confessing God before people (14:22). The book of Hebrews in the New Testament applies this account to Jesus, identifying Him as a high priest in the order of Melchizedek.

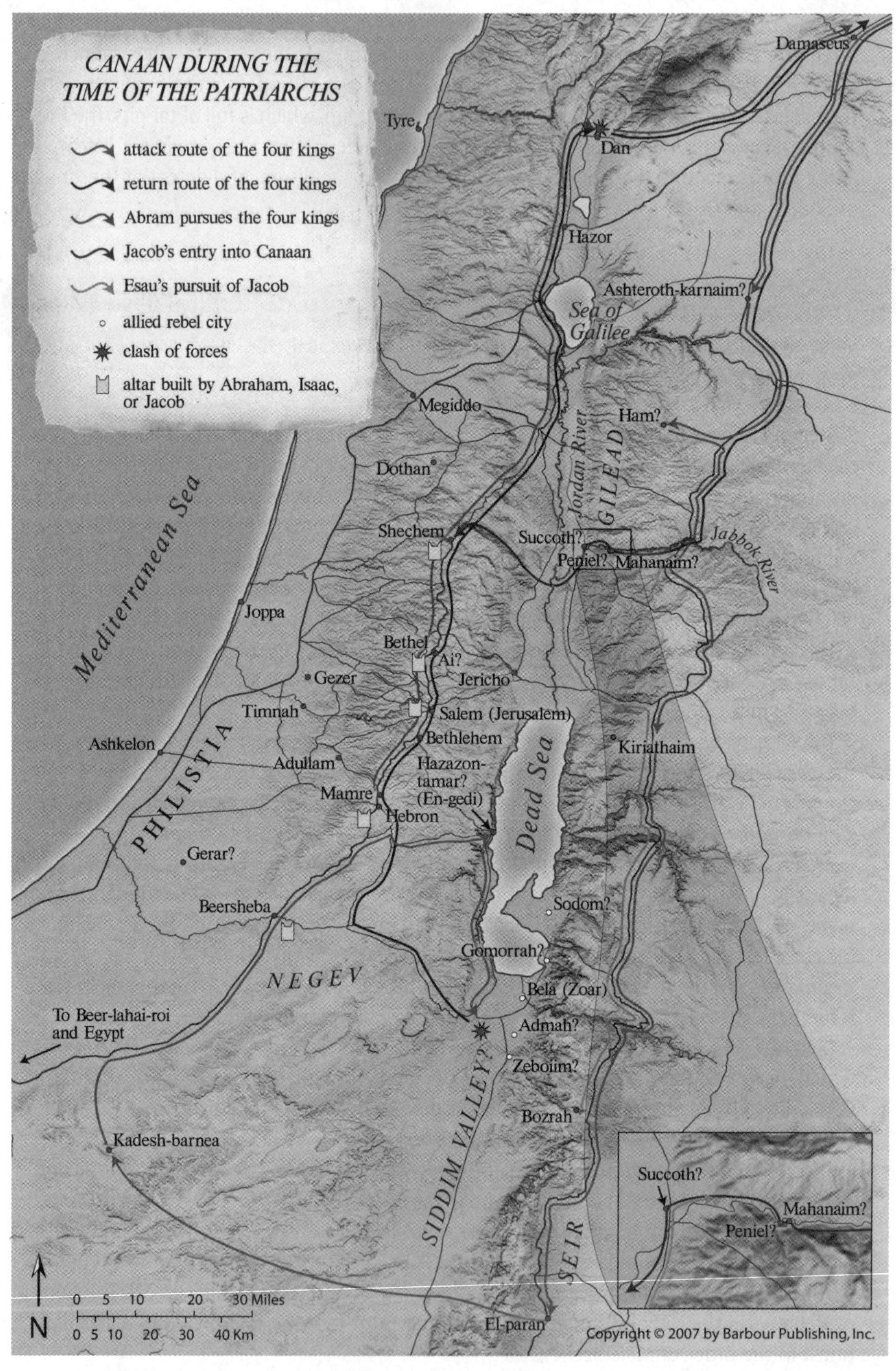
CANAAN DURING THE TIME OF THE PATRIARCHS
attack route of the four kings
return route of the four kings
Abram pursues the four kings
Jacob's entry into Canaan
Esau's pursuit of Jacob
allied rebel city
clash of forces
altar built by Abraham, Isaac, or Jacob
Damascus
Tyre
Dan
Hazor
Ashteroth-karnaim?
Sea of Galilee
Megiddo
Ham?
Dothan
Jordan River
GILEAD
Mediterranean Sea
Shechem
Succoth?
Jabbok River
Peniel?
Mahanaim?
Joppa
Bethel
Ai?
Gezer
Jericho
Timnah
Salem (Jerusalem)
Ashkelon
Bethlehem
Kiriathaim
PHILISTIA
Adullam
Hazazon-tamar? (En-gedi)
Mamre
Dead Sea
Hebron
Gerar?
Sodom?
Beersheba
Gomorrah?
NEGEV
Bela (Zoar)
To Beer-lahai-roi and Egypt
Admah?
Zeboiim?
SIDDIM VALLEY?
Bozrah
Kadesh-barnea
Succoth?
Mahanaim?
Peniel?
SEIR
0 5 10 20 30 Miles
0 5 10 20 30 40 Km
N
El-paran

15:1–21

ABRAM'S COVENANT

Though Abram turns down the reward offered by the king of Sodom, he receives a promise that God Himself will be his reward and his shield (15:1).

The shield was the primary defensive weapon of the Old Testament warrior. It was a portable fortress, a defensive wall that could be taken with the warrior into battle. It provided a barrier between the vulnerable flesh of the soldier and the dangerous impact of the enemy's weapons.

Verses 2–3 record, for the first time, Abram's response to God. Inherent in his response is the pain of having wealth and success, but no heir to pass it on to. It was a common practice in the ancient Near East for a childless couple to adopt a son, who would care for them in their old age and inherit their possessions and property. Abram suggests that he adopt his chief servant, Eliezer.

Amidst Abram's doubt and despair, God encourages him. He not only gives Abram the promise again (12:2; 13:15–16), but He confirms it by stating that Abram's descendants will be as numerous as the stars of heaven.

Critical Observation

Some consider Genesis 15:6 to be the most important verse in the Old Testament: God declares Abram righteous (clean, morally right) on the basis of Abram's faith. The idea is that God is crediting Abram's faith as righteousness. While this connection between faith and righteousness is most often considered a New Testament concept, this verse confirms that God has always desired faith from His people.

Genesis 15:7–21 recounts God's making of the covenant with Abram. The emphasis in this section shifts to the land promised by the Lord to Abram's descendants.

God encourages Abram with the fact that He had brought him out of Ur of the Chaldeans to give him the land of Canaan as his inheritance. This statement is virtually identical to the opening statement of the Sinai covenant in Exodus 20:2: "I am the LORD your God, the one who brought you out of Egypt where you were slaves" (CEV). The expression "Ur of the Chaldeans" refers back to Genesis 11:28, 31, and grounds the present covenant in a past act of divine salvation from Babylon, just as Exodus 20:2 grounds the Sinai covenant in an act of divine salvation from Egypt.

The sacrifice that God instructs Abram to make involves the same ceremonially clean animals that are used later in the sacrificial system under the Law of Moses. The use of five different kinds of sacrificial animals underlines the solemnity of the occasion.

The text implies that Abram is familiar with the ritual to take place, because God does not explicitly state what to do with the animals. His command is only to bring the animals, but Abram not only brings the animals; he also sacrifices them and lays them out as an offering (15:9–10).

In Abram's day, legal agreements were formalized by means of a very graphic covenant ceremony: the dividing of an animal sealed the covenant. The animal was cut in half and the two parties would pass between the halves while repeating the terms of the covenant. By doing so, the two parties were stating, "If I fail to fulfill my commitments to this covenant, may I suffer the same fate as this animal."

In one of the most dramatic scenes in Abram's life, he is depicted as a passive observer. In this case, though, he faces terror. This is often the response in the Bible when someone faces God's presence (15:12).

God makes a seven-fold prophecy concerning the nation of Israel (15:13–16). Abram did not live through this period of slavery, but it is the story found in the book of Exodus.

The smoking oven and flaming torch represent the presence of God. The Lord Himself passes between these pieces of animals, sealing a covenant with Abram (15:17). As He makes this covenant with Abram, God gives the geographical boundaries and the nations that will belong to Abram. The borders of this land, promised to Abram's descendants, appear to coincide with the borders of the Garden of Eden (Genesis 2:10–14). The land consists of ten nations in which God would grant Abram's descendants victory.

16:1–16

ISHMAEL

Chapter 16 gives the account of Abram and his wife, Sarai, attempting to fulfill God's promise on their own.

God had promised Abram a son (12:2). But in Abram's impatience, he adopts his servant girl's son, Eliezer, so he will have an heir (15:2–3). However, God rejects Eliezer and reaffirms His promise to give Abram a son of his own (15:4). But ten years later, Abram is still waiting.

In another attempt for an heir, Sarai suggests following a custom through which Abram would have a child through Hagar, Sarai's servant. Ancient documents reveal that when a woman could not provide her husband with a child, she could give her female slave as a wife and claim the child of this union as her own.

There is an ironic reversal here. When in Egypt, Abram gave Sarai over to the Egyptian Pharaoh, and Hagar joined their entourage (12:10–20). Here in Canaan, Sarai gives Abram over to the Egyptian servant.

While Hagar is not on equal standing with Sarai, her status does change when she becomes a slave wife. If she produces the heir, she could be the primary wife in the eyes of society. According to verses 4–5, in Hagar's opinion Sarai had been demoted. The Hebrew word translated *despise* (NET) means to "treat lightly or with contempt." A contemporary rendering of Sarai's closing threat in verse 5 would be: "God will get you for this." According to verse 6, the mistreatment goes both ways as Sarai begins treating Hagar *harshly*—same word used later to describe how cruelly and unfairly the Egyptian slave masters treated Israel.

In verse 7, the angel of the Lord appears to Hagar. This is the first of this kind of appearance described in the Bible. There is debate about who this angel is; some believe him to be the preincarnate Christ. In the conversation between the two, the angel of the Lord instructs Hagar to submit not only to Sarai's authority, but to whatever mistreatment the situation involves. This requires Hagar to humble herself (16:9). Hagar's son, Ishmael, will grow up in Abraham's household because of these instructions.

It is only in association with her return and submission to Sarai that the Lord offers Hagar a blessing, the promise that she will have many descendants (16:9–12). Abram, Isaac, and Jacob are given a similar promise, but Hagar is the only woman that is given a promise like this. She is also told to name her son *Ishmael*, which means "God hears," or "God has heard."

The prophecy of verse 12 is not an insult. The wild donkey lives a solitary existence in the desert away from society. Ishmael would be free-roaming and strong. His free-roaming lifestyle will put him in conflict with those who follow social conventions. This is not a prophecy of open warfare, only of friction because of his antagonism to others' ways of life.

Verse 13 is the only place in the Bible where a person names God. Hagar names God *El Roi* the God who sees. The name given to the well in verse 14 reflects the same thing: "The well of the living One who sees me." The text suggests that God takes up the cause of those who are oppressed.

According to verses 15–16, Hagar obeys the Lord and returns to the household. There is no mention of Sarai in these closing verses of chapter 16.

17:1–27

ABRAHAM'S CIRCUMCISION

The account in Genesis 17:1–27 reveals a mixture of divine sovereignty and human responsibility. The idea of a *covenant* between God and Abram is central to this narrative (see 12:1–3).

Thirteen years have passed since the last conversations recorded between Abram and God (chapter 15). In the newest revelation, God refers to Himself as God Almighty (*El Shaddai*). The word *El* means "the strong one." This suggests that God is the One from whom Abram is to draw strength and nourishment.

This is the first time God is called by this name. So far, the primary name by which the Lord has revealed Himself is *Elohim. El Shaddai* is used exclusively in scripture relating God to His children.

The word translated *blameless* in verse 1 has the sense of wholeness when used of attitudes and is translated "without blemish" when used in the context of sacrifice (see Exodus 12:5; Leviticus 1:10).

The word translated *establish*, or *confirm*, means "to set in motion." The covenant has already been established; here God is restating it to Abram.

Abram's response, prostrating himself before God, is a typical act of worship (17:3; Leviticus 9:24; Joshua 5:14; Ezekiel 1:28).

It is at this time God changes Abram's name. *Abram* means "exalted father," a name that probably refers to God's nature more than Abram's. Here God changes Abram's name to *Abraham*, which means "father of a multitude."

God makes five "I will" statements in Genesis 17:6–8.

God also outlines the obedience He expects from Abraham; circumcision will be the sign of the covenant (17:7–14). Circumcision is an outward sign of an inward commitment.

It is to an Israelite what a wedding ring is to a bridegroom.

Abraham is to circumcise himself and every male in his household. From then on, baby boys were to be circumcised on the eighth day of life.

Demystifying Genesis

The word *circumcision* means "cutting around." It refers to a minor operation that removes the foreskin from the male organ. Only males underwent circumcision. In the patriarchal society of the ancient Near East, people considered that a girl or woman shared the condition of her father if she was single, or her husband if she was married.

Why was the circumcision to be performed on the eighth day (17:12)? We know today that on the eighth day the infant's immune system is at the optimum level for such a procedure. Important blood-clotting agents, vitamin K and prothrombin, are at their highest levels in infants on precisely the eighth day of life, making the eighth day the safest day to circumcise an infant.

Verse 14 says that an uncircumcised male will be cut off from his people. Typically, this is a reference to execution, sometimes by the Israelites but usually by God, in the form of premature death.

Sarai's name is changed as well, to Sarah (17:15–16). The names are two different forms of a word meaning "princess."

When the Lord had appeared, Abraham fell on his face, exhibiting respect and reverence (17:3). After God's promise that Sarah will bear a son, he again falls on his face, but this time to hide his laughter (17:17). When Abraham hears that God will greatly increase his descendants, he responds with respect and submission. But when he hears *how* God will carry out His plan, his respect contains a tinge of laughter.

Abraham's plea on behalf of Ishmael reveals a kind of "if only" agony. He is being asked to believe the seemingly preposterous, when a sure thing is already a part of the family.

In verses 19–22, we read God's outline of the future for both of the sons of Abraham. Abraham's son will be named *Isaac*, which means "laughter," an ironic name in light of Abraham's response (17:3, 19). God promises blessings on Ishmael as well as on Isaac. As the Hebrew people would have twelve tribes, so Ishmael's people would also have twelve families. (The list of Ishmael's twelve sons is given in Genesis 25:13–15.)

This chapter concludes with Abraham's obedience to the demand for circumcision (17:23–27). It is important to note that circumcision is not a condition of the covenant, but a sign of Abraham's participation in it.

18:1–19:38

SODOM AND GOMORRAH

God's appearance to Abraham recorded in chapter 18 is apparently only a few weeks or months after the appearance recorded in chapter 17. In Genesis 17:21, God said Sarah would give birth one year later, and the account in chapter 18 gives us no indication that she is pregnant yet.

Abraham's reaction to the three visitors is typical of ancient Middle Eastern hospitality.

He hurries to serve them and bows before them (18:2–5). He also makes his best food available (18:6–8). In the ancient world, a person's hospitality was often determined by the ability to provide extravagant hospitality. Also, though Abraham has servants available to him (14:14), he is personally involved in the care of these guests.

Though many believe that one of Abraham's visitors was Jesus, preincarnate, the fact that there were three visitors should not be pressed to represent the Trinity. It's unclear whether Abraham recognized the identity of any of the men, but many scholars believe he did because he addresses one of them as "my lord."

In the next seven verses, the narrative pans to Sarah, Abraham's wife (18:9–15). The Lord affirms His promise that Sarah will have a child the following year. He even promises He will show up for the birth (17:21; 18:10).

It was customary in Abraham's day, as in some cultures today, for women to be neither seen nor heard while male guests are entertained. Yet, Sarah listens from where she is (18:10).

Verse 11 offers background information that reveals that what the guest proposes—Sarah's pregnancy—is a natural impossibility. Sarah certainly believed it to be impossible, and her laughter is not simply from being caught off guard by the idea; it reveals her unbelief (18:12).

Critical Observation

If this were the entire story, we would be tempted to say that Sarah is no example to follow. Verses 12–15 reveal a woman who doubts God and lies about it. But in the book of Hebrews, we get the rest of the story. Hebrews 11:11 reveals that Sarah does consider God faithful to keep His promises. Eventually, she finds the answer to the Lord's question, "Is anything too hard for the Lord?" (18.14 NIV).

After feeding his guests, Abraham walks with them awhile (18:16). It is during this time that Abraham learns about Sodom, and the theme of the account takes a turn from faith and fellowship to judgment.

Critical Observation

The Lord chose to disclose His intentions toward Sodom and Gomorrah because He had chosen Abraham to be a channel of blessing to all the nations of the earth, and because of Abraham's relationship with God. The Bible certainly doesn't represent Abraham as a perfect man, yet his faith in God put him in relationship with God; Isaiah 41:8 even refers to Abraham as His friend. Therefore, God trusted him with this information about Sodom and Gomorrah.

Verses 20–21 reveal God's basic plan for Sodom and Gomorrah. The word translated *outcry* in verse 20 is used to describe cries of the oppressed and brutalized. In this case, the term may have two meanings: (1) It may mean the outcry against Sodom caused by its injustice and violence, or (2) the cry of its rebellion against God (19:13).

The Lord speaks of personally observing sin (18:21). The Hebrew text here could be rendered, "I will go down personally and see if their sin is made complete."

Abraham's conversation with the Lord recorded in verses 22–33 is a prayer-negotiation for the righteous people of Sodom and Gomorrah. This is the first time in the scriptures so far that a man has initiated a conversation with God.

Keep in mind that these wicked cities are where Abraham's nephew Lot has settled. Abraham's primary purpose seems to be to secure justice (or deliverance) for the righteous minority in their wicked cities. Secondarily, he wants God to spare the cities. This interpretation finds support in Abraham's appeal to the justice of God rather than to His mercy (18:23–25).

Why does Abraham stop at the number ten? He probably felt there were at least ten righteous people in Sodom.

Take It Home

Why does God allow Abraham to intercede for Sodom? Some of the answers to that question may be seen in these last verses of chapter 18. God is a God of mercy as well as of judgment; He takes no pleasure in destroying the wicked. This narrative also shows us the power righteous people can have, and the value of intercession on the behalf of others. Abraham stands as an example of someone who desires mercy for others just as he has received mercy.

After this negotiation, two angels approach Lot at the gate of Sodom. The city gate is where the civic leaders met to finalize legal and business transactions. It is a place of prominence and influence. The implication is Lot had achieved not only his goals but also his social and political ambitions.

While there is no indication that Lot recognizes these visitors as angels, as Abraham does, he treats them with hospitality (19:1–3). The phrase "urged them persistently" (NET) is a translation of the Hebrew verb meaning "to press; to insist." This word ironically foreshadows the hostile actions of the men of Sodom, where they pressed hard against Lot and came near to break the door (19:9).

Verses 4–9 provide a chilling testament to the wickedness of both the Sodomites and even Lot himself, as the Sodomites demand to be given access to the guests and Lot offers his daughters instead. Though there is some debate on this account, the verb traditionally translated *know* in verse 5 is most often translated *sexual intercourse* in more modern-language Bibles. This idea seems to be confirmed by Lot's offer of his virgin daughters to the men. These citizens of Sodom meant to do harm.

Lot's offering of his daughters is unfathomable to a modern society. We understand it a little more when we consider the low place of women in the pre-Christian world and the high standing of any guest in terms of Middle Eastern hospitality.

The word used to describe the blindness the men of Sodom experienced (19:11) is a rare word that may indicate "a dazzled state," or a combination of partial blindness and a kind of mental bewilderment. Yet, despite their physical blindness, these men and boys persist to the point of weariness in their effort to satisfy their sexual cravings.

When the guests explain to Lot the fate of the city, the word translated *destroy* is the same word used twice in Genesis 6:13 of the judgment of the flood (19:13).

Lot has lost such credibility with his sons-in-law that they treat his message as a joke. Ironically, the Hebrew word that is translated *joking* (NIV) is the same root from which the name *Isaac* is derived, meaning "laughter."

The angels warn Lot by telling him there are great consequences for sin, but he delays responding to God. Lot is so attached to his present world of family, friends, power, and material things that he just cannot bear the thought of leaving it all behind (19:15–16; 1 John 2:15–17).

Even as the angels are rescuing Lot from the cities, he is fighting for his own self-preservation. Rather than trusting these messengers, he fights to stay within his comfort level (Genesis 19:18–22).

The destruction of the cities is described in verses 23–29. Archaeologists believe that today these cities are buried under the Dead Sea. As for Lot's wife, the Hebrew verb translated *looked back* signifies an intense gaze, not a passing glance, even though their rescuers had warned them to keep moving ahead (19:17, 26).

The follow-up account in verses 30–38 is remarkably similar to the story of the last days of Noah after his rescue from the flood (9:20–27). In Noah's case, he became drunk with wine and uncovered himself in the presence of his children. In both narratives, the act has grave consequences. Thus, at the close of the two great narratives of divine judgment—the flood and the destruction of Sodom—those who are saved from God's wrath subsequently fall into a form of sin reminiscent of those who die in the judgment. This is a common theme in the prophetic literature (Isaiah 56–66; Malachi 1). The mention of the Ammonites and Moabites is significant since these neighboring nations are mentioned in the nation of Israel's later journey to occupy the promised land.

20:1–18

ABIMELECH

The account described in Genesis 20 is quite similar to another account, described in Genesis 12:10–20, where Abraham and Sarah devise a scheme to avoid potential problems with the Pharaoh in Egypt. There are some scholars who find these similarities so striking that they wonder if this is the same account recorded a second time.

As with the similar event in chapter 12, the information Abraham gives is factual. Sarah is his half-sister. Even if factual, though, he is concealing the whole truth that Sarah is also his wife. This, combined with the conversation recorded in verses 4–6 between God and Abimelech, leaves readers with the impression that Abimelech is more righteous than Abraham. In fact, according to verse 6, the Lord Himself preserved Abimelech from falling because of Abraham's deceit.

Abraham even blames God for his vulnerable condition, complaining that God made him wander away from home (20:13). The implication is that if God had not told him to leave his father's house, he would have never ended up in Abimelech's kingdom. If he had never arrived in Abimelech's kingdom, he would have never lied.

To make matters worse, the last part of verse 13 reveals that Abraham pushes Sarah into his deception.

Verses 17–18 reveal that the women in Abimelech's household are unable to have children because Sarah had become a part of the household. God heals them, yet Sarah remains childless.

GENESIS 21:1–25:18

ISAAC

Setting Up the Section

Chapters 21–25 offer the accounts of Isaac's birth and Abraham's death. This period of time is the beginning of the fulfillment of God's promise that Abraham would father a nation.

21:1–34

ISAAC'S BIRTH

Verses 1–7 record the birth of Isaac. Upon the birth of Isaac, Abraham immediately obeys by calling the boy *Isaac* (17:19; 21:3). *Isaac* means "he laughs," or "may [God] smile." Abraham also obeys God by circumcising his son on the eighth day (21:4). This was God's command to Abraham and His covenant with him (see 17:7–14).

In 21:6–7, the scene shifts to Sarah, alluding to her laughter of unbelief when the Lord announced that she would give birth (18:10–15). In verses 8–9, the Egyptian Hagar again has a role in the narrative. Fourteen years earlier, Hagar had given birth to Ishmael, and for most of the intervening period, Abraham had treated Ishmael as the heir. By this point Ishmael is a teenager.

At Sarah's demand that Abraham banish Ishmael (21:10), Abraham receives a direct word from God for the sixth time since coming to the land of Canaan (21:11–13).

Take It Home

When Abraham slept with Hagar, he actually was following an accepted custom of the day. But it certainly appears in retrospect that it was an act of unbelief. God had promised an heir, and this was a way to help God's promise along. In sending Ishmael away, Abraham faced the consequences of that act of unbelief. His story stands as a reminder to trust God to fulfill His promises.

Verses 15–16 describe the plight of an ancient single mother without the support of family or friends. While Hagar does cry out to God, it is the boy's cries that God hears. This offers special meaning to the fact that *Ishmael* means "God hears" (16:11; 21:17–19).

The account closes with an example of God's sovereignty and compassion. Even though Hagar suffers, her need for support is met (21:17–21). God does not forget His promise to greatly multiply her descendants (16:10). God has compassion on Hagar's plight and becomes like a father to Ishmael.

At verse 22, Abimelech reenters the account, arriving with his enforcer, Phicol, to sign a treaty with Abraham (21:22–24). The term *Phicol* may be a title rather than a proper name. The same name is used in Genesis 26:26 of Abraham's military commander.

In contrast to Abraham's previous fear of Abimelech, he now boldly stands up to this powerful king. Abraham brings up the matter of the well that Abimelech's servants had seized from him (21:24–26). Wells were of extreme importance to seminomadic people like Abraham. The Hebrew verb translated *complained* implies that Abraham had to complain several times.

In their last conflict, it is Abimelech who models generosity, sending Abraham away with gifts (20:14–16). Here, Abraham returns the favor in a small way (21:28–30). Abraham and Abimelech also show great patience with each other.

The passage concludes with the men naming the well *Beersheba*. By granting Abraham rights to a well, Abimelech has made it possible for Abraham to live there permanently and acknowledged his legal right, at least to water.

By planting a tree, Abraham indicates his determination to stay in that region. Tamarisk trees were long-lived and evergreen. The tree is meant to be a lasting landmark to God's provision and a focal point of Abraham's worship. It serves as an appropriate symbol of the enduring grace of the faithful God (21:33).

The Hebrew phrase translated *eternal God* is only used here and carries with it a distinction for this account. This name stresses God's never-ending nature. God's promises and covenant are everlasting because God Himself is eternal. This perhaps reflects growth in Abraham's understanding of God.

Abraham now owns a small part of the land God promised him.

22:1–24

AN OFFERING

In Genesis 22, we come to one of the greatest crisis chapters in the Bible—the crisis of obedience.

Notice in verse 1 that God tested Abraham. There is a vast difference between God's purpose in testing a person and Satan's purpose in testing a person. God tests to confirm and strengthen; Satan tests to corrupt and weaken.

God makes His impossible demands. The repetition of the word *son* and *only son* reiterates the severe nature of this test. This same term can refer to an infant (Exodus 2:6) or a young man (1 Chronicles 12:28). Abraham obeys God's commands immediately and unquestioningly (Genesis 22:3–4).

The name of the land, *Moriah*, means "where the Lord provides," or "where the Lord appears." It was a three-day journey from Beersheba to Moriah, about fifty miles (22:2–4).

In the biblical world, three days was a typical period of preparation for something important (for example, Genesis 42:17–18; Exodus 19:10–11; Numbers 31:19; Esther 5:1; Hosea 6:2; Matthew 12:40; 1 Corinthians 15:4).

This site is the location where the temple was later built (2 Chronicles 3:1).

In Genesis 22:5–8, we see that Abraham's obedience is based on faith. He believes God will provide the sacrifice. The word *worship* in verse 5 means "to bow oneself close to the ground."

In 22:9–10, we see that Abraham's obedience is thorough and complete. Keep in mind, though, that Abraham could not have offered Isaac without Isaac's consent and cooperation. Isaac, as the bearer of the wood, is the stronger of the two. As a young man he is also the faster of the two. Clearly, he is strong enough and big enough to resist or subdue his father.

Verses 11–12 don't imply that God is just now learning that Abraham fears Him. God is omniscient. The angel of the Lord is saying to Abraham, "By your faithful actions I experientially know that you fear God." The language is accommodated to the human understanding, uttered, as it were, from a human point of view.

Critical Observation

Verse 15 is the final recorded instance of God speaking to Abraham. God spoke directly to Abraham eight times (12:1, 7; 13:14; 15:1; 17:1; 18:1; 21:12; 22:1, 15).

Abraham's obedience is rewarded in three ways. First, God provides the very thing He demands from Abraham (22:13–14). Fittingly, Abraham names this place "The Lord will provide." Second, God provides assurances of His promises (22:15–19). It is unusual for God to speak with an oath. Abraham's supreme act of obedience draws forth God's supreme assurance of blessing. Finally, God provides for future needs (22:20–24). The narrative closes with the happy news that Abraham's brother Nahor has become the father of twelve sons. They will later become the ancestors of twelve Aramean tribes. Most of the other names in this genealogy are the ancestors of cities and tribes around Israel. They are precisely the peoples who are to be blessed through Abraham's offspring. The central purpose of this list is to introduce the future bride of Isaac, Rebekah (22:23).

Take It Home

Remember, total obedience is not only measured by what you give God; God also takes into account what you keep for yourself. Can God get close to the most important things in your life—your possessions, business, plans and dreams, and relationships? Are you willing to let go (Luke 14:26–27)? Sometimes the supreme test of our faith will be a matter of putting obedience to God above something we have lived for all of our lives. Sometimes it will involve something that might seem foolish and ridiculous to everyone else. Are you willing to be sacrificially obedient to God in every area of your life?

23:1–20

SARAH'S DEATH

The first two verses of Genesis 23 record Sarah's death, and the next eighteen verses have to do with the purchase of the plot where Sarah is buried. The focus of this story is that Sarah is buried in Canaan (23:2, 19), and that Abraham goes to great lengths and cost to make this a certainty. This demonstrates how Abraham's actions reflect a faith for the future.

As commentators over the centuries have noted, Sarah is the only woman in the Bible whose age is revealed (23:1). Sarah is also the only woman whose name God changes (17:15).

Sarah dies in Hebron, the center of the land of promise (23:2). Kiriah Arba was its original name, named after Arba, the greatest man of the Anakites, a frightening group of warriors (Joshua 14:15).

Abraham mourns and weeps, indicating that, in addition to crying, he goes through the traditional mourning customs of his day: tearing clothes, cutting his beard, spreading dust on his head, and fasting. This is all done in the presence of the dead body. The Israelites had a very elaborate and intense process that they went through when someone died (23:2). This is the first record of a man's tears in the Bible.

In verses 3–5, some English translations (ESV, NIV, NRSV) render the Hebrew term *Heth* as *Hittites* (also in Genesis 23:5, 7, 10, 16, 18, 20), but this gives the impression that these people are the Hittites of Anatolia. However, there is no known connection between these sons of Heth, who are apparently a Canaanite group and the Hittites of Anatolia. The sons of Heth call Abraham a mighty prince. Apparently, Abraham's influence and reputation has spread (21:22–23).

Demystifying Genesis

The ancient Israelites placed great importance in the location of their own and family members' burial sites. It was normally important to be buried in one's homeland. Verses 20–24 remind us that Abraham and Sarah's family roots were in Ur (11:31). Despite the importance of burial location, family roots, and Abraham's current alien status, he insists on burying Sarah in Canaan, even though doing so is costly. Why? Because Abraham is not looking backward to where he came from, nor is he looking at his present situation—living in a tent because he does not possess even one acre of the promised land. Abraham is looking forward.

In Abraham's day, bargaining was done from a seated position. When Abraham stands, it signals something important. Abraham has a specific grave in mind. Abraham, in faith, wishes to stake his claim in the promised land by buying a cave used traditionally as a tomb. The sons of Heth are currently in control of this area of Canaan, so Abraham makes the request of them (23:7–11).

Critical Observation

Even though Ephron offers to give Abraham the land free of charge, he still places value on the "gift" that he offers. It is extortion, pure and simple. All Abraham wants is the cave, but Ephron adds the field. More real estate, more money! Ephron is certainly not being generous to a grieving man. In fact, the price and terms of the sale indicate that Ephron is greedy and unfair. This cave of Macphelah is very well attested to archaeologically. Abraham was buried there, Sarah was buried there, and their children were buried there. Currently a mosque stands on the burial site.

Sarah's grave is the first mentioned in scripture. Later, Abraham is buried there (25:8–9), and so are Isaac, Jacob, Rebekah, and Leah (49:30–33; 50:13). The crucial element in this chapter is not Sarah's death, but Abraham's acquisition of land from outsiders.

24:1–67

ISAAC'S MARRIAGE

Genesis 24 contains a great love story. The Lord, who never speaks in this chapter, is nevertheless the main character. He is mentioned seventeen times (24:1).

The threefold description in verse 2 leads many to the conclusion that this servant is Eliezer, who is mentioned in Genesis 15:2, and whose name means "God of help" or "helper."

The oath Abraham makes with his servant seems a little bizarre, as does the servant's placing his hand under Abraham's thigh. Yet this is customary in Abraham's day (see also 47:29).

Abraham's mind-set seems to be that it is better to have no wife than to have a Canaanite wife. In the Old Testament period, the family is the most important educational unit (Deuteronomy 6:6–7; Proverbs 1:8).

A point of tension arises when the servant asks if Isaac can go to the land to meet his future wife (Genesis 24:5). It's a legitimate question. What Abraham is seeking to do requires blind faith from any woman; leave home to marry a man sight unseen. Nevertheless, twice Abraham warns his servant not to take Isaac back to Ur (24:6, 8). Abraham knows God has called him out of Ur and has promised him abundant descendants and land, so he is willing to trust the Lord in whatever He chooses to do.

Verse 10 begins a new section. The description of the servant's travels actually encompasses hundreds of miles and several months, as the servant assembles a caravan and makes his way to Mesopotamia. The city of Nahor could refer to a city by that name, or could simply mean that Abraham's brother Nahor lives there. The servant's arrival at the proper place is all a part of the divine blessing. God's hand is in the events of this story.

Although a number of English translations understand the servant's prayer as a request for success in the task (24:12 NASB, NIV, NRSV), many feel that it is more likely that the servant is requesting an omen or sign from God (24:14). Culturally, it was a normal act of hospitality to provide water to thirsty travelers. But providing water for ten thirsty camels was going far beyond what would normally be expected (24:13–14). In praying this prayer, the servant actually stacks the deck against finding someone. It would take a remarkable woman to volunteer for this lowly and backbreaking task.

Verses 15–21 record Rebekah's appearance and her family connections; they also record that she does exactly what the servant had prayed, exhibiting a servant's heart by going beyond his request and watering his camels.

Critical Observation

A typical ancient well was a large, deep hole in the earth with steps leading down to the spring water. Each drawing of water required substantial effort. Camels can consume up to twenty-five gallons of water in ten minutes, and the servant had ten camels with him. One more fact: A typical water jar held about three gallons of water. All of this together means Rebekah made many descents into the well. Her labors could have taken well over an hour.

Verses 22–27 point out the obvious: God is behind the scenes but directing the acts. God sovereignly works through the circumstances of those who are acting in faith.

Rebekah returns home and shares everything with her family (24:28–33). The servant's urgency is evident since he considers his master's business more important than the food his hosts place before him.

Critical Observation

A third tension-filled episode occurs in 24:34–49, as the servant seeks to obtain the approval of Rebekah's family. Genesis 24, as a whole, is an excellent example of the ancient storyteller's art. In those days people enjoyed repetition—in fact, they preferred it—as they listened to tales or read them. Far from being signs of inept editing or dual authorship, the servant's repetition of the details that leads up to his search are probably deliberately employed as effective literary devices.

In 24:50–54, the tension is resolved by the family's approval. Again, the servant responds appropriately by bowing to the ground in worship and gratitude. The gifts the servant offers (24:53) may have been the bride price, which would finalize the agreement.

Abraham's servant does not want to delay his leaving, which presents a difficult choice for Rebekah. She would leave her family and everything familiar and go away with a man whom she had just met in order to marry another man whom she had never seen (24:55–61). Rebekah's courageous willingness seems to be another testimony to God's leadership in this situation.

The scene now switches to where Isaac lives and meditates. This is a place where God has previously answered the prayer of Hagar, Sarah's handmaiden, after she became pregnant with Abraham's son, Ishmael (16:14; 24:62). Since Ishmael and Isaac are pitted against each other, this is an ironic twist in the account.

A final episode of tension is found in 24:62–67. The question is: How will Isaac and Rebekah respond to each other? After a play-by-play of their initial encounter, verse 67 says Isaac loves Rebekah.

Ultimately, this entire story is about God's faithfulness. He protects and guides the servant on his journey, and He brings Rebekah, along with just the right servant-spirit, at just the right time. From our historical perspective centuries later, we can see how God used the remarkable obedience of a few family members to accomplish His purposes.

25:1–18

ABRAHAM'S DEATH

Before he dies, Abraham passes on his legacy: the promises he received from God. According to verses 2–4, the six sons that Abraham has with Keturah become the descendants of several Far East tribes.

Abraham wills everything he owns to Isaac, because he is the legal firstborn. But while he is alive, he honors his other sons with gifts (25:5–6).

Genesis 25:7–11 relates the account of Abraham's death. The reference to a full life carries the idea of a sense of satisfaction.

Demystifying Genesis

In the Old Testament, those who have already died are regarded as still existing. The event of being "gathered to one's people" is always distinguished from the act of burial, which is described separately (35:29; 49:29, 31, 33). In many cases, only one ancestor was in the tomb (1 Kings 11:43; 22:40), or there were none at all (Deuteronomy 31:16; 1 Kings 2:10; 16:28; 2 Kings 21:18), so the idea of being gathered to one's people or joining one's ancestors does not mean being laid in the family sepulcher.

Abraham is buried in the field that he purchased from Ephron the Hittite (Genesis 23:1–20; 25:9–10), once again affirming that he believed God would grant the land to Abraham's descendants.

Isaac dwelt near Beer-Lahai-Roi, which means "well of the living One who sees me" (25:11). Here, God delivers Hagar (see 16:14), and Isaac has come to meditate as he awaits Rebekah (24:62). Isaac later prays again, this time for his barren wife (25:21).

Critical Observation

In between the major sections of Genesis dealing with Abraham (11:27–25:11), Jacob (25:19–35:29), and Joseph (37:2–50:20), there are smaller sections dealing with Ishmael (25:12–18) and Esau (36:1–37:1). Genesis 25:12–18 looks briefly at Ishmael before continuing the story.

In this small passage about Ishmael, there is reference to God's promise that twelve princes will be born to Ishmael (17:20). God had pronounced that Ishmael would live in hostility toward his brothers (16:12). The description in verse 18 of Ishmael's descendants seems to confirm that pattern.

Like his father, Abraham, Ishmael is also gathered to his people, indicating that he is a believer in God and shares in the spiritual blessings of all who die in the faith (25:17).

GENESIS 25:19–36:43

ISAAC'S FAMILY

Twins: Esau and Jacob	25:19–34
Isaac and Abimelech	26:1–35
Jacob's Blessing	27:1–28:9
Jacob's Departure	28:10–30:43
Jacob's Return	31:1–35:29
Esau	36:1–43

Setting Up the Section

The entire book of Genesis emphasizes the sovereignty of God and the wisdom of His "delays." Chapters 26–36 trace this sovereignty through the generation following Isaac. The struggles that Jacob and Esau face, as described in retrospect in Genesis, reveal God's plan rising to the surface against the odds.

25:19–34

TWINS: ESAU AND JACOB

Just as Sarah before her, and Rachel after her, (29:31; 30:1–2), Rebekah seems unable to provide the male heir that was so important to this ancient culture—despite the promise God made to Abraham, Isaac's father, to give him a nation of descendants. At this point, twenty years have passed since Isaac and Rebekah married. Isaac is approaching sixty.

The word used to describe Isaac's prayer does not connote a simple formality of prayer; instead, it implies a fervent plea (25:21). Out of that plea, Rebekah becomes pregnant with twins (25:22). Jewish legends say the twins, eventually named Jacob and Esau, tried to kill each other in the womb. According to some of the legends, every time Rebekah went near an idol's altar, Esau would get excited in the womb, and when she went near a place where the Lord was worshiped, Jacob would get excited.

More than legend, though, the words describing the struggle of the twins in Rebekah's womb carry the idea that they smashed themselves inside her. In retrospect, this struggle of the children foreshadows the fact that these twins would father conflicting nations. And, we learn in verse 23, the older son will serve the younger.

Critical Observation

This idea of the younger serving the older appears in several places in scripture:

- The offering of Cain, the older brother, is rejected, whereas the offering of the younger brother, Abel, is accepted (4:1–5).
- The line of Seth, the younger brother of Cain, is the chosen line (4:26–5:8).
- Isaac is chosen over his older brother, Ishmael (17:18–19).
- Rachel is chosen over her older sister, Leah (29:18).
- Joseph, the younger brother, is chosen over all the rest of Jacob's sons (37:3).

The intention behind each of these reversals is the recurring theme of God's sovereign plan of grace. The blessings given to these younger sons and daughters are not the natural rights of the firstborn. Instead, they are blessings associated with the call of God.

At last the twins are born. Esau's name means "hairy one"; Jacob's name means "God will protect." The Hebrew word for *Jacob* is similar to "heel," reminiscent of Jacob grasping Esau's heel during the birth. From this comes the nickname "heel holder," which has a connotation of a wrestling term, but also indicates a scoundrel. While Esau's name reflects his appearance, Jacob's name later comes to reflect his character.

There's a contrast right at the beginning between these two twins—one is outdoorsy while the other prefers a more orderly life (25:27). According to verse 28, Isaac and Rebekah each have a favorite. The verb translated *love* is indicative of favor, choice, and preference.

Isaac knows God's desire to pass on the physical and spiritual blessing of the inheritance to Jacob, but he fails to obey God's will.

Verses 29–34 recount the well-known story of Esau's trading his birthright for some stew. In the original Hebrew, there is a bit more texture revealed in this account than in modern English. Esau's so-called request is actually a forceful demand. Not only does Esau demand food, but he demands to devour it. The word translated *swallow*, or better yet, *gulp down*, is a word that normally describes the feeding of cattle.

Jacob's counterdemand, on the other hand, suggests that he has long premeditated his act and is exploiting his brother's weakness.

Demystifying Genesis

What is the birthright, and why does Jacob want it so badly (25:32–33)? Deuteronomy 21:17 and 1 Chronicles 5:1–2 tell us the birthright involves both a material and a spiritual blessing. The son of the birthright receives a double portion of the inheritance, and he also becomes head of the family and the spiritual leader upon the passing of the father (Genesis 43:33). And, in the case of this family, the birthright determines who will inherit the covenant God made with Abraham—the covenant of a land, a nation, and the Messiah.

26:1–35

ISAAC AND ABIMELECH

Genesis 26 is the only chapter of Genesis devoted exclusively to Isaac. While he is mentioned in other chapters, he is not the focus of attention. Here Isaac's life is summed up in the events described, all of which have a striking parallel in the life of his father, Abraham.

Isaac travels to Gerar to escape a famine (26:1–6). Gerar is the same place Abraham and Sarah went after the destruction of Sodom and Gomorrah (20:1). It was in the land of the Philistines. While in Gerar, or perhaps even before, Isaac decides to go down to Egypt just as his father had done (12:10–20).

When the Lord appears to Isaac to instruct him not to go to Egypt, He uses the same covenant language that He had used with Abraham (12:1–3; 13:14–17; 15:18–21; 17:6–8, 16; 22:17–18).

In verse 5, the word *because* seems to suggest that Abraham received the covenant as a result of works, yet nothing could be further from the truth. Granted, for Abraham and Isaac to enjoy the practical benefits of the covenant, obedience was imperative, but the covenant would be upheld despite their unfaithfulness.

The charge that Abraham kept was the office of patriarch and leader of God's people. The commandment included the mandate to leave Ur and to separate from family and land. The statutes include the rite of circumcision, and the laws refer to the practice of righteousness. Together, these terms reveal Abraham's wholehearted obedience.

Critical Observation

Chronologically, Genesis 26 precedes Genesis 25:21–34. For another example of this, see Genesis 10–11 (table of nations and tower of Babel). If Isaac and Rebekah had Jacob and Esau by this point, the fact that they were husband and wife would have been obvious. Here, the promised seed is with Isaac and Rebekah, but no child has yet been born.

Verses 7–11 continue the parallel between Isaac's and Abraham's lives: Isaac lies about Rebekah's identity out of a fear for his own survival. The Abimelech mentioned in verse 8 is probably the son, or even the grandson, of the Abimelech who ruled over Gerar in Abraham's time (20:2).

The parallel between Isaac's life and that of his father is again evident in this account of the disputes over the wells (26:12–22). Due to their growth, Abraham and Isaac need much room for their flocks, as well as a source of water. Prosperity had brought contention between Lot's herdsmen and those of Abraham (13:5), just as it has between Isaac's herdsmen and the herdsmen of Gerar. Isaac, like his father, chooses to keep the peace by giving preference to the other party.

The names of the wells in verses 20–22 reflect the situations. *Esek* means "argument" in Hebrew, a reminder of the conflict its discovery created. *Sitnah* comes from a Hebrew verbal root meaning "to oppose; to be an adversary," and signals that the digging of this well causes opposition from the Philistines. *Rehoboth* comes from a verbal root meaning "to make room," and reminds all how God has made room for them. Since he finally has a well that is uncontested, Isaac might logically have decided to stay there. Instead, he moves on to Beersheba (26:23).

We read in 26:23–25 that God appears to Isaac in Beersheba (His second revelation), calming Isaac's fears and reviewing the promises He had given previously (26:2–5). Isaac's response is to build an altar, worship the Lord, and settle down there. These verses seem to confirm the fact that Isaac's decision to move out of Philistine territory pleased God.

This account in Isaac's life closes with good news in verses 26–33. Abimelech again testifies to God's blessing of Isaac and gives God glory.

Critical Observation

Like many biblical passages, the next section of scripture has bookends. Two reports of Esau's pagan marriages (26:34–35 and 28:6–9) frame the major account regarding Isaac (27:1–28:5). These Esau accounts provide a kind of prologue and epilogue. The main account then centers on Isaac's giving the blessing to Jacob.

Genesis 26:34–35 is best read as an introduction to Genesis 27. Esau marries at age forty, just as his father Isaac did (25:20). Esau, however, marries two Hittite women from the land of Canaan (36:2).

Abraham had warned his servant not to take a wife for Isaac from among the wicked Canaanites, who would not give up their gods for their husbands (24:3). Thus, the servant finds Rebekah from the country and family of Abraham (chapter 24). Note that Isaac seems to have had no hand in Esau's wife-taking, though Esau is, at one point, his favorite son, according to Genesis 25:28. Compare this with Isaac's own experience with his father, Abraham, who sent a servant five hundred miles to get a suitable wife for Isaac (24:1).

27:1–28:9

JACOB'S BLESSING

This lengthy passage is like a theatrical play in five scenes, though these scenes are broken down differently by different commentators.

- **Act One: Isaac Asks Esau for a Meal (27:1–4)**

In the willfulness of his old age, Isaac is determined to pass on the blessing to Esau, despite what the Lord has said (25:23) and what the boys have shown with their lives. The fact that he attempts to make this transaction—which should have been a family event—without the knowledge of his wife, Rebekah, and his son, Jacob, compounds his sin.

Isaac's insistence on a good meal before the blessing recalls Esau's own trading of the birthright for a pot of stew, and thus casts Isaac in a similar role to that of Esau (25:27–34).

Critical Observation

The words *my son* and *here I am*, which also appear along with the words *my father* in Genesis 27:18, set this story up as a parody of Genesis 22:1–19, where the same words are used. In the Genesis 22 story, both Abraham and his young son, Isaac, employ the words *here I am* to convey trusting availability. Abraham obeys God, and Isaac obeys Abraham. Here Isaac takes the role of God but orders an unholy dish of food instead of a holy sacrifice. Esau is the obedient son in Isaac's ill-conceived plan, which blows up in both of their faces.

- **<u>Act Two:</u> Rebekah's Scheme (27:5–17)**

In 27:5–10, the story intensifies. The word used to describe Rebekah's listening suggests that this is a habit, a pattern of behavior, not happenstance. Her behavior gives us an idea of the level of mistrust and poor communication in the family.

Critical Observation

The plan is carried out with garments and the skins of goats. Jacob himself would later be deceived when his sons dip the garment of Joseph, his favorite son, in the blood of a goat to make him think Joseph has been killed (27:16; 37:31–33).

Rebekah, not Jacob, is the mastermind behind the plot to outwit Isaac and obtain his blessing for Jacob, a plot that seems to reveal some forethought. She volunteers to absorb any curse that Jacob will incur (25:13). This would be impossible, of course, but it reveals her sense of urgency.

- **<u>Act Three:</u> Jacob's Esau Imitation (27:18–29)**

The relationship between Jacob and Esau is like a boxing match. The first round occurs at birth (25:21–28), and the second round is over the birthright (25:29–34). Here we have the third round of Jacob's battle with Esau. In all three rounds, Jacob manipulates his brother.

In this scenario, who is deceiving whom? On one hand, Jacob is definitely deceiving his father, Isaac. However, Isaac—because he thinks Jacob is really Esau—thinks he is deceiving Jacob by giving the blessing to Esau. Both intend to deceive the other, yet only Jacob succeeds. Even through this act of deception, God's will is done, and the family blessing continues through Jacob.

Jacob has already received the blessing of the promised land through the birthright that he obtained. In Genesis 27:28, Isaac blesses Jacob with fruitfulness in the promised land (Deuteronomy 7:13). The dew of heaven provides irrigation. The fatness of the earth is rain. Grain and new wine evoke the image of a banquet, overflowing with joy (Psalm 4:7).

Isaac also blesses Jacob with dominion over the nations and his family. The people and nations refer specifically to the Gentile people and nations. He is also granted dominion over Rebekah's descendants through Esau, who would also become Gentiles. The curses and blessings equate to God's protection and are particularly linked to dominion (Numbers 24:9).

- **<u>Act Four:</u> Esau's Horror and Revenge (27:30–45)**

When Esau discovers the ruse, he is enraged. Once the blessing was given, it had the force of a legal contract and could not be revoked.

The two losses that Rebekah feared may have been Isaac's death and then Jacob's death at the hand of Esau, or Jacob's death at the hand of Esau, then Esau's necessary departure.

- **<u>Act Five:</u> Jacob's Departure (27:46–28:9)**

When Rebekah fears for Jacob's life, she manipulates Isaac into sending Jacob away. In effect, she gives Isaac a cover story. Her real goal is to protect him, not to find him a wife. Isaac agrees, calling Jacob to his side, repeating the Abrahamic blessing, and sending him off to Haran to find a wife.

In one sense, the plot to receive the blessing from Isaac is a great success. However, in another sense, it is a terrible failure. Jacob receives the blessing, but he has to leave the inheritance with Esau.

The best move that Esau could think of reveals his character. Given that he has already displeased his parents by marrying Hittite brides, he disappoints them further by marrying an Ishmaelite to bring into the family. The families of Isaac and Ishmael have been in contention since Isaac received Abraham's blessing rather than Ishmael (17:18–20; 25:14–18).

28:10–30:43

JACOB'S OTHER LIFE

Jacob's journey retraces the steps of his grandfather, Abraham, who came from Haran to the promised land many years before. It is natural that Jacob's mother, Rebekah, would think of Haran when she cast about for a safe haven for her wayward younger son. The trek from Beersheba to Haran was far enough that Esau wouldn't follow Jacob there. Yet there was family at Haran, so Jacob wouldn't be alone.

The two most significant events in the life of Jacob are the visitations from God, both while he is sleeping. The first visitation happens in a dream. Angels are taking messages from earth up to heaven, and messages from heaven down to earth, on some kind of stairway, though the Hebrew word for *ladder* is used here (28:13–15).

The stairway is reminiscent of the tower of Babel, in which rebel humanity attempted to build a tower that reached into heaven (11:4). The ladder in Jacob's dream, by contrast, brought heaven to earth.

Jacob wakes up amazed by his experience, sure that the God of his fathers is the source of it (28:16–17). He had received the blessing passed down from his grandfather, Abraham. Why does Jacob raise a pillar and not just build an altar like his grandfather, Abraham? Perhaps it is a connection with the stairway in his dream. Nevertheless, Jacob is acknowledging God. Pouring oil on the pillar constitutes an act of consecration. The pillar becomes a monument marking the place and the event. The name given to the place means "house of God."

Jacob's vow is understood by some to be another form of his scheming nature (28:20–22).

Others suggest that he is simply making a commitment, acknowledging the need for God's help in order to keep that commitment.

After many days of traveling, Jacob arrives in Haran. He plans to stay there a few months, find a wife, and then return home to Beersheba. Little does he know that Haran will be his home for twenty long years.

The phrase describing Jacob's journey carries the suggestion that Jacob has a new lease on life now that God has promised him the blessing he had so desperately tried to gain by his own efforts.

In Haran, Jacob meets Rachel and her family. She is attractive and is a shepherdess in her own right, a sign of wealth in this era (29:9, 17).

According to verse 11, after Jacob meets Rachel, he kisses her. Most likely, he kisses her on both cheeks, a traditional greeting. However, it is worth adding that this appears to be the only case in the Bible of a man kissing a woman who is not his mother or wife. So it is possible that this was more than just a "holy" kiss.

According to verses 12–15, Jacob works for Rachel's father, Laban, for over a month before they negotiate any payment for Jacob's labor.

Verses 16–17 introduce Laban's other daughter, Leah. In Hebrew, *Leah* means "cow," and *Rachel* means "ewe lamb." There is some mystery regarding Leah's eyes. A few English translations understand Leah's eyes to be her best quality, so they translate the Hebrew word for "soft" (*rak*) as *lovely* (NRSV), *pretty* (NLT), or *delicate* (NKJV). However, most scholars suggest that Leah's eyes are a detriment in some way. The point is, she does not measure up to her gorgeous sister.

In 29:18–20, we learn that Jacob offers to work for seven years to earn the right to marry Rachel. Verse 20 is often misunderstood. It doesn't necessarily mean that the time passed quickly. More likely it means that the price seems insignificant when compared to what he is getting in return.

Finally, the wedding ceremony takes place (29:21–25), but Jacob wakes up with the wrong sister. According to contemporary Western customs, no man could be fooled in this way. The most likely explanation is that when Laban brings his daughter, Leah, to Jacob, it is late and dark, and she is veiled from head to toe. It seems that the wedding feast hosted by Laban is an intentional ploy to dull Jacob's senses with wine (29:22). We are not given information as to Rachel's and Leah's roles or even perspectives on the situation, but Genesis 30 leads one to conclude that sisterly jealousy is part of this deception. Laban's explanation that he must see his firstborn daughter marry first seems ironically appropriate in this story. Jacob had dishonored the principle of the firstborn by cheating his brother out of the birthright and the blessing. Now, God forces him to honor the principle he had violated by marrying Leah first. The deceiver is deceived. God trains Jacob by allowing him to meet his own sins in someone else.

Jacob receives Rachel seven days after he consummated his marriage to Leah (29:28–30). Jacob marries two women in eight days.

When verse 31 refers to Leah as unloved, this does not mean that Jacob hates her, but rather that he loves her less than Rachel. Leah's becoming a mother ensures that her importance will increase in Jacob's estimation, as well as in the estimation of her family and society in general.

The name of her firstborn, *Reuben*, means "see, a son" (29:32). The name of her second born, *Simeon*, means "hear" or "listen" (29:34). The name of her third born, *Levi*, means "attached" or "associated" (29:34). Levi is an influential child. The tribe of Levi supplies the royal priesthood (Numbers 3:5–13). The name of her fourth born, Judah, means "praise." The Messiah would come through the line of Judah (29:35).

Demystifying Genesis

Is Jacob's situation a case for multiple wives? Not necessarily. It is a description of the facts as they happened. There are other men in the Bible who took more than one wife, including the notable examples of King David and King Solomon. Exodus 21:10–11 also makes provision for the first wife if a man takes another wife. There is no text that presents multiple spouses as God's preference, though it is an accepted custom in some cultures. Jacob's life story stands more as a testimony against the practice. His wives are in conflict over their shared husband throughout the account.

Chapter 30 begins with a dramatic moment: Although her husband loves her, Rachel does not consider her life worth living without children. Jacob responds in anger. In fact, the word translated *anger* here is quite graphic. It means "to breathe hard, be enraged, flare the nostrils." Jacob's anger is heated as he, in essence, says Rachel's childlessness is not his fault.

Rachel's solution is an ancient custom that allows an infertile woman to offer her female servant as a wife, then claim the child of this union as her own. This is culturally acceptable and completely legal, and, in fact, it was a solution that had been employed by Abraham and Sarah, Jacob's grandparents (16:1–3; 20:4).

When Bilhah, the servant, becomes pregnant, Rachel falsely assumes that God is pleased with her schemes. She adopts Bilhah's first two sons as her own.

Since Leah is no longer conceiving, according to 30:9–13, Leah offers her maid, Zilpah, to Jacob to increase their brood. This joining provides two sons: Gad, whose name means "fortune," and Asher, whose name means "happy."

The story shifts gears in 30:14–21. Little Reuben comes upon some mandrakes, a plant that bears bluish flowers in winter and yellowish, plum-size fruit in summer. In ancient times, mandrakes were reputed as aphrodisiacs (Song of Solomon 7:13) and for aiding in conception. The fruit was even called "love apples." Leah gives Rachel the mandrakes in exchange for nights with Jacob. Thus, Leah's fifth and sixth sons are born, and finally a daughter.

Critical Observation

Rachel, who takes the mandrakes, remains barren for three more years; Leah, who doesn't have the mandrakes, has three more kids. She has a total of seven children—the number of perfection. This is more than the other three women in this story. However, she never receives what she desires most—Jacob's love. Leah spends years trying to win her husband's approval, but it never happens. She spends the rest of her life in a loveless marriage, even though she has half of the sons who would be the fathers of half the tribes of Israel.

In this story, both women want what the other has. Leah feels that having sons for Jacob will somehow earn his love, while Rachel is as desperate for children as Sarah had been before her.

This particular portion of the story concludes in 30:22–24. After fourteen years, Rachel conceives a son named Joseph. The theme of the entire narrative is the movement from barrenness (29:31) to birth (30:22). For all the maneuverings of the sisters, it is still God who opens the womb.

After the birth of Joseph, Jacob asks to be released from Laban's authority. Unlike today, Jacob could not simply pack his bags and leave. The authority structure in this Eastern, extended family is far more complex and restrictive–as it is still today in some Eastern cultures. There is a shared ownership of Jacob's wives and children. To leave without his father-in-law's permission and blessing could lead to outright war within the family clan.

Jacob had been living with Laban in Paddan-aram for twenty years (31:38). For fourteen years, he had worked for Laban, keeping his agreement in exchange for Laban's two daughters (29:30; 31:41). Another six years elapse before Jacob finally makes the break. During that time, eleven sons and one daughter are born.

Laban is averse to Jacob's leaving, not because he loves his nephew, or son-in-law, but because he knows his prosperity is dependent on Jacob's presence.

Jacob lets Laban know rather candidly that it doesn't call for an act of divination to discover why he has experienced material prosperity. It is fairly obvious that this is the product of a combination of factors–Jacob's faithfulness and hard work and God's favor and blessing resting upon him (19:29–30).

Verses 31–33 suggest that Jacob has prepared for this moment. Why the speckled and spotted sheep and goats? It is a foolproof way to distinguish between the flocks of Laban and Jacob. It appears to favor Laban, since goats in the Middle East are generally black or dark brown (Song of Solomon 4:1), and the sheep are nearly always white (Psalm 147:16; Song of Solomon 4:2; 6:6; Daniel 7:9). It gives Jacob an opportunity to put his trust in God. And as we'll discover in Genesis 31, Jacob selects the spotted and speckled because of the Lord's instruction (31:10). Furthermore, Jacob's dream from God ensures him that the Lord will protect him from the dishonesty of Laban.

From every angle it seems a great deal for Laban, yet Laban's actions in verses 35–36 are an attempt to make sure Jacob does not get even the speckled animals.

Jacob counters with a plan from God. It was generally believed that, by placing the kind of visuals described here before the animals as they were mating, it was possible to influence the appearance of their offspring (30:37–43). Interestingly, the Hebrew words for *poplar* and *white* are puns on the name *Laban*, which means "white."

31:1–35:29

JACOB'S RETURN

Jacob's plan seems to be working (30:37–43), and both Laban and his sons are unhappy about Jacob's growing herds. Essentially, Laban's sons are accusing Jacob of stealing their inheritance. From their perspective, it is disappearing right before their eyes. As a result, they become envious and bitter toward Jacob. Laban also treats Jacob differently.

The last recorded revelation that Jacob received from God was twenty years earlier, while he was still in the land of promise (28:10–22). God had promised to bring Jacob back to the land (28:15); now, at last, God gives Jacob the divine directive to return to the promised land (31:3).

Jacob lays out the facts to Rachel and Leah about Laban—the family tension and the unhealthy work environment—and God's divine providence (31:4–13). Despite Jacob's challenges, God proves Himself faithful.

Rachel and Leah agree with Jacob's assessment. Seven times in 31:4–16, Jacob and his wives mention God by name. The sisters uncharacteristically agree and submit themselves to Jacob's leadership. After all, their father Laban had stolen their inheritance, treated them like foreigners, sold them, and used up the money from their dowry.

So the trip begins. It was nearly three hundred miles from Haran to the mountains of Gilead. Jacob travels with the knowledge that Laban might be pursuing him from behind in order to kill him, and Esau, his brother, might be waiting ahead, also wanting to kill him.

Jacob and Rachel deceive Laban in their departure (31:19–21). Rachel steals his household idols while he is busy at work shearing his sheep. These idols are small figurines (probably 2–3 inches long) used in divination and to bring good luck. Why does she steal them? No exact reason is given, but it may have been simply for protection and "luck," which would have revealed some attachment to the religion of her father.

Critical Observation

It is curious that Rachel—the wife he most loved and wanted—most often turns out to be Jacob's greatest hindrance. In spite of the fact that Rachel has a growing trust in God, she is reluctant to make a complete break from her idolatrous past.

Jacob leaves without informing Laban. Jacob is doing God's will by returning to the land of promise, but he is not doing it in God's way.

Laban catches up to Jacob, a journey that takes seven days since Jacob had a three-day head start. It is interesting that God reveals Himself to Laban, a man who, thus far in this account, has not expressed the kind of faith we associate with messages from God (31:22–55). God will accomplish His purposes in whatever way is necessary.

After an uneventful search in which Rachel sits on the idols to hide them, Jacob unleashes twenty years of pent-up frustration (31:36). In his rebuke to Laban, Jacob shows himself to be a man of faith (31:31–42).

This part of the story concludes in 31:43–55. Jacob takes a stone and sets it up as a pillar (31:45). This may have been in the form of a heap of stones that functioned both as a table for the meal and as a memorial of the event. Standing stones sometimes marked supposed dwelling places of the gods (28:17–18) or graves (2 Samuel 18:17). In this case, it seals a treaty.

It seems Jacob gives two names to this place of agreement. *Galeed*, meaning "witness heap," is the name from which the name Gilead came. *Mizpah*, meaning "the witness or watchtower" (Genesis 31:47–48), recalls that both of these men said the Lord would be the watchman between them. Both names signify what had taken place between Jacob and Laban.

Laban has two deities in mind, as the Hebrew plural verb translated *judge* indicates. Jacob worships the God of his fathers; Laban swears by the pagan god his fathers worshiped (31:53).

Verse 55 is the last mention of Laban in the Bible.

Jacob leaves Laban and goes on to Canaan. He does this in obedience to God's command (31:3). The angels that meet him join Jacob's company of travelers for his protection. This is the reason for the name *Mahanaim* ("double host" or "double camp"). These angels were apparently intended to reassure Jacob of God's protective presence (32:1–2).

Genesis 32:2–21 describes Jacob's preparations for meeting Esau. At the news that Esau has four hundred men with him, Jacob becomes afraid. Esau may have had a large army because he had had to subjugate the Horite (Hurrian) population of Seir (32:6). His soldiers probably consisted of his own servants, plus the Canaanite and Ishmaelite relations of his wives.

After Jacob cares for the physical concerns of the journey, he turns to the spiritual concerns, offering up the first recorded prayer and the only extended prayer in Genesis (32:9–12). At the end of the prayer, he offers back to God the only thing he has—God's promise to his family.

Jacob's wording in his instructions to his servants (32:7–18) is important. He first humbles himself by calling himself Esau's servant. He also calls Esau "lord." Jacob seems to want to impress Esau with his greatness.

Demystifying Genesis

Why does Jacob send such an impressive gift to Esau? As a bribe or payoff for his sin of deception and theft? Possibly, but it could also have been an act of restitution and reconciliation. It also could have been for the practical reason that he wants Esau to know he is wealthy (verses 14–15 list over 550 animals given as gifts) and is not returning for the inheritance.

Hebrew narrative style often includes a summary statement of the whole passage, followed by a more detailed report of the event. In this case, verse 22 provides a summary statement while verse 23 begins the detailed account.

It is when Jacob is alone, having done everything he could to secure his own safety, that God comes to him. God has arranged the circumstances so that He could get Jacob alone at a moment when he felt completely helpless. God comes to Jacob as a wrestler to teach him how to fight like a man.

Why does he touch Jacob's thigh? Because the thigh is the largest and strongest muscle connection of the body. The man is deliberately crippling Jacob at the point of his greatest strength (32:24–30).

The new name Jacob receives, *Israel*, means either "God strives," or "he who strives with God." If the latter interpretation is the one intended by the wrestler who blesses Jacob, then the name fits well with Jacob's character as one who, throughout his life, struggles with God (32:28).

The name given to this place, *Peniel*, means "the face of God" (32:30).

Genesis 33 is a pivotal chapter in Jacob's life—facing Esau after twenty years. Jacob has every reason to believe that twenty years has not diminished Esau's anger, as he sees Esau marching toward him with four hundred men.

By going ahead of his family to meet Esau, Jacob shows that he has overcome the fear that had formerly dominated the old Jacob. He also shows valor in protecting his family. Bowing to the ground before Esau demonstrates humility. This is ancient court protocol for approaching a lord or king (33:3, 6–7).

In Esau's culture, men walked; they didn't run. By running to Jacob (33:4–5), Esau is breaking the cultural norms and humbling himself. His kiss seems to be an indication of forgiveness (33:4–5).

The fact that Esau refuses Jacob's herds as gifts is significant. Esau is not the taker that Jacob has been.

Jacob's comparison of seeing Esau to seeing God's face (33:10) may seem like flattery or overstatement. It could also have been recognition on Jacob's part of God's character in the life of his brother.

The word translated *gift* is the word "blessing." When Esau finally accepts Jacob's gift, he gives Jacob the opportunity to feel forgiven.

Jacob claims to be going to Seir, but he goes to Succoth instead (33:12–17).

Succoth is to the north and the west; in other words, it is in the exact opposite direction from Esau. Perhaps Jacob did not want to face his father, or perhaps reconciling with Esau was a different matter than living side-by-side. It could have also been a practical concern regarding pastures for the herds.

Critical Observation

As a result of Jacob's choice to settle away from his brother, he never saw his father again. The next time we find Jacob and Esau together in scripture is twenty-seven years later at the graveside of their father, Isaac (35:29).

Jacob settles near the city of Shechem (33:18), even though God had commanded him to settle in Bethel (28:21; 31:3, 13). This may have been fear-based. In spite of Esau's warm greeting, Jacob probably didn't trust him. Nevertheless, he builds his first altar, as Abraham had also done at Shechem, when he had first entered Canaan (12:6–7).

This is the first instance in which an altar is named (33:20; see also 35:7; Exodus 17:15; Judges 6:24). *El-Elohe-Israel* means "the mighty God is the God of Israel." Jacob uses his own new name, Israel (Genesis 32:29). Here he acknowledges God as *the* God, his own God.

In Genesis 34, we come to a horrific account. This story serves to warn us of the high price of compromise. The tragedies that take place in this chapter are the result of Jacob's failure to be obedient to God's command to return to Bethel.

Dinah is in her early teens and is Jacob's only daughter—his daughter by Leah, the wife he did not love (30:21). Dinah's name means "justice." The Hebrew word translated *went out* in 34:1 bears a sense of impropriety.

The account can be a bit confusing in that the place is called Shechem, and the man Dinah encounters is also named Shechem. He is the son of Hamor, who is the leader of that part of the world. As Hamor's son, Shechem could have whatever he wanted.

Jacob seems far less affected by the news of Dinah's assault than her brothers (30:5–7).

In verse 7, the name *Israel* is used here for the first time as a reference to God's chosen people. The family of Jacob had a special relationship to God by divine calling, reflected in the name *Israel* (prince with God).

Neither Hamor nor Shechem offers an apology. Apparently, they assume that the offense is no big deal. Hamor offers an alliance between the two peoples to include intermarriage, trade, and land deals (34:8–12).

As was customary in their culture, Jacob's sons take an active part in approving their sister's marriage (34:13; see 24:50). They were correct in opposing the end in view: the mixing of the chosen seed with the seed of the Canaanites. Yet they were wrong in adopting the means they selected to achieve their end (34:13–17); thus, the description "Jacob's sons" rather than "Dinah's brothers." The sons are following in their deceitful father's footsteps (34:13).

Regarding the proposal made by Jacob's sons, the men of the city become convinced on financial grounds. While Shechem has fallen in love with Dinah, to these men circumcision seems a small price to pay if it results in a huge financial windfall from the alliance (34:13–24).

The slaughter described in verses 25–29 outrages Jacob on an unexpected level. He seems to think only of his lowered standing among the local inhabitants. His selfish response (34:30–31) reflects his focus on himself.

It is interesting that Simeon and Levi refer to Dinah as their sister rather than Jacob's daughter, which would have been appropriate in addressing Jacob. This could imply that Jacob had not showed enough concern for Dinah, so her blood brothers felt compelled to act in her defense.

Chapter 35 opens with God's renewed command to Jacob to go to Bethel. It is at Bethel that Jacob has his first real encounter with God and is told about God's plan to bless him.

It is also at Bethel that Jacob first builds an altar of worship to the Lord.

Jacob's instructions to his entourage to wash and change their clothes are the kind of instructions that often signify spiritual preparation for a new beginning (35:1–5).

The inclusion of the phrase "the sons of Jacob" suggests that the other cities fear Jacob's boys (35:5; Deuteronomy 11:25) because of what they had done to the people of Shechem. Yet, it also seems evident that, as Jacob obeys the Lord, the Lord protects Jacob and his family by causing a fear to fall on the surrounding cities.

Jacob faithfully fulfills his vow to God at Luz (Genesis 35:7–15), which he renames Bethel, or "house of God." The insertion of the story of Deborah's death and burial probably is an indirect reference to Jacob's mother, Rebekah, and perhaps an allusion to her death (35:8).

At Bethel, the Lord reconfirms His covenant with Jacob, again affirming Jacob's new name (already pronounced by the angel; see 32:24–28) and promising him many descendants and land (35:9–12). God's promise of land was first given to Abraham and then to Isaac, and here it is renewed with Jacob.

Jacob solemnizes this occasion by setting up a second pillar (28:18; 35:13–15) that perpetuates the memory of God's faithfulness for the benefit of his descendants. He not only sets the stone apart by pouring oil on it, as he had done thirty years earlier, but he also makes an offering to God and reaffirms the name Bethel.

Rachel's death is recorded in verses 16–20. She, who had so longed for a child, dies bearing her second son. She gives him the name *Ben-oni,* which can mean "son of my sorrow"; but the name that Jacob gives is *Benjamin,* which means "the son of the right hand."

The tower of Eder (or Migdal Eder) mentioned in verse 21 is simply a watchtower built to help shepherds protect their flocks from robbers (2 Kings 18:8; 2 Chronicles 26:10; 27:4). Since the time of Jerome, the early church father who lived in Bethlehem, tradition has held that Eder lay very close to Bethlehem.

Verse 22 mentions Reuben, now an adult. He was the son that brought the mandrakes to Rachel, hence playing some small part in the all too brief restoration of his mother's conjugal rights (Genesis 30:14).

A *concubine*, as Bilhah is described in verse 22, was sometimes a slave with whom her owner had sexual relations. She enjoyed some of the privileges of a wife, and people sometimes called her a wife in patriarchal times, but she was not a wife in the full sense of the term.

Reuben's relations with Bilhah are a power move as much as anything else. In that culture, a man who wanted to assert his superiority over another man might do so by having sexual relations with that man's wife or concubine. It may have included a play for asserting his mother's role as "first wife." With the death of Rachel, who had been Jacob's favorite, Bilhah, Rachel's servant, may have been able to move into a favored role. Reuben's actions make Bilhah detestable to Jacob; thus Leah has a better chance for power in the household.

While Reuben's actions may have been on behalf of his mother, they are an affront to his father as the head of the family. In the end, though, according to 1 Chronicles 5:1–2, Reuben's actions cost him.

Chapter 35 closes with a list of Jacob's sons and the account of his father Isaac's death. The use of Israel rather than Jacob in verse 22 may suggest that, here, the patriarch responds rightly (not the old Jacob but the new) to this situation.

Benjamin is not born in Paddan-aram but near Bethlehem (35:16–18). Therefore, the statement that Jacob's twelve sons were born in Paddan-aram (35:26) must be understood as a general one.

With the record of Jacob entering into his father's inheritance, the history of Isaac's life concludes. Isaac lives for twelve years after Jacob's relocation to Hebron. He shares Jacob's grief over the apparent death of Joseph, but dies shortly before Joseph's promotion in Egypt. He is buried in the cave of Machpelah, near Hebron (49:29–31).

36:1–43

ESAU

Chapter 36 is the account of Esau, Jacob's twin, and his descendants. The name *Esau* means "red." This is a reference and reminder of Esau's foolish decision to trade the birthright and blessing of his father, Isaac, for a pot of red stew (25:30).

Esau takes his wives from the Canaanites, even though this was considered a religious mixed marriage and was strictly forbidden by his family. But Esau, in open defiance, takes wives from the idolatrous Hittites and brings them to his tents within the camp, where they make life miserable for Esau's parents, Isaac and Rebekah (26:35). He later adds a third wife from the descendants of Ishmael (28:9).

Demystifying Genesis

The names of Esau's wives present a problem, in that the names given in earlier chapters do not correspond with the names listed here. In 26:34, it is said that Esau marries Judith and Basemath. Genesis 28:9 reports that he adds Mahalath. But in 36:2–3, the names are different, though the fathers associated with them are the same. The wives probably took different names, either when they moved from Canaan to Edom, or because of changes over time (a common practice; Esau became known as Edom over the incident with the red stew which he traded for his birthright).

Since infertility has been a large theme in the stories of Abraham's family, it is significant that there is no mention of infertility when it comes to Esau's line.

The dividing of territory between Esau and Jacob described in verses 6–8 is reminiscent of the episode between Abraham and Lot in 13:1–13. There are two reasons for Esau's move: (1) There isn't sufficient water and pasture for both Esau's and Jacob's flocks and herds, and (2) Esau has finally come to accept that the promised land of Canaan is to be passed on to Jacob.

Critical Observation

Esau's name is also Edom, thus the reference to his descendants as Edomites. These people are important neighbors to Israel, though not always agreeable ones. Even so, God commands special treatment for the Edomites among Israel.

Esau and his descendants are men of great political power (36:8–43). They are called chiefs (36:15) and kings (36:31). These men reign as kings in Edom before any king reigns in Israel.

Some have hailed verse 31 as an indication that Genesis must have been written after the beginning of the monarchy, some three hundred years after Moses. But in the previous chapter, God prophesied to Jacob that kings would come forth from him (35:11), a promise that had also been made to Abraham (17:6, 16). Put into that context, the information contained here would not have been an unreasonable forecast for Moses to make.

Esau's sons, who walked away from God, had the distinction of being kings long before Jacob's sons to whom it was promised. While Esau's sons and grandsons become rulers, Jacob's sons remain lowly shepherds for generations (47:3).

GENESIS 37:1–50:26

JACOB'S SONS

Joseph's Journey to Egypt	37:1–36
Judah	38:1–30
Joseph's Success in Egypt	39:1–41:57
Joseph's Brothers in Egypt	42:1–47:31
Jacob's Blessings	48:1–49:33
Jacob's and Joseph's Final Days	50:1–26

Setting Up the Section

For the final time, Genesis introduces a new series of generations. This marks the final section in the book of Genesis. The storyline of the last fourteen chapters focuses on Jacob's sons. Of those twelve sons, most of the focus is on Joseph. This whole section reveals how God's plan for His people triumphs over human frailties to guide and strengthen those who follow Him.

37:1–36

JOSEPH'S JOURNEY TO EGYPT

Chapter 36 reveals that Esau's descendants are mighty chieftains; in contrast, by Moses' day (over four hundred years later), Israel is still a fledgling nation of slaves, recently escaped from Egypt, owning no land of their own. Edom, on the other hand, is an established kingdom that has the power to refuse Israel passage over their land.

While the last fourteen chapters of Genesis include Jacob, the storyline focuses on Jacob's sons. And of his twelve sons, special interest is spent on Joseph, who is mentioned twice as much as Jacob. This means a quarter of the book of Genesis is devoted to Joseph.

Elsewhere, the word *report* is used in the negative sense of an untrue report (37:2; Proverbs 10:18). This may imply some exaggeration or inaccuracies on Joseph's part, which would have added fire to the rivalry between him and his brothers.

Jacob's favoritism, signified by the special tunic he gives his favorite son, is no help. The tunic was probably a long robe extending all the way down to the wrists and ankles, as opposed to the ordinary, shorter one with no sleeves that working men wore.

While it's not clear exactly what the tunic looked like, the idea that it is a coat of many colors comes from the Greek translation of the Old Testament. The tunic sets Joseph apart as the favored one.

Critical Observation

Favoritism and rivalry have a long history in Jacob's family. Jacob's father, Isaac, preferred Esau. His mother, Rebekah, claimed Jacob as a favorite. In Jacob's own family, his preference for Rachel set up resentment between not only Rachel and her sister (also Jacob's wife) Leah, but probably between their children as well.

Verses 5–11 recount two of Joseph's dreams. Dreams in this narrative concerning Joseph always come in pairs (chapters 40–41). One dream seems to confirm that the other is not a fluke or a one-time event.

Joseph's first dream involves sheaves, which subtly points to his future role in overseeing all of Egypt's grain distribution. Amazingly, twenty-three years later, in fulfillment of Joseph's dream, all eleven of his brothers prostrate themselves in submission to Joseph on at least five different occasions (42:6–7; 43:26, 28; 44:14–16; 50:18). Joseph's second dream is far more graphic. It involves celestial imagery bowing down to him. Joseph probably reveals part faith and part foolishness in sharing these dreams with this already contentious family.

Later, according to verses 12–14, Joseph is sent to check on his brothers. It is not uncommon for shepherds to lead their flocks many miles from home in search of pasture. Shechem was about fifty miles north of Hebron. Jacob owned land there.

When he doesn't find his brothers at Shechem, Joseph goes to Dothan, a location fifteen miles north of Shechem. In verse 18, when Joseph finds his brothers, there is a shift in perspective. Suddenly the story is told from his brothers' point of view.

Reuben, who advocates for Joseph's life, is the firstborn and the decision-maker in the family (27:21–24). He is apparently not part of the family group that was plotting to kill Joseph. That group consisted probably of Dan, Naphtali, Gad, and Asher—the four sons against whom Joseph brought a bad report (37:2).

Verses 23–28 record how the brothers capture Joseph and subsequently sell him to the Midianite merchants for twenty pieces of silver. Slave-trading was common in Egypt. The price agreed on for Joseph was the same price that was later specified for a slave between the ages of five and twenty years under the Mosaic economy (Leviticus 27:5).

When Reuben returns to find Joseph gone, he knows that as the oldest, he will have to answer to his father for whatever has happened (Genesis 37:29–32). Thus evolves the brothers' scheme. Notice that the brothers never actually say Joseph is dead. They simply deceive their father.

The boys live for years without ever telling their father what they had done. Had Jacob believed more strongly in God's revelations through Joseph's dreams, he might not have jumped to the conclusion that Joseph was dead, and his sorrow might not have been as great (37:33–35).

Joseph ends up in Egypt, in the home of one of the most responsible officers of Pharaoh's administration (37:36).

Take It Home

God is never defeated by anyone's deceit. Jacob deceived and was deceived. The brothers hated, envied, plotted, and lied. And when you get to the end of the chapter, God has placed Joseph exactly where he needs to be to accomplish God's purposes. All of this points to the sovereignty of God. When you and I sin and go against the will of God, we don't thwart the purpose of God; we thwart ourselves. Our job is not to work out the details. Joseph didn't. Our job is to remain pure and usable. God will work out the details. He did in the case of Joseph, and He will do it for you, too.

38:1–30

JUDAH

Genesis 38 records a scandalous story from the life of Judah, Joseph's brother.

Verses 1–11 tell us that Judah leaves home and moves to Canaan. This means he is living among people that his family considered unclean. There, he marries and raises children to adulthood. When Judah's oldest son Er dies, Er's wife, Tamar, becomes a childless widow. Since carrying on the bloodline is of the highest value in this culture, the custom of the day is for Er's brother to marry Tamar and supply Er with an heir. This custom, called levirate marriage, is described in Deuteronomy 25:5–10. The word *levirate* comes from a Latin word meaning "husband's brother."

The downside of this agreement for the second brother is that the son born is considered the heir to the deceased. His birth does not increase the wealth of the younger brother at all. This is why Onan does not cooperate in providing Er with an heir.

After Onan dies, Tamar expects that the third son of Judah will provide her an heir when he is old enough, but that is never Judah's intent.

According to verses 12–19, when Tamar realizes that Judah lied to her, she plans a ruse to make him take responsibility for the situation. Sheep-shearing was a time for partying and celebration (1 Samuel 25:11, 36; 2 Samuel 13:23, 28), and the place Judah was going to shear his sheep was a place with abundant sexual temptation. This is an ideal situation for Tamar to trick Judah into having sex with her in exchange for three distinctive items: his personal seal, the cord with which it probably hung around his neck, and his staff—probably carved and one-of-a-kind.

When Judah finally hears the stories of pregnant Tamar, the so-called prostitute, he calls for her judgment by burning (Genesis 38:20–24). In the Mosaic Law, the penalty of burning was only for a priest's daughter who had become guilty of prostitution (Leviticus 21:9). The usual mode of death was by stoning (Deuteronomy 22:20–24; John 8:4–5).

Going to execute judgment on Tamar, Judah faces the woman who has his personal belongings and is pregnant with his twin sons. There is evidence that among ancient Assyrian and Hittite peoples, part of the levirate responsibility could pass to the father of the widow's husband, if there were no brothers to fulfill it. Thus Tamar was, in one sense, claiming what was due her. She had tricked Judah into fulfilling the levirate responsibility and now would bear his children.

Tamar and Judah have two sons: Perez and Zerah (38:27–30). *Perez* means "a breach" or "one who breaks through." Perez becomes the ancestor of David (Ruth 4:18–22), who in turn becomes the ancestor of Jesus Christ (Matthew 1:3). *Zerah* means "a dawning or brightness."

The struggle between the twins at birth is reminiscent of the struggle of Jacob and Esau, Judah's father and uncle (Genesis 25:24–26; 38:27–30).

39:1–41:57

JOSEPH'S SUCCESS IN EGYPT

The account of Joseph's life in Egypt begins with chapter 39. The theme of this narrative is found in the statement in verse 2: The Lord is with Joseph (39:2).

After Joseph's brothers sell him into slavery, the Midianites take him down to Egypt and sell him to Potiphar (37:36). Potiphar is the chief executioner or chief of police.

Even in these less-than-ideal circumstances, Potiphar notices God's hand on Joseph (39:3).

Critical Observation

Verse 6 describes Joseph's outward appearance. The Bible rarely offers this kind of description. The only other men who are referred to in this way are David (1 Samuel 16:12) and Absalom (2 Samuel 14:25).

Verses 7–20 describe Joseph's life in Potiphar's house, and particularly his interaction with Potiphar's wife. According to verse 7, she carefully scrutinizes Joseph, and then eventually propositions him. When he refuses, she manipulates the situation to make it appear that Joseph has acted inappropriately, and so he is thrown in jail.

In this time and place, attempted rape was a capital offense. The milder punishment Joseph receives suggests that Potiphar does not believe his wife. Furthermore, the king's prison was a place for political prisoners and would hardly have been expected to accommodate foreign slaves guilty of crimes against their masters. Another very telling observation is that the prison was in the basement of Potiphar's house (40:3, 7). Joseph was thus demoted.

Verses 21–23 reveal Joseph's persistent good character. He is not enslaved by his circumstances.

While Joseph is in Potiphar's jail, God brings some influential and unexpected guests: Pharaoh's cupbearer, or butler, and baker. The cupbearer and baker are not guilty of some minor indiscretion or inadvertent offense against Pharaoh; they had greatly offended him (40:1–3).

Joseph's role is to act as a servant to these men, and in the course of serving them, he also interprets some dreams for them (40:4–11). He recognizes that their dreams are revelations from God and invites the two prisoners to relate their dreams to him. He is careful, however, to give God the glory for his interpretative gift (40:8; 41:16, 25, 28, 39).

Verses 14–19 relate Joseph's interpretations—one having a positive outcome and the other having a harrowing outcome. In some translations, Joseph is credited with saying that the baker's head would be lifted up, but that is actually a reference to a hanging. The baker would not simply suffer execution, but his corpse would be impaled and publicly exposed.

Joseph's predictions come true just as God had said (40:20–23). One of the men is reinstated by Pharaoh, and the other is executed. Between the end of chapter 40 and the beginning of chapter 41, however, two years pass without the cupbearer fulfilling his promise of remembering Joseph and his interpretative gifts.

Take It Home

Joseph is an excellent example to follow regarding life's disappointments. Nowhere in this narrative do we see Joseph feeling sorry for himself or blaming others. He simply took each situation as it came and made the best out of it. The biggest problem in life is not having problems. Our problem is thinking that having problems is a problem.

Two years after the cupbearer's return to court, Pharaoh has two dreams symbolic enough to require interpretation (41:1–7). In the first dream, seven fat cows are eaten by seven gaunt cows (41:1–4). In the second dream, seven plump ears of grain are eaten by seven thin ears (41:5–7).

The magicians that Pharaoh sends for shouldn't be confused with contemporary magicians, who wear tuxedos and pull rabbits out of hats. These were the wise, educated men of Pharaoh's kingdom. They were schooled in the sacred arts and sciences of the Egyptians. Yet they are unable to help Pharaoh (41:8).

Though it was two years before that the cupbearer (or butler) had promised to remember Joseph, it is these troubling dreams that finally make it happen (41:9–13). He summons Joseph for the Pharaoh. Notice that part of Joseph's preparations for meeting Pharaoh is to shave. The Egyptians preferred to shave all the hair off their bodies and wear wigs (41:14).

Once in Pharaoh's presence, Joseph makes it clear that he can interpret the dreams only in God's power (41:15–16). In essence, Joseph tells Pharaoh (who is considered a god in his own country) that his God is superior to and sovereign over Pharaoh and the gods of Egypt. This is quite a stand to take.

Pharaoh explains his dreams to Joseph (41:17–24), and Joseph interprets the dreams and discusses a plan of action with the great king of Egypt (41:25–36). Three times in this section, Joseph attributes the outcome of Pharaoh's dreams to God (41:25, 28, 32).

Because of these events, Joseph becomes an advisor to and an officer of the Egyptian government (41:37–45). To naturalize Joseph, Pharaoh gives him an Egyptian name (41:45; Daniel 1:7) and an Egyptian wife from an appropriate level of society. Joseph's name, *Zaphenath-paneah*, is probably Egyptian for "God speaks; He lives."

Critical Observation

Joseph's marriage to an Egyptian seems out of place. The patriarchs generally avoided marriage to Canaanites, but this was a marriage to a non-Canaanite Gentile, which was less serious.

Under the circumstances, it doesn't seem that Joseph is given much choice. Perhaps more important, it's clear from the names given to their two sons that Joseph doesn't allow his wife's pagan background to influence him away from God. It is this falling away that is the issue with mixed religious marriages in the Old Testament.

This chapter of Joseph's life closes with his preparing Egypt for the seven years of famine (41:46–49). During this time, God blesses Joseph with two sons (41:50–52). Joseph names his firstborn *Manasseh*, which means "making to forget." He names the second *Ephraim*, meaning "God has made me fruitful in the land of my affliction." If the name of Joseph's first son (Manasseh) focuses on a God who preserves, the name of Joseph's second son (Ephraim) focuses on a God who blesses. Joseph gives his boys Hebrew names that are testaments of God's faithfulness.

42:1–47:31

JOSEPH'S BROTHERS IN EGYPT

In chapter 42, the scene switches to Canaan. The seven years of famine that Joseph predicted are now in full force (41:54–57). The famine has spread to Joseph's family in Canaan (42:1–2).

Demystifying Genesis

What would have kept Jacob's sons from going to Egypt until their father instructed them? For one thing, the trip was long (250–300 miles) and dangerous, and a round trip could consume six weeks' time. Even after arriving in Egypt, the brothers couldn't be certain of a friendly reception. As foreigners from Canaan, they would be vulnerable and could even be arrested and enslaved.

It's evident that Jacob is a man controlled not only by favoritism but also by fear. He has already lost his favorite wife and his favorite son. He was determined to prevent the loss of Benjamin, who was his final link to Rachel, his favored wife. It also appears that over the years since the death of his eleventh son, Joseph, Jacob may have grown suspicious of his ten older sons. This suspicion manifests itself in 42:4, where Jacob refuses to send Benjamin with his brothers into Egypt to buy food for the family.

When the brothers arrive in Egypt and are ushered into Joseph's presence, the predictions of Joseph's dreams from long ago (37:5–7) are fulfilled as his brothers bow before him.

The last time the brothers had seen Joseph, he was a seventeen-year-old boy who was in a position of weakness, being carried off into slavery by the Midianites (37:2). At this point in the story, though, Joseph is nearly forty, the governor of Egypt, wearing the royal clothing of a king; and to top it off, he is powerful and confident in his role.

The brothers are astounded at Joseph's accusation that they are spies. What spy would travel with his brothers and in a group of ten? A good spy wants to be inconspicuous.

Demystifying Genesis

Why does Joseph do this? Was it just a cruel act of vengeance—the product of twenty years of bitterness and resentment? No! The Bible is very clear that Joseph never indulges in any resentment against others who had injured him (45:5; 50:18–21). Joseph's purpose in speaking harshly and accusing his brothers of spying is not motivated by bitterness, but by a desire to covertly discover information regarding the health and well-being of his father, Jacob, and his younger brother, Benjamin. He also is testing their character—have they changed in how they care for each other?

Joseph gives his brothers a glimmer of hope when he tells them he fears God (42:18). The name he uses for God is the name of the Hebrew's God (*Elohim*). The brothers would not have expected this from the seemingly harsh Egyptian prime minister. But there is enough hope of fair treatment in those words to keep them from despairing.

According to verse 24, Joseph's pent-up emotions simply had to come out, so he leaves the room and weeps privately. This is the first of six such experiences. Joseph also weeps when he sees his brother Benjamin (43:29–30), when he reveals himself to his brothers (45:2), when he meets his father in Egypt (46:29), when his father dies (50:1), and when he assures his brothers that they are truly forgiven (50:17).

The scripture does not say why Joseph chooses to imprison Simeon rather than any of the other brothers (42:24). Perhaps the reason is in the brothers' discussion of their guilt in having sold Joseph into slavery. In that discussion, Joseph learns for the first time that Reuben, the oldest son of the family, had kept the other brothers from killing Joseph. If Joseph had intended to imprison the oldest brother, he may have had a change of heart. Simeon, being the second oldest, would have been the one responsible for their collective wickedness.

There's a good chance that Simeon had been the ringleader in throwing Joseph into the pit, where his intention was to kill him. Simeon had been the leader in the slaughter of the Shechemites. In Jacob's final words to his sons, he refers only to Simeon's violence and anger (49:5–7). By putting Simeon in prison, Joseph may have intended to eliminate Simeon's influence on the others on the return journey, or perhaps he hoped that the time in prison would break Simeon's hardened heart. At the very least, Joseph chooses to keep him as leverage and to see if his brothers are willing to desert Simeon as they had him.

Before his brothers leave, Joseph hides their payment for the grain in their grain sacks (42:25–28). Perhaps this is to test his brothers to see if they could still be bought with money. Joseph wanted to know if they would do to Simeon what they did to him. The brothers panic because they could be accused of stealing this money. Interestingly, Joseph's brothers never mention God until now.

When they return home, Jacob's sons share with their father what happened (42:29–36). Unfortunately, Jacob's response only serves to prolong their return, Simeon's imprisonment, and his reunion with his long-lost son.

Reuben's offer in verses 37–38 may have made sense to Reuben, but basically he is only offering to increase his father's sense of bereavement by losing two grandsons in addition to his youngest son.

Genesis 43–45 describes what happens when Joseph's brothers return to Egypt. In chapter 43, Joseph exhibits tender love; in chapter 44 he exercises tough love; and in chapter 45 he lives out God's sovereignty.

Even after some time has passed, Jacob still isn't willing to make the hard decision to send Benjamin. First he suggests they just buy a little food, in hopes that the governor in Egypt won't require Benjamin to go there with his brothers (43:2).

Fortunately, Judah steps up and lovingly puts Jacob in his place, as well as offers to be the collateral for Benjamin (43:3–10). This is the first evidence of real character we find in Judah so far in Genesis. Up until now, he has been like his father, self-centered and self-absorbed.

When Jacob finally allows the brothers to make the trip with Benjamin, he employs his gift-giving strategy of diplomacy. It is the same strategy he had employed when he was preparing to meet his brother, Esau (33:10–16). Jacob's gift-giving isn't motivated by love or friendship; it is intended to soften the heart of the Egyptian leader.

When the brothers are reunited with Simeon (43:15–25), they go from agony to ecstasy in a matter of moments. Then Joseph hosts a meal for the brothers, who years before had callously sat down to eat while he languished in a pit (37:25). We aren't told whether Joseph even acknowledges the gifts that Jacob sent.

Verse 33 marks the second occasion that the brothers bow down before Joseph. They are seated in order by age by a host who presumably is entirely ignorant of their birth order. The chances of that happening are approximately one in forty million. It must have seemed like magic.

Joseph shows respect to Benjamin as his distinguished guest by giving him larger and better servings of food than his brothers receive. Special honorees frequently received double portions, but a fivefold portion was the sign of highest privilege. With this favor, Joseph is not only honoring Benjamin but is also testing his other brothers' feelings toward Benjamin. He may have wanted to see if they would hate him as they had hated his father's former favorite. Evidently they pass this test.

Genesis 44 reveals Joseph's effort to discover the truth—to find out whether his brothers are still the selfish, godless, wicked men who sold him into slavery twenty years earlier. A silver cup like the one he had placed in Benjamin's sack is, of course, valuable. But Joseph's decision to put silver in the bags probably also stems from his personal recollection that his brothers had sold him into slavery for twenty pieces of silver. Now he is testing them.

When the accusation of theft is made, the brothers are no doubt indignant because they are confident in their righteousness. But when the silver cup is discovered in Benjamin's sack, they are broken and show evidence that they had become a family (44:3–9).

In verses 5 and 15, divination is mentioned. This practice of determining information from the movements of liquids was not a practice of the Israelites. But even in the Egyptian culture of this time, a cup was not a standard tool for divination. If you read closely, Joseph does not actually claim to practice divination.

Genesis 44:18–34 is the longest and most moving speech in the book of Genesis. Fourteen times in this speech, Judah mentions his father, Jacob. Jacob would eventually crown Judah with kingship (49:10), because he demonstrates that he has become fit to rule according to God's ideal of kingship—that the king serves the people, not vice versa. Judah is transformed from one who sold his brother as a slave to one who is willing to be the slave for his brother.

In 45:1–15, this account comes to a resolution. Joseph reveals his identity. The response of the brothers to Joseph's revelation of his identity is a term translated *dismayed* or *dumbfounded.* This is a term used of paralyzing fear as felt by those involved in war (Exodus 15:15; Judges 20:41; 1 Samuel 28:21; Psalm 48:5). But after a threefold expression of Joseph's goodwill toward his siblings (weeping, explaining, and embracing), his brothers are finally able to talk to him.

Critical Observation

Throughout the course of Joseph's life, he has discerned God's providential control of events. Four times he states that God, not his brothers, is behind what has happened (45:5, 7–9).

Upon parting, Joseph's admonition to his brothers not to quarrel on their journey is a bit unclear (45:24). Probably he means just that; not to become involved in arguing and recriminations over the past. The brothers had already quarreled over their sin against Joseph (42:21–22). Joseph may have known that as soon as these men left his presence they would be tempted to assign blame to one another.

Take It Home

How is Joseph able to forgive his brothers? First, he sees his situation from an eternal perspective (50:19–20). Then he prepares in advance to forgive. Finally, he receives their confession and repentance for their sins.

Whom do you need to forgive? Do you want restitution? Can you let someone who offended you off the hook in the way that Joseph did? Will you see that God's sovereignty allows you to forgive others for whatever sin they have committed against you?

Jacob is stunned to receive news that his favorite son, Joseph, is alive. At the age of 130, he prepares the family to leave Canaan and head out to join Joseph in Egypt. Jacob's sacrifices at Beersheba (46:1) are not burnt offerings, but offerings of thanks that Joseph is alive, and perhaps also vows to God. The fact that the names *Israel* and *Jacob* are used interchangeably in verses 46–47 indicates that the earlier negative connotations of the name Jacob have faded (31:11; 32:28; 35:10).

Demystifying Genesis

Why sacrifices at Beersheba? Beersheba was at the southernmost boundary of Israel. In essence, it was the point of no return. Furthermore, Beersheba was a significant place to Jacob's family. This is where Abraham had dug a well, planted a tamarisk tree, and called on the name of the Lord (21:30–33). Abraham even lived in Beersheba after offering Isaac on Mount Moriah (22:19). Isaac also lived in Beersheba (26:23, 32–33) and built an altar there (26:24–25). It is perhaps at this altar where Jacob presents his sacrifices.

God appears once more to Jacob (46:2–4), as He had to Jacob's grandfather, Abraham (22:11). God identifies Himself in virtually the same way as when He spoke to Jacob during his vision of the stairway up into heaven (28:13). He also offers the fourth and final "do not be afraid" consolation recorded in Genesis (see 15:1; 21:17; 26:24).

After hearing directly from the Lord, Jacob and his family leave Beersheba and travel to Egypt (46:5–7).

To the first readers of this book, the names in verses 8–27 mean something. This is a list of every tribe (and every major family group within that tribe) that later formed the nation of Israel. Every Hebrew knew his family ancestry. The division of labor, the organization of the army, and the parceling of the land all were done according to tribe. This list of names reminds original readers of their identity as God's people in fulfilling His purposes; in the four hundred or so years from Jacob's time to Moses', the number of Israelites had mushroomed from seventy to more than two million!

In verses 28–30, the fact that Jacob chooses Judah to be the guide indicates that he trusts his son, which suggests that the men had told their father everything and were in his good graces again. Now Jacob can see the hand of God in all that has happened.

In spite of his past failures, Judah now proves he is faithful, and his descendants are eventually named the royal tribe (49:8–12).

The reunion between Jacob and Joseph recalls Jacob's former meeting with Esau (32:3). In both situations, after a long period of separation, Jacob sends a party ahead to meet the relative. Previously, Jacob had said that the loss of his sons would bring him to his grave in mourning (37:35; 42:38). But finding Joseph alive enables his father to find a measure of peace.

Critical Observation

Joseph encourages his family to be completely honest with Pharaoh when asked about their occupation so that he would send them to live in Goshen (46:34). Goshen had some of the best pastureland in all of Egypt. It would be a place to keep the Hebrews isolated and insulated from the culture and religion of Egypt, since the Egyptians considered sheep unclean and Hebrews detestable (43:32).

One of the greatest dangers to the covenant promises of God was intermarriage between the Hebrews and the Egyptians, because intermarriage would inevitably lead to spiritual compromise and the worship of the false gods of the Egyptians.

Joseph explains to Pharaoh the needs of his family (47:1–6). He even introduces five of his brothers to Pharaoh. After the brothers answer Pharaoh's questions, they ask his permission to live in Goshen. Pharaoh agrees to their request and even offers any capable brothers a job—to be put in charge of Pharaoh's livestock.

Jacob's blessing of Pharaoh (47:7) is unusual in that it implies Jacob is superior, even though Pharaoh is a man of immense worldly power and influence. The precise meaning of the Hebrew verb translated *blessed* is difficult in this passage, because the content of Jacob's blessing is not given. The expression could simply mean that he greets Pharaoh, but that seems insufficient. Jacob probably praises Pharaoh, for the verb is used this way for praising God. It is also possible that he pronounces a formal prayer of blessing, asking God to reward Pharaoh for his kindness.

Verses 13–27 demonstrate the fulfillment of Jacob's blessing on Pharaoh (46:31–47:10). Joseph is able to save Egypt and its neighbors from a severe famine and alleviate the desperate plight of the Egyptians. God blesses Pharaoh because he has blessed the Israelites with the best of Egypt.

According to verse 22, Joseph gives preferential treatment to the Egyptian priests. More than a sign of religious support, this concession is probably due to the powerful lobby that the priests have with Pharaoh.

The tax described in verse 24 is not out of line with what was common in that day in the ancient Near East. It was lower than the average 33.3 percent.

The account of Jacob begins to draw to a close in verse 28. Jacob enjoys the blessings of God for seventeen more years—ironically, the same number of years he enjoyed Joseph until Joseph was sold into slavery to Egypt by his older brothers (37:2).

Why does Jacob insist on being buried in Canaan (47:29–31)? It isn't because he has already invested in a family plot. Knowing that the day of his departure is drawing near, Jacob makes his death a testimony to his faith and a stimulus to the faith and obedience of his descendants. This would serve as a reminder to his descendants that Egypt was not home, but only a place to sojourn until God brought them back to their true home, Canaan, the land of promise (Hebrews 11:22).

48:1–49:33

JACOB'S BLESSINGS

Jacob is coming to the end of his life. He has not always honored God, but is an example of a man who finishes well. Before he dies, Jacob passes the torch on to those who follow.

It is likely that in the seventeen years Jacob lived with Joseph in Egypt, he invested in Joseph's sons Manasseh and Ephraim. These sons were born during the seven years of abundance, before the first year of the famine (41:50). Jacob went down to Egypt somewhere around the end of the second year of the famine (45:6) and lived seventeen years after he arrived (47:28). Since Jacob is near death, the sons of Joseph must have been about twenty years old.

Jacob might have been losing his health, but he was not losing his memory. In verses 3–4, he shares his testimony. Twice, God had appeared to Jacob at Luz (28:10–17; 35:9–12), and in both appearances God promised him that he would become a great nation and that he would possess the land of Canaan. While it is not recorded that God specifically promises Jacob the land will be an everlasting possession (48:4), God does make that promise to Abram (17:7). This was probably orally passed on through Isaac.

Jacob effectively adopts his grandsons (48:5–6). Ephraim and Manasseh go from being Jacob's grandsons to his number one and two sons. Keep in mind that Joseph's sons are half-Egyptian. This is a large step for a full-blooded Israelite like Jacob. It is also a step that displaces Reuben and Simeon as the two oldest sons. Thus, in future lists of the twelve tribes of Israel, Ephraim and Manasseh are normally included in the place of Joseph.

Normally, the birthright would have been given to the firstborn son. But Reuben and Simeon had disqualified themselves from positions of status and leadership in Israel's family because of their sin: Reuben due to his sin of lying with Bilhah, Jacob's concubine (35:22; 49:4; 1 Chronicles 5:1–2), and Simeon due to his violent murder of the men of Shechem (Genesis 34:25). In essence, Jacob is giving Joseph the double blessing that is generally reserved for the firstborn (Reuben). In the future, Joseph's other children will be incorporated into the tribes of Ephraim and Manasseh (48:6).

Jacob's words in verse 7 are a reminder of his love for Rachel, the wife for whom he worked seven years and then seven more.

When Israel asks, "Who are these?"(48:8), the question is not an indication of Jacob's blindness but the initiation of the ceremony.

Genesis 48:13–20 is the first of many scriptural instances of the laying on of hands. By this symbolic act, a person transfers a spiritual power or gift to another. In this case, Jacob symbolically transfers a blessing from himself to Joseph's sons. Ephraim and

Manasseh do become great tribes. At one time, Ephraim was used as a synonym for the kingdom of Israel.

Jacob's blessing of Ephraim and Manasseh also carries prophetic significance and force (48:19–20). This is the fourth consecutive generation of Abraham's descendants in which the normal pattern of the firstborn assuming prominence over the secondborn is reversed: Isaac over Ishmael, Jacob over Esau, Joseph over Reuben, and Ephraim over Manasseh.

In verse 15, Jacob calls God his shepherd. This is the first mention in the Bible of God as a shepherd to His people.

Critical Observation

Jacob testifies of an angel who had redeemed him from all harm (48:16). The Angel of the Lord appears frequently in the Old Testament. He appears to Hagar when she flees from Sarai (16:7–13), wrestles with Jacob (33:22–32; Hosea 12:4), and appears to Moses in the burning bush (Exodus 3:2). Many believe this angel is a preincarnate appearance of Jesus Christ. This is further supported by the first use of the word *redeemed* in the Bible.

Jacob's prophetic promise to Joseph in Genesis 48:21–22 is a play on words. The word for *portion* means "ridge," or "shoulder (of land)," and is the same as *Shechem*, the name of a city in Manasseh's territory. The Israelites later bury Joseph at Shechem (Joshua 24:32). In Jesus' day, people spoke of Shechem (near Sychar) as territory Jacob had given to Joseph (John 4:5).

Jacob speaks as though he has taken Shechem from the Amorites by force, but no such battle is recorded (48:22). He may have viewed Simeon and Levi's slaughter of the Shechemites as his own taking of the city (34:27–29). Jacob gives Joseph Shechem, which he regards as a down payment of all that God would give his descendants as they battle the Canaanites in the future.

Like Jacob, Joseph also had remarkable faith. In giving his two sons to Jacob, he is virtually consenting to their being rejected for a future and position in Egypt. By identifying his sons with the despised shepherding people, Joseph seals them off from ascendancy. It is madness from the perspective of the Nile. But like his father, Jacob, Joseph believed the word of promise—that God was building a great people who would one day return to the land of promise.

Take It Home

The first 28 verses of Genesis 49 record Jacob's last words to his twelve sons. All twelve of Jacob's sons, regardless of their faithfulness, have a future and a blessing. But *only* the faithful sons would have an inheritance in the land. This is an example of a principle that continues even today: The actions of believers determine their future blessings in God's program.

Jacob's prophecies refer to the distant future (49:1). The double exhortation to give attention to Jacob's words stresses the importance of what he is about to say (49:2). The prophecies included here are not the spontaneous thoughts of a dying man, but the carefully prepared words of a prophetic poet.

Jacob's three oldest sons are disinherited for their unfaithfulness (49:3–7). The firstborn son normally has two rights. First, he becomes the leader of the family, the new patriarch. Second, he is entitled to a double share of the inheritance. But Reuben is not to receive this blessing because he is reckless and destructive. The picture painted with these descriptive words is of water that floods its banks and goes wildly out of control. The result is an evaluation of Reuben that points to wildness and weakness, an undisciplined life. This is a reference to Reuben's misconduct in Genesis 35 (49:3–4).

True to Jacob's prophecy, the Reubenites never produce a leader of any kind for Israel. They never enter the promised land (Numbers 23). They build unauthorized places of worship (Joshua 22:10–34). The tribe produces no significant man, no judge, no king, and no prophet.

When Jacob says that Simeon and Levi are brothers (Genesis 49:5–7), it is not a statement simply about their family relationship as brothers as much as their similarity in character—they are two of a kind. Interestingly, Jacob still characterizes his sons as angry men. He doesn't say their anger *was* fierce; instead, he says it *is* fierce. These men have remained angry.

Jacob's prophecy that these tribes will be scattered is fulfilled, as the tribe of Simeon later inherits land scattered throughout Judah's territory (Joshua 19:1–9; see also 1 Chronicles 4:28–33, 39, 42). The tribe of Levi becomes priests with no inheritance, but scattered throughout the rest of the tribal lands.

Even though these first three tribes suffer loss for their sins, Jacob's prophecies about them are still a blessing. They retain a place in the chosen family and enjoy the benefits of God's promises as Jacob's heirs. Yet, they are disqualified from the reward that could have been theirs because of their failure to repent of their sin (Numbers 32:23–24; Ezekiel 18:30).

Jacob gives the seven acceptable sons responsibilities, and the two most faithful sons receive greater responsibility. True to the poetic qualities of the text, the images of the destiny of the remaining sons are, in most cases, based on wordplays of the sons' names (Genesis 49:8–27).

Judah will be preeminent among his brothers, and they will praise him. Judah's hand will be on the neck of his enemies, and his brothers will bow down to him. But leadership of his descendants will not be fully realized until the days of King David, some 640 years later (49:8).

In some translations, the word *Shiloh* appears in verse 10. There's been much discussion about the exact meaning of this word, but modern translations simply translate it as *he*. Many believe this is a reference to the Messiah, and that it functions as a confirmation that He will come through Judah's bloodline (Zechariah 10:4; Hebrews 7:14).

Zebulun is promised territory between the Mediterranean Sea and the Sea of Galilee (Genesis 49:13). It is possible that Zebulun and Issachar share some territory (Deuteronomy 33:18–19), so Zebulun could have bordered the Sea of Galilee.

Issachar will prefer an agricultural way of life rather than political supremacy among the tribes (Genesis 49:14–15). Evidently, Issachar is strong and capable, but also passive and lazy. In contrast to Judah, who subdues his enemies like a lion, Issachar submits to the Canaanites.

According to Jacob's prophecy, Dan will judge Israel (49:16–18). This prophecy comes to reality partially during Samson's era in ancient Israel (Judges 13:2). Dan's victories benefit all Israel. Yet this tribe leads Israel into idolatry (Judges 18:30–31; 1 Kings 12:26–30) and becomes known as the center of idolatry in Israel (Amos 8:14).

The tribe of Gad will become tenacious fighters and be victorious over all the foreign armies they face (Genesis 49:19; Jeremiah 49:1).

Asher will enjoy some of the most fertile land in Canaan (Genesis 49:20; Deuteronomy 33:24–25; Joshua 19:24–31).

The tribe of Naphtali will be well-known for producing eloquent speakers and beautiful literature (Genesis 49:21). The most famous of these is Deborah, who composes a beautiful poem of military triumph (Judges 5:1–31). Along with the land of Zebulun, Naphtali's territory is near the Sea of Galilee, the region where Jesus carries out much of His teaching and ministry (Matthew 4:15–16).

Joseph's blessing is especially abundant (Genesis 49:22–26). Judah receives the leadership of the tribes, but Joseph obtains the double portion of the birthright (1 Chronicles 5:2). The two tribes bearing his sons' names will see the fulfillment of the blessing, even though during his lifetime Joseph faced much opposition.

The tribe of Benjamin has a reputation for being fierce and aggressive (Judges 19–21). We have a number of examples of the tribe of Benjamin's aggressive leaders: Ehud (Judges 3:15–23), King Saul (1 Samuel 9:1; 14:47–52), and Paul the apostle (Acts 8:1–3). The tribe demonstrates a warlike character (Judges 5:14; 20:16; 1 Chronicles 8:40; 2 Chronicles 14:8; 17:17).

The rest of chapter 49 has to do with Jacob's death. In verses 29–33, a repeated phrase serves as bookends: Jacob is going to his people (Genesis 49:29, 33). This ancient expression describes Jacob's reunion with those who had preceded him in death and had exercised faith in God. Jacob's specific instructions reveal that he probably reflected on his death; he wanted to make sure that everything was in place.

50:1–26

JACOB'S AND JOSEPH'S FINAL DAYS

Joseph was a man of faith and a man of sensitivity. The only tears recorded in Joseph's life are not for himself but for the plight of his brothers and the loss of his father (50:1–7).

The Egyptians show great honor to Jacob and to Joseph in their seventy days of mourning after Jacob's death. This length of time is only two days short of the length of mourning for a Pharaoh.

When Joseph goes to bury his father, all of Pharaoh's servants and elders, and all of the elders of Egypt, accompany him (50:7–8).

The location of the threshing floor at Atad is not certain (50:10). The expression "the other side of the Jordan," used in several Bible translations, could refer to the eastern or western bank. However, it is commonly used in the Old Testament for Transjordan. This would suggest that the entourage came up the Jordan Valley and crossed into the land at Jericho, just as the Israelites would in the time of Joshua.

God's promises are all connected to Canaan, but Joseph does not choose to stay there (50:14). He knows his calling concerns Egypt. He takes one look at the land of promise, which he has not seen since he was seventeen years old, and then goes back to the place where God had called him.

Joseph's brothers exhibit some negative and positive responses when their father dies (50:15–18). Initially, they respond negatively due to guilt, fear, and paranoia. They assume that Joseph has been simply biding his time out of respect for his father Jacob. But now that Jacob is gone, they are gripped with the terrifying expectation of punishment for their sins. So they falsely claim that Jacob has issued a charge for Joseph to forgive his brothers. However, Jacob never did this, because he recognized that Joseph had completely forgiven his brothers.

Positively though, the brothers own their sin against Joseph. They beg for forgiveness, bow down before Joseph, and offer themselves up as slaves (50:17–18).

In response, Joseph recognizes God as the only One who is able to judge. While not diminishing the manner in which his brothers wronged him, he recognizes God's greater purpose (50:19–21). Joseph's claim that God meant for good what his brothers meant for evil is the theme of the entire Joseph narrative.

Joseph was a man who experienced God's blessing (50:22–26). More than fifty years elapse between verses 21 and 22. During this period, God abundantly blesses Joseph with a long life, the privilege of seeing his great-great-grandchildren, and a remarkable faith. It is only fitting that the book of Genesis ends on a note of blessing, since it has been a consistent theme throughout the book.

Although God's people would spend four hundred years in Egyptian bondage, Joseph already saw the day when God would bring them back to the promised land. In light of this faith, Joseph makes his wishes known to be buried in the promised land (50:25). This is an expression of faith and confidence that God's covenant promises will come to pass. Joseph dies and is placed in a coffin in Egypt (50:26). Unlike his father, Jacob, Joseph's body isn't buried immediately. Instead, his coffin lay above ground for over four hundred years, until the people of Israel take it back to Canaan as they leave Egypt under Moses' leadership. So there it sat, in Egypt, for four hundred years, as a silent witness to Joseph's confidence that Israel was going back to the promised land, just as God had said (Exodus 13:19). Joseph's faith in God's promises to his forefathers provides a fitting climax for the book of Genesis.

EXODUS

INTRODUCTION TO EXODUS

Exodus tells the story of the birth of the nation of Israel through their deliverance from bondage in Egypt and the receiving of God's instructions, based on His covenant, for building their nation to honor Him.

AUTHOR

Though there is debate among scholars about the authorship of Exodus, Moses is considered the author by most evangelical scholars.

PURPOSE

The main purpose of the book of Exodus is to describe God's rescue of His enslaved people and His making them a nation. This book chronicles God's faithfulness to His people—in spite of their sin.

OCCASION

The book of Genesis closes with the family of Israel making a home in Egypt under the leadership of Joseph. Exodus picks up centuries later in Egypt after the family of Israel has grown into the nation of Israel. While Joseph had saved the Egyptians from starvation, his family's descendants had become slaves. Exodus follows the story of God's people from the birth of Moses, the leader of Israel during this period in their history, through their deliverance from bondage, the giving of the law, and the construction of the tabernacle in the desert.

THEMES

Exodus is rich in themes which will recur in the Old and New Testaments—the burden of bondage to sin, God's faithfulness and deliverance in spite of stubbornness, and the radical vision that He has for His people.

CONTRIBUTION TO THE BIBLE

In many ways, Exodus expands on what Genesis teaches us about God's character and His intentions for creation. We witness both His judgment in the plagues on the Egyptians and His mercy in the deliverance of the Israelites from slavery. The Exodus introduces the Law of the Lord, which will bring both blessing and suffering to the nation of Israel until it is fulfilled by the work and person of Jesus Christ. Exodus establishes how Israel is going to be set up, and much of the rest of the Old Testament recounts their struggle to meet God's requirements. The book also describes God dwelling with His people in the tabernacle, which is ultimately an image for the kingdom of heaven. It is rich in relevance to the New Testament with its many symbols of the sacrificial lamb, the holiness of God, and the fatal consequences of people's failure to keep His commandments.

OUTLINE

EXODUS 1:1–22

PHARAOH'S FEARS AND ISRAEL'S FAITH

Setting Up the Section

There are times when God is there, but He is, at least from our perspective, silent. The period of time depicted in the first chapter of Exodus is a time when, from all appearances, God is silent. Nevertheless, God is present and His hand is at work in the lives of His children.

1:1–7

LINKING THE PAST TO THE PRESENT

The beginning of Exodus links the events of Genesis to those recorded in Exodus—two books intended to be understood in relationship to each other. Genesis provides an excellent backdrop for Exodus, reminding Israel of her roots and of the basis for God's blessings, which were soon to be experienced. Exodus 1:1–6 sums up the history of Israel as a clan, as described more thoroughly in Genesis 12–50. These six verses remind us that all that is going to take place in this book is directly related to what has gone before. Verse 7 fills in a nearly 400 year gap, covering the period from the death of Joseph to the time of the Exodus.

Most importantly, this portion of the introduction to the book of Exodus (1:1–6) links the existence and rapid growth of Israel as a nation to the covenant that God made with Abraham (Genesis 12:1–3; 15:12) and reiterates to the patriarchs (Genesis 26:2–5, 24; 28:13–15). The sons of Israel and their families are seventy in number (Exodus 1:5) when they arrive in Egypt. But when the sons of Israel leave Egypt, they do so as a great nation (1:7, 12, 20; 12:37).

Demystifying Exodus

Periods of silence similar to the gap in the history of Israel (1:7) exist throughout scripture. During these periods, God is at work behind the scenes, and in ways that at the time are not immediately apparent. Verses 8–22 demonstrate that during periods of apparent silence, God is at work providentially, bringing His purposes to pass and preparing history for another of His dramatic interventions into the affairs of people.

1:8–14

A NEW KING'S POLICY

There is considerable disagreement among the scholars as to the identity of this new king who does not know about Joseph (1:8). Much of the problem hinges on the date of the Exodus (see intro). Keeping with an early date for the Exodus, it is most likely that the king referred to here is new in a very significant sense. He represents not only a new person, but also a new dynasty.

The fears of the Pharaoh are of interest. He fears the numerical strength of the Israelites and seeks to diminish them. He fears that they will become allies with the enemy, overcome them, and leave Egypt. Interestingly, everything Pharaoh fears comes to pass, in spite of his diligent efforts to prevent it. But Pharaoh's plans are contrary to the purposes and promises of God with regard to His people.

Pharaoh's plan is to enslave the Israelites and tighten control over them. A substantial part of this plan seems to be that of intimidation and oppression, so demoralizing and frightening to the Israelites that they will not dare to resist their masters. Yet just as Israel had greatly multiplied during the time of Joseph (Genesis 47:27), and after his death (Exodus 1:7), so they continue to multiply under the cruel hand of their taskmasters. The Egyptians came to dread the Israelites and worked them ruthlessly (1:12–13).

The Egyptian response to the phenomenal numerical growth of the Israelites is to increase the workload and intensify the harassment and cruelty imposed on them by their taskmasters (1:14). These tactics do not work, which leads to an even more evil plot directed against the people of God, as outlined in verses 15–21.

Critical Observation

The curse of God in Genesis 3 includes hard toil, which is surely the lot of Israel in Egypt. The salvation of mankind, as promised also in Genesis 3, is through the birth of a child. So, too, it is through the birth of a child (Moses, in Exodus 2) that God provides a deliverer for His people. As people strove to provide themselves with security and significance, Egypt sought to secure herself by forcing the Israelites to build cities with bricks and mortar (compare Genesis 11 with Exodus 1:14; 5:1).

1:15–22

PHARAOH AND THE MIDWIVES

Pharaoh's demands of the midwives are quite abominable. Not only does he propose acts of violence on the innocent, he also passes on all responsibility for the death of these Hebrew infants. He wants the midwives to solve this national dilemma of the Hebrew birthrate. But the midwives fear God more than Pharaoh, so they refuse to put the infant boys to death (1:17). Pharaoh's plan backfires.

God rewards the midwives for fearing Him by enabling them to be fruitful themselves (some scholars suggest that barren women were often made midwives). God also records names of two of these God fearing Hebrew midwives—as an example to believers throughout the centuries.

Take It Home

God cares not about your position or your prestige in life. He cares only if you fear Him and trust in His Son, Jesus Christ, for the forgiveness of your sins and eternal life. The fact that the writer of Exodus names the midwives but leaves Pharaoh unnamed is a good picture of God's value on those who obey Him. If you are His child, He knows you by name. If not, no matter what your earthly splendor or power, you are nameless to Him, and you will spend eternity apart from Him.

EXODUS 2:1–25

MOSES: ISRAEL'S DELIVERER

Setting Up the Section

Few stories in the Bible are more familiar than that of Moses set afloat in the waters of the Nile and his rescue by the daughter of Pharaoh. Exodus 2 shows how God's hand is at work in the history of Israel, preserving the life of one child who will become Israel's deliverer.

2:1–10

MOSES—OUT OF THE WATER

We see from verse 2 that Moses is exceedingly well formed and beautiful, and that his parents perceive that God has a special purpose for their child. But Moses is not suggesting that God moved his parents to hide him because they were convinced that he was particularly special in appearance or in purpose, but rather that they saw something special about him as a child of God. Exodus 2:2 could simply be rendered, "she saw that he was good." The Hebrew word meaning "good" is frequently used by Moses in the five books of the Law, and in most it has the sense of goodness which is the result of being made (or given) by God, and of being declared good by Him. The frequent expressions in Genesis 1 and 2, "it was good," employ the same term.

The biblical perspective is that children come from God (Psalm 127). Every child is the product of divine creation (Psalm 139:13–14) and is thus "good" in the eyes of God. Moses' parents refuse to put their child to death because God created him, and because this means he (like every other child ever born) is special to God. They feared the God who created their son more than the Pharaoh who wished to kill him.

Pharaoh's daughter comes face-to-face with the implications of her father's policy of genocide (Exodus 2:6). What Pharaoh had commanded was not only unthinkable, it was undoable. She names the boy *Moses*, a name rooted in the event of her finding him as a baby at which time she drew him out of the Nile.

Critical Observation

The deliverance of Moses is significant in that it is a beautiful illustration of the truth declared in Ephesians 3:20–21. Not only was Moses spared and protected by Pharaoh's daughter's love, but his parents were allowed to keep him for a time, train him in the ways of their God, and then, in addition to all these blessings, they were paid for it. Now, in the palace of the Pharaoh whose orders were, "Throw them in the water!" there is a Hebrew boy whose name means "Taken from the water." Once again, God providentially preserved and prospered His people. Not only was Moses spared, but now there is a Hebrew living in the palace, part of the royal family. What a challenge to the limits of our faith! What a gracious God we serve!

2:11–25

MOSES FLEES TO SAFETY

Verse 11 passes over nearly forty years (see Acts 7:23), taking up the story of Moses as an adult. Moses makes the critical decision to identify with his people before he goes out to observe the affliction of his brethren (as described in Hebrews 11:24–26), which informs us that the reason Moses visits his brethren is due to his decision to identify with them and even suffer with them. Thus, Moses does not lose his status as a son of Pharaoh's daughter by the killing; he gives it up before the killing. Moses' visit to his brethren backfires, in one sense, but it is used providentially to prepare him for his future calling.

Demystifying Exodus

Moses' premeditated murder (Exodus 2:12) cannot be defended. Yet while Moses' method of dealing with this problem is wrong, we see that his motivation is commendable. Moses sought to defend the oppressed. When he sought to rebuke his Hebrew brother for wrongly mistreating another Hebrew (2:13), Moses reveals, once again, the disposition of a deliverer.

Rather than taking his place as a deliverer of his people, at this point Moses flees to find himself delivering the oppressed elsewhere. At the well, Moses does not like how the women are being pushed in line by the shepherds (2:15–17). Moses enforces the policy of "ladies first," and once again delivers the oppressed. Moses can not look the other way, even when advantage is being taken of strangers.

With great economy of words, Moses briefly records that this chance encounter leads to a lengthy stay in Midian, his marriage to Zipporah, and the birth of a son, Gershom. Moses names the child Gershom because he felt like an alien in a foreign land (2:22). In Midian, a land closer to Canaan than Egypt, Moses thought of himself as an alien and a sojourner. He still thought of Egypt, not Canaan, as his homeland. One can hardly think of this time as that of great faith or purpose in Moses' life. The faith and commitment to the people of God with which verse 11 began has somehow eroded into something far less.

Verse 25 tells us that in spite of all these appearances, God is at work. Humanly speaking, it looks as though everything is working against Israel, yet this reiterates that God is very much informed, involved, and intent upon fulfilling His purposes and promises. This section ties together the agony of God's people in Egypt (described in chapter 1, but overshadowed by the personal account of Moses in chapter 2) with the deliverance about to take place in the following chapters.

Take It Home

We can easily acknowledge the fallibility of those who do not know or serve God. But having acknowledged the depravity of mankind in general, we should not forget also the fallibility of the faithful. Every detail of our lives, every incident, every failure, is employed by God providentially to further His purposes. While this should in no way make us lax in our desire to know God's will and to obey Him, it should serve to assure us that even when we fail, He does not. How do you see this to be true in your own journey? And what can you learn from Moses' experiences?

EXODUS 3:1–22

THE BURNING BUSH

The God of the Burning Bush	3:1–15
Moses' Marching Orders	3:16–22

Setting Up the Section

Chapter 3 introduces a significant change in the drama of the deliverance of God's people from Egypt. From God's providential dealings in the life of the nation of Israel, we move to God's direct intervention through Moses and the miracles He performs. We move from the silence of God over the past four hundred years to God's speaking directly to Moses from the bush, and later on, from the same mountain.

3:1–15

THE GOD OF THE BURNING BUSH

The revelation of God to Moses is the basis for Moses' obedience, as well as for the entire nation. It is also the basis for all of God's actions with regard to Egypt and to His people. In many ways, the incident of the burning bush is critical to our understanding of God.

The burning bush made not only a profound impact upon Moses and the nation of Israel, but it also continued to serve as a key event in history—the significance of which is not lost on Israel in the generations that followed. This passage of scripture is one that must have been well-known to the Jews of Jesus' day. The account of the burning bush is so central to the thinking of the Gospel writers, Mark and Luke, that they (perhaps like most men in their day) came to call this section of scripture "the bush" portion (Mark 12:26; Luke 20:37).

The bush is apparently a typical common desert bush, but the fire is far from ordinary. The closer Moses gets to the bush, the more incredible the scene becomes. Moses surely had to wonder about this phenomenon. Scholars have offered numerous "natural" explanations for the burning bush over the years, not wanting to acknowledge a full-fledged miracle. Yet we know from the biblical account that this is truly a unique intervention of God in time and space.

Demystifying Exodus

Attempts to explain the burning bush as something other than miraculous abound. Some of the most common include that it was a natural phenomenon called "St. Elmo's fire," which is a discharge of electricity that causes a kind of glow, or firebrands of light which often occur in dry lands with an abundance of storms. Others suggest that it may have been a volcanic phenomenon, or simply that this account is a myth, like other ancient accounts of burning objects that were not consumed. Still others say that it may have been a beam of sunlight piercing through a crack in the mountain, or a purely psychological experience. The author (Moses) himself, however, provides a wholly supernatural explanation—the burning bush that would not be consumed was aglow with the angel of the Lord (Genesis 16:7; 22:11; Exodus 3:2; Judges 6:11; 13:3), the preincarnate manifestation of the second person of the Godhead.

The character of the God who is calling and commissioning Moses is the basis for Moses' faith and obedience. The God of the burning bush is a holy God, an object of fear and reverence. At the time the law is given on Mount Sinai, God's holiness is the basis for Israel's conduct, which the law prescribed. But how is the holiness of God a significant factor in the Exodus? The sins of the Egyptians must be dealt with, and additionally, the possession of the land of Canaan by the Israelites (Exodus 3:8, 17) is a judgment on these peoples for their abominations in the sight of God (see Genesis 15:16; Leviticus 18:24–28).

The God of the burning bush is the covenant-making, covenant-keeping God of Abraham, Isaac, and Jacob. In verse 6, God identifies Himself to Moses in this way. He is the God who made a covenant with Abraham and reiterated it to Isaac and Jacob. There is no new plan, but simply the outworking of the old plan, revealed to Abraham in Genesis 15.

The God of the burning bush also reveals Himself to be a compassionate, imminent God who commissions people to participate in His purposes. Some of the richest revelation concerning the character of God is found in verses 11–15, where God responds to two questions raised by Moses. In essence, these questions can be summarized: "Who am I?" (3:11), and "Who are You?" (3:13). God's response to these questions serves to clarify His character even further.

Forty years before, Moses made a critical decision concerning his identity—he was an Israelite, and thus could not be known any longer as the son of Pharaoh's daughter. Moses determined that he would attempt to deliver his people, but at the time Moses had assumed authority which had not yet been given him. Moses had forty years to ponder his presumption and its consequences. Here, his question reflects caution and a desire to receive a clear commission from God.

God's answer seeks to refocus Moses' attention from looking at himself to having faith in God. What is important is not the instrument in God's hand, but the One in whose hand the instrument is being held. God promises Moses that His presence will go with him as he obeys his calling. Moses' authority is wrapped up in the presence of God, which is assured when he is obedient to God's command.

Critical Observation

It has been observed that the Great Commission of the New Testament is strikingly similar to the commission of Moses. The Great Commission begins with the statement, "All authority in heaven and on earth has been given to me" (Matthew 28:18 NIV), and ends with, "Surely I am with you always, to the very end of the age" (Matthew 28:20 NIV). Divine authority is inseparably linked with divine presence. Many of us are waiting for God to give us a sign before we are willing to step out in faith. God may well require that we act in faith before we are given a sign of His presence and His power.

Scholars have spent a great deal of effort to determine the exact meaning of the expression, "I AM WHO I AM" (3:14). Predictably, they do not all agree. As the "I AM," God is not the God who *was* anything, in the sense that He changes. Whatever He was, He continues to be, and He will be forever. God exists independently and unchangeably. Therefore, whatever God has begun to do He will bring to completion, because there are no changes which necessitate any alterations in His original plans and purposes.

How can Moses and the people of Israel be assured that God will deliver them from Egyptian bondage and lead them into the promised land? Their confidence is well placed in the God whose nature and character is that of the "I AM" in Exodus 3. Isaiah 43:1–3 references this same idea and is intended to comfort Israel and assure the nation of God's promises. Just as Israel was not swallowed up by the sea, neither will she be swallowed up by her present and future affliction. Just as the burning bush was not consumed by the fire, so Israel will not be consumed by the fires of affliction and adversity, now or forever (see Malachi 3:2–3, 5–6).

Take It Home

The basis for the call of Moses and for his obedience to that call is an assurance as to the character of God. The measure of our faith is proportionate to our grasp of the greatness and the goodness of our God. No person's faith will be any greater than his or her grasp of the greatness of God as the object of faith. For the Christian, there is no thought more comforting than the eternality of God and His unchanging character. It assures us that His purposes will be fulfilled.

3:16–22

MOSES' MARCHING ORDERS

Now that God has revealed Himself, He reveals His plan for Moses and for Israel. Moses is to repeat the words which God has spoken to him from the burning bush, request a three-day "leave" for the Israelites to worship God in the desert, and finally, collect the wages that are owed to the people of God for their hard work in Egypt.

These commands are all based on the promise and the prophecy which God had previously given Abraham in Genesis 15:12–20. The real struggle now is between Moses and God, and whether he will do what God commands. As the next section reveals, Moses will learn that God's commands are not to be refused.

EXODUS 4:1–31

BEATING AROUND THE BURNING BUSH

Signs for a Reluctant Leader	4:1–17
Signs for the Exiled Israelites	4:18–31

Setting Up the Section

Moses seeks to prove that he is not the man for the task which God has given him. The essence of Moses' argument is, "Send someone else!"

4:1–17

SIGNS FOR A RELUCTANT LEADER

In the past, Moses doubted his calling; now he is doubting the Word of God, for the Lord has just told him the leaders of Israel will accept him (3:18). From the words which follow this assurance, we know that Moses is not only told that the leaders of Israel will accept his leadership, but that it will all work out, just as God has said. Moses is guilty of unbelief.

God still graciously deals with the weakness of Moses by granting him the ability to perform three signs. For the Israelites, these signs are visible evidence that God did appear to Moses in the burning bush. Not only do these signs emphatically prove the existence of the God of the Hebrews, but they give evidence of His superior power.

Rather than acting on the basis of who God is, Moses retreats on the pretext that he is not a gifted communicator. This is indeed a piece of false humility. Moses does not have a speech problem, as some might suppose. According to Stephen, he is eloquent (Acts 7:21–22). Moses is not only doing a disservice to God (by refusing to believe Him and obey in faith), but to himself. Moses should not trust in his own abilities, but neither should he deny the abilities which God has given him.

God reminds Moses that, as his Creator, He fashioned him precisely as He intended, and he is therefore fully able to carry out his commission. The problem of what to say is one that the Lord will handle in due time (Exodus 4:12). While Moses is worrying about what he will say when he gets to Egypt, God is spurring him to get going. Moses is looking too far down the path. Verse 13 reveals the bottom line: Moses does not want to go. It is not that he lacks the assurance or the authority; he simply lacks the courage to act.

God is longsuffering and patient, but now He is angry. God's anger is not only reflected in a visible way, but it is evident in His answer to Moses (4:14–17). Aaron could speak fluently, so why not let him speak for Moses? As later events indicate, the presence of Aaron is a burden for Moses and at times a stumbling block for others (Exodus 32:1–5; Numbers 12:1–12).

4:18–31

SIGNS FOR THE EXILED ISRAELITES

Jethro, who seems to be a wise and gracious man, grants Moses' request, wishing him well (4:18). It almost seems as though Moses rearranges the facts God has given when he asks for Jethro's permission to leave, so as to suggest that Moses needed to see if his own people were, in fact, alive and well. Does Moses inadvertently confuse the facts, or does he deceptively rearrange the facts so as to gain the permission of Jethro to take his family to Egypt? The text does not tell us.

Critical Observation

Here, for the first time, the nation of Israel is referred to as the firstborn son of God (4:22–23). Because Pharaoh would not release Israel, God's firstborn son, to worship Him in the desert, God would have Moses tell Pharaoh that He will kill his firstborn. The mention of Israel as Yahweh's firstborn is significant in this larger context. The firstborn son was to the Egyptians not only special, but in many respects sacred. It is therefore most interesting that the people of God are regarded as firstborn in this passage.

One's initial impression of verses 24–26 is that they are inappropriate or out of place, an idea that is not worth entertaining. This action on God's part seems so unusual and so harsh that some have even suggested the "deity" mentioned here was demonic. What does this action on Zipporah's part mean, and what is the purpose of including this story in Exodus? Many believe this enigmatic event explains Moses' deeply rooted resistance to obeying the call of God to return to Egypt to rescue the Israelites.

To the Israelite, the covenant God made with Abraham and reiterated to the patriarchs and Moses was their "gospel." Circumcision was the sign of the covenant—evidence of the parents' faith in the promise of God to Abraham that through his seed blessings would come to Israel and to the whole world (see Genesis 12:1–3). As a testimony of the parents' faith in God's covenant promise, every male in Israel was to be circumcised.

The basis of Israel's preservation (as pictured by the bush that doesn't burn) is the covenant made with Abraham by the eternal God who is, from now on (Exodus 3:15) the "I AM." The covenant was the "gospel," the promise of blessing and salvation which every Israelite was called upon to believe and whose belief was symbolized by the circumcision of his sons and all the males in his household. Moses was to go to Egypt and tell the Israelites that God was about to fulfill His promises, based upon His covenant. And yet Moses had not yet circumcised his son. And if this son is his firstborn, he has had many years in which to do so.

The conclusion of chapter 4 serves as a divine commentary on the fivefold objection of Moses to the call of God. The last verses of the chapter, which report the belief of the people and their worship of God, inform us that Moses' fears were unreal and unreasonable. All of his objections as reported in chapters 3 and 4 have no foundation and are based more on his fears than on reality.

Critical Observation

Moses, with all his fancy royal Egyptian and personal experience with God, failed to obey God in the simplest area of his life—to circumcise his son. He cannot challenge men and women to step out in obedience, based upon their faith in God's covenant promises, when he has not yet circumcised his son as an evidence of his faith. Thus, Moses' problems in relation to his public work are rooted in his personal walk. No wonder Paul writes this to Timothy: "Pay close attention to yourself and to your teaching; persevere in these things, for as you do this you will insure salvation both for yourself and for those who hear you" (1 Timothy 4:16 NASB).

The leaders portrayed in the Bible are not the giants we would like to find, but people whom God has used in spite of their weaknesses and failures. Surely we must admit that Moses, like Elijah, was a man of "like passions" (see James 5:17), a man who had the same fears and failures as we do. It is not the greatness of the man which is the key to his success, but the character of the God who calls and uses fallible people to do His will.

Take It Home

It is hard to call others to faith when one's own is deficient. The gospel is the bedrock foundation on which our personal walk and our public work is based. This is one reason why we as a church believe that the remembrance of the Lord's death is necessary on a weekly basis—and why sacraments like the Lord's Supper and baptism still have such significance. They are not just rituals, but touchstones to remind us what is essential and foundational to our faith and walk. It is unbelief that keeps us from realizing God's purposes. We must remind ourselves that the things of this life are momentary and that eternity will expose what is both lasting and enjoyable.

EXODUS 5:1–6:13

THE REALITY OF BONDAGE

Setting Up the Section

After Moses has met with God, he returns to Egypt where his fears that Pharaoh would resist God's demands to let the Israelites go are realized.

5:1–21

DEMANDS OF DELIVERANCE

In this passage, Moses first uses God's powerful (and now popularized) phrase: "Let my people go." God desires to be alone with *His* people, but Pharaoh is annoyed by the arrogance of the request. He even says he suspects Moses is lying about receiving divine revelation. Even though Pharaoh is warned there will be consequences, he remains arrogant himself–without any fear or reverence for the God of the Israelites. His heart is already hardened to the plight of the Hebrews. In response to the Israelites' request, he further complicates their situation by demanding bricks without providing straw for them to be made.

Critical Observation

Historical records show that Egyptian serfs around this era were allowed to take time off for religious festivals and celebrations. This fact underscores how proud Pharaoh was in his dealings with the Israelites. In the ancient world, the foreman was typically held accountable and responsible for the conduct of the group of slaves in his charge. Thus the foremen were beaten for the Israelites' inability to make enough bricks and, according to the custom that all slaves could make direct petitions even to Pharaoh, they complained.

5:22–6:13

GOD PROMISES DELIVERANCE

God reiterates to Moses His commitment to deliver the Israelites from bondage in Egypt—these are the promises of the Abrahamic Covenant. Yet even the promise of deliverance does little to raise the hopes of the beleaguered people. The Hebrew word for *redeem* is the same word used in the story of Ruth, when she is redeemed by the house of Boaz. It refers to the right of family members to acquire persons or property belonging to other family members that are at risk—just as God redeems His people during their time of need in Egypt and ultimately purposes to save their souls through the work of Jesus Christ.

EXODUS 6:14–7:13

GOD'S PEOPLE: MOSES AND AARON

Genealogy of Moses and Aaron 6:14–27
Aaron to Speak for Moses 6:28–7:7
A Slithering Staff and a Hard Heart 7:8–13

Setting Up the Section

God often uses genealogies to testify to His faithfulness and work across generations in space and time.

6:14–27

GENEALOGY OF MOSES AND AARON

Evidently the genealogy of Moses and Aaron is partially truncated since only four generations are recorded for the 400-year period during which the Israelites wander in the desert. This record introduces the team that God has chosen to lead His people, His children, out of slavery. The genealogy testifies to how intimately connected the Israelites would always be with Egypt, because scholars note that it includes Egyptian names—like Phinehas and Putiel.

6:28–7:7

AARON TO SPEAK FOR MOSES

God likens the relationship between Moses and his brother, Aaron, to the one between God and His prophet. Aaron will speak for Moses. Later on in this story, when the Israelites commit idolatry under Aaron's watch (chapter 32), Moses will discover what a frustrating and disappointing relationship this can often be! Aaron is Moses' mouthpiece in part because of Moses' own lack of faith in himself. Another significant description here is the hardening of Pharaoh's heart. Throughout the story of Israel's deliverance, both God and Pharaoh play a role in this process, which will ultimately bring great sorrow and destruction to the Egyptians through the plagues and defeat in the Red Sea.

7:8–13

A SLITHERING STAFF AND A HARD HEART

The miracle of turning the staff into a snake is a demonstration of Moses and Aaron's God-given powers. Though the Egyptian sorcerers were able to imitate the miracle to a point—changing their staffs to serpents—their power was inferior to the power God gave Aaron and Moses.

The point of this supernatural ability on the part of Moses and Aaron is also to demonstrate to Pharaoh, who was considered a god himself, that Moses has been divinely appointed and anointed and is an opponent to be reckoned with. The demand increases from the request for an opportunity for communion with God to a demand for release of the Israelites from slavery. Again Pharaoh's heart is hardened. Eventually, even the sting of the plagues and the death of his firstborn cannot penetrate Pharaoh's heart to be humble before God.

EXODUS 7:14–10:29

THE FINGER OF GOD

Plague One: The Nile Turns into Blood	7:14–25
Plague Two: The Frogs	8:1–15
Plague Three: The Gnats	8:16–19
Plague Four: The Flies	8:20–32
Plague Five: Livestock Killed	9:1–7
Plague Six: Boils	9:8–12
Plague Seven: The Storm	9:13–35
Plague Eight: Locusts	10:1–20
Plague Nine: Darkness	10:21–29

Setting Up the Section

The plagues which God brings upon the Egyptians are a unique kind of tragedy—part of God's judgment of Pharaoh and his people for their oppression of the Israelites (see Genesis 15:13–14; Deuteronomy 11:1–4; Psalm 78:44–52).

7:14–25

PLAGUE ONE: THE NILE TURNS INTO BLOOD

There are some tragedies in life which are simply that—part of the suffering and sadness of life. There are also tragedies which have a very positive and beneficial purpose—the tragedies of Job's life, for example, or the tragedy of the cross of Christ. The sufferings of the nation of Israel during the four hundred years of their slavery in Egypt also will, in the drama of Israel's history, prove to be beneficial.

The Nile is virtually the lifeblood of Egypt. Without the silt it provides during its times of overflow and the water it provides to sustain life, Egypt would be almost uninhabitable. The meaning of the miracle of turning the Nile to blood can best be understood in light of God's later prophecy, recorded in Ezekiel 29:2–6, where He concludes that by this miracle all of Egypt will know that He is the Lord.

This plague serves as an attack on one of the Egyptian gods. The Egyptians believed that Hapi, a god of fertility, was also the god of the Nile.

8:1–15

PLAGUE TWO: THE FROGS

Frogs were common in Egypt, especially around the Nile River, but there had never been this many. From this account, one can visualize frogs hopping and croaking all over Egypt, and even overrunning the palace of the Pharaoh. The frogs got into the food, into the kneading troughs, and ovens. When Egypt is finally rid of the frogs, thanks to Moses, huge heaps of dead frogs are piled all over the country, creating a stench that is a plague in and of itself. God is making the Israelites' presence a real nuisance to the Egyptians. Soon, it is their groaning, not the Hebrews', that will accomplish God's purpose.

Critical Observation

Frogs were also regarded as having divine power. In the Egyptian pantheon, the goddess Heqet had the form of a woman with a frog's head. From her nostrils, it was believed, came the breath of life that animated the bodies of those created by her husband, the great god Khnum, from the dust of the earth. Therefore frogs were not to be killed.

8:16–19

PLAGUE THREE: THE GNATS

It is not altogether certain what is meant by the Hebrew term translated *gnat*. The King James Version renders the term *lice*, which is also possible. Some have suggested that it was a plague of mosquitoes. It does not really matter exactly what is meant. The gnats plagued both humans and animals. The significance of this plague is that the magicians of Egypt are unable to produce these gnats themselves, which leads them to tell Pharaoh that it is the work of God (8:19). From the other places where this same expression is found (Exodus 31:18; Deuteronomy 9:10; Psalm 8:3; Luke 11:20), it seems to refer primarily to the power of God directly intervening in the affairs of men and women. Nevertheless, Pharaoh's heart is hardened, and he refuses to listen.

8:20–32

PLAGUE FOUR: THE FLIES

With this plague, the second sequence of three plagues is commenced. Here, discrimination is made between the Egyptians and the Israelites. While the exact species of flies that plagues Egypt is not certain, one can assume that they are bigger and more difficult than the gnats previously set loose on the Egyptians. Because the flies are so bothersome, Pharaoh is willing to negotiate with Moses. Pharaoh's request, "Pray for me" (8:28), indicates his self-centered interests. Moses leaves, but with the warning that there must be no more deceit on Pharaoh's part regarding his promise to let Israel go. But when the flies are gone, so is Pharaoh's motivation to release Israel.

9:1–7

PLAGUE FIVE: LIVESTOCK KILLED

The fifth plague is directed against the livestock of the Egyptians, but not the cattle of the Israelites. There is only speculation as to the cause of death. By whatever means, God virtually wipes out the cattle of the Egyptians. Since wealth was measured largely in terms of cattle, this was an economic disaster. The gods of Egypt were once again proven to be lifeless and useless.

9:8–12

PLAGUE SIX: BOILS

There is a subtly humorous note here. The magicians are not only unable to rid the land of Egypt of the boils, they are also so afflicted themselves that they cannot even show up to stand before Moses.

9:13–35

PLAGUE SEVEN: THE STORM

God often uses weather to humble people and to demonstrate His power. Remember the instance where the disciples were caught in a storm on the sea and Jesus walked on water? Describing this as the plague of hail is only partly true. In reality, the plague is the worst thunderstorm in Egypt's history (9:18), and the death and destruction that occurs is the result of both hailstones and lightning (9:24).

This plague begins the third and final trilogy of plagues. Things get considerably worse as the plagues continue to progress. These last plagues begin with the warning that unless Pharaoh releases the Israelites, God will send even more plagues against Pharaoh and Egypt (9:14). God could have legitimately and easily wiped out all of Egypt in one blow, but He does not (9:15). However if Pharaoh persists in his hardness of heart, things will get considerably worse.

In verse 16, Moses explains why God has allowed Pharaoh's stubbornness to persist. God raised Pharaoh up for the purpose of hardening his heart and thus providing the occasion for God to manifest His power to mankind.

10:1–20

PLAGUE EIGHT: LOCUSTS

The previous plague of the thunderstorm had destroyed the flax and barley crops, but the wheat and spelt crops were not destroyed since they matured later (9:31). The locusts, however, would wipe out the remaining crops. This plague brings Pharaoh to a point of humility before Moses and God, but still there is no deal made between them.

10:21–29

PLAGUE NINE: DARKNESS

The darkness of the ninth plague is so intense that it produces dread in the hearts of the Egyptians. God often refers to His way and Himself as "the light," particularly in the incarnate Christ. Consider how striking the frightening plague of darkness must have been. Some have suggested that the darkness described here is only a partial darkness, created by a dust storm. This can hardly be the case, for the darkness described is much more intense. The three days of darkness had a tremendous emotional and psychological impact on the nation as a whole. The experience may have been something like the three-day period of blindness that Saul experienced prior to his conversion (see Acts 9:8–12).

Critical Observation

The plague of darkness struck hard at one of the chief Egyptian deities, the sun god Re, of whom Pharaoh was a representation. Re was responsible for providing sunlight, warmth, and productivity. Other gods, including Horus, were also associated with the sun. Nut, the goddess of the sky, would have been humiliated by this plague. It was God's way of demonstrating that He alone has power over any other being in His creation. The plagues were an indictment and judgment of the gods of Egypt and demonstrated God's existence and power.

The ninth plague, like the third and the sixth plagues, comes upon the Egyptians without warning, which gives them no opportunity to prepare for the disaster—physically or psychologically. Pharaoh offers to allow the Israelites to leave Egypt to worship God, but insists that the cattle must remain behind (10:24). When this offer is rejected, Pharaoh hotly warns Moses that he must leave his presence, and to return will be to his death. Moses agrees, but he has yet one more plague to proclaim before his final exit from Pharaoh's presence. This tenth plague, he threatens, will bring about the release of the Israelites.

These plagues are a prototype, a sample, of God's future judgment. They are like those which Israel will experience (Deuteronomy 28:27) if they disobey the law God is soon to give. There is much similarity between the plagues of Egypt and the plagues described in the book of Revelation, which are poured out upon the earth in the last days, preceding the return of the Lord. Thus, in Revelation we find the victorious tribulation saints singing the "song of Moses" (Revelation 15:3).

Take It Home

Obviously, not all calamities are the result of sin and evidence of God's judgment. Job's adversity was not the result of his sin, but a means of Job's growth in his walk with God. Job's affliction is also a teaching tool for Satan, who cannot fathom why a saint would continue to worship God when it's not profitable, but painful, to do so. When God is punishing men and women for sin, He is not silent about it. When He is silent at the time of the suffering of a saint, this is a test of faith, not an evidence of God's judgment. The plagues on Egypt remind us of the seriousness of sin.

God's actual judgment of sin is something false religionists seek to deny. Judgment is not easy to believe in or dwell upon. Thus the plagues against Egypt are not popular reading, but are nonetheless a vital part of divine revelation. The psalmist in Psalm 73 looks about and senses that the wicked are not suffering for their sin, but are prospering, while the righteous seem to be the ones who suffer. In this present day, it may seem that sin is profitable, while righteousness is painful. At such times we must remember that we accept the fact of God's future judgments (as we do His future rewards) by faith.

God's judgment of the Egyptians is severe, so it's instructive to consider several perspectives. God judged the gods of Egypt more than He did the Egyptians. Just as hell is the place prepared for Satan and his angels, so judgment here is for the Egyptian gods and whoever chooses to serve these gods. God's judgment may be intended to bring some of the Egyptians to a saving faith. The fact that some Egyptians leave Egypt with the Israelites (Exodus 12:38) gives substance to this possibility. Also, God's judgment upon the Egyptians is the means of delivering His people from terrible bondage. Finally, God's judgment is poured out upon His own Son on the cross of Calvary, so that all mankind might be saved. God's "severity" extended to His own Son. There was an alternative provided by God to suffering the plagues of Egypt—heeding God's warning and doing as He commanded. God's judgment could be avoided by faith and obedience.

EXODUS 11:1–13:16

THE PASSOVER AND THE PLAGUE OF THE FIRSTBORN

The Tenth Plague Foretold	11:1–10
The First Passover	12:1–36
Israel's Exodus	12:37–13:16

Setting Up the Section

The slaughter of the firstborn of the Egyptians raises tremendous moral issues. God uses the tenth plague as the means to release His people from slavery. This text insists that we examine and accept the meaning and application of God's judgment at work in His creation and in the lives of His people.

11:1–10

THE TENTH PLAGUE FORETOLD

Throughout this account, Moses' purpose is not merely a chronological review of historical events, but to explain theologically the significance of what happens to Egypt and Israel as a result of the plague of the firstborn and the first Passover. Thus, he sacrifices chronological smoothness in deference to theological explanation. Verses 4–8 are Moses' final retort to Pharaoh, made immediately after his demand that Moses leave. Verses 1–3 are cited before the announcement of Moses to Pharaoh that the firstborn of Egypt will be slain. This explains how Moses knew that this was the final plague, and why Pharaoh will nonetheless reject the warning. Verses 9–10 are also a parenthetical explanation of why Pharaoh stubbornly refuses to heed the warning of the plagues. This plague is the final blow, which will compel Pharaoh to release the Israelites.

12:1–36

THE FIRST PASSOVER

Like the Feast of Unleavened Bread and the redemption of the firstborn, the Passover was to become a permanent part of Israel's religious liturgy (12:24–25). There were several purposes for the Passover celebration, some of which were to be understood at a later time. The Passover is a memorial of the deliverance of Israel, accomplished by the mighty power of God (3:20; 13:9, 14, 16). The Passover and its related celebrations, the Feast of Unleavened Bread and the redemption of the firstborn, were intended to serve as occasions for instruction for the future generations of Israel (12:26–27; 13:8, 14–16).

The Passover celebration is a means of incorporating or excluding the Gentiles in the covenant of God to Abraham (12:38, 43–49). No uncircumcised person could partake of the Passover. The Passover lamb is a model of the Messiah, the Lamb of God, through whom God would bring redemption to both Israel and the Gentiles (12:5–7, 46–47).

Critical Observation

The similarities between the Passover lamb and the Lamb of God are perhaps not immediately perceived, but consider what we know about the Passover lamb and the Lamb of God today: The lamb was to be without defect (12:5), just as Jesus was without blemish (1 Peter 1:19); the shed blood of the lamb saved Israel's firstborn (Exodus 12:12–13, 22–23), just as the blood of Christ saves mankind from God's judgment (1 Peter 1:18–19; Revelation 5:9); and just as no bone of the Passover lamb was broken (Exodus 12:46), so no bone of Jesus was broken (John 19:32–36). Thus, the Old Testament prophet, Isaiah, spoke of Israel's Savior as a Lamb (Isaiah 53:6–7).

For the Israelites, the Passover and the tenth plague serve as a judgment on the gods of Egypt, whom the Israelites had worshiped (Joshua 24:14), and as evidence of the grace of God in the lives of His people. The plagues point out the sin of the Egyptians and their need to repent and believe in the God of Israel.

The firstborn of Israel are not spared because they are more worthy or more righteous than the Egyptians, but because of the grace of God alone. God made provision for non-Israelites to partake of the Passover if they were circumcised (acknowledging their faith in the Abrahamic Covenant; see Genesis 17:9–14; Exodus 12:48–49). Since there were many non-Israelites who left Egypt with Israel (Exodus 12:38), it is likely that a number were converted and physically spared from death through the process of the plagues and the provision of the Passover.

12:37–13:16

ISRAEL'S EXODUS

Verses 31–42 give a historical overview of the Exodus, from the command to leave issued by Pharaoh to an account of the departure, showing that God's promises have been carried out in accord with His schedule—to the very day. Verses 43–51 conclude with further instructions for the Israelites regarding the celebration of the Passover in the future, especially focusing on the participation of foreigners. God would have Israelites (and the readers of New Testament times as well) know that the institution of the Passover was done in accordance with direct divine revelation—designed and prescribed by God.

The Passover is proof of God's possession of Israel. The firstborn of Israel belonged to God as a result of the Passover, and all of Israel was God's possession as a result of the Exodus. All of the commandments and requirements which God placed upon the Israelites were predicated upon the fact that they were a people who belonged to Him.

EXODUS 13:17–14:31

THE RED SEA: ISRAEL'S DELIVERANCE AND EGYPT'S DEFEAT

Charting Israel's Course	13:17–22
Changing Israel's Course	14:1–9
Calming Israel's Fears	14:10–14
Divine Instruction and Intervention	14:15–20
Israel's Deliverance and the Egyptians' Destruction	14:21–31

Setting Up the Section

This text portrays the hardness of humanity's heart, which leads ultimately to destruction. The sea, which destroyed the Egyptians, is the instrument of God's wrath, but it is also the instrument of Israel's deliverance.

13:17–22

CHARTING ISRAEL'S COURSE

Israel's passing through the Red Sea is one of the most dramatic events recorded in the Old Testament. It rid the Israelites, once for all, of Pharaoh's dominion and released them from their obligation to return to Egypt, after traveling a three-day journey into the wilderness to worship God (as had been described by Moses to Pharaoh). This was, in fact, the birth of the nation of Israel.

There were three possible land routes for Israel to take to reach Canaan. The shortest route would have been to cross the land belonging to the Philistines, but they would have encountered war and lost heart (13:17). It may seem strange that God wants to avoid a military confrontation, when in verse 18 (see also 6:26; 12:41) it reads that the Israelites are armed for battle. The expression used here has been understood to refer only to the orderly way in which the Israelites (nearly two million people, counting women and children; see 12:37) departed Egypt. Others understand that the Israelites did come out of Egypt at least partially armed, but all seem to agree that Israel was not at all prepared to fight a full-scale battle at this point in time. Instead, the nation moved in a southeasterly direction, avoiding the Philistines.

Verses 21–22 describe a cloud and fire in which God is present (14:24; 40:38; Numbers 9:15–23; 14:14; Deuteronomy 1:33; Nehemiah 9:12, 19; Psalms 78:14; 105:39; 1 Corinthians 10:1). This provides the Israelites with a visible manifestation of His presence, protection, and guidance.

14:1–9

CHANGING ISRAEL'S COURSE

Moses' leadership (beyond the guiding pillar and cloud) was to bring about a change of course for the Israelites, one that would perplex the people. The Israelites are instructed to turn back and camp near Pi Hahiroth, between Migdol and the sea. God's instructions explain that this change of course, while it puts the people in a seemingly vulnerable position, is intended to encourage Pharaoh's pursuit. God knew Pharaoh would think the Israelites were miserably lost or misguided and that recovering them would be easy. Pharaoh's attack would result in his defeat, to the glory of God (14:4).

14:10–14

CALMING ISRAEL'S FEARS

The Israelites are terrified by the sight of the rapidly approaching Egyptians (14:10). They begin to reason that God has failed them. Moses, confident that God will deliver them from the Egyptians, tries to reassure the people. Even Moses begins crying out to God, not unlike the Israelites before him (14:10, 15), anxious for deliverance.

14:15–20

DIVINE INSTRUCTION AND INTERVENTION

Why does God rebuke Moses (14:15)? Because Moses knows that God has guided the Israelites to this place—between the Red Sea and the Egyptians. The pillar has led them there (13:21–22; 14:19), and God has explained His plan to Moses—so that He could gain glory through Pharaoh and his army (14:1–4). Moses knew that God had promised to bring the Israelites into the land of Canaan, which was across and beyond the Red Sea (Genesis 15:13–21; Exodus 3:7–8, 16–17; 6:4; 12:25; 13:5). Moses also knew that God had given him power through the use of his staff. God's gentle rebuke of Moses implies that Moses should have understood these things.

In spite of Moses' lack of faith, God graciously responds to his cry for help. He instructs Moses to raise his staff and stretch out his hand over the sea, making it possible for the Israelites to pass through on dry ground (14:16). The Egyptians, God informs Moses, will enter the sea behind them, resulting in their destruction and God's ultimate glory (14:17–18). God does more than just speak; the angel of the Lord, manifested in the pillar of cloud and fire, moves from the front of the Israelites to the rear, giving light to them and paralyzing the Egyptians in darkness (14:20).

14:21–31

ISRAEL'S DELIVERANCE AND THE EGYPTIANS' DESTRUCTION

Stretching forth his hand over the sea, Moses brings about a strong wind, turning the seabed to dry ground (14:21). Even more amazing than the courage of the Israelites to enter the seabed is the fact that the Egyptians follow them there. The Egyptians are blind to the incredible dangers of doing so by the hardness of their hearts.

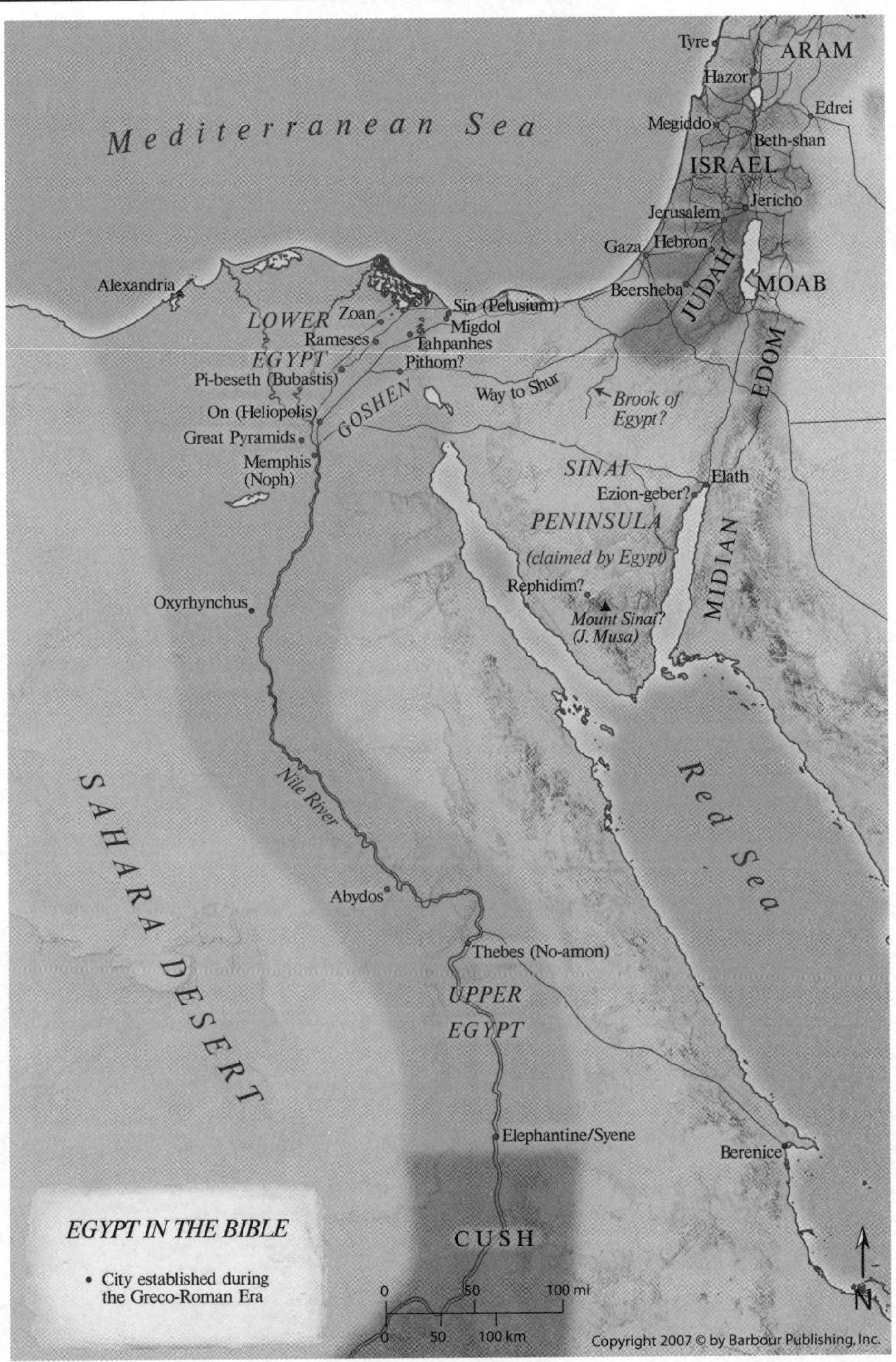
Mediterranean Sea
Tyre
ARAM
Hazor
Edrei
Megiddo
Beth-shan
ISRAEL
Jericho
Jerusalem
Gaza
Hebron
Beersheba
JUDAH
MOAB
Alexandria
Zoan
Sin (Pelusium)
LOWER
Migdol
Rameses
Tahpanhes
EGYPT
Pithom?
Pi-beseth (Bubastis)
Way to Shur
Brook of Egypt?
EDOM
On (Heliopolis)
GOSHEN
Great Pyramids
Memphis (Noph)
SINAI
Elath
Ezion-geber?
PENINSULA
(claimed by Egypt)
MIDIAN
Rephidim?
Oxyrhynchus
Mount Sinai? (J. Musa)
SAHARA DESERT
Nile River
Red Sea
Abydos
Thebes (No-amon)
UPPER
EGYPT
Elephantine/Syene
Berenice
EGYPT IN THE BIBLE
• City established during the Greco-Roman Era
CUSH
0
50
100 mi
0
50
100 km
N
Copyright 2007 © by Barbour Publishing, Inc.

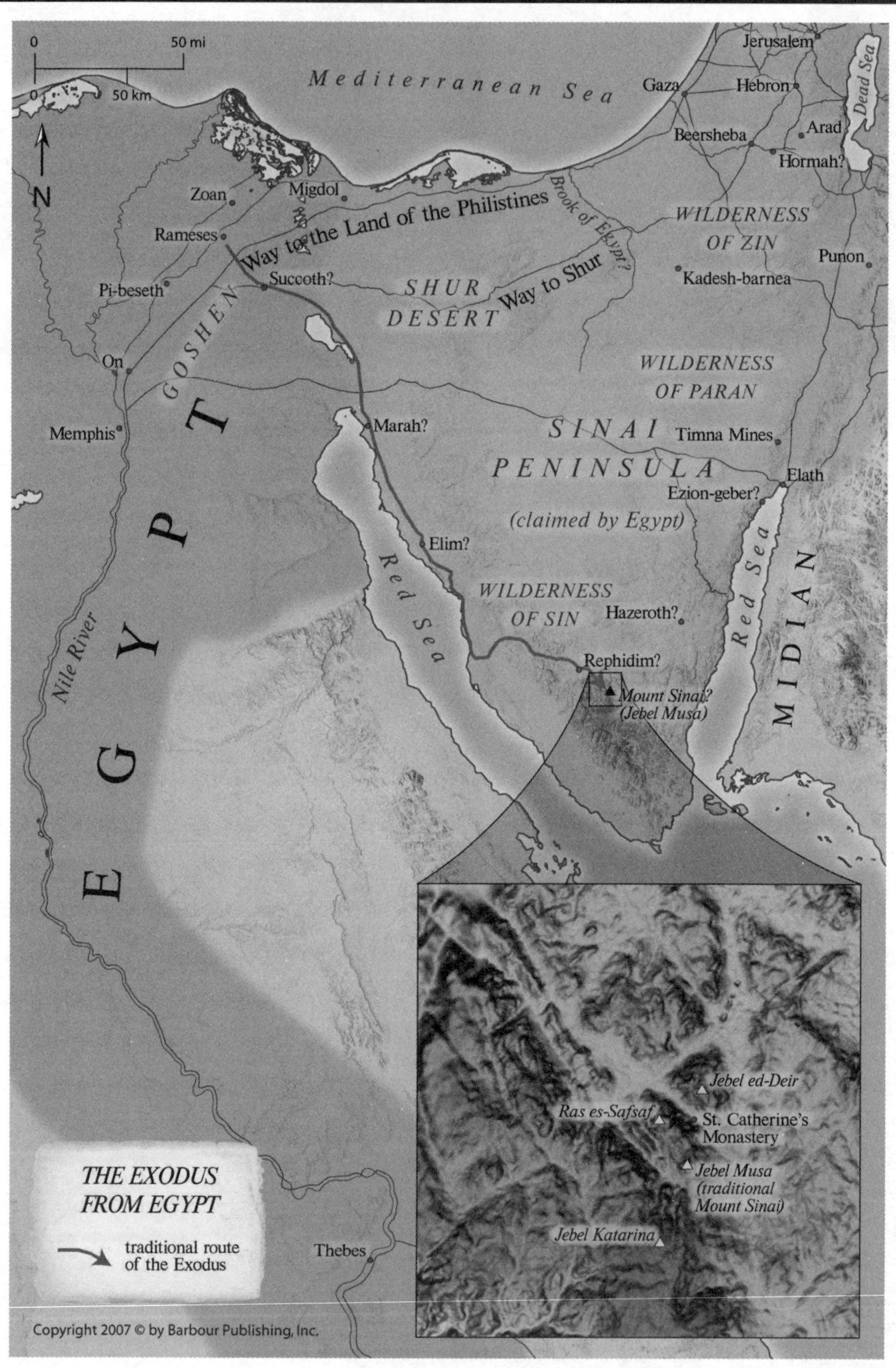

0
50 mi
0
50 km
N
Mediterranean Sea
Jerusalem
Dead Sea
Gaza
Hebron
Arad
Beersheba
Hormah?
Zoan
Migdol
Brook of Egypt?
Way to the Land of the Philistines
WILDERNESS OF ZIN
Rameses
Punon
Succoth?
Kadesh-barnea
Pi-beseth
SHUR DESERT
Way to Shur
GOSHEN
On
WILDERNESS OF PARAN
Memphis
Marah?
SINAI PENINSULA
Timna Mines
Elath
Ezion-geber?
(claimed by Egypt)
Elim?
EGYPT
Red Sea
WILDERNESS OF SIN
Hazeroth?
Nile River
Rephidim?
Mount Sinai? (Jebel Musa)
MIDIAN
Jebel ed-Deir
Ras es-Safsaf
St. Catherine's Monastery
Jebel Musa (traditional Mount Sinai)
Jebel Katarina
THE EXODUS FROM EGYPT
traditional route of the Exodus
Thebes

In the morning watch, which is from 2:00 a.m. until dawn, God brings confusion to the Egyptian troops (14:24). The poetic description of Psalm 77:16–19 makes it seem that a thunderstorm causes the confusion. The Egyptians try to retreat, but instead plunge headlong into the waters (14:27–28).

Critical Observation

The destruction of the Egyptians in the Red Sea is the culminating act of divine judgment that began with the hardening of the Egyptians' hearts. God began to judge the Egyptians at the time that Moses returned to Egypt and appeared before Pharaoh. Each plague was a judgment of the gods of the Egyptians (12:12). The Bible references the hardening of Pharaoh's heart (and sometimes his officials' or his army's hearts) fourteen times in Exodus. Of these fourteen instances, six refer to God hardening Pharaoh's heart (9:12; 10:1, 20, 27; 11:10; 14:8), three refer to Pharaoh hardening his own heart (8:15, 32; 9:34), and five are indefinite (7:13, 22; 8:19; 9:7, 35).

EXODUS 15:1–27

THE SONG OF THE SEA

Setting Up the Section

Israel's first great affirmation of faith is expressed in a song. Some have titled this song the "Song of the Sea." The mood of the song is triumphant. The structure has two parts: what God has done for Israel at the Red Sea and what God will surely do for Israel in the future (15:11–21).

15:1–12

GOD'S VICTORY OVER THE EGYPTIANS

Moses apparently wrote the song and led Israel as they sang it. In psalmlike fashion, the acts of God are viewed as evidence of His nature and character. With dramatic poetic strokes, God's sovereignty is evidenced by His control over the forces of nature (wind) and His ability as the Creator to cause nature to act unnaturally (the piling up of the water). In spite of the Egyptians' power and confidence, God simply blew them away, causing them to sink in the sea (15:10). The greatest army on the face of the earth is no match for the God of Israel. The greatness and the goodness of God are recognized by the Israelites as they reflect on God's victory over their enemies.

Demystifying Exodus

This song reveals the fulfillment of God's plan for the deliverance of Israel. God told Moses that Pharaoh would not release the Israelites until God's mighty hand compelled him to by performing miracles (3:19–20; 6:1). Now, after their passing through the Red Sea, Israel praises God for what He has done (15:6, 9, 12). God revealed through Moses that He was going to judge the gods of Egypt (12:12). Now, after the Exodus, Israel proclaims God as the one unique God (15:11). By the Exodus, God said that Israel would know He was the God who delivered them (6:7). Here, the Israelites sing their praises to Him for deliverance (15:2). This praise song reveals that God accomplished what He had sought to accomplish in the events of the Exodus.

15:13–21

GOD'S FUTURE VICTORY OVER ISRAEL'S ENEMIES

The second half of the song focuses on Israel's deliverance that is yet to come, and the defeat of the enemies who will resist Israel in Canaan. The NIV underscores the shift from the past defeat of the Egyptians to the future defeat of Israel's enemies by rendering the verbs of verses 13 and following in the future tense. The plagues and passing through the Red Sea are the beginning of Israel's journey home.

The "Song of the Sea" provides the Israelites a mechanism for recalling God's great act of deliverance at the Red Sea, and it directs their attention to the character of God, producing hope and confidence in His future protection and blessing.

15:22–27

ISRAEL'S PROTESTS AT THE WATERS OF MARAH

The Israelites travel into the Desert of Shur, and for three days they find no water. When they realize the water at Marah is bitter, they quickly turn to anger at Moses for leading them to such a place. This reveals their lack of faith and hardness of heart. The transformation of the waters of Marah, which means "bitter" (Ruth 1:20), is a miracle. No one knows of any wood which could produce the result described here. The casting of the wood into the water must have been a symbolic act, like Moses raising his staff over the waters of the Red Sea.

Take It Home

The Israelites failed to see the relationship between the affirmation of their faith in their worship (15:1–21) and the application of their faith in their daily walk (15:22–26). Israel had just proclaimed her faith in God as her warrior (15:3), but she was unable to trust in God as her provider (15:22–26). If God could deal with the waters of the Red Sea, surely He could be trusted to deal with the waters of Marah.

When we gather to worship God, we sing many hymns and choruses which express our faith in God, and yet too often we forget the truths that these hymns affirm. We must learn to apply in our daily walk those truths which we affirm in our public worship.

EXODUS 16:1–36

OBEDIENCE BOOT CAMP

Setting Up the Section

In the passage, Israel is guilty of two sins: greed and grumbling. Both of these sins are symptomatic of an even more serious underlying sin. Exodus 15:26 provides the background for God's provision of manna for His people. God's instructions regulating the gathering and use of the manna serve as a test of Israel's faith and obedience.

16:1–3

GROWLING STOMACHS AND GRUMBLING SAINTS

In this passage, there is a definite relationship between the Israelites' growling stomachs and their grumbling lips. In verse 3, Israel greatly exaggerates the benefits of Egypt and the direness of their current predicament, and they fail to perceive the hand of a sovereign God in their sufferings. They are struggling with submitting to the wisdom of their leaders, and they are complaining because they feel like they have no control over their situation.

16:4–36

THE BREAD OF HEAVEN

God reveals His glory to the Israelites by manifesting Himself in the cloud (16:10) and satisfies their physical needs by providing quail and manna (16:11–14). God's daily provision of manna in the wilderness teaches the Israelites to look daily to God for their sustenance. The regulations for collecting the manna—gathering only the needs of the day—taught them self control that kept their hope for deliverance in God and not in the manna. The greatest danger Israel faced was not starvation in the midst of a wilderness, but the wrath of God.

Take It Home

The tension here is a part of the broader tension between divine sovereignty and human responsibility. God provided the manna that Israel needed, but He commanded them to collect, cook, and keep it in accordance with His instructions. This illustrates the fact that divine sovereignty and human responsibility are related. God provides, but we must obey. In this relationship, God asks us to have self-control, but also provides the catalyst to produce it.

EXODUS 17:1–16

GOD'S GRACE TO ISRAEL

Massah and Meribah: Water from the Rock	17:1–7
The Lord Is My Banner	17:8–16

Setting Up the Section

Leaving the Desert of Sin, where the provision of manna had commenced (Exodus 16), the Israelites went from place to place as the Lord directed them. While Israel's later wandering in the wilderness is the result of their sin at Kadesh-barnea (Numbers 13–14), the wanderings in this chapter are designed to serve as Israel's "boot camp" experiences.

17:1–7

MASSAH AND MERIBAH: WATER FROM THE ROCK

Moses names the place where he draws water from the rock *Massah* (test) and *Meribah* (quarrel). This incident is typical of Israel's stubbornness and rebellion against God (Deuteronomy 9:6–8, 24; Hebrews 3:10). The grumbling of the Israelites in the wilderness is a persistent problem. Furthermore, the sin of this first generation of Israelites is almost identically reproduced by the second generation of Israelites some years later (Numbers 20:1–13). The problem of grumbling is common to every generation, in every age. Thus, we find the events of Massah and Meribah frequently referred to throughout scripture (Numbers 20:1–13; Deuteronomy 6:16–17; 8:15, Psalm 95:7–9; 1 Corinthians 10:1–13; Hebrews 3, 4).

Israel's lack of water is by divine design, for God is testing them by their response to adversity (Deuteronomy 8:2, 16; Psalm 81:7). It reveals the sinful condition of their hearts and is a reminder that God is always blessing them on the basis of His grace, not their works.

17:8–16

THE LORD IS MY BANNER

Scripture often reveals one dramatic event immediately after another. The attack of the Amalekites right after the Israelites' testing of God is an opportunity for them to demonstrate their confidence in God's desire for their good. The image of Moses holding up his staff to call on the power of God to defeat the Amalekites is a powerful one. What a simple but powerful picture of the interplay between our limited strength and God's all-powerful might. The image of the Lord as His people's Banner is used elsewhere in the Bible.

Take It Home

Is it possible that you are in a kind of wilderness? God may have purposed this season so that you could come to know Him in a much more intimate way than you have previously. Just as God meant Massah and Meribah for Israel's good, He means your wilderness experience to be for your good as well.

EXODUS 18:1–27

THE TYRANNY OF THE URGENT

Setting Up the Section

Moses' father-in-law, Jethro, having heard of God's protection and deliverance of the Israelites, comes to visit in order to reunite Moses with his wife and children. The first half of the chapter reveals several symptoms of a serious problem in Moses' life, which prompts not only Jethro's arrival, but also his advice about achieving balance.

18:1–12

JETHRO'S ARRIVAL

The arrival of Jethro, accompanied by Zipporah, Gershom, and Eliezer, is apparently a pleasant surprise for Moses. We are not told precisely when or why Moses and his family are separated, but the last mention of them is in chapter 4. One might conjecture that Moses sent his family back to Jethro at a time when he feared for their safety. Perhaps, too, he felt that the pressures of confronting Pharaoh and of leading Israel were too great to have the additional responsibilities of a husband and father.

Jethro acts out of wisdom, compassion, and concern for Moses' best interest. This is a magnanimous act, especially after the deceptive explanation Moses gave for his return to Egypt (Exodus 4:18). Jethro rejoices with Moses, praising God for His grace manifested toward Israel, as evidenced by Moses' report (18:9–10). Also, Jethro seems to acknowledge, for the first time, the superiority of God over all other gods—unique in that Midianites were generally idolaters (Numbers 25:17–18; 31:16). Jethro demonstrates his newfound faith by offering sacrifices to God and sharing the sacrificial meal (Exodus 18:12).

Critical Observation

There is a tendency among Christians to minimize the failings of a man like Moses in this situation. The assumption is that the saints who are described in the Bible always do the right thing for the right reasons. Instead, we should interpret Moses' actions in light of the fact that, while we know he is God's chosen leader, he is also an imperfect human being. The text here is not extolling Moses' virtues, but his vices. Here is a person who we can identify with, an individual with flaws just like us. Yet he is used by God nonetheless and blessed by the keen advice of those who care about him.

18:13–27

JETHRO'S ADVICE

Jethro is baffled by the inefficiency he has witnessed. It is apparent from his questioning that he does not agree with the way Moses is handling things. Moses' response reveals his distorted perception and several misconceptions regarding his role as a leader.

While Moses deals with the Israelites individually, Jethro advocates dealing with them collectively (18:19–20). Moses is unable to manage because he fails to see that he needs a strong team to support him. He is dealing with nearly two million people, and he is trying to do so by himself. He is, according to Jethro, wearing himself out (18:18). Moses has allowed his sense of public duty to overshadow his sense of personal responsibility.

Jethro's advice is that Moses rearrange his time so that priority is given to teaching the people God's principles and precepts, and prescribe guidelines for solving problems when they arise.

Take It Home

Jethro's advice is good for all. How can you facilitate the ministry of others by encouraging and equipping them to do what they do best? Faith is required to trust God to enable you to do what He has called you to do. Faith is also required to enable you to leave what you should not do to others.

EXODUS 19:1–25

THE PREAMBLE TO ISRAEL'S CONSTITUTION

God's Purpose for the Decalogue	19:1–6
Preparing for the Appearance of God	19:7–15
The Manifestation of God on the Mountain	19:16–25

Setting Up the Section

Chapter 19 serves as a preamble to the commandments given by God to Israel. It reveals the purpose of the commandments, as well as the perspective we should have toward them.

19:1–6

GOD'S PURPOSE FOR THE DECALOGUE

Apparently, it is not necessary for God to summon Moses (19:3). This may be due to the fact that it is on Mount Horeb (synonymous with Mount Sinai) where Moses first encounters God (chapters 3 and 4). At the burning bush, God promises Moses that the nation will come to worship Him "at this mountain" (3:12). Thus, Moses seems to know that he is to ascend the mountain to speak with God. From the mountain, God speaks some of the most significant words found in the Old Testament (19:4–6). God's statement declares to the Israelites His faithfulness to His covenant, their distinction from the Egyptians, and His promise to keep Israel the special object of His care.

God uses an image of the eagle's care for its offspring. In the book of Deuteronomy, Moses explains the image more fully (Deuteronomy 32:11). While there are times when God seems (to the Israelites) to have abandoned His people, in reality God is simply stirring up the nest, forcing the Israelites to try their wings.

This declaration also describes how Israel's deliverance is for the purpose of being brought to God so that the nation could be His prized possession. In the Abrahamic Covenant, God promises Abraham that Israel will become a great nation and the special object of His blessing. The blessing of Israel is also meant to be a source of blessing to all nations (Genesis 12:2). While this would ultimately be fulfilled by the coming of the Messiah, there is also a more immediate application. God purposed to bless the nations by establishing Israel, His servant, as a mediatory people, sharing with the nations the way of entering into fellowship with God.

Israel must keep God's covenant (as defined by the law) to maintain their status as God's people. Israel's calling is to a position of both privilege and responsibility. To whom much is given, much is required. Israel is given the commandments as a distinction from other nations so that they can fulfill their priestly calling.

19:7–15

PREPARING FOR THE APPEARANCE OF GOD

To this point, God has only indicated that the people must keep their covenant by obeying the laws which He is about to set down. The Israelites anticipated the law with eagerness, demonstrating their implicit trust in the character of God. Verses 10–15 outline the steps which the Israelites must take in order to purify and prepare themselves for the appearance of God on the third day.

Why are these boundaries so serious to God? To press past the barriers which were constructed to satisfy one's curiosity would be to demonstrate an attitude of irreverence. It is this irreverence which God finds as such a serious sin. Remember, it is irreverence which results in Uzzah being struck dead, even though his intentions (to keep the ark from falling from the ox cart) are well meaning (2 Samuel 6:6–7). It is also Moses' irreverence (in the striking of the rock) that keeps him from entering into the promised land (Numbers 20:12).

Irreverence is the by-product of an inadequate sense of the holiness of God. The Israelites do not yet have an adequate grasp of the holiness of God. The manifestation of God on Mount Sinai is a spectacular demonstration of God's power and majesty. His coming necessitates preparatory consecration, and it also motivates continual consecration, as people could see themselves in the light of His glory and grace (Exodus 19:23).

19:16–25

THE MANIFESTATION OF GOD ON THE MOUNTAIN

This text describes the splendor and the majesty of God as He manifests Himself to Israel on the mountain. Exodus 19 prepares us for the glorious giving of the law by God to His people—an occasion marked by God's purity, power, and holiness.

The law contained not only the regulations of God, but also the account of God's mercy and grace in saving and keeping His people. Each generation is to teach the next generation the goodness of God, and each new generation is to ratify the covenant for itself (Psalm 78:5–7).

Critical Observation

The Mosaic Covenant was never given as a means of earning righteousness by law keeping. The new covenant is promised because the Mosaic Covenant could not be kept by Israel (Jeremiah 31:31–34). Whenever Israel failed with regard to the law, it was not just a matter of violating the law in some minute particular, but it was a result of unbelief (Psalm 78:21–22, 32–33, 37).

The proper interpretation and application of the law is best determined by a study of the Old Testament prophets, who focus on the essence of the law rather than the particulars of its expression (Hosea 6:6–7; Micah 6:6–8). The law (in its broadest form—the Pentateuch, the first five books of the Bible) is intended to serve as a record of God's faithfulness to His promises and to His people. The Ten Commandments, along with the rest of the laws of God, are given to serve as the covenant between God and His people, and as their national constitution, by which the nation would be guided and governed.

Critical Observation

When Paul or the other apostles speak disparagingly of the law, it is not the law as given by God and properly interpreted and applied, but the law as interpreted and applied by the Judaizers, who sought to pervert it into a system of works oriented righteousness. In order to refute their false teaching, Paul finds it necessary to teach the proper perspective of the law. The law, writes Paul, is provisional and preparatory, and is superseded by the new covenant. The law was good—but the new covenant is far better.

Take It Home

The law is a gracious provision for the nation of Israel, albeit a temporary one. The new covenant would be far better, but the old covenant is a necessary prerequisite and preparation. In the first covenant, God's majesty and might are manifested to all, but only a select few could draw near. In the new covenant, all who wish to can draw near, but only a few behold His majesty. The first manifestation of God on Mount Sinai portrays the marvelous truth of the holiness of God, and the separation which that demands. The second manifestation of the Lord (on Mount Calvary) reveals the marvelous grace of God, by which He draws near to us and by which we may draw near to Him. How careful we must be to keep both the holiness and the grace of God in perspective.

EXODUS 20:1–26

THE TEN COMMANDMENTS

Setting Up the Section

The Decalogue, also called the Ten Commandments, is one of the keys to understanding the Old Testament. It is the central core of the lengthy Mosaic Law.

20:1–17

THE CHARACTERISTICS OF THE COMMANDMENTS

In Exodus 20, God expresses the essence of the Old Testament law in ten principle statements. In chapter 19, we learn that the giving of the law is directly related to Israel's calling to be a kingdom of priests and a holy nation (19:6). If Israel is to represent God, they must be like God. The law defines how God's holiness is to be manifested in the lives of men and women.

The Ten Commandments are both a corporate constitution for Israel and an intensely personal revelation from God to His children. The *you* in the commandments is not plural, but singular. Each individual is therefore urged to enter into the joy of service by adopting this covenant and by obeying the laws which are contained therein. The Decalogue is not only a constitution, it is God's standard for Israel's culture.

20:18–26

PURE WORSHIP

Verses 18–21 contain the account of the Israelites' reaction to the giving of the law. It also offers God's reason for giving it as He did—to keep the people from sinning (20:20).

While God evidently spoke the Ten Commandments in the hearing of all the Israelites (19:9; 20:19, 22) the people were so struck by the revelation that they asked Moses to act as a go-between for them from then on, which he did (20:21).

Verse 20 mentions two kinds of fear. First, the people are told not to fear, but then they are told the fear of God will be with them. The first fear is a tormenting fear (which enslaves). The second is a respectful fear (which demonstrates trust with acknowledgement of power). The latter is the fear that will keep the people from sinning.

Verses 22–26 include specific instruction regarding worship. Idolatry is clearly prohibited, but also there seems to be a prohibition against making images to represent God (20:22). An altar, on the other hand, was an acceptable form of worship. The Israelites built altars both at a central location once they settled and along the way when God revealed Himself (Genesis 35:7; Joshua 8:30). The specific instruction regarding uncut stones was probably to distinguish the Israelite altars from the Canaanite altars.

Another distinction between the two was the prohibition of stairs leading up to the altar. This seems to be simply to keep the priest from exposing himself as he went to the altar to make a sacrifice.

The simple description of the altar—made of earth or stone—could serve to keep the emphasis of the worship on God rather than man's efforts.

EXODUS 21:1–23:33

BEYOND THE TEN COMMANDMENTS

Setting Up the Section

The Ten Commandments set out in broad strokes God's law for His people, outlining how we are to relate to Him and honor His image in others. The Mosaic Law continues for two more chapters in Exodus, outlining God's design for protecting servants, persons, and property, and further explaining the role of social responsibility, mercy, and justice in the nation of Israel.

21:1–22:15

PROTECTION FOR SERVANTS, PERSONS, AND PROPERTY

The laws in this chapter relate to the commandments in which God prohibits killing and stealing. Though they differ from contemporary times and customs, they do explain the moral law and the rules of natural justice. God's people are to have a unique approach to everything, including their servants and other property. God commands the Israelites to respect their servants as human beings—even preserving their family bonds and allowing their families to go free with them in the Year of Jubilee. In being made free, servants become a picture of God's mercy and a living example of the eventual freedom that is possible in Christ, through His own sacrifice and grace.

Demystifying Exodus

Who were servants in ancient Israel? Foreign slaves were often war prisoners. However, impoverished Israelites sometimes sold themselves or their children so that they could work and be cared for. In other cases, judges sold some persons for their crimes, and creditors were, in some cases, allowed to sell debtors who could not pay. Forced Hebrew slavery for any reason was not practiced and is ranked in the New Testament with the greatest of crimes.

God gives and maintains life. In these laws dealing with murder, we see how fiercely He protects and values it. God's harsh punishment for ungrateful and disobedient children is designed in part to encourage parents to be very careful in training their children and setting a good example in learning self-control and respect.

22:16–31

SOCIAL RESPONSIBILITY

The people of God answer to God, not only for what they do maliciously, but for what they do without intent. In this portion of the law, God calls His people to always be ready to show mildness and mercy, according to the spirit of these laws. When one does harm to a neighbor, he or she should make it right, even when not compelled by law. God calls upon the Israelites to honor those around them and God Himself by being generous and living justly.

23:1–9

LAWS OF MERCY AND JUSTICE

The Law of Moses includes many straightforward, practical requirements. Every element of the law enables the Israelites to act as God's people and to worship Him with their conduct, thus separating themselves from the pagan world. The Israelites are called to remain fair and honest, allowing nothing to compromise God's justice by lessening faults, aggravating small ones, excusing offenders, accusing the innocent, or misrepresenting the truth in any way.

23:10–19

SABBATH LAWS AND FESTIVALS

The Sabbath laws require that both the seventh day of each week and each seventh year are treated as sacred opportunities for rest and rejoicing in God's provision and power. It teaches not only the importance of mercy, but the need for dependence on God by forcing people to trust that God will bless their faithfulness with plenty.

The Israelites have a weakness for idolatry, and therefore God requires them to be rigorous in honoring Him during three annual festivals. They are required to come together before the Lord, rejoicing in and honoring His faithfulness. They are not to arrive empty-handed but with sacrifices that demonstrate their loyalty and love for God.

23:20–33

GOD'S ANGEL TO PREPARE THE WAY

In the closing verses of Exodus 23, God promises to prepare the way for the nation of Israel, drive out their enemies, and bring them into the promised land. He commands the Israelites to be sensitive and attentive to the angel He is sending ahead of them and to worship Him alone. He promises to provide for them and make them prosper in their new home.

Take It Home

Have you allowed your life to crowd out time for worshiping and celebrating God's goodness? This is the blessing intended for all of God's children—to come together in gratitude and to enjoy and honor Him on a regular basis. Indeed, periodic rest from the duties of the world helps us anticipate the heavenly rest which we all crave—when all earthly labors and cares shall cease. How can you seize upon the blessing of a day of rest and worship more practically amidst a hectic life?

EXODUS 24:1–18

THE MAGNIFICENT MEAL ON MOUNT SINAI

The Call and the Confirmation	24:1–11
The Tablets of Stone	24:12–18

Setting Up the Section

Centuries before the scenes described in this text, God promised Abraham a seed (a son, which would become a great nation), a land (the land of Canaan), and the promise that this nation would be blessed and be a blessing to all nations (Genesis 12:1–3). The promises God made were ratified as a covenant between Himself and Abraham in Genesis 15. Now the Mosaic Covenant, which has been spelled out in the Ten Commandments, is formally imposed upon Israel by the God who has delivered her out of Egypt.

24:1–11

THE CALL AND THE CONFIRMATION

The ratification of the Mosaic Covenant is the key to the remainder of the book of Exodus. God is the initiator of this covenant with His people Israel. A distinction is drawn between the Israelites and God, but there is also a distinction made between Israelites. These same distinctions are paralleled in the tabernacle, where the priests have greater access to God than the people, and the high priest alone can enter the Holy of Holies, once a year. Such distinctions are abolished in the new covenant.

Demystifying Exodus

Covenants had several common elements. Usually they involved promises or commitments to which the parties bound themselves. There was often a sacrifice made, followed by a meal, which included some of the sacrifice. There was also a memorial, some kind of physical token of the oath, which served to remind the parties of their commitments. There was a curse attached to the one who broke the covenant which he had made. There was always a sense of solemnity in the making of a covenant, for it was a serious step of commitment.

Moses understood that the covenant God was making with Israel needed to be ratified by the nation. Once the Israelites have verbally ratified this covenant, Moses carries out the ratification process by the use of symbols and representatives. Moses offers covenant sacrifices (these are not sin offerings), making an altar with twelve pillars for the twelve tribes of Israel. The blood sprinkled upon the altar and upon the people links the people with the covenant sacrifices.

The covenant meal, eaten by the seventy-five leaders of Israel in the presence of God, is the final act of ratification. The leaders (seventy elders, plus Nadab and Abihu, Aaron, Moses, and his servant, Joshua) are representatives who act on behalf of the entire nation, teaching and interpreting the law.

On the mountain, the elders of Israel see God enthroned, but from a distance. This perhaps explains why there's no account of fear on the part of the elders. This also helps to explain why Moses could later ask to see God, as though he had not seen Him earlier (33:17–23).

The ratification of the Mosaic Covenant had great meaning for the Israelites of that day. It clearly defined Israel's relationship with God, and what was expected of each Israelite. The covenant also spelled out the consequences, both of obedience and of disobedience. Israel could always know where she stood with God.

24:12–18

THE TABLETS OF STONE

The second call of Moses to the top of Mount Sinai is for the purpose of giving him the commandments written on stone by the finger of God (24:12). It is also for the purpose of revealing the blueprints for the tabernacle. From chapter 25 to the end of Exodus, the tabernacle is the principle subject. The tabernacle was designed to institutionalize God's presence among His people on an ongoing basis, as the mountain had served on a one-time basis.

While Moses puts Aaron and Hur in charge as he prepares for his trip, note that it is not until later (Numbers 11; Deuteronomy 1) that Jethro's advice of a team of leaders helping him (Exodus 18) is actually put into practice. Once again, the seventh day is set apart from the other six, this time by God's personal arrival in a cloud. Unfortunately, the forty days of Moses' absence provide a test which Israel fails (see Exodus 32).

The wonder of the revelation of God to the elders of Israel is that God does not strike them dead. The wonder of the revelation of God to Moses is that it is described from the perspective of the Israelites, at the base camp, rather than from Moses himself. Why didn't Moses give a firsthand account? We know Moses was a very humble man (Numbers 12:3), who was not intent upon glamorizing his own experiences. Perhaps Moses simply had too much awe and reverence for the things he experienced to try to recreate or capture it.

Take It Home

As we consider the Mosaic Covenant, we are reminded of the gospel. The gospel is the news that God has provided as a means of relating to people, through the new covenant, which was achieved through the sprinkling of the blood of Christ. The gospel is the message of an everlasting covenant, which men and women can enter into with God.

EXODUS 25:1–31:18

A PLACE TO WORSHIP

Setting Up the Section

Now that Israel has been delivered from Egypt, they need a place where they can worship their God, a place where He can be present among them. Once God gives Moses the law, He follows with specific instructions for such a place—the tabernacle.

25:1–9

OFFERINGS FOR THE TABERNACLE

The gifts for the tabernacle are given voluntarily, as an act of gratitude. God also required compulsory giving and sacrificing by the Israelites, however in this instance, there is no need to compel the people to get excited about building God's dwelling place among them. And as we see later, their giving actually exceeds what could be used.

In verses 8–9, Exodus refers to the structure that was to be built as a *sanctuary* ("place of holiness") and a *tabernacle* ("dwelling place"). These words stress the fact that God is worthy of worship and that He is choosing to live with His people.

25:10–26:37

THE FURNISHINGS OF THE TABERNACLE

The tables on which God describes His will for the Israelites are called *the Testimony*. In the New Testament, Christians associate this same word with the good news of Christ's work that the disciples and apostles testify to in the Gospels. Here the law, God's testimony to His people, is placed in an ark overlaid with gold that is kept in the Holy of Holies. Above the ark, God's visible glory hovers.

The *ark of the covenant* (25:10–22) functioned as God's throne. The solid gold lid of the box was called the mercy seat (25:17). This is where the high priest made his yearly offering on the Day of Atonement (Leviticus 16).

The table for the bread of the presence was replenished weekly (25:23–30). This was a constant thank offering placed before God. Some think it was also a reminder of the testimony that Israel was to be to the world around them.

The lampstand (25:31–40), the *menorah*, is often seen today as a symbol of Israel. Some see the place of the lampstand in the original tabernacle as a symbol of God's Word which lights the darkness. Others see it as a symbol of Jesus, light of the world.

The curtains and the veil were similarly constructed (26:1–35). The curtains outlined the tabernacle while the veil provided a boundary for the innermost holy chamber. The screen served as a front door (26:35–37).

Take It Home

While many elements of the tabernacle are attributed with symbolic properties, the mercy seat is seen by some as the most rich. As the lid of the ark of the covenant (seen as God's throne), it provided temporarily what Jesus' sacrifice permanently offered to believers. It was the place of a blood sacrifice that atoned for sin. In fact, the same word that is translated *mercy seat* in verse 17 is the word used to describe Jesus in 1 John 2:2—atoning sacrifice.

27:1–20

OTHER CRUCIAL INSTRUCTIONS

God is very specific in His description of the other elements of the tabernacle; nearly everything is not only functional but also symbolic and instructive in its form.

The altar of burnt offerings stood just inside the entrance to the court (27:1–8). Some see this as an apt picture of this sacrifice being the first step to fellowship with God.

The curtain around the courtyard was an added boundary, though a shorter one, to protect the innermost holy place of the tabernacle (27:9–19). It was in the courtyard that the priests did their work and the people offered their sacrifices.

These instructions regarding the oil that was in the lamps form a transition from this information about the tabernacle furnishings to the following information about the priests' ministry (27:20–21).

28:1–43

THE PRIEST'S CLOTHING

Chapter 28 describes the clothing of the priest: "a breastpiece, an ephod, a robe, a fitted tunic, a turban, and a sash" (28:4 NET). The *ephod* was an apron-like piece of clothing that fit over the robe. Verses 6–14 describe the ephod in detail.

Verses 15–30 describe the breastplate. While we often think of military metal breastplates, this one was made from the same material as the ephod.

Demystifying Exodus

Verse 29–30 outline the decision-making function of the breastplate. There is much we do not know about the Urim and Thummim. We know they helped with decisions, probably yes or no kinds of decisions, and were kept in the pockets of this breastplate. They are usually compared to casting lots or throwing dice, but we don't have enough details to understand the exact process the priest used for them.

29:1–46

CONSECRATION OF THE PRIESTS

In the consecration of the priests—Aaron and his sons—God demands solemnity and ceremony. Ultimately, the model for the priesthood is Jesus, called by God to intercede for His people and anointed by His Spirit clothed with glory and beauty (Hebrews 3:1–2). Hebrews 2:10 instructs that in the new covenant all believers are priests, offering spiritual sacrifices and relating directly to God. For the Israelites, the priesthood established here would be their intercessors and their representatives before God for generations to come.

30:1–38

INCENSE, ATONEMENT, WASHING, AND ANOINTING

The priests are instructed to burn incense every morning and evening, the same time that the daily burnt offerings are made. The incense is to be left burning continually throughout the day and night as a pleasing aroma to the Lord. It is made of an equal part of four precious spices (stacte, onycha, galbanum, and frankincense) and is considered holy. The offering of incense foreshadows the gifts brought to the infant Jesus ("God with us") by the wise men.

31:1–18

THE PRIESTS AND THE SABBATH

This passage reveals how God gifts His servants. God chose Bezalel and Oholiab and anointed them with His Spirit "with skill, ability, and knowledge in all kinds of crafts" (31:3 NIV). Indeed, God has made these two skilled artists so that they can construct the temple exactly according to His commandments. The example of these two artists commissioned and gifted by God Himself reminds us that whatever our life's work or calling, we can use it to honor God.

Critical Observation

The importance of keeping the Sabbath has already been described in detail, yet God returns to it. He goes one step further saying that the Sabbath signals the special relationship that exists between God and Israel—it is a sign of the Mosaic Covenant, just as circumcision is a sign of the Abrahamic Covenant. Immediately after God issues this reminder, Moses encounters the Israelites in the full swing of their rebellion—too impatient to wait to rest in God's true presence. God's emphasis on His people's need for ritualistic rest and worship has obviously not been honored by the impatient Israelites.

EXODUS 32:1–35

THE REJECTION OF GOD AND THE REVELATION OF MAN

Israel's Idolatry	32:1–6
Divine Indignation and Human Intervention	32:7–14
Moses and God Respond	32:15–35

Setting Up the Section

In the story of the golden calf, Israel is guilty of impatience for God's manifestation in the tabernacle, but it is her idolatry that condemns her.

32:1–6

ISRAEL'S IDOLATRY

There is a cause and effect relationship between the absence of leadership and the practice of idolatry. While Moses is gone for forty days and nights (24:18), receiving instructions about building the tabernacle, the Israelites use his absence as a pretext for taking immoral action, seizing the opportunity for creating an image of God.

32:7–14

DIVINE INDIGNATION AND HUMAN INTERVENTION

The Mosaic Covenant, ratified approximately one month before Israel's idolatry, defines the relationship Israel has with God. In Moses' appeal for his people on Mount Sinai, he does not refer to the Mosaic Covenant, because the law can only condemn; it cannot save.

When Moses appeals to God, he appeals to the Abrahamic Covenant, made centuries before. The law is God's provisional covenant, given to humanity because of its depravity, but it is not the cure. If the promises of the Abrahamic Covenant are to be fulfilled, it would have to be by some other covenant than the Mosaic Covenant.

The Mosaic Covenant could not change human hearts—the root problem of sin. Striving to keep the law in order to be saved or sanctified is true folly, because we all suffer from the same ailment—sin. Idolatry seeks to replace what cannot be seen with something that can be seen—it is physically oriented. Thus, the underlying issue of idolatry is faith, since faith focuses on what is not seen (Hebrews 11:1).

32:15–35

MOSES AND GOD RESPOND

The irony of the dialogue between Moses and God (Exodus 3–4), in which God provides Aaron as Moses' spokesman, is shown here. Moses is empowered by his fear of God, whereas Aaron is fumbling because of his failure. God reveals His righteousness in response to the sins of the Israelites; Aaron reveals his unrighteousness. It is not enough for us to recognize merely the depravity of humanity; we must resist it.

Take It Home

This is Israel's first great act of rebellion and sin since the ratification of the covenant. The Mosaic Covenant was based on the righteousness of men, and thus served only to condemn. The new covenant is based on the righteousness of the Messiah, Jesus Christ, and thus can be counted on to forgive humanity and save them from their sin. The old covenant gave no assurance of the forgiveness of sins; the new gives us absolute confidence and boldness.

EXODUS 33:1–34:9

THE PRESENCE OF GOD WITH HIS PEOPLE

33:1–11

OUTSIDE THE CAMP

Because of Israel's sin, God deals with His people from a distance as they travel through the wilderness. Although this is a fulfillment of Israel's first inclination and request (20:18–21), when it actually happens the nation mourns.

Israel's removal of ornaments and jewelry is an appropriate act of repentance, because these ornaments are similar to those which had been contributed to make the golden calf (32:2–4) and were associated in the ancient Near East with pagan gods. To put off these ornaments demonstrates Israel's sincere repentance over their idolatry in the preceding chapter.

The grace of God is seen even in God's threat to remove Himself from Israel's midst. God states that the purpose for keeping a distance between Himself and the Israelites as they travel on toward the promised land is that their sinfulness would require Him to destroy them. The threatened consequence for Israel's idolatry is losing God's intimate presence among them. God's grace is evident as well in the provision of Moses as the mediator for the people.

In the midst of Israel's sin, and the threat of God withholding His presence, God provides a tent where not only Moses, but all the people, can go to seek God. This provides the people a means of worshiping God and offers them a hope for a future fellowship with God.

Take It Home

The Israelites mourn because they have only the promise of prosperity, but not God's intimate presence among them. In our day and time, prosperity is touted as the proof of God's presence. It's simply not true. Learn from the Israelites to desire the presence of God more than mere prosperity.

33:12–34:9

MEETING GOD

The remainder of this text is divided into Moses' three petitions to God. Each request is followed by God's response, which then becomes the basis for a further petition of Moses. Once he is assured of the presence of God in the midst of His people, Moses makes a personal request to see the glory of God.

Moses has already faced war with the Amalekites, a war only won by prevailing prayer (Exodus 17). Now more than ever, he is aware of the rebelliousness and waywardness of the Israelites. And Aaron has so far proven to be a liability. Also, the Mosaic Covenant, which gave such hope initially, is now known to pronounce only a curse and not to promise blessing, due to the sinfulness of the people. No wonder Moses is concerned about setting out for Canaan. Moses wants to know not only the person God is sending with him, but also the plan God has for the people. He is also seeking to know God more intimately, to know God's character in order to better understand how to please Him.

God promises Moses He will be with him and provide the means to get the Israelites to Canaan. Furthermore, He promises Moses that the Israelites will ultimately live safely in Canaan. This is indicated by the term *rest*, used here and elsewhere in the Old Testament. This word conveys the end of an evil, an enemy, hostility, or adversity. When God promises Moses rest, He assures him that the things Moses fears most will be overcome, and that the task which God has given him will be completed.

Moses is not willing to enjoy God's favor alone while Israel's destiny hangs in the balance. So in his second request, he petitions God's presence not only be with him, but with everyone. Notice how Moses twice links himself with Israel in order to associate God's favor for them with His favor for Moses. God assures Moses that He will be present with Israel, as well as with him.

Later, after Moses' request to see the glory of God (33:18), the glory of God will fill the newly constructed tabernacle (40:34–35). On various occasions during Israel's sojourn in the wilderness, God's glory is manifested to the people. On a number of these occasions, the glory of the Lord appears to stop the people from sinning.

The glory of God is almost always some visible manifestation of God's presence and of His splendor. For Moses, and ultimately with the entire nation, the sight of God's glory would serve as an assurance of God's presence,.

The Bible consistently teaches that no person is able to see God face-to-face and live. God speaks of Moses as being able to see His back, but not His face. In the context of the passage, this means that Moses will be able to see all of God's goodness, but not some of His other attributes. Let us not fail to appreciate the wonder and the honor of this revelation of God to Moses. While it is only the back of God, it is all Moses can survive—and it is more than any man had yet been privileged to see.

Critical Observation

While Moses met with God at the tent of meeting (33:7), the renewal of the Mosaic Covenant took place at the top of Mount Sinai. The revelation of God's glory to Moses took the place of the manifestation of God to the seventy elders of Israel. The dimension of God's character that encourages Moses is the goodness of God. It is this side of God that gives Moses (and Israel) hope of forgiveness and God's renewed presence among them. God grants Moses this vision of His glory along with Israel's forgiveness, reclaiming them as His own people once again.

EXODUS 34:10–35

A NEW BEGINNING

Setting Up the Section

Moses returns from the mountain with a radiantly beaming face, a reflection of the glory of God. Every time he speaks to God face-to-face, the radiance will be renewed. Every time he speaks to Israel with his beaming face, the people know that God is speaking to them through Moses, giving him credentials that they dare not ignore.

34:10–28

THE "NEW" OLD COVENANT

The covenant made here is virtually a renewal of the former covenant; however, there are some differences. The first covenant was based on the miracles God had done in delivering the Israelites from Egyptian bondage, while this covenant looks forward to the miracles that are instrumental in Israel's possession of the land of Canaan (34:10–11).

Ironically, the miracles God formerly accomplished in Egypt resulted in the Egyptians driving the Israelites out of their land; now, the miracles God promises to accomplish will drive the Canaanites out of Israel's land.

There are a number of differences between the way this new covenant is given and the way in which the former was given. Moses goes alone to the mountain, apparently not even accompanied by Joshua. No promises are made this (second) time by the Israelites, although the blessings of this covenant are still conditional.

The "code of the covenant" given here is significantly shorter than that found in chapters 20–23. The first code emphasizes social matters, such as the treatment of slaves and just compensation for losses caused by negligence or theft. In this abbreviated code of the covenant, the emphasis falls on Israel's walk with God, which had quickly been interrupted by Israel's idolatry and apostasy.

34:29–35

THE TRANSFIGURATION OF MOSES

Predictably, the people are at first frightened by the brightness of Moses' countenance, but then they are eventually able to draw near enough to hear Moses speak and to accept his words as from God Himself. Moses begins to employ a veil that he will remove when he speaks with God and will leave it off until he has conveyed God's words to the people. Then, the veil will be put on until the next time he speaks with God. The text indicates that Moses does this on a number of occasions, with some degree of regularity.

The greater intimacy of Moses with God is apparent by the people's actions here. In the past, the manifestations of the glory and majesty of God were more distant, so that the people wanted to keep their distance from God and have Moses to be their intermediary (20:18–20).

Take It Home

Moses' authority is evident in his radiant face, a sign that he had been speaking with God. Christians today have the ministry of the Holy Spirit, who dwells within and bears witness internally to those to whom the new covenant is proclaimed (John 16:8–16). Whenever we speak the Word of God in truth, the Holy Spirit bears testimony within the listener, validating the truth of what has been said, just as Moses' radiant face gives the Israelites confidence that his testimony and leadership are from God.

EXODUS 35:1–36:7

ISRAEL'S OFFERINGS

Setting Up the Section

Chapters 35–40 conclude by describing the construction of the tabernacle, and climax at God's descent into the midst of the camp. The theme of this section is the presence of God in the midst of His people.

35:1–36:7

ISRAEL'S OFFERINGS

The excitement and enthusiasm of the Israelites is evident by the abundance of their gifts. In fact, the text informs us that the gifts exceed the need, so much that Moses is asked to command the people to stop giving. The Israelites' giving includes both material goods and technical services—both of the highest quality.

Because giving is done willingly, joyfully, and unanimously, it is not mandatory—the motivation of the Israelites is extremely high. The tabernacle is the means of God personally dwelling among His people (25:8), and the people are eager to have this promise fulfilled. This is a onetime need, for which the people have been amply enabled to contribute. With such motivation, God could easily allow the nation to provide the skills and materials for the tabernacle voluntarily.

There were other ongoing needs in Israel, however, which were not so glamorous, and of a much longer duration. To insure these needs are met, God makes giving a compulsory matter. There is an ongoing need for the support of the priests and Levites, who devote themselves to the service of God in the tabernacle.

EXODUS 36:8–39:43

THE TABERNACLE, THE DWELLING PLACE OF GOD

Characteristics of the Tabernacle 36:8–39:43

Setting Up the Section

The description of the tabernacle provides the first biblical revelation as to how God dwells among His people, and what this suggests for the church today.

36:8–39:43

CHARACTERISTICS OF THE TABERNACLE

When the people left Sinai for Canaan, they would need some portable place for God's presence to be manifested. The tabernacle serves as a meeting place between God and humans, and is known as the "tent of meeting" (35:21). Since the tabernacle is a tent, the problem of portability is solved.

The tabernacle also solves the problem of having a holy God dwell in the midst of sinful people. The tent curtains, and especially the thick veil, serve as a dividing barrier between God and the people. Beyond this, the tabernacle is sanctified and set apart as a holy place. Also, the tabernacle is a place of sacrifice so that the sins of the Israelites could be atoned for. While the solution is not permanent, it does facilitate communion between God and His people.

The tabernacle displays wealth and beauty in a reflection of God's glory within. According to this calculation, there would be some 1,900 pounds of gold, 6,437 pounds of silver, and 4,522 pounds of bronze. The excellence of the tabernacle, both in its materials and its workmanship, is a reflection of the excellence of God. The tabernacle is also a holy place, because abiding in it is a holy God (30:37–38).

While the tabernacle is composed of varied elements, it is its unity—in design, function, and purpose—that is celebrated and emphasized in the text. It is God's masterwork amidst His people, proclaiming His presence and hinting at His glory.

Take It Home

The tabernacle and, eventually, the temple of God are the forerunners for the modern church. The New Testament Epistles teach us that the dwelling place of God's Holy Spirit is now the church—not the church building, but each Christian who is part of the body of Christ (Ephesians 2:19–22). In the new covenant, believers are called to consider their body a temple of the Lord, and treat it with appropriate reverence, just as the Israelites were called to approach the tabernacle and the temple with great reverence for God's holiness (1 Corinthians 6:18–20).

EXODUS 40:1–38

THE CONSECRATION OF THE TABERNACLE AND THE PRESENCE OF GOD

Setting Up the Section

This is the climax of the story of Exodus: The tabernacle is completed, and the glory of God descends upon it. It is also an introduction to Leviticus. God commands the anointing of the priesthood, who will dominate the next story in the history of the Israelites and receive God's instructions regarding the use of the carefully constructed tabernacle.

40:1–16

DIVINE INSTRUCTIONS: ARRANGING AND ANOINTING

There is a distinct change in the personal pronoun employed in chapter 40 from *they* (39:43) to *you* (40:2). The shift is from the construction of the tabernacle, in which all the people were involved, to the setting up of the tabernacle and the anointing of it, which was the responsibility of Moses (40:1, 16).

There is a descending order of holiness of the items referred to in the chapter. We begin in the Holy of Holies, the most holy place in the tabernacle, and end in the courtyard, the least holy place.

40:17–33

THE TABERNACLE IS ASSEMBLED AND RAISED

There is a mood of excitement and anticipation among the Israelites who have spent months carefully following God's specific instructions. Amazingly, the tabernacle is constructed on Israel's first anniversary as a free nation (12:2), and just about nine months from the time of her arrival at Mount Sinai. It also appears that the tent is erected on this one day, since the materials are all made and ready before this time (39:32–43). God's precise timing emphasizes how far the Israelites have come since they escaped Egypt.

Moses' role finally seems to have evolved into something more provisional (almost priestly), which continues until Aaron and his sons are anointed and installed as the official priesthood of Israel. Moses offers incense (40:27), burnt and grain offerings (40:29), and washes himself (40:31), like Aaron and his sons.

40:34–38

THE GLORY OF GOD DESCENDS UPON THE TABERNACLE

Since the cloud has been present with the Israelites from the time they left Egypt and never departed from them, there is a sense in which nothing new occurs here. What was once distant (either before or behind the nation, or far away, atop Mount Sinai) is now in the very midst of the camp. The second fact is even more significant. The appearance of the glory of God in the tabernacle takes place after Israel's great sin (the golden calf), which is reported in chapter 32. Finally, the glory of God settles on the tabernacle to abide there, not just as a momentary manifestation of God.

Imagine the Israelites' delight in seeing the tabernacle set up for the first time and intensified by the splendor of God's glory descending upon it. The cloud, the visible manifestation of the glory of God, descends upon the tabernacle to dwell in the midst of the people and to guide them into the promised land. The joy of God's presence is all the more glorious in the light of Israel's "fall" in chapter 32.

The glory of God descending upon the tabernacle is the realization of Israel's highest hopes, of Moses' most noble and impassioned petition. The glory of God in the tabernacle is so awesome that even Moses could not enter it. Remember that Moses had seen more of God's glory than any other human being alive—in the burning bush (chapter 3), in the plagues and exodus of Israel, and from inside the cloud atop Mount Sinai (chapters 19, 24). At his request, he had seen even more of God's glory when he was privileged to view the back of God (33:17–34:9). But the glory of God in the tabernacle is greater than that which Moses (or any other Israelite for that matter) could behold.

Take It Home

The presence of God is indeed dear to the Israelites, who had never had the presence of God closer to them. Nevertheless, God is still separated from the people. Even Moses could not enter into the presence of God in the tabernacle, and only the high priest could enter into the Holy of Holies once a year. Christ has torn the veil away—He dwells within each individual believer, not just in the midst of the nation.

LEVITICUS

INTRODUCTION TO LEVITICUS

Though many see Leviticus as a book addressing the priests of Israel, the information here was actually written for the people, yet includes specific instructions for the priests. The laws relate to the entire nation of Israel, but it was the priests who were to teach others how to live as God's holy people and to regulate worship in the tabernacle (also called *sanctuary*, or *tent of meeting*), where God's holy presence dwelled.

AUTHOR

Moses is generally ascribed as the author of the first five books of the Old Testament, or the Pentateuch (which means "five books" or "five scrolls"). These books are also known as the Law of Moses, or Mosaic Law. It is most likely that Moses wrote during the time when Israel was wandering and intermittently camping in the desert for forty years during the second half of the fifteenth century BC.

PURPOSE

In the Hebrew text, the first word of the book of Leviticus, translated "and He called," serves as the title of the book, though its English title means "of the Levites." The book served as a handbook for the priests God put in place after the institution of the Mosaic Covenant at Mount Sinai. The specific details are many, and this preciseness was to ensure the Israelites that the continuing presence of God was with them. The laws on both ceremonial holiness and personal holiness were supposed to teach the Israelites about their holy God and how to live set apart as His people. Not only does God tell the Israelites how to worship, but He gives them practical ways to live out holiness in everyday life.

THEMES

The book of Leviticus is comprised of twenty-seven chapters including many regulations and guidelines. The rules are not arbitrary, though. Each of the seemingly minute details in Leviticus deals with the main theme of holiness.

The phrase that is repeated most often in Leviticus is a variation of God's command, "Be holy as I am holy." During this time, Israel was a new nation. God's laws were designed to teach them how to become set apart—holy people who imitated God's character.

The tent of meeting was built by the Israelites as a holy place to house the presence of a holy God. Sinful people could not approach their God, though, because He was the essence of holiness. The rituals and offerings detailed in Leviticus are God's compassionate design to allow His people to find atonement so that they could approach Him in worship and experience a covenant relationship with Him.

Leviticus can be divided into two major sections, separated by chapter 16, which deals with the annual Day of Atonement. Chapters 1–15 deal with what we might call priestly holiness, by giving instructions about sacrifices and rituals that relate to one's holiness. Chapters 17–27 deal more with what we could call practical holiness—that which is worked out in daily life.

HISTORICAL CONTEXT

During the writing of Leviticus, the Israelites were camped at the base of Mount Sinai in the desert after their deliverance from Egypt and before their entrance into the land of Canaan. It was at Mount Sinai that God entered into a covenant relationship with the Israelites. He would be their God, and they would be His people. God communicated to His people through their leader, Moses, how they should live out their covenant responsibilities.

Leviticus is the third book in the Pentateuch. It is closely connected with the book of Exodus and often repeats or expands on instructions God gave through Moses there. Exodus records God's detailed instructions to the Israelites for how to build His holy tabernacle. Leviticus follows up with regulations God communicated from that tabernacle. The laws of Leviticus did not initiate sacrificial offerings, but they did serve to regulate them.

CONTRIBUTION TO THE BIBLE

The book of Leviticus is quoted or referred to in the New Testament at least forty times (more than any other book in the Bible). Many of Jesus' teachings, particularly those on the Great Commandment, come from Leviticus (19:18). New Testament teachings on holiness tie directly to Levitical teachings (1 Peter 2).

The greatest theological contribution of Leviticus is an introduction to atonement. The sacrificial system detailed in Leviticus reveals human sinfulness and introduces atonement through a substitutionary blood sacrifice. To fully understand the reason for and importance of Jesus' ultimate sacrifice, a student of the Bible would need to understand the Old Testament system's purpose and flaws.

OUTLINE

THE BURNT OFFERING 1:1–17

- The Command 1:1–2
- Bulls 1:3–9
- Sheep and Goats 1:10–13
- Birds 1:14–17

THE GRAIN OFFERING 2:1–16

- Uncooked Grain 2:1–3
- Cooked Grain 2:4–10
- Yeast and Salt 2:11–13
- Firstfruits 2:14–16

THE PEACE OFFERING 3:1–17

- From the Herd 3:1–5
- From the Flock 3:6–17

THE SIN OFFERING 4:1–35

- Unintentional Sins 4:1–2
- The Priest's Sins 4:3–12
- The Community's Sins 4:13–21
- A Leader's Sins 4:22–26
- An Individual's Sins 4:27–35

THE GUILT OFFERING 5:1–19

- More on the Sin Offering 5:1–13
- The Guilt Offering 5:14–19

MORE OFFERING RULES 6:1–30

- More on the Guilt Offering 6:1–7
- More on the Burnt Offering 6:8–13
- More on the Grain Offering 6:14–23
- More on the Sin Offering 6:24–30

EVEN MORE RULES 7:1–38

- The Guilt Offering Again 7:1–10
- The Peace Offering Again 7:11–38

THE DAY OF ATONEMENT 16:1–34

Preparation 16:1–5
Sacrifice 16:6–19
Cleansing 16:20–34

PRECIOUS IS THE BLOOD 17:1–16

Sacrificial Blood 17:1–9
Lifeblood 17:10–16

RELATIONSHIP RULES 18:1–30

A Covenant Relationship 18:1–5
Relational Boundaries 18:6–23
Consequences 18:24–30

HOLY, HOLY, HOLY 19:1–37

Being Holy 19:1–8
Loving Others 19:9–18
Living Holy 19:19–37

CAPITAL CRIMES 20:1–27

Molech and Mediums 20:1–6
Family Business 20:7–21
Follow the Rules 20:22–27

HOLINESS: TRUE/FALSE, PART 1 21:1–24

Mourning and Marriage (Priest) 21:1–9
Mourning and Marriage (High Priest) 21:10–15
Stay Back 21:16–24

HOLINESS: TRUE/FALSE, PART 2 22:1–33

Keep It Clean 22:1–9
The Priest's Food 22:10–16
What to Give/Not Give 22:17–33

ALL IN GOOD TIME 23:1–44

The Weekly Sabbath 23:1–3
Spring Holy Days 23:4–22
Fall Holy Days 23:23–44

LAMP, LOAVES, AND LOUDMOUTH 24:1–23

Keep the Fires Burning 24:1–4
Give Us Our Weekly Bread 24:5–9
The Peril of Profanity 24:10–23

SUPER SABBATH 25:1–55

Sabbath Year 25:1–7
Jubilee Year 25:8–34
Neighborly Ways 25:35–46
Strange Company 25:47–55

A WELCOME WARNING 26:1–46

Blessings 26:1–13
Curses 26:14–39
Assurance 26:40–46

THE VALUE OF A VOW 27:1–34

People 27:1–8
Animals 27:9–13
Property 27:14–25
Prohibitions and Tithes 27:26–34

LEVITICUS 1:1–17

THE BURNT OFFERING

Setting Up the Section

In Exodus, God gives Moses instruction for how to build the tabernacle (2:1–8; 38:1–7). In Leviticus, He gives Moses instruction for how to offer sacrifices at the tabernacle. The burnt offering illustrates God's principle of atonement, where humanity's sin is answered through a sacrificial shedding of blood.

1:1–2

THE COMMAND

The Israelites were camped at the base of Mount Sinai when Moses received their instructions. The burnt offering is a voluntary and personal offering, and instructions are given for individuals (1:2). The sacrifice is not for specific sins, but rather for the general state of sinfulness. The purpose of the burnt offering is to make atonement for the sin of the offerer and to gain God's acceptance.

1:3–9

BULLS

The sacrificial animal had to be the best quality (without defect) and male (1:3). Bulls were valuable livestock, and the male would be able to produce additional offspring. It would be a true sacrifice for an Israelite to offer a young, productive animal.

Both offerer and priest participate in the sacrifice (1:4–9). The offerer is responsible for the slaughter, and the priest handles the sprinkling of blood and burning of the offering on the altar of sacrifice. By laying his hands on the animal, the offerer identifies his sins with the offering. The animal becomes a substitute for the individual. While many sacrifices benefit both the offerer and the priest, because both are allowed to eat from the sacrificed animal, the burnt offering is completely consumed by fire.

When an Israelite wanted to find acceptance with God in order to worship, he had to come with a burnt offering. This is to acknowledge and make provision for his sinfulness. The sacrifice allowed the Israelites to come into the presence of a holy God in the tent of meeting.

1:10–13

SHEEP AND GOATS

Sheep and goats were livestock of considerable value, and the best male of the flock was required as the offering. One of the unique contributions of the burnt offering is that it illustrates sacrifice in its purest form. A valuable animal is given up wholly to God without expectation of anything in return, other than the benefit of finding acceptance with God.

Demystifying Leviticus

The Israelites of Moses' day understood the burnt offering in terms of what they already knew about it, not its future fulfillment. The key to understanding the meaning was what had already been revealed (see Genesis 8, 22; Exodus 10, 18, 20). Through Noah's example, the Israelites saw that God's blessing came after an offering, not after good deeds. In Abraham's story, they saw the sacrifice as substitution. So when the Israelites placed their hands on the head of a sacrificial animal, they would have known it was dying in their place.

1:14–17

BIRDS

God gives three options for animal sacrifices (herd, flock, or bird). This is because the poor could not afford a bull, sheep, or goat. God did not keep people from coming into His presence because they could not afford to sacrifice (14:21–22, 30–32). A dove or young pigeon was a true sacrifice for those who were poor, just as a bull or goat was a sacrifice for those who owned livestock, making it pleasing to God (1:17).

Take It Home

Real sacrifice is seldom practiced today in the church. We tend to give away our leftovers, while we keep what is new and best for ourselves. The kind of costly sacrifice seen in the burnt offering is what God expects from true disciples who give up all to follow Christ. When we give ourselves to God, as living sacrifices (Romans 12:1–2), it is completely as a pleasing offering. May God enable us to practice this kind of sacrifice in our own lives.

LEVITICUS 2:1–16

THE GRAIN OFFERING

Setting Up the Section

The second offering explained in Leviticus is the grain offering. This name *grain offering* refers to the material most often used, but the Hebrew name for this offering indicates its primary function, which is "gift." At this time, the Israelites were camped in the desert, where they could not grow grain, so this offering (most likely wheat or barley) was a great sacrifice. To sacrifice this seed to God was an act of faith because they would have to depend on God to provide more.

2:1–3

UNCOOKED GRAIN

Like the burnt offering, the grain offering required the highest quality sacrifice (2:1–3). The grain had to be fine, meaning finely ground flour. To make fine flour entailed a great deal of extra effort. The grain offering was also sacrificed by fire and produced a pleasing aroma to the Lord (2:2).

The Israelites are instructed to make the grain offering after the burnt offering (Numbers 28; Joshua 22:23, 29; Judges 13:19, 23). Since there is no blood shed in this offering, it does not atone for sin. Contribution to the grain offering is allowed because a person's sinfulness has already been atoned for in the burnt offering.

2:4–10

COOKED GRAIN

The oil used in this offering (2:4) would probably have been olive oil, also a sacrifice since it was not readily available in the desert. All the sacrificial materials were difficult to obtain in the days of Moses, though of course, these laws would continue on into the settlement of the land.

Critical Observation

The Israelites had to depend on God for even basic needs while camped at Mount Sinai, but when they were in Canaan, it would be easy to enjoy their blessings and forget to depend on God. The grain offering was one way for the Israelites to remember that God is both Creator and Sustainer.

Only a handful of the grain offering was burned on the altar; the rest was given to the priests, Aaron and his sons (2:2–3, 9–10). The greater portion of the offering served as the livelihood of the priests, just as the tithe was God's means for supporting the Levites (Numbers 18:21–24). The sacrificed portion was called the "memorial portion" (Leviticus 2:2, 9, 16 NET), and the other portion was called "a thing most holy" (2:3, 10; 5:17 NASB).

Demystifying Leviticus

The grain offerings in the King James Version of the Bible are referred to as "meat offerings." The word *meat*, as it was used by the translators of the King James Version, did not have the same meaning as the term today. This was a term that simply referred to food, and in a general way could refer to grain (either in its raw or cooked form).

2:11–13

YEAST AND SALT

Through the grain offering the Israelites acknowledge God's provision for their needs. Since the purpose of the grain offering is worship, not atonement, the offerer could contribute. However, only certain additions were allowed. Salt was allowed, but leaven and honey were forbidden. The Hebrew word translated *honey* indicates fruit (not bee) honey. When this kind of honey is burned, it ferments—a form of decay which is associated with death and thus is to be avoided (the same is true of yeast).

The grain offering was associated with the burnt offering, and the blood sacrifice could not be associated with leaven, which was known to corrupt.

Known to preserve and purify, salt was added to the grain offering. Salt may have reminded Israel of the enduring covenant with God, since salt does not burn or turn into a gas but basically stays the same through fire (2:13).

Demystifying Leviticus

The salt added to the grain offering has significance as "the salt of the covenant of your God" (2:13 NIV). A "covenant of salt" is also found in Numbers 18:19 and 2 Chronicles 13:5. Salt was used symbolically in covenants in the ancient Near East. The salt used in the grain offering represents purity and longevity, reminding Israel of their long-lasting covenant with God.

2:14–16

FIRSTFRUITS

The grain offering of firstfruits (Leviticus 2:14–16) was that which was first harvested from a crop (Exodus 23:19). The offering was accompanied by incense as a sensory symbol of the pleasure the offering would bring God. Again, the expense was a reminder that sacrifice is costly, but pleasing God is the highest good.

Here's a review of the offerings and the laws that governed them:

First Regulations:	Additional Regulations:
(More "laity" directed)	(More priestly in orientation)
Burnt Offering, ch. 1	Law of Burnt Offering, 6:8–13
Grain Offering, ch. 2	Law of Grain Offering, 6:14–23; 7:9–10
Peace Offering, ch. 3	Law of Peace Offering, 7:11–34
Sin Offering, ch. 4	Law of Sin Offering, 6:24–30
Guilt Offering, ch. 5, 6:1–7	Law of Guilt Offering, 7:1–10
Ordination Offering, 6:19–23	Ordination Offerings, 8:1–9:24 Priests and offerings, 10:1–20

Take It Home

How do we develop real trust in God? Leviticus suggests it is by giving sacrificially. This is the kind of giving we see when the Israelites offer their firstfruits, trusting God to provide an additional harvest. Sacrificial giving requires faith in God as the One who faithfully supplies our needs and who gives us our daily bread.

LEVITICUS 3:1–17

THE PEACE OFFERING

Setting Up the Section

The burnt offering focuses on God's righteousness and an individual's atonement through an animal sacrifice. The grain offering focuses on the Israelites' dependence on God. The peace offering is made on top of the burnt offering (3:5) and focuses on the Israelites' peace with God—the peace of mind and wholeness that comes with knowing God is at peace with us. There is also a strong element of fellowship signified by the sharing of the meal together. This is why some translations translate it "fellowship offering."

Three principle passages in Leviticus deal with the peace offering: 3:1–17 (the mechanics of the sacrifice); 7:11–34 (the meaning of the sacrifice); and 19:5–8 (the law of leftovers).

3:1–5

FROM THE HERD

In the day of Moses, an Israelite would begin to make a peace offering by selecting an animal without any defect (male or female) from his herd or flock (3:1, 6). He would then take this animal to the doorway of the tabernacle, where he would lay his hand on its head, identifying his sin with the animal and himself with its death, and slaughter it. Inside the tabernacle, the priests would collect the shed blood and sprinkle it around the altar (3:2, 8, 13). After skinning the animal and cutting it into pieces, the priests would then burn the fat, kidneys, and part of the liver on the altar (3:3–5, 9–11, 14–16).

The process is much like that of the burnt offering, except in the peace offering the entire animal is not consumed. The blood, fat, and organs are burned (3:3–5, 9–11, 14–16), but the rest is given to the priests and the offerer (7:30–34; 10:14–15).

Critical Observation

Some Bible versions have translated *peace offering* as *fellowship offering*. Both *peace* and *fellowship* are appropriate. The word *peace* has the connotation of "wholeness" or "completeness." The Israelites became whole when they were accepted by God in worship (19:5). The meal that the offerer enjoyed, along with fellow Israelites, signified the peace that the sacrifice brought about. Today, through Christ's death, we can have peace and fellowship with God and peace and fellowship with others.

3:6–17

FROM THE FLOCK

The process for a sacrifice from the flock is the same as one from the herd. At the end of the chapter, though, Israelites are instructed never to eat the fat or blood of an animal (3:16–17; 17:10–13).

Critical Observation

Each sacrifice by an Israelite was a certain type for a specific purpose. Every offering had exact rules. Because of the consequences for failing to observe the rules, individuals had to be certain about the specifics of each offering. In part, this was a safeguard against mindless ritual. People could not go through the motions of sacrifice without thinking about the purpose.

LEVITICUS 4:1–35

THE SIN OFFERING

Unintentional Sins	4:1–2
The Priest's Sins	4:3–12
The Community's Sins	4:13–21
A Leader's Sins	4:22–26
An Individual's Sins	4:27–35

Setting Up the Section

Offerings in Leviticus 1–3 are organized by sacrificial animal. The sin offering in chapter 4 is organized by categories of people: high priest (4:3–12); congregation of Israel (4:13–21); leader (4:22–26); and individual Israelite (4:27–35). The sin offering is for a specific sin, as opposed to a state of sinfulness addressed by the burnt offering. Also, while chapters 1–3 are concerned with the process of sacrifice, chapters 4–6 emphasize the result of the process: forgiveness. (The sin offering is further explained in 5:1–13 and 6:24–30.)

4:1–2

UNINTENTIONAL SINS

The sins addressed through the sin offering are those that, for some reason, are not immediately apparent but are eventually known. The text notes that the sin offering is to be made immediately after the knowledge of sin is present (4:14, 23, 28).

4:3–12

THE PRIEST'S SINS

If the high priest sinned, he would bring guilt on the entire congregation of Israelites (4:3), so the offering was necessary to atone for the sin for everyone. The priest himself would bring a bull to the tabernacle, lay his hand on it, and slaughter it (4:3–4). He would then sprinkle some of the blood on the tabernacle veil and some on the altar of incense (4:5–6). The remaining blood was poured at the base of the altar of burnt offering (4:7). The fat of the offered bull was burned as with the peace offering, but its body was burned completely outside the camp (4:11–12, 21). The offerer received none of the meat.

4:13–21

THE COMMUNITY'S SINS

When the entire community sins, there is a sin offering to atone for the collective sin (4:14). The process is the same as the sin offering of the priest.

4:22–26

A LEADER'S SINS

Even unintentional sin makes a person guilty (4:22). When a leader is aware of his sin, he is to sacrifice a male goat as a sin offering. The process is similar to that of the priest's offering, with two exceptions: Blood is not sprinkled at the veil, and the animal's body is not burned. (The meat of these sacrificial animals could be eaten in a holy place by the male priests [6:24–30].)

With each category, the person or people involved are found guilty due to sin. In each case, a blood sacrifice is needed for atonement.

Demystifying Leviticus

The Old Testament prophecy of Isaiah spoke of the Messiah, whose shed blood would atone for our sins (Isaiah 53:4–6). When John the Baptist saw Jesus, he proclaimed, "Look, the Lamb of God, who takes away the sin of the world!" (John 1:29 NIV). Hebrews demonstrates that Jesus is the sinless Lamb of God (Hebrews 9:11–14; 1 Peter 1:13–21). Jesus is the sin bearer, who died once for all, so sin could be cleansed and we could approach a holy God.

4:27–35

AN INDIVIDUAL'S SINS

An individual Israelite could offer a male goat or a female lamb as a sin offering. The process would have been the same as that of the leader's sin offering.

In chapter 4 we see a repeated sequence: There is sin, resulting in guilt; there is a blood sacrifice, resulting in atonement and forgiveness. This explains why only the blood and fat of the sin offering are used and the rest is thrown away. God is demonstrating in a dramatic way that only blood can atone for Israel's sin.

Take It Home

The ancient sin offering has something to say to Christians today. Whenever we sin, we need to remember that God used Christ's shed blood to provide forgiveness. Confession and repentance is the means for experiencing that forgiveness. Every sin, no matter how insignificant it seems, requires the blood of Christ to be shed. Let us not forget that while forgiveness is free, it is not cheap.

LEVITICUS 5:1–19

SIN AND GUILT OFFERINGS

Setting Up the Section

Leviticus 5:1–13 continues to explain the sin offering (see chapter 4) and begins to address sins specifically. In verses 14–19, the sin offering and the guilt offering are combined.

Critical Observation

Leviticus 4–7 presents both sin and guilt offerings. The two themes intermingle throughout. The Bible closely ties sin and guilt together. Take, for example, 5:5–6 and 5:15. If a person is *guilty* he may need to bring a *sin offering*, but if a person *sins* he may need to bring a *guilt offering*. The two concepts are seemingly inseparable.

5:1–13

MORE ON THE SIN OFFERING

Chapter 5 addresses specific sins such as ignoring a call to testify, touching something or someone ceremonially unclean, or speaking without thinking (5:1–5). The guilty person would confess his or her sin and give a female lamb or goat as a sin offering (5:6).

Verses 7 and 11 show God's grace in providing an exception for those who are poor. They could offer a less expensive blood sacrifice (doves or pigeons), or even fine flour. So while not everyone could afford a peace offering, everyone was afforded the opportunity to experience forgiveness. (In fact, Psalm 69:30–33 seems to imply that all the poor really need to bring is a "song.")

5:14–19

THE GUILT OFFERING

The guilt offering is similar to the sin offering. The guilt offering seems to have been used for a breach of God's commandments, even if unintentional or for a sin where restitution could be made. Just as with the sin offering, atonement could be found through a guilt offering. Unlike the sin offering, restitution was also necessary to make up for what a person did or did not do by giving part of the value of the sacrificial ram to the priest.

Take It Home

One of the reasons we sometimes continue to carry our guilt is that we refuse to recognize that the debt has been paid. For the believer, our guilt offering is Jesus Christ. But God doesn't ask us to pay for our guilt; He only asks for confession and repentance. We can confess sin and leave the guilt behind.

LEVITICUS 6:1–30

MORE OFFERING RULES

More on the Guilt Offering	6:1–7
More on the Burnt Offering	6:8–13
More on the Grain Offering	6:14–23
More on the Sin Offering	6:24–30

Setting Up the Section

Chapter 6 flows directly out of chapter 5, including additional details related to the guilt offering, burnt offering, grain offering, and sin offering.

6:1–7

MORE ON THE GUILT OFFERING

A guilt offering was necessary in the case of disobedience against God's laws, specifically those relating to other people. If, for example, an Israelite cheated his neighbor, he would need to make a guilt offering. The same goes for a number of sins that affected others (6:4–5). A sin against one person was seen as a sin against the entire community, and ultimately God. The penalties teach that restitution is necessary before forgiveness (6:6).

6:8–13

MORE ON THE BURNT OFFERING

Priests would sacrifice burnt offerings every morning and evening for the congregation of Israel. These verses focus heavily on how to make sure sacrifices are completely consumed by not allowing the fire to go out (6:9), and how to handle disposing of ashes (6:11).

6:14–23

MORE ON THE GRAIN OFFERING

These details show priests how to burn the memorial portion of the grain offering and what to do with the leftovers (6:15–16). The priests could eat what remained, but only in a consecrated area since it was still a holy offering (6:16). The seemingly tedious details ensure that priests are obedient to God rather than following their own way.

Critical Observation

The Israelites brought their offerings to the Lord, but the priests served as His representatives. With the coming of Christ and His death and resurrection, we no longer need an earthly intermediary; we have direct access to God through Jesus (Hebrews 4:14–5:10).

6:24–30

MORE ON THE SIN OFFERING

These additional rules relate to holiness. The tabernacle is a holy place because the presence of God dwells there, and the sin offering is a serious, sacred ritual that the priests are not to take lightly.

Demystifying Leviticus

The passages in Leviticus 6:8–7:38 address Aaron and his sons, the priesthood, directly. They form a kind of handbook of priestly procedures. The priests were keepers and protectors of the law, so these specific and serious words would have been written, not handed down through oral tradition.

LEVITICUS 7:1–38

EVEN MORE RULES

Setting Up the Section

After a few more rules about the guilt offering, the majority of chapter 7 gives additional regulations for the peace offering, including the grain offerings that should accompany it and how to handle the leftovers.

7:1–10

THE GUILT OFFERING AGAIN

The first verses give additional regulations concerning the guilt offering. The focus is on keeping it holy; it is not something to be taken lightly. Because of the offering's holy nature, only the priests (or males in their family) could partake in eating the meat of a sacrificed animal after the kidneys and the fat around them were burned on the altar to God (7:3–6). Likewise, the cooked grain offering belonged to the priests (7:9–10). Even then, they could be eaten only in a holy place (7:6).

7:11–38

THE PEACE OFFERING AGAIN

Verse 11 begins the additional rules to help the priests administer the peace offering. Along with the fat of a sacrificial animal that is offered to God, an appropriate grain offering is also necessary. If the peace offering is out of thanksgiving, both leavened and unleavened cakes are to be offered. Part is burned on the altar, and the rest goes to the priests (7:12–13).

Since the fat and blood of the animal are offered to God, and the breast and the right thigh go to the priest, the rest of the sacrificial animal is left for the offerer. So after the ceremonial sacrifice, the Israelite would eat a festive meal with what remained. This is perhaps the most striking feature of the peace offering.

Critical Observation

Throughout scripture, the meal has a deeply religious significance. The festive meal that was part of the peace offering added to this significance. Here, the meal is a symbol of the peace the Israelite has with God and with others through the sacrifice.

Considerable emphasis is placed on what happens to the leftovers from the peace offering (7:15–18; 19:5–8). They had to be eaten on the day of the sacrifice in the case of thanksgiving (7:15), or by the next day in the case of a vow or freewill offering (7:16–18; 19:5–8). Anyone who was unclean or had touched something unclean could not eat of the meal; disobedience meant being cut off from the rest of the Israelites (7:20), a severe consequence.

Demystifying Leviticus

For an Israelite to be cut off from his people (7:20, 25) was the ultimate punishment. The Israelites were a communal people, so to be cut off signified loss of identity and covenant relationship. The phrase "cut off" indicates the offender was taken outside the camp and put to death or possibly banished forever.

Verses 22–26 offer another reminder that the Israelites are absolutely not to eat any of the fat or blood of sacrificed animals (or any other animals, for that matter). Eating fat means the possibility of an Israelite being cut off from his people (7:25), and eating blood means he will certainly be cut off (7:27).

The fat of the sacrificial animal, along with its breast meat and thigh, are offered to the Lord, but the priests keep the meat after burning the fat. This is one of the ways that God provides for the physical care of the priests (7:28–35).

LEVITICUS 8:1–36

PRINCIPLES OF PRIESTHOOD: ORDINATION

The Choice	8:1–4
The Clothes and the Oil	8:5–13
The Sacrifice	8:14–36

Setting Up the Section

Leviticus 8 describes the origin and ordination of the Aaronic priesthood. This chapter portrays the fulfillment of God's commands pertaining to the ordination of Aaron and his sons, as detailed in Exodus 29.

8:1–4

THE CHOICE

God announces Aaron's ordination through Moses. Aaron was made high priest and his sons were made priests because God had chosen them, not because of any merit they possessed on their own.

Demystifying Leviticus

The Aaronic priesthood is just being formally established in chapter 8, but the concept of priesthood is not new to the Pentateuch, the first five books of the Bible. In a curious incident in the life of Abraham, a priest king by the name of Melchizedek is introduced (Genesis 14:18–20). Also, Joseph's wife is the daughter of an Egyptian priest (Genesis 41:45, 50; 46:20), and Jethro, Moses' father in law, is known as "the priest of Midian" (Exodus 2:16; 3:1; 18:1). At Mount Sinai, God proclaimed that He had delivered Israel from bondage and set her apart to be a "kingdom of priests" (Exodus 19:6). Instead of creating the concept of priests, Leviticus 8 is the first mention of Israelite priests.

8:5–13

THE CLOTHES AND THE OIL

Worship of God is a serious matter, shown in part through the detailed preparation in verses 5–13. While other Israelites are often purified through washing their hands, the priests are symbolically purified through full-body baths (8:6). The elaborate ceremonial garments would have set apart the priests in appearance and in service to God. The oil represents a divine anointing (8:10–13).

Critical Observation

God took the sin of His priests very seriously. Being in close proximity to God brought with it correspondingly high standards of conduct. This is indicated in several ways in Leviticus. God frequently indicates that disobedience to His commands could bring death (8:35; 10:6–7, 9; Exodus 28:35, 43; 30:20–21). Chapter 10 shows this played out with two priests, plus the implications it has for the entire priesthood.

8:14–36

THE SACRIFICE

Before the priests could be accepted into God's holy presence, they would have to make sacrificial offerings (8:34). Moses had been serving in the high priest function before Aaron's ordination, so he performs the sacrificial rites of the sin offering and burnt offering (8:14–21; see chapters 1, 4). In a special ordination ritual, a second ram is used to symbolize how the priest should hear God's voice, do righteous deeds with his hands, and walk in the ways of God (8:24). Additional offerings are made, and the portions that are not burned are given to Aaron and his sons for a ceremonial meal (8:31). The ordination is complete seven days later, only after the priests show their obedience to God (8:35-36).

Take It Home

Aaron and his sons were obedient to the things God asked of them, and God sanctified them. First Peter 1:2 reminds us that obedience is still a mark of personal holiness.

LEVITICUS 9:1–24

PRINCIPLES OF PRIESTHOOD: MINISTRY

Preparation	9:1–14
Service	9:15–24

Setting Up the Section

Leviticus 9 turns the focus from Moses to Aaron. Aaron and his sons are now commanded to offer sacrifices, first for their own sins and then for the sins of the nation.

9:1–14

PREPARATION

After the ordination of Aaron and his sons is complete, Moses calls them and the leaders of Israel. He tells Aaron to make a sin offering and burnt offering for his own atonement, and then he tells him to educate the Israelites about their responsibilities (9:3–4). The Israelites obeyed and drew near to God (9:5).

Aaron and his priestly sons perform their first ritual duties. Aaron makes a sin offering and burnt offering for himself and his family (9:8–14). They would have to be pure before God before they could offer sacrifices on behalf of the people.

9:15–24

SERVICE

As God's representative of the nation of Israel, Aaron makes a sin offering, burnt offering, grain offering, and peace offering for the people (9:15–18; see chapters 1–4).

The purpose of these offerings is to make preparations for the revelation of God's glory to the people (9:23–24). The Israelites' response to God's presence is joyful worship (9:24).

Demystifying Leviticus

At the sight of God's glory, the people fell facedown (9:24). This was a typical symbol of submission in the Near Eastern cultures.

Take It Home

The Old Testament priests had to be washed in order to carry out their priestly duties. This terminology is now applied to all who are in Christ as a royal priesthood (1 Peter 2). Priests are those whose sins have been atoned for, so that they are free to minister to other sinners. This atonement for the New Testament priest is that which Christ, our great High Priest, has made through the shedding of His blood on the cross (Hebrews 4:14–5:10).

LEVITICUS 10:1–20

PRINCIPLES OF PRIESTHOOD: A DANGEROUS JOB

Setting Up the Section

At the end of chapter 9, fire consumes what is left of the people's sacrifice, and at the beginning of chapter 10, fire comes from God's presence, consuming two of Israel's priests. Nadab and Abihu are sons of Aaron who die because they exercise their priestly duties in a way that dishonors God. The priesthood was an exceedingly dangerous job, for those who drew near to God in service dared not do so casually or irreverently.

10:1–5

PLAYING WITH FIRE

The exact sin committed by Nadab and Abihu, the two oldest sons of Aaron, is not clear; the text says they were offering unauthorized fire before God (10:1). What is clear is that their actions were in direct disobedience to God's commands.

The death of Nadab and Abihu dramatically conveys that priests were allowed to approach God, but that privilege demanded corresponding honor toward Him and His laws (10:3).

10:6–11

FOLLOWING THE RULES

After taking Aaron's oldest sons outside the camp, Moses gives additional rules (10:6–7), so Aaron and his other sons do not become unclean as a result of improper mourning.

In verses 8–11, God speaks directly to Aaron. His words indicate that Nadab and Abihu may have sinned as a result of drinking while on duty (10:9), and He makes a clear distinction between what is holy and what is common (10:10). He also emphasizes the priests' role of teaching the Israelites God's law (10:11).

10:12–20

UNDERSTANDING HOLINESS

Verses 12–15 are instructions to the Aaronic priests conveyed through Moses. They provide a backdrop for understanding Moses' anger when he suspects the sin offering is not properly carried out (10:16–18). Typically, when a goat is given for a sin offering, the breast meat is eaten by the priests. When Moses does not see the meat, he thinks Aaron's other sons have disobeyed God's instructions, but the situation is answered successfully by Aaron. Because of the recent tragedy, Aaron thinks eating of the offering is inappropriate, so it is burned.

Demystifying Leviticus

At the beginning of chapter 8, Moses is the prominent leader, as he has been throughout the account of the Exodus. In chapter 10, however, Aaron is installed as high priest, and he very much comes into his own. Moses' provisional priestly role seems to come to an end here. He is the great prophet, but Aaron is the great priest.

LEVITICUS 11:1–47

CLEAN AND UNCLEAN: FOOD RULES

Land Creatures	11:1–8
Water Creatures	11:9–12
Flying Creatures	11:13–23
The Solution	11:24–47

Setting Up the Section

The third major section of Leviticus (chapters 11–15) defines what is clean and unclean. The label *clean* and its counterpoint *unclean* comprise a prominent theme in Leviticus. The importance of distinctions between the holy and the profane is introduced in 10:10. To get a good grasp on Leviticus, it is important to understand what clean and unclean mean and how they relate to holiness.

11:1–8

LAND CREATURES

Chapter 11 explains clean/unclean food regulations in particular. (There is no clear reason for why certain creatures were considered clean and others were not.) Three animal categories are listed: land, water, and flying creatures. These same distinctions are found in Genesis 1, where God creates all life that is in the heavens, on earth, and under the waters.

Demystifying Leviticus

Various Bible translations name different animals as clean or unclean in chapter 11, and the names of the animals listed may not point to the exact creature we think of today. When a translator deals with Hebrew terms and attempts to isolate and identify a specific creature, it is not always easy, or even possible, to do so with exact accuracy. However, that should not affect the understanding of the principles of cleanness and uncleanness.

Two basic stipulations must be met before a land animal can be considered clean and, therefore, something an Israelite could eat: The creature must have a divided split hoof and chew its cud (11:3). Of course, some animals fit one category but not the other, but the rules are clear that both are necessary (11:4–8).

11:9–12

WATER CREATURES

To be considered clean, animals that live in the sea have to meet two qualifications as well: They must have fins and scales (11:9). The Israelites are not only to avoid unclean creatures, but they are to detest them (11:10–12).

11:13–23

FLYING CREATURES

Instead of qualifications for birds, God provides a list of unclean birds to avoid. The list includes birds that eat other animals or feed off dead carcasses (11:13–19). Flying insects are also mentioned. Essentially, all flying insects are unclean, unless they have jointed jumper legs (11:20–23).

11:24–47

THE SOLUTION

An additional category of unclean animals includes ones that creep or swarm, such as mice and lizards (11:29–31, 41–43).

Touching an unclean creature that is dead would make an Israelite categorically unclean. Even eating a clean animal without going through the proper sacrificial procedure would do the same thing (11:39). The last half of the chapter provides solutions for the problem of uncleanness.

Critical Observation

Essentially, the death of even a clean creature made it unclean, which would, of course, make it difficult to eat since generally all animals are killed before they can be eaten. So all meals that include meat would become an act of worship, since the only way an animal could be killed and stay clean is if it were offered as a sacrifice to God in front of the door of the tent of meeting (see Leviticus 17).

The offenses in chapter 11 are relatively minor, so a person or object could be made clean with water, and the state of uncleanness lasted only until evening (11:32). The exception is a clay pot or oven; it had to be destroyed (11:33, 35).

"Clean" and "unclean" are categories more than conditions. There is a direct relationship between what is clean and what is holy in scripture. Only what is clean can become holy. God emphasizes the Israelites' identification as His people by reminding them, "I am the LORD who brought you up from the land of Egypt to be your God; thus you shall be holy, for I am holy" (11:45 NASB).

Take It Home

In the Levitical system, those declared unclean by priests suffered both humiliation and isolation. The practical result meant a person could not approach God in worship until made clean again. Being unclean restricted fellowship with both God and other people. In the new system, we have been made clean and acceptable through Christ. We can draw near to God (James 4:8), and we can be holy as God is holy (1 Peter 1:15–16).

LEVITICUS 12:1–8

CLEAN AND UNCLEAN: MOTHERS ONLY

Setting Up the Section

Chapters 12–15 continue to define what is unclean, along with the process of purification. Chapters 12 and 15 address uncleanness related to sexual reproduction, and chapters 13 and 14 address skin ailments.

12:1–5

UNCLEAN MOTHERS

These verses describe the categorical uncleanness a woman experiences after childbirth. The act of having a child itself is not considered sinful, but the flow of blood and other discharges associated with birth cause uncleanness. It may be that reproductive blood and semen are seen as holy fluids. When one comes into contact with something holy it renders one temporarily unclean (note, for instance, that handling the scrolls of scripture make one's hands unclean). (See chapters 15 and 17.)

After the birth of a boy, a woman is isolated at home for seven days. After the child's circumcision on the eighth day, she is required to wait another thirty-three days before worshiping at the sanctuary (12:2–4). After the birth of a girl, a mother's period of uncleanness doubles, with fourteen days at home and sixty-six days before she is allowed to go to the sanctuary (12:5). The reason for this discrepancy is unclear, though some think that "life" is the issue here and the longer one is unclean it means the longer one is in contact with principles of life—so, since a baby girl has a womb, the period of uncleanness is twice as long.

12:6–8

PURIFICATION

An unclean mother has to sacrifice both a burnt offering (lamb) and a sin offering (pigeon or dove) to be considered clean again. Provisions are made for mothers without much money by allowing them to substitute two birds for a lamb (12:6–8).

LEVITICUS 13:1–59

CLEAN AND UNCLEAN: PROBLEM SKIN, MILDEW

Rashes and Infections	13:1–23
Spots and Balding	13:24–46
Mildew	13:47–59

Setting Up the Section

The laws in chapters 13 and 14 declare that serious skin disease (physical evidence of decay) made an individual unacceptable before a holy God and unacceptable within the Israelite community. Chapter 13 in particular helps the priests identify these skin disorders.

13:1–23

RASHES AND INFECTIONS

If an Israelite had any kind of symptom of a skin disease, he was taken to a priest to be examined through clinical-type instructions (13:1). A deep sore or raw skin would indicate decay and, therefore, cause a person to be unclean (13:3, 15).

Infection also indicated decay and made a person unclean (13:6–8, 18–23). If a priest was unsure, the affected Israelite was quarantined (13:5), followed by additional examination (13:5–7, 21). A condition that did not spread was purified through water, but a spreading rash or other disorder pointed to infection (13:6–8). A chronic disease was also considered infection and made a person unclean for the duration of the disease (13:9–11). If a disease was cured or shown not to be infectious, the person was considered clean (13:12–13, 23).

While the practices described in this section certainly have potential for health benefits, it appears that, at the most fundamental level, the issue is "wholeness." Notice in verse 12 that if a person is covered from head to toe, he is considered clean.

Demystifying Leviticus

The term *leprosy*, used in many Bible translations, is most likely not used to describe the disease we know as leprosy. It is more likely a generic term referring to a number of skin disorders rather than a specific disease. The NIV better translates the original term as "infectious skin disease."

13:24–46

SPOTS AND BALDING

The same rules apply for suspicious spots or burns (13:24–40). A man who experiences normal balding is clean (13:40–41), but a disorder on the skin of his head is examined the same way other disorders are examined by a priest (13:42–44).

Any person found to have an infectious skin disease is to be put outside the camp to live. He was also forced to announce his unclean state to anyone he encountered and to take on the posture of a mourner (13:45–46). He would also be cut off from fellowship with other Israelites and could not approach God in worship.

13:47–59

MILDEW

The Israelites are instructed to deal with mildewed clothing in a similar way to diseased skin. Just as infectious diseases could spread, so could mildew. Priests examined and isolated contaminated clothing (13:49–51). Clothes with spreading mildew, or mildew that would not wash out, were burned (13:52, 55, 57).

LEVITICUS 14:1–57

CLEAN AND UNCLEAN: CLEANING INFECTIONS AND MILDEW

Outside Camp	14:1–8
Inside Camp	14:9–32
Mildew Matters	14:33–57

Setting Up the Section

The laws in chapters 13 and 14 declare that serious skin ailments make an individual unacceptable before a holy God and even within the Israelite community. Chapter 14 in particular outlines the purification process.

14:1–8

OUTSIDE CAMP

Those with symptoms of skin disease were sent outside the camp in a kind of quarantine, presumably so others would not catch the disease (14:3). This would have been significant, as it separated an individual from both his community and the sanctuary of God.

Critical Observation

The Old Testament law says the unclean could never come into the presence of the holy God, yet God's Son took on human flesh and lived among humanity. In His ministry, He avoided the self righteous, who considered themselves clean by their own merits, and He sought out those who were regarded unclean. The new covenant, in the person of Christ, broke down the barrier that the Old Testament law and its sacrificial system could not. Jesus Himself went "outside the camp," seeking to save the unclean. As Christians, we are called to do likewise (Hebrews 13:12–13).

If the priest finds the condition to be healed after a week, there is then a cleansing ceremony including hyssop, known for healing properties (Psalm 51:7; Matthew 27:48), and two clean birds (Leviticus 14:4–7). Additional bathing and washing then took place, along with shaving all hair to allow the person back into the camp (14:8).

Demystifying Leviticus

The killing of a bird in the ceremony was not so much a sacrifice as a symbol. The life of one bird is exchanged for the life of the other, who is given freedom from death and decay and "new" life.

14:9–32

INSIDE CAMP

After the ceremonial cleansing, the affected person has seven days of additional examination that includes additional shaving (14:9). That is followed by the sacrifice of three lambs for guilt, sin, and burnt offerings (14:10–13), along with a grain offering. The ceremonial smearing of blood (14:14) is similar to the priestly consecration ritual (see 8:24). The oil ritual (14:14–18) accompanied the atonement that made the unclean person clean.

Three sacrificial lambs would have been expensive, so special exceptions were made for the poor, as with other offerings (14:21–22).

14:33–57

MILDEW MATTERS

Rules relating to mildew (a general term for anything from mold to dry rot), which was something that would cause decay in the home, are similar to those relating to human skin disease (14:33–57). These instructions deal with the homes the Israelites would build once in Canaan (14:34). Verse 34 likely indicates that God is the Creator of all living things, not that He is sending mildew as some kind of test or punishment.

The examination periods (14:37–42) are similar to those for skin disease in chapter 13. In the same way an unclean person is sent out of the camp, contaminated building stones are put outside the city (14:40). The cleansing ritual for a home (14:49–53) is the same as for the person who is unclean (14:4–7).

Take It Home

While the priests could pronounce a person unclean or clean, he could not heal a person with a disease. We see the same thing as the focus in the New Testament turns from external symptoms to what is going on in a person's mind and heart. The scribes and Pharisees of Jesus' day did not have this grasp of the meaning of "clean" and "unclean." They could not understand why He spent time with people considered unclean. They failed to see Him as the One who could make humans clean, the One who could bring wholeness. Let us focus more on what's going on inside ourselves and others, and let us point others toward the restoration found in Christ.

LEVITICUS 15:1–32

CLEAN AND UNCLEAN DISCHARGES

The Male Kind	15:1–18
The Female Kind	15:19–32

Setting Up the Section

Chapter 15 picks up where chapter 12 leaves off, declaring certain discharges as unclean. Both men and women have what might be called normal (15:16–18, 19–24) and abnormal (15:2–15, 25–30) discharges. Aside from practical hygienic concerns, the laws once again address the subject of holiness.

15:1–18

THE MALE KIND

Verses 1–12 refer to a man with a discharge from his body as unclean. The word translated *body* could mean a person's body, but it is also used as a euphemism for a man's sexual organ. The nature of this particular discharge is not clear, but it is likely some kind of infection. Because infections often contain dead matter, the man would be considered unclean. And since some infections can spread, anything or anyone the man touched would also be unclean.

Verses 13–15 address his purification. Those who touch the unclean man could become clean simply by washing their clothes and bathing (15:5–12). The man himself has a period of isolation (15:13) and then can renew relationships with God and fellow Israelites after sacrificing birds as a sin offering and burnt offering (15:14–15).

Verses 16–18 address semen discharge, a normal male function. The answer to the day-long unclean condition is to bathe and wash any affected clothing. Even intercourse between a married couple resulted in both the man and woman being unclean until evening and having to bathe (15:18).

15:19–32

THE FEMALE KIND

A woman's regular menstruation would make her unclean for seven days (until the period is completely over). Anything she sat on was considered unclean, and anyone who touched her or anything she had touched would be unclean for a day (15:19), requiring bathing and washing (15:20–23). If the woman's husband had sex with her, then he would also be unclean for seven days (15:24). Purification came through water.

Verses 25–30 address an unusually long period or other associated discharge, which are considered to make a woman unclean. The same rules apply as with normal menstruation (15:25–27), but the woman has to go through the same sacrificial ceremony as the man with the abnormal discharge (15:14–15, 29–30).

Critical Observation

The laws concerning the unclean state during abnormal discharges (15:25–30) shed light on the story of the hemorrhaging woman who sought healing from Jesus in Luke 8:43–45. Not only was she seeking physical wholeness, but the healing would bring her relational wholeness as well.

Take It Home

Verse 31 of this chapter emphasizes the reason for the clean/unclean laws. Since the tabernacle housed the presence of a holy God, those who were declared categorically unclean could not enter into that presence. In addition, the laws reminded the Israelites that they were a people who had been set apart by God. As Christians today, our holiness is not judged by these kinds of laws, but it is good to remember that when we approach God through prayer or worship, we are approaching a holy God.

LEVITICUS 16:1–34

THE DAY OF ATONEMENT

Setting Up the Section

Chapter 16 serves in part as a kind of addendum to chapters 8–10, as it addresses the expectations of the Aaronic priesthood. It opens with instructions God gives Moses to give to Aaron after the death of Aaron's two sons in chapter 10. The focus of these regulations is to make the people of Israel clean (a topic explained in detail in chapters 11–15). The chapter ends with a command for the high priest to make atonement for all the sins of Israel once a year. This is the introduction of the annual Day of Atonement.

16:1–5

PREPARATION

Even the high priest could not enter into the Holy of Holies whenever he wanted (16:3), so the opening instructions are to prepare Aaron to enter into that sacred place (Exodus 28, 39; Leviticus 16:4). Before he could enter into the Lord's presence, Aaron would have to make a sin offering for himself and his family, as well as a burnt offering. He would also go through an elaborate bathing and dressing process (Leviticus 16:4) to illustrate the contrast between God's purity and human sinfulness.

Critical Observation

In the course of his daily sacrifices, Aaron, the high priest, represented God, so his clothing was beautiful and extravagant. But when he entered the Holy of Holies to perform the annual atoning ritual, he went before God in simplicity and humility.

16:6–19

SACRIFICE

The two goats Aaron brings on behalf of the people serve a special purpose. One will become the sacrificial sin offering for the people; the other will provide atonement by symbolically taking on the people's sin and then being sent away (16:7–10, 15). The bull sacrifice is a sin offering for Aaron and his family (16:11), and the subsequent goat sacrifice is a sin offering for the people (16:15).

God's dwelling place (the tabernacle) is emphasized with the cloud of incense (16:12–13) to veil the glory of God so that Aaron can enter into His presence. Atonement is made for the holy place, including the altar, since the sin of the people defiles the tabernacle (16:16–19).

16:20–34

CLEANSING

After taking care of the holy place, Aaron symbolically lays the sins of the entire nation on the head of the second goat and sends it away in the desert so it can not return (16:20–22). Atonement is made complete with burnt offerings for Aaron and the people (16:24) and with completing the sin offerings (16:25–27).

The people participate in the day through solemn rest and intentional humility (16:31).

Take It Home

Unlike the other Jewish holidays, the Day of Atonement was not a festive event. It was a day of national mourning and repentance. The Israelites were told to humble themselves (16:31), which most likely included fasting. No work was done since it was on the Sabbath. This would thus be the only appointed holy day characterized by mourning, fasting, and repentance. The Day of Atonement was a time for dealing with unknown sins that had gone unaddressed in the past year. Even unknown sins hinder our fellowship with God and others. This kind of reflection and repentance should be a regular part of the Christian life.

LEVITICUS 17:1–16

PRECIOUS IS THE BLOOD

Sacrificial Blood 17:1–9
Lifeblood 17:10–16

Setting Up the Section

Leviticus 17 is a transitional chapter. It concludes the previous sixteen chapters, which focus on the sacrificial process, by applying the value of blood to the daily practices of the Israelites. It also introduces the following chapters that deal with the practice of holiness in the everyday life of the Israelites. If the first sixteen chapters of Leviticus were addressed primarily to the priests of Israel, this chapter is addressed mainly to the people of Israel. If the previous chapters dealt with the sacred—the tabernacle, the sacrifices, and the priests—this chapter deals with the secular, the normal course of life for the Israelite.

17:1–9

SACRIFICIAL BLOOD

The regulation of verses 3–7 presupposes that an Israelite will be tempted to slaughter one of his animals for its meat. Slaughtering any animal had to take place as an offering at the tabernacle (17:4, 8–9; see chapters 1–7, 16); otherwise it is considered bloodshed. An Israelite has to make a peace offering in order to voluntarily slaughter and eat an animal.

Demystifying Leviticus

The people of Moses' day had learned a killing ritual from surrounding pagan cultures. There was no purely secular slaughter, but only a sacred ritual. An Israelite who slaughtered an animal was performing some type of worship, either of God or of a goat idol (17:7). God commands the Israelites to exchange past practices for those that worshiped Him.

17:10–16

LIFEBLOOD

The regulation of verses 10–13 prohibits anyone living in Israel to eat the blood of any animal (17:10–11, 13). Blood is equated with life and God's atonement of the Israelites (17:11), so anyone who ate it would be "cut off" from his people, an expression that, at best, means expulsion from the nation and, at worst, execution.

Hunters are instructed to cover the blood of game they kill (17:13). An animal killed by another animal could be eaten, but the one who does so will become unclean (11:39–40; 17:15).

Critical Observation

Any animal that was slaughtered had to be offered to God as a sacrifice. Any blood that was shed was shed as a part of a sacrifice. Thus, any meat an Israelite ate (even from his own herd or flock) had to be first offered to God as a part of a sacrifice at the tent of meeting. And since the peace offering is the only sacrifice that the Israelite could eat, every time the Israelite wanted to eat meat, he had to make a peace offering.

LEVITICUS 18:1–30

RELATIONSHIP RULES

Setting Up the Section

The Israelites had been the slaves of Pharaoh. The Exodus freed the Israelites from bondage to Egypt, but it also brought them under the yoke of their God, who had delivered them. These people were to live under a new order, spelled out in the covenant that God made with them. God spells out clearly what kind of behavior He expects from His people. This chapter begins a new section of Leviticus that offers practical guidelines for how the Israelites are to live as a holy people.

18:1–5

A COVENANT RELATIONSHIP

Verses 1–5 address the Israelites' motivation for obeying the laws that God is going to lay down in the following chapters. God reminds the Israelites of their relationship to Him. Knowing they had a tendency to mimic the cultures around them, He also gives specifics for how they should live as the people of God by following His ways and statutes (18:3–4).

18:6–23

RELATIONAL BOUNDARIES

These verses define for the Israelites the boundaries of God-honoring relationships (see chart). The progression is from inner boundaries that prohibit sexual relationships with close relatives (18:6–18) to middle boundaries that limit sex within and outside of marriage (18:19–20) to outer boundaries of unnatural relationships (18:21–23).

Demystifying Leviticus

The regulations concerning sex related uncleanness serve in part to clearly separate sex from religious worship. The separation is particularly important to the Israelites because of the pagan worship rituals of the Canaanites, whose fertility cult engaged in sexual union as an act of worship (Numbers 25:1–9). Since the Israelites had been known to imitate other people (Exodus 32:6), these laws set apart the Israelites' worship from that of their pagan neighbors.

Verses 6–18 begin with the closest relationship (mother and child) and progress from there to a man and his sister-in-law. In ancient Israel, familial relationships were the social cornerstone of the community, so keeping them pure would have been extremely important.

Verse 19 reiterates the law found in chapter 15, and verse 20 is a reminder of the seventh commandment. Verses 21–23 remind the Israelites not to imitate the pagan people around them.

18:24–30

CONSEQUENCES

For the Israelites, the land of Canaan represents God's blessings. The last part of this chapter stresses the fact that the sins of the Canaanites defiled the land and would lead to their expulsion (18:24–25). It also warns the Israelites that if they fail to live according to God's laws when in Canaan, then they will lose the blessing of the land (18:28). At the conclusion of Leviticus, God spells out in greater detail the blessings of obeying Him (chapter 26).

Critical Observation

After God led the Israelites out of captivity in Egypt, He made a covenant with His people, known as the Mosaic Covenant because it was communicated through Moses. God introduced the Ten Commandments, part of the covenant, with the words "I am the LORD your God" (Exodus 20:2). When the covenant was reiterated to the next generation, the same phrase was used (Deuteronomy 5:6). In Leviticus 18, it shows up again. The words, used forty-seven times in chapters 18–26, are a reminder to the Israelites of their identity as people of God.

Take It Home

Sexual boundaries matter to God, and they should matter to us as Christians. Still, God offers renewed purity and forgiveness. Look at the love Jesus shows the Samaritan woman at the well (John 4), the woman caught in adultery (John 8), and the prostitute who honored Him (Luke 7). We can let our pasts be in the past. We can receive Christ's words, "Go and sin no more" (John 8:11), and also receive His love and grace.

LEVITICUS 19:1–37

HOLY, HOLY, HOLY

Setting Up the Section

The Mosaic Covenant was established so Israel would be a holy nation (Exodus 19:6), set apart as God's people. Leviticus hammers home the importance of holiness for the Israelites. The book provides instructions for holiness involved with special ceremonies, holy days, and how to approach the tabernacle. Chapter 19 provides detailed, specific ways to practice everyday holiness that include respect for God and for others.

19:1–8

BEING HOLY

God had Moses assemble all the Israelites to offer this command: "You shall be holy, for I the Lord your God am holy" (Leviticus 19:2 NASB). The law is God's standard of holiness, instructions on how to imitate His character. What follows is a refresher course on the Ten Commandments (19:3–4) and a repeat of ceremonial law surrounding the peace offering (19:5–8).

19:9–18

LOVING OTHERS

After the reminders, God inserts new instructions that lead to God's second overarching command: "You shall love your neighbor as yourself; I am the Lord" (19:18 NASB). Holiness would be practiced as the Israelites loved their neighbors. This includes the vulnerable (19:9–11, 14–15), fellow Israelites (19:11–13, 15–16), foreigners (19:10, 33–34), and even enemies (19:17–18).

Critical Observation

Leviticus 19 is important because of the prominence of its teaching in the New Testament. Both our Lord (Matthew 5:43; 19:19; 22:39; Mark 12:31, 33; Luke 10:27) and the apostles (Romans 13:9; Galatians 5:14; James 2:8; 1 Peter 1:16) make a great deal of the two great commandments that are given here: "You shall be holy, for I the Lord your God am holy" (Leviticus 19:2), and "You shall love your neighbor as yourself" (19:18). In the context of this chapter, it becomes clear that the Israelites' enemies are included in the broad category of "neighbor," something Jesus also taught (Matthew 5:44–48).

19:19–37

LIVING HOLY

The rest of the chapter lists miscellaneous laws. They are reminders to be a set-apart people who do not mix with other cultures (19:26–29). The people are reminded to create God-honoring relationships (19:20–22), to maintain fairness (19:36), and to practice compassion rather than oppression (19:33–34).

Demystifying Leviticus

The holy behavior that God required was seen in acts He had already performed on behalf of His people. God's holiness was manifested by His compassion on the Israelites when they were oppressed in Egypt. So, too, holiness is to be manifested by the people of God by the way they treat others.

LEVITICUS 20:1–27

CAPITAL CRIMES

Molech and Mediums	20:1–6
Family Business	20:7–21
Follow the Rules	20:22–27

Setting Up the Section

Chapter 20 falls into the broader context of chapters 18–20, which stress practical holiness in the everyday life of the Israelite. Chapter 18 has focused primarily on the family, chapter 19 instructs Israel to love their neighbor, and chapter 20 follows up by detailing the capital punishment for serious sins forbidden in the previous chapters. The actions highlighted become crimes as well as sins.

20:1–6

MOLECH AND MEDIUMS

Verses 1–6 show a co-participation between God and His people in condemning those who are guilty of capital crimes. In fact, those who close their eyes to sin also become guilty (20:4–5). The child sacrificed here is a reflection of the surrounding pagan cultures.

Critical Observation

These capital crimes are violations of God's covenant with Israel. The crimes in Leviticus that call for a death penalty are all crimes against God's covenant, which emphasizes that God set Israel apart from the surrounding nations to distinguish them by means of holiness as His people (Exodus 19:5–6). The Mosaic Covenant is the definition of the holiness that God requires in order for Him to dwell among His people and for them to be His holy nation.

20:7–21

FAMILY BUSINESS

The relational sins listed in chapter 18 are repeated here, this time with the penalty. (See chart.)

Verse	Relationship	Penalty
18:7	Mother and son	Death, 20:11
18:8	Stepmother and son	Death, 20:11
18:9	Brother and sister/Brother and maternal half-sister	Cut off, 20:17
18:10	Father and granddaughter	Burned, 20:14
18:11	Brother and paternal half-sister	Cut off, 20:17
18:12	Nephew and aunt (father's sister)	Barrenness, 20:20
18:13	Nephew and aunt (mother's sister)	Barrenness, 20:20
18:14	Nephew and aunt (wife of father's brother)	Barrenness, 20:20
18:15	Father and daughter-in-law	Death, 20:12
18:16	Brother and sister-in-law	Barrenness, 20:21
18:17	Father and stepdaughter/Father and step-granddaughter/ Husband and mother-in-law	Burned, 20:14
18:18	Husband and sister-in-law	None

20:22–27

FOLLOW THE RULES

When God made certain sins crimes as well, the Israelites were strongly motivated to obey God's laws and to avoid sin. In these verses, God gives a general exhortation to follow His laws (20:22). The result of disobedience will be loss of their promised land in Canaan. God had promised the Israelites a land flowing with milk and honey, a symbol for blessing (20:24), but He requires obedience and sanctified (set apart) lives that imitate His own character (20:26). As an example, He lists another crime that is influenced by pagan culture and deserving of the death penalty.

Take It Home

There is a difference between crimes and sin. Chapter 20 highlights capital crimes, but in God's eyes all sin brings death (Romans 6:23). There is no room for self-righteousness if God views all sins as capital offenses. If we are not guilty of one form of sin, we are surely guilty of another; and seen from God's point of view, the kind of sin we commit matters little. As James explains, to be found guilty of offense at one point is to fall short in all points (James 2:1–13).

LEVITICUS 21:1–24

HOLINESS: TRUE/FALSE, PART 1

Setting Up the Section

Chapters 17–20 are addressed to the Israelites in general, defining how holiness is to be practiced in the everyday activities of life. Chapters 21 and 22 return to addressing the Aaronic priesthood. Of particular importance is how they are to avoid being defiled and to remain holy. Each section is marked by the statement, in slightly modified forms, "I am the Lord, who sanctifies you" (21:8, 15, 23; 22:9, 16, 32).

21:1–9

MOURNING AND MARRIAGE (PRIEST)

Priests had to remain ceremonially clean so that they could approach God and make offerings on behalf of the people. This meant they could not bury the dead, except in the case of close blood relatives (21:1–3). All Israelites (especially priests) were forbidden to shave their heads or the edges of their beards or to cut their skin as a sign of mourning (19:27; 21:1–5, 10–12; Deuteronomy 14:1). An ordinary Israelite had greater freedom in choosing a wife; priests could marry a widow but not a divorcee (21:7). Even a priest's daughter was held to higher standards (21:9).

21:10–15

MOURNING AND MARRIAGE (HIGH PRIEST)

If there is a high standard for the priests (21:1–9), there is an even higher standard for the high priest (21:10–15). The high priest could not participate in standard mourning traditions (21:10), or even leave the tabernacle to take part in burying near relatives (21:10–12). And the high priest could marry only a virgin of his own people (21:13–15).

21:16–24

STAY BACK

The Aaronic priesthood began with Aaron and his sons and would continue through his line of descendants. Those who had physical defects would not be able to participate in sacrificial offerings (21:16–21). The sacrificial animal had to be without defects, and so did the priest doing the offering. The priest with the defect could eat the food the priests were allowed, but he could not approach the altar (21:23).

Critical Observation

Aaron's position as high priest did not make him holier than others, though it did hold him to a higher standard. God chose Aaron and his descendants, just as God chose the Israelites. A look at Aaron's life reveals that neither he (Exodus 32) nor his sons (Leviticus 10) were holy by their own merit. Even though a priest was ceremonially pure, he still could approach God only by means of sacrifice and atoning blood.

LEVITICUS 22:1–33

HOLINESS: TRUE/FALSE, PART 2

Keep It Clean	22:1–9
The Priest's Food	22:10–16
What to Give/Not Give	22:17–33

Setting Up the Section

As with chapter 21, chapter 22 addresses the Aaronic priesthood with a continued emphasis on how to avoid being defiled and how to remain holy. Each section is marked by the same statement, in one form or another, "I am the Lord, who sanctifies you" (21:8, 15, 23; 22:9, 16, 32).

22:1–9

KEEP IT CLEAN

Priests were tasked with approaching God's holy presence in the tabernacle and offering blood sacrifices that would atone for sin. This means they had to remain clean. Attempting priestly duties while unclean would cause defilement, and that person would be cut off from God (22:3). The priests were to respect the rules for cleanness and uncleanness in chapters 11–15 (22:4–9).

Demystifying Leviticus

The nature of defilement is not that of specific sin, but of external ceremonial defilement. Leviticus begins by defining defilement in very concrete terms, but as the Old Testament revelation unfolds, the prophets emphatically teach that God is not nearly as interested in the external ceremonial acts of people as He is in the attitudes of their hearts and the resulting righteousness.

22:10–16

THE PRIEST'S FOOD

These verses add a few details regarding how priests are to handle the food left over after sacrificial offerings (see chapters 2–7).

22:17–33

WHAT TO GIVE/NOT GIVE

Verses 17–33 are additional regulations for sacrificial offerings (see chapters 1–7). Because the blood is atoning or purifying in nature, a sacrificial animal has to be without defect (22:19–22, 24–25). Those who had defects, some simply in their appearance, were not to be offered. The priests followed laws related to holiness in order to teach the Israelites that God is holy (22:31–33).

Critical Observation

Since chapters 21–22 were addressed to Israel's priests, the priests of Jesus' day would have seen the teachings directed at them. It was their misunderstanding of the text, and their misapplication of it, that resulted in their immediate and intense opposition to Jesus' teachings and practices.

Take It Home

In chapters 21–22, God says six times, "I am the LORD, who sanctifies you." He set Israel apart from the nations, and He set the priests apart from the people. God commands the priests to avoid outward defilement because they are already holy, by God's sanctification. They are to avoid the prohibited things, not because avoidance would make them clean, but because these things would make them unclean. There is a world of difference between avoiding something to keep yourself from sin and avoiding something to make yourself holy. May God grant us to understand and to apply the principles of Leviticus and the law as our Lord taught us to do, for His sake.

LEVITICUS 23:1–44

ALL IN GOOD TIME

Setting Up the Section

The Lord's appointed times are festivals and holy days that commemorate significant times and events in Israel's history. The commemorative holidays show truths of God's salvation, love, and plans. The appointed times create a sacred rhythm in the lives of the Israelites.

23:1–3

THE WEEKLY SABBATH

Sabbath means "rest." The Sabbath celebration has its roots in the creation of the world (Genesis 2:1–3). God blessed the seventh day and sanctified it, separating it from the others in kind and character. The Sabbath becomes a day of rest in a week otherwise filled with toil and work.

23:4–22

SPRING HOLY DAYS

The Israelites celebrate Passover (Leviticus 23:4–5) and the Feast of Unleavened Bread (23:6–8) together. The first month in the sacred Jewish calendar is marked by Passover, a day celebrating Israel's deliverance from captivity and birth as a nation. It is the most important festival. The Feast of Unleavened Bread is an extension of Passover. This is a time for the Israelites to remember their identity as God's people.

The Festival of Firstfruits (23:9–14) is a time for the Israelites who were camped in the desert to be reminded of the hope of future blessings in Canaan (23:10). On this day, the first sheaf of barley is harvested, but nothing can be eaten until the sheaf is waved before God as an act of thanksgiving for His provision. The priest would also make a burnt offering together with a grain offering and a drink offering of wine (23:12–13).

The Festival of Pentecost, or the Feast of Weeks (23:15–22), gets its name from the counting of fifty days from the Sabbath following Passover. It coincides with and celebrates God's giving of His law at Mount Sinai. The feast also includes several offerings to God, and the Israelites are instructed to leave the edges of their crops unharvested for the poor and the foreigner as well (23:22).

Demystifying Leviticus

The Jewish calendar is based on the relative motion of both the moon and the sun. Each month is defined by phases of the moon. The first of every month coincides with a new moon, and the fifteenth of every month coincides with a full moon. The calendar keeps the months and their respective seasons together by inserting a leap month, meaning most years have twelve months, but some have thirteen. The primary markers in the calendar are the sacred holidays.

23:23–44

FALL HOLY DAYS

The Festival of Trumpets (23:23–25) is known today as Rosh Hashanah. It is a day marked by assembling together, doing no regular work, and commemorated by blowing trumpets with fanfare. It is a reminder that the Day of Atonement is approaching and a time for the Israelites to reflect on the year and their relationship to God.

Following the somber reflection of the Day of Atonement, the Feast of Tabernacles (23:33–43) is the joyous holiday of the manifest presence of God. As a reminder to younger generations of God's deliverance of the Israelites in Egypt, they are all to live in booths (temporary shelters made of tree branches and palm leaves) for seven days.

Take It Home

The story of God's deliverance and salvation is told without words through the tastes of Passover, waving of the sheaf during Firstfruits, waving of loaves on Pentecost, the sound of trumpets, and temporary tabernacles. These days speak of past and future deliverance, and they provide markers each year in the life of a Jew. Do you have any kind of sacred rhythm in your own life? Are there any visual markers that help you remember God's presence?

Religious Month	Canaanite Name	Babylonian Name	Gregorian Placement	Holy Day
First	Abib	Nisan	March or April	Passover; Feast of Unleavened Bread; Wave Offering of Firstfruits
Second	Ziv	Iyyar	April or May	
Third		Sivan	May or June	Pentecost
Fourth		Tammuz	June or July	
Fifth		Ab	July or August	
Sixth		Elul	August or September	
Seventh	Ethanim	Tishri	September or October	Trumpets; Day of Atonement; Feast of Tabernacles
Eighth	Bul	Cheshvan	October or November	
Ninth		Chislev	November or December	
Tenth		Tebeth	December or January	
Eleventh		Shebat	January or February	
Twelfth		Adar	February or March	
Thirteenth		Adar II	March	This is the leap month

LEVITICUS 24:1–23

LAMP, LOAVES, AND LOUDMOUTH

Setting Up the Section

Leviticus 24 addresses how the Israelites should care for the dwelling place of God and how they should deal with someone who blasphemes God's name. The first nine verses concern the ritual of maintaining the lamp and the loaves. Justice is also to become a matter of consistency (24:10–33). In all three sections, the element of continuity in ritual is present.

24:1–4

KEEP THE FIRES BURNING

The golden lampstand has already appeared in the Pentateuch several times (Exodus 25:31–40; 27:20–21; 37:17–24; 40:25–26). It is housed in the holy place to provide light in the darkness of the tabernacle. Even in the daytime, the many layered coverings of the tent would keep out sunlight, so the light of this lamp is required. The emphasis of these verses is that the light must be kept burning at all times. The key word is *continually* (Leviticus 24:2–4). Virtually the entire nation plays a role in this task of keeping the golden lamp burning.

24:5–9

GIVE US OUR WEEKLY BREAD

There are two reasons the continual changing of the loaves is important. First, they are a part of the sacrificial offerings (24:7). To fail to provide fresh loaves each week would hinder the sacrificial process, which is symbolic of an everlasting covenant (24:8). Second, these loaves (or, more accurately, what remained of them) are a part of the food that sustains and nourishes the priests (24:9). To fail to provide for the priesthood would be to hinder the priestly process, so the loaves are always to be on hand.

24:10–23

THE PERIL OF PROFANITY

The next group of verses addresses the case of a man who had blasphemed God's name. The Israelites were not sure how to interpret God's law, so they asked for a ruling (24:10–12). In clarifying the law as it applies to this man's offense, Israel is taught how the law applies to them personally. In addition, God's people are taught some important principles that apply to a much wider range of offenses.

The one who defames God's character is to be taken outside the camp. All the witnesses lay their hands on his head as an act of recognizing their part in the crime, and then the entire congregation of Israelites would stone the offender as a way to identify with God and His holiness (24:14–15).

Critical Observation

God's instructions to the Israelites relating to blasphemy are such that justice would be carried out consistently, without variation, without deviation, and without cessation. The principle of equality in punishment is consistently taught in the Old Testament. In Deuteronomy 17:2 and 17:7, the principle of equality in punishment is applied to men and women. It is most clearly taught in the book of Numbers (Numbers 15:13–16; Deuteronomy 29:10–13; 31:11–12).

God then gives general rules for how to deal with blasphemy. God's holiness is emphasized by the severe punishment prescribed for someone who blasphemes. The other rules in verses 17–22 show that the punishment provided should match the crime committed.

LEVITICUS 25:1–55

SUPER SABBATH

Setting Up the Section

Leviticus 25 reveals God's compassion for the poor and oppressed. The Sabbath Year and the Year of Jubilee are part of God's gracious provisions for all His people. The two events are interrelated, so they are dealt with at the same time. Verses 1–34 lay down God's law pertaining to the land, while verses 35–55 apply to people.

25:1–7

SABBATH YEAR

During the Sabbath Year, the land is given its rest (25:2–3, 5). Following these commands would require great faith since letting fields lie fallow for a year would mean trusting God to provide as He promises (25:18–22). The land regulations are also a provision for the poor, since anyone is allowed to eat from the crops but no one could harvest them for sale (25:6–7). This provided them with food in times of need and the possibility of a new beginning.

Demystifying Leviticus

The "laws of the land" were designed to hinder greed by keeping in check those who would try to accumulate vast land holdings at the expense of others.

25:8–34

JUBILEE YEAR

The Year of Jubilee was like a super Sabbath. Every fifty years, God proclaimed a year of freedom and liberation from bondage following the Day of Atonement (25:9–10). On the Sabbath Year, all debts are canceled (Deuteronomy 15:1–2), but in the Year of Jubilee, the Israelite who has sold himself to another is released, and the land that has been leased to another is restored to its original owner. The Year of Jubilee is a reminder that God owns the land (25:23).

Loans were to be made without any consideration of how many years were left to repay the loan (Deuteronomy 15:7–11), but leases were made by calculating the number of years remaining until the Jubilee (Leviticus 25:14–16, 26–28). One is an act of generosity, considered more a gift than a loan, and the other is a business arrangement that is regulated to ensure a fair deal.

25:35–46

NEIGHBORLY WAYS

The first type of poverty addressed (25:35-38) is temporary. God's solution is a no-interest loan. In verses 39–46, God instructs the Israelites how to help a fellow Israelite who is so poor he has to sell himself. That person is to be treated not as a slave, but with dignity as a hired worker who could leave his employment if treated unfairly (see Deuteronomy 15:16–17; 24:15). At the Year of Jubilee, the servant has to be released so he can return to the property of his forefathers (Leviticus 25:41).

While an Israelite could not be a slave because he was ultimately God's servant, not another person's (25:42), non-Israelites could be bought as slaves. However, they were also to be treated well.

Critical Observation

One of the most significant prophecies of Israel's restoration, couched in Jubilee terminology, is found in the book of Isaiah: "The Spirit of the sovereign Lord is upon me, because the Lord has chosen me. He has commissioned me to encourage the poor, to help the brokenhearted, to decree the release of captives, and the freeing of prisoners, to announce the year when the Lord will show his favor" (Isaiah 61:1–2 NET). It is this text that our Lord read in His hometown synagogue (Luke 4).

 25:47–55

STRANGE COMPANY

A poor Israelite could sell himself to a wealthy foreigner, but he kept the right to redemption (25:47–48) at any time by a relative or himself (because he ultimately belonged to God). If that did not happen, though, the nation of Israel was responsible to make sure he was not mistreated (25:53) and that he was released in the Year of Jubilee (25:54).

Take It Home

Israel was to show compassion to the poor and the oppressed in order to imitate God. The instructions given to the Israelites concerning the poor among them was to ensure that God's people imitated Him, both in attitude and action. While this is an Old Testament text, the principles here are relevant today. Loving our neighbor as ourselves is part of living out God's character.

Verses:	35–38	39–46	47–55
Problem:	Cash flow shortage	Poverty	Dire Poverty
Solution:	Loan	Slave of Israelite	Slave of Stranger
Conditions/ Obligations:	No interest to be charged	No harsh treatment A day laborer Released (Jubilee)	Right of Redemption Not deal harshly Released (Jubilee)
Goal/Purpose:	So he can dwell in the land	So he can dwell in the land	So he can dwell in the land (implied)
Motivation:	God's deliverance from Egypt	They are God's servants	They are God's servants

LEVITICUS 26:1–46

A WELCOME WARNING

Setting Up the Section

Leviticus 26 is one of the clearest warnings in the Pentateuch (and is reiterated more emphatically in Deuteronomy 28). God's standards for Israel's conduct and the results of obedience or disobedience are given well in advance of punishment or blessing. This chapter does not contain just words of warning, though. It also reveals some of the greatest words of hope found in the Bible.

26:1–13

BLESSINGS

God reminds the Israelites that they are His people (26:1–2) and then promises blessings if they will act as His people (26:3–13). In its broadest definition, God's blessings are conditioned by Israel's keeping of the Mosaic Covenant (26:3–4). At the heart of that covenant is worshiping God alone and observing the Sabbath (26:1–2).

The blessings God promises Israel are directly related to her possession of the land of Canaan: peace (26:6), prosperity (26:4–5, 9–10), and the presence of God (26:11–12). Those promises end with a reminder of past blessings and of God's faithfulness (26:13).

26:14–39

CURSES

The curses are virtually a reversal of the promised blessings. Instead of prosperity, disobedience will bring poverty (26:16, 26). Instead of peace and security, disobedience will bring insecurity, peril, and fear (26:16, 17, 21–22, 25, 31–32, 36–39). Instead of God's presence, disobedience will bring separation (26:17, 21, 23–24, 28, 34–35).

Demystifying Leviticus

There are a number of passages that are parallel to Leviticus 26. Exodus 23:22–33 is the first recording of the promise of blessings and curses, based upon Israel's obedience to the Mosaic Covenant. In Deuteronomy 28, the blessings and curses are repeated in greater detail for the second generation of Israelites who are about to possess the land of Canaan. Joshua 24:20 is a brief summation of the warnings of this chapter, and the writings of the prophets reveal some direct dependence on it (Isaiah 49:1; Ezekiel 34:25–30; 37:21–28). Leviticus 26 is key to understanding the history of Israel.

26:40–46

ASSURANCE

God deals with Israel's sin and with repentance at its roots, at the level of motivation. Israel's disobedience is the result of her hatred of God's laws (26:15). But God's motivation in discipline is to have Israel turn back to Him (26:41). God assures Israel of an ultimate hope by reaffirming His love for them. In the end, God assures Israel that He will restore her not based on obedience to the Mosaic Covenant, but because of His own faithfulness (26:40–45).

Take It Home

The benevolence of God is underscored in this chapter, even with its gruesome warnings. God's desire is for restoration; to have Israel turn back to Him (26:18, 21, 23, 27). And in the end, despite their unfaithfulness, God assures Israel that He will restore them based on His faithfulness, not their deeds (26:40–45). Israel is always assured of God's love and of His good purposes for His people. May we find hope in the faithfulness and mercy of God in our own situations.

BLESSINGS (26:1–13)	CURSES (26:14–39)
God Confirms Covenant (9)	God's Vengeance for Covenant (25)
God's Presence	**God's "Absence"**
God turns toward His people (9)	God sets His face against them (17)
God will dwell among them (11)	God sends them into captivity (38–39)
God walks among them (12)	God becomes their adversary (33)
Peace	**Peril**
Security (5)	Soul pines away/sudden terror (16)
Peace of mind (6)	Terror, fear, panic (36–37)
Beasts won't harm them (6)	Beasts destroy and decimate (22)
Prevail over their enemies (7–8)	Attacked by enemies—raids (16) Struck down by enemies (17) Ruled by enemies (17) Flee, but none pursue (17) Delivered into enemy hands (25) Scattered among nations (33) Destroy themselves—cannibalism (29)
Prosperity	**Poverty**
God gives rains in season (4)	God withholds the rains (19)
Crops will grow abundantly (4–5) Old grain cleared out for new (10)	Crops don't grow (20) Enemies raid and steal crops (16) Famine—lack of bread (26) Land is desolate (32)
Israelites fruitful and increase (9)	Consumption, fever, waste away (16) Wild animals decimate (22) Pestilence in cities kills (25) Israelites kill and eat their own (29)

LEVITICUS 27:1–34

THE VALUE OF A VOW

People	27:1–8
Animals	27:9–13
Property	27:14–25
Prohibitions and Tithes	27:26–34

Setting Up the Section

The key to the structure of chapter 27 is found by the categories of things that are vowed as offerings to God. In a systematic way, this chapter deals with the various kinds of things that men and women may promise to dedicate to God. Regulations appropriate to each are then specified. The vows of Leviticus 27 are voluntary promises to offer a particular gift to God. But God, knowing human nature, makes provisions for vows that are made irresponsibly.

27:1–8

PEOPLE

People could be devoted to God (Judges 11:30–31; 1 Samuel 1:11) to serve in ministry or to serve the priests in non-ceremonial roles. The monetary values set for these different categories of people (based on age and gender) serve to discourage vows that are not well thought out, as the money would have to be presented if the offered person was not presented to fulfill what had been promised.

27:9–13

ANIMALS

In these verses, regulations are given regarding the gift of clean and unclean animals that could be offered to God (27:9–13) and used or sold. The vowed animals had to meet sacrificial standards and could not be replaced with a less valuable offering. If a man wanted to renege on a vow, he had to buy back the animal and pay a penalty.

27:14–25

PROPERTY

The house in verses 14–15 is not attached to family land but is a piece of property that would not revert to the owner in the Year of Jubilee. The value of the house would be established by the priest, and if the offerer wanted to redeem the house, he had to pay that value plus a penalty.

A portion of inherited family land could be dedicated to God (27:16–21), but it would revert to the owner or his heirs in the Year of Jubilee. To redeem the field, the donor would be required to pay fifty shekels of silver for every certain amount of seed required for planting. The number of years remaining until Jubilee would determine the value of the gift. If the man who dedicated this field attempted to negate his vow by selling this property to another, then it would become property of the priests in the Jubilee year.

Someone could purchase another person's fields and devote them to God (27:22–25). In that case, the priest determines the property value and expects payment the same day, but the land would revert to the original owner at Jubilee.

27:26–34

PROHIBITIONS AND TITHES

Unacceptable gifts include things that already belong to God (27:26), including tithes (27:30–33).

Demystifying Leviticus

Simply viewed, offering a vow is practicing a kind of credit card act of worship. It is a promise to worship God with a certain offering in the future, motivated by gratitude for God's grace in the life of the offerer. There is a delay in making the offering if the offerer is not able, at that moment, to follow through. The vow is made, promising to offer something to God if God will intervene on behalf of the individual, making the offering possible. Often the vow was made in a time of great need (see Genesis 28:20–22; Numbers 21:10–3; Judges 11:29–40; 13; 1 Samuel 1:10–11; Jonah 2:9).

While earlier chapters of Leviticus deal largely with compulsory offerings and obedience, the last chapter concludes by focusing the Israelites' attention on voluntary worship. The voluntary act of worshiping God by means of vows is the highest form of Old Testament worship. The legislation of this chapter assumes that people will make offerings in response to love, not to law.

Take It Home

These regulations taught the Israelites that it is a costly matter to break a vow. How many promises or commitments have been made to you—by a parent, friend, or business associate—that have been forgotten or ignored? How many times can you recall making a commitment you later regretted? This chapter highlights the importance of following through on promises and thinking them through before committing.

NUMBERS

INTRODUCTION TO NUMBERS

The book of Numbers derives its name from the two censuses taken of the nation of Israel at the beginning and the end of this book. Before being referred to as *Numbers*, this writing had also been known as *In the Desert* (or *Wilderness*), referring to the fact that the Israelites spent forty years in the desert.

AUTHOR

Many evangelical scholars consider Moses the author of Numbers. Additional support for Moses as the author is found in the fact that Jesus calls the first five books of the Bible "the book of Moses" (Luke 24:27, 44).

PURPOSE

The instructions included in the book of Numbers are intended to prepare the people to travel to Canaan. The families are counted and they are organized. Numbers accounts for the forty years the Israelites wandered in the wilderness and moves from the judgment that fell on the first generation that left Egypt to the hope of the second generation who would see God's promise come true.

OCCASION

This book covers a history of thirty-nine years in the travels of the Israelites from Mount Sinai to the border of the promised land. Throughout this book, Israel is sometimes seen as a complaining and rebellious nation, often needing God to intervene with discipline. In the midst of His discipline, however, this book also clearly establishes the reality that God will still keep His covenant and will continue to provide for the needs of His people. Thus, Numbers does not end with failure but with a generation ready to enter the promised land because of God's mercy and grace.

THEMES

Numbers highlights certain critical theological themes, including God's covenant with Abraham and His power to deliver. Along with that is the essential theme of the obedience (or disobedience) of the people. In addition, many of the laws that are described in Exodus are either restated or expanded upon in Numbers.

CONTRIBUTION TO THE BIBLE

Numbers is an important part of the first five books of the Old Testament. It links the book of Exodus to the book of Deuteronomy. Exodus shows the movement of Israel from Egypt to the early years of Sinai. Numbers picks up the next forty years, taking the Israelites from Sinai to the plains of Moab. Then Deuteronomy picks the story up in the plains of Moab and the final preparations to enter Canaan.

OUTLINE

NUMBERS 1:1–12:16

ISRAEL AT SINAI AND THE JOURNEY TO KADESH

Setting Up the Section

The book of Numbers opens with a census, a counting of the people. The nation of Israel is organized by tribes. This census prepares the tribes for their march, identifying those who will be fit for battle once the people enter the land. As a number of scholars have pointed out, this number is really more of a military registration than a simple census.

Verse 1 gives us a telling reference point. This census takes place in the second month of the second year after the Israelites have left Egypt. The Passover described in Numbers 9:1 was to have happened in the *first* month of the second year. So, while the facts and figures are included at the beginning of the book of Numbers, the census actually happens after the first Passover feast is commemorated.

1:1–54

THE CENSUS PREPARATION AND RESULTS

The Lord commands Moses to take a census of all the Israelites, with an exclusive emphasis on those who will be able to function as soldiers (1:1–4). This census is taken by tribe, with a tribal leader listed (1:5–16). Each tribe is identified by the son of Jacob from whom they descended. Jacob was the grandson of Abraham. His name is later changed to Israel, thus the people as a whole are referred to as *Israelites*.

In verses 17–46, Moses provides the results of the census, with the numbers rounded off to the nearest hundred. The total is 603,550 men.

Following is the summary of each tribe:	
Reuben: 46,500	Ephraim (son of Joseph): 40,500
Simeon: 59,300	Manasseh (son of Joseph): 32,200
Gad: 45,650	Benjamin: 35,400
Judah: 74,600	Dan: 62,700
Issachar: 54,400	Asher: 41,500
Zebulun: 57,400	Naphtali: 53,400

Notice that Ephraim and Manasseh are both sons of Joseph. This means actually only eleven of Jacob's sons are represented. The missing son (and tribe) is Levi. God has a special purpose for the descendants of Levi (1:47–54). The Levites are not to be included as soldiers, but are to care for the tabernacle and all that belongs to it. They are to camp around it, protect it, and be responsible for dismantling it and setting it back up as the camp moves. This assignment elevates the role of the Levites and puts a priority on the role of worship among the people.

Take It Home

God orders the Levites to be set apart for the worship of God, which surely indicates a priority on worship. How important is worship to you? How much of your life do you set aside for it? Do you prepare for the role worship will play in your life, or do you leave it to the "professionals?"

2:1–34

THE ARRANGEMENT OF THE CAMP

In order for the Israelites to live their nomadic lifestyle without falling into complete chaos, there would have to be some structure. In this case, the tabernacle becomes the hub around which the tribes are organized. The campsites are described in relation to the tabernacle—north, east, south, or west (2:1–31). Each tribe has a banner, or standard, that displays the tribe's symbol (2:1–2).

Campsites

^ NORTH ^

	Naphtali	Asher	Dan	
Ephraim				Judah
Manasseh		TABERNACLE (surrounded by Levites)		Issachar
Benjamin				Zebulun
	Gad	Simeon	Reuben	

SOUTH

This order held significance not only for camping and breaking camp, but also for traveling. The ark of the covenant always leads the way, carried by the priests, and the tribes to the east and south march ahead of the tabernacle, while those to the west and north march behind it.

Marching Diagram

Rear of the Column>>>>> Front of the Column>>>>>>

Dan Asher Naphtali	Ephraim Manasseh Benjamin	Kohathites Carry the Tabernacle Furnishings	Reuben Simeon Gad	Gershonites and Merarites Carry the Tabernacle	Judah Issachar Zebulun	Levites Carry the Ark

3:1–4:49

THE RESPONSIBILITIES OF THE LEVITES

Setting Up the Section

The Levites are given the care of the tabernacle. Once the people enter Canaan, the Levites will have no specific piece of land. Instead, they will be scattered throughout the land and will live off a portion of the offerings brought by the people.

The opening verses of chapter 3 include the names of the sons of Aaron: the first high priest, Nadab (the firstborn), and Abihu, Eleazar, and Ithamar. We don't know the exact nature of the error that causes Nadab and Abihu to be killed in the line of duty, but we know it was an improper worship connected to the censors (3:1–4).

The remainder of chapters 3 and 4 offers a double census of the descendants of Levi and a description of their responsibilities. The organization of the Levites through the rest of Numbers is according to the three sons of Levi. The priests, however, are a subset of the descendants of Kohath, those who would descend specifically from Aaron's family line.

- Descendants of Gershon: the curtains and coverings (3:21–26)
- Descendants of Kohath: the furniture and utensils (3:27–32)
- Descendants of Merari: the boards and bars (3:33–37)

Demystifying Numbers

Verses 40–51 discuss the substitution of the Levites for the firstborn sons and cattle of each of the other tribes. Traditionally, the firstborn belonged to the Lord, so they could be expected to be offered to the tabernacle for service (the sons) and sacrifice (the livestock). In this case, though, the Levites stand in the place of these firstborn, offering their service to the tabernacle instead.

When a family came to offer their firstborn to the tabernacle, or later, the temple, they had the opportunity to give money to redeem their son back into family life. The same thing happens here with the 273 firstborn who outnumber the Levites. A price is paid for their redemption—1,365 shekels, which is given to Aaron and his sons.

This practice of redeeming provides a kind of foreshadowing picture of the ransom that Christ paid in being the only begotten Son of God, who took our place and became the sacrifice.

While chapter 3 lists the duties of each family of Levi's descendants, chapter 4 delves deeper into their ministries.

The Kohathites between thirty and fifty years of age numbered those who could care for the holy objects of the Tent of Meeting after the priests had prepared them for removal (4:1–20). Rather than loading these objects onto wagons or animals, the Kohathites carry them. The items had to be covered before the Kohathites dealt with them, so they wouldn't be killed by touching them or looking at them. This is not an affirmation of the worth of these items as much as the purity of God.

The census of the Gershonites between thirty and fifty years of age numbered those who would carry the curtains of the tabernacle under direction of Aaron and his sons, especially Ithamar (4:21–28).

The census of the Merarites between thirty and fifty years of age numbered those who could carry the poles and tent pegs of the tabernacle, also under direction of Ithamar (4:29–33). These items would have been quite burdensome.

Verses 34–39 summarize the census, which numbers the Levites for service at 8,580.

Demystifying Numbers

Why put so much effort into the breakdown of the tabernacle? Partly because it highlights the seriousness with which God's holiness should be taken. In this scenario, this meticulous amount of care is an expression of respect.

5:1–31

CLEANSING THE CAMP

Setting Up the Section

As the Israelites prepare to go on the move, they must purify themselves. This pursuit of purity is meant to impact all their social interactions. In this chapter, God focuses the attention of the nation on dealing with three specific issues: physical impurities, moral impurities, and marital impurities.

In verses 1–4, Moses is to identify the ceremonially unclean people: any man or woman who has a skin disease (often wrongly interpreted as leprosy), a discharge (whether natural or related to infection), or is unclean because of contact with a dead body—human or animal. While the purpose here is associated with purity rather than health, the actions probably benefited the whole community.

Next are moral impurities (5:5–10). The Lord orders anyone who has wronged another to make full restitution to the one who was wronged. This restitution involves more than simply returning the offended person to the point before the loss, but also adding 20 percent. If the restitution can't be made directly to the person, then it is made to the family. If not the family, then to the priest. Under these guidelines, there is no excuse for not making wrongs right again. This is more than a matter of community; it is a matter of cleansing oneself before God who sees all.

Finally there is the issue of marital impurity. Verses 11–31 outline a test by which a man can ferret out suspected infidelity on the part of his wife. The test requires an offering and a drink of holy water with tabernacle dust (some consider this to imply a bitter herb) mixed in. The result of the test depends on how the woman's body responds to the liquid.

While this test seems foreign to contemporary minds, the first purpose it serves is to put the man and his wife in the midst of spiritual leadership—the tabernacle priest. An important point of this procedure is that it places the woman before God for Him to determine if she is guilty or innocent. The husband isn't free to act on his suspicions any way that he chooses.

Critical Observation

The test for infidelity described in verses 11–31 seems like a double standard to the contemporary mind. Where was the man with whom the woman was unfaithful? What if the woman suspected her husband of infidelity? The hard truth is that in this tribal culture, women were not given the same rights as men. There seems to be no demands made, for instance, on the husband who falsely accuses his wife. There are elements of this practice, however foreign it sounds to us, that did serve to protect women to a certain point.

In reality, the point of this test is to protect paternity rights so that a child by another man does not inherit the estate of the husband. That is why the negative consequences involve the shriveling of the "thigh" (a euphemism for the womb), which would result in a miscarriage.

6:1–27

THE NAZIRITE VOW AND AARON'S BLESSING

Verses 1–20 outline the vow of the Nazirite. This is typically a temporary vow of spiritual dedication.

There are three marks of this vow, called a separation to God: abstaining from wine and grape products (6:3–4), not touching dead bodies (6:6–8), and not cutting one's hair (6:5).

The first two conditions are similar to the rules for priests during their terms of service. Wine would hinder the priests' vigilance (Leviticus 10:6–11), and the high priest could not even enter the place where a relative's corpse lay, although the ordinary priests could attend to a close relative (Leviticus 21:1–4, 11). Uncut hair, however, is peculiar to the Nazirite and symbolizes his commitment (Numbers 6:7). The word translated *Nazirite* is related to the Hebrew term which carries the idea of both a vow and a crown. This may contain a deliberate suggestion that the long hair functions as a crown—evidence of the vow.

If the vow is broken, for instance if someone can't escape touching a dead body, the Nazirite must pay a penalty and start fresh (6:9–12). When the period of dedication ends, he has to shave his head and burn the hair in the flames of the fellowship offering (6:13–21).

Critical Observation

Jesus is referred to as a Nazarene because he was from a town called Nazareth. This is an entirely different matter than the Nazirite vow discussed here.

There are examples of Nazirites in the Bible though. Samson was a Nazirite from birth (Judges 13; 16:17–20), and many think Paul made such a vow as well (Acts 18:18; 21:20–26). Apart from the priesthood, the Nazirite expressed the highest form of separation to the Lord. He was a token of Israel's dedication to God. Unlike some contemporary vows, the law was clear that vows had to be fulfilled (Deuteronomy 23:21–23), so the Nazirite vow, though temporary, was binding.

Numbers 6:22–27 contains the blessing God gives the Israelites. It is a frequently quoted spiritual blessing. God's face, described in this blessing as shining on His people, is a symbol of His presence. His favor is implied by the picture of Him turning His face toward the Israelites. Thus, this blessing is a prayer for God's presence and favor.

7:1–89

THE DEDICATION OF THE TABERNACLE

Setting Up the Section

Chapters 7–9 describe the dedication of the tabernacle. The events of chapters 7–9 actually precede the events described in chapters 1–6.

Numbers 7 is the second longest chapter in the Bible. It describes the twelve-day festival in which the people bring gifts to be used in the tabernacle. Each day different tribes send a representative to offer the gifts. There is much repetition, but to the original readers of Numbers, this repetition is understood as an emphasis.

Moses completes the tabernacle setup as he has been instructed (7:1). In verses 2–11, the leaders of the tribes offer six covered carts (one for every two leaders) and twelve oxen (one for every leader). Moses daily accepts the carts and oxen for twelve days. He gives two carts and four oxen to the sons of Gershon, to carry the curtains and coverings of the tabernacle (3:21–26). He gives four carts and eight oxen to the sons of Merari, to carry the heavy boards and bars of the tabernacle (3:33–37). None are offered to the sons of Kohath, though. They are required to carry the holy objects on their shoulders (3:27–32). Even though the tribes offer the same gifts, Moses lists them separately, honoring each one (7:12–83).

Verses 84–89 serve as a summary of the gifts, and then God speaks to Moses. His message begins with chapter 8.

8:1–26

GOD DIRECTS MOSES

In verses 1–4, God gives instructions regarding the lampstands. They are to be mounted so their light falls forward, resembling a tree. This symbolizes the fact that God is the giver of life to mankind. It also may symbolize the fact that Israel is to be a light to the world. The light from this lamp also shines brightly upon the showbread, which symbolizes the daily provision of God.

Verses 5–26 prescribe how the whole Levite workforce (in place of the firstborn Israelites; 3:40–51) is dedicated and purified for their work, and how those who retire at age fifty may continue to help the younger Levites as guards in the tabernacle. The male members of the Levites are to be set apart by

- being cleansed by water and shaving their hair;
- washing their clothes;
- offering burnt, sin, wave, and grain offerings.

Without being made clean through an offering and a spiritual washing, the Levites could not serve God.

Take It Home

In this passage of Numbers, God is establishing what it means to be set apart for His service. Though we worship differently today, this issue of seeing ourselves as God's servants is still important. First Peter 2:9 tells us that all believers are a holy priesthood. We are set apart unto God for His purposes and glory. When Jesus Christ came, He did not do away with the priesthood; instead, He widened it so that all those who come to God through faith in Him become a holy priesthood, set apart for the work of God.

9:1–23

OBSERVANCE OF THE PASSOVER

Setting Up the Section

In Numbers 9:1–10:10 there are three very important aspects of life in Israel established—the Passover celebration, the presence of God in the cloud covering the tabernacle, and the silver trumpets that function as a kind of public address system.

On the first month of the second year after the people had come out of Egypt, God commands them to commemorate the Passover (9:1–14). Comparing Numbers 9:1 with Numbers 1:1 makes it obvious that this celebration must have preceded the census described at the opening of Numbers.

There are provisions made for those who are unable to celebrate the Passover at the appointed time, but the death penalty awaits those who do not celebrate at the appointed time if they are able (9:13). This underscores the priority on worship that runs throughout Numbers.

Critical Observation

The Passover is the celebration that remembers God's faithfulness in protecting the Israelites from the angel of death. The Passover also shows the grace of God. God not only spared the firstborn, but He also rescued the people and brought them out of slavery to the promised land.

The Israelites are to celebrate the Passover annually, as a way of remembering the grace and the mercy of God. These two great themes come to their fullest expression on the cross of Jesus, where Jesus stood as the Passover Lamb for mankind.

The means of guidance for the sons of Israel is the movement of the cloud over the tabernacle (9:15–23) and the sounding of two silver trumpets (10:1–10). Despite the failings of the nation, the cloud is always present. In fact, the presence of the Lord is seen all day: a cloud by day and fire by night. The Israelite people are not only reminded of the past, they also have the daily reminder of the present: God is with them. He is their God and they are His people.

Take It Home

When the cloud moves, the Israelites are to move. God directs the people to go where He wants them to go, when He wants them to go. The people, then, had to respond by obeying His direction. This passage contains eight references to God's orders and the Israelites' obedience (9:18, 20, 23). This underscores a subtheme of Numbers: It is a dangerous thing to know what God demands and not do it.

10:1–36

THE DEPARTURE

God commands Moses to make two hammered trumpets of silver (10:1–10). They are to be blown for several reasons: to gather the people, to sound an alarm for the camps to begin to move, and to mark celebrations (like the monthly festival mentioned in verse 10).

According to verse 9, these trumpets also act as a kind of prayer that God will hear His children and rescue them from their enemies.

On the twentieth day of the second month of the second year, Israel sets out in military array for the first time. The cloud leads them from the wilderness of Sinai to the wilderness of Paran (10:11–36). Because of the organization described in the previous chapters (instructions about which families would care for what parts of the tabernacle, and in what order they would travel), all the people have to do is follow the directions they have been given (10:13–17).

Verses 11–12 give a quick summary of the journey, then verse 13 begins a more detailed account.

Moses talks his brother-in-law, Hobab, into continuing on in the journey. Hobab understands the places to camp and how to function in the desert, so his presence has some advantages. Moses even promises Hobab that if he comes along, he will share in the blessings promised to the Israelites. (Though Hobab initially resists, he apparently changes his mind because his descendants are listed with the Israelites in Judges 1:16 and 4:11.)

Though Hobab's expertise is certainly useful to the Israelites, God does the leading. Verses 35 and 36 include two short hymns that celebrate God's direction. The first is a prayer for protection as the group moves. The other is a prayer for fellowship as the group settles.

11:1–35

DISSENSION IN THE RANKS

Setting Up the Section

The people have now become frustrated with their circumstances. The inconveniences and sacrifices required of them are great, and they begin to complain. They have lost sight of God's promises and have become focused on their immediate suffering.

In verses 1–3, only three days into their journey from Sinai, the people begin to complain about their difficulties—and God responds. Fire from the Lord may imply lightning, but the text is not that specific. When the people cry for help, Moses intercedes for them. The place is called *Taberah*, which means "burning." Yet, in the following verses, the complaining continues.

In verses 4–9, the Israelites still don't return their attention to God, and instead keep their focus on the next problem in their lives. In this case they complain about the food God has provided: manna. It seems that they forget the sweat, labor, pain, and enslavement that had been a part of their lives in Egypt and remember only the food.

Critical Observation

The manna God provides is like a seed of grain, and looks like small, clear drops. The name is commonly thought to be derived from an expression of surprise, "What is it?" More probable is it derives from a word that means "to allot," denoting an allotment or a gift. Generally, manna has been associated with a byproduct of the tamarisk tree found in northern Arabia.

The mixed multitude of verse 4, sometimes interpreted *rabble*, or *riffraff*, that seems to instigate this round of grumbling is not clearly defined here, though it likely refers to the non-Israelites who traveled with the group out of Egypt (Exodus 12:38).

Upon hearing the cries of widespread dissatisfaction from the people, God is considerably angered, and Moses is distressed (Numbers 11:10–15). The dissension is so great that Moses becomes exasperated at the people for making his role as a leader unbearable, and resentful toward God for assigning him this overwhelming burden of leadership. Prior to this, Moses worked hard to intercede for the people. Now, temporarily, his focus is on finding an end to his own misery.

The conversation between God and Moses in verses 16–35 deals with the situation on two levels—the immediate problem of feeding the people and the long-term problem of leading the people.

The first strategy is for Moses to appoint seventy elders among the Israelites (11:16–17). Seventy of these men, a number suggestive of a full complement of persons, are to be endowed with the Spirit of God for assisting Moses in bearing the burdens of the people as spiritual leaders. This spiritual dimension differentiates this group from those appointed for administrative and judicial tasks in Exodus 18:25–26.

The next strategy is a double-edged sword. God provides directions for the larger populace to consecrate themselves prior to receiving the blessing from the Lord (Numbers 11:18–23). In this case, though, the so-called blessing described in verses 19–20 is one that will wear out its welcome. Notice the emphatic nature of the description in verse 19—not one, two, five, ten, or even twenty days, but for an entire month (more than twenty-nine days) they will receive meat.

Demystifying Numbers

Consecration is a term used here to describe the process of purification through bathing. The purpose, which is what makes it a spiritual process, is to be prepared to receive the presence of the Lord. Ritual purity was necessary before offering sacrifices and as preparation for celebrating festivals such as Passover. Here, it is to prepare for God's blessing.

In verses 21–23, Moses reminds God of the numbers of the people. The promised meat would need to be in astronomical quantities. In his disbelief, Moses challenges God's ability to meet the needs of the people in the wilderness. Still, in verses 24–25, he follows through with the first stage of the instructions (11:16).

The promise God gives in verse 17 is fulfilled in verse 25, but according to the text, it seems to be a one-time event that proved God's presence.

Two of the men—Eldad and Medad—who had been registered among the seventy elders remained in the camp and prophesied there. An unknown young man (perhaps Joshua, who voices the complaint of 11:28) gives witness of this phenomenon back to Moses, who is still gathered at the Tent with the other sixty-eight. The generosity that Moses exhibits here seems to imply that he has gathered his spiritual and personal resources after his lack of faith evidenced in verses 16–35. While there aren't many specifics about why these two men didn't join the others, the fact that they face no judgment from God makes it appear benign, though it doesn't seem so to Joshua.

Critical Observation

Joshua, the son of Nun, is introduced in the account of the Israelites as a leading warrior in the first battle against the Amalekites (Exodus 17:8–14). When Moses meets with the Lord at the Tent of Meeting, which is at first outside the camp of Israel (Exodus 33:7–11), the young Joshua remains at the Tent even after Moses departs. Here, Joshua acts as an assistant to Moses, calling for Moses to force Eldad and Medad to cease their prophesying. Joshua perhaps sees these two men as a threat to Moses' leadership.

Moses' response to Joshua contrasts considerably with that of his earlier expressions of complaint and despair (11:28–31). Instead of feeling threatened, Moses commends the event. An undercurrent in Moses' response may be his own desire for further relief from the heavy responsibility of leadership, but it also reveals a heart open to God's leadership.

Verses 31–32 describe the wind that brought the quail to the camp. The magnitude of the quail is measured in three ways:

- The breadth of distribution: a day's journey in each direction, or twelve to fifteen miles
- The depth of the piles: about 3 feet high (though some interpret this as the level at which the quail flew)
- The amount individually collected: at least ten homers over a two-day period, a volume estimated at between thirty-eight and sixty-five bushels. The homer is the largest dry volume measure in the Hebrew vocabulary.

Some of the birds are eaten right away, while most of them are spread out around the camp, presumably for drying the meat after cleaning and salting it. While the people are processing and eating the quail, the Lord's anger burns against many of those who had gathered too much, and they are struck down and die, possibly from food poisoning.

In verse 35, the journey continues toward Hazeroth. This precise location is conjecture.

Take It Home

Grumbling is a form of rebellion against God. It comes from losing sight of His promises and is an attack against His nature and character. If you forget the promises of God, the only thing you can look at is the problems of the present. Where are your eyes today?

12:1–16

FROM DISSENSION TO TREASON

In Hebrews, the grammar of the opening verses of chapter 12 suggests that Miriam is the one leading the attack against Moses, but she is backed by her brother Aaron. This conflict is bigger than a family squabble. Miriam and Aaron have national religious positions of leadership, and they are challenging the leadership of Moses as sole mediator between God and Israel. Though the question seems to be about Moses' wife's ethnicity, it is really Moses' right to lead that is at the heart of the issue.

Critical Observation

Ethnic purity was an important issue in ancient Israel, but only in the protection of religious purity. This is evidenced in the instructions of Ezra to his countrymen to separate themselves from their pagan foreign wives before they could lead their husbands into idolatry.
Throughout the law of the Old Testament, however, there are explicit instructions that there is one code of law for the native Israelites and the sojourning foreigners in the land. In Numbers 9:14, aliens living among the Israelites could celebrate the Passover if they do so according to the statutes. So while Miriam and Aaron's charge against Moses has some foundation, it isn't entirely valid.

The gravity of Miriam and Aaron's objections is amplified in the last words of verse 2—God heard. Verse 3 interjects a kind of character witness on behalf of Moses.

In verses 4–8, all three siblings are summoned to come out to the tabernacle, a central locale that offers a reminder of the presence of the Lord. In verses 6–8, the Lord affirms Moses' unique commission as a prophet of God, a man who stands above the others among the Israelites, such as the recently endowed seventy elders, as well as above Miriam and Aaron. He is also the mediator of the covenant, hearing from God directly. Since this is the case, how could Miriam and Aaron dare to speak against him? To speak against God's servant is tantamount to speaking against God Himself.

The immediate response of the Lord to Miriam is one of anger, followed by withdrawal (12:9–13). The charges against Moses are dismissed and judgment meted out. When the cloud of God's presence withdraws, Moses and Aaron witness their sister's skin disease that requires her separation from the tabernacle and from the community itself.

Critical Observation

That Miriam rather than Aaron is plagued by the disease reinforces the idea that Miriam is the chief instigator of the dispute. Whatever the skin disease Miriam contracted, she would become an outcast from society, forced to live outside the holy camp. The laws regarding various skin diseases required the afflicted to live on the outskirts of the camp or town so as to not defile the purity of the community (Leviticus 13:45–46).

Aaron immediately apologizes to Moses, addressing him as lord and submissively confessing his sin of rebellion. This may have been an attempt to lighten the potential judgment against himself in the face of Miriam's judgment. But out of concern for his sister, he begs Moses for her healing, and Moses begs God for the same (12:11–13).

Moses' request is that she be given the kind of punishment she would have experienced if her father had spat on her face in contempt—seven days. This is also the standard period for the purification process for a leper (Leviticus 14:1–32).

Israel will not disembark on the next stage of the journey until the Lord leads them by the cloud. The rebellion of Miriam has consequences for the entire community as they wait for her purification.

Verse 16 marks the departure from Hazeroth toward the Desert of Paran in the modern southern Negev, or northeast Sinai region. The Paran wilderness is the goal of the first phase of the journey (10:11), and from that area the spies are to be sent to explore Canaan (13:3).

NUMBERS 13:1–21:35

ISRAEL DELAYED AT KADESH AND THE JOURNEY TO MOAB

Setting Up the Section

The events recorded here took place while Israel was camped at Kadesh. The sending of the spies and all that came from this event became engraved on the corporate memory of God's people. Later writers refer back to these incidents with a sense of painful disappointment (see Deuteronomy 1:26–46; Psalm 95:10–11).

13:1–14:45

FROM TREASON TO REJECTION TO REBELLION

This account records one of the biggest mistakes made by the nation of Israel. At the heart is the question of whether circumstances can outpower God's plan.

In Exodus 3:8, Moses had been told by God that Canaan would be spacious and have an abundance of food. Here in Numbers, Moses chooses twelve leaders from the tribes of Israel to explore Canaan (13:1–16). While these leaders were chosen from the tribes, they weren't the tribal leaders. These spies were to evaluate the people, the land, and the cities (13:17–20). The twelve spies travel from the south (wilderness of Zin) to the north (Rehob) and return after forty days with their report (13:21–24).

Except for Caleb, the spies report that although the land is rich, it also is inhabited by mighty people who could outpower them (13:25–33). Ten of the spies report that in relation to these giants, the people of Israel look like grasshoppers. The spies who make the majority report only saw the giants, whereas Joshua and Caleb saw victory.

Demystifying Numbers

The descendants of Anak, the giants, are noted for their great size and strength (13:28). They are described as being related to the Nephilim (13:33), who lived on the earth before the flood (Genesis 6:4). Since the Nephilim would have been wiped out by the flood, however, these descendants of Anak were only associated with the Nephilim because of their great size.

The people responded to the spies' report with despair, prompting Moses and Aaron to prostrate themselves in the presence of God (14:1–10). The people's despair is a rejection of faith. When God is rejected, people become disillusioned and turn toward their past bondage.

Take It Home

To Caleb and Joshua, God is bigger than their enemies (14:6–9). These two see the land through the eyes of faith. To the other ten spies, the problems seem bigger than God. They minimize the greatest resource they have—the fact that God has already promised them the land. When a person acknowledges the power of God, he or she will not minimize the divine resources available.

After Joshua and Caleb stand against the majority, the people want to stone them. Then God appears. The Israelites' actions are actually a rebellion against God Himself—more than a rejection of the two men.

When God speaks of destroying the people, Moses intercedes on the basis of God's character (14:11–19). He reasons that the nations will hear about this destruction and it would impugn God's character. Moses declares God's glory and seeks to protect it.

The people are pardoned, but because of their sin, the generation from age twenty and older (except for Caleb and Joshua) would wander for forty years (one year for every day of the spies' investigation) and die in the wilderness (14:20–35). These people had treated God with contempt. Although He provided them with proof over and over again that He is their deliverer, they still refused to believe Him.

After the plague that attacks the spies, only Joshua and Caleb remain of the group that had investigated Canaan (14:36–45). Taking matters from bad to worse, the people continue to demonstrate their rebellion by entering the land against all instruction from Moses (14:39–45). This is an attempt to reverse their consequences, but of course they are soundly defeated by the Amalekites and Canaanites. Only through God's strength do they find victory.

Take It Home

From a spiritual point of view, the value of sending in the spies was not to determine if the conquest was possible, but to show Israel what God was going to give His people. This was not intended to be a joint decision, but a time of excitement and revelation. They were to see all that God was providing for them. Instead, they looked at the land through faithless eyes and sent the nation into a tailspin. Their story reminds us to notice how we are viewing the promises God has made in our lives. Do we believe or do we question?

15:1–41

RENEWING WORSHIP

Setting Up the Section

Though we often think of the book of Numbers as the Israelites' journey across the wilderness, Numbers 15 marks the beginning of the only five chapters of this book that provide narratives of that journey (15–19).

This chapter also marks the first set of instructions for the people who now know they will wander in this wilderness until their deaths. Notice that this section begins with the reaffirmation of worship. The first thing God does after the pronouncement of the consequences of Israel's sin is reestablish the worship He wants from His people.

When the Israelites enter Canaan, they are to provide meal, oil, and wine as their thanksgiving offering (15:1–16). Today, we offer money because that is the fruit of our labors. In the case of these Israelites, who would eventually settle into farming and cultivating vineyards, these offerings were a gift of their labors.

Verses 3–10 describe a number of different styles of sacrifices and offerings. Leviticus 1–7 provides the guidelines for these rituals.

Just as the foreigners living among the Israelites are able to take part in the Passover, verses 14–16 include these foreigners in worship. While the Israelites are considered the people of God, their God accepts worship from anyone who is willing to be in right relationship with Him.

When the Israelites enter Canaan, they are to offer from the food of the land the first of their dough throughout their generations (15:17–21). This is an expression of gratitude for the harvest of grain.

The next instructions, listed in verses 22–29, change gears to deal with unintentional sins—sins of omission rather than commission. When the nation or an individual (native or alien) inadvertently sins against the commands of God, they are to make a sin offering.

On the other hand, if one sins defiantly, it is considered blasphemy, a capital crime. Verses 32–36 give an example of a man who is found gathering wood on the Sabbath. He is brought before Moses and Aaron, and then stoned by the congregation outside of the camp as God commands. While this is an extreme and uncomfortable example for the contemporary mind, it is the full knowledge with which the man committed the sin, rather than the details, that prompted his judgment.

In verses 37–41, God commands Moses to tell the Israelites to put tassels on the corners of their garments with a cord of blue through each. These tassels are to be constant reminders, not of one particular law, but of the relationship they solidified with God by their obedience. The color blue is related to both heaven and royalty in the minds of the Israelites.

16:1–50

THE REBELLION OF KORAH

This chapter marks the fifth complaint of the Israelites in the desert, this time against the authority of Aaron and his priestly line. In verses 1–3, the chief rebel is Korah, who descended from Levi through his son Kohath. As a Kohathite, he has high duties at the tabernacle—but he isn't a priest. Just as Korah wants more power, so do Dathan, Abiram, and On (who is not mentioned again). The rebels rise up against Moses and Aaron with 250 leaders of the community. The heart of their accusation is Moses' arrogance in claiming a special relationship with God. These rebels want the same privilege.

When the leaders accuse Moses and Aaron of exalting themselves in verses 4–7, Moses does not try to convince the rebels of his calling. Although it's clear that he's angry, he will let God defend him, if God so chooses.

Critical Observation

The test described here involves offering incense because this was one of the most holy responsibilities of the priests. The fatal disaster of Nadab and Abihu, priests who died by offering strange fire, seems to confirm this (Leviticus 10:1–3).

In Numbers 16:8–11, Moses also rebukes the Levites under Korah and his company, making it clear that their rebellion is against God, because they want to exalt themselves rather than wait for Him to exalt them. In verses 12–15, Moses summons Dathan and Abiram to come to him, but they refuse.

In the confrontation recorded in verses 16–24, the glory of God appears with the intention to destroy the entire congregation, save Moses and Aaron. Moses quickly asks God to spare those who did not follow the sin of these men. In verses 25–35, Moses announces the severity of what will happen—the Lord opens the ground and swallows up the households of the rebels and the 250 men who were offering incense. This event leaves no question as to God's stance on the rebellion, nor do His orders to Eleazar, to use the censers of the rebels to plate the altar—an ongoing reminder.

Demystifying Numbers

There is much we still don't know about Korah's rebellion. We don't know exactly when it took place. It could have occurred soon after the spies returned, or sometime during the four decades of wandering in the desert. What kind of disaster ended the rebellion is also unclear. Some speculate that the rebels' tents were pitched on a mudflat, common to the area, that's hard on the surface but boggy underneath. If the crust breaks, anything on its surface can be swallowed up. Whatever the details of the event, its record here stands as a reminder of the importance of surrendering to God's plan.

Perhaps not surprisingly, the next day the people complain again, accusing Moses and Aaron of causing the death of Korah and his men. The truth, however, is that Moses and Aaron had asked for the survival of the same people who are continuing to complain against them (16:41). Thus follows a plague (16:43–49) that kills 14,700. The deaths only stop because of Aaron's intercession. We aren't given a lot of details about the nature of this plague or what Moses' actions may have been in the midst of it, but the account serves to set up a transition to the next passage regarding Aaron's leadership.

17:1–13

AARON'S ROD—GOD'S AFFIRMATION OF HIS MEN

The story of Aaron's rod is the third in a series that demonstrates the divine sanction of the priestly leadership of Aaron and the Levites. This incident, though, is inverted in structure compared with the first two (Korah's rebellion and the plagues at the end of chapter 16). Rather than people's complaints precipitating the threat of destruction, here God seeks to prove Aaron's call once and for all, and the people end up crying out to God for fear of destruction.

Demystifying Numbers

Each of the twelve tribal leaders has a staff with the name of the current leader carved into the wooden rod. These staffs symbolize the tribe and the authority of the leader.

In verses 1–7, the staffs of the twelve tribal leaders are to be brought inside the innermost holy chamber and placed before the throne of God. This placement demonstrates the gravity of the occasion. The staff that sprouts leaves, then, will represent the leader whom God has appointed to stand before Him. Only God can impart life to that which is dead, and this test will show the combined tribes of Israel that God has conferred a special blessing upon the tribe whom He chooses.

The following morning, Moses enters the inner Tent of the Testimony and finds that not only has Aaron's staff sprouted, but God has caused it to bud, blossom, and produce almonds (17:8–13).

Critical Observation

The almond is one of the earliest trees to bud and blossom in the spring, and the fruit ripens in early to mid summer. But for a dead limb to sprout, bud, blossom, and produce ripe almonds overnight is a remarkable wonder, a natural process made supernatural. The almond branch in Israelite art and literature was a symbol of life that derived from their Maker. The bud and flower were shaped so elegantly that the three golden bowls on each side of the tabernacle lampstand were patterned after them (Exodus 25:31–40).

Moses subsequently returns with the twelve staffs so that the Israelites can observe the results. The priority of the Aaronic priesthood is vindicated.

The unanswered question closing Numbers 17—Are we all going to die?—will be resolved in the following two chapters, which contain the instructions from God concerning a proper approach to a holy and just God.

18:1–32

RENEWED COMMITMENT TO THE LEVITICAL ORDER

Israel's high priests (Aaron's family line) and the Levites in general, as guardians of the tabernacle, are called to a dangerous and crucial task. After affirming their position to the Israelites, God now spells out to Aaron the Levites' roles, responsibilities, regulations, and rewards.

Numbers 18:1–7 reiterates (and builds upon) certain aspects of the priestly roles outlined in Numbers 3–4 (also Leviticus 8–10). The most basic responsibility is to be accountable for any potential sacrilege against the innermost holy place in the tabernacle. The priests must monitor their own purity as well.

The priests are allowed to keep some of the offerings given by the people (Numbers 18:8–19). This priestly tribute is divided into two levels of sanctity, the *most holy* offerings and the generally *holy* offerings. The holiest of the offerings, which are to be consumed by the priests, are cereal offerings, sin (purification) offerings, and guilt (reparation) offerings. The cereal grain offering, as described in 2:1–13 and 6:14–23, is an unleavened mixture of fine flour, oil, and incense. A memorial portion is burned on the altar as a sweet aroma to God, and the remainder is eaten by the priests.

The second level of tribute consists of the variety of firstfruits and firstborn gifts. The first fruit from the trees and offspring from the womb (people and livestock) are treated as special gifts from God that are to be returned to Him. Verses 12–18 provide guidelines for these offerings.

Critical Observation

God has much to say about firstborn gifts. The firstborn are the first male from the womb of the mother, whether human or animal. Animals defined by Levitical law as clean—such as cattle, sheep, and goats—are to be offered as sacrifices. Since humans cannot be sacrificed (nor unclean animals), a redemption price is established to be given instead of the firstborn. The process of human and animal redemption has a teaching purpose, too. It reminds the Israelites of their redemption from Egypt.

Numbers 18:19 restates the fact that the tribute from Israel is a gift from God for the priestly families, both male and female. God calls it "an everlasting covenant of salt" (NIV). Though the origin of this covenant is unknown, the function of salt in ancient Near Eastern society included the concepts of preservation and permanence.

Though the Levites receive no land, God is their inheritance. This is not to say that the priests and Levites somehow owned God (18:20–24). Instead, what physically accrued to God from the territorial inheritance of the Israelites would belong to them. These gifts become the Levites' birthright instead of territorial grant.

Critical Observation

The tithe, or *tenth*, is the required percentage of the productivity of Israelite labors that is to be rendered to God at the tabernacle (18:21). The statutes on tithing and the relationship between the Levites and the other Israelites are expanded in Deuteronomy 12:17–19 and 14:22–29.

During the wilderness journey, the Levites camp immediately around the tabernacle, serving as a barrier between the tabernacle and the community at large. This responsibility was a perpetual one. The contributions of the Israelites to God are, in turn, His gifts to these Levites for their dedicated service.

The previous accounts involve rules and regulations found elsewhere in the Pentateuch. Starting in verse 25, however, a new law emerges (18:25-32). The Levites are responsible to tithe to God, and thus to the priesthood, out of the tithes they receive. Furthermore, they are to contribute, in this tithe of the tithe, the very best of what is bestowed upon them. The original tithe, designated as the Levite inheritance in exchange for their service in the tabernacle, is treated like income. Like the other Israelites, the Levites are to tithe on this income.

19:1–1:22

PURIFICATION

Setting Up the Section

Numbers 19 offers the cleansing process for those who have been in contact with a dead body. This is an important ceremony for the Israelites, because the nation will encounter many deaths on a daily basis for several decades. Thus, they must be prepared as to how they are going to remain ceremonially clean after dealing with a dead body.

Verses 1–13 outline a ritual involving an unblemished red cow. The cow is to be brought to Eleazar, the priest, and slaughtered outside of the camp. Eleazar then is to sprinkle some of the cow's blood toward the front of the tabernacle before the cow is completely burned. After burning, its ashes are to be mixed with cedar wood, hyssop, and scarlet material, then it is to be used to clean those who have touched a corpse.

The animal designated for sacrifice is a young cow. The color red may symbolize blood, but that is uncertain. The exact age of the animal is not made clear by the Hebrew, but the fact that it is not to be allowed to pull the plow or do any other type of work suggests it may have just reached maturity.

Eleazar is the one who is to receive the animal. He is the second, or deputy, high priest, and he is selected for this duty because the job causes the participant to incur temporary defilement, which the high priest can not.

Some details that set this ritual apart from the sacrifices at the tabernacle are that the animal is led out of the camp rather than being slaughtered at the altar. Also, every part of the cow is consumed by fire except the blood used in sprinkling.

The ingredients mixed with the ashes are the same as those employed in the sprinkling of lepers (Leviticus 14:4–7). Numbers 19:14–22 explains the use for this mixture. Anyone who even enters the tent of a dead person needs to be sprinkled with this mixture of water and ashes from the red cow on the third and seventh days (after the contact with the dead body) in order to be cleansed. In addition, the one who performs the sprinkling, as well as all the things that the unclean person touches, will be considered unclean until evening. These rituals for dealing with the dead, though mysterious, helped preserve the sanitary conditions of the camp.

20:1–29

A SAD DAY

Setting Up the Section

In Numbers 20, Moses faces a series of sad events, beginning with the death of his sister, Miriam. This chapter highlights the seriousness with which we must treat the Word of God. In addition, it shows how God is faithful to Israel, in allowing a next generation to emerge so that His work might continue.

When the Israelites come in the first month to the wilderness of Sin, or Zin in some translations, and stay at Kadesh, Miriam dies and is buried there (20:1). Miriam is the leading female character in the story of the Exodus. This account of her death sets the somber mood for the rest of the chapter.

At Kadesh, the people resume their murmuring about lack of water, and rebel against Moses and Aaron because of it. They again lose sight of the plan of God and are caught in the misery of the moment. God commands Moses to take the rod, gather the community, and speak to the rock; then it will bring forth water (20:2–13)

For unknown reasons, Moses instead takes the rod, gathers the community, speaks to them with a hasty and passionate voice, and then strikes the rock twice.

There are two things that Moses and Aaron get wrong: the first is their unbelief, and the second is their lack of obedience. Believing is not just mentally agreeing with God; it is actually doing what God says. The consequence of their actions is severe—they will be prevented from bringing the people into Canaan.

The waters are called *Meribah* because the meaning of this name reflects the fact that Israel contended with God, but God proved Himself holy among them. Naming locations like this is meant to teach future generations about the history of Israel, and about all that God did in that region.

Following the two great blows already described in chapter 20—Miriam's death and the conflict at Meribah—Moses has to deal with the Edomites, who will not allow them to pass to Canaan (20:14–21).

Moses makes a diplomatic request to go through the land of Edom, but the Edomites state they will attack Israel before letting them pass through. Moses counters: What if they only pass via the main roads? And if any of the livestock drinks any of their water, they will pay for it. Edom still refuses, and the Israelites find another way.

Critical Observation

The Edomites are descendants of Esau, who was the twin brother of Jacob, forefather to the Israelites. The story of these brothers, told in Genesis 25–27, is filled with conflict. Understanding the distant family history, generations past, adds to the conflict described here in Numbers 20.

Chapter 20 opens with the death of Miriam and closes with the death of Aaron (20:22–29). When the Israelites come to Mount Hor, near the border of Edom, Moses, in obedience to God, takes Aaron and his son, Eleazar, up the mountain. (Scholars are not certain where Mount Hor is located, despite an early tradition identifying it with Jebel Nebi Harun near Petra.) There he gives Aaron's garments to Eleazar, and Aaron dies. When Moses places Aaron's vestments on Eleazar's shoulders, he is also transferring his responsibilities as Israel's high priest, the supreme mediator between God and Israel. The people mourn for Aaron for thirty days.

This point in the lives of the Israelites seems to be the lowest so far. Yet, God is allowing the next generation to take over, to carry on the work. God is still working and preparing the next generation to live in Canaan.

21:1–35

SO NEAR, YET SO FAR: LESSONS ALONG THE WAY

After Aaron's death, Moses alone leads the Israelites closer to Canaan. Moving northward, the king of Arad attacks them and takes captives (21:1–3). This is an important first battle because it establishes a pattern. God will do the winning. The Israelites acknowledge that unless God gives their foes into their hands, they will not have any success.

The Israelites vow that if God will give the Canaanites into their hands, they will obey Him by completely destroying the cities. After this battle, the location is called Hormah, which means "destruction." *Hormah* became an ancient town on the southernmost borders of Palestine, not far from Kadesh. Tell Arad marks the spot today.

Later, when the people are traveling from Mount Hor to the Red Sea, they begin to grumble again about their circumstances and food (21:4–9). Remember that they are on this longer road to the promised land because the king of Edom refused to allow them to travel through his land (10:14–21). Perhaps because this journey is long, morale sinks.

When one complains, he or she is essentially saying that God has not provided the way He should have. It is an attack. This is why God responds by sending fiery serpents. The desert near the head of the Gulf of Aqabah is known for being infested with venomous reptiles. In fact, there are lizards, that raise themselves in the air and swing themselves from branches, and scorpions, which are particularly dangerous because they lie hidden in the grass. The people now face a threat, and in humility, they admit their misstep and ask for help from Moses.

According to God's instructions, Moses fashions the brass serpent and elevates it in plain sight of everyone in the camp. Every bitten Israelite who looks to it will be healed. Why this method? It is not that the brass snake or the pole is magical; it is the people's opportunity to choose faith and obey. Thus salvation is brought to the nation for their sin.

This is the last recorded occasion in which Israel grumbles about the food and yearns for Egypt.

Critical Observation

This form and method of salvation—the brass snake raised high—has become a picture of Jesus, hung on the cross, able to save those who look upon Him in faith (John 3:14, 15; 2 Corinthians 5:21).

In verses 10–21, Israel moves to the eastern frontier of the Edomites, in the valley of Zared. Then they pitch their tents on the other side of Arnon (now called El-Mojib). This is a deep, broad, and rapid stream, dividing the land of the Moabites and Amorites. In both places, God provides camp space and water.

Demystifying Numbers

In addition to the Bible, other sources written from this era record the history of Israel. Two sources were *The Book of Jashar* (see Joshua 10:13; 2 Samuel 1:18) and *The Book of the Wars of God*, mentioned in Numbers 21:14. Based upon these three short mentions, these two books were collections of victory songs and stories of the powerful acts of God working through His leaders during the early formation of Israel. Unfortunately, neither book survived, but their mention shows some of the alternate ways that God worked in spreading the word of His mighty power in calling, forming, growing, and protecting the nation of Israel.

The song of the well in Numbers 21:17–18 may also have come from *The Book of the Wars* (mentioned in verse 14). For those living in the desert, finding water is the most essential act for survival. In this song it appears as if princes, using their official rods only, not spades, find a well that is concealed by the brushwood or the sand. This song is a song of praise for the great provision of God.

In the account of Sihon, king of the Amorites, Israelite messengers request permission to march through their land, promising not take anything and to leave the city and its supplies alone (21:21–32). In addition, they will stay on the king's highway, which is the ancient trade route used by many merchants. This request is rejected, and Sihon sends troops to fight Israel. Unlike the similar situation with the Edomites (20:14–21), Israel has no alternate route, so they must stand and fight. In this case, they are victorious.

It is meaningful to note Genesis 15:16 here: "In the fourth generation your descendants will come back here, for the sin of the Amorites has not yet reached its full measure" (NIV). This is a promise that the Israelites will be brought back to the land of the Amorites, and as a form of judgment, they will defeat the Amorites and take their land, just as it happens here.

Critical Observation

The song of Heshbon was an old Amorite taunt song in which the Amorites taunt the Moabites because they had lost in battle. In it, an earlier Amorite conquest was celebrated over the Moabites. According to this song, Chemosh, a Moabite god, did not deliver the Moabites from the hands of the Amorites. The Jews are using this as their own taunt song, thus giving praise to God.

The Israelites make their way through various villages, clearing out many of the Amorites. God then directs them to turn and go up by the way of Bashan, a hilly region east of the Jordan, lying between the mountains of Hermon on the north and those of Gilead on the south (21:33–35). There lies an intimidating foe, Og, who is a giant (see Deuteronomy 3:11). This likely describes the size of the inhabitants that scare the spies in Numbers 13. The Lord tells Moses not to fear this man and gives Og over to the Israelties. God clearly shows the Israelites that they need Him at every turn on this journey.

The idea here in verse 14 is that God is celebrated as being a great warrior who has settled on the edge of the promised land with strength, power, and victory. In short, the Israelites are worshiping God for His great power and strength as they sit on the edge of Canaan waiting to go in.

NUMBERS 22:1–36:13

ISRAEL AT MOAB ANTICIPATING THE PROMISED LAND

Setting Up the Section

The deceptively simple but profound story of Balaam and his donkey begins a period in which the Israelites—poised on the border of the promised land—encamp for an apparently lengthy time at the foot of the mountains of Moab, not unlike their encampment four decades prior at Sinai.

These accounts are humorous as well as somber. Some characters are stupid and stubborn, and there is more spiritual awareness in the donkey than in the humans. Structurally, watch for threes: the donkey avoids the angel three times, Balaam arranges for three sets of sacrifices, he has three encounters with God, and so on. The narrative itself extends over six days, through Numbers 24.

22:1–24:25

BALAAM'S STORY

As this account begins, Israel is about four months away from the end of the forty years' desert exile. When the sons of Israel camp in the plain of Moab, Balak, son of the king, becomes afraid. He has heard about Israel's victory over the Amorites.

Balak comes up with a plan. He seeks to defeat Israel by having Balaam, a Mesopotamian prophet, proclaim a curse upon Israel. An ancient text, the *Tell Deir 'Allah*, suggests that Balaam is a soothsayer of great renown in this region. The local text of that region suggests that he sees visions and dreams. Thus, he is an obvious choice for Balak to turn to for spiritual help. Balak sends a message requesting help and a fee.

When Balaam seeks direction from God, it is clear that the children of Israel are a blessed people and that it would be wrong to put a curse upon them. Yet, Balak sends another, more impressive delegation with a promise of more money in payment for the curses. In the end Balaam goes, but with the determination to only speak God's words.

Verses 21–35 tell the story of Balaam's journey. As he begins to leave with the leaders of Balak, he is stopped by his donkey. An angel of the Lord is in the road with a sword in his hand. This signifies that if Balaam tries to go to Balak, he will be killed. Balaam's donkey saves his life by not walking, despite being beaten.

Three times the donkey tries to avoid the angel. Then the donkey is given the ability to speak and converses with Balaam. Finally, Balaam sees the angel, who reveals that the donkey saved his life and that Balaam must speak only God's words.

This is not to say that God tells Balaam to go and then gets mad at him for going. The account probably implies that Balaam was not planning to carry out what God had requested.

In verses 36–41, Balak comes to meet Balaam, a gesture of some import, because the son of the king could have waited until Balaam came to him. Balak is upset with Balaam for not coming when first invited. He may have wondered if Balaam didn't believe Balak could pay—"Am I not able to honor you?" (22:37 NET).

Balak holds a banquet for Balaam and takes him to the high place of Baal to see a portion of Israel, perhaps hoping that this will make Balaam's curses stronger.

Critical Observation

Some scholars portray Balaam as a saintly seer; others as a money-hungry heathen sham. In the beginning of the story, he appears positive, intent on listening to God. Other Bible passages aren't so flattering, for instance Deuteronomy 23:4–5; 2 Peter 2:15; Jude 11; and Revelation 2:14.

Each of Balaam's blessings concerning Israel reiterates and confirms one of the promises of the Abrahamic covenant. What is about to take place in the life of Israel is a part of the fulfillment of what was spoken to Abraham in Genesis 12.

- **The first oracle (23:7–10):** Israel will be multiplied like the dust of the earth.
- **The second oracle** (23:18–24): Balaam proclaims that with God as their strength, Israel is indestructible and mighty. God cannot change His promise.
- **The third oracle (24:3–9):** Israel will inherit the land, and nothing will stop this from happening. The fact that Agag, the Amalekite king, is mentioned confirms specifically that Canaan is in mind here. This blessing also states that Israel will devour hostile nations. This fulfills the promise that they will possess their enemies' cities. The last words of this blessing bring home a key point of the Abrahamic covenant: May those who bless you be blessed, and those who curse you be cursed!
- **The fourth oracle (24:15–19):** This vision promises a king in the distant future who will defeat Israel's enemies and crush the foreheads of Moab. This passage seems to anticipate King David's victories, and the promise of his throne: the promise of the Messiah whom the Gentiles will obey. By this point, Balaam knows that the curse is not coming to Israel but to Balak. This fourth oracle is actually a series development of the third one, explicitly describing the distant future.

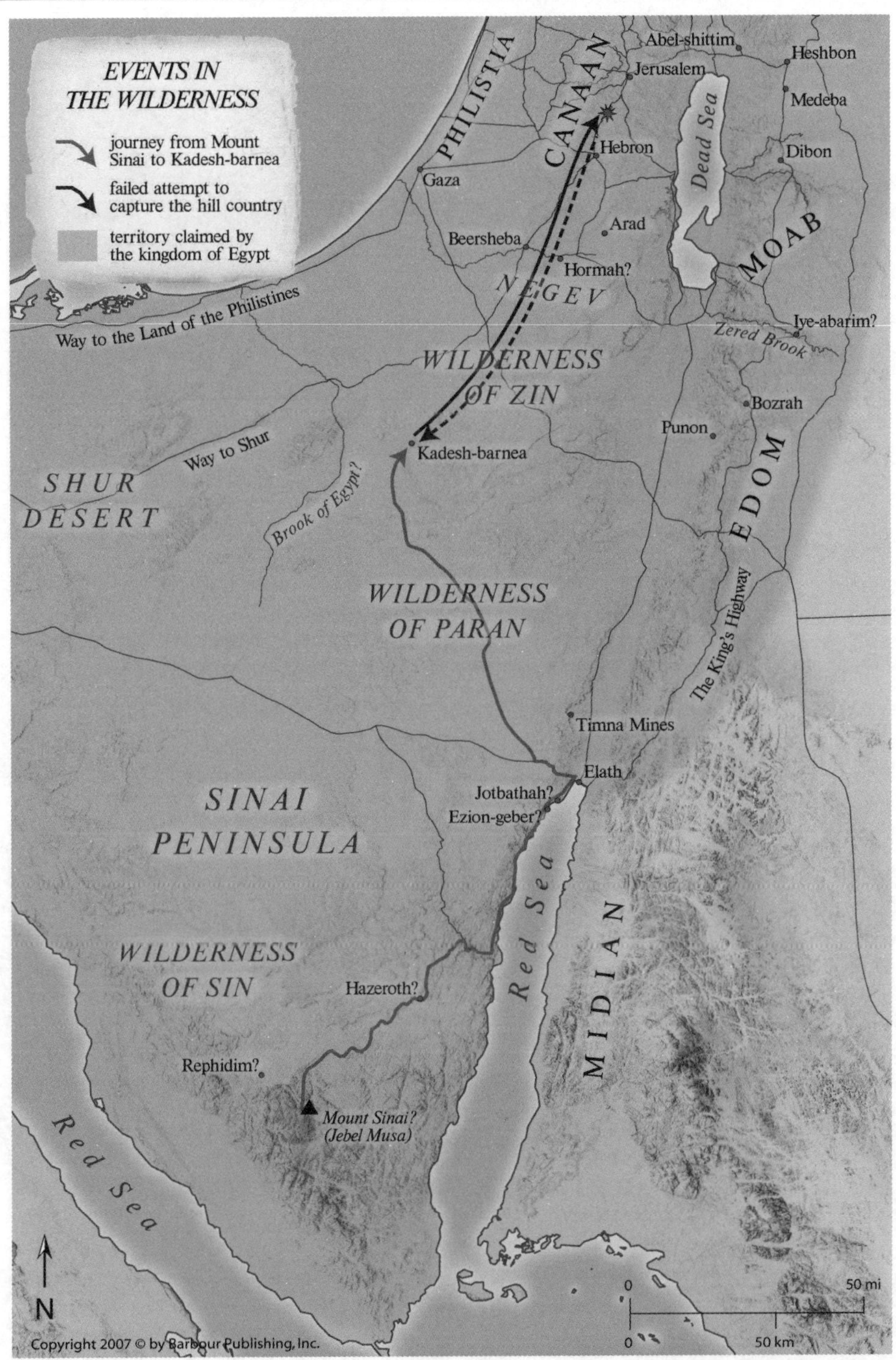
EVENTS IN THE WILDERNESS
journey from Mount Sinai to Kadesh-barnea
failed attempt to capture the hill country
territory claimed by the kingdom of Egypt
PHILISTIA
CANAAN
Abel-shittim
Heshbon
Jerusalem
Medeba
Dead Sea
Hebron
Dibon
Gaza
Arad
MOAB
Beersheba
Hormah?
NEGEV
Way to the Land of the Philistines
Iye-abarim?
Zered Brook
WILDERNESS OF ZIN
Bozrah
Punon
Kadesh-barnea
Way to Shur
EDOM
SHUR DESERT
Brook of Egypt?
WILDERNESS OF PARAN
The King's Highway
Timna Mines
Elath
Jotbathah?
Ezion-geber?
SINAI PENINSULA
Red Sea
MIDIAN
WILDERNESS OF SIN
Hazeroth?
Rephidim?
Mount Sinai? (Jebel Musa)
Red Sea
N
0
50 mi
0
50 km

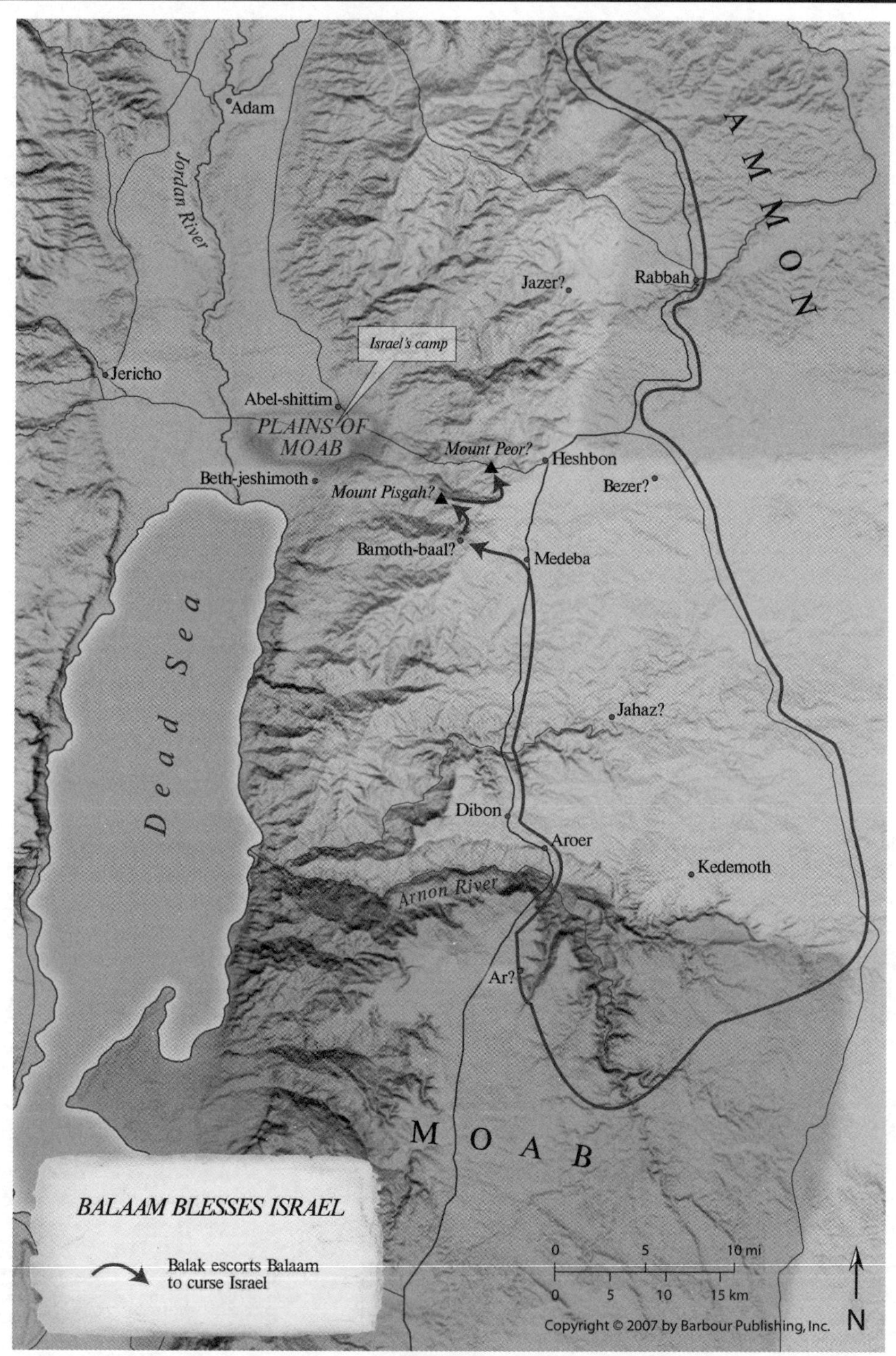
Adam
Jordan River
AMMON
Rabbah
Jazer?
Israel's camp
Jericho
Abel-shittim
PLAINS OF MOAB
Mount Peor?
Heshbon
Beth-jeshimoth
Mount Pisgah?
Bezer?
Bamoth-baal?
Medeba
Dead Sea
Jahaz?
Dibon
Aroer
Kedemoth
Arnon River
Ar?
MOAB
BALAAM BLESSES ISRAEL
Balak escorts Balaam to curse Israel
0 5 10 mi
0 5 10 15 km
N
Copyright © 2007 by Barbour Publishing, Inc.

Finally, Balaam describes the future destruction of those leaders who are present: Amalek, Kain, Asshur, and Eber (24:20–24).

25:1–18

THE THREAT FROM WITHIN

Setting Up the Section

After Balaam goes home, a new and more subtle assault on Israel spreads through the immense population. And, as we find out later (31:8, 16), Balaam is tied to it.

This strategy uses Moabite women—possible temple prostitutes—to seduce the men of Israel and lead the whole nation to ruin through idolatry. God hates sexual immorality, especially when it is tied to idol worship. Therefore, if Moab could not take down Israel through a curse from Balaam, it hoped to use the lust of the flesh.

While the Israelites are at Shittim, the region across the Jordan from Jericho, they are drawn into the worship of Moab's god, Baal of Peor, through Moabite women (25:1–3). Baal is a fertility god whose worship often involves sexual immorality. Israel would be drawn into sin with Baal more than once in its history.

The Lord commands Moses to slay all of the leaders of Israel so that He might turn His anger away from the entire people. Moses orders the judges to slay the men who have coupled themselves with Baal of Peor.

When one of the leaders of Israel blatantly brings a Midianite woman into the camp to have sexual relations with her, Phinehas, the grandson of Aaron through Eleazar, spears them both with one stroke. This stops the plague of apostasy and sexual immorality, which leads to the death of 24,000 Israelites–a number even larger than the 14,700 who died in Korah's rebellion (chapter 16). (There is some debate over whether 25:10 also refers to an actual plaque.)

Critical Observation

How is Phinehas' slaying of the offending couple meritorious? The high priest represents God before the people. That's why God compares Phinehas' zeal to His own. The execution of the sinners illustrates in a brutal way just how much God hates sin.

In addition, the high priest represents the people before God. As such, Phinehas restores the covenant between God and Israel, which had been broken by worshiping false gods. That's why he is awarded the covenant of peace.

As a result, in verses 10–16, God affirms Phinehas, offering him a perpetual priesthood. Phinehas shows that he shares in God's jealousy for uprightness among the people. Therefore, the Lord proclaims that Phinehas has His covenant of peace. This means that he possesses a perpetual priesthood, having made atonement for the sons of Israel.

The Israelite who committed the sexual sin was Zimri, a leader of the Simeonites. The Midianite woman who participated was Cozbi, a daughter of Zur, who was a leader in Midian. Because this woman was a Midianite, the Lord commands Moses to be in perpetual war with the Midianites, who are closely associated with the Moabites. Moses is to attack them because they had been a part of this plot at Peor, to lead the Israelites away from God into idolatry and sexual immorality.

Take It Home

Right after the magnificent prophecies of Balaam comes this depravity, reflecting a common pattern of spiritual lows after high points. Think of the golden calf right after Moses is given the Ten Commandments, and the ordination of Aaron followed by the disobedience of his sons. Perhaps we are most vulnerable after a mountaintop experience. Israel's journey stands as a warning to seek consistent obedience in our walk with God.

26:1–65

PREPARATIONS BEGIN

Preparations are now beginning for the Israelites to take the land. The first thing that must take place is a census, in which men age twenty and older within each tribe are counted.

The counting of the people provides several things for the Israelites:

- It confirms the reality of God's promise of the land in Genesis 12:7. God makes good on His promises.
- It focuses the people on the step before them. They are going to get land that will be big enough for their clan, but they are going to have to fight for it. Thus, numbering the men for war makes that point abundantly clear.
- It reaffirms God's faithfulness to Israel. Even though people from every tribe rebelled against God, He did not wipe out every tribe. Therefore, this walk down memory lane reminds the people that God is trustworthy, just, kind, and reliable.

In Numbers 26:1–2, the Lord tells Moses and Eleazar to take a census. So, in verses 3–51, we see the results. On the plains of Moab by the Jordan, across from Jericho, Moses and Eleazar carry out the command. The census is to be of men twenty years and older who are able to go to war. It is important that a breakdown of the nation, its family distribution, and its military size be established.

The total amount numbers the men at 601,730 and the Levites at 23,000. Now that the census has been taken, the land can be distributed, and the leadership knows the size of the army.

Summary

- The families of Reuben number 43,730 men.
- The families of Simeon number 22,200 men.
- The families of Gad number 40,500 men.
- The families Judah number 76,500 men.
- The families of Issachar number 64,300 men.
- The families of Zebulun number 60,500 men.
- The sons of Joseph—Manasseh and Ephraim
  Manasseh: The families of Manasseh number 52,700 men.
  Ephraim: The families of Ephraim number 32,500 men.
- The families of Benjamin number 45,600 men.
- The families of Dan number 64,400 men.
- The families of Asher number 53,400 men.
- The families of Naphtali number 45,400 men.

In verses 52–56, the Lord commands Moses that the land is to be divided by lot. The larger inheritance is to go to the larger families; the smaller inheritance is to go to the smaller families. Because God is in charge of the outcome of the lots, there will be no fighting over who gets what land.

Demystifying Numbers

Many understand these lots to resemble a specially-made set of dice. The people could not control the way these dice fell, so it seemed to the people that God had room to lead.

Some consider these lots to be the Urim and Thummim (Exodus 28:30). According to the Jewish historian, Josephus, the Urim consisted of two stones, each contained in a pouch in the breastplate worn by the high priest. These stones would be thrown, and God would move them into certain combinations to make His will known. When decisions were made in this way, no one could argue that the decision was the result of politics, nepotism, or favoritism.

In the first census, the Levites are numbered separately because they are not to serve in the army. For the census described in verses 57–62, the Levites are omitted from the main census because they are neither going to serve in the army nor receive any land. Thus, we see a post-census count of the Levites. The Levites numbered 23,000 from a month old and upward.

In verses 63–65, with the exception of Moses, Joshua, and Caleb, there is no one left from the first census. The punishment on the people for their disbelief when they first faced the border was not entering the land (chapters 13–14). That original generation has died in the journey through the wilderness.

Compare the censuses of Numbers			
Tribe	**Second Census**	**First Census**	**Change**
Reuben	43,730	46,500	- 2,770
Simeon	22,200	59,300	-37,100 •
Gad	40,500	45,650	- 5,150
Judah	76,500	74,600	+ 1,900
Issachar	64,300	54,400	+ 9,900
Zebulun	60,500	57,400	+ 3,100
Ephraim	32,500	40,500	- 8,000
Manasseh	52,700	32,200	+20,500
Benjamin	45,600	35,400	+10,200
Dan	64,400	62,700	+ 1,700
Asher	53,400	41,500	+11,900
Naphtali	45,400	53,400	- 8,000
• Simeon's decimated population number may be attributable to its support for Dathan and Abiram, and to the recent catastrophic "affair of Peor," as Zimri (25:14) was a leader of a Simeonite family.			

27:1–23

RESOLVING THE ISSUES

The first issue is one of inheritance among the daughters of Zelophehad (27:11). These five women approach the Tent of Meeting to implore Moses, an unprecedented act of courage and conviction.

Zelophehad had died without sons. Therefore, when the land distribution plan was set, his daughters would be left without land. Facing Moses, they want to know if it is fair for them to not have any land because they have no brothers. They also are concerned about the preservation of their father's name. Zelophehad apparently was one of the followers of the skeptical spies; therefore he died in the wilderness (14:10–12; 27:5).

Moses seeks the Lord (27:5–8), who commands him to allow the daughters to receive their father's inheritance. Then God prescribes a set of rules for the succession of the inheritance when other difficult cases arise: If a man dies without any sons, his inheritance is to be transferred to his daughter. If he has no daughter, then the inheritance goes to his brothers. If he has no brothers, the inheritance goes to his father's brothers. If his father has no brothers, the inheritance goes to his nearest relative in his own family to posses it. This ensures that everyone will get the land that was promised to Abraham.

In the second half of chapter 27, the Lord commands Moses to go up to the mountain of Abarim to see the land which He is giving to the nation of Israel (27:12–23). After

Moses views his final destination, he will die.

At Moses' request, God appoints Joshua as Moses' successor. Before all the people, Moses brings Joshua before Eleazar, the high priest, and transfers some of his authority to Joshua.

Joshua is to have the same leadership characteristics as Moses: faith in God, a heart of intercession for the people, strength to lead into battle, love for the children of God, and no fear to carry out God's plans for the nation.

28:1–29:40

PATTERNS FOR WORSHIP

The Lord prescribes specific daily and yearly observances for the sons of Israel to keep when they enter into the land. The entire calendar for the nation is to be governed by worship.

The Lord commands Moses to be careful to present the various offerings at their appointed times, not as rote actions, but as prayers of dependence.

The Daily Offering (28:1–8): Two spotless male lambs are to be offered each day as burnt offerings to the Lord. One is to be offered in the morning and the other at twilight, with a grain offering and a drink offering.

The Sabbath Offering (28:9–10): In addition to the daily offering, two one-year-old male lambs without defect are to be offered to the Lord on the Sabbath. They are to be accompanied with a grain offering and a drink offering.

The New Moon (28:11–15): In addition to the daily offering, the nation is to offer two bulls, one ram, seven one-year-old male lambs without defect, and a male goat. These are for a sin offering, along with appropriate grain offerings and a drink offering at the beginning of each month.

The Passover (28:16–25): The Passover is to be celebrated on the fourteenth day of the first month. This is in association with the Feast of Unleavened Bread (Leviticus 23:4–8), which begins the next day and runs for the next seven days. On Passover, Israel is to rest and to present an offering of two bulls, one ram, and seven male, one-year-old lambs without defect along with their grain offering, and a male goat for a sin offering to make atonement for them in addition to the offerings above.

The Feast of Weeks (28:26–31): Fifty days after the Feast of Unleavened Bread, on the day of Firstfruits, the sons of Israel are to rest. In addition, they are to offer two young bulls, one ram, and seven one-year-old male lambs with their grain offerings and drink offerings, as well as one male goat to make atonement. This is to be done in addition to the offerings mentioned above.

The First Day of the Seventh Month (29:1–6): On this day, they are to rest as well as offer one bull, one ram, seven one-year-old male lambs without defect, the appropriate grain offerings, and one male goat as atonement for them. This is to be offered in addition to the other offerings and drink offerings.

The Day of Atonement (29:7–11): On the tenth day of the seventh month, they are to rest and offer one bull, a ram, seven one-year-old male lambs without defect, appropriate grain offerings, and a male goat for atonement, in addition to the other offerings and drink offerings.

The Feast of Tabernacles (29:12–38): This feast runs the fifteenth to the twenty-first of the seventh month. On the first day, they are to rest and offer thirteen bulls, two rams, fourteen one-year-old male lambs without defect, the appropriate grain offerings, and a male goat as atonement. These sacrifices are to be repeated on the second through seventh days, minus one bull each day.

The Eighth Day (29:35–8): On this day, they are to rest and offer one bull, one ram, seven one-year-old male lambs without defect, the appropriate grain offerings, and one male goat for a sin offering in addition to the regular offerings.

There is not a season, month, or week that goes by that does not have a time of worship associated with it. These offerings of worship are to be seen as prayers—prayers of dependence, repentance, salvation, and sanctification.

Take It Home

There are a few things that are important to observe in all of these sacrifices:

- Worship is to be seen as a part of daily life. There is not a moment or an experience that is to be divorced from worship.
- Excellence must be part of worship because God is worthy of it. All of these sacrifices and offerings are to be done with excellence. Only the best is to be given to God.
- God is pleased and honored with our obedience. When the children of Israel offer their sacrifice to God, it is a pleasing aroma to God. God loves obedience.
- God truly does pardon our iniquities. God put this system in place to provide a means for people to have their sins covered. This entire system anticipates the coming of the perfect sacrifice, Jesus Christ, who will take away the sins of the world (John 1:29).
- God planned for days of rest, which allow His children to have the rest they need. Every seventh day they rest. God provides for our needs because He loves us.

30:1–16

VOWS

Setting Up the Section

Vows are commitments made to God that are over and above what is required by the law. Moses introduces the topic in 30:1–2, by reminding the leaders of Israel that vows obligate us to follow through

If a young woman makes a vow to the Lord while she is still at home under her father's authority, her father can undo the vow and release the girl from all responsibility. Girls only are mentioned in verses 3–5, but many theologians believe that all minors who reside under the parental roof are included.

If a woman who has taken a vow to the Lord marries, or binds herself with any form of obligation, there is still a way out. She is bound by the vow unless her husband hears of it and forbids it on the day that he learns of it. If this happens, the Lord will release her.

On the other hand, in verses 9–12, we learn that if a widow or divorced woman makes a vow to the Lord, she is bound by it. The only way she can get out of it is if she takes it in her husband's house, and he hears of it and forbids it on the day that he learns of it.

A husband may confirm or annul an oath of his wife, according to verses 13–15. If he does not annul the oath upon hearing it, the vow remains binding. If he does annul the vow some time after he has heard of it, he will be held responsible. In other words, he must not wait to annul it or he will be guilty before the Lord for breaking the vow.

Take It Home

The seriousness with which an oath is to be taken should motivate us to take a serious look at all our speech. The intent of this law is to teach us to watch what we say as unto the Lord. Whenever one considers oaths, pledges, and vows, he or she should not forget the words of Jesus on this issue, found in Matthew 5:33–37.

31:1–54

GOD VINDICATED

Setting Up the Section

This chapter is a call to war. The Israelites are to go to war with the Midianites. The Midianites were the principle instigators of the wicked scheme of seduction in Numbers 25, in which they planned to entrap the Israelites into the double crime of idolatry and licentiousness. The Lord tells Moses that he is to treat the Midianites as enemies and to kill them. Now is the time for their destruction.

The Lord tells Moses exactly what to do in 31:1–16. Moses speaks the command of God to the people, and says prepare for war. They gather twelve thousand men (one thousand from each tribe), as well as Phinehas, the son of Eleazar, the priest with the holy vessels and trumpets, to fight against the Midianites. This war is to be fought in the manner that God prescribes because the offense was not against Israel but against God.

When the sons of Israel go to war against the Midianites, they gain an incredible victory (31:7–12). They

- kill every Midianite male;
- kill the five kings of Midian;
- kill Balaam, the son of Beor (from chapter 25);
- capture the women and children;
- plunder Midianite livestock;
- burn Midianite cities;
- take all the spoil and prey, which they present to Moses, Eleazar, and the entire Israelite camp at the plains of Moab.

In 31:13–24, the army returns to the sons of Israel; Moses is angry that they have returned with Midianite women. Earlier, the Midianite women had brought a plague upon Israel by leading the people into idolatry. Moses commands that all of the male children be killed, that only the virgin girls be allowed to live, and that the army purify itself (for contact with the dead) and wait seven days before they reenter the camp.

The judgment of God is very thorough. He does not take sin lightly, and the sin that drives the heart of this people brings about certain death to their city.

The Lord commands Moses, Eleazar, and the leaders of the tribes to divide the booty between the warriors and the congregation in verses 25–47. Moses also must issue a tax—one out of every five hundred captured persons and animals goes to the Lord. Half of the booty from the warriors goes to Eleazar, the high priest, and one out of fifty from the congregation going to the Levites. The priests and the Levites are not to go to war, and the only way that they will ever get any spoils is from taxation.

Booty	Total Amount	Half to Soldiers	Tithed to God	Half to Congregation	Tithed to Levites
Sheep	675,000	337,500	675	337,500	6,750
Cattle	72,000	36,000	72	36,000	720
Donkeys	61,000	30,500	61	30,500	610
People	32,000	16,000	32	16,000	320

Not one of the sons of Israel is found to be missing in action. As a result, in verses 48–54, the warriors provide a memorial offering of thanksgiving (6,700 ounces of gold) to the Lord. They want to celebrate God's goodness, as well as make atonement for all that they did in going to war.

Take It Home

When the Midianites sought to remove the blessing of the Lord from Israel, they joined those who cursed Israel and were, thus, cursed themselves. This chapter shows with great clarity the incredible seriousness with which God takes His people, His plan, and those who would try to stop Him. This should drive us to understand the importance of pursuing holiness, as well as the great value of taking God, His mission, and His plan seriously.

32:1–42

AN INTERESTING TWIST

As the entire nation looks across the river to the promised land (32:1–5), there are two tribes, Reuben and Gad, who see that the land in the Transjordan region will be suitable for their numerous livestock. They request that they be allowed to settle in this region rather than going across the Jordan.

In verses 6–15, Moses severely rejects Reuben and Gad's proposal. He perceives it to be a sin like that of their fathers, who did not want to enter the promised land (chapters 13–14). He sees it as

- selfishness;
- discouragement to others;
- failure to learn from the sins of their forefathers;
- failure to walk in the path of obedience;
- failure to live for the will of the Lord.

The leaders of Gad and Reuben modify their request in 32:16–19. Even though they would like for their inheritance to be in the Transjordan, they will go and fight with the rest of the Israelites to help them acquire their inheritance. All they want is to be able to live in this spot after the land has been taken. Moses agrees to let them settle in the Transjordan if they will keep their word and go to war (32:20–27). If they do not fight, then they will be sinning against the Lord.

In verses 28–30, Moses tells Eleazar, Joshua, and the heads of the fathers' households that the sons of Gad and Reuben say they will fight with the sons of Israel in the promised land if they can be given the land of Gilead. Moses says that if they do not fight, they will be apportioned a possession in Canaan, and will have to accept what they are given. Moses puts in place a contingency for their disobedience, just in case they get too comfortable where they are.

The sons of Gad and Reuben agree to the plan (32:31–38). Moses gives to the sons of Gad, Reuben, *and* the half-tribe of Manasseh the kingdoms of Sihon, king of the Amorites, and Og, the king of Bashan, with all of its cities and territories. The first land is distributed to these families.

The sons of Machir, the son of Manasseh, take Gilead from the Amorites, and Moses gives the land to them. More land is being taken and these tribes are getting settled in their new home. The problem has been averted, obedience to God's plan is still going to be carried out, and the nation is about to experience what God promised to Abraham many years ago.

33:1–56

A REVIEW OF GOD'S FAITHFULNESS

Before the Israelites take the promised land, Moses reviews the hand of God in leading the children of Israel out of Egypt to Canaan.

In the first four chapters of Numbers, we see how many of the generation that is entering the promised land were babies when the Lord delivered the Israelites from Egypt. They would not have remembered the great miracle of the Lord delivering them from their bondage, the most powerful event in the entire forty-year period. (Time and time again God refers to Himself as "I am the God who delivered you out of Egypt." One of the main ways God wants to be defined is as the God *who delivers.*)

Perhaps that's why God commands Moses to make this record, starting in 33:1–4. This new generation of followers needs to be reminded that God delivered them from Egypt and will deliver them from the enemies in the promised land. Their God is dependable.

The beginning of the journey, recorded in verses 5–15, following their deliverance from Egypt, is a time of intense testing.

As they travel from the Sinai Wilderness to Kadesh (33:16–36), the people are reminded of their grumbling against Moses and his leadership. It is here where the discontent of the people's heart is put on display—and as a result they reject God's will for entering the land and suffer a great consequence for their rebellion. The children entering the land need to be reminded of this colossal failure so that they will not make the same mistake as their parents.

Then, in the journey from Kadesh to Moab, even the leaders of Israel sin and suffer for their sin. Miriam, Aaron, and Moses all sin and face grave consequences in verses 37–49. None of them are allowed to enter into the promised land. Here we see that no one is exempt from following God in the manner and fashion that God determines.

Critical Observation

It would be horrible for the next generation to enter the promised land ignorant of their history and of the mistakes made before them. The power of God's hand of deliverance, the wildness of God's grace and mercy, the serious consequences of sin, and the extreme importance of obedience to God all must be embraced by the next generation.

The Lord speaks to Moses to tell the people to take the land (33:50–56). As they take the land they must drive the inhabitants out of the land and destroy all their false worship. If they do not do this, the current inhabitants will be a snare to the Israelites. In other words, the people who are in the land will draw them away from God.

After just receiving the history of their people, they must not take lightly this command found in verses 50–56. God calls His people to be separated from the world in order to be a light to the world about His great plan of salvation. Thus, the Israelites must be called out from these people, and they must ensure that the idolatry is cleared completely from the land. God makes it clear that He will do to Israel what He plans on doing to the idolaters if they do not drive them from the land. The consequences will be great if they fail to take God seriously.

When they take possession of the land, they must do it by lot, assigning to each tribe their portion as the Lord delineates. God is going to give each tribe what He determines they need. Even though the land is God's gift to the people, they still need to distribute the land according to lots so that there is impartial distribution. No doubt high levels of emotion would surface if they all have to pick their own land. God is going to give the land to the nation exactly in a manner that He wants so that all will be able to worship God for what He has provided.

Take It Home

Just as it is important that the next generation of Israelites not lose sight of the mighty hand of God in delivering them through such a journey, we, too, must remember how God has worked in our lives. When the work of God in the past is forgotten, then the character of God is overlooked in the present. The fallout of this is people who do not trust in God, live for God, and depend on God in the future.

34:1–29

DISTRIBUTION OF THE LAND

Throughout Numbers, God has reiterated in multiple ways His promise that the people would reach Canaan (See 13:2; 14:8, 16, 23, 30; 15:2, 18; 27:12; 32:7, 9, 11). Now, the children of Israel are about to hear what portions of the land will be assigned to each tribe. This continues to affirm the certainty of this promise. God will distribute the land before they take it, because it is a sure thing that they will have the land.

The Israelites never occupy the entire land—they do not drive out all the inhabitants. One of the main enemies that emerges after Israel takes the land is the Philistines. They have strongholds in the western frontiers. This keeps the nation from enjoying all that God has provided for them.

The two and a half tribes of Gad, Reuben, and Manasseh would not be included in the apportionment of the land, since they already have their portion in the Transjordan (34:13–29). For the rest of the tribes, who divides the land? The job is given to Eleazer the priest, Joshua the son of Nun, and a chosen leader from each of the remaining nine and a half tribes.

Demystifying Numbers

Looking at the chosen leaders' names, it is important to read them with a method called *Theophoric naming.* Theophoric naming is a method of naming someone after God. In this list, the names given carry the idea of the greatness of God. Here's an example:

- Shemuel (heart of God)
- Hanniel (grace of God)
- Elidad (God loves)
- Kemuel (God establishes)
- Elizaphan (God protects)
- Paltiel (deliverance is God)
- Pedahel (God ransoms)

Naming people in this fashion was a way of declaring the greatness of God.

35:1–34

SPECIAL LAND PROVISIONS

The Levites are to be given a portion of each tribe's inheritance (35:1–8). This is because the Levites are to devote their lives to the worship of God. The Levites are not to be given just one specific area of land; instead, they are allocated forty-eight towns with pastureland around them. The surrounding land extends around the city 500 yards (1,000 cubits) and extends 1,000 yards (2,000 cubits) around the city walls.

Six of the forty-eight Levites' towns are to be set apart as cities of refuge, to which a person who has killed someone may go for safety (35:9–34). The Lord is fully aware that there will be conflict between people. Thus, if someone kills another accidentally, he may flee to this place of refuge for protection until he can stand trial for his action.

To ensure that everyone understands what these cities are for, God explains in verses 16–21. A person who commits deliberate murder—if he strikes someone with an iron object, a stone, a wooden object, or his hand, by lying in wait or in enmity—is not allowed a place of refuge, but instead, the blood avenger is to put the murderer to death.

If a person commits involuntary manslaughter, if he pushes his victim suddenly without enmity, throws something at him without lying in wait, or strikes him with any deadly object without being his enemy or seeking his injury, then that person is allowed to have protection until a trial can be given.

Here is the way it works: If someone commits involuntary manslaughter, the congregation sends him to the city of refuge, where he is to stay until the death of the high priest. The victim's family is not allowed to hurt the person. If he leaves the city of refuge before the death of the high priest, the blood avenger is allowed to take the life of the one who committed the act.

Critical Observation

In Summary:

- First, if anyone is accused of a murder, two witnesses are to testify concerning the crime—no one is to be put to death on the basis of one witness.
- Second, the accused person is to surrender his life if he is convicted of murder.
- Third, the murdered person's kinsman is to be the avenger of the wrong, and thus they must carry out the execution.
- Fourth, there is no other penalty than the blood of another. Since murder is an attack on the very life that God gives, it is important that, if life is going to be held in regard, the person who takes the life must forfeit his life.

God takes life seriously. Therefore, the people must understand how to hold life in the same high esteem while allowing for accidents to occur.

36:1–13

FUTURE OWNERSHIP OF THE LAND

In Numbers 27:1–11, there is land that is to be distributed to the daughters of Zelophehad, who had died without sons. The daughters want to know if they will get land since there are no men left in their family. God says they will. Now the question arises, what happens if these girls marry? Do they lose their land?

This brought up a question about marriage and land being inherited by other families. Could one family begin to marry women in another family, and thus begin to amass a giant amount of land? It would be a very natural way of thinking for individuals to become self-centered and try to acquire wealth and take from others, to their own detriment.

God speaks to this issue to ensure that there will be fairness. People must marry within their own tribe so that the land will remain distributed in the same fashion as it was first given. No inheritance is to pass from tribe to tribe. Land ownership is something that is very important to the nation. God does not want one family member to lose out on the inheritance, and He protects each family to ensure that each generation will have what their forefathers originally received.

This also highlights the significance of the family. God wants to ensure that each generation will be able to survive and not lose out due to land issues. It is important to note how Numbers ends. The daughters of Zelophehad do marry within their tribe: They obey the Word of the Lord. One of the great themes of the book of Numbers is the importance of obedience. God must be taken seriously, and obedience to Him must be more than a goal; it must be a lifestyle.

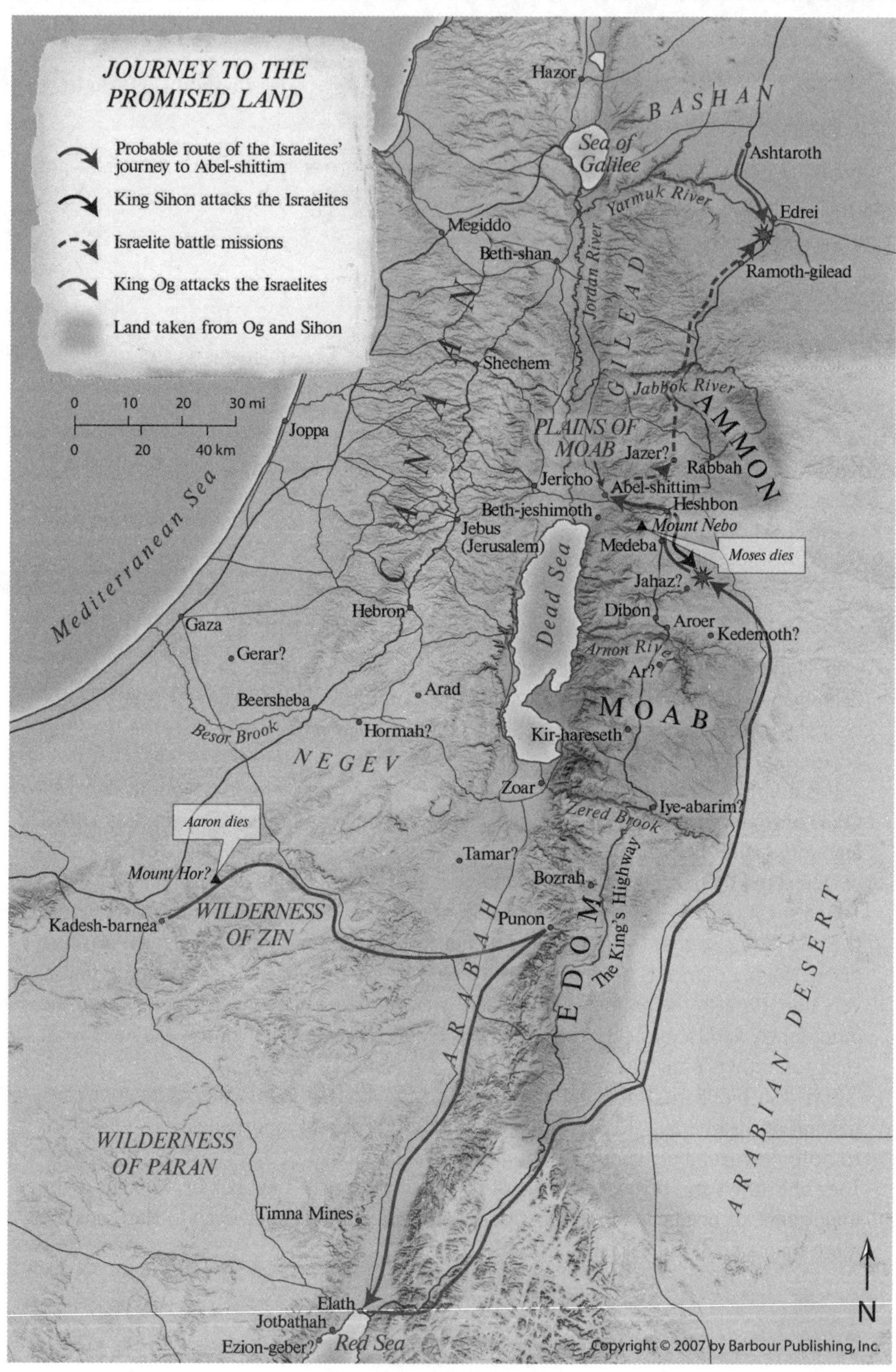
JOURNEY TO THE PROMISED LAND
Probable route of the Israelites' journey to Abel-shittim
King Sihon attacks the Israelites
Israelite battle missions
King Og attacks the Israelites
Land taken from Og and Sihon
0 10 20 30 mi
0 20 40 km
Mediterranean Sea
Hazor
BASHAN
Sea of Galilee
Ashtaroth
Yarmuk River
Edrei
Megiddo
Beth-shan
Jordan River
GILEAD
Ramoth-gilead
CANAAN
Shechem
Jabbok River
AMMON
Joppa
PLAINS OF MOAB
Jazer?
Rabbah
Jericho
Abel-shittim
Heshbon
Beth-jeshimoth
Mount Nebo
Jebus (Jerusalem)
Medeba
Moses dies
Dead Sea
Jahaz?
Dibon
Aroer
Kedemoth?
Hebron
Gaza
Gerar?
Arnon River
Ar?
Arad
Beersheba
MOAB
Besor Brook
Hormah?
Kir-hareseth
NEGEV
Zoar
Iye-abarim?
Zered Brook
Aaron dies
Tamar?
Mount Hor?
Bozrah
The King's Highway
WILDERNESS OF ZIN
Kadesh-barnea
Punon
ARABAH
EDOM
ARABIAN DESERT
WILDERNESS OF PARAN
Timna Mines
Elath
Jotbathah
Ezion-geber?
Red Sea
N

DEUTERONOMY

INTRODUCTION TO DEUTERONOMY

Deuteronomy might be called the Romans of the Old Testament. It is chock-full of the great themes of scripture. It is a wonderfully down-to-earth and practical book that provides counsel about both the large and small issues and questions of life. It addresses itself both to private matters such as the inner conflicts of the believing soul, the way of faith under trial, marriage and family, and to such public and corporate issues such as worship and the proper stewardship of the environment.

AUTHOR

Moses is clearly identified as the author of Deuteronomy in verse 1. Moses' authorship is claimed throughout Deuteronomy (1:5, 9; 5:1; 27:8; 29:2; 31:1, 30) as well as in other Old Testament books (1 Kings 2:3; 8:53; 2 Kings 14:6; 18:6, 12). Jesus also identified Moses as the author of Deuteronomy (Matthew 19:7–8; Mark 10:3–5; John 5:46–47), as did Peter (Acts 3:22), Stephen (Acts 7:37–38), and Paul (Romans 10:19; 1 Corinthians 9:9).

The final chapter, recording Moses' death and burial (34:1–12), was most likely added by another writer after Moses' death.

PURPOSE

The title *Deuteronomy* means "second law." In this book, Moses reiterates and expands on the laws God has already given Israel and calls them to renew their covenant with God by pledging their obedience.

OCCASION

The book of Deuteronomy records Moses' last words to the people of Israel as they are poised to enter the promised land after forty years of wandering in the wilderness. Moses reminds the people of all that the Lord has done for them to this point and calls them to a life of faithful obedience in the land they are about to receive.

STRUCTURE

At the time that Deuteronomy was written (around 1400 BC), "suzerainty treaties"—treaties of sovereignty of a stronger king over a weaker one—were common. Deuteronomy appears to be an almost perfect example of the ancient Middle Eastern treaty, a literary form that would have been easily appreciated and understood in Moses' day:

- Opening preamble (paralleled in 1:1–5)
- Historical introduction (1:6–4:49)
- The particular stipulations of the treaty (chapters 5–26)
- What blessings and curses would result from keeping or breaking the treaty (chapters 27–28; 32–33)
- Some form of oath taking (chapters 29–30)
- Provisions for the perpetuation of the covenant after the death of the particular kings who signed it (chapter 31)

OUTLINE

FAITH BEFORE WORKS	**1:1–46**
Preamble	1:1–5
God's Faithfulness Comes First	1:6–18
The Necessity of Faith	1:19–46
FROM WANDERING TO CONQUEST	**2:1–37**
Mercy over All His Works	2:1–23
Hard Sayings	2:24–37
MOSES' LAST BATTLE	**3:1–29**
Holy War	3:1–11
Division of the Land	3:12–23
Unanswered Prayer	3:24–29
LAWS AND ORDERS	**4:1–49**
The Grace of Law	4:1–14
Keep Yourselves from Idols	4:15–31
Our History	4:32–40
Some Unfinished Business	4:41–49
LOVE, FEAR, AND OBEDIENCE	**5:1–33**
The Ten Commandments	5:1–22
How Blessed Are They Who Fear the Lord	5:23–33
GOD-FEARING CHILDREN	**6:1–25**
Talk the Talk	6:1–9
Walk the Walk	6:10–25
GIFTS AND REWARDS	**7:1–26**
God's Electing Grace	7:1–11
The Gospel of Prosperity	7:12–26
FORGET NOT ALL HIS BENEFITS	**8:1–20**
Remember What God Has Done	8:1–5
Give God Credit	8:6–14
Keep Remembering	8:15–18
Follow God's Way	8:19–20

LIVING BEFORE THE HOLY GOD 25:1–19

Disputes 25:1–3
Working Oxen 25:4
Levirate Marriage 25:5–10
How Not to Stop a Fight 25:11–12
Honest Business Dealings 25:13–16
The Destruction of the Amalekites 25:17–19

PRESENTATIONS 26:1–19

Firstfruits 26:1–11
The Presentation of the Tithe 26:12–15
The Declaration of Intent 26:16–19

BLESSINGS AND CURSES, PART 1 27:1–26

The Law Displayed and an Altar Built 27:1–10
The Announcement of the Curses 27:11–26

BLESSINGS AND CURSES, PART 2 28:1–68

The Blessings 28:1–14
The Curses 28:15–68

AN APPEAL TO OBEY 29:1–29

Review of the Lord's Faithfulness and Israel's Disobedience 29:1–8
The Covenant 29:9–15
The Curses for Disobedience 29:16–29

BLESSINGS FOR OBEDIENCE 30:1–20

Restoration 30:1–10
Choose Life 30:11–14
The Call to Obey 30:15–20

TRANSITIONS 31:1–29

The Transition from Moses to Joshua 31:1–8
The Public Reading of the Law of God 31:9–13
The Commissioning of Joshua 31:14–23
The Placement of the Law as a Witness 31:24–29

THE SONG OF MOSES — 31:30–32:52

Moses Begins	31:30
The Themes	32:1–3
A Faithful God and a Foolish People	32:4–9
The Goodness of God	32:10–14
From Prosperity to Idolatry	32:15–18
Judgment	32:19–27
Lack of Discernment	32:28–33
God's Justice and Mercy in Judgment	32:34–43
Moses' Final Charge	32:44–52

THE BLESSING OF MOSES ON THE TRIBES — 33:1–29

The Man of God	33:1
All Blessing Flows from Praise	33:2–5
The Blessing of the Tribes	33:6–25
Final Words of Praise	33:26–29

THE DEATH OF MOSES — 34:1–12

A Glimpse of the Promised Land	34:1–4
The Death of Moses	34:5–9
The Epitaph of Moses	34:10–12

DEUTERONOMY 1:1–46

FAITH BEFORE WORKS

Setting Up the Section

When Deuteronomy commences, Israel as a nation is poised on the eastern bank of the Jordan River opposite Jericho. Two months later, she will cross the river, on dry land, into the promised land for the first time. It is at this juncture in her history that God initiates a renewal of the covenant He had established with the Israelites when they were camped at Sinai (Exodus 19–24). Chapter 1 records the preamble to this renewal and the beginning of a lengthy review of God's dealings with Israel. The historical prologue, which begins here in chapter 1, serves to provide a rationale for obedience to the commandments which occupy the largest part of the book.

1:1–5

PREAMBLE

Deuteronomy appears to be an almost perfect example of the ancient Middle Eastern treaty form. It begins, as did the treaties of that time, with a preamble (1:1–5), giving the geographical and historical setting.

Critical Observation

Archaeological discoveries of international treaties have shed new light on the literary structure of the book of Deuteronomy. Ancient Middle Eastern treaties had a standard form:

- Opening preamble (paralleled in 1:1–5)
- Historical introduction (1:6–4:49)
- Particular stipulations of the treaty (chapters 5–26)
- What blessings and curses would result from keeping or breaking the treaty (chapters 27–28; 32–33)
- Some form of oath (chapters 29–30)
- Provisions for the perpetuation of the covenant after the death of the particular kings who signed it (chapter 31)

1:6–18

GOD'S FAITHFULNESS COMES FIRST

Moses begins by reminding Israel that their favored status as God's children and their wonderful prospects as a people have nothing to do with them or anything they have done. They can take no credit for the land and prosperity that is soon to be theirs—or for the spiritual life and bounty of which the promised land is a sign and seal. The promise being fulfilled was made generations before to their forefather, Abraham. God is faithful to His promises.

The Lord had promised Abraham that his descendants would be as numerous as the stars in the sky (Genesis 15:5; 22:17; 26:4). Moses observes that this promise has come true (Deuteronomy 1:10) and with it the conclusion that leading the people is more work than one man can do (1:9–12). Moses reminds the people that they approved the appointment of leaders and agreed to be subject to their authority (1:13–18). Chapters 16–18 will further refine the system of leadership in Israel.

1:19–46

THE NECESSITY OF FAITH

The account of Israel's cowardly refusal to enter the land that God had promised is an instructive beginning to the book of Deuteronomy, because it shows that God's fundamental requirement is not obedience to the law, but faith.

The event that Moses recounts had happened thirty-eight years earlier at Kadesh Barnea (1:19). As Moses recollects in verse 21, the Lord has already given them the land, as it were, and all they have to do is walk in and take possession. But they are unnerved by the spies' reports of fortified cities and warlike people (1:22–28). The Lord has already proved His might and His faithfulness to His people by bringing them out of Egypt and providing their food and water in the wilderness (1:29–33). Now they stand poised to enter the promised land, but they do not do so. Verse 32 indicates it's a faith issue: "You did not believe the LORD your God" (ESV).

Demystifying Deuteronomy

Most ancient Middle Eastern treaties were "suzerainty treaties," or treaties of sovereignty of a stronger king over a weaker one. The Lord had given Moses this covenantal revelation in the form drawn from the custom of ancient Middle Eastern diplomacy. It provides a wonderful example of God's condescension, of His employing a literary form that would have been easily appreciated and understood in Moses' day. He wanted to be understood and wanted His covenant to be kept.

When the people realize that as a result of their lack of faith they will never be permitted to enter Canaan (1:34–40), they see the error of their ways and march across the border (1:41–43). The Lord does not go with them, and they are soundly thrashed by Canaanite armies and chased back into the wilderness (1:44). They gather in the camp and weep before the Lord, but He will not relent (1:45–46).

It is clear enough that what lies behind the Lord's unwillingness to listen to Israel's cries is His knowledge that their hearts are far from Him. They are bitterly sorry for the consequences of their stupidity, but they still have neither true faith in the Lord nor true reverence for Him. Numbers 14:24, the original account of this episode, reveals that the Lord does not punish Caleb the same way, because Caleb has a different spirit. It is not the disobedience itself that is so important; God is always forgiving the disobedience of His people. The problem is the people do not obey God, because they neither trust His Word nor love Him for His goodness to them.

Take It Home

First things first: faith then obedience. First the glad acceptance of God's gracious salvation; then a life lived in demonstration of undying gratitude to God. Deuteronomy spends most of its time teaching us how to live so as to demonstrate our love and gratitude to God—how God would have us think and speak and act. But it begins by reminding us that the only obedience that pleases God is that which flows from the love and gratitude of a person who knows full well that he or she has been saved by the grace and mercy and goodness and power of God alone. To a very great degree, what kind of Christian you are will be determined by just how fully you appreciate the grace of God.

DEUTERONOMY 2:1–37

FROM WANDERING TO CONQUEST

Setting Up the Section

Moses, at the end of the forty years of desert wanderings, is recalling for the people their history. Chapter 1 ends with the Lord's decree that the generation who left Egypt will not enter the promised land of Canaan. Chapter 2 begins the saga of Israel's forty-year sojourn in the wilderness.

2:1–23

MERCY OVER ALL HIS WORKS

Poised on the brink of the promised land, the Israelites now have to turn around and retrace their steps toward the Red Sea (2:1). Hidden in this narrative of Israel's travels through the wilderness from Kadesh Barnea to the Arnon Gorge is a lovely and profoundly important truth: The Lord shows kindness to the large part of humanity that lies beyond the boundaries of the church and His kingdom.

Verses 1–8 show the Lord's concern for the people living in Seir. The Lord gives careful instructions to Israel that she is not to engage them in battle, for God has no intention of letting Israel take the land from them (2:5). What is more, all the food and water they consume while passing through is to be paid for in cash, which they could easily afford because God has provided; they lack nothing (2:6).

Similar instructions about how to treat the Moabites (Deuteronomy 2:9, 17–19) bracket the three short verses relating the passage of thirty-eight years and the death of an entire generation of fighting men (2:14–16). Historical asides about the previous inhabitants of the land (2:10–12, 20–23) remind the readers that in these cases, as in the case of Israel's conquest of Canaan, it is the Lord who drives out the nations (2:21–22) and who gives ownership of the land (2:7, 9, 12, 19).

Critical Observation

The mercy of God toward all people, not just believers, often goes by the name of "common grace," to distinguish it from particular and saving grace.

2:24–37

HARD SAYINGS

Verse 24 signals a change in the way God commands Israel to deal with other nations. They *will* engage in battle, but according to God's plan (2:24–25). The Lord is telling them what will occur. Peace can still be genuinely offered (2:26–29).

Deuteronomy 2:30–37 not only recounts the first victory recorded in the book, but also introduces some hard sayings. Verse 30 states that God hardens Sihon's heart so that he will not allow Israel to pass through his territory peacefully, because God had determined to give Sihon and his kingdom into Israel's hand. This is the only explanation given of this statement.

Critical Observation

The word translated *destroyed* in verse 34 is the Hebrew term which means "to dedicate or devote something to God." Sometimes it has a positive sense—such as when objects are devoted for use in the temple and its worship—but more often it refers to the compulsory devotion of something which impedes or hinders God's work. In that case, the object is devoted to utter destruction. That is the idea here.

It is clear that it is the Lord who wins the battle for Israel (2:31–33, 36). Verses 34–37 are the account of the utter annihilation which Israel bestowed upon Sihon's kingdom. No one is left; not men, not women, not even children. That God would use these means is a tough truth to understand.

Demystifying Deuteronomy

Why would a holy God condone such annihilation? Such destruction is a judgment on the wickedness of the people destroyed (see 9:4). Keep in mind that God had already given the nations ample time to repent. In fact, He had delayed Israel's conquest for some four hundred years for this reason (Genesis 15:16). In the end, however, Israel was not spiritually strong enough to withstand the influence of pagan nations, and judgment fell (see Deuteronomy 20:17–18).

Take It Home

The Lord tests our faith intellectually by forcing us to reckon with realities we find difficult to accept. When faced with such hard sayings, we either subject His Word to our own thinking and pass judgment on God and His ways, or we acknowledge that, though we cannot comprehend it, if God has said it, it must be true and right.

The hard sayings here in Deuteronomy 2 are good examples. Will we believe that God is infinitely pure, unstained by sin in any way? Or will we reason that God's sovereign disposal of even the hearts and minds of humanity, as here He hardens Sihon's heart, must impeach the divine purity and make God a partner in sin?

Will we take God at His word? That is the test such a hard saying puts to our faith. We must live each day in the certainty that everything we read in scripture is absolutely true and to be practiced and trusted in, even though much of it is beyond our full comprehension.

DEUTERONOMY 3:1–29

MOSES' LAST BATTLE

Setting Up the Section

Chapter 3 continues the historical prologue that precedes the covenant laws and decrees that make up the bulk of Deuteronomy. The Israelites' desert wanderings have come to an end, and they are engaged in the business of conquering and claiming the land.

3:1–11

HOLY WAR

It is essential for a true estimation and appreciation of this history to realize that the destruction of Bashan (3:1–11) is, in fact, God's judgment and God's doing. Israel is His instrument. This point is made in verse 2, where it is clear that, in the campaign against Og, Moses and Israel are acting on orders given them by God. It isn't Moses' idea to destroy the women and children; it is a direct order from the Lord Himself.

Demystifying Deuteronomy

The conquest of Bashan took the Israelites off their route somewhat, as they went north of the point where they would cross the Jordan into Canaan. From a military point of view, the conquest of Bashan was necessary to protect Israel's right flank as she crossed the river for her main assault on the cities of Canaan. History records that several other armies conquering Palestine from the same direction proceeded on the same military principle.

In respect to both the specific instructions Moses is given and to the general instructions God gave Israel for waging her wars, Israel does precisely as she is told by the Lord God when she exterminates the population of Bashan. Therefore, whatever we may at first think about what Israel does here, we are forced to reckon with the fact that it is done under God's instruction.

The word rendered "destroyed" in verse 6 is in fact a technical term and means, more precisely, "devoted"—separated for a holy use. It is true that these people were devoted to destruction, but they were destroyed precisely to further the interests of the kingdom of God. They are destroyed because they stand in the way of God's good purpose. That is the sense of the word *destroyed*, which is also used in much more positive ways to refer to things which are consecrated to the service of God.

Critical Observation

Leaving no survivors was not always the outcome of an Israelite conquest. Outside of Canaan (the land the Israelites were in inhabiting), the women and children were spared. The men (who would serve as warriors against the Israelites) were killed. Inside Canaan, all were destroyed; but keep in mind that even in those situations, should the people surrender, they were spared (see 20:10–15).

Bashan had always been an idolatrous and crudely sinful people. Centuries before this incident, they had been notoriously evil in their ways. But God had been patient with them. He had endured their unbelief and the ugly corruption of their life for hundreds of years. Indeed, He consigned His own chosen people, Israel, to live in bondage in Egypt for four hundred years, in large part because He was unwilling to move against these Amorite peoples until the cup of their iniquity was full to the brim, as He tells Abraham (see Genesis 15:16) some six hundred years before Moses moved against Og, king of Bashan.

Christians who know that God's judgment is always just and righteous will know that the wickedness of this people must have been very great to be judged so severely. The warfare described here is a preview of hell where all God's enemies—men, women, and children—will suffer.

Demystifying Deuteronomy

The culture of Bashan appealed to the bestial in human nature in a very direct way. Not only were their gods particularly violent and vicious, but the people's worship of these gods was idolatrous and utterly debauched. Cult prostitution and fertility rites were a major feature of what they called "worship." Whether child sacrifice was also a feature at this time has not been certainly established, but it was in later years. One of the goddesses of the Canaanite pantheon, Anat, is represented laughing with joy over the dismemberment of young and old alike, gleefully collecting the heads and the hands.

In the laws governing Israel's warfare, given in Deuteronomy 20, the Lord says plainly why He wants certain peoples devoted in this way, especially the peoples who would be Israel's neighbors, if left to live in the land Israel is to occupy and possess (see 20:18). It is to keep Israel from catching the moral and spiritual diseases of these people. God knew that a pure, devout, and faithful people of God could not long exist if thoroughly mixed with a radioactively wicked, corrupt, and sensually powerful culture.

As it happens, Israel does not destroy all of these peoples, and their influence does terribly corrupt the people of God, to the spiritual death of vast multitudes of them.

3:12–23

DIVISION OF THE LAND

The accounts of Israel's history that precede the law-giving conclude with a summary of the allotment of land Israel had conquered up to this point (3:12–17). All the land that had been taken was east of the Jordan River; Israel had not yet crossed into Canaan proper. Only the tribes of Reuben, Gad, and the half tribe of Manasseh receive land east of the Jordan—perhaps because they had a lot of livestock (3:19) and needed a large range for them.

Verses 18–23 detail the trans-Jordan tribes' responsibilities to the rest of Israel. They are to accompany the other tribes across the Jordan and fight alongside them. Only after all the tribes have received their territories may any man settle down in his new home.

q 3:24–29

UNANSWERED PRAYER

We have in verses 12–29 one of the most striking and important examples of God saying "no" to the prayer of one of His children. Moses' prayer recorded here (3:24–25), asking God to relent and allow him to set foot in the promised land, is apparently not his first. During the months, perhaps years, that had passed from striking the rock (see Numbers 20:1–13) to this point, with Israel poised on the west side of the Jordan, ready at last to enter Canaan, Moses had apparently often pled with the Lord. That is the suggestion of Deuteronomy 3:26, where we read that the Lord says, "That is enough. Do not speak to me anymore about this matter" (NIV).

In this particular case, the Lord seems to have decided it was necessary to say no to Moses so that the people of Israel, already suffering from a seriously inadequate view of their own sinfulness, would not be further confirmed in their tendency to take sin lightly. Moses reminds the Israelites that it is because of them that he was provoked to commit the sin for which now he is paying so steep a price (3:26). In Moses' punishment, the Lord is sending a message to Israel concerning the seriousness with which He takes their disobedience.

Further, the Lord forbids Moses to cross the Jordan in part because He wants Joshua properly prepared for the task that will fall to him when Israel enters the promised land (3:28). Once Moses understands that he is not to cross the river, he can devote all his energy to preparing Joshua to take his place.

DEUTERONOMY 4:1–49

LAWS AND ORDERS

Setting Up the Section

The first three chapters of Deuteronomy recall God's faithfulness and power. Now Moses begins to lay out the commandments that God calls Israel to obey in response to what He has already done.

q 4:1–14

THE GRACE OF LAW

Before setting out any specific laws, Moses speaks more generally about the importance of obedience (4:1–8). The obedience which Israel is here summoned to give to God is not for the purpose of making them God's children; it is not for earning salvation. This obedience they owe to God *because* God has saved them and because they are already His children. Throughout the chapter, beginning with verse 2, the law is referred to as "the commands of *the LORD your God*." The Israelites are already God's people.

While obedience does not earn salvation, it does convey certain benefits. Obedience removes the threat of punishment (4:3–4). Living by the commandments of God will make this people wise and understanding, so wise as to be the envy of their neighbors (4:5–8). The law is God's good gift and blessing to His people, demonstrating His nearness and involvement in their lives (4:7).

Just as the Lord is the God of Israel's forefathers (4:1), He is the God of the generations yet to come as well. This generation is to teach God's law to their children (4:9).

There is a significant difference in obeying commandments to earn God's approval and acceptance and obeying commandments because one has already been graciously given God's approval and acceptance. The latter is the case here, very clearly. Israel does not receive the law of God at Mount Sinai (4:10–13) until after she is delivered from her bondage in Egypt. Salvation comes first, then obedience; grace first, then the believer's grateful response to God's goodness.

God's law is not some set of unreasonable and onerous requirements which God imposes simply to test His people's loyalty or fortitude. God's law is His wisdom, His instructions for how human life should be lived if it is to be lived right. It is God's fatherly counsel to His children so that they might live happily, fruitfully, and safely in the land He is giving them (4:14).

4:15–31

KEEP YOURSELVES FROM IDOLS

There is no particular reason why Israel should be so captivated by idols, but Moses here clearly regards this as the standing danger of her religious life. God has never appeared to His people in a form that they could pattern an idol after. They had never seen God—a point Moses reminds them of (4:15). They are not to make or worship an image of any shape—not images of humans, birds, animals, or fish (4:16–18). Nor are they to worship any object of God's making, such as the sun, moon, and stars (4:19). As Moses points out, having delivered them from bondage in Egypt as He did, God has every right to demand that He be worshiped by His people in the way that He deems right and proper (4:20, 23–24).

Demystifying Deuteronomy

The peoples of the ancient Middle Eastern world made and worshiped idols of every kind. Gods and goddesses were represented as animals—fish, bulls, calves, and the like—or as human beings in figurine form, or as poles and pillars. What is more, as indicated in Deuteronomy 4:19, they not only worshiped gods through images which represented them, but they also actually considered heavenly bodies as gods themselves. Idolatry was a universal institution and a part of the fabric of life for all of these people, save one: Israel herself.

Despite God's clear command, Israel drifts toward idol worship over and over again. Indeed, while Moses is still at the top of Mount Sinai, receiving the law from the hand of God, Israel is at the foot of the mountain cavorting before a golden calf, with bitter consequences, as Moses reminds them (4:21–22).

Critical Observation

Old Testament history is the long story of Israel's partial success and then complete failure to live up to the true understanding of God she had been given. She was always being lured into idol worship. First, it would be the worship of the Lord her God but with the use of idols. After all, all the other nations worshiped their gods by means of idols. But it would eventually cease altogether to be the worship of the Lord and become instead the worship of the idols and the gods they represented: Baal, Ashtoreth, Molech, and the like. One of the great themes of the Old Testament prophets is their condemnation of Israel and Judah for taking over the worship of idols from neighboring nations. But it took the destruction of the nation of Israel and the long bitter years of captivity in Babylon before that kind of idolatry was finally exterminated in Israel.

Moses warns Israel not to forget what kind of God the living and true God is: invisible, immortal, transcendent in glory, infinite in power and might (4:24–25). All idolatry thus becomes both dangerous and utterly foolish. It will bring God's punishments instead of His blessings—for Israel it means that they will lose the promised land (4:26–27)—and it will turn the idolaters into fools, spending their lives chasing after the ridiculous. That is the dripping irony of verse 28. Idolatry practiced long enough will finally bring a person to a state of complete blindness about life. It will bring people who know better to worship objects they themselves have made; it will make people who have long since learned that money cannot buy happiness to seek after more of it still more avidly; it will make people who have sought the meaning of life in pleasure or power or fame completely incapable of serving another master. It is a form of madness. And it is what happens when God finally, as an act of judgment, hands idolaters over to their idolatry.

Take It Home

Idolatry is by no means a problem for Old Testament Israel only. It is a constant danger to God's people still today. By our very nature, we all worship something. It is in our nature to give our allegiance to something or someone. God made us this way so that we might worship and serve Him. Sin has corrupted this tendency, but it did not remove or destroy it. If a man or woman will not worship the living God, then he or she will worship someone or something else.

The Bible takes full account of the fact that one can be an idolater in many other ways than by bowing down to figurines representative of an imaginary god. An idol is anything which claims from us the loyalty and the service we owe to God alone. Today, as in former times, many people worship many idols at the same time: pleasure, power, money, fame, political ideas, and so on. The church is likewise crammed full of idolaters. Every time we give loyalty to something else over God, we are idolaters.

Yet this warning is not without hope. Those who look for the true God will find Him (4:29). Those who repent will learn the mercy of the faithful, covenant God (4:30–31).

4:32–40

OUR HISTORY

We have in verses 32–40 the climactic conclusion of the historical prologue and some of the most beautiful prose in the book of Deuteronomy. The elevated style is the result of the subject matter: the glorious works of Almighty God.

The answer to the rhetorical questions in verses 32–34 is clearly, "No." Christians today, however, can answer, "Yes," and speak of the historical events of Christ's incarnation and resurrection of which these Old Testament events are foretastes.

The monotheism alluded to in verse 35 is an essential implication of Israel's history. They never thought to ask, as people have often since, whether God exists. They had seen Him at work.

The discipline of verse 36 is that of a father disciplining his child. (This is made explicit in 8:5.) God has established a parent-child relationship between Himself and His people.

Moses here speaks to the people as if they were personally present at the Exodus and Mount Sinai, even though many of them clearly had not been. The oldest among those to whom Moses is speaking had been children during those days of the deliverance from Egypt and the two years at Sinai, but many more would have been born in the years since Israel left Sinai and began her wanderings in the wilderness.

Moses has a very practical purpose in speaking this way to his contemporaries. Reminding them of their history, he expects them (and us) to live according to it. He wants them to consider the past, take it seriously, and draw from it courage to face the challenges of life in the promised land. He desires his listeners to fear God and develop a solemn determination to keep His commandments, to be ever thankful and hopeful, and possess a sense of great obligation to pass this history on to future generations (4:40).

4:41–49

SOME UNFINISHED BUSINESS

At the conclusion of this historical prologue, Moses tends to some logistical details for the tribes receiving territories east of the Jordan. He establishes cities of refuge, one for each tribe (4:41–43).

Verses 44–49 once again describe the geographical locations of the territories Israel has taken possession of, anchoring this account firmly in historical time and place.

DEUTERONOMY 5:1–33

LOVE, FEAR, AND OBEDIENCE

Setting Up the Section

The book of Deuteronomy follows the pattern of ancient Middle Eastern treaties. The preamble in chapter 1:1–5 gives the historical and geographical setting. The historical prologue in chapters 1:6–4:49 comprises a lengthy review of God's dealings with Israel and serves to provide a rationale for obedience. In chapter 5, we begin the particular stipulations of the covenant: the commandments which occupy the largest part of the book.

5:1–22

THE TEN COMMANDMENTS

Moses' words recorded in Deuteronomy 5:1–5, like those in chapter 4, address the people as if the Ten Commandments have been given directly to them, rather than to the generation before (The Lord made a covenant with *us* at Horeb [5:2]; He spoke to *you* from the mountain [5:4]; *you* were afraid of the fire on the mountain [5:5]). In the statement recorded in verse 3, Moses seems to draw special attention to this foreshortening of history by saying that God made His covenant at Sinai not with the people who were present there at the time, but with those who would come after them.

The Ten Commandments recorded in verses 6–21 are already familiar to the Israelites. Moses repeats them as a summary of the covenant the people had to affirm for themselves. As Moses conveys in verses 1–5, the people could not simply inherit the covenant of their forefathers; they had to own it for themselves.

Critical Observation

The Ten Commandments are not simply ten of the many laws that God gave His people; they are not even the ten most important of those laws. The Ten Commandments are a summary of the *entire* law of God. All the rest of the commandments in God's Word are applications or elaborations of these fundamental duties. Their character as a general summary is further indicated by the fact that both in the Old and the New Testaments these ten can be further summarized by only two commandments: to love God with all your heart and soul and to love your neighbor as yourself (see, for example, Deuteronomy 6:5; Luke 10:27).

5:23–33

HOW BLESSED ARE THEY WHO FEAR THE LORD

After repeating the Ten Commandments that God had delivered to the people through him (5:22), Moses recalls the scene at the foot of Mount Sinai after the law had been given. The glory of God's presence continued to surround the mountain through the majesty of fire, thunder, and darkness, and the people cowered in fear (5:23–24). They felt they could not stand any further exposure to the glory of God or it would literally kill them (5:25–26), so they pleaded with Moses to approach the Lord and to speak on their behalf (5:27).

Some of this fear is clearly the result of their faithlessness. They did not have a true and living trust in God; they feared God for His justice and His wrath and His power. But that is not the whole explanation. God does not dispute the request the people make of Moses. Indeed, He commends it, as it reads in verse 28. And then He goes on to say that His people will always fear Him as they feared at Sinai. It is only through this fear that they will be blessed and things will go well with them and their children forever (5:29).

Critical Observation

What does it mean to fear the Lord? True fear of God is a positive, not negative, thing; it is an expression of high regard for God, not of alienation or repulsion. It is taking God as seriously as His majesty requires, not hating to be near or with Him.

Holy fear does not drive out all other emotions before it or displace all other emotional states. The fear of the Lord coexists with joy.

The fear of God spoken of here could be defined as an apprehension of the true majesty and glory of God. It is the awe one should have in the presence of God's greatness and wonder; it is high reverence, which is appropriate to creatures before their Creator, finite persons before the infinite and Almighty God.

It is easy for Israel to have such reverence and fear; they have, with their own eyes, seen terrific, breathtaking, heart-shuddering manifestations of the divine majesty. They know the vastness that separates them from God and how it feels to be so small before something so infinitely great.

If God's people truly fear Him as they should, that fear will bring them blessing and prosperity (5:30–33). Nothing leads to obedience more certainly than a true reverence for God, than some sense of His majesty, His immensity. Before such a God, a God who sits enthroned in the heavens, any and all disobedience seems absurd, irrational, and unquestionably wicked. Sin is not likely to find much welcome in a soul often overwhelmed with God's sublime splendor.

Take It Home

God gave Israel the law after He had already delivered them from their slavery in Egypt. They did not need to earn their deliverance by obeying the law. Rather, the law served another purpose: to show God's people how they ought to live out love and gratitude to their Redeemer.

In the same way, Christians keep the commandments of God not in order to be saved—that would be legalism and not the gospel of grace—but because they have been saved by grace and wish to live a life that glorifies God. The law of God shows us the way. Obedience is a response of love to a God who has not only delivered us from the wrath to come by the death of His Son, but has given us such wise and sound counsel that our lives might be rich and full and good. God has given His laws to us and laid us under obligation to keep them because we are His children—He loves us and wants the very best for us.

DEUTERONOMY 6:1–25

GOD-FEARING CHILDREN

Talk the Talk	6:1–9
Walk the Walk	6:10–25

Setting Up the Section

Deuteronomy 5 looked to the previous generation and emphasized how essential it was for the current generation to inhabit as their own the covenant made with their parents and grandparents. Deuteronomy 6 takes a forward view to the next generation. In it we read of God's exhortations for parents to nurture their children in the faith of the covenant God.

6:1–9

TALK THE TALK

After exhorting the people to fear the Lord as had the generation at Sinai (4:29), Moses extends that charge—and the promised blessings—to their children and the children after them (6:1–3).

Two essentials form the core of what each generation must know: the truth about who God is (6:4) and how the people are to relate to Him (6:5). This covenant succession from parents to children is too important to be left to chance. Parents must be intentional and passionate about passing on the faith. The picture is not of disinterested parents who set their children to memorizing the catechism or who suppose their obligation is satisfied by taking the children to church. The picture is of parents who are eager and determined to see their children enter into an ever deeper understanding of God's Word and gratitude for God's great works. Here are parents who, with remarkable diligence and great affection, teach the truth of God to their children until they are sure their children understand it and apply it to the practical issues of life, until it is written indelibly in their hearts (6:6–7).

Critical Observation

Most of the significant characters of biblical history were sons and daughters of the covenant and were raised in the faith. Godly successions of faith and love litter the pages of scripture: Seth, Enoch, Noah; Abraham, Isaac, Jacob, Joseph; Boaz, Jesse, David, Solomon; Lois, Eunice, Timothy; and so on. The godly Hebrew kings, the heroes of faith listed in Hebrews 11, and John the Baptist all were children once in homes where fathers and mothers faithfully kept the command to nurture their children in the faith.

Verses 7–10 say it plainly. The Word of God is never to be far from the lips and should often be popping into the conversation that fathers and mothers have with their children. What are the commandments that parents are to impress upon the hearts of their children? They are the commandments, we read in verse 5, which are summed up in this: that they are to love God with absolutely everything they have.

Demystifying Deuteronomy

Many observant Jews take literally the injunctions in Deuteronomy 6:8–9. They bind small, scripture-filled leather cases, called *tefillin*, on their arms and foreheads, and post small cases containing the words of Deuteronomy 6:4–9, called *mezuzahs*, on their doorframes.

6:10–25

WALK THE WALK

Children cannot follow where their parents do not lead. So parents are called upon to maintain their own close walk with God. In prosperity, they must not let materialism crowd out God (6:10–12). In a secular culture, they must not follow the crowd (6:13–15). In times of deprivation, they must not succumb to ingratitude (6:16). At all times, they are to do what is right and trust the Lord with the consequences (6:17–19).

And how will parents know if the grace of God is impacting their children's lives? Their children will begin turning to them to ask the great questions of life (6:20), giving them the opportunity yet again to recount the mighty works of God by which He saved His people (6:21–23) and to teach them nothing is more important than keeping every one of God's commands, in the fear of God, holding nothing back.

Take It Home

Are your children learning from your words, example, and expectations that you care for nothing more than this: that their lives be joyfully spent serving the Lord Christ? Do they know that your primary and ultimate goal for them is to do all they can for the sake of their Redeemer and yours?

DEUTERONOMY 7:1–26

GIFTS AND REWARDS

Setting Up the Section

Some refer to the book of Deuteronomy as the Romans of the Old Testament. Well, then, we should not be at all surprised to find in it such a strong statement of the doctrine of divine election, the very doctrine to which Paul devotes such considerable and famous attention in his letter to the Romans.

7:1–11

GOD'S ELECTING GRACE

Verse 1 of chapter 7 establishes once again that it is God who drives out the nations so that Israel may possess the land. Here we find a strong statement of the principle of sovereign and electing grace. Out of all the peoples of the world, God chose Israel to be His own people. He chose her, not because she deserved His favor—she most certainly did not—but entirely and mysteriously because He loved her. As the apostle Paul would later put it: "It does not, therefore, depend on man's desire or effort, but on God's mercy" (Romans 9:16 NIV).

Critical Observation

The doctrine of election is that God has been pleased from all eternity to choose certain men and women out of fallen humanity whom, and for His love's sake, He has determined to save by Jesus Christ. This is a controversial doctrine; those who disagree with it contend that

1) election makes God unjust, choosing to save some and not others;
2) this doctrine of divine election robs humans of their free will and thus destroys human responsibility.

Election is given a double aspect here in Deuteronomy 7. If it is true that God has chosen Israel, it is also true that He has not chosen the other nations (7:1–5). God makes this distinction between sinful and unworthy people, to call some to Him and to leave others unsummoned (7:7–10). The election of Israel as a people was the first step in that process by which God set apart to Himself those who would be saved. It is His gracious choice in each case, not human action or merit, that is the final explanation for anyone's salvation.

As verse 11 makes clear, Moses' point is not merely that God has chosen His people, but that they should be deeply grateful for the salvation they do not deserve but have been given as a gift, and that in their gratitude they ought to seek the Lord's pleasure by keeping His commands.

7:12–26

THE GOSPEL OF PROSPERITY

Verses 12–15 contain the remarkable promise of blessing that the Lord makes to His people if they walk faithfully and obediently before Him. If they are faithful to His covenant, He will make their lives rich and happy in every way. They will enjoy good health. Their farms will prosper and they will become very successful, while all their enemies will suffer ruin. It is a dramatic passage in its extravagance and in the absence of all qualification or limitation.

In the most literal sense, these words—this promise of blessing for covenant faithfulness—are true. The fact of the matter is that, as a general rule, those who live godly lives by a living faith in the Lord, and by careful and scrupulous obedience to His commands, do prosper in the kinds of ways that are mentioned here in Deuteronomy 7. This is the constant theme of the book of Proverbs. A person who lives faithfully and responsibly before the Lord will say and do those things which make for a fruitful life. It is a simple fact often and everywhere to be observed. The English Puritans, for example, became a prosperous people as a direct consequence of their faithfulness to the way of life and ethics taught in scripture, which they embraced because they loved and trusted the Lord.

A faithful member of God's covenant community—who has, by the grace of God, come to trust the Lord and commit himself to the Word of God—will be an honest and hard-working man, a kind and generous man, and a man who sees life as rich with opportunity and possibility because it is under the rule of his Father in heaven. Such a man does well in this world and finds great reward in it.

Demystifying Deuteronomy

While chapter 7 was being written, Israel was poised on the brink of entering the promised land. But Canaan was not only a fertile and beautiful land which God had given His people; it also represented their spiritual inheritance, the blessings of the eternal promised land. A great point of this is made in the New Testament letter to the Hebrews, especially in chapter 11. There we read that Canaan was never as significant as a piece of real estate as it was as a figure, an enacted prophecy of the heavenly country which God's people, by faith, were headed. The promise of great blessing for covenantal faithfulness is also true in the sense that it will eventually be perfectly fulfilled, in even the most literal way, in the life of God's faithful people in the world to come.

This promise of great blessing for covenantal faithfulness is also true in the sense that the physical blessings mentioned here, as often in scripture, represent spiritual blessings and the general blessedness of God's people who live under His favor. When the Lord promised physical blessings, He meant much more than that, and any spiritual man or woman would want and seek more than that.

Critical Observation

The great problem posed by such promises as this one in Deuteronomy 7:12–16 is, of course, that the Bible itself bears abundant witness to the fact that godly and righteous people do not always enjoy such a wealth of worldly riches and reward; often they experience the reverse. Sometimes it is for a time that a godly man undergoes great tribulation and must walk heavily in this world, such as Job. But often the faithful of the Lord have lived their whole lives in comparative poverty, suffering trials of various kinds. What is more, contrary to the expectation of Deuteronomy 7:17–26, the scripture itself more than once raises the point that the wicked seem to enjoy a greater prosperity than the righteous.

Scripture points the way to a proper understanding. Very often the blessings of salvation, the far greater blessings of peace with God, the forgiveness of sins, eternal life, and the joy of salvation and communion with the Lord are represented under the figure of physical prosperity. When we read in verse 13, for example, of wine and oil being the blessing of the Lord, we are reminded how many times in the scripture wine and oil are symbols of happiness and joy and fulfillment in life (see Job 29:4–6).

In verses 16–26 we read the flip side of the promises in verses 12–15: Not only will God's faithful people prosper, but the wicked nations around them will suffer defeat at their hands. This defeat is also a part of Israel's faithfulness: God's people are to destroy the idols in Canaan so that they will not be tempted into idolatry (7:25). Those who are not faithful in rejecting these rival "gods" will not receive the promises of the faithful, but rather destruction (7:26).

Take It Home

The extravagant promise that was made to Israel in Deuteronomy 7 is also made to God's people today. We are to understand it as a general promise of prosperity for those who trust and obey the Lord, a promise of still far greater blessings of the soul and heart which are represented by these physical blessings spoken of, and a promise of literal and complete fulfillment and prosperity of life in the world to come, the true and eternal promised land.

Are the choices you make day by day based on your conviction that what God will give you for faithfulness to Him will always vastly surpass what you could get for yourself if you sought your own pleasure, success, or prosperity? Is it obvious to those who watch you that what is supremely important to you is to love and serve the Lord? Do you invest your money, your time, and your effort according to this promise in Deuteronomy 7 and many others like it in scripture? Or do you seek first the other things and give only partial and divided attention to the kingdom of God?

DEUTERONOMY 8:1–20

FORGET NOT ALL HIS BENEFITS

Setting Up the Section

You would think that Israel's escape from Egypt and desert wanderings would have been so indelibly printed on every Israelite heart that forgetting it would be nearly impossible. But Moses knew human nature too well to think that. He knew that when they entered the lush and fruitful land that God was giving them, and settled down into their new homes and began enjoying their wealth and prosperity, it would be entirely natural for them to forget all about the desert and all that God had done for them, even forget that the new land and prosperity was His gift to them. Moses knew full well what the human heart is capable of, and how it can so quickly begin to take credit itself for the Lord's achievements.

8:1–5

REMEMBER WHAT GOD HAS DONE

In this chapter of Deuteronomy, Moses warns the people of God of the ease with which they can forget the Lord and His great kindnesses to them. He urges them to be careful not to do so, but to remember the Lord and all that He has done (8:1).

This generation has much to remember. They have just finished long years in the wilderness, which were necessary, after all, only because their parents had rebelled against the Lord and faithlessly refused to trust His promise to bring them into Canaan in triumph, even though He had brought them so miraculously and triumphantly out of bondage in Egypt (8:2). They should also remember how often they had tested the Lord and complained against Him and how, nevertheless, He patiently and generously met their needs with manna, clothing, and with fatherly discipline (8:3–5).

8:6–14

GIVE GOD CREDIT

The appropriate response to what God has done, Moses points out, is to obey Him, walk with Him, and give reverence to Him (8:6–8). And God's blessings are not simply part of Israel's history; at that moment God was in the process of bringing Israel into a good land of their own (8:7–9). The blessings of prosperity, it seems, come with their own temptations: to become proud and forget God (8:10–14).

Critical Observation

This pattern of remembering God's work and responding in gratitude parallels in miniature the entire book of Deuteronomy, in which Moses first recounts God's history of faithfulness to Israel and then calls Israel to obedience.

8:15–18

KEEP REMEMBERING

To emphasize his point, Moses again reiterates what God has done and that which Israel is to remember. How true had all of God's promises proven themselves to be; how safely Israel had lived according to the Word of God. It was not by their own skill or effort or endurance that they had managed those long years in the desert, but by the goodness and provision of God. All of this was fresh in their minds as they sat poised on the eastern bank of the Jordan, ready to cross and possess the promised land.

Demystifying Deuteronomy

While the land of Canaan may not seem like a fertile land by North American standards, it was more fertile and verdant in antiquity especially before the land was raped by the Ottomans. Also keep in mind that the Israelites were seeing the land compared to desert, where Israel had wandered for forty years, and to Egypt, which depended on irrigation. It was indeed a good land (8:7–8).

Moses warns the people that they must resist this natural tendency to forget the Lord and His works. Instead, they must set themselves to remembering them, every day and in every way calling to mind the Lord and all His benefits. Moses doesn't think that Israel will actually forget the Exodus and the wilderness in the sense that the people will no longer know that these things happened. But what Moses means is that they must remember them in a spiritual way, being forever impressed on their hearts so that the Exodus and the wilderness continue generations afterward to awaken faith, hope, and love in the hearts of God's people.

8:19–20

FOLLOW GOD'S WAYS

If you are going to live a faithful life, Moses tells the Israelites, then make a determined and heartfelt effort to keep God's commandments, for love's sake (8:19–20).

The kind of remembering Moses is speaking of here is that which stirs the heart, breaks pride and willfulness, and awakens faith, hope, and love.

Take It Home

What we read here in Deuteronomy 8 we will often read in the Bible. Remembering has a great deal to do with living the Christian life—remembering what God has done for us in the distant past and remembering our own lives and our own experience of the Lord. And the Christian man or woman, boy or girl, who keeps the Lord and His works in remembrance is the person who will most joyfully and zealously live the Christian life.

How will you keep the memory of the Lord, His word, and His works in front of you? With a verse stuck to the door of your refrigerator? Through keeping a journal? In weekly worship with other believers?

DEUTERONOMY 9:1–29

UNRIGHTEOUSNESS

Setting Up the Section

Interestingly, all of the examples Moses uses to demonstrate how unworthy Israel is of the gift she is about to receive are from the life of the previous generation, not this generation about to cross into the promised land. Those who aroused the Lord's anger at Mount Sinai, who cavorted before the golden calf, and then who later rebelled at Kadesh Barnea—they all lie dead and buried back in the wilderness. They had forfeited the promised land by their faithlessness. But, with that sense of family solidarity which is so common to the Bible, the present generation is addressed as if they, too, had been at Horeb, they, too, had worshiped the golden calf, they, too, had participated in the cowardly refusal to enter the promised land at Kadesh Barnea.

9:1–6

NOT FOR YOUR RIGHTEOUSNESS

Moses again assures the people that they will be successful in conquering the land—successful even against the fearsome Anakites (9:1–2). And he reminds them yet again that their success will not be a result of their own strength but of the Lord's power and faithfulness (9:3).

Critical Observation

It is significant that Moses assures the people they will conquer the Anakites. These are the very people that terrified the Israelites so much that they refused to enter the land forty years earlier (see Numbers 13:26–33). The Anakites were very tall and very strong, and some thought they were descended from a race of giants.

This ought to be a cause of humility for the Israelites, but Moses recognizes that Israel may turn it into a source of pride (9:4). So Moses clearly states, not once, but twice, that God's driving out of the nations is not because of Israel's righteousness, but because of the nations' unrighteousness and because of God's faithfulness to His covenant promises (9:5–6). The fact is, they, too, are guilty of the sins of their parents. Their parents were unworthy of the promised land, but the current generation is as well. They, too, are stubborn people, always saying and doing things that offended the Lord. And here the Lord is reminding them, in the most emphatic way, that the land He is about to give them they do not deserve.

Demystifying Deuteronomy

Israel is described as a "stiff-necked" people (9:6, 13 NIV). The description is a farming expression for an animal that would not be led by a rope around its neck. It portrays Israel as stubborn and resistant to God's leading.

9:7–29

THE GOLDEN CALF

In chapter 8, we read the charge to remember what God has done. Now the charge is to remember what Israel had done (8:7). It is not a list to be proud of. At the very moment that God is carving His covenant with Israel into stone (9:8–11), Israel is making a golden statue and calling it the God who had led them out of Egypt (9:12–22).

Demystifying Deuteronomy

The full account of the golden calf is in Exodus 32. The calf could have been modeled after the Egyptian god Apis, which the Israelites knew from Egypt, or after the Canaanite god Baal, both of which took the shape of a calf or bull.

Next, Moses lists three other places where the people had angered the Lord: Taberah, Massah, and Kibroth Hattaavah. In each of these places, the people doubted God's provision and complained about what He did provide. At Taberah, the people's complaints angered the Lord so much that He sent fire to burn the outskirts of the camp (Numbers 11:1–3). Massah is the place where the people claimed that Moses (and, by implication, God) had led them into the desert to die of thirst (Exodus 17). Kibroth Hattaavah was the place where the people complained that they were sick of manna and whined that the food had been better in Egypt (Numbers 11:4–35).

Finally, Moses reminds the people of the sin that led to forty years of desert wandering: the refusal to enter the promised land because their fear of the Canaanites was greater than their trust in the Lord (Deuteronomy 9:23–24). They escaped destruction, Moses explains, only because God was faithful to His promises to Abraham, Isaac, and Jacob (9:25–29). Again, the message is that the gift of the promised land is because God is faithful, not because Israel is deserving.

Take It Home

In Deuteronomy 9, the spirit of God is speaking as surely to us as He was speaking at that moment to the people of Israel. We, too, are an unrighteous people who have been given a great gift—a still more wonderful promised land—which we do not deserve. We, too, are always forgetting and slighting that tremendously important fact.

DEUTERONOMY 10:1–22

A FAITHLESS PEOPLE; A FAITHFUL GOD

Setting Up the Section

The Bible was written in largest part not to the world but to the people of God. Most of its contents, both in the Old Testament and the New Testament, are directly addressed to the church and the people of God. And for that reason one of its greatest themes is the possibility and the temptation, and the frequent reality and danger, of formalism in the Christian faith—of a faith which is not a matter of the heart.

The tragic story of the Old Testament is of a people who were religious in an outward way but whose hearts were far from God. Moses has repeated some of that history to the people; now he calls them specifically to give their whole hearts to God.

10:1–11

TWO MORE TABLETS

Verses 1–5 continue the account of what happened immediately after Israel's blatant unfaithfulness when they made the golden calf (chapter 9). Israel had broken covenant with God when they made that calf, and any other treaty-maker would have considered that covenant over. But God does not turn away; instead, He rewrites the very same words of covenant treaty that He had written on the stone tablets that Moses had broken. God gives the people another chance—exactly the same opportunity He had given them before they turned to idolatry, just as if they had never betrayed Him.

Verses 6–9 are a parenthetical summary not only of the people's travels but of the development of the priesthood. Aaron, the original priest, dies (10:6), and the Lord sets apart the tribe of Levi to serve as priests (10:8).

Demystifying Deuteronomy

Deuteronomy 10:9 states that the Levites would inherit no land. Their needs were provided for in the stipulations about offerings: Part of the meat and grain offered to God was to feed the priests (see Leviticus 6:18; 7:28–36).

Verses 10–11 provide a flashback to the time at Horeb and return the focus back to entering the promised land.

10:12–22

WITH ALL THE HEART

Moses reiterates the earlier theme of the importance of the heart in a true and right relationship with God. He tells Israel that they must serve the Lord with all their heart and soul (10:12). Verse 13 elaborates on that: Serving God involves observing God's commands and decrees.

Verses 14–15 reiterate once again both God's supremacy—everything belongs to Him—and His gracious choice to love Israel above all other nations. Verse 16 returns to the issue of the heart. The first part of circumcising hearts is to practice dependence upon the Lord for sanctification, for, as Deuteronomy 30:6 will show, it is really the Lord who does the circumcising. For this work of making hearts right before God, they are utterly dependent upon the Lord. He calls His people to do something, but He must bless what they do, and He alone can make it effective.

Critical Observation

Circumcision was the original sign of God's covenant with Abraham and Abraham's descendants (Genesis 17). It was an outward, physical sign, but the command in Deuteronomy to circumcise one's heart indicates that circumcision was always intended to reflect an internal reality, not merely external obedience.

Moses seems to be saying that it is the heart that matters and there will never be true loyalty to God and faithfulness to His covenant unless it comes from the heart.

Critical Observation

What Moses says here in Deuteronomy 10, about the circumcision of the heart, Paul will later say in Romans 2:28–29: "For you are not a true Jew just because you were born of Jewish parents or because you have gone through the ceremony of circumcision. No, a true Jew is one whose heart is right with God" (NLT).

Take It Home

Christianity is uniquely, among the religions of the world, a matter of the heart. It condemns in no uncertain terms religious activity and performance which is not as much a matter of the heart as it is of outward behavior. From the beginning to the end of the Bible, we are reminded that the living God sees the heart, inspects the heart, and judges according to what is in the heart. The life of true faith is not the doing of certain religious acts, but rather, in one's heart, the fear of God, love for God, desire for God, joy in God, and gratitude to God.

DEUTERONOMY 11:1–32

LOVE AND OBEDIENCE

The Call to Love God	11:1–7
The Call to Obey God	11:8–25
The Consequences for Obedience and Disobedience	11:26–32

Setting Up the Section

It is imperative that the Israelites understand that the key to staying in the land is to obey God. All obedience to God starts with love. A person who does not love God cannot obey God. For this reason, Moses reiterates the call to love.

11:1–7

THE CALL TO LOVE GOD

Everything that happened in the history of Israel had been for the purpose of motivating the people to love God with their whole hearts. For this reason, as they are called to love God (11:1), they are to remember all that He has done for them (11:2). He rescued them (11:3–4), provided for them (11:5), and disciplined them (11:6–7) so that they would grow in their obedience to Him. The call to love is grounded in the love that God had given to them.

Critical Observation

This chapter is laid out in a logical sequence. It begins with the call to love God, then moves to the call to obey God, and ends with the consequences for both obedience and for disobedience. This order is theologically important. To work it backward would look like this:

- If you obey, you are blessed; if you disobey, you are cursed.
- Therefore, you must obey.
- The only way to obey is to love God, for all obedience is motivated by love.

11:8–25

THE CALL TO OBEY GOD

The strength of the Israelites to take possession of the land and to secure for themselves a place to live in peace, safety, and security is directly related to their obedience. Their abilities to conquer stronger enemies and to live long in the land (4:40; 5:16; 6:2; 25:15; 32:47) are ultimately matters of obedience, not military skill or sound military leadership (11:8–9). This is the uniqueness of this nation. Their focus is not to be on becoming better soldiers or leaders; their focus is to be on loving God and following all He says.

Mentioning the contrasts between the promised land and Egypt (11:10–12) was no doubt prompted by those who wanted to return there, as Dathan and Abiram had (11:6). The land of Canaan had far more potential than Egypt ever had. What God provided clearly exceeded what Egypt offered. The people in Egypt had to depend on irrigation; God's people would have rain from heaven (11:11). Unlike human irrigation, rain is in the complete control of God. Thus, God is again showing the people that He will care for them and give them what they need to survive (11:12).

Because of the importance of obedience and the seduction of false religion, Moses again warns Israel against worshiping other gods (11:16). Many of the gods worshiped in Canaan were fertility gods (gods of grain, oil, rain, etc.). If the people transfer their trust for the prosperity of their land to one or more of these false gods, the Lord will withdraw His gifts of rain and produce (11:17).

These commandments about staying away from false gods are so important that the people are to have them always in their hearts and minds (11:18). God's laws are to be always in front of them and their children (11:19–21).

In return for their obedience, the Lord will grant Israel supernatural success against all her enemies—no matter how large and strong they are (11:22–24). He will put terror and fear in their enemies so that they are not able to fight successfully against Israel (11:25). God will deliver this nation and provide for her in extraordinary ways.

Demystifying Deuteronomy

Moses was very clear that love and obedience are intrinsically connected (6:5–6; 7:9; 10:12–13; 11:13, 22; 19:9; 30:6, 8, 16, 20). In Hebrew, the command to love the Lord carries with it something more than just a feeling; it carries the idea that a person will follow God in a very personal and intimate relationship and then express that desire to follow in obedience to His revealed will. Thus, it means more than just a close relationship; it is a relationship that causes one to be united with God in intent and purpose.

11:26–32

THE CONSEQUENCES FOR OBEDIENCE AND DISOBEDIENCE

The Lord clearly set before the people the simple reality for obedience: If you obey, you will be blessed; if you disobey, you will be cursed (11:26–28). Longevity, prosperity, and security are not based on following pagan practice, but on loving God and following Him all the days of their lives. A formal proclamation of blessings and curses will reemphasize this truth once the people enter the land. (The blessings and curses proclaimed from Mount Ebel are recorded in 27:9–26.)

Take It Home

Many people take these words to ancient Israel to mean that obedience is the key to all business success today. In other words, *if I want to get rich, I must follow these commands.* This is an inappropriate application. The proper application is that God blesses obedience and punishes disobedience. The fact is that Israel could not obey God. Early on they began serving other gods. Therefore, what we must look at is *how do we obey God?* The answer is found in trusting the person and work of Jesus Christ. When the love of Christ takes residence in one's life, then he or she will have the right motivation to obey God, and God will bless the person for His glory (Galatians 4–5).

DEUTERONOMY 12:1–32

FORM AND FREEDOM IN WORSHIP

Destruction of Idols	12:1–4
One Place of Worship	12:5–28
Avoiding Snares	12:29–32

Setting Up the Section

This chapter opens the next major section of Deuteronomy. The first four chapters are a historical introduction, or prologue, an account of the previous relationship between the Lord and His people Israel. Chapters 5–11 set out the general commandments or stipulations of the covenant with repeated exhortations to Israel to keep the covenant which God had made with her. Chapter 12 begins the third and longest section of the book, stretching from 12:1 to 26:15. These chapters contain the specific stipulations, or legislation, covering matters as diverse as worship and the management of criminal cases in court.

12:1–4

DESTRUCTION OF IDOLS

Chapter 12 begins and ends with brief sections of warning, serving as bookends to the larger sections of positive instructions in between. These laws are designed for the life of Israel once she is resident in the promised land (12:1). Pluralism and religious tolerance is not to be a part of Israel's experience. The people are not only to avoid pagan forms of worship; they are to destroy both the places of worship and the instruments used in that worship (12:2–3). This introductory section concludes with the summary prohibition, "You must not worship the LORD your God in their way" (12:4 NIV).

Demystifying Deuteronomy

The sacred stones referred to in 12:3 are stone monuments used in Canaanite worship, probably engraved to represent Canaanite gods. Asherah poles were wooden poles set up to honor Asherah, the Canaanite goddess of love and war.

12:5–28

ONE PLACE OF WORSHIP

Verses 5–28 contain regulations governing the right worship of God. Verse 5 refers to the yet unidentified place where the sacrifices are to be offered to the Lord. Eventually, of course, this would be Jerusalem with its temple.

The Lord here tells His people that in true worship there is no conflict between form and freedom. That is, though they must worship God in a certain way, according to rules He has laid down, the worship does not need to be without vitality and sincerity and pleasure.

Worship itself in this chapter is identified with the sincere and joyful engagement of the heart. The worship of Israelite people at the sanctuary is described as an act of joy. In verse 7, the people who brought their sacrifices—and note that, characteristically, they worshiped not as individuals but as families—are to come and rejoice. Again in verse 12, when they come to offer sacrifices and pay their tithes, they were in those acts of worship to rejoice before God. Once again, in verse 18, as they eat their sacrifices and special offerings at the tabernacle and temple, they are to rejoice before the Lord with their families, servants, and the Levites who are there to assist their worship.

The worship God desires from His people is not to be a mere performance, a going through of motions, a series of acts done in a spirit of mere duty or obligation. The God who looks upon the heart and weighs the heart has from the earliest times demanded that the honor and worship which His people pay Him be as much a matter of their heart as of their performance of certain rituals and duties. He has done great things for them and is giving them the land as inheritance (12:9–10). What they celebrate when they come to worship Him is nothing less than the forgiveness of their sins and God's gift to them of Himself and of everlasting life. Surely any true worship, any true thanksgiving, would be offered with joy.

Notice another concern in this chapter about the right worship of God: that worship must be offered according to the directions and the specifications of God's law. The Holy Spirit, through Moses, insists that worship be joyful, but He is still more insistent that Israel's worship of God be offered according to the many laws and regulations which have been laid down. They may not worship in various places as the pagans do, but only where God says (12:5). They must worship the Lord in the specific ways they have been taught, with certain kinds of offerings and gifts to be given in a certain way (12:6, 9). More regulations follow regarding these sacrificial meals and the proper way they are to be taken (12:15–28).

Verse 8 summarizes all of this material in a nutshell: "Your pattern of worship will change. Today all of you are doing as you please" (NLT).

12:29–32

AVOIDING SNARES

The second bookend to this passage again warns against the problem and the temptation Israel would face upon entering the promised land (12:29). True worship of the true God might not appear nearly as exciting or as entertaining as the worship of the Canaanites (12:31). That kind of worship is easy to find—they were fully engaged in sexual and violent acts (12:31).

Critical Observation

Unfortunately, not all of God's people listened to these warnings. No sooner had Israel settled in the promised land than there were people attracted and lured into Canaanite worship. It was this problem, this running after Canaanite worship, which finally ruined the faith of Israel in the Old Testament. In chasing after the worldly way, they finally stopped worshiping God altogether and began to worship only themselves and false gods—though still claiming to be true Israelites.

These warnings are all brought to a conclusion in verse 32, where the Lord says again that Israel is to worship Him only as He has taught them.

Take It Home

God wants our worship of Him to be full of true joy in our hearts, but He wants it to be offered according to His Word and law. He clearly does not see the two things to be in contradiction at all: True worship is to be at the same time both joyful and lawful.

True worship requires preparation and determination. And one must practice true joy in the Lord so that nothing is done as a mere duty, but all is happily a work of love and thanksgiving to God. It is work, hard work, but those who have learned to worship God this way will attest to its ultimate satisfaction. It is work so rewarding as not to be thought work at all.

DEUTERONOMY 13:1–18

CONTEND OR DIE

Setting Up the Section

Deuteronomy 13 continues the warnings about worshiping other gods. Here, however, the source of temptation is not the Canaanites, as in chapter 12, but rather people among the Israelites themselves.

13:1–5

AMONG RELIGIOUS LEADERS

Deuteronomy 13 contains the same warning repeated three different times, but each time with reference to a different group of people within the covenant community who may tempt the people to infidelity to God and His Word.

Critical Observation

The New Testament is just as severe as the Old in its condemnation of false teaching and in the steps it requires to be taken to protect the church from it. Execution has been changed to excommunication, but the issue is the same: The heresies that people foster in the church destroy the soul and bring the wrath of God. No one is to toy with eternal damnation.

In verses 1–5, the Israelites are warned that their own prophets may undermine the truth and that Israel must stand ready to oppose even those with authority and reputation if they contradict the Word of God. The remarkable warning in verse 2, that false teachers may be able to work miraculous signs, reminds us that Moses is writing in an age of miracles—even Egyptian magicians had performed at least one miracle. It is a further demonstration of the general fact that falsehood will always have its powerful inducements and arguments—if not miracles, then through the appearance of compassion or broadmindedness or the approbation of the world.

We read that these false teachers will entice God's people to follow other gods. But this is the biblical judgment as to the true meaning of their message. Very few false teachers come out and say, "Let's abandon God's truth and follow this new way." They almost always say that they are really the defenders and promoters of God's truth, as Aaron does when he calls the revelry around the golden calf a festival to the Lord (Exodus 32:5).

13:6–11

WITHIN THE FAMILY

Verses 6–11 warn the people even against members of their own families, whose wanderings from the truth they would be most likely to excuse and whose punishment they would be most reticent to impose. It would not be a difficult thing to name any number of sons (or husbands, or wives, or brothers) of godly people whose teaching led God's people astray through the generations.

The Lord requires the most severe punishment for those who are found guilty of infidelity to the Word of God: execution (13:5, 9–11, 15). The reason is just this: This falsehood will kill the souls of many others who turn away from the Lord (13:10). As Moses says in verse 11, only punishments as severe as this will serve to prevent others from embracing the same deadly errors and evils.

Demystifying Deuteronomy

It is characteristic of the Lord's teaching in the Bible to devote Himself to one aspect or part of a subject in one place and to leave other aspects of the same theme for consideration in another place and time. Here in Deuteronomy 13, the Lord is instructing His people that they are to contend for the truth and that any disloyalty to the Word of God, any effort to weaken the church's commitment to God's revealed will in the Bible, is to be vigorously and thoroughly exposed and punished.

13:12–18

IN THE TOWNS

Finally, in verses 12–18, Moses warns that in the towns especially there may be a general revolt that takes place against the Word and law of God as fashions and tastes change from time to time. One commentator speaks of "urban revolutionaries," but he is probably referring to people with modern ideas who appear in every generation, arguing that in one way or another the Word of God is out-of-date and needs revision.

If the Israelites catch even a whiff of the scent of such infidelity, they are to take immediate action to find out whether the rumors and reports have substance (13:12–14). They are not to wait to see if heresy comes to full flower; they are to make every effort to locate it and nip it in the bud.

Take It Home

We live in a relativistic age in which the greatest sin is to judge and condemn the convictions of others. In an age like ours, which in some important ways is very similar to that of Canaan in the time of Moses, there will be constant pressure on the truth. And Moses' point is that pressure will be everywhere: in the teaching ministry of the church itself, in our own Christian families, and in new consensuses forming in the Christian population. If we are not constantly on guard, we will be overwhelmed by falsehoods insinuating themselves into the body of the church.

And so that we are not and cannot be seen to be hypocrites, let us first promise the Lord again that before we defend that truth and contend for it in every part, we will first obey it and believe it ourselves. The best defenders of God's truth are always those who truly believe that "Man does not live on bread alone, but on every word that proceeds from the mouth of the LORD" (Deuteronomy 8:3 NIV; Matthew 4:4 NIV).

DEUTERONOMY 14:1–29

A HOLY, GIVING PEOPLE

The Holiness of the Laity	14:1–21
To Tithe or Not to Tithe	14:22–29

Setting Up the Section

Deuteronomy, in its recapitulation of the commandments about clean and unclean animals, gives but a brief account of the laws of cleanliness. This paragraph in Deuteronomy 14 should be understood as representing the much longer legislation touching ceremonial cleanliness in Leviticus 11–15.

14:1–21

THE HOLINESS OF THE LAITY

There is much that remains obscure in these particular laws distinguishing between clean and unclean animals, recorded here in 14:1–21. In fact, the identity of some of the animals named in the verses is not certain. But, more important, the principle of why one animal is clean and another unclean is also by no means certain.

Demystifying Deuteronomy

Leviticus 11–15 records not only the laws distinguishing between clean and unclean animals, but about uncleanness contracted by a woman through childbirth, uncleanness from skin diseases, uncleanness in one's home from the appearance of mildew, and uncleanness contracted by men and women from discharges from the sexual organs. In each case, the law describes how Israelites became unclean, what the consequences of that uncleanness are, and how they are to remove the uncleanness.

There are at least five major theories to explain this distinction between clean and unclean animals.

First, there are those who maintain that the division is entirely arbitrary. God divided the animals this way and gave these laws as a test of obedience. But this distinction between clean and unclean animals is of very great antiquity. It already existed in the days of Noah, as we learn from Genesis 7:2. This suggests that there was some basis for this distinction and that this basis was known to various peoples of the ancient world.

Second, others argue that the division between clean and unclean animals is due to the use of the same animals in pagan worship, but this explanation hardly accounts for all the facts. Pagan religions also made extensive use of the bull, sheep, and goat, even in sacrificial ritual, and these are all considered to be clean animals.

Third, one of the most popular explanations for this distinction between clean and unclean animals is that it is rooted in hygienic considerations. Many of the unclean animals were, in fact, carriers of diseases, and would have been known to be so in the ancient world. But this explanation likewise leaves much unexplained. Why, for example, is the camel unclean? And if hygiene is the right approach, why does Jesus do away with the distinction?

Others argue a fourth theory, namely that animals are categorized as clean or unclean according to a symbolic significance: the clean animals representing traits Israel is to emulate. For example, chewing the cud reminds one of contemplative meditation upon God's law. Sheep remind one of the shepherd. Pigs, on the other hand, suggest nothing positive. This explanation, however, leaves much more unexplained than it can account for.

Finally, there is a new interpretation gaining ground among biblical scholars. One might describe it as the "sociological explanation." It argues that in any culture there is an instinctive recognition of certain things as the standard or ideal against which other things are judged. Birds with wings and two bent legs that eat seeds are proper, or normal, birds. Killer birds and straight-legged birds do not conform to the ideal, and are thus improper and unclean. Fish with scales and fins conform to the ideal concept of fish. Others that do not are unclean. Because the cow, sheep, and goat are the standard fare in the ancient Near East, and hence normal, those animals that do not conform to their pattern of cud-chewing and cloven hoof are abnormal and unclean.

It does not appear, then, that any perfectly satisfactory explanation has been yet advanced to explain why certain animals are clean and certain unclean. Perhaps the true explanation lies in a combination of several of these theories. But it is not necessary for us to know everything about the origin of such laws in order to receive instruction from Deuteronomy 14.

Moses himself indicates the general significance of this legislation about clean and unclean animals with the statement he makes in verses 1–2 and again in verse 21: "You are a people holy to the LORD your God." God's people are to live as a mirror in which God's own holiness is reflected in the world. All of God's people—not just priests—are to be holy.

These laws bring the demands of divine holiness into every aspect of a faithful Israelite's life. At every turn, he or she is faced with the demand that God's people be holy because God is holy and in their midst. God's holiness is to prevail also at their tables and at the taking of meals; they are the people of God, and in their eating and drinking, as in every other part of their lives, they are to be holy as their God is holy. The family could not sit down to a meal without the requirements of their heavenly Father's holiness impinging upon them. In this way, Israel is constantly impressed with the need to be fit for God's service, fit to approach Him, to worship Him, and fit to reflect something of His glory in the world.

Take It Home

While the purpose of the distinction between clean and unclean animals functioned primarily to distinguish between Israelite (Jew) and Gentile, there is significance behind the regulation that still has meaning for us today. We, too, are required to be holy, because our heavenly Father is holy. And though the demands of God's holiness upon us are not illustrated and taught and recollected in the same way they were in the days of Moses, the demands themselves are just as comprehensive, searching, and universal as they were in that ancient time when, no matter where an Israelite turned, he bumped into reminders of the fact that he had to behave as a child of the holy God.

14:22–29

TO TITHE OR NOT TO TITHE

The Israelites are required by the law of God to tithe (14:22). As verse 23 makes clear, they are to tithe not only from their harvested crops, but also from their livestock. One-tenth had to be given as an actual gift to the Lord (Leviticus 27:13).

In this passage, Moses spells out three purposes of tithing. First, it provides for worship for the entire household (14:13–16). The sanctuary meal would have been one of the great occasions of the year for an Israelite family (14:23, 26), and their tithe is put against the cost of the meal. Moses spells out the lesson of the tithe in verse 23. God's people are to tithe in order to learn to revere Him.

A second purpose of tithing is to provide for others (14:27–29). The Levites are able to devote themselves to the priesthood because the people's tithes provided for them (14:27, 29); they did not have to work in the fields or tend flocks in order to make a living. Also, tithing provided a communal storehouse from which to feed the needy—the outsiders, the fatherless, and the widows (14:29).

And finally, regular tithing is God's appointed way to drive home to His people that their prosperity does not depend, as appearances might suggest, on the bounty of the land or their own skill as farmers and herdsmen, but upon the blessing and the provision of their heavenly Father (14:29). The people, with their produce and income, give back a portion to the One who has given it all to them in the first place; year after year they must reckon with the fact that everything they have is a gift from God.

DEUTERONOMY 15:1–23

HOLY EXTRAVAGANCE

Setting Up the Section

Deuteronomy 15 flows thematically from the previous chapter. Deuteronomy 14 concludes with a concern for the poor and the tithe as a means of providing for the poor. Deuteronomy 15 continues the concern for the disadvantaged—in this case, those in debt and those who have to sell themselves as servants.

15:1–11

CANCELING DEBTS

God weaves mercy into the fabric of Israel's life by commanding that debts be canceled every seven years (15:1–2). Opinions vary as to whether the entire debt was to be permanently terminated, or whether payments were only suspended for the seventh year. It's likely the latter is more probable, and this provision has to do with the fact that according to the Law of Moses, in that same seventh year the land was to lie fallow. Many poor people, without the income of the land, would be unable to make payments on their debt and would, therefore, experience even greater hardship, such as being forced into servanthood, which is discussed in verses 12–18.

Critical Observation

Debts were to be canceled every seventh year. The number seven was significant among many ancient Near Eastern peoples—possibly having to do with the cycles of the moon. But for the Israelites, the number seven stood for something that was complete—reflecting the seven days of creation.

If the Israelites follow this law, there will be no poverty in Israel (15:4–8).

Verses 7–11, however, acknowledge that this condition will not be faithfully met. Therefore, the people need instruction about being generous to the poor. The requirement of charity extends past the letter of the law to the attitude of the heart (15:9–10).

15:12–18

FREEING SERVANTS

The servanthood referred to in verses 12–18 could as easily be called slavery. Unlike slavery as we think of it today, this form of slavery provided a solution to the person who could no longer support himself. He could sell himself with the assurance that his servitude was only temporary (15:12) and that he would not go away empty-handed when his time of service ends (15:13–14). Lest the wealthy think this freeing of servants is too much to ask, God reminds them that they were slaves in Egypt and were given their freedom by God (15:15). God's lavish love for them has become the pattern of their lives; loving God and wanting to honor Him, they seek to imitate Him in the extravagance of love.

Demystifying Deuteronomy

One of the unique and remarkable features of the Mosaic Law is its genuine concern for the individual member of society, and especially the poorer and weaker members. Elsewhere in the ancient Near East, men were treated according to their social and economic status. In the Code of Hammurabi, for example, the slave and the underprivileged counted less before the law. But in Israel, the needy were the special concern of the Lord, and the covenant community was expected to ensure their welfare.

The Israelites' laws were wonderfully different from those of the people around them, because they were the people of God. God required things of them that a worldly calculation would never think of or approve. But then, by faith, Israel could enter a world and see a truth that was hidden from unbelievers.

A servant can choose to forgo emancipation and remain in service to his master (15:16). David later describes the custom of piercing a servant's earlobe to show his willingness to serve God (Psalm 40:6), and the writer of Hebrews quotes David when describing Jesus' willingness to become a servant (Hebrews 10:5–10).

This section concludes with a practical word: "Do not consider it a hardship to set your servant free, because his service to you these six years has been worth twice as much as that of a hired hand" (Deuteronomy 15:18 NIV).

15:19–23

FIRSTBORN ANIMALS

Verses 19–23 briefly touch on setting aside the firstborn animals for the Lord. Like the tithed animals (14:22–29), these animals belong to the Lord and may be eaten only by those who offer them. This section, along with the section on tithing in chapter 14, frames the instructions on debts and servants, putting concern for the impoverished in the context of what is owed to God.

Take It Home

The simple question posed to us by these commandments in Deuteronomy 15 is this: What in your life is the equivalent to this extravagance and immoderation? In what way have you cancelled debts, freed slaves, and given up the firstborn of your flocks and herds? What do you do for no other reason than God's grace to you demands a lavish response from you? As is mentioned three times in this chapter (verses 6, 10, 18), God reserves His blessing for those who serve Him in this abandoned way.

DEUTERONOMY 16:1–17

THE GOD OF HOLIDAYS

Passover	16:1–8
Feast of Weeks	16:9–12
Feast of Tabernacles	16:13–17

Setting Up the Section

The chapter gives only a summary statement on the three great yearly feasts of the Israelite calendar. More complete legislation is found in Exodus 12; 23:14–17; Leviticus 23; and Numbers 28:16–31.

16:1–8

PASSOVER

The month of Abib (16:1) is later called *Nisan*. On today's Jewish calendar, it marks the beginning of the religious year. The festival of Passover (16:2–4) celebrates the Angel of Death passing over the homes of believing Israelites in Egypt (Exodus 12:14–20).

While only the adult males are required to attend the Passover ritual at the central tabernacle, and later the temple in Jerusalem (Deuteronomy 16:5, 16), every Israelite family participates in their homes, starting in the evening (16:6) as on the first Passover. The tents to which the men are to return (16:7) are their temporary lodgings at the sanctuary where they stay for the six days of the festival (16:8).

Critical Observation

The Hebrew word for "feast" used in these verses is *Hag*, which reminds us of the Muslim annual pilgrimage to Mecca, the Haj. The idea of pilgrimage belongs to the Hebrew word as well.

16:9–12

FEAST OF WEEKS

The Feast of Weeks is so called because it begins seven weeks after the offering of a sheaf of new grain (16:9). The date is given more precisely in Leviticus 23:15–16 as fifty days after the beginning of Passover, which is the reason the festival is also called Pentecost (*pente* means "fifty"). In Exodus and Numbers, it is also called Harvest and Firstfruits, because the freewill offering (16:10) comes from the first produce of the harvest.

The celebration includes a trip to Jerusalem and the temple, wonderful food, grand ceremonies, and no normal labor, allowing free time for sightseeing and recreation—and all of it is made more special because of the sacred and holy connotations in the festival itself (16:11–12).

Demystifying Deuteronomy

The three feasts described here (Passover, the Feast of Weeks, and the Feast of Tabernacles) are still celebrated by observant Jews today. Passover begins on the fifteenth day of the month of Nisan on the Israelite calendar—sometime in March or April of the Gregorian calendar. The Feast of Weeks begins on the sixth of Sivan (in May or June), and the Feast of Tabernacles on the fifteenth of Tishri (late September through October).

16:13–17

FEAST OF TABERNACLES

The Feast of Tabernacles (16:13–15), or Booths, is celebrated at the autumn harvest of produce (grapes, olives, dates, figs). In Exodus it is also called the Feast of Ingathering. Part of the festival is camping out for the week, living in booths as a reminder of their camping in the wilderness following the exodus from Egypt. Every Israelite man is required to celebrate these three feasts every year (16:16). Giving to God (via the tabernacle or temple offerings) is an essential part of all three festivals (16:17).

Take It Home

Isn't it remarkable that God should require of His people that they take so many holidays? That He should want to be remembered by His people over a meal? That He should seek to build their faith in such a happy and festive way? This is a point hardly confined to the Old Testament pilgrimage feasts; it's a theme woven through all the Bible. We are to be a festive people.

Deuteronomy 16 is a call to all of us to live festive lives, in our families and in our church fellowship. It is our inheritance as the people of God, part of our calling, ministry, witness, and most importantly, it is to God's honor.

DEUTERONOMY 16:18–17:13

UNDER AUTHORITY

Judges	16:18–20
Responsibility of Every Believer	16:21–17:7
Law Courts	17:8–13

Setting Up the Section

In this section, God is saying that His people must be under His authority and live their lives under that authority. These verses are about judges, trials, and punishment, but that is all to demonstrate that God requires His will be done in the community of His people. All of this instruction is to that end and purpose.

16:18–20

JUDGES

Each town has its own legal system, though there is also a central, or national, system. The officials referred to in verse 18 likely hold a role similar to that of police officers. Judges and officials must rule according to the will of God. They are to enact justice—which is to enforce the laws and commandments of God and those only (16:19). If by the faithful exercise of their office the judges ensure that God's people are living according to God's Word, the people of God will live and prosper in the land (16:20). Contrarily, if they do not, as we read often in Deuteronomy, they will lose both God's blessing and the land.

Demystifying Deuteronomy

The judges referred to in 16:18 are the leaders whose appointment was described in Deuteronomy 1:9–18.

16:21–17:7

RESPONSIBILITY OF EVERY BELIEVER

The judges and officials, along with other government officials of Israel, are appointed by the Lord precisely to ensure that His people remain faithful and obedient to Him. The people have already been commanded to tear down the Asherah poles at Canaanite centers of worship when they enter the land (chapter 12), and now they are told not to set up any of their own, nor to offer defective sacrifices (16:21–17:1).

Deuteronomy 17:2–7 is closely related to 4:15–24 and 13:1–8 in its discussion of God-pleasing worship. Disloyalty to God is equivalent to treason and undermines the security of the people. When God's people refuse to live in submission to God's authority, terrible consequences ensue (16:5–6). By casting the first stone, the witnesses are laid under the onus of murder if they testify falsely (17:7).

17:8–13

LAW COURTS

It isn't at all hard to imagine what the difficulties in judgment (17:8) might be, for they were the same as we face today. Difficulties arise when courts are faced with a set of complex circumstances that the law doesn't precisely address. Such cases are to be submitted to priests for judgment (17:9–11). The priest's comprehensive knowledge of the scripture helps ensure that the judgment rendered is in keeping with God's Word. No doubt, after a time, a body of precedents will be compiled to aid judges in adjudicating cases, just as in modern times.

Critical Observation

In Deuteronomy 17:10–11, the command to obey the priests and judges is, "Do not turn aside from what they tell you, to the right or to the left." This is exactly the same kind of language used for obedience to the law of God: "So be careful to do what the Lord your God has commanded you; do not turn aside to the right or to the left" (Deuteronomy 5:32 NIV); "Do not turn aside from any of the commands I give you today, to the right or to the left, following other gods and serving them" (Deuteronomy 28:14 NIV). The use of this language reinforces the message that obedience to God's appointed leaders is obedience to God Himself.

In verse 12, the point is made again that priests and judges are ministers of the Lord. A minister is one who does not act for himself or in his own name but carries the authority of another and speaks and acts in His name and with His authority.

The whole reason for priests and judges is to ensure that God Himself is obeyed. When sin is tolerated and wickedness goes unpunished, the commitment of the whole community to the law of God and the life of obedience is undermined. This is the point of verse 13. Faithful discipline, correction, and, if necessary, even the most extreme punishments, are carried out so that the obedience and faithfulness of others will be preserved and fostered. If unfaithfulness is tolerated, it will soon become the normal way of life. This is why God is so severe in His demand for the punishment and the correction of such conduct among His people.

Take It Home

God calls His people to obey Him by obeying His officers, those entrusted to rule on His behalf and in His name. In the Christian church today, you will quickly run into individuals who make a great show of their submission to the Lord and their zeal to keep His commandments but who won't heed or obey any particular church government or any particular group of elders. These people are defying the Word of God in this unwillingness to submit to those who have been given authority within their church. And their claim to be submissive to God Himself is, in this way, demonstrated to be pretence and hypocrisy.

DEUTERONOMY 17:14–18:22

THE THREE OFFICES

The King	17:14–20
The Priests	18:1–8
The Prophet	18:9–22

Setting Up the Section

Deuteronomy 17:14–18:22 is a highly interesting passage of scripture for the way in which it places together the three great offices of the Old Testament religious structure. God communicates His presence directly to the hearts of His people by His Spirit, and He also uses people as instruments of His presence. He speaks to His people through prophets, He grants forgiveness of sins and maintains fellowship with them through priests, and He rules over them through kings.

17:14–20

THE KING

The instructions here assume that in the future Israel will want a king (17:14). In these guidelines, God is not *recommending* that Israel have a king, but rather *allowing* her to have one. The instructions that follow (17:15–20) will provide for a godly king and a godly reign. This passage makes clear that, like the judges and courts, the king is God's officer, intended to rule on God's behalf. Unfortunately, the many wives and much gold that Moses warns against (17:17) do indeed lead future kings astray.

Demystifying Deuteronomy

Deuteronomy 17:14 says that the Israelites will want to appoint a king over the land. First Samuel 8 records that, although God warned the Israelites about the hardships of serving a king, they insisted, just as God had predicted: "We want a king over us. Then we will be like all the other nations. . ." (1 Samuel 8:19–20 NIV).

18:1–8

THE PRIESTS

Every man in the tribe of Levi is part of the priesthood (18:1). Rather than working the land, they are to offer sacrifices on behalf of the people. Since their work does not produce a livelihood, the Levites are to be supported by the rest of the people (18:2–8). Like the judges, courts, and king, priests exercise their office for the Lord's sake and in His name (18:7, 15).

18:9–22

THE PROPHET

Between sections devoted to Israel's priesthood and prophecy, several verses forbid them to recognize or make any use of the priestly and prophetic practices of Canaan (18:9). God forbids sacrifices offered to false gods, and here He specifically forbids human sacrifice as well (18:10). Divination, interpreting omens, and consulting the dead (18:10) are ways of trying to predict the future or discover things through human intervention, rather than God's divine intervention through His prophet. Israel is to separate herself from these practices (18:12–14).

Critical Observation

Peter (in Acts 3:22–23) quotes Deuteronomy 18:15 about the prophet to come. He says Jesus is a prophet like Moses but greater than Moses.

Moses promises that God will raise up a prophet like him (18:15). A prophet's job is to deliver God's messages to God's people. Moses reminds Israel that he fulfilled this prophetic role at Horeb (18:16–20). Prophecy that is proven wrong or that conflicts with God's Word is evidence of a false prophet (18:21–22).

Critical Observation

This is not information of mere historical importance. The offices of prophet, priest, and king—and the officers who filled them in the ancient epoch—were enacted and living prophecies of Jesus Christ. These offices are one of the most important ways God chose to reveal in advance what the Messiah would be, what He would do, and how He would save His people from their sins.

All of this about the Savior being a prophet, priest, and king is taken up in detail in the New Testament and applied to Jesus Christ (Matthew 27:11; Luke 4:17–19; Hebrews 5:5–6). All the other prophets in the Bible were a part of the prophetic work of Jesus Christ, but He Himself is its culmination and completion. He is the Word of God. All that we need to know, He has taught us by His Word and Spirit.

In our guilt, we are estranged from God and subject to His wrath. And so Christ, the High Priest, came and offered a sacrifice to satisfy divine justice and make us friends with God again. And, when the work was done, He ascended to heaven and there continues to be our High Priest by interceding for us.

Take It Home

In the old days in Israel, if people got wind that there was a prophet in the area, they dropped what they were doing and ran to hear him speak so that they might know what God was saying to them. People went to the priest to unburden themselves of their sins and their problems and to request prayer. The people also gathered before their king to declare their allegiance to him and to promise him their obedience. We ought to do no less today, for One who is far greater in every way, and far better able to help us, is now our Prophet, Priest, and King

DEUTERONOMY 19:1–21

LEST INNOCENT BLOOD BE SHED

Setting Up the Section

The apparent subject of the chapter is the laws governing murder and its punishment. But, really, the subject of the chapter is the purpose of all of these laws, which is stated in Deuteronomy 19:10—that innocent blood not be shed in the land. This is the purpose of all that we read in this chapter.

19:1–14

CITIES OF REFUGE

In addition to the three cities already set aside east of the Jordan mentioned in Deuteronomy 4:41–43, the people are to establish three cities on the west of the Jordan. This is an expansion of the law of Exodus 21:12–14, according to which the altar is a sanctuary, or asylum, for someone who has accidentally killed another. There he cannot be molested by anyone bent on vengeance. But when Israel enters the land, the altar is too far away, and a person fleeing to it might not reach it before being overtaken by the avenger of blood. Hence three centrally located cities (Deuteronomy 19:1–7).

Demystifying Deuteronomy

The term "cities of refuge," which many translations use as a paragraph heading, does not appear in this chapter, but it is used in Numbers 35:6, 11 for these same cities.

The avenger of blood (19:6) is not merely a hotheaded relative bent on revenge but the kinsman who by culture and law is responsible to see that justice is carried out.

The cities of refuge are not only for the purpose of asylum; they are also places of punishment, for while manslaughter may not be murder, in many cases it is still wrong. In Numbers 35:25–28, where the more comprehensive explanation of these cities is found, the law states that in some cases, once a person is found to be guilty of manslaughter, he is to be returned to the city of refuge and remain there until the death of the high priest. If he leaves that city, the avenger of blood is free to take his life. In effect, the city of refuge then becomes a prison, though certainly not like modern prisons.

The purpose of these cities of refuge is that no innocent blood is shed. Executing an innocent man is equivalent to murder, making the community as a whole guilty of bloodshed (19:10). Another way that innocent blood might be shed is to let a murderer go unpunished (19:11–12). If executing an innocent man is a crime to be avoided at all costs, so is the failure to punish a murderer by execution. Failure in that case also renders the community guilty of bloodshed (19:13).

A boundary stone marks the edge of a person's property (19:14). To move it is essentially to rob a person of that portion of land.

19:15–21

WITNESSES

All of this information about cities of refuge and trials to discriminate between what is truly murder and what is something less is to ensure that no one be executed for anything other than a capital crime.

Trials are to be conducted in every case. One witness, even an eyewitness, is not sufficient to prove the guilt of an accused murderer. There must be two or three, which is a cryptic way of saying that the evidence must be incontestable (19:15). The scripture clearly entertains the possibility that guilty men might go free for want of adequate evidence.

Witnesses are sworn to the truth upon the most serious penalty should they be found to have perjured themselves (19:16–17). If a witness's lie results in the condemning of an innocent man to death, the witness is executed (19:18–19).

The point made in verse 20 is the principle of deterrence. Swift, sure, and just punishment is to deter others from the commission of the same crime. Failure to provide such punishment, by implication, will lead others to a greater willingness to commit such crimes.

Critical Observation

The law of retaliation in verse 21 is also found in Exodus 21:23–25 and Leviticus 24:17–20.

The principle of justice by equity is stated in Deuteronomy 19:21—punishments are to be, as far as possible, the exact equivalent of the crime. An eye for an eye, a hand for a hand, and a life for a life means that justice requires a murderer forfeit his own life. Anything less or more is not retribution in proportion to the crime. Other ancient Near Eastern law codes (famously, the Code of Hammurabi) sometimes insisted on excessive punishments, so the guidelines here function to guard from that excess.

Take It Home

The perspective of scripture is twofold. First, being made in the image of God, the life of a human is sacred, and this in itself makes it a crime of unimaginable proportion for one person to murder another. Because we are made in the image of God, it is a form of deicide (of God-killing) as well as homicide to lift up our hand against our neighbor.

Second, justice is a matter of equity and, in the case of a criminal, his receiving what is due. Humans instinctively, if not always consistently, recognize the wrong of a small crime being punished with a great penalty—a man being sent to Devil's island for stealing a loaf of bread for his hungry family—or contrarily, of a great crime being punished with a small penalty. This is the principle expressed in the statue of justice as a woman with eyes blindfolded holding balances or scales in her hand. Crime lies on one side of the balance, punishment on the other, and the scales are to be even at the end of the matter. Justice requires an impartial reckoning of a punishment which fits the crime.

DEUTERONOMY 20:1–20

THE COMMANDS OF GOD ARE NOT A BURDEN

Exemptions from Military Service	20:1–9
Offering Peace	20:10–20

Setting Up the Section

Chapter 20 begins a section of the book of Deuteronomy devoted to particular laws addressing many different issues. In certain cases, they reiterate points that have already been made in previous chapters. This chapter, for example, recapitulates some of what was already stated in chapter 7: laws governing the conduct of war.

20:1–9

EXEMPTIONS FROM MILITARY SERVICE

Israel's strength lay not in the size or equipment of her army, but in her God, and this is a matter not only of faith, but of her own experience. Egypt has a far greater army than the ill-equipped and untrained Israelite people, but it is the vaunted army of Egypt that is destroyed in the Red Sea (20:1). Before the battle, the priest is to remind the soldiers of the fact that God is worth many armies (20:2–4).

The officers mentioned in verse 5 probably refer to officials of the tribes of Israel, not to army officers, as is confirmed in verse 9. These men, knowing their tribe, would know which ones qualify to be exempted from service (20:5–8). God thinks it important to ensure that no man dying in battle should be deprived of the pleasure of seeing his new vineyard begin to bear fruit, and that no young man miss the joy of marrying his bride. God doesn't require the same thing of the fainthearted that He does of the brave.

Demystifying Deuteronomy

The point briefly made in verse 6 is made with more detail in Leviticus 19:23–25, with reference to fruit-bearing plants in general—trees as well as vines. For the first three years, no fruit was to be taken. The fourth year, the fruit was to be dedicated to the Lord, and from the fifth year on, the fruit was to be harvested and sold or eaten. Those who were engaged in this lengthy process—one which was very important for the long-term production of the land—were exempted from army service. God is always after His people's welfare. He didn't want farms and orchards and vineyards ruined because the men who had to cultivate and care for them were absent at the critical period.

It is clear that Israel, at least at this early stage, does not maintain a standing army or has very little of one. For each war, the army has to be recruited separately (20:9).

Take It Home

Chief among the lessons taught by the laws on exemption from military service is this: As the apostle John would later say, God's commandments are not burdensome. These verses are simply teaching in another way that the law of God is one of God's great gifts to His people, and it is intended to lead them into a life that is rich, secure, satisfying, and fruitful.

All of us chafe under the commandments of God. We have a rebellious streak, and, much like little children, we resent being told what to do. God's commands are kindly given and well-meant, and the one who lives by them is going to find a great reward. In Deuteronomy 20:1–9, we are being taught to love and cherish the laws and commandments of God as not only right, but good and health-giving.

20:10–20

OFFERING PEACE

It is often overlooked that outside of the promised land, God commands that the Israelites offer peace before attacking cities (20:10). Only if the rulers of the city reject the offer of peace are the Israelites to attack (20:11–13). Even then, the women and children are to be spared (20:14–15). Deuteronomy 15 outlines rights of the captives and provisions for incorporating them into the Israelite community.

The rules are different for the neighboring cities, however (20:16). The laws laid out in Deuteronomy 7:1–6 are summarized here (20:17), along with the reason for them: to keep Israel from being led astray (20:18).

Ancient military powers often destroyed everything they found on the land they conquered. But God's covenant with Noah extends to the earth as well; the trees are not to be destroyed (20:19–20). This provision allows the land to remain productive.

DEUTERONOMY 21:1–23

LAWS FOR DIFFICULT SITUATIONS

Setting Up the Section

This chapter gives laws that govern three sets of issues. The first is what to do on the discovery of a murdered body when there is no way to ascertain who committed the crime. The second set of laws governs family life, and the third set of laws governs how to handle the remains of a person who has been executed for a crime.

21:1–9

UNSOLVED MURDER

The point of mentioning a field in the land from God (21:1) is that a person murdered in the promised land is killed on sacred soil. For this reason, the sin is elevated—it isn't just a sin against this person who dies and his family, but also a sin against God because it desecrates His land. The process is set up to preserve the honor of God and make right what has been desecrated. In this, the holiness of God is seen as something to take very seriously.

Having determined the nearest town by measurement (21:2), the elders and judges of the district (see 16:18) will instruct the elders of that town the prescribed duties for making things right.

The fact that the animal and field have never been worked (21:3–4) suggests that they are undefiled, never having been ritually contaminated by humans. Something clean has to be offered for the unclean act of a murder. The heifer is to be killed in a very specific manner—it must have its neck broken (21:4).

Critical Observation

By breaking the heifer's neck, there would be no blood shed, for this offering was different from a traditional sin offering, which requires the shedding of blood (Leviticus 17:11). Blood sacrifices always had to be offered on altars at recognized centers (see Deuteronomy 12), therefore shedding this blood at a random town would not be acceptable.

The priests, chosen by the Lord not only to offer sacrifices and pronounce blessings but also to function in judicial capacities (see 17:9; 19:17), assume a role in the proceedings (21:5). Since the murderer is unknown, it is the guilt or innocence of the community at large that is at stake. The entire point of this ritual is to make the community clean.

The town elders, on behalf of all the people, are to symbolize the innocence of the community by washing their hands over the carcass of the heifer, state their collective innocence of the deed, plead with the Lord to accept their act of exculpation, and absolve them of any blame for the death of the victim (21:6–9).

21:10–21

WIVES AND CHILDREN

A bride taken as a captive is to shave her head, trim her nails, discard her native clothing, and fulfill a month of mourning for her parents before becoming a wife of an Israelite (21:10–13). All these procedures represent cutting off all ties to the former life. It is important that the bride enter into her new life fully and unreservedly.

Demystifying Deuteronomy

The cities attacked in this scenario would be distant cities (20:10–15)—which probably means they were not Canaanite cities (for it was against the law to marry Canaanites—see Exodus 34:16; Deuteronomy 7:3).

The reality is, because of the sinful nature of humanity, not all relationships will be successful. The husband could therefore end the marriage by simply releasing his wife to go wherever she wishes. He is forbidden to sell her as property or regard her as a slave.

Critical Observation

It is important to note that Deuteronomy 21:14 is not endorsing divorce. Jesus says (in Mark 10:5) that these laws are in place to protect the women, not to endorse a behavior. The laws were in place so that a woman would be treated in a respectable manner even if her husband chose to send her away.

A husband's attitude toward his wife is not to affect his legal responsibilities to her and her children. If he has two wives and the one he does not love gives him the firstborn male, he cannot favor the firstborn son of the wife that he does love (21:15–16). The matter of law that is pertinent here is the proper bestowal of inheritance rights. On the basis of what appears to be a long-standing custom, the eldest son is to receive a double portion of his father's estate (21:17). This is a stipulation first recorded here in biblical law.

The motive for this is clearly articulated: The firstborn is the first sign of his father's strength (21:17). What this means is that a man first gives indication of his virility and capacity to sire succeeding generations when his first son is born (see Genesis 49:3; Psalm 105:36). It is only fitting that the son who gives the father such recognition be recognized himself for what he symbolizes. Therefore, the rights of the firstborn are not based upon feelings or relationships but on what the firstborn son represents.

At the basic level of civil society is the family. A child who cannot obey his parents shows that he or she does not possess the fundamental skill to function properly in a society. In this case, the parents have a responsibility to the society at large to deal with this issue.

Specifically, the charge is that a child who is stubborn-minded (21:18) against his father and mother is disobeying the fifth commandment (to honor your father and your mother, Deuteronomy 5:16). This rebellious son is to be brought to the gate (21:19), that is, the broad plaza just outside the gate where matters of public interest are conducted. The court before which the case is presented consists of elders (21:20), not those of a district or the whole nation but the rulers of the local village. It is they who hear the evidence and rule on the case.

Once the case is heard and the elders judge the child to be guilty as charged, the townsmen execute the felon by stoning. Only by this drastic means can the evil be purged (21:21) from the community. Since this child proves to be nothing more than a plague on the society, he has to be removed. This is the last step in dealing with a child's rebellion—not the first step. It is done only after evidence of uncontrollable and dangerous rebellion that would cause the whole of society to be hindered.

21:22–23

CAPITAL PUNISHMENT

The cause of death might not be by hanging, for in this text the act of hanging follows the person's having been put to death (21:22). The purpose of such a postmortem hanging is to provide a sober warning to the community of the serious consequences of the crime committed.

The corpse is to be brought down and buried before sunset because the curse applied to the criminal would otherwise accrue to the community and the land as a whole (21:23).

Take It Home

Why an individual who was put on display on a tree was considered especially cursed is not clear. What is clear is that God wanted the people to recognize that someone hanging from wood was under God's curse. This is a foreshadowing of the cross. The apostle Paul quotes Deuteronomy 21:23 when talking about Jesus: "Christ redeemed us from the curse of the law by becoming a curse for us—for it is written, 'Cursed is everyone who is hanged on a tree'" (Galatians 3:13 ESV). When Jesus was hanging on the cross, cursed, He took on our guilt and the punishment that we deserved. Imagine the love that inspired Jesus to willingly take God's curse upon Himself!

DEUTERONOMY 22:1–30

LAWS ABOUT LOVE AND SEX

Setting Up the Section

The laws here deal with the sixth and seventh of the Ten Commandments and the themes that lie beneath them—the sanctity of life and marriage.

22:1–8

ONE'S BROTHER'S KEEPER

The brother referred to in verse 1 is not related by blood but by membership in the same spiritual community. There is to be no "finders, keepers" among brothers; possession is not nine-tenths of the law. Any straying animal or lost possession is to be returned (22:1–3), and each person is to be responsible for caring for his neighbor's animals if the owner is away (22:4).

Take It Home

Our natural tendency is to reduce the obligation we owe to others to doing them no harm. In these laws in Deuteronomy 22:1–4, we indeed are forbidden to harm our neighbors; but far more than that, we are required actually to do them good. We are not simply to leave them in the condition we find them in, but we are to improve their lot and help them. They are to be the better for our encounter with them.

There is nothing in it for the one who keeps these laws. At least, there is no gain in any outward or material sense. If you find a lost animal you are to catch it, take it home, care for it—perhaps at some considerable expense to yourself—and then when you locate the owner or he finds you, you are to return the animal to him at no charge! Your neighbor's need has become your obligation.

Not many of us have cows, but we all have lost things we need others to help us find. All of us in one way or another need a bit more of what others have in abundance. How different might the community of believers be, and how much more powerful might our witness to the world be, if only we would make one large step forward in loving one another and caring for one another heartily and positively as God commands us here in Deuteronomy to do.

The command about clothing (22:5) is not a statement about fashion so much as it is about real confusion of genders, specifically transvestism. Some suggest this command is related to pagan practices in the nations around Israel at that time.

The instruction to leave a mother bird on the nest (22:6) is a law of conservation. The potential for future supply is not to be destroyed for the sake of immediate gain. Only if the Israelites take care of the resources around them will it be well with them (24:7).

Roofs were flat and used for sleeping in the summer, for certain chores, and for entertaining, so it is not inconceivable that someone could fall off an unfenced roof (22:8). Protecting people from this danger is the homeowner's responsibility.

22:9–30

MARRIAGE VIOLATIONS

Although many Bible translations put verses 9–12 with the commands in verses 1–6, simply classifying them as "various laws," their relationship to the laws about marriage are closer than it might appear at first reading. Maintaining a separation between different kinds of seeds (22:9), animals (22:10), and fabrics (22:11) reflects the separation Israel is to maintain between herself and the nations around her. Failure to stay separate eventually leads to God's charge of spiritual adultery (see, for example, Jeremiah 3).

Critical Observation

The distinctions in verses 10–11 are more than random examples. The ox (22:10) was a symbol of the Israelites, while the Canaanites were represented by the donkey. Israelite priests wore clothes of wool (22:11); Canaanite priests wore clothes of linen. The imagery here, like the prohibition elsewhere against intermarrying with the Canaanites, illustrates Israel's call to maintain purity and an identity distinct from the pagan nations around her.

If a man slanderously accuses his wife of not being a virgin when they married (21:13–14), her parents can bring proof of her virginity (blood on the bedclothes—verse 17) to the city elders (21:15–17), who will require the husband to pay a fine to the girl's father and deny the right to divorce (21:18–19).

Should the charge be true, however, the woman will be stoned (21:20–21). Note that the men of the village, not just the husband, carry out the execution, indicating, as does the comment about purging Israel, that the sin affects the entire community. The same holds true for those caught in adultery (21:22).

The laws about sex between single, unmarried people take into account a number of factors. First, the offense is more serious if the woman is engaged to another man (21:23, 25, 28). If the liaison took place in the city, both the offending man and the woman are considered equally deserving of execution (21:24), on the assumption that the sex was consensual (if the woman had cried for help in a city, someone would have heard and rescued her). She could not get away with falsely accusing her lover of rape. In the country, however, the woman is given the benefit of the doubt; she may have resisted without anyone being close enough to hear her. In this case, only the rapist receives the death penalty (21:25–27).

Demystifying Deuteronomy

Engagement in ancient Israel was more like marriage than engagements in Western cultures today. The engaged woman described in Deuteronomy 21:23–27 is also referred to as her fiancé's wife (21:24). Unfaithfulness to her betrothed received the same penalty as adultery—death. Likewise, a man who had intercourse with a woman engaged to another man—whether consensually or by rape—was also accounted an adulterer.

A man who raped a woman who was not engaged (21:28) did not receive the death penalty, but he was responsible both to marry the woman and to pay a bride-price to her father (Exodus 22:16–17; Deuteronomy 21:29).

Although in some cases a man's father's wife might not have been the man's mother (if his father had been widowed and remarried, for instance, or in the case of polygamy), marrying her was forbidden; it would dishonor the father (Deuteronomy 21:39).

DEUTERONOMY 23:1–25

VARIOUS LAWS

Exclusion from the Assembly of the Lord	23:1–8
Uncleanness in the Military Camp	23:9–14
Slavery	23:15–16
Prostitution	23:17–18
Loans and Interest	23:19–20
Vows	23:21–23
Eating in a Neighbor's Fields	23:24–25

Setting Up the Section

Chapter 23 continues the laying out of laws relating to a variety of situations.

23:1–8

EXCLUSION FROM THE ASSEMBLY OF THE LORD

These laws were established for those who were being excluded from the corporate worship services of God. The assembly of the Lord (23:1–3) refers to the gathering of the people for corporate worship.

First, no castrated man is allowed (23:1).

Verse 2 can be translated to exclude either those born of a forbidden marriage or those of illegitimate birth. In either case, it refers to a child of an incestuous relationship, a child born out of pagan worship, or a child born outside of marriage. Such a child comes from that which is an affront to God's laws and is thus not allowed at the ceremonies.

The Ammonites and Moabites (23:3) are not allowed to join the worship of Israel because they refused to provide a break and water to the Israelites as they were moving toward the promised land (23:4). In addition, Balak the Moabite king hired Balaam to curse Israel (Numbers 22:2–6; Deuteronomy 23:4–5). Because of their rejection of the children of God, the Israelites are not to seek any reconciliation with these people (23:6). The Moabites and the Ammonites descended from the incestuous relationship between Lot and his daughters (Genesis 19:29–38) and so would have been excluded as those of illegitimate birth as well.

Critical Observation

A later exception to this prohibition against relationships with Moabites is the case of Ruth, a Moabite woman who married into an Israelite family. After being widowed, she returned to the land of Israel with her also widowed mother-in-law, Naomi. Ruth embraced Naomi's people and Naomi's God. Her story can be read in the Old Testament book of Ruth (Ruth 1).

Edomites, however, are considered the Israelites' brothers (Deuteronomy 23:7–8) because they descended from Esau, the brother of Israel's patriarch, Jacob.

Critical Observation

The key to understanding the laws about exclusion from the assembly is that they dealt with the ceremonial aspects of worship. These were not laws excluding people from believing in God, loving God, or having eternal life. These laws were in place to govern the ceremonial worship for the nation of Israel. Since that worship dealt with Israel's sin and redemption, it had to be done in a way that was according to the holiness of God.

23:9–14

UNCLEANNESS IN THE MILITARY CAMP

God wants the army to remember that He is the One who fought for them, and He is in their presence (23:14). With this in mind, they must not be trite about the way they handle their human waste (24:12–13). If a man has nocturnal emissions, out of respect for God, he is required to stay outside the camp until he has bathed himself (23:10–11). This way the camp of the Lord remains clean—for both health reasons and also so that the people will remember that God must always be treated with respect and dignity (23:14).

23:15–16

SLAVERY

The slaves referred to in verse 15 are not Israelites. In most Middle Eastern treaties there is a provision that slaves seeking refuge are to be returned to their owners. But Israel is not to have allegiances to other nations. Slaves from other countries who come to seek sanctuary (refuge) in Israel are to be accepted (23:16). This law no doubt reminds Israel that their treaty is with God, and they do not need any political alliance with another nation.

23:17–18

PROSTITUTION

Another way that Israel is to be different is in the way that they reject the practice of temple prostitution (23:17). This practice was common in the Near East. God rejects this type of religious practice because it degrades sex and it degrades holy worship.

Demystifying Deuteronomy

Unfortunately, Israel failed to observe the command against temple prostitution (1 Kings 14:24; 15:12; 22:46; 2 Kings 23:7; Hosea 4:14). This unfaithfulness was one of the reasons that God later let Israel be conquered and taken into exile.

In addition to temple prostitution, the nation is not to practice prostitution at all. The money that is gained from this is degraded money, and therefore a vow is not to be paid with money obtained in this manner (23:18).

23:19–20

LOANS AND INTEREST

The context of this law is of a brother who has become poor or is in severe need (see Exodus 22:25; Leviticus 25:35–37); he is not borrowing money to engage in a capitalistic endeavor. The point is that to charge a poor brother interest will only worsen his condition. Mercy, kindness, and grace are all virtues that must mark this nation (Deuteronomy 23:19).

An Israelite is permitted to charge a foreigner interest (23:20). This is because he is not a member of the covenant community. Most likely the loan is for business purposes, and it isn't unreasonable to charge interest in this case.

23:21–23

VOWS

In this law (23:21), God wants the Israelites to make sure that when they speak, they speak with honesty and integrity. The vow is a commitment that is not forced upon anyone—it is made out of the volition of the person (23:22–23). Yet, once it is made, it is to be kept without question.

23:24–25

EATING IN A NEIGHBOR'S FIELDS

A traveler is given the right to revive himself from a vineyard or grain field but is not given the right to take grapes with him or to harvest in the field (23:24–25). Since the Lord has been gracious in providing for the farmer, the farmer in turn should be gracious to a stranger traveling through his land. Yet the person in need must not take advantage of the one giving; he must show proper respect for the one from whom he is taking food.

DEUTERONOMY 24:1–22

VARIOUS LAWS CONTINUED

Setting Up the Section

Deuteronomy 24 continues the rather lengthy section devoted to various laws touching many different aspects of life. There is no clearly discernible principle of organization in these chapters. The laws are not even grouped together according to theme, as is clear from the English versions that use paragraph titles such as "Various Laws" and "Miscellaneous Laws."

24:1–5

LAWS ABOUT MARRIAGE

The Old Testament always regards divorce as a tragedy (see Malachi 2:16). The commands in Deuteronomy 24:1–4, then, are given to regulate an already existing practice rather than introducing a new idea. The idea of indecency (24:1) cannot refer to adultery, for which the penalty is death (22:22). It cannot refer to the wife's premarital intercourse with another man, for which the penalty is also death (22:20–21). The precise meaning of the phrase is unknown. If a man finds something indecent, the certificate of divorce he writes is apparently given to the woman for her protection under the law. This certificate keeps her from being completely rejected by society. She is allowed to be free and cared for by another man or her father (24:2).

If after being divorced, a woman remarries and her second husband divorces her or dies, her first husband is not permitted to remarry her since she has been defiled. The word translated *defiled* is often used to describe a man who has committed adultery (Leviticus 18:20). So the use of this word to describe a woman who has been divorced and remarried to the same man suggests that divorce is viewed in a negative light, even though Moses permits it. A remarriage to her former husband is equal to adultery and, therefore, detestable to the Lord (Deuteronomy 24:3–4). The purpose of this law seems to be to prevent trivial divorce and to present divorce in its proper light.

Critical Observation

Jesus' interpretation of Deuteronomy 24:1–4 indicates that divorce (like polygamy) goes against the divine ideal for marriage (see Matthew 19:3–9).

Marriage is held in high honor. Thus the nation is to allow a man to get settled into his new relationship after marriage. It is considered cruel to send a recently married man to war (20:7; 24:5). If he is killed in combat, he will probably have no children to preserve his name in Israel. A newly married man is also to be free of other responsibilities in order to have time to adjust and bring happiness to his wife.

Demystifying Deuteronomy

Deuteronomy 25:5–10 shows how important it was for a man to leave a child to preserve his name.

24:6–22

LAWS MOSTLY ABOUT THE NEEDY

Millstones (24:6) were used daily in homes to grind grain in preparing meals. To take both or one of these as collateral for a debt would deprive a man of his daily bread and therefore contradict the spirit of generosity. Thus, when a loan is made, collateral should never be something that will hurt someone.

The crime of kidnapping (24:7) was common in the ancient Middle East. The law codes of Mesopotamia and the Hittite Empire both mention this issue. In fact, it is still an issue today in this area. Since the kidnapper is depriving his victim of his freedom, the kidnapper is to be punished by death—as though he has taken the victim's life.

Leprous diseases (24:8) refer to a broad range of skin diseases, not exclusively leprosy. Instead of repeating the legislation concerning these diseases, Moses refers the people to his original instruction in Leviticus 13–14. Motivation to obey this ceremonial legislation is furnished by Miriam (24:9), who opposed Moses and is struck with leprosy (see Numbers 12).

A borrower typically gives something to the lender as collateral (Deuteronomy 24:6, 10). For a lender to go inside the borrower's house suggests that the borrower is not trustworthy—as if the lender needs to keep an eye on him to ensure that he will hand over the collateral. By keeping the lender outside the house (24:11), both the borrower's dignity and his possessions are safeguarded—the lender does not have the option to take anything he might want as a pledge.

If the borrower is so poor that all he can offer as a pledge is his cloak (which serves as a blanket at night), then the lender is to return it before nightfall (24:12–13). By acting in this manner, the lender shows love, kindness, and mercy, which must govern all civil relationships in Israel.

This kindness is to be extended to resident aliens as well as to fellow Israelites (24:14). If a man is so poor that he is making ends meet day-to-day, he has the right to receive his wages every day (24:15). This is not merely a suggestion about how an employer should act; it is a requirement. Not to do so is a sin.

The edict that fathers should not be executed for their children's crimes (24:16) must be held in tension with other teaching and laws. This refers primarily to legal responsibility, but even then, there are exceptions (such as Achan's family in Joshua 7).

Verse 17 instructs God's people to pay special attention to protecting the powerless in society: foreigners without a say in the governance in the community, those without fathers to speak and act on their behalf, and widows, who have no voice in society. Lest they forget, Moses reminds the people that they were all once powerless slaves in Egypt (24:18). Just as the Lord looked out for them, they are to look out for others.

Another way of looking out for the needy is by making it possible for them to provide for themselves honestly. Women, in particular, have few vocational options other than prostitution. The practice of leaving part of every harvest—whether it be in the field (24:19), the orchard (24:20), or the vineyard (24:21)—allows those who do not own land to work honestly for their food.

Demystifying Deuteronomy

The practice of leaving part of the harvest for the needy is key to the story of Ruth. God rewarded Boaz, who was so generous that he left extra sheaves, by putting him in the family line of both King David and Jesus Christ.

As in verse 18, Moses again reminds the people that they are not so different from those who are in need of their help (24:22).

Take It Home

The deliverance from Egypt, mentioned in verses 18 and 22, is the great Old Testament picture of our redemption in Jesus Christ. As the Israelites were to respond to God's mercy to them by being merciful to others, so we are to be merciful, kind, and generous to others, because Christ is immeasurably kind and merciful and generous to us. Because He became poor for us, then impoverishing ourselves for others not only makes eminent sense, but it is what we most desperately want to do.

These laws, then, dig down into our motives and absolutely require us genuinely to love others and to love mercy. Without God's grace and mercy animating our hearts, these laws will never be kept. On the other hand, as the Bible says, if God's grace is alive in our hearts, if we love Christ because He first loved us, it is inevitable that the love of others will follow in turn.

DEUTERONOMY 25:1–19

LIVING BEFORE THE HOLY GOD

Disputes	25:1–3
Working Oxen	25:4
Levirate Marriage	25:5–10
How Not to Stop a Fight	25:11–12
Honest Business Dealings	25:13–16
The Destruction of the Amalekites	25:17–19

Setting Up the Section

All of the details of the laws in Deuteronomy 25 point to two important things: God is holy and He is everywhere. Thus these laws highlight the incredible detail with which God's holiness should be taken and how much every person should recognize God's presence every day and everywhere.

25:1–3

DISPUTES

Vigilante justice has no place in Israel. They are to allow a judge to handle disputes (25:1) and determine the appropriate punishment (25:2). The guilty party is not to be flogged more than forty times, so as to provide a consequence without permanently hurting the person (25:3).

25:4

WORKING OXEN

The command not to muzzle an ox while it is treading grain (25:4) stresses kindness and fairness to the animals that help the people survive. Mercy and kindness should extend to animals.

Critical Observation

Deuteronomy 25:4 is quoted in two New Testament books: 1 Corinthians 9:9 and 1 Timothy 5:18, where the use of the passage makes the point that if God cares about a working ox, how much more must He care about human laborers, especially those laboring for His kingdom.

25:5–10

LEVIRATE MARRIAGE

The marriage described in Deuteronomy 25:5–10 is also called *levirate*, from the Latin word that means "brother-in-law." This marriage happens when the deceased relative has died without a male heir. The point of the levirate marriage is to provide a male heir who, in turn, can care for the parents in their old age and keep the property in the family.

God is so concerned about people not losing their family line that the first son born from the levirate marriage is given the deceased brother's name (25:6). This shows that God cares about family legacy.

Take It Home

For God's New Testament people, biological bloodlines are no longer what determine family; the true Israelites, or children of Abraham, are those who believe in Jesus Christ (Galatians 3:7). In what ways do God's people today demonstrate the value of adding new believers to the family of God? What will be your personal legacy?

If a widow's brother-in-law refuses to fulfill his duty, she is to tell the elders of his town about it (25:7). She could then remove one of his sandals and spit in his face (25:9). This would mark him, for the entire town to see, as a man who does not care for others (25:10).

Demystifying Deuteronomy

The levirate law and a variation of the ritual with the sandal are played out in the life story of Ruth (Ruth 4:1–8).

25:11–12

HOW NOT TO STOP A FIGHT

This law is the only time when physical mutilation serves as punishment (25:11–12). This command intends to protect both womanly modesty and the capacity of a man to produce heirs. This also shows God's seriousness in regard to the next generation, which is probably why this law follows the one on levirate marriages.

25:13–16

HONEST BUSINESS DEALINGS

Israel is to be content with what God has provided for them. For this reason, they are to be totally honest in their business dealings (25:13–14). This form of business dealing is a way of proclaiming one's faith in the Lord's ability to support him and give him long life (25:15–16).

25:17–19

THE DESTRUCTION OF THE AMALEKITES

The Israelites are to wipe out the Amalekites when they enter the land. The reason is clear: Since the Amalekites have shown no mercy to Israel (25:17–18), they are to receive none. Israel is to blot out the memory of Amalek from under heaven (25:19).

Demystifying Deuteronomy

The Amalekites were a nomadic desert tribe ranging from Sinai northward to upper Arabia. Their genealogy is traced to Amalek, son of Eliphaz, and grandson of Esau (Genesis 36:12). God wanted the Israelites to punish these people for what they had done in showing no mercy to the Israelites (Exodus 17:8–16; Numbers 14:39–45).

DEUTERONOMY 26:1–19

PRESENTATIONS

Firstfruits	26:1–11
The Presentation of the Tithe	26:12–15
The Declaration of Intent	26:16–19

Setting Up the Section

The book of Deuteronomy is a reiteration of the law for the children of those who were brought out of Egypt and allowed to enter into the promised land. Since all that is said here is a reiteration of the law for those entering the land, it is stated in its simplest form. Chapter 26 describes some of the rituals that are to be followed as soon as they enter the land.

26:1–11

FIRSTFRUITS

When Israel takes possession of the promised land, they are to celebrate the first ritual of taking the firstfruits (the initial produce of the harvest; see Leviticus 23:9–14) to the priest at the central sanctuary (26:1–2). The declaration "I have entered the land" (26:3 NASB) is a testimony to the Lord's faithfulness in bringing the nation into the land He had promised. In this way, at the very beginning of their new life, each one has the opportunity to come before God and acknowledge His great deliverance while presenting the basket of firstfruits (26:4).

The second part of the ritual is declaration of the Lord's faithfulness. This confession highlights both God's faithfulness and the miraculous nature with which Israel received the promised land. This confession is quite a confession. It includes Israel's heritage—her father Jacob, a wandering Aramean (26:5); Israel's growth (26:5); Israel's bondage in Egypt (26:6–7); deliverance from Egypt (26:8); and God's provision in the promised land (26:9). At this point the basket is again presented (26:10) and celebration ensues (26:11).

Critical Observation

Tithing and giving firstfruits were not unfamiliar requirements for the Israelites. Legislation regarding firstfruits and the tithe had already been given in Deuteronomy (14:28–29; 18:3–5). What is unique in this passage, however, is the declaration ritual for each offering (26:3, 5, 13). It seems that these declarations were meant to be practiced only once: for the firstfruits after Israel's first harvest and for the tithe after being in the land three years. They were given in order to celebrate Israel's transition from a nomadic existence to a settled community through the power of the Lord.

26:12–15

THE PRESENTATION OF THE TITHE

After the third year in the land, the people are to pay a tithe to the Lord. This tithe is to be given to those in need (Levite, strangers, orphans, widows) so that there will be food for them to eat in their towns (26:12). It is a sacred offering, intended to show the same mercy and kindness that they themselves had received (26:13). Because of its sacredness, the offering could be given only by someone who is ritually clean, as described in the declaration accompanying this offering (26:14).

The prayer for blessing in verse 15 emphasizes Israel's dependence on the Lord and on His grace. He is so transcendent that He dwells in heaven, but at the same time He is so near to His people that He hears their prayers on earth. God is good and provides for His people.

Take It Home

The provision of the Lord is the subject of celebration in the ceremonies associated with both firstfruits and tithes. Since God provided for His people, they should in turn provide for others. The same is true for God's people today. All that God does for us is intended to shape our ethics. In this way, we will reflect the image of God that we were created to bear (Genesis 1:26).

26:16–19

THE DECLARATION OF INTENT

This section is very important because it ends with a call for commitment. Everything that will happen in Israel depends upon adherence to the law of God. This nation is to be different. Their ethics, morality, practices, business, and their entire infrastructure are to derive their ethical moorings from God. As a result, the nation must be committed to God.

Demystifying Deuteronomy

Deuteronomy 26:16–19 is the conclusion to the entire section that began in chapter 5:1, where Moses begins to reiterate the law (see the "Critical Observation" at Deuteronomy 1:1–5).

Two things are mentioned here: the responsibility of Israel and the responsibility of God.

Israel is to devote herself to obey carefully and unreservedly the Lord's decrees and laws (26:16). Israel is formally accepting the terms laid out in the law of God that have just been restated for her (26:17). In other words, the people are saying that they want to be bound by this structure and framework. By this, they are accepting the responsibility to love and serve God by obeying all of His statutes.

With the same type of terminology, the Lord formally acknowledges His obligation to Israel: to be her God and to make her His most valued nation on earth (26:18). God is committed to this nation, and He will provide all that they need to grow and prosper. The reiteration of Israel's responsibility (26:18) reminds Israel that her special status of honor depends on her obedience to Him. To be the Lord's treasured possession means that He will exalt Israel high above all the nations (26:19).

DEUTERONOMY 27:1–26

BLESSINGS AND CURSES, PART 1

Setting Up the Section

Deuteronomy 27 begins a new section in the ancient Near Eastern treaty form that structures the book (see the "Critical Observation" note at 1:1–5). Following the opening preamble (1:1–5), historical introduction (1:6–4:49), and the particular stipulations of the treaty (chapters 5–26), chapter 27 opens the section of blessings and curses that will result from keeping or breaking the treaty.

27:1–10

THE LAW DISPLAYED AND AN ALTAR BUILT

Moses and all the leaders of Israel command the people again to obey all the commands of God (27:1). They must remember that the entire key to their success depends upon their obedience to God.

They are to write all the words of the law on large stone tablets coated with plaster.

The meaning of the phrase "all the words of this law" (27:3, 8) probably refers to the entire book of Deuteronomy rather than just parts of it.

Demystifying Deuteronomy

The writing of laws on large stones coated with plaster was a common practice in Egypt. It was a way of preserving the words of important documents for generations.

The stones are to be set up on Mount Ebal (27:4–6), at the base of which lies the city of Shechem. The altar will commemorate God's faithfulness in giving them the land. There are two possible reasons for not using any iron tools (27:5). Because the nation probably did not have any access to iron, they had to get it from the surrounding nations. This would put them into contact with the nations and might cause them to stumble. A second reason could be that the altar should not have any human additions that would cause humans to get the glory.

Critical Observation

Shechem was the place that the Lord first appeared to Abraham. It was also the place where Abraham built his first altar to the Lord (Genesis 12:6–7). The choice of this location emphasizes God's faithfulness to the original promises to Abraham and highlights that the time for God to make good on this promise is near.

The covenant is to be renewed not only by writing the law but also with sacrificial offerings (27:7). The burnt offerings express the people's total dependence on the Lord. The fellowship offerings express their thankfulness to Him and their joy in His provision.

The final reminder to write the law very clearly (27:8) emphasizes the supreme importance of the role of God's law in the promised land. It is important that God's law be central to all that happens. This section, then, ends with a second call to obey God (27:9–10).

27:11–26

THE ANNOUNCEMENT OF THE CURSES

After the altar is set up on Mount Ebal, six tribes are to assemble on Mount Gerizim to bless the people (27:12), and six are to assemble on Mount Ebal to pronounce curses (27:13). The six tribes on Mount Gerizim are from Jacob's wives, Rachel and Leah. Four of the six tribes on Mount Ebal are descended from Jacob's concubines, Bilhah and Zilpah. The other two are Reuben, Jacob's firstborn who forfeited his birthright through incest (Genesis 35:22; 49:3–4), and Zebulun, Leah's youngest son.

A curse is a condemnation by God. In other words, it is a divinely made consequence in which a person who has violated the law of God must face the discipline that God ordains for the violation of that law. Deuteronomy 27:15–26 records twelve curses. Many of them pertain to actions done by individuals in secret. Eight of the twelve are violations of the Ten Commandments.

Deuteronomy 27:15 addresses idolatry. God hates idolatry, both public and private. If a person tries to keep his or her idolatry secret, the Lord will see it and the idolater will be cursed.

Critical Observation

All the people, by responding with *Amen* to each curse, are acknowledging that they understand and agree to the proclamation.

Verse 16 has to do with parents. Anyone showing dishonor to parents is cursed. This again shows that God is a God who believes that authority should be respected. God takes the family lineage seriously.

Verse 17 deals with honesty. Anyone who steals from his or her neighbor by moving the landmark is cursed. Some might try this by moving the boundary markers in the middle of the night.

Verse 18 concerns abuse. A blind man cannot care for himself. If someone comes along pretending to care for a blind man but really seeks to take advantage of him, this person is cursed. This curse probably applies to all who mistreat the weak and oppressed members of the community (Leviticus 19:14).

Verse 19 declares a curse for oppression. It would also have been easy for an Israelite to take advantage of these generally poor classes of people. But God will defend them. Strength and power are to help, not hurt, the weak.

Verses 20–23 have to do with immorality. These four curses are directed to one who engages in one of four forbidden sexual relationships. The marriage bed is to be held in high honor, and sexual relations are not to be perverted by taking them out of a proper marriage context. Some of these perversions show that when sexual relations are taken outside of God's context, they turn into horrible and degrading practices.

The tenth and eleventh curses deal with an attempt to violate the sixth commandment, which prohibits murder (27:24–25). Human life is to be preserved. Taking someone's life is an action that is cursed by God.

Verse 26 spells out a final curse against disobedience to any of God's laws. God desires a wholehearted obedience to the law in every area of life. God wants the people to understand that all disobedience to His law will be punished.

Take It Home

There are Christians, alas, who come to think of the Christian life as some heavy task that must be done in order not to get hammered with some heaven-sent punishment. What a weary way to live! But that entirely misses the point. To think this way is to behave as children who pout and sulk because their parents refuse to let them grab the pan on the stove while the soup is boiling in it. They cannot see the love in the warning!

God's punishment for disobedience reveals His love, care, and interest in our welfare.

DEUTERONOMY 28:1–68

BLESSINGS AND CURSES, PART 2

The Blessings	28:1–14
The Curses	28:15–68

Setting Up the Section

In this chapter, Moses sets before Israel the blessings and curses of the covenant they are renewing. The curses section (28:15–68) is about four times longer than the blessings section (28:1–14). This underscores the importance of obedience. God is making the point that if you fail to obey, there is no such thing as success; every area of life will be impacted in a great way. This commitment is intended to make a strong point—they should obey God.

28:1–14

THE BLESSINGS

God's gift of the promised land is an act of grace and mercy. But Israel's continued success in the land is conditioned on the people's obedience. This covenant was made with a people who had already been redeemed by God's gracious deliverance from Egypt (as will be spelled out again in 29:1–8). Their deliverance was not conditioned by their obedience; only their blessing in the land was conditioned in this way (28:1–2). This covenant enables Israel to enjoy unhindered fellowship with God in the fullness of His blessing. One of those blessings is the exalting of Israel above all other nations (28:1). God will make this nation great. God outlines some very specific blessings for their obedience.

If Israel obeys the Lord, then every aspect of life will be blessed greatly by God. Both the merchant and the farmer will be blessed (28:3). Israel can expect fertility in both humanity and animals (28:4). There will always be food in her homes for daily meals (28:5), the land will never experience a famine, and in all their daily work, Israelites will enjoy God's blessings (28:6). In their obedience they will find happiness and fulfillment.

Critical Observation

Verses 3–6 were probably read aloud in covenant-renewal ceremonies in order to state the blessings of covenant obedience. What follows in verses 7–14 is probably Moses' elaboration of those blessings.

Three areas of blessing are singled out.

The first one deals with Israel's relationship to the nations around them. Israel will have supernatural military success and financial prosperity that will cause them to be above other nations (28:7). The fruit of this is that they will never borrow from other nations, and they will always lead and never follow (28:12–13).

The second deals with agricultural endeavors. Israel will experience abundant prosperity in her farming and family life (28:8, 11).

Take It Home

It can sometimes trouble believers that God promises such earthly blessings to those who prove faithful to His covenant. Large families, large harvests, good health, political and military security, and the like, are the blessings promised here. Should He not instead have promised such things as peace and purity of heart, the nearness of God, and eternal joy in the world to come?

Of course, those things are promised to those who trust and obey the Lord; and in the context of the Bible, we ought to take these promises of earthly prosperity as containing in themselves and pointing to the more spiritual blessings which God pours out on those who love Him. God does, of course, reward His faithful children with many earthly benefits. But the Bible also teaches clearly enough that a faithful Christian can suffer ill-health or financial reverses that are in no way the curse or punishment of God.

All through the Bible, the physical and the earthly is taken to stand for the spiritual and the heavenly—in large part because we respond better to what we can see, touch, and taste. The faithful in Old Testament days understood well enough that the promised land, Canaan, stood for the blessings of eternal life and the heavenly country. When God spoke to His people of their earthly life in the promised land, He was saying much more to them about spiritual good and heaven.

The Lord Jesus spoke the same way. He promised that those who sacrifice houses and fields for His sake would receive in this life one hundred times as many houses and fields. But He was not speaking literally of houses and fields. The apostles, for example, who had made such sacrifices of property and earthly possessions, did not finish their lives as wealthy landowners. The outward blessing—which God does give as a general rule—is still more important as a sign of the unseen and everlasting blessings God gives to those He loves.

The third deals with Israel's reputation. By being God's obedient and holy people, the Israelites will enjoy such a close relationship with God that they will be a testimony to all the peoples on earth who witness it (28:9–10).

All three of these blessings will come to Israel if they obey God (28:14). What if they do not obey God?

28:15–68

THE CURSES

Just as obedience will bring blessings, so disobedience will bring curses. No middle ground exists (28:15).

The four curses in verses 16–19 are the exact opposite of the four blessings cited in verses 3–6. The point here is that all the great blessings will be undone with disobedience to God. Disobedience is ultimately rejection of God and His ways. If you reject God, there are grave consequences.

In addition to reversing the blessings mentioned above, there will also be eleven more major judgments that will come upon Israel for disobeying: destruction (28:20), disease (28:21–22), drought (28:23–24), defeat in battle (28:25–26), diseases of Egypt (28:27–29), oppression and robbery (28:30–35), exile (28:36–37), crop failure and economic destruction (28:38–48), siege by the enemy (28:49–57), and disease that brings death and exile (28:58–68).

Demystifying Deuteronomy

Keep in mind that these curses were written specifically to Israel in Canaan. We cannot expect these literal curses to come our way if we disobey. Nevertheless, we must take obedience to God seriously. We must know that blessings do follow obedience, and consequences follow disobedience.

Each of these judgments essentially has one goal: to turn Israel from disobedience. God's heart is to turn the nation back to Him through these punishments. The point here is that the process that leads to this level of pain and destruction is disobedience. Israel must know that she has to obey God. If they fail in this area, then all the blessings will be taken away, and pain and destruction will follow. They should take this seriously.

DEUTERONOMY 29:1–29

AN APPEAL TO OBEY

Setting Up the Section

Chapter 29 opens with the conclusion of the reiteration of the covenant. At this point, Moses begins to unfold a summary of the covenant to highlight what the Israelites should keep foremost in their minds.

29:1–8

REVIEW OF THE LORD'S FAITHFULNESS AND ISRAEL'S DISOBEDIENCE

This review (29:2–8) is unique for one reason—it makes the point that Israel has not really understood the significance of what God has done for them. They do not understand the real significance of the deliverance from Egypt or the hand of God in their life. Because their minds do not fully grasp what God is ultimately doing, it is easy for them to rebel against God (29:4). To miss the heart of God is to miss the motivation to obey.

Critical Observation

The two places mentioned in verse 1 are significant. Horeb is the same location as Mount Sinai, where God gave the Ten Commandments at the beginning of the Israelite journey. Here, in Moab, the people are at the end of the journey, almost to their destination.

29:9–15

THE COVENANT

In verse 9, Moses brings the nation back to the most fundamental of all issues, one that is a running theme in Deuteronomy—obedience. The people must obey God in order to prosper. The word *today* occurs several times (29:10, 15), as well as *this day* (29:12–13 NIV). Moses is focusing on the present. He wants the people at that moment in time to realize they need to commit themselves to God, and God is going to commit Himself to them. This moment is all a part of God's plan to make good on His promise to Abraham.

Yet, there is more than just the moment focused on in this text. The scope of this covenant renewal also includes future generations ("those who are not here today"; 29:15 NIV). Therefore, the obedience of that present generation has a great effect on those not yet born. They are to pass on to the next generation the importance of obedience to God. With this great call to multigenerational obedience, Moses will again focus on the curses that befall disobedience.

Take It Home

This multigenerational principle is true for us today. We, too, must make sure that we pass on to the next generation their role and focus on obedience to God.

29:16–29

THE CURSES FOR DISOBEDIENCE

Moses reminds the Israelites that they are not naive concerning idolatry. They witnessed it in Egypt and had fallen into idolatry on the way to Canaan (Exodus 32; Numbers 25). These people understood how one act of idolatry was a bitter poison. For this reason, they are told to be diligent against this sin when they enter the land of Canaan. Once they enter this land, they will face new temptations to idolatry over and over again.

Demystifying Deuteronomy

The word *poison* in verse 18 refers to wormwood, a plant known for its bitter pulp. Wormwood is often associated with poison in scripture (Jeremiah 9:15; 23:15; Amos 5:7; 6:12).

These words are reminders that if the people are not vigilant, then an idolatrous foothold can take place through a single person who might think he or she is safe from judgment because the Lord has said Israel is His people. In other words, a deceiver might come in and think that Israel is off limits from the judgment of God. If they allow this person to come in, this foothold could flower into a downfall of faith that will certainly bring God's judgment. If this happens, everyone in Israel will suffer in the judgment that God will bring to the nation, and anyone who brings such sin into Israel can never escape the consequences of that sin (29:19–21).

Not only will judgment fall on the one who introduced idolatry, but also on the whole nation, because they let themselves be swept away by the false worship. The judgments will be so severe that it is compared to the judgment that fell on Sodom and Gomorrah, and Admah and Zeboiim (Genesis 14:2). The land will be covered with salt and sulfur and thus destroyed and unable to support life.

The devastation will be so intense that the nations will ask why Israel's God allowed it to happen. The judgment will be so severe that it will seem almost unlikely that God would bring such a harsh punishment upon His own people. The point is that God hates all rebellion, no matter who does it. Therefore, God will make good on His word—if the people use the land for idolatry, then the people will be taken from the land (Deuteronomy 29:22–28).

In verse 29, the secrets probably refer to future details that God has not revealed to the nation. There are many things that God has not yet revealed to Israel—things according to His will that no one knows. God is bigger and working with a view of history that no one can see or understand. Yet what He has revealed (future judgment for disobedience, future blessing for obedience, His requirements for holiness, etc.) is enough to encourage the Israelites to follow all the words of the law. Even though they do not know it all—they know enough to obey.

Take It Home

As with the Israelites, people today also want to know more than God reveals, and because they do not have exhaustive knowledge, they fight God. Yet, what God has revealed is enough to be accountable for. This is what Israel needed to remember and what the modern church should never forget.

DEUTERONOMY 30:1–20

BLESSINGS FOR OBEDIENCE

Setting Up the Section

In chapter 29, the language seems to assume the reality that the people of Israel will fall into exile because of their tendency toward idolatry. Chapter 30, then, is the good news—they will eventually be brought out of exile. God will not abandon His people, even in the midst of the worst punishment—that of losing the land they believe God had promised them.

30:1–10

RESTORATION

While chapter 30 sheds some light on the end of the journey the Israelites have set out upon, their repentance from idolatry will be insufficient to reverse all the effects. For this reason, God Himself will intervene and with tender compassion gather the nation and bring her back to her land. This restoration will be a time of spiritual prosperity greater than the nation has ever known. During this time, God will work a miracle that will change the fortunes for people forever (30:1–3, 8–10).

God is going to deal with their hearts—the very source of the problem. God promises to circumcise their hearts (30:6). Circumcision is the requirement God put on Abraham. It was one of the ways the Hebrews were set apart from the nations around them. Here, the idea of circumcision is used as an image of God claiming the people's hearts for Himself, marking them irrevocably. He will give them a new will to obey.

With this new heart they will experience the abundant blessing that comes from obedience. In fact, the ultimate goal of God's covenant with the Israelites is to bring about this new heart. God is at work in the lives of this nation, not just to give them a land, but to give them a heart that will obey Him (30:6; Jeremiah 31:31; Ezekiel 36:24–32).

According to verse 7, when this restoration happens, all the enemies of Israel will receive all the curses mentioned in this book.

30:11–14

CHOOSE LIFE

According to verse 11, God's commands are not beyond the Israelites' ability to understand. Though the law has a heavenly origin, God clearly reveals it to Israel directly. Israel did not need a special interpreter before they could obey the law. For this reason, verse 14 says the word is very near. The people can speak it (it is in their mouth) and they know it (it is in their heart). When God laid out His will and His plan for the nation, He communicated it and recorded it in a manner for all to see, hear, and understand. The problem with their disobedience has nothing to do with the structure, form, communication, and recording of the law—the problem is with their hearts.

Take It Home

Paul quotes this passage in Romans 10:6–8. He makes the point that just as God revealed His law in a very clear way, and it was near them and accessible to them, so, too, Jesus came and fulfilled the law and revealed God's righteousness, and it is near to humanity in the same manner.

Our God is a speaking God who communicates to us rather than forcing us to find Him and force Him to speak. All that He does He puts out there to communicate to us in all clarity.

30:15–20

THE CALL TO OBEY

The point of this passage is not the salvation of the souls of the nation. Instead, it is about the fellowship of these people with God. Genesis 15:6 makes it clear that a person is made righteous by faith. Deuteronomy 30:15–20 explains how a believing people can then have fellowship with God. For the Israelites, their full enjoyment of life depends on their obedience to God's Word. Though no one can be justified by the law, the people can be blessed under the law. The quality of their lives in the land is based on what they do with this law of God (30:15–16).

Critical Observation

Inherent in Deuteronomy 30 is the truth that humans cannot obey God's law without divine intervention, thus reaffirming the reality that without God circumcising the heart of humanity, no one can be right with God.

On the other hand, according to verses 17–18, anyone who disregards the law can easily be drawn back into idolatry (see also 29:18) which would bring catastrophic judgment into that person's life. In this way, the law serves the purpose of keeping the nation (as well as the individuals) in check and providing a barrier to unfettered sin.

So the life of the nation as they lived in the land is to consist of obeying the Lord. This obedience can be passed down from one generation to another. Parents who choose to obey the Lord are also making a significant choice for their children—t hey will be passing on to the next generation a heart of obedience (30:19).

Since the Lord is the One who gave life to Israel and provided all the blessings that they have and will have in the future, this chapter concludes by again urging the people to love the Lord, to listen to and obey Him, and to cling to Him (30:20). In fact, this is a key theme of the entire book of Deuteronomy.

DEUTERONOMY 31:1–29

TRANSITIONS

Setting Up the Section

Here, at the end of their journey through the wilderness and at the doorstep of the conquest, Moses prepares to step out of the way. He is now going to transfer leadership from himself to Joshua. Moses' priority is ensuring that the next generation places a priority on their relationship with God.

31:1–8

THE TRANSITION FROM MOSES TO JOSHUA

Moses has been forbidden to enter Canaan because of an earlier act of unbelief (Numbers 20:1–13), but God's plan does not depend on any one human leader. Instead, God's plan depends only on God's power to fulfill His own promises to His people. Therefore, in light of God's past faithfulness, Moses charges the nation to be obedient and fearless. There is nothing that they should be afraid of—God will make good on His promises.

After his strong charge to the people, Moses commissions Joshua with the same charge: Be strong and courageous! God will bring victory to this nation. Joshua is not the one responsible to take the land; he is the one responsible to lead the nation to be faithful to the God who will take the land for them.

31:9–13

THE PUBLIC READING OF THE LAW OF GOD

Moses records God's law and then commissions the priests to ensure that it is read every seven years to the entire nation. The priests are to read the law during the Feast of Tabernacles. Entire families are required to attend this holiday, which means the most people possible will hear the reading. As a nation, they will be reminded of what God requires for them to remain an acceptable nation before Him.

Critical Observation

The reading of the law every seven years was important for two reasons. First, not everyone had a copy of the entire law in their homes. Therefore, it would be a time for the whole nation to hear the entire law read in its context.

Second, the celebration of the Feast of Tabernacles (with its tradition of the Israelites leaving their homes) would remind them of the exodus from Egypt and the forty years of wandering their ancestors experienced. This event is central to the theology of Israel as well as her history. Because of this, the people would hear the law within the context of God's deliverance.

31:14–23

THE COMMISSIONING OF JOSHUA

The commissioning of Joshua begins rather ominously. After Joshua is called to the tent of meeting, God addresses both him and Moses. He tells Moses that the people are going to rebel after they enter the land. Their idolatry will bring on God's judgment (31:14–18).

In hearing God's revelation to Moses, Joshua is prepared for what will come. As a leader he will understand the full spiritual context of what is about to take place.

God commissions Moses to write a song to outline the rebellion of the people. This way, when the people rebel and run from God, the song will serve as a reminder and a point of accountability (31:19–22).

Demystifying Deuteronomy

In this account, God is clearly showing the Israelites their need for Him. Unfortunately, even in the face of this information, the people do not cry out to God for help.

God is making the point here that they need Him in order to set the stage for their eventual repentance. Even after they fall, they can return to God for deliverance.

Moses' song includes both the path of repentance as well as a warning of the judgment to come when the people fall away from their faith (31:19–22). God is fully aware of the tendency of the human heart to stray from Him and the extent to which these people will stray. Yet rather than rejecting the nation outright, He will use them and provide hope that they can have a changed heart (30:6).

In spite of this knowledge that the people will fall, the Lord formally commissions Joshua, giving him a charge to be strong and courageous and assuring him of success—God will be true to His plan.

31:24–29

THE PLACEMENT OF THE LAW AS A WITNESS

The Book of the Law is to be placed beside the ark, rather than inside of it. Only the Ten Commandments are placed inside (Exodus 25:16; 31:18). This placement of the law is a witness that the people are not going to follow this law. Though this is a harsh reality, it is also an expression of God's grace.

Take It Home

God will bring a Savior, One who will deal with the rebellion in the hearts of these people (30:6). Thus, this accountability—the placement of the law—is a beginning of God dealing with the people and their sin. It is only by knowing that they are sinners that they will be able to turn to God for forgiveness and redemption. As faithful as God is in revealing the sin of His people, He is equally as faithful in dealing with sin and overcoming it through Jesus Christ (Colossians 2:13–15).

DEUTERONOMY 31:30–32:52

THE SONG OF MOSES

Setting Up the Section

Deuteronomy 31:19–21 tells us that Moses' song is to be used to remind Israel of God's law within the context of God's deliverance. It will remind the people of their sin and rebellion and of the fact that their hearts are far from God.

31:30

MOSES BEGINS

The account of Moses' song actually begins at the end of chapter 31. Based on the information given thus far, Israel's future seems gloomy. Yet, the consequence of the people seeing the seriousness of their spiritual condition is to place them in the right position to be delivered spiritually—deliverance greater than the physical deliverance they had experienced from Egypt.

Critical Observation

A true understanding of Moses' song must come within the context of Deuteronomy 30:6, a verse of hope in the midst of disappointing news. This verse tells that God is going to show the people of Israel their sin so that they can embrace the salvation that the Messiah is going to bring.

32:1–3

THE THEMES

There are seven themes in Moses' song. These seven themes take us on a journey from the great goodness of God to the horrible sin of humanity to the grace and kindness of the Lord.

At the opening of the song, we are told that it is for everyone in the entire world to hear and learn from. In other words, these historical events reveal eternal and binding truth for all humanity. These words are to water the earth and give meaning for all creation, for the God of all creation is going to be declared to the entire world.

32:4–9

A FAITHFUL GOD AND A FOOLISH PEOPLE

In verse 4, God is described as a rock and as faithful and just. This description is presented in contrast to humanity in verse 5. The faith of His people had become so skewed that they bore no family resemblance to their Father. Even with the deliverance God has already provided in a variety of ways, the people still rebel, highlighting how extremely foolish and faithless humanity really is.

32:10–14

THE GOODNESS OF GOD

As this nation is growing and developing in some rather difficult circumstances, God is there. The metaphor of the eagle speaks of God's wise and loving parental care. Like an eagle, the Lord remains ready to catch them when necessary.

Demystifying Deuteronomy

In verse 13, the idea of getting honey and oil from the rock suggests that even the most barren places will become fertile. In the goodness of God, the people will be blessed in miraculous ways!

32:15–18

FROM PROSPERITY TO IDOLATRY

Throughout the centuries, many lives have revealed that prosperity is often more dangerous for the faithful than adversity. In adversity, a person calls out to God as a way of life, while in prosperity it is easy to give lip service to faith but not make it a true priority. Israel (in verse 15, ironically referred to as *Jeshurun*, "the upright one") abandoned the Lord, their only hope for salvation, when they became prosperous. The mention of *kicking* builds on the metaphor of an animal kicking at its owner. It suggests the mindless nature and complete foolishness of Israel's rebellion against God.

The downfall of Israel took shape in idol worship. They actually made sacrifices to something that God created rather than to God Himself. Put in its proper perspective, this is demon worship (32:16)—pure evil. In verse 18, Moses compares God to both a father and a mother. Yet, in spite of His provision, the people scorn Him and His great love.

32:19–27

JUDGMENT

Israel's idolatry provokes God to anger, which He expresses in judgment. God's anger is not like the anger of humanity. Human anger is based on selfish emotions. God's anger, in this case, is based on His righteous indignation toward children who are unfaithful and perverse (32:20), who follow worthless idols and scorn the only way of salvation. The rebellion of the nation is such that they are leading countless generations into a path of destruction.

Demystifying Deuteronomy

In His righteous indignation, God withdrew His presence and judged Israel with a foreign nation (32:21). This means that while God may have provided protection to Israel from the attacks of surrounding enemies, because of Israel's lack of faithfulness, God would remove His protection. The consequences, then, would be the defeat of Israel and hopefully the repentance of the nation in light of that defeat.

God's judgment will touch every area of Israel's life. The devastation from the attacks of armies and plagues will be so great that Israel will almost be completely wiped out. Though the nation deserves to be wiped out, the Lord will not allow it. Why? Because her complete destruction will cause her enemies to question His sovereignty and power (32:22–27).

32:28–33

LACK OF DISCERNMENT

Even after all the signs of God's power, displays of God's holiness, and warnings of judgment, Israel continues unaware down her destructive path (32:28–29).

The evidence of God's supernatural judgment through other nations will be clear. Those coming against Israel will have such strength and power that only God could be behind them (32:30–31). This judgment could not be attributed to the gods of Israel's enemies. In fact, according to verses 32–33, the enemies who will execute God's judgment on Israel are as evil as Sodom and Gomorrah. God allows the worst of the worst to come against Israel so that the people can see how far they have fallen.

32:34–43

GOD'S JUSTICE AND MERCY IN JUDGMENT

Though the Lord will use Israel's enemies to execute His judgment, He will still hold those enemies accountable for their wickedness and repay them for their evil. God will use their evil to chastise Israel, but He does not condone that evil.

In bringing judgment on Israel, God will have compassion on them. The statement in verse 36 that God will judge His people is interpreted by some to mean that He will judge *for* them, or vindicate them. Yet, Israel will not experience God's compassion until they abandon all trust in their own efforts and in the false gods to which they have turned. In verses 37–38, Moses calls on Israel to turn for help to the false gods so that they can plainly understand that these gods cannot help them.

God's goal in judging Israel is not to extinguish the nation. Instead, it is to bring her to understand that there is no god besides the Lord. He wants Israel to understand that God alone has power over death and life (32:39). He is the only hope for humanity, the only power for salvation, and the only God to trust in for help and deliverance. When Israel comes to this realization, then God will take vengeance on her adversaries (32:41, 43). The turning point will be the nation's true repentance.

32:44–52

MOSES' FINAL CHARGE

After reciting all the words of the song, Moses tells the people to consider them seriously. If the people will meditate on the certainty and severity of the judgment that the Lord will bring, this song could serve as a powerful deterrent for their rebellion. If they will repent of the sin that is in their hearts right then, God will forgive them. The threat of the Lord's discipline is a warning for them to turn from their wicked ways. This fear of the judgment set forth in the song would also enable them to teach their children the need to obey the words of this law (32:46).

At the close of chapter 32, Moses goes up to view the land that he had earlier in his life hoped to enter with his people. Because of his break with faith, the view from Mount Nebo is as close as he will get to Canaan.

Demystifying Deuteronomy

The breaking of faith God refers to in verse 51 is a reference to an incident in Meribah, in which Moses was instructed to speak to a rock to miraculously draw water from it. Instead Moses struck the rock and seemed to claim that he and Aaron were responsible for the miraculous water, rather than following God's specific instructions and letting Him get the glory for the incident.

DEUTERONOMY 33:1–29

THE BLESSING OF MOSES ON THE TRIBES

Setting Up the Section

The blessing of Moses given here, just before his death, is very important and common for that day. It was typical for a father to impart a blessing just before his death. Moses, leader of the Exodus and mediator of the covenant, served in a fatherly capacity for the nation. As they were being birthed into a nation, Moses was there to provide the earthly fathering that they needed.

33:1

THE MAN OF GOD

In verse 1, Moses is referred to as the "man of God" (NIV). This is a term used throughout the scriptures to denote a man set aside to serve God. After this passage, the phrase is used in the Old Testament to refer to messengers of God (1 Samuel 2:27; 1 Kings 13:1; 2 Kings 4:7). It is also used in the New Testament in the same way (1 Timothy 3:16–17). Moses was not just a leader, but he was a servant of God, a man set apart for the purpose of leading people in the will and Word of the Lord.

33:2–5

ALL BLESSING FLOWS FROM PRAISE

Moses begins this blessing with praise for the greatness of God, including a description of the Lord's appearance at Sinai when He gave the Ten Commandments (Exodus 19–20; Deuteronomy 33:1–2). Verse 2 is written in poetic language that describes the light of God shining on Sinai in the south, and then on Seir in the northeast, and then on Paran in the north. The idea is that God's law engulfed the land.

The fact that God came surrounded by angels (33:2) made the giving of the law not just a transaction, but a moment of worship.

Critical Observation

The giving of this law was more than just a moment when the glory of God shined upon the world; it was also a moment of love. This moment served to be the time when God's love came to the earth in the form of the revelation of His will and His heart. Thus, the response of all the followers of God was a response to this love.

The proclamation of the Lord's kingship over *Jeshurun* (a name for Israel; 32:15; 33:26) is a reference back to the nation's deliverance from Egypt and the giving of the law (when the leaders and the tribes assembled to receive God's commands). When God brought the law to the people, they gathered under His rule, and He became their official king. The giving of the law was then the event that ratified His kingship over the nation.

33:6–25

THE BLESSING OF THE TRIBES

Moses pronounces a blessing on each tribe. The names of these tribes represent the son of Jacob from whom the tribe descends:

Reuben (33:6). The prayer for the tribe of Reuben to survive suggests that it will face some unique adversity that might bring a disaster. While this tribe, descendants of the firstborn son of Jacob, would have typically been in a position of honor, this is clearly not the case. Genesis 49:4 and Judges 5:15–16 reveal that the tribe of Reuben is not going to excel. The dishonor found its root in the affair Reuben had with Bilhah, his father's concubine (Genesis 35:22).

Judah (Deuteronomy 33:7). When the order of the tribes was given for the journey to Canaan, the tribe descended from Judah marched first (Numbers 2:9) and therefore was first in battle. Moses' blessing here is a prayer for Judah's military success through the power of God.

Levi (Deuteronomy 33:8–11). The tribe of Levi was set apart to care for the tabernacle and to provide priests to serve there. The Thummim and Urim are used by priests to cast lots, a method of receiving direction from God (some compare their use to throwing dice in order to leave the outcome out of human hands). Thus, the tribe of Levi was entrusted with the great work of mediating between God and humanity. At first, the faithfulness of Levi is praised because they are faithful at Massah, also called Meribah (Exodus 17:1–7). Then the tribe is praised collectively (Deuteronomy 33:9) for their faithfulness to execute God's judgment in the matter of the golden calf (Exodus 32:25–29). Moses' blessing here is a prayer for supernatural ability so that the Levites will use their skills in God's work.

Benjamin (Deuteronomy 33:12). Moses prays that this tribe will have security and peace through being shielded by the Lord. This prayer reflects Benjamin's special status as Jacob's youngest and particularly loved son (Genesis 44:20).

Joseph (Deuteronomy 33:13–17). Moses prays first for Joseph's material prosperity—that the crops will grow as they receive water from above and below. God wants this tribe to experience true earthly blessing.

Moses then prays for the military success of Joseph. This tribe is eventually divided into the two tribes named after Manasseh, Joseph's firstborn, and Ephraim, Joseph's younger son. Though Manasseh was the older son, Jacob gave Ephraim the blessing of the firstborn (Genesis 48:17–20). That is why Moses mentions Ephraim first and credits ten thousands to him, and only thousands to Manasseh (Deuteronomy 33:17).

Zebulun and Issachar (33:18–19). Zebulun and Issachar, mentioned together here, are also mentioned together in Jacob's original blessings over his sons (Genesis 49:13–15), as well as in the Song of Deborah (Judges 5:14–15). The prayer here is that these tribes will receive blessing in their daily lives and especially in their trade upon the sea. Though the

Canaanite territories assigned to these tribes apparently do not touch the Mediterranean Sea, Issachar is near the Sea of Kinnereth (Galilee), and Zebulun is only a few miles from the Mediterranean. What this probably means is that merchants traveled through both tribal territories with products from the sea and the coast, and the tribes benefited from the trade.

Gad (Deuteronomy 33:20–21). Even though this tribe held choice land east of the Jordan, they still fought valiantly in the conquest of Canaan. In this way the tribe of Gad carries out the Lord's will.

Dan (33:22). The image of Dan as a lion's cub implies a potential for great strength. The tribe has the possibility for doing great things. However, though the tribe could be strong, it remained timid, not reaching full potential. The tribe of Dan did not stay in the land allotted to them, but instead established a colony in the north. For this reason some say that Dan not only was timid, but also acted like a snake in taking land that did not belong to him (Genesis 49:17–18).

Naphtali (Deuteronomy 33:23). Naphtali's blessing describes the tribe's assigned land as extending southward to the lake, probably the Sea of Galilee. This was a fertile area. Thus this blessing is similar to Joseph's sons Ephraim, Manasseh (33:16), and Asher (33:24)—the tribe will enjoy material blessings from God.

Asher (33:24–25). The name *Asher* means "blessed, happy." This blessing will be great material prosperity. To bathe one's feet in oil rather than simply to anoint them is something only a person of extreme wealth can do. Thus the tribe of Asher will experience abundant prosperity. The bolts of iron and bronze indicate the tribe's military security will be outstanding.

33:26–29

FINAL WORDS OF PRAISE

Jeshurun ("the upright one") is a name for Israel. Verse 26 honors the God of Israel as incomparable in power. He rides on the heavens and the clouds (33:26). Because God is eternal and a refuge for His people, His everlasting arms will protect Israel in times of trouble. God will destroy her enemy (33:27). Having such a wonderful and powerful God, the nation can walk in the full assurance that God will provide for them the promised land. They also can have the confidence that, once in the land, they can live in both safety and prosperity (33:28).

Take It Home

This chapter closes with a strong reminder of God's provision. Moses claims God as the Great Deliverer. With the descriptions given here, we are left with the clear idea that the God of Israel is worthy of our trust.

DEUTERONOMY 34:1–12

THE DEATH OF MOSES

Setting Up the Section

At the close of the book of Deuteronomy, Moses ascends to Mount Nebo as the Lord told him to do. Though Moses is not to lead the people into the land, God allows Moses to see the land.

34:1–4

A GLIMPSE OF THE PROMISED LAND

In verses 1–4, the places Moses sees from the mountain start in the north and follow to the south in a counterclockwise direction. Though one could not normally view the western sea (the Mediterranean) from Mount Nebo, God may have allowed Moses to supernaturally do so in order to see the great promise that was made years before.

God's mention of the oath (34:4) reminds Moses that He will still be faithful to His promise to the great ancestors of the Israelites—Abraham, Isaac, and Jacob (Deuteronomy 1:8; 6:10; 9:5, 27; 29:13; 30:20)—and bring Israel into her new land.

34:5–9

THE DEATH OF MOSES

Though Moses' inability to enter Canaan is a form of discipline for his act of unbelief at Meribah (Numbers 20:1–13), he still dies as a man of faith. This one act of rebellion is not the defining characteristic of his life and ministry.

God bestows an honor on Moses by being the One who buries him. Moses' last moments on earth were evidently spent in fellowship with God. The place of his grave is unknown today. In Jude 9 we learn that there might have been a supernatural struggle over the body of Moses. Moses' death, at the age of 120, was an ending of an era for Israel. It was time for a new beginning.

The typical mourning period for a loved one at this time was seven days (Genesis 50:10). But the Israelites mourn for thirty days after Moses' death.

After Moses' death, Joshua is empowered with the wisdom necessary to take Israel to the next step in experiencing the fulfillment of God's promise. Since this job is truly a spiritual job, Joshua will need the supernatural insight and power to carry out the will of God. According to verse 9, the Israelites accept Joshua's leadership, and in a sense, even this is an honor to Moses' leadership.

34:10–12

THE EPITAPH OF MOSES

Moses is unique among the prophets for his intimacy with the Lord and for his miraculous works. From his early days facing the king of Egypt with the plagues to the miracles of the desert such as speaking water out of a rock, Moses displayed the power of God. This becomes even more significant when you remember that early in Moses' life, when God called him to lead the people, he felt himself the least likely candidate for the job (Exodus 3:11–14; 4:10).

Take It Home

After Moses, the Israelites longed for another leader like him, and God did provide one. Hebrews 3:1–6 tells us that One came who was greater than Moses to bring a covenant even greater than the one given on Sinai. This new covenant would be one in which our hearts are made right with God (30:6)—and that leader is Jesus Christ.

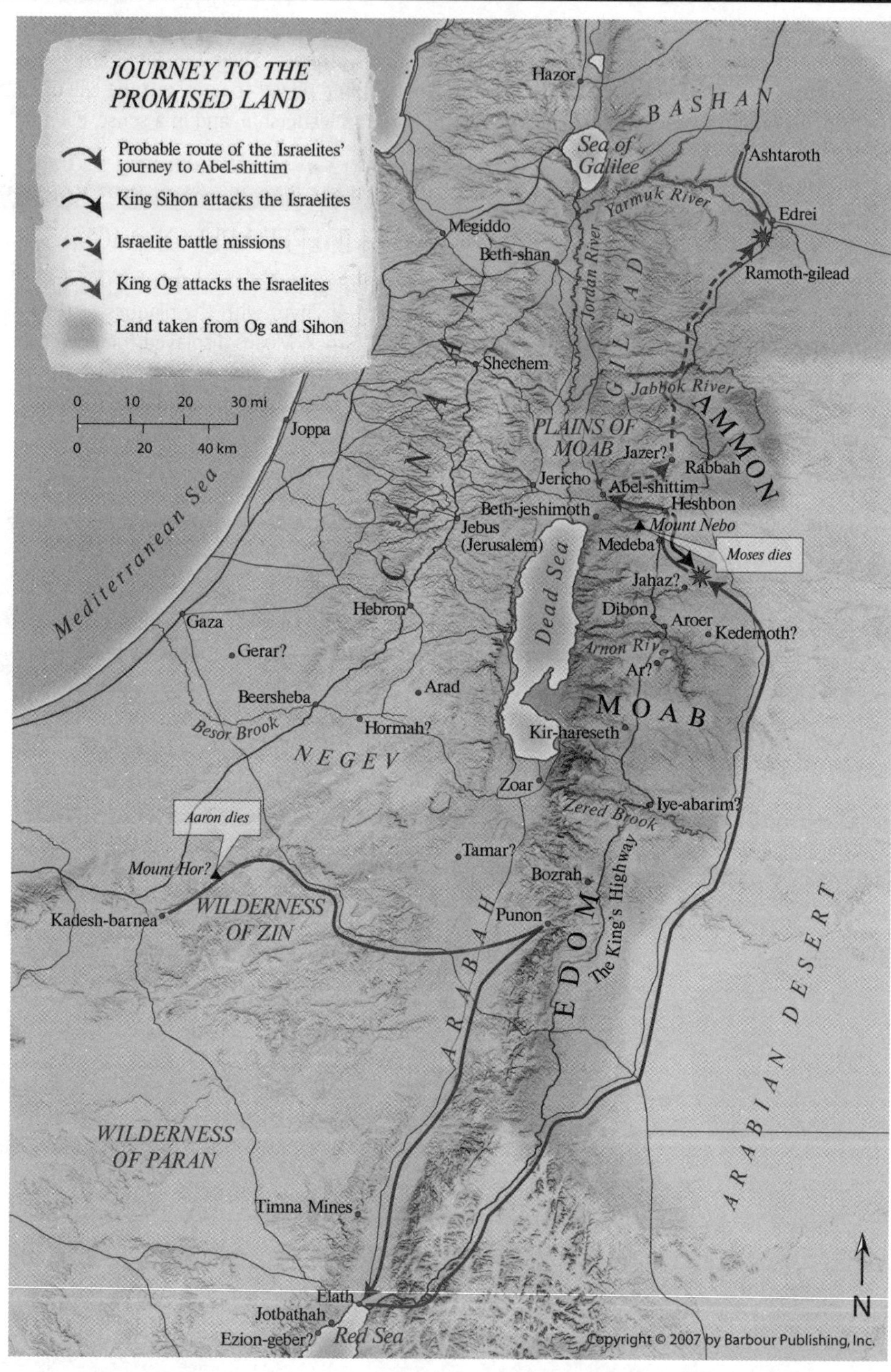
JOURNEY TO THE PROMISED LAND
Probable route of the Israelites' journey to Abel-shittim
King Sihon attacks the Israelites
Israelite battle missions
King Og attacks the Israelites
Land taken from Og and Sihon
0 10 20 30 mi
0 20 40 km
Hazor
BASHAN
Sea of Galilee
Ashtaroth
Yarmuk River
Edrei
Megiddo
Beth-shan
Jordan River
GILEAD
Ramoth-gilead
CANAAN
Shechem
Jabbok River
AMMON
Joppa
PLAINS OF MOAB
Jazer?
Rabbah
Mediterranean Sea
Jericho
Abel-shittim
Beth-jeshimoth
Heshbon
Jebus (Jerusalem)
Mount Nebo
Medeba
Moses dies
Dead Sea
Jahaz?
Hebron
Dibon
Gaza
Aroer
Kedemoth?
Gerar?
Arnon River
Ar?
Arad
Beersheba
MOAB
Besor Brook
Hormah?
Kir-hareseth
NEGEV
Zoar
Iye-abarim?
Zered Brook
Aaron dies
Tamar?
Mount Hor?
Bozrah
The King's Highway
Kadesh-barnea
WILDERNESS OF ZIN
Punon
ARABAH
EDOM
ARABIAN DESERT
WILDERNESS OF PARAN
Timna Mines
N
Elath
Jotbathah
Ezion-geber?
Red Sea
Copyright © 2007 by Barbour Publishing, Inc.

JOSHUA

INTRODUCTION TO JOSHUA

For centuries, the descendants of Abraham had anticipated possessing the land God had promised to the patriarch in the Abrahamic Covenant (Genesis 12:1–3; 15:5–8) and then reiterated to Isaac and Jacob. Joshua is the compelling history of the fulfillment of that promise.

AUTHOR

There is some tradition that claims Joshua as the author of this book. But the author is unknown, as is the date of writing.

PURPOSE

This is an account written to reveal God's faithfulness and how, by faith in God's promises, God's people can overcome and experience His life-changing deliverance.

OCCASION

The book of Joshua describes the conquest and possession of the land of Canaan. This is the land God had promised Israel through Abraham, Isaac, and Jacob. Here God fulfills that promise, though not exhaustively, since there still remains a rest for the people of God. Joshua describes the military triumph of God's people through faith and obedience. However, unlike most military histories, Joshua's focus is on the commander's Commander, the Captain of the Lord's host (5:15). Repeatedly, as Joshua's name illustrates ("Yahweh saves"), the book demonstrates that Israel's victories are due to God's power and intervention.

THEMES

The primary theme of the book of Joshua is God's faithfulness to His promises, that He has done for Israel exactly what He promised (Genesis 15:18; Joshua 1:2–6; 21:43–45). The events recorded in Joshua set forth God's special intervention on behalf of His people against all kinds of tremendous odds. The fulfillment of God's promises, as is evident in the birth of Isaac to Abraham and Sarah (Genesis 17:19–21; 21:1–5) and in possessing the land with its fortified cities, is the work of God, which cannot be accomplished without God's blessing no matter how hard one tries (see Romans 4).

HISTORICAL CONTEXT

Joshua is the history of Israel's conquest of the land of Canaan in fulfillment of God's promises for the people of Israel. In Joshua, the nation of Israel crossed over Jordan and took possession of the land God had promised them. If Moses is the symbol of deliverance, then Joshua is the symbol of victory. Joshua teaches us that faith is the victory that overcomes the world (1 John 5:4).

CONTRIBUTION TO THE BIBLE

God's Word continually shows our need of deliverance that only God can provide. This story reminds us of the absolute necessity of looking to God for salvation. The Israelites were brought into the promised land, which was an image of the eternal inheritance we now claim in the saving work of Jesus Christ. The book of Joshua portrays the rest that comes to the believer who experiences the blessings of salvation through a faith that overcomes the various trials, temptations, and difficulties of life that are faced in our three enemies: the world, the flesh, and the devil. The battle belongs to the Lord.

OUTLINE

THE PERIL OF WALKING BY SIGHT 9:1–27

The Alliances against Israel 9:1–2
The Deception of the Gibeonites 9:3–17
The Decision of the Leaders 9:18–27

DESTRUCTION OF THE COALITION 10:1–43

The Amorite Coalition 10:1–5
Miraculous Deliverance 10:6–15
Further Victories 10:16–43

THE CONQUEST OF THE NORTH 11:1–23

An Attempt to Stop Israel 11:1–5
God's Promise for Victory 11:6–15
God's Victories Reviewed 11:16–23

KINGS CONQUERED 12:1–24

The Record of Moses 12:1–6
The Record of Joshua 12:7–24

THE DIVISION OF THE LAND 13:1–33

The Command to Divide the Land 13:1–7
The Special Land Grant 13:8–33

CALEB'S PORTION 14:1–15

Dividing the Land 14:1–5
Caleb's Request 14:6–15

LAND FOR THE TRIBE OF JUDAH 15:1–63

Judah's Land 15:1–12
Caleb's Portion 15:13–19
The Towns of Judah 15:20–63

EPHRAIM AND MANASSEH 16:1–17:18

The Sons of Joseph 16:1–4
Land for Ephraim 16:5–10
Land for Manasseh 17:1–13
The Complaint 17:14–18

JOSHUA 1:1–18

THE COMMISSIONING OF JOSHUA

Setting Up the Section

In Joshua, we are introduced to the leadership of Moses' successor. Joshua is first mentioned in Exodus as a military leader fighting the Amalekites (Exodus 17:9–13). The book of Numbers reveals that he served as Moses' aide (Numbers 11:28). What better preparation could there be to lead the Israelites? Israel's preparation for taking control of the promised land proceeds out of God's commission and charge. Here we see God's people behaving well, responding to His revelation according to His will.

1:1–5

THE CHARGE FROM GOD

God's powerful words of commission here are a direct result of the fact that His people, lead by Joshua, hear and respond to His charge. Apart from God's Word there is no chance for God's people to experience the blessings of either the old covenant (as seen here in the promised land) or of the new covenant—blessings of a rich life in the kingdom of heaven through Christ. Whenever anyone begins to turn away from God's Word through indifference or apathy, they are turning away from His power into defeat.

The commission of Joshua and the continuation of God's purposes for Israel happen immediately after the death of Moses. In many ways, Moses represented God's law as revealed atop Mount Sinai. The law was a guide, a measure that would be fulfilled by Christ. Thus, the conclusion of God's revelation of His standard (the law) and the death of that standard bearer (Moses) opens the scene for God to introduce the Israelites to a new leader and a new era as He delivers the promised land to their possession.

Demystifying Joshua

Joshua's name means "Yahweh is salvation." As the Hebrew equivalent of the name *Jesus*, Joshua typifies the saving work that would later come for all people through Jesus, whose saving life provides believers with redemption and the power to enter into the possession of our inheritance in Christ.

With the command to cross the Jordan, the Lord is saying, "get out of the desert and move on into Canaan." God's will is never for His children to languish in the wilderness. This command is repeated to the New Testament believer—take up your armor and trust God (Ephesians 6:10–17).

Take It Home

While the Christian life involves obedience to the principles and imperatives of the Word, it is more than just that. It is a faith relationship with God to be lived out in the power of the Spirit and in the light of the Word. The abundant Christian life is God's plan and will for every single one of us; it is only limited by our lack of availability to His constant availability to us. Every believer is blessed with every spiritual blessing and is a priest of God with abundant grace, available for every situation if we simply seek God in faith.

In verse 5, Joshua is given the promise, "no one will be able to stand up against you" (NIV), but this promise is also a warning. While the land is theirs for the taking, it would not be taken without conflict or battle. This is a wake-up call, a reality that must be faced: Life is full of battles and conflicts, even for God's people.

1:6–18

THE CALL TO COURAGE

The issue before Joshua and the people is God's call to be strong and courageous. God is calling Joshua to a special yet difficult ministry, one with tremendous challenges and obstacles far beyond his own skill or abilities. In the same way, God has called each of us to ministry in some way—we are all gifted priests of God called to live out the gospel among those around us.

This passage reminds us that moral strength and courage come from faith in the sovereignty and provision of God. Courage is that quality of mind that enables people to encounter danger and difficulty with firmness and resolve in spite of inner fears (1 Corinthians 2:3; 2 Corinthians 7:5). Strength and courage come through recognizing and relating to God's pleasure (His will) and having a sense of God's calling and destiny (Joshua 1:1–2).

Joshua's courage is the direct result of knowing God's will (see Ephesians 5:9–10). Also, Joshua is reminded that he has already been prepared for this as the servant of Moses (Joshua 1:1). Regardless of the obstacles, Joshua is commanded to act on God's will by faith in the Lord's person, promises, and provision. Now Joshua begins to survey the land, size up the enemy, and prepare the people for battle.

In verses 10–15, the keynote is Joshua's immediate and obedient response, regardless of the obstacles that lay before them. There is a note of urgency, certainty, expectancy, and faith in Joshua's commands to the people. As God commanded, the new leader is taking charge and following the Lord's orders with confidence.

Joshua delegates specific tasks promoting the concept of the people of God as a team, which was first given to Moses in Exodus. This principle shows up repeatedly in the kingdom of God: Each person is needed and each person has a crucial role. The people are not only willing to obey, but they are willing to deal with any disobedience in their midst because of the demoralizing effect on others and the dishonor it brings to the Lord.

Take It Home

Israel got into the promised land the same way they got out of Egypt—with God as their deliverer. Likewise, we enter into the abundant life of Christ the same way we were delivered from wrath—by faith in the saving life of Christ. Just as we trusted in Christ and the accomplishments of the cross for redemption, so we must rely on God's salvation as the basis for our security and the foundation of our courage (Romans 6:4–11; Colossians 2:6–3:3).

JOSHUA 2:1–24

FAITHFUL PREPARATIONS

Israel's Spies	2:1–3
The Faith of Rahab	2:4–14
The Scarlet Thread	2:15–24

Setting Up the Section

Joshua and the people are called to accomplishments far beyond their ability. Regardless of these obstacles, Joshua, believing the promises of God, courageously moves ahead preparing to lead the Israelites into the promised land.

2:1–3

ISRAEL'S SPIES

While Joshua has the promise of God's deliverance, he has not been given instruction on just how God plans to defeat the enemies they will face. As a wise military leader, he is simply gathering information concerning the layout of the enemy's defenses, the condition of their morale, and other important factors. Moreover, he is not to presume on the Lord. He is to trust the Lord implicitly; but in that trust, he is also to use the resources God gave him: the training, the men, and the wisdom he had gained.

Critical Observation

Jericho lay just five miles on the other side of the Jordan and was one of the most formidable fortresses in the land. Conquering this city would not only give them a strong foothold into the land, but it would literally split the forces of the Canaanites by hindering their communication and supply lines. This would have a further demoralizing effect on the rest of the inhabitants.

Rahab is mentioned eight times in scripture (Joshua 2:1, 3; 6:17, 23, 25; Matthew 1:5; Hebrews 11:31; James 2:25), and in six of these occurrences, her name is found with a specific descriptive noun—*harlot* or *prostitute*. To remove this stigma, some have argued that she was only an innkeeper. That is unlikely, but there is some evidence that inns in the ancient world doubled as brothels, so both could be true.

Very likely, Rahab's house is the only place where the men can stay with any hope of remaining undetected; plus they will be able to gather information. Rahab's house also offered an easy way of escape since it was located on the city wall (Joshua 2:15). This story illustrates God's amazing grace—how He accepts and forgives us not because of what we are or might be, but because of who He is.

Demystifying Joshua

The king may have assumed that the spies were staying with Rahab, but he would have had reason to expect that she would do her patriotic duty and turn the spies in. The ancient law code of Hammurabi contains a provision for putting prostitutes who harbor felons to death. And yet Rahab had faith in God's ability to deliver her against all odds.

2:4–14

THE FAITH OF RAHAB

Rahab is saved because she believes in the God of Israel (see 6:17; Hebrews 11:31; James 2:25). Hiding the messengers is an outworking of her faith. She has come to believe that the God of Israel is indeed "God of the heavens above and the earth below" (Joshua 2:11 NLT).

Rahab's faith, which gives her strong convictions about God, causes her to act to the point of putting her life on the line. She knew Israel would eventually attack the city and destroy it, and she wanted to be delivered and to be on God's side. She does not know much about Israel's God—His laws of righteousness or the way of salvation—but she knows He is God.

Was Rahab's lying justified? Most commentaries approve of her faith but disapprove of her lie. In essence, they approve of her hiding the spies, but not telling the lies. In 6:17 Joshua explains that Rahab is to be spared because she hid the spies, and she did this as an ally. The question of whether her lie was justified by God because it was a matter of warfare is debated by theologians. Obviously, her faith was recognized as sincere regardless of whether or not her lie was excused by the circumstances.

Rahab is confident in the Lord's power. Somehow she knew what had occurred at the Red Sea and that it was the product of the sovereign power of Israel's God. Rahab is not only concerned about herself but also her family (2:12–13). This attitude of concern demonstrates God's plan for evangelism—sharing the hope we have in the Lord with those closest to us.

The inhabitants of the land are terror stricken. Three times in this chapter, the word *melted* is used to describe the emotional condition of the people (2:9, 11, 24). Mentally and emotionally, they are defeated. God had already given the people of Jericho into their hands. Note the irony: The inhabitants are looking at Israel's God and shaking in their sandals. The Israelites, who have seen the mighty works of God over and over again, are looking at their problems instead of focusing on God and are terrorized into unbelief.

2:15–24

THE SCARLET THREAD

Joshua and the men of Israel see the words and actions of Rahab as clear evidence of the sovereign providence and blessing of the Lord. This passage demonstrates God's concern and work to deliver each person who calls on Him (2 Peter 3:9). The story also demonstrates that the only thing that can hinder us in doing the will of God and fulfilling our calling is our own unbelief. Our faith should lead to action and ministry to and for others. Rahab reaches out to both the spies and to her household (John 1:35–51; 4:28–29, 39).

From this passage, we see that God's mercy and grace is powerful enough to overcome even His own wrath. Rahab was an Amorite, and according to the Law of Moses there is to be no pity or covenant with any inhabitants—only judgment (Deuteronomy 7:2). Yet through her genuine faith, Rahab becomes an exception and an archetype of God's purpose to save anyone who comes to God in faith to partake with Israel in the blessings of the kingdom.

Take It Home

The story of Rahab echoes the deliverance we have seen of God's children before. In the days of Noah, there was safety and refuge for those who entered into the door of the ark. In Egypt, there was safety and refuge for those who were gathered behind the doors that were sprinkled with the blood of the Passover lamb. The scarlet thread is a picture of Christ's redemptive work on the cross. For you and me, there is safety and refuge from eternal judgment—only if we enter the right door: Jesus Christ alone (see John 10:9).

JOSHUA 3:1–17

CROSSING THE JORDAN

Setting Up the Section

Life in a fallen world necessitates our need for strength from above, even for God's chosen people. The battle is really the Lord's, and this is what Israel is being taught in this chapter. With their hopes high, they prepare to confront the challenges ahead.

3:1–6

CAREFUL PREPARATIONS

Aside from the miraculous way the river is crossed, the most important feature of this chapter is the ark of the covenant. Its prominence is stressed in the number of times it is mentioned in chapters 3 and 4 (nine times in chapter 3 and seven times in chapter 4) and by the nature of the commands and statements given in its regard.

The ark represents the person and promises of God. It points to the fact that, as the people of Israel set out to cross the Jordan and invade and possess the land, they must do so not in their own strength, but in God's. Indeed, it is God Himself going before them as their source of victory.

In verse 5, Joshua commands the people to consecrate themselves in view of the wonders God would work among them on the next day—not exactly the preparations we might expect from a military standpoint. But God's ways are not our ways. For God's people, spiritual preparation is the vital element; for it is being rightly related to God that brings the power of God on our work and ministry.

Demystifying Joshua

Consecrate means "to set apart, prepare, or dedicate." Here it has reflexive meaning, "to prepare yourselves." This word is often used (in Exodus and Leviticus) in connection with cleansing of sacrifices, washings, and offerings. It underscores the need for God's people to deal with their own sin. It sets them apart for the Lord and His purposes. When there is a lack of consecration, we hinder the power of God. And there is even more included here—the people are preparing themselves for a miracle. Israel is to *expect* God to work wonders.

The consecration of Israel reminds us of God's holiness and the cleanliness He insists on in His servants. God is absolute holiness, completely set apart from sin. He is a holy God who cannot have fellowship with sinful man or allow sin in His presence without a solution to the sin problem. For believers, God's call for consecration demonstrates the necessity for cleansing through confession. To experience God's power, protection, and deliverance, we need to prepare our hearts and deal with the known sin in our lives through confession (Exodus 19:10, 22; Joshua 7:13).

This command also reminds us of the necessity of understanding our purpose as God's people along with a commitment to God and His purpose. It means the Israelites are to set themselves apart to Yahweh to cross the Jordan so they can enter the land, defeat the enemies, and become a testimony to the nations (Exodus 19:4–6).

3:7–13

THE PROMISE OF SAFETY

These verses reinforce the concept of grace. They show that crossing the Jordan and dispossessing the enemies (as in all aspects of our salvation and sanctification) is the work of God. The things we do in consecration are not works of righteousness that merit God's favor or overcome our enemies. Rather, the acts of consecration (like confession) remove the barriers to God's power and to fellowship, and so prepare our hearts to receive God's grace; they build our faith so we will put our feet in the water, cross over, and go up against the enemy.

To be effective, leaders need the right credentials—solid biblical training under people of God who truly know His Word. So it is time that God establishes Joshua as His representative to guide the nation (3:7). It is significant that it is God who does the exalting (4:14). The natural tendency is to exalt ourselves, but Joshua, in reporting God's communication to him, says nothing about this promise of being exalted. Instead, he focuses their attention on the fact that it is the living God who is among them, and it is He and He alone who will dispossess the enemies of the land (3:10).

Since the priests carry the ark of the covenant, and since the ark represents God's person and power, they alone are to take it to the edge of the water and stand still. What do we gather from this? It reminds us of our part in the plan of God. We must learn to step out in faith and obedience to the principles and promises of scripture. (This passage reminds us of the words of Moses in Exodus 14:13–14, when the Israelites are hemmed in with the Red Sea in front of them and Pharaoh and his chariots behind them.)

God's people are reminded to focus on hearing the words of their Lord (Joshua 3:9; Romans 10:17). We learn here that the authority of leaders among God's people needs to be the scripture rather than their personality, charisma, or whatever happens to appeal to people. The ark of the covenant helps the Israelites focus on the fact that it's God's battle.

3:14–17

PASSAGE BY GOD'S POWER

After breaking camp, as instructed, the priests carrying the ark of the covenant lead the way and walk to the Jordan, which is swollen over its banks. This must have been a fearful sight; but resting in the presence of God, they step into the waters. Immediately, a miracle occurs.

Many insist that this is no miracle since the event can be explained as a natural phenomenon. Earthquakes on record have caused the high banks of the Jordan to collapse and dam up the river for extended periods of time, however, never during flood season. Admittedly, God could have employed natural causes such as an earthquake and a landslide, and the timing would have still made it a miraculous intervention. But considering all the factors involved, it seems best to view this occurrence as a special act of God brought about in a way unknown to humans. The most important point about the event, however, is that it is to remind the people of the crossing of the Red Sea when God opened up a path. This would have clearly communicated that the God of power who was with their fathers against the Egyptian enemy is still with this next generation.

Crossing the Jordan at flood stage with two million people has several immediate results: God is magnified and Joshua is exalted (3:5). God's people are energized and motivated, and the people of the land, the Canaanites, are terrorized (just as in 1:9 and 5:1). God is indeed giving His people the promised land. Providentially speaking, He had already done so (1:2–6; 2:9), but the people of the land were not going to simply lie down. The inhabitants of the land would resist with all the resources at their disposal.

Crossing the Jordan meant two things for Israel. First, they must be totally committed to going against armies, chariots, and fortified cities. But then, if they are to be successful, they must also be committed to a focused walk of faith in Yahweh rather than, as they had done in the wilderness, a walk according to the flesh and their own resources.

Take It Home

For believers today, crossing the Jordan represents passing from one level of the Christian life to another. It is a picture of entering into spiritual warfare to claim what God has promised. This should mean the end of a life lived by human effort and the beginning of a life of faith and obedience.

JOSHUA 4:1–24

LEST WE FORGET

Prepared to Remember	4:1–7
Significant Stones	4:8–24

Setting Up the Section

God is often wisely concerned over our proneness to forget His faithfulness. Here we see His reminder for the Israelites by building a physical monument to their crossing of the Jordan.

4:1–7

PREPARED TO REMEMBER

Exodus 15 describes a relevant story in the history of God's people—how in only three days the Israelites, although they had just seen and sung of the mighty works of God, are quick to forget God's faithfulness. Rather than having confidence in God, we read of their grumbling (Exodus 15:24). The memorial of stones in this passage serves to promote encouragement and reverence in all Israel and for all time (4:6, 7, 24); in the context of the Israelite's former forgetfulness, we see God's great wisdom.

Critical Observation

The name *Gilgal* means "a circle of stones." Every time Israel returns to Gilgal, they will see the circles of stones and remember what God has done to roll away the waters of the Jordan. The very site of the stones was to be an encouragement, but also a reminder of the sovereign power of the Lord over nations and creation so they might fear the Lord forever and remain faithful to their purpose in the plan of God.

4:8–24

SIGNIFICANT STONES

The memorial is significant for many reasons. It is a permanent sign to future generations (4:6–7, 21–23). In two places in the chapter, covering five verses, parents are reminded of their responsibility to communicate God's Word and His calling to their children, generation to generation, whenever they ask about the stone monument. Parents dare not and cannot abdicate this to others. God charges parents with this privilege and responsibility. Finally, the stones are a testimony to other nations (4:24). Here, God is again reminding Israel of her purpose as a nation of priests (Exodus 19:4–6; 1 Peter. 2:5, 9–11).

Take It Home

Christians are living stones of a holy temple, living memorials of the power of God (1 Peter 2:4–5). But we, too, face the threat of forgetting the Lord by forgetting our pilgrim character through preoccupation with the world. All of God's children are regularly called to do things that form memorials of the saving grace of God such as assembling together, partaking of the sacraments, meditating on scripture, praying, and fellowshipping with other believers.

JOSHUA 5:1–15

CONSECRATING THE PEOPLE

Setting Up the Section

This chapter bridges the crossing of the Jordan and the beginning of the military campaigns. Israel needed a preparation of heart and willingness to submit to God's directions that they might experience His power and overcome the enemy.

5:1

THE CONDITION OF CANAANITES

The Canaanites are, in essence, already defeated. They are fearful of the nation of Israel because of the mighty works of God. God's people need to recognize and understand that the Lord is mightier than all their enemies (John 16:33; 2 Corinthians 2:14). God calls us to be strong in the Lord and in the strength of His might (Ephesians 6:10). The Lord leads Israel through a number of important experiences to spiritually fortify and prepare them for battle.

5:2–10

RENEWING THE COVENANT SIGNS

As a nation, this is the second time a group circumcision is observed among the Israelites, the first being while the older generation was still in Egypt. Circumcision was not unique to the Israelites. For instance, it was an Egyptian practice with religious connotations reserved for the priests and upper-class citizens. In associating it with God's covenant, however, the Israelites gave significance to circumcision that other nations did not.

The renewal of the rite of circumcision is necessary again because none of the men born after they came out of Egypt had been circumcised—that generation of men had died. Circumcision symbolized their faith that God would enable them to posses the land. At Gilgal the people are to remember God's covenant promises and past deliverance in order that they might live as His people in the days ahead.

This instance (5:10) is only the third Passover God's people have kept. The first was in Egypt (Exodus 12:1–28), and the second was at Mount Sinai (Numbers 9:1–5). By partaking of the Passover, they reexperience their deliverance and redemption out of Egypt and look forward to other victories—to the defeat of the Canaanites and also to the victory to come in Christ's work on Calvary.

5:11–15

THE CAPTAIN OF THE LORD'S ARMY

The Passover stands for God's deliverance out of Egypt. The promised land speaks of their new beginning, their new life as the people of God delivered from judgment into the place of blessing.

The manna had begun as a provision during a time of God's judgment of the people's disobedience when they rebelled and failed to believe God's promises. But now the new generation had left the wilderness by faith in the power of God. Now they are able to appropriate the blessings of the land and taste the goodness of the Lord.

For forty years, manna had served as God's special supply for His people in the wilderness, even after their acts of rebellion and unbelief. Israel's feasting on the fruits of the land is a demonstration of faith and a lesson from the Lord of the saving life of God through fellowship with Him. After eating of the land, the manna is no longer necessary because their time of wandering in the desert is over—the people are coming into the promised land.

The blessings of the promised land are only a foretaste of what is to come. Experiencing God's blessings leads to a two-fold expectation: Through fellowship and faith, there is always more for us to taste of the goodness and mercy of God in this life (1 Peter 2:1–3), but this is only a taste of richer and more abundant blessings that await us in eternity as the people of God.

In verse 13 Joshua looks up and sees a man armed with a sword. Joshua's question (of whose side this man is on) expresses his concern as well as his courage. It reveals a mindset that poses a threat to his effectiveness in the service of the Savior—the tendency to see the battles we face as *our battles* and the forces we face as forces marshaled *against us*. From the commander's answer, we learn (with Joshua) that the Lord is there with the armies of heaven to secure Jericho.

Joshua needs to acknowledge God's claim over him for God's purposes.

Certainly, the battle is a joint venture between God and the people of Israel under Joshua's leadership as appointed by the Lord (1:1–9), but Joshua must be following the Lord, submitting to His authority, taking orders from Him, and placing the battle in His hands.

The Lord reminds Joshua of God's personal presence and His powerful provision. Joshua responds how each of us should respond when confronted with God's power—in worship and submission. He quickly gets the picture after being confronted by the divine commander; he is reminded of a truth he heard Moses declare many years earlier when they stood on the banks of the Red Sea. "The LORD will fight for you; you need only to be still" (Exodus 14:14 NIV). Joshua learns afresh the truth that David will learn and declare when facing Goliath: This is the Lord's battle (1 Samuel 17:47).

Critical Observation

God is not present to fight our battles or help in our causes when we get in trouble as though He were a genie in a bottle. The battle is His, and our role is that of soldier-servants: We are here to serve Him, do His will, follow Him, and depend on Him completely. The warfare of God's people is a holy calling, but it's also a divine undertaking accomplished by those who humble themselves under the mighty hand of a present and powerful God (1 Peter 5:6–7).

Joshua's worshipful response to this figure shows this is a vision of God Himself. If this was only an angel, he would have repelled Joshua's worshipful response. Joshua is reminded here that he is merely the leader of God's army for whom God abundantly supplies the most important kind of armor—the armor of God (Ephesians 6:10–18).

Take It Home

Joshua had an encounter with the very revelation of God. It was an encounter that lifted a great burden from his shoulders. Like Joshua, we need to go into battle mindful of the Lord and mindful of His Word, which must guide our thoughts, direct our actions, and fortify our hearts. As we look over the battles in our own lives, we must look up and see the Commander of the Lord of Hosts, in awe of our glorious guide.

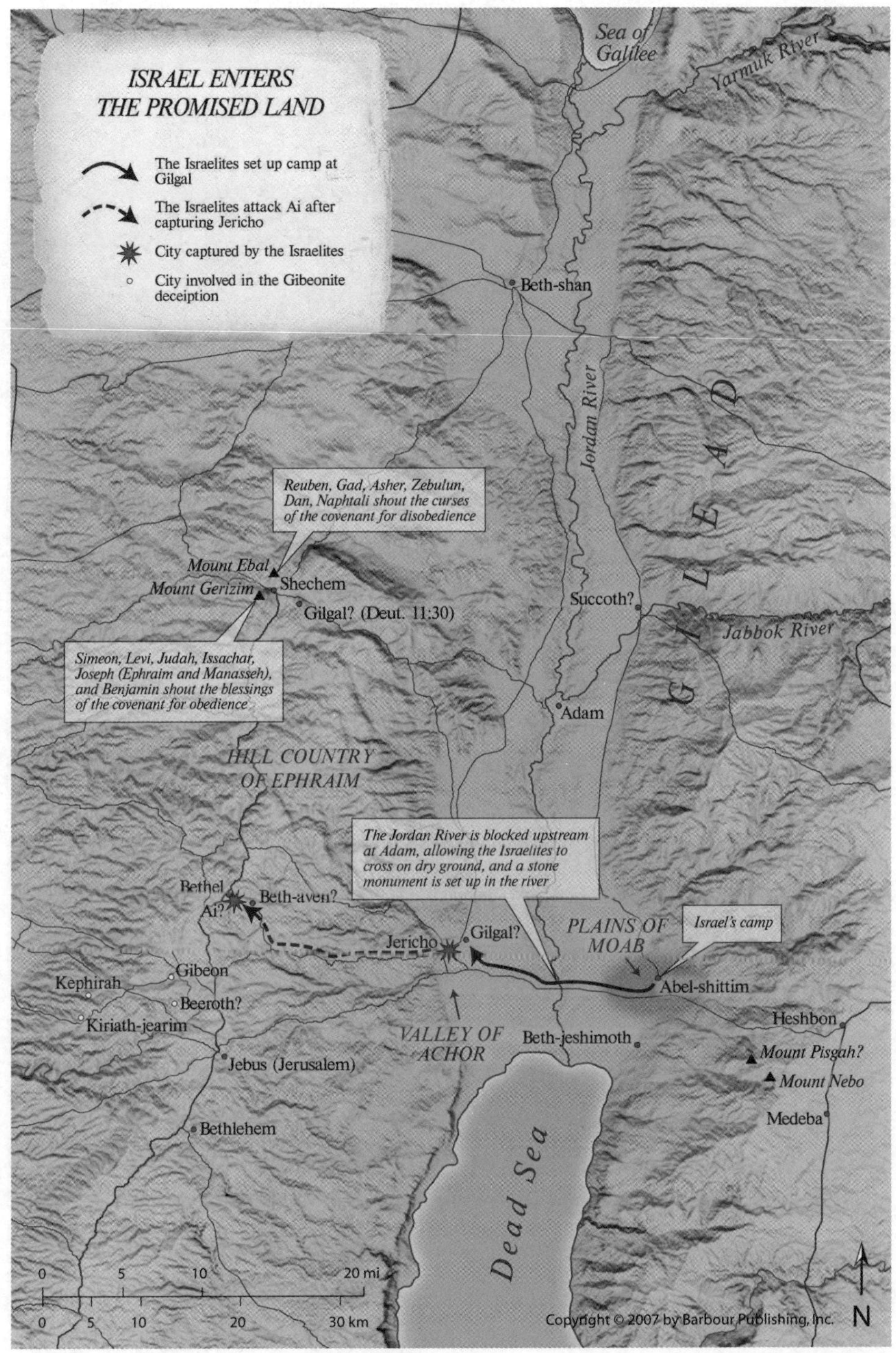
ISRAEL ENTERS THE PROMISED LAND
The Israelites set up camp at Gilgal
The Israelites attack Ai after capturing Jericho
City captured by the Israelites
City involved in the Gibeonite deceiption
Sea of Galilee
Yarmuk River
Beth-shan
Jordan River
GILEAD
Reuben, Gad, Asher, Zebulun, Dan, Naphtali shout the curses of the covenant for disobedience
Mount Ebal
Shechem
Mount Gerizim
Gilgal? (Deut. 11:30)
Succoth?
Jabbok River
Simeon, Levi, Judah, Issachar, Joseph (Ephraim and Manasseh), and Benjamin shout the blessings of the covenant for obedience
Adam
HILL COUNTRY OF EPHRAIM
The Jordan River is blocked upstream at Adam, allowing the Israelites to cross on dry ground, and a stone monument is set up in the river
Bethel
Ai?
Beth-aven?
Jericho
Gilgal?
PLAINS OF MOAB
Israel's camp
Abel-shittim
Gibeon
Kephirah
Beeroth?
Kiriath-jearim
VALLEY OF ACHOR
Beth-jeshimoth
Heshbon
Mount Pisgah?
Mount Nebo
Jebus (Jerusalem)
Medeba
Bethlehem
Dead Sea
0 5 10 20 mi
0 5 10 20 30 km
N
Copyright © 2007 by Barbour Publishing, Inc.

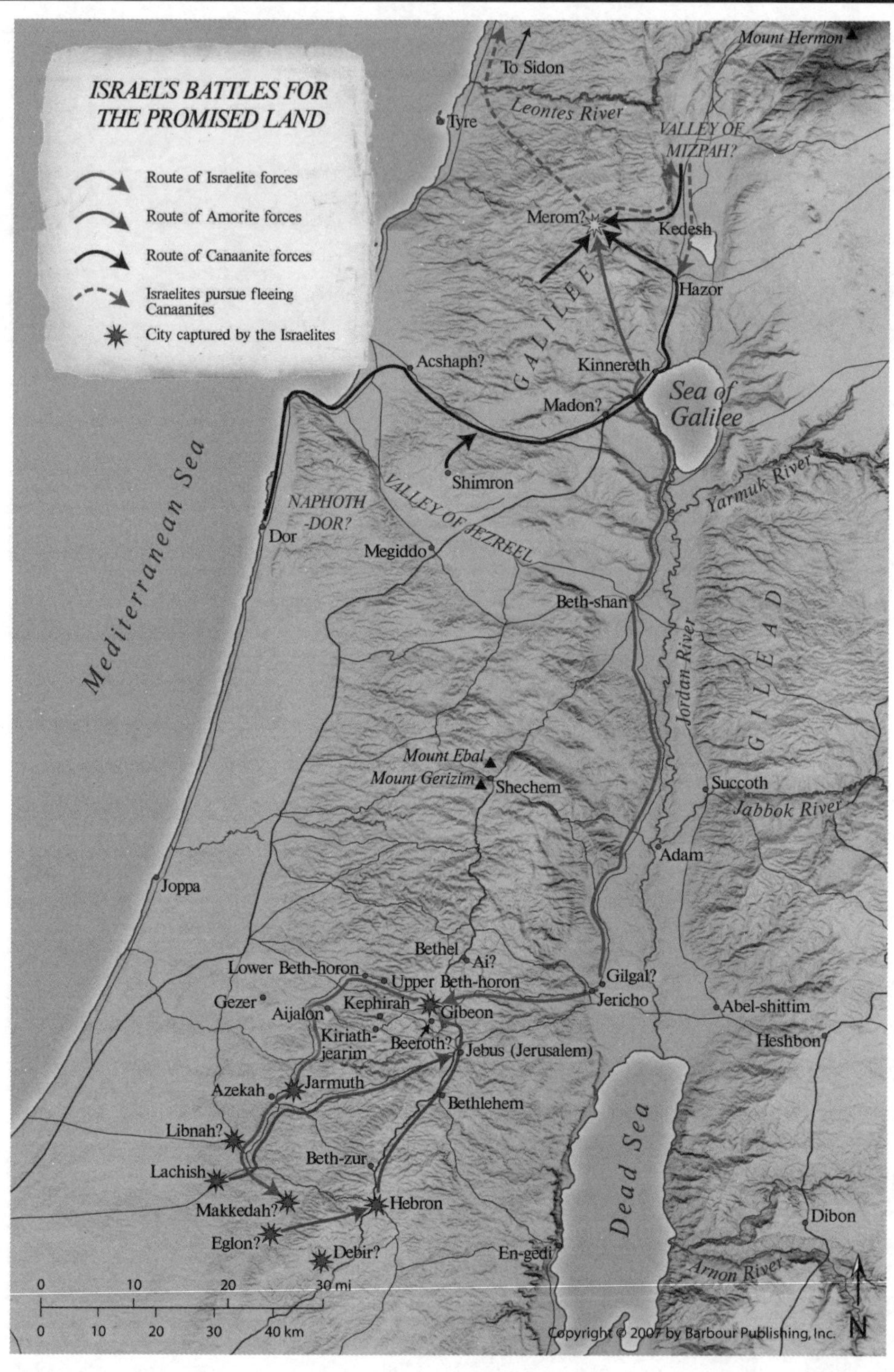
ISRAEL'S BATTLES FOR THE PROMISED LAND
Route of Israelite forces
Route of Amorite forces
Route of Canaanite forces
Israelites pursue fleeing Canaanites
City captured by the Israelites
Mount Hermon
To Sidon
Leontes River
Tyre
VALLEY OF MIZPAH?
Merom?
Kedesh
Hazor
GALILEE
Kinnereth
Acshaph?
Madon?
Sea of Galilee
Shimron
Mediterranean Sea
NAPHOTH -DOR?
VALLEY OF JEZREEL
Yarmuk River
Dor
Megiddo
Beth-shan
GILEAD
Jordan River
Mount Ebal
Mount Gerizim
Shechem
Succoth
Jabbok River
Adam
Joppa
Bethel
Ai?
Lower Beth-horon
Upper Beth-horon
Gilgal?
Jericho
Gezer
Aijalon
Kephirah
Gibeon
Abel-shittim
Kiriath-jearim
Beeroth?
Jebus (Jerusalem)
Heshbon
Azekah
Jarmuth
Bethlehem
Libnah?
Dead Sea
Beth-zur
Lachish
Makkedah?
Hebron
Eglon?
Debir?
En-gedi
Dibon
Arnon River
0 10 20 30 mi
0 10 20 30 40 km
N

JOSHUA 6:1–27

VICTORY AT JERICHO

Setting Up the Section

God guides the Israelites into a miraculous victory with an unlikely strategy.

6:1–7

THE PLAN FOR VICTORY

The directions given to Joshua by God for the conquest of Jericho obviously seem strange, but only if we fail to think in biblical terms of the life of faith and mankind's inherent inability to accomplish God's plan on our own. Before the Lord outlines His plan, He graciously assures Joshua of victory. Victory is always by the Lord's hand, and we should expect it to be something that bypasses dependence on human strength and ability.

The words *have given* (6:2) describe a future event or action as having already been accomplished. Future victory was already assured by the promise of an omnipotent, faithful, and immutable God. God's plan for victory will serve to teach Israel and God's people for all ages. Though we have human responsibilities in tearing down the strongholds raised up against the knowledge of God, our victory is dependent on two things: God's power and faithfulness to His plan.

Critical Observation

The number seven is used eleven times in this chapter. Seven signifies perfection or completion, which reminds us that God's plan is always perfect and cannot be improved upon (Romans 11:33–36; 12:2; 1 Corinthians 1:18). Further, the number seven shows that the conquest is part of a spiritual exercise designed to set the people apart (sanctify them) for the Lord as a holy people who belong to a holy God. Because of the significance of the number seven to creation and the Sabbath, and the fact they were entering into their inheritance, it also signifies the beginning of a new order and the land as a picture of the believer's rest in the Lord (Hebrews 4).

6:8–21

THE PATH TO VICTORY

The statement about the men being able to charge straight ahead (6:20) calls our attention to the fact that they are able to charge in from all around the city. The whole wall around the city collapses with the exception of the portion where Rahab's house is located. Some interpreters claim that an earthquake caused the destruction. If so, it was a miracle of timing and location since the camp at Gilgal (a little more than a mile away) and Rahab's house remain intact.

We should not forget that these instructions and the events of this chapter are preceded by a number of things God used to prepare the people to believe and obey Him. Israel had been prepared to trust the Lord by the events of the first chapters and their consecration to the Lord, especially in chapter 5. Spiritual preparation is fundamental to our ability to appropriate God's strength in exchange for our weakness.

The passage does not tell us why they are to be silent (6:10), but perhaps it illustrates and teaches the principle of being silent before God and resting in Him (Exodus 14:14; Psalm 46:10–11).

Take It Home

Hebrews 11:30 says that the walls of Jericho fell down by faith. In spite of the taunts that were perhaps hurled down at them from the walls as they marched silently around Jericho, they were willing to look foolish for the Lord. He was their source of strength. If we want to overcome our obstacles, we must submit to God's way by faith (Galatians 5:5).

Joshua does not unfold the entire plan at first, but day by day gives the people instructions. Each day they go out and march silently around the city. Though nothing seems to happen, they do not murmur or complain or question Joshua's instructions. They simply obey, day after day, until the seventh day when they give the great shout and the walls come tumbling down by their faith in the mighty hand of God (Hebrews 11:30). This reminds us that the Lord often works slowly. We want immediate deliverance, but the Lord often tests our faith and in the process builds our character and our relationship with Him so we find the Lord to be what we really need (James 1:2–4).

6:22–27

THE PROMISE FULFILLED

In these final verses, we see some marvelous facts about God and His dealings with people. First, they demonstrate God's faithfulness to His Word (James 1:17). The promises to Rahab are kept—she and her family are delivered. While it is not stated, evidently that part of the wall on which Rahab's house was built did not collapse. Second, they demonstrate God's grace and mercy. God's love and plan of salvation are open to anyone who calls on His name (John 3:16; Romans 10:11–13; 2 Peter 3:9).

The prophecy against any who would seek to rebuild Jericho (6:26) demonstrates God's severity and the surety of His Word. This prophecy came to be fulfilled in the days of Ahab (1 Kings 16:34), keeping with God's faithfulness to keep His promises. Jericho was occupied sporadically after its destruction, but never to the previous degree.

JOSHUA 7:1–26

THE AGONY OF DEFEAT

Disobedience and Defeat	7:1–5
The Dismay of Joshua	7:6–9
God's Direction	7:10–15
Learning from Sin	7:16–26

Setting Up the Section

The distance between a great victory and a terrible defeat is one step and often a short one at that. Ai is the next objective in the path of conquest because of its strategic location.

7:1–5

DISOBEDIENCE AND DEFEAT

This chapter reminds us of the reality of the ever-present threats and contrasts of life—victory is always followed by the threat of defeat. Never is the child of God in greater danger of a fall than after a victory (1 Corinthians 10:12).

Jericho has been placed under a ban, a phrase which comes from the Hebrew word *herem*, meaning "a devoted thing, a ban." The verb form, *haram*, means "to ban, devote, or destroy utterly." Basically, this word refers to the exclusion of an object from use or abuse, along with its irreversible surrender to God. So, to surrender something to God meant either devoting it to the service of God or putting it under a ban for utter destruction.

The problem facing the Israelites as a nation is not their enemies as much as their own unfaithfulness. The Lord holds the whole camp of Israel accountable for the act of one man, and He withholds His blessing until the matter is dealt with. This does not mean that the rest of the nation is sinless, but this sin is of such a nature (a sin of direct disobedience and rebellion) that God uses it to teach Israel and remind them that they are a community, a family, a body—like the church is today. Sin contaminates the whole assembly—like yeast in dough (1 Corinthians 5:6).

Nothing escapes the omniscience of God, especially sin (Numbers 32:23). God sees the sin in our lives and desires for us to deal with it, not hide it. Even though the Lord died for our sins and stands at God's right hand as our advocate and intercessor, God does not and cannot treat sin in our lives lightly (James 4:5–6).

Critical Observation

There is an irony of the defeat of Ai. The name itself means "ruin," so it is being contrasted with the powerful city of Jericho. Jericho falls easily because God fights for obedient Israel, whereas Ai, the dump, defeats them because of Achan's sin.

The defeat at Ai demoralizes God's people. It creates misgivings and a lack of hope in the Lord. Rather than examine their own lives as the source of their defeat, they begin to doubt the Lord. People are quick to blame, make excuses, and hide, but they often fail to honestly examine their own lives.

7:6–9

THE DISMAY OF JOSHUA

Joshua's dismay shows us his humanity and encourages us in our own failures to know that God will still accept us if we turn to Him for forgiveness. God can greatly use us if we will trust Him. Failure is not the end—often it is a test. Most leaders fail God at some point but refuse to continue lying in the dust. Failure and repentance teach the human heart a more ample conception of the grace of God. We learn that God is slow to anger and abounding in love, even when we are not. Defeat and failure often enable people to grow in faith.

7:10–15

GOD'S DIRECTION

While the Lord understands and sympathizes with our problems and fears, and while humbling ourselves before the Lord is always needed, He never condones our being prostrate in despair or excuses us from appropriating His grace and moving out in obedience. Instead He calls us to turn back to Him.

The consequences of unconfessed sin are weakness and an inability to serve and live for the Lord. We each have the capacity to live victoriously for the Lord, but the ability to do so always depends on fellowship with the Savior in the power of the Spirit; we must walk in the light (1 John 1:5–9).

God calls for a restoration to fellowship and faith in the power of God (Luke 22). Joshua is to call their attention to the sin of someone taking things that are under the ban, which is also the cause of their failure in the battle against Ai. As the Lord had emphasized to Joshua, he is to call the people's attention to both the cause and the consequences of the sin.

7:16–26

LEARNING FROM SIN

As 1 Corinthians 10 reminds us, what happens to Achan is recorded for our warning and instruction. Achan's sin was a familiar one. He saw, he coveted, and he took. It was the same with Eve and with King David, and it is the same with us.

As with Satan and Eve, Achan is dissatisfied, impatient, and self-reliant. He is trusting in his own strategies to get what he wants. Ironically, God is in the process of taking Israel into the land filled with abundant blessings. Yet Achan does not trust or believe in God's power to give him every good thing. As with Ananias and Sapphira, Achan is put to death to exemplify the seriousness of sin and to strike the fear of God into the hearts of the people.

Had Achan voluntarily cast himself on the mercy of God, his life might have been spared, as in the case of David. When Achan sins, the blessing and strength of God is halted, and the nation is met with discipline and failure. But once the sin is dealt with as the Lord commanded, by His grace, the blessing and strength of God resume.

Take It Home

Our failure to find contentment in the Savior and His love and grace is surely the cause of a great deal of our own self-made misery and sinful behavior (Matthew 6). Jesus defined the pursuit of the details of life at the expense of seeking first the kingdom of God and His righteousness as a simple matter of not truly trusting in God's supply. The issue is one of having too little faith. Known sin in one's life creates a barrier between one and God. Sin involves seeking from other things what only God can give. So, we seek contentment in the Lord (Philippians 4:12–13).

JOSHUA 8:1–35

VICTORY AT AI

The Battle	8:1–29
The Covenant Renewed	8:30–35

Setting Up the Section

Often God engineers defeat before He engineers victory. Sometimes success comes through the back door of failure. In this chapter we again see the grace of God and the truth of restoration. Defeat never has to be the end.

8:1–29

THE BATTLE

God's new revelation to Joshua is meant to both encourage him and give him directions for victory. God uses significant words to encourage God's people—the same ones He used with Moses at Kadesh-barnea, as he sent out the twelve spies (Deuteronomy 12:21). These are also the words Joshua heard from Moses forty years later (Deuteronomy 31:8) as he turned over the reins of leadership. Joshua hears similar words directly from the Lord as He commissions him to lead the people into the land (Joshua 1:9). Joshua uses these same words to encourage the nation in the face of their enemies, and they are used on three other occasions when Judah faces the enemy and terrible odds (Joshua 8:1; 10:25; 2 Chronicles 20:15, 17; 32:7). These words remind us that God is a God of comfort and that He wants to encourage us through His Word.

With God's blessing assured through words of comfort, a few specific directions are given: Don't make the same mistake twice. Though the primary cause of the defeat at Ai is Achan's sin, a secondary cause is underestimating the enemy, overestimating themselves, and presuming on the Lord (7:3–4). By trusting Him, God promises they can turn a place of defeat into a place of victory.

Still, the basis of victory is the same: Just like at Jericho, victory at Ai will come by the power of God. The irony of God's blessing is that the spoils of Ai and its livestock can now be taken by Israel. As the firstfruits of the land, Jericho has been placed under the ban, but this is not the case with Ai. Achan's dissatisfaction actually causes him to miss precisely what he longs for and much more.

With the battle at Ai, we are reminded that we should not expect God to work the same way always. We need to be open and sensitive to the various ways God may lead. As the sovereign God of the universe, He is never limited to one particular method to accomplish His purposes.

The strategy for the capture of Ai is ingenious (8:3–9). The plan works like clockwork (8:14–22). Thus Israel, out of their failure, comes not only to a second chance but to a great victory along with some much-needed lessons. Though we should never seek to fail, failure can be the back door to success; for God is willing to forgive and restore us if we will deal with our sin appropriately and sincerely.

8:30–35

THE COVENANT RENEWED

Instead of further pursuing the military campaign following the victory at Ai, Joshua leads the Israelites on a spiritual pilgrimage for a special time of worship. Moses had commanded it (Deuteronomy 27:1–8) because of what this event would stand for in the lives of the Israelites. This counterintuitive strategy illustrates the principle of first priorities: Our capacity in life is always dependent on our spiritual capacity and orientation to the plan of God.

Joshua leads the entire nation—men, women, children, and cattle—to the place specified by Moses, the mountains of Ebal and Gerizim. This is a march of about thirty miles and evidently is not difficult or dangerous because they pass through an area that is sparsely populated. These mountains are located in the geographic center of the land. This place represents all the land, both at the time of entrance into Canaan and also when Joshua's leadership comes to a close (24:1).

Critical Observation

The place where Joshua led the people had outstanding acoustical properties, kind of like a natural amphitheater, and one person standing on one mountain could be easily heard by someone standing on the other mountain. Mount Ebal stood for cursing, and Gerizim stood for blessing. These mountains formed a huge object lesson. What happened to the Israelites in the land was going to depend on where they lived, as it were—on Mount Ebal, in disobedience and under the curses, or on Mount Gerizim, in obedience and under God's blessing.

When there is obedience to the law of God, there is victory. But when there is disobedience, the result is defeat. We are reminded in this object lesson of God's grace and provision that obedience brings blessing and disobedience brings cursing.

At Mount Sinai, God gave the Ten Commandments and the judgments, and He also gave the ordinances, the sacrifices. The altar here is for those who acknowledge their sin and come not as righteous, but as sinners to the place of sacrifice. The altar, constructed of uncut stones without any human workmanship (8:30–31), is a negation of humanism and salvation by works. It shows that human beings can add nothing to the work of God for salvation or for spirituality. It is by God's work that we are saved.

Take It Home

The law pointed Israel to those moral statutes that are so vital to justice and order within nations. But it did more. It demonstrated the holiness of God and man's inability; it showed how sin separates people from God. Through the tabernacle, the sacrifices, and the priesthood, it pointed forward to a suffering Savior, the Lamb of God, who must die for humanity's sin that we might have a relationship with God and be His people in a fallen world.

JOSHUA 9:1–27

THE PERIL OF WALKING BY SIGHT

Setting Up the Section

This passage describes the danger of failing to commit to the Lord, the peril of prayerlessness, and the peril of walking by sight—making decisions on the basis of how things appear rather than trusting in God for guidance. As we have seen, Israel's failure at Ai was to a large degree the result of failing to consult the Lord.

9:1–2

THE ALLIANCES AGAINST ISRAEL

The record given here is typical of Satan's strategies. Powerful alliances begin immediately to form in both the north and the south of Canaan. Where tribal warfare had gone on for years, suddenly deadly enemies come together in alliances as they unite against the invasion of God's people into the land.

Critical Observation

When righteousness becomes aggressive and bent on an objective, it has a way of uniting the forces of righteousness and the enemies of righteousness. It happened this way when Jesus Christ launched His earthly ministry. His aggressive ministry of healing, preaching, and the confrontation of sin galvanized His own followers; but it also welded together three groups who had formerly been enemies—the Pharisees, the Sadducees, and the Herodians.

It appears that all the city-states in mountainous regions join forces against Israel as a means of keeping Joshua and his army from attacking one city at a time, as had been done with Jericho and Ai. In resisting Israel, however, these kings are resisting God. Their stubborn rebellion against God is an eloquent testimony that the sin of the Amorites had reached its full measure.

9:3–17

THE DECEPTION OF THE GIBEONITES

Not all are willing to openly go against Israel in view of Israel's victories. The Gibeonites, which include a league of cities (9:17), concoct a clever ruse designed to deceive the Israelites and hide their true identity—a typical strategy of Satan, the deceiver. They evidently somehow know that God had commanded the Israelites to totally destroy all the inhabitants of the land.

Their claim is that they are impressed with the great things Joshua has done, and so they want a treaty allowing them to live because they are not of the land of Canaan.

The Gibeonites play on the Israelites' sympathies by appearing as weary travelers who have been on a long journey. They also play on their egos and their sense of pride. They insist they came from a great distance to show their respect for the power of the God of the Israelites and want to be allowed to live as the servants of Israel. Caught off guard, Joshua and the leaders of Israel listen to the ruse of the Gibeonites.

The primary mistake here is a failure to seek counsel from the Lord. The Israelites should have sought direction from the Lord through the Urim and Thummim. Here we see the peril of presumption through prayerlessness. It is always a mistake for us to lean on our own wisdom or judgment and make our own plans apart from God's direction.

9:18–27

THE DECISION OF THE LEADERS

The text tells us that once the ruse is discovered, the people grumble against their leaders because they judged them to be responsible. Though the Israelites erred by leaning on their own understanding rather than consulting the Lord, they honor their agreement with the Gibeonites. To break the covenant would dishonor God's name and bring down His wrath.

While they could not go back on their pledge, the Gibeonites had deceived them, so a punishment fitting their sin must be prescribed. First, Joshua rebukes them for their dishonesty and then sentences them to perpetual slavery. In the ruse of the Gibeonites, they had offered to be the subjects of the Israelites (9:8, 11). By this they are merely offering to become Israel's vassals. In return they expect Israel, the stronger of the two, to protect them from their enemies (10:6). Their plan backfires and they become woodcutters and water-bearers for the Israelites, especially in relation to the tabernacle service. In God's grace, this turns out to be a great blessing.

The very thing the Gibeonites hoped to retain—their freedom—was lost. But the curse eventually becomes a blessing. It is on behalf of the Gibeonites that God later works a great miracle (10:10–14). Later, the tabernacle of the Lord will be pitched at Gibeon, and the Gibeonites (who may have been later known as Nethinims) will replace the Levites in temple service (Ezra 8:20). That is the amazing way the grace of God works. God not only forgives, but in many cases He actually overrules our mistakes and brings blessing out of sin.

The Gibeonites have the privilege of being brought close to the Lord on a regular basis. It is interesting that in later years, when the Israelites go into idolatry, the Gibeonites are still standing at the altar where the true God ordains that sacrifices should be made for sins. As a result of what they have seen God do for Israel, they become convinced, like Rahab, that Israel's God is the true God. Like Rahab, they become loyal believers.

Take It Home

As Christians, we are involved in deadly spiritual warfare with a power far superior to our own strength. To be delivered from our opponent and his nefarious schemes, we must clothe ourselves with our spiritual armor as given us in Christ. The offensive weapons given to us by the Lord are the Word of God and prayer. Without the Word and prayer, we are sitting ducks. When God's people are victorious or prosper, it seems Satan doubles his efforts in attacks against them. Be ever on your guard! (Read 1 Samuel 12:23; Proverbs 3:5–6; 1 Corinthians 10:12; Ephesians 6:10–18.)

JOSHUA 10:1–43

DESTRUCTION OF THE COALITION

The Amorite Coalition	10:1–5
Miraculous Deliverance	10:6–15
Further Victories	10:16–43

Setting Up the Section

During Israel's campaign and victory over the southern portion of Canaan, something miraculous happens that provides Joshua with a great military opportunity for a quick victory over a number of enemies at once.

10:1–5

THE AMORITE COALITION

The defection of the Gibeonites is cause for great alarm for three reasons: (1) It is discouraging to see such a large city surrender to the enemy, (2) without Gibeon the southern coalition is severely weakened, and (3) they constitute a fifth column to fight with Israel in time of war. Though it has no king, Gibeon is like a royal city; it is just as strong and influential as any city-state (11:12).

10:6–15

MIRACULOUS DELIVERANCE

Faced with the armies of the coalition and certain destruction, the Gibeonites send a messenger to Joshua asking for help based on their treaty with Israel. Humanly speaking, this is the perfect opportunity for Joshua to get rid of the Gibeonites. Yet Joshua is a man of integrity who honors his word and does not consider that an option. The Israelites had given their word and are duty bound to honor it. Plus, the situation now provides a unique military opportunity to defeat and destroy several armies at once.

The fact that God now gives this promise might suggest that Joshua had inquired of the Lord and had received this answer and promise. With all these kings coming together, there was surely a certain amount of concern in Joshua's heart. The situation was urgent, and God's word of encouragement and His promise of victory were certainly needed.

This passage provides an excellent example of the interplay between the work of God and the work of humanity in achieving victory. Here a man's efforts and God's sovereign intervention cooperate with the clear emphasis on the fact that it is the Lord who gives the victory. God gives us responsibilities and talents to serve Him, yet ultimately, we must understand that victory is the Lord's.

The Canaanites worshiped gods in the image of natural forces. What a shock when it seems that their gods, in which they have placed their faith, are helpless against the God of Israel, who sends a hailstorm to defeat them.

This battle includes the greatest of four miracles found in the book of Joshua (10:12), often called "Joshua's long day," or "the day the sun stood still." It is noon, and the hot sun is directly overhead when Joshua utters his prayer. The petition is quickly answered by the Lord. Joshua prays in faith and a great miracle results. The record of this miracle has been called the most striking example of conflict between scripture and science because, as is well-known, the sun does not move around the earth causing day and night. Instead, light and darkness come because the earth rotates on its axis around the sun. Why, then, does Joshua address the sun rather than the earth? He is using the language of observation; he is speaking from the perspective and appearance of things on earth.

Demystifying Joshua

Obviously, this was a unique day in the history of creation. Views concerning this phenomenon fall into two categories. The first assumes a slowing or suspending of the normal rotation of the earth so that there were extra hours that day. God did this so that Joshua's forces could complete their victory before the enemy had a night for rest and regrouping. The Hebrew for *stood still* (10:13) is a verb of motion, indicating a slowing or stopping of the rotation of the earth on its axis. The second category includes views that assume no irregularity in the rotation of the earth. One view argues for the prolonging of daylight by some sort of unusual refraction of the sun's rays. While the details of how it took place are not described in scripture, what is made clear is that God did something completely amazing to give the Israelite armies a complete and decisive victory.

10:16–43

FURTHER VICTORIES

The five kings and their armies have left the safety of their fortified cities to fight Joshua and his army out in the open, which gives Joshua a great advantage. He is determined to keep them from escaping to the safety of their walls, which will prolong the campaign against that portion of the land.

Joshua's thinking of human responsibility and tactical wisdom combines with his faith in the One who ultimately delivers victory. Our need is to keep our eyes on Him, to obey Him, and above all, to trust in His strength rather than in our own. This will usually mean expending great effort, as we see Israel doing here, all the while knowing that the Lord is also at work to enable and to fight for us. Most of us learn, early in our Christian experience, that we do not just face one enemy. We face a coalition of evil forces that have banded together in an attempt to destroy us. Those enemies are commonly called the world, the flesh, and the devil.

Together the world, the flesh, and the devil make an unbeatable combination—or they would be unbeatable, if not for the saving intervention of God. Without God, victory against such an alliance is impossible. With God, victory is assured. Joshua was a man who knew God above all else; the impressive results are told in this history.

Take It Home

Joshua and the Israelites take possession of their God-given inheritance, but not without having to go up against hostile forces. The Christian life is precisely like this. In Christ we have been given every spiritual blessing (Ephesians 1:3). In Him, we are complete (Colossians 2:10), but the appropriation of those blessings requires faith in the accomplished work of Christ, along with personal effort through the disciplines of godliness—things such as prayer, Bible study, meditating on God's Word, and regular fellowship with other believers for encouragement.

JOSHUA 11:1–23

THE CONQUEST OF THE NORTH

An Attempt to Stop Israel	11:1–5
God's Promise for Victory	11:6–15
God's Victories Reviewed	11:16–23

Setting Up the Section

Joshua has a decisive victory over the south of Canaan. Now the rulers of the cities in the north have become scared. Although earthly rulers are quick to devise plans to stop Israel, they underestimate the power of God being on one's side. The victory He promised Israel will be realized, even if the battle is long and grueling.

11:1–5

AN ATTEMPT TO STOP ISRAEL

King Jabin believes the only hope for the kingdoms in north Canaan is to unite into one powerful army to fight off the coming Israelites. This strategy provides yet another opportunity for God to demonstrate that it is His power and His plan that will prevail.

Strategically, it allows Joshua and the Israelites to fight a collective army rather than having to go through the work of taking each city one at a time.

The threat of annihilation forces the kings of the north into an unlikely partnership. Prior to Israel's imminent threat, the kings of the north were hostile to each other and had no alliances. This new united force made an impressive army—militarily speaking, they have a distinct upper hand. The text uses hyperbole to describe the numbers—soldiers as numerous as the sand on the seashore and horses and chariots in great numbers—suggesting that the army is a formidable, overwhelming enemy for the worn-out Hebrews to face.

Demystifying Joshua

Josephus, a Jewish historian of the first century AD, estimated that this northern alliance included 300,000 infantry soldiers, 10,000 cavalry troops, and 20,000 chariots. With such a huge army, it would appear from outside observation that Joshua and his army had good reason for fear.

11:6–15

GOD'S PROMISE FOR VICTORY

As the remaining Canaanite forces gather and take position, Joshua is moving, too. The Israelites are not staying in one place waiting for the battle to come to them. They are marching directly toward Merom, a five-day trek from their home base. It is during this journey that God speaks to Joshua and reminds him again that God will deliver provision and victory. The promise God gives Joshua echoes what He has been saying to Joshua from the very beginning of his time as the leader of Israel: "Do not be afraid; your enemies will be delivered to you" (1:9; 8:1). Joshua's courage flows from faith in the power of God to deliver the promised land to His people.

Not only is Israel going to see this army delivered over to them, but God even tells Joshua specifically to cripple their horses and burn their chariots. These acts may seem brutal, but they send a strong message to the Canaanite kings. Not only have the Israelites defeated their spectacular force, but they destroyed their hope and resources for future attacks. Destroying these weapons holds a lesson for Israel as well: not to depend on superior weaponry, but on the Lord.

Through Israel's conquest of the north, God sends a signal both to Israel and the world that He is the One who provides victory, and His victory is complete and thorough. Never again will these people be able to use their horses to attack God's nation.

Demystifying Joshua

Hazor alone among the northern cities is both seized and burned. This city was by far the largest and most prominent city of ancient Palestine (200 acres in size, compared with Megiddo at 14 and Jericho at 8). Hazor was also ruled by King Jabin—the instigator of the alliance among the northern cities. It was strategically positioned at the center of several branches of an ancient highway which led from Egypt to Syria, Assyria, and Babylon. Because it was the hub of a trade route, Hazor was a very wealthy city. If Hazor could not escape the power of God, the remaining cities would be forced to acknowledge their own vulnerability to the Israelites.

11:16–23

GOD'S VICTORIES REVIEWED

With the victory in the north, the formal end of the conquest occurs. Before giving the record of how the land is distributed among the tribes, the author reviews Israel's triumphs in Canaan. He includes a description of the conquered geographic areas (11:16–23) and a list of the defeated kings (chapter 12). This is done to make sure that everyone knows and understands the great work that God has done. Reviewing God's provision builds faith and serves as a reminder of God's blessings.

The battles fought by Joshua and his troops ranged over lands that stretched from border to border, from south to north, and from east to west (11:16–17). The entire land was covered in Israel's amazing conquest. Understandably, it takes time for Israel to gain victory through this vast geography. Conquest of the enemy was neither easy nor quick. Even though God promised them victory, His people were still required to participate, work, and struggle along the way.

One amazing fact is that during the entire conquest, amidst all their confrontations, only one city, Gibeon, sought peace and salvation. The rest were so given over to their depravity that God led His people to take them in battle. Remarkably, even when faced with the ultimate, supernatural power of God, the Canaanites were willing to die rather than submit to God's will or ask for mercy.

Critical Observation

Forty-five years before, the Israelites failed to enter the land for fear of giants—the Anakites Numbers 13:33). Under Joshua, those fearful enemies were almost completely destroyed. Only a few remained in Gaza, Gath, and Ashdod.

The final verse of this chapter (11:23) concludes a major section in Joshua—the conquest. This verse looks backward to where the people have come and forward to where they must go. Even though there are still areas that need to be secured, the victory is now decisive. The battles in the north are the end of this rigorous war schedule.

JOSHUA 12:1–24

KINGS CONQUERED

Setting Up the Section

The list in this chapter is the only complete list of the kings Israel conquered. This list is a testimony to the power of God to accomplish His purposes, overcome earthly powers, and provide for His people in a magnificent manner.

12:1–6

THE RECORD OF MOSES

The conquest of the promised land does not begin with Joshua—it began with Moses. It is important to recount the deliverance of God under the leadership of Moses. What Joshua records here are the victories Israel had—over Sihon and Og—under Moses' leadership on the east side of the Jordan. These were important victories because they signified the beginning of Israel establishing itself as a God-empowered powerhouse. Additionally, they remind us just how long ago—more than a generation—this battle for the promised land had begun.

Sihon was the king over a piece of land about ninety miles south to north from the Arnon Gorge at about the midpoint of the Sea of the Arabah (today called the Dead Sea) up to the Sea of Kinnereth. Og ruled over a piece of land extending north from Sihon's northern boundary for about sixty miles (Numbers 21:21–35; Deuteronomy 2:24–3:17). This territory was given to the tribes of Reuben and Gad and the half-tribe of Manasseh (Numbers 32; Joshua 13:8–13).

12:7–24

THE RECORD OF JOSHUA

The sixteen kings of southern Canaan who the Israelites defeated under Joshua's leadership are listed first (12:9–16). This is followed by the list of the fifteen kings of northern Canaan (12:17–24). Not only is this list impressive because of the number of kings, but it serves to highlight the power of God to carry out His promises.

For the Israelites, these kings' names bring back a flood of memories of specific experiences, faces, and events from battles they had participated in personally or from the stories that had been passed down to them from generation to generation. Imagine how hearing a list of names at a graduation ceremony can flood the graduates with memories of the individuals they know who are crossing the stage. This list does much more. It is as poignant and moving as the reading of a list of names at a war memorial service; this list is a memorial to the goodness of God.

Critical Observation

Consider the number of kings who reigned in the small region which would be Israel: thirty-one kings in a land approximately 150 miles from north to south and 50 miles from east to west. This may seem strange considering the nation-states we are familiar with today. However, these kings reigned over city-states and were more like governors or mayors over cities than kings of a nation.

In addition to the significance of the list of names, Joshua calls out the land itself. While the geography of this region is not something many of us have experienced firsthand, the promised land had been traversed by the nation of Israel. When Joshua mentions the hill country, the western foothills, the Arabah, the mountain slopes, the desert, and the Negev, the people had literally walked over those various areas and they could picture precisely what God's provision included. Indeed, this land is the backdrop for their nation's history. These are the same hills and valleys that Jesus and His disciples will travel through, the same territory that Rome will conquer, and later still, the Muslims. It is a setting that has significance not just to the generation of Israelites that had fought alongside Joshua, but for all generations to come.

These kinds of lists remind the people that their victory in the Lord does not come without tremendous cost—indeed thirty-one conquered kings represent a vast swath of humanity whose lives were completely interrupted and destroyed so that Israel might be given the inheritance the Lord had promised to Abraham. This list reminds the people of a crucial truth: There is no one more powerful than God, and no one can stand in His way.

Take It Home

The list in Joshua 12 was a great reminder for the Israelites of where they had been, who God had helped them overcome, and His enduring faithfulness in the face of thirty-one formidable enemies. We all benefit from being reminded of how God has taken us out of the wilderness of our unbelief and into the promised land of a rich life in Christ. Take a few moments to reflect on the enemies that God has allowed you to defeat during your journey as His child. How has He changed you and enabled you to conquer sins and grow in grace? Write down your vanquished enemies by name and keep the list to remind you of God's faithfulness and provision and just how far you've come.

JOSHUA 13:1–33

THE DIVISION OF THE LAND

Setting Up the Section

This chapter deals with an exciting time for the Israelites—the distribution of the land. After four hundred years in bondage in Egypt, forty years of wandering in the desert, and years of long hard fighting, they now are able to enjoy and possess the promised land.

13:1–7

THE COMMAND TO DIVIDE THE LAND

Joshua is now growing old. God changes his title, and Joshua becomes more of an administrator for the nation of Israel rather than a military leader. The land has to be assigned to the various tribes, and Joshua is instructed to oversee these important transactions.

To many people this section of the book of Joshua, with its detailed lists of boundaries and cities, seems boring to read. Keep in mind that this is not just some boring list of boundaries; instead, it is the complete and literal fulfillment of the promise of God. When God gives a promise, He fulfills it perfectly and literally. As you read this section, do not forget that God is a promise-keeping God.

We know from later in the text that Joshua dies at the age of 110 (24:29). Given the timing of events between this point and his death, he probably is at least 100 at this time. Because of his age, it is important that Joshua begin the distribution of the land. Even though there are some military threats still facing Joshua, he must begin the distribution and encourage the people to begin settling and enjoying the land.

The land that remains to be taken is described from south to north and includes Philistia, Phoenicia, and Lebanon (13:5–6). All this land is now to be allotted to the nine and a half tribes because God promised to drive out all the enemies (13:6).

13:8–33

THE SPECIAL LAND GRANT

In verses 8–13, Joshua confirms the provision and land division that had already been done by Moses on the east side of the Jordan. The tribes of Reuben, Gad, and the half-tribe of Manasseh, possessing large herds of cattle, had been anxious to settle in the rich grazing lands of the Jordan River valley. They are given this privilege only after their men agree to fight alongside their brothers to win Canaan proper (Numbers 32).

The text provides a survey of the area of Transjordan (13:9–12). It is interesting to note that Geshur and Maacah (already mentioned in 12:5) are not defeated by the Israelites.

It is not stated as to why, but it is something that was a present reality for the original readers of the book. These countries were located east and northeast of the Sea of Kinnereth (the Sea of Galilee).

We are told that the tribe of Levi receives no specific territory of land (see 13:33; 14:3–4; 18:7). Instead, the Levites receive forty-eight towns with pastureland for their flocks and herds (14:4; 21:41) as Moses had specified (Numbers 35:1–5). God wanted to make sure that the Levites were set aside as servants of Him and therefore, freed from the cares of the land. They are given cities to raise their animals and provide housing for their families.

Joshua emphasizes more than once that the tribe of Levi did not acquire any land (13:33, 14:3–4; 18:7). The reason for the repeated reminder of this is that it highlights why God set them aside. The Levites were given the important task of managing the worship of God. The tribe of Levi served particular religious duties for the Israelites and had political responsibilities as well. In return for their special calling and service, the landed tribes were expected to give 10 percent of everything they had (a tithe) to the Levites. The tithe is known as the Maaser Rishon, or Levite Tithe.

Reuben (as we see in 13:15–23) receives the territory previously occupied by Moab, east of the Dead Sea. The tribe of Gad inherits the portion in the center of the region, in the original land of Gilead (13:24–28). The allotment to the half-tribe of Manasseh (13:29–31) is the rich tableland of Bashan, east of the Sea of Kinnereth.

Demystifying Joshua

In Genesis 35:22 and 49:3–4, as he was dying, Jacob had uttered prophecies regarding his sons. His prophecy about his firstborn, Reuben, was intensely emotional and judgmental. According to Hebrew tradition and law, the firstborn is entitled a double portion of land (Deuteronomy 21:17). Yet his father's dying prophecy was that neither he nor his tribe received it, because he had defiled his father's bed by sleeping with his father's concubine. As Joshua is dividing the land up, more than four centuries later, Reuben's punishment is passed on to his descendants. The right of the firstborn passed over to his brother, Joseph, who received two portions, one for Ephraim and the other for Manasseh (Genesis 48:12–20).

JOSHUA 14:1–15

CALEB'S PORTION

Setting Up the Section

This chapter describes the process by which the land is distributed to the rest of the nine and a half tribes. The first inheritance is given to Caleb. This is fitting because Caleb, along with Joshua, is one of the only two left from those who are freed from Egypt, and they had been the only two who believed all along that God was powerful enough to give the land to Israel. Here, Caleb gets his reward.

Demystifying Joshua

After the Israelites first escaped Egypt, they traveled across the desert to the border of Canaan and sent twelve spies (one from each of the twelve tribes) across the border to do reconnaissance. Caleb and Joshua were two of the twelve spies and were the only two who brought back a good report. Rather than being fearful of the task ahead, Joshua and Caleb encouraged the people to believe that God would help them conquer the land.

Unfortunately, the people were not convinced, and because of their lack of faith they wandered for forty more years before reapproaching the border for entry. During that forty years, the generation that originally left Egypt died out except for Joshua and Caleb, the only two who made it across the border (Numbers 13:1–14:38).

14:1–5

DIVIDING THE LAND

The beginning of this chapter introduces how Joshua is going to the divide the remainder of the promised land. The explanation is repeated regarding the dealings with the Reubenites, the Gadites, the half-tribe of Manasseh, and the arrangements for the tribe of Levi (13:14, 33; 18:7). The method by which the land is to be distributed is by lot (14:2; 18:8; 19:51).

It is important to note that the Lord had instructed Moses that each tribe was to receive territory proportionate to its population, while the casting of lots would serve to determine the land's location (Numbers 26:54–56). To cast a lot meant that dice from the breastplate of the priest were used. They were thrown on the ground, and if a certain combination emerged, then God's will would be known (Exodus 28:30; Numbers 27:21).

14:6–15

CALEB'S REQUEST

When the time for distribution arrives, the tribe of Judah, receiving the first portion, assembles at Gilgal. Before the lots are cast, Caleb steps forward to remind Joshua of a promise the Lord had made to him forty-five years earlier: "I will give him and his descendants the land he set his feet on, because he followed the LORD wholeheartedly" (Deuteronomy 1:36 NIV).

Caleb then reviews the highlights of his life and makes his request. It is important that Caleb stand up at this point—not just so he will get the land, but so all will remember the lack of faith in their forefathers set in contrast to the great hand of deliverance of God. This moment speaks volumes about how the hand of God provides and rewards His faithful servants.

The autobiographical story continues as Caleb reminisces about God's faithfulness to him over many years (14:10–11). Caleb bears testimony that God kept him alive the past forty-five years as He had promised. Caleb was given two divine promises: one, that his life would be prolonged, and the other, that he would someday inherit the territory he had bravely explored near Hebron.

Demystifying Joshua

Caleb's remarks provide important information to help us determine the length of the conquest of Canaan by the Israelites. Caleb states that he was forty years old when he went to spy the land (14:7). Then he adds that the years Israel spent wandering in the wilderness lasted thirty-eight years. Finally, at the time of the conquest, Caleb was eighty-five years old. That tells us that the conquest lasted seven years. This is confirmed by Caleb's reference (14:10) to God's sustaining grace for forty-five years since Kadesh-barnea (thirty-eight years of the wanderings plus seven years of the conquest).

Caleb concludes his speech to Joshua with a very important request: that he and his family be given the same section of land whose inhabitants had struck fear into the hearts of the ten spies so many years before. This was the inheritance he desired. Imagine how meaningful it must have been to see his faith come to fruition forty-five years later. He wants that land as a testimony of God's power and his own faith.

In order to take possession of this particular portion of land, Caleb still has some battles to win. Yet even at eighty-five, he feels as strong and confident in the Lord as he did years before. Thus, Caleb is ready to fight the Anakites at Hebron and take that city for his own inheritance. His faith is steadfast and sincere, and he wants to see God deliver that land to Israel.

A historical note explains that the previous name of Hebron was *Kiriath Arba* (14:15). Arba was a giant among the Anakites, a nation of giants. Yet, although these giants scared most of Israel, they were taken down by God through Caleb, and thus Hebron was renamed. The giants proved no match for God or the faith of His servant Caleb.

Take It Home

The examples of Caleb's faithfulness and God's provision remind us of how mysteriously God often works in the lives of His children—and it also underscores the fact that divine timing is not always what we might expect (2 Peter 3:8). God requires that our hearts be in the right place even when His plan involves years of waiting. In our journey of faith we are often asked to expect good things from God, but the when and the how are not always made clear to us as quickly. Isaiah 40:31 reminds us that "those who trust the Lord will find new strength" (cev). As you learn to wait on God's provision faithfully, remember to, like Caleb, claim His strength along the way.

JOSHUA 15:1–63

LAND FOR THE TRIBE OF JUDAH

Setting Up the Section

After Caleb's allotment, Joshua now turns to the distribution of the land for the tribe of Judah. Judah receives the largest portion because they are the largest tribe. In the distribution of the land to Judah, there are some things already spoken by Jacob that have a remarkable bearing on this tribe.

15:1–12

JUDAH'S LAND

The great patriarch Jacob had prophesied several specifics concerning his sons. In regard to Judah, Jacob had predicted that his tribe would grow to be strong and fierce because they would be surrounded by their enemies (Genesis 49:8–9). With the land they are given, Judah's tribe is surrounded by the Moabites to the east, Edomites to the south, Amalekites to the southwest, and the Philistines to the west.

Jacob also noted that Judah would be a place flowing with wine and milk (Genesis 49:11–12). The placement of this land is ideally suited for vineyards and cattle. In fact, it was from this region that the spies cut down the huge cluster of grapes (Numbers 13:24).

Jacob also made it clear that Judah was to be a royal line (Genesis 49:10). This prophecy can be understood in two ways. Most immediately, it looks for the rise of kingship in Judah, namely David and his descendants. Also, it looks forward to the coming of the Messiah.

With the allotment of this tribe we begin to see the fulfillment of what Jacob said years ago. If you were looking at the boundaries of this land on a map, you would see that the territory conquered by Joshua in his southern campaign is included in Judah's inheritance (Joshua 10:1–43).

15:13–19

CALEB'S PORTION

This passage is unique in its position. In fact, it seems a bit out of order. It is here, either in anticipation of what will happen later (Judges 1:12–15), or the Judges passage is a flashback to this event. If it is in anticipation of a future event, it is probably included here by the author to bring completeness to the land distribution.

Included in Judah's portion of land is the city of Hebron (Kiriath Arba; 14:15). This city has been granted to Caleb. Caleb has to drive out the Anakites in order to take possession of his land, specifically their three leaders: Sheshai, Ahiman, and Talmai (15:14). These three kings are mentioned earlier (Numbers 13:22) as having been at Hebron when Caleb and the other spies were sent by Moses to scope out the land forty-five years earlier. Do you see the way that God works? Caleb is able to attack and drive out the kings that should have been driven out by a previous generation—a very redemptive victory indeed.

After his victory over Hebron, Caleb turns his attention to the nearby city of Debir (10:38–39; 11:21). Caleb puts an offer out to his men—whoever helps him take this city will be given his daughter Acsah's hand in marriage. Othniel captures the city and he receives Acsah as his wife. Othniel is part of the Kenizzite clan, and he is also Caleb's nephew (15:17), which keeps the land in the family. Othniel is later one of the twelve judges whom God uses in delivering the Israelites from foreign oppressions during difficult years ahead (Judges 3:9–11).

According to the text, Acsah urges someone to seek a piece of land from Caleb. It is not entirely clear who she is asking, but it seems that she is asking her husband, Othniel, to acquire a piece of land for them. This is the second time someone has specifically requested a portion of the land (15:18–19)—ironically, the first had been Caleb. This account is set apart from the rest of the text, forming an aside to the main story.

The text moves abruptly to a conversation between Acsah and Caleb. The father asks his daughter what she wants, and she adds two more things to the land: a blessing and some springs. Natural springs would give her and her new husband the resources to prosper. The Negev is noted as being a place where there is little water. The blessing that she seeks is the special favor of God upon her so that she will truly prosper in the land. Her father, Caleb, complies.

Critical Observation

Many interpret this as a sign of a woman of faith who was seeking what was best for her family. Others have suggested that her request was presumptuous, even greedy. Whatever your opinion of her boldness, this is a very unique moment, and it shows the extreme amount of passion that existed for the Israelites regarding the land. Here was a couple who had fought to conquer the land (and win each other) and then who persisted in expecting God to give them good things.

15:20–63

THE TOWNS OF JUDAH

God is clearly providing for each tribe as He promised. But there is one thing in the list that seems to be a contradiction; the number of towns in the Negev is said to be twenty-nine (15:32), but thirty-six are listed (15:21–32). The reason for the difference is that seven of these towns were separated out later and given to Simeon's tribe (19:1–7).

It is interesting to note that Judah inherits well over one hundred cities and occupies almost all of them with little difficulty. The only city that is difficult for them to possess is Jerusalem. The distribution for the tribe of Judah ends on a dark note: Judah could not remove the Jebusites, who were living in Jerusalem (15:63). Was this lack of victory because they simply weren't strong enough, or was it because they failed to trust God? Joshua does not say. Unfortunately, the Jebusites will prove to be a snare for Israel later.

JOSHUA 16:1–17:18

EPHRAIM AND MANASSEH

The Sons of Joseph	16:1–4
Land for Ephraim	16:5–10
Land for Manasseh	17:1–13
The Complaint	17:14–18

Setting Up the Section

Years before, while Joseph was away in Egypt, he had two sons: Ephraim and Manasseh. When his father Jacob discovered Joseph was not dead (Genesis 48:21), he included these two children in the blessing of the promised land. In his joy, Jacob brought Ephraim and Manasseh into his direct inheritance. Thus, they were considered heads of tribes with their uncles (Joseph's brothers).

16:1–4

THE SONS OF JOSEPH

The boundary line for the sons of Joseph began in the east, near Jericho, which was north of Judah's boundary. Ephraim's territory does not butt up against Judah, because sandwiched in between Ephraim and Judah is Benjamin. The territory given to Ephraim in Canaan is in many respects the most beautiful and fertile. They are centrally located and have a wonderful piece of land.

The borders outlined here are for the tribes of both Manasseh and Ephraim. The text is giving us the overall picture of what both tribes receive. This overall picture gives us a clearly defined southern border—the area that makes up the southern part of Israel.

Demystifying Joshua

The unified treatment of the two Joseph tribes ends (15:1–4), completing the common southern boundary that separated them from the southern tribes of Benjamin and Judah. From this point on, the boundaries are given for each of Joseph's son's tribes individually, almost foreshadowing how significant this southern border would soon become. The southern border is significant because it marked a real geographical division between the north and south, which already had significant cultural and political ones. It is noteworthy that even at this early stage of being a landed nation, God's people were experiencing some divisions. These divisions surface with a vengeance during the reign of David before Israel and Judea split into two separate nations. You can see in the scriptures where Judah is distinguished from Israel, even before there had been an official split (2 Samuel 2:9–10; 3:10; 4:1). It's possible that hints of this division were already at play when the author was writing the history.

16:5–10

LAND FOR EPHRAIM

The specific allotment for the tribe of Ephraim is located immediately north of the territory to be assigned to Dan and Benjamin. The allotment of Ephraim stretches from the Jordan to the Mediterranean and includes the sites of some of Joshua's battles as well as Shiloh. Shiloh is the sacred place where the tabernacle will remain for close to three hundred years. To foster unity between the two tribes, some of Ephraim's towns are located in the territory of Manasseh (16:9).

Just like the men of Judah, the men of Ephraim do not completely drive out the Canaanites from their region. In fact, they greedily keep the Canaanites around as forced laborers. This provides a labor force for free and fostered economic growth—for a season. Moses had warned the Israelites against failing to drive out the Canaanites (Deuteronomy 20:15–18). Ultimately, this decision proves to be a fatal mistake for the tribe of Ephraim. In the time of the judges, the Canaanites rise up and enslave the Israelites.

17:1–13

LAND FOR MANASSEH

Half of the tribe of Manasseh had settled in the Transjordan region (13:29), while the other half settled in Canaan proper. Machir is Manasseh's firstborn (Genesis 50:23; Numbers 26:29). His descendants represent the half-tribe of Manasseh that had already received a separate portion east of the Jordan, in Gilead and Bashan (Joshua 13:29–31). The rest of Manasseh's allotment is west of the Jordan. The remaining heirs settle in Canaan proper and are given the territory north of Ephraim, extending from the Jordan River to the Mediterranean Sea (17:7–10).

Machir had been given land in Gilead and Bashan. The text refers to him as a "man of war" (17:1); many years later, the same fighting streak would be ascribed to Machir's descendants in Gilead (Numbers 32:39). A portion of Manasseh's descendants inherit the lands east of the Jordan, and this fact forms the backdrop for understanding why the rest of Manasseh's descendants receive their inheritance west of the Jordan (17:2).

The allotment to Manasseh's other descendants was to be west of the Jordan. All six sons are named, and we learn later that all are descendants of Gilead (Numbers 26:30–32). For these six male descendants of Manasseh, Jewish tradition allows them to inherit the land with no problem. Yet one descendant, Zelophehad, a great-great grandson of Manasseh, had already died with no male heirs.

In fact, Zelophehad had five daughters, but no sons. Hebrew culture demands that the inheritance go to the son, not to the daughter. This is because women entered into a new family when they were married and were not able to own land or receive inheritance. The Lord declared that because their father died without any sons, the daughters could receive his inheritance (Numbers 27:1–11). The only requirement is that they not marry outside the tribe so that the land would not switch out to another tribe.

These girls go to the high priest Eleazar (Aaron's son; 24:33), who with Joshua and the tribal leaders oversee the allotments to the tribes (19:51). These five women receive their portion within the territory of Manasseh. This incident shows God's concern for the rights of women at a time when most societies regarded them as mere chattel. God was committed to being fair with the entire tribe—men and women. God's faithfulness to the women reminds us that a custom should never be held to such a degree that it hurts the very people it was intended to protect.

Critical Observation

The daughters' names and Zelophehad's genealogy are carefully recorded (17:3) to show the legal legitimacy of their claim. It was important to keep all the division of the land legal to prevent any misunderstandings or misinterpretations arising from confused identities in the future. The details with which the tribes' boundaries and cities are recorded extend down to the inheritance for individuals because this was God's gift to the whole nation. The daughters presented their case to Eleazar, the priest, and Joshua precisely for this reason. With their approval, no one could take this land away from this family.

This text reinforces the point stated that daughters could—and indeed did—inherit land, under the conditions mentioned (Numbers 27). Their portion was fair and allowed this line of Manasseh to be cared for in the new land. Manasseh's actual inheritance is outlined, but just general boundaries are given (17:7–10)—including a few cities that outline the boundary list properly. Two cities in its boundary description became Levitical cities: Shechem (17:2, 7; 21:21) and Taanach (17:11; 21:25).

Several cities located in the tribes of Issachar and Asher are given to Manasseh (17:12–13). Apparently it is considered necessary for military purposes that these cities be held by a strong tribe. The sons of Manasseh, like the Ephraimites, however, choose tribute over triumph: Rather than driving out the Canaanites, they enslave them. This proves to be a major issue for Israel in the future. Going outside God's instruction can be deadly.

17:14–18

THE COMPLAINT

In this passage, the sons of Joseph speak as one (16:4 and 17:14). These two tribes are discontented with their allotted territory, challenging Joshua for more land. The episode unfolds through two verbal exchanges between Joshua and the tribes (17:14–15, 16–18). This is the fourth narrative of people wanting to talk about land.

Joshua handles their complaint with skill. He challenges them to clear the trees and settle in the forested hill country (17:15). He suggests that they combine their energies to drive out the Canaanites (17:18). This shows how much land there is yet to possess. Joshua's advice is wise—if they need more land, then they should clear out land from the forests where the Perizzites and Rephaites live. In short, there is more land; they just need to possess it.

This complaint evidences a degree of arrogance and greed in the Joseph tribes' confrontation with Joshua. Compare this attitude with the tone of Caleb (14:6–12) and the daughters of Zelophehad (17:4). In both instances, the requests are made based on the Lord's promises. The sons of Joseph had no promise to appeal to. Instead, they were just dissatisfied with what God had provided for them. At the heart of this is more than just a complaint against Joshua—it's a complaint against God.

The response of the sons of Joseph further reveals their hearts. They say that the entire hill country is not enough and that they fear the Canaanites. Thus we see that their faith is weak. God had promised to give them the land and told them to trust in Him as their deliverer. At this point, the sons of Joseph are not trusting in God. Joshua agrees that they should have more land, but that they must take the hill country and drive out the Canaanites.

Take It Home

The sons of Joseph had a remarkable lack of faith. Their pride backed them into a corner and the result was fear. The point to see here is that without faith in God, it is impossible to take the promised land. The ten spies learned this in Numbers 13 and 14, and now the sons of Joseph are learning the same lesson. What are the things that frighten you? How can you learn to trust God, unlike the sons of Joseph, to provide all you need?

JOSHUA 18:1–28

THE ALLOTMENT OF THE REST OF THE LAND

Setting Up the Section

The context of chapter 18 is very simple. There are still seven tribes that need to receive their allotment. The story now reaches a turning point in the land distribution lists for the nation of Israel. The nation is now moving to Shiloh. It is at this new location that the Tent of Meeting is mentioned for the first time in the book. The Tent of Meeting is going to be set up in a place where the presence of God will be close to the center of the entire nation.

18:1–10

THE NATION PREPARES TO SETTLE

Prior to this point, Israel's central encampment in the land appears to have been at Gilgal, near Jericho. It is at this camp where the nation observes several ceremonies (4:19–20; 5:2–12) worth commemorating. Now the people are moved about fifteen miles northwest of Jericho to Shiloh. This place will remain an important Israelite religious center for several hundred years. In fact, it will remain the center of religious worship until the taking of Jerusalem by David (2 Samuel 5–6).

The tabernacle was a large portable tent where the presence of God dwelt when the Israelites were in the wilderness. In it was the ark of the covenant as well as other holy items that were to be kept clean and sacred. It was made of fine boards that were covered with layers of fabrics according to specific instructions given to Moses by God (Exodus 26).

Demystifying Joshua

Joshua calls the land "a land which the God of your fathers has given you" (18:3). The phrase "your fathers" refers to the patriarchs of Israel: Abraham, Isaac, and Jacob. This expression, "the God of your fathers," was an important one, for it had a rich history in Israel. God used it with Moses at the burning bush (Exodus 3:13). Moses used it often in Deuteronomy when he would speak to the people (1:11; 4:1; 6:3; 21:1: 27:3). This is the first time we see it in Joshua, and it reminds the nation of the historical importance of this moment. God had made a promise a long time ago that He has now fulfilled (Genesis 12:7; 15:18–21; 26:3–4; 28:4, 13; 35:12).

To begin the process of dividing the rest of the land, Joshua instructs that three men from each of the seven remaining tribes be appointed as surveyors. The role of these surveyors will be to travel throughout the land and record its description (18:4). They are to write down their findings. This is highlighted three times (18:4, 6, 8); God is making sure that all generations will know the land division.

The previous allotments are reviewed to remind the remaining people how God has provided for all the people of Israel (18:5–7). The Lord was with the nation, not only in the tabernacle, but also in the casting of lots for the remaining allotments. The Levites' special inheritance is important, so Joshua mentions it again. He will make sure that those set apart for God's service are cared for and given everything they need.

18:11–28

THE ALLOTMENT FOR BENJAMIN

Of the seven remaining tribes, Benjamin's allotment is given in the most detail (eighteen verses). This is probably because Benjamin's geographical location is between Judah on the south and Joseph (Ephraim) on the north.

Benjamin's northern boundary is the same as the Joseph tribes' southern boundary (16:1-4). Every place mentioned in this passage is found already in 16:1-5, except for the desert of Beth Aven. Beth Aven is between Jericho and Bethel, but its exact location is not fully known. Benjamin's southern boundary is given in the most detail in this passage. This is no doubt because it is bordered by Judah. Judah is the most prominent of all the tribes.

Critical Observation

Several of the cities mentioned in Joshua's lists have the same name as others. Therefore it is important not to confuse the cities. Ophrah (18:23) is also found in Manasseh (Judges 6:24; 8:27). Ramah (18:25) is also found in Asher's northern border (Joshua 19:29), in Naphtali's territory (19:36), and in Simeon's territory (19:8). The name *Ramah* means "height," and for this reason it is not unreasonable that several cities shared that name. Mizpah (18:26) is found in Judah (15:38). Gibeah (18:27) is also found in Judah (15:57).

JOSHUA 19:1–51

THE REST OF THE LAND

Allotment for Simeon	19:1–9
Allotment for Zebulun	19:10–16
Allotment for Issachar	19:17–23
Allotment for Asher	19:24–31
Allotment for Naphtali	19:32–39
Allotment for Dan	19:40–48
Joshua's Allotment	19:49–51

Setting Up the Section

Joshua is now ready to allot the rest of the land to the remaining tribes. God deals with each tribe according to their lot.

19:1–9

ALLOTMENT FOR SIMEON

The tribe of Simeon's inheritance is unique because they are not given an independent allotment, but rather receive land scattered within Judah's allotment. Judah's portion was more than they needed (19:9). Simeon's tribe was small relative to Judah's (1 Chronicles 4:27).

Jacob's prophecy describes why Simeon does not inherit any land. Simeon and Levi are brothers who were bent toward violence. Both men committed acts of violence against the inhabitants of Shechem, when they annihilated every man in the city while the men were recuperating from circumcision (Genesis 34:24–30). Simeon and Levi's landless status is a punishment for their taking violent, personal vengeance against the men of Shechem.

Critical Observation

The tribe of Levi is favored by the Lord. They received a special inheritance far greater than Simeon's. Forty-eight cities throughout the land were all components of their inheritance (chapter 21). One possible reason God deals with these two tribes differently is that the Levites vindicated themselves in the episode involving the golden calf. When Moses discovered the golden calf, he called those who believed in the Lord to follow him, and only the Levites responded (Exodus 32:26). Moses then told the Levites to kill the offenders among them, which they did, killing about three thousand people. Therefore, Moses blessed the Levites and declared them to be set apart to the Lord (Exodus 32:27–29).

Simeon's cities fall into two groups: thirteen cities in the southern portion, the Negev (19:2–6), and four additional cities—two in the Negev and two in the western foothills, the Shephelah (19:7). One additional city in the far south is mentioned (19:8) for a total of eighteen. It is not long before Simeon loses its individual identity as a tribe, as the scattered people become incorporated into the tribe of Judah. As this incorporation begins, many in the tribe of Simeon migrate north to Ephraim and Manasseh (2 Chronicles 15:9; 34:6).

19:10–16

ALLOTMENT FOR ZEBULUN

Zebulun's lot is cast third, and it is the first of five small tribes in the north whose territories are now listed. The text provides very few details about the inheritance of these five smaller tribes beyond standard boundary and city lists for each. Zebulun was a small tribe whose territory nestled between Issachar, western Manasseh, Asher, and Naphtali. According to Jacob's prophecy, Zebulun would live by the seashore and become a haven for ships. In this text we see that Zebulun is assigned land in lower Galilee. This land extends to the Mediterranean Sea, forming an enclave in Issachar's territory.

Demystifying Joshua

The city named *Bethlehem* mentioned here is not the same as the one in Judah—famous for being the birthplace of the Messiah (Judges 17:7; Ruth 1:1; 1 Samuel 16:1; Micah 5:2; Matthew 2:1). Rather, it is in Zebulun, the site where Ibzan, the judge, is buried (Judges 12:8–10). Three cities within Zebulun's boundaries later became Levitical cities: Jokneam (Joshua 19:11; 21:34), Nahalal (19:15; 21:35), and Daberath (19:12; 21:28).

19:17–23

ALLOTMENT FOR ISSACHAR

Issachar is the second small tribe in the north, in the region of Galilee. Its boundary description consists of only three cities (19:22), and its city list contains thirteen cities. Issachar's general location is clear: It is north of western Manasseh, east and south of Zebulun, west of the Jordan, and south of Naphtali.

19:24–31

ALLOTMENT FOR ASHER

The tribe of Asher's territory lay in a long, narrow strip in the far northwest. The land is bordered on the west by the Mediterranean Sea and the tribe of Zebulun, and on the east by Manasseh's western boundary. This territory, by virtue of its position, serves as a major land of protection from northern coastal enemies (including, for example, the Phoenicians). By the time David is king, this tribe had lost much of its significance. One significant fact connects this tribe to the Messiah; Anna, the prophetess who blesses Jesus, is from this tribe (Luke 2:36–38).

19:32–39

ALLOTMENT FOR NAPHTALI

Naphtali receives the rich, forested land in the heart of the Galilee region. Asher is to the west, Zebulun to the south, and the Jordan River and eastern Manasseh to the east. This region does not play a highly significant role in the Old Testament period. Yet in the New Testament, this is the region where Jesus centers His Galilean ministry. It is in this region where Jesus fulfills the prophecy of Isaiah (Isaiah 9:1).

Naphtali's allotment includes a list of fortified cities (Joshua 19:35). To be fortified means that these cities were built up with strong fortresses and surrounding walls. This layer of protection was necessary, because a branch of an international trade route from Egypt to Mesopotamia ran through the territory of Naphtali. The city of Hazor guarded a section of that important route. Because of these well-protected cities, the tribe of Naphtali enjoys periods of prosperity, especially when Israel's kings are strong.

19:40–48

ALLOTMENT FOR DAN

The final lot is cast for the tribe of Dan. The Danites' territorial allotment is in the south, abutting Judah and other tribes. Yet they are listed in this chapter with the northern tribes in Galilee. They are unable to take their own land, so they move north and attack the city of Leshem, which is opposite of the northern part of Naphtali, and settle there (Genesis 49:17; Judges 1:34; 18). Thus they are included among these smaller tribes with allotments in Galilee, because this is where they eventually settled.

19:49–51

JOSHUA'S ALLOTMENT

Caleb's inheritance is settled first (14:6–15); Joshua's is last. Joshua evidently wanted to make sure that his work had been accomplished before he would take what belonged to him. He allows all of the land to be distributed and takes from what is left over. In no way does he exercise his position for selfish gain; his choice of land demonstrates his humility.

Joshua asks for Timnath Serah, a region that promised to be difficult to settle because of its rugged mountainous terrain. The region is within the allotment of his own tribe of Ephraim. Joshua could have taken land in the fairest and most productive area of Canaan, but he did not. Instead, he chooses an area that may otherwise have been overlooked and builds from the ground up. Joshua had an amazingly wide skill set. He is a wise military leader, a fair chief administrator, and now we see that he is also a skilled builder.

God grants Joshua his own personal inheritance. Both of the faithful spies, Caleb and Joshua, have not only entered the land, but they both also receive special portions in it. Yet only Joshua is given his own city. No other Israelite receives any inheritance in this way—not even Caleb. Joshua is an extraordinary leader who is blessed by God.

The most difficult work has been accomplished; the land has been conquered, and the regions have been distributed. All that remains is the marking out of cities for the Levites and the establishment of cities of refuge. Now that the greatest work is behind them, the people are finally in possession of the promised land. Their faithful and powerful God has made good on His promise to their forefathers (19:51).

JOSHUA 20:1–9

CITIES OF REFUGE

Setting Up the Section

God knows that all murder should not be treated in the same manner; thus He commands the Israelites to set up cities of refuge for people who have accidentally killed another person.

20:1–6

A PLACE OF GRACE

The instructions governing the cities of refuge are based upon legislation established by Moses. In the Pentateuch, the Israelites were instructed that six cities should be established within their nation as cities of refuge, where a man could flee if he accidentally kills someone (Exodus 21:12–14). The all-knowing God of the Israelites recognizes that people are often victims of the fallen world in which they live. These cities provided a place where people could flee if they had accidentally murdered someone—they were establishments of grace and mercy in a nation where murderers were normally condemned to death.

The Israelites were instructed to select six cities, three on each side of the Jordan (Numbers 35:9–29). Thus Moses had established three cities for the tribes east of the Jordan (Deuteronomy 4:41–43). He had also given instructions that the same should be done with three cities west of the Jordan (Deuteronomy 19:1–10). By establishing these cities, the law is making distinctions in degrees of guilt. God's law recognizes that motive or intention set some murders apart from accidents, and He makes gracious provisions for such cases.

A man who flees to one of these cities is to state his case before the elders of the city. The elders have the power to return him to his original city and into the hands of the blood avenger (Deuteronomy 19:12). When the refugee's story is credible, innocence is presumed, and the refugees are able to live in the city under the protection of the elders. The refugee is to remain in this city until he has a chance to make his case and defend his innocence, and also until the reigning high priest dies (20:6). Then he is free to return home with no fear of being executed. There is still a consequence for the accidental killing—refugees are bound to their city of refuge—yet their lives are spared.

Demystifying Joshua

Some suggest that refugees had to wait for the death of the high priest before returning home, because the high priest represented the sacrificial system and his death atoned for the sins of the manslayer. No ransom was to be accepted for a murderer or for a manslayer (Numbers 35:30–31). In this rule, God allowed for there to be proper justice (one life for another) for the death. The justice of Old Testament law was taken even further by Jesus Christ in His famous Sermon on the Mount, when He called believers to sacrifice themselves, turn the other cheek, and love their enemies for the sake of the gospel (Matthew 5:38–42).

20:7–9

CITIES OF REFUGE

No place in the land was more than a day's journey from one of these cities of refuge. All six of these cities are mentioned again in the next chapter, since they also were Levitical cities. Despite their importance here and in the Pentateuch, however, they do not appear again in the Old Testament. The six designated cities were located on both sides of the Jordan River. On the west side were Kedesh in Galilee, Shechem in Ephraim, and Hebron in Judah. The cities on the east side were Bezer in the south, Ramoth in the region of Gilead in the tribe of Gad, and Golan in the northern territory of Bashan in Manasseh's tribe.

Take It Home

God takes justice very seriously—consider the example He made of Achan (chapter 7). Yet He is also abounding in love and aware of the challenges that are present in this world. The God of the Old Testament is often considered harsh and unloving, and yet this is the same God who sends His Son to make the ultimate sacrifice for sinful people. This passage reminds us that the God of the Bible is the same throughout all time. As you consider the grace and mercy exemplified in these cities of refuge, consider how God has called you to give grace and mercy to those refugees that come into your world. Also, remember that Christ's standards of justice call each of us to follow His example and sacrifice vengeance for mercy as a means of witnessing the gospel to our enemies.

JOSHUA 21:1–45

CITIES FOR THE LEVITES

The Final Task	21:1–3
Provision for God's Servants	21:4–42
God's Faithfulness	21:43–45

Setting Up the Section

The Levites are not to possess land but are to be given cities and pasturelands to raise their families and care for their cattle (Numbers 35:1–8). They are to be set apart to the Lord for the service to God.

21:1–3

THE FINAL TASK

The last act of distribution is now taking place. Because the Levites are not given an allotment of their own territory, they are scattered (like Simeon's tribe; see 19:1–9). The Levite's inheritance is the honor that they have been set apart to serve God. The call to service is a gift greater than wealth or territory, and the Levites are reminded here to treasure what God has already blessed them with so abundantly.

The leaders of the tribe of Levi claim the towns that had been promised to them by Moses. These forty-eight towns with pasturelands, including the six towns of refuge, are now assigned to the Levites and are the final act of laying claim to the land.

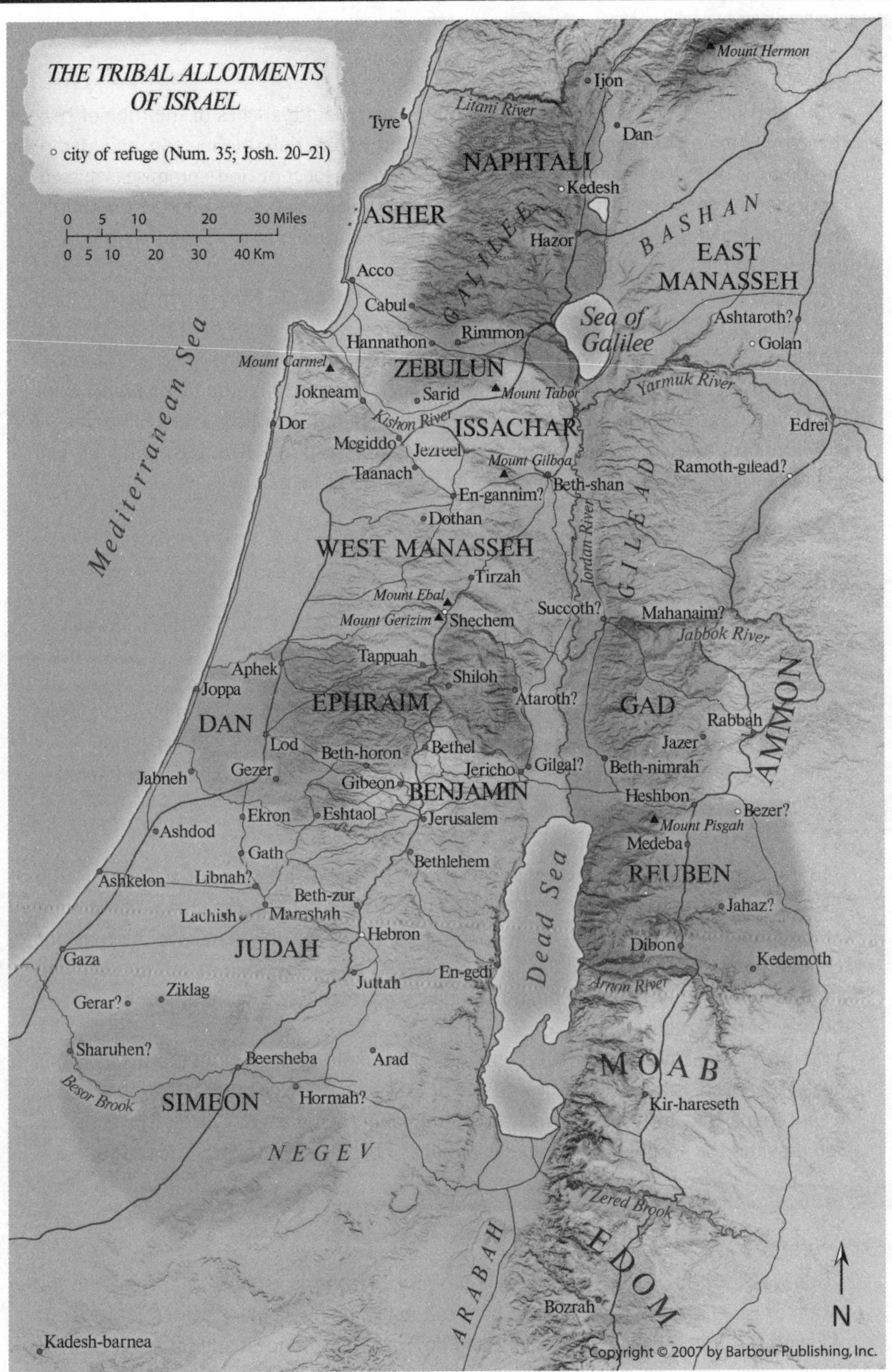
THE TRIBAL ALLOTMENTS OF ISRAEL
○ city of refuge (Num. 35; Josh. 20–21)
0 5 10 20 30 Miles
0 5 10 20 30 40 Km
Mount Hermon
Ijon
Litani River
Tyre
Dan
NAPHTALI
Kedesh
ASHER
GALILEE
BASHAN
Hazor
EAST MANASSEH
Acco
Cabul
Sea of Galilee
Ashtaroth?
Golan
Hannathon
Rimmon
Mediterranean Sea
Mount Carmel
ZEBULUN
Yarmuk River
Jokneam
Sarid
Mount Tabor
Dor
Kishon River
ISSACHAR
Edrei
Megiddo
Jezreel
Mount Gilboa
Ramoth-gilead?
Taanach
Beth-shan
En-gannim?
GILEAD
Dothan
WEST MANASSEH
Jordan River
Tirzah
Mount Ebal
Succoth?
Mahanaim?
Mount Gerizim
Shechem
Jabbok River
Tappuah
Aphek
Shiloh
AMMON
Joppa
EPHRAIM
Ataroth?
GAD
DAN
Rabbah
Lod
Bethel
Jazer
Beth-horon
Jericho
Gilgal?
Beth-nimrah
Jabneh
Gezer
Gibeon
BENJAMIN
Heshbon
Ekron
Eshtaol
Jerusalem
Bezer?
Ashdod
Mount Pisgah
Medeba
Gath
Bethlehem
Dead Sea
REUBEN
Ashkelon
Libnah?
Beth-zur
Jahaz?
Lachish
Mareshah
Hebron
JUDAH
Dibon
Gaza
Kedemoth
En-gedi
Juttah
Arnon River
Ziklag
Gerar?
Sharuhen?
Beersheba
Arad
MOAB
Besor Brook
SIMEON
Hormah?
Kir-hareseth
NEGEV
Zered Brook
ARABAH
EDOM
N
Bozrah
Kadesh-barnea

21:4–42

PROVISION FOR GOD'S SERVANTS

The distribution takes place according to the three main branches of the tribe of Levi. These three main branches correspond to Levi's three sons: Kohath, Gershon, and Merari. This detail is included to show the reader that not one aspect of God's promise is missed. Every clan of every branch receives what was promised—God does fulfill His promises. This should give us great hope as we consider the future promises waiting for us in heaven (1 Peter 1:3–9; Revelation 19–22).

Thirteen towns for the Kohathites are listed first (21:8–19). Nine are in the territory belonging to the tribes of Judah and Simeon. Hebron is listed as a city of refuge because the Levites are responsible for these cities. Ten more cities, including Shechem (another city of refuge), are listed (21:20–26). These cities are assigned to the other branches of the Kohathites in Ephraim, Dan, and western Manasseh. The priestly cities fall primarily within the southern kingdom of Judah. It is in the southern region where the temple will be built in Jerusalem, so it makes sense for the Levites to be nearby.

Critical Observation

To understand the distribution described here, it is important to be reminded of the history of the Levites. The tribe of Levi was cursed by Jacob (Genesis 49:5, 7) for their senseless murder of the Shechemites (Genesis 34). God overruled this curse in Levi's descendants to preserve their tribal identity and make them a blessing to all Israel, because the Levites stood with Moses when the rest of the tribes desired to worship at the feet of the golden calf (Exodus 32:26). God was also pleased with Phinehas (a Levite and Eleazar's son) because he vindicated God's righteous name in the plains of Moab (Numbers 25).

To have the Levites dispersed within the land is a great blessing for the nation. The Levites are to instruct Israel in the law of the Lord, to maintain the knowledge of His Word among the people. The blessing of this inheritance allows the nation to have the constant reminder and the continual discipleship of the way of God. God is, in essence, sending His ministers all throughout the land to build up, protect, and equip all generations in the way of the Lord.

No one in Israel lives more than ten miles from one of the forty-eight Levite cities. This means that every Israelite has access to one of God's men who could shepherd the people. Keep in mind that for the nation to stay in the land, they must obey God (Leviticus 26). God provides the shepherd and leadership that the people need to obey the Lord.

21:43–45

GOD'S FAITHFULNESS

God was, as He always is, faithful to His promise. Not one aspect of God's promise to the nation of Israel is unfulfilled. Looking back to the beginning of the Israelites' journey out of Egypt, through the wilderness years, and now into the conquest and possession of the promised land, Joshua is impressed by the theme that resonates through each experience in the nation's history: God always keeps His promise. God had kept His promise to give Israel the land, rest from their wanderings, and victory over their enemies.

Critical Observation

Though God had fulfilled His promises, every corner of the land was not yet in Israel's control. God had told Israel they would conquer the land gradually (Deuteronomy 7:22). Additionally, God's faithfulness does not guarantee that the people will not walk away from Him in the future. The unfaithfulness of Israel is not dependent in any way on the faithfulness of God. Even though Israel would fail God in the future, God remained faithful.

JOSHUA 22:1–34

HOME TO THE EAST

Setting Up the Section

As the eastern tribes returned home and got settled, something occurred that almost disrupted the unity of the nation. The eastern tribes acted so inappropriately that a civil war almost overtook the newly formed nation. In the midst of this tension, God protected the nation and taught them some serious lessons about true worship.

22:1–8

SERVICE

The eastern tribes of Reuben, Gad, and the half-tribe of Manasseh have served the rest of the nation and fought alongside their brothers. Now it is time for them to return to their land. Joshua praises them for their efforts and for their commitment to their promise—to fight with the rest of the nation before they took their land (Numbers 32; Joshua 1:16–18; 4:12–14). They had been faithfully fighting for seven years, and during this time they had been away from their family and their homes. These men are being honored for their service.

Leaving for home, the men from the eastern tribes take with them much of the spoils from the enemy. They are instructed to share the spoils with those who remained at home to care for and protect the land (22:8). The rule that is being established here surfaces again in the history of the Israelites (1 Samuel 30:24). The principle is that those who serve in support of war but who do not actually do the fighting are able to share in the full spoils of war. Support roles are of equal importance.

The returning soldiers are given six commands by Joshua before they leave: First, be very careful to keep the commandment and the law. Second, love the Lord your God. Third, walk in all His ways. Fourth, keep His commands. Fifth, cling to Him. And finally, serve Him with all your heart and all your soul. The message is that just because their military commitment to God is complete, their spiritual commitment is not. In exchange for their service, God promised that they will be allowed to stay in the land to the east. God desires for His people to have a heart to work and fight for Him and love and serve those around them (Micah 6:8).

22:9–20

MISUNDERSTANDING

As the eastern tribes return to their new home, the realization hits them that they will be separated from their brothers on the other side of the Jordan. This creates fear of what this separation might cause them. The mountains that surround the river rise to heights above two thousand feet. The Jordan Valley is a huge trench, five to thirteen miles wide. When it is hot, this valley becomes impassable. Thus, the Jordan River creates a difficult barrier that truly does separate the eastern tribes from the rest of Israel. The eastern tribes become afraid that this separation will cause the next generation to be excluded from the worship of the Lord.

The solution to this problem is to build a huge altar, one that can be seen from a great distance. This will keep the worship of God front and center for all generations. The eastern tribes erect such an altar on the Israelite (western) side of the Jordan River. The motive that drives these men is the fact that they prioritize the worship of God, and they know that the true basis of their unity is their common worship of the one true God.

The act of building this altar is interpreted as an act of apostasy. The rest of the tribes of the western side of the border meet at Shiloh. This is significant because this is where the one true altar is located. It is here that they decide to go to war against the armies of the eastern tribes. They conclude that this new altar is rebellion against God. From their perspective they believe that the others have set up a second altar of sacrifice contrary to the Mosaic Law (Leviticus 17:8–9).

The western tribes believe that if their brethren are going to mock God and set up an alternate place of worship, then they will go to war to defend the integrity of worship. As difficult as this must have been, the rest of the tribes are prepared to go to war against their own brothers. Eleazar's son, Phinehas, is passionate for the Lord (Numbers 25:6–18). He heads a force to confront the eastern tribes.

God has always treated rebellion with severe consequences, and the leaders know that obedience to Him is very important (Joshua 22:20). Phinehas warns the people of the eastern tribes that they are in jeopardy because of apparent rebellion. He then offers a solution to the problem: If the land east of the Jordan is defiled because of this altar, the western tribes will make room for their brethren on their side of the Jordan. They take the holiness of God seriously enough to relocate these two and a half tribes in order to help them walk with God.

22:21–29

SEEKING PEACE

Notice that the eastern tribes do not fight back or act in a defensive manner. Rather, the eastern tribes respond with humility to the charge that the altar they erected is in rebellion against God. They present their hearts before God as a witness and they swear twice by His three names—El, Elohim, Yahweh (the Mighty One, God, the Lord), strongly stating that if their act was in rebellion against God and His commands then they deserved His judgment. Despite their initial misunderstanding, we see in this account that both tribes handle this situation correctly—with humility and a willingness to listen.

The eastern tribes make it clear that they are fully aware of God's laws governing worship. The point of this altar is not to replace the place for burnt offerings, but instead it is intended to show all generations that the eastern tribes have the right to worship God with the western tribes; in short, they are a part of the community.

Critical Observation

Every generation loses the heart and the understanding of the first generation. Inevitably the battle wounds, lessons, and wisdom of the past must be relearned again and again by the younger people. It is important to make sure that things are in place to help protect future generations, to remind them of history's lessons. It is not unreasonable to assume the next generation will have a breakdown because pride and conflict are sewn within the sin nature that all humans carry around in them.

God ordains the law that all Israelite males are to appear at the sanctuary three times a year (Exodus 23:17). Thus, what they erect is not necessary. This law preserves the unity of all the tribes if followed. God had already anticipated this problem and put in place a way of avoiding it. The bigger concern of this altar would have been that rather than driving people to the real altar at Shiloh, it would replace it; though this was not the heart of those who erected it.

22:30–34

PEACE PRESERVED

The explanation of the eastern tribes is fully accepted by Phinehas and his delegation. Indeed, this response causes the western tribes to rejoice and praise God. Phinehas expresses joy and thankfulness that no sin has been committed and that the wrath of God is not going to be called down upon their eastern brothers.

Take It Home

Look for God's solution rather than picking your own fight. Sometimes things appear one way and yet turn out to be another. We don't always interpret the people around us appropriately, so it is important to seek understanding and peace before launching into conflict. Israel learned a lesson about listening. What appeared as a separation was really an act of unity. One person can do one thing to keep unity, and someone else may interpret it as an act of separation and rebellion. God's children need to commit to communication.

JOSHUA 23:1–16

JOSHUA'S CHARGE

Setting Up the Section

Joshua ends with his farewell address. His parting words express his deep concern for a potential danger emerging in Israel—a growing complacency on the part of Israel toward the remnants of the Canaanites. Joshua feels compelled to warn the people that obedience to God is essential to His blessing, including enjoying all the fruits of the land.

23:1–8

BE ON YOUR GUARD

Some years after the end of the conquest and distribution of the land, Joshua summons Israel's leaders, probably to Shiloh where the tabernacle is located. This gathering serves a very serious and solemn purpose—to warn the leaders of the dangers of not taking God and His commands seriously.

Joshua has one theme that he repeats three times: God has been faithful to Israel, so Israel must serve and obey Him all the days of their lives (23:3–8, 9–13, 14–16). There is no more important message for followers of God in any age. God must be taken seriously, obedience must be a way of life, and sin must be treated as an abomination to the Lord.

Joshua reminds the people that their enemies have been defeated solely because the Lord had fought for them. The battles that they fought were the Lord's, and God provided the victories. Scripture tells us repeatedly that every good and perfect thing we have is from God (James 1:17).

Joshua reminds the leaders that the Lord will push the Canaanites, who are still scattered throughout the country, out of the land entirely if they rely on God. God remains committed to creating their nation if they rely on His strength, and He has promised to enable them to carry out the task of taking full possession of the land.

All leaders are called to establish for the next generation what God has taught them. Joshua passes on to the next generation the very words that he was instructed with at the beginning of His time as leader of Israel: Be strong and courageous and careful to obey (1:6–9). Courage and obedience are the virtues that led to the success of conquering Canaan, and they are no less essential now (22:5). Joshua is also concerned about Israel's conformity to the people around them. For this reason, he forbids all contact and marriage with these nations. Joshua knows that his people will walk away from God if they become engaged with the nations around them.

This is the very definition of complacency—once a person becomes comfortable with sin, it becomes easier to fall headlong into a sinful way of living rather than remaining sensitive to the Spirit of God. Knowing this, Joshua wants to make sure that the leaders take obedience to God seriously.

23:9–16

DISOBEDIENCE HAS CONSEQUENCES

To make sure that they understand the seriousness of this, Joshua reminds the leaders that God will not tolerate a nation that mingles with the sin of the Canaanites. God is faithful, but if the Israelites unite themselves with the Canaanites in sin, God will not bless them with His strength.

At the heart of Joshua's message is the reminder of the faithfulness of God and the command to love Him with all their hearts (22:5). The type of love that Joshua speaks of requires diligence and watchfulness. The Israelites must keep an eye on their hearts, because they are in the presence of corruption.

Take It Home

This is true for all of God's followers. Believers must remember that loving the things of this world is the same as loving what God has sent His Son to transform. God loves sinners for the express purpose of changing them—not keeping them in their state of depravity, but bringing them into right relationship with Him. To use the grace and mercy of God to pursue sin is to treat God with contempt.

Israel's greatest danger was not military; it was spiritual. The key to the success of Israel was not in their strength but in how dedicated they were to the will and glory of God. This is true for us today as well.

JOSHUA 24:1–33

THE COVENANT RENEWED

Setting Up the Section

Joshua's last meeting with the people takes place at Shechem. In this significant city, Israel's covenant with God is renewed.

24:1–13

GOD'S WORDS REVIEWED

Shechem is the place where Abraham first received the promise that God would give his seed the land of Canaan. Abraham responds by building an altar to demonstrate his faith in the one true God (Genesis 12:6–7). Jacob, too, stops at Shechem on his return from Paddan Aram and buries the idols his family had brought with them (Genesis 35:4). After the Israelites complete the first phase of the conquest of Canaan, they journey to Shechem where Joshua builds an altar to Yahweh, inscribes the law of God on stone pillars, and reviews these laws for all the people (Joshua 8:30–35).

Critical Observation

The location is one of importance, because this spot symbolizes the covenant that God made with Israel. Consider what would be in this location: The stones on which the law had been written were still there reminding people of their theological heritage and that their calling as a nation serves something higher than just being a nation. They serve the one true God to whom all the glory for their victory is owed. This place had been dedicated as the spot for worshiping the Lord and remembering His holiness.

Joshua is reminding the people what God Himself has said. In other words, this is God speaking to the people, reviewing with them what He has done and reminding them what lies at the heart of their covenant. First, He brought them out of Ur of the Chaldees (24:2–4). Then, they were delivered out of the bondage to Gentile worship and brought to the land of blessing. Next, they were brought out of Egypt (24:5–7) and into Canaan (24:8–13). Again, they were delivered from the bondage and slavery of the Egyptians and brought to the freedom of the promised land.

God uses "I" eighteen times to underscore that these good things, these amazing deliverances and victories, were performed by Him and not the Israelites. God is the One who pulled them out of every mess, out of every conflict, and out of every problem. God is the One who delivered them from all of their trials and the One who brought them into the land flowing with milk and honey.

Any greatness, prosperity, or blessing that Israel ever received was not by her own effort but through God's grace and power. From the first call of Abram, to the conquest, to the present moment, everything they have and all that they are is because of God's good mercies.

24:14–24

THE RESPONSIBILITY

Israel must fear the Lord and serve Him. Joshua personalizes this command, saying that whatever the leader's choice is in regard to serving God, his own mind was made up. He declares, "But as for me and my household, we will serve the LORD" (24:15 NIV).

The initial response of the people is good. They are still so close to the time of the conquest that they despise the very thought of forsaking God. They had the firsthand experience of being delivered by God.

But Joshua is not at all satisfied with their verbal commitment. He knows the human heart and how people can easily be led astray, and he knows how deceptive sin can be. He is quite aware that an emotional commitment made at a moment in time does not mean as much as it might appear. Joshua bluntly declares to the Israelite leadership that they are not able to serve the Lord. He is a holy God and a jealous God. He will not forgive their rebellion and their sins.

Joshua does not mean that God is not a God of forgiveness. He means that God is not to be worshiped or served lightly. To forsake Him deliberately and to serve idols will be willful sin against God, and to sin in this manner under their circumstances will be unforgivable under the law (Numbers 15:30). This type of sin will result in disaster. Again the people respond to Joshua's probing words, earnestly reaffirming their purpose to serve the Lord.

Joshua speaks a third time and calls Israel to serve as witnesses against themselves if they do turn aside from God. The people immediately reply "yes." Joshua then speaks a fourth and final time, coming again to the point he had mentioned at the beginning—that they must get rid of their idols. They have already begun the slow and steady slide to disobedience. Joshua challenges them to prove their sincerity by their works and get rid of the idols. It is interesting to note that without the slightest hesitation, the people shout, "We will serve the LORD our God. We will obey him alone" (24:24 NLT).

There can be no mixing of allegiance to God with idol worship. Every generation has to make this decision in life—*Will we be completely committed to God, or will we adopt the practices of the nations around us?* Every individual today must also make a strong commitment to serve the Lord above anything or anyone else.

24:25–28

THE REMINDER

Joshua makes a covenant with the people this day. He writes down their agreement in the book of the law of God, which is probably placed beside the ark of the covenant (Deuteronomy 31:24–27).

As a final reminder, Joshua also inscribes the statutes of the covenant on a large stone slab, which is set up beneath the oak at this sacred location. Joshua says that the stone is a witness to this covenant. It bears the words of the covenant for all generations to see.

All of this again underscores the seriousness with which God is to be taken. Fast-forward to the book of Micah, and one will see the great cost the nation pays for completely rejecting God.

24:29–33

GOD KEEPS HIS PROMISE

Three burials—each of them in Ephraim—mark the close of the book of Joshua. First it is recorded that Joshua dies at the age of 110 years. He is buried in his own town (19:50). No greater tribute can be paid to him than the fact that he is called the servant of the Lord. Such should be the highest goal of every person who lives.

The burial of Joseph's bones is also recorded. Joseph's dying request was that he be buried in the promised land (Genesis 50:25). Moses, knowing of this request, took Joseph's bones with him in the Exodus (Exodus 13:19). Finally, Joseph's remains, which had been embalmed in Egypt more than four hundred years earlier, are laid to rest in Shechem (Genesis 33:18–20; 50:26).

The third burial mentioned is that of the high priest Eleazar, son and successor of Aaron. These burials testify to the faithfulness of God. Joshua, Joseph, and Eleazar once lived in a foreign nation where they received God's promise to take His people back to Canaan. Now all three are laid to rest within the promised land. God kept His word to these men, just as He had kept His promise to the Israelites.

Take It Home

The responsibility to serve God is a great gift, not a burden. The call to the Israelites to serve God comes after the great blessings of life, freedom, and autonomy. Our service is a response to His love, kindness, and mercy. Therefore, God's call in our life, like the command of Joshua, should be seen as the only appropriate response to the gift of freedom. God is faithful with all of His children to the end.

JUDGES

INTRODUCTION TO JUDGES

The book of Judges gets its name from its main characters: the people God graciously selected to save ancient Israel from itself. It tells the stories of colorful and imperfect individuals with charismatic qualities God uses to break the yoke of oppression that Israel experienced, time after time, as a result of its own sinfulness. Through these types of saviors, God calls His children back to Himself.

AUTHOR

Although Samuel was traditionally thought to be the author of Judges, no one knows who put it together. Experts say it could have been a single author, because the material is well-shaped into a coherent whole; or there may have been more than one compiler.

PURPOSE

Judges is a compilation of selected independent stories, mostly centered on one individual. But there is one overall message: Israel's repetitive cycle of sin, and God's consistent and merciful response.

THEMES

In Judges we see Israel's continual cycle of unfaithfulness:

1) Obedience to the law of God
2) Moral complacency
3) Moral compromise as a result of their complacency
4) A falling away from their faith and religious roots
5) Oppression from other nations as their weakening faith results in a weakened nation
6) Deliverance from these consequences and a temporary return to faith

It is in the deliverance that God provides at the turn of each cycle that reveals His righteousness, mercy, and long-suffering nature. The individuals God chooses, though certainly imperfect deliverers, can be seen as temporary models of the great deliverance that will one day come through Jesus, the perfect and permanent deliverer of the people of God.

HISTORICAL CONTEXT

Judges is known as one of the books of the "former prophets," and it reveals God working throughout the history of His people. The book covers approximately 350 years, from the time of Joshua's death until the rise of Samuel, the last judge before the kings of Israel begin to lead as the formal monarchy is established.

The era that Judges recounts is a period of transition—from the conquest of Canaan in the latter part of the thirteenth century to the beginning of the monarchy with King Saul, perhaps in 1020 BC. There is a direct correlation between the decisions Israel makes during these centuries and her downfall later.

OUTLINE

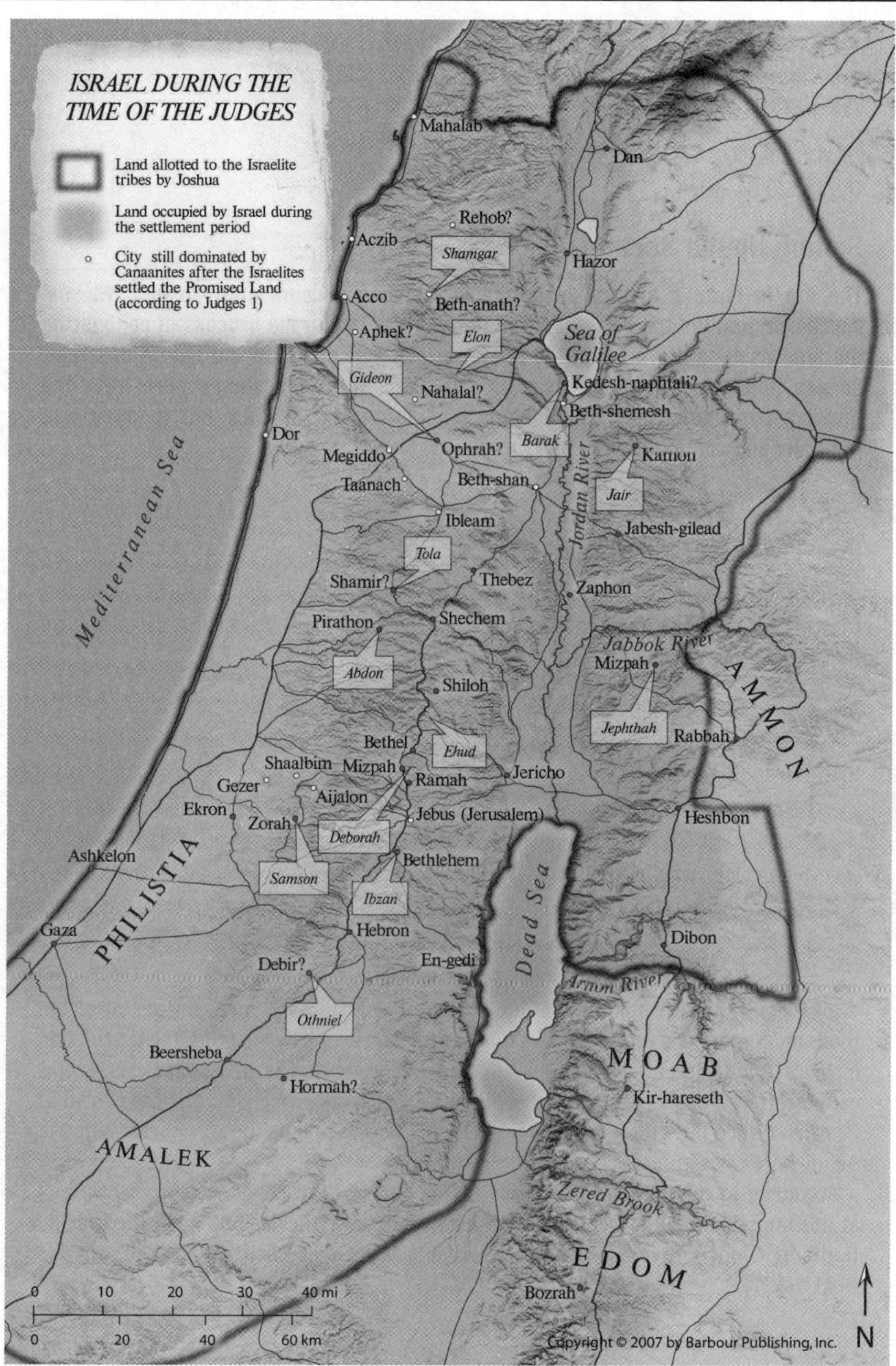
ISRAEL DURING THE TIME OF THE JUDGES
Land allotted to the Israelite tribes by Joshua
Land occupied by Israel during the settlement period
City still dominated by Canaanites after the Israelites settled the Promised Land (according to Judges 1)
Mahalab
Dan
Rehob?
Aczib
Shamgar
Hazor
Acco
Beth-anath?
Aphek?
Elon
Sea of Galilee
Gideon
Nahalal?
Kedesh-naphtali?
Beth-shemesh
Dor
Barak
Mediterranean Sea
Megiddo
Ophrah?
Kamon
Taanach
Beth-shan
Jordan River
Jair
Ibleam
Jabesh-gilead
Tola
Shamir?
Thebez
Zaphon
Pirathon
Shechem
Jabbok River
Mizpah
Abdon
AMMON
Shiloh
Jephthah
Rabbah
Bethel
Ehud
Shaalbim
Mizpah
Jericho
Gezer
Ramah
Aijalon
Ekron
Jebus (Jerusalem)
Heshbon
Zorah
Deborah
Ashkelon
Bethlehem
PHILISTIA
Samson
Ibzan
Dead Sea
Gaza
Hebron
Dibon
Debir?
En-gedi
Arnon River
Othniel
Beersheba
MOAB
Hormah?
Kir-hareseth
AMALEK
Zered Brook
EDOM
Bozrah
0 10 20 30 40 mi
0 20 40 60 km
N
Copyright © 2007 by Barbour Publishing, Inc.

JUDGES 1:1–36

AFTER JOSHUA

Setting Up the Section

The era in Israel's history described in this book occurs after Joshua, Moses' successor, had led the Israelites into Canaan and begun the process of conquering the land assigned to each of the twelve tribes that make up the nation of Israel. Judges then describes the occupation of Canaan. The accounts here track the growing consequences of the people's compromises as they fail to obey God faithfully and completely in this process.

1:1–21

INITIAL FAITHFULNESS

Judges begins with several short accounts of victory by the Israelite tribe of Judah. This tribe (from which the royal line of King David eventually will descend) is called to lead the battle into Canaan.

Critical Observation

The tribe of Simeon mentioned in verse 3 would have lived in close proximity to the tribe of Judah. Simeon was given territory within the boundaries of the southern kingdom, taking land out of Judah's territory (Joshua 19:1–9). This connectedness to Judah, while it may have had advantages, also meant that the tribe of Simeon lost some of its distinct identity. Many trace this loss back to the curse that Jacob put on his son Simeon, the ancestor of this tribe, in Genesis 49.

In verses 4–7, we're told of the destruction of ten thousand men. This count of ten thousand is more of a representative number than an actual head count. The destruction includes Adoni-Bezek (lord of Bezek). While their treatment of Adoni-Bezek seems extreme, it also has a sense of justice. He is receiving the same kind of treatment that he often dished out—for instance, rendering his victims unable to run or bear weapons. Adoni-Bezek dies in Jerusalem.

According to verse 8, Jerusalem is set on fire; but the Israelites did not occupy the city at this time. Eventually, of course, Jerusalem will become the capital city of the Israelite territory of Judah. The day will come when King David, a descendant of Judah, will rule from there.

Kiriath Arba is mentioned in verse 10. This name means "the city of Arba." It is so named because Arba was the great man among the Anakim who spawned a population of giants (see Joshua 14:13–15). This same city later came to be known as Hebron, a city mentioned often throughout the Israelite monarchy.

Critical Observation

Caleb, mentioned first in verse 12, is one of the twelve spies who, forty years earlier, entered Canaan on reconnaissance to report back to Israel before they entered the land. Of the twelve spies, only Joshua and Caleb believed that God could and would give them the land He had promised. As a result of their faith, these two men were the only two of the spies who actually entered Canaan (Numbers 14:21–24).

In verses 11–15, Othniel, to win his bride, destroys a great city of wickedness. Caleb, the father figure, gives the bride to his nephew and grants them a land of peace. The bride seeks a blessing, an outpouring of water, from the father.

Moses had persuaded some of his father-in-law's (Jethro) family to come with him to the land of promise. Those who believed and followed Moses came through his line of Levi and found a place to flourish in the land of Judah (1:16).

Hormah in verse 17 means "placed under the ban, totally destroyed." If this utter destruction described in verse 17 is done according to God's decree (see Deuteronomy 20:16–18), then it is considered a whole burnt offering to the Lord. Simeon may be mentioned, because this time (as opposed to his actions in Genesis 34) he is faithfully bringing God's wrath to bear.

In verses 19–21, Judah takes several Philistine cities and the hill country; but he cannot take the valley due to the strength of the Canaanites' iron chariots. Judah initially takes Jerusalem (also called Jebus), which is in the land given to Benjamin, but Benjamin is not able to drive out the Jebusites living there. In the end, they allowed these pagans to dwell with them.

In both of these cases, only a partial victory is obtained. This is significant in that it represents only a partial obedience to what God told the tribes to do. The land was supposed to be claimed for God entirely. Any non-Israelites who remained there should have been incorporated into the worship of the Israelite God Yahweh rather than taken on as simply co-inhabitants.

Demystifying Judges

The lessons of the book of Judges are taught not through a systematic recounting of theology, but through stories. These stories teach us about a purity of faith in the midst of a culture that is often in opposition to that faith. They also teach us that victory has nothing to do with the size of the enemy, but rather with the size of our faith in the promises of God.

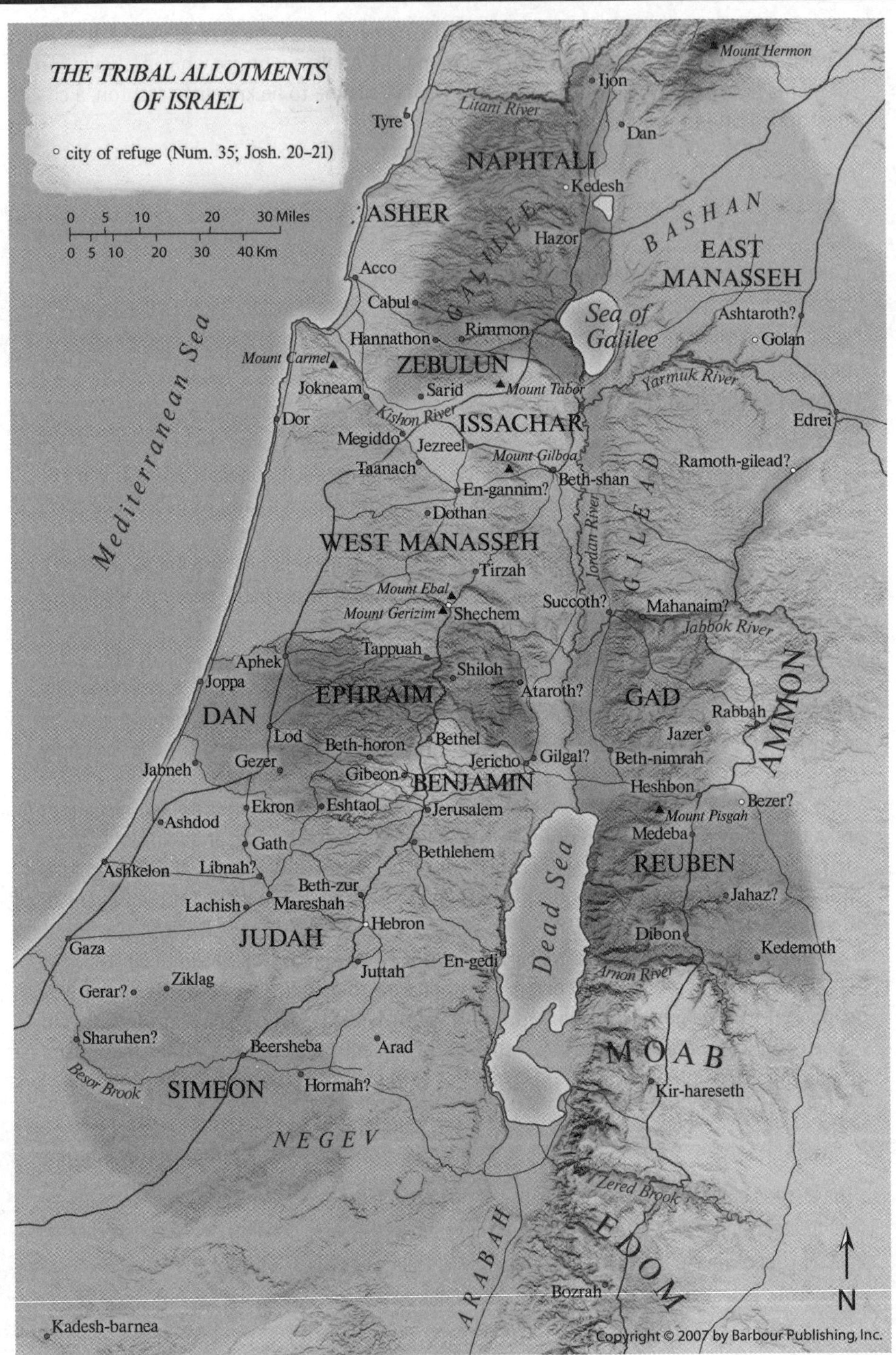
THE TRIBAL ALLOTMENTS OF ISRAEL
○ city of refuge (Num. 35; Josh. 20–21)
0 5 10 20 30 Miles
0 5 10 20 30 40 Km
Mount Hermon
Ijon
Litani River
Tyre
Dan
NAPHTALI
Kedesh
ASHER
GALILEE
BASHAN
Hazor
EAST MANASSEH
Acco
Cabul
Sea of Galilee
Ashtaroth?
Rimmon
Hannathon
Golan
Mediterranean Sea
Mount Carmel
ZEBULUN
Yarmuk River
Jokneam
Sarid
Mount Tabor
Dor
Kishon River
ISSACHAR
Edrei
Megiddo
Jezreel
Mount Gilboa
Ramoth-gilead?
Taanach
Beth-shan
En-gannim?
GILEAD
Dothan
Jordan River
WEST MANASSEH
Tirzah
Mount Ebal
Mount Gerizim
Shechem
Succoth?
Mahanaim?
Jabbok River
Tappuah
Aphek
Shiloh
Joppa
EPHRAIM
Ataroth?
GAD
AMMON
DAN
Rabbah
Lod
Beth-horon
Bethel
Jazer
Jabneh
Gezer
Jericho
Gilgal?
Beth-nimrah
Gibeon
BENJAMIN
Heshbon
Ekron
Eshtaol
Jerusalem
Bezer?
Ashdod
Mount Pisgah
Medeba
Gath
Bethlehem
Dead Sea
REUBEN
Ashkelon
Libnah?
Beth-zur
Lachish
Mareshah
Jahaz?
Hebron
JUDAH
Dibon
Gaza
Kedemoth
Juttah
En-gedi
Arnon River
Gerar?
Ziklag
Sharuhen?
Beersheba
Arad
MOAB
Besor Brook
SIMEON
Hormah?
Kir-hareseth
NEGEV
Zered Brook
ARABAH
EDOM
Bozrah
N
Kadesh-barnea
Copyright © 2007 by Barbour Publishing, Inc.

1:22-36

THEOLOGICAL GEOGRAPHY

In the description in verses 22–36, the author of Judges provides a verbal journey across the land. Here we see pragmatic victories and theological compromises made by the tribes. These compromises are spelled out in a list of progressive failures. Seven times in these verses, the tribes are charged with not driving others out. The significance of this is that by not driving out the inhabitants, the Israelites leave themselves open to the influence of other religions. As the rest of Judges plays out, that influence is a crucial factor in the faith of the nation.

In verses 22–26, spies are sent to Luz (Bethel), and they find help from within. But this time (unlike the story of Rahab in Joshua 2:1–13; 6:17), when the city is taken, the saved family does not repent and join Israel, but flees and sets up another pagan city.

Manasseh does not drive out the Canaanites but puts them under tribute, clearly against the Lord's commands (see Exodus 23:32). Ephraim and Zebulun act similarly (Judges 1:27–30). In this way, these tribes have not only ignored God's commands, they have put themselves at risk spiritually by allowing the current religions to still be practiced. Keep in mind that Israel was not yet a monarchy. Rather than being guided by the kings, they were still governed by religious leaders. The religious health of these tribes was in direct correlation to their political health.

In verses 31–33, Asher and Naphtali allow the previous inhabitants to dwell among them. What this means is that the Canaanites predominate these lands. Rather than Asher and Naphtali allowing the Canaanites to live there under each Israelite tribe's dominion, this situation is closer to the other way around. This is a great evidence of weakness for these tribes.

The tribe of Dan is forced to live in the mountains. The wickedness of this tribe is revealed in much more detail in chapters 17–18.

JUDGES 2:1–3:6

VICIOUS CYCLE

Yahweh's Judgment	2:1–5
Generation to Generation	2:6–15
Spiritual Adultery	2:16–3:6

Setting Up the Section

At this point, though God had commanded them to enter the land and drive out any peoples there that refused to follow Yahweh, the Israelites are convinced that their half attempts and compromised efforts in claiming their territories are justified and, in fact, represent practical victories. They are at least in the promised land, and they are settling down. The story of the Exodus, the mission the people set out upon, and the amazing works God performed seem to be a distant memory.

2:1–5

YAHWEH'S JUDGMENT

The angel of the Lord is specifically charged to bring judgment upon sinful Israel (see Exodus 23:20–23). The charges in this passage suggest that this angel visitor is the Lord Himself, probably a preincarnate visitation of Jesus.

Critical Observation

There are several events in the Old Testament in which an angelic visitor seems more like an appearance of Jesus than simply an angel. You can observe some other visitations like this in the accounts of Hagar (Genesis 16:7–12) and Abraham (Genesis 22:15–16).

The Lord had been with the children of Israel at Gilgal (Joshua 5), where the next generation had been circumcised, signifying their transition into the same covenant that God had made with Abraham—one that was sealed with the act of circumcision (Genesis 17:10–14). Now, at Bochim (or Bokim, which means "weepers"), they grieve over the fact that they had not stayed true to that covenant.

God had brought the people out of Egypt. Enemies with iron chariots were no match for Him. God had made good on His promises, but the Israelites made covenants with the Canaanites, defying the Lord's command (see Exodus 23:32). It also appears that they did not tear down the idols that already existed in the land, even in cities where they had some control (Judges 1:33), again disobeying the Lord (Exodus 34:13).

The result? In rejecting the Lord's commands, what the Israelites may have thought would be pleasures in their new lives in Canaan would become deep thorns in their sides. True mourning can produce comfort (Matthew 5:4), but it is unclear whether it occurs at this place. On the one hand, it appears the Israelites repent—they offer up sacrifices, acknowledging their sin and need for an atonement. Unfortunately, if there is true repentance, it does not get passed on to the next generation.

2:6–15

GENERATION TO GENERATION

The passage from 2:6 to 3:6 is a second introduction of sorts, picking up from the end of the book of Joshua. The theme emphasizes the ongoing spiral—of compromise to faithlessness to slavery to God's deliverance—that defines the period of Judges in the history of the old covenant.

Take It Home

Joshua is buried in a place called "Portion of the Sun" in some translations. This may be reminiscent of one of God's great works during Joshua's conquest of Canaan when He made the sun stand still during the great battle at Gilgal (Joshua 10). Joshua was a great leader for the Israelites. His faithfulness influenced all the elders of his generation. His life is a reminder that the faithfulness of one person can have a great impact upon a family or a nation.

In stark contrast to the life of Joshua is the generation that follows after his death. In the historical review found in Judges 2:10–15, it is clear that the basic failure of Israel is that they do not pass on to their children the stories of the Lord nor the loyalty He requires of them. Faithfulness only lasts as long as one generation if it is not passed on to children.

The consequences of Israel's disobedience are devastating. After their great journey and the building of the tabernacle, carrying it with them to every camp, here when they settle in the land, they seem to forget God's presence. They had been commanded in Deuteronomy 6:4–9 to keep God's commands ever before them, even placing them on their hands, foreheads, and doorposts. It is evident from this account, and much of the book of Judges, that the people did not fashion a life for themselves in this new land that followed those guidelines.

2:16–3:6

SPIRITUAL ADULTERY

Later in the life of Israel, the prophet Jeremiah describes the people as those who had given up living water for their own broken cisterns, faulty water-catchers dug into the earth (Jeremiah 2:13). Certainly the roots of that accusation can be seen here in the Judges description of a nation that is departing from their faith for a life that does not support the values that had provided them their roots.

As expected, this angers God. However, this godly anger does not produce thoughtless rage from the Lord. He is faithful to His Word. He promised that if His children worship Him solely and properly, their fruitfulness would be supernatural, as would their strength against any enemy (Leviticus 26:1–13). And if they do not keep this covenant with Him, He promised the very consequences the tribes were beginning to experience in Judges (Leviticus 26:17; Judges 2:15).

Judges 2:16–19 describes a terrible cycle. God's children do not listen to judges God raises up for them. Instead, they spiritually prostitute themselves to other religions such as Baal worship. Then they *groan*, a word used before only in Exodus 2 and 6, under oppression. Each time, the Lord raises up a man to judge and deliver them again, but once he dies, the people quickly fall again into spiritual adultery. And unfortunately, each generation of Israelites falls more deeply into this cycle than the one before.

Critical Observation

The gods Baal and Ashtoreth, mentioned in verse 13, were the male and female counterparts of the representation of the power of nature. These two powers interacted (had intercourse, thus the sexual rituals included in Baal worship), and the fruit of their union was considered creation. Adherents to the worship of these deities believed religious orgies in the temples would motivate Baal and Ashtoreth to once again bring forth better crops in the land. These false deities were seen as hard taskmasters, as Psalm 106:34–42 describes.

Many times when God's judgments come into play, the very means of compromise becomes the means God uses to chastise His children (2:20–23). This is not merely the impassioned rage of God, but probably an ordained means of revealing humanity's sin in terms that are easily accessible.

Though they seem to say two different things, there is no contradiction between Judges 2:22 and 3:2. This generation has indeed not experienced war in the way the previous generation had (those who were first entering the land). Perhaps because of that, this generation has grown too quickly accustomed to having the Canaanites and their idols around. But it is also true that God used the battles with the Canaanites as a form of consequences for the Israelites, reminders that they needed God's power and presence.

Demystifying Judges

The judges were deliverers of Israel. This was their life's work. Their position was not hereditary (in most circumstances). While some believe the judges had legislative authority, much like elected officials today, there is not strong evidence that this is the case. Their special work was to act as avengers for Israel—being anointed to destroy God's enemies and deliver His people. In this way, they foreshadowed the redemptive work of Jesus Christ.

JUDGES 3:7–31

OTHNIEL AND EHUD

Setting Up the Section

We now turn to the first of two stories of exemplary judges: Othniel and Ehud. The story of Othniel is given to us without much detail. In this simple story, we see the sovereign goodness and grace of God in both His chastisements and in His deliverance. The story of Ehud is a violent comedy, but also in some ways a picture of the gospel.

3:7–11

THE FIRST JUDGE

The first evil mentioned in verse 7 (intermarrying when God specifically instructed the people not to) draws the Israelites into the second and more visible evil—forgetting God and worshiping idols. It is not that the people simply worshiped and served Baal, but they forgot about God. This forgetting was a sin. But, while the people may forget their God and their covenant with Him, God does not forget. Thus, the people experience consequences of this breaking of their spiritual covenant.

In the Hebrew, the name listed in verse 8, *Cushan-Rishathaim, king of Aram Nahariam,* is a play on words. Roughly, it means "the Cushite of double-wickedness, king of Syria of the double-river." This attack described here is from the north.

In this case, since the people do not want to follow God, He is sending them back, giving them over to their sin. Interestingly, this is also the place where one day, further down the line in Israel's story, Assyria and Babylon will come and take the people into exile, one that will be far worse than their famous bondage in Egypt. Through these eight years of subjection to a foreign power, the Israelites have an opportunity to experience life without God, since they seem to be choosing that life, after all.

As expected, the children of Israel cry out to God, who raises up a deliverer: Othniel. Othniel's victory is due to the work of the Spirit (3:10). The result of this victory is a full generation of rest (which most likely indicates a rest from war): forty years, until Othniel dies.

3:12–30

THE SECOND JUDGE

After Othniel dies, Israel falls away from the God of their salvation once again and faces some ironic twists of circumstances that should draw their attention back.

According to verse 12, through God's hand, Eglon, king of Moab, overpowers Israel. He takes Jericho (the City of Palms) and forces Israel to pay tributes to him. These tributes may very well have been the firstfruit sacrifices, first harvests of crops and herds, which should have been rendered to the Lord.

Joining Eglon are the people of Ammon and the Amalekites. After they conquer the Israelites, it is eighteen long years of oppression before the Israelites meet their next deliverer.

Demystifying Judges

The Moab and Ammon people-groups are descendants from Lot, Abraham's nephew. Thus, they are distant relatives of the Israelites. These groups had a dark history. After the destruction of Sodom and Gomorrah, which had been Lot's home, he and his family were displaced. His two daughters conspired together, got their father drunk, and conceived children with him. The son born to Lot's oldest daughter became the ancestor of the Moabites. The younger daughter's son was the ancestor of the Ammonites (Genesis 19:31–38).

The Amalekites, who also partnered with Eglon, were sworn enemies of God and Israel. Exodus 17:8 describes a time when Israel defeated Amalek, but here in Judges 3 the roles are reversed.

Ehud, a Benjamite introduced in verse 15, is a left-handed warrior. He is also trusted by Eglon to present the required tribute. Ehud makes a dagger for himself and hides it on his right thigh. As unexpected as this might be, Ehud's unconventional actions have only just begun.

The stone idols mentioned in verses 19 and 26 either refer to the altar of stones built in Gilgal in Joshua's day (Joshua 4:20) or to idols placed there by Moab.

This shrewd deliverer takes advantage of his situation to bring about the salvation of his people from the tyranny of Eglon. This is not the act of an individual in a domestic dispute. Ehud is at war, and Eglon is an unlawful king in Israel's homeland. Ehud leaves the rest of his people and deals with the head of the enemy himself. He declares that he has a word from God and then drives the dagger into Eglon where it disappears, leaving the Moabite king helpless in a scene that becomes a mockery at Eglon's expense. Having crushed the political head of the enemy, Ehud summons his army and leads them to victory, killing ten thousand.

The day began with a tribute to an enemy king and ended with that kingdom routed and ashamed, and the people of God set free.

3:31

SHAMGAR

In what can seem like a strange and out-of-place addendum, this story ends with a single verse about another judge, Shamgar. Although we know little of his story now, he was apparently well-known in the days of Deborah, the one female judge mentioned in this book (chapters 4–5).

Shamgar's name reveals that he was most likely not an Israelite, but a convert to the Lord. Apparently, this farmer-turned-warrior was a big surprise to his Philistine opponents.

Because the account following Shamgar's in chapter 4 still mentions Ehud, it may be that Shamgar's listing here doesn't relate to a linear time line. But we cannot know for sure when Shamgar's defeat of six hundred philistines took place. His weapon of choice, an oxgoad, was a long, thin tool, taller than a man when held upright. Among other uses, the tool probably had one end whittled to a point to be used to keep oxen moving along.

Take It Home

The Spirit of God was given to Othniel, Israel's temporary deliverer, in a limited way; but to Christ, the once-for-all deliverer, God's Spirit will be given without limits (see John 3:34). Othniel's victory was only partial (in time and space), but Christ's is, and will be, complete in eternity (see Isaiah 11:1–5; 42:1–4). Only in the Spirit-anointed Christ can we be strong against our enemies (Ephesians 6:10–13). The Spirit makes the preaching of the Word effective. The Spirit makes our work and prayers effective. The Spirit gives us strength to triumph over our sin.

JUDGES 4:1–24

DEBORAH AND JAEL

Setting Up the Section

In the account described in this section, a woman raises a man to lead an army against the enemy of Israel. Then a second woman completes the victory by crushing a wicked leader.

4:1–3

JABIN AGAIN

When the Israelites continue their cycle of spiritual downfall—again—God lets them fall into the hand of a wicked king called Jabin. This may have been a title instead of a personal name, much as the Egyptians called their kings Pharaoh.

Jabin's commander, Sisera, cruelly oppresses the Israelites in Harosheth of the Gentiles. This area, in the north, is the land of Zebulun and Naphtali, north and west of the Sea of Galilee. Sisera commands nine hundred iron chariots, the same tools of battle that Judah had feared generations before according to 1:19 (4:2–3).

4:4–5

DEBORAH, THE MOTHER OF ISRAEL

During Jabin's twenty-year rule, Deborah, a prophetess whose name means "bee," acts as a judge in Israel. According to verses 4–5, she held court under a tree. Deborah stands out simply because of her gender. It is unusual (though not unheard of) in this era in the history of Israel to find a woman filling the role of prophetess or judge. Though Deborah may be unlikely, she is effective in her role, providing a way to deliver her people by calling Barak.

Critical Observation

The image of trees is a significant one in the Bible. Trees were a source of comfort and shade. They provided not only shelter, but sometimes food as well. They are often included in important biblical events and images. Humanity was first judged at a tree, and that judgment is paid by a Savior who hangs on a tree. The tabernacle is pitched under a great tree where the Book of the Law of God was kept (Joshua 24:26). It was a place that represented a gate to heaven, a place of righteousness and justice, and (later) a place of healing and food (Revelation 22:2). In this chapter, Deborah judges under the Palm of Deborah, and Jael's husband moves away from the Lord and pitches a tent under a great tree.

4:6–10

OBEY YOUR MOTHER

Barak is most likely a Levite from the northern city of Kedesh and therefore a priest of some sort. Barak's faith is tested as Deborah pronounces the command of the Lord. The plan, with no contingencies for the cutting edge iron chariots and the great army they will face, is a great test for Barak.

4:11–24

ANOTHER BATTLE, ANOTHER WOMAN

Deborah's response to Barak's struggle to believe is a rebuke, but a gentle one. Barak does believe, raises up an army of ten thousand, and leads them to victory (more details are revealed in chapter 5). He is included in a list of faithful ancestors in Hebrews 11 as an example to follow.

According to verses 17–22, Jael's husband, Heber the Kenite, has moved away from his fellow Kenites' alliance with Israel and made peace with Sisera. Apparently Jael, whose name means "goat," does not approve. When she recognizes the fleeing Sisera, she courageously deceives this enemy of the Lord into coming into her tent, where she offers him milk (perhaps goat's milk) and then slays him. Then she faces up to Barak and shows him her handiwork—an honor Barak was told would not be his.

We have already seen with Ehud that deception and killing are not unlawful in times of war. Deborah, the prophetess of God, commends Jael (5:24–27) with a blessing similar to that given to Mary in Luke 1:28. Others have condemned Jael for disobeying her husband. But her story illustrates where the lines of matrimonial submission are to be drawn. A wife is to submit to and honor her husband, but when times of crisis and real choosing are required, she must side with the Lord.

JUDGES 5:1–31

THE SONG OF DEBORAH

Setting Up the Section

In chapter 5, Deborah and Barak praise God for His victorious strength. They exalt those who keep their word and serve the Lord in battle, and chastise those who fall back in their comfortable religion. They contrast the true and living God with Baal, the false god, and mince no words in describing the violent victory of the righteous and the violent debauchery of the fallen.

5:1–9

PRAISE TO THE LORD

God is blessed when kings and their people choose to follow Him. Deborah recalls the battle from Mount Tabor in terms reminiscent of the historic coming of the Lord to Mount Sinai (compare Exodus 19:9–19 and Judges 5:4–5). The song recalls threatening scenes of normal life before the arrival of Deborah, a mother of Israel (5:7). And following this maternal motif, Deborah does bring new life to the nation of Israel.

5:10–12

SPEAK! AWAKE! SING!

Verses 10–11 are somewhat obscure but appear to be summoning all of the people—the rich and the poor, men in arms and the common people at the watering places. All are to recount the righteous acts of God and thus stir one another up to serve God by coming down to the gates of the city. Deborah is to awaken the people with her song of deliverance (her prophecy of the Lord's promises), and Barak is to then call upon and lead a remnant, those who will believe the promises and obey the commands (5:12).

Critical Observation

Though Deborah's song celebrates those who came to fight, it is clear that the Lord does not need help to win a battle. God's assistants are not the point of this account. The point is that in a time of crisis and judgment, such as the fight against Sisera, events often conspire to test the people involved to see who is on the Lord's side.

5:13–23

THE WORK OF MEN AND THEIR GOD

Deborah praises those who respond in faith and join the battle (5:13–15, 18), and she mocks those who are too comfortable, too busy, or too frightened to fight (5:16–17, 23).

Also, according to the song, Baal is impotent compared to the true Lord of the stars and clouds (5:20–21). This mention of stars and clouds may be a dig at the Canaanite astrologers. We have no record of the village of Meroz, cursed in verse 23.

5:24–31

A TALE OF TWO WOMEN

Verses 24–31 celebrate the story of Jael, the Kenite woman who assassinated Sisera. In contrast to Meroz, Jael shows more zeal, courage, and faith. Jael refuses to compromise with her husband, and when the Lord grants her the opportunity, she serves Him honorably. Conversely, Deborah's words toward Sisera's mother are a form of mockery toward the woman for sitting and wondering why her son has not returned home (5:28).

Take It Home

Like Deborah, we applaud faithfulness, bravery, and obedience, and shun apathy, schisms, and hypocrisy. But most importantly, we acknowledge that it is God who wins the battle and stands as final judge. It is God who has led forth His captives and who crushes His enemies. More than anything else, this leads us to bless His name for His great mercy.

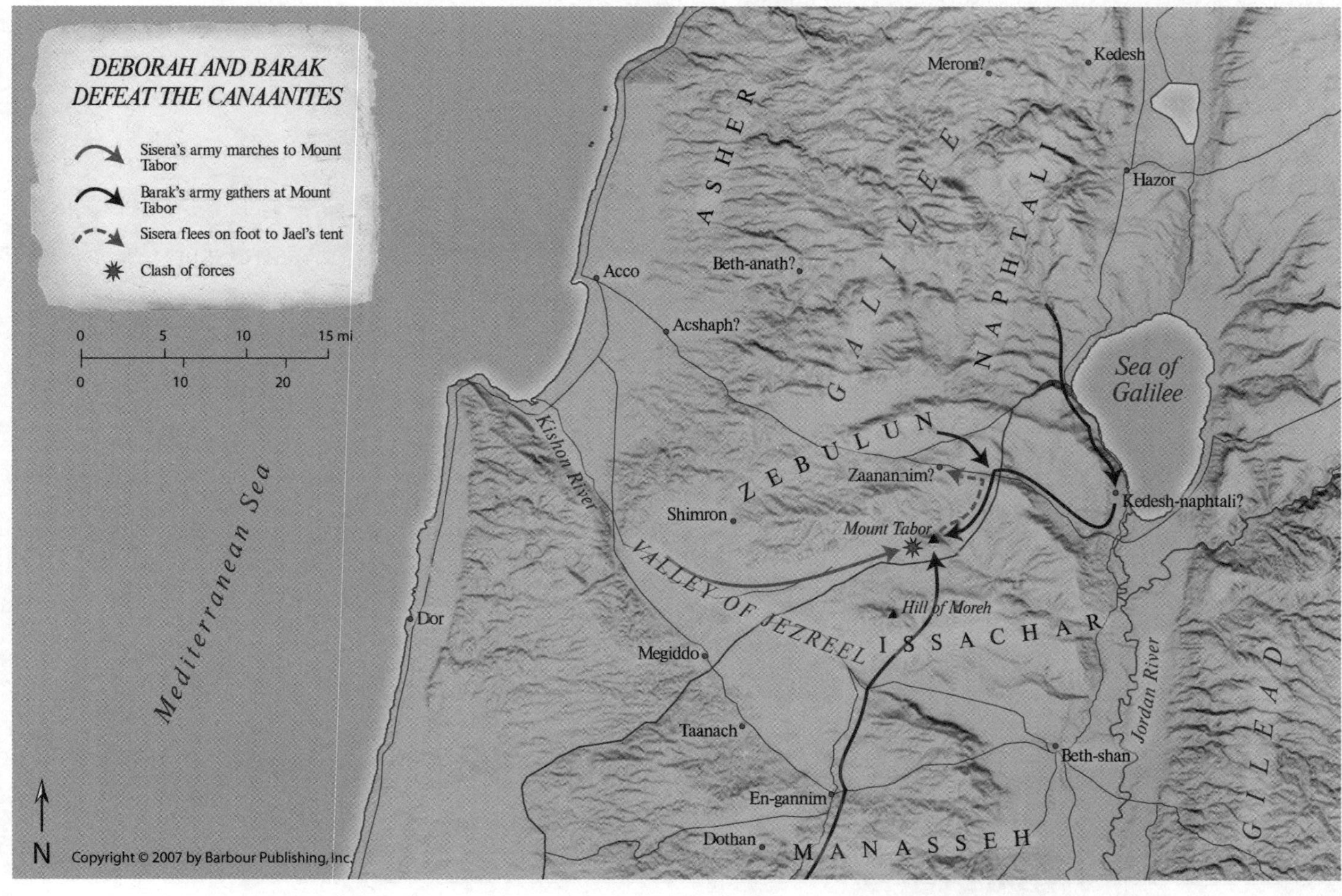
DEBORAH AND BARAK DEFEAT THE CANAANITES
Sisera's army marches to Mount Tabor
Barak's army gathers at Mount Tabor
Sisera flees on foot to Jael's tent
Clash of forces
0 5 10 15 mi
0 10 20
N
Copyright © 2007 by Barbour Publishing, Inc.
Mediterranean Sea
Dor
Kishon River
Acco
Acshaph?
Beth-anath?
ASHER
GALILEE
Merom?
Kedesh
Hazor
NAPHTALI
Sea of Galilee
ZEBULUN
Zaanannim?
Shimron
Mount Tabor
Kedesh-naphtali?
VALLEY OF JEZREEL
Hill of Moreh
ISSACHAR
Megiddo
Jordan River
GILEAD
Taanach
Beth-shan
En-gannim
Dothan
MANASSEH

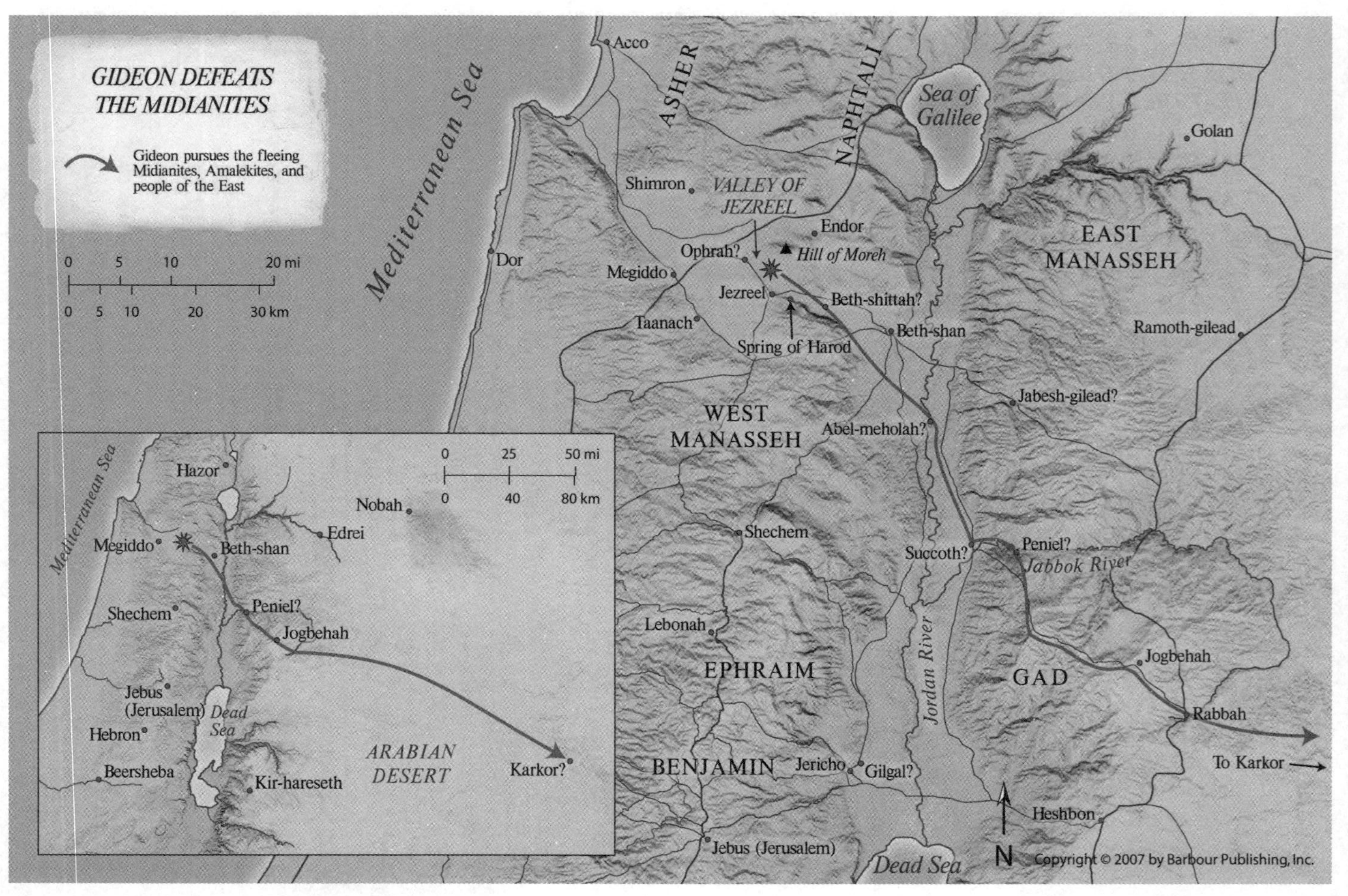

GIDEON DEFEATS THE MIDIANITES
Gideon pursues the fleeing Midianites, Amalekites, and people of the East
0 5 10 20 mi
0 5 10 20 30 km
Mediterranean Sea
Acco
ASHER
NAPHTALI
Sea of Galilee
Golan
Shimron
VALLEY OF JEZREEL
Endor
Hill of Moreh
Ophrah?
Dor
Megiddo
Jezreel
Beth-shittah?
Taanach
Spring of Harod
Beth-shan
EAST MANASSEH
Ramoth-gilead
Jabesh-gilead?
WEST MANASSEH
Abel-meholah?
Shechem
Succoth?
Peniel?
Jabbok River
Lebonah
EPHRAIM
Jordan River
GAD
Jogbehah
Rabbah
To Karkor
BENJAMIN
Jericho
Gilgal?
Heshbon
Jebus (Jerusalem)
Dead Sea
N
Copyright © 2007 by Barbour Publishing, Inc.
Mediterranean Sea
Hazor
0 25 50 mi
0 40 80 km
Nobah
Edrei
Megiddo
Beth-shan
Shechem
Peniel?
Jogbehah
Jebus (Jerusalem)
Dead Sea
Hebron
ARABIAN DESERT
Beersheba
Kir-hareseth
Karkor?

JUDGES 6:1–40

THE CALL TO GIDEON

Setting Up the Section

The cycle of falling away from faith, becoming oppressed, and then praying for deliverance starts again. This section begins the literary center of Judges, involving Gideon and his idolatrous son, Abimelech; and it emphasizes the central issues: the worship of Baal and the Lord's kingship over His covenant people.

6:1–6

TERRIBLE OPPRESSION

Doing evil is a phrase used in the book of Judges to refer to idolatry. Israel strays again, which brings the typical consequences—the nation weakens, and the people have to leave their homes and hide in caves as foreign invaders come in and wipe out their crops and livestock. When Israel lives according to God's laws, they live under God's blessing—the Israelites get to reap what others sow (Joshua 24:13). On the other hand, when the Israelites live in disobedience, others reap what Israel has sown (Deuteronomy 28:29, 31). And true to form, in verse 6 we are told that Israel finally cries out to God again for deliverance (6:6).

6:7–10

OBVIOUS WORDS

Before He sends them a deliverer, God sends them a prophet. This unnamed prophet, in essence, prepares the way for the deliverer. This prophet does not bring new prophecies; he declares what has been forgotten. Verse 10 again makes clear that the main problem is not oppression, but false worship, false gods, and disobedience to the Lord.

6:11–13

GOD IS WITH YOU

The angel of the Lord appears at the foot of a tree—sometimes translated as a *terebinth*, or *oak*. Gideon is threshing in a winepress, trying to hide what little wheat his father has from the marauding band. All of this symbolism points to a lack of communion with God.

The angel declares that the Lord is with Gideon. Because God is with him, Gideon will be a valiant warrior. Gideon's response is one of faith, for he acknowledges that the oppression is from the hand of God.

6:14–16

THE PROMISE OF STRENGTH AND VICTORY

The source of Gideon's might, according to verse 14, is that God is sending him. Gideon is dumbfounded at this idea. He is of the weakest clan in a half-tribe of Israel, he is the least in his father's house, and he is down in an empty winepress threshing wheat like an ox. In the history of Israel, however, there have been other situations in which a younger (and thus weaker in position) son was chosen: Abel over Cain, Isaac over Ishmael, Jacob over Esau, Joseph over his ten older brothers. Strength comes from God's appointment of a person rather than his or her human rank or glory.

The Lord rewards Gideon's humility with yet a third promise. Because God is with him, Gideon's victory will be total. Moses was considered the meekest man in the old covenant, and like Moses, Gideon now asks for a sign.

6:17–24

THE SIGN OF RESTORED COMMUNION

Why does Gideon choose this sign? What is his nagging question? It is this: Is God with us? Have we been reconciled to Him? Only then can we have confidence that He will deliver us. So he prepares an offering (a modified peace offering), and the fire that consumes it leaves no room for doubt—Gideon has been with God.

Critical Observation

Having witnessed a picture of Israel's atonement, one might expect Gideon to be filled with joy. Instead, he is scared to death: No one sees the Lord and lives. This sounds so strange to us; we no longer have a sense of terror in the awesomeness of God. But many would say that if there is nothing terrifying about God's holiness, then there is really nothing amazing about His grace.

Here, having received this sacrifice, God declares peace with Gideon. Gideon builds a memorial-altar, which is visible for generations to come, reminding the people of God's judgment and God's peace. In much the same way today, the ritual of the Lord's Supper is a contemporary reminder of God's judgment and peace through Jesus Christ.

6:25–27

CLEANING HOUSE FIRST

Gideon's first task is to tear down an altar to Baal, which apparently is on his father's property. This task by itself reveals that Gideon grew up in an idolatrous home.

The second bull (which may be a sacrifice representing Gideon and his family) is seven years old (which may correlate with the seven years of oppression). The bull may have been considered sacred in Baal worship, which may add even more significance to this choice for a sacrifice. Gideon was instructed to use the wood of idols for the altar and to make the sacrifice publicly. Every connection between the outside oppression and the internal idolatry is to be declared. Notice that Gideon is not chastised for his fear of the mob and his decision to do this during the night. Apparently obedience is required, but boldness is optional (John 3:2; 19:39).

6:28–32

JERUBBAAL

The morning after Gideon's sacrifice, everyone knows what has happened. Baal's altar is wrecked, Lady Asherah's pole is now ashes, and Joash's prize bull has been sacrificed as a sign of the Lord's favor. The men of the town demand that Joash turn over his son, but Joash, in biting sarcasm, reveals that his household is now following Gideon and the Lord. Then, Gideon's father renames him *Jerubbaal*, the Baal-fighter.

Critical Observation

The delivering judges in this book are types of our great Deliverer, the Lord Jesus Christ. On the cross, Christ made a mockery of all the false gods that lay a claim over the people He came to redeem (Colossians 2:15). And in Christ, our victory comes when His work continues through us: We are promised final and complete victory over all idols and sin (Romans 16:20; Philippians 1:6). We must tear down our idols (Colossians 3:5–7) not in our own strength, but by the same Spirit that came upon Jerubbaal, the Baal-fighter (Romans 8:12–14).

6:33–35

AN ANOINTED ONE

In verses 34, the Spirit is imparted to Gideon. The idea is that the Spirit is "put on him" like clothing. Here we see also a pattern—a sacrifice for sin and the gift of repentance, followed by the equipping of God's people by His Spirit to finish the work which was already definitively accomplished by God in the sacrifice. Gideon is now clothed as a new man, re-created after the image of God. He calls upon the people of God to battle. The Midianites have come again, but this time God has sent messengers who gather the people back to Himself, back to the battle at hand.

Demystifying Judges

The Midianites have a long history with the Israelites. Where did they come from? This people group actually descended from Abraham (like the Israelites), but the Israelites were descended from Isaac, Abraham and Sarah's son. The Midianites were descended from Abraham and his second wife Keturah.

It was the Midianites who bought Joseph from his brothers and sold him as a slave in Egypt. Generations later, Moses married a woman who was a Kenite, a subset of the Midianites. Her Kenite father was Moses' father-in-law and advisor.

The Midianites were severely routed under Moses in Numbers 31. Here in Judges, some two hundred years later, the tables are turned. God is now using the Midianites as a judgment upon Israel.

6:36–40

PUTTING OUT A FLEECE

To understand the prophetic meaning of these signs, it is important to keep the context in mind. Gideon has faith in God, but it is weak. His very need for the confirmation of the fleece reveals that. There is a battle about to take place between the Lord (who has been perceived as weak) and Baal (who has been perceived as strong). The Midianites are used to fighting; the Israelites are used to hiding. It will take a miracle. Does the Lord intervene in miraculous ways? And can Israel trust Him this time? How much does Gideon believe this?

The dew and fleece may represent Gideon being anointed and then, through him, all of Israel being blessed. As to miracles, the triune God of scripture is eternally active in His providence of all things.

Take It Home

Should we "put out the fleece" like Gideon? At one time, the ability to ask God for a miraculous sign was a function of only the prophets and apostles. It validated their ministry and gave a sign to the people that they were in fact speaking the very words of God (2 Corinthians 12:12). When Gideon asked for his sign from God, however, it was the request of a weak faith, not the sign of a strong faith.

Our faith needs to be more than asking God to reveal Himself in a miraculous way over and over. While God does do miracles still today, we don't depend on these miracles alone to validate our faith. We are also encouraged by the community of other believers, truthful Bible teaching, and meaningful rituals like the sacraments of baptism and the Lord's Supper.

JUDGES 7:1–8:17

GIDEON'S BATTLES

Setting Up the Section

The theme of weakness in people and strength in God is paramount to the story of Gideon's battle over the Midianites, foreshadowing what the apostle Paul taught in 2 Corinthians 12:9–11: that God's strength is made perfect in our weakness.

7:1–8

GOD-MADE WEAKNESS

Gideon's messengers gather a fighting force of some 32,000 men. That may seem like a lot, but the Midianites have more than 135,000. Nevertheless, the Lord wants to make clear that He alone is delivering Israel, and He alone is to receive the glory.

Gideon first reduces the troops to 10,000. This is in line with God's commands in Deuteronomy 20:8. Holy war cannot be fought except by men of faith, who have confidence in the Lord and no fear. Incredibly, though, God further reduces the number. The second reduction comes through choosing men who drink water in a unique way. This leaves Gideon with the 300 men God wants. The ratio is now 450:1. God's providence has made His people recognize their utter dependence on Him for their salvation.

7:9–15

GOD'S ENCOURAGEMENT IN WEAKNESS

When Gideon accepts God's offer of assurance, God kindly strengthens his faith. God's message of encouragement comes through a Midianite private, who correctly interprets his friend's dream. Note that Gideon's reputation is known among his enemies. This soldier recognizes that the barley loaf—the bread of the poor—flattening the Midianite tent means doom. Overhearing this, Gideon bows in worship before the Lord.

7:16–22

GOD'S GLORY THROUGH WEAKNESS

Gideon has received special instructions from the Lord for the battle plan. It would be missing the point to simply say it was psychological warfare. The dew-drenched, Spirit-anointed men and their deliverer are now images of the coming of God's glory cloud, complete with fire, a trumpet, and a voice.

7:23–25

IRONIC JUDGMENT

Two commanders of the Midianite army are captured and killed by Ephraim. The places where they are killed become landmarks of God's ironic and holy humor. The Israelites used to hide in rocks (6:2), but now Oreb is killed, possibly trying to hide in a rock himself. Gideon once hid in a winepress (6:11), but now Zeeb is killed at a winepress. Their heads being cut off remind us of the theology of the crushing of Satan's head.

8:1–3

JUDGMENT IN A SOFT ANSWER

Ephraim's concern is for personal glory. But Gideon decides to turn away their anger with a soft answer (Proverbs 15:1). Ephraim can be commended for what they have done right, even if it is wrapped in seeking personal gain (see Philippians 1:15–18). Gideon does mildly rebuke them, noting that God delivered these princes into their hands.

8:4–17

JUDGMENT FOR UNFAITHFULNESS

Succoth refuses to risk their immediate safety by openly trusting God's promise of deliverance in the light of risky circumstances. They will not side with the Lord in His blessing, and so they come to know the Lord in His discipline (8:16). Even worse is the city of Penuel. They are not afraid of the enemy, but their trust is not in the Lord. Their trust is in their big tower. Gideon's judgment upon them is not only to destroy their tower, but to kill the men of the city as well. God is a jealous God, and He will not share His glory with any other.

Take It Home

God is not in the business of making life more secure or more comfortable. That is not His goal. His goal is His glory—revealing Himself to humanity. Sometimes, in order to share this glory, He makes us weak—so that in our weakness we are able to see Him more clearly.

JUDGES 8:18–32

SHADOWS ON GIDEON

Setting Up the Section

Gideon is a man of faith. He is listed in the "hall of faith" in Hebrews 11. He has the kind of faith we are to imitate, the kind of faith that perseveres to the end. But there are other lessons to learn from Gideon. God does not give us stories like fairy tales, where the good prince goes off and lives happily ever after. In fact, one of the greatest lessons to learn from the end of Gideon's life is that we must never rest on our laurels or think that we are no longer susceptible to temptation. We must learn the importance of finishing well and the incredible covenantal connection between us and future generations.

8:18–21

SHADOWS OF SLIPPING IN GIDEON

Gideon, as Jerubbaal, the servant of the Lord for the people of Israel, has the right and obligation to put to death these princes of Midian. But in this short discourse, we see the beginnings of something dark taking place. Gideon does not correct Zebah and Zalmunna when they imply he is a king (8:18). Perhaps misusing his power for vengeance, he seeks to disgrace them by having his young son slay them (and, like his father was earlier, Jether is afraid).

8:22–23

SHADOWS OF SLIPPING IN ISRAEL

The people now seek to establish a dynasty in Gideon. But he only judges as one appointed by God, and it was the Lord who delivered them. The people's trust is moving away from the Lord again, toward an earthly throne. Unfortunately, the story doesn't end after Gideon's faithful answer.

8:24–27

COMPROMISED WORSHIP, COMPROMISED GOVERNMENT

What happens next, though, is a small picture of the real problem. When we are faithful in our worship of God, then the Lord truly is the King, and human kings are no threat to God's glory or to the liberty of the people. But in 8:24–27, Gideon starts changing the rules for worship and starts acting like one of the pagan kings.

8:28–32

GIDEON'S DEATH AND POSTERITY

Verses 28–29 and 32 emphasize the fact that Gideon's life was blessed by God, and that overall, his service to the Lord was faithful. Nevertheless, notice the name change from *Jerubbaal* to *Gideon* between verses 29 and 32. This suggests that Gideon does not end up acting as a Baal-fighter, but a pagan king, influenced by Baal-like gods.

Abimelech, Gideon's son of a concubine, is named "my father is king." Most of us know the struggle of making our practice as holy as our theology. Gideon has denied the throne, but in his dreams, and in some of his actions, he has been letting this temptation simmer, slowly and quietly permeating the aroma of his life.

Demystifying Judges

Gideon probably justifies making a new ephod out of the Midianite plunder because God had instructed him to sacrifice and had spoken to him specifically. The original ephod, in the distant tabernacle, was a golden tunic worn by the priests. It bore the Urim and Thummim, used by the high priest to determine the word and will of God. With this new object, located in Gideon's hometown of Ophrah, the Israelites begin to follow Gideon as a pseudo-king and priest.

JUDGES 8:33–9:57

GIDEON'S EVIL SON

Faithlessness, Again	8:33–35
The Conspiracy of Abimelech and Shechem	9:1–6
The Curse upon Abimelech and Shechem	9:7–21
The Judgment upon Abimelech and Shechem	9:22–29
Fire of the Bramble upon Gaal	9:30–41
Fire of the Bramble upon Shechem	9:42–45
Fire of the Bramble upon Baal	9:46–49
Fire of the Bramble upon Abimelech	9:50–57

Setting Up the Section

Following Gideon's forty years of peace, the consequences of sin and compromise weave a web of great judgment upon the next generation. The story of Abimelech is a warning.

8:33–35

FAITHLESSNESS, AGAIN

Gideon's time as a judge is a mixed bag, but he must have restrained the worship of Baal effectively, because it isn't until after his death that the Israelites begin engaging in Baalism again. *Baal-Berith* is literally "lord of the covenant." Much like "God bless America," this title could appeal to God-fearing Israelites and Baal-worshiping Canaanites alike. But this mushy theology leads to a terrible curse and judgment from the true Lord of the covenant.

9:1–6

THE CONSPIRACY OF ABIMELECH AND SHECHEM

Gideon's half-Canaanite son Abimelech ("my father is king") confronts Shechem's leaders, his uncles on his mother's side. He calls for loyalty to Baal-Berith and not to the Baal-fighter and his God. Implied is Abimelech's argument that for Shechem to make a clean break, all of Jerubbaal's sons must be killed, for surely their intent is to rule over them.

Shechem's citizens agree and give Abimelech seventy shekels (perhaps one for each son) out of Baal's treasure. The thugs Abimelech hires with it capture all seventy sons (minus one who escapes), and one by one they are executed upon a stone, like sacrificial animals. Abimelech is then crowned king at the very place Joshua had set up a memorial stone for the people of Israel (Joshua 24:1, 24, 26), most likely employing a bit of historical revisionism to a people who have forgotten God.

9:7–21

THE CURSE UPON ABIMELECH AND SHECHEM

Gideon's youngest son, Jotham, proclaims a parable from the mount of blessing, Gerizim. It is a curse and a call to repentance. The people have obviously been seduced to believe that what they have done is right and just, and that they have acted in truth and sincerity. Jotham warns them that if they do not turn from their loyalty to Abimelech, they will be burned by this same tyrant. Once again, rebellious sin becomes the very instrument of judgment upon a people.

9:22–29

THE JUDGMENT UPON ABIMELECH AND SHECHEM

Evil is self-destructive; evil people will be at one another's throats soon enough. But in His graciousness to His own people, God sends an evil spirit to speed things along. The people of Shechem turn against Abimelech, who has ruled them for three years, and begin to rob travelers passing by.

Gaal, in the midst of a great harvest festival (remember, Baal is a god of the harvest), calls for pure devotion to the god and people of Shechem. In the drunkenness of the feast, he calls on Abimelech to come out and fight.

9:30–41

FIRE OF THE BRAMBLE UPON GAAL

Zebul, a city leader, hears about Gaal and warns Abimelech, who then plans a preemptive strike. Gaal spots movement, but Zebul convinces him he sees shadows until it's too late. In 9:38, we see that Zebul gets the last laugh before the battle. Gaal and his Canaanite followers are chased from town. But like a brush fire, Abimelech's wrath has just begun.

9:42–45

FIRE OF THE BRAMBLE UPON SHECHEM

The people of Shechem figure that the crisis is over and head back out to the harvest. But Abimelech, fresh from one victory, comes down upon the field and the city, destroys, kills, and curses the land with salt (see Deuteronomy 29:23). We begin to see the hand of the Lord bringing His judgment on the land using the instrument of Abimelech, who is himself an enemy of the Lord.

9:46–49

FIRE OF THE BRAMBLE UPON BAAL

The leaders of the tower flee to the inner chamber of El-berith ("God of the covenant"). Just as Gideon had burned the altar of Baal, so Abimelech now brings bramble-fire judgment upon Baal's house.

9:50–57

FIRE OF THE BRAMBLE UPON ABIMELECH

Abimelech's lust for power presses him further, to what appears to be an easier target: Thebez. God's irony is everywhere. Another tower, another woman, another stone—but this time, his own head (perhaps representing the serpent) is crushed.

Although we clearly see the chastisement of God upon Gideon's family, still these verses declare that God is at work avenging the family of Gideon, the Baal-fighter.

Critical Observation

In Jotham's parable of the trees and the bramble (9:7–15), the trees represent Israel; they are seeking for a king to rule over them. The three fruitful trees (olive, fruit, and grapevine) are associated with Israel throughout scripture. There is a strong contrast made between the fruitfulness and blessing of these trees working according to their calling and the bramble's worthlessness; he is a fire hazard. The bramble is an emblem of the curse that came upon humanity because of sin (Genesis 3:18). Part of the practical consequences of this curse is the tyrannical reigns of evil men over others. Of course, in this case, this is God's description of Abimelech.

JUDGES 10:1–18

RETURN TO APOSTASY

Setting Up the Section

Following the accounts of Gideon and Abimelech, passages like 10:1–5 (and 12:8–15, at the end of this section) seem to be filled with minor details, but that is not always the case. Consider their placement in light of the greater passages and the whole book to make sense of what they offer.

10:1–5

TOLA AND JAIR

Verses 1–5 provide a quick description of two judges of Israel. Tola served as judge for twenty-three years, yet no children are listed. Jair's description includes thirty sons.

Critical Observation

What we can see in this opening description, as with the account of Gideon, is the struggle to establish a dynasty. Keep in mind that there was not a prohibition against having many wives in the Old Testament, and having many children was a sign of blessing. This is why the count of children is significant here.

The Lord grants rest after the work of the first judges (3:11, 30; 5:31; 8:28). With these regimes following Abimelech, though, there is no mention of rest for the people. Life goes on, but it is as if the people are constantly falling away from their faith. Instead of rest, there is only more human activity.

In the opening description, you also see an emphasis on burials, which actually began in the account of Gideon. Gideon was buried in Ophrah; Tola in Shamir; Jair in Kamon; Jephthah in Gilead; Ibzan in Bethlehem; Elon in Aijalon; and Abdon in Pirathon. With the judges listed here in verses 1–5, we know nothing of their battles. They are described as judges, but we hear nothing of the people crying out or of the Lord sending these men as deliverers or saviors. Their graves are reminders of the temporary nature of their reigns.

The fact that God keeps raising up judges to rescue and protect and lead His people is a sign of His grace. Judges 10:6 and 13:1 both point to the fact that after these judges rule, Israel falls back into idolatry. This seems to tell us that, during their administrations, they kept the people from idolatry.

10:6–9

FORSAKING THE LORD AGAIN

Verses 6–9 reveal yet another forsaking of faith. It seems every time a judge dies, the people fall back into idolatry, but the situation described here is to the fullest extent. Seven gods are named, yet this may imply more gods than this since it seems to include the gods associated with these deities. The issue at hand is that the Israelites have forsaken God.

Critical Observation

While our modern view of sin often boils down to breaking a set of laws or rules, here we see that sin is also the offending of a personal and jealous God. The object of God's wrath was not simply at Israel's sins, but upon Israel herself (10:7). His anger was evidenced in the life of the nation; from that year on they were shattered and crushed as the land was invaded (10:8–9). This oppression lasted for eighteen long years and came from both the northeast (Ammonites) and the southwest (Philistines).

10:10–14

SORROW UNTO DEATH

Apparently, Israel's cry of repentance is received by the Lord as just another song and dance (10:10–14). The Lord reminds Israel that seven times (a number denoting completeness) He delivered them, yet each time they fell away and served other gods. God sees no change in their hearts and responds with the chilling words of verses 13–14. God has given fair warning that He will respond in kind (Deuteronomy 32:37–38). These frightening words, however, are used by God as a means to give Israel true repentance (Judges 10:15–16). They once again put away their false gods and serve the Lord.

10:15–18

A GODLY SORROW

Notice that in verse 16 it does not say God is impressed or moved by the repentance of the people. In fact, it says that God's soul cannot endure their misery. This is a reminder that hope in the mercy of God does not rest in the sincerity of a person's repentance but in the intensity of God's compassion. Repentance, like faith, is never the ground of our salvation or pardon. Instead, that ground is the mercy of God.

Critical Observation

We get a glimpse in verse 16 of the personality of God. The God who decrees everything that comes to pass is also the living God of scripture. It is possible for Him to be sovereign over the earth and the people in it yet respond authentically to the events at hand.

JUDGES 11:1–12:15

JEPHTHAH

Setting Up the Section

The beginning of the story of Jephthah is full of comparisons and contrasts. First, notice that Jephthah looks a lot like Abimelech. Both are sons of a mix representing faithfulness and unfaithfulness. Both are surrounded by worthless men. But Jephthah is listed as a believer, a man of great faith (Hebrews 11:32), a mighty man of valor (Judges 11:1), one who speaks with and worships the Lord (11:11). In addition, this part of the story (Gilead and Jephthah) closely parallels the exact situation of Israel and the Lord.

11:1–11

AS GOD WAS REJECTED

In verses 1–3 Jephthah is rejected, much as God is rejected in chapter 10 (10:6). Then Gilead comes to Jephthah (11:4–6), much as Israel made an attempt to return to the Lord (10:10).

Considering that parallel, in the same way that God rejected Israel's cry for help after they fell away from faith (10:11–14), Jephthah at first rejects the cry of his family who calls out to him because they need his help (11:7). And in the same vein of comparison, when Gilead appeals, Jephthah does return to his family (11:8–11)—in some fashion like the second cries of Israel and the answer of the Lord (10:15–16). The parallel here is more flawed, for Jephthah is imperfect in his motives.

11:12–28

JEPHTHAH'S MESSAGE OF PEACE

In sending messengers to Ammon, Jephthah is revealed to be a man of peace (11:12). The Ammonites claim that Israel has taken their land, and they want it back (11:13). Jephthah responds with a series of diplomatic arguments.

First Argument (11:14–18): As Israel passed through the eastern side of the Jordan, she always attempted to remain at peace with the nations of Edom, Moab, and Ammon, respecting their borders.

Second Argument (11:19–22): The disputed land that Israel took was the territory of the Amorites under King Sihon, not the Ammonites.

Third Argument (11:23): The Lord gave this land to Israel.

Fourth Argument (11:24): Jephthah charges them to live with what their god, Chemosh, has given them. One God is greater than another, and Jephthah makes that case clear.

Fifth Argument (11:25): Jephthah also attempts to avoid war with threats. Balak couldn't contend with Israel, so what makes Ammon think they will?

Sixth Argument (11:26): Israel has occupied the land for three hundred years.

Seventh Argument (11:27): Jephthah's true faith is seen here. His final appeal is to the Lord, who is the true judge of Israel.

Even faced with these arguments, however, Jephthah's diplomacy is rejected (11:28). When Ammon rejects the proposal for peace, the nation brings judgment upon itself. In this case, rejecting Jephthah's words is, in effect, rejecting the Word of God Himself, because Ammon refuses to surrender to God's will as defined by the Israelite judge.

11:29–33

JEPHTHAH'S VOW AND CONQUEST

Jephthah is given a great victory over Ammon, but we are given very little information on the battle. Rather, the focus of the story is on the vow that Jephthah makes and the results of that vow. He has declared his faith in the Lord. Now, the Spirit of the Lord comes upon him.

The commitment Jephthah makes in verse 31 is similar to a tithe-offering. In essence, it is a kind of firstfruit. In most cases this term refers to the first of a harvest, but in this case it reflects the first product of this newly established peace. By offering this firstfruit, Jephthah is dedicating the peace, the result of his conquest, to God. (Jacob made a similar vow in Genesis 28:20.)

11:34–40

JEPHTHAH'S DYNASTY

Verses 34–40 constitute one of the most debated passages in the Old Testament. Did Jephthah actually take his daughter to the tabernacle, where the Levites would kill, skin, and section her, offering her up as a burnt offering? Some would argue that this is the only interpretation this scripture allows. Others disagree.

Another perspective is that the word translated *burnt offering* is not a Hebrew word that necessarily implies the *burning* of the offering (other offerings not referred to as burnt offerings were indeed burnt). Instead, an offering that is burnt up can carry with it the idea that the entire offering ascends to God. No portion is reserved back, even for the priests.

Another insight that seems relevant is that Leviticus 27:1–7 describes the redemption contract for those who have been consecrated by a vow to the Lord. There are those who are irrevocably devoted to God and cannot be redeemed, however, as in this case (11:28). In a holy war ban, also, those who had been irrevocably devoted to God would be killed (11:29). (These deaths were not considered human sacrifices.)

However one interprets Jephthah's vow, it is a vow of dedication to the Lord for victory, and it includes the promise to devote the firstfruits of peace coming from his home to the Lord. Jephthah promised to give him or her entirely away to the Lord. Consequently, however, Jephthah is shocked when God appoints his only daughter to be the one. This would seem to stand in the way of Jephthah establishing any kind of dynasty in Gilead.

Both father and daughter, in faith, submit to the vow and, as she is Jephthah's only child, sacrifice the hopes of the continuing reign of the family line. The young woman bewails her virginity with friends who would have been in her wedding party. Then Jephthah fulfills his vow. Some believe that this means his daughter then went to serve at the tabernacle as other women did (Exodus 38:8; 1 Samuel 2:22). Many others believe it means she was killed as a sacrifice.

The chapter closes with the resulting annual Israelite custom in commemoration of the great sacrifice made by this judge and his only daughter.

12:1–7

THE REBELLION OF EPHRAIM

This is the second time in the book of Judges that Ephraim claims they have been left out of the action and the resulting glory (8:1–3). Here, in verse 1, they actually threaten Jephthah, God's appointed judge, something the law condemns (Deuteronomy 17:12).

Judges 12:5–6 reveals a kind of humorous irony on God's part. Jephthah's men capture the fords of the Jordan where the Ephraimites had to cross to return to their home (after they had made an offensive attack on Gilead). The irony of this event is that this is the same tactic Ephraim had used against Midian (6:3). Because of the ingenuity of Jephthah's men, 42,000 Ephraimites fall under God's judgment.

Jephthah's reign was a mere six years (12:7). Perhaps the six years of judging (contrasted with the idea of seven, which is often associated with completeness in the Bible) represents the shortcoming of man's rule to bring about God's kingdom and rest.

12:8–15

MINOR JUDGES

As with the opening of chapter 10, chapter 12 closes with a brief history of three judges: Ibzan, Elon, and Abdon. The last in this list of minor judges, Abdon, has seventy sons (or grandsons), yet Elon has no children listed. Ibzan, like Jair in the opening of chapter 10, has thirty sons listed.

Also, as with the list at the opening of chapter 10, these short histories give facts regarding not only the number of children, but also the places of burial. While these judges rule for a time, theirs is not an ongoing dynasty.

JUDGES 13:1–25

SAMSON'S PARENTS

Setting Up the Section

Over a thousand years before the birth of Jesus, an angel appeared to a woman. He told her that she would conceive in a miraculous way and give birth to a son. He said that her son would be set apart for the Lord from his birth on and that he would start to save his people from their enemies. We have learned from our study in Judges that these are not simply coincidences. The background of the birth of Samson reveals that this unintentional deliverer is a gift from God.

13:1

THE HAND OF THE PHILISTINES

The oppression of the Philistines is mentioned in Judges 10:7, but it is in the story of Samson (along with Samuel, and later, David) that we hear of the conflict. Samson is born and raised during these years of oppression.

The Danites lived in great compromise (1:34–36; also chapters 17–18). This time, there is no narrative of the people crying out for deliverance. Instead, they are a people seemingly so used to bondage that they do not even call out for relief (15:11). But here is a picture of the grace of God. He doesn't wait for us to make the first move. His grace is greater than all of our senseless sin. He takes the initiative, even if it requires a miracle.

13:2–7

THE NAZIRITE AND THE PROMISE

In these verses, and also in Numbers 6:1–8, we learn that *nazar* generally means "to be separated, consecrated," and can be used as a crown of sorts, signifying the one set apart for something special. Nazirites are like priests, set apart for a particular service for the Lord, either for a particular time, or as we see in some cases, for their entire lives.

Demystifying Judges

The Nazirite abstained from any product made from vine fruit—wine, juice, or even the grapes themselves. This act of abstinence signified the idea that he was set apart for special service. This text regarding Samson is not a biblical argument for everyone abstaining from drinking wine, but rather a description of a specific scenario (Judges 9:13; Psalm 104:15). In this case, Samson is representing Israel and is not in a time of rest until he has finished his vow (Numbers 6:20).

Manoah's wife is to keep the Nazirite vow herself, until the child is born, for her son has been consecrated to the Lord from the womb. Here is more proof from the scriptures that an unborn child is a living person, a person who can even be in relationship with his mother and with God.

By his life and by his death, Samson will begin a process of deliverance. But it will take Samuel and, finally, David before the Philistines will be completely crushed.

The Nazirite's holiness is connected to long hair (Numbers 6:5). A man or a woman who takes a Nazirite vow represents the whole nation to God as a bride, one set apart and devoted to her husband. The long hair is a crown, and at the end of the time of the vow, the Nazirite cuts his long hair and offers it up as a sacrifice to God, much as we will take our crowns and cast them before the Lord in heaven (Revelation 4:10).

In addition, the Nazirite is to ceremonially separate himself from death (Numbers 6:6–8), a sign of uncleanness.

13:8–14

MANOAH AND HIS WIFE

The Lord continues to show His distance with Manoah, even while answering his prayer. This savior will not come in a natural way. In one sense, Manoah has nothing to do with it (although his wife will conceive by Manoah).

Manoah wants to know about this boy, what they will do for him, and what his work will be. The angel of the Lord returns and answers, coming first to the woman and answering Manoah's questions about the boy by speaking about the requirements for his mother (13:12–13). God is not going to give Manoah any more details for now.

13:15–16

GETTING YOUR OFFERINGS STRAIGHT

There is a clear contrast in this scene to Gideon in Judges 6. Gideon's offering (a peace offering of sorts) was accepted. But God refuses Manoah's (and thus, Israel's) offer of a meal.

Communion, the peace-meal with God, could not occur because in Manoah's day, the people had not cried out to the Lord; there was no peace with God and mankind (13:1). First, an *olah*—a whole burnt offering, an ascension offering—must be made. The writer parenthetically tells us that Manoah is not confused regarding the order of offerings (as we might be). Rather, it is only because he does not yet know that this is the angel of the Lord that he wrongly offers to sit and eat in peace with this man.

13:17–23

THE NAME OF GOD

Manoah has another question: *What is your name?* The God whose name is *Wonderful* (Isaiah 9:6) did wondrous things in the sight of Manoah and his wife. The angel of the Lord (who is the Lord Himself) ascends in the flame of the offering. Then Manoah knows that he has seen the Lord (13:22).

Critical Observation

We do not realize all that we are asking when we—like Manoah in chapter 13—ask God for His name, for we do not think of names in the same ways that the ancients did. When a person was named, his or her character was revealed and, in a way, dominion was claimed over that person in that they were defined by that name. Parents take some kind of dominion over their children by naming them—the act of naming is a part of the parents laying claim to their little ones. In the account of creation, Adam expressed the dominion God gave him in part by naming the animals. It is telling, then, that the angel of the Lord says that God's name is wonderful (or secret). It is beyond our ability to fully comprehend and certainly beyond our ability to have any kind of dominion.

When God reveals who He is and what He is doing, the result is never simply an ascent to truth. Dull religion (in your heart) betrays your presumptive spirit. Those who realize they have seen God fall on their faces.

13:24–25

ONE MORE SIMILARITY IN GOD'S STORYTELLING

While so much attention is given to the events surrounding the birth of Samson, after his birth we learn very little about him until his adult ministry is initiated. We are told that from this point, God's Spirit began to move in him. God's wonders will be displayed not only on behalf of this deliverer, but actually through him.

JUDGES 14:1–20

SAMSON

Setting Up the Section

The account of Samson is one of the strangest stories in the book of Judges. He is surprising in his actions and in his strength. At first it doesn't seem that Samson is acting as a judge but rather just doing his own thing. But we are told that the Lord raised up Samson to begin to deliver Israel (13:5) and that the Spirit of the Lord had begun to move upon him (13:25). To understand the stories of Samson, we should keep in mind three things: first, Samson's association with Philistine women; second, Samson's Nazirite vow; and third, Samson's ministry of stirring up a sleeping Israel and his work of beginning a deliverance from the Philistines.

14:1–4

SAMSON'S DESIRES

Instead of getting ready for war, Samson is in the mood for a wedding. Against his parent's desires, he finds a woman among the Philistines. We find ourselves easily siding with the parents on this one. But that would be siding against the Lord, who is intending to do something about the dominion of the Philistines over Israel even with as unwitting an accomplice as Samson seems to be.

14:5–9

SAMSON'S SURPRISING MIGHT

The Nazirite finds himself in the vineyards of Timnah, where the fruit of the vine is to be enjoyed in this glorious land given to Israel by the Lord. But it has been taken from them. A lion (an unclean beast) attacks Samson, but the Spirit of the Lord comes mightily upon him, and he tears the lion apart with his bare hands. Later, Samson comes back and finds honey in the carcass, scrapes some out and eats it, and then gives some to his parents. But he keeps these strange events to himself.

As a Nazirite, Samson is not supposed to touch the unclean carcass. Yet he enjoys and shares a token of what is promised by his deliverance in that the land would again be a land of milk and honey for God's people.

14:10–18

SAMSON'S RIDDLE

Samson's father provides a wedding for his son, and a seven-day feast ensues. During this time, the occasion comes to move against the Philistines, but with a riddle. Samson really wins because the Philistines have to coerce his wife through fear to squeeze the information out of Samson. The point is not Samson's weakness, but his wife's unfaithfulness. The bride is supposed to forget her own people (Psalm 45:10), come out, and be made one with her husband. How often does Christ's bride, the church, forget or betray her husband?

14:19–20

SAMSON'S VENGEANCE

Like the lion, the Philistines have attacked Samson in the contest of the riddle, and the Spirit of the Lord comes mightily upon Samson again. This isn't a fit of rage—this is the Lord's administration of justice upon the Philistines. Afterward, Samson's anger is roused (toward his wife) and he leaves her, going back up to his father's house.

JUDGES 15:1–20

SAMSON'S BATTLES

Judgment Fire	15:1–5
A Heap of Vengeance	15:6–8
Judah's Betrayal	15:9–13
Jawbone Hill	15:14–17
"I'm Thirsty"	15:18–20

Setting Up the Section

Holy violence sounds like an oxymoron and brings to some an image of religious fanaticism. The story of Samson is neither for the squeamish pacifist nor the Victorian prude. But the story is for the people of God, that they might fear a mighty and holy God and rest alone in the life, provision, and vengeance of the Savior.

15:1–5

JUDGMENT FIRE

We are not told why Samson returns to his father's home without his wife. The story picks up as Samson returns to have relations with her. It is important to note this because it bears upon the eye-for-an-eye justice he will bring. The problem lies with the Philistines of Timnah. They have robbed him of his wife and fertility, and so he responds by attacking their fertility. The choice of foxes (wild animals—possibly jackals), three hundred of them, sent in pairs, all lead to questions that are hard to answer. It is clear that this is not a fit of rage on Samson's part when we hear his words in verse 3.

15:6–8

A HEAP OF VENGEANCE

Samson's wife has been afraid of being burned by her own people, and so she betrays her husband (14:15). She ends up receiving the very judgment she sought to escape. But she is Samson's wife, and so he brings vengeance with a great slaughter. Those who do not turn in repentance after receiving a slighter judgment will find that God has been patient in withholding His full wrath.

15:9–13

JUDAH'S BETRAYAL

Like Samson's wife, the men of Judah fear the Philistines more than God. In fact, they are quite bothered for the ruckus that Samson has raised. They may have been enslaved by the Philistine culture, but at least they are at peace. Judah is the tribe that originally had faithfully gone into battle (1:1–20); they have now become cowards. But something else is being pictured here. God's own people are betraying their messiah, and this messiah is going along with it, with a greater plan of judgment and deliverance.

15:14–17

JAWBONE HILL

Once again, the Spirit of the Lord comes upon Samson, frees him, and sets him on a holy war. Picking up the fresh jawbone of a donkey (another unclean animal), Samson kills a thousand Philistines, one by one. Then the Nazirite throws the jawbone away, separating himself from that which is unclean.

15:18–20

"I'M THIRSTY"

If we do not have water, we die in a matter of days. God, in a clear reference to the forty-year wilderness wanderings, humbles this deliverer to show him that God alone must provide for all his needs. Just as the rock was Christ in the desert, so this rock is Christ, the water of life. This is more than physical refreshment. As Samson represents Israel, we are reminded that we are always in need of God for the water of life. As Samson represents Christ, remember we sing in Psalm 110 of our Messiah drinking from a brook and lifting up His head.

Critical Observation

Over and over, Judah and Israel turn their back on the deliverers God sends to them. Even in the first century, Jesus' rejection and His trial and execution are an extension of this same pattern (John 11:49–52).

JUDGES 16:1–31

SAMSON AND DELILAH

Setting Up the Section

There are many literary parallels between Judges 14–15 and Judges 16. In both, a woman is approached by Samson, she obtains and betrays a secret, Samson is bound, and there is a great slaughter of Philistines. But there is a significant contrast. Three times in Judges 14–15 the Spirit of the Lord comes upon Samson. In Judges 16, amidst Samson's sin, the Spirit is not mentioned and then later is mentioned as having departed.

16:1–3

SAMSON LOOKS FOR A BRIDE

In chapter 14, Samson has pure motives as he looks for a woman to be his bride (14:1). But this time he approaches a woman with eyes of lust. And Samson is representing Israel again. Judges 15 concludes as each story of deliverance in the book of Judges concludes: with judgment on Israel for many years. The first verse of Judges 16 begins with the same pattern established back in 2:16–17. Samson is being led by his lusts just as Israel has been led by hers.

Samson goes deep into Philistine territory where he sleeps with a harlot. When he finds out that he is going to be attacked, he thwarts the attackers' plans with a preemptive strike. He picks up the gates of the city and puts them where Hebron can see that Gaza is ripe for the picking. And then he leaves, and sleepy Israel does nothing. While Samson remains strong, there is no mention of the Spirit. Samson may think he escaped this mess, but he is clearly on the wrong trajectory.

16:4–5

DELILAH THE BETRAYER

Samson continues to forsake his calling and his vows. Delilah will be the one who betrays him this time. She turns him over for silver.

Samson is probably not all that big and muscular, because Delilah and Samson begin to play guessing games with what kind of magic has brought this amazing power upon him. But the Philistines are not playing a game.

16:6–14

PLAYING GAMES WITH SIN

Samson has fun ridiculing the Philistines' belief in magic. But we also see Samson playing around with his vow. He mentions the number seven and later mentions his hair. Samson does not need to fear magic, but he does need to fear compromise, and Delilah playfully pouts and seduces her way to the truth.

16:15–21

BLINDED WITH LUST

Samson's focus is primarily upon his lusts, and he has lulled himself into thinking he is invincible. Giving in to Delilah's vexing, Samson tells her that if his hair is shaved, his strength will leave him. Delilah lulls him to sleep upon her knees (a veiled allusion to his sexual immorality), and like the harlot in Proverbs, her "feet go down to death" (Proverbs 5:5 NIV). Like Israel, Samson has been raised up out of a barren womb, set apart to be holy, received grace after grace, and deliverance after deliverance. Like Israel, Samson chases after other lovers, taking God's grace as license for any sin that pleases him. And like Israel, Samson is sent into exile.

16:22–27

PROVOKING THE LORD

Verse 23 mentions that Samson's hair is growing back. This is a sign of the stupidity of the Philistines, but also a sign of Samson's strength returning

The Philistines call for a great party, and their victory is their theme. But Dagon has nothing to do with their victory; it is not Dagon's power, but the Lord's absence. They bring out Israel's great deliverer and publicly mock him (16:25), and we should see the foreshadowing of another Deliverer, betrayed for silver, blinded and mocked by the Roman guards (Luke 22:64).

16:28–31

VENGEANCE IS MINE

The servant of the Lord will be avenged, for the Lord's name will be avenged. The Lord answers the prayer of His suffering servant—Samson's death does not picture a suicide, but a victorious self-sacrifice. Once again we are told of the burial of a judge, a memorial of sorts, until the day that the greater Samson will come, die, and leave His grave empty in complete victory over His enemies.

Take It Home

Samson's life was not a life typified by humility. His life can serve as a reminder to us where our strength and our accomplishments find their source. It is not a difficult thing to lose sight of that reality and begin to view our accomplishments as our own. Whether individuals or nations—those who trust in their own strength are setting themselves up for a fall.

JUDGES 17:1–13

FALSE PRIESTS

Setting Up the Section

The book of Judges begins with two introductory passages and concludes with two appendices. The accounts in chapters 17–21 most likely took place before the first judges came upon the scene. Moses' grandson is mentioned in Judges 18:30 and Aaron's grandson in Judges 20:27–28. Their placement here at the end of the book is to emphasize what went wrong in Israel and why she fell into idolatry so often. The first appendix is contained in chapters 17–18.

Some see Judges 17 and 18 as a parody of the story of Moses. Moses delivered the people of Israel, and through him God established a house of worship, a priesthood, and the promise of conquest of a land. Judges 17 perverts this history of an established worship and priesthood, and Judges 18 will pervert the story of the conquest. This parody displays for us why Israel falls into such apostasy time and time again throughout the following generations (described in the first 16 chapters of Judges) and is told through the life of the priest who is the grandson of the same Moses.

17:1–6

A FALSE TABERNACLE

In Judges 16, Samson has been betrayed with 1,100 pieces of silver (16:1–4), and in the opening of Judges 17, we see 1,100 pieces of silver again surrounding a betrayal. Micah steals the silver from his mother but returns it because he fears her curses. While Micah returns what he has taken, he makes no restitution as required by laws, such as those in Leviticus 6:1–7, nor is any trespass offering made.

Micah's mother, unnamed in this passage, dedicates the silver to the Lord, but then uses it to make a carved image and a molded image, openly breaking the second commandment. According to verse 5, Micah has a shrine (a false tabernacle), an ephod (a false garment for fortune-telling), and household idols. These idols are *teraphim*—little messengers to gods—as opposed to the seraphim who serve God. Micah also sets up his son as the priest of his own worship house.

Verse 6 reveals Israel's lack of a king. Had there been a king who loved and kept God's laws, actions like Micah's would have been stopped. Deuteronomy 13 and 17 confirm that idolatry (including idolatry that is combined with true religion) is not only a sin, but a crime against society. Rather than adhere to the laws of their religion, the people of Israel do whatever they think is right in their own eyes.

17:7–13

A FALSE PRIESTHOOD

From Micah's perspective, things seem to get better. A Levite from Bethlehem (which means "the house of bread") comes looking for work. This maverick priest is hired to serve in Micah's false tabernacle before false idols in false worship. This priest will even get a suit of clothes (contrasted with the first high priest's garments of glory and beauty).

Critical Observation

Part of the role of the Levites in Israel's history was as a substitution for the firstborn of Israel. By the laws of God given to these ancients, the firstborn always belonged to God, as well as the firstfruits of a crop. (This practice carries over today in the practice of offering a tithe or offering to God first from our income.)

In this substitutionary role, the Levites gave up certain freedoms. They lived in appointed cities because they had no land, and they also served in the towns of Israel, more or less like pastors of synagogues. The Levites were to reveal God's truth and lead true worship. Unfortunately, in the first 16 chapters of Judges, the Levites are conspicuously absent.

As presented in the Old Testament, priests are also to be like fathers, leading and protecting and teaching their flock. But Micah's priest becomes like a son, manipulated by Micah rather than rebuking him (Malachi 2:7–9). Micah manipulates the gods he owns rather than submitting to the true Lord. Once he determines that he has this perverted form of religion under control, he believes that the Lord will bless him for sure.

Take It Home

The tabernacle at Shiloh and, later, the temple in Jerusalem are simply shadows of the true temple of God. In actuality, we are the reality: The temple of God is the body of Christ. More than that, we are the priesthood, under our High Priest, Jesus.

We still can be tempted to worship God however we see fit, without regard for His commands. We still can be tempted to attempt to manipulate God with our accomplishments or outward rituals of worship. These externals are not where God observes us, though. God sees right into the temple of our hearts (Matthew 15:8–9).

JUDGES 18:1–31

DAN'S DECEIT

Setting Up the Section

In the days of Moses and the Exodus, the Lord led His people out of Egypt, established His priesthood, sent His spies, and conquered the land, burning the first city, Jericho. This section is similar to that story but is more of a distorted parody. This account reveals how the people of Israel, during the times of the judges, continue to miss the mark, fall into the sin of idolatry, and find themselves under God's wrath. Their story is a reminder of the importance of walking in faithfulness.

The account here gives the details of the Danites' compromise, something that has already been mentioned in Judges 1:34 and even in the account of Joshua, the first Israelite leader in the land of Canaan (Joshua 19:47).

18:1–2

THE DANITES IN THE HOUSE OF MICAH

In the days when there was no king in Israel, and long before the mighty Samson, the Danites were unable to conquer the portion of the land that had been given to them when the Israelites returned to the land. When they didn't establish their promised inheritance, they made an attempt to establish their own, sending spies in to explore possible sites.

18:3–6

THE DANITES WITH THE PRIEST OF MICAH

Verses 3–6 describe these spies' interaction with Micah's personal priest. Even though the priest readily admits that he is Micah's priest (rather than God's), the spies ask him to predict their future. Rather than go to Shiloh, the place where the Israelites worshiped, these men go to this priest, who tell them just what they want to hear.

18:7–12

RECRUITING THE PEOPLE TO TAKE THE LAND

The spies return with news that the land is good and an attack could be successful. In contrast to the first spies during the Exodus, who were afraid to trust the Lord and go into the land, these spies are not afraid. Unfortunately, what looks like trusting the Lord is really a justification to disobey. This becomes obvious when they arrive at Micah's house.

18:13–21

RECRUITING THE PEOPLE TO TAKE THE GODS

The spies recruit Micah's Levite. The law requires that they burn Micah and his shrine to the ground. But what do they do? Their perspective seems to be that since they are going to take a land, they will need a priest and an altar. In some twisted way, they can construe this Levite as God's provision. There is even a great promotion for their good friend, the priest. Verse 20 says the priest was happy in his place among the Danites (contrast this with Numbers 2:17).

18:22–26

MANHANDLING MICAH

Micah was a thief and an idolater. In the end, he could not stop his gods from being stolen. The thief is robbed, and the idolater's gods are in the control of men.

18:27–29

MANHANDLING LAISH

Just like Jericho, the Danites come in and burn the first city of their conquest to the ground. The Lord calls for holy war, and in certain cases, whole cities are to be utterly destroyed. The people are to represent the Lord's holy fire of judgment.

18:30–31

FINAL TRIBUTE TO DAN

Verses 30–31 describe a final tribute to Dan that includes an element of irony given the mention of the house of God in Shiloh along with the idols Micah had made. The carved images that the Danites set up are idols clearly prohibited by the Law of Moses. Yet the people remained successful even though they openly worshiped these idols. This is a good example of the fact that the consequences of breaking God's law are not always immediate. Eventually, at the hand of the Philistines, the Danites' "luck" ran out.

Take It Home

The account of the spies holds a lesson for all of us. Whose voices do we listen to? These spies were not only attracted to the priest's voice, but to his worldview. Like these spies, we, too, can convince ourselves that we are serving God, but we are listening to the voices that say what we want to hear.

JUDGES 19:1–30

THE LEVITE'S CONCUBINE

Setting Up the Section

This section includes one of the most shocking stories in the Bible, a horror story of sorts. But God has a purpose in it for us. One structure that has been applied to these appendices is this:

1) Chapters 17–18 show us that the Levites fail to protect the people from idolatry.

2) Chapters 19–21 show us that the Levites fail to protect the people from immorality.

In the Bible, idolatry leads to immorality. If we don't love God exclusively, we will not love others.

19:1–3

UNFAITHFUL WIFE

Verses 1–3 give the account of a concubine. In this era and culture, in places where polygamy was practiced, a concubine was like a second-class citizen, a second wife. The male head of the household was still considered her husband, but she wasn't always referred to as his wife.

In this case, the Levite's concubine is unfaithful and finally deserts her husband to return to her father's household. After he waits for her return for four months, he seeks to win her back to himself by traveling to the father's house.

Critical Observation

The story of the Levite following his second wife to bring her back is seen by some as reminiscent of God's wooing of Israel, though the nation was spiritually unfaithful over and over again. Israel played the part of an unfaithful bride throughout Judges, rejecting her Lord as husband and returning to the gods of her ancient forefathers (Joshua 24:2, 14).

19:4–13

DELAYING THE RETURN

According to verses 4–9, the Levite's father-in-law repeatedly delays the departure. There is nothing wrong with this display of hospitality in itself. But the way the story is told, we sense the Levite's anxiousness to be on his way, and so the repeated delay seems awkward. The Levite needs to return, but we do not know why.

Jerusalem is referred to as Jebus in verse 10. This is the name of the city before the Israelites settled there. The traveling family should have been able to stay in Jebus, but the fact that it had not yet become an Israelite city is troublesome for the Levite.

19:14–24

SODOM IN ISRAEL, NOT GIBEAH OF THE BENJAMITES

They travel on to Gibeah, an Israelite city, but find it empty, dark, and ominous (19:14–15). Their choice to wait in the city square is not unusual in this day. Hospitality, even to strangers, was expected. They would have expected to be invited to someone's home for the night. When they finally do receive a single offer, it is not from a citizen of Gibeah but from an old man transplanted from Ephraim (19:16–21).

Critical Observation

From this point on in the story of the Levite, the storyline becomes somewhat reminiscent of the angelic visitors of Genesis 19, who call on Lot to warn him of the coming destruction of Sodom and Gomorrah. In both accounts, the response of the townsmen to the newcomers is a chilling example of wickedness.

In the Genesis account of Lot in Sodom, the wicked men who attack the household are struck blind, and the attack ends. Here in Judges, there is no such rescue. The woman is victimized and killed.

Once the Levite and those traveling with him settle into the old man's home, wicked Gibeanites pound the doors requesting the Levite have sex with them. The response from within is awful. First, the old man offers his daughter and the Levite's wife. Then the Levite forces his wife out to be victimized by the men (19:22–24). The fate of the virgin daughter and especially of the concubine is so horrible that it is remembered throughout Israel (Hosea 9:9; 10:9).

Demystifying Judges

It's important to understand the account of the Levite in a broader context. When the Israelites entered Canaan to claim it as their inheritance from the Lord, each tribe was assigned a territory. It was that tribe's responsibility to conquer the territory and drive out all those who would threaten the faithful worship of the Israelites. The Benjamites had failed to trust God and follow Him to battle against the Canaanites. They never conquered the land or claimed it for their religion. By this point in their history, they have come to live like Canaanites rather than forcing the Canaanites to adopt the Israelite way of life.

19:25–30

THE CRUELTY OF THE LEVITE, THE WICKEDNESS OF MEN

In Judges 17–18 we see the consequences of a Levite living for himself. Here in verses 25–28 we see the consequences of a Levite failing to protect his wife, even if she is a concubine. And in 29–30, he makes the corpse of his bride some kind of message to Israel. What is the point of the Levite's actions here? He creates a kind of picture of Israel. She is dead, torn apart, in her sin and treachery. Idolatry has given birth to immorality, and that has resulted in captivity and death.

Take It Home

What application can we make for our own lives out of this horrific story? While the events are grotesque, the hearts that allowed those actions are not unfamiliar.

When we fall away from worship, our lives change. As idolatry leads to immorality, we are numbed to the ways in which we start looking out for our own interests, sometimes to the deficit of others. While we may stay within acceptable moral standards for our culture, the heart issue is the same. First we fall away from the Lord, and in doing so, we fall away from one another.

JUDGES 20:1–48

RESPONDING TO THE CRIME

Setting Up the Section

At the close of chapter 19, a Levite responds to the brutal death of his concubine, or second wife, by cutting her corpse into twelve pieces and sending each piece to a tribe of Israel. Judges 20 records the response of the tribes of Israel against the tribe of Benjamin on behalf of the crime committed against the Levite and his concubine.

Some consider the Levite's decision to act in this way to be a picture of Israel that is torn apart by sin and unfaithfulness.

20:1–11

A QUICK REVIEW

At the opening of Judges 20, the tribes gather to hear the Levite's story and to decide how to respond. All of Israel, from the northernmost city, Dan-Laish, to the southernmost, Beersheba, gather as one (20:1, 8, 11) in full fighting force to respond to the evil the Levite and his concubine endured.

20:12–17

ALL EXCEPT ONE

While all the rest of Israel has gathered together in Mizpah, a city in Benjamin, the tribe of Benjamin remains absent. An offer of peace is made to them if they will turn over the men who are guilty of raping and killing the woman, following the laws of war in Deuteronomy 20:10–11. But Benjamin refuses and instead prepares for battle. This reveals the hearts of the people of Benjamin, that they would fight for those who had victimized the powerless.

20:18–25

FIRST AND SECOND BATTLES

The campaign against Benjamin begins just as the battles against the Canaanites began in Judges 1. Judah is selected to go first. Two battles and two terrible losses later, we are reminded of the battle of Ai in Joshua. The problem is not that they shouldn't be fighting the battle, but that Israel is sinful and does not have God's blessing.

20:26–28

THE LORD PURIFIES HIS PEOPLE

In verses 26–28, the Lord purifies His people. This time there is weeping and fasting. Also, this time there is an ascension offering and a peace offering. The fasting portrays their need for God over anything else. Their ascension offering is the atonement granted by a substitute, wholly offered to God. Their peace offering is the communion meal when fellowship is restored. The Lord purifies and nourishes His people. The covenant with Yahweh is renewed. Now they are ready for battle.

Critical Observation

Sometimes in reading a biblical account, the details provided in one book reveal context for the information in another book. Verse 28 is such a case, where the mention of Phinehas, son of Eleazar, helps to put this event in a historical context. Phinehas is mentioned in Numbers 25:10–13.

Demystifying Judges

The ark of the covenant, mentioned in verses 27–28, was Israel's most holy shrine, a box made to God's specifications that held artifacts like the first high priest's rod and a sampling of the manna that provided food for the Israelites in the desert. The ark was usually kept in the national place of worship and was naturally where the people would go to seek God's will. It was considered God's presence, and there were even times when the armies would carry the ark into battle with them in the hopes that it would imbue them with God's power (1 Samuel 4:2–3).

20:29–36

THE BATTLE OF BENJAMIN

The battle of Benjamin described here is reminiscent of a previous battle at Ai, at least in terms of strategy (Joshua 8:1–26). This battle, however, is not only a battle against the Benjamites, but a victory for Israel over the spirit of the Canaanites. Verse 35 offers a theological summary of the battle when it states that it is God who won the battle. The strategy of the battle is an ambush (Judges 20:36–48).

20:37–48

IMPORTANT DETAILS

Drawing the Benjamites out of the city, Gibeah is burned to the ground (20:40).

There is a relentless pursuit of the fleeing Benjamites. The word translated *struck down* in verse 45 is the same word that is used with regard to the abuse leveled at the concubine in Judges 19:25. In both situations, the idea of a brutal, awful, and complete harvest is in mind. Her life was cut down, and Gibeah is cut down. A small remnant finds refuge in the battle at the rock of Rimmon and stays there four months. Besides them, the destruction is total—men, women, beasts, and cities fall under the wrath of the Lord.

Take It Home

Gibeah (similar to Sodom) faced God's wrath and was destroyed with fire. There are several lessons we can learn from their fate:

1) Every individual and every people group will face God's judgment for the way they have lived their lives. Either they will face it through faith in the work of Jesus, or they will face it by themselves.
2) The people were judged because they became like the Canaanites. In other words, rather than spreading God's way of living to the people around them, they took on the lifestyle of those people. We face the same temptation today to become like the evil we are exposed to rather than transforming and influencing change in the culture around us.
3) The tribe of Benjamin was judged, but Israel was saved. Even in this unfortunate incident, God's grace was evident in the stand that the eleven tribes took against Benjamin. God disciplines His people and calls them back to righteousness.

JUDGES 21:1–25

THE REBELLION OF BENJAMIN

Setting Up the Section

As we end this story of the rebellion of Benjamin, we see the grace of God in this final chapter. The Levites have been unable to protect the people from Idolatry and immorality, and thus the judgment of the Lord falls hard upon the house of the Lord in chapter 20. The tribe of Benjamin is dead. And God, in His extraordinary and unpredictable ways, resurrects the tribe.

21:1–4

THE FAILURE OF BENJAMIN

In verses 1–3, there are six hundred men of Benjamin left at the rock of Rimmon (20:47), but they have no wives. Why? Israel had sworn an oath, a curse upon herself if she gave any daughters to Benjamin (21:1, 18). In light of the wicked heart of Benjamin, this was an honorable vow (Deuteronomy 7:3–4). But the excommunication of the tribe of Benjamin brings no joy to Israel (Judges 21:3); it is not a moment of triumph. Instead, it is heartbreaking for even one tribe to fail. Their question—*Why?*—is in essence a prayer for restoration.

Take It Home

Israel had already offered sacrifices for their sins, but in verse 4 they do so again for all of Israel, including Benjamin, as they cry out to the Lord for Benjamin's restoration. While the motivation had some national interest unique to this situation, it still stands as an example of the kind of covenant connection that would serve the church well when a member has fallen away from the faith (1 Corinthians 5:6; Ephesians 4:4–6).

21:5–9

ANOTHER VOW

The sacrifices described in verses 2–4 provide a basis for the tribe of Benjamin's forgiveness and restoration, but they don't provide one practical need—wives so that the remnant of the tribe can repopulate. Therefore, Israel is still mourning (21:6). But the nation had taken another vow as well (21:5). Jabesh Gilead became the loophole that could solve the puzzle. This tribe had refused to come to Israel's assistance when every other city had sent men to battle the Benjamites. In this way, Jabesh Gilead had stood against the efforts of Israel—and thus the perceived efforts of the Lord—by doing nothing.

Critical Observation

Was the vow to shun the tribe of Benjamin a typical response in this situation? When Deborah judged Israel, the city of Meroz was cursed but not utterly destroyed (5:23). Both of these scenarios are an example of internal conflict and thus an internal judgment call. Deuteronomy 17:7 certainly seems to support the action taken against the Benjamites as an effort to rid Israel of the evil that had risen up from within the nation.

21:10–14

UTTER DESTRUCTION

In verses 10–14, another Hormah is carried out (1:17). In the days of Phinehas, twelve thousand men are gathered together and all are killed, leaving only the virgin women. This is a repeat of yet another slaughter against the Midianites described in Numbers 31. After the destruction, there were four hundred women to give as wives to the six hundred Benjamites.

21:15–25

EXTENDING PEACE

A peace offering has already been made (21:4), and peace has been extended to the remnant of Benjamin (21:13). In verses 16–24, the Benjamites are brought to Shiloh, the place of rest (peace), to receive the first four hundred wives and to provide them with this third episode of peace and reconciliation with God and with His people.

Verses 16–18 reveal that the remainder of Israel wants to see the full restoration of Benjamin in spite of the curse placed upon these men.

This dance of virgins described in verses 18–24, the festival in Shiloh, must have declared the desire of these women to be married or their father's declaration to give them in marriage, maybe in a way similar to when we see a group of women scrambling to catch the bouquet at a wedding (21:19–24). The fathers had declared that they would never give their daughters to Benjamin, but the fact that the men took the women during the festival provided an end run around that declaration. In an unexpected way, the tribe of Benjamin is reborn.

Take It Home

On the one hand, the book of Judges is a history of dark days for the people of Israel. We see their constant rebellion, the Levites' failure to protect and lead the people out of idolatry and immorality, and the recurring consequences of oppression by God's enemies. On the other hand, the cycle of God's deliverance reveals His overriding grace for those He had promised to protect.

The broad context of this book is the rule of Israel without a king (21:25). If Samuel, or someone in Samuel's day, is writing, he is contrasting the lack of a godly king to the eventual rule of David as king of Israel. While David was a righteous king, he was still a man. David's own family will lead the people back into sin. The history of Israel is evidence of the fact that humanity needs more than itself to be righteous. This is why God sent Jesus, to do the work in the hearts of His people that neither they nor their leaders could do for themselves.

Consider the modern church. She experiences God's grace, yet struggles with temptations. God brings reformation. She grows. She falters again and again. God continues to raise up modern leaders to call the church back to true faith, but the struggle continues. On an individual level, we face the same dilemma—the struggle with falling away from the grace and faith we've been given. But God continues to bring voices into our lives to call us back. And ultimately, Christ's sacrifice stands in for our failings. God will not leave you, just as He did not leave Israel. And after all of your struggle with sin and failure and falling, He will give you salvation for all eternity.

LIST OF BIBLICAL JUDGES

Judge	Biblical Reference	The Enemy They Fought
Othniel	Judges 3:9–11	Mesopotamia
Ehud	Judges 3:15–30	Moabites
Shamgar	Judges 3:31	Philistines
Deborah and Barak	Judges 4:4–5:31	Canaanites
Gideon	Judges 6:7–8:35	Midianites
Tola	Judges 10:1–2	None listed
Jair	Judges 10:3–5	None listed
Jephthah	Judges 10:6–12:7	Ammonites
Ibzan	Judges 12:8–10	None listed
Elon	Judges 12:11–12	None listed
Abdon	Judges 12:13–15	None listed
Samson	Judges 13:2–16:31	Philistines
Eli	1 Samuel 1–4	None listed
Samuel	1 Samuel 7–9	Philistines

RUTH

INTRODUCTION TO RUTH

Ruth is a small book, only four chapters, that reveals God's work of providence in the details of people's lives.

AUTHOR

Even though there has been speculation about possible authors, no one knows who wrote the book of Ruth. We do believe, however, that the book was written during the time of King David. This seems reasonable because of the genealogy included at the end of the book, a genealogy that includes David's ancestors.

PURPOSE

One option for the purpose of this book is to reveal how a Moabite—a non-Jew—can become a faithful follower of Yahweh, Israel's God. Another option is that it is meant to be a contribution to the genealogy of David, an ancestor to Jesus. Just as likely, however, the primary purpose of the book of Ruth is to illustrate how simple, obedient people can be saved by God's providence and become part of His larger plan.

OCCASION

It's unclear when the book of Ruth was written, though it likely was written during King David's reign, thus the genealogy at the end of the book. In the English Old Testament, it comes right after the book of Judges. This placement may allow Ruth to provide a stark contrast to the greed and disobedience displayed by God's people during the time of the judges. In the Hebrew Old Testament, this book follows Proverbs, displaying Ruth as an example of the virtuous woman described in Proverbs 31.

THEMES

The book of Ruth focuses on divine providence. Through obedience and lovingkindness, God's people continue in His plan even in the face of obstacles and mistakes.

HISTORICAL CONTEXT

Throughout Christian history, the book of Ruth has been considered part of the historical record of God's people. In addition to a story about love and obedience, Ruth reveals the workings of religious laws related to widowhood, as well as a part of the genealogy of Christ—even through a Moabite woman.

OUTLINE

RUTH 1:1–22

THE JOURNEY

Setting Up the Section

This chapter has a poignant lesson: God's providence is certain and He makes no mistakes. As He unfolds the intricacies of His divine purpose in our lives, He does so with a goal in mind. We also see how the saving purposes of God often begin in the sometimes dark periods in someone's life.

1:1–5

FROM BETHLEHEM TO MOAB

At the opening of chapter 1, Bethlehem faces a lack of food, but there is also a famine in spirituality, faith, and morals. The book of Ruth describes an era in Israel's history before the monarch was established. The people were ruled by judges or national champions. It was described as a time when, rather than following the laws of God, every person did what was right in his or her own eyes. Within that context, this famine could be seen as a judgment on Israel for wandering from the faith.

Elimelech's family leaves Judah, the only land to which God has given specific promises of blessing, for the neighboring country of Moab. Soon Elimelech dies, leaving Naomi with her two sons, Mahlon and Kilion, and their Moabite wives, Orpah and Ruth (1:3–4). After about ten years, Naomi's sons die, leaving her alone with her daughters-in-law. Naomi is away from the land of her God, her immediate family, and any extended family. Naturally she would long for her home and for the company of people with similar faith.

1:6–18

RUTH'S CHOICE

Naomi hears that the Lord has returned blessing to Bethlehem but sees a problem with her daughters-in-law returning there. They cannot be guaranteed marriage partners. According to Jewish customs, the women would be married to their nearest relative in order to continue the family inheritance of their deceased husbands. But as Naomi points out, she has no other sons and is too old to have more (1:6–7). As widows, all three would be poverty-stricken beggars, eking out an existence. As foreign Moabites, the daughters-in-law would struggle even more than Naomi herself (1:8–9).

At first, both daughters-in-law refuse to leave Naomi despite her recommendation that they stay in Moab (1:10), but Naomi explains that their best chance for remarriage is to stay. Naomi, even in difficult circumstances, believes in the faithfulness of God's providence (1:9–13).

While Orpah decides to stay in her Moabite culture (1:15), Ruth's choice to return to Bethlehem with Naomi (1:14) reveals her depth of family commitment. Commentators believe Ruth learned some of the principles of God's people by watching Naomi persevere in her beliefs despite great odds (1:16–18) and that her decision reflects Naomi's impact in her life. Ruth is prepared to forsake her past and future and put her trust in Naomi's God and people (1:15–17).

1:19–22

GOD'S HUMBLING POWER

As Naomi returns home, her look has changed (1:19); pain and sorrow have etched their way into her very visage. She had gone away full, but she has come back empty, even requesting she be called by the name *Mara*, which means "bitter," rather than *Naomi*, which means "pleasant" (1:20–21).

Critical Observation

The last sentence of this chapter gives a hint of promise by mentioning the barley harvest (1:22). Troubling things have happened in the lives of the main characters so far, but a harvest is coming. This harvest may not be accomplished without hard work, but the narrator is hinting that a time of blessing and abundance is near.

RUTH 2:1–23

THE COUPLE

Ruth Gleans in Boaz's Field	2:1–3
Boaz Provides for Ruth	2:4–17
Ruth's Harvest	2:18–23

Setting Up the Section

In discovering how Naomi and Ruth are to survive, we are introduced to Old Testament laws of gleaning, which were meant to provide for the poor and for the widow.

2:1–3

RUTH GLEANS IN BOAZ'S FIELD

The opening information about Naomi's relationship to the family of Elimelech implies Naomi has a plan (2:1). When Ruth offers to go glean in Boaz's field, a man related to Elimelech, Naomi encourages her (2:2–3).

Demystifying Ruth

The national religious laws of Israel state that after harvesting a field, a certain amount must be left on the side of the field and in the corners of the field for the poor and for those who cannot provide for themselves (Leviticus 19:9–10; Deuteronomy 24:19–22). Often women and widows used this provision to find sufficient grain to make food for one, two, or even three days, but no more than that. To survive only from the grain gleaned from a harvested field was a menial and difficult existence.

2:4–17

BOAZ PROVIDES FOR RUTH

Boaz is a businessman, yet his first words to his workers are of God. The writer presents Boaz as a man of character (2:4). His inquiry about Ruth alludes to an attraction toward her (2:5). His workers explain that she has asked to be allowed to glean and is currently resting (2:6–7).

Boaz finds Ruth and advises her to stay in this particular field and to follow his maids (2:8). He tells her he has ordered his servants not to touch her, an indication that such fields can be dangerous, but he is providing for her safety. He also allows her to drink from his servants' water jars (2:9). Boaz is providing for Ruth beyond what is required by Levitical law.

When Ruth inquires about Boaz's kindness toward her, he explains that he has heard of her widowhood and her devotion to her mother-in-law, particularly in her leaving her homeland to join Naomi's people (2:10). This story has all the elements of romance and an awakening of interest as Boaz sees in Ruth a character that is attractive to him (2:11).

Boaz asks God's blessing on Ruth's work, noting that Ruth has come to Israel to seek God's shelter. He uses the metaphor of being under God's wings, a protective gesture that mother hens provide for their baby chicks. And as the narrative unfolds, similar language is used about Boaz's relationship to Ruth; Boaz takes a surrogate role of protector and responsibility for Ruth. He takes her under his wing, just as he prays God will do for her (2:12).

Ruth acknowledges that Boaz is treating her like one of his own maidservants, even though she is a stranger (2:13). When Boaz invites Ruth to eat dinner with the reapers, Ruth not only gets full, but has leftovers. What a gift for a woman who is usually dependent upon the leftovers of others for her daily sustenance.

When it is time for Ruth to go back to gleaning, Boaz commands his servants to expand the areas where she is allowed to glean, and specifically orders them not to harass her, but to leave extra (2:15–16). Again, Boaz is going well beyond the requirements of the law. Because of his generosity, Ruth is able to work in the field all day, with access to water and a full meal, and leave the field that evening with about thirty pounds of barley (2:17).

2:18–23

RUTH'S HARVEST

The text tells us that Ruth takes her thirty pounds of barley back to Naomi and shares it with her (2:18). Naomi must have known that the volume of the harvest is more than expected, because she asks God's blessing on the generous person. When Ruth tells her it is Boaz's field, Naomi repeats her blessing and explains that he is one of their closest relatives (2:20).

Demystifying Ruth

In addition to the law of gleaning, the Hebrew people also operated under the law of the kinsman redeemer: If a woman was left as a widow and childless, the nearest relative would take her as his wife, yet any children that she bore would be considered the heirs of her previous husband (Deuteronomy 25:5–6). In this way, the kinsman redeemer was helping continue that family line rather than his own. Naomi may have been already hoping that this kinsman's kind treatment of Ruth would lead to a marriage.

When Ruth tells Naomi that Boaz instructed her to work with his servants until the end of the harvest (2:21), Naomi supports this instruction. Several times in the book of Ruth, the narrator hints that the harvest fields can be a dangerous place for women. Harvest time could also be a time of drinking and celebration, intensifying the risk for vulnerable workers. Thus, Naomi agrees that staying near Boaz's servants would decrease the risk of someone attacking or mistreating Ruth (2:22–23).

Take It Home

Ruth does her duty to her mother-in-law by moving to Israel with her and gleaning in the fields. By doing so, God's plan to connect her to Boaz will be fulfilled. Sometimes it's not in the extraordinary things that we find the guidance of God, but in the small business of going about our ordinary, day-to-day work.

RUTH 3:1–18

THE AGREEMENT

Naomi's Plan	3:1–5
Boaz's Response	3:6–18

Setting Up the Section

The narrative of the book of Ruth is clearly leading to Ruth and Boaz's marriage, which will fulfill God's plan for the line of David, leading to the birth of Jesus. Also of note is the setting of daytime and nighttime. Chapter 3 begins in daytime, then moves to night, and ends in daytime again. In the middle of the night, the greatest risk occurs.

3:1–5

NAOMI'S PLAN

Naomi presents a plan to Ruth that would ensure Ruth's future (3:1). As a widow and a nonnative of Israel, the future most likely consists of gleaning for survival. Naomi reminds Ruth of the kinsman relationship to Boaz and the promising relationship between Ruth and his maids (3:2). On a night when Naomi knows that Boaz will be at the threshing floor, she instructs Ruth to wash, anoint herself, put on her best clothes, and go to him. Knowing the dangers of harvest time, her suggestion that Ruth go to the threshing floor both after dark and after the men have been eating and drinking carries some risk (3:3).

The risk in this plan isn't solely for Ruth. In addition to placing Ruth in a vulnerable position, following Naomi's instructions to lie down at Boaz's feet could put Boaz in a compromising position as well. The events of the evening described here will require faith on the part of all three people (3:4–6).

3:6–18

BOAZ'S RESPONSE

According to the Hebrew, there is a shudder in the middle of the night, and Boaz awakens to find Ruth at his feet. It is astonishing that Boaz, after food and drink, reacts to this situation with such composure (3:7–8).

In response to Boaz's question about her identity, Ruth's answer is pointed. She identifies herself as one of his maids and uses a phrase that asks him to take her under his wing, a word picture he has already used with her. In this case, Ruth's request is a pledge of marriage. She even uses the language that will remind him that he is a close relative with a right and possibly a responsibility in this situation (3:9).

Boaz asks God's blessing on Ruth and suggests that her gesture of interest in him, even though he is not a young man, impresses him (3:10). He continues, telling her not to fear, referring to her reputation as an honorable woman (3:11). Could Boaz be assuring Ruth that she doesn't have to fear the rumors of what can happen to vulnerable women on the threshing floor?

Boaz's response to Ruth's presence indicates his intention to treat her with honor. However, he explains that while he is, indeed, a close relative, there is someone even more closely related to Ruth who, according to the law of kinship, has first claim to her. Boaz will defer to this relative (3:12–13). In other words, while Boaz's heart has been won over by Ruth, he will do what is right according to God's law.

Demystifying Ruth

Naomi and Ruth's closest kinsman is under obligation to make sure that Naomi's lineage (the lineage of her deceased son) is maintained (Deuteronomy 25:5–6). In this case, the redeemer also bought the land belonging to Elimelech's sons. This would have provided financially for Naomi as well as provide for her son's inheritance.

When morning arrives, Boaz makes sure no one knows he came to the threshing floor (3:14). The message here is that Boaz wants Ruth's reputation to remain unblemished. Boaz, however, also wants his commitment to Ruth and Naomi to be clear. He sends Ruth home with another significant load of barley (3:15–17). Hearing Ruth's summary of the night, and seeing this message from Boaz, Naomi assures Ruth that Boaz will move to marry her (3:18).

Take It Home

It's only through the grace of God that this chapter ends with the reputations of all the major players intact. Ruth's obedience to her superiors and Boaz's obedience to the law ensured both emerged safely from temptation.

RUTH 4:1–22

THE LEGACY

Setting Up the Section

In chapter 4, the fulfillment of God's plan is evident for not only Naomi and Ruth, but also for the beginning of the line of David. Boaz has fallen in love, but he's not the nearest kinsman.

4:1–15

RUTH AND BOAZ MARRY

Boaz waits at the town gate, the place of business in the ancient world, and finds the man who is related to Naomi's deceased husband, Elimelech—her closest relative (4:1). Boaz also finds ten men to witness the transaction (4:2–3).

Demystifying Ruth
In ancient times, the city gate was the place where justice was administered. If you had a case that needed to be resolved in some way, you would go to the city gate and call upon the elders to make a judgment.

Boaz explains his interest in Naomi's land, but defers this option to the nearest kinsman, who agrees to purchase it from Naomi, until he realizes that the land comes with the widow, Ruth (4:4). Because this man would jeopardize his own family's future by taking on another, he hands over the right of redemption to Boaz. In this culture, the passing on of this responsibility is symbolized by handing over a sandal (4:6–7). For the record, Boaz announces to all the witnesses the result of the transaction: He has acquired everything that belongs to Naomi, and Ruth will be his wife in order to continue Elimelech's line (4:9–10).

When the people ask that the Lord make Ruth like Rachel and Leah (wives of Jacob), they are stating their hopes for a large family (4:11). Rachel and Leah bore Jacob twelve sons. The reference to Perez here is because he is the ancestor of Boaz, revealing the family connection (4:12). This section reveals the answer to Naomi's prayer in Ruth 1:8 for her daughter-in-law.

Boaz and Ruth marry and have a son. The narrator's phrasing emphasizes the belief that children are a gift from God (4:13). The women of Bethlehem respond to Naomi, and it is significantly more hopeful than when she returned from Moab. They ask God's blessing on Naomi's grandson, and call Ruth the Moabitess, describing her as someone who is better to Naomi than seven sons, a powerful indication of Ruth's standing in the eyes of the community (4:14–15). Naomi becomes the nurse to her grandson, Obed, whose name means "servant," and who will become grandfather to King David (4:16–17).

Take It Home

God will stop at nothing for those whom He has determined to bless, even when we seem at times to get in the way through our choices. The story of Ruth is also the story of Naomi. God's blessing came to them both through a variety of twists and turns, some of which could have drawn them further from God's plan rather than closer.

4:16–22

THE LINE OF DAVID BEGINS

The genealogy here traces the line of Judah from Perez, son of Tamar, through Boaz to David (4:16–22). These names hold significance; they show that God's plan of sending the Messiah through the house of David will be fulfilled and that God can work through all kinds of circumstances to ensure His plan of salvation.

1 SAMUEL

INTRODUCTION TO 1 SAMUEL

The book of 1 Samuel is best understood after a thorough review of the book of Judges. This was a dark era of history for the nation of Israel. God had delivered the Israelites from slavery in Egypt to the promised land in Canaan. The transition had not been a smooth one, yet under the leadership of Joshua the people had done reasonably well. However, after the death of Joshua, Israel went through repeated cycles of blessing and discipline—the result of their obedience or rebellion. Judges ends with the bleak statement: "In those days Israel had no king; everyone did as he saw fit" (Judges 21:25 NIV). That is the situation as 1 Samuel begins.

AUTHOR

What we know as 1 Samuel and 2 Samuel were originally a single book (along with 1 and 2 Kings in its final form), and Jewish tradition credits Samuel as the author. But since Samuel's death is included halfway through the (combined) book, other sources clearly were involved. Several resources were available to other authors at that time, which are mentioned in Samuel and related passages (1 Samuel 10:25; 2 Samuel 1:18; 1 Chronicles 29:29). Even assuming that Samuel made a major contribution to the book that bears his name, no one can state with certainty who authored the other portions. The date of writing is also questioned. Some suggest that since David's death is not included in 1 or 2 Samuel, the writing may have been concluded prior to that time. Others believe Samuel could have been written considerably later—after the kingdom was divided (based on clues such as "kings of Judah" in 1 Samuel 27:6).

PURPOSE

The books of Samuel deal with the transition between Israel's judges and their kings. This was a period when word from the Lord was rare (1 Samuel 3:1). Samuel was just the leader the nation needed to remind them of their spiritual commitments and help them move forward. Even though they would eventually reject Samuel's advice regarding their leadership, he continued to faithfully mediate between the people and the Lord.

OCCASION

The books of 1 and 2 Samuel were recorded to provide historical accounts of a crucial period of Israel's past. The book of 1 Samuel spans Samuel's life from birth to death, chronicles Saul's entire reign as the first king of Israel, and reveals the lengthy transition David underwent from shepherd boy to heir to the throne.

THEMES

Numerous times throughout 1 Samuel, the significance of *obedience* is emphasized, as are the consequences of disobedience. The Israelites would reject both Eli's sons and Samuel's sons as leaders because they did not obey God. We are also shown Saul's recurring tendency to be almost (but not quite) obedient. Closely related is the issue of *receiving guidance from God.* Some of the improper methods attempted include using the ark of God like a good luck charm (4:1–11) and seeking spiritual advice through a medium (28:4–25). In contrast, we see Hannah's fervent prayer (1:1–20), Samuel's ability to discern God's voice (3:1–21), the use of the priestly ephod with the Urim and Thummim, and other methods not fully explained (14:18–19).

HISTORICAL CONTEXT

The previous era of Israel's judges had been a downward spiritual spiral as Israel's numerous enemies dominated them until the people repented and God responded with a leader who would free them (temporarily). As the people moved from judges to kings, the reign of Saul wouldn't be much better. The rules of David and Solomon were, in part, bright spots of repentance, spiritual renewal, and prosperity. But the series of kings would soon drift away from God (with only a few exceptions), resulting in eventual capture and captivity for Israel and Judah.

CONTRIBUTION TO THE BIBLE

The book of 1 Samuel contains some of the favorite stories familiar to children's Sunday schools and Bible story books: Hannah and the boy Samuel, Samuel hearing God speaking to him, Israel's first king, and David and Goliath, to name a few. It is also enlightening to reflect on the stories of people who come into contact with the ark of the covenant when it is not in its traditional location in the tabernacle (or temple). Both the Philistines and the Israelites learn some hard lessons about misusing the holy things of God in this book. Additionally, it is in 1 Samuel where we find an explanation of the cryptic line in the older versions of the hymn, "Come Thou Fount of Every Blessing." When we sing, "Here I raise my Ebenezer," it is a reference to 1 Samuel 7:12–13.

OUTLINE OF 1 SAMUEL

THE SON AND THE PSALM OF HANNAH 1:1–2:10

Hannah's Dilemma 1:1–8
Hannah's Desire 1:9–20
Hannah's Dedication of Samuel 1:21–2:10

THE RISE OF SAMUEL 2:11–4:22

A Contrast of Leadership 2:11–26
A Grim Prophecy 2:27–36
The Voice of God Is Heard Again 3:1–14
Samuel's Accreditation as a Prophet of God 3:15–21
Israel's Defeat 4:1–22

THE PHILISTINES ENCOUNTER ISRAEL'S GOD 5:1–7:17

The Consequences of Capturing the Ark 5:1–12

1 SAMUEL 1:1–2:10

THE SON AND THE PSALM OF HANNAH

Setting Up the Section

The book of 1 Samuel is known for its grand accounts of Samuel (the great prophet, priest, and judge), Saul (Israel's first king), and the rise of the great King David. But it begins with the story of a humble and burdened young woman. Hannah's story is a model of the value of ongoing faithfulness and prayer, even when life's circumstances seem overwhelming.

1:1–8

HANNAH'S DILEMMA

Hannah is one of two wives of a man named Elkanah, the other being a woman named Peninnah. Elkanah is a godly descendant of Levi, designated as an Ephraimite because of his place of residence. Peninnah had borne a number of children to Elkanah, but Hannah was barren.

Each year the family traveled some twenty miles or so north of Jerusalem to Shiloh, where the tabernacle was stationed. Three annual feasts (with required attendance for Jewish males) attracted many visitors. The event referred to in this passage may have been the Feast of Tabernacles (Leviticus 23:33–36), a time to rejoice and recall the Exodus from Egypt.

Critical Observation

It is unlikely that Hannah and Peninnah would have had much contact on a daily basis. They probably lived and ate in separate tents, well distanced from each other. But on journeys they would be thrown together, and Hannah would be forced to endure Peninnah's provocations.

1:9–20

HANNAH'S DESIRE

Hannah's inability to conceive a child is bad enough, but traveling with Elkanah's taunting wife makes things worse. On arrival at Shiloh, Hannah hurries off to the tabernacle, where she pours out her heart to God. Eli, the priest, sees her distressed body language but hears no verbal prayer, and jumps to the conclusion that she is drunk (which suggests incompetence on his part). He has no idea she is making a solemn vow to God as she pleads for a son.

After a short conversation, however, Eli sends her away in peace with his endorsement of whatever she has been praying for. Immediately Hannah is able to eat, and she feels much better (1:18). Meanwhile, Elkanah is consistently attentive to Hannah's feelings, and before long she conceives and has a son whom she names Samuel.

1:21–2:10

HANNAH'S DEDICATION OF SAMUEL

The year after Samuel's birth, Hannah doesn't go on the annual trip to Shiloh. Her child is still weaning, and she is not yet able to honor her promise to God. But after Samuel is weaned, and still quite young (1:24), she takes him to Shiloh and presents him to God, leaving him in the care of Eli.

Despite knowing that she will give up her long-desired firstborn son, Samuel's birth gives Hannah great joy. Her prayer (2:1–10) in response to his birth has a number of features worth noting. It employs parallelism and symbolism, indicative of the format of a psalm. Like other biblical psalms, Hannah's prayer is addressed to God and reflects her praise and thanksgiving. What began as her personal expression of gratitude has become part of scripture for all to read and repeat as edification of the soul. Her words of praise seem to reflect Israel's past experiences, particularly the Exodus. (Note her use of *rock* in 2:2 [Deuteronomy 32:30–31] and *horn* in 2:1 [Deuteronomy 33:17].) Hannah's psalm does not concentrate on her sorrow, her suffering, or even her blessings. Rather, it focuses on her God who is holy (1 Samuel 2:2), faithful (2:2), omniscient (2:3), gracious (2:8), all-powerful (2:6), and a sovereign reverser of circumstances (2:6–10). Hannah's is a magnificent expression of faith at a time when she is giving up her (at the time) only child.

Demystifying 1 Samuel

Hannah speaks of God giving strength to His king (2:10), although Israel had never had a human king at this time. In this sense, her song is prophetic. Her son, Samuel, will eventually anoint the first two kings of Israel.

The positive, righteous example of Hannah (and Elkanah) stands out in contrast to the sad spiritual state of Israel during the time of the judges as well as the state of the priesthood at that time, as will be seen in the next section.

Take It Home

When it comes to responding to criticism, jeers, and similar unpleasant circumstances of life, it would be difficult to find a better example than Hannah. We find no evidence that she retaliated toward Peninnah in any way. Though hurt and humiliated, she remained hopeful and faithful. In God's timing, her sorrow is turned to joy, and her son will be instrumental in turning Israel from its self-indulgent mentality into a powerful nation that once again has a godly leader and receives abundant blessings of God.

1 SAMUEL 2:11–4:22

THE RISE OF SAMUEL

A Contrast of Leadership	2:11–26
A Grim Prophecy	2:27–36
The Voice of God Is Heard Again	3:1–14
Samuel's Accreditation as a Prophet of God	3:15–21
Israel's Defeat	4:1–22

Setting Up the Section

After the birth of Samuel, it doesn't take long for Eli and the people of Israel to see that he is a special person with a rare (in those days) call from God. As Samuel moves into the office of the priesthood and the role of a prophet, his spiritual integrity is clearly evident in contrast to those around him.

2:11–26

A CONTRAST OF LEADERSHIP

Eli had committed to raising Hannah's child, Samuel, but he already had sons of his own. Eli's sons, Hophni and Phinehas (1:3), are wicked men who have no regard for the Lord (2:12). Their priestly responsibilities should include maintaining the tabernacle (Exodus 27:21; Leviticus 24:1–7; Numbers 18:1–7) and the altar (Leviticus 6:8–13). They should also set good examples by avoiding strong drink when serving in the tabernacle (Leviticus 10:8–11), maintaining sexual purity (Leviticus 21:1–9), and remaining ceremonially clean (Leviticus 21:10–22:9). But these sons of Eli do not take their service or responsibilities seriously. They are greedy and insensitive, and they regularly take advantage of others.

Critical Observation

Hophni and Phinehas should have known better than to abuse their sacred positions. The sons of the first high priest, Aaron, had acted improperly and had been judged and killed as a result (Leviticus 10:1–3; Numbers 3:4; 26:60–61).

The maturity of Samuel—physically and spiritually—is seen in stark contrast to Eli's sons. It is worth noting that each year Hannah makes not just clothes to take to Samuel, but she makes *priestly garments*. It might be presumed that she and Elkanah continue to have a positive influence on their son, even as he is growing up in the shadows of Hophni and Phinehas. Their offenses (detailed in 1 Samuel 2:17, 22–25) go beyond the liturgical abuse of the priesthood into moral corruptions. Their disregard for God's law is blatant.

Samuel's first assignment as a prophet is to tell Eli something that isn't pleasant to hear (3:17–18). Yet it seems that his mentor Eli cannot do the same with his own sons. If he attempts to rebuke them, he lacks force and authority. Eli learns of everything they are doing, yet allows the problem to continue. Again, Samuel is a direct contrast (2:26).

2:27–36

A GRIM PROPHECY

The situation with the priesthood is, of course, evident to God. He makes known His displeasure and intent by sending a prophet to Eli—a rare event (3:1). The prophet addresses the priesthood in a proper historical and theological perspective. He first recalls the Exodus, when the Aaronic and Levitical priesthood had been established and respected. Then he looks to the future, when God will build a new house of priests. As for the present, judgment is in store for Eli and his sons—they will all die on the same day, after which God will establish a faithful priest (2:34–35). (The accusation that the priests are fattening themselves on the offerings [2:29] may have hit home with Eli; he is later described as a heavy old man [3:18].)

The problems with the priesthood will be resolved with a new dynasty of priests. The house had been strong under Aaron, but it is crumbling under Eli. Samuel will begin to restore the integrity that has been lost. It will become an enduring house (2:35) that will continue under Zadok, the high priest during the reign of David. Then, ultimately, the fulfillment of this prophecy is found in Jesus. No other priest in Israel's history is worthy to serve as priest eternally.

3:1–14

THE VOICE OF GOD IS HEARD AGAIN

In this passage Samuel is called a *boy*—a term flexible enough to refer to a newborn or a young man. Most likely, several years have passed between chapter 2 and chapter 3, and Samuel is probably entering his teen years.

During this period in Israel's history, the people have stopped listening to God, so God does not communicate with them very often. Therefore, when God speaks to Samuel, the youngster assumes the voice is that of his mentor, Eli. It takes three times before the more experienced priest suspects what is happening (evidencing again his incompetence) and instructs Samuel to reply directly to God.

The lamps burn throughout the night in the temple (2 Chronicles 13:11) and burn out around daybreak. So this setting, where the tabernacle residents are sleeping while the lamps are burning, suggests the early morning hours.

When Samuel finally acknowledges God's voice, God gives him a solemn message concerning Eli. God is about to bring judgment on Eli and his house because Eli has done nothing to hinder the offensive behavior of his sons. Judgment is now imminent. No longer will sacrifice or atonement set the record straight (1 Samuel 3:14).

Demystifying 1 Samuel

Some Bible translations say that Eli does not *rebuke* his sons (3:13), yet it certainly appears that he verbally reprimands them (2:22–25). Other versions offer the translation that Eli does not *restrain* his sons, which seems to be a better word choice. In either case, the result is that Eli and his sons have passed the point of no return.

3:15–21

SAMUEL'S ACCREDITATION AS A PROPHET OF GOD

Not surprisingly, the young Samuel is reticent to approach Eli with the message he has received from God. He doesn't bring it up until Eli confronts him. (Eli, of course, has already heard a similar message from a different prophet [2:27–36].) When pressed by Eli, Samuel reluctantly tells him the entire message.

Eli's response to the prophecy is disturbing. Even after hearing of the impending judgment of God, he doesn't repent of his own sin of neglect. His words have a pious ring of submission to the sovereign will of God, yet are actually an expression of fatalism couched in religious terms.

God continues to speak to Samuel (3:21) and Samuel speaks for God. The people soon notice his evident call as a true prophet (Deuteronomy 13:1–5; 18:14–22; 1 Samuel 3:19). As Samuel continues to listen and respond, the young prophet will soon become a righteous priest and judge as well.

4:1–22

ISRAEL'S DEFEAT

At this point the Philistines have dominated the Israelites for some time (4:9). In a previous battle, Israel lost 4,000 soldiers (4:2), after which they questioned why God would allow such a thing to happen. But rather than consulting God and praying and fasting, they decide to carry the ark of the covenant into the next battle, assuming it will guarantee God's presence with them.

When the ark first arrives at the Israelite camp, a great shout goes out. The soldiers are confident and assured of victory. In fact, the cheering is so loud that it is heard in the Philistine camp. After the Philistines discover the ark has been summoned, they presume that they will be doing battle against Israel's gods as well as their soldiers. (They are well aware of Israel's past victories where the ark is prominent.) But rather than causing them to cower, the news motivates the Philistines to fight harder and die like men, if it comes to that. As fighting ensues, the tragedies accumulate for Israel: They lose the battle, 30,000 men die (including both of Eli's sons), and the ark is captured and carried away by the Philistines.

The news is equally grim on the home front. Eli has stationed himself by the road, anxiously awaiting word. A Benjamite who had escaped eventually comes by. His clothes are torn and he has dust on his head—signs of mourning and defeat. Eli's vision is poor and he may not have detected the visible signs, but he could certainly hear the commotion (3:11). When the messenger confirms the worst, the news is more than Eli's 98-year-old body can handle. He collapses and breaks his neck. As had been foretold, he and his sons die on the same day.

In addition, tragedy also strikes Eli's pregnant daughter-in-law (the wife of Phinehas). The deaths of Eli and her husband, Israel's defeat, and the loss of the ark all hasten her labor. She refuses comfort or help from others, and dies during the delivery. But before she does, she names her son Ichabod ("no glory"). She comments that the glory of God departed with the capture of the ark. In reality, due to Israel's ongoing problematic spiritual condition, God's presence had not been felt by Israel for a long time.

Take It Home

This section of scripture describes three different responses the people had toward God, which are still evident today. The Israelites callously act as if God is their servant, rather than vice versa. But God is not a good luck charm. Eli responds with fatalistic resignation. At least twice God speaks to him through other people, but in spite of the repeated warnings, he does absolutely nothing. Samuel, on the other hand, responds in faith to God's call. He did nothing to prompt God's appearance yet does not take for granted the grace and sovereignty of God. Every Christian is called to faith in Christ and called to proclaim the Word of Christ to others. May we respond as Samuel does—immediately, faithfully, and continually.

1 SAMUEL 5:1–7:17

THE PHILISTINES ENCOUNTER ISRAEL'S GOD

Setting Up the Section

The Israelites appear to be in a bleak situation. The Philistines have just routed the army, with thirty thousand casualties. Their priests are among the dead. Worst of all, the ark of the covenant was captured. But as will become evident in this section, God is still in control and remains active on behalf of His people.

5:1–12

THE CONSEQUENCES OF CAPTURING THE ARK

As the Philistines carry off the ark of the covenant, it may appear to the Israelites that their God is being held hostage. But they—and the Philistines—are in for a few surprises.

The Philistines first take the ark to Ashdod, the northernmost of their five principle cities, where they place it in a temple before one of their primary gods, Dagon. Imagine their surprise the next morning as they come to celebrate Dagon's victory, only to find his image fallen and prostrate before the ark of God. They reposition Dagon and return the next day. The situation is even worse. Dagon has fallen again, and this time its hands and head have broken off. The ark of God may be in Philistine hands, but the god of the Philistines is in the hands of the only true God, the God of Israel.

Prior to the battle, the Philistines had been fearful of Israel's God because they knew He had inflicted the Egyptians with all kinds of plagues (4:8). After the incident in Dagon's temple, a plague begins to spread throughout Ashdod. The local citizens quickly reason that the only way to be rid of the plague is to get rid of the ark, so they send it on to another of their cities, Gath.

Demystifying 1 Samuel

The exact nature of the plague is unknown. Some people have suggested the outbreak of tumors was a widespread bout of severe hemorrhoids, although the number of deaths might indicate something more serious. Since the tumors and deaths appear to be associated with rodents, another likely possibility is that the epidemic might have been a manifestation of the bubonic plague, or something similar.

The citizens of Gath immediately experience the same plague faced by the Ashdodites, and they attempt to forward the ark on to the city of Ekron. By then the Philistines have determined that the plagues seem to be directly associated with the presence of the ark. They strongly suspect that their trouble is the result of God's judgment on them and their god, Dagon. Yet they make no effort to renounce Dagon, cease their idolatry, or worship the God of Israel. Instead, they simply want to distance themselves from Israel's God.

6:1–7:2

THE RETURN OF THE ARK

After seven months of plagues, the Philistine priests are more than ready to discuss the best way to return the ark to Israel. In their eagerness to be rid of the ark, they still want to exercise caution. They fashion a guilt offering of five gold tumors and five gold mice to send back with the ark. They transport the ark on a cart pulled by two milk cows, whose nursing calves have just been separated from them. The mother cows should not be willing to leave their calves under any circumstances, so when they pull the cart straight toward Israel without turning aside, it is a clear sign that the plagues are no coincidence. The Philistines follow at a distance and see the cart and its cargo come to a halt in Israel.

If the Philistines are glad to be rid of the ark, the Israelites of Beth Shemesh are ecstatic when they realize it has returned. The people reaping in the fields use the wood from the cart as fuel and the cows as an offering. But what begins as a festive occasion quickly comes to an end when some of the people look into the ark—a serious violation of the law. As a result, a plague breaks out and a significant number of people are struck dead.

The ark is transferred to Kiriath-jearim, where it remains for twenty years. David eventually arranges for its transport to Jerusalem.

7:3–17

POSITIVE CHANGE BEGINS

Samuel is strangely absent from the accounts in 1 Samuel 4–6. But while the ark is set aside for two decades, Samuel is an essential part of Israel's spiritual revival. With the absence of the ark as a "security blanket" (as Israel had attempted during the battle), the people have to look elsewhere for security.

They gather with Samuel at Mizpah, where Samuel promises to pray to the Lord on their behalf as the people fast. While they are there, the Philistines prepare to attack. Samuel offers a burnt offering to God and asks for His deliverance. In response, God sends thunder that creates great confusion among the Philistines and enables the Israelites to overcome them.

Critical Observation

After the Israelites chase the fleeing Philistines, Samuel erects a stone between Mizpah and Shen. He calls it *Ebenezer* ("stone, rock of my help"). It served as a lasting commemoration that the battle had been won with God's help.

After the battle, the Philistine domination over Israel ends for a while. Peace is also established between the Israelites and Amorites, all largely because of the influence of Samuel. From his home in Ramah, he will travel throughout Israel as a kind of circuit rider, fulfilling the roles of priest, prophet, and judge.

Take It Home

The account of the Philistine god Dagon falling before the ark of God is almost comical. But the story quickly turns tragic as the Israelites—people who should have known better—disregard the holiness of the ark. It is a reminder to regularly evaluate the way we approach the holy things of God. Some, like the Philistines, treat holy things almost as superstitions. Others are far too familiar with things that should be regarded with great respect. We can be sure that God invites us to come boldly to His throne (Hebrews 4:16), but we should never take for granted His grace and mercy that allow us to do so.

1 SAMUEL 8:1–11:13

ISRAEL INSISTS ON A KING

Setting Up the Section

In spite of Israel's recurring tendency to fall away from God, He has faithfully called a series of judges to free them from the oppression of various enemies. Now, even though the people have been pleased with the leadership of Samuel, they want to have a king like the nations around them. Samuel will be specific about the potential drawbacks, but the people are insistent.

8:1–22

THE DEMANDS OF A KING

Considerable time has passed as 1 Samuel 8 begins. Samuel has adult sons and is old enough that the people are already beginning to discuss who will replace him. He has gained the respect of the Israelites, but his sons are corrupt. Perhaps Samuel deals with his dishonest offspring because the problem is never mentioned again, yet the Israelites are unwilling to support them as leaders of the nation. Since all the other nations around them have kings, the Israelites want one, too. They don't just make a request to Samuel—they *demand* a king. The people's desire for a king is not only equivalent to firing Samuel as a judge; they are also firing God as their king.

Samuel is disappointed in the people, not because of the personal affront, but because their request is wrong and sinful. But rather than spout off a quick retort to the elders of Israel, he affirms his godly character by turning to God in prayer. God's response confirms Samuel's assessment of the situation.

Critical Observation

The Exodus from Egyptian bondage demonstrates that God is truly the King over Israel. . .or is supposed to be (Exodus 15:16–18). God had allowed for the possibility of a human king—with clearly stated expectations—in the Mosaic Law (Deuteronomy 17:14–20), but that does not negate the fact that the Israelites' demand is from evil intent, rooted in idolatry. During the leadership of previous judges, the people had at least waited until after the death of the judge to revert to their disobedient and rebellious ways. But with Samuel, they seem eager to see him step aside. They had not properly valued the ark, and had lost it. They didn't respect Samuel and his close connection to God. What makes them think anything will be different if they place their trust in a human king instead?

In response to the people's demand for a king, Samuel is explicit about the demands a king will place on the people (8:10–18). Clearly, a king will require a costly and demanding government. Everyone will feel the effects. But the Israelites will not be dissuaded (8:19–22).

9:1–10:9

A KING IS CHOSEN

Oblivious to the seriousness of their sin and all related warnings, the Israelites remain ecstatic about their future king. Yet while Israel is being granted its request, their first leader will not be chosen in the same manner as other human kings. Israel's king is supposed to be a person of God's choosing (Deuteronomy 17:15). Since Samuel has a spotless record in speaking for God, all eyes are on him to see whom God will select.

The events of 1 Samuel 9 bring Saul into contact with Samuel in a manner that makes the prophet certain that Saul is God's choice for Israel's king. Saul's father, Kish, is a Benjamite of some reputation. A "mighty man of valor" (9:1 ASV) can refer to courage, military skill, success, or even wealth. Saul is physically impressive, but many other qualities are yet to be determined.

Saul is sent off with a servant to find some lost livestock. After covering a lot of ground on an unsuccessful three-day search, the servant realizes they are near the home of a man of God. Neither of them appears to have known Samuel by name, but the servant, at least, is aware of his reputation as a prophet. They ask for directions and some young women tell them they have arrived at an opportune moment. From the women's point of view, Saul and his servant are lucky, but the biblical account makes it clear that Saul was expected at Samuel's—even after three days of aimless wandering.

Samuel has been told to anticipate the person God will choose as Israel's first king, but Saul has no such knowledge. As Saul sits down to eat, Samuel even sends for a choice piece of meat that has already been set aside for the guest of honor (9:22–23). The next morning Samuel assures Saul that his father's donkeys have been found. He then has Saul send the servant ahead, and he anoints Saul as ruler over Israel (10:1). He also gives specific instructions and tells Saul exactly what to expect on his way home, including where he will find provisions for the journey.

10:10–27

THE KING IS CONFIRMED

Samuel's words and actions must have been affirming to Saul. Moreover, as soon as Saul leaves Samuel to return home, God changes him (10:9). Upon meeting a group of prophets along the way, Saul joins them in prophesying, giving rise to a new proverb (10:11–12).

Demystifying 1 Samuel

The significance of Saul's prophesying with the prophets is to publicly demonstrate that God has empowered him to judge the nation. When Moses had appointed seventy judges to share his workload (Exodus 18), all of them prophesied before the eyes of the nation, demonstrating that the Spirit of God was upon them (Numbers 11:16–17, 24–25). Saul's similar experience is the first public indication that he is to be Israel's king.

When Saul arrives home, people naturally want to hear about his journey. His uncle seems especially interested to learn that Saul had an encounter with Samuel. Saul provides only sketchy details about the trip, focusing on the search for the donkeys rather than his being anointed. Saul's silence is telling. He was probably supposed to attack the Philistine garrison. Instead, when the Spirit comes upon him, he simply returns home. It will be Samuel who publicly introduces Saul as Israel's king.

Samuel summons all of Israel to Mizpah—the location where they had repented and turned to God at the beginning of his ministry (chapter 7). His audience is enthusiastic and optimistic, eager to hear the coming announcement. But first Samuel reminds them once more that their demand for a king is a manifestation of unbelief and disobedience. No human king will deliver them from their difficulties. Their source of deliverance has always been God, and always will be. Yet God is graciously giving them the king they have demanded.

Although Samuel already anointed Saul, God's designation of Saul is confirmed through the casting of lots. But when Saul's name is chosen, he is nowhere to be found. Further inquiry of the Lord reveals that he is hiding among the baggage. He is then brought forward to the acclaim of (most of) the nation. From a merely physical perspective, Saul is an impressive king.

Samuel presents Saul to the nation, clarifies all the ordinances that pertain to kingly rule, and then sends the people home. One group of valiant men accompanies Saul, not unlike a secret service unit. Another group, however, voices disdain for Saul and refuses to offer gifts. Saul chooses to remain silent and do nothing for the moment.

11:1–13

THE KING'S FIRST TEST

What the Israelites really want is a king who will deliver them from their enemies. The immediate threat is from Nahash, the king of the Ammonites (12:12), who had besieged the Israelite town of Jabesh-gilead. He had told the city's men that they could avoid all-out conflict only by agreeing to lose their right eyes (both humiliating them and rendering them unable to fight effectively).

When Saul is informed of the situation, he takes immediate (and attention-getting) action to recruit an army (11:6–7). He soon has 330,000 soldiers, whom he leads to deliver a crushing defeat of the Ammonites.

Saul becomes an instant hero. His qualifications of being among the prophets and chosen by lot have certainly been impressive proofs of his designation as king. But his ability to rally the nation and defeat an imposing enemy really gets everyone's attention. In fact, the majority want to execute the group of naysayers who have refused to support Saul from the beginning. But Saul earns even more credibility and respect by giving God credit for the victory and granting amnesty to those who opposed him.

Take It Home

This text is a remarkable demonstration of the wonderful grace of God. On a personal level, it shows what can happen when someone is going about mundane, even irksome, tasks. Saul goes out looking for lost donkeys and is anointed king by the time he returns home. Who knows to what end God will use someone's daily tasks? And on a larger level, we see how much more God provides beyond what is requested. The Israelites wanted a king like the kings of other nations. But the person of God's choosing was *unlike* other kings—an exemplary human, transformed in heart and supernaturally empowered by God's Spirit (at least, for the time being). God regularly provides more for us than we ask or imagine (Ephesians 3:20).

1 SAMUEL 11:14–12:25

RENEWING THE KINGDOM

Samuel's Innocence and Israel's Guilt	11:14–12:5
Lessons from History	12:6–18
The People's Response	12:19–25

Setting Up the Section

The Israelites have asked for a king in spite of Samuel's clear warning about what their request would eventually entail. In essence, the people are rejecting the leadership of both Samuel and God. As Saul assumes leadership of the nation, Samuel gives his farewell address and offers a final challenge for the Israelites.

11:14–12:5

SAMUEL'S INNOCENCE AND ISRAEL'S GUILT

Saul's impressive victory over Nahash and the Ammonites is hardly concluded when Samuel summons the people to Gilgal to renew the kingdom (11:14). Saul is confirmed as king, sacrifices are offered to God, and there is much rejoicing (11:15).

Samuel had previously summoned people to Mizpah, and the shift to Gilgal is significant. Gilgal is located just west of the Jordan River where the people had camped before entering the promised land. It's where the second-generation Israelites were circumcised and had renewed their covenant with God, and where Joshua erected a memorial of twelve stones. It was also one of the cities on Samuel's circuit (7:16) and the place where Saul was to wait for Samuel (10:8). The city of Gilgal is closely related to God's covenant with Israel.

Samuel is in a potentially uncomfortable, perhaps embarrassing, situation. Israel had previously implied that his leadership was not sufficient, and they had demanded a king (8:1–9). Rather than tiptoe around their charges, Samuel brings them out in the open. He publicly challenges anyone to accuse him of wrongdoing, especially in regard to his official duties.

He begins by pointing out that he had listened to them and granted their request, but they should not expect the same compliance from a king. He then makes a reference to his age (12:2). The Israelites' implication had been that he was too old to judge the nation. But as is true with many Supreme Court justices, age carries with it much experience. Samuel is not "over the hill"; he will continue to serve the people for a long while.

Demystifying 1 Samuel

The Israelites' accusations against Samuel's sons were true (8:1–5), but Samuel could not be accused of such behavior (12:3–5). In addition, it appears that Samuel may have attended to the problem with his sons. Unlike his predecessor, Eli, there is every indication that Samuel is without fault in the discipline of his children.

The people agree that Samuel has done nothing improper (12:4–5). Since Samuel is found not guilty of the charges, then the Israelites' accusations must have been false. Consequently, Samuel is still qualified to judge Israel, and he continues to confront them and call the wayward nation into account for the sin of rejecting him and God.

12:6–18

LESSONS FROM HISTORY

Israel's history as a kingdom began at the Exodus. Samuel points out that their present demand to have a king like the rest of the nations is just one more instance of their rebellion against God. He emphasizes that it had not been Moses and Aaron who had delivered Israel from Egyptian bondage—it was God (12:7). God works through human leaders, but He is the one who delivers His people.

So Samuel summons the Israelites to take their stand before God (12:8). In a sense they are on trial and he is their prosecutor. History is a witness to the fact that the blessings they have received are not the result of their own righteousness. Rather, history shows that the nation's deliverance has been achieved thanks to God's righteous deeds, performed on Israel's behalf, and always in context of their sin. Repeatedly, God has graciously delivered the people from their enemies, but the people persistently forget the

Lord and turn to other gods.

Samuel briefly scans Israel's history, citing illustrations from the major periods (the Exodus, the wilderness wanderings, the possession of the land under Joshua, and the periods of the judges) to demonstrate a consistent pattern. Then he links Israel's past with their current situation. Like the Israelites of old, they are once again oppressed by a neighboring nation. Yet while previous generations had realized that outside oppression was a result of sin and had repented before crying out to God for deliverance, this time they have not acknowledged their sin or repented. Instead, they have blamed their circumstances on bad leadership and demanded a king so they will be like all the other nations.

Critical Observation

Notice that Samuel tells the people that this will be *their* king—not God's king. God is giving them what they asked for (12:13). With or without a king, they will suffer the consequences if they rebel against God. The king is not the key to the success of the nation; the key is Israel's trust in and obedience to God.

Samuel underscores the importance of what he is saying with a sign of divine intervention. It is not the rainy season. The people have no reason to expect showers, much less storms. Yet in response to Samuel's prayer, a great thunderstorm immediately blows in—right at harvest season. This would have frightened the people because it would have threatened to destroy the crop. The unexpected rain reminds Israel that both calamity and blessing come from the Lord (Isaiah 45:5–7).

12:19–25

THE PEOPLE'S RESPONSE

Samuel's message—punctuated by the sudden storm—results in great fear among the people. They are beginning to comprehend the severity of their sin in general and their demand for a king in particular. They want no further discipline, and they plead with Samuel to pray for them. Suddenly they are looking not to a king for deliverance, but to Samuel (12:19).

Yet Samuel is not holding grudges. He tries to assure the people with words full of mercy, grace, and hope. Without minimizing the magnitude of their sin, he gives them good reason for faith, hope, and endurance. It is not wrong, per se, to have a king, but it *is* wrong to trust any human for salvation and deliverance from the guilt of sin.

Samuel never suggests that Israel's salvation is based on faithfulness or good works. Nowhere does he tell the people to try harder in order to receive God's blessings. Israel's obedience and service to God is spoken of as the *result* of God's grace, not its *source*.

Take It Home

Like the Israelites, many in today's society—and even within the church itself—may have become accustomed to defining sin in secular terms and then looking for the solution through human means. Individually and corporately, believers may be swayed by secular methods of giving (fund-raising), evangelism (marketing), counseling (psychological methodology), and such. May Samuel's words to Israel be a reminder to us as well that we have a gracious and merciful God. When we sin, He disciplines us so that we might once again turn to Him in faith, obedience, love, and gratitude.

1 SAMUEL 13:1–23

THE BEGINNING OF THE END FOR SAUL

Setting Up the Section

Most of what has been written about Saul so far has been quite complimentary. He has displayed physical strength, spiritual experience, and military skill. He has the full support of the people. But soon things begin to go wrong for Saul—not in major ways, but in numerous little situations where he doesn't quite obey God as he should.

13:1–7

THE BATTLES BEGIN

Saul's first battle against Nahash and the Ammonites had resulted in an inspiring victory, but this section reveals that Israel is by no means free of its enemies. The Israelites remain under Philistine control. In fact, it appears that the Philistines have no intention of wiping out the Israelites, who are positioned as a buffer between the Philistines and other more aggressive nations. So even though Saul has a standing army of three thousand soldiers (13:2), Israel remains in subjection to the much larger Philistine force. (The Philistines regulated the number of Israelite weapons by controlling the blacksmith trade [13:19–22].)

Demystifying 1 Samuel

Portions of this passage are incomplete in the original text, which creates some variation in interpretation. For example, 13:1 in the original language reads, "Saul was a year old when he began to reign, and he reigned two years over Israel"—obviously, this was a textual error. The New King James Version interprets: "Saul reigned one year; and when he had reigned two years over Israel, Saul chose for himself three thousand men of Israel." Other translations attempt to fill in the blanks with logical estimates. For example: "Saul was [thirty] years old when he began to reign, and he reigned [forty-] two years over Israel" (NASB), or "Saul was [thirty] years old when he became king, and he reigned over Israel for [forty-] two years" (NIV). The number of Philistine charioteers is also questioned. Some scholars suggest the thirty thousand quantity should actually be three thousand, but the larger number makes more sense in conveying the hopelessness of the Israelite situation.

The delicate détente between the two nations ends when Saul's son, Jonathan, attacks a Philistine garrison without his father's permission. Jonathan's reasoning is not provided, though it is logical to assume from other passages that he is acting on faith, believing that God still wants His people to drive out the nations inhabiting the land He has given Israel.

Regardless of Jonathan's motivation, the Philistine response is predictable. Perhaps Jonathan both expected and desired to provoke a conflict. But the result is an angry swarm of 30,000 chariots, 6,000 horsemen, and countless Philistine foot soldiers bearing down on Saul and his relatively miniscule army.

The scene in 1 Samuel 13 is much different than the one previously described in 1 Samuel 11. Before, Saul was Spirit-empowered and forcefully summoned 330,000 soldiers. Here, however, nothing is said about God's Spirit, and it appears that the number of fighting men is much lower. The soldiers who *do* show up are tentative at first and then terrified when they discover the size of the opposing force. They begin to desert, hiding in caves, thickets, cliffs, cellars, and pits.

Saul has specific instructions from Samuel: Go to Gilgal and wait seven days for the prophet to arrive. When he arrives there, Samuel will offer sacrifices to God and provide further instructions (10:8). But as the seven days go by, Saul agonizes while he watches his army shrink. Some flee across the Jordan River (13:7) while others join the Philistines (14:21). Those who remain are trembling with fear.

13:8–23

SAUL'S ACT OF DESPERATION AND ITS CONSEQUENCES

Saul manages to make it through six days and most of the seventh. But when Samuel still hasn't shown up, Saul calls for the burnt and peace offerings. It appears that he makes the offerings himself. No mention is made of a priest.

Saul may have recalled the previous instance when Israel was gathered to repent and renew their covenant to God. The Philistines had perceived the gathering as a military threat and prepared to attack (7:7). On that occasion Samuel had presented a burnt offering to God as the Philistines approached, and God had sent great thunder that confused the Philistines and allowed Israel to rout them.

Critical Observation

Perhaps Saul perceived that the offering itself had been the means to Israel's deliverance (in much the same way the Israelites had believed taking the ark into battle would ensure God's blessing). If so, it is no wonder Saul is so determined to get the sacrifice offered—with or without Samuel.

Yet it appears that just as Saul makes the offering, Samuel arrives—in plenty of time to have made the offerings himself. Rather than Saul being able to rebuke Samuel for being late, it is Samuel demanding an explanation from Saul. Saul's excuse falls flat.

Samuel's response is direct and stern. Saul's actions are foolish and willfully disobedient to Samuel's instructions. If Saul had obeyed the command of God, his kingdom would have endured forever. But his disobedience costs him a dynasty. God has already sought out and chosen another leader whose heart is in tune with His. Although Saul's kingdom will last for a number of years, it will end with him.

Samuel departs without giving Saul any guidance for how to handle the Philistine threat (10:8). Saul takes a count of his troops and discovers he has only six hundred men ready for battle. In addition, of all the Israelites, only Saul and Jonathan have a spear or sword. The Philistines control all the ironwork in the territory, keeping more sophisticated weapons out of Israelite hands.

And if the difficulty with the main Philistine army isn't enough of a challenge, the Philistines are sending raiding parties in various directions throughout the land. Those destructive raiders appear to be a special force of troops whose task is to destroy human life, cattle, buildings, and crops. If the Philistines are not soon defeated and driven out of the land, much trouble is ahead for Israel.

A shift in power is about to take place, but the motivating force this time will not be Saul. It will be someone who is able to exhibit more faith.

Take It Home

It may appear from a casual reading that Saul makes one little mistake and loses his kingdom as a result, which could infer that God is vindictive or petty. But it was Saul's duty as king to know God's laws and carefully observe them (Deuteronomy 17:18–20). He ignores those general commands along with the very specific instructions of Samuel (1 Samuel 10:8). Like Saul, if we have no sense of our calling, we are headed for trouble. The emergencies of life are not excuses to disobey God's commands; they are tests of our faith and obedience. God often works through less-than-perfect people like Saul—and like us. If we can learn from Saul's mistakes to be more obedient throughout our own difficulties, we can become much more effective in our individual ministries.

1 SAMUEL 14:1–52

JONATHAN'S DISPLAY OF FAITH

Setting Up the Section

Outnumbered and without a plan of action, the Israelites are facing the Philistines. Driven by desperation and self-interest, Saul has made an offering to God, and Samuel has rebuked him and left. But Saul isn't the only leader of Israel's army. His son, Jonathan, is also in charge of some troops. In this section the emphasis shifts to him.

14:1–14

A SIGN THAT INSPIRES ACTION

This account of Jonathan should be considered in light of the preceding actions of his father. Saul has been chosen by God to be the king the Israelites demanded. He is divinely enabled to serve as king by God's Spirit who came upon him (10:5–10). Israel's decisive victory against the Ammonites was hardly initiated by Saul; it had been accomplished by the Spirit of God. Then two years passed with no mention of action on Saul's part, although a later summary of Saul's reign suggests he had a rigorous military career (14:47–48).

It seems that Israel had demanded a king in hopes that he would deliver them from their enemies as the judges had done. As long as Saul trusted God and obeyed His commandments, God would give him victory. The Spirit of God initially came upon Saul as He did upon Samson and other judges, enabling Saul to lead the Israelites victoriously against their enemies.

Yet Saul doesn't appear to be a particularly spiritual man. His hometown (Gibeah) is only three miles from Samuel's hometown (Ramah), yet he has apparently not heard of Samuel when the prophet first approaches him. One also wonders why, after Saul recruits an army of 330,000 and defeats the Ammonites (11:1–11), he doesn't continue on to battle the Philistines. Instead, he sends most of the men home and keeps a standing army of only 3,000. It seems that Saul might have been satisfied with the status quo, not wanting to irritate the powerful Philistines.

It's no wonder that Samuel goes to such great lengths to remind Israel that it has always been God—not their human leaders—who has delivered them from their enemies. Saul may have been slow to comprehend this simple truth, but his son, Jonathan, certainly seems to understand it.

Quite a contrast of these two leaders is shown in this passage. With Israel at war, desperately outnumbered, and miserably equipped, Saul is seen under a pomegranate tree—out of the sun and safely out of reach of the Philistines. Samuel has given him no guidance after his disobedience at Gilgal (13:1–14), but he has with him a priest wearing the ephod—one of the means of determining the will of God (see 23:9–12; 30:6–8). Yet Saul never inquires of God what he should do.

Jonathan, on the other hand, has a definite sense of God's will that prompts him to take action. He is troubled by the influence the Philistines hold over Israel, and he is eager to do something about it. He recruits his armor-bearer to go out on a mission with him. He neither asks permission from nor informs his father. While Saul doesn't want to cause trouble with the Philistines, Jonathan wants to be troubled by them no longer.

Jonathan appears to know much about the will of God from Israel's history and from the nature of God Himself. His words to his armor-bearer (14:6) are filled with a sense of faith and duty. The question in Jonathan's mind is not whether God can deliver the Philistines into the hands of the Israelites, but whether it is God's intent to do so at the time. So he determines another way to discern the will of God.

Critical Observation

Jonathan's reference to the Philistines being uncircumcised (14:6) means that they do not have a covenant relationship with God as the Israelites do. In fact, the Philistines were one of the few people groups in this Old Testament time period that did not practice circumcision. Their uniqueness as an uncircumcised people highlighted Israel's uniqueness as a circumcised people.

Because of the Philistines, the Israelites are not experiencing the freedom from surrounding nations they should. Jonathan realizes that Israel's victory will not be limited by the number of their troops or the kind of weapons they possess if it is God's will to prevail.

A group of Philistines is stationed at Michmash, atop a very narrow pass. Jonathan's plan is to make his presence known, risking the possibility that the Philistine soldiers will come down and fight. But if they invite him to climb up to where they are, he will take it as a sign that God will give him victory.

After approaching with only his armor-bearer, the Philistines do indeed tell the two of them to come on up. Imagine the soldiers' surprise when Jonathan begins wielding his sword as soon as he has climbed to the top. Before long twenty Philistines are dead, and the Michmash pass is opened, allowing the Israelites to pursue the fleeing enemy.

Demystifying 1 Samuel

Why would the Philistines ever invite enemy soldiers into their camp? Why not kill the two Israelites with boulders while they are climbing up? Perhaps it was a boring night and they wanted a little excitement. But more likely, maybe the Philistines were so confident of their superiority that they expected the two Israelites to defect. Either way, Jonathan doesn't conform to their expectations.

14:15–23

GOD JOINS THE BATTLE

A close reading of 1 Samuel 13–14 reveals an interesting wordplay. In 13:7 we read that the Israelites are trembling because of the Philistines. But by 14:15, the *ground* is trembling beneath the Philistines as God sends an earthquake. Their smug sense of security on top of the Michmash pass must have quickly disappeared when that former position of safety became the most dangerous place in the area.

To describe the confusion among the Philistines, the NIV calls it "a panic sent by God" (14:15). The Philistines are disabled and terrified, but the Israelites are also confused at first. They may not have known about the earthquake, since it seems to be limited to the places where the Philistines are stationed, but they can see and hear that something marvelous is happening.

Saul does a quick inventory of his army and discovers that, sure enough, Jonathan and his armor-bearer are missing. It doesn't appear that Saul is happy to confirm this fact. Previously, Jonathan had attacked the Philistine garrison at Geba (13:3), upsetting Saul's tentative truce with them. As the two armies were encamped and at war with each other, Saul was positioned under a pomegranate tree (14:2), managing to avoid further action. But then Jonathan again initiated conflict involving the entire army.

At long last, Saul decides to consult God. Apparently the method involves the ark of God and the outstretched hand of Ahijah the priest, and it seems as though the process is time-consuming. However, as has already been seen, Saul is not a patient person. The commotion in the Philistine camp convinces Saul to act right away, so he instructs the priest to withdraw his hand.

The Israelite army goes in pursuit of the panic-smitten Philistines, with Jonathan and his armor-bearer leading the charge. The ranks of Israel's army swell that day as the six hundred soldiers are joined by the deserters who had been hiding and the Israelites who had previously gone over to the Philistines (14:21).

14:24–35

SAUL'S FOOLISH OATH

Even though the Israelites are taking advantage of the situation, their victory is not what it could have been. Their soldiers are hard-pressed that day, largely because of Saul. He had long been intimidated, if not humiliated, by the Philistines. When he sees his enemies begin to suffer defeat, he determines to make them pay. He places his soldiers under an oath, forbidding them to eat until evening. His reasoning appears to be to avoid wasting valuable time and daylight by stopping for a meal. (The action had begun suddenly and spontaneously, so neither he nor his men are prepared.)

But Saul is wrong on two counts. If he hoped to maximize daylight to kill Philistines, the battle doesn't conform to his expectations. The fighting spreads eastward, first to Beth-aven (14:23) and then to Aijalon (14:31). The Israelites have to pursue the Philistines over twenty miles of mountainous territory. Without food, they become weary and weak. Second, Saul assumes there will be no food for his soldiers. But God has provided the fastest food available—a reserve of honey. A soldier could have dipped his staff into the honey and transferred it to his mouth for a boost of energy in no time at all. There was no faster or finer food around.

Jonathan benefits from the honey because he hasn't heard his father's prohibition. He says what many other soldiers must have been thinking: Saul is not the source of Israel's military successes, but a hindrance to them.

The other Israelites comply with Saul's senseless order not to eat until evening, but fewer Philistines are killed as a result. Additionally, the Israelites are famished. When they come upon the Philistine cattle that evening, they kill them and eat the meat while it is still dripping with blood, in clear defiance of the Mosaic Law (Leviticus 17:10; 19:26). It is unfortunate that they fear disobeying Saul's commands more than breaking God's law.

When their grievous behavior is brought to Saul's attention, he self-righteously points an accusing finger at his famished men (1 Samuel 14:33). Saul's foolish demand has initiated the damage, and now he attempts damage control. He builds an altar of stone where the soldiers can sacrifice their offerings. Yet this can hardly be considered sincere worship. It is merely an attempt to sanctify the appetites of the soldiers so they do not sin further.

Ironically, this is the first altar Saul builds. Did it take a crisis for him to seek to worship his God? This is not exactly a holy moment in Israel's history. In addition is the irony that Saul had forbidden eating in the attempt to save time. Yet to correct the situation, Saul takes the time to build an altar and then ensure that each person's sacrifice is properly slain and prepared.

14:36–52

JONATHAN'S CLOSE CALL

At long last the meal is over and Israel is again ready to fight. But when the priest tries to get direction from God, the Lord provides no answer. Saul immediately jumps to a number of conclusions: that someone has sinned, that the sin is the violation of his (foolish) order rather than God's law, and that the sin is worthy of death. Perhaps it is no coincidence that he singles out Jonathan (14:39). It seems he feels that in the area of war, Jonathan is a nuisance at best and a liability for sure. It also appears that Saul *expects* Jonathan to be selected by lot, and perhaps he even feels the situation is perfectly suited to do away with his son.

After Jonathan is identified by the casting of lots he confesses that he has indeed eaten a bit of honey. Although Jonathan had no knowledge of his father's command and had not affected the army in any negative way, Saul supposes that he is the reason for Israel's failure to finish the battle. He feels it is better to kill his son than to admit his own sin and foolishness. Jonathan makes no excuses for himself or any indictments against his father.

With great flair, Saul pontificates about the certainty of Jonathan's death (14:44). But the other soldiers recognize the foolishness of Saul's actions and are unwilling to let him put Jonathan to death. It is Jonathan, not Saul, whom they credit with their deliverance (14:45). Clearly Jonathan has been working *with* God, not against Him. So Jonathan is allowed to live, and with this incident the battle with the Philistines ends—sooner and less decisively than it should have. But the war continues. For the rest of Saul's life, Israel and the Philistines will be in conflict (14:52).

Despite Saul's shortcomings exposed in this passage, he has a reputation as an excellent fighter. Like Samson and other judges, God's chosen leader over Israel could be a moral and spiritual failure, yet still be a great military leader. God is not restricted to using godly people to accomplish His promises and purposes. In addition, from a historian's point of view, all Israel's victories are credited as Saul's victories. For example, he received credit for defeating the Philistine garrison when it had been Jonathan's doing (13:4). This and other victories are by the grace of God, and often in spite of the inaction and foolishness of Saul.

Take It Home

Saul had the title of king and the responsibility for leading the nation, but it was Jonathan who consistently demonstrated faith and character. With this early insight into Jonathan's qualities, it should come as no surprise later on to discover Jonathan's powerful and almost immediate bond with David. Contemporary Christians may find themselves in similar positions—lacking official power or control of a situation, yet in a position to act faithfully and exert a godly influence. Perhaps taking appropriately bold actions in such circumstances will have surprisingly beneficial results.

1 SAMUEL 15:1–35

THE CONSEQUENCES OF PARTIAL OBEDIENCE

The Amalekite Problem	15:1–3
Saul's Disobedience	15:4–9
Saul Loses His Kingdom	15:10–26
Saul Loses His Mentor	15:27–35

Setting Up the Section

Saul got off to a pretty good start as Israel's first king. But as time passed, he began to make some poor decisions, including issuing a foolish oath that almost resulted in the death of his son, Jonathan, and overseeing an offering that Samuel should have made. In this section he again is given some specific instructions to follow, but he doesn't quite obey them fully. The results will be worse than he ever anticipated.

15:1–3

THE AMALEKITE PROBLEM

Saul had done battle against the Ammonites, Philistines, Moabites, Edomites, and others (14:47). This time God instructs him to attack the Amalekites, a group dwelling in the southern part of Canaan. Saul is to render God's judgment in return for the hostility they had shown toward Israel during the Exodus.

Critical Observation

Israel already had a lengthy history with the Amalekites. In addition to the conflict that took place under Moses' leadership (Exodus 17:8–13; Numbers 14:25, 43, 45), the Midianites and Amalekites had joined forces to plunder Israel during the time of Gideon (Judges 6:3, 33; 7:12). Later they would create problems for David as well (1 Samuel 27:8; 30:1, 18; 2 Samuel 1:1).

God's instructions to Saul appear harsh to modern sensibilities. But Saul, and anyone familiar with the history of Israel, would have had a different perspective. The law provided the reasoning behind the intentional deaths of entire nations, and even their cattle (Leviticus 27:28–29). Joshua had the same instructions as Saul after the walls of Jericho fell. Not long afterward, as a result of failing to fully eliminate the inhabitants of the promised land, the Israelites found themselves regularly in subjection to other powers.

When a predominantly sinful nation is not totally destroyed, the native peoples would usually teach the Israelites their sinful ways and thus bring them under divine condemnation. In cases such as this one with the Amalekites, the annihilation is retribution for not only the sinful condition of the current generation, but also for their predecessors who had sinned greatly (1 Samuel 15:18, 33). Those who cursed Israel were to receive a curse in return (Genesis 12:1–3). The Amalekites had already been singled out to perish (Numbers 24:20). God had not forgotten what the Amalekites had done, and Israel was not to forget either (Deuteronomy 25:17–19). If we are unsettled by the just wrath of God, we should also note that God takes no pleasure in meting out punishment (Jonah 4:9–11).

15:4–9

SAUL'S DISOBEDIENCE

Saul has specific instructions to attack and destroy the Amalekites without sparing anyone or anything. He doesn't fully comply with the order, and we might be tempted to excuse his disobedience because of the harshness of the order. But that is not the case.

He cannot be faulted for warning the Kenites ahead of time to detach themselves from the Amalekites. The Kenites, closely associated with the Midianites, had an ongoing association with Israel. Moses' wife was from a Kenite family, and some Kenites had traveled to Canaan along with the Israelites (Judges 1:16).

But as for the Amalekites, Saul slaughters everyone there except their king and some of their best sheep and cattle. His disobedience to God's command, therefore, appears to be self-serving rather than mercy-based. He would have gained a measure of popularity among the Israelites—they could use Amalekite animals for their sacrifices (without killing their own), and they could feast on the meat. Meanwhile, Amalekite king Agag would have been a living trophy of Saul's prowess and power.

Saul will defend his partial obedience to Samuel, attempting to justify his actions as doing what God had instructed. Samuel (and God), however, will interpret Saul's partial obedience as disobedience.

15:10–26

SAUL LOSES HIS KINGDOM

God speaks to Samuel before dealing with Saul, expressing disappointment in Saul's performance as king. From God's perspective, Saul has turned away from Him and has not followed clear instructions. Samuel is so troubled that he cries out to God all night. He gets up early the next morning to deal with Saul, who can't be found at first because he is busy setting up a monument in his own honor. When Samuel finally catches up with him, Saul speaks first, proudly affirming that he has carried out God's instructions.

Samuel's reply is classic: "Then what is all the bleating of sheep and lowing of cattle I hear?" (15:14 NLT). It is hard for Saul to claim that he has killed all the flocks and herds of the Amalekites when the best of the bunch are standing there making noise.

After Saul discovers his level of obedience is unacceptable to God, he first tries to blame the soldiers of Israel (15:21). But Samuel is hearing no excuses. God prefers obedience to sacrifice. Saul's lack of obedience is tantamount to arrogance and rebellion (15:23). It is severe enough for God to reject Saul as king of Israel.

Saul next tries a brief (and unconvincing) confession of sin and attempts to quickly guide the discussion back to the blessings of God. He is looking for an ally in Samuel, but the prophet will have nothing more to do with Saul. He is emphatic that God will not change His mind about Saul's ability to rule as king.

Demystifying 1 Samuel

Saul's earlier sin of making the offering himself instead of waiting for Samuel (13:11–14) resulted in Samuel's warning about Saul's losing the kingdom. At that point, God's proposed action might have been conditional (see Jeremiah 18:6–8). If Saul had sincerely repented at that point, perhaps his story would have had a different ending. But in this second similar offense, Saul's motives and attitudes are more clearly exposed. In 1 Samuel 13 God decides not to grant Saul a dynasty, and in chapter 14 He decides to send Samuel to anoint David and bring Saul's reign to an end.

It is sad to read the biblical account of Saul's disobedience. His concern is not that he has sinned against a righteous God, but that his public image will be damaged if Samuel openly severs his relationship with Saul. He lacks a deep conviction concerning the vileness of his sin; he only fears that he will look bad if the situation is not handled properly.

15:27–35

SAUL LOSES HIS MENTOR

When Samuel turns to leave, Saul grabs the hem of the prophet's robe, and it tears. Samuel uses the incident as an illustration of how God had torn the kingdom away from Saul. It will soon be given to another.

And rather than attempting to mollify Saul, Samuel turns his attention to finishing what Saul started by calling for Agag. The Amalekite king is confident that since he has not been executed by now, the danger is over. But if God's command had been to annihilate the Amalekites, how could the one spared be the one who had led them in their wickedness? Samuel kills him on the spot. The text doesn't say, but it is likely that Samuel also saw that all remaining Amalekite cattle were also put to death.

We are not informed that Saul ever truly grieved over his sin, or even this final separation from Samuel. But God was grieved that He had ever made Saul king. Even though Samuel never goes to see Saul again, he continues to mourn for him. The cost of Saul's disobedience will continue to be felt for the rest of his lifetime.

Take It Home

The plight of Saul in this passage is a reminder of the danger of stratifying sins. Many people tend to strongly condemn sins that don't pertain to them, while downplaying their own transgressions. (Telling "little white lies" sounds much better than being a chronic liar.) But to know what God commands, and then to disobey, is to willfully rebel against Him—regardless of the "level" of the sin. Saul's story also reminds us that spiritual leaders must first and foremost be followers of God, determined to please Him before worrying about whether or not they are pleasing other people.

1 SAMUEL 16:1–17:58

THE RISE OF SAUL'S SUCCESSOR

Setting Up the Section

In the previous section, Samuel walks away from Saul, never to visit him again.

But it isn't long until God sends Samuel on another assignment, this time to anoint Saul's replacement as king of Israel. Samuel will follow God's instructions, but this time he isn't told in advance exactly who the person will be. And although it isn't emphasized, this section begins with a lot of fear and nervous tension.

16:1–13

THE CEREMONY OF SELECTING A KING

It isn't long after God has rejected Saul as king that He sends Samuel to anoint the next ruler of Israel. The Lord has narrowed His choice down to a certain family—the sons of Jesse of Bethlehem—but does not designate a specific individual.

However, Samuel isn't particularly eager to take on this assignment. He fears that Saul will kill him. After all, Saul has just annihilated (nearly) all the Amalekites, and previously had been willing to put his own son to death. (Saul's future behavior will demonstrate that Samuel's concerns are well-founded.) To make things more interesting, Samuel will have to travel through Saul's hometown of Gibeah to get from Ramah to Bethlehem. Saul may not know exactly what Samuel is doing, but it is logical to assume that if God had rejected Saul as king, then Samuel would be assigned to designate his replacement.

God gives Samuel a legitimate reason to travel to Bethlehem. He tells the prophet to take a heifer, offer a sacrifice there, and invite Jesse's family to the dinner that follows. When Samuel arrives, it is the townspeople who are frightened. When a prophet shows up unannounced, he doesn't always have good news. The elders are trembling, and they want to know if Samuel has come in peace. He assures them that everything is fine and has them prepare for the sacrifice.

When he had been instructed to anoint Saul, Samuel knew exactly what to expect (9:15–17). This time, however, he has no idea which of Jesse's sons God will choose. The oldest, Eliab, appears to be an ideal candidate, but is not chosen. Neither are the next six sons who stand before Samuel. It is the youngest, the one out doing the childish, mundane chore of shepherding, who is chosen. It is David. Samuel (and all those present) would have chosen someone else. But God wasn't looking at outer qualities; He was looking at David's heart. If David's heart is right, God will provide everything else Israel's king will need. When Samuel anoints David in the presence of his other family members, God's Spirit falls powerfully upon him.

16:14–23

TWO PATHS BEGIN TO MERGE

In terms of logistics, how does a young unknown shepherd even begin to replace an established and paranoid king? It will be a lengthy and difficult transition, but this section explains how God providentially begins to bring about the change. With Samuel no longer available to the king, Saul is at a loss for spiritual guidance. And it is at this point when an evil spirit begins to terrorize Saul.

Demystifying 1 Samuel

Not only does God remove His Spirit from Saul, but He also sends an evil spirit that torments the king. God is sovereign, and nothing can take place without His permission. After God sends the spirit to Saul, He sends David to serve as a court musician to provide Saul some relief.

One of Saul's attendants knows of David's musical ability and arranges to have him come to the royal court on a regular basis. In addition to being a gifted musician, David is already a courageous warrior (against bears and lions [17:34–35]) and a person of godly wisdom. The same characteristics that enable David to serve the king are traits that qualify him to serve *as* king. So ironically, David's initial contact with Saul is made in response to Saul's personal request (16:19–22). Before long, he is one of Saul's armor-bearers—someone with a close and trusted relationship with the king.

17:1–16

BIG TROUBLE IN THE VALLEY OF ELAH

Jesse's three oldest sons join the Israelite army, and occasionally David delivers things from home for them (17:13–15, 17–19). The Philistines are still the primary threat to Israel, and one particular Philistine is especially threatening. Twice a day for forty days, a towering individual named Goliath has challenged Israel to send someone out to fight. The winner of the one-to-one combat will determine which nation will serve the other.

Forty days seems like a lengthy standoff. Saul and his army don't really want to fight, and they seem content with the stalemate. But the Philistines aren't in an ideal position for battle either. Their chariots work well on level ground, but not on mountain slopes. Both sides apparently want to avoid a full-scale battle.

Yet the Israelites are growing more and more intimidated by Goliath. He stands between nine and ten feet tall, and his armor seems impenetrable. It gets to the point where, when the Israelites see him, they run in fear (17:24). Their lack of faith is reminiscent of former generations who had sent spies into the promised land and had been fearful of the giants there (Numbers 13:27–33).

Note what a contrast is made when David is introduced to the story. Goliath is described in physical terms: appearance, weaponry, aggressiveness, and so forth. But nothing is said of David's stature, strength, or weapons. Rather, he is introduced in the context of his family. One reason has already been mentioned: David was chosen because of his *heart*, not his outer physical qualities (1 Samuel 13:14; 16:7). Another reason is that the Messiah will come from the tribe of Judah and from Bethlehem (Genesis 49:8–12; Micah 5:2). Jesus will eventually trace His human ancestry back to David.

17:17–58

DAVID VS. GOLIATH

David, as the youngest son of Jesse, is still doing the shepherding and errands. Jesse is quite old at this point (17:12) and surely doesn't intend to place David in harm's way. Most likely he expects David to arrive while the soldiers are encamped rather than when they are rushing toward the battle line a few miles to the west.

Critical Observation

In 1 Samuel 16, David is summoned to work in Saul's court, yet in 1 Samuel 17 he is back with Jesse, and Saul even inquires about his identity (17:55, 58). Various solutions have been proposed to resolve this apparent discrepancy. Perhaps David has grown considerably. Saul might have had a poor or disturbed memory. Or upon a closer reading, we see that Saul asks about David's *father*, not David himself. Also, with Saul and the army off at war, it is likely that David might have taken a break as court musician.

David witnesses Israel's army shouting a war cry while running toward the Philistines (17:20), but then running away as soon as they get close to Goliath (17:24). He keeps asking why someone doesn't do something about Goliath. He learns that Saul has issued a call for a volunteer to fight the Philistine and has offered a number of substantial rewards for any takers. David's oldest brother overhears David talking to the soldiers and rebukes him with a series of false accusations (17:28). No doubt Eliab still feels the sting of rejection from seeing his youngest brother anointed in front of him (16:13). David pays Eliab little mind, responding with a short defense, and goes to ask King Saul's permission to fight Goliath.

Fortunately for Israel, David is neither devastated nor deterred by Eliab's sarcastic retort. He is acting like the king of Israel should act. He trusts God, inspires his fellow Israelites to do likewise, and takes action to defeat the enemies of God. Saul gives David every opportunity, first to excuse himself and go back home, and then to arm himself before fighting, but David has a faith-based confidence. His faith is contagious. Somehow Saul believes there is a good chance David will prevail over Goliath, and he gives him permission to fight. So David takes his shepherd's staff and his sling, and he picks up five smooth stones from the stream on the way to face the giant.

The next section (17:40–50) contains one of the best-known stories in the Bible—the confrontation between David and Goliath. Goliath first tries to intimidate David verbally, but his empty boasts do not faze David. The young shepherd speaks right back to the giant. David understands it will not be his own strength that will win the contest, but God's strength. His faith is rewarded. Although Goliath is armored from head to foot, protected by shield and armor-bearer, he still needs an opening around his eyes so he can see. David's accuracy with a sling sends the first stone into Goliath's exposed forehead, and the giant falls. David, who had no sword, uses Goliath's own weapon to cut off his head.

There must have been a silent and still moment in time as both Philistines and Israelites slowly comprehend what has just happened. With the loss of their champion, the Philistines lose all courage and will to fight, and they turn and run. The Israelites, in pursuit, are able to kill many more of their enemies.

Saul immediately wants to find out more about David's family (17:55, 58). He should have known David, who was one of his armor-bearers and musicians (16:21, 23). But perhaps Saul is interested in knowing exactly where David acquired the wherewithal to face off against Goliath as he had done. One might raise the question, however, of why Saul (the king) and Abner (the commander of the army) are standing around discussing genealogy while the rest of the soldiers are in pursuit of fleeing Philistines.

This is a big day for Israel and the first introduction to David for most of them. But David's instant popularity will soon create problems for him.

Take It Home

The account of David and Goliath is always a graphic reminder of how God has promised to care for and protect His faithful people. When Saul's fear became evident, Israel's soldiers were also frightened (13:5–8; 17:11, 24). But after David stood up to Goliath, the other troops became courageous. It shouldn't matter how large (or numerous, well-armed, mean, etc.) our enemies are. If we remain in a proper relationship with God, He will continue to go before us as He has always done (Deuteronomy 20:1–4). And as we learn to demonstrate faith, it may indeed inspire others.

1 SAMUEL 18:1–20:42

DAVID AMONG SAUL'S FAMILY

Setting Up the Section

David's courageous defeat of Goliath is an impressive moment that changes the course of Israel's history as well as the dynamic within Saul's family. David's instant fame creates jealousy in Saul, even as his display of faith cements a bond between David and Saul's son, Jonathan. After David becomes a member of Saul's family, loyalties change and rivalries intensify.

18:1–5

THE DAVID/JONATHAN CONNECTION

Previous passages have shown that Jonathan has an outstanding faith and eagerness to serve God (13:2–3; 14:1–14), so it should come as no surprise that he is impressed with David's stand against Goliath. He overhears David's conversation with Saul, and an immediate bond forms. We aren't told exactly what it is about David that affects Jonathan so greatly, whether it is David's humility, his willingness to give God credit for the victory, his concern for the people of Israel, or a combination of things. But for some reason, David and Jonathan become kindred spirits from this point onward.

The depth of Jonathan's commitment to David is demonstrated by Jonathan's gift of clothing and armor. A similar transfer of clothing might be made in the transfer of authority from one priest to another (Numbers 20:25–29) or one prophet to another (1 Kings 19:19–21; 2 Kings 2:7–14). Jonathan's symbolic gesture may have demonstrated his awareness that David is the person God has chosen to be Israel's next king—and his personal endorsement of God's choice.

Jonathan isn't the only one intrigued by David. From that day onward, Saul does not let David return home. David will have other things to do besides tend sheep and make deliveries. In fact, David excels at whatever assignment Saul gives him, which impresses both the army officers and the people of Israel (1 Samuel 18:4).

18:6–19

THE DAVID/SAUL SEPARATION

David's heroism is soon depicted in song. Women come out to greet the returning army singing, dancing, and playing instruments. But the lyrics (18:7) are irksome to Saul. Most likely the singers have no intent to compare Saul with David. They are simply elated that

David and Saul have rid the nation of so many of their enemies. Yet Saul interprets their comments literally and becomes jealous of David (18:8–9).

Saul's envy grows quickly. The inspired writer of scripture alerts the reader to Saul's thoughts and motives, which probably aren't as apparent to onlookers at the time. But what began as subtle hypocrisy (chapter 18) soon becomes outright hostility (chapter 19).

When God once again sends a spirit that troubles Saul, David returns to playing the harp with the intent of soothing the king as before (16:23). But this time, Saul attempts to kill David with his spear. David twice escapes without harm (18:10–11). Then Saul's strategizing becomes more subtle. He gives David a big promotion, placing him over 1,000 soldiers. The battlefield is a dangerous place where Saul hopes David will meet his death and be forgotten. But God is with David and gives him great success in all he attempts, which increases David's popularity with the people even more.

Saul even offers David one of his daughters in marriage, on the condition that David continues to fight (18:17). Whether or not this is intended as part of the reward for fighting Goliath (17:25) is uncertain. But Saul is not prepared for David's response. David rejects Saul's offer, not because he is reluctant to endanger himself in battle, but because he is a truly humble man who considers his station in life unworthy of such a gift. After David declines the offer, Saul allows that daughter to marry another man.

18:20–30

THE DAVID/MICHAL CONNECTION

But another of Saul's daughters, Michal, loves David. Saul takes the opportunity to offer David another deal. If David feels he lacks the wealth or social status to be the king's son-in-law, Saul will consider another dowry altogether: one hundred Philistine foreskins. Saul sends word of this offer to David, who responds with enthusiasm. Saul's stated intent is to take revenge on his enemies, but his real desire is to have David killed by the Philistines (18:25). Saul's hopes are dashed again as David returns with twice the dowry Saul had demanded.

Everything Saul attempts backfires. Jonathan has made a covenant of love and friendship with David (18:3), and now Michal is united with David through the covenant of marriage. And the more David goes out to fight the Philistines, the more successful and famous he becomes (18:30).

19:1–24

SAUL'S HOSTILITY INCREASES

When Saul's subtle attempts to kill David continue to fail, the king tries to recruit help from others. He instructs his attendants to kill David, but he also tells Jonathan, who immediately warns David. Rather than openly defy his father, Jonathan wisely sets out to convince Saul to rescind the order. He has David lie low while he tries to reason with his father. Jonathan's plan works (this time), and Saul again welcomes David (19:1–7). But Saul's tolerance doesn't last long.

Critical Observation

If Jonathan had any desire to set himself over David as the next leader of Israel, this would have been the ideal time to do so. Yet he willingly subordinates himself and his own personal interests to those of David. He remains a faithful and submissive son to his father, yet is courageous enough to confront Saul when it was not always safe to do so. Saul quickly reverts to his hatred of David, but the incident says much about Jonathan's character.

Scripture provides no indication that Saul is going out to do battle against the Philistines. Yet when David goes out to fight and comes back a hero, Saul is overcome with jealousy and anger. Perhaps Saul's powerful negative emotions are somehow connected with the arrival of the evil spirit that came upon him (19:9). As David is attempting to minister to Saul by playing the harp, Saul again tries to kill him with a spear, and again misses.

This time, however, Saul follows up by ordering a stakeout of David's home. Soldiers are ordered to kill David when he comes out in the morning. But Michal knows her father well and emphatically urges David to escape during the night. Her instincts are good. After David leaves, she uses a household idol and some goat hair to make it appear that David is sick in bed. By the time Saul's soldiers question her, hear her cover story, report to Saul, and return to find they have been deceived, David has had plenty of time to escape.

David goes to Ramah, where he finds Samuel and informs him of his experiences with Saul. The two of them then go to nearby Naioth, where apparently a number of prophets gathered. The king soon learns of David's whereabouts and sends three successive groups of soldiers to retrieve him. But each time, as soon as the group of soldiers approaches the group of prophets, the Spirit of God causes the soldiers to begin to prophesy. After three failed attempts, Saul decides to go in person to get David. But as he approaches, he too begins to prophesy, lying naked half the day and through the night. What had originally been a sign of God's endorsement of Saul as king of Israel (10:9–13) had become God's method of protecting His new choice of king. (We aren't told *what* Saul is prophesying, but could it possibly have included godly insight into Israel's next king?)

20:1–42

DAVID AND JONATHAN RECONNECT

David leaves Naioth and goes to see Jonathan. After a short initial conversation, the two friends discover that Saul is not being completely honest with either of them. To David's credit, he assumes potential blame for the problem with Saul. Jonathan can hardly believe his father was so intent on doing harm to David, but is immediately convinced by David's urgent persuasion.

Demystifying 1 Samuel

One might wonder why David flees from Naioth at Ramah (20:1). He had been pursued by three squads of Saul's soldiers, and then Saul himself. Yet while in the environment of Samuel and the other prophets, he appears to be untouchable. So it seems likely that rather than fleeing from Samuel, he is fleeing to Jonathan. Perhaps he simply needed a friend at this point in his life.

David also has a plan to confirm that what he is telling Jonathan is true. On the next day is a special festival (Numbers 10:10; 28:11–15) that David will be expected to attend with the members of Saul's family. He plans to be absent. If Saul asks why he isn't there, Jonathan will say that David's family in Bethlehem is making a special annual sacrifice and that David asked to be excused to be with them. It should be no big deal to Saul. If the king is to get angry, it is likely because he has malicious intent. Twice already David has dodged Saul's spear. He had escaped from Saul's soldiers, both in his own home and in Ramah with Samuel. It is only natural to be suspicious that perhaps Saul is looking for yet another opportunity to kill David.

Of course, if Saul does turn out to be angry, Jonathan needs a way to inform David. The gravity of the situation seems to register with Jonathan at this point. Before even answering David, he waits until the two of them have gone to a nearby field, out of range of curious eyes and finely tuned ears. In the field, Jonathan can also point to landmarks as he explains what he intends to do. After speaking to Saul, Jonathan will shoot three arrows. If he yells to his assistant that the arrows are short of the mark, then all will be well and David will be safe. But if he remarks that they are beyond the mark, David needs to leave for his own safety (1 Samuel 20:18–23).

The first day of the festival goes by without incident. David isn't there, but Saul assumes he might be ceremonially unclean—unable to participate for some reason. But when David is gone again the second day, Saul asks Jonathan directly where David is. Jonathan gives Saul the excuse he and David had rehearsed. It is a reasonable, logical reason for David to be absent, but Saul goes into a rage, with his anger focused on Jonathan. He starts with offensive name-calling (20:30). Next he tries to enlist Jonathan's help in finding and killing David (20:31). And when Jonathan tries to reason with him instead, Saul hurls a spear at his own son, attempting to kill him (20:32–33). Saul's aggressive behavior removes any doubt Jonathan might have had about his intentions.

Jonathan's emotions reflect his maturity. He is supposed to be enjoying a feast, but has completely lost his appetite (20:34). He isn't feeling the humiliation his father had tried to heap on him or fear because of his father's rage. Instead, Jonathan is angry and grieved on David's behalf.

The next morning Jonathan goes out with a young boy to the place where he knows David is hiding and watching. He shoots an arrow and gives the verbal signal that lets David know Saul indeed wants him dead. The young lad retrieves the arrow, and Jonathan sends him back to the city.

Most likely, the plan had been for David to escape unnoticed into the forest, but both friends realize their lives will never be the same. If they ever see each other again, it will have to be in secret, and for only a brief time. So David comes out of hiding to say goodbye. Both are sorrowful, but David weeps more than Jonathan.

David's fleeing from Saul had always been temporary. But from this point on, he will never again sit at Saul's table, never play his harp to soothe the king's troubled spirit, never again fight for Saul in the Israelite army. David will be a fugitive constantly on the run. Yet he will know that the friendship he and Jonathan had forged will be ongoing, extending to their descendants forever (20:42).

Some people attempt to read more into this account than mere friendship between David and Jonathan, but there is no justification for doing so. David and Jonathan are two men who love each other as friends and brothers. There is no cause to suggest a relationship that is romantic, sexual, or homosexual.

Take It Home

In this section, Saul tries about a dozen times to kill David, including the times he throws his spear at him, sends soldiers out to get him, and sends him into dangerous battle conditions. If Saul had worked as hard to kill Israel's *enemies*, he would have been a much better military leader and king. But David was so devoted to serving God that he escaped every incident unscathed. While believers should never presume to have any kind of special protection from worldly pains and problems, an ongoing closeness to God can have a remarkably calming effect during hard times. God can provide a peace that transcends all understanding (Philippians 4:7).

1 SAMUEL 21:1–23:14

DAVID THE FUGITIVE

Priestly Support	21:1–9
Living on the Run	21:10–22:5
Saul's Wrath Intensifies	22:6–23
David Saves a City	23:1–14

Setting Up the Section

At one time, Saul had felt very warmly toward David, but the closeness ends soon after David's victory over Goliath. Saul's jealousy of David's instant fame creates a rift between David and Saul. Envy soon gives rise to outright hostility, with Saul attempting to kill David a number of times. David has become a fugitive, and this section describes a number of events that take place as Saul pursues him, still hoping to end his life.

21:1–9

PRIESTLY SUPPORT

David is a political refugee, a man without a country. He feels the pain of separation from his wife, from his position in Saul's administration, and from his friend, Jonathan. He is in continual danger, yet he maintains faith in God. It is a time of growth and preparation that will help prepare David for the day he will rule over Israel as God's anointed king.

He travels a few miles north and east of Jerusalem to Nob, the city of the priests. Ahimelech, the high priest, is no fool. He does not know about the schism that has formed between David and Saul, but he does know David is supposed to have a number of troops. When he sees David coming alone, he is troubled. But David has a story prepared. Aware of Saul's influence and potential for violence, David does not disclose all the details of his sudden appearance, perhaps hoping to avoid involving the priests in his feud with Saul. Instead, he tells Ahimelech he is on a secret mission for Saul, and that his men are hidden nearby. If Ahimelech doubts David's cover story, he has the tact not to say anything.

David then comes to the reason for his visit. First, he needs some provisions. The only food available is the showbread (Exodus 25:30)—sacred bread normally eaten only by the priests. Ahimelech is willing to share the bread with anyone who is ceremonially clean, and he gives David what is available. The gift is witnessed by the chief of Saul's shepherds, an Edomite named Doeg.

Next David asks Ahimelech for a weapon, which again may have raised the priest's eyebrows. What kind of soldier on a special mission would be without a sword or spear? At the time few weapons could be found in the entire kingdom—much less in the city of the priests. In fact, the only sword on the entire premises is the sword of Goliath, a trophy/memorial of the victory God gave Israel through David. It belongs to David anyway, so Ahimelech willingly gives it to him. David takes the sword and bread and promptly leaves.

21:10–22:5

LIVING ON THE RUN

David's next move is a bold one. He leaves Israel and goes into Philistine territory. In fact, the city of Gath is Goliath's hometown, and David boldly enters carrying Goliath's sword. The Israelites had recently pursued fleeing Philistines right up to the cities of Gath and Ekron (17:51–52), leaving bodies in their wake, but this time David is a political refugee seeking asylum from King Achish. The fact that David is willing to take such a risk illustrates how strongly Saul desires to kill David. Yet whatever David's reasons for going to Gath, it becomes quite obvious that God doesn't want him there. It is not unusual for kings to receive political refugees from nearby nations (1 Kings 11:40; 2 Kings 25:27–30). If they are given sanctuary, they might become grateful allies, if not loyal subjects. But if those are Achish's thoughts, his servants quickly bring him back to reality. David has killed the Philistine hero, Goliath, and people have written songs about him (1 Samuel 21:10–11).

Critical Observation

In both 21:10–15 and chapters 27–29, the Philistine leader Achish is presented as gullible and less than astute. Somehow, he takes a liking to David. He seems overly confident of David's loyalty to him and of his value as an ally. He does not willingly entertain thoughts that David may still be a loyal Israelite, soon to take the throne of Israel.

While Achish begins to rethink his offer of sanctuary, David also gives some thought to *his* predicament. If Achish takes the advice of his people seriously, he might have David put to death. So David feigns madness, slobbering and scribbling on the gates.

Achish is convinced. He hadn't wanted to kill David in the first place, and if the Israelite poses no threat, there is no need to do him harm. The Philistines are glad to get rid of David, and by then David appears ready to leave. He escapes with his life, but not with his dignity.

David leaves Philistine territory and goes into Judah, but just barely. The exact site of the cave of Adullam (22:1) is unknown but appears to have been a safe, secluded hideout not too close to either Gath or King Saul. Word begins to spread that David is there. Among the first to find him are his family members. They are soon joined by Israelites who are in distress, in debt, or out of favor with Saul. They come to David as their new leader, despite the danger of being associated with him. He soon has a band of about four hundred people.

His next stop is the territory of Moab, where he arranges for his elderly parents to stay. Moab is out of Saul's realm of influence, and it had been the homeland of Ruth, David's great-grandmother (Ruth 1:4; 4:13–17). The move appears to put David's parents out of harm's way during the years he is fleeing from Saul.

A prophet named Gad then directs David back to Judah from the land of Moab. The location of the forest of Hereth is not entirely clear, but forests could be dangerous and forbidding places, especially for soldiers (2 Samuel 18:8).

22:6–23

SAUL'S WRATH INTENSIFIES

Word of David's movements are bound to reach Saul eventually. The scene in this passage is a somewhat sinister one, with Saul seated under a tree in his hometown, spear in hand and ranting to nearby officials. He blames them for everything. He had found out too late about Jonathan's covenant with David. Even worse, he accuses them of conspiring against him.

But Saul's chief shepherd, Doeg, speaks up with some information that Saul might find useful. He had seen David in Nob, receiving help from Ahimelech and the priests. Doeg tells Saul that he had seen Ahimelech equip David with provisions and Goliath's sword. These things are true. And from Doeg's observation that David had inquired of the Lord (22:10), it would seem that the reason David went to Nob was primarily to seek God's will by using the Urim and Thummim in the priest's ephod (Exodus 28:30).

But what Doeg *doesn't* say (and perhaps he does not know) is that David never informed the priests that he was fleeing from Saul. Neither David nor the priests had ever said or done anything to conspire against the king. But Saul's blinding jealousy and devotion to protecting his throne took precedence over getting the facts straight.

Saul doesn't even need to move; he has all the priests summoned to appear before him. In his mind, Ahimelech and all the other priests are already guilty of conspiracy.

It should have been the responsibility of the priests to enlighten Saul and others in Israel about the judgments of God. But here it is Saul who presumes to pass judgment on the entire priesthood. The king had shown little respect for the priesthood in the past when he offered sacrifices himself instead of waiting for Samuel (13:7–14). Here he shows outright disdain by not even using the priest's name in the conversation (22:12). He doesn't even ask *if* Ahimelech has betrayed him, but *why*.

With remarkable poise, Ahimelech speaks on David's behalf, reminding Saul that David is the king's most faithful servant, honored by the people, the one whom Saul had appointed to positions of authority, and, in fact, Saul's son-in-law. Ahimelech also speaks in his own defense. Yes, he had assisted David, but it wasn't the first time. Ahimelech knows he has done nothing inappropriate, and he knows Saul has no idea what has actually gone on in Nob.

However, Saul is not listening to reason. His mind is apparently already made up. He commands his guards to kill Ahimelech and all the other priests. But no one moves. As much as these men fear Saul, they are not willing to act on his heinous command. Saul then turns to Doeg, a non-Israelite, who doesn't appear to have the same qualms about killing God's priests. But he and Saul don't stop with that terrible crime. Doeg then travels to Nob where he also kills the priests' families and cattle. Eighty-five priests die that day. And how ironic it is that while Saul had defied God's order to annihilate the people and property of the Amalekites (15:1–3, 7–9), he readily wipes out his own spiritual leaders.

Only one priest escapes Saul's wrath: one of Ahimelech's sons named Abiathar. He runs to David and tells him what Saul has done. David assumes full responsibility. He had seen Doeg at Nob, but who could have predicted how far Saul would go in his hatred of David? David could do nothing more for those who had been killed, but he does offer sanctuary to Abiathar.

23:1–14

DAVID SAVES A CITY

David learns that the Philistines are looting a town near their border called Keilah. The problem *should* have been Saul's concern (9:16), but David is already thinking like the king of Israel. Thankfully, when Abiathar fled from Nob, he had taken the high priestly ephod with him. With a priest and the ephod, David can receive God's direction for what to do. After he gets instructions to rescue Keilah, he asks again to be sure. His men aren't eager to come out of hiding to go fight in the open where they will be targets for Saul's army as well as the Philistines.

Still, they go to Keilah. By now David has six hundred followers—a ragtag group of discontents who have fled from Saul (22:2). They aren't trained soldiers, yet they win a decisive victory.

Their fears about Saul prove to be valid, however. Saul learns of David's whereabouts and is pleased to discover that David is in a city with gates and bars. Those protections won't keep Saul out for long, but they will keep David trapped. When David gets word of Saul's intent, he again has Abiathar bring the ephod to consult God. One would think that the citizens of Keilah would be grateful to David and offer him some protection. But God lets him know that Saul is indeed on his way and that the people of Keilah will turn him over to Saul when the king arrives. So before that can happen, David leaves.

Demystifying 1 Samuel

When David seeks direction from the Lord, the answers he receives are hypothetical. For example, God tells him that he will be turned over to Saul, but that is conditional on his staying in the city. He can take action to avoid that ominous result. After David leaves with his men, Saul doesn't bother making the trip. But if David had remained in Keilah, both of God's messages would have come to pass: Saul would have gone to the city, and the city's inhabitants would have handed David over to Saul. It is overwhelming to consider that God not only knows all things that will be, but He also knows all things that *could* be, under any set of circumstances. He is both in control of every situation (sovereign), and He knows all the options of each one (omniscient).

David takes his troops to the desert where they can hide in various strongholds and hilly areas. Saul keeps looking for him, but God is watching over him, and Saul is never able to find him.

Take It Home

David's world is much like our own in terms of spiritual action and risk. Many people tend to be like David's followers, believing that safety is best achieved by isolation or by hiding out from the dangers of the world. But David knew he could calculate his safety in terms of his nearness to God. Believers should not seek to hide when God calls them to be salt and light in dark places, even though risk is still involved. Believers are not immune to the injustices of the world, as Ahimelech and his priests discovered. However, no one is safer than the believer who trusts and obeys God, even during the most dangerous of circumstances.

1 SAMUEL 23:15–26:25

A FUGITIVE MODELS MERCY, PATIENCE, AND FORGIVENESS

A Brief Reunion	23:15–18
A Narrow Escape	23:19–29
David's Ideal Opportunity #1	24:1–22
A Great Loss	25:1
A Rich Fool and His Wise Wife	25:2–44
David's Ideal Opportunity #2	26:1–25

Setting Up the Section

David has been hiding from Saul, moving from place to place to avoid being killed. People are beginning to support his leadership, and he has already freed one city from a threatening Philistine presence. In this section, we see David's faith in God

demonstrated in a number of difficult situations. His dependence on God allows him to show forgiveness to those who offend him and repeated mercy to the person who is most eager to see him dead—King Saul.

23:15–18

A BRIEF REUNION

At this point in David's life, his outlook must have been a bit dark and foreboding. He had gone from the champion who slew Goliath to Israel's most-wanted fugitive. He had recently received help from the high priest, and as a result, eighty-five priests and their families had been killed at Saul's order. He had come out of hiding to save a city from Philistine attack, only to discover that the people were quite willing to turn him over to Saul. While on the run from Saul's forces, he was trying to ensure the safety of his family and followers. It had to be an emotionally and physically challenging time.

David has just gotten word that Saul has again pinpointed his location and is on the way. The location of Horesh is unknown, but the Hebrew word means "forest," so it is presumed that David is in a forested area in the Wilderness of Ziph. With all the bad news he has been receiving and the uncertainty of his day-to-day situation, what a pleasant surprise it must have been when Jonathan shows up unexpectedly. Not much is said of their reunion, but what is said is significant.

Jonathan does all he can to affirm David. It is more than a pep talk; he helps David renew his strength in God (23:16). Jonathan encourages David not to be afraid. Yes, Saul is doing everything in his power to find and kill David. But Jonathan—and even Saul—realizes that God is protecting David because David is certain to be the next king of Israel. Jonathan reaffirms that he is secondary to David—his most loyal servant and supporter.

David and Jonathan conclude their short meeting with another covenant, or perhaps a renewal of their earlier one (18:3; 20:16–17). Then Jonathan returns home while David goes back into hiding.

23:19–29

A NARROW ESCAPE

At this time some of the locals (the Ziphites) report David's location to King Saul. Perhaps they want to curry his favor, or maybe they simply want to avoid his anger. But their willingness to betray David is particularly grievous because they, too, are from the tribe of Judah.

Upon receiving the report from the Ziphites, Saul responds with pious-sounding language (23:21). Yet his holy-sounding words are only a front for the wickedness of his intended actions. Such misuse of God's name is one way of taking God's name in vain—a violation of the third commandment (Exodus 20:7).

This time Saul doesn't go rushing out with his army. David has escaped his efforts several times already, and it won't look good to come back empty-handed. Instead, he instructs the Ziphites to watch David closely, making note of his habits and hiding places. When he feels the time is right, Saul makes the journey himself.

David is told of Saul's intention (1 Samuel 23:25), and he moves on a few miles to the desert of Maon. The situation again looks bleak for David as Saul's forces are coming around a mountain and gaining on him. But Jonathan had been right. Saul will not lay a hand on David (23:17). As it seems that David and his forces have no way of escape, a messenger appears to tell Saul that the Philistines are attacking and his help is needed. Saul responds immediately, allowing David to escape again. This location becomes known as the Rock of Parting (23:28), and David moves on to En Gedi where there are protective strongholds.

24:1–22

DAVID'S IDEAL OPPORTUNITY #1

As soon as Saul deals with the Philistines, he returns to his pursuit of David. He takes three thousand trained soldiers to fight David's six hundred men. But before Saul has even found David, he stops at a cave to have some privacy for a restroom break. Little does Saul know that he has chosen the very cave where David and his men are hiding.

Perhaps David's crew grew fearful as the king approached their hiding place because they were trapped and had no place to go. If so, however, their fears are soon alleviated as they discover why Saul has entered the cave. Saul has probably thrown his robe aside for the moment, and David uses the cover of darkness to slip over and cut off a piece of cloth. David's soldiers want to do much more, of course. They are surely weary of being on the run and in perpetual danger, and they interpret the remarkable coincidence of Saul's appearance—alone and defenseless—as God's way of delivering David's enemy into his hands.

Critical Observation

In light of David's subsequent remorse (24:5), some people have interpreted his slashing of Saul's robe as an intentional act of defiance that symbolically challenges or undermines Saul's right to rule. That conjecture doesn't seem to be supported by the facts, however. David has nothing but respect for Saul in this passage. More likely, he came to realize that what had been intended as a trivial action had greater weight because it was committed against his king. By raising his hand against God's king, David feels he has raised his hand against God. To David's credit, he doesn't merely persuade or rebuke his men (24:7) when they want to kill Saul. The original word means "tear apart." David tears into his men (verbally), insisting that none of them will harm the king.

They are surely perplexed when David refuses to take advantage of the situation to kill Saul. Even more astounding is what David does next. All they have to do is keep quiet for a few minutes until Saul and his troops go on their way. But David follows Saul from the cave, out into the light, abandoning all efforts at self-protection or evasion. David addresses Saul first as his lord the king (24:8) and later as father (24:11). He shows reverence and submission to Saul. He appeals to Saul to set aside any rumors he might have heard and to judge David's guilt or innocence for himself, based on David's actions.

Saul must have been shocked to hear a familiar voice from behind. He quickly determines that David is not seeking his defeat or death. David isn't attempting to gain the throne by removing Saul from it. Saul can also see the sliver of his robe in David's hands. His life had been in David's hands, and now David is placing his life in Saul's hands. David quotes a proverb to assure Saul he has no evil intent (24:13), and he likens himself to a dead dog or a single flea (24:24)—no threat at all to Saul and his kingdom. Then David rests his case, looking to God for justice and protection, and waits for Saul's response.

Saul begins to weep, responding to David's affectionate address (my father) by calling him his son (24:16). And for the first time, Saul acknowledges the truth. He had heard from Samuel that his kingdom will not endure (13:14) and that God has rejected him as Israel's king (15:26). He had seen that David's popularity could easily allow David to possess his kingdom (18:8–9). He had privately admitted that as long as David was alive, Jonathan would never become king (20:31). Yet he had resisted all those truths, treating David as a traitor to the nation and pursuing him with the intent of killing him. Here, however, Saul publicly admits that God is taking his kingdom away from him and that David's ascent to the throne is a certainty.

In light of this reality, Saul wants David to swear that he will not kill off all of Saul's descendants. It is common practice of the time for new kings to kill off every other possible heir to the throne—especially descendants of the preceding king. Saul doesn't realize that David has already made that promise to Jonathan (20:14–17, 41–42). Nevertheless, David affirms to Saul that he will not destroy all of his descendants.

Saul goes home, but David returns to his stronghold. He is probably hoping that his troubles with Saul are over, but he knows Saul's previous instances of repentance hadn't lasted long (19:1–7). David will remain at a safe distance to see what Saul's long-term response will be. Then again, David's intent may have been for Saul's benefit as well. If the people are ready to turn to David rather than Saul, David's remaining out of the public eye will not prematurely undermine Saul's popularity.

25:1

A GREAT LOSS

The death of Samuel is succinctly summarized at this point—without much fanfare, considering his significance to the nation. He had listened to and followed God from childhood. He had defended the people against the Philistines (7:7–14). He served as judge throughout his life (7:15). He had designated and anointed Saul as Israel's first king. He also spoke with God's authority to inform Saul that his kingship was going to be taken away. He anointed David as Saul's successor and was a source of wisdom and comfort for David during Saul's pursuit (19:18–24). The Israelites mourn Samuel's death and bury him in his hometown of Ramah.

Samuel's death must have been particularly hard on David, who had just said good-bye to Jonathan for the last time (23:18) and had left his parents in care of the king of Moab (22:3). He will eventually discover that while he was keeping his distance from Saul, the king had taken David's wife Michal and given her to another man (25:44). And David is about to encounter other problems.

25:2–44

A RICH FOOL AND HIS WISE WIFE

Since David is going from place to place with a following of at least six hundred (23:13), they can't remain in complete isolation. They are bound to run into various people from time to time, and this passage describes one such encounter. David's group is staying in the desert where they come to know some shepherds in the service of a rich man named Nabal. It is sheep-shearing season, when the work is followed by a time of celebration and relaxation.

David sends ten of his group to Nabal to report that they have been treating Nabal's shepherds with great respect and to ask for any provisions Nabal could spare. However, Nabal refuses to acknowledge that David's men have helped protect his shepherds and their flocks. He doesn't even send a token gift. Instead, he insults David, inferring that he is no better than a runaway slave, and he sends the messengers back empty-handed.

Demystifying 1 Samuel

Nabal's insensitivity to David's crew is made worse in light of some of the facts he reveals. If David were an absolute stranger, Nabal might have been somewhat justified in rejecting his request. But he knew David was the son of Jesse (25:10), and Nabal himself was a Calebite (25:3). Caleb had been from the tribe of Judah (Numbers 13:6), as was Jesse. So Nabal must have realized that he and David were distant relatives, yet arrogantly denied him anything, even though much food would have been on hand for the sheep-shearing celebrations.

When David is told what transpired with Nabal, he becomes irate. David has acted honorably. His men could easily have taken whatever they needed from Nabal's flocks, but had not done so. David expected a positive response in return for his positive actions. When he determines that Nabal is being unjust, David determines to achieve justice himself. He orders his men to arm themselves, and he sets out to kill Nabal and every male in his household (25:12–13, 22).

David had tolerated Saul's mistreatment, but Saul was the anointed king of Israel. David considers himself Saul's servant, in spite of Saul's inappropriate behavior. Nabal is a different story. Nabal is not David's superior, and David does not appreciate the demeaning treatment he has received. Furthermore, David is not thinking or behaving as a man of faith as he sets out to kill Nabal and all the males associated with him. He is eager to take action in response to how he is feeling.

Nabal would have suffered dire consequences had it not been for his wise wife, Abigail. One of Nabal's servants had gone to her with an account of what had happened, including a warning that David is likely to retaliate. She wastes no time gathering generous portions of food (bread, wine, grain, raisins, figs, and sheep), packing everything on donkeys, and sending it ahead to David. (One might wonder how she could gather so much food so quickly. The timing is convenient because Nabal had planned a fit-for-a-king banquet [25:36]. He probably never missed what Abigail sent to David.)

Abigail works her way down the mountain, out of sight of David and his men. David likewise comes from higher ground, still grumbling about Nabal's insults and rehearsing what he will do when he finds the ungrateful despot. Without either party realizing what is happening, David and Abigail converge and suddenly find themselves face-to-face with each other.

Abigail is everything Nabal is not: polite, well-spoken, submissive, honest, and ready to take responsibility and blame. Six times she refers to herself as David's maidservant, and fourteen times she calls David her lord. She doesn't try to cover for her husband; she calls him a fool (25:25), and in doing so she may have saved his life. David knows from experience there is no honor or status in killing fools. Perhaps Abigail's comment prompts him to recall feigning insanity while in Philistine territory, which caused the citizens to perceive him as non-threatening. Abigail isn't attempting to exaggerate her husband's faults through name-calling: *Nabal* literally means "fool," and there is little doubt that he lives up to the name.

Next Abigail tactfully points out how taking vengeance will be detrimental to David. God had prevented him from shedding blood for personal revenge (25:26). Abigail acknowledges the hand of God on David, and she exhorts him to avoid wrongdoing (25:28–31). She pleads with David to accept the gift she has brought and asks him to forgive *her* transgression.

Abigail's words stop David in his tracks. He knows she is right, and he praises her in front of his men. She has literally been a godsend, used by God to prevent David from taking vengeance on Nabal and shedding other innocent blood. Had she not acted so quickly, David would have carried out his plan. He thankfully accepts her gift and sends her home in peace.

David leaves vengeance in God's hands, and it comes rather quickly. Nabal is drunk when Abigail gets home, so she waits until the next morning to tell him about her encounter with David. Upon hearing the news, his heart fails, and he dies ten days later.

David rejoices in the news, not so much that Nabal is dead, but that thanks to Abigail, David hadn't acted hastily and done something he would always regret (25:39). And David wastes no time asking Abigail to marry him. Her action had been selfless, and it is quickly rewarded.

During this time, Saul has a change of heart and is about to take up the pursuit of David once more. He even gives his daughter Michal (David's wife) to another man while David is gone. But David's marriage to Abigail counteracts Saul's action. Whatever Saul attempts to deny David, God will amply provide.

26:1–25

DAVID'S IDEAL OPPORTUNITY #2

The events of this section are similar to those of 1 Samuel 24, so much so that some people have suggested it is an alternative account of the same incident. In both cases Saul is pursuing David after being informed of his location by the Ziphites, and in both instances Saul has three thousand men. These are not unusual repetitions. If the Ziphites gained Saul's favor for giving him David's location once, it shouldn't be surprising if they do so again. And it's reasonable to assume that Saul's army is three thousand strong (13:2). Other details of this second account are quite different from the previous one.

David's first close encounter with Saul had been in a cave where David was hiding. This time David seeks out Saul's position and finds him out in the open, asleep and surrounded by his entire army. Saul and Abner, the commander of his army, are in the center of a large circle. David doesn't realize that the entire army is in a divinely induced slumber (26:12), yet he is willing to approach the king anyway. He and a volunteer, Abishai, walk through the sleeping soldiers, right up to Saul. The king's spear is stuck in the ground nearby, and his water jug is near his head.

Abishai is a stouthearted soldier (2 Samuel 23:18–19). Every instinct tells him to take the spear and do away with Saul with one good thrust. After the cave incident, perhaps Abishai thinks David might be squeamish about killing Saul, and he is more than willing to do the job himself. But David had not spared Saul out of fear, but out of respect for the king's position and reverence for God's right to remove the king whenever He deems that the time is right. In addition, David's recent encounter with Abigail may have strengthened his resolve not to be hasty in bloodshed. He tells Abishai to take Saul's spear and water jug, and they go to a neighboring hillside, within earshot of the Israelite army.

David shouts over, but to Abner, not Saul. As commander of the army, Abner is primarily responsible for Saul's protection. David points out the absence of the spear and water jug, and he makes it clear that if his intent had been to destroy the king, Saul would be dead by now. Indeed, David prevented Saul's murder by Abishai, making him a more reliable defender of Saul than anyone else in Israel.

Still groggy, Saul finally recognizes the voice as David's and calls over to him. David then begins to address Saul, giving a personal defense much as he had done previously (1 Samuel 24:8–15; 26:17–20). In essence, David accuses the king of listening to other people who endeavored to make David serve other gods. (As soon as someone left Israelite soil, he or she was quickly exposed to the various gods of the various peoples of the area, and David was being kept away from his community of worship.)

Saul again is quick to confess and repent. He invites David to return. David arranges for someone to come over and retrieve Saul's property. Then the king goes home as David again goes on his way, no doubt anticipating another encounter.

Take It Home

This section contains repeated illustrations of mercy in light of what many would consider reasonable justice. The most obvious examples are perhaps the two times David spares Saul's life when it would have been just as convenient to kill him. Less apparent, but just as emphatic, is Abigail's confrontation with David. Her example is nothing less than an illustration of Christ's salvation for humankind: She saw that many were about to die, she took immediate action that did not personally benefit her in any way, she took the blame upon herself, and she appeased the wrath of one about to judge. Even David's actions in the final story reflect mercy and salvation. Had Saul been put to death that night, Abner and all the rest would have been guilty of failing to protect their king. In that sense, David saves not only Saul's life, but also those of all the soldiers. Such stories should inspire each reader of scripture to act with greater effort to extend mercy and grace to others in life's everyday encounters.

1 SAMUEL 27:1–31:13

THE FINAL DAYS OF KING SAUL

Setting Up the Section

After Saul is told his kingdom is being removed by God and given to another, a considerable amount of time passes before the prediction is fulfilled. In the meantime, David has already been anointed to take Saul's place. Although Saul is trying hard to put David to death, David has twice had Saul's life in his hands and refused to harm him. But after long months of conflict and turbulence, Saul finally runs out of time—seemingly farther away from God than ever. The book of 1 Samuel concludes with his death and burial.

27:1–28:2

DAVID'S PHILISTINE QUANDARY

David has just gotten a reprieve from Saul's persistent pursuit (26:21), but he knows it will only be a matter of time until Saul renews the manhunt. Until this point, David has been sounding confident and faithful (24:15; 26:23–24), and Abigail confirmed those qualities (25:28–29). David's change of heart (27:1) is not explained.

If David primarily wants to stop worrying about Saul, he succeeds. After he arranges with King Achish to live in Philistine territory, David has no more trouble from Saul. However, the move will soon create other problems.

David had hidden out among the Philistines before (21:10–15). He survived, but left the city perceived as a scribbling, slobbering lunatic. This time he is not alone; he has his six hundred men, their wives and families, and his own two wives. At first their accommodations seem ideal. Achish gives David the city of Ziklag, where his group resides. Ziklag is about twenty-five miles from Gath, so Achish won't be privy to David's every activity.

David and his men regularly fight enemies of Israel, killing all the people (to eliminate any witnesses) and accumulating livestock and clothing. Anytime Achish asks about their raids, David tells him they have been fighting the Israelites. It also appears David may have given Achish a portion of the spoils (27:9). In time, Achish comes to trust David. He assumes that David can never go home again, and it seems that Achish will always benefit from having David as an ally.

During this time David's life is relatively carefree. He goes wherever he wants, he associates with the king, he has no fear of Saul or Israelites who might betray him, he and his men live well on the spoils of his raids, and he keeps reducing the influence of the enemies of Israel. His life is good, that is, until one day when King Achish decides to join a larger Philistine coalition marching against Israel, and he enlists David's help. Though taken by surprise, David tells Achish what he wants to hear, and the king responds by bestowing David an honored position (28:2). How amazing that David has gone from being armor-bearer for King Saul (16:21) to being bodyguard for a Philistine king. Of course, now David has the dilemma of how to keep from actually fighting against Israel without Achish discovering his true loyalties.

28:3–25

SAUL'S PHILISTINE PROBLEM (AND UNUSUAL SOURCE OF ADVICE)

Before the writer of Samuel relates the rest of David's story, he shifts to some problems Saul is having in the meantime. The Philistines have harassed the Israelites throughout Saul's lifetime, but this time they seem determined to break Israel's resolve once and for all. It appears their strategy is to divide and conquer by separating Israel's forces and then focusing on the northern and southern halves independently. The numbers of the Philistine forces are staggering, and Saul may have also heard that David was among them. Samuel is now dead, and Saul receives no guidance from the Lord. God doesn't provide an enlightening dream. He doesn't send a prophet. The priests can't even discern God's will with the Urim and Thummim in the priestly ephod (28:6).

Demystifying 1 Samuel

This account of the story says that Saul inquires of the Lord (28:6); the Chronicles account says he does *not* inquire of the Lord (1 Chronicles 10:13–14). Based on Saul's previous spiritual habits, one has to wonder if this inquiry is less a genuine desire to know God's will than a desperate attempt to get God to bail him out of the trouble he has gotten himself into. Either way, he receives no answer.

Saul's uneasiness progresses from fear to terror to sheer panic, and he doesn't always make good choices when he is under pressure (13:7–14). This time he hits a new low. Even though he has been responsible for removing everyone involved in occult practices (28:9), he decides to find a medium and seek some direction. His prior action had been in compliance with God's law (Leviticus 19:31, 20:6, 27; Deuteronomy 18:10–14), so this decision reflects clear disregard for God's will.

His servants know of a medium, but it isn't easy for Saul to arrange a meeting. Getting to her location requires an eight-mile trek from Gilboa to En-Dor (at risk of encountering the Philistines). Saul's disguise (1 Samuel 28:8) serves a couple of purposes. If he runs into enemy soldiers, he certainly doesn't want to be identified as the king of Israel. Nor does he want the medium to discover who he is. Since she is working undercover, she is already suspicious of anyone she doesn't know—and he is the one who has forced her underground.

But after arriving, his secret identity doesn't last long. Saul asks the woman to contact Samuel, but when she does, she grows alarmed. Her response suggests that this is no ordinary conjuring. She immediately discerns Saul's identity, and she sees Samuel as a divine being (28:13) coming up out of the ground. (Other Bible versions translate the Hebrew word as *spirit* or *god*.)

Saul falls on the ground before Samuel, and the two have a short conversation. Saul wants to know what to do. Samuel has frequently spoken to Saul for God, and his messages have been consistent: Because of Saul's disobedience, he is going to lose his kingdom (13:13–14; 15:27–29). If Saul is hoping for a different message this time, he is sorely disappointed. In fact, Samuel says that the next day the Philistines will soundly defeat the Israelites, and Saul and his sons will be with him (28:19).

Saul hasn't eaten all day, and the news literally floors him. The medium is still worried because her client has been the king, but she musters the courage to offer him a meal. He refuses at first, but his companions convince him to eat before returning home.

29:1–11

DAVID'S PROVIDENTIAL SOLUTION

At this point the flow of 1 Samuel returns to David's dilemma. Not only are David and his men marching out with Philistine King Achish to do battle against Israel, but they are honored with the crucial position of rear guard, where the bravest and most highly skilled warriors are placed (29:2). Apparently each of the five key Philistine cities had its own king and troops. But this time the Philistines are combining forces to march against Israel.

When the other leaders discover that King Achish has included David among his troops, they are incensed. They feel that Achish is being deceived (which he is), and that David will be a real threat if the Philistines go into battle and he starts fighting for Israel. They even remind Achish of the song that has been written about David concerning how many people he has killed (29:5), and they insist that David return to Ziklag.

In an almost comical scene, the Philistine king gives David the disappointing news that he will not be allowed to fight against Israel. Achish even invokes the name of David's God (Yahweh) in praise of David. With the matter already settled by the Philistines, David even protests their decision (29:8). In reality, it is the best thing that could have happened to extract him from a delicate situation.

Critical Observation

It might not have been the best idea for David to hide out among the Philistines, especially after his deceit of Achish was about to be exposed. It seems clear that God is working to deliver David from a dilemma of his own creation. Yet it is left to the reader to acknowledge God's deliverance in this situation. The only person who actually talks about God in this passage is the Philistine king (29:6).

30:1–31

DAVID AND THE AMALEKITES

David and his men must have celebrated all the way back to Ziklag. But approaching their base city, the group sees, and perhaps smells, smoke. On arrival, they find the city burned. Missing are all their family members and livestock, and many of their possessions. Their initial emotion, naturally, is grief. They all weep until they have no more strength. But the next emotion is bitterness, and they begin to blame David for all that has gone wrong. They even talk of stoning him (30:6).

But this event seems to turn David back to God (30:6). He calls for the priest and the ephod to determine whether God will have them pursue the raiders. God assures him of success in rescuing everything.

The trouble is that David's group had been physically challenged during the almost sixty-mile march from Aphek back to Ziklag. Then the emotional toll of finding their city in ruins and families absent makes things worse. Not everyone is up to marching off with David right away. They all start, but a third of them are too exhausted to continue. The other two-thirds leave some of their gear with the two hundred staying behind in order to move faster (30:24).

The trail is indeed cold. David doesn't even know whom he is chasing. But then his men find an Egyptian slave who hasn't had food or water for three days. They feed him and discover it had been the Amalekites who had raided Ziklag. After being promised protection, the Egyptian even agrees to lead David to the Amalekite camp.

The timing couldn't have been better. When David's men arrive, the much larger group of Amalekites is celebrating their easy conquest—drinking and disorganized. David and his men attack, resulting in a slaughter that lasts many hours. Four hundred young men escape on camels, but every other Amalekite soldier is killed. The next day David recovers *everything* that had been taken from Ziklag—wives, families, animals, and possessions—not to mention plunder from the Amalekites.

When David's fighting men return, there are those among them who don't want to share the plunder they have accumulated with the two hundred men who remained behind (30:22). But David steps in and sees that his soldiers all get equal shares. In addition, David sends some of their new wealth to friends and elders at various places throughout Judah (30:26–31). His decision will have far-reaching effects. Many of the recipients are men of considerable influence who will soon be among the first to embrace David as king.

31:1–13

THE DEATHS OF SAUL AND HIS SONS

As has already been shown several times in 1 Samuel, when life is going well for David, it is taking a downturn for Saul. The book concludes with one final, graphic example. At about the time that David is in pursuit of the Amalekite raiders, Saul and the Israelite army are fighting the Philistines. David returns with only good news, but the Israelites are soundly defeated. Among the casualties are Saul and his sons (31:2–3). News of the defeat causes neighboring Israelites to flee the area and allow the Philistines to inhabit their cities (31:7), so the loss of the battle not only reduces the size of Israel's army, but also reduces the size of Israel.

Saul is critically wounded and asks his armor-bearer to kill him so he will avoid any torment by his enemies. His armor-bearer is afraid and refuses, so Saul falls on his own sword. The armor-bearer follows suit. A passing Amalekite later takes credit for delivering the death blow to Saul (2 Samuel 1:8–10), though he might have been lying in hopes of receiving a reward from David.

When the Philistines discover Saul's body, they cut off his head, place his armor in the temple of Ashtoreth, and hang his body on the wall of one of their cities. But the inhabitants of Jabesh-gilead remember how Saul had previously kept them from humiliation at the hands of the Ammonites (1 Samuel 11:1–11). When they hear what has happened to Saul, many of their brave men march through the night, retrieve the bodies of Saul and his sons, and return them to Israel for a proper burial. Saul's boldness toward the Ammonites at Jabesh had been his finest hour, and it was not forgotten by those whom he had saved.

The book of 1 Samuel appears to end rather abruptly at this point, because 1 Samuel and 2 Samuel were originally one single book. So the story will continue as 2 Samuel begins.

Take It Home

The final contrasts between David and Saul in this passage highlight the significance of the daily decisions we make, especially as they pertain to spiritual development. Saul makes a series of choices that are not quite obedient to what God has instructed him to do. He has moments of clarity where he sees that he is wrong, yet he never makes a conscious decision to get back on the right path. Eventually, he turns to the occult for guidance and ends up committing suicide. David, on the other hand, tries to consciously make the right decisions even when it is difficult to do so. Both Saul and David face suffering and difficulty, and both have their failures. But because David is slow to anger, quick to repent, and perseveres in his faith, he and Saul come to quite different ends.

2 SAMUEL

INTRODUCTION TO 2 SAMUEL

AUTHOR

There is no mention of the author in the book of Samuel, though Jewish tradition states that Samuel wrote the first twenty-four chapters of what was originally one book of Samuel. In fact, 1 and 2 Samuel and 1 and 2 Kings are thought to be a single historical work edited by the same theological circle during the exile.

PURPOSE

This book tells the story of how David sets out to establish his throne with God's blessing following King Saul's death. David is a man after God's own heart, but he is still simply a man with real shortcomings, and his sin with Bathsheba has a myriad of truly tragic consequences. The text recounts the events of the second half of King David's life during which his reign unites Israel and testifies to God's faithfulness to His servant David and to all His children.

OCCASION

The book of 1 Samuel ends tragically, with King Saul a virtual madman. He turns against David, his loyal servant and friend, and seeks to kill David as though he is a traitor. He fails to obey God's Word, and so brings about his own downfall and demise. Saul even goes so far as to consult with a medium. The closing chapter of 1 Samuel is the account of his death at the hand of the Philistines and his own hand as well. As sad as it is, we breathe a sigh of relief, for now David's days of fleeing from Saul as a fugitive are over. Second Samuel starts immediately afterward to tell how David will reign in Saul's place.

THEMES

Second Samuel is a study in contrasts—of the blessing and curse of power, of the sinfulness that is present even in God's greatest servants, and of the power that temptation, lust, and covetousness have against even the mightiest kings. In this book we are reminded of how even a man of God can fail in major ways, including adultery and murder. And yet, we are struck again and again by God's forgiveness and grace even in the midst of some harsh consequences from David's sinfulness. The resounding theme of 2 Samuel is that even the greatest world leaders must remember that the kingdom, the power, and the glory belong to the Lord alone.

HISTORICAL CONTEXT

Israel is divided when David first comes to power, thanks to the intrigue of men like Abner and Joab. This division is a foreshadowing of future times for the nation of Israel. It is not without some challenge that David becomes king of all Israel.

CONTRIBUTION TO THE BIBLE

Second Samuel leaves us with an appreciation for the greatness of David and also a realization of his human weaknesses. If there is to be a king who will dwell forever on the throne of David (2 Samuel 7:12–14), it must be one who is greater than David. If David is the best king who ever ruled over Israel, then God will have to provide a better king. And so He will; Jesus is the perfect king that David cannot be.

OUTLINE

THE DEATH OF A MENTOR AND A FRIEND 1:1–27

News of Saul and Jonathan's Deaths 1:1–16
David's Lament 1:17–27

DAVID BECOMES KING 2:1–32

David Anointed King over Judah 2:1–11
War with the House of Saul 2:12–32

KING DAVID'S HOUSE 3:1–39

Taking Sides 3:1–21
Joab Murders Abner 3:22–39

WAITING ON THE LORD 4:1–12

DAVID: KING OF ISRAEL 5:1–25

Jerusalem: A Place of One's Own 5:1–16
David Defeats the Philistines 5:17–25

GOD RAINED ON DAVID'S PARADE 6:1–23

The Ark Brought to Jerusalem 6:1–15
Judging Joy 6:16–23

BUILDING GOD'S HOUSE 7:1–29

God's Promise to David 7:1–17
David's Prayer 7:18–29

WAR AND PEACE 8:1–10:19

David's Victories 8:1–18
David and Mephibosheth 9:1–13
David Defeats the Ammonites 10:1–19

2 SAMUEL 1:1–27

THE DEATH OF A MENTOR AND A FRIEND

Setting Up the Section

David and his men are certainly grateful for the defeat of the Amalekites and the recovery of their families and possessions. But this victory must be overshadowed by David's concern for what is taking place in Israel. When David left Achish to return to Ziklag, the Philistines had mounted a massive fighting force to attack Israel. David knows very well how awesome this military effort is, because he and his men marched in review at the end of the procession. On his third day back in Ziklag, a young man approaches David with news of Israel's defeat.

1:1–16

NEWS OF SAUL AND JONATHAN'S DEATHS

From the time he parted ways with the Philistines, David has been greatly concerned for Saul and his beloved friend Jonathan, not to mention the rest of his countrymen. During his pursuit of the Amalekite raiding party and the ensuing battle, David had little time to think about how things were back in Israel. Now, for three days David and his men have been back in Ziklag, wondering how the war is going, or perhaps, how it concluded (1:1–2).

The Amalekite messenger who brings David the news ran some one hundred miles to reach him at Ziklag. His clothing is torn and dust is upon his head. It is a sign of mourning. Reaching David, this young man falls on the ground before him, prostrating himself as though approaching royalty. He brings David news of the death of many Israelites, including Saul and Jonathan (1:3–4).

Demystifying 2 Samuel

The transition from 1 to 2 Samuel is virtually seamless, which is actually the case in the original Hebrew text. In the original text, both 1 and 2 Samuel were contained in one book. The book was divided by the translators of the Septuagint. Since the division, all subsequent Bibles have followed this precedent, calling these two books 1 and 2 Samuel. It is therefore very natural for us to move from 1 Samuel to 2 Samuel without noticing much change.

David is unwilling to accept this man's report without some verification and immediately begins to question him. The young man explains how he came upon Saul, mortally wounded, on Mount Gilboa. There he obliges the king's request to slay him. The messenger seems to think that David will be ready to reward him, even for his role in Saul's death (1:5–10).

The young man sees Saul as David's enemy, an obstacle to his rise to the throne. He sees Saul's death as good news to David and killing Saul as putting him out of his misery. But David sees it much more simply: This man killed the Lord's anointed. It does not matter that Saul would have died anyway and that he made David's life difficult. It does not matter that Saul was suffering or wanted to die. And it does not matter that the Philistines may soon have been upon him. This man killed the Lord's anointed, and now David wants him put to death.

David's response is quite different than the young Amalekite expects it to be. He is grief-stricken over the defeat of Israel and the death of Saul. He is devastated by the death of his closest friend, Jonathan. Any thought of personal gain at the expense of others is cast aside. David sets the pace in the mourning, and his men promptly follow his lead (1:11–16).

1:17–27

DAVID'S LAMENT

This eulogy, or dirge, is a special labor of his love. David's eulogy is a psalm that mourns the deaths of Saul and Jonathan. It says nothing negative about Saul, but instead honors both Saul and Jonathan as fallen heroes. David not only restrains himself from speaking ill of the dead, he honors Saul and Jonathan as war heroes, as men worthy of respect and honor. David's psalm begins by focusing on Saul and ends with the focus on Jonathan.

David's psalm appears to be an expression and consequence of the covenant between David and Jonathan. We have seen the covenant made between these two men (1 Samuel 18) implemented (1 Samuel 19:1–7) and then extended and reaffirmed (1 Samuel 20; 23). By his eulogy, David is already blessing Jonathan and his descendants. David's psalm has been written for a much wider audience than David and his six hundred men. Not only does David wish to honor Saul and Jonathan, he wants all of the sons of Judah to join him (2 Samuel 1:18), and thus instructs that this song be taught to them.

Take It Home

David sets an example of trusting that God will write history, and as God's servant, he must bring proper honor to Saul and Jonathan. His eulogy reflects the forgiveness that he had already exercised toward Saul. The book of Proverbs teaches that the wise person carefully chooses what to say, and how and when to say it. The New Testament reminds us that we should speak only that which edifies the hearers (1 Corinthians 14:4–5, 17, 26).

2 SAMUEL 2:1–32

DAVID BECOMES KING

Setting Up the Section

Now that the grieving is over, it is time for David to take his rightful place as king of Israel. Yet there are some obstacles that still remain in his way, as the next several chapters reveal.

2:1–11

DAVID ANOINTED KING OVER JUDAH

David seeks divine guidance and is divinely directed to go up to the city of Hebron. After David, his wives, and the rest of his followers arrive at Hebron with their families, the men of Judah anoint David as king (2:1–4). David's graciousness toward the men of Jabesh-gilead (2:4–7) gives the people of Israel an excellent opportunity to make David their king as well. It seems from Abner's words in 3:17–19 that the men of Israel not only know David has been designated as Saul's replacement, but that they want this. The problem is Abner. This cousin of Saul opposes David's reign in Saul's place and orchestrates events so that Ish-bosheth, a surviving son of Saul, becomes king over the rest of Israel. This delays David's reign for several years (2:8–11).

Demystifying 2 Samuel

Abner is the commander of Saul's army, but even more important, he is Saul's cousin. As Abner has much to gain from Saul's appointment as Israel's king, he also has much to lose if Saul is removed. Abner knows that David is the one Samuel anointed as Saul's replacement. Once Saul is dead, Abner is the one who actively resists David's appointment as king in Saul's place. It would not be a stretch to assume Abner fed Saul false information—information that made David look like an adversary who must be hunted down and put to death. Abner is no friend of David's, nor is he a good friend to his cousin Saul.

2:12–32

WAR WITH THE HOUSE OF SAUL

The rivalry between the Benjamites and the house of David continued to grow. Their military leaders are Abner (Benjamites/Israelites) and Joab (Judah).

In the midst of the fighting, Asahel, brother of Abishai and Joab, is hot on the heels of Abner. Abner does not wish to kill Asahel, but the young man is not willing to give up the chase. Finally, after failing to talk Asahel out of his pursuit, Abner kills him. It is almost an act of self-defense, but Joab will never accept the death of his brother at the hand of Abner. He is intent upon revenge (2:18–25).

Both Abner and Joab pave the way for a future division. This text describes the origin of one of many cracks in the foundation of the united nation of Israel, and this crack will develop over time into a gaping chasm, one which seems almost impossible to bridge (2:26–3:1).

Take It Home

How many relationships are shattered because of ego and competition? How many marriages are ruined and churches split because we fail to be peacemakers? Many times small decisions and actions can lead to major issues down the road. Something initially seems like such a small thing, but it causes cracks that grow and swallow us whole over time. Let us beware of the rifts that appear in our own relationships because of neglect and begin repairs in earnest before it becomes something too big to mend.

2 SAMUEL 3:1–39

KING DAVID'S HOUSE

Setting Up the Section

The conflict between Abner and Joab continues, and David is forced to wait on the Lord to reunite Israel.

3:1–21

TAKING SIDES

God brings blessing on the house of David, and it grows stronger and larger even in the midst of trial and waiting for David to become king of a united Israel. This family register of births also fleshes out what we know of David's household, mentioning (in addition to the two wives he brought with him) four more wives. Also notable is the introduction of Amnon and Absalom, who later play a prominent role in the tumultuous period of David's kingship following his sin with Bathsheba (3:1–6).

David and Abner have a long history together. In 1 Samuel, we are introduced to Abner, who is not only the commander of Saul's army, but also Saul's chief of security. While pursuing David, Saul sleeps in the center of his troops, with Abner right beside him. If anyone attempts to harm Saul, they have to get past his troops and Abner. On one occasion Saul and his men are divinely anesthetized (1 Samuel 26:12), allowing David to obtain Saul's spear and water jug. David specifically calls out Abner and accuses him of dereliction of duty, and thus he is worthy of death (1 Samuel 26:14–16). David's words publicly humiliate Abner.

Despite his role in Saul's army, Abner is not mentioned from 1 Samuel 26 to 2 Samuel 2. Here in chapter 3, however, Abner approaches David with the offer to make him king. He claims that the land is his and that he is in charge. If David will but make a covenant with Abner, Abner will handle the rest. He promises to bring all Israel over to David (2 Samuel 3:6–12). David initially accepts Abner's offer of the kingdom with one condition: that he be given back his wife, Michal. David has loyalty to his wife (1 Samuel 25:44) and regards her return as an important reunion for his household, especially because she is from the house of Saul. Ish-bosheth grants this request to David (2 Samuel 3:13–16).

Before his death, Abner meets with the leaders of both sides. There is an agreement in principle. All that is left to do is finalize it. It seems that if he had lived, he would have done as he promised (3:17–21).

3:22–39

JOAB MURDERS ABNER

Joab returns from a raid and discovers that David has formed an alliance with Abner, who he is still angry with over the death of his brother, Asahel. He does not kill Abner in the context of war—which would not be viewed as a murder but a necessary part of war (see 3:28–34; 1 Kings 2:30–33). Instead, Joab clearly believes his own position is threatened and calls Abner back. In a private conversation of which David is unaware, Joab murders Abner to avenge the blood of his brother (2 Samuel 3:22–27).

When David learns of the murder of Abner by Joab, he publicly renounces the actions of Joab as reprehensible. There is no excuse for what he has done. David condemns the murder and calls down divine judgment on Joab and his family (3:28–29). David then mourns the death of Abner, seeing to it that his burial is honorable, even if his death is not (he dies the death of a fool). David not only walks behind the bier, weeping loudly and chanting a lament for Abner, he also refuses to eat all day long. It is obvious to all that David had no part in the death of Abner (3:31–39). David's standing with the people continues to increase.

Critical Observation

God providentially removes Abner so that David will not become king because of him. Abner's reasons for switching his allegiance from Ish-bosheth to David are questionable. Abner's approach to David seems similar to Satan's approach to our Lord in His temptation (Matthew 4:1–11; Luke 4:1–12). Like Satan, Abner claims that the kingdom he offers is really his (compare 2 Samuel 3:12; Luke 4:5–7). Abner wants David to enter into a covenant with him (2 Samuel 3:12), but when David does become king of all Israel, he enters into a covenant with the people with the Lord's favor (2 Samuel 5:3).

2 SAMUEL 4:1–12

WAITING ON THE LORD 4:1–12

Setting Up the Section

As the conflict continues to sort itself out, David exemplifies patience during a tough time of transitioning power.

4:1–12

WAITING ON THE LORD

Although the Lord had anointed David as the next king, Abner had installed Ish-bosheth as Saul's replacement. With the death of Abner at the hand of Joab, Ish-bosheth loses all his courage. He could hardly stand up to Abner, let alone even think about standing up against David. Now Ish-bosheth is on his own, knowing that Abner had already set up David to rule in his place (4:1).

Two men think they are the solution. These men are fellow members of the tribe of Benjamin and commanders of divisions of Israelite soldiers (4:2–3). They take matters into their own hands and proceed to brutally kill Ish-bosheth in his own home while he is lying in bed (4:5–8). They do not understand David's love for Saul or his commitment to protect the lives of his offspring and the honor of his name (1 Samuel 24:16–22). David refuses to look the other way when others do evil to facilitate his ascent to the throne. He understands what being God's king is all about and trusts that God will make him king as long as he honors Him (4:9–12).

Here we are introduced to Mephibosheth, Jonathan's lame son, who will be honored with David's blessing in chapter 9 (4:4).

Critical Observation

David waits fifteen years from the time he is first anointed by Samuel to the time he becomes king over Judah. Even after David is anointed as king of Judah, he must wait a full seven years to be anointed king of all Israel. This means David waited more than twenty years of his life to be made king. How David handled this two-decade delay is the subject of this message. As David waits on the Lord, the divisions around him splinter and crackle relationships even among his closest friends and family. This is a reoccurring theme in his life—how sin can come between even the closest allies to make them enemies. David has gone through many different experiences, all of which will make him a better king for having endured them. He is now much better prepared to reign as Israel's king (5:4–6).

The promise God made to Israel and to David took a long time being fulfilled. David becomes king of Israel after a considerable delay and with a great deal of adversity. This is typical of the way God brings about His promises and purposes. God is not in a hurry. It is in times of waiting for God that many have failed in their faith and obedience. Waiting tests our faith and endurance. Like David, waiting is a significant part of each of our lives, and God will reward us if we are patient and faithful as we await His blessing.

2 SAMUEL 5:1–25

DAVID: KING OF ISRAEL

Setting Up the Section

Ish-bosheth has just been murdered in what concludes a bloody and difficult phase of David's coming to power as king of Israel. Now God has new lessons for the king to learn as he takes over Jerusalem and meets with an old enemy, the Philistines.

5:1–16

JERUSALEM: A PLACE OF ONE'S OWN

The Israelites are the ones who come to David in Hebron and the ones who recognize and anoint him as their king (5:1–3). The people are the initiators, just as they were the initiators when Saul became their king. The significance of the submission of the Israelites to David as God's king is best understood in comparison and contrast to 1 Kings 8–12, where the people demand a king, and Saul is given to them as their first king.

In the earlier situation, the Israelites were rebelling against God, demanding a king without being willing to repent (1 Samuel 8). Here, in stark contrast, the Israelite leaders are acting out of obedience to God, not in rebellion against Him. The king they gain in David is, in some measure, the king they deserve. When they approach David, they acknowledge several vitally important truths, which are the basis for David's kingship and thus their submission to him. They recognize that they share a common heritage with David—that they are under the same original covenant with God and that God desires unity for His people. The Israelites also recognize that David has provided leadership for many years now, and they accept David as God's anointed choice for the throne. Thus, David becomes king of all Israel.

At the same time, he finally obtains a place of his own. The place has been known as *Jebus* up to this point in time, and its inhabitants are called the *Jebusites*. But from this text onward, Jebus becomes Jerusalem, and Zion is called the City of David. God continues to bless and increase David's power and his household (5:6–16). In the next chapter, Jerusalem will become the dwelling place of God, as the ark of the covenant is brought to the city where Solomon will later build the temple and where Israel's coming king, Jesus Christ, will eventually ride in triumphantly on a donkey one week before His crucifixion.

Demystifying 2 Samuel

Jebus is first mentioned as a city occupied by true Canaanites (Genesis 10:15–16), the descendants of Canaan, the third son of Ham (Genesis 10:6). It is this Ham who saw the nakedness of Noah (Genesis 9:22) and who brought a curse upon himself and his descendants (Genesis 9:25). Also in Jebus is Mount Moriah, where Abraham offered up his son, Isaac, which is the same mountain on which Solomon will later build the temple (2 Chronicles 3:1). When the Israelites took over the promised land, they failed to completely drive out the Canaanites from Jebus (Joshua 15:63). This leads to a kind of coexistence, which results in the Israelites embracing the sins of the Jebusites and oppression from their neighbors as a divine chastening (Judges 3:1–8).

David recognizes that no kingdom can be viewed with fear (or even respect) if it is not able to expel its enemies from its midst. The Jebusites need to be dealt with, and David knows it. It is time for these enemies of God to be defeated. The defeat of the Jebusites and the taking of Jebus is the first step in Israel's conquest of their enemies—a conquest that is partial in the times of Joshua and the judges. This victory will overshadow the victory of Saul and the Israelites over the Ammonites (1 Samuel 11).

The possession of Jebus as David's new capital will unite Israel. The city is virtually on the border of Judah and Benjamin. It is a city that neither the sons of Judah nor the sons of Benjamin have been able to capture. Thus, taking this city as his capital will not seem to favor either of these two tribes. In addition to all of this, its natural setting makes it difficult to defeat (which is why the Israelites had not taken and held it before). It is in the hill country, on the top of more than one mountain, and is surrounded by valleys. With a little work, it is a virtual fortress (2 Samuel 5:9).

5:17–25

DAVID DEFEATS THE PHILISTINES

The Philistines, unlike the Israelites, will not submit to David as God's king. They attack David, seeking to kill him and to remove the threat that he and a united Israel pose. Not once, but twice, these Philistines come against David and the army of Israel. And twice God gives David the victory over his enemies. Those who receive David as God's king are blessed; those who reject David as God's king are crushed (5:17–22).

It is interesting to note that once David is established as king of Israel, the first enemy he meets is the Philistines. It parallels the first battle that David ever finds himself in after he is anointed by Samuel as the future king—his battle with Goliath, the giant Philistine who had frightened all of Israel's forces (1 Samuel 17). The picture here is of God going ahead of David into the battle—as indicated by the sound of marching in the tree tops—and delivering the victory to His servant (2 Samuel 5:23–25).

2 SAMUEL 6:1–23

GOD RAINED ON DAVID'S PARADE

Setting Up the Section

Some days, no matter how carefully we plan and orchestrate events, things just have a way of going wrong. And sometimes even the most well-intentioned actions can inflict the wrath of God.

6:1–15

THE ARK BROUGHT TO JERUSALEM

God gave very clear instructions about the ark of God. He not only gave specific instructions about how it should be made, He also indicated who should carry it and how it should be transported from one place to another. In Numbers 5, God tells exactly how the tabernacle should be taken down and carried to its next resting place.

No wonder Uzzah is struck dead for having laid hands on the ark. The ark is holy. It is not be touched. By using poles, men could transport the ark without touching the ark itself. And these men, walking in step with one another, give the ark stability. Putting the ark on the ox cart made it susceptible to the movements of the cart and less stable, and thus more likely to fall off the cart. The only way to keep this from happening is to grab hold of the ark, as Uzzah does, and to die. Uzzah is a reminder to us that God's holiness is such that sinful people cannot draw near to Him unless He provides the means to do so (6:1–8).

David is struck with fear of the Lord and decides to let the ark remain outside the city in the house of Obed-edom, the Gittite. God's blessing on the house of Obed-edom, where the ark rests for three months, assures David that the nearness of the ark is a blessing, but that it must be brought to Jerusalem in accordance with God's directions. David resumes bringing the ark into the city—this time being careful to observe God's instructions.

The ark is carried six steps, and then a sacrifice is offered. Those first six steps are no doubt the tensest steps of the entire journey. As the journey continues, the men's courage and joy increase. Soon there is great celebration as they make their way to the holy city.

Along the way, David and his entourage dance and worship God and offer sacrifices as signs of humility before God (6:9–15).

Critical Observation

The ark had accompanied the Israelites wherever they went while they were in the wilderness. It went before the Israelites when they crossed the Jordan River (Joshua 3:14–17). We find the ark mentioned quite often in 1 and 2 Samuel. Samuel sleeps near the ark as a child (1 Samuel 3:3). When the Israelites are being beaten by the Philistines, they unwisely take the ark into battle with them as a kind of magic charm. They not only lose the battle, they lose the ark as well (1 Samuel 4). The next two chapters (5–6) of 1 Samuel are the account of how God plagues the Philistines, and how they finally decide they do not want the ark among them. In Exodus 25, God tells Moses He will meet with him and speak to him from above the ark, between the cherubim (Exodus 25:22). God chose to manifest His presence in the tabernacle, specifically from the ark. When God's glory first filled the tabernacle, even Moses was not able to enter (Exodus 40:34–35). Sinful men cannot get too close to a holy God.

6:16–23

JUDGING JOY

It seems there is only one person in all of Israel who does not and will not enter into the spirit of rejoicing and celebration, and that person is Michal, David's wife. The author of the Chronicles makes very little of this, devoting only one verse to the subject and informing us that as Michal looks on, she despises her husband in her heart for his role in the celebration (1 Chronicles 15:29).

Michal has no intention of being a part of the celebration, and she proceeds to distract from David's praise and blessing. She is not angry with David for doing something wrong and standing out from the rest of the people. She is angry with David for behaving like the common people and not acting like a king as he worships God. He had humbled himself, demeaned himself, and lowered himself. And Michal judges David for his joy (2 Samuel 6:16–23).

David serves as a prototype of Christ in this text and beyond. He is both a king and a priest (he wears a linen ephod). David lays aside his royal robes and humbles himself, just as our Lord lays aside His royal robes and humbles Himself (see John 13; Philippians 2:5–8).

Critical Observation

Michal serves as a kind of prototype of the self-righteous scribes and Pharisees of Jesus' time. As Michal had come to enjoy her position as daughter of the king, so the scribes had come to enjoy their privileged position as religious leaders in Israel. They fear losing their power and status. They challenge Jesus about His authority. They look upon the Lord with disdain because He associates with the lowly. Just as Michal bears no fruit (in other words, children), neither do the scribes and Pharisees. Those who worship God must come to Him in humility, not in pride. Michal is the only person not joyfully worshiping God. No wonder, since she is preoccupied with herself.

2 SAMUEL 7:1–29

BUILDING GOD'S HOUSE

Setting Up the Section

David begins to formulate a plan to build a house for God. However, Nathan reveals that God will build for David, and it surpasses the temple-house David wants to build for God.

7:1–17

GOD'S PROMISE TO DAVID

To the people of Israel (and those outside Israel for that matter), David is the highest authority in the land. But in relation to God, David is merely a servant. David is living In a palace, and God is living in a tent, at least in David's mind. David almost appears to want to give God a helping hand. David has a bright idea, but it does not correspond with God's plan as revealed to Nathan. David is referred to as the *king* (7:1–3), but when God refers to David, He calls him His *servant* (7:5). The question God asks David sets the tone for what is to follow: Are you the one who should build my house?

God gave Israel the tabernacle; the temple is David's idea. God explains that as the Creator of all things, He neither requires nor can be confined by a dwelling made by human hands. In short, God does not need a temple, and He does not ask for one. God reminds David who is taking care of whom. God gently rebukes David for this heady plan. David has taken the wrong posture of helping out God, rather than being the one who has constantly been helped *by* God (7:5–7).

After pointing out all that He has done for David and Israel in the past, God goes on to tell David that he hasn't seen the best of it yet. God promises to appoint a place for His people where they will be planted. They will have a place of their own (as David intended to give God a place of His own), and they will dwell in peace there because the wicked will no longer afflict them. God has been behind all of David's successes, and now He is promising even greater glory. God announces to David that He is going to build a house for him by blessing his descendants and ultimately bringing the Messiah through his bloodline (7:8–15).

David will have sons, and these sons will become sons of God in that they will rule over Israel. But there will be one very special Son, and through Him all of the promises God has made here and elsewhere (pertaining to the kingdom of God) will be fulfilled, either in His first coming or in His return to the earth. It is in this Son that all of David's hopes, all of Israel's hopes, and all of humanity's hopes are fulfilled—this is the essence of what is often called the Davidic Covenant (7:16–17).

7:18–29

DAVID'S PRAYER

David now stands in awe of the fact that God takes him, a man of no status or standing, and makes him king of Israel. This, too, is what God has reminded David through Nathan (7:8–9). David sees his standing and status as Israel's king as the result of God's sovereign grace, and not as the recognition of his potential greatness. It is amazing how pride and arrogance can distort one's thinking. No wonder humility is the starting point, the prerequisite, for wisdom (Proverbs 11:2; 15:33; 18:12; 22:4; 29:13).

God has done great things for David, but these were not done for David alone. God has worked in David and through David to bring about the fulfillment of His promises to the entire nation of Israel. Verses 23 and 24 recount the greatness of God as revealed in His acts on behalf of His people, Israel. The reason for David's confidence is God, not himself (7:18–24).

The presumptuous self-confidence that characterizes David in the early verses of this chapter is gone, replaced by a humble confidence based in the God who made it. God has promised this good thing to His servant (not to the king). The promise is clear, and any promise made by God is a sure thing. Thus David petitions God for its fulfillment (7:25–29).

Take It Home

We need to be on guard against prideful thoughts of our own contribution to the kingdom of God. It is always He who will be carrying us, rather than us carrying Him. How easily we begin to focus on what we have done and can do for God, rather than on all He has done and will do for and through us.

2 SAMUEL 8:1–10:19

WAR AND PEACE

Setting Up the Section

David uses his newfound power at war with the enemies of Israel in chapters 8 and 10. In chapter 9, we learn of how David's kindness toward Mephibosheth allows him to use his power to fulfill his covenant commitment to his beloved friend, Jonathan, and his promise to Saul.

8:1–18

DAVID'S VICTORIES

The Philistines, located to Israel's west, are troublesome to Israel (Genesis 26:1, 8, 14–15, 18), especially from the time of the judges onward (Judges 3:3, 31; 10:6–7). Samson fought with the Philistines (Judges 13–16). It was the Philistines who took the lives of Eli's two sons and indirectly caused the death of Eli, as well as taking the ark of God (1 Samuel 4–7). Jonathan attacked a Philistine garrison in Israel, precipitating another confrontation with the Philistines (1 Samuel 13:3–14).

David killed Goliath, a Philistine, and then led the pursuit of the Philistines (1 Samuel 17). It was the Philistines who eventually defeated the army of Israel and killed Saul and his two sons (1 Samuel 31). It was also among the Philistines that David sought and found sanctuary (1 Samuel 21:10–15; 27). Once David becomes king, the Philistines think it's best to attack quickly in an attempt to nullify the threat he will pose to them. They fail, and now David will subdue them, ending their tyranny for some time. We know from the parallel passage in 1 Chronicles 18:1 that the chief city is actually Gath. No wonder David is able to capture it; he knows it well.

The killing of the Moabites seems amazingly harsh and barbaric. But standard warfare rules during this era usually dictated killing all of one's enemies. So the fact that David spares one-third of the Moabites (2 Samuel 8:2) demonstrates his mercy. As king of Israel, David is God's representative. These Moabites are enemies of Israel, and therefore they are enemies of God. As such, they all deserve to die. The wonder is not that two-thirds of the Moabites are killed, but that one-third is left to live. And in the killing of the two-thirds, any thought of resisting David or rebelling against him is laid to rest.

This is a period for David where Israel celebrates many victories. The outcome of all of David's activities is that he defeats his enemies (8:1–13). Israelite garrisons are found among the neighboring nations (8:14), whereas foreign garrisons had once been in Israel (1 Samuel 10:5; 13:3–4). This means they will no longer be able to resist, harass, or oppress Israel for some time. There will be peace in the land, just as God promised.

All of the success David achieves is from the hand of God (2 Samuel 8:6, 14). David's dominion grows such that he has to add administrative and secretarial personnel to his staff, recorded in verses 15–18. Where David rules, there is justice and righteousness (8:15). As a result, David's name becomes great (8:13), just as God had promised (7:9). In addition, the tribute paid to David is great. He obtains great quantities of silver, gold, and bronze (8:7–12). These riches are stored, and at least some become building materials for the temple that Solomon will construct (1 Chronicles 18:8).

9:1–13

DAVID AND MEPHIBOSHETH

David is a man who makes promises and keeps them. Before he became Israel's king, he made promises to both Jonathan and Saul. To Jonathan, he promised to protect his life and to show loving-kindness to his house forever (1 Samuel 20:12–17). To Saul, he vowed not to cut off his descendants after him (1 Samuel 24:21–22). Now Saul and Jonathan are dead, and David is king.

David not only remembers his commitment to Saul, he goes far beyond it. It seems as though all of Saul's descendants are dead. No descendant of Saul approaches David, seeking his favor. David is now in a position to carry out his promise to Jonathan—all he needs is one of his descendants. David inquires as to whether there is a descendant of Saul to whom he may show kindness for Jonathan's sake (2 Samuel 9:1). David speaks of this act of kindness as the kindness of God (9:3).

Only one of Jonathan's sons is still living—Mephibosheth, who is crippled in both feet. Ziba doubts David will want him to be the one to whom he shows favor. Yet David summons him and promises to restore to Mephibosheth all the land which had belonged to his father, and which he had evidently lost sometime after the death of Saul and his father. Not only will David restore all that to which Mephibosheth is heir, he will make him his regular guest at the palace. Mephibosheth is overcome with gratitude and relief, falling prostrate before David once again, calling attention to the fact that he is a dead dog (9:8). David uses this very expression to refer to himself in speaking to King Saul (1 Samuel 24:14).

Demystifying 2 Samuel

At this time, when one king prevailed over another by winning in battle, he would cut off the thumbs and the big toes of his opponent, and then keep them as a kind of showpiece. These incapacitated kings would sit under the table of the victorious king, getting the scraps, like dogs. These defeated kings were not honored guests; they were trophies of war. David would have none of this with regard to Mephibosheth. He does not want him at his table as a subjected foe, but as an honored guest, the son of his beloved friend, Jonathan. It is an amazing act of grace (9:7–13).

10:1–19

DAVID DEFEATS THE AMMONITES

Hanun is the Son of Nahash, who as king of the Ammonites has been on good terms with David. When David hears of Nahash's death, he sends a delegation to Ammon to convey his respect for Nahash and to mourn his death. The advisors of this newly installed king give him some bad counsel. They assure Hanun that David's intentions cannot be honorable. He is only sending these men as spies to obtain intelligence so that he can attack them, as he has so many other nations. This explanation of events gives Hanun the excuse he is looking for—a reason to break the alliance his father made with David and Israel.

David receives word that his delegation has been abused and humiliated. Their beards are, for the Hebrews, a mark of dignity. Hanun has half of the beard of each man shaved off. In addition, he has their garments cut off to embarrass them. David takes pity on the dishonored delegation. He sends to meet them and then instructs them to wait in Jericho until their beards grow back, and then to return to Israel.

We are not told that David summoned his troops, intending to go to war. We are told that the sons of Ammon recognize that they have angered David (10:6). Rather than apologize or attempt to reconcile with David, the sons of Ammon seek to make an alliance which will strengthen them in their conflict with Israel. Syrians from several regions are hired as mercenaries (10:6). Only after David learns of this military buildup does he call his army into active duty.

David and his forces draw up to battle with the Ammonites and their Syrian mercenaries. This coalition army divides into two groups, intending to attack the Israelites from the front and the rear. When Joab sees this, he divides the army of Israel into two forces. He leads one division, and his brother Abishai leads the other. Joab sets himself against the Syrians, and Abishai is to fight the Ammonites. If either of the two becomes hard-pressed by their opponent, the other is to come to their aid.

Critical Observation

The political and military intrigue in 2 Samuel 8 and 10 are used providentially by God to give Israel the land and the victory God had long before promised His people (Genesis 12:1–3). The tribute that David obtains from his subjected enemies seems to provide the raw materials that will be required for the building of the temple. These events fulfill not only the promise of God made to David in 2 Samuel 7, but also the promises God made long before to Abraham and the patriarchs and to Moses.

Take It Home

In chapters 8–10, David serves as a prototype of Christ. He establishes his kingdom by prevailing over the enemies of Israel, subjecting them to himself. On the other hand, David shows mercy toward Mephibosheth, the son of Jonathan and the grandson of Saul. Mephibosheth is the sole heir of Saul, the last candidate for king. Usually, a king in David's place would kill such potential contenders to the throne, but David seeks this man out and shows mercy to him. This is not because of what he can contribute to David and to his kingdom (he is handicapped, which in those days makes him useless in the eyes of men). It is because of David's love for his friend, Jonathan, Mephibosheth's father. This serves to remind us how the two dimensions of God—sovereignty and grace—combine perfectly. God's grace is sovereign grace, not earned or deserved.

2 SAMUEL 11:1–27

DAVID COMMITS ADULTERY

Setting Up the Section

The picture of David at the pinnacle of his success in chapters 8–10 sets the scene for David's fall to the depths in chapters 11–12. David's experience is proof that spiritual highs do not assure that we cannot fall, but may in some ways prepare us for a fall.

11:1–4

DAVID WITH BATHSHEBA

Up until this point, David has been leading his men in battle. But here, as spring returns and the Israelites go back to fight the Ammonites, David suddenly steps back from his duty and stays in Jerusalem. David is failing to lead the people in subduing their enemies and instead has become arrogant in his victories. David is starting to become like Saul in that he is willing to let others go out and fight his battles for him. Among those David is willing to send in his place are Joab and Abishai.

Joab is not the commander of the army of Israel by David's choice. David had distanced himself from Joab and Abishai because of the death of Abner (2 Samuel 3:26–30). Joab became the commander of Israel's armed forces because he was the first to accept David's challenge to attack Jebus (1 Chronicles 11:4–6). Suddenly, David is willing to stay at home and leave the whole of Israel's armed forces under Joab's command. David is probably not motivated by trust in Joab as much as he is by his disdain for the hardship of the campaign to take Rabbah (2 Samuel 11:1–2).

A relaxed and aimless King David, shirking his duties in battle, spies a beautiful woman bathing one evening while strolling on his rooftop. He learns that she is married to a Hittite named Uriah, who is a soldier in his army. Bathsheba is perhaps the most famous object of desire in the whole Bible because David, a man after God's own heart, is brought down from a place of glory because of his adultery with her and the resulting cover-up (11:3–5).

Many wish to view this text in a way that forces Bathsheba to share David's guilt by assuming that she somehow seduced him. In fact, when Nathan pronounces divine judgment upon David for his sin, Bathsheba and Uriah are depicted as the victims, not the villains. The tragedies that take place in David's household are the consequence of his sin, just as Nathan indicates (12:10–12).

The root of David's sin is not low self-esteem; it is arrogance. He has come to see himself as better than the rest of the Israelites. They need to go to war; he does not. They need to sleep in the open field; he needs to get his rest in his palace bed. They can have a wife; he can have whatever woman he wants.

David's sin is the abuse of power. In the previous chapters, David employs his God-given power to defeat the enemies of God and of Israel. He uses his power as Israel's king to fulfill his covenant with David and his promise to Saul by restoring to Mephibosheth his family property and by making him a son at his table. Now, David, drunk with his power, uses it to indulge himself at the expense of others. Sexual abuse and sexual harassment are two common ways people, even today, abuse their power, and just as David quickly discovers, they remain some of the most destructive sins.

Take It Home

Prosperity is as dangerous—if not more dangerous—as poverty and adversity. Often when it appears everything is going right, we are in the greatest danger, because we forget that we need God and that we must rely on His power. No longer on our guard, we can easily become drunk with our own power and control. Yet this will backfire just as it does for King David. How can you remember God when times are good? What can we learn from David's sins of omission as well as his sins of commission? (Examine 1 John 1:7–9; 2:1–2; 3:4–9 for some New Testament guidelines for avoiding sin.)

11:5–27

DAVID AND URIAH

One of the tragic aspects of this story is that the sequence of sin in David's life does not end with his adulterous union with Bathsheba. It instead leads to a deceptive plot to make her husband, Uriah, appear to be the father of David's child with Bathsheba and culminates in David's murder of Uriah and his marriage to Bathsheba (11:5–27).

Throughout history, many attempts have been made to cover up incompetence, immorality, and even crimes. In the Bible, cover-ups appear early: Adam and Eve sought to cover their nakedness and to hide from God, not realizing their efforts betrayed their sin and guilt. Second Samuel 11 is one of the great cover-up attempts of all time, and like so many, it fails miserably.

It seems likely that David and Uriah are not total strangers, but that they know each other to some degree. Uriah is listed among the mighty warriors of David (2 Samuel 23:39; 1 Chronicles 11:41). Some of these mighty men came to David early, while he was in the cave of Adullam (1 Samuel 22:1–2), and likely among them were brothers Joab, Abishai, and Asahel (2 Samuel 23:18, 24; 1 Chronicles 11:26). Others joined David at Ziklag (1 Chronicles 12), and still other great warriors joined with David at Hebron (1 Chronicles 12:38–40).

It seems unlikely that Uriah is ignorant of what David has done and of what he is trying to accomplish by calling him home to Jerusalem. Rumors must have been circulating around Jerusalem about David and Bathsheba and could easily have reached the Israelite army which had besieged Rabbah. Uriah not only refuses to go to his house and sleep with his wife, he sleeps at the doorway of the king's house, in the midst of his servants. He has many witnesses to testify that any child borne by his wife during this time is not his child. Bathsheba is not said to have any part in David's scheme to deceive Uriah or to bring about his death, much less any knowledge of what David is doing (2 Samuel 11:6–13).

When the deception of making the child appear to be Uriah's fails, David, instead of repenting, escalates the sin by ordering to have Uriah sent to the front lines of the battle—a virtual death sentence for an innocent man. Certain biblical figures may cause us to question whether they really ever came to faith in God, such as Balaam, Samson, and Saul. But we have no such questions regarding David. He is not only a believer, he is a model believer—a man after God's heart. Nevertheless, David, in spite of his trust in God, in spite of his marvelous times of worship and his beautiful psalms, falls deeply into sin. If David can fall, anyone can (11:14–26). And that is precisely what Paul warns believers about in 1 Corinthians 10:11–12.

Take It Home

Uriah is a reminder to us that God does not always deliver the righteous from the hands of the wicked immediately, or even in this lifetime. In the Old Testament, as in the New, God sometimes delivers His people from the hands of wicked men, but often He does not. Their deliverance comes with the coming of the Messiah, the Lord Jesus Christ. Uriah, like all of the Old Testament saints, dies without receiving his full reward, and that is because God wants him to wait. Uriah is not immediately delivered from the hands of the wicked.

2 SAMUEL 12:1–31

DAVID AND GOD

Setting Up the Section

In this section God sends the prophet Nathan to confront David about his sin.

12:1–6

A POWERFUL STORY

Nathan is a prophet and a friend to David. Even one of David's sons is named Nathan (5:14). David informs Nathan of his desire to build a temple in 2 Samuel 7. Nathan will name Bathsheba and David's second son (12:25). He will remain loyal to the king and to Solomon when Adonijah seeks to usurp the throne (1 Kings 2). Nathan does not come to David only as God's spokesman; he comes to David as his friend.

Nathan confronts David about his sin by telling him a story about sheep—one greedy shepherd has taken everything from a lowly farmer who had only one sheep. The story, of course, parallels the actions of David with Bathsheba and Uriah. David, a former shepherd himself, immediately recognizes the wrongfulness of the actions of the greedy murderous shepherd in the story (2 Samuel 12:1–4). David identifies two evils that have been committed by this fictional rich man. First, the man has stolen a lamb, for which the law prescribes restitution (Exodus 22:1). Second, David recognizes what he views as the greater sin, and that is the rich man's total lack of compassion (12:5–6).

David does not see what is coming. The story Nathan tells makes David furious. David is furious because a rich man stole and slaughtered a poor man's pet. He does not yet see the connection to his lack of compassion for stealing a poor man's beloved companion, his wife. The slaughtering of Uriah is most certainly an act that lacks compassion. The crowning touch in David's display of righteous indignation is found in the religious flavoring he gives it by the words, "as surely as the LORD lives" (12:5 NLT).

12:7–12

NATHAN'S INDICTMENT

David has just sprung the trap on himself, and Nathan is about to let him know about it. The first thing Nathan does is dramatically indict David as the culprit. In stunned silence, David now listens to the charges against him. Through Nathan, God speaks to David as though he has forgotten all the things God has given him, or rather as though he has come to take credit for them himself. God reminds David that He has given everything he possesses to him. Has it been so long since David himself was a lowly shepherd boy?

David is a rich man because God has made him rich. And if he does not think he is rich enough, God will give more to him. David has begun to cling to his riches rather than to the God who has blessed him (12:7–8).

David was thinking only in terms of the evils the rich man committed against his neighbor, stealing a man's sheep and depriving him of his companion. Put another way, David thinks only in terms of crime and socially unacceptable behavior, not in terms of sin. God wants David to understand that David's evil actions violate God's revealed Word (12:9–10). Nathan draws David's attention to his sin against God and the consequences God has pronounced for his sin (12:11–12).

Critical Observation

First and foremost, David's sin is against God. He has ceased to humbly acknowledge God as the giver of all he possesses. He has ceased to look to God to provide him with all his needs and his desires. David has not only stopped relying on God for his needs, he has disobeyed God's commands by committing adultery and murder. David's sin against God manifests itself by the evils he commits against others. Nathan outlines these, employing a repetitive *you* as he speaks to David.

12:13

REAL REPENTANCE

Remember that David's repentance is the culmination of a painful process, climaxing in the confrontation of David by Nathan. David's confession follows shortly after the account of his sin. But the text itself indicates that David's sin took place over a considerable period of time, slightly more than nine months by estimation. David knew what he did was wrong, but he chose to persist for a time. He does not confess his sin, and the result is torturous (Psalm 32). While sin has its momentary pleasures (Hebrews 11:25), it eventually grieves the Spirit who indwells us, and thus the believer's spirit can no longer take pleasure in that sin.

Demystifying 2 Samuel

Psalm 32 is one of two psalms (along with Psalm 51) in which David himself reflects on his sin, his repentance, and his recovery. Verses 3 and 4 of Psalm 32 fit between chapters 11 and 12 of 2 Samuel. The confrontation of David by Nathan the prophet, described in 2 Samuel 12, results in David's repentance and confession. But this repentance is not just the fruit of Nathan's rebuke; it is also David's response to the work God has been doing in David's heart before he confesses, while he is still attempting to conceal his sin.

David confesses his sin, without any excuses, without any finger-pointing toward others. He sees that he has sinned against God. Psalms 32 and 51 (both written by David) indicate that David gave his sin a great deal of thought, and the more he reflected on it, the more heinous it became to him. Since these psalms are preserved for worship and for posterity, David's sin and his confession become public knowledge. Ultimately, his sin is against God and God alone. This is not to diminish the evil he had done to Uriah and Bathsheba, but sin is ultimately the breaking of God's law. Crimes are offenses against people, but sin (in this highly specific sense) is only against God, in that it breaks His laws. David had broken at least three laws. He coveted his neighbor's wife, he committed adultery, and he committed murder (Exodus 20:13–14, 17).

David does not presume upon God's grace, expecting to be forgiven and to have his life spared. He knows what he deserves, and he does not ask to escape it. From Psalm 51, we know that David's repentance results in a renewed joy in the presence and service of God, and a commitment to teach others to turn from sin (Psalm 51:8, 12).

Drawing near to God and clinging to Him alone changes David's heart. According to the law, David should have died for his sins. Based upon divine grace through the coming death of Christ, David is forgiven for his sins and assured that he will not die. These words from Nathan must have been a huge relief to David, who knew he did not deserve anything but God's wrath (2 Samuel 12:13).

12:14–31

THE DEATH OF A CHILD

David's sense of relief is short-lived, however, because Nathan is not finished with what he has to say. The child conceived by Bathsheba with David will not live. By taking the life of this child, conceived in sin, God makes a statement to those looking on about how seriously He takes transgression of His law (12:14–15).

In spite of David's sorrow, sincerity, and persistence in petitioning God to spare the child's life, his request is denied. The child indeed dies. David must not have been with the child when it happened, or he would have seen this for himself. David does, however, see his servants whispering to one another, perhaps furtively glancing in his direction as they do so. They are afraid to tell David because they fear he might cause harm. The text is not altogether clear about whom the servants fear David might hurt (12:16–18).

Still David has a remarkable peace about the death of his first child by Bathsheba, a peace which causes those who witness it to marvel and to question David about it. And, as we can see from David's response to the questions posed by his servants, he is able to praise and worship God at a time of loss and sorrow for his child (12:19–23).

Take It Home

The Christian's hope and joy in the midst of trials and tribulations is witness to faith in Jesus Christ. David's servants expect him to react to the death of his son in a very different way. His peace surpasses understanding and his joy and desire to worship God in the midst of tragedy amaze them. David is able to give a reason for his hope (1 Peter 3:15). Even in the worst of circumstances, we must cast ourselves upon the God to whom we have entrusted our souls and our eternal destiny. Our confidence and our joy are in the Lord.

Following the death of their son, David goes to comfort Bathsheba; and as a result of their union, God blesses them with the birth of a second child, Solomon, who will become the next great king of Israel. Nathan prophetically names the son Jedidiah, which means "loved by the Lord." Again, the story of David's life is a study in stark contrasts and how God uses them to teach, train, and refine His servant king (12:24–25). It is significant that the closing action of this section describes David returning to his place as the leader of Israel's army claiming victory over Rabbah of the Ammonites on the people's behalf. This role is the one David had originally shirked when he fell into sin with Bathsheba (12:26–31).

2 SAMUEL 13:1–15:12

TRAGEDY IN THE ROYAL FAMILY

Setting Up the Section

God gives King David power, riches, and prosperity, not because of David's greatness, but because of God's grace. Following the death of David's first son with Bathsheba, David's family continues to experience serious tragedies and trials as a consequence of his sin. Soon, David's sin will divide the nation and deprive David of his throne for a time.

13:1–36

AMNON'S SIN AGAINST TAMAR

The character of Amnon warns about the pursuit of fleshly lusts (compare 1 Corinthians 10). Jonadab warns about the danger of using the sins of others to further our own interests, making them a part of our own agenda, rather than paying the price for rebuke and correction. David instructs us concerning passivity toward sin (2 Samuel 13:1–11).

This story of betrayal, lust, rape, and murder demonstrates the divisive power of sin—breaking bonds between individuals, families, and, most seriously, with God. Sin is the root of disunity and division. Amnon has confused his "love" for his sister Tamar with his desire to have sex with her. Obviously, Amnon's love does not stand the test of 1 Corinthians 13. Love is not synonymous with sex. Amnon's brand of love is not at all concerned about respecting the other person or doing what is right, both of which characterize the love that God encourages and prescribes (13:12–16).

Tamar is one of the strongest women in the Bible—and yet she suffers terribly as a result of her brother's sin. She begs him to spare her and still he rapes her and then sends her away to fend for herself. Her brother Absalom takes her in, but because of the sexual crime against her, she remains desolate (13:15–20).

David is furious about the crime committed against his daughter, yet it seems that he does nothing about it. His tangled web of loyalty paralyzes him. David's inaction facilitates the sin of others (13:21–22). Absalom is not willing to deal with Amnon biblically; he wants to get his revenge in his own way. This he does, and in doing so becomes a murderer and a fugitive who will famously challenge his father's throne. From Absalom, we learn the danger of resentment and bitterness even in the midst of righteous anger (13:23–36).

Take It Home

As we examine the tough realities that David's family is dealing with, we are reminded that no one is worthy of eternal life—except Jesus Christ. Every single person is born in sin and fails to live up to God's standard of righteousness (Romans 3:23; 6:23). We all deserve the penalty of death. God, in His mercy and grace, has provided a solution in the person of His Son, Jesus Christ. He came to this earth, adding perfect humanity to His undiminished deity by revealing Himself as God's only way to heaven and eternal life (John 14:6).

13:37–14:33

ABSALOM, ABSALOM!

After Absalom murders Amnon, he chooses political asylum in Geshur with his grandfather. David is not wrong to still love this son and yearn to see him. But it would not have been right for David to pardon him so he could return. It would not even have been right to visit him in Geshur. God uses Absalom to continue to draw David closer to Him (13:37–39).

Using trickery and deception, Joab pursues his own self-serving agenda in seeking to manipulate David into bringing Absalom back to Israel. Presumably using Joab's words, a woman from Tekoa is able to get David to commit himself to the safety of her son. Finally, David rules with a divine oath that this son is not to be harmed. Now the woman can appeal to the precedent David has just set (which it seems cannot be changed) and press David to deal similarly with his own son (whose guilt is much more clear [14:1–20]).

David gives in, reluctantly, to Joab's prodding. He tells Joab that he can bring Absalom back to Israel. The assumption is that he will not allow anyone (any avenger) to take Absalom's life. But somewhere along the line, David considers what he has done and makes a change in plans. Absalom is not to be brought back to Israel as though an innocent man, free to come and go as he pleases. Absalom is to be under house arrest, confined to Jerusalem and his own house (14:21–23).

There is a kind of poetic justice in this confinement, as it is Absalom who had confined his sister Tamar to quarters. By confining Tamar to his house, Absalom kept her quiet. He also kept her desolate. All of this enabled him to carry out his evil plan to murder Amnon. Now, David confines Absalom to the same quarters in which he confined his sister.

Absalom has a great deal going for him. He is a good-looking man, without a single flaw. His hair is his crowning glory, and everybody knows it. He has three sons and a beautiful daughter, who also adds to his standing. He is a celebrity of that day. He requests to see the king's face, accepting that the consequence may be death. Even though he is a murderer, his actions prove that he believes he is on the side of justice and that his heart is not repentant (14:25–33).

15:1–12

DAVID HUMILIATED

Absalom is very charming and wins the hearts of the Israelites by promises of justices and displays of affection. Absalom uses his freedom to undermine David's reputation and standing with the people. Absalom's betrayal is the ultimate tragedy—much like Saul's attempts to kill David or Judas's kiss that betrays Christ (15:1–6). Soon, Absalom is in full rebellion, which leads to the division of Israel, and finally the death of Absalom at the hand of Joab. Absalom's life is truly a trail of tears.

We must be careful not to say that God is punishing David for his sins through the suffering of others. Many people will suggest that whenever a person suffers, it is because they are being punished for their sin. Job's friends believed this and continually sought to compel him to repent (Job 4 and 5). Our Lord's disciples assumed the man born blind was this way because of someone's sin (John 9:1–2). There are those whose suffering is the direct result of their sin (Deuteronomy 28:15), but this is not always the explanation for suffering. Sometimes the righteous suffer for being righteous (1 Peter 4).

This text has much to say about parenting. The Bible is amply clear that there are no perfect parents—that nature and nurture are surely two parts of the human condition. Even the godliest men and women parent children who rebel against God (think of Eli, Samuel, Saul, and now David). Obviously, parents honor God by being good to their children and teaching them the way of the Lord, but each person is ultimately responsible for his or her own choices.

Absalom is a man who "bites the hand that feeds him." He lacks any sense of debt to his father, and there is no evidence of gratitude on his part. But more than this, there is absolutely no true submission to his father-king. Absalom sees himself as next in line for the throne. He does not submit himself to his father. Instead he uses his position and power to undermine his father's authority and to disrupt his kingdom. Behind his father's back, he speaks ill of his father, making him look bad in the eyes of others. And all of this is done to get ahead (2 Samuel 14:7–12).

Critical Observation

Through Absalom's rebellion, God allows David to see his own sin from a different point of view. The story provides powerful perspective. Absalom is a warning to us all about submission and its counterpart, rebellion. David cannot save his son Absalom any more than we can save our children. For the appropriate reconciliation to occur, Absalom needs to submit to God in repentance. To be reconciled to God, one must acknowledge his or her sin and rebellion against God and accept the free gift of eternal life that He offers in the gospel of grace.

2 SAMUEL 15:13–16:19

TRAIL OF TEARS

At the Palace in Jerusalem	15:13–16
At the Last House	15:17–22
Just Over the Brook Kidron	15:23–29
The Ascent of the Mount of Olives	15:30–37
The Summit of the Mount of Olives	16:1–4
At Bahurim—Stoned by Shimei	16:5–14
Back in Jerusalem	16:15–19

Setting Up the Section

Word comes to David that the people's allegiance has turned to Absalom and that a full-scale rebellion is about to occur. It is at this point that David decides to flee from Jerusalem, along with many of his followers. Those who will be numbered among his followers (and who will remain behind in Jerusalem) will be determined by whether or not they are true friends of David.

15:13–16

AT THE PALACE IN JERUSALEM

Notice that the messenger's report, as conveyed to the reader, does not indicate that Absalom has already sounded the trumpet, declaring himself king (15:10). Nor is it said that Absalom is actually marching on the city. But it is apparent that this is assumed. If it has not already happened, it will happen very soon. This is the time to act.

Instead of giving the order to prepare for battle, David gives the order to prepare to flee from Jerusalem. Here is the man who did not hesitate to stand up to Goliath when no one else was willing to do so, including Saul himself. Here is the man who, when insulted by Nabal (1 Samuel 25), was provoked to anger and set out to kill this man and every male member of his household. Why is David so eager to flee rather than fight?

It is important to understand that in fleeing from Jerusalem, David has not indicated his intention to abdicate the throne. This is why he leaves ten concubines behind to keep his house (2 Samuel 15:16). He is leaving town, but he is not leaving his throne. Absalom may seize it, but this will not be because David has handed in his resignation. The concubines are a symbol of David's continuing reign over Israel.

There are a number of reasons David makes the decision to flee. First, David knows that God will bring about troubles in his kingdom from within his own family. If the rebellion of Absalom is a part of the divine discipline he has brought upon himself, David is not sure whether he should resist it. If this is of God, will David be fighting against God to fight against this rebellion? David clearly indicates his intention to wait until he has a sense of certainty about what he should do.

Additionally, David loves Absalom. He does not want to precipitate a fight with him because he does not wish to kill him (chapter 18). Why start a fight you are not willing to win? And so it is that David chooses flight over a fight.

15:17–22

AT THE LAST HOUSE

David pauses at the last house and allows those going with him to pass him. This last house may refer to the last of the houses that his wives and children inhabit in Jerusalem, but it appears to be the last house they come to before leaving the town. David stops at the outskirts of Jerusalem, pausing as those fleeing with him pass by. This gives David the opportunity to allow some to accompany him and to encourage others to turn back.

Demystifying 2 Samuel

The first major group of those loyal to David, who will accompany him as he flees from Jerusalem, are loyal foreigners—Gentiles. These all seem to be men whose association with David goes back to his days spent hiding out from Saul in the land of the Philistines. Among these are the Cherethites, Pelethites, and Gittites. The Cherethites and Pelethites are mentioned earlier (8:18) and later (23:22–23) in 2 Samuel. They are foreigners led by Benaiah. These men were probably a kind of honor guard for David who protect his life. Many kings had foreign mercenaries who served as their personal bodyguards.

A Gittite is a person from the Philistine city of Gath. Goliath was probably the most famous Gittite (21:19).

In addition to this larger group of faithful Gentiles, there is one who is a relative newcomer: Ittai the Gittite (15:19–22). This man must have been both loyal and capable for David to make him commander of a portion of his troops in chapter 18. There are a number of reasons why Ittai should have felt little obligation to follow David. He is a foreigner–it isn't his fight. He is a relative newcomer. He is accompanied by a number of children, who will certainly be a burden and be in danger if Absalom pursues David. So David pulls him aside to suggest that he turn back. Ittai responds with an outpouring of loyalty–in a speech that is notably similar to the response of Ruth to Naomi (Ruth 1:16–17).

15:23–29

JUST OVER THE BROOK KIDRON

David demonstrates that he has learned something valuable by commanding Zadok to return the ark of the covenant to Jerusalem. He knows that if God is truly with him, then He will bring David back to Jerusalem, back to the place where God has chosen to dwell. If God is not with him, David knows the ark will do him no good.

This is a far cry from the mindset seen in 1 Samuel 4. There, when the Israelites suffer a defeat at the hands of the Philistines, the people fetch the ark, assuming it will somehow magically give them victory. Instead, the Israelites are defeated, Eli's two sons are killed, and the ark is taken by the Philistines. On top of this, Eli falls dead with the news that his sons are dead and the ark is in enemy hands. David does not see the ark as some kind of magic charm that assures him of God's presence or of divine deliverance. Jerusalem is where the ark belongs, and David is not going to attempt to take it with him.

15:30–37

THE ASCENT OF THE MOUNT OF OLIVES

David ascends the Mount of Olives, weeping as he makes his way toward the top. His head is covered and his feet are bare, as is the case with all those accompanying him. The report reaches David that Ahithophel has joined Absalom in his revolt. This is a devastating blow because Ahithophel's counsel is so reliable (16:23).

Critical Observation

While the loss of Ahithophel is a devastating loss for David's administration, it should not come as a great surprise because of his relationship to David—Ahithophel is Bathsheba's grandfather (11:3; 23:34). Ahithophel very likely feels toward David as Absalom feels toward Amnon, so it is little wonder that he decides to side with Absalom at this point.

David's response is to utter a prayer that God will somehow thwart the counsel of Ahithophel. The answer to his prayer is not that far off, for David has hardly begun praying when his trusted friend, Hushai the Arkite, arrives. His coat is torn and he has cast dust on his head, both signs of mourning. This is indeed a most terrible thing that has happened. Hushai is ready to accompany David wherever he is going. David changes Hushai's plans. The king informs Hushai that if he does accompany him into hiding, he will only be an added burden. Hushai can perform a much more valuable service to David by returning to Jerusalem and pretending to become one of Ahithophel's loyal supporters. This way, Hushai will be in a position to counter the counsel of Ahithophel. David informs Hushai that Zadok and Abiathar are also loyal supporters. When Zadok or Abiathar hear something from the palace, they can send a message to David by their sons: Ahimaaz, Zadok's son, and Jonathan, Abiathar's son.

16:1–4

THE SUMMIT OF THE MOUNT OF OLIVES

David and his followers have just passed the summit of the Mount of Olives. There he is met by Ziba, the servant of Mephibosheth. Ziba was a servant of King Saul. In order for David to fulfill his covenant with Jonathan, he needed to find an heir of Saul to whom he could show favor for Jonathan's sake. He was told of Ziba, who was formerly Saul's servant. Ziba was summoned, and there he informed David about Mephibosheth. When David brought Mephibosheth into his home, to eat at his table, he also restored to Mephibosheth all that was his as the heir of Saul and Jonathan. David also appointed Ziba and his family to serve Mephibosheth as his servant, as they had done before Saul's death.

Now we meet Ziba again. This time Ziba meets David with provisions for the journey ahead. David inquires of Ziba as to why he is bringing these supplies, and Ziba tells him that it is for the king and those with him, since the journey will prove difficult. David then asks Ziba where his master, Mephibosheth, is. Ziba tells David that Mephibosheth has gone to Jerusalem, hoping that his father Saul's kingdom will be restored to him. On the basis of Ziba's account, David gave to Ziba and his sons all that had been given to Mephibosheth.

16:5–14

AT BAHURIM—STONED BY SHIMEI

Bahurim is a small town not far from Jerusalem. This is the place where the two spies, Ahimaaz and Jonathan, were hidden in a well until Absalom's men gave up searching for them (17:17–20). Here, a man named Shimei appears, not to mourn with David nor to provide supplies for his journey, but to mock and curse him, throwing dirt and stones at David and his followers.

Shimei's accusations are interesting. He accuses David of being a man of bloodshed. We immediately think in terms of Uriah and his death, ordered by David himself. But this is not what Shimei mentions specifically. He speaks of David's shedding of blood in terms of Saul and his house (16:8). Abishai wants to shut this man's mouth permanently by cutting off his head, but David refuses permission, convinced of the sovereignty of God in all these matters. He knows that Shimei's actions are wrong, even that his accusations are inaccurate. In spite of this, David believes that it is possible that God is speaking to him through this man, and thus he will not seek to silence him. Instead, he proceeds, looking to God for his vindication.

16:15–19

BACK IN JERUSALEM

David's flight from Jerusalem certainly prompts Absalom's bold advance to the city and his possession of it. Once in the city, Absalom turns to Ahithophel for counsel as to what he should do next. Ahithophel counsels Absalom to symbolically declare himself king in a way that will make a statement to David and to all Israel. Ahithophel recommends that Absalom take the ten wives (or concubines; the terms seem to be used almost interchangeably here) and publicly sleep with them, as a symbol of his possession of the throne (along with the harem). The taking of a king's harem certainly symbolizes the taking of his place. Ruben does this by taking one of Jacob's concubines (Genesis 35:22; 49:4). Adonijah will attempt to do this with Abishag, one of David's concubines (1 Kings 2:13–25).

Absalom's actions regarding David's wives are not only a gesture that symbolically proclaims his taking of the throne; it is also the fulfillment of Nathan's prophetic words (2 Samuel 12:9–12). There is never any doubt that God will bring about that which He had spoken through Nathan. The author of this text does not want us to miss the fact that this event is, in part, the fulfillment of Nathan's words. David sinned with one woman, taking her as his wife when she was the wife of another. Now, Absalom takes ten wives of David and makes them his own wives by sleeping with them.

David sinned in private; Absalom purposely makes a spectacle of his. David's humiliation in this situation is great. Let us never deceive ourselves into thinking that our sin is worth the price. If David could have seen where his sin was leading, he would never have chosen the path he did.

Take It Home

In the tragedies of David's flight from Jerusalem and his son's humiliation of him, we are reminded that people betray one another in terrible ways—even ones bound by bonds of family or friendship. The one friend who does not desert Moses or Joshua or Paul or David is God. He is not intimidated by anyone, nor is He deterred by suffering and sorrow. His love is not based on what we can give to Him or what we have to offer through friendship. His love is unconditional. He is the model, the benchmark, for a true friend, whose life calls us all to go the extra mile and turn the other cheek even for our enemies.

2 SAMUEL 16:20–19:8

DARKEST DAYS

Ahithophel's Counsel	16:20–17:4
Hushai's Counsel	17:5–14
David's Escape to Mahanaim	17:15–29
The Defeat and the Death of Absalom	18:1–18
Proclaiming the Good News	18:19–33
Joab Rebukes His King	19:1–8

Setting Up the Section

This passage is filled with intrigue and drama and more tragedy for David. David is overwhelmed by sorrow and suffering. Still, there is deliverance and hope for David in these dark hours as he passes through the valley of the shadow of death (Psalm 23).

16:20–17:4

AHITHOPHEL'S COUNSEL

Ahithophel's counsel is exceedingly shrewd in several ways. It offers an appealing course of action to Absalom. He, not unlike his father David, can stay home from the battle with his wives while Ahithophel and his army are at war with David (16:20–22). Absalom can quickly enter into his possession of the throne, yet without the dangers or discomforts of going into battle. As an added incentive, he can indulge himself with David's wives in a way that gets back at David and hurts and humiliates his father. Only David, Absalom's real enemy, will be killed.

Ahithophel proposes a quick, easy victory for Absalom. It is almost too good to be true, but Absalom (like his father) believes that Ahithophel speaks wisely (16:23–17:4). The fact is it is a plan that would have worked, but God has other plans for David and for Absalom. These plans are brought to pass through David's friends: Hushai, Zadok, and Abiathar, their sons Ahimaaz and Jonathan, a farmer's wife in Bahurim, and a number of other faithful friends and supporters of David.

17:5–14

HUSHAI'S COUNSEL

Hushai has one great handicap: Absalom and everyone else in Israel know he is David's friend. How can Absalom trust a man who has been David's friend for so long? His counsel must be suspect. Rather than try to avoid this issue, Hushai uses his friendship.

Hushai challenges the assumptions on which Ahithophel's plans are based. He proposes a very different plan. Hushai insists that Ahithophel has dangerously underestimated David and his ability to defend himself and his kingdom. Hushai reminds Absalom and the elders of Israel about the kind of man David is. He is no mental weakling, but a tough and seasoned warrior. Absalom's rebellion will not break David's spirit; it will antagonize him. David will be fighting mad and fighting ready (17:7–9).

If Ahithophel comes into the wilderness to attack David, they will fight him on his turf. After all, David has spent years hiding from Saul in the wilderness. Does Ahithophel really think David can easily be found sitting among the rest of the people? He will be hiding out, and when Ahithophel and his small army arrive, David will pounce on them, giving them a humiliating defeat. It will be Absalom's soldiers who will lose heart and run, not David or his men (17:10).

Hushai's plan brings about a bigger battle, so that not only will many of Absalom's supporters die, but Absalom himself will be killed, thus ending the revolution. In reality, Hushai's plan gives David the time he needs to plan his battle (17:11–13). It allows David to fight on his turf. Hushai's plan makes Ahithophel's counsel seem foolish, which is exactly what David had prayed for (15:31). It brings about the deliverance of David and the defeat of his enemies (17:14).

17:15–29

DAVID'S ESCAPE TO MAHANAIM

As Absalom prepares to cross the Jordan in hot pursuit of David, David and his men flee to the gates of Mahanaim. This is indeed a city with history. It was Jacob who gave this city its name. As he returned to the land of promise, fearful of what would happen when he met his brother Esau, Jacob is met by angels, prompting him to say, "This is God's camp" (Genesis 32:2 NASB). And so it is that Jacob names that place Mahanaim (meaning "two camps").

Is David fearful about meeting up with his son Absalom? We know from later events that he wishes to avoid a confrontation that will end in death. He should have remembered that God always protects His people, His promises, and His purposes, even by the use of angels if needed.

Ahithophel remains in Jerusalem only long enough to be convinced that his counsel is not going to be heeded by Absalom. Once it is clear that Hushai's counsel has prevailed, he knows he is finished. He has gambled everything on the assumption that Absalom will prevail over David. Now he knows that Absalom is destined to be defeated. He makes his way to his own home, sets his business in order, and kills himself. What a tragic end for a man with such great potential (2 Samuel 17:23).

Critical Observation

God provides for David at Mahanaim in more tangible and visible ways as well. When he and his faithful followers arrive, there are those ready and willing to help. Particularly amazing is the help that David receives from Shobi, the son of Nahash, and now king of the Ammonites. David and Nahash had been on relatively friendly terms, but when Nahash died and his son, Hanun, took the throne, he foolishly humiliated the delegation David sent to mourn Nahash's death (10:1–5). This disgrace led to war between Israel and the Ammonites. In fact it is this war with the Ammonites (and specifically the besieging of Rabbah) that David decided to avoid, leaving the battle to the Israelites under Joab's command; and during his stay in Jerusalem David fell into sin with Bathsheba (11:1–5). David finally defeated the Ammonites (12:26–31). Now Shobi is on the throne and eager to come to David's aid when he is opposed by Absalom. The Lord provides allies for David in unusual ways.

The second supporter to come to David's aid at Mahanaim is Machir, the son of Ammiel from Lo-debar (17:27). This is the man who takes in Mephibosheth after the death of King Saul and of Jonathan (9:4–5). Finally, Barzillai the Gileadite, an elderly man of great wealth, brings supplies for David and those with him. We learn even more about this man in 19:31–40. What an encouragement these men and their assistance must be to David.

18:1–18

THE DEFEAT AND THE DEATH OF ABSALOM

David is wisely advised—because of his status as the priority target—to stay behind while his men go to battle. As David's men head off to fight Absalom's men, David charges them to deal gently with Absalom (18:5). Everyone hears these words. How different from the advice of Ahithophel, who intends to kill David alone and let the rest of the people live. David allows his men to kill any other Israelite, but not his son, the leader of the revolution. He commands those who are risking their lives for him to fight, but not to fight to win. It underscores how sensitive and loyal David is to the fact that though he is his mortal enemy, Absalom is also his son (18:1–5).

Absalom's forces suffer a great defeat, not only at the hand of David's men, but even from the forest itself. Absalom's men are not cut out for this kind of warfare. A total of twenty thousand men die in this slaughter, which spreads out over the whole countryside, as Absalom's men begin to turn and run for their lives. It is a great victory for David, and a devastating defeat for Absalom (18:6–8).

We do not know whether Absalom is running for his life or not, but he does seem to be alone at the time his mule runs under the branches of a great oak tree and Absalom's head is wedged in the branches. None of Absalom's men seem to be around to rescue him. (They may have been fleeing for their lives.) One of Joab's men comes upon Absalom and mentions it to his commander. Joab is incensed that this young man has not killed Absalom on the spot. Would he not have been rewarded for doing so? The young man is taken back by Joab's rebuke.

He reminds Joab that David, their commander-in-chief, has specifically forbidden anyone to harm his son Absalom. No matter what Joab may promise to do for him, this soldier knows that when David learns he has killed his son, there will be no protection for him.

It is ironic that it is Joab who kills Absalom, since it was Joab who had orchestrated amnesty for Absalom and brought him back to Jerusalem. It was Joab who obtained greater freedom for Absalom and brought him into the king's presence. And yet, for all Joab had done for Absalom, this man set out to take the throne away from his father, and to set another as commander over Israel's forces (16:9–18).

Joab has played a major role throughout the story of David's kingship. It was likewise Joab who, under orders from David, had Uriah killed in battle, without raising a word of protest. And now this military commander, who would kill a righteous man at David's request, kills David's own son in direct violation to his orders. Joab is not averse to doing dirty work. David, who abused his almost absolute authority to take Uriah's wife and have him killed at Joab's command, is powerless to save his own son from death at the hand of Joab (or anyone else).

Demystifying 2 Samuel

Both Absalom and Ahithophel fail to correctly answer the most important question any person will ever answer in their lifetime: "Who will I serve as king?" Absalom and Ahithophel do not want David for their king. Both, in effect, want to be king of their own lives. But in rejecting David as their king, they are rejecting God's king, and thus they are rebelling against God Himself. Both of these men have great ability, but in the end, their talents are of no eternal profit because they refuse to submit to God's authority and His chosen king.

18:19–33

PROCLAIMING THE GOOD NEWS

Joab knows his king well. He knows that David will not take the news of Absalom's death lightly. That is why he is reluctant to send Ahimaaz to David with the news. This is also why Ahimaaz hedges his answer to David's specific question about Absalom's well-being. David has been waiting for news of the outcome of the battle (18:19–28).

There is more space devoted to the messengers who report to David than there is about the war between the two opposing armies, including the account of the death of Absalom (18:28–33). Besides the space devoted to the relaying of the message, the text emphasizes the term good news, using it four times. When the translators of the Septuagint rendered this term in Greek, they used the term that we often find in the New Testament in reference to the proclamation of the gospel. The good news that Ahimaaz proclaims to David is that God has given him the victory by the death of his son. But this news is not good for David. It is a strange parallel to the New Testament gospel, which hinges on the death and resurrection of the Son of the eternal King, God (18:33).

19:1–8

JOAB REBUKES HIS KING

The scene of this victorious army returning to Mahanaim must have been jubilant. There would be shouting and celebration. What a great day of victory. But King David is not with his army. Instead, the triumphant soldiers learn that David is grieving over the death of his son. Now, instead of feeling proud of what they have done, David's men feel ashamed. David's warriors, who risked their necks to save their king, now hang their heads in shame. A day of victory is suddenly transformed into a day of mourning. The soldiers begin to sneak into the city, as though they have done something wrong (19:1–4).

Joab rightly rebukes David for putting everyone who has come with him from Jerusalem to shame, not just his soldiers, but his wives, children, and his concubines as well. By his response to the day's events, David reveals that he loves his enemy more than his friends and family. He loves those who hate him more than those who love him. He has shown total disregard for those who are willing to give their all for their king. Joab puts it as bluntly: David would rather have heard that his entire army was slaughtered and that his son Absalom was alive than to learn that his army had prevailed, but that Absalom was dead (19:5–7).

Take It Home

Many of David's psalms are written in a time of despair, possibly even during this time of exile from his throne and war with his own son. David uses the psalms to express his fears, despair, depression, and to cry out to God for strength. He finds hope and help in remembering the God to whom he speaks. And in the process of writing these psalms, David has also ministered to many people from his own despair. It is often from our times of mourning and sorrow that we begin to see life more clearly, to trust in God more completely, and to recognize our profound need for Him. If this is the case, then suffering and sorrow and even depression may at times be our friend and not our enemy. Anything that draws us more closely to God is something in which we should rejoice (James 1).

2 SAMUEL 19:9–20:26

RETURN TO JERUSALEM

Setting Up the Section

David is about to return to Jerusalem to resume his reign over the nation of Israel. To win the favor of the people (and perhaps to remove a thorn in his own flesh), David removes Joab as commander of his armed forces, replacing him with Amasa.

19:9–18

CONVINCING ISRAEL

The people who had supported Absalom as king and remained in Israel need to be handled carefully in order to convince them to accept David as their king again. Word of their reluctance to accept him reaches David while he is still residing in Mahanaim. He acts in a way that makes it easier for the Israelites to welcome him back. David sends word to Zadok and Abiathar (the priests who were in Jerusalem and had remained loyal to him), instructing them to speak to the elders of Judah. This is David's tribe, the tribe which first anointed David as their king when he was in Hebron. These are David's closest kinsmen. It is logical that they should take the lead in bringing David back to Jerusalem.

David makes it even easier for the people of Judah by announcing that he is firing Joab as commander of his army and replacing him with Amasa. This action on David's part does the trick. Word comes from the elders of Judah, inviting him to return. David and all those with him make their way from Mahanaim to the banks of the Jordan River. The people of Judah assemble at Gilgal to assist David and those with him in crossing the river, and to welcome him back as their king. In addition to the people of Judah, a good-sized delegation of Israelites is present, representing the other tribes as well. Among these are Mephibosheth, Ziba (his servant, along with his sons and servants), and Shimei, accompanied by a thousand Benjamites.

19:19–23

REPENTANCE AND FORGIVENESS

Shimei is no stranger to David. He is the descendant of Saul who harasses David and those with him when they flee from Jerusalem (16:5–14). He hurls rocks, dirt, accusations, and insults at David. Abishai had wanted to shut this man's mouth permanently then, but

David refused, assuming God was, in some way, rebuking him through Shimei. Now, on his return, David must pass through Bahurim, Shimei's hometown. Shimei knows he is in serious trouble. David is once again the king of Israel, and he may reasonably view Shimei as a traitor who needs to be removed.

19:24–30

DAVID DEALS WITH MEPHIBOSHETH AND ZIBA

Ziba, his sons and servants, and Mephibosheth are there to greet David and help him on his journey through the Jordan and on to Jerusalem (19:24). While Ziba is somewhere around, the conversation here is between David and Mephibosheth. Ziba is the one who appears to have forsaken David, while Mephibosheth seems to be in good standing. David asks Mephibosheth why he did not accompany him when he fled from Jerusalem. The accounts he receives do not match. Rather than trying to reconcile them, David divides the land he had given to Mephibosheth.

David declares that Mephibosheth's land (which David had given him earlier, and then given to Ziba) will be divided evenly between him and his servant Ziba. Once again, it is a day of rejoicing and reunion. David will give both men the benefit of the doubt and make a judgment that might facilitate their reconciliation.

Mephibosheth acknowledges David's graciousness to him in the past and also that he is unworthy and undeserving of any special consideration from David. He then seems to waive his rights to what David has given him, signing them over (as it were) to Ziba. Whether he actually does this is another matter. But the impression he seeks to give David is that he is more than happy to live in the king's presence and that further benefits are unnecessary and unwanted (19:28–30).

19:31–39

BLESSING BARZILLAI

Barzillai is an elderly man, eighty years old to be precise. He is also a very wealthy man. He must have lived close to Mahanaim, for it is there where this generous old man provides for the needs of David and those with him while in exile. Now that David is going back to Jerusalem, Barzillai goes to great efforts to extend his friendship and hospitality to him on his return. It is some twenty-five miles (approximately—we don't know exactly where Mahanaim was located) back to the Jordan where David will cross, and another twenty to twenty-five miles to Jerusalem. This old man accompanies David to the Jordan and beyond to Gilgal (not far from where ancient Jericho would have been).

David wishes to show his gratitude to this elderly man and invites Barzillai to accompany him to Jerusalem, where the king promises to abundantly provide for him. Barzillai graciously declines David's offer. He is too old, he admits, to appreciate the difference between filet mignon and mush, or between the concert soprano voice of one of David's musicians and his own singing in the shower. David's delicacies would be wasted on him; and besides, he does not have all that much time left. He prefers to stay in his own home, near the place where his parents are buried and where he, before long, will be buried as well.

Barzillai does not wish to personally benefit from the generous offer David makes him, but he does propose an alternative. Barzillai commends a young man, Chimham, to the king, asking David if he will confer his blessings on this lad, as if upon him. From what we are told in 1 Kings 2:7, we know David intends not only to keep his promise to Barzillai in his lifetime but to continue it after his own death. David instructs Solomon to continue to be kind to Barzillai's sons (note the plural). It is assumed that Chimham is a son of Barzillai and that either at this time or later he is joined by another son or more. David generously provides for these men as Barzillai has cared for him.

19:40–20:2

THE GREAT DIVIDE

As David and his men return to Jerusalem, the quarrelling continues between the men of Judah and the other ten tribes of Israel. Petty jealousy and strife prevail, so much so that the ten tribes become angry and embittered toward the men of Judah. Tensions are at an all-time high. Any precipitous action here could cause the situation to ignite.

Something precipitous does happen. There just happens to be a man among the people of Israel whose name is Sheba (20:1). The author makes it known that he is trouble (the text literally reads, "son of belial"). Sheba would not be taken seriously under normal circumstances. But in the heat of this argument, Sheba loses his temper (or sees the opportunity to assume leadership here) and blurts out, "Down with the dynasty of David!" (20:1 NLT). These words are all it takes for these Israelites to turn on their heels and leave with Sheba. And so this once joyful procession turns sour with a bitter debate and now a major schism. One moment these Israelites claim David as their leader; the next they are following Sheba, a worthless man. David has not even reached Jerusalem, and his kingdom is already a divided one. It looks as though he is starting all over again, as the king of the tribe of Judah.

Critical Observation

When the people of Israel are arguing with the people of Judah, the Israelites claim ten times the ownership of David since they have ten tribes. In other words, David is ten times more obligated to them. But when the people of Judah speak of their relationship to David, their claim to him is that he is near kin. Neither the ten tribes of Israel nor the tribe of Judah speak of David as God's anointed king. Both tribes follow David for self-serving reasons. Thus, Judah is hardly better for following David than the men of Israel are for leaving him.

20:3–13

BACK TO BUSINESS

The first thing David does after arriving in Jerusalem is deal with the ten wives (or concubines) he left behind to keep the house. Absalom has slept with these women in public; there is no way David can go back to the way things were. He will never sleep with any of these women again. He appoints a place for them to stay and provides generously for them, but they have been defiled by Absalom.

The next item of business for David is the rebellion that is under way, led by Sheba. For some unexplained reason, Amasa does not assemble the armed forces of Judah in the three-day time frame David sets down. You can imagine how uneasy David must be, knowing that every hour Sheba is free that the threat to his kingdom increases. It must pain David greatly to finally admit Amasa is not coming, at least not for a while, and to call for Abishai, the brother of Joab and a long-time pain-in-the-neck for David (1 Samuel 26:6–11; 2 Samuel 16:9–12; 19:21–22). David would not ask Joab to do the job, for it would appear to be an admission that he has erred in firing Joab and replacing him with Amasa. But when Abishai goes out from Jerusalem, leading David's select warriors (the Green Berets or Navy Seals of his day) in pursuit of Sheba, he is accompanied by Joab.

When Joab and Amasa meet, Joab promptly kills him. It does not seem to be at Joab's initiative that a certain soldier takes it upon himself to address the rest. He is one of Joab's men, so we would expect him to be loyal to Joab and one of his supporters. Seeing Amasa lying there dead, it is obvious to him that there needs to be a new commander of the army. After all, someone needs to give the orders. It seems clear that next in the chain of command is Abishai. He is the oldest son (1 Chronicles 2:16), but most importantly, he is the one David sends to pursue Sheba when Amasa does not return. In spite of this, the young man urges the rest of his colleagues to acknowledge Joab as their new commander, and it seems this is precisely what happens. There is no mention of any protest, and Joab is spoken of as the leader from here on.

20:14–26

THE DEMISE OF SHEBA

Joab and his forces finally track down Sheba at Abel Beth-maacah. When they hear that Sheba has sought refuge in this fortified city, they put the city under siege. A wise woman sizes up the situation and takes the initiative. She goes to the wall, calls down, and asks to speak to Joab. He comes near, and she recounts to him how this city has been highly esteemed as a source of wisdom and counsel. It is a place known for ending disputes. Why then would Joab want to destroy such a place? She goes on to tell Joab that she is among those in the city who are peaceable and faithful in Israel. They have done nothing to deserve what Joab is dishing out. This is a part of the inheritance from God. Does Joab really wish to be responsible for destroying it?

Joab assures the woman that he does not wish to destroy the city. He then informs her why the city is being besieged. They are seeking but one person, Sheba the son of Bichri, who is guilty of rebellion against King David. If the woman will arrange to have this man handed over to them, they will go on their way in peace. The woman assures Joab that Sheba's head will be thrown over the wall to him. The woman then convinces the people of the city to execute Sheba, and his head is thrown down to Joab and his army. With this, Joab blows the trumpet, indicating the cessation of hostilities (20:20–22).

Take It Home

The events of 2 Samuel 19–20 underscore the reality of divine providence. There are times when God intervenes in the lives of His people in direct ways. The roots of division between Judah and the other tribes of Israel run deep in Israel's history, but it is evident that Israel is divided for a very short time in David's day. This division is never completely healed. It lays dormant for the years of Solomon's reign, but it comes to life after his death. In all of this, God is preparing the nation for the division He purposes. We must remember to submit to God's anointed King in our own lives just as the Israelites were called to. In the new expanded kingdom of God's chosen people, God has appointed Jesus as our sovereign King. Let us submit to Him as Savior and Lord, and let us live as His loyal subjects, for His glory and our eternal good.

2 SAMUEL 21:1–22

PROMISE BREAKERS AND KEEPERS

Setting Up the Section

King Saul had violated a covenant with the Gibeonites that was more than four centuries old. His actions with regard to the Gibeonites bring a famine upon the land of Israel some time after he dies. Now David must deal with Saul's covenant breaking and make things right.

21:1–14

RIGHTING A WRONG

The Gibeonites are an interesting people. Our author refers to them as Amorites (21:2), but they are more technically known as the Hivites (Joshua 9:1, 7; 11:19). These Gibeonites were among those living in Canaan, whom God had commanded Israel to annihilate (Exodus 33:2; 34:11; Deuteronomy 7:1–2). This would have been the case except for a strange turn of events, which is described in the book of Joshua (chapter 9).

Demystifying 2 Samuel

Under the leadership of Joshua, the Israelites had just crossed the Jordan River (Joshua 3) and captured the city of Jericho (Joshua 6) and then Ai (Joshua 7–8). The next city to come under attack by Israel almost certainly would be Gibeon, and the Gibeonites knew it. Gibeon was a great city, and its warriors were among the best (Joshua 10:2). But rather than fighting the Israelites, they were allowed to stay in Canaan as their slaves (Joshua 9:16–17). The treaty the Israelites made with the Gibeonites also assured these people of Israel's protection (Joshua 10:8).

As we come to our text, some four hundred years have passed since the leaders of Israel made their covenant with the Gibeonites. God is angry with Israel because of the sin of Saul and his bloody house against the Gibeonites. Saul and his house commenced a program of genocide against the Gibeonites.

The Gibeonites must bless Israel, the people of God, in order for God to once again bless Israel. It seems to be almost an exact reversal of the Abrahamic Covenant, where God promises to bless those who bless the Israelites. Here the Israelites have violated the Gibeonites, however, which deeply angers God. Being God's chosen people does not give anyone a license to sin. God hears the cries of the oppressed and judges sin, even when that sin is committed by His chosen people.

Critical Observation

This passage emphasizes the importance of covenants. Throughout Old Testament history, God deals with people through covenants (Genesis 9:1–17; 12:1–3; 17:1–22; Exodus 19–20; 31:12–17; Deuteronomy 5; 2 Samuel 7:12–17). Then, in the New Testament, He ushers in the New Covenant by the Lord Jesus Christ through the shedding of His blood (Jeremiah 31:31–34; Luke 22:20; 1 Corinthians 11:25; 2 Corinthians 3:6; Hebrews 9:11–22). God has not dealt with His people capriciously; He has always dealt with them in accordance with a covenant. David's dealing with the Gibeonites, at its roots, is a matter of keeping covenants. Israel had made a covenant with the Gibeonites. Even though this covenant is four hundred years old, it is still to be honored. No matter how good Saul's intentions might have been, the covenant must be kept. The breaking of that covenant had serious consequences.

This passage foreshadows the gospel in so many ways. Not only does it remind us that God relates to His people by means of His covenants, but it speaks to us particularly of the New Covenant. Saul's sins had to be atoned for or God's blessings could not be enjoyed. Saul's sin brought adversity in the form of a famine. Money could not atone for this sin—only the shedding of blood. It is the shedding of this blood that brings about atonement and appeases both God and the Gibeonites. The story of Saul, David, and the Gibeonites reminds us not only that sin must be atoned for by the shedding of blood, but that there is a payday, according to God's timing, for sin.

21:15–22

WAR WITH GIANT ENEMIES

This chapter describes the end of David's military career. It is not yet the end of his reign as king of Israel, but it is the end of his military career. David will no longer go out to fight with his men (21:17). David's military career began with a contest with Goliath and a victory over the Philistines (1 Samuel 17). The ending of David's military career is a final battle with one of Goliath's offspring and the defeat of the Philistines.

This is a story of closure and transition. The task of leaders is not to do everything, but to facilitate ministry, to train, equip, and encourage others who will take their place to do an even better job. If this is what Christian leadership is to be, then David is a great leader. Under Saul, not one man is willing to stand up to Goliath. In David's ministry, there are many willing and able to do so. David is now free to step aside (first as commander of the military and later as king) because he has done his job well.

2 SAMUEL 22:1–51

DAVID'S SONG OF SALVATION

Setting Up the Section

This passage records David's reflections, penned at the outset of his reign as Israel's king. The text is virtually identical to (and possibly quoting) Psalm 18.

22:1–3

DAVID'S DELIVERER

In the first verse of the psalm, we are given the historical background for this song of David. David wrote this psalm after God delivered him from the hand of his enemies and from the hand of Saul. It would seem then that the psalm was written shortly after Saul's death and at the outset of David's reign as king. David now occupies the throne, and from this vantage point, he reflects on God's gracious dealings in his life to fulfill His promise that he would be Israel's king.

God is David's fortress and his stronghold. He is David's shield and the horn of his salvation. These are not mere images; these are the very means God employed to save David's life from the hand of his enemies. And now, David urges us to look beyond these means which God employed to God Himself. It is God who delivers; He is our place of safety.

22:4–20

CRY FOR HELP

David called to God for deliverance, and God responded in a way that signaled His sovereignty over all creation. When God heard David's cry, He responded, as evidenced by all of His creation. God is angered by the enemies who have endangered His anointed king, and all of creation reflects God's anger. This is not just a description of a God who is eager to save His king, but a God who is intent upon destroying the enemies who threaten His king.

God reaches down and plucks His servant from the waters, delivering him from his strong enemy and setting him down in a broad place on solid ground. Though David's enemies are stronger, God delivers him from their hand. He is David's support when they confront him.

22:21–51

DIVINE DELIVERANCE

In the Law of Moses, God made it clear to His people that He would bless them as they trusted in Him and kept His law (Deuteronomy 7:12–16). On the other hand, it was also clear that their righteousness attained by their works was not the basis for God's grace. David understood that God saves the righteous and condemns the wicked. It is for this reason that God hears David's cry for help and comes to his rescue from his wicked enemies. Not only does God save the righteous, but He saves the afflicted, while He condemns the proud.

Very often God will have us play a role in His deliverance. In such cases, it is God who gives us the strength and ability to prevail over our enemies. David stood up to Goliath and prevailed, but it was God who gave the victory. David describes the strength God supplies in terms of waging warfare. God's strength enables him to leap over a wall and to overrun a troop of men (2 Samuel 22:30). Military strength begins in the mind. David had the moral courage to stand up to Goliath as well as the God-given skill to strike him down with his sling.

The basis for this strength of courage (faith) is God's Word. God's Word (both direct and indirect revelation) guides David's actions. He not only sets David on the high places (the place of military advantage), He gives David the sure-footedness that enables him to fight from this position (22:34). God is the one who trains David's hands for battle, who gives him the strength to bend the difficult bronze bow (22:35). He gives him the shield of His salvation, and then gives him firm footing with which to stand and fight (22:36–37).

Reflecting on God's deliverance and enabling strength, David's conclusion is one full of hope and anticipation. David is God's anointed king, but his reign is soon to end. God has proven to be David's deliverer, but it is not over. Because of the covenant God made with David, he will have an eternal throne. David's psalm reminds us that if God is our refuge, there is no need to fear.

2 SAMUEL 23:1–24:25

EPILOGUE

Setting Up the Section

As David continues to reflect on his time as king of Israel, we are reminded to celebrate the greatness of other people.

23:1–39

PROFILES IN COURAGE

David confidently speaks of a reign of righteousness for his house. This is not due to David's merits or self-righteousness, but rather to the grace of God, assured through His covenant with David (7:14). Based upon God's covenant with him, David is assured of an eternal reign of righteousness, signed, sealed, and delivered in the covenant of God as fulfilled (ultimately and permanently) in the person of Jesus Christ. This is David's ultimate salvation and desire, brought about by God, the author and finisher of all salvation. David's song of salvation is centered in God. The message of the Bible is not the promise of salvation and eternal life for all people; it is the offer of salvation to all people. David celebrates God's offer of universal salvation in this passage.

David is a man of courage. When a lion or a bear threatened his father's flock, he refused to allow any losses. When Goliath blasphemed the name of God, David killed him. David constantly proved himself to be a man of courage. Is it any wonder he attracted like-minded men? The man who stood up to Goliath was surrounded by courageous men who would gladly take on Goliath's descendants (21:15–22). Courage inspires courage—it's no wonder we find so many heroes among those closest to him.

Considering the heroes of courage remembered here, we are reminded that God uses an army of followers to accomplish His purposes. The church is the body of Christ, composed of those Jews and Gentiles who are believers through faith. Each member of the body has a unique function, which they carry out by means of their spiritual gifts. No one should think of themselves as independent of the rest of the body (1 Corinthians 12:21–22), nor should anyone think of themselves as nonessential (1 Corinthians 12:14–19).

24:1–25

FIGHTING MEN AND AN ALTAR

Divinely incited, David decides to number the fighting men of Israel and Judah. Numbering is not necessarily wrong. Moses numbered the fighting men of Israel in preparation for battle (Numbers 1:1–4). Moses also numbered the Kohathites (Numbers 4:2) and the Gershonites (Numbers 4:22) for priestly service. Saul numbered the Israelites to defend the people of Jabesh-gilead by fighting the Ammonites (1 Samuel 11:8). David numbered those loyal to him in preparation for defending himself against an attack by his son, Absalom (2 Samuel 18:1). In none of these cases is numbering wrong.

Numbering Israel seems to produce the knowledge that David is forbidden to have, a knowledge of his greatness and military strength (compare Deuteronomy 17:14–20). He wants to see his strength and power, and even though forbidden, it is what his heart desires. The Lord is angry with Israel, and the pestilence which came to His people was justly deserved—not only because of David's sin but because of Israel's sin. How ironic that David seeks to learn how many Israelite warriors are at his disposal, and as a result of his finding out, the numbers are changed by seventy thousand men.

David's faith in God for judgment is well-founded. God had poured out His wrath on His people, but now He takes compassion on them. The angel of the Lord is standing by the threshing floor of Araunah the Jebusite when he was ordered to halt.

1 KINGS

INTRODUCTION TO 1 KINGS

First Kings was originally joined with 2 Kings in one book. The narrative covers almost five hundred years, tracing the history of Israel and Judah from the last days of the monarchy under David to the disintegration and capture of the divided kingdoms.

AUTHOR

The author of this book is unknown. While there is a Jewish tradition that points to the prophet Jeremiah as the author, there is more evidence that the book evolved over a long period of time.

PURPOSE

The purpose of 1 Kings is not explicitly stated. However, the fact that Kings doesn't mention the return of the exiles to Jerusalem suggests that the book is written in order to answer the question, "Why are we in exile?" This book serves as a kind of warning about the consequences of falling away from faith and the practice of that faith. In the same way, it serves as an encouragement toward consistent obedience.

Many scholars believe that the exilic author(s) of Kings is looking at the history of Israel and Judah through the prism of Deuteronomy. They are evaluating how well they have observed the law, and of course the answer is not well at all.

HISTORICAL CONTEXT

While today 1 and 2 Kings appear as two separate yet related books in the Bible, it is important to remember that they are actually two parts of the same book. The date of both should be considered at the same time. The last event mentioned in 2 Kings 25 is the release of Jehoiachin from Babylonian prison during the reign of Evil-Merodach (Amel-Marduk) who reigned from 562–560 BC, thus the book had to be completed in its final form between this date and the end of the exile (which is not mentioned in the book of Kings) in 539 BC.

THEMES

There is no single theme in 1 Kings. It instead offers historical events and theological commentary that continues biblical themes consistent with earlier books. For example:

God in history as sovereign Lord
God in judgment
God as deliverer
God's promise to David
God's prophecy

STRUCTURE

The writer of 1 Kings provides a framework for the histories of each kingship recorded. The beginning resume includes dates, length, place of reign, and theological appraisal (whether the king did right in the eyes of the Lord). The ending may include a citing of sources, additional historical notes, notice of the king's death and burial, and successor. In between is the drama of the reign itself.

OUTLINE

1 KINGS 1:1–53

SOLOMON BECOMES KING

Setting Up the Section

The first section begins dramatically in the twilight of King David's glorious reign, with the question of his successor hanging in the air. His oldest living son, Adonijah, wants to reign. But the throne of Israel will not be left to the rules of hereditary succession; God will determine the next king.

1:1–10

ADONIJAH'S BID FOR THE THRONE

In verse 1 we learn that David is now so old that he can't even keep himself warm, much less rule the nation. He seems even older than seventy; but for David, it isn't just the years—it is the mileage.

The selection of a beautiful virgin to warm David up may sound strange or even immoral, but it was a recognized treatment in the ancient world. When Josephus describes this in his *Antiquities of the Jews*, he says that this was a medical treatment, and he calls the servants of 1 Kings 1:2 "physicians."

Also, David almost certainly makes this young woman, Abishag the Shunammite, his concubine, which is not at this time illegal or prohibited by God. Later, in chapter 2, Adonijah will condemn himself to death for asking for Abishag as a wife. His request would only be so outrageous if Abishag had belonged to David as a concubine.

Critical Observation

A concubine in ancient culture was not a simple mistress; she was a wife of secondary rank. Still, David's relationship with Abishag the Shunammite is disputed, and many have associated her with the Shulamite addressed in the Song of Solomon (Song of Solomon 6:13), concluding that she became romantically involved with David's son, Solomon. This is conjecture.

In 1 Kings 1:5–6 we meet Adonijah and his ambitions. In exalting himself, he violates a basic principle in the scriptures: that we should let God exalt us and not exalt ourselves (Psalm 75:6–7; James 4:10).

Adonijah gathers a personal military force of chariots and fifty men to run ahead of him. He may have remembered his charismatic older brother, Absalom, who did the same thing (2 Samuel 15:1) and whose bid for the throne was similarly doomed. In fact, the writer notes that Adonijah is very handsome (as Absalom was) and was born right after Absalom. It seems clear that Adonijah hopes that if he puts forth the image of a king, he will become king in reality.

Critical Observation

Second Samuel 3:2–5 describes the sons of David and lists Adonijah as the fourth son. We know that two of the three sons older than Adonijah are dead (Amnon and Absalom), and we suspect that the other older son (Chileab) either died also, or he was unfit to rule because he is never mentioned after 2 Samuel 3:3. Thus by many customs, Adonijah would be considered the heir to the throne. But it is God who would determine the next king, not heredity.

The writer of 1 Kings observes (1:6) that David doesn't challenge Adonijah on his behavior. Sadly, David did not do a very good job raising his sons.

In 1 Kings 1:7, Adonijah gains the key support of Joab (David's chief general) and Abiathar (the high priest of Israel). It is sad to see these once trusted associates of David turning on him late in his life. Joab may have sought revenge for David's choice of Amasa over him (2 Samuel 19:13). Abiathar might have been jealous of Zadok, the high priest (2 Samuel 8:17).

But some remained loyal to David (and to the Lord's plan for the throne), including his mighty men, or special guard (1:8).

Adonijah throws both a feast and a sacrifice (1:9), inviting all his brothers except for Solomon. The idea is that he will burn the fat of these animals as a sacrifice to the Lord and use the meat to hold a dinner honoring and blessing his supporters.

1:11–27

NATHAN AND BATHSHEBA INTERCEDE FOR SOLOMON

David is clueless to everything going on (1:11). Nathan, David's old friend and prophet, knows that if Adonijah does become king, he will immediately kill every potential rival to his throne, including Bathsheba and Solomon. He instructs Bathsheba what to do.

Nathan knows that David is indulgent toward his sons and finds it hard to believe that Adonijah would act out the way he has. So Nathan (1:13–14) describes a message to be presented in a convincing way—Bathsheba will remind him of a promise.

The specific promise Nathan and Bathsheba refer to is not recorded before, but we know from 1 Chronicles 22:5–9 that David does in fact intend for Solomon to succeed him as king. (It is a remarkable display of grace, really, that a son of the wife David took through adultery and murder in the most infamous scandal of his life should be his heir.)

Bathsheba begins by telling David the facts about Adonijah's actions. Then she uses this tender appeal, reminding David that her life and the life of Solomon are in grave danger if Adonijah should become king.

Critical Observation

The latest mention of the prophet Nathan was in 2 Samuel 12, where he rebuked his friend David over the scandal with Bathsheba and murder of Uriah. Yet now, at the end of his days, David receives Nathan, and it seems he remains a trusted friend. David did not treat Nathan as an enemy when he confronted him with the painful truth, and he responds again when Nathan informs him of Adonijah's rebellion.

1:28–40

SOLOMON IS MADE KING

David finally sees what's happening and moves quickly to confirm Solomon. He calls in Bathsheba, and with a solemn oath (1:28) confirms the previous promise he made that her son Solomon would be the next king.

Bathsheba's response in verse 31 is a customary expression of thanks and honor. Since David knows that death is near, it may have sounded strange in his ears.

David next orders arrangements for Solomon's anointing, calling in three prominent leaders in Israel who do not support Adonijah as king: Zadok the priest, Nathan the prophet, and Benaiah. David knows who is loyal to him.

In the scene of 1:32–35, we have a rare glimpse of all three offices in cooperation—prophet, priest, and king. Each of these offices is gloriously fulfilled in Jesus.

David wants the proclamation of Solomon as successor to be persuasive. He has five points to the plan for Solomon: (1) Solomon is to ride David's own mule; (2) Zadok and Nathan are to anoint him; (3) they will blow the horn; (4) they will say, "Long live King Solomon"; (5) Solomon will sit on David's throne.

Take It Home

Benaiah reacts with an exuberant, "Amen!" (1:36), underscoring an important principle: Unless the Lord God blesses the selection of Solomon, he will not stand. Benaiah senses that this is the Lord's will and offers the prayer that God would in fact declare it. His wish in verse 37, that Solomon's reign would be greater than David's, is on a human level fulfilled. But on a spiritual level, it is not.

Zadok, Nathan, Benaiah, and the Cherethites and the Pelethites (foreign mercenaries who served under David) escort Solomon to Gihon (1:38). Gihon is outside Jerusalem and its major source of water, making it a popular place for the people to gather.

Demystifying 1 Kings

The mule in ancient Israel was rare and expensive. It had to be imported and was ridden only by royalty. (Everyone else rode donkeys.)

No one could use anything owned by royalty without permission. Thus Solomon riding on David's mule was a sign that David had appointed him his successor.

1:41–53

SOLOMON'S MERCY TO ADONIJAH

Adonijah's party is over before Solomon is proclaimed king. Bathsheba and Nathan act quickly and it is rewarded. At the sight of Solomon's anointing, the people rejoice so loudly (1:40–41) that Adonijah and his followers ask what is happening. Despite Adonijah's best marketing campaign, he could not win the hearts of the people. They sense that Solomon is the man, not Adonijah.

The trusted messenger, Jonathan (1:42), reports the events in 1:43–48, including King David's own words of praise to God (1:48). This tells Adonijah that even his father David is completely behind Solomon. There is no hope for his future as king.

In verses 49–50, we see Adonijah's guests scatter, and Adonijah flees to Jerusalem to the altar, a traditional place of refuge. Everyone now knows he fears for his life and is asking for Solomon's mercy. Word gets to Solomon (1:51), who grants amnesty unless Adonijah does evil (1:53). He sends men to get Adonijah, allows him to show allegiance, and then sends him home.

1 KINGS 2:1–46

THE SECURING OF SOLOMON'S THRONE

Setting Up the Section

After his father, King David, bids farewell with final instructions, Solomon takes care of old business as a way to secure his reign.

2:1–12

THE FINAL ACTS OF KING DAVID

In his final charge to his son Solomon, David—Israel's greatest king, apart from the Messiah—acknowledges that he is just a man who shares the common destiny of all the earth. (See 1 Chronicles 28 and 29 for an expanded account of David's last speech, which emphasizes Solomon's duty to build the temple.)

David's advice to be strong was a typical exhortation for new leaders, not just in Israelite literature but more broadly ancient Near Eastern literature. See Joshua in Joshua 1. In verse 4, David alludes to the covenantal promise that as long as David's sons walked in obedience, they would keep the throne of Israel.

Take It Home

God's promise to David is an amazing one. No matter what the Assyrians or the Egyptians or the Babylonians did, as long as David's sons were *obedient* and followed God, He would establish their kingdom. He would take care of the rest. (Unfortunately, they didn't hold up their end of the bargain.) All children of God have a similar promise (Matthew 6:33). God says that if we put Him first, He will take care of the rest.

David wants Solomon to begin his reign in justice. First on the list of actions concerns Joab, his former commander, who was guilty of the murder of both Abner, the general of Israel's army under Saul (2 Samuel 3:27), and Amasa, one of David's military commanders (2 Samuel 20:9–10).

David doesn't mention Joab's killing of Absalom, which David commanded him not to do (2 Samuel 18). Perhaps by this time David recognizes that Absalom in fact had to die for his treason and attempted murder against David.

David charges Solomon to use wisdom but to not let Joab die in peace.

Demystifying 1 Kings

Joab was one of the more complex characters of the Old Testament. He was David's nephew (1 Chronicles 2:16–17), and while fiercely loyal to David, he was not strongly obedient. He disobeyed David when he thought it was in David's best interest, and he was cunning and ruthless in furthering his own position.

Many scholars think that David did not command Joab's execution during his lifetime because Joab knew about the murder of Uriah, the husband of Bathsheba (2 Samuel 11:14–25). Joab may have used this knowledge as blackmail against David. However, it appears others knew of David's sin with Bathsheba and against Uriah also (such as Nathan the prophet and servants in David's court). It would seem that Joab's knowledge would only be effective as blackmail if no one else knew it.

David orders Solomon to show kindness to the sons of Barzillai the Gilead, who supported him when he was fleeing Absalom. In saying that they should be allowed to eat at the king's table, David is providing them the equivalent of having a pension, food and clothing, and a house and land to support him and his family.

But Shimei son of Gera, the angry follower of Saul whom David had vowed not to kill, doesn't fare as well. David orders Solomon to kill the obnoxious rebel (2 Samuel 16:5–13).

In verse 10 the author simply records the end of the earthly life of David. Appropriately, David is buried in the City of David. His tomb is known in the time of Jesus and the apostles, according to Acts 2:29. What is currently labeled in Jerusalem as David's tomb is almost certainly *not* the genuine one known in ancient times.

2:13–46

SOLOMON SECURES HIS THRONE

The phrase in 2:12 shows that the establishment of Solomon's kingdom is a fulfillment of the promise made to David in 2 Samuel 7:12–16. That promise is ultimately fulfilled in Jesus, the Son of David; but it also has a definite and partial fruition in Solomon and all of David's heirs down to Zedekiah.

Immediately, the author puts Adonijah back on stage, approaching Bathsheba. She wisely asks if he comes peacefully, since Adonijah has reason to wish revenge.

By claiming that the kingdom is his and all Israel looks to him, Adonijah seems to suffer from delusions of grandeur. In reality, he only has a handful of influential malcontents to support him, and they quickly deserted him when it was evident that David favored Solomon.

His audacious request to take the concubine widow, Abishag from Shunem, as his wife is more than it seems. In 2 Samuel 16:20–23, Absalom—the brother of Adonijah—asserts his rebellious claim on David's throne by taking David's concubines unto himself. Adonijah wants to build a claim to Solomon's throne by taking David's concubine as his wife. Bathsheba agrees to bring the request to Solomon. She may have felt that it is best that Solomon knows what Adonijah wants to do.

Demystifying 1 Kings

Why would Adonijah, knowing the warning Solomon made in 1 Kings 1:52, make the outrageous request for King David's concubine? Perhaps he felt that Solomon was too young, too inexperienced, or too timid to do the right thing. He soon found out that Solomon was a decisive leader.

When she says she has one small petition, she is being at least a little sarcastic to make the request of Adonijah seem even more offensive to the ears of Solomon.

Solomon reacts immediately. Solomon understands that this is Adonijah's attempt to declare claim to the throne of Israel. He is zealous to give justice to Adonijah because he knows that God gave him the throne of Israel.

He acts according to the parole terms granted to Adonijah in 1 Kings 1:52. Adonijah made a wicked, treasonous request and is executed because of it.

Abiathar, the priest who supports Adonijah as the next king, in defiance of the will of God and the will of King David (1:7), deserves death. This is treason against both God and the king of Israel.

Yet Solomon shows wisdom and acts with mercy toward Abiathar in light of his past standing as a chief priest and supporter of David. But Solomon lets Abiathar know that he can still be executed.

When Joab hears of Adonijah's execution and Abiathar's banishment, he knows he's next. Now he imitates Adonijah's attempt to find refuge by taking hold of the horns of the altar (as Adonijah does in 1 Kings 1:50–53).

Although it was almost a universal custom in the ancient world to find sanctuary at a holy altar, Solomon knows that this tradition is not used in Israel to protect a guilty man (Exodus 21:14). Since Joab refuses to leave, Solomon has his rival, Benaiah, execute him right at the altar.

When it comes to the rebellious Shimei, who is associated with the household of the former King Saul and shows himself as a threat to the house of David (2 Samuel 16:5–8), Solomon again shows mercy.

David instructs Solomon to not allow Shimei to die in peace (1 Kings 2:8). Solomon begins dealing with Shimei by placing him under house arrest, perhaps to eliminate any opportunity to plot with others against the throne. Shimei knows that Solomon is being merciful and generous to him. He not only agrees with the arrangement, but he is grateful for it.

However, three years later (2:39–40) he abuses the mercy to retrieve runaway slaves. It seems to have mainly been a matter of neglect or forgetfulness, but it is criminal to neglect a royal covenant. Shimei pays with his life.

1 KINGS 3:1–28

SOLOMON IS GIVEN GREAT WISDOM

Setting Up the Section

God gives Solomon the opportunity to ask for anything, and Solomon wisely asks for wisdom, even after unwisely bringing a new Egyptian wife into his court. He then famously uses his godly wisdom to decide a conflict between two mothers claiming one baby.

3:1–15

GOD GIVES SOLOMON WISDOM

First Kings 3 opens with Solomon marrying an Egyptian princess, as part of an alliance with the Pharaoh, and bringing her to Jerusalem.

Marriage to fellow royalty was a common political strategy in the ancient world and continues to the modern age. It was not only because royalty wanted to marry other royalty, but also because conflicts between nations were avoided for the sake of family ties.

Demystifying 1 Kings

This is not Solomon's first marriage. First Kings 14:21 tells us that his son, Rehoboam, came to the throne when he was forty-one years old, and 1 Kings 11:42 tells us that Solomon reigned forty years. This means that Rehoboam was born to his mother—a wife of Solomon named Naamah the Ammonitess—before he came to the throne and before he married this daughter of Pharaoh.

Critical Observation

Marrying a foreign woman was not against the Law of Moses—if she became a convert to the God of Israel. Ruth was an example of this. A Moabite, she returned to Bethlehem with her mother-in-law Naomi and adopted Naomi's faith. Ruth then married into Naomi's family (Ruth 1–4).

Solomon eventually collects a thousand foreign wives and concubines, which makes him more than just a bad example. They ruined his spiritual life. First Kings 11:4 says Solomon turns away from the Lord when he is old, but the pattern is set with this first marriage to the Egyptian princess. It perhaps makes political sense, but not spiritual sense.

Nehemiah, five centuries later—after the disintegration and captivity of Israel and Judah—is angry and frustrated because the people of Israel marry with the pagan nations around them. He charges them to remember Solomon's bad example (Nehemiah 13:25–27).

In 1 Kings 3:2–4, we see how the people are making sacrifices at the high places—shrines meant for worship. These shrines are allowed in Israel as long as the altars are built for worship of the one true God and not corrupted by idolatry (as commanded in Deuteronomy 16:21). When the temple is built, sacrifice is then centralized at the temple (Deuteronomy 12). Solomon in 3:3 is described as walking according to God's law, but there is a contrasting "except" when it comes to his sacrificing at the high places.

Solomon goes to Gibeon, where there is a most important high place. He offers a thousand burnt offerings. This huge amount of sacrifice demonstrates both Solomon's great wealth and his heart to use it to glorify God.

This is an important event marking the beginning of Solomon's reign. According to 2 Chronicles 1:2–3, the entire leadership of the nation goes with Solomon to Gibeon.

Critical Observation

What set Gibeon apart was that the tabernacle was there, even though the ark of the covenant was in Jerusalem. How did that come to be? Saul moved the tabernacle to Gibeon (1 Chronicles 16:39–40), but David brought the ark to Jerusalem and built a temporary tent for it (2 Samuel 6:17; 2 Chronicles 1:4).

Why didn't David bring the tabernacle from Gibeon to Jerusalem? There are a few possibilities: (1) He may have believed that if the tabernacle was in Jerusalem, the people would be satisfied with that and lose the passion for the temple God wanted built; (2) it may be that the tabernacle was only moved when it was absolutely necessary, as when disaster came upon it at Shiloh or Nob; (3) or David simply focused on building the temple, not continuing the tabernacle.

Solomon's dream recorded in 1 Kings 3:5–15 is one of the more significant dreams in the Bible. God offers him an amazing opportunity, with an amazing promise. This isn't because Solomon sacrificed a thousand animals; it is because his heart is surrendered to God.

Take It Home

The natural reaction to reading this promise of God to Solomon is to wish we had such promises. We do (see Matthew 7:7; John 15:7; 1 John 5:14).

Solomon praises God before asking for anything, and he remembers God's faithfulness to both his father David and himself. He acknowledges that he comes to God in great humility, and especially considering the job in front of him.

With that, Solomon asks for more than great knowledge; he wants understanding, and he wants it in his heart, not merely in his head. Actually, the ancient Hebrew word translated *understanding* is literally, "hearing." Solomon wants a hearing heart, one that will listen to God.

God is pleased by Solomon's request. God knew his great need for wisdom, discernment, and understanding. God is also pleased by what Solomon does not ask for: riches, fame, or power for himself.

God answers Solomon beyond all expectations (3:11–14). Solomon doesn't ask for riches and honor, but God gives him these things. Solomon experiences God's ability to do far beyond all that we ask or imagine (see Ephesians 3:20).

Then Solomon awakes and realizes it is a dream (1 Kings 3:15). But at the same time he knows it is a message from God. God does answer Solomon's prayer and makes him wise, powerful, rich, and influential. His reign is glorious for Israel.

Critical Observation

We can fairly say that Solomon tragically wasted the gifts God gave him. Though he accomplished much, he could have done much more—and his heart was led away from God in the end (1 Kings 11:4–11).

3:16–28

AN EXAMPLE OF SOLOMON'S GREAT WISDOM

One of the most famous stories in the Bible is found in 1 Kings 3:16–28. That Solomon would take the time to settle a dispute between two prostitutes is testimony to his goodness and generosity.

The problem of two mothers claiming one baby seems impossible to solve. It's one woman's word against another's.

Solomon's solution to the problem (a sword) at first seems foolish, even dangerous. The wisdom of his creative approach is only understood when the matter is settled. In the same way, the works and the judgments of God often first seem strange, dangerous, or even foolish. Time shows them to be perfect wisdom.

The true mother's love is revealed in verse 26. She would rather have the child live without her than to die with her. She puts the child's welfare above her own.

Solomon issues his ruling in 3:27, rewarding the baby to its mother, and causing all of Israel to hold him in awe because they know Solomon has wisdom from God.

1 KINGS 4:1–34

SOLOMON'S ADMINISTRATION

Solomon's Cabinet and Governors	4:1–19
The Prosperity of Solomon and Israel	4:20–28
Solomon's God-Given Wisdom	4:29–34

Setting Up the Section

Solomon's leadership is organized, creative, and, initially at least, non-oppressive, perpetuating the prosperity established by his father David.

4:1–19

SOLOMON'S CABINET AND GOVERNORS

Solomon is a leader of leaders. No wise leader does it all himself; he knows how to delegate responsibility and authority and get the job done.

Solomon's great wisdom enables him to see the need to acquire, train, and employ the right people to meet those needs.

In verses 2–6, we learn how the government is structured—much like that in modern nations. There are chief officials who serve as ministers, or secretaries, over their specific areas of responsibility.

Jehoshaphat also served under David (2 Samuel 8:16; 20:24; 1 Kings 4:3). The role of recorder is more than a historian. Scholars say he was like a chief of protocol, or even a secretary of state.

Critical Observation

Abiathar is listed as a priest (4:4). Including him after his exile (2:26) seems to be a problem. But scholars remind us that Solomon could not take away his title as priest, even if he banished him.

In 4:7–19 we learn of Solomon's twelve district governors over Israel. These men are responsible for taxation in their individual districts. The districts are strictly separated by tribal borders, as had been done in the past, but often according to mountains, land, and region. Thus, Solomon's leadership is creative. He is willing to try new things.

Each governor is required to make provision for one month of the year. It doesn't seem too much to do one-twelfth of the work, so each of these governors likely doesn't feel overwhelmed by the burden of raising so much in taxes. Taxes are paid in grain and livestock, which are used to support the royal court and the central government.

4:20–28

THE PROSPERITY OF SOLOMON AND ISRAEL

Under Solomon's leadership, Israel is described as large, happy, and expansive (4:20–21). It is a golden age for Israel as a nation. The population has grown robustly, and it is a season of great prosperity, allowing plenty of leisure time and pursuit of good pleasures.

Solomon's reign encompasses all kingdoms from the Euphrates River to the border of Egypt, well beyond what Abraham was promised. Solomon is not a warrior or a general. This peace was achieved by King David and is enjoyed by King Solomon. It is also assisted—under God's providence—by a season of decline and weakness among Israel's neighbor states.

Such an empire requires a lot. The daily provision described in 4:22–23 is of course not for Solomon only. This is for Solomon's entire household, his royal court, and their families. Some estimate that this much food every day could feed 15,000 to 36,000 people.

Demystifying 1 Kings

The kor, or cor, equaled 220 liters or about 55 gallons. We can accurately picture thirty 55-gallon drums full of fine flour being delivered for every day.

Part of the prosperity encourages Solomon's collection of horses and chariots. His famous stables show what a vast cavalry he has assembled for Israel. Second Chronicles 9:25 is a parallel passage and has 4,000 chariots instead of 40,000: The smaller number seems correct, and the larger number is probably due to copyist error.

Unfortunately, it also shows that Solomon does not take God's Word as seriously as he should. In Deuteronomy 17:16, God speaks specifically to the future kings of Israel about acquiring horses for themselves. One may argue if twenty or one hundred horses violate the command, certainly forty thousand stalls of horses do.

Yet at this point, there is order, and each officer meets his obligation to provide what is expected of his district (1 Kings 4:27–28).

Take It Home

Each follower of Jesus Christ has a charge to fulfill in the kingdom of God, and we should be diligent to perform it—and expectant in being supplied for it.

4:29–34

SOLOMON'S GOD-GIVEN WISDOM

Because of God's gift of wisdom, Solomon becomes a prominent and famous man, even among kings (4:29–34). In a strong sense, this is the fulfillment of the great promises to an obedient Israel described in Deuteronomy 28:1, 10.

Ethan the Ezrahite and Heman are mentioned in 1 Kings 4:31. Ethan is the author of Psalm 89, and Heman is the author of Psalm 88. The other names are only mentioned in this passage.

Only some of Solomon's three thousand proverbs are preserved in the book of Proverbs. He composes songs (1 Kings 4:31), but few psalms.

Solomon's wisdom more so concerns science and nature (4:32–34). He knows much about plant life, animals, birds, reptiles, and fish—the spectrum of created things.

1 KINGS 5:1–18

PREPARATIONS TO BUILD THE TEMPLE

Setting Up the Section

Solomon nurtures his father's friendship with the king of neighboring Tyre, who helps supply him with needed materials and manpower for the building of the temple.

5:1–12

SOLOMON'S ARRANGEMENTS WITH HIRAM OF TYRE

Hiram, the king of Tyre, reaches out to Solomon, son of his friend, King David. David was a mighty warrior against the enemies of Israel. But he did not regard every neighbor nation as an enemy. David wisely built alliances and friendships with neighboring nations, and the benefit of this reaches Solomon.

Solomon's reply in verses 3–6 refers to Hiram's knowledge of David's wish to build a temple. This means that David told Hiram spiritual things.

David couldn't build the temple until he had vanquished his enemies and no natural disasters threatened (5:4). Now Solomon enjoys that peace and intends to take advantage of it.

He proposes to build a house to honor God. He wants to show reverence by setting the plan apart from pagan practices, as Solomon notes in 2 Chronicles 2:6, where builders construct actual residences for their gods.

So Solomon begins to obtain the materials needed for the temple. He doesn't start from scratch, though. David had already gathered some supplies (2 Chronicles 22:4).

The cedar trees of Lebanon were legendary for their excellent timber. This means Solomon wants to build the temple out of the best materials possible.

The king of Tyre is pleased by Solomon's message and request (1 Kings 5:7). We can't say if Hiram is a believer, but he certainly seems to have respect for the God of Israel—perhaps due to David's godly influence. He sets a plan in motion.

Solomon offers Hiram whatever he wants as payment for the timber to build the temple. The arrangement is for Hiram to send logs by sea in exchange for payment and food.

In 5:10–12 the two leaders enjoy peace and a good business arrangement leading to a treaty.

5:13–18

SOLOMON'S LABOR FORCE

Solomon's wisdom is evident in the way he employs this great workforce. First, in verse 14, he wisely delegates responsibility to men like Adoniram. Second, instead of making the Israelites work constantly away from home, he works them in shifts, as described in 5:13–14.

In addition, verses 15–18 seem to suggest that those who carry burdens and quarry stone are Canaanite slave laborers.

Three hundred from the chiefs of Solomon's deputies form the middle management team, administrating the work of building the temple.

The fact that the stones are quality shows that Solomon is determined to use the best materials, even in the temple's foundation where the stones cannot be seen.

The men of Gebal (5:18) may refer to the inhabitants of Biblos, north of Sidon, on the coast of the Mediterranean Sea.

Take It Home

Solomon's use of quality stones in the foundation of the temple speaks to the way we should work for God. We don't work for appearance only, but also to excel in the deep and hidden things.

It also speaks to the way God works in us. He works in our hearts, when others are concerned with appearances. It also speaks to the way God builds the church. He wants to do a work of strong foundations instead of a work a mile wide but an inch deep.

1 KINGS 6:1–38

THE CONSTRUCTION OF THE TEMPLE

Setting Up the Section

Solomon begins to build the temple four hundred years after the Israelites began worshiping God at His tabernacle. Solomon uses only the very best skills, men, and materials of his day.

6:1–10

BASIC DIMENSIONS AND STRUCTURE

According to the first verse of chapter 6, Solomon begins to build the temple in the fourth year of his reign. This shows just how long Israel lived in the promised land without a temple. The tabernacle served the nation well for more than four hundred years. The temple being built, then, was prompted more from divine instruction than out of absolute necessity.

The actual construction begins in the second month of the fourth year, but Solomon probably began organizing the work right away, building on the preparation his father David had already completed. There is some evidence that it took three years to prepare timber from Lebanon for use in building. If Solomon began the construction of the temple in the fourth year of his reign, he probably started organizing the construction in the very first year of his reign.

The work is carefully organized and planned even before Solomon becomes king. In fact, 1 Chronicles 28:11–12 reveals that David gave Solomon the plans for the temple that the Holy Spirit had given him. They included plans for the vestibule, treasuries, upper chambers, inner chambers, the mercy seat, the courts, and the chambers. Everything was planned.

Demystifying 1 Kings

The temple's length is 60 cubits, its width 20 cubits, and its height 30 cubits. Assuming that the ancient cubit was approximately 18 inches (perhaps one-half meter), this means that the temple proper was approximately 90 feet (30 meters) long, 30 feet (10 meters) wide, and 45 feet (15 meters) high. This was not especially large as ancient temples go, but the glory of Israel's temple was not in its size.

Allowing for the outside storage rooms, the vestibule, and the estimated thickness of the walls, the total size of the structure was perhaps 75 cubits long (110 feet, 37 meters) and 50 cubits wide (75 feet, 25 meters).

The dimensions of the temple tell us that it was built on the same basic design as the tabernacle, but twice as large. This means that Solomon meant the temple to be a continuation of the tabernacle. The difference, however, is that the temple was a permanent structure. The last of the internal enemies of Israel had been conquered, and the people were permanently established in the land.

Take It Home

During the temple's construction, no hammer or chisel or any iron tool was heard at the site itself (6:7). The stones used to build the temple were all cut and prepared at another site. The stones were only assembled at the building site of the temple.

This speaks to the way God wants His work done. The temple had to be built with human labor. Yet Solomon did not want the sound of man's work to dominate the site of the temple. He wanted to communicate, as much as possible, that the temple is of God and not of man.

6:11–38

GOD'S PROMISE AND SOLOMON'S BUILDING

At some point during the building, the word of the Lord comes to Solomon (6:11–13). We might say that there is nothing particularly new in this promise. These are essentially the same promises of the old covenant made to Israel at Sinai. But this is an important reminder and renewal of previous promises.

God says that if Solomon walks in His statutes, He will fulfill His promises to David through Solomon. Notice it is conditional.

God promises an obedient Solomon that he will reign and be blessed, fulfilling the promises God made to David about his reign (2 Samuel 7:5–16). He also promises that His special presence will remain among Israel as a nation. He seems to be careful to not say that

He will live *in* the temple, the way pagans believe their gods live in temples. He will dwell among the children of Israel. The temple is a special place for people to meet with God.

In 6:14–38, we learn of the beautiful finishing touches Solomon installs. For example, he panels the temple with beams and boards of cedar; these are some of the finest building materials available. The impression is of a magnificent building.

He also builds side chambers against the entire temple. This describes the rooms adjacent to the temple, surrounding it on the north, west, and south sides. These side chambers are built in three stories.

The inner sanctuary is 20 cubits long, 20 cubits wide, and 20 cubits high: Special attention is given to the Holy of Holies, or Most Holy Place. It is a 30-foot (10 meter) cube, completely overlaid with gold. It also has two large sculptures of cherubim (15 feet or 5 meters in height), which are overlaid with gold.

It is mentioned that gold chains are hung across the veil separating the Holy Place from the Most Holy Place, accentuating the idea that the Most Holy Place is inaccessible (6:21).

The two cherubim—angels—made of olive wood are large sculptures inside the Most Holy Place, facing the entrance to this inner room, so as soon as the high priest enters he sees these giant guardians of the presence of God.

There is gold everywhere in the temple. The walls are covered with it (6:20–22), the floor is covered with it (6:30), and gold is hammered into the carvings on the doors (6:32).

The walls all around the temple, both the inner and outer sanctuaries, are carved with figures of cherubim, palm trees, and open flowers. This is modeled after the pattern of the tabernacle, which had woven designs of cherubim on the inner covering. The curtain was a deep blue with cherubim—the person who saw it would know that they were in heaven on earth

In 6:36 we see the inner court is the court of the priests, where the altar and laver are set and sacrifices conducted. Outside it is the great court, where the people come to pray.

Critical Observation

It must always be remembered that under the old covenant, the temple was not for the people of Israel; it was only for the priests to meet with God on behalf of the people. The people gathered and worshiped in the outer courtyard.

Demystifying 1 Kings

The writer of 1 Kings never tells us exactly where the temple was built, but the writer of 2 Chronicles tells us it was built on Mount Moriah (2 Chronicles 3:1), the same place where Abraham went to sacrifice Isaac, and—on another part of the hill—where Jesus would be sacrificed.

It takes Solomon and his thousands of workers seven years to finish the temple (6:38). It is a spectacular building. It is easy for Israel to focus on the temple of God instead of the God of the temple. Yet without continued faithfulness to God, the temple's glory quickly fades. This glorious temple will be plundered just five years after the death of Solomon (14:25–27).

1 KINGS 7:1–51

SOLOMON'S PALACE AND THE TEMPLE FURNISHINGS

Setting Up the Section

Solomon may have taken seven years to build the temple, but he puts almost twice that into building his palace. Meanwhile, a skilled bronze worker crafts the temple's furnishings.

7:1–12

THE CONSTRUCTION OF SOLOMON'S PALACE

The writer notes in the first verse of 1 Kings 7 that it takes Solomon almost twice as long (thirteen years) to build his palace as to finish the temple. The temple is glorious, but it seems that Solomon wants a house that is more glorious than the temple.

Its magnificence is described in verses 2–12. Noteworthy is the prevalence of cedar wood from Lebanon—so much so that the structure comes to be known as the Palace of the Forest of Lebanon. Walking in the richly paneled walls of the palace is like walking in a forest. The roof is cedar also (7:3).

Critical Observation

First Kings 10:16–17 says that five hundred gold shields hang in the House of the Forest of Lebanon. Isaiah specifically calls this building an armory in Isaiah 22:8.

At the end of the detailed, magnificent description of Solomon's palace, the writer mentions that some of the great architectural features of the palace are also used in the house of the Lord.

Take It Home

The magnificent cathedrals of old Europe were mostly built hundreds of years ago at great labor and cost to poor people who could never dream of living in such spectacular places. When their most magnificent buildings were churches, it said something about their values. When Solomon made his palace more spectacular than the temple, it said something about his values.

7:13–51

HURAM MAKES THE TEMPLE FURNISHINGS

In verse 13, Solomon hires the best bronze craftsman in the business: Huram from Tyre, who is half Israelite and half Gentile. Huram makes the needed furnishings for the temple after the pattern of the tabernacle furnishings.

Critical Observation

Huram from Tyre casts two pillars of bronze (7:15), structures so impressive that they are given names: *Jachin*, meaning "He shall establish" and *Boaz*, meaning "in strength." Some take this to mean they are a reminder that kings rule by God's appointment and with God's strength. They're mentioned also in 2 Chronicles 3:17.

Others believe that the pillars are meant to remind Israel of the twin pillars from the Exodus. The pillar of fire by night and the pillar of cloud by day are constant reminders of the presence of God in the wilderness.

Regardless, every time someone comes to the house of the Lord in the days of Solomon, they are reminded of these truths and put in the right frame of mind to worship God.

Huram makes the sea of cast bronze, 10 cubits from one brim to the other. The huge laver is more than 15 feet (5 meters) across and is to be used for the ceremonial washings connected with the temple. In addition, Huram makes ten identical lavers of bronze, with each laver containing forty baths. It is significant that the sea was a symbol of chaos, and here God has tamed chaos.

On the golden table sits the bread (7:48). Second Chronicles 4:8 says there are ten individual tables of showbread, though here they are referred to as one.

All these great works of art and articles of great value go inside the temple. This includes the ten carts and the shovels, bowls, and other needed utensils for sacrifices.

When all is finished Solomon brings in the silver and gold furnishings that his father David already had dedicated. God told David that he could not build the temple, but David was still able to collect furnishings and treasures for the temple that his son would build (1 Chronicles 29).

1 KINGS 8:1–66

THE DEDICATION OF THE TEMPLE

Setting Up the Section

In what must have been a celebration on the scale of our modern installation of a new pope, Solomon assembles the elders of Israel, the heads of the tribe, and the chiefs of the families for the dedication of the temple.

8:1–21

THE ARK OF THE COVENANT IS BROUGHT TO THE TEMPLE

Solomon chooses the seventh month (8:2) for the dedication, eleven months after the temple is finished (6:38). This may have been because it was the time for the Feast of Tabernacles.

By making it clear that the priests are the ones who carry the ark, the author of 1 Kings shows how Solomon is carefully obeying what God commanded about transporting the ark of the covenant. He will not repeat the error of his father David in 2 Samuel 6:1–8.

The ark, which David had already brought up to Jerusalem (2 Samuel 6), is the most important item in the temple—it represents God's presence—but it is not the only item. The book of Exodus records God's instruction about the items kept in the tabernacle (Exodus 30:25–29). The priests bring these other items into the temple: the lamp stand, the table of showbread, and the altar of incense.

Demystifying 1 Kings

First Kings 8:9 says that the ark holds nothing but the two tablets of stone that Moses put there at Horeb. Yet earlier in Israel's history the ark held the golden pot that had the manna (Exodus 16:33) and Aaron's rod that budded (Numbers 17:6–11), as well as the tablets of the covenant (Exodus 25:16). We don't know what happened to the golden pot of manna and Aaron's rod, but they are not in the ark when Solomon sets it in the Most Holy Place.

The description of sacrificing so many sheep and cattle (8:5) sounds as if Solomon goes overboard in his effort to honor God on this great day.

The reminder of the deliverance from Egypt (8:9) is significant, because there is a sense in which this—some five hundred years after the Exodus—is the culmination of the deliverance from Egypt. Out of Egypt and into the wilderness, Israel, out of necessity, lived in tents—and the dwelling of God was a tent. Now, since Solomon built the temple, the dwelling of God among Israel is a *building*, a place of permanence and security.

After the ark is in place, the priests withdraw from the Holy Place, and the temple fills with the cloud of glory (8:10).

Demystifying 1 Kings

The cloud of God's glory that filled the temple in the Most Holy Place—later called the Shekinah Glory—is hard to define. We might call it the radiant outshining of His character and presence. It's so intense that the priests have to stop performing their service.

This glory remained at the temple until Israel utterly rejects God in the days of the divided monarchy. The prophet Ezekiel sees the glory depart the temple (Ezekiel 10:18).

Take It Home

We know that God is good and that God is love—why should an intense presence of goodness and love make the priests feel they could not continue? Because God is not only goodness and love, He is also *holy*. And the holiness of God made the priests feel that they could no longer stand in His presence.

The intense sense of the presence of God is not a warm and fuzzy feeling. Men like Peter (Luke 5:8), Isaiah (Isaiah 6:5), and John (Revelation 1:17) felt *stricken* in the presence of God. This is not because God forced an uncomfortable feeling upon them, but because they simply could not be comfortable sensing the difference between their sinfulness and God's holiness.

In his response in 8:12–13, Solomon senses that the cloud means that God dwells in the temple in a special way. It is good to recognize a special place to come meet with God, as long as it doesn't turn into something superstitious.

Solomon goes on to make a short speech in which he recognizes that the temple is the fulfillment of God's plan, not David's or Solomon's. They were just the instruments of God's work.

In verse 16 Solomon presses the remembrance of the Exodus. Though it happened five hundred years before, it is just as important and real for Israel as the day it happened.

8:22–53

SOLOMON'S PRAYER

Solomon does not dedicate the temple from *within* the temple. It would be inappropriate for him to do so, because he is a king and not a priest. The Holy Place and Most Holy Place are only for chosen descendants of the high priest.

As Solomon prays he spreads out his hands toward heaven. This is the most common posture of prayer in the Old Testament. Solomon recognizes God is unique and incomparable, and the maker and keeper of promises. He thanks God for His past fulfillment of promises. Then he calls upon God to keep the promises that He made.

In 8:27–30, Solomon recognizes God as transcendent and asks God to dwell in this place and honor those who seek Him here. From statements in verses 12–13 we might think Solomon had a superstitious idea that God actually lived *in* the temple. That makes his comments here even more important. God cannot be restricted to a structure built by human hands—even heaven itself is not big enough for Him.

He asks God to forgive in verses 28 and 30. Next, Solomon asks God to incline His ear toward the king and his people when they pray from the temple. For this reason, many observant Jews still pray facing the direction of the site of the temple in Jerusalem.

He also asks that God hear when the people take an oath at the temple.

Take It Home

This is the great secret to power in prayer—to take God's promises to heart in faith and then boldly and reverently call upon Him to fulfill the promises. This kind of prayer takes possession of God's promise. Just because God made promises doesn't mean we possess them. Through believing prayer like this, God promises and we appropriate. If we don't appropriate in faith, God's promise is left unclaimed.

Demystifying 1 Kings

The temple grounds were used as a place to verify and authorize oaths. When a dispute came down to one word against another, Solomon asked that the temple would be a place to properly swear by.

In 8:33–40, Solomon asks God to hear when the people are defeated, whether due to their own sin, attack from enemies, or during plague and famine.

Take It Home

Solomon recognizes that some plagues are easily seen, but other plagues come from the heart. Solomon asks God to answer such a plague-stricken person when he or she humbly asks, since God knows the heart. A person does not have to be sinless or righteous to have prayer answered. The guilty can find a gracious God if He is sought in humble repentance.

Solomon doesn't forget the people outside Israel who seek God. In 8:41–43, he asks God to hear the prayer of the foreigner out of a missionary impulse. He knows that when God mercifully answers the prayers of foreigners, it draws those from other nations to the God of all nations.

Critical Observation

The temple was in Israel, but it was always intended to be a house of prayer for *all* nations (Isaiah 56:7). The first-century temple included a court of the Gentiles to be a place where the nations could come and pray.

The violation of this principle made Jesus angry in Matthew 21, when He came to the temple and found the outer courts—the only place where the Gentile nations could come to pray—more like a swap meet than a house of prayer. He drove out the money changers and the merchants.

Solomon states in 1 Kings 8:46 what Paul reiterates in Romans 3:23: All human beings sin and fall short of God's glory.

Solomon wraps up his magnificent prayer by asking God to hear Israel's prayer in war and to recognize their sin and offenses in defeat.

8:54–66

SOLOMON BLESSES THE PEOPLE

Solomon praises God for past fulfillment of promises and asks Him to be with Israel now and forever—that all the people of the earth may know the Lord.

As part of the feast surrounding the dedication of the temple, Solomon offers a staggering amount of sacrifice (8:62–66). It is such a great amount of sacrifice that they just specially consecrate the area in front of the temple to receive sacrifices, because the bronze altar is too small.

Demystifying 1 Kings

The sacrifice of 22,000 cattle and 120,000 sheep and goats is enough to feed a vast multitude for two weeks. It appears that the celebrations are followed by the regular observance of the Feast of Tabernacles.

The dedication of the temple ends where the story of the temple begins: with David, not Solomon, with the people glad in heart for what the Lord had done for His servant David and His people Israel (8:66). The writer remembers that it was David's heart and vision that started the work of the temple (2 Samuel 7:1–3 and following).

1 KINGS 9:1–28

GOD'S WARNING TO SOLOMON

Setting Up the Section

God again visits Solomon and gives him a promise and a warning. Meanwhile, the king negotiates with his old friend and neighbor, King Hiram of Tyre, and we are told of the forced labor for his other major projects.

9:1–9

GOD APPEARS TO SOLOMON AGAIN

Approximately twenty-four years after Solomon came to the throne, he has finished his greatest accomplishments: the temple and the palace in Jerusalem. Some experts comment that the verb in verse 1 conveys a desire like a bridegroom toward his bride, and this obsession may have been the start of Solomon's fall.

God's second appearance to Solomon is more crucial. (The first is in 3:5–9.) He assures Solomon in verse 3 that He heard his great prayer at the temple dedication. God also confirms that He consecrated the temple. The building was Solomon's work, done in the power and inspiration of God. The consecration of the building was God's work. Solomon can build a building, but only God can hallow it.

But then God turns to Solomon himself. God's answer to Solomon's previous prayer has a great condition (9:4–5). If Solomon walks before God in obedience and faithfulness, he can expect blessing on his reign and the reign of his descendants, and the dynasty of David will endure forever. God does not demand perfect obedience from Solomon. David certainly did not walk perfectly before the Lord, and God tells Solomon to walk before Him as his father David walked. This is not out of reach for Solomon.

God warns Solomon (9:6–9) if the condition is not met. If Solomon or his descendants turn from following Him, God promises to correct a disobedient Israel.

God's previous answer to Solomon's prayer in 1 Kings 8 was not an unqualified promise to bless the temple in any circumstance. With such a glorious temple, Israel will be tempted to forsake the God of the temple and make an idol of the temple itself. Here God makes it known that He will never bless this error. He will cast it out of His sight if the kings of Israel forsake Him.

Critical Observation

Under the old covenant, God promised to use Israel to exalt Himself among the nations one way or another. If Israel obeyed, He would bless them so much that others can't help but recognize the hand of God upon Israel. If Israel disobeyed, He would chastise them so severely that the nations would know that the Lord has brought all this calamity on them.

9:10–28

THE WAYS AND MEANS OF SOLOMON'S BUILDING PROJECTS

Solomon next makes a new arrangement with his old friend and neighbor, King Hiram of Tyre, who had supplied him with cedar and pine and gold for the temple and palace. Tyre, the prominent city of the land just north of Israel, in what is now modern Lebanon, was noted for its fine wood.

The twenty settlements Solomon mortgages to Hiram do not please the king. Hiram nicknames the cities *Kabul* or *Cabul*, which literally means "good-for-nothing." It's not clear why, but they appear to be fairly insignificant towns. Solomon, apparently a shrewd dealer, receives a large amount of gold in return, an estimated four tons (9:14).

The forced labor described in verses 15–24 came from remnant Canaanite peoples. Solomon gathered the workforce to complete massive building projects. Archaeology is a witness to the ambitious and successful building projects of Solomon.

This is another apparent compromise by Solomon. God strictly commanded that the remnants of these tribes be driven out of the land, not used as slave laborers in Israel. Solomon doesn't make Israelites forced laborers, but he uses them to oversee the remnants of the Canaanite tribes.

Demystifying 1 Kings

Hazor, Megiddo, and Gezer were three prominently fortified cities in the days of Solomon. Hazor controlled the north, and Megiddo was the great fortress that controlled the major passes from the Plain of Sharon on the coast into the Valley of Jezreel through the Carmel range. (It figures in prophecy as the staging area for Armageddon, in which Christ will defeat the forces of the Antichrist.) Gezer, on the great north-south trade route, was given to Solomon as a wedding gift by Pharaoh to his daughter.

The reference in verse 25, describing that Solomon offered burnt offerings three times a year, may have been a transgression by Solomon. It may be that he took upon himself the exclusive duties of a priest. But it also could be that the phrase refers to him initiating the ceremonies through a priest properly. The three festivals likely are Passover, Pentecost, and Tabernacles (Exodus 23:14–17; Deuteronomy 16).

Solomon also builds ships (1 Kings 9:26–28), perhaps under the influence of Hiram, who sends him sailors. The fleet sails to Ophir and brings back 420 talents of gold.

Critical Observation

No one knows where Ophir was located. Suggestions have included southern Arabia, the eastern coast of Africa, and India.

1 KINGS 10:1–29

THE QUEEN OF SHEBA VISITS SOLOMON

Setting Up the Section

The queen of Sheba travels thousands of miles to see Solomon's riches and wisdom for herself, and indeed the reader of 1 Kings 10 is given a taste of his vast wealth and possessions.

10:1–13

THE QUEEN'S VISIT

The queen of Sheba visits Solomon and Israel at their material zenith. But Solomon's kingdom is famous not only for its prosperity but also for the king's great wisdom. The queen comes to test him with hard questions (10:1). She travels in the manner of queens—with a large royal procession, heavily laden with gifts and goods for trade (10:2).

Demystifying 1 Kings

Sheba, also known as Sabea, was where modern day Yemen is today in southern Arabia. We know from geography this was a wealthy kingdom, with much gold, spices, and precious woods. History also tells us that they were known to have queens as well as kings.

The trip to Israel was long, about 1,500 miles, or 2,400 kilometers. The queen probably came as part of a trade delegation, as implied in 10:2–5, but there is no doubt that she was highly motivated to see Solomon and his kingdom.

The queen challenges Solomon with questions, perhaps diplomatic and ethical in nature, which Solomon answers fully (10:2–3). That, and all that the queen sees of his kingdom, is overwhelming (10:5).

She obviously is familiar with the world of royal splendor and luxury. Yet she says Solomon's court is twice as magnificent as she expected (10:7). Not only that, but she notices that his staff and servants are happy (10:8).

Then she draws the connection to Solomon's God in verse 9. It is fair to ask if this is a true confession of faith, expressing allegiance to the God of Israel. Taken in context, her beautifully phrased language may only be a diplomatic response to the astonishing blessing evident in Solomon's Jerusalem.

Critical Observation

The queen of Sheba's reaction to God's blessing on Solomon and Israel is an example of what God wanted to do for Israel under the promises of the old covenant. God promised Israel that if they obeyed under the old covenant, He would bless them so tremendously that the world would notice and give glory to the Lord of Israel (Deuteronomy 28:1, 10). If Israel did not obey, then God would speak to the nations through a thoroughly disciplined Israel.

Take It Home

If we take the queen of Sheba as an example of a seeker, as Jesus did in Matthew 12:42, we see that Solomon impressed her with his wealth and splendor and also impressed her personally. But she returned home without an evident expression of faith in the God of Israel. This shows that impressing seekers with facilities, programs, and professionalism isn't enough.

Yet, if the queen of Sheba sought Solomon and the splendor of his kingdom so diligently, how much more should people today seek Jesus and the glory of His kingdom?

She acknowledges how Solomon was chosen by God (10:9). This statement is especially meaningful because Solomon is not necessarily the most logical successor of his father David. There were several sons of David born before Solomon.

10:14–29

SOLOMON'S GREAT WEALTH

Solomon is an extremely wealthy ruler (10:14–15). The 660 talents of gold itself is a vast amount of gold even by today's standards.

The writer of 1 Kings gives a warning here. He assumes that we know of the instructions for future kings of Israel in Deuteronomy 17:14–20, specifically verse 17. In that passage God tells rulers not to multiply silver and gold for themselves.

God blesses Solomon with great riches, but Solomon allows that blessing to turn into a danger because he disobediently multiplies silver and gold for himself.

In 1 Kings 10:16–26, we are given examples of Solomon's wealth and prosperity. He is so rich that silver holds no value (10:21, 27). In fact, verses 24–25 imply he is the richest man on earth, and the whole earth wants an audience (and is willing to bring gifts to get one).

His golden shields are beautifully displayed in the House of the Forest of Lebanon, Solomon's palace, but they are of no use in battle. Gold is too heavy and too soft to be used as a metal for effective shields. This shows Solomon in the image of a warrior king, but without the substance.

Solomon still recognizes the need for a strong defense, despite not being a warrior. In verses 26–29 we are told of his immense collection of chariots, horses, horsemen, stables, and fortresses.

Critical Observation

When we think of Solomon's great wealth, we also consider that he originally did not set his heart upon riches. He deliberately asked for wisdom to lead the people of God instead of riches or fame. God promised to *also* give Solomon riches and fame, and God fulfilled His promise.

We also consider that Solomon gave an eloquent testimony to the vanity of riches as the preacher in the book of Ecclesiastes. He powerfully showed that there was no ultimate satisfaction through materialism. We don't have to be as rich as Solomon to learn the same lesson.

Demystifying 1 Kings

In 10:28–29, Solomon's horses are imported from Egypt, in direct disobedience to Deuteronomy 17:16, which prohibits it. Yet, perhaps the importation of horses from Egypt began as trading as an agent on behalf of other kings. From this, Solomon could say, "I'm importing horses from Egypt, but I am not doing it for myself. I'm not breaking God's command." Many examples of gross disobedience begin as clever rationalizations.

1 KINGS 11:1–43

SOLOMON'S DECLINE AND DEATH

Solomon's Apostasy	11:1–13
Two Foreign Adversaries	11:14–25
Jeroboam—A Special Adversary	11:26–43

Setting Up the Section

Solomon's love of foreign women leads to his downfall, and adversaries begin to rise as he approaches death.

11:1–13

SOLOMON'S APOSTASY

The writer of 1 Kings confronts two obvious problems in verse 1: Solomon loves foreign women who worship other gods—from nations God specifically told Israel not to intermarry with (11:2)—and Solomon loves many women, rejecting God's plan from the beginning for one man and one woman to become one flesh in marriage (Genesis 2:23–24; Matthew 19:4–6).

Critical Observation

Seven hundred wives, princesses, and three hundred concubines is an almost unbelievable number of marriage partners. Solomon had so many marriage partners because he followed the bad example of his father David, who had many wives and concubines himself (2 Samuel 5:13–16). Why would he do that? It is likely a combination of two types of lust, sexual and the lust for power. In those days a large harem was a status symbol.

Solomon's wives turn him away from God. Age does not make Solomon wiser. He seems to be wiser in his youth, and old age has hardened the sinful tendencies that were present in his younger days. Age and experience should make us more godly and wise, but they do not automatically do so.

Not only does Solomon wander from the Lord, but he participates in worship of the false gods of the day: Ashtoreth, the goddess of the Sidonians, and Molech of the Ammonites (11:5, 7). Probably Solomon does not see this as a *denial* of the Lord of Israel. In his mind, he probably thought that he still honored God and just simply added the honor of these other gods to it. But this is never acceptable to God. He demands to be the *only* God in our life.

Take It Home

If this apostasy was the case with the wisest man who ever lived, then what hope do we have to remain faithful, apart from constant dependence upon Jesus Christ? Let the example of Solomon drive you to greater dependence and abiding with Jesus.

God's judgment comes to Solomon (11:9–13). God has special reason to be displeased with Solomon: He had appeared to him twice and warned him explicitly, and still Solomon went after other gods. Solomon's sin shows ingratitude and a waste of great spiritual privilege.

The Lord says in verses 9–13 that the kingdom will be divided; part of it will be loyal to the descendants of David, and part of it will be under a different dynasty. God promised the entire kingdom of Israel to the descendants of David forever, *if* they remained obedient. David reminded Solomon of this promise shortly before his death (2:4). Yet Israel could not remain faithful even one generation.

Yet for the sake of the memory of David, God delays this judgment until after Solomon's generation (11:13). Even in this great judgment, God mingles undeserved mercy with deserved judgment.

Demystifying 1 Kings

Many passages in the Old Testament (such as 2 Chronicles 11:12) tell us that the southern kingdom was made up of two tribes, Judah and Benjamin. Several times in this chapter the southern kingdom is referred to as one tribe. This is because either Benjamin is swallowed up in Judah, or the idea is one tribe *in addition* to Judah.

11:14–25

TWO FOREIGN ADVERSARIES

Solomon's reign has been glorious, but God has not allowed it to be without problems. There are adversaries like Hadad and Rezon. Rezon is mentioned in 11:23–25. He causes problems out of Aram in the north country.

We are not told specifically how the two warriors attack Solomon, only that they trouble his reign.

11:26–43

JEROBOAM—A SPECIAL ADVERSARY

Jeroboam is a fellow Israelite, which sets him apart from the previously mentioned adversaries. In fact, Solomon himself had chosen him (11:28) to oversee the labor force from the tribes of Ephraim and Manasseh (the house of Joseph) during the major projects listed in 11:27.

It is not immediately apparent why these construction projects cause Jeroboam to rebel against Solomon. But it is obvious from the comments from his visitors in verses 1–3 that the oppression of these projects was a reality.

Jeroboam receives a prophecy from Ahijah, perhaps a newly appointed prophet (wearing a new coat). Ahijah, in an acted-out prophecy, shows Jeroboam that he will lead ten tribes of a divided Israel after the death of Solomon.

Critical Observation

This is the first we hear of the divided kingdom, which became Israel's history for hundreds of years after the death of Solomon. At this first description we would expect that the ten tribes under Jeroboam would be larger, greater, and more enduring than the one tribe left unto the house of David. As it works out, just the opposite happens, because the ten tribes forsake the Lord, while the one tribe is more obedient.

God promises to make a lasting dynasty for Jeroboam *if* he will do what is right in the sight of the Lord (11:35). An obedient Jeroboam has the opportunity to establish a parallel dynasty to the house of David. Both Jeroboam and David are appointed by God to follow after disobedient kings. David waited upon the Lord to make the throne clear, and God blessed his reign. Jeroboam does not wait on God and makes his own way to the throne, and God does not bless his reign.

Solomon seeks to kill Jeroboam. This is more startling evidence of Solomon's decline. God specifically says the breakup of the kingdom will happen *after* the death of Solomon and i*n judgment* of Solomon's apostasy. Solomon doesn't want to hear it, so he seeks to kill Jeroboam. Solomon thinks he can defeat God's will in this, but he is unsuccessful. God's word through Ahijah proves true.

In verses 41–43 we learn of Solomon's death. Many commentators believe that Solomon became king when he was about twenty years old and died around 932 BC, after forty years (a generation) of reign. This means that Solomon did not live a particularly long life. Some scholars also believe that Solomon wrote the book of Ecclesiastes at the very end of his life as a renunciation of his fall into vanity.

1 KINGS 12:1–33

REHOBOAM AND JEROBOAM

Setting Up the Section

Solomon's son, Rehoboam, is made king and opens the door for the breakup of the kingdom. His opponent, Jeroboam, begins his idolatrous rule over the northern kingdom.

12:1–24

REHOBOAM AND THE DIVISION OF ISRAEL

After Solomon dies, the leaders of Israel gather at Shechem to make Rehoboam king (12:1). This is the logical continuation of the Davidic dynasty. Solomon succeeded David; now his son shall succeed him. Although Solomon had a thousand wives and concubines, we read of only one son by name, Rehoboam, and unfortunately he is a fool.

Demystifying 1 Kings

Shechem is a city with a rich history. Abraham worshiped there (Genesis 12:6). Jacob built an altar and purchased land there (Genesis 33:18–20). Joseph was buried there (Joshua 24:32). It was also the geographical center of the northern tribes. Having to meet the ten northern tribes on *their* territory instead of demanding that representatives come to Jerusalem is a weak start for Rehoboam.

Naturally, since God tells Jeroboam through a prophet that he will rule over a portion of a divided Israel when Solomon dies, he returns from Egypt when he hears of the gathering in Shechem. He was in Egypt hiding after Solomon sought to kill him. He joins the elders who address Rehoboam in 12:3–7.

Solomon was a great king, but he took a lot from the people. Israel seeks relief from the heavy taxation and forced service of Solomon's reign, and they offer allegiance to Rehoboam if he agrees to this.

Sadly, the elders of Israel make no spiritual demand or request on Rehoboam. Seemingly, Solomon's gross idolatry and apostasy doesn't bother them enough to seek a change.

Rehoboam sends the group away for three days (12:5-6) and consults with his father's advisors. Their response would be valuable for any ruler, but they also know that Rehoboam is not Solomon and cannot expect the same from the people that Solomon did. Rehoboam has to relate to the people based on who *he* is, not on who his father was. If he shows kindness and a servant's heart to the people, they will serve him forever.

Unfortunately, Rehoboam does not listen. He turns to the young men he grew up with. By turning to those likely to think just as he does, it shows that Rehoboam only asks for advice for the sake of appearances.

The younger advisors' response in 12:10–11 suggests a harsh approach—to make Rehoboam more feared than Solomon. That's how Rehoboam responds in verses 12–15, setting up destruction. God of course knew beforehand what would occur (12:15) but did not *make* Rehoboam take this unwise and sinful action. God simply left Rehoboam alone and allowed him to make the critical errors his sinful heart wanted to make.

Rehoboam's foolishness makes Israel reject him and the entire dynasty of David. They reject the descendants of Israel's greatest king.

Apparently, Rehoboam does not take the rebellions seriously until his chief tax collector, Adoniram, is murdered by an angry crowd and he himself barely escapes (12:18–19). Adoniram was the wrong man for Rehoboam to send. He was famous for his harsh policy of forced labor (4:6; 5:14). Rehoboam probably sent him because he wanted to make good on his promise to punish those who opposed him. His tough-guy policy doesn't work.

Demystifying 1 Kings

From this point (12:19) on in the history of Israel, the name *Israel* refers to the ten northern tribes, and the name *Judah* refers to the southern tribes of Benjamin and Judah.

There was a long-standing tension between the ten northern tribes and the combined group of Judah and Benjamin. There were two earlier rebellions along this line of potential division in the days after Absalom's rebellion (2 Samuel 19:40–43), which developed into the rebellion of Sheba (2 Samuel 20:1–2).

Now Israel turns to Jeroboam and makes him their king (12:20–24). At the time the prophecy of Ahijah (11:29–39) was made, it seemed unlikely that Jeroboam would prevail; but here we see God's word fulfilled.

Demystifying 1 Kings

King Jeroboam is sometimes called Jeroboam I to distinguish him from a later king of Israel also named Jeroboam, usually known as Jeroboam II (2 Kings 14:23–29).

Rehoboam makes plans to reunify the nation by force, but God speaks through a prophet, Shemaiah, and stops him. To his credit, or perhaps due to a lack of courage, Rehoboam listens to God this time.

12:25–33

JEROBOAM'S IDOLATRY

In his first acts as leader of the northern kingdom, Jeroboam makes Shechem his capital, because Jerusalem is in the territory of Judah and Benjamin. Then he builds the strategic defensive town of Penuel across the Jordan River.

But instead of following Ahijah's prophecy, in which God promises him an enduring house if he follows God's ways, Jeroboam next promotes false religion to serve his purposes (12:26–29).

The fact that the kingdom is divided does not mean that the northern tribes are exempt from their covenant obligations; they are still under the Law of Moses as much as the southern tribes. Jeroboam fears the *political* implications of yearly trips down to the capital city of the southern kingdom of Judah. So he appeals to a natural desire for convenience in 12:28 and sets up idols in Bethel and Dan.

Demystifying 1 Kings

Jeroboam repeats the same idolatrous words of Aaron about five hundred years before his time: "Here are your gods, O Israel" (Exodus 32:4). It is bad enough for Jeroboam to pervert obedience to the one God Almighty, but it's even more of a sin when the people follow him. He continues to make more places of worship than the main centers at Bethel and Dan. He then goes so far as to establish a priesthood of his own liking, rejecting the commandments of God regarding the priesthood of Israel. He even serves as a priest himself.

Critical Observation

The legitimate priests and Levites who lived in the northern ten tribes did not like Jeroboam's actions. They, along with others who set their hearts to seek God, moved from the northern kingdom of Israel to the southern kingdom of Judah during this period (2 Chronicles 11:13–16). Spiritually speaking, Israel was struck twice: by the ungodly religion of Jeroboam and by the departure of the godly and faithful. There were few godly people left in the northern kingdom.

1 KINGS 13:1–34

THE MAN OF GOD FROM JUDAH

Setting Up the Section

A prophet comes up from Judah to prophesy against Jeroboam, and then he himself becomes an object of God's judgment.

13:1–10

A PROPHECY FROM A MAN OF GOD

As the chapter opens, a man of God comes up from Judah to prophesy at the false altar at Bethel. Apparently, there are no qualified messengers within the northern kingdom of Israel. This is a sad commentary on the spiritual state of Jeroboam's kingdom.

This man of God says a child named Josiah will be born to the house of David (13:2). Addressing the altar, he says Josiah will sacrifice false priests on it. This remarkable prophecy will be precisely fulfilled 340 years later (2 Kings 23:15).

Critical Observation

The man of God's prophecy is more than a pronouncement of judgment against the altar; it also announces that the judgment will come through a ruler of Judah (the house of David). This is a special rebuke and source of concern to Jeroboam, who has always been aware of the threat from his neighbor to the south (1 Kings 12:27).

The man from Judah says the sign to confirm the prophecy will be this: The altar will split and its ashes will pour out (1 Kings 13:3). This will be a direct rebuke to the idolatrous worship at that altar.

Immediately, Jeroboam stretches out his hand and commands his men to seize the prophet. He seeks to silence the messenger rather than respond to the message. What a surprise to see his own hand seize up so that he cannot pull it back. God judges him at the precise point of his most glaring sin: ordering, with illegitimate authority, action against a man of God.

The altar splits as prophesied (13:5), and in the next verse Jeroboam turns not to his golden calf but to the Lord. As the subsequent chapters will show, Jeroboam doesn't really repent here; or if he does, it is only for a moment. Wanting to receive something from God is not the same as repentance.

To his credit, the man of God shows great grace to Jeroboam in verse 6. He quickly moves from being under arrest to being an intercessor for his persecutor. This mercy reflects the great mercy of God, who answers his prayer.

Jeroboam quickly, and naturally, given the circumstances, embraces the man of God as a friend. He wants to refresh and reward him, without any repentance for the sin the man of God denounced. But the man of God refuses the invitation, based on a prior warning from God. To accept Jeroboam's invitation would demonstrate fellowship with his idolatry.

13:11–34

THE MAN OF GOD'S DISOBEDIENCE AND DEATH

An old prophet in Bethel invites the man of God to dinner. Apparently not every godly person has left Israel for Judah; some still remain behind. The old man hears about what the man from Judah did in Bethel and rides to meet him on his way home. He finds him under an oak tree, perhaps tired from fasting and travel.

The old prophet asks the man to come home with him and eat, an invitation he refuses under the same reason he refused Jeroboam—that God had specifically told him to return to Judah without accepting hospitality, and to return a different way.

The old man's deception, that he, too, is a prophet and that an angel told him to bring him home, persuades the man from Judah to give in. Perhaps the angel was a deceiving angel. Satan and his messengers can appear as angels of light (2 Corinthians 11:14–15).

Nevertheless, no matter how natural and enticing this gesture was, it is the duty of the man of God to resist it. He had a word from God to guide his actions and should receive no other word accept through dramatic and direct confirmation by God's Spirit. God does not contradict Himself. His failure at this point ends his usefulness as a man of God.

The man here lives much like Israel, being drawn to the prophets who say what they want to hear, rather than the truth, however harsh.

The old prophet of Bethel will be used for one more prophecy now. At his table God uses him to foretell the man's doom (13:20–22). God judges the man of God far more strictly than He seems to judge Jeroboam or the prophet from Bethel. They are guilty of worse sins (leading national idolatry and a deliberate false prophecy), yet the man of God receives the most severe verdict.

Demystifying 1 Kings

An unburied body is a curse, and it was a disgrace to be buried among strangers, away from family.

The results are swift. In verses 23–25, the old prophet gives the man from Judah his donkey to ride, but he doesn't get far. A lion pounces and kills him, leaving the donkey unharmed. Passersby report the scene in Bethel.

This demonstrates that this is no mere accident, but something unique from God. The lion does not attack the donkey (the donkey stood by it), nor does it attack the men who pass by.

The old prophet hears of the incident in verse 26 and guesses rightly who the victim is. He is sympathetic to the man of God from Judah, even in his disobedience and resulting judgment. The old prophet himself appears not to be a particularly righteous man or good prophet, having used a deceptive prophecy to lead the man of God into sin and judgment. He recognizes the common weakness of this fellow servant of God.

In 13:27–32 the prophet retrieves the body, buries it in his own tomb, and confirms that the judgment is of the Lord. It's not the tomb of the fathers of the man of God, in fulfillment of the previous prophecy. But although he lied to him, led him into sin, and prophesied judgment against him, perhaps the old man from Bethel still respected the man of God, recognizing he had courage to speak against Jeroboam that he himself did not have.

Even after all this, Jeroboam does not repent. Instead he keeps consecrating anyone who wants to be a priest, leading to the destruction of his name from the face of the earth.

Take It Home

Jeroboam had great opportunity, especially in light of the promise of God through Ahijah, recorded in 1 Kings 11:38. But he does not obey God and honor His commandments, and he never fulfills his potential or promise.

The same principle works in servants of God today. We are not called because of our obedience or used out of merit; our disobedience hinders our potential for full use. God uses vessels of honor, separation, usefulness, and preparation to their fullest potential (2 Timothy 2:21).

1 KINGS 14:1–31

THE END OF JEROBOAM AND REHOBOAM

The End of Jeroboam, King of Israel	14:1–20
The End of Rehoboam, King of Judah	14:21–31

Setting Up the Section

In this section we see the end of both Jeroboam and Rehoboam. One started as a populist with a shining prophecy of success and ended terribly, the other governed as a tyrant but humbled himself toward the end (2 Chronicles 12:6–7).

14:1–20

THE END OF JEROBOAM, KING OF ISRAEL

Jeroboam in 14:1–4 sends his wife to the prophet Ahijah to ask him the fate of their son, Abijah. Even kings have troubles common to all people, and consulting prophets was a common practice (2 Kings 1:2; 4:22, 40; 5:3).

This is a familiar pattern for Jeroboam. In his time of need, he turns to the true God and men of God. He knows that idols cannot help him in any true crisis. Yet he also knows that he had rejected God and His prophets, and so he tells his wife to wear a disguise.

Yet he does not tell his wife to pray for the boy or to ask Ahijah to pray. He wants to use Ahijah the prophet as a fortune-teller more than seek him as a man of God.

The woman's disguise and Ahijah's blindness (1 Kings 14:4) don't matter, because God has told Ahijah what is going on. When Ahijah greets the woman, he informs her that though she was sent to Ahijah by her husband, in truth Ahijah was sent by God with a message to her and Jeroboam (14:6). She also learns right away that the news will be bad.

Indeed it is bad news. God recounts in 14:7–11 that Jeroboam could have had a lasting dynasty, but he wasted the promise of God with his unbelief, idolatry, and outright rejection of God. Jeroboam is worse than all who have ruled before him. Saul was a bad man and a bad king. Solomon was a good king but a bad man. Jeroboam is far worse. He has thrust God behind his back, a powerful description of contempt (see Ezekiel 23:35).

In verses 12–16, Jeroboam's wife hears an immediate judgment and a distant one. First, their son will die. Yet his death will be a demonstration of mercy, because at least he will be buried in honor and properly mourned. Such great judgment is coming upon the house of Jeroboam that all will see that, by comparison, this son was blessed in his death.

Second, God will uproot Israel from the land He gave them and scatter them, a judgment that will be fulfilled some three hundred years later. God knew that the root of Jeroboam's apostasy would eventually result in the bitter fruit of national exile.

The immediate judgment is fulfilled in 14:17–18, demonstrating the future prophecy to be true.

The rest of Jeroboam's reign is recorded elsewhere (14:19). According to 2 Chronicles 13:20, the Lord strikes him down, and after twenty-two years of rule, he dies (1 Kings 14:20).

14:21–31

THE END OF REHOBOAM, KING OF JUDAH

Meanwhile, under King Rehoboam's reign, Judah has sinned and angered God. The sins involve idolatry (14:23) and prostitutes associated with the worship of idols (14:24). In fact, the people of Judah have sunk to practicing the abominations of those nations the Lord had cast out. Considering the depth of depravity among the Canaanite nations, this is a strong statement.

The debauchery leads to God's chastisement. Only five years into Rehoboam's rule—not that long from the years of security in Israel—the king of Egypt attacks (14:25). God chastises Rehoboam through Egypt.

No foreign enemy ever did as much against God's people during the time of David and Solomon as during Shishak's aggression in 945–924 BC. Both 2 Chronicles and archaeology confirm it (see 2 Chronicles 12).

Shishak takes the treasures of the house of the Lord and the treasures of the king's house (14:26). Solomon left great wealth to his son Rehoboam, both in the temple and in the palace. After only five years, that wealth is largely gone.

Rehoboam replaces the gold shields of his father Solomon with bronze shields, a perfect picture of the decline under the days of Rehoboam. He places them in the hands of the commanders of the palace guard, hidden away in a protected guardroom until they are specifically needed for state occasions.

The writer of 1 Kings sums up Rehoboam's account by mentioning continual warfare with Jeroboam (14:30) and repeating that his mother is Naamah, an Ammonite—reminding readers that it was Solomon's marriages to foreign wives that started Israel's decline.

1 KINGS 15:1–34

ABIJAM, ASA, NADAB, AND BAASHA

Setting Up the Section

Of the four next kings of Judah and Israel, only Asa does right before God, and God grants him a long reign.

15:1–24

TWO KINGS OF JUDAH: ABIJAM AND ASA

In 15:1–8 we learn that the son of Rehoboam, Abijam, rules Judah for three years. The brevity of his reign indicates God did not bless him.

Yet by comparing the 1 Kings 14 account with 2 Chronicles 13, we can tell that Abijam knows something of the Lord and even knows how to preach. But he does not uproot the idolatry and sexual immorality that was introduced by his father, Rehoboam. His heart is not devoted to God, as was David's (15:3). This is his real problem. David sinned during his reign, but his heart stayed loyal to his God.

God allows his rule, not because of the character of David's descendants (15:4), but to preserve David's dynasty.

Demystifying 1 Kings

Second Chronicles 13 fills in more interesting details about the reign of Abijam (called Abijah in Chronicles). It tells us how there is war between Jeroboam of Israel and Abijam of Judah, and how Abijam challenges Jeroboam on the basis of righteousness and faithfulness to God.

Jeroboam responds with a surprise attack, and victory seems certain for Israel over Judah, but Abjiam cries out to the Lord, and God wins a victory for Judah that day.

Abijam's son, Asa, succeeds him and reigns forty-one years. Unlike his father, Asa does right as measured against David and begins a series of reforms (15:12–15).

He banishes the state-sanctioned temple prostitutes who were introduced into Judah during the reign of Rehoboam (14:24). He deposes his own grandmother, Maacah, because she keeps a repulsive pole associated with the fertility cult of Asherah. This demonstrates the thoroughness of Asa's reforms. He is able to act righteously even when his family is wrong.

Asa's heart remains dedicated to the Lord, and in verse 15 he restores to the temple some of the displaced silver and gold.

Meanwhile, the struggle with the northern kingdom of Israel for dominance continues. The current king of Israel, Baasha, gains the upper hand in the days of Asa because he effectively blocks a main route into Judah at the city of Ramah. He hopes this military and economic pressure on Judah will force Asa into significant concessions.

Asa counters by gathering the silver and gold from the palace treasuries to buy the favor of Ben-hadad of Syria so that he will withdraw support from Israel. Apparently, Baasha of Israel could not stand against Judah by himself; he needs the backing of Syria.

The plan works. Ben-hadad moves against Israel, forcing Baasha to withdraw from Ramah. Asa uses the materials Baasha had gathered to rebuild two key towns, Geba and Mizpah. Asa's actions are condemned as he lacked reliance on God.

Critical Observation

Second Chronicles 16:7–10 tells us that God is not pleased by Asa's deal with Ben-hadad. He sends the prophet Hanani to tell Asa this and to prophesy that because of his foolishness, Asa will face wars from that point on.

Sadly, Asa reacts badly and throws the prophet in prison. Asa shows us the tragedy of a man who rules well and seeks God for many years, yet fails in a significant challenge of his faith and then refuses to hear God's correction. (See 2 Chronicles 14–16 for additional details about Asa's reign.)

All in all, Asa is a good man who does not finish well (15:23–24). The last years of his life are marked by unbelief, hardness against God, oppression against his people, and disease.

15:25–34

TWO KINGS OF ISRAEL: NADAB AND BAASHA

In the northern kingdom, the short reign of Nadab, king of Israel (15:25–32), does not go well. This son of Jeroboam does as his father did, continuing in his idolatry and hardness toward God. His assassination by Baasha, and the murder of all his family (15:29–30), effectively fulfills God's prophecy that the house of Jeroboam will be destroyed.

Baasha, the son of Ahijah, becomes king over all Israel (15:33–34) and ushers in a dreadful period for the nation, both spiritually and politically. He does evil in the sight of the Lord and walks in the way of Jeroboam. Though Baasha is not a genetic descendant of Jeroboam (having murdered his family), he is certainly a spiritual descendant of Jeroboam.

1 KINGS 16:1–34

FIVE SUCCESSIVE KINGS OF ISRAEL

Setting Up the Section

Sinful kings come to power in Israel, culminating in Ahab and his wicked wife, Jezebel.

16:1–20

TWO SHORT DYNASTIES OVER ISRAEL: BAASHA AND ZIMRI

God's rebuke and judgment of Baasha reveals the behind-the-scenes way God moves, even through the conspiracy of Baasha against Nadab (chapter 15).

Because Baasha is a wicked king after the pattern of Jeroboam, he will face the same judgment as Jeroboam and his house (16:3–4). This has special relevance to Baasha because he is the instrument of judgment God uses to bring justice to the house of Jeroboam. It is considered a special disgrace to have your dead corpse desecrated and be kept from proper burial.

Demystifying 1 Kings

The word of God came by the prophet Jehu. Apparently Jehu had a long career as a prophet. Second Chronicles 19:2 mentions another work of Jehu the son of Hanani. Some fifty years after this word to Baasha, he speaks to Jehoshaphat, the king of Judah.

Jehu also wrote specific books of history regarding kings of Israel (2 Chronicles 20:34). His father, Hanani, is also mentioned in 2 Chronicles 16:7–10, where it describes how he suffered imprisonment because he was a faithful prophet in speaking to King Asa.

Critical Observation

In 1 Kings 16:2, God says that He lifted Baasha out of the dust and set him as ruler over Israel. In doing this God used Baasha to bring judgment upon the house of Jeroboam; yet God did not *cause* Baasha to do this. He rightly judged Baasha even though God used Baasha's wickedness to bring judgment upon Jeroboam.

God did not need to coerce a reluctant Baasha to conspire against and assassinate Nadab the son of Jeroboam. That wicked desire was already in the heart of Baasha. In using Baasha to bring judgment on the house of Jeroboam, God only needed to let Baasha do what he wanted to do. Therefore, it was proper of God to judge Baasha for something that ultimately furthered God's eternal plan.

Next, Elah, son of Baasha, becomes king (16:8–10) for two years. But before we are told much about Elah, a man named Zimri, an officer in the army of Israel, assassinates him. Even as Baasha gains the throne through assassination, so the son of Baasha is assassinated.

Zimri kills all Baasha's household, a common practice in the ancient world (and exactly what Baasha did to the house of Jeroboam in 1 Kings 15:29). David's treatment of the house of Saul was a glorious exception to this common practice. The massacre is an exact fulfillment of the word of God through the prophet Jehi, the son of Hanani (16:2–4).

But Zimri is destined to reign all of seven days (16:15–20). The army revolts and names their commander, Omri, king (16:16). Omri's rise shows that the democratic influence in Israel is greater than many realize. The people—especially the army—simply do not want Zimri to reign as king over them. They therefore reject his authority and appoint Omri in his place.

Omri and the army lay siege to Tizrah, where Zimri is located. The rejected ruler, who walked in the ways of Jeroboam (16:19) even if for a short time, goes to the citadel of the palace, sets it ablaze, and dies.

Critical Observation

Zimri is one of the few suicides in the Bible, along with Samson (Judges 9:54), Saul (1 Samuel 31:4), and Ahithophel (2 Samuel 17:23).

16:21–34

THE FOURTH DYNASTY OF ISRAEL: THE HOUSE OF OMRI

Civil war breaks out as soon as Zimri dies, with half of Israel supporting Omri and the other half supporting Tibni, son of Ginath (16:21–28). Scholars say the conflict continues for five years, until Omri's forces defeat those loyal to Tibni. Tibni dies, presumably killed by Omri, whose rise to full power is the beginning of another dynasty in Israel.

In verse 24, Omri builds a city on the hill, the new capital of the northern kingdom, and calls it Samaria. His aim is to have a capital that is politically neutral (being a new city with no previous tribal associations) and in a strong defensive position (on top of a hill).

In the records of secular history, Omri—the sixth king of Israel since the once-unified kingdom's split—is one of the more successful and famous kings of ancient Israel. But in 16:25–26 it's clear that Omri follows Jeroboam's evil ways. He dies and is buried in Samaria (16:28).

While Asa is ruling for forty-one years in Judah, there are seven different kings in Israel. Omri's son, Ahab (16:29–34), distinguishes himself in being worse than Jeroboam.

Omri is a political and economic success for Israel but a spiritual failure. Ahab picks up where his father left off. Ahab introduces the worship of completely new, pagan gods. In his disobedience Jeroboam said, "I will worship the Lord, but do it my way." Ahab said, "I want to forget about the Lord completely and worship Baal."

Ahab takes as his wife Jezebel, the daughter of Ethbaal, king of the Sidonians (16:31). *Ethbaal* means "with Baal." Jezebel is famous for her hostility and cruelty. Their marriage is also politically expedient, as the alliance with the Sidonians, or Phoenicia, gives Ahab a powerful ally.

Critical Observation

In his later years, King Solomon worshiped pagan gods. Yet Omri and Ahab were far worse in that they *commanded* the worship of idols (see Micah 6:16).

Ahab sets Hiel of Bethel to work (16:34) rebuilding Jericho, in disregard of Joshua's prophecy that anyone rebuilding the city shall lose his firstborn and his youngest (Joshua 6:26). If Ahab does think that he can fortify Jericho without being affected by this curse, he is wrong. Hiel lays its foundation at a cost of losing Abiram, his firstborn; and with his youngest son, Segub, he set up its gates.

1 KINGS 17:1–24

THE EARLY MINISTRY OF ELIJAH

Setting Up the Section

The prophet Elijah comes on the scene, challenges Ahab, and then encounters a widow with a dying son.

17:1–7

ELIJAH EXPERIENCES GOD'S PROVISION

At this crucial time in the history of Judah and Israel—when it looks as if the worship of the true God might be eliminated from the northern kingdom—the prophet Elijah suddenly appears (17:1). He will become the dominant spiritual force in Israel during these dark days of Ahab's apostasy.

Demystifying 1 Kings

The name *Elijah* means, "Yahweh is my God." In the days when Ahab's government officially supported the worship of Baal and other gods, even the name of this prophet told the truth.

Elijah confronts Ahab with the dramatic pronouncement that there will be no dew or rain in the next few years, until Elijah gives the word. This is a challenge to the pagan god Baal, who was thought to be a storm god, thus his association with lightning. Elijah is not merely the prophet of this drought; in the sense of prayer, he is the cause. James 5:17–18 makes this clear.

Elijah's bold statement gives us an understanding of the source of his strength. Everyone else lives as if the Lord is dead, but for Elijah, the Lord lives. He is the supreme reality of Elijah's life.

The Lord sends Elijah to Cherith, or the Kerith Ravine, east of the Jordan, for his safety. God is leading Elijah one step at a time. (He does not tell him to go to Cherith until he first delivers the message to Ahab, and He does not tell him to go to Zarephath until the brook dries up.) Elijah follows in faith, practicing dependence upon the Lord (17:5).

Critical Observation

God sends Elijah away, just as he had become famous as an adversary of Ahab, so mighty that his prayers could stop the rain. At the moment, God wanted Elijah to hide and be alone with God. There is a time for the hidden life.

Every bit of food that comes to Elijah is from the beak of an unclean animal (17:6). Elijah has to put away his traditional ideas of clean and unclean or he will die of starvation. Through this, God teaches Elijah to emphasize the spirit of the law before the letter of the law.

Just as He faithfully provided manna for Israel in the wilderness, God provides for Elijah's needs, morning and night. Elijah comes to trust more than ever in the miraculous provision of God.

Elijah stays by the brook until it dries up (17:7), the start of the drought Elijah prayed for. He does not pray for rain to come again, even for his own survival. He keeps the purpose of God first, even when it adversely affects him.

q 17:8–16

GOD PROVIDES FOR ELIJAH THROUGH A WIDOW

Next God calls Elijah to go to Zarephath (17:8–9), a Gentile city in the general region of the wicked Queen Jezebel. He is entering enemy territory. There a widow will supply him with food.

Widows were notorious for their poverty in the ancient world. When He is rejected by His own people, Jesus uses this example of Elijah's coming to the widow of Zarephath as an illustration of God's right to choose a people to Himself (see Luke 4:24–26).

Once in Zarephath (1 Kings 17:10–11), Elijah sees a woman gathering sticks, a sign she is poor. Elijah perhaps thought that God would lead him to an unusual rich widow, but God leads him to a poor Gentile widow.

Critical Observation

God tells Elijah that He commanded a widow to feed the prophet. Yet this woman seems unaware of the command. This shows how God's unseen hand often works. She goes to gather fuel, not meet a needy guest. She is planning to feed herself and her son, not a hungry man. Yet in her obedience, faith, and service she is blessed.

Elijah boldly requests, in faith, water and bread from the woman. Common sense and circumstances tell him that the widow will not give so generously to a Jewish stranger, but faith makes him ask.

She responds in verse 12 with a polite statement, showing that she respects God, yet recognizes that the God of Israel is Elijah's God and not her own. Elijah quickly finds out that she is not only poor, but desperately poor. Elijah encounters her right before she is going to prepare her last morsel of food for herself and her son and then resign themselves to death (17:12).

Elijah makes an audacious request (17:13), after encouraging the widow not to be afraid. He asks the destitute woman to feed him first, perhaps with her last bit of food. But he goes on to prophesy that her source of flour and oil will not be used up.

The widow obeys in faith and is immediately rewarded with food every day (17:16) for both Elijah and her family. God uses her as a channel of supply, and her needs are met as a result.

q 17:17–24

ELIJAH RAISES THE WIDOW'S SON

This happy time of sustenance is replaced by a dark cloud as the widow's son grows ill and dies (17:17–18). She indirectly blames Elijah and more directly blames herself and her unnamed sin. Whatever her sin is, the guilty memory of it is always close to her.

Demystifying 1 Kings

The death of the son is a double blow to this widow. Not only does she suffer as any mother who loses a child, but she also suffers as one who lost her only hope for the future. The expectation is that her son would grow and provide for her in her old age. Now that expectation is shattered.

Elijah takes the dead son out of the widow's arms (17:19). This vivid detail shows that the widow clutched the dead child tightly in her arms. He takes him to the upper room where he is staying and cries out to God (17:20–21).

Elijah prays with great heart and intimacy with God. He brings the seemingly unexplainable and irredeemable sadness to God in prayer. Since he knows God lead him to this widow, Elijah asks Him to remedy it.

The Lord answers Elijah and raises the boy from the dead. God provides for the widow on every level—not only with the miraculous supply of food but also with the resuscitation of her son.

1 KINGS 18:1–46

ELIJAH'S VICTORY AT CARMEL

Elijah Meets Ahab	18:1–17
Elijah's Victory on Mount Carmel	18:18–40
Elijah Goes to Jezreel	18:41–46

Setting Up the Section

Elijah returns to Israel and meets faithful Obadiah in Ahab's court. He arranges the dramatic confrontation on Mount Carmel between Baal's prophets and Elijah, the prophet of the true God.

18:1–17

ELIJAH MEETS AHAB

God tells Elijah to go back to Ahab, and God will end the severe drought which has lasted three and a half years by Elijah's fervent prayer.

Earlier God told Elijah to *hide* himself. Now it is time to *present* himself. There is a time to hide and be alone with God, and there is also a time to make ourselves active in the world.

Ahab had previously summoned a man named Obadiah, a brave believer who stood for God, to work for him (18:3). In fact, he was so brave that while Ahab's wife, Jezebel, was killing the Lord's prophets (18:4), Obadiah was hiding a hundred of them in two caves, secretly supplying them with food and water.

The drought is so bad that the king himself is out searching for pastureland for his horses and mules (18:5–6). Ahab goes one direction and Obadiah goes another. Elijah then encounters Obadiah in verse 7. Obadiah recognizes him and bows, calling him lord.

Reverence turns to fear (18:9–14) when Elijah asks Obadiah to announce to Ahab that he wants an audience. Obadiah knows that King Ahab conducted an exhaustive search for Elijah, to punish him for the drought that his prayers imposed on Israel. Obadiah fears that if he announces that he met Elijah and the prophet disappears again, Ahab will kill Obadiah for letting Elijah get away.

Kindly and wisely, Elijah responds to Obadiah's legitimate fears and assures him that he will meet with Ahab. He will not make Obadiah a martyr for Elijah's deeds.

At their meeting (18:17–19), Elijah and Ahab trade accusations. According to his theology, it makes sense for Ahab to blame Elijah. Ahab believes in Baal, so much so that his government promotes and supports Baal worship and persecutes the worshipers of Yahweh. Ahab believes that Elijah has angered Baal, and therefore Baal withheld rain. Ahab probably thought that Baal would hold back the rain until Elijah was caught and executed.

Elijah challenges King Ahab to gather the idol prophets of Baal and Asherah—those who eat at Jezebel's table, or in other words, are supported by the government of Israel—for a meeting at Mount Carmel.

It is important to confront and eliminate these prophets of Baal before God sends rain to the land of Israel. It is crucial that everyone understands that the rain comes from Yahweh, not from Baal.

18:18–40

ELIJAH'S VICTORY ON MOUNT CARMEL

Ahab obeys Elijah, sending word throughout Israel of the impending confrontation. Perhaps he hoped that the people would be so angry with Elijah for the last three years of drought that they would turn against the prophet.

Elijah addresses the people of Israel in verse 21, asking them how long they will waffle between two worldviews. This is a logical and useful question. The people of Israel want to give some devotion to *both* Yahweh and Baal. But the God of Israel is not interested in such divided devotion.

The people do not answer (18:21). They lack the courage to either defend their position or to change it. They are willing to live unexamined lives of low conviction.

Critical Observation

The appeal of Elijah makes it clear that there is a difference between the service of Baal and the service of Yahweh. Perhaps in the minds of many, there is not a great difference. The only important thing is to have *some kind* of religion, and to be sincere about that, following your heart to whichever god you feel led to follow. Yet Elijah knows it can never be this way; you either serve Baal *or* you serve Yahweh. There is a difference.

In verses 22–24, Elijah says he alone is left as a prophet of the Lord. He knows this is not literally true, since Obadiah had told him of the sheltered one hundred, but perhaps Elijah means the last prophet able to confront Baal in public.

He proposes a test between God and Baal on Mount Carmel. He gives the prophets of Baal the advantage: They can pick which bull to sacrifice—they get to go first. The deities will answer by fire from the sky—another apparent advantage, since it was thought that Baal was the sky-god, lord of the weather and the sender of lightning.

The prophets of Baal take up the challenge and pray for fire from their god (18:25–29). They pray long and with great passion. Yet because they do not pray to a *real* God, their prayer means nothing.

Elijah cannot resist the opportunity to mock the prophets of Baal for their foolish faith, and the prophets work even harder. They cry louder and cut themselves, a common practice to arouse the deity's pity.

Take It Home

The prophets of Baal were utterly sincere and completely devoted to their religion. They were so committed that they expressed it in their own blood. They had zeal, but without knowledge—therefore their zeal profited them nothing.

This is the sad result of worshiping an imaginary god or a god of our own making. We may dedicate great sincerity, sacrifice, and devotion to such gods, but it means nothing. There is no one there to answer.

When it is Elijah's turn to make the sacrifice, he first wants to get the attention of the people. This is for their benefit, not his own or for God. They need to pay attention so they can see that the Lord is the true God, in contrast to the silent Baal.

He repairs a broken altar with twelve stones, one for each tribe of Israel. Elijah is looking to revive something that once was. Then he prepares the altar so that there can be no question of trickery. In wanting to make a deep impression upon the people, Elijah requires more of Yahweh than he does of Baal. Elijah does not even suggest to the prophets of Baal that they wet down their sacrifice once or twice, much less three times. Yet Elijah does this, confident that it is no harder for God to ignite a wet sacrifice than it is for Him to set a dry one ablaze.

Everything is prepared in time for the evening sacrifice. Some fifty years before this, Jeroboam, the king of Israel, officially disassociated the citizens of the northern kingdom from the worship of the God of Israel at the temple in Jerusalem. Nevertheless, Elijah still remembers the evening sacrifice that is offered according to God's commandment every day at the temple in Jerusalem.

In his prayer in verses 36–37, Elijah wants it known that God is God and he is His servant. He also wants the people to know that everything Elijah has done is at God's instruction. Elijah does this according to the Word of God. It isn't prompted because of his own cleverness, because of presumption or vainglory. God led Elijah to this showdown with the prophets of Baal.

Within what appears to be minutes, God answers. Fire falls from the sky, consuming the burnt sacrifice, the wood, the stones, and the dust. And it licks up the water that is in the trench (18:38–40).

Critical Observation

When the fire of God fell, its work was beyond expectation. It would have been enough if only the cut-up pieces of the bull on the altar were ignited, but God wanted more than simple vindication—He wanted to glorify Himself among the people.

The people fall on their faces (18:39). At this moment, the people are persuaded. Asked to choose between Baal and Yahweh, there is no choice to make. Obviously the Lord is the one true God. Tragically, this is only a momentary persuasion. The people are decidedly persuaded, but not lastingly changed.

Elijah has them seize the prophets of Baal, who now face the same fate they promoted for the prophets of Yahweh. They were dealt with according to the Law of Moses (Deuteronomy 13:5, 13–18; 17:2–5; 18:9–22).

18:41–46

ELIJAH GOES TO JEZREEL

Elijah knows that once the official worship of Baal has been defeated, the purpose for the drought is fulfilled and rain is on the way. Elijah and Ahab will now each do what they want to do: Ahab will eat and Elijah will pray.

Elijah prays persistently. He sends his servant to look for rain seven times. Elijah will not take "no" for an answer, because he has confidence that God's will is to send rain. Elijah obviously senses this is the will of God, yet it is his fervent prayer that brings the rain. The evidence of the rain comes slowly and in a small way, but out of this small evidence God brings a mighty work.

Elijah sends his servant to tell Ahab to get moving to Jezreel before the rain stops him. This is a word of faith from Elijah to Ahab. Based only on the sighting of a small cloud, he knows a torrent is on the way.

The amazing day ends with dark clouds and heavy rains and a supernaturally empowered fourteen-mile, cross-country run. We don't know exactly why it is important to God for Elijah to reach Jezreel first.

1 KINGS 19:1–21

GOD ENCOURAGES ELIJAH

Setting Up the Section

In this famous chapter, we see Elijah go from the high point of winning a contest with the prophets of Baal to the low point of post-traumatic depression. God ministers to him, though, and sends him to anoint a new king and his own successor, Elisha.

19:1–4

ELIJAH FLEES TO THE WILDERNESS

Ahab tells his wife, Jezebel, the champion of Baal and Astarte worship in Israel, of all that Elijah has done. She thought so much of these priests that she supported them from the royal treasury—and now they are dead at the hand of Elijah.

So she sends a messenger to Elijah and vows to kill him within twenty-four hours. Elijah's response? He flees in fear (19:4). We cannot say for certain if this is led by God or not. It is clear that God wants to protect Elijah, but we cannot say if God wanted to protect him at Jezreel or by getting him out of Jezreel. Nevertheless, Elijah flees about eighty miles south to Beersheba.

Once at the distant city of Beersheba, Elijah secludes himself even more, lies down, and prays to die. This mighty man of prayer—mighty enough to make the rain and the dew stop for three and a half years, and then mighty enough to make it start again at his prayer—has given up.

Demystifying 1 Kings

Thankfully, Elijah's prayer to die is not answered. In fact, Elijah is one of the few men in the Bible to never die. We can imagine that as he is caught up into heaven, he smiled and thought of this prayer—and the blessed no that answered his prayer. To receive a no answer from God can be better than receiving a yes answer.

In his depression Elijah cannot take any more. The work is stressful, exhausting, and seems to accomplish nothing. The great work on Mount Carmel did not result in a lasting national revival or return to the Lord.

Perhaps Elijah had especially hoped that the events on Mount Carmel would turn Ahab and Jezebel and the leadership of Israel in general around. If so, Elijah forgot that people reject God *despite* the evidence, not *because* of the evidence.

19:5–21

GOD'S MINISTRY TO THE DESPAIRING ELIJAH

God rejects Elijah's request to die and ministers to his physical needs (19:5–8). This is not always His order, but physical needs are important.

The angel God sends twice orders Elijah to eat and drink and then sends him on his two-hundred mile journey to Mount Horeb, also known as Mount Sinai. Elijah takes forty days, four times as long as needed for a straight trip. This shows that God does not demand an immediate recovery from Elijah. He allows the prophet time to recover from his spiritual depression.

Once at Horeb, God allows Elijah to vent his frustrations. Elijah goes into a cave, perhaps the cave or cleft of the rock in which Moses hid when God appeared to him (Exodus 33:22).

God asks him what he is doing there. God knows the answer, of course, but it is good for Elijah to speak to the Lord freely and to unburden his heart. So Elijah vents.

Elijah recounts the bad situation he's in and says he's the only prophet left. This is not accurate, but it reflects how Elijah feels. Discouraging times make God's servants feel more isolated and alone than they truly are.

God knows what the depressed and discouraged Elijah needs (19:11–12). He needs a personal encounter with God. There is nothing fundamentally wrong with Elijah's theology, but at the time there is something lacking in his experience.

God brings His presence before Elijah, but first to show where He is *not*. The Lord is not in the wind, He is not in the earthquake, He is not in the fire. Like many others, Elijah probably only looked for God in dramatic manifestations. Certainly, God sometimes appears in such ways, but He often appears in less dramatic surroundings.

Then, after the fire, a still small voice: This final phenomenon is in marked contrast to the previous manifestations. God actually meets Elijah in the quiet whisper of a voice instead of the earth-shaking phenomenon that had gone before. Because he senses the special presence of God, Elijah immediately humbles himself and wraps his face in his mantle.

Take It Home

Elijah perhaps thought that the dramatic display of power at Mount Carmel would turn the nation around. Or perhaps he thought that the radical display of God's judgment against the priests of Baal, following the vindication at Mount Carmel, would change the hearts of the nation. Neither of these worked. This example is important for Christian leaders, especially preachers, today. It shows that displays of power and preaching God's anger do not necessarily change hearts. Instead, the still small voice of God speaking to the human heart is actually more powerful than outward displays of power or displays of God's judgment.

Immediately after ministering to Elijah, God gives him work to do (19:14–15). The prophet needs a task to focus on. He needs to stop looking at himself and his own (admittedly difficult) circumstances. He needs to get on with what God wants him to do.

God sends him to anoint three servants: Hazael, to be king over Aram (19:15); Jehu, king over Israel (19:16); and Elisha, his own successor (19:16).

Critical Observation

Elijah needs a friend; the core of his complaint before God is that he is alone. God lets him know that there is a man ready to learn from the great prophet and be his disciple and companion.

Elijah also needs hope, and since Elisha will be raised up as a successor to Elijah's prophetic office, Elijah knows that his work will continue even after his death.

The three will provide justice by putting to death all who have followed Baal (19:16–17). This is another source of encouragement to Elijah. With this promise he knows that ultimately justice will be carried out, and God will not allow the institutionalized persecution and promotion of idolatry to go unpunished.

The final encouragement to Elijah is God's promise that He has reserved seven thousand in Israel, all whose knees have not bowed to Baal (19:18). Elijah repeatedly bemoans that he is alone among the true followers of God. This assures Elijah that he is not alone and that his work as a prophet has indeed been fruitful. His quiet ministry through the years actually bears more fruit than the spectacular ministry at Mount Carmel.

Elijah finds Elisha at work and commissions him to ministry (19:19–21). The mantle is the symbol of Elijah's prophetic authority. This act signifies that Elijah is calling Elisha as his successor.

Demystifying 1 Kings

We are told that Elijah finds Elisha first, doing what the voice of God told him to do but perhaps in reverse order. Perhaps Elijah believed that he *first* needed a friend and apprentice.

Elisha begs to say good-bye to his parents. It appears that Elijah begrudgingly gives permission. Elisha sacrifices his twelve oxen (having that many indicates his relative wealth), burns his equipment as fuel to cook the meat, and shares it with the community. This demonstrates Elisha's complete commitment to following Elijah. He destroys the tools of his trade in a going-away party for his family and friends.

1 KINGS 20:1–43

ISRAEL'S VICTORIES OVER SYRIA

Ben-hadad Comes Against Samaria	20:1–12
Victory for Israel	20:13–22
A Second Victory over Syria	20:23–43

Setting Up the Section

God gives Israel two victories over the attacking Syrians to the north, and Ahab is condemned for letting the ruler Ben-hadad go free.

20:1–12

BEN-HADAD COMES AGAINST SAMARIA

The writer of 1 Kings now turns from Elijah to accounts of war between Israel and Aram. Ben-hadad, king of Syria, rises against Israel (20:1–6) and makes demands. Thirty-two kings are with him, a formidable military force. Though the Israelites are outwardly strong politically and militarily during the reign of Ahab, they are not strong enough to discourage such an attack.

Ahab's response to Ben-hadad (unconditional surrender) fits his general personality. He is a man concerned with the luxuries and comforts of living, and so he does not have the character to stand in the face of such a threat. Indeed, the national and military might of Israel is greatly weakened by the three-and-a-half year drought and famine that had just ended.

Ben-hadad makes further demands (20:5). Officials will come and search Ahab's house and those of his servants, to take away anything valuable. This is a greater demand than what Ben-hadad makes at first.

The king of Israel calls the elders of the land. It would have been wiser for Ahab to seek the counsel *before* he surrendered to the Syrians. Now, in the brief time between the message of surrender and the actual abduction of his women and the plundering of his goods, he seeks counsel.

The elders of Israel rightly see that such surrender to Ben-hadad and the Syrians is the first step to a total loss of sovereignty for Israel. If they want to remain a kingdom at all, they have to resist this threat.

Ahab tells Ben-hadad that he will do most of what he requested, but not all. But to deny a tyrant on one point is to deny him on every point. Ahab could expect a harsh reaction.

Critical Observation

Though it was an uncharacteristically bold speech from Ahab, his response to Ben-hadad (20:11) is a wonderful piece of wisdom. The idea is that you should do your boasting *after* the battle, not before.

20:13–22

VICTORY FOR ISRAEL

The two sides prepare for war, and a prophet approaches Ahab (20:13–14). This nameless prophet does not seem to be either Elijah or Elisha. He is one of the seven thousand in Israel who are quietly faithful to Yahweh.

God promises victory, a generous gesture to an idolatrous ruler. Israel's hardened rejection of God deserves divine abandonment. God has every right to leave them alone and let them perish without His help. Yet God is rich in mercy, and He shows His mercy to Ahab and Israel.

Ahab asks who will make it happen (20:14). He is looking around at his army and military leaders and wondering how God can bring a victory against a mighty enemy. Ahab also asks who will lead the battle, and God answers that Ahab himself will. God wants to win this victory by working through the unlikely people Ahab already has on his side.

Take It Home

Whenever a work for God is to be done, we often ask Ahab's question: "By whom?" When many Christian leaders ask God that question, they expect God will answer by bringing someone new to them, a leader or champion that can do the work or at least help with it. However, many times God's way of working is to use those who are already there, even if it seems unlikely.

Israel claims the victory over Ben-hadad, who at the start of the conflict is seen getting drunk at the command post. (In part, he is defeated by his own weak character.)

God blesses the army of Israel and the leaders that Ahab has, even blessing Ahab's own leadership of the army. Despite great odds, they win the battle.

Soon after, the same nameless prophet advises preparation again. The victory over Ben-hadad does not end the conflict between Israel and Syria. He tells Ahab to prepare for a Syrian attack in the coming spring. The prophet knows that God works through the careful preparation of His people.

20:23–43

A SECOND VICTORY OVER SYRIA

The Syrians indeed try again in the spring (20:23–34). They strategize to meet the Israelites on the plains, where they think Israel's God is weakest. The idea of the *localized deity* was prominent in the ancient world. The ancients felt that particular gods had authority over particular areas. Because the recent victory is won on hilly terrain, the servants of the king of Syria believe that the God of Israel is a localized deity with power over the hills, not the plains. The action they recommend is logical, given their theology. Their theological belief directs their advice and action.

Take It Home

Sometimes we pick and choose God's domain as the Syrians did—the God of the hills but not of the plains. At times we think He is the God of the past but not always of this present moment. Some think He is the God of a few special favorites but not of all people. But God is over everything, everywhere, forever.

The armies muster, and Israel routs Ben-hadad in an even more spectacular victory (20:26–30). A casualty count of one hundred thousand Syrian foot soldiers in one day is clearly a miracle, yet it is a miracle working through the existing Israelite army, not by another outside agency. God wants to show that as unlikely as it seems, God *can* work through this outwardly weak and ineffective instrument.

Those who escape to the city of Aphek are killed when a wall falls on them. Ben-hadad hides with his officials. They decide to beg for their lives (20:32).

Ahab feels a kinship toward this pagan king with exceedingly pagan ideas of God. Perhaps Ahab wants Ben-hadad and Syria's friendship as protection against the powerful and threatening Assyrian Empire. If so, he looks for friends in the wrong places. Ahab has no business making a treaty with Ben-hadad, as Israel's victory is the Lord's.

In verses 35–38, a new prophet prepares to confront the king about Ben-hadad.

The prophet prepares himself to become an object lesson. When what appears to be a fellow prophet declines to strike him as requested (20:35–36), the first prophet pronounces God's judgment on him (death by lion).

The prophet disguises himself and waits for Ahab to pass by. He brings God's message through a story. He tells Ahab of a man who was responsible to guard the life of another and proved himself unfaithful. In the story, the guilty man's excuse was that he was busy here and there. But he should have paid attention to the job he had to do.

Ahab rightly judges that the fictional man should be held responsible for his failure to guard what was entrusted to him. That's when the prophet reveals his identity, because Ahab otherwise would not listen.

Now he is forced to hear God's judgment (20:41–42). God intends that Ben-hadad should be utterly destroyed, but He also intends that this happen by the hand of the army of Israel. God is interested in more than the mere death of Ben-hadad; He is interested in the way that death is carried out.

Ahab goes home sullen but not repentant (20:43). He has the sorrow of being a sinner and knowing the consequences of sin, without having the sorrow for the sin itself.

1 KINGS 21:1–29

THE MURDER OF NABOTH

Setting Up the Section

Ahab and Jezebel arrange the death of Naboth to obtain his land. Elijah strongly condemns the murder.

21:1–16

NABOTH IS MURDERED FOR HIS VINEYARD

The account of Naboth and his land begins as an attempted simple real estate transaction. Ahab wants the vineyard near his royal house in Jezreel so that he might have it as a vegetable garden. He says he is willing to trade for the land or pay for it.

Naboth's response is an emphatic *no.* His rejection of the otherwise reasonable offer is rooted in the ancient Israelite idea of the land. They believed that the land was an inheritance from God, parceled out to individual tribes and families according to His will. Therefore land was never really sold, only leased—and only under the most dire circumstances. Real estate offices in ancient Israel didn't do very good business.

Ahab pouts before Jezebel (21:4–7) for being refused this small portion of land. This seems entirely characteristic of Ahab, a man who reacts this way when he meets any kind of adversity.

Jezebel's manner of speech in verse 7 reveals who really exercises authority in the palace of Israel. She begins to plot Naboth's murder with Ahab's collusion, since he allows letters in his name to be sealed with his seal (21:8).

Jezebel lays the groundwork for the idea that some evil or calamity has come upon Israel, and a scapegoat has to be found for the evil. Jezebel intends for Naboth be revealed as the scapegoat. She has him seated in honor, then destroyed.

Two scoundrels accuse Naboth of blasphemy, worthy of stoning. Jesus is charged with similar crimes, accused of offending both God and Caesar. Naboth, just like Jesus, is completely innocent of such accusations and is murdered without cause. The stoning of Naboth over a piece of land for a vegetable garden shows the brutal and immoral character of Jezebel and Ahab.

Demystifying 1 Kings

Second Kings 9:26 indicates that the crime is even worse than this, connecting the murder of Naboth with the blood of his sons. It is likely that the entire family of Naboth was murdered, so no heirs were left to claim his property.

In 1 Kings 21:15–16, Ahab takes possession of Naboth's land, which adds evil to evil. Even with Naboth dead, the land does not belong to Ahab or the royal house of Israel. It belongs to the family of Naboth. Ahab probably claimed the land as a royal right because the crown seized the land of any executed criminal.

21:17–29

ELIJAH CONFRONTS AHAB

God sends Elijah to confront Ahab as he is enjoying his new possession (21:17–24). Elijah does what few other men have the courage to do: confront this wicked, brutal, and immoral king and queen of Israel. He pointedly charges them with the two crimes: murder and theft of Naboth's land.

Notice that Elijah confronts Ahab over the sin of Jezebel and her wicked associates. God clearly holds Ahab responsible for this sin as husband, as king, and as beneficiary of this crime. He predicts that dogs will lick Ahab's blood on the same field on which Naboth died.

God continues to prophesy through Elijah. He tells Ahab that disaster is coming, and He will consume every descendant of Ahab's (21:21–22).

This is a severe judgment against anyone, in particular against a king. A king's legacy is in his posterity succeeding him on the throne, and here God announces an end to the dynasty of Omri (Ahab's father). His dynasty would come to a dead end just like the dynasties of Jeroboam and Baasha.

In addition, the dogs shall eat Jezebel by the wall of Jezreel. Her end will be horrible and disgraceful.

The writer of 1 Kings here summarizes Ahab's great wickedness (21:25–26), likening his sin to the sin of the Amorites. Thus, God prepares the ground for the future eviction of Israel from the promised land. Just as the Amorites were cast out of Canaan for their continued idolatry and rejection of God, the northern kingdom of Israel will meet a similar fate.

For all his wickedness, though, Ahab receives this prophecy of judgment exactly as he should (21:27–29). He understands that the prophecy is in fact an invitation to repent, humble one's self, and to seek God for mercy. However, it's clear that the repentance is outward and superficial, arising from terror and not from sincere belief.

God nevertheless honors Ahab's actions. This shows the power of both prayer and humble repentance. If Ahab did not humble himself in this way, then the judgment would have come in his own day. This shows that God gave the prophecy of judgment as an invitation to repentance, and God opened the door of mercy when Ahab properly responded to that invitation.

There is no record of Jezebel's humility or repentance. Therefore we can expect that God's judgment will come upon her exactly as He first announced.

Take It Home

God's response to Ahab shows us the character of God's mercy: It is given to the undeserving. By nature, the innocent do not *need* mercy. Ahab was a great sinner, but he won great mercy (in this life) through humble repentance. The worst sinner should not disqualify himself from receiving God's mercy if that sinner should only approach God in humble repentance.

1 KINGS 22:1–53

THE DEATH OF AHAB

God Foretells Ahab's Doom	22:1–28
Ahab Dies in Battle	22:29–40
The Reigns of Jehoshaphat and Ahaziah	22:41–53

Setting Up the Section

The book of 1 Kings ends with Ahab's death and Jehoshaphat's reign in Judah.

22:1–28

GOD FORETELLS AHAB'S DOOM

During a visit from Judah's king, Jehoshaphat, Ahab sets his eyes upon Ramoth-gilead in the north (22:1–4).

Previously, the king of Syria promised to return certain cities to Israel (20:34) in exchange for leniency after defeat in battle. Apparently this was a city that Ben-hadad never returned to Israel, and it is in a strategically important location.

Ahab asks Jehoshaphat to help him in this dispute against Syria. Ramoth-gilead is only forty miles from Jerusalem, but there is probably another reason for Ahab's request. It seems clear that Jehoshaphat is in a treaty relationship with Ahab, and Jehoshaphat is the subordinate partner in the alliance.

Jehoshaphat responds by proposing that they seek God in the matter. Considering the generally adversarial relationship between Ahab and the prophets of Yahweh, this is a bold request of Jehoshaphat to ask of Ahab. It isn't surprising that Ahab picks prophets who will tell them what he wants to hear.

Jehoshaphat still wants to hear from a prophet of Yahweh (22:7). Ahab knows of one more, Micaiah, whom he hates because he never says anything good. Yet he is willing to call him when the king of Judah responds that Ahab should listen to Micaiah (22:8).

Demystifying 1 Kings

It was an ancient custom to hold court and make decisions at the gates of the city. There were even thrones for high officials to sit on at the gates of the city of Samaria. Ahab and Jehoshaphat are there, surrounded by the unfaithful prophets (such as Zedekiah) who are prophesying in the name of the Lord, but not truthfully. Perhaps these were true followers of Yahweh who were seduced by Ahab's sincere but shallow repentance three years before (21:27–29). After that, they began to align with Ahab uncritically. Three years later they were willing to prophesy lies to Ahab if that was what he wanted to hear.

The prophet Zedekiah uses a familiar tool of ancient prophets, an object lesson, to convey his prophecy (22:11). He uses horns of iron to illustrate the thrust of two powerful forces, armies that would rout the Syrians. Zedekiah has the agreement of four hundred other prophets (all the prophets prophesied so).

Into this dramatic scene comes Micaiah, the faithful prophet, in rags and chains straight out of prison (see 22:26). The messenger who retrieved him has already told him what's happening and advised him to go along with the basic message (22:13). Micaiah assures him that he will simply repeat what God says to him.

But first he mimics the false prophets (22:15). King Ahab recognizes the mocking tone of Micaiah's prophecy and demands that Micaiah tell nothing but the truth.

Micaiah now changes his tone from mocking to serious. He says that not only will Israel be defeated, but also that their leader (the shepherd) will perish.

Ahab turns to Jehoshaphat with a quick, "See? I told you he never says anything good." Ahab can't handle the truth.

King Ahab and others at the court may have found it hard to explain how one prophet could be right and four hundred wrong. Micaiah goes on to reveal the inspiration behind the four hundred prophets (22:19–23).

He describes the throne of God, with God asking who will entice Ahab to attack Ramoth-gilead and die. Apparently, one of the fallen angels volunteers for this task. Since Ahab wants to be deceived, God will give him what he wants, using a willing fallen angel who works through willing unfaithful prophets.

Zedekiah responds to Micaiah's vision (22:24–28) the way many do when they are defeated in argument: with violence. He slaps and taunts him. And Ahab responds the way tyrants do when they are confronted with the truth: He sends him back to prison.

Micaiah's final appeal indicates that he is willing to be judged by whether his prophecy comes to pass or not (22:28).

22:29–40

AHAB DIES IN BATTLE

So Jehoshaphat and Ahab go into battle. It is easy to understand why King Ahab of Israel attacks; it is less easy to understand why King Jehoshaphat of Judah follows the false prophecy. He should have believed Micaiah and known that the battle would end in disaster and the death of at least Ahab.

Going into the battle, Ahab does not want to be identified as a king and therefore be a special target. Perhaps he thought this would help protect him against Micaiah's prophecy of doom. The fact that Jehoshaphat agrees to go into the battle as the only clearly identified king is evidence that Jehoshaphat was the subservient partner in his alliance with Ahab.

The result? Jehoshaphat is saved and Ahab dies in battle. Ahab's previous mercy to Ben-hadad does not win any lasting favor with the rulers of Syria.

Finding himself as the only identifiable king in the battle, Jehoshaphat realizes he is in mortal danger. He cries out (22:33) to God and is saved when his attackers see that he is not the king of Israel. Second Chronicles 18:31 makes it clear that the Lord hears Jehoshaphat's cry and rescues him.

Demystifying 1 Kings

After the close escape at Ramoth-gilead, Jehoshaphat rededicates himself to the spiritual reform of Judah. He goes out again among the people from Beersheba to the mountains of Ephraim and brings them back to the Lord God of their fathers (2 Chronicles 19:4).

A bowman at random strikes Ahab, as if the arrow is a sin-seeking missile. God orchestrates unintended actions to result in an exercise of His judgment.

Ahab orders his body propped up in his chariot, facing his enemies, to inspire his troops. All day long he lingers, but by evening he dies, and the battle is over.

The word through the prophet Micaiah proves true. King Ahab never returns to Samaria or Israel in peace.

When they go to wash Ahab's chariot, the dogs lick his blood (22:38). This is almost the fulfillment of God's word through Elijah in 1 Kings 21:19, where Elijah prophesies that dogs will lick the blood of Ahab. This proves true, but not in the place Elijah said it would happen. God relents from His original judgment against Ahab, but because of Ahab's false repentance and continued sin, a very similar judgment comes upon him.

There is another prophecy fulfilled in the death of Ahab. It was the word from the anonymous prophet of 1 Kings 20:42, that Ahab spares Ben-hadad's life at the expense of his own.

By materialist standards, the reign of Ahab was a success. He was generally militarily successful and enjoyed a generally prosperous economy. Yet spiritually his reign was a disaster, one of the worst ever for Israel.

22:41–53

THE REIGNS OF JEHOSHAPHAT AND AHAZIAH

The focus now turns to Jehoshaphat (22:41–50) and his reign. Jehoshaphat, son of the good king Asa, follows in his footsteps and does what is right in the eyes of the Lord.

Jehoshaphat does not take away all the high places, though (22:43), a serious shortcoming.

Jehoshaphat builds ships at Ebion-geber, a territory of the Edomites, who are without a king at the time (22:47). After a disastrous shipping venture, Jehoshaphat is tempted to make an alliance with Ahaziah of Israel, Ahab's successor (22:49), but Jehoshaphat will not. This is to his credit. He learned the lesson of not entering a partnership with the ungodly.

The book of 1 Kings ends with mention of the son of Ahab, Ahaziah, who reigns for two years (22:51–53), walking in the same evil ways as his father and his grandfather, Jeroboam.

With this, 1 Kings ends on a low note. It began with the promise of the twilight of Israel's greatest king, David. It ends with the sad reign of one of the most wicked kings reigning over a divided nation.

2 KINGS

INTRODUCTION TO 2 KINGS

The books of 1 and 2 Kings were originally joined in one book. The narrative covers almost five hundred years, tracing the history of Israel and Judah from the last days of the monarchy under David to the disintegration and capture of the divided kingdoms.

AUTHOR

The author of this book is unknown. While there is a Jewish tradition that points to the prophet Jeremiah as the author, there is more evidence that the book evolved over a long period of time.

PURPOSE

First and Second Kings were written to the people of the southern kingdom of Judah to explain that the fall of the northern kingdom of Israel was God's judgment on their idolatry, to call the southern kingdom to repentance for following Israel's example, and to remind them of the hope promised through the royal—and ultimately messianic—line of David.

THEMES

The book of 2 Kings repeatedly demonstrates the judgment that results from unfaithfulness and idolatry. Over and over, kings and commoners are charged with worshiping false gods or worshiping the true God in false ways.

The book also highlights the way God uses other nations to execute His judgment: Israel falls to Assyria in 722 BC, and Judah falls to the Babylonians in 586 BC.

Along with God's judgment, however, 2 Kings underscores God's patience. He sends prophets to call His people to repentance, warns them over and over of the consequences of disobedience, and hears the prayers of faithful people.

HISTORICAL CONTEXT

The compilation of 1 and 2 Kings began before Babylon invaded Judah in 586 BC, but since the final chapters tell of events that occurred midway through the Babylonian captivity, obviously the book could not have been completed until then.

STRUCTURE

The commentary for this book is laid out by chapters for ease of use, but here is a look at the broader structure of this book of the Bible:

- The Divided Kingdom 1:1–17:41
  - Elisha's Ministry
  - Kings of Israel and Judah
  - Israel's Exile to Assyria
- The Surviving Kingdom 18:1–25:30
  - Kings of Judah
  - Judah's Exile to Babylon

OUTLINE

2 KINGS 1:1–18

AHAZIAH AND ELIJAH

Setting Up the Section

The book of 1 Kings ends with King Ahab's death and his son Ahaziah's ascension to the throne. The reign of Ahab had been a spiritual disaster for Israel, the northern kingdom, but it was a time of political security and economic prosperity. Moab, the land just south of Israel and west of the Dead Sea, had been under Israelite domination since the days of David (2 Samuel 8:2, 11–12). After Ahab's death, the kingdom of Moab finds a good opportunity to remove their nation from the domination of Israel. This is where the book of 2 Kings picks up the story.

1:1–9

AHAZIAH'S INJURY

After Ahab's death, the land of Moab rebels against Israel (1:1). This rebellion of Moab in the days of Ahaziah is significant of the decline of Israel's power and the judgment of God.

King Ahaziah apparently leans against a wooden lattice on a second-floor balcony or room. When the lattice gives way, Ahaziah falls to the ground below (1:2). This is surely an unexpected crisis. Such accidents happen to kings and peasants both. Ahaziah shows that he is a true worshiper of the pagan god Baal-zebub, because he turns to this god in his time of trouble.

Demystifying 2 Kings

The god identified as Baal-zebub was originally named Baal-zebul, "Baal, the prince." This god was believed to have great power. The Israelites used the name Baal-zebub, "lord of the flies," as a jab or parody of this false god. The name stuck however—in the New Testament, Beelzebub is a common name for Satan, or the prince of devils. If the wooden lattice was intended to screen out flies, it would have made sense to Ahaziah to call on this god when the lattice failed.

There is little doubt that King Ahaziah believes that Yahweh lives, but Elijah's question (1:3) points out that Ahaziah *lives* as if there is no God in Israel. He is a practical atheist, and the way he seeks Baal-zebub instead of the Lord demonstrates this.

Since Ahaziah does not seek help from the real God, he will receive no real help. Instead this will be an occasion for God to send a message of judgment to King Ahaziah. When ancients sought their gods about medical issues, the response was considered to be a medical diagnosis. It was as if Elijah said, "Here's your diagnosis Ahaziah: Your condition is fatal and irreversible" (1:4).

Although Ahaziah had sent the messengers to seek a word from the pagan priests of Baal-zebub, the word from Elijah persuades them so much that they do not follow through on their original mission (1:5–6).

Ahaziah clearly suspects it is the prophet Elijah who spoke this word. His suspicion is confirmed when the man is described as being hairy and wearing a leather belt around his waist (1:7–9). The Hebrew words translated *hairy man* literally mean, "possessor of hair." Most likely this description refers to clothing made of hairy animal skins.

Critical Observation

Identifying Elijah by his clothes also connects him to the ministry of John the Baptist, who dressed in hairy skins from animals (Matthew 3:4). When the priests and Levites saw him they asked, "Are you Elijah?" (John 1:19–21).

1:10–18

ELIJAH APPEARS BEFORE AHAZIAH

The king sends a captain with fifty men (1:9). This should have been plenty of men to capture one prophet. Clearly, Ahaziah sends more men than are normally required. There are many reasons why Ahaziah wants to arrest Elijah, even though he already heard the prophecy through Elijah. Perhaps he wanted Elijah to reverse his word of doom and was willing to use force to compel him to do it. Perhaps he just wanted to show his rage against this prophet who had troubled him and his father Ahab for so long. Perhaps he wanted to dramatically silence Elijah to discourage future prophets from speaking boldly against the king of Israel.

The captain admits Elijah's righteousness when he calls him a man of God. The implication is that they are wrong in doing this, even though they are following orders from their king.

Elijah puts the issue in stark contrast. If he really is a man of God, then the captain and his men are on an ungodly and immoral mission. Since Elijah cannot bring down fire from heaven without divine approval, he asks God to evaluate these men and the rightness of their actions against God's prophet (1:10). Essentially Elijah says, "You say I am a man of God even though you are not acting like it. Maybe I am and maybe I am not. Let's let God decide by fire."

The captain commands Elijah to come down. The man of God doesn't come down, but the fire of God does (1:11). God brings judgment on these men who act as if Yahweh is not a real God and as if Elijah is not truly His servant.

The second captain repeats the same error as the first captain, but with even more guilt because he knew what happened to the first captain. The judgment upon the first group should have warned this second captain and his fifty men, but the specific request of the second captain ("Come down quickly!") shows that the second captain makes his request even more bold and demanding (1:11).

Elijah leaves the matter in God's hands, and God again responds in dramatic judgment (1:12).

The third captain approaches his mission in a completely different manner. He comes to Elijah humbly, recognizing that he really is a man of God (1:13–14). Perhaps the third captain looked at the two blackened spots of scorched earth nearby before he spoke to Elijah!

The problem isn't that God does not want Elijah to go to King Ahaziah; it is that Ahaziah, his captains, and their soldiers all act as if there is no God in Israel. When the request is made wisely and humbly, Elijah goes (1:15). God assures Elijah that he has nothing to fear from Ahaziah.

Again, Elijah asks, "Is there no God in Israel" to answer your question? (1:16 NLT). This is the same message Elijah gave to the men Ahaziah sent to inquire of Baal-zebub. The message from God does not change just because Ahaziah doesn't want to hear it the first time.

The proof of Elijah's credibility is in the result. Elijah is demonstrated to be a man of God because his prophecy is fulfilled just as spoken. Ahaziah does not recover from his fall through the lattice (1:17).

Jehoram, who succeeds Ahaziah, is also the son of Ahab (3:1) and therefore the brother of Ahaziah. Ahaziah has no descendant to pass the kingdom to, so the throne goes to his brother. The account becomes a little confusing here, because the king of Judah at that time is also named Jehoram (the son of Jehoshaphat).

The Book of the History of the Kings of Israel, referred to in 1:18, is not the books of 1 Kings and 2 Kings, but a nonbiblical book.

2 KINGS 2:1–25

ELIJAH'S ASCENSION

Setting Up the Section

Chapter 1 of 2 Kings relates Elijah's confrontation with King Ahaziah and concludes with Ahaziah's death. Chapter 2 picks up the story at the end of Elijah's ministry and tells the account of his miraculous departure in a whirlwind and of Elisha's succession as prophet.

2:1–12

ELIJAH ASCENDS TO HEAVEN

The Lord is about to take Elijah into heaven by a whirlwind (2:1). Apparently, this is somewhat common knowledge. Elijah, Elisha, and the sons of the prophets each knew that Elijah would soon be carried into heaven by a whirlwind (2:2–3); presumably there was a prophecy announcing this that at least some knew.

Elijah knows that God has a dramatic plan for the end of his earthly life, yet he is perfectly willing to allow it all to take place privately, without anyone else knowing. He seems to test the devotion of Elisha by telling him to stay behind (2:2). Since it is known that Elijah will soon depart to heaven in an unusual way, Elisha wants to stay as close as possible to his mentor. Elijah continues to test the devotion of Elisha, and Elisha continues to stay with his mentor until his anticipated unusual departure (2:4–6).

When Elijah and Elisha reach the Jordan, Elijah takes his mantle, rolls it up, and strikes the water. The water divides so that the two of them cross over on dry ground (2:7–8). This is a strange and unique miracle, though it was reminiscent of the crossing of the Red Sea during the Exodus and the stopping of the waters of the Jordan when the Israelites entered Canaan. Elijah walks in the steps of Moses and Joshua as those whom God uses to miraculously part waters.

After testing Elisha and finding him faithful, Elijah is now able to give him whatever he asks for (2:9). When invited to make a request, Elisha asks for a big thing—a double portion of the mighty spirit of Elijah. Elisha sees how greatly the Spirit of God worked through Elijah, and he wants the same for himself.

Demystifying 2 Kings

The idea of a double portion is not to ask for twice as much as Elijah has, but to ask for the portion that went to the firstborn son, as in Deuteronomy 21:17. Elisha asks for the right to be regarded as the successor of Elijah, as his firstborn son in regard to ministry. Yet Elisha has already been designated as Elijah's successor (1 Kings 19:19). This is a request for the spiritual power to fulfill the calling he already received.

Elijah tests the devotion of his protégé one more time by seeing if he will persistently stay with him through these last remarkable hours. If the devotion of Elisha remains strong through the testing, his request to be the successor of the first prophet will be fulfilled (2:10).

As the two prophets walk, a fiery object separates the two of them, and then a whirlwind carries Elijah up to heaven (2:11). This is a strange and unique miracle. Elijah is taken up to heaven in the whirlwind, not in the chariot and horses of fire (2:12). These chariots and horsemen symbolize the forces of God's spiritual presence. In them, Elisha recognizes that the strength of Israel has been that of the presence of the prophet of God. When Elisha himself dies, Joash, the reigning king, has the same vision and cries out the same words (13:14).

Elisha sees it: This fulfills the requirement mentioned in 2 Kings 2:10. Elisha will indeed inherit the prophetic ministry of Elijah. Yet Elisha isn't happy when this happens; he takes hold of his own clothes and tears them into two pieces as an expression of deep mourning (2:12).

2:13–25

THE BEGINNING OF THE MINISTRY OF THE PROPHET ELISHA

Elijah takes up the mantle of Elijah that had fallen from him (2:13). Since the mantle is the special mark of a prophet, this is a demonstration of the truth that Elisha truly has inherited the ministry of Elijah.

Take It Home

Think of what it was like for Elisha to pick up that mantle. The mantle did not fall from heaven and rest on his shoulders; he had to decide to pick it up and put it on. He had to decide: *Do I really want to put this on?* Elijah's ministry was one of great power, but also of great pressure and responsibility. What mantles lay waiting for you to pick them up?

When Elisha strikes the water, it is divided (2:14). This shows that Elisha immediately has the same power in ministry that Elijah had. He goes back over a divided Jordan River the same way that he and Elijah first came over the river.

Elisha asks, "Where is the God of Elijah?" Elisha knows that the power in prophetic ministry does not rest in mantles or fiery chariots. It rests in the presence and work of the living God. If the God of Elijah is also with Elisha, then he will inherit the same power and direction of ministry.

The succession of Elisha to the power and office of Elijah is apparent to others (2:15). Elisha doesn't need to persuade or convince them of this with words. God's blessing on his actions is enough to prove it.

The sons of the prophets wonder if the chariot of fire had not merely taken Elijah to another place in Israel (2:16). Elisha knows that it had carried him to heaven, so he is hesitant to give permission for what he knows will be a futile mission (2:17).

At this time Jericho had a poor water supply. This made agriculture impossible and life very difficult (2:19). When the water is purified, it is not because Elisha wants to impress others or because he thinks it will be good to do it. This is a work of the Lord that announces the healing of the water (2:20–22).

The ancient Hebrew word translated *youths*, or *boys*, refers to young men in a very broad sense (2:23). This term applied to Joseph when he was thirty-nine (Genesis 41:12), to Absalom as an adult (2 Samuel 14:21; 18:5), and to Solomon when he was twenty (1 Kings 3:7). These youths are from Bethel, and their mocking shows the continuing opposition to a true prophet in Bethel, the chief center of pagan calf-worship.

The young men mock Elisha both because of his apparent baldness and because of his connection with the prophet Elijah. The idea behind the words *go up* (2 Kings 2:23) is that Elisha should go up to heaven like Elijah did. It mocks Elisha, his mentor Elijah, and the God they serve.

Demystifying 2 Kings

Elisha's baldness isn't the result of old age; since he lived about fifty years after this incident, he must have been relatively young at the time. His baldness may have been all the more noticeable by comparison with Elijah's hairiness.

Elisha leaves any correction of these young men up to God but pronounces a curse on them in the name of the Lord (2:24). In response to the curse of Elisha, God sends two female bears and they maul (cut up, not kill) the young men. Forty-two in all are mauled. The bear attack has the effect of breaking up the gang, while Elisha continues on his way unharmed (2:25).

2 KINGS 3:1–27

WAR AGAINST MOAB

Setting Up the Section

King Ahab dies, leaving the throne of the northern kingdom of Israel to his son Ahaziah. When Ahaziah dies without a son, his brother Jehoram (or Joram) succeeds him. There has also been a change in the prophets: Elisha succeeded Elijah after Elijah is carried to heaven in a whirlwind.

3:1–10

THREE KINGS GATHER AGAINST THE MOABITES

King Jehoram (or Joram) comes from a family that is far beyond dysfunctional. His father, Ahab (3:1), was one of the worst kings the northern kingdom of Israel ever knew, and his mother, Jezebel, was certainly the worst queen Israel ever knew. Jehoram is better than his father and mother, but he is still a wicked man (3:2–3). He is the ninth consecutive bad king over the northern kingdom, which never had a godly king.

The sin of Jeroboam that Jehoram perpetuates includes setting up golden calves for the people to worship in Bethel and Dan (1 Kings 12:25–32). Possibly Jehoram tears down the sacred pillar of Baal out of bad motives—either because he is frightened when he remembers the judgment that came against his father Ahab and his brother Ahaziah, or because he wants to impress Jehoshaphat so the Judean king will agree to an alliance. Either way, Elisha isn't impressed with Jehoram's putting away of Baal (2 Kings 3:13).

The Moabites live on the eastern side of the Dead Sea and are under tribute to Israel. The rebellion that began when King Ahab died (1:1) continued under Jehoram (3:4–5). Jehoram asks Jehoshaphat, king of Judah, for help (3:6–7). Jehoshaphat is a godly king (1 Kings 22:41–43), who followed in the godly footsteps of his father Asa (1 Kings 15:9–15).

Yet Asa had fought against Israel (1 Kings 15:16) while Jehoshaphat made peace with the northern kingdom (1 Kings 22:44). Though the kingdom of Israel was long since separated by a civil war, the two nations (Judah and Israel) are now willing to come together to fight this common foe.

Demystifying 2 Kings

The Moabite Stone (also called the Mesha Stele), discovered in 1868, contains a Moabite inscription that confirms many of the events of 2 Kings 3, but it gives a distinctly pro-Moabite spin.

Jehoram of Israel asks Jehoshaphat of Judah for military advice because Jehoshaphat is more experienced in battle than Jehoram. The king of Judah advises Jehoram that they attack Moab from the south, going through the dry desert of the Edomites (2 Kings 3:8).

The combined armies of Judah, Israel, and Edom have to travel a considerable distance to attack Moab from the south, and they find themselves in the wilderness with no water (3:9). Jehoram's guilty conscience convinces him that this calamity is the judgment of God. His own sin makes him think that everything that has happened against him is the judgment of God (3:10).

3:11–27

ELISHA SPEAKS FOR THE LORD

Both Jehoram and Jehoshaphat believe there is a divine element to their current crisis. Jehoram believes that God is to be *avoided* because of the crisis, while Jehoshaphat believes that God should be *sought* because of the crisis (3:11).

The description of Elisha in verse 11 has been translated as "personal assistant." This is a wonderful title for any servant of God. Elisha is the humble and practical servant of Elijah. This is spiritual service that prepares him for further spiritual service.

The kings' decision to go to Elisha (3:12) is encouraging humility on the part of these three kings. Normally, kings demand that others come see them. These three are willing to go to the prophet.

Elisha's call is to continue the ministry of Elijah, and in verse 13 we see that he imitates Elijah's plain speaking to powerful people. Elisha's plain speaking strikes the conscience of the king of Israel. Elisha is willing to speak to these three kings for the sake of Jehoshaphat, the godly king of Judah (3:14).

Elisha wants to become more sensitive to the leading and speaking of the Holy Spirit, so he asks for the service of a musician (3:14–15). This demonstrates the great spiritual power in music. One way to be open to the Spirit is through psalms, hymns, and spiritual songs.

God makes a strange promise: Water will be provided, but not through just any rain or storm. The people must dig ditches in order to catch what God will provide (3:16–17). They must dig the ditches before the water comes so they can benefit from it.

Critical Observation

What many versions translate as the command, "Dig ditches," in 2 Kings 3:16 is in some versions translated as a statement that the valley or streambed will hold water. The injunction to dig, however, is in keeping with the principle that God wants us to prepare for the blessing He wants to bring. Listening to Him, we are to anticipate His working and to get ready for it.

Digging ditches was something the people of God could do. God didn't ask them to do more than they were able to do. When God wants us to prepare for the blessing He will bring, He gives us things that we can really do.

The kings come to Elisha inquiring about water. God wants to give them more than their immediate need. He wants to give them complete victory over their enemies (3:18–19).

It seems that God sends an intense downpour in the nearby mountains, and this causes a flash flood though the desert of Edom (3:20). God meets their need for provision when mysterious water flows through the camp. The water is available only because they are obedient to dig the ditches. The ditches collect the water from the flash flood.

Take It Home

If Israel and Judah had disobeyed God and failed to dig the ditches, then God's blessing would have passed them by. God told them to get ready and prepare to receive and catch His blessing. God often moves us to do things that may or may not make much sense for the moment, but they are things that will prepare us for what He will do in the future.

The measure of water available to these thirsty men is directly connected to how faithful they are to dig the ditches. The more ditches and the bigger the ditches, the more water provided. Though it was hard and unpleasant work, the more they did the more blessing they received.

The ditches are not the blessing, and they are not the victory, though they are essential parts of both the blessing and the victory. Without the miraculous blessing of God, the ditches mean nothing.

The ditches that catch the water and save the armies of these three kings from dehydration are also the means of confusion and defeat to the enemies of the people of God. When they see the sun shining on the water collected in the ditches, they think it is blood from the three kings fighting one another (3:21–23).

When they come to the camp of Israel, Israel rises up and attacks the Moabites, so that they flee before them. God uses the ditches in a completely unexpected way to supply the need *and* to defeat the enemy (3:24–25).

That the king of Moab is willing to sacrifice his own son and heir (3:26–27) shows how desperate he is. He does this to honor his pagan gods and to show his own people his determination to prevent defeat. The radical determination of the king of Moab convinces the kings of Israel, Judah, and Edom that they cannot completely defeat Moab. They leave content with their near-complete victory.

2 KINGS 4:1–44

GOD WORKS MIRACLES THROUGH ELISHA

Miracles Connected with a Widow and a Barren Woman	4:1–37
Miracles Connected with the Provision of Food	4:38–44

Setting Up the Section

We are not told precisely when the events recorded in chapter 4 occurred. In contrast to the faithlessness of King Ahaziah and King Jehoram described in 2 Kings 1–3, here we read of simple people with profound faith.

4:1–37

MIRACLES CONNECTED WITH A WIDOW AND A BARREN WOMAN

This woman in verse 1, the widowed wife of one of the sons of the prophets, has debts and no means to pay them. The legal system in Israel does not allow her to declare bankruptcy; she has to give her sons as indentured servants to her creditor as payment for the debts.

Elisha makes this woman commit herself in faith to God's provision. To borrow vessels in this manner (4:3–4) invites awkward questions, but she does as the Lord through His prophet commands her (4:5). Elisha tells the woman to take what she has—one jar of oil (*all* that she has)—and to pour that out in faith into the borrowed vessels. As she does this, the oil miraculously continues to pour from the original vessel until all the borrowed vessels are filled. At the end of it, she has a lot of oil—enough to pay the debt and provide for her future (4:6–7).

We notice that Elisha makes *her* do this. Perhaps Elisha was tempted to gather the vessels and pour the oil himself, but he knew that she had to trust God herself.

Take It Home

The miracle is given according to the measure of the widow's previous faith in borrowing vessels; when the vessels are full, the oil ceases. Had she borrowed more, more would have been provided; had she gathered less, less would have been provided.

The oil does not pour out on the ground or simply flow about. It is intended for a prepared vessel. Each vessel had to be prepared by being gathered, assembled, emptied, and then put in the right position. When there are no more prepared vessels, the oil stops.

The principle of this miracle is the same as the principle of the ditches (chapter 3). The amount of one's work with the miracle determines the amount of blessing and provision actually received. God's powerful provision invites our hard work and never excuses laziness.

A remarkable relationship between Elisha and the Shunammite woman begins when the woman seeks to do something for the prophet and offers him a meal (4:8). Elisha doesn't seek anything from this woman; she simply offers her hospitality. The Shunammite woman then seeks to do more for the prophet. With the approval of her husband, they make a room for Elisha to stay in on his frequent travels through the area (4:9–10). Still she asks for nothing in return (4:13).

It is Gehazi, Elisha's servant, who identifies what the woman needs: a son to care for her in her old age (4:14). To this barren woman this promise seems too good to be true. The stigma associated with barrenness was harsh in the ancient world, and this promised son would answer the longing of her heart and remove the stigma of barrenness (4:15–16).

The woman who so generously provides material things for the prophet of God is now blessed by the God of the prophet, blessed beyond material things (4:17).

Yet the son granted by miraculous promise, in reward to the faithful service of the Shunammite woman, tragically dies on the lap of his mother after a brief but severe affliction (4:18–20).

When the woman lays her son on Elisha's bed and prepares to fetch Elisha (4:21–24), she shows her faith. She prepares for the resurrection of the boy, not his burial. Perhaps she heard that Elijah had raised the widow of Zarephath's son to life (1 Kings 17).

The Shunammite woman doesn't want Elisha to learn of her grief through his assistant Gehazi (2 Kings 4:25). She wants the man of God to hear it from her own lips and sense her own grief. Elisha seems mystified that this woman (who he presumably often prays for) is in a crisis that he is not aware of. In this circumstance, Elisha is more surprised that God *didn't* speak to him than if God had spoken to him (4:27).

Instead of going directly himself, Elisha sends his servant Gehazi with his staff (4:29). This seems to follow the previous pattern in Elisha's ministry: He does not do things for people directly but gives them the opportunity to work with God and to trust Him for themselves. God tells the alliance of kings to have ditches dug (3:16). God tells the widow to gather vessels and pour the oil herself (4:1–7).

It may be that the Shunammite woman fails under this test, because she thinks that the power to heal is more connected with Elisha himself, and she refuses to leave his presence (4:30). The child is not healed by the laying on of the staff (4:31), though (hypothetically) the child may have been healed with only the staff if the Shunammite would have embraced this promise with full faith.

God does heal the Shunammite's son in response to Elisha's prayer (4:32–37). He prays after the pattern shown by his mentor Elijah (1 Kings 17:20–23). Elisha prays with great faith because he knew God worked in this way in the life of his mentor Elijah. He also prays with great faith because he senses that God wants to raise this boy from the dead.

Critical Observation

There is a significant contrast between the stretched-out supplication of Elijah and Elisha and the authoritative command of Jesus in raising the dead (as in John 11:43). Elijah and Elisha *beg* God to raise the dead. Jesus *commands* the dead to be raised.

4:38–44

MIRACLES CONNECTED WITH THE PROVISION OF FOOD

The famine mentioned in verse 38 may be the seven-year famine referred to in 2 Kings 8:1–3. Elisha feels a special responsibility to help in this situation because he tells the men to gather ingredients for the stew, and they gather the wild vine that poisons the pot (4:38–40).

Demystifying 2 Kings

It's probable that the poisonous gourds were *colocynth*, also known as wild cucumber. These vines still grow near the Dead Sea. The dried pulp can be used to induce vomiting, and too much of it can be fatal.

There is nothing inherently purifying in the flour Elisha puts in the pot (4:41). The real purification is a miraculous work of God.

The twenty barley loaves are bread of the firstfruits (4:42). Normally anything from the first harvest, like these loaves, is reserved for God (Leviticus 23:20) and the Levitical priests (Numbers 18:13; Deuteronomy 18:4–5). But religious practices had been corrupted under King Ahab and his sons. The farmer probably brings his firstfruits to Elisha because he knows Elisha to be a man of God.

In a miracle that anticipates Jesus' miracle of feeding the five thousand, Elisha commands that a small amount of bread be served to one hundred people, quoting God's promise not only to provide, but to provide beyond the immediate need (2 Kings 4:43). Elisha trusts the promise of God, acts upon it, and sees the promise miraculously fulfilled (4:44).

2 KINGS 5:1–27

NAAMAN THE LEPER

Setting Up the Section

The miracle recounted here in 2 Kings 5 does not occur chronologically between the events described in chapter 4 and those in chapter 6. Rather, this account, grouped with other miracles that Elisha performs, demonstrates his credibility as a prophet of God.

5:1–8

NAAMAN COMES TO ELISHA

Naaman is the chief military commander of Syria (translated as Aram in some versions), a persistent enemy to both Israel and Judah. Not long before, in the days of Ahab and Jehoshaphat, Syria had fought and won against Israel (1 Kings 22:35–36). His position and success make him a great and honorable man, and personally he is a mighty man of valor (2 Kings 5:1).

Naaman has a lot going for him, but what he has against him is devastating. He is a leper, which means that he has a horrible, incurable disease that will slowly result in his death. No matter how good and successful everything else is in Naaman's life, he is still a leper.

Demystifying 2 Kings

The disease called leprosy at this time began as small, red spots on the skin. Before too long the spots got bigger and started to turn white, with sort of a shiny or scaly appearance. Pretty soon the spots spread over the whole body and hair began to fall out—first from the head, then even from the eyebrows. As things got worse, fingernails and toenails became loose, started to rot, and eventually fell off. Then the joints of fingers and toes began to rot and fall off piece by piece. Gums began to shrink until they couldn't hold the teeth anymore, so each tooth was lost. Leprosy ate away at the face until literally the nose, the palate, and even the eyes rotted—and the victim wasted away until death.

The girl who serves as a maid to Naaman's wife (5:2) is an unwilling missionary, taken captive from Israel and now in Syria. She was probably raised in a godly home, yet taken from her family at a young age. God allows the tragedy of her captivity to accomplish a greater good, illustrating the mysterious ways God works.

This young girl is an outstanding example of a faithful witness in her current circumstance. She cares enough to speak up, and she has faith enough to believe that Elisha will heal Naaman of his leprosy (5:3).

Considering the record of wars between Israel and Syria described in the previous chapters, it seems strange that the king of Syria would send a letter of recommendation with his general Naaman (5:4–6). It seems that 2 Kings is not necessarily arranged chronologically, so this probably occurred during a time of lowered tension between Israel and Syria.

Naaman took over one million dollars worth of gold, silver, and merchandise with him to Israel. All this together shows how desperate Naaman's condition is and how badly the king of Syria wants to help him.

When the king of Israel (Jehoram) reads the letter, he is understandably upset. First, it is obviously out of his power to heal Naaman's leprosy. Second, he has no relationship with the prophet of the God who does have the power to heal. He thinks the king of Syria seeks a quarrel (5:7).

Elisha gives a gentle rebuke to the king of Israel: "This is a crisis to you, because you have no relationship with the God who can heal lepers. But it is a needless crisis, because you *could* have a relationship with this God." Sadly, Naaman will never know there is a prophet in Israel by hanging around the royal palace. The true prophet in Israel isn't welcome at the palace (5:8).

5:9–19

NAAMAN IS HEALED

Naaman takes the trouble to come to the home of Elisha, but Elisha refuses to give him a personal audience. He simply sends a messenger (5:9–10). This is humbling to Naaman, who is accustomed to being honored. The messenger brings simple, uncomplicated instructions. Yet as Naaman's reaction demonstrates, these are humbling instructions. Naaman has it all figured out. In his great need, he anticipates a way in which God will work, and he is offended when God doesn't work the way he expects. Because his expectation is crushed, Naaman wants nothing to do with Elisha. If the answer is washing in a river, Naaman knows there are better rivers in his own land (5:11–12).

Thank God for faithful subordinates who will speak to their superiors as Naaman's men do (5:13). Naaman is obviously angry, yet they are bold enough to give him the good advice he needs to hear. They use a brilliantly logical approach. If Elisha had asked Naaman to sacrifice one hundred or one thousand animals to the God of Israel, he would have done it immediately. Yet because his request is easy to do and humbling, Naaman refuses.

Naaman does exactly what Elisha tells him to do (5:14). Therefore, each dunk in the Jordan is a step of faith, trusting in the word of God through His prophet. Naaman's response of faith is generously rewarded. God answers his faithful actions with complete and miraculous healing. Elisha's absence makes it clear that the miracle is from God, not from Elisha.

Before, Naaman expected the prophet to come to him. Now he returns to the man of God and stands before him. The healing, connected with the word of the prophet, is convincing evidence to Naaman that the God Elisha represents is the true God in all the earth. Naaman's desire to give a gift to Elisha is a fine display of gratitude (5:15). We can say that Naaman only means well by this gesture. He feels it is appropriate to support the ministry of this man of God whom the Lord had used so greatly to bring healing. However, Elisha steadfastly insists that he will take nothing from Naaman (5:16).

Like many new believers, Naaman is superstitious in his faith. He holds the common opinion in the ancient world that particular deities have power over particular places. He thinks that if he takes a piece of Israel back with him to Syria, he can better worship the God of Israel (5:17). As an official in the government of Syria, Naaman is expected to participate in the worship of the Syrian gods. He asks Elisha for allowance to direct his heart to Yahweh even when he is in the temple of Rimmon (5:18). Some commentators believe that Naaman asks forgiveness for his previous idolatry in the temple of Rimmon, instead of asking permission for future occasions. Apparently, the Hebrew will allow for this translation, though it is not the most natural way to understand the text.

By generally approving, but not giving a specific answer, it seems that Elisha leaves the matter up to Naaman and God (5:19). Perhaps he trusted that the Lord would personally convict Naaman of this and give him the integrity and strength to avoid idolatry.

5:20–27

THE GREED OF GEHAZI

As Gehazi hears Naaman and Elisha speak, he is shocked that his master refuses to take anything from such a wealthy, influential, and grateful man. He figures that someone should benefit from such an opportunity, and he takes the initiative to run after Naaman and take something from him (5:20–21).

Gehazi may have thought that God was blessing his venture. After all, he asks for one talent of silver, and Naaman is happy to give him two talents (5:22–23). The fact that he hands them to two of his servants shows that this is a lot of silver. But the fact that Gehazi deliberately hides the silver from Elisha (5:24–25) suggests that he knows that he has done wrong.

Elisha knew what Gehazi had done (5:26). We don't know if this was supernatural knowledge, or simply a familiarity with Gehazi's character. At any rate, all Gehazi's attempts to cover his sin fail.

It seems that Elisha had no absolute law against receiving support from those who were touched by his ministry. Yet it is spiritually clear to Elisha, and should have been clear to Gehazi, that it is not appropriate at this time and circumstance (5:26). Obviously, Gehazi does not bring home all of the things Elisha lists: vineyards, cattle, and servants. Yet he wants all of these things, and Elisha exposes his greedy heart.

Gehazi receives a severe judgment (5:27), but as a man in ministry he is under an even stricter judgment. When he allows himself to covet what Naaman has, he thinks only in terms of the money. God allows him to keep the riches, but also gives him something else Naaman has—severe leprosy.

2 KINGS 6:1–33

GOD'S PROTECTION OF ELISHA

Setting Up the Section

Chapter 6 of 2 Kings deals with needs both great and small. The recovery of a lost ax head is a miracle of provision. The miracle of protection from the Samarian army is a dramatic demonstration of God's invisible but very real power. Chapter 6 concludes with a situation even graver: a siege that threatens to destroy the population of an entire city.

6:1–7

THE RECOVERY OF THE AX HEAD

At this time Elisha has a significant impact on the nation. The old facility for housing the sons of the prophets is not large enough to meet the needs of all those who want to be trained in ministry (6:1–2). Elisha does not initiate or lead this work of building a new center for training the prophets, but it cannot happen without his approval and blessing (6:3).

Losing the iron ax head in the water (6:4–5) is a significant loss. Iron was certainly present at this time in Israel, but it was not common enough to be cheap. The man who loses the ax head is rightly sensitive to the fact that he lost something that belongs to someone else, making the loss more acute.

This is an obvious and unique miracle. There is no trickery in the way Elisha puts the stick in the water; it is simply an expression of his faith that God honors (6:6).

Conceivably, God could have arranged a way for the ax head to appear right in the man's hand without any effort on his part. But this miracle works in a familiar way—God does the part only He can do, but He leaves to man the part that he can do (6:7).

6:8–23

GOD PROTECTS ELISHA FROM THE SYRIANS

Elisha does not support the corrupt monarchs of Israel, but he knows that it is even worse for Israel to be conquered and subjugated under Syria. Therefore, he gives the king of Israel information from divinely inspired espionage (6:8–10).

The king of Syria is naturally mystified by the way the king of Israel knows all of Syria's plans beforehand. He is convinced there is a traitor among them, until one servant reveals that Elisha, the prophet in Israel, knows and reveals these things (6:11–13).

When Elisha's servant sees the horses and chariots and the great Syrian army that has come to seize Elisha, he is naturally afraid (6:13–15). He knows that there is little chance of escaping or surviving an attack from so many. But Elisha says not to fear, for they have more men (6:16). This is not empty hope or wishful thinking; it is a real reason for confidence, even if the servant cannot see it. This seems unbelievable to Elisha's servant. He sees the horses, the chariots, and the great army surrounding them. He cannot see anyone who is with himself and Elisha.

Elisha does not pray that God will change anything in the situation, nor does he try to persuade the servant of the reality of those who are with them. His only request is that his servant can actually see the reality of the situation (6:17). When a person is blind to spiritual reality, only God can open his or her eyes.

When his eyes are opened, the servant sees what he could not see before. He sees that there really are more with him and Elisha than those assembled against them.

The previous lack of perception on the part of Elisha's servant does not make the reality of the spiritual army any less real. If there are fifty people who do not see something, it doesn't invalidate the perception of one who does see.

Critical Observation

Horses and chariots were the most sophisticated and mighty military instruments of the day. But the invisible army of God had literally more firepower than the horses and chariots of the Syrians. The spiritual army had chariots of fire all around Elisha.

The Syrian soldiers could not see the spiritual army, so they do not hesitate to approach Elisha. But just as he previously prayed that God would give sight to his servant, he now asks God to strike this people with blindness. God answers this prayer, just as He previously answered the prayer to give perception to the servant (6:18).

When Elisha tells the army to follow him, he tells a technical truth but certainly intends to deceive. He does in fact bring them to the man whom they seek (when their eyes are opened, Elisha is there with them). However, he leads them back to Samaria—the capital city of the kingdom of Israel and an unfriendly place for a group of Syrian soldiers (6:19–20).

Elisha commands the king of Israel to treat the soldiers with kindness and generosity (6:21–22). This practice of answering evil with good successfully changes the policy of freelance raiders from Syria, and the bands of Syrian raiders no longer invade the land of Israel (6:23).

6:24–33

THE SIEGE OF SAMARIA

Though the kindness of Elisha and the king of Israel changes the heart of the Syrian raiders, it does not change the heart of the king of Syria. He launches a large, full-scale attack against his neighbor to the south (6:24).

Demystifying 2 Kings

The king of Syria used the common method of attack on securely walled cities: He besieged Samaria. A siege was intended to surround a city, prevent all business and trade from entering or leaving, and eventually to starve the population into surrender.

The siege strategy successfully starves Samaria, and there is a great famine. The famine is so bad that a donkey's head or dove droppings become so expensive that only the rich can afford them. Their price of five shekels of silver is more than a month's wages for a laborer. Mothers are so hungry that they even eat their own children (6:25–29).

The king is deeply grieved and angry—but not with himself, with Israel, or with their sin. The king is angry against the prophet of God—and with God Himself (6:30–33).

Critical Observation

Deuteronomy 28 contains an extended section where God warns Israel about the curses that will come upon them if they reject the covenant He made with them. Part of that chapter describes the horrors fulfilled in this chapter (see Deuteronomy 28:52–53).

2 KINGS 7:1–20

GOD'S MIRACULOUS PROVISION FOR SAMARIA

God's Promise and What the Lepers Discover	7:1–9
The Plundering of the Syrian Camp	7:10–20

Setting Up the Section

Chapter 7 of 2 Kings picks up the account of the Syrian's siege of Israel's capital, Samaria.

7:1–9

GOD'S PROMISE AND WHAT THE LEPERS DISCOVER

Though the king of Israel blames God for the calamity that came upon Israel and Samaria (6:33), God still has a word for the king and the nation—and it is a good word. God's promise through Elisha is that in twenty-four hours the economic situation in Samaria will be completely reversed. Instead of scarcity, there will be such abundance that food prices will radically drop in the city (7:1).

Demystifying 2 Kings

By the standards of that time, the prices listed were not cheap, but they were nothing compared to the famine conditions associated with the siege.

The king's officer doubts the prophecy, and his doubt is based on several faulty premises (7:2). First, he doubts the power of God. If God wills it, He can drop food from the sky. Then he doubts God's creativity, that He can bring provision in a completely unexpected way. Finally, he doubts the messenger of God who has an established track record of reliability.

Through Elisha, God pronounces a harsh judgment upon the king's doubting officer. He will see the word fulfilled, but he will not benefit from its fulfillment.

The four lepers introduced in verse 3 stay at the entrance of the gate because they are not welcome in the city. Their leprous condition makes them outcasts and untouchables. Their logic is perfect. They will soon die from the famine if they stay in the city. If any food becomes available, they will certainly be the last to receive it. So they decide that their chances are better if they surrender to the Syrians (7:4).

When they come to the outskirts of the Syrian camp, to their surprise, no one is there. This huge army surrounded the city of Samaria for many months, and the camp was the home and supply center for thousands of men. When the lepers come upon it that morning, they discover an empty army camp—fully supplied. The words translated "to the outskirts of the camp" (7:5 NASB) imply that they came not only to the edge of the camp, but that they walked around to the furthermost part of the Syrian camp, the part away from the city. They came to the camp as someone from afar would approach, not as someone from Syria. They figured that this was their best chance, coming as if they were not from the besieged city and to the least fortified positions of the camp.

Israel is powerless against this besieging army, but God isn't powerless. He attacks the Syrian army simply by causing them to hear noises of an army (7:6–7). Perhaps God does this by putting the noise into the air; perhaps He simply creates the perception of the noise in the minds of the Syrian soldiers. The same God who struck one Syrian army so they could not see what was there (6:18) now strikes another Syrian army so that they hear things that are not there. As a result, the siege for Samaria is over—even though no one in the city knows it or enjoys it.

Everything is left behind, leaving the unlikely lepers to spoil the camp. They go into one tent and eat and drink. After the long period of famine, this is the answer to every hope and prayer they had. They know that their discovery of the camp can't remain secret forever, so they hide some of the valuables so they can profit from them even when the camp is discovered by others. After enjoying it all, the lepers realize their responsibility (7:8–9).

7:10–20

THE PLUNDERING OF THE SYRIAN CAMP

The lepers call to the gatekeepers of the city (7:10). Since the lepers are not welcome in the city, they can only communicate with the gatekeepers. There are many people they cannot speak to, but they are faithful to speak to the ones whom they can speak to. The good news from the lepers is communicated in the simplest way possible. It goes from one person to another, until the news reaches the king himself (7:11), whose officers go to check the accuracy of the report (7:12–15). This is the sensible reaction to the good news that started with the report of the lepers. The report might be true or it might not be; it only makes sense to test it and see.

When the good news is found to be true, there is no stopping the people. Because they know their need, they are happy to receive God's provision to meet that need (7:16–17). Through Elisha, God had announced the exact prices in the Samarian markets, and the prophecy is proven to be precisely true (7:18).

The officer who earlier had said provision would never come (7:2) has to personally supervise the people responding to that provision. Not only does the prediction about the prices come true, but so does the prediction Elijah made about the officer himself (7:2). Because of his unbelief, others enjoy God's blessings, but he does not (7:19–20).

2 KINGS 8:1–29

NEW KINGS IN SYRIA AND JUDAH

Setting Up the Section

The story of the kings of Judah pauses at 1 Kings 22:50, where Jehoshaphat the son of Asa ends his twenty-five-year reign and his son Jehoram comes to the throne. This chapter picks up the story of Jehoram again. But first we read of the king of Israel and the assassination of Ben-hadad, king of Syria.

8:1–6

THE RESTORATION OF THE SHUNAMMITE'S LAND

Second Kings 4 describes Elisha's previous dealings with the woman mentioned in 8:1. She and her husband are godly, generous people who help the prophet. Through Elisha's prayer they are blessed with a son, who is also brought miraculously back to life.

On the advice of the prophet, the woman and her family leave Israel because of a coming famine. In the land of the Philistines, they are spared the worst of the famine (7:2). When she returns, she appeals to the king for the return of her land (7:3).

Demystifying 2 Kings

Upon leaving Israel and going to the land of the Philistines, the woman forfeits her claim to her ancestral lands. To regain them requires intervention from the king.

The king is talking with Gehazi (8:4). This is the same servant of Elisha who was cursed with leprosy (5:20–27). It seems strange that a severely afflicted leper would be a counselor to a king, so it seems that either Gehazi is granted healing from his leprosy or that this actually takes place before the events of 2 Kings 5. Of course, it is still possible that the king has this conversation with Gehazi when he is a leper and the king simply keeps his distance.

The woman comes to make her request at the exact time Gehazi tells the king about the miracles associated with her life (8:5). This is perfect, God-ordained timing. The king understands that if God is obviously supportive of this woman, then it also makes sense for him to support her and to answer her request (8:6). In the end, her obedience to God is not penalized by losing her land.

8:7–15

A NEW KING IN SYRIA

The leaders of Syria had at one time tried to capture or kill Elisha. But since God has miraculously delivered the prophet so many times, he is now respected and welcome in the courts of the Syrian king. He is especially welcome on account of the king's illness (8:7). Wanting to know the outcome of his present illness, the king of Syria asks the prophet—and with his extravagant gift does whatever he can to prompt a favorable message (8:8–9).

God gives Elisha insight into more than the health of the king of Syria. He also sees the inevitable and ultimately God-ordained political machinations that will unfold. Elisha rightly says that the king will certainly recover from his illness, and he does (8:10). However, Elisha also sees that the same servant he speaks with at that moment will engineer an assassination and take the throne. This is how Elisha's statement is true. The king certainly does recover from his illness, and he really does die soon—but not from the illness.

This is a dramatic, personal confrontation between this prophet and the high official of the king of Syria. Elisha stares at him because he has prophetic knowledge of future events and of how this man will trouble Israel in the future. God tells Elisha more about the coming situation than he wants to know. He shows the prophet that the messenger of the king (Hazael), after he takes the throne from the present king of Syria, will do evil to the children of Israel (8:11–12). Elisha's prophetic calling and gift is at times more of a burden than a blessing. He can clearly see what will befall Israel through Hazael, but he is powerless to prevent it.

Perhaps Hazael had planned this assassination and simply pretends to be ignorant at Elisha's announcement (8:13). Perhaps he has not yet planned it and does know the evil capabilities in his own heart. Either way, his offence is inappropriate. He should have taken this warning as an opportunity to confront himself and to do right, instead of turning an accusation back upon Elisha.

Hazael takes an evil inference from Elisha's prophecy and seizes the throne (8:14–15). Instead of taking the prophet's announcement as a warning to check his own heart, he acts on that evil—and is fully responsible for his own actions.

8:16–29

TWO NEW KINGS IN JUDAH

The fact that Jehoram followed the example of the kings of Israel (8:16–18) is not a compliment. While the southern kingdom of Judah had a mixture of godly and wicked kings, the northern kingdom of Israel had nothing but evil, God-rejecting kings. The wickedness of Jehoram is not a surprise, considering how much he allows himself to be influenced by the house of Ahab. Arranged by his father, Jehoram marries the daughter of Ahab and Jezebel—her name is Athaliah. In order to consolidate his throne, he murders his many brothers and many other leaders (1 Chronicles 21:1–6). Perhaps his marriage to Ahab's daughter makes sense politically or socially, but it is a spiritual calamity for Judah.

Demystifying 2 Kings

It is easy to confuse the variation between Jehoram and Joram in verses 21–23, but in this case, they are two variants for the same name. On the other hand, it's also easy to confuse Jehoram of Judah with the King Jehoram of Israel, mentioned in 2 Kings 3. That Jehoram is called *Joram* in 8:16.

Yet God will not destroy Judah, for the sake of His servant David (8:19). The implication is that Jehoram's evil is great enough to justify such judgment, but God withholds it out of faithfulness to his ancestor David.

The Edomite revolt against Judah (8:20–22) is evidence of the weakness of the kingdom of Jehoram. He thinks that the marriage alliance with Ahab and the kingdom of Israel will make Judah stronger, but this act of disobedience only makes them weaker.

Critical Observation

According to 2 Chronicles 21:12–15, Elijah writes Jehoram a letter, condemning him for his sins and predicting that judgment will come upon him and disaster upon the nation. At the age of forty, Jehoram is struck with a fatal intestinal disease, and he dies in terrible pain (2 Chronicles 21:19).

The short life and reign of Jehoram (he reigns only eight years and dies at age forty) should have warned his son Ahaziah. His brief reign (one year) shows he was even less blessed than his father (8:25–26). His close association with the wicked house of Ahab develops into a war alliance with Israel against Syria. His connection with his mother's family (she is a daughter of Ahab and Jezebel, 2 Kings 8:18) is so strong and sympathetic that he pays a visit to the injured and sick King Joram of Israel (8:27–29).

2 KINGS 9:1–37

JEHU TAKES THE THRONE OF ISRAEL

Setting Up the Section

After the account of kings Jehoram and Ahaziah of Judah in chapter 8, the story shifts back to the northern kingdom of Israel in chapter 9. Joram, the king of Israel identified in 2 Kings 3, is king at the time the events of this chapter take place.

9:1–13

JEHU IS ANOINTED AND DECLARED KING

Elisha summons a young man from the association for training prophets in Israel (9:1–3). We might imagine that Elisha gives him this duty as a class assignment. Though Israel has abandoned God, God has not abandoned Israel. He still has the right to interfere among them. He will appoint and allow kings as He chooses, either to bless an obedient Israel or to curse a disobedient nation, according to the terms of His covenant with them at Mount Sinai.

So the young man, the servant of the prophet, goes to Ramoth-gilead. There he finds the captains of the army and Jehu, a commander in the army of Israel, under King Ahab and his son, King Joram (9:4–5). Jehu is anointed but is not to take the throne immediately (9:6). Both Saul and David were anointed as king over Israel before they actually possessed the throne.

Critical Observation

Jehu had previously been anointed as a future king of Israel who would overthrow the dynasty of Omri and Ahab (1 Kings 19:16–18). But that was a long time ago, and now he is anointed again to show that the time of fulfillment of the previous prophecy is at hand.

The young prophet's message about the destruction of Ahab's family (9:7–10) is more than Elisha tells this man from the school of prophets to say (9:1–3). Either Elisha told him to say this and it was not recorded previously, or he came under the inspiration of the Spirit when he did what Elisha told him to do and spoke this in spontaneous prophecy to Jehu. Clearly, God intends to use Jehu as a tool of judgment against the royal house of Ahab.

When Jehu emerges from the tent with his head drenched with oil, it is easy to think that the man who did it is a madman (9:11). It is easy for both Jehu and his associates to think of any God-honoring man as demented. Yet Jehu knows—and the others soon do also—that the man is a true prophet of God. When Jehu repeats the prophet's message, they take his word seriously and proclaim the reluctant Jehu as the king of Israel (9:13). This shows the sense of dissatisfaction they have with Joram.

9:14–37

JEHU BRINGS GOD'S JUDGMENT TO THE HOUSE OF OMRI

Upon seeing the company of Jehu approaching, King Joram wants to know if this mysterious group comes in peace (9:14–17). As he waits to recover full strength in Jezreel, Joram is fundamentally insecure in his hold on the throne and easily suspects threats. Jehu's reply (9:18) means that the soldier should not regard this as a time of peace, but a time of conflict—a time to violently overthrow the throne of Joram and the dynasty he comes from. When two messengers do not return but instead join the company of Jehu (9:19–20), it shows that he enjoys popular support among the troops of Israel, and King Joram does not.

Jehu is such an intense man that his personality can be easily seen in the way he drives a chariot (9:20).

The property of Naboth the Jezreelite (9:21) is the land that Ahab and Jezebel had so wickedly obtained by murdering the innocent owner of the land (1 Kings 21:1–16). On this very land—which, as far as God is concerned, still belongs to Naboth—the dynasty of Omri will meet its judgment.

The wicked, compromising Joram wants peace with Jehu (9:22). But none of the dynasty of Omri wants peace with God; nor do Ahab and Jezebel want peace with Naboth.

Jehu's condemnation of Jezebel shows that he takes his previous anointing by Elijah (1 Kings 19:16–17) and his more recent anointing by one from the school of the prophets seriously. Jehu's words as he has Joram's body dumped on Nabal's property confirm that Jehu sees himself as a fulfiller of God's will in bringing judgment on the house of Ahab (9:25–26).

Take It Home

Jehu's mind is not filled with thoughts of political gain and royal glory. He acts for the honor of God, as a conscious executor of divine judgment against the house of Ahab. While we today are not likely to be called to execute kings, we are called to do everything not for our own gain, but for the glory of God (1 Corinthians 10:31).

Jehu receives no direct command or commission from God to bring judgment upon the king of Judah, but he does anyway. Consciously or unconsciously, he is guided by God and he kills Ahaziah. Ahaziah is happy to associate himself with the northern kingdom of Israel and their wicked kings. Therefore he dies in the same judgment that came upon the king of Israel. Ahaziah is also a blood relative of Ahab (Ahab is his grandfather), therefore making him liable under the judgment that came upon Ahab and his descendants (9:27–29). When

Ahaziah is killed in battle, they give him a dignified burial—not for his own sake, but only because his ancestor Jehoshaphat was a godly man (2 Chronicles 22:9).

Jezebel compares Jehu to Zimri (2 Kings 9:30–31), who assassinated King Baasha of Israel (1 Kings 16:9–12) when Zimri was also the servant of Baasha, a commander in his army. It is her way of calling Jehu a despicable rebel. It is also an implied threat, because the brief reign of Zimri is ended by Omri, who is the father of Ahab and the father-in-law of this same Jezebel. By implication, Jezebel says "The dynasty of Omri will defeat you just like it defeated Zimri."

The eunuchs at the window probably work for Jezebel, but they quickly respond to Jehu's command to throw the queen down. In ancient Near Eastern cultures, the desecration of the dead body—Jezebel's body being trampled under the horse's hooves—was a fate worse than death. Yet Jehu is completely untroubled by the ugly end of Jezebel; he eats and drinks after trampling over her dead body and passing over the pavement splattered with her blood (9:32–35).

Verses 36 and 37 record Jehu's conviction that God's promise against Jezebel and the house of Ahab is exactly and righteously fulfilled (1 Kings 21:19, 23–25).

2 KINGS 10:1–36

THE REFORMS OF JEHU

Setting Up the Section

Jehu, anointed king of Israel at God's command, has executed the wicked queen mother, Jezebel, her son, Joram, who is Israel's king, and her son-in-law, Ahaziah, who is Judah's king—all in fulfillment of the judgment the Lord had sworn against them. But seventy sons of King Ahab, the patriarch of this idolatrous family, remain alive.

10:1–17

JEHU EXECUTES THE HOUSE OF AHAB

Ahab's seventy sons are a significant danger to the anointed King Jehu. First, they are the descendants of Ahab and have a great interest in battling to keep the throne of Israel among the dynasty of Omri. Second, they are in Samaria, the capital city of Israel—meaning they are away from Jehu, who killed King Joram in Jezreel. Jehu challenges any partisans of the house of Omri to declare themselves and prepare to fight for their master's house (10:1–3).

Instead, terrified, they send a message back to Jehu, promising not to put any of the princes on the throne as king (10:4–5). Jehu's letter—and his previous bold action against Joram and Ahaziah—powerfully persuades the leaders of Israel to execute the sons of

Ahab on behalf of Jehu. The nobles are so afraid of Jehu that they send grim evidence of their obedience: the princes' heads in a basket (10:6–7). Jehu has the heads piled at the gate of the city (10:8).

Demystifying 2 Kings

Jehu doesn't ask for the severed heads on a whim. It is the custom at the time to display the heads of rebels at the city gate as a public warning against rebellion.

When the people see the severed heads of seventy descendants of Ahab, they fear that judgment has gone too far and they will be punished for it. Jehu assures them that they have done right and that none have the right to accuse him, because he acted at the command of God (10:9–11).

On his way to Samaria, Jehu meets relatives of Ahaziah, king of Judah. This is to the great misfortune of these men. Since Jehu is committed to execute all those connected with the house of Ahab, these men are also targets of judgment. Ahaziah is a descendant of King Ahab through his mother (who is the daughter of Ahab and Jezebel). Therefore, their mention of the queen mother does not help them. None of them escape (9:12–14). This is characteristic of Jehu—whole-hearted and energetic obedience.

Next Jehu encounters a man named Jehonadab. Jehu wants to know if Jehonadab is on his side (10:15). Jehonadab is optimistic about this energetic reformer, and Jehu is hungry for the approval of this popular religious leader and reformer. It isn't too cynical to think that Jehu wants to use Jehonadab to add legitimacy to his reign as king.

Jehu's zeal is evident in his complete and energetic obedience to the Lord, to the disregard of his own safety and comfort (10:17). Yet he seems to boast of his dedication (10:16), revealing a dangerous root of pride.

Demystifying 2 Kings

Jehonadab, the son of Rechab (10:15–16), was the mysterious founder of the Rechabites, a reform movement among the people of God protesting the immoral and impure lives of many in Israel and Judah. In Jeremiah 35, God uses the Rechabites and the memory of Jehonadab as an example of faithfulness and obedience to rebuke His unfaithful and disobedient people.

10:18–31

JEHU STRIKES AGAINST BAAL WORSHIP

Jehu feigns devotion to Baal to lure the priests and worshipers of Baal into a trap. The priests of Baal believe the deception (10:18–21). Jehu gathers all the Baal-worshipers in one temple and makes certain that all the worshipers of the true God are put out of the place (10:22–23).

Jehu chooses to offer the sacrifice to Baal first and then to call for the execution of the worshipers of Baal. Ahab had built this temple for his wife Jezebel (1 Kings 16:32); Jehu tears it down. He works to completely eliminate the worship of Baal from Israel, making him a unique king among the other rulers of the northern kingdom (10:24–28). However, he promotes the false worship of the true God after the pattern of Jeroboam, who set up the golden calves that were at Bethel and Dan (10:29).

Critical Observation

Beginning with the first king of Israel—Jeroboam—Israel was steeped in idolatry. Jeroboam began with false representations of the true God (the golden calves described in 1 Kings 12:25–33). The successive kings of Israel continued his idolatry (Nadab, Baasha, Elah, Zimri, and Omri) until the reign of Ahab. Under King Ahab, Israel moved from the false worship of the true God to the state-supported worship of Baal (1 Kings 16:29–34). The son of Ahab (Jehoram/Joram) continued this practice until he was assassinated by Jehu, who destroyed the infrastructure of state-sponsored Baal worship in Israel.

Clearly, there was some good in the reign of Jehu—standing against Ahab and driving out Baal worship. For this, he is rewarded with a dynasty that will last four generations (10:30). Yet, Jehu did not obey or serve God with all his heart (10:31).

10:32–36

A SUMMARY OF JEHU'S REIGN

Syria captures large portions of Israel's territory. This is the work of God. For hundreds of years before this—since the time of the entry into the promised land more than six hundred years before—Israel held substantial portions of land on the eastern side of the Jordan River. This land was held by the tribes of Gad, Reuben, and Manasseh. Now this land is taken by the enemies of Israel because of their sin and unfaithfulness to the covenant. These neighboring rulers and their kingdoms are prompted and made successful by God (10:32–33).

Though incomplete in his own goodness, this man is the best of a bad group. Jehu's goodness is rewarded with a twenty-eight-year reign (10:34–36). This is a long reign, but notable only at its beginning. Jehu has the energy and influence to truly turn the nation back to God, but his half-commitment to God leaves that potential unfulfilled and points to a lack of any real relationship with the Lord.

2 KINGS 11:1–21

THE YOUNG KING JOASH

Setting Up the Section

King Ahaziah of Judah has been executed by Jehu, as recorded in 2 Kings 9:27–29. We don't know how many sons he leaves as heirs, but Ahaziah's mother has plans of her own for the throne of Judah.

11:1–12

THE PRESERVATION OF JOASH

Athaliah uses the occasion of her son's death to take power for herself. Athaliah is from the family of Ahab, and Jehu has completely destroyed all of Ahab's descendants in Israel. Now, after Jehu's coup, Athaliah tries to save something for Ahab's family by trying to eliminate the house of David in Judah (11:1).

Demystifying 2 Kings

Athaliah is the daughter of Ahab and Jezebel and is given to Jehoram, king of Judah, as a bride. She is a bad influence on both her husband (Jehoram of Judah) and her son (King Ahaziah of Judah).

Jehosheba, a little-known woman, had an important place in God's plan. Through her courage and ingenuity, she preserves the royal line of David through which the Messiah will come (11:2). Evil people like Athaliah will begin their work, but God can always raise up a Jehosheba.

Though Ahaziah is a bad king who makes evil alliances, he is still a descendant of David and the successor of his royal line. For the sake of David, God remembers His promise and spares this one young survivor from the massacre of Athaliah. The line of David is almost extinguished and continues only in the presence of a small boy, but God does preserve that flickering flame.

Like the boy Samuel, Joash grew up in the temple (11:3). Like Samuel, he probably found little ways to help the priests, whatever could be done without attracting too much attention, while Athaliah reigned over the land for six years.

Jehoiada is a godly man who is concerned with restoring the throne of David to the line of David and taking it away from this daughter of Ahab and Jezebel. From the place—the temple—where Jehoiada charges the guards with an oath of loyalty, and from the context of the oath, we learn that the worship of the true God is not dead in Judah. These captains and bodyguards and escorts respond to their responsibility before the Lord (11:4).

It is a dramatic moment when Jehoiada brings out the young prince, Joash, secret heir to David's throne. Jehoiada chooses the Sabbath for the day of the coup, because that is the day when the guards change their shifts, and they can assemble two groups of guards at the temple without attracting attention (11:5–8). It is fitting for these soldiers to use weapons that had belonged to King David himself (11:9–11).

11:13–21

THE DEATH OF THE QUEEN MOTHER ATHALIAH

Athaliah rushes to the temple and sees the newly-crowned king (11:13). For the usurper queen mother, this is a horrifying sight. For six years she ruled because she believed there were no legitimate claimants to the throne of David. Now she sees that one son of Ahaziah—Joash, her own grandson—escaped her murderous intent.

All the people of the land rejoice (11:14). They were obviously weary of the wicked reign of Athaliah.

Athaliah's charge of treason is not unfounded. This is treason against her government, but it is a well-founded and godly treason against a tyrannical, wicked ruler.

The execution of Athaliah is both righteous and prudent. It is a just sentence against this woman who had murdered so many, and prudent precautions are taken so she cannot mount a resistance. As a priest, Jehoiada has a great concern for the sanctity and reputation of the temple, so Athaliah is not executed there but in the place where horses enter the palace grounds (11:15–16).

Then Jehoiada establishes a new covenant. The covenant is between the Lord, the king, and the people. They commit themselves to honor, obey, and serve God. He also makes a covenant between the king and the people (11:17). Both kings and citizens have mutual obligations toward the other; neither have absolute rights over or against the other.

Previously, Jehu had supervised the destruction of the temple of Baal in Samaria (chapter 10). Here the temple of Baal in Jerusalem is destroyed. They don't stop at destroying the building itself; they go on to destroy both the sacred objects dedicated to Baal and to kill Mattan, the priest of Baal (11:18).

Critical Observation

One reason the people resent the worship of Baal in Jerusalem is because, according to 2 Chronicles 24:7, Athaliah had directed that sacred objects from the temple of the Lord be put into the temple of Baal.

After more than six dark years, the rightful king of Judah once again rules over his grateful people (11:19–21).

2 KINGS 12:1–21

THE REIGN OF KING JOASH OVER JUDAH

Setting Up the Section

Chapter 12 of 2 Kings chronicles the reign of King Joash, who comes to the throne at the age of seven (2 Kings 11). The Hebrew text uses the variant spelling *Jehoash*. Some translations use this spelling, while others use the name *Joash*. Both refer to the young king introduced in 2 Kings 11.

12:1–16

JOASH REPAIRS THE TEMPLE

Joash has a long and mostly blessed reign (12:1). Joash falls short of full commitment and complete godliness, but he does advance the cause of God in the kingdom of Judah. Verse 2 implies that when the priest Jehoiada dies, Joash no longer does what is right in the sight of the Lord. Second Chronicles 24:15–23 tells us that he turns to idolatry when Jehoiada dies, and judgment follows.

Joash implements a halfway reformation but not a total reforming of Israel's worship. He does not take on the difficult job of removing the high places of worship (2 Kings 12:3).

There is a regular income coming into the temple from several different sources—census (Exodus 20:13), assessments or taxes (Leviticus 27:2), and voluntary gifts. King Joash wants to put that money toward a particular purpose: repairing the temple (12:4–5). The temple needed restoration because it had been vandalized by Athaliah and her sons (2 Chronicles 24:7). It is natural for Joash to have a high regard for the condition of the temple, because it was his home as a young boy (2 Kings 11:3).

King Joash has to wait a very long time until the damages of the temple are repaired. The work is going far too slowly (12:6); the priests and the Levites have taken the money for their own use (12:7). Under the direction of King Joash, the priests give the people the opportunity to give (12:8–9).

King Joash gets to the heart of the problem—poor administration and financial mismanagement. Through Jehoiada the priest, he implements a system where the money will be set aside, saved, and then wisely spent for the repair and refurbishing of the temple (12:10–13). Through good administration of the project, they are able to find men who can be trusted to use the money wisely and honestly (12:14–15). In the end, the project succeeds without taking anything away from the priests. They still receive money from the trespass offerings and from the sin offerings (12:16).

12:17–21

THE DECLINE OF KING JOASH

At this time, the kingdom of Syria attacks Judah (12:17). Instead of trusting God, Joash trades prior blessing—the sacred treasures of the temple—to protect his capital and kingdom against the attacking Syrians (12:18). There is no record of repentance on Joash's part. He never comes back to fulfill his early promise (12:19).

The officers' conspiracy against Joash is startling, and it shows that the blessing of God long before vanished from the compromised king who began so well but failed to finish well (12:20–21).

2 KINGS 13:1–25

THE DEATH OF ELISHA

The Reigns of Jehoahaz and Jehoash, Kings of Israel	13:1–13
The Death of Elisha	13:14–21
God's Mercy to Israel	13:22–25

Setting Up the Section

When Jehoahaz, the king who opens this chapter, comes to the throne, it is the beginning of the fulfillment of a promise made to Jehu, recorded in 2 Kings 10:30. God promised him that his descendants would sit on the throne of Israel to the fourth generation. This dynasty—though founded on a violent overthrow of the previous royal house—continues because Jehu came to the throne doing the will of God.

13:1–13

THE REIGNS OF JEHOAHAZ AND JEHOASH, KINGS OF ISRAEL

Jehoahaz follows in the footsteps of both Jeroboam and his father Jehu—two wicked kings (13:1–2). So the Lord delivers the kingdom of Israel into the hand of Hazael, king of Syria (13:3). Israel retains its own name and king, but it is a tributary and subservient nation to Syria.

Demystifying 2 Kings

In the general history of this time, the Assyrian Empire kept the Syrians weak and unable to expand their domain into Israel. But there was a period when internal problems made the Assyrians bring back their troops from the frontiers of their empire, and the Syrians took advantage of this time of Assyrian distraction.

Jehoahaz is an ungodly man, and his prayer does not mark a lasting or real revival in his life. Yet God listens to his prayer because of His great mercy and because of His care for Israel (13:4–5). The identity of the deliverer in verse 5 is unknown.

Though God answers their prayer and sends a deliverer, Israel continues in their false worship of the true God (13:6). Israel's repentance is only halfhearted; they repent because they suffer rather than because they regret their sin (13:7).

After Jehoahaz's death, his son Jehoash becomes king over Israel (13:8–10). He is the grandson of King Jehu, founder of this dynasty. He continues in the same sins as his father and grandfather (13:11).

The reign of Jehoash sees a civil war among the people of God, with the southern kingdom of Judah and the northern kingdom of Israel at war (13:12). On Jehoash's death, his son Jeroboam II becomes king of Israel (13:13).

13:14–21

THE DEATH OF ELISHA

Elisha has become ill and will die (13:14). The reaction of King Joash of Israel might seem strange, in light of the sin and evil that marks his reign. However, Joash is not a worshiper of false gods; he is a *false* worshiper of the true God. He has some respect for the true God and therefore some regard and honor for Elisha.

Critical Observation

"The chariots of Israel and their horsemen!" Elisha says these words to Elijah at the end of the elder prophet's days on this earth (2:12). In saying this, he recognizes the true strength of Israel, which is really in the presence of the prophet of God. Now Joash sees the same strength slipping from this earth and mourns it.

Joash is concerned that the true strength of Israel is about to depart from this earth. Therefore, Elisha uses this illustration of the arrow shot through the window to show him that the arrow of the Lord's deliverance is still present, and all Joash has to do is to shoot the arrow in faith (13:15–17). Elisha makes it clear that there is a connection between the shooting of the arrows toward the east and a strike against the Syrians that will bring deliverance to Israel.

The phrase "strike the ground" (13:18) can be used for arrows hitting the ground. Elisha asks Joash to shoot the arrows through the window at no particular target, not to pound them on the floor. Joash timidly receives this invitation. He shoots three arrows and stops, not sensing what he should—that the arrows represent victories in battle over the Syrians. Because King Joash does not seize the strategic moment, Israel will enjoy only three victories over the Syrian army instead of the many more they could have enjoyed (13:19).

Perhaps Elisha expected or hoped that he would be carried up into heaven after the dramatic pattern of his mentor Elijah. Yet that is not God's plan or will for Elisha. Like many others, he simply becomes old, sick, and then dies.

There is little explanation for the resurrection of the corpse that touches the bones of Elisha (13:21). The silence of the record suggests that there is not inherent power in the bones of Elisha to resuscitate others. This seems to be a one-time miracle bringing honor to the memory of this great prophet.

13:22–25

GOD'S MERCY TO ISRAEL

God allows—even plans—King Hazael's oppression of Israel to discipline this wayward nation (13:22). Second Kings 8:12 records Elisha's prior knowledge of the calamity Hazael will bring upon Israel. Israel deserves this discipline, yet God refuses to forsake them. He has given them many blessings and saved them from many problems and will not yet destroy them or cast them from His presence (13:23).

Elisha had promised Joash these three victories over the Syrians (13:24–25). We can suppose that especially after the third victory, King Joash wished he had shot more arrows through the window at the invitation of Elisha.

2 KINGS 14:1–29

THE REIGNS OF AMAZIAH AND JEROBOAM II

Setting Up the Section

The parallel and intersecting histories of the southern kingdom of Judah and the northern kingdom of Israel continue in this chapter. Chapter 12 of 2 Kings outlined the reign of Joash in Judah; chapter 13 highlighted the reigns of first Jehoahaz, then Jehoash in Israel. The next chapters relate the reigns of their successors.

14:1–22

THE REIGN OF AMAZIAH OVER JUDAH

Amaziah, son of the great reformer Joash, continues the policies begun by his father. Yet some of those policies allow compromises regarding idolatry. Compared to David, Amaziah does not match up favorably (14:1–4).

Amaziah's execution of the servants who had murdered his father eliminates those who would find the assassination of the king a reasonable way to change the kingdom. It also fulfills God's command to punish murderers with execution, first given in Genesis 9:5–7. It is the standard practice of the ancient world to execute not only the guilty party in such a murder, but also their family. Amaziah goes against the conventional practice of his day and obeys the Word of God instead (Deuteronomy 24:16; 2 Kings 14:5–6).

Amaziah's victory over the Edomites (14:7) shows the military might of Amaziah and that he successfully subdues the weaker nations surrounding Judah.

Critical Observation

Second Chronicles 25:5–16 gives more background to the battle against the Edomites. Amaziah gathers a huge army in Judah to go against Edom (three hundred thousand). He also hires one hundred thousand mercenary soldiers from Israel. But a prophet comes and warns him to *not* use the soldiers from Israel, because God is not with that rebellious and idolatrous kingdom. Amaziah is convinced to trust God, send the mercenaries from Israel away, and accept the loss of the money used to hire them. God blesses this step of faith and gives them a convincing victory over the Edomites.

Proud from his success against Edom, Amaziah decides to make war against the northern kingdom of Israel (14:8). He has reason to believe he will be successful. He had recently assembled an army of three hundred thousand men that killed twenty thousand Edomites in a victory over Edom (2 Chronicles 25:5, 11–12). Jehoahaz seems very weak, having only fifty horsemen, ten chariots, and ten thousand foot soldiers after being defeated by the Syrians (2 Kings 13:7).

The reply of Jehoash, king of Israel, is both wise and diplomatic. He counsels Amaziah to glory in his previous victory over Edom but then to stay at home (14:9–10). Instead, Amaziah provokes a fight he should have avoided and does not consider the effect his defeat will have on the whole kingdom (14:11–18).

The embarrassing loss against Israel undermines Amaziah's support among Judah's leaders. He flees to Lachish, but he meets a similar end to that of his father—assassination (12:20–21; 14:29–30).

This signals the start of the illustrious reign of Azariah (also known as Uzziah). He is the greatest king of Judah after David (14:21–22).

14:23–29

THE REIGN OF JEROBOAM II IN ISRAEL

King Jeroboam II of Israel is a wicked king who continues the politically-motivated idolatry of his namesake, Jeroboam the son of Nebat (14:23–24). During his reign, the prophets Jonah and Amos spoke for God (14:25). This is almost certainly the same Jonah who is famous for his missionary trip to Nineveh.

Out of great mercy, God shows kindness to a disobedient Israel ruled by an evil king (14:26–27). The reign of Jeroboam II is a time of prosperity for Israel because of God's mercy. Around the year 800 BC, the mighty Assyrian Empire defeated Syria and neutralized this power that hindered Israel's expansion and prosperity. With Syria in check, Israel can prosper (14:28).

Zechariah, Jeroboam's son, succeeds to the throne after his father's death (14:29). It was prophesied that the dynasty of Jehu would continue for four generations—Zechariah is the fourth generation (10:30).

2 KINGS 15:1–38

UNSTABLE MONARCHY IN ISRAEL

Setting Up the Section

This section of 2 Kings 15 begins the story of five kings over Israel and anticipates the final dissolution of the northern kingdom. The kings, families, and dynasties ruling Israel change quickly during this period. Yet there is an amazing continuity of evil through these dynasties. Each is evil and each continues the state-sponsored idolatry in Israel.

15:1–7

THE REIGN OF AZARIAH (UZZIAH) OVER JUDAH

The reign of Azariah (also called Uzziah in 2 Kings 15:13 and many other places in 2 Kings, 2 Chronicles, and Isaiah) is largely characterized by the good he does in the sight of the Lord. His godliness is rewarded with a long reign of fifty-two years (15:1–3). As with Jehoash (12:3) and Amaziah (14:4), however, the reforms of Azariah do not reach so far as to remove these traditional places of sacrifice (15:4).

Demystifying 2 Kings

Second Chronicles 26 tells us much more about the successful reign of Azariah:

- He began his reign when he was only sixteen years old (26:3).
- He reigned during the ministry of Zechariah the prophet (26.5).
- He defeated the Philistines and took many of their cities and also kept the Ammonites in tribute (26:6–8).
- He was internationally famous as a strong king (26:8).
- He was an ambitious builder and skilled in agriculture (26:9–10).
- He built up and organized the army, introducing several new items of military technology (26:11–15).

Azariah comes into the temple as an arrogant king, and he leaves—indeed, he hurries to get out, because the Lord has struck him (2 Chronicles 26:20)—as a humbled leper (2 Kings 15:5). And so he is to the day he dies. His son Jotham becomes the next king (15:6–7).

15:8–31

FIVE KINGS OVER THE KINGDOM OF ISRAEL

The reign of Zechariah is both short and wicked, and he continues in the state-sponsored idolatry began by Jeroboam (15:8–9). Zechariah is so despised by his own people that Shallum assassinates him in public. This is the end of the dynasty of Jehu, which began with such potential but ends (as God has foretold) in great darkness (15:10).

Shallum's reign is even briefer—four weeks. The violence that marks Shallum's rise to and fall from power shows that he does not reign with the blessing of God (15:13–15).

When Menahem's enemies fail to surrender, his soldiers rip open the pregnant women (15:16). This brutal act is commanded by Menahem himself—the next king of Israel. Menahem's reign is evil and a continuation of the state-sponsored idolatry of Jeroboam (15:17–18). He puts the kingdom of Israel under tribute to the Assyrian Empire, purchasing the backing of the Assyrian king with money raised from the wealthy people in his kingdom. Therefore he rules with the strength of Assyria supporting him (15:19–21).

The previous two kings of Israel (before Menahem) do not establish any kind of dynasty to pass to a son. Menahem rules well enough to pass the kingdom to Pekahiah (15:22–23). The blessing of God is obviously not on Pekahiah, whose reign ends with assassination after only two years (15:24–26).

For chronologists, the twenty-year reign of Pekah is difficult to place. It perhaps includes time that Pekah rules as an antigovernment rebel in certain regions of Israel (15:27–28). The Assyrian king, unlike in the days of Menahem, will not be paid off by the king of Israel this time. He comes and takes some of the best land of the kingdom and carries the Israelites as captives to Assyria (15:29). This is an official state policy of the Assyrian Empire. Upon conquering a land, if necessary, they relocate by force the best and the brightest of the conquered nation, bringing them to Assyria.

Pekah is another king and another dynasty to end with assassination (15:30–31), as a powerful demonstration of the great instability in the northern kingdom.

15:32–38

JOTHAM'S REIGN OVER JUDAH

King Jotham of Judah does what was right in the sight of the Lord (15:32-34). This stands in strong contrast to the evil done by the previously mentioned kings of Israel. Among the kings of Judah, there are good and godly kings.

Rebuilding in the temple is always a positive sign in Judah (15:35). When kings and leaders are concerned about the house of the Lord, it reflects some measure of spiritual revival. Jotham's father Azariah (Uzziah) had misunderstood the link between the royal house and the house of God, demanding priestly authority (2 Chronicles 26:16–21). Many kings before him wanted no link between the royal house and the house of God. Jotham understands that he is a king and not a priest, yet he wants a good, open link between the palace and the temple. The building of this link between the palace and the temple is one of the chief ways that he prepares his way before God.

At this time, Judah begins to be chastened for their partial obedience. Under the inspiration of the Holy Spirit, the writer of 2 Kings tells us that it is the hand of the Lord that sends these foreign rulers who trouble Judah (15:36–38).

2 KINGS 16:1–20

THE COMPROMISE OF AHAZ

Setting Up the Section

Chapter 15 closes with an account of King Jotham of Judah. Chapter 16 is devoted entirely to the reign of Jotham's son, Ahaz. Ahaz may well have been the worst king of a nation ruled by bad kings.

16:1–4

A SUMMARY OF THE REIGN OF AHAZ

This account briefly describes the reign of an unfaithful king of Judah. Whereas many previous kings fall short in some area or another (typically, allowing idolatry), of Ahaz it is simply said that he does not do what was right in the sight of the Lord.

Ahaz not only rejects the godly heritage of David, he embraces the ungodly ways of the kings of the northern kingdom of Israel. The southern kingdom of Judah had a mixture of godly and ungodly kings; the northern kingdom of Judah had only ungodly kings, and Ahaz follows their pattern. Ahaz participates in the worship of Molech, which includes child sacrifice (16:3–4).

Critical Observation

In Leviticus 20:1–5, God pronounced the death sentence against all who worship Molech.

One of the great crimes of the northern tribes of Israel was their worship of Molech (17:17). King Manasseh of Judah gave his son to Molech (21:6). God will bring judgment upon Judah for their continued practice of these sins.

16:5–9

AHAZ MAKES JUDAH A SUBJECT NATION TO ASSYRIA

King Pekah of Israel joins forces with King Rezin of Syria against Judah (16:5). This is part of Pekah's anti-Assyria policy. He thinks that with Judah defeated, Syria and Israel together can more effectively resist the resurgent power of the Assyrian Empire. The combined armies of Syria and Israel are strong enough to capture many cities of Judah but not strong enough to defeat Jerusalem and overthrow the government of Ahaz.

Critical Observation

Judah suffers terrible losses from this attack. King Ahaz loses 120,000 Judean soldiers and 200,000 civilian hostages in these battles with Israel and Syria (2 Chronicles 28:5–8). It is a dark time for Judah, and it looks as if the dynasty of David will soon be extinguished, as so many dynasties in the northern kingdom of Israel had ended.

When this great number of captives is taken to Samaria (the capital city of the northern kingdom of Israel), a prophet named Oded calls on the army to return them to Judah. These leaders in Israel respond, realizing that they have already offended the Lord and risk offending Him even further. So they clothe and feed the captives (who had before this been treated terribly) and return them to Judah (2 Chronicles 28:8–15).

Ahaz sends messengers to Tiglath-pileser, king of Assyria, asking for help (2 Kings 16:7–9). In this way, he surrenders to one enemy in order to defeat another. He refuses to trust in the God of Israel and instead submits himself and his kingdom to an enemy of Israel, making Judah a subject kingdom to Assyria. Ahaz now takes his orders from the Assyrian king, sacrificing the independence of the kingdom of Judah.

Take It Home

What blessing might have come if Ahaz would have surrendered and sacrificed to God with the same energy and whole heart that he surrendered to the Assyrian king? It is true that the Assyrian king answers and delivers Ahaz, but it is short-lived deliverance. He could have really secured his kingdom by surrendering and sacrificing to God in the same way.

16:10–20

AHAZ PERVERTS WORSHIP AT THE TEMPLE

It is unusual for the kings of Judah to make official visits to other kingdoms; they generally stay within the borders of the promised land. Yet Ahaz's trip is much more than a visit—this is an official act of submission to Tiglath-pileser, king of Assyria (16:10). Using the plans sent from Ahaz, Urijah imitates the pagan altar at Damascus and has it ready by the time Ahaz returns from the Syrian capital (16:11). He does this both to please Tiglath-pileser and to incorporate the latest trends in altar design into the national worship of Judah. Of course, Ahaz bears the greater blame in this matter, but the high priest Urijah also bears significant blame in the replacement of the Lord's altar with this one of pagan design.

Ahaz serves as a priest at the altar of his own design, a direct disregard for God's commands regarding priests (Numbers 18:7; 2 Kings 16:12–13). Urijah not only allows Ahaz to do this, he participates.

Critical Observation

Ahaz's grandfather Azariah (Uzziah) dared to enter the temple and serve God as a priest (2 Chronicles 26). Yet at least Azariah falsely worshiped the true *God*. Ahaz falsely worshiped a false god of his own creation.

Ahaz cannot bring in his pagan, corrupt innovations without also removing what had stood before at the temple (16:14–18). This is an ungodly exchange, taking away the good and putting in the bad—including the king's outer entrance built in the days of his father, King Jotham. Collectively, all these things serve to discourage the worship of the true God. All this takes place at the temple Solomon built for the Lord, but the location does not make it true worship.

So ends the reign of an unfaithful king of Judah (16:19–20). Micah—who prophesied during the reign of Ahaz—describes a man who works to successfully do evil with both hands (Micah 7:3). The idea is that the man pursues evil with all his effort. He may very well have had King Ahaz in mind.

2 KINGS 17:1–41

THE FALL OF ISRAEL

The Fall of Samaria	17:1–6
The Reasons for the Fall of the Northern Kingdom of Israel	17:7–23
The Resettlement of Samaria	17:24–41

Setting Up the Section

Two hundred years and nineteen kings after the time of Solomon (the last king over a united Israel), the northern kingdom of Israel falls. It is not because the God of Israel is unable to help them, but because they have so forsaken God and ignored His guidance and correction that He finally stops actively protecting them and allows them to degrade according to their desire.

17:1–6

THE FALL OF SAMARIA

We last saw Hoshea, in 2 Kings 15:30, as the man who led a conspiracy against Pekah, the king of Israel. After the successful assassination, Hoshea takes the throne and starts his own brief dynasty (17:1). Hoshea is an evil man, but by no means the worst of the kings of Israel (17:2). Sadly, his bloody overthrow of the preceding king and violent ascent to power do not make him unusually evil among the kings of Israel. Yet it is during his reign that the kingdom of Israel is effectively destroyed. This reminds us that judgment may not come at the height of sin. When God judges a nation or a culture, He has the big picture in view. For that reason, the actual events of judgment may come when things are not as bad in a relative sense.

In the pattern of Menahem before him (15:17–22), Hoshea accepts the status of vassal unto the king of Assyria. If he pays his money and does as the king of Assyria pleases, he will be allowed to continue on the throne of Israel (17:3). King Hoshea hopes to find help among the Egyptians, who are in a constant power struggle with the Assyrian Empire. On account of this conspiracy, and the failure to pay the yearly tribute money, Hoshea is imprisoned by the king of Assyria (17:4).

The king of Assyria embarks on a long, dedicated campaign to finally crush the rebellious kingdom of Israel, who had defied the power of the Assyrian Empire. Though it takes three years, it is worth it to the Assyrians (17:5). When Samaria finally falls and the northern kingdom is conquered, the Assyrians implement their policy toward conquered nations. They deport all but the very lowest classes back to the key cities of their empire, either to train and utilize the talented or to enslave the able (17:6).

Demystifying 2 Kings

When the Assyrians depopulate and exile a conquered community, they lead the captives away on journeys of hundreds of miles, with the captives naked and attached to one another with a system of strings and fishhooks pierced through their lower lips. (See also Amos 4:2–3.)

17:7–23

THE REASONS FOR THE FALL OF THE NORTHERN KINGDOM OF ISRAEL

In the following verses, the divine historian explains the fundamental reasons for the conquering and captivity of the northern kingdom. At the root, it is a problem with sin. It isn't geopolitical changes or social causes.

First, they had feared other gods (17:7). In the central act of redemption in Old Testament history, God brought Israel up out of the land of Egypt. Remembrance of this act alone should prompt Israel to a single-hearted commitment to the Lord. Yet they do not remember this and instead they fear other gods, breaking the covenant God made with His people.

Second, they conform themselves to the godless nations around them (17:8). Before Israel occupied Canaan in the days of Joshua, the promised land was populated by degenerate, pagan peoples who practiced the worst kinds of idolatry and human sacrifice. One of the fundamental sins of Israel was that they followed in these ancient Canaanite ways. God cast out the Canaanite nations in the days of Joshua because of these sins. Now He has cast out the northern kingdom of Israel for the same sins. God's judgment is not against the ancient Canaanites because of race or ethnicity; it is because of their conduct.

Third, they practice idolatry both secretly and openly (17:9–12). Rebellion and sin cloud the judgment of people, and clearly the judgment of Israel is affected. Their judgment is impaired enough to think they can sin secretly against the God who sees everything.

Fourth, they reject the repeated warnings from God (17:13–15). In love, God sends prophets to the northern and southern kingdoms. Their message is a warning against the sins that corrupt God's people and separate them from their God. They invite God's people with the theme, "Turn from your evil ways." Nevertheless, the people will not hear. God sends these messengers to help Israel and to spare them the judgment that will come if they do not turn from their evil ways. Yet God's people become more stubborn when God brings this call to repentance, and they sink deeper into sin.

Fifth, they forsake God and serve idols—until judgment finally comes (17:16–23). The two calves mentioned here refer to the infamous sin of Jeroboam (1 Kings 12:26–29). This state-sponsored idolatry does not immediately ruin the kingdom—the northern kingdom of Israel lasts as an independent nation for another two-hundred years following the time of Jeroboam. Yet it certainly was the beginning of the end. The people participated in the abominable worship of the idol Molech, to whom children were burned in sacrifice. They embraced the same occult practices as the Canaanite tribes before them. Collectively, these great sins of idolatry provoke God to anger.

This is the end of the ten northern tribes as an independent kingdom (17:18–23). When they are dispersed by the Assyrians, some assimilate into other cultures, but others keep their Jewish identity as exiles in other lands.

Critical Observation

It is a mistake to think of these ten northern tribes as *lost*, though they are indeed lost as a separate entity. Far back in the days of Jeroboam and his original break with the southern kingdom of Judah, the legitimate priests and Levites who lived in the northern ten tribes did not like Jeroboam's idolatry. They, along with others who set their hearts to seek the God of Israel, then moved from the northern kingdom of Israel to the southern kingdom of Judah (2 Chronicles 11:13–16). So actually, the southern kingdom of Judah contained Israelites from all of the ten tribes.

Spiritually speaking, Judah is more faithful to God than the northern kingdom of Israel. Yet they also begin to imitate their sinful neighbors to the north (17:19). Judah had the lesson right in front of them—the conquered nation of Israel is evidence of what happens when hearts turn from God. Yet they ignore these plain lessons and imitate the sins of Israel.

17:24–41

THE RESETTLEMENT OF SAMARIA

The policy of the Assyrian Empire is to remove rebellious, resistant people and to resettle their former lands with people from other parts of the empire (17:24). These newcomers do not fear God, so He sends lions among them (17:25–26). This shows that there is not only something special about the kingdom of Israel, but also something special about the *land* of Israel. God demands to be feared among the people of the land, even if they come from other nations.

These Assyrian officials seem to know what the recently conquered kingdom of Israel does not know—that they have to honor the God of Israel. Yet, any faith in God among these resettled people is founded in simple fear of the lions, leading to an inadequate relationship with God.

The priesthood of the kingdom of Israel was corrupt, but the king of Assyria does not know and is not interested in the pure religion of Israel. Therefore this nameless, corrupt priest teaches the new inhabitants of the land a corrupt religion (17:28). Certainly, it has elements of the true faith in it, but at the same time it is corrupted by the centuries of state-sponsored idolatry that reigned in Israel.

The priest-for-hire brought in by the Assyrians does not tell the new inhabitants of the land that they must *only* worship the God of Israel. He does not teach it because, coming from Israel, he does not believe it. The new residents of Israel give a measure of respect to the God of Israel—after all, they do not want to be eaten by lions. Yet they also serve their own gods and pick and choose among religious and spiritual beliefs as they please (17:29–34). This accurately describes the pagan peoples who repopulate Israel. This accurately describes the northern kingdom of Israel before they are conquered and exiled. This accurately describes common religious belief in the modern world.

This mixed religion first promoted by the Assyrians continues for many centuries in Samaria, existing even until New Testament times.

The writer restates God's covenant with His people (17:35–41) to remind us that if Israel had been faithful—even moderately faithful—to their covenant with God, they would still stand. God would have delivered them from all of their enemies. Instead, they are conquered by the Assyrian Empire after their own self-destruction in sin and rebellion.

2 KINGS 18:1–37

HEZEKIAH'S REIGN; ASSYRIA'S THREAT

Setting Up the Section

Hezekiah, the subject of chapter 18, comes to the throne of Judah at the very end of the kingdom of Israel. Three years after the start of his reign, the Assyrian armies lay siege to Samaria, and three years after that the northern kingdom is conquered. The sad fate of the northern kingdom is a valuable lesson to Hezekiah. He sees firsthand what happens when the people of God reject their God and His Word and worship other gods.

18:1–12

THE RIGHTEOUS REIGN OF HEZEKIAH

Hezekiah is one of the better kings of Judah and thus has a long and mostly blessed reign (18:1–2). He is one of Judah's most zealous reformers, even prohibiting worship on the high places (18:3–4). These are popular altars for sacrifice set up as the worshiper desires, not according to God's direction. He also breaks apart the bronze snake from the time of Moses.

Critical Observation

Numbers 21:1–9 describes how, during a time of a plague of fiery serpents upon the whole nation, Moses makes a bronze serpent for the nation to look upon and be spared death from the snake bites. This statement in 2 Kings tells us that this particular bronze serpent had been preserved for more than eight hundred years and had come to be worshiped as Nehushtan. Hezekiah, in his zeal, breaks this bronze artifact into pieces and puts an end to the idolatrous worship of this object.

This bronze serpent is a wonderful thing—when the afflicted people of Israel looked upon it, they were saved. It was even a representation of Jesus Christ, as Jesus Himself said in John 3:14–15.

Sometimes good things become idols and therefore must be destroyed. For example, if the true cross of Jesus or His actual burial cloth are to be discovered, and these objects become idolatrous distractions, then it is better for those objects to be destroyed.

Hezekiah is unique in his passion and energy of his personal trust in God and for promoting the true worship of God (18:5). This is even more remarkable when we consider that his father, Ahaz, was one of the worst kings to have reigned in Judah (16:10–20).

Because of Hezekiah's faithful trust in the Lord, God blessed him thoroughly (18:6). This fulfills a long-standing promise to David and his descendants: that if they obey God, their reign will always be secure (1 Kings 2:1–4).

At this time Assyria is mighty enough to completely conquer the northern kingdom of Israel. Yet the kingdom of Judah stands strong, because God blesses the trusting and obedient king (18:7). Hezekiah also finds success in subjugating Judah's aggressive neighbors (18:8). He works for a strong, free, and independent Judah.

The fall of Samaria, the capital of the northern kingdom of Israel, is a sobering experience for the southern kingdom of Judah to see. The cruel devastation brought by the Assyrians shows what calamities can come upon disobedient people of God (18:9–12).

18:13–37

THE ASSYRIAN THREAT DURING THE REIGN OF HEZEKIAH

Approximately five years after the fall of Samaria, King Sennacherib of Assyria brings his force against Judah, who had successfully resisted him before (18:7). He captures all of the fortified cities of Judah and needs only Jerusalem itself to completely conquer Judah (18:13).

Demystifying 2 Kings

The mention of Lachish in verse 14 is important historically. Lachish was thirty miles southwest of Jerusalem. Archaeologists have discovered a pit there with the remains of about fifteen hundred casualties of Sennacherib's attack. In the British Museum, you can see the Assyrian carving depicting their siege of the city of Lachish, which was an important fortress city of Judah.

Hezekiah offers tribute money in exchange for peace (19:14–16). This is a clear lack of faith on the part of Hezekiah. He feels it is wiser to pay off the Assyrian king and become his subject than it is to trust God to defend Judah against this mighty king. We can suppose that Hezekiah thought that since the northern kingdom had been recently conquered and all the fortified cities of Judah had been captured, God had demonstrated that He would not intervene on behalf of Judah. Therefore Hezekiah feels he must do something himself. Perhaps this idea is strengthened in Hezekiah when he remembers the wickedness of his own father, Ahaz, and when he considers that, because of their prior sin, Judah deserves such judgment.

Hezekiah hopes that this policy of appeasement will make Judah safe. He is wrong, and his policy only impoverishes Judah and the temple and makes the king of Assyria more bold than ever against Judah.

The word *Rabshakeh* in verse 17 is not a name but a title. It describes the field commander for the Assyrian army, who represents the Assyrian king, Sennacherib, and is translated "chief of staff" in some versions. The Rabshakeh seems to be in complete command of the situation. He is able to walk right into the city of Jerusalem and stand at the crucial water supply—which is Jerusalem's lifeline in a siege attack. As he stands there, three officials from Hezekiah's government come to meet him (18:17–18).

From the perspective of the unbeliever, Sennacherib asks a valid question: "What are you trusting in that makes you so confident?" (18:19 NLT). Instead of trusting the Lord, Hezekiah has put his hope in an alliance with Egypt, and the Rabshakeh wants him to lose confidence in that alliance (18:20–21). In this sense, the Rabshakeh speaks wisely. God wants Judah to have no confidence in Egypt at all. But the Rabshakeh does not do it to bring Judah to a firm trust in God, who can and will deliver them from the Assyrians. He does it to completely demoralize Judah and drive them to despair.

Strangely, the Rabshakeh can see the truth of Egypt's weakness better than many of the leaders of Judah can. Hezekiah's trust-in-Egypt policy will indeed be trouble for Judah.

The Rabshakeh anticipates the response of the leaders of Judah. "Rabshakeh, you say that we can't trust in Egypt. All right, we won't. But we can trust in our God" (18:22). The Rabshakeh knows that King Hezekiah has implemented broad reforms in Judah, including the removal of the high places (18:3–4). Yet in the Rabshakeh's thinking, Hezekiah's reforms displease God, so he should not expect help from the God of Israel. The Rabshakeh will say, "Look at all the places there used to be where people would worship the God of Israel. Now, since Hezekiah came in, there is only one place. More is always better, so the God of Israel must be pretty sore at Hezekiah!"

Take It Home

The Rabshakeh's whole strategy is to make Judah give up. This is the entire reason the Rabshakeh is at the aqueduct, speaking to these leaders of Hezekiah's government. He had the superior army—he could have just attacked Jerusalem without this little speech. But the Rabshakeh prefers Judah to surrender out of fear, discouragement, or despair.

The enemy of our soul uses the exact same approach. Many of us picture Satan as one who is itching for a fight with us. Really, Satan doesn't want to do battle with you. First of all, there is the strong chance you will win. Second of all, win or lose, the battle can draw you closer to God. Thirdly, what God does in your life through the battle can be a great blessing for others. No, Satan would much rather not fight you at all! He would rather you just give up.

We see this exact strategy used against Jesus during His temptation in the wilderness. When Satan promises Jesus all the kingdoms of the world in exchange for Jesus' worship, Satan is trying to avoid the fight and trying to talk Jesus into giving up (Luke 4:5–8). It doesn't work with Jesus, and it shouldn't work with us.

The Rabshakeh mocks Judah's weak army. His basic message is, "We could beat you with one hand tied behind our backs!" (18:23–24). The Rabshakeh saves his best thrust for last: "Admit it, Hezekiah. You know that *your* God is on *my* side" (18:25).

It would have been easy for Hezekiah and his men to believe this. After all, hadn't the Assyrians been wildly successful, and don't they have the most powerful army? Surely, God must be on their side. We can just imagine how difficult this is for these leaders in Hezekiah's government. They must have thought, "It's bad enough we have to hear this. But since he is speaking in Hebrew, everyone will hear, and soon the people will become so discouraged they will rise up against us and make us surrender!" (18:26).

The Rabshakeh doesn't care if the common citizens of Jerusalem can hear him. That is one of his goals. The more fear, discouragement, and despair he can spread, the better. He points forward to what conditions will be like in Jerusalem after an extended siege. He wants this to offend everyone who hears it and magnify their sense of fear (18:27).

Then the Rabshakeh stands and calls out with a loud voice in Hebrew (18:28–33). He can't wait to speak to the people of Jerusalem. His speech is intended to glorify the enemy facing God's people, to make God's people doubt their leaders, to build fear and unbelief in God's people, and to make surrender an attractive option. The Rabshakeh refers to the policies of ethnic cleansing and forced resettlement practiced by the Assyrians. When they conquer a people, they forcibly resettle them in faraway places, to keep their spirits broken and their power weak. The Rabshakeh's speech is intended to make this terrible fate seem attractive.

The Rabshakeh's speech is intended to destroy their trust in God. His message is simple: "The gods of other nations have not been able to protect them against us. Your God can't protect you either" (18:34). For anyone who had the spiritual understanding to see it, Judah could have started planning the victory party right then. It is one thing to speak against Judah, its people, and its leaders; it is another thing altogether to mock the God of Israel this way and count Him as just another god. The Rabshakeh's speech is going well until he simply oversteps his bounds. There is no way God will let him off the hook for this one. He has offended God in a way he will soon regret.

The people don't try to argue with the Rabshakeh. Often, it is useless—if not dangerous—to try and match wits with this demonic logic. It is almost always better to keep silent and trust God, instead of trying to win an argument with Satan or his servants. King Hezekiah is wise enough to make this command, and his officials and the people are wise enough to obey him (18:36).

Though they are silent, they are still deeply affected by this attack (18:37). They have the same experience Paul describes in 2 Corinthians 4:8–9. Times are tough, but the battle is not yet lost.

2 KINGS 19:1–37

GOD DELIVERS JERUSALEM FROM ASSYRIA

Hezekiah's Prayers and Sennacherib's Threats	19:1–19
God Speaks Concerning the Situation	19:20–34
God Defends Jerusalem	19:35–37

Setting Up the Section

Hezekiah's response to the current national crisis reveals a king who was wise enough to seek God's guidance.

19:1–19

HEZEKIAH'S PRAYERS AND SENNACHERIB'S THREATS

The tearing of clothes and the wearing of sackcloth (a rough, burlap-type material) are expressions of deep mourning, usually for the death of a loved one. Hezekiah receives this report regarding the Rabshakeh seriously, knowing how dedicated this enemy is to completely conquering Jerusalem (19:1).

Hezekiah's initial reaction is good. He sees the situation for what it really is. Jerusalem's situation is desperate and Hezekiah knows it.

Hezekiah's second reaction is even better. He does not allow his mourning and grief to spin him into a rejection of the Lord's power and help. He knows it is more necessary than ever to seek the Lord at this time, so he goes to the temple.

Demystifying 2 Kings

When verse 1 says that Hezekiah goes into the house of the Lord, that doesn't mean the holy place itself, which is forbidden for all except priests. It simply means that Hezekiah went to the courts, to seek God in the place which was open to him as a man of Israel.

A previous king of Judah, King Uzziah, saw his reign tragically end when he broke this command to stay out of the holy place of the temple (see 2 Chronicles 26:16).

The third thing Hezekiah does is also good. The king seeks out the Word of God, given through His prophet (19:2).

Hezekiah puts the words about childbirth in the mouth of his messengers to Isaiah to express the total calamity of the situation (19:3). This is a proverbial expression for a disaster—a woman so exhausted by labor that she cannot complete the birth, so both mother and child die. Hezekiah knows their only hope is that God will take offense at the blasphemies of the Rabshakeh and rise up against him (19:4).

Without hesitation, Isaiah speaks as if he is speaking for the Lord (19:5–6). How these words must have cheered Hezekiah! We can be sure that Isaiah does not take this lightly. The fate of the nation, and his entire credibility as a prophet, is riding on what he says. Isaiah, speaking for the Lord, is about to make a bold prediction (19:7). His prophecy will be entirely provable. It will either happen or it will not happen. Isaiah will either be known as a true prophet or a false prophet. The Lord assures Hezekiah that He will indeed deal with the Rabshakeh. He has heard his blasphemy and will bring judgment against him.

Significantly, in this initial word from the prophet Isaiah, there is no mention of Jerusalem's deliverance or the defeat of the Assyrian army. God focuses this word against the Rabshakeh personally.

The Rabshakeh leaves Jerusalem, and Hezekiah likely thinks this is the fulfillment of the Lord's promise through the prophet Isaiah (19:8).

The Rabshakeh is not in Jerusalem, but that doesn't stop him from trying to build fear, discouragement, and despair in Hezekiah. He sends a letter to the king of Judah to attack him from a distance. Yet if read with an eye of faith, the words of the letter must have been trust-building to Hezekiah. In counting God of Israel among the gods of the nations, the Rabshakeh again blasphemes the Lord and invites judgment (19:10–13).

Hezekiah does exactly what any child of God should do with such a letter. He takes it to the house of the Lord (to the outer courts, not the holy place) and spreads it out before Him (19:14). In this, Hezekiah boldly and effectively fulfills the later command of 1 Peter 5:7: casting all your care upon Him, for He cares for you.

As Hezekiah prays using the title, "God of Israel," it must have reminded him that God is indeed the covenant God of Israel and that He will not forsake His people (19:15).

Critical Observation

As recorded in Isaiah 37:16, Hezekiah also uses another title when he addresses God, crying out "O Lord of hosts." This title for God essentially means, "Lord of armies." Hezekiah is in a crisis that is primarily military in nature, so it makes sense for him to address God first according to the aspect of God's nature that is most needful for him.

Hezekiah sees the great majesty of God. Surely, the One who dwells between the cherubim (19:15) will never allow the Rabshakeh's blasphemies to go unpunished. Hezekiah realizes the most fundamental fact of all theology: God is God, and we are not!

In recognizing God as Creator (19:15), Hezekiah sees that He has all power and all rights over every created thing. We can almost feel Hezekiah's faith rising as he prays this!

Hezekiah knows very well that the Lord did in fact hear and see the blasphemies of the Rabshakeh. This is a poetic way of asking God to act upon what He has seen and heard, assuming that if God has seen such things, He will certainly act (19:16).

In his prayer, King Hezekiah draws the contrast between the living God and the false gods of the nations the Assyrians had already conquered. Those false gods are not gods, but the work of human hands, so they are not able to save them from the Assyrians. But Hezekiah prays confidently that the living God will save them, that all the kingdoms of the earth may know that He alone is God (19:17–19).

19:20–34

GOD SPEAKS CONCERNING THE SITUATION.

The glorious answer that fills the rest of the chapter comes because Hezekiah prays (19:20). What if he had not prayed? Perhaps there would have been no answer, and Jerusalem would have been conquered. Hezekiah's prayer was critically important.

The Lord, speaking through Isaiah, simply says to the Rabshakeh, "Do you know whom you are dealing with?" (19:22). The Rabshakeh obviously does not know. Curiously, this prophecy may have never reached the ears of the Rabshakeh. After all, Isaiah doesn't exactly have free access to him. But perhaps before his terrible end, God finds a way to get this prophecy to him. At the very least, this prophecy would have been hugely encouraging to Hezekiah and all of Judah, even if the Rabshakeh never heard it. Sometimes God speaks to the enemy more for the sake of His people than for the sake of the enemy himself.

The Lord describes the great pride the Assyrians have in their own conquests. But they forget that the Lord is really in charge. Even if the Assyrians don't know it, they owe their success to the Lord (19:19–26).

Verses 27 and 28 make an especially dramatic statement, because this is exactly how the Assyrians cruelly march those whom they force to relocate out of their conquered lands. They line up the captives and drive a large fishhook through the lip or the nose of each captive, stringing them all together. God will do the same to the Assyrians.

The invasion has interfered with planting crops, but the Lord promises that enough will grow on its own to provide for the people until they can plant again (19:29).

As much as the Assyrians would like to crush Jerusalem and Judah, they are not able to. God will preserve His remnant (19:30–31). Although the Assyrian military machine is poised to lay siege to Jerusalem and ultimately crush them, they won't. The king of Assyria will not come into this city because God promised to defend it (19:32–34).

Critical Observation

It is hard for modern people to understand the ancient horror of the siege, when a city is surrounded by a hostile army and trapped into a slow, suffering starvation. King Hezekiah and the people of Jerusalem lived under the shadow of this threat, but God's promise through Isaiah assured them that Sennacherib and the Assyrian army would not only fail to capture the city, but would not even shoot an arrow or build a siege mound against Jerusalem. God promised that they wouldn't even begin a siege.

God would defend Jerusalem, not for the city's sake at all—Jerusalem deserved judgment—but for His own sake and for the sake of David. In the same way, God the Father defends and blesses us, not for our own sake but for His, and for the sake of Jesus Christ.

19:35–37

GOD DEFENDS JERUSALEM

Simply and powerfully, God destroys the mighty Assyrian army in one night. At the hand of the angel of the Lord, 185,000 die. Against all odds, and against every expectation, the Assyrian army is turned back without having even shot an arrow into Jerusalem. The unstoppable is indeed stopped, the undefeated defeated (19:35–36).

Between 2 Kings 19:36 and 2 Kings 19:37, twenty years pass. Perhaps Sennacherib thought he had escaped the judgment of God, but he hadn't. He meets death at the end of swords held by his own sons.

2 KINGS 20:1–21

GOD EXTENDS HEZEKIAH'S LIFE

Setting Up the Section

Chapter 20 is set at the time of the Assyrian invasion of Judah; Jerusalem has not been delivered from the Assyrian threat yet (20:6). The events of this chapter are also recorded in Isaiah 38.

20:1–11

HEZEKIAH'S RECOVERY

We are not told how Hezekiah becomes sick. It may have been through something obvious to all, or it may have been through something known only to God. However it happened, it was certainly permitted by the Lord. God is remarkably kind to Hezekiah, telling him that his death is near (20:1).

Critical Observation

We know from comparing 2 Kings 18:2 with 2 Kings 20:6 that Hezekiah is thirty-nine years old when he learns he will soon die.

Hezekiah is earnest in his prayer. He turns his face toward the wall to direct his prayer in privacy to God (20:2–3). Hezekiah lived under the old covenant, and at that time there was no confident assurance of the glory in the life beyond. Also, under the old covenant Hezekiah would have regarded his fatal illness as evidence that God was displeased with him.

God hears Hezekiah's prayer (20:4–5). By all indications, if Hezekiah had not made his passionate prayer, then his life would not have been extended. This is another demonstration of the principle that prayer matters.

In response to Hezekiah's prayer, God grants him fifteen more years (20:6). In fact, God gives two gifts to Hezekiah: the gift of an extended life and the gift of knowing he only has fifteen years left. This gives King Hezekiah the motivation to walk right with God and to set his house in order.

Because Hezekiah recovers, was God's Word in 20:1 proven false? No. First, Hezekiah does in fact die—just not as soon as God first announced. Second, when God announces judgment it is almost always an invitation to repent and to receive mercy.

The Lord's promise to defend Jerusalem (20:6) is in accord with the previous prophecies of deliverance and dates this chapter as being before God destroys the Assyrian army (Isaiah 37:36–37). The connection of the two promises indicates that one will confirm the other. When Hezekiah recovers, he can know that God will also deliver him from the Assyrians.

Apparently, God uses the medical treatment with the figs to bring Hezekiah's healing (20:7). God can, and often does, bring healing through medical treatments, and apart from an unusual direction from God, medical treatment should never be rejected in the name of faith.

Hezekiah wants a sign that will allow him to go up to the house of the Lord (20:8). This is because he cannot and will not go up to the house of the Lord until he is healed, so the two are connected.

God shows even more mercy to Hezekiah. God is under no obligation to give this sign. In fact, God would have been justified in saying, "How dare you not take My word for truth?" But in real love, God gives Hezekiah more than he needs or deserves. God promises to do something completely miraculous as a confirming sign. He promises to make the shadow on the sundial move backward instead of forward (20:9–11). This is a wonderfully appropriate sign for Hezekiah. By bringing the shadow of the sundial backward, it gives more time in a day—just as God gave Hezekiah more time to live.

20:12–21

HEZEKIAH'S RECEPTION OF THE BABYLONIAN ENVOYS

Shortly after Hezekiah's illness, the king of Babylon sends letters and a present to Hezekiah (20:12). Apparently this is a gesture of kindness from the king of Babylon, showing concern to Hezekiah as fellow royalty. Most likely it is also an attempt to bring the kingdom of Judah to the side of the Babylonians against the Assyrians. We can imagine that this is flattering for King Hezekiah. After all, Judah is a lowly nation with little power, and Babylon, while a vassal state of Assyria, was far more powerful.

We can imagine Hezekiah wanting to please these envoys from Babylon and wanting to show them that they have good reason to be impressed with him and his kingdom. So he does everything he can to impress them and shows them the very best riches of the royal household (20:13). As the coming rebuke from Isaiah will demonstrate, this is nothing but proud foolishness on Hezekiah's part. He is in the dangerous place of wanting to please and impress others, especially ungodly men.

Isaiah probably already knows the answer to the questions he asks Hezekiah (20:14–15). It is likely that his questions are guided by God to allow Hezekiah the opportunity to answer honestly (which he does) and to see his error himself (which he apparently does not). There is the flavor that Hezekiah is *proud* to tell Isaiah this.

Hezekiah thinks that this display of wealth will impress the Babylonians. All it does is show them what the kings of Judah have and what they can get from them. One day the kings of Babylon will come and take it all away (20:16–17). This prophecy is fulfilled under the Babylonian king Nebuchadnezzar (24:10–13; 25:11–17).

Worse than taking the material riches of the kings of Judah, the king of Babylon will take the sons of the king of Judah—his true riches (20:18). Some think the word *eunuchs* means simply household servants to the king.

Critical Observation

One fulfillment of Isaiah's prophecy is the taking of Daniel and his companions into captivity. Daniel was one of the king's descendants taken into the palace of the king of Babylon (Daniel 1:1–4). Because of this promise of God through Isaiah, many think that Daniel and his companions were made eunuchs when they were taken to serve in the palace.

Hezekiah welcomes the prophecy about his sons (20:19). This is a sad state of heart in the king of Judah. God announces coming judgment, and all he can respond with is relief that it will not happen in his lifetime. In this, Hezekiah shows himself to be self-centered. All he cares about is his own personal comfort and success.

The pool and tunnel bringing water into the city (20:20–21) is an amazing engineering feat. Hezekiah builds an aqueduct to insure fresh water inside the city walls even during sieges. It was more than 650 yards long through solid rock, begun on each end and meeting in the middle. It can still be seen today, and it empties into the pool of Siloam.

There is no doubt that Hezekiah starts out as a godly king, and overall his reign is one of outstanding godliness (18:3–7). Yet his beginning is much better than his end; Hezekiah does not finish well. God gave Hezekiah the gift of fifteen more years of life, but the added years do not make him a better or a more godly man.

2 KINGS 21:1–26

THE WICKED REIGNS OF MANASSEH AND AMON

The Reign of Manasseh, Son of Hezekiah	21:1–18
The Reign of Amon, Son of Manasseh	21:19–26

Setting Up the Section

After the death of Hezekiah (2 Kings 20), Manasseh takes the throne in Judah. This is about twenty-five years after the fall of the northern kingdom of Israel. The kingdom of Judah will survive one hundred more years, but already an unfaithfulness like that of Israel's is apparent.

21:1–18

THE REIGN OF MANASSEH, SON OF HEZEKIAH

Manasseh is twelve years old when he becomes king (21:1). This means that he is born in the last fifteen years of Hezekiah's life, the *additional* fifteen years that Hezekiah prayed for. Those additional fifteen years bring Judah one of its worst kings. Manasseh's reign is both remarkably long and remarkably evil. A long career or longevity is not necessarily evidence of the blessing and approval of God.

Manasseh imitates the sins of both the Canaanites and the Israelites of the northern kingdom (21:2). Since God brings judgment on these groups for their sin, casting them out of their land, then similar judgment against an unrepentant Judah should be expected.

Manasseh opposes the reforms of his father Hezekiah and brings Judah back into terrible idolatry (21:3). This shows that repentance and reform are not permanent standing conditions. Manasseh does not want to imitate his godly father. Instead, he imitates one of the worst kings of Israel: Ahab. He embraces the same state-sponsored worship of Baal and Asherah (honored with a wooden image) that marked the reign of Ahab. Manasseh not only brings back old forms of idolatry; he also brings new forms of idolatry to Judah. At this time the Babylonian Empire is rising in influence, and they have a special attraction to astrological worship. Manasseh probably imitates this.

It is bad enough for Manasseh to allow this idol worship in Judah. Worse, he corrupts the worship of the true God at the temple and makes it a place of idol altars, including those dedicated to his cult of astrological worship (20:4–5). He sacrifices his own son to the Canaanite god Molech, who is worshiped with the burning of children (21:6), and he invites direct satanic influence by his approval and introduction of occult arts.

He even sets a carved image of Asherah in the temple (21:7). Asherah is the Canaanite goddess of fertility, worshiped through ritual prostitution. This means that Manasseh makes the temple into a brothel, dedicated to Asherah.

The people of Judah pay no attention to the generous promises of God, promising protection to His obedient people (21:8–9). This describes the basic attitude of the people throughout the fifty-five-year reign of Manasseh. In addition, they are willingly seduced by Manasseh's wickedness and are attracted to do more evil. Manasseh is indeed a wicked king, but perhaps the greater sin is on behalf of the people who accept this seduction willingly. God speaks to both the people and the leader, but they reject His Word (2 Chronicles 33:10).

When the leaders and the popular culture abandon God, He still has a voice to Judah. He speaks by the prophets to His disobedient people (21:10).

Manasseh acts more wickedly than all the Amorites who were before him (21:11). This is a remarkable achievement of evil. The Amorites were among the Canaanite tribes who populated the promised land before Israel captured it, and they were infamous for their violent, immoral, and depraved culture.

If Judah insists on imitating the sins of the northern kingdom, then God will answer their similar sins with a similar judgment. God will cleanse Jerusalem, subjecting them to their enemies (21:12–15).

Manasseh persecutes the people of God (21:16). This puts Manasseh, king of Judah, in the same spiritual family as Ahab, king of Israel. Under both of these kings—among others—the people of God are persecuted by the religion of state-sponsored idolatry. The extent of it is so great that it can be metaphorically said that he filled Jerusalem from one end to another with the blood of his victims.

Second Chronicles 33:11–19 describes a remarkable repentance on the part of Manasseh. Because he and his people will not listen to the warnings of God, the Lord allows the Babylonians to bind King Manasseh and take him as a captive to Babylon. There, he humbles himself before God, and God answers his prayer and restores him to the throne. Manasseh then proves that his repentance is genuine by taking away the idols and the foreign gods from Jerusalem (2 Chronicles 33:16).

This is a wonderful example of Proverbs 22:6. Manasseh was raised by a godly father, yet he lived in defiance of his father's faith for most of his life. Nevertheless, at the end of his days, he truly repents and serves God. In this way, we can say that it is true that Manasseh rests with his fathers (2 Kings 21:18).

21:19–26

THE REIGN OF AMON, SON OF MANASSEH

Amon's unusually short reign (21:19) is an indication that the blessing of God is not upon it. Amon sins as Manasseh had sinned (21:20–22), but without repentance.

This story of conspiracy and assassination seems more like something that would happen among the kings of Israel, not Judah (21:23). Yet when the kings and people of Judah begin to imitate the sins of their conquered northern neighbors, they slip into the same chaos and anarchy that marks the last period of Israel's history.

But the people of the land execute all those who have conspired against King Amon (21:24). This is a hopeful sign. Up to this point, the people of Judah have largely tolerated some fifty-seven years of utterly wicked kings who led the nation in evil. Now it seems that they want righteousness and justice instead of the evil they have lived with for so long.

God gave them the leaders they wanted and deserved. Now, as the people of the kingdom turn toward godliness, God will give them a better king. God does not yet allow Judah to slip into the same pit of anarchy that Israel has. Because of the righteous action of the people of the land, there is no change of dynasty, and the rightful heir to the throne of David receives the throne (21:24–26).

2 KINGS 22:1–20

KING JOSIAH FINDS THE BOOK OF THE LAW

Setting Up the Section

With the death of King Amon, Josiah becomes king in Judah. He is one of the few kings who is obedient to the Lord throughout his reign.

22:1–10

THE BEGINNINGS OF JOSIAH'S REFORMS

The young king Josiah comes to the throne at eight years of age (22:1). This is because of the assassination of his father, Amon. Josiah does what is right in the sight of the Lord (22:2).

Critical Observation

It is possible that Josiah is motivated to rebuild the temple after hearing (or remembering) that this was the workings of King Jehoash many years before (chapter 12). Josiah understood that the work of repair and rebuilding the temple needed organization and funding. He paid attention to both of these needs when he commanded Hilkiah to begin the work on the temple (22:3–7).

The fact that Hilkiah has to find the Book of the Law (22:8) makes it clear that it has been lost. It seems remarkable that this is even worthy of mention—that the high priest finds the Word of God and a scribe reads it. Yet the Word of God is so neglected in these days that this is an unusual event. According to Deuteronomy 31:24–27, there is to be a copy of the Book of the Law beside the ark of the covenant, beginning in the days of Moses. The Word of God was with Israel, but it was greatly neglected in those days. This neglect could only happen because Judah was in prolonged disobedience to God.

Shaphan reads the book before the king (22:9–10). It had been forgotten and regarded as nothing more than an old, dusty book. Now it is found.

22:11–20

KING JOSIAH IS CONFRONTED WITH THE BOOK OF THE LAW

The hearing of God's Word does a spiritual work in King Josiah. It is not merely the transmission of information; the hearing of God's Word has an impact of spiritual power on Josiah. The tearing of clothing is a traditional expression of horror and astonishment. In the strongest of displays, Josiah shows his grief on his own account and on account of the nation (22:11). This is an expression of deep conviction of sin, and a good thing. This conviction of sin is the special work of the Holy Spirit.

Demystifying 2 Kings

Scholars believe that the particular portion of the law that was found and read before King Josiah was the book of Deuteronomy or a portion of it.

King Josiah is so under the conviction of sin that he does not know what to do next. He knew that the kingdom of Judah deserved judgment from God. He could not hear the Word of God and respond to the Spirit of God without seriously confronting the sin of his kingdom (22:12–13).

We know little of Huldah the prophetess other than this mention here (and the similar account recorded in 2 Chronicles 34:22). With the apparent approval of King Josiah, Hilkiah the priest consults this woman for spiritual guidance (22:14). She is not sought out because of her own wisdom and spirituality, but she is recognized as a prophetess and can reveal the heart and mind of God.

Judah deserves judgment, and that judgment will indeed come. Judah and its leaders had walked against God for too long and will not genuinely repent so as to avoid eventual judgment (22:15–17). God's Word is true, even in its promises of judgment. God's faithfulness is demonstrated as much by His judgment upon the wicked as it is by His mercy upon the repentant.

Josiah's heart is tender in two ways. First, it is tender to the Word of God and is able to receive the convicting voice of the Holy Spirit. Second, it is tender to the message of judgment from Huldah in the previous verses (22:18–19). So the Lord promises that Josiah will die in peace before judgment falls on Judah (22:20).

2 KINGS 23:1–37

THE REFORMS OF JOSIAH

Setting Up the Section

Chapter 22 recounts the finding of the Law and Josiah's response to it. Chapter 23 highlights some of the outcomes of Josiah's convictions.

23:1–27

THE COVENANT AND THE REFORMS OF KING JOSIAH

Josiah hears the promise of both eventual judgment (22:16) and the immediate delay of judgment (22:20). He does not respond with indifference or simple contentment that he will not see the judgment in his day. He wants to get the kingdom right with God, and he knows that he can't do it by himself—he needs all the elders of Judah to join in broken repentance with him (23:1).

Josiah is so concerned that the nation hear the Word of God that he reads it to them himself. He stands before the people and publicly declares his commitment to obey God to the very best of his ability. The people take a stand for the covenant in response to the example and leadership of King Josiah. We do not read of any command for the people to do this; they do it spontaneously as they follow the king's example and leadership (23:2–3).

Take It Home

This kind of mass response and commitment to God cannot be commanded, but that does not mean there is no part for people to play. It is clearly the work of God among the people, but God works through the example and leadership of King Josiah.

The fact that this happens among all the people means that this is a special work of the Holy Spirit. The Bible tells us that there are times when the Holy Spirit comes upon people as a *group*, which is a different work than the individual filling of the Spirit (see Acts 2:4; 4:31; 10:44).

Verses 4–7 show just how deep idolatry is in Judah. There are idols dedicated to Baal, to Asherah, and to all the hosts of heaven in the very temple itself. From this account, it seems that Josiah began the cleansing reforms at the center and worked outwards. Josiah's reforms do not only remove sinful things but also the sinful people that promote and permit these sinful things. The idols that fill the temple do not get there or stay there on their own—there are idolatrous priests who are responsible for these sinful practices.

Demystifying 2 Kings

Throwing the ashes of the idols on the graves outside the city is not intended to defile their graves. Any contact with death was believed to be an act of defilement, so scattering the dust on the graves serves to defile the idols.

Verses 8–14 reveal something of the extent of official idolatry in Judah. It is widespread, elaborate, and heavily invested in. Previous kings of Judah had spent a lot of time and money to honor these pagan idols. It takes a long, dedicated commitment on the part of King Josiah to do this work.

King Josiah is so diligent in his reforms that he takes down altars located in the former kingdom of Israel. He removes the pagan altar at Bethel that Jeroboam set up hundreds of years earlier (23:15).

Verses 16–17 record the remarkable fulfillment of a prophecy made hundreds of years earlier. The words of this anonymous prophet are recorded in 1 Kings 13:1–2. Josiah is careful to honor the gravestone of this anonymous prophet, but he executes the pagan priests (2 Kings 23:18–20).

Josiah can't command heart obedience to God, but he can establish a national holiday to observe the Passover. The celebration of the Passover had become so neglected that this was a remarkable observance (23:21–23).

Demystifying 2 Kings

Passover remembers the central act of redemption in the Old Testament: God's deliverance of Israel from Egypt in the days of Moses. Their neglect of Passover proves that they had neglected to remember God's work of redemption for them. It would be like a group of modern Christians completely forgetting the celebration of the Lord's Supper, which remembers Jesus' work of redemption for us.

King Josiah also fulfills the commandment of God to put away those who practice the occult (23:24). His passion is to perform the words of the Law which were written in the book. Josiah is one of the most remarkable kings of Judah, unique in the strength of his obedience and commitment. He stands as a wonderful example of what a leader can and should be (23:25). There were other great kings of Judah and the united kingdom of Israel—such as David and Hezekiah. Yet one thing that makes Josiah unique is his godliness *in his day*. He lived in a remarkably wicked time, so his godliness was remarkable against the backdrop of his times.

Nevertheless, not long after Josiah's reign, Judah is severely judged by the Lord (23:26–27). There is an outward conformity among the people of Judah, yet their hearts are not really turned toward God. God does not turn from His wrath because, despite Josiah's personal godliness and his righteous example and leadership, the people of Judah still provoke Him, loving the sins introduced during the wicked days of Manasseh, Josiah's father.

23:28–37

JOSIAH'S END AND HIS SUCCESSORS

The alliance between Egypt and Assyria is part of the geopolitical struggle between the declining Assyrian Empire and the emerging Babylonian Empire. The Assyrians make an alliance with the Egyptians to protect against the growing power of the Babylonians. When Josiah leads his army against the king of Egypt, he is killed and his body is brought back to Jerusalem for burial (23:29).

The reforms of King Josiah are wonderful, but they are not long-lasting. His own son Jehoahaz does not follow in his godly ways (23:31–32). After the defeat of King Josiah in battle, Pharaoh is able to dominate Judah and make it effectively a vassal kingdom and a buffer against the growing Babylonian Empire. He imposes on the land a tribute, imprisons King Jehoahaz, and puts on the throne of Judah a puppet king, Eliakim, (renamed Jehoiakim), a brother of Jehoahaz (23:33–34).

Jehoiakim is nothing more than a puppet king presiding over a vassal kingdom under the Egyptians. He imposes heavy taxes on the people and pays the money to the Egyptians, as required. Like his brother Jehoahaz, Jehoiakim does not follow the godly example of his father Josiah (23:35–37).

2 KINGS 24:1–20

JUDAH SUBJECTED UNDER BABYLON

The Reign of King Jehoiakim of Judah	24:1–7
The Reign of Jehoiachin	24:8–16
The Reign of Zedekiah	24:17–20

Setting Up the Section

As the book of 2 Kings comes to a close, this chapter recounts the reigns of the last three kings of Judah before Judah is taken into exile.

24:1–7

THE REIGN OF KING JEHOIAKIM OF JUDAH

Nebuchadnezzar, king of the Babylonian Empire, is concerned with Judah because of its strategic position in relation to the empires of Egypt and Assyria. Therefore it is important to him to conquer Judah and make it a subject kingdom (his vassal), securely loyal to Babylon (24:1). This happens in 605 BC, and it is the first (but not the last) encounter between Nebuchadnezzar and Jehoiakim. There will be two later invasions (597 and 587 BC).

Demystifying 2 Kings

This specific attack is documented by the Babylonian Chronicles, a collection of tablets discovered as early as 1887 and held in the British Museum. Excavations also document the victory of Nebuchadnezzar over the Egyptians at Carchemish. Archaeologists found evidences of battle, vast quantities of arrowheads, layers of ash, and a shield of a Greek mercenary fighting for the Egyptians.

This campaign of Nebuchadnezzar is interrupted suddenly when he hears of his father's death and races back to Babylon to secure his succession to the throne. He travels about five hundred miles in two weeks—remarkable speed in that day. Nebuchadnezzar only has the time to take a few choice captives (such as Daniel), a few treasures, and a promise of submission from Jehoiakim.

When Nebuchadnezzar has to make a hurried return to Babylon, Jehoiakim takes advantage of his absence and rebels against him.

It might seem that God will honor the Judean independence movement of Jehoiakim, but He does not bless it. God sends against him many adversaries because Jehoiakim is a patriot of the kingdom of Judah, but not a man submitted to God. One of Jehoiakim's great sins is that he persecutes the godly and fills Jerusalem with innocent blood (24:2–6).

The various peoples mentioned in verse 2 are probably allies who are willing to fight with him. In the geopolitical struggle between Egypt and Babylon, Nebuchadnezzar defeats the army of Egypt and then becomes the dominant power in that part of the world (24:7).

Critical Observation

The fall of Jerusalem occurs in stages:

- Nebuchadnezzar's initial subjugation of the city
- Destruction from Nebuchadnezzar's marauding bands
- The siege and fall of Jerusalem under Nebuchadnezzar's main army
- Nebuchadnezzar's return to completely destroy and depopulate Jerusalem

24:8–16

THE REIGN OF JEHOIACHIN

Jehoiachin succeeds his father, Jehoiakim. He carries on in the tradition of the wicked kings of Judah (24:8–9).

The previous king of Judah, Jehoiakim, had led a rebellion against Nebuchadnezzar. Now the king of Babylon comes with his armies against Jerusalem, and Jehoiachin hopes to appease Nebuchadnezzar by submitting himself, his family, and his leaders to the Babylonian king. But God allows Jehoiachin to be taken as a bound captive back to Babylon (24:10–12, 15).

On this second attack against Jerusalem, Nebuchadnezzar takes whatever valuables remain in the temple or in the royal palaces of Jerusalem, including the gold from the furniture and the precious things of Solomon's temple. Some ancient traditions tell us that Jeremiah hides the ark of the covenant before this, so that it is not among the things that are cut up and carried back to Babylon (24:13).

Nebuchadnezzar not only takes the material treasures of Judah, but also the human treasures. Anyone with any skills or abilities is taken captive to Babylon (24:14–16). Among these captives is the prophet Ezekiel, who compiles his book of prophecies while in captivity in Babylon.

24:17–20

THE REIGN OF ZEDEKIAH

Since Nebuchadnezzar has completely humbled Judah, he puts a king on the throne whom he thinks will submit to Babylon. He chooses Mattaniah, an uncle of Jehoiachin and a brother to Jehoiakim, and changes his name to Zedekiah (24:17). The name *Zedekiah* means "the Lord is Righteous." The righteous judgment of God will soon be seen against Judah.

Zedekiah, like so many kings before him, does evil in the sight of the Lord (24:18–19). Second Chronicles 36:11–20 tells us more of the evil of Zedekiah, specifically that he does not listen to Jeremiah or other messengers of God. Instead, he mocks and disregards the message. God's patience and longsuffering has finally run its course, and He allows—even instigates—the conquering of the kingdom of Judah (24:29).

2 KINGS 25:1–30

THE FALL OF JERUSALEM AND THE CAPTIVITY OF JUDAH

Setting Up the Section

The book of 2 Kings opens with Elijah being carried to heaven. It ends with the people of Judah being driven into exile. God's judgment has fallen on His disobedient people.

25:1–21

JERUSALEM IS CONQUERED

When Nebuchadnezzar attacks Jerusalem, he uses the common method of attack in those days of securely walled cities (25:1). A siege was intended to surround a city, prevent all business and trade from entering or leaving, and to eventually starve the population into surrender. After a year and a half, the famine has become severe (25:2–3), and Nebuchadnezzar and the Babylonians are at the point of victory over Jerusalem.

At this desperate point for Judah at the siege of Jerusalem, Zedekiah makes a last-chance effort to escape the grip of the nearly successful siege. He plans a secret break through the city walls and the siege lines of the Babylonians (25:4). The enemy army pursues the king, and they overtake him in the plains of Jericho. This is a considerable distance from Jerusalem. Zedekiah probably thought that his strategy was successful and that he had escaped the judgment that prophets such as Jeremiah had promised. Yet God's Word is demonstrated to be true, and he is captured in the plains of Jericho (25:5).

The Babylonians are not known to be as cruel as the Assyrians, who conquered the northern kingdom of Israel some 150 years earlier, but they are still experts in cruelty in their own right. They make certain that the last sight King Zedekiah sees is the murder of his own sons, and then he spends the rest of his life in darkness (25:6–7).

Critical Observation

Zedekiah's capture fulfills the mysterious promise God makes through Ezekiel regarding Zedekiah shortly before the fall of Jerusalem (Ezekiel 12:13).

The captain of Nebuchadnezzar's guard returns to Jerusalem and sets fire to it (25:8–9). Solomon's great temple is now a ruin. It will stay a ruin for many years, until it is humbly rebuilt by the returning exiles in the days of Ezra. He destroys the walls of Jerusalem—the physical security of the city (25:10). Jerusalem is no longer a place of safety and security. The walls will remain a ruin until they are rebuilt by the returning exiles in the days of Nehemiah.

Then he carries away the rest of the people who remain in the city (25:11–12). This is the third major wave of captivity, taking all the remaining people except for the poor of the land. As the remaining people are taken captive to Babylon, so also the remaining valuables from the temple are taken (25:13–17). Jerusalem is left desolate, completely plundered under the judgment of God.

The last leaders of Jerusalem and Judah are captured and put to death. The king of Babylon has what seems to be complete rule over the former kingdom of Judah. This is the land God gave to His people, the tribes of Israel. They had possessed this land for some 860 years; they took it by faith and obedience, but they lose it through idolatry and sin (25:18–21).

25:22–30

JUDAH AND JERUSALEM UNDER THE BABYLONIANS

The king of Babylon has made Gedaliah governor in what remains of Judah (25:22). It seems that Gedaliah is a good and godly man who is a friend of the prophet Jeremiah (Jeremiah 26:24; 39:14). He advises the people to live peacefully and serve the king of Babylon (25:23–24). It seems unpatriotic and perhaps ungodly to do this, but it is the right thing to do. The best they can do under this situation of deserved and unstoppable judgment is to simply accept it from the hand of God. The Babylonians are doing the work of God in bringing this judgment upon the deserving kingdom of Judah. In this situation, to resist the Babylonians is to resist God.

Critical Observation

This situation greatly bothers the prophet Habakkuk. Even though Judah is wicked and deserves judgment, how can God use an even more wicked kingdom like Babylon to bring judgment? Habakkuk deals with these difficult questions in Habakkuk 1:5–2:8.

Because Gedaliah leads the remaining people of Judah to submit to the Babylonians (also called the Chaldeans in some versions), he is assassinated as a traitor to the resistance movement (25:25). Afraid of what the Babylonians will do to them, the people of Judah flee to Egypt (25:26).

King Jehoiachin, mentioned in verses 27–30, is not the last king of Judah; Zedekiah comes after him. Jehoiachin had previously been taken away to Babylon in bronze fetters (24:10–12). These last events of the book of 2 Kings occur after Jehoiachin has been a captive for many years.

The final words of the book of 2 Kings describe small kindness and blessings given in the worst circumstances. Judah is still depopulated, the people of God are still exiled, and the king of Judah is still a prisoner in Babylon. Yet, looking for even small notes of grace and mercy as evidences of the returning favor of God, the divine historian notes that King Jehoiachin begins to receive better treatment in Babylon. This is small, but evidence nonetheless that God is not done blessing and restoring His people, foreshadowing even greater blessing and restoration to come.

1 CHRONICLES

INTRODUCTION TO 1 CHRONICLES

In the Hebrew, 1 and 2 Chronicles are one single book. The title means, "the events of the times." The book of 1 Chronicles covers the same time period and many of the same events as portions of 1 and 2 Samuel and the first chapters of 1 Kings, but has a unique perspective. While the books of Samuel and Kings focus more on the political history of Israel and Judah, the Chronicles dwell more on the religious history and stay focused primarily on Judah. The information included in the Chronicles helps the people of Judah understand their history so they can live well in the present.

AUTHOR

Many scholars believe that Ezra wrote 1 and 2 Chronicles, which is quite possible. The book of 2 Chronicles flows smoothly into the book of Ezra, and the time frame (450 to 430 BC) is reasonable. However, the author's identity cannot be proven beyond reasonable doubt, so it has become traditional to refer to him as "the Chronicler."

PURPOSE

In Jewish thought, genealogies were extremely important. The firstborn of each family was entitled to a double portion of the inheritance. The land was portioned out first by tribe, and then by family, and would never permanently leave that family. Levites had to prove their family credentials in order to serve in the temple. Priests had to show they were descendants of Aaron. Jewish people would consult these genealogies frequently, for various reasons. Genealogies were particularly important to post-exilic Judeans returning from exile after a disruption of their cultural history.

The Chronicler focuses his genealogies on the tribe of Judah, which eventually leads to the reign of David. Late in life, David is promised a "house" in which one of his offspring will reign forever (17:10–14). The Chronicler realizes the importance of such a promise and verifies the line of Judah both before and after David. For an audience who no longer has a temple or a Davidic king, 1 Chronicles is both a reminder of God's faithfulness in their past and an optimistic look toward the future.

OCCASION

The Israelites are captives of a powerful foreign empire, but some of the citizens are being allowed to return home. Their current status seems uncertain, so the Chronicler goes back to Adam (1:1) and reviews their history up to the current time (2 Chronicles 26:23). In doing so, he supports his outlook with various citations from the books of law, the Psalms, the prophetic books, and other sources. His repeated emphasis is on the covenants, the temple, and other reminders of how God has always provided for and delivered His people. As they look to return home and rebuild the temple that the Babylonians left in ruins, the Chronicler wants to assure them that God will continue to be with them.

THEMES

The Chronicler is fond of the term *all Israel*, and he uses it frequently, downplaying the divided kingdom of Israel/Judah, while highlighting the perspective that the kingdom is indeed intended to be a single nation.

Associated with Israel are the temple, priests, and Levites—all ongoing concerns of the author.

Most of 1 Chronicles, aside from a lengthy series of opening genealogies, focuses on David as God's chosen king over the united nation. In conjunction is the prominence of Judah over the northern tribes.

HISTORICAL CONTEXT

The Chronicles were written for a Hebrew audience no longer completely in control of their lives. They have recently undergone captivity at the hands of the Babylonians, but control has quickly shifted to the Persians. It is a time of uncertainty, if not despair, for the Jews, who have always taken for granted that they are God's chosen people. The book of 1 Chronicles, therefore, is a review of the best of their past history: the beginning of the kings, David's eventual rise to power, his desire and plans to build a temple for God, and the transition from his reign to that of Solomon.

CONTRIBUTION TO THE BIBLE

One of the interesting aspects of Chronicles is not so much what it adds to scripture but what it leaves out. (The translators of the Septuagint titled the book, "the things omitted.") While covering much of the same content as 1 and 2 Samuel, the author streamlines the story to make it a targeted look at God's ongoing involvement in honoring the covenants He had made with Abraham and David. The Chronicler has a distinct perspective. While the books of Samuel and Kings were written during the exile and answer the question "What did we do to deserve the exile?" Chronicles addresses the questions, "What do we do now?" and "What is our connection with the past?"

There are a few things unique to 1 Chronicles involving some of the names in genealogies (much of 23–27, for example) and a number of orations found nowhere else. The Chronicler identifies a Shalleketh Gate of the temple (26:16) that is mentioned nowhere else in scripture. And the Jabez who sparked a bestselling book in the early 2000s is not mentioned anywhere else in the Bible except 1 Chronicles 4:9–10.

OUTLINE

IMPORTANT FAMILY HISTORIES 1:1–7:40

The Family of Noah 1:1–27
The Family of Abram (Abraham) 1:28–34
The Family of Israel: Judah 2:1–4:23
The Family of Israel: Simeon 4:24–43
The Family of Israel: Reuben, Gad, and Manasseh 5:1–26
The Family of Israel: Levi 6:1–81
The Family of Israel: Issachar, Benjamin, Naphtali, Manasseh, Ephraim, and Asher 7:1–40

THE BEGINNING AND END OF THE ERA OF THE KINGS 8:1–10:14

The Family of Saul 8:1–40
Back from Captivity 9:1–34
A Brief Look at Saul 9:35–10:14

THE RISE OF DAVID 11:1–12:40

David Unites a Nation 11:1–9
David's Fighting Men 11:10–12:40

DAVID AND THE ARK OF THE COVENANT 13:1–16:43

An Early Misstep 13:1–14
David's Fame Begins to Spread 14:1–17
The Ark Is Carried to Jerusalem 15:1–16:6
David's Expression of Thanksgiving 16:7–43

DAVID THE WARRIOR 17:1–20:8

David's Plan and God's Response 17:1–27
David's Military Achievements 18:1–17
The Ammonite Incident 19:1–19
Subjugating the Philistines 20:1–8

THE SIGNIFICANCE OF THE TEMPLE SITE 21:1–22:19

David's Offense 21:1–8
The Immediate Consequence of David's Offense 21:9–17
The Long-Range Results of David's Offense 21:18–22:1
Plans for the Temple 22:2–19

ORGANIZING PEOPLE TO SERVE IN THE KINGDOM — 23:1–27:34

Organizing the Levites	23:1–32
Organizing the Priests	24:1–19
Organizing the Other, Non-Priestly Levites	24:20–31
Organizing the Singers	25:1–31
Organizing the Gatekeepers	26:1–19
Organizing the Other Temple Staff	26:20–32
Organizing the Soldiers	27:1–15
Organizing the Other National Leaders	27:16–34

DAVID'S FINAL DAYS — 28:1–29:30

Creating Support for the Temple	28:1–21
Funding the Temple	29:1–9
David's Response	29:10–20
The Coronation of Solomon	29:21–25
The Death of David	29:26–30

1 CHRONICLES 1:1–7:40

IMPORTANT FAMILY HISTORIES

Setting Up the Section

The first nine chapters of 1 Chronicles cover a number of genealogies going all the way back to Adam. While such lists of family histories are sometimes perceived to be insignificant (or even boring) to modern readers, the Hebrew mindset was quite different. Such lists helped define who they were as a people and were a reminder of the blessings of their past. In particular for this group of exiles returning home, the genealogies grounded them in their history. This section contains family lines for Noah, Abraham, and Israel.

q 1:1–27

THE FAMILY OF NOAH

When approaching any section of biblical genealogy, many people automatically assume it will be dry and essentially meaningless. However, God does not place anything in His Word that is unimportant. With a little effort, the significance of many of these names will become both apparent and relevant to our modern faith. It has been said that some of the greatest treasure is found in the driest places.

The primary focus of the genealogies in Chronicles is the line of the Messiah. Other genealogies are included but usually run through a few names and are then dropped. Those that connect Adam to David to the ancestors of Jesus, however, will be much more prominent.

The sequence from Adam to Noah is brief but afterward becomes more detailed because it is the sons of Noah who are assigned to repopulate the earth after the Flood. Noah has three sons (1:4). Japheth (1:5–7) and his descendants live in the area of the north—what is now Europe and some of the former Soviet states. Ham's descendants (1:8–16) settle on the continent of Africa and the area known as Canaan. Perhaps the most prominent name in his progeny is Nimrod, a mighty hunter and warrior whose name is connected with both Babylon and Nineveh (Genesis 10:8–12). The Jewish Targum, a paraphrase of the Old Testament, attributes no small measure of wickedness to Nimrod, crediting him with creating the false religious system at the Tower of Babel.

The messianic line goes through Noah's remaining son, Shem (from where we get the word *Semites*). His descendants (1 Chronicles 1:17–27) take up residence in the Middle East.

The mention of the dividing of the earth during the days of Peleg (1:19) has created varying schools of thought. Some believe the reference is to the dividing of Earth's land masses into continents, but how could this be? They would have no knowledge of this in antiquity. Others feel it means that during the time of the Tower of Babel God divided languages, and thus people, into separate groups.

q 1:28–34

THE FAMILY OF ABRAM (ABRAHAM)

The final entry in Shem's list of descendants is Abram, and the genealogy picks up there with his families. Ishmael, the son Abraham had with Hagar, has a number of sons (1:29–31). Abraham himself has a number of additional children after Sarah dies (1:32–33). But the son whose line the Chronicler will follow is Isaac, the only son of Sarah.

Isaac has two sons: the twins, Jacob and Esau. However, Jacob's name isn't even used in this section of Chronicles. Instead, he is identified as *Israel*, the name he receives from God and by which the entire nation eventually comes to be known. (*Jacob* means "heel catcher"; *Israel* means something like "wrestling or struggling God.") Esau has several sons and many grandchildren. His line eventually comes to be called the Edomites (1:43). But it will be the children of Jacob—the Israelites—who will get the most attention in this genealogical list. And Judah will be the one of whom most is written because he is the one in the messianic line.

2:1–4:23

THE FAMILY OF ISRAEL: JUDAH

Israel has twelve sons (2:1). Judah is fourth in birth order but rises to prominence after Jacob's oldest sons commit harsh actions that prevent them from receiving their father's blessing (Genesis 34:25–30; 35:22; 49:1–12). Still, Judah is hardly a perfect son or citizen.

Judah's first two sons, Er and Onan, are killed by the Lord for their wickedness (Genesis 38:6–10). Judah is reluctant to let his third son marry the same woman, Tamar, which was the tradition of the time. Tamar is therefore unable to remarry or have children. Seeing a unique opportunity, she poses as a prostitute and is approached by Judah himself, who unknowingly impregnates her without ever discovering her identity. Months later, when she is discovered to be pregnant, Judah wants to have her killed, but she produces some of his possessions as collateral. Only then does he realize he is the father of her child, which turns out to be *children*—twins (Genesis 38:13–30). One of the offspring is named Perez, and as it turns out, he is in the messianic line (1 Chronicles 2:3–9).

Another notorious member of Judah's family is Achar (2:7). Known in Joshua as Achan, he plunders Jericho after Israel's victory, in defiance of God's and Joshua's explicit instructions (Joshua 7). His life is summed up in Chronicles in one phrase: a troubler of Israel (1 Chronicles 2:7).

Other memorable names of a more honorable reputation are Boaz, the kinsman-redeemer and husband of Ruth, and his grandson, Jesse, who was the father of David

(2:12). The account of Samuel anointing David as king in 1 Samuel 16:6–13 provides the names of David's three oldest brothers, but Chronicles provides the names of those three and three more (2:13–15). David has seven older brothers, but only six are listed in 1 Chronicles. Perhaps the difference is to promote David to seventh position, since seven is a significant number throughout scripture.

David's nephews (2:16–17) are decent warriors, yet they create a lot of unnecessary stress during David's conflict with Saul. Saul's commander, Abner, kills Asahel. Later, even though David has established a peace treaty with Abner, Joab kills Abner out of revenge. David tries to remove Joab as general, but Joab holds on to his job, although he is not a man to be trusted (2 Samuel 19:11–13). It is Joab who later kills David's son, Absalom, in direct disobedience to David's orders (2 Samuel 18:14–15).

Backing up a bit, the Chronicler records the family of Caleb (1 Chronicles 2:18–54). Caleb had represented the tribe of Judah when Moses selected one person from each tribe to spy out the promised land before entering (Numbers 13:3–16). Of the twelve spies, only Caleb and Joshua return with the recommendation to move ahead in faith. Sadly, they are outvoted. The other spies are terrified of the inhabitants of the land, and their fear spreads to the entire nation. As a result, all the tribes are forced to wander in the wilderness for forty years because of their unbelief. Caleb, however, has a strong and consistent faith throughout his lifetime (Judges 1:8–20).

Historically, perhaps the most famous Old Testament character who comes through the line of Judah is David. David's descendants are listed in this section (1 Chronicles 3:1–9), and after the opening genealogies of 1 Chronicles (1–9), most of the rest of the book reviews his life (11–29).

Even a brief mention of David's sons and daughters, however, tends to trigger recollections of tragic stories. David's daughter, Tamar (3:9), is raped by David's son, Amnon (2 Samuel 13:1–22; 1 Chronicles 3:1). In response, Tamar's full brother, Absalom (1 Chronicles 3:2), bides his time for two years before assassinating Amnon (2 Samuel 15:23–39). Absalom later leads a revolt against David in an effort to take the throne but is killed in the process (2 Samuel 18:1–18). Still later, another son named Adonijah (1 Chronicles 3:2) attempts a coup and is also put to death (1 Kings 1; 2:13–25). All these events follow the declaration of the prophet Nathan that "the sword will never depart from [David's] house" (2 Samuel 12:10 NIV), a prophecy that was delivered immediately after David's adultery with Bathsheba and his murder of her husband, Uriah (2 Samuel 11).

Yet the Chronicler's list of David's sons also includes Solomon (1 Chronicles 3:5), which serves as a reminder of God's grace and forgiveness. Even after David's sins, his son would sit on the throne of Israel during the most peaceful and prosperous era in their history.

Demystifying 1 Chronicles

After the kingdom is divided, the northern tribes will have eight different families/dynasties on the throne. The southern kingdom of Judah, however, had only one dynasty: David's. And it is from David's lineage that the Messiah will eventually come.

The kings of Judah who follow David are listed in 3:10–16. All the kings of Judah are descendants of David, up to Zedekiah, the last king before the majority of the people are taken away captive to Babylon. A curse is placed on Jehoiachin because of his great wickedness, averring that he will never have a descendant on the throne (Jeremiah 22:28–30). Zedekiah, who follows Jehoiachin, is a son of Josiah (Jeremiah 37:1), but Jehoiachin outlives Zedekiah to become the last surviving king in the line of David—until the arrival of Jesus.

The kingdom had originally been divided for a short time in the transition from Saul's kingship to David's (2 Samuel 2–5). During that time David reigned in Hebron for seven and a half years, with only Judah supporting him as king. Meanwhile, Saul's son Ish-bosheth ruled over Israel for two years. David continued to grow stronger and soon united the kingdom, after which he ruled over all of Israel for thirty-three years. He is the one who established Jerusalem as the capital city and planned the building of the temple.

Two of David's children born to Bathsheba, Nathan and Solomon (1 Chronicles 3:5), continue David's lineage in the messianic line. Nathan's descendants continue to the family of Mary, the mother of Jesus (Luke 3). Solomon's descendants go to Joseph, the adopted father of Jesus (Matthew 1), which links Jesus to the royal line of David, but avoids the blood curse that had been placed on Jehoiachin and his descendants (Jeremiah 22:28–30).

Hezron (1 Chronicles 4:1) is the father of Caleb, who had been an exemplary soldier and follower of God. Yet he is not included in the messianic line. The line runs through Perez instead. (The listing of Judah's descendants [4:1] is not a group of siblings, but rather a sequential series of families.)

The account of Jabez (4:9–10) is short but fascinating. He is a man in pain who seeks the Lord, and his prayers are answered. God honors his request and blesses him.

After spending much time detailing the family of Judah, the son of Israel through whose line the Messiah will eventually come, the Chronicler moves on to the other sons of Israel and their family lines. These non-messianic lines are considerably more abbreviated.

The Chronicler's extensive coverage of the family of Judah (2:3–4:23) is due to both David's involvement and the anticipation of the Messiah to come from that line. Reuben is actually the oldest son of Jacob (Israel), but he loses the privileges that were usually bestowed on the firstborn (5:1–2). He not only misses out on the birthright that would connect him with the Messiah, he also forfeits the double portion of the inheritance that traditionally would have been his. That honor goes to Joseph. (This is why there is no tribe of Joseph. Instead, there are two tribes named for Joseph's sons, Ephraim and Manasseh.) Reuben isn't even listed first after Judah in this genealogy. Next comes Simeon, the second oldest.

Critical Observation

When Jacob was blessing his sons, he made a somewhat cryptic statement that the scepter would not depart from Judah and that there would not cease to be a lawgiver until Shiloh comes (Genesis 49:10). The reference to the *scepter* brings to mind a king with the right to execute capital punishment. (Perhaps the best-known biblical example is King Xerxes in the book of Esther [see Esther 4:10–11].)

The Jewish nation eventually loses the right to govern themselves as they always had, which is why the Jewish leaders appeal to Pilate to have Jesus put to death. After the Romans deny Israel the right to pass a death sentence, rabbis walk through the streets of Jerusalem in sackcloth and ashes. They perceive that the scepter had been taken away before the Messiah had come, and they weep because they believe the Word of God has been broken. They do not realize that some seventy miles to the north, in a town called Nazareth, a young boy is working in his father's carpenter shop. The Messiah *has* come before the scepter departed, but He is not yet revealed to them.

4:24–43

THE FAMILY OF ISRAEL: SIMEON

Simeon, along with his brother, Levi, had offended their father in an incident involving their sister, Dinah (Genesis 34). However, in this example provided by the Chronicler, the Simeonites are good models of faith and action. Their families have grown, along with their flocks and herds. They feel restricted and need more room, so they seek to destroy their enemies and enlarge their borders. Too frequently the problem with the Israelites (as well as with believers of all ages) was that they became complacent during good times. After they entered the promised land, they settled and stopped struggling as soon as they had acquired a little personal comfort—before they had dealt with the problems around them. Consequently, they remained vulnerable to the attacks of their enemies. The Simeonites are an admirable exception in this instance.

5:1–26

THE FAMILY OF ISRAEL: REUBEN, GAD, AND MANASSEH

The tribes of Reuben and Gad and the half tribe of Manasseh have the common bond of settling on the east side of the Jordan River. In one account recalled by the Chronicler, these tribes go into battle and are victorious—not because of their own strength, but because they cry out to God (5:18–22). God gives them victory because they express confidence and trust in Him. In addition to their victory, they receive the spoils of battle, including land and numerous animals.

In time, however, this cluster of tribes became unfaithful to God. When the Assyrian army invades, led by Tiglath-pileser (or Pul), they are easily defeated and taken into exile. They had not crossed the Jordan River, a line of defense, to settle in Canaan, so they were easily the first to be taken away captive.

6:1–81

THE FAMILY OF ISRAEL: LEVI

The Levites are placed in charge of the tabernacle and matters of worship, with each of the sons of Levi given a specific duty. Gershon and his descendants are responsible for the fabrics of the tabernacle, the coverings, tents, clothes, curtains, cords, and so forth. Kohath and his descendants (including Aaron) are to care for the ark, the table of showbread, the oil-burning lamp, the altars of burnt offering and incense, the sacred vessels, the veil, and related furnishings. The Merarites (descendants of Merari) take care of the boards, sockets, walls, floors, and such.

Critical Observation

It was important for those who planned to work in the soon-to-be-built temple to trace their genealogy back to Levi to prove their authenticity. The Gershonites, Kohathites, and Merarites will be mentioned repeatedly throughout 1 Chronicles to identify those qualified to serve in various specific duties.

The assignment of specific responsibilities is akin to the Spirit's assignment of spiritual gifts in the New Testament. When everyone is doing what they have been assigned to do, worship goes smoothly. But it can be disastrous when someone attempts to be something he or she is not. When Korah and some of his followers rebel against the leadership of Moses (Numbers 16), God causes the earth to swallow them up.

The Gershonites, Kohathites, and Merarites are still going strong as David becomes king (1 Chronicles 6:31–48). David is a man of worship who is determined to provide qualified people to worship. Imagine being able to walk by the temple day or night and hear the worship of God being sung out.

The descendants of Aaron become the priestly line in Israel (6:49–53). The Levites do not inherit any land because the Lord is to be their inheritance. (It is important to note as well that Jacob cursed Levi's tribe in Genesis 49.) Instead, forty-eight cities are designated throughout Israel in which the Levites live and minister (6:54–81). Under this arrangement, no one in the other tribes is more than a day's journey from one of the Levitical cities.

7:1–40

THE FAMILY OF ISRAEL: ISSACHAR, BENJAMIN, NAPHTALI, MANASSEH, EPHRAIM, AND ASHER

Biblical genealogies aren't altogether unlike the average family tree: Some members are going to be more prominent than others. In this section of Israel's family tree there are fewer familiar names. And while some of the tribes have lengthy sections with name after name and generation after generation, the tribe of Naphtali gets but a single verse with four names (7:13). But interesting tidbits are recorded for some of the biblical families, just as every modern family has its favorite stories that are told and retold. For example, two men in the line of Ephraim are killed in an altercation over livestock (7:21–24). The father grieves for them many days but then has other children and goes on with life.

One noteworthy name in Ephraim's family is Joshua, the assistant to Moses, spy of the promised land, and leader of the nation when the Israelites conquer Jericho and march triumphantly into the land. Here, however, he appears as just another name in the series (7:27).

In Manasseh's section (in this case, the western portion of Manasseh as opposed to the previously listed Transjordanian section) is mention of a man named Zelophehad, who had only daughters (7:15). More of that story is provided in Numbers 27:1–11, where the daughters go to Moses and the other leaders of Israel upon the death of their father, pointing out that the law made no provision for inheritances of families without sons. Moses took their case to the Lord, who determined that the daughters certainly did have a right to inherit their father's land.

The Chronicler has a few more lists of names to record (1 Chronicles 8–9), and then he moves into some history of Israel during the reigns of Saul and David.

Take It Home

How far back can you trace your family tree? Unless someone has an interest in genealogy, most people can't go back more than a generation or two. Aside from a relative who might be famous, notorious, or eccentric, we tend to forget our previous generations of family members. Yet Chronicles reveals in the ancient Hebrew mindset a devoted, intense commitment to trace one's ancestry back for dozens of generations. The importance placed on family lines might appear strange or useless to modern readers, yet it needs to be acknowledged in order to better understand Chronicles.

1 CHRONICLES 8:1–10:14

THE BEGINNING AND END OF THE ERA OF THE KINGS

Setting Up the Section

The lengthy opening list of genealogies in 1 Chronicles concludes in this section with an account of some of the people who return to Judah after being released from captivity. The author then backtracks to the first king of Israel and explains why, in spite of all his potential, King Saul falls far short of what God wants him to be.

8:1–40

THE FAMILY OF SAUL

When Samuel first approaches Saul about being the first king of Israel, Saul's initial response is skepticism. He is well aware that he is not only from Israel's smallest tribe, but he is also from the least significant clan within the tribe (1 Samuel 9:21). Since that time, however, it appears that being the source of the first king of Israel had helped the tribe of Benjamin increase in status. The Chronicler has already included a short genealogy of the tribe, and here he inserts another, more detailed, family line.

The list begins with a background of the Benjamites in general (1 Chronicles 8:1–28). The note that they all lived in Jerusalem (8:28) indicates the author's awareness that David had eventually conquered the city and established it as Israel's capital. That act had not yet taken place during the lifetime of Saul.

The names that follow (8:29–40) are the Benjamites to whom Saul is specifically related. Similar lists of names are found elsewhere in scripture and do not always coincide exactly. Sometimes the term *son* might actually refer to a grandson or perhaps even a more distant relative. And depending on the writer's intent, he might be selective in how many names he provides. Not all lists will be complete. However, this particular section is more comprehensive than others of a similar nature (Genesis 46:21; Numbers 26:38–40).

9:1–34

BACK FROM CAPTIVITY

After Solomon forsakes the worship of the Lord to pursue other gods (1 Kings 11:1–13), the kingdom begins a long spiritual deterioration. First it splits, with ten tribes forming the northern kingdom (Israel) and the remaining two comprising Judah. Each kingdom has a succession of kings, but very few show any kind of genuine devotion to God.

The northern kingdom is first to fall as the Assyrian Empire rises to power. More than a century later the Babylonian Empire begins making incursions into the southern kingdom, each time carrying away segments of the more trained and useful people. The first invasion was in 605 BC, the second in 597 BC. By 586 BC, they would tolerate no more of Judah's revolts and they level the city of Jerusalem, destroying the temple in the process. The invaders also take the majority of the leaders back to Babylon, leaving only the poor to take care of the land.

In 539 BC the Persian Empire conquers Babylon. The Persians allow the Israelites to go back to their homeland. However, by then not many of them *want* to return because they have become very comfortable in Babylon. The religious leaders are the first to return (9:2).

The priests (9:10–13) would normally have attended to and ministered in the temple, but the temple was no longer standing. They are assisted by the Levites (9:14–16). The gatekeepers (9:17–32) are a specified group of Levites in charge of opening and closing the gates of the temple. They ensure that only those who are permitted to be in the temple area are allowed in, and they keep out those who do not belong there.

Critical Observation

Although the official position of gatekeeper is not found in most churches today, that role has been assigned to the pastors and church leadership. The overseers of the church are not only to provide spiritual direction but also are to watch over and warn their congregations of danger, ensuring that "wolves" don't get in to harm the flock (see Acts 20:27–30). False teachers can be overt or subtle; either way, they need to be confronted and dealt with.

Some of the people in this group have no responsibilities other than being in the temple and singing worship songs to the Lord. Music and worship could be heard day and night. The Chronicler will have more to say about the priests, singers, gatekeepers, and other groups in chapters 23–26.

9:35–10:14

A BRIEF LOOK AT SAUL

A portion of Saul's genealogy is reviewed as a prologue to the story that follows. First Chronicles 9:35–44 repeats 8:29–38.

Conflict with the Philistines escalates throughout Saul's lifetime, and they are victorious in the battle at Mount Gilboa. Saul's sons are killed, and Saul himself is severely wounded by an arrow. He knew he could not escape in his condition, and he did not want to be tortured and/or killed at the hands of his enemies. Saul appeals to his armor bearer, requesting to be killed, but the armor bearer refuses. As a last resort, Saul falls on his own sword, and the armor bearer follows suit. A young Amalekite takes credit for ending Saul's life in hopes of impressing David, and David has him killed as a result (see 2 Samuel 1:1–16).

Demystifying 1 Chronicles

The Chronicler covers only Saul's ancestry (1 Chronicles 9:35–44) and his death (10:1–14). A much more extensive account of Saul's life is found in 1 Samuel 9–31.

The Philistines are brutal. They cut off Saul's head and take his body, along with those of his sons, back to their town. Saul's head and armor are displayed as trophies in their temples (10:10). But one of Saul's first acts as king had been to rescue the men of the Israelite city of Jabesh-gilead from hostile Ammonites (1 Samuel 11:1–11). When the citizens of that city hear of the Philistines' despicable treatment of Saul and his family, they conduct a night raid, heroically retrieve the bodies, and carry them back to Jabesh for a decent burial (1 Samuel 31:11–13; 1 Chronicles 10:11–12).

The Chronicler adds an editorial note about Saul's life that isn't included in Samuel (10:13–14). The author of Samuel implies that Saul's consultation with a medium is entirely inappropriate. But here (10:13–14) the author provides three specific reasons why Saul falls short of what God wants him to be:

1) *Saul is unfaithful to God.* The Lord had instructed Saul to wipe out the Amalekites, but Saul uses his own discretion to determine who and what should be spared (1 Samuel 15:1–26).
2) *Saul disregards God's Word.* Only priests were permitted to sacrifice animals to God. Yet in a moment of desperation and panic, Saul makes an offering himself without waiting for Samuel, as he had been instructed (1 Samuel 13:5–14).
3) *Saul fails to seek God properly.* After the death of Samuel, Saul no longer receives direction from God. Again motivated by fear, he seeks counsel from a medium where he learns of his impending death (1 Samuel 28:4–25).

This section of 1 Chronicles recalls both the first king of Israel, who hadn't performed his duties very well, and the captivity of the people, which ended their long line of kings. Neither the beginning nor the end of the era of the kings in Israel is an exemplary time of spiritual faith or national security. But in between is the reign of David—a period when God blesses His people spiritually and in every other way. David's reign paves the way for Solomon to rule in an atmosphere of peace and prosperity, yet it is Solomon who begins the idolatry that eventually brings down the entire nation.

When Israel demands a king, God gives them Saul and promises to bless the new king if Saul will be obedient (1 Samuel 12:13–15). Saul, however, does not obey God. Consequently, his dynasty lasts only some forty years. He is replaced by David, a leader divinely ordained by God, whose dynasty lasts more than ten times as long—from 1011 BC until 586 BC.

Take It Home

It is easy to criticize someone like King Saul, who began his reign as king with God's full endorsement and a green light to lead, but ends up completely estranged from God. Yet Saul is not unlike many believers today. He was somewhat obedient—but not totally—and it was his lack of total commitment that eventually cost him his kingdom. What is recorded in 1 Chronicles is not his occasional courage or good intentions, but his ultimate failure. Believers will benefit by reminding themselves frequently that their spiritual journey is a lengthy race, and they need to pace themselves in order to *finish* (1 Corinthians 9:24).

1 CHRONICLES 11:1–12:40

THE RISE OF DAVID

Setting Up the Section

After providing all the opening genealogies and the brief account of King Saul, the Chronicler in this section turns his attention to the primary focus of this portion of his writing: the life story of King David. We need to remember that 1 and 2 Chronicles were originally a single book; the rest of what we know as 1 Chronicles (11–29) will be about David, concluding with his death.

11:1–9

DAVID UNITES A NATION

By the time Saul dies, David is more than ready to be the next king. He had already been anointed years before, yet he was always insistent on leaving the timing of the transition in God's hands. He had had two ideal opportunities to kill King Saul, but refused each time (1 Samuel 24; 26).

In the meantime, he continues to serve God and his nation. His victory over Goliath and subsequent battles against the Philistines garner him national attention. It is not only evident that he is a great military figure, but the people also recognize the hand of God in David's life. Even as a shepherd, God had been training David to be king.

After Saul dies, the people in Judah immediately turn to David as their next leader, and he establishes a headquarters in Hebron (2 Samuel 2:1–4). The rest of the nation, however, recognizes Saul's son, Ish-bosheth. (They had wanted a king in order to be like the other nations, and the other nations tended to pass down their royal status through family lines.) For a long while, war rages between the supporters of David and the supporters of Saul (2 Samuel 3:1). As time passes, David's influence expands as the house of Saul gets weaker. It takes seven and a half years, but finally the entire nation gathers to endorse David's leadership as king (1 Chronicles 11:1–3).

David's next step displays good political sense, insightful wisdom, and military courage. Rather than choose an established city in Israel as a capital (which would likely upset some of those in Judah) or a city from the south (that could reignite the still-delicate feelings of Saul's supporters), David chooses the city Jebus, located between Judah and the northern tribes. But unfortunately the city is inhabited by Israel's enemies.

The citizens of Jebus had withstood all former assaults for hundreds of years and were not worried about David's desire to conquer them (11:4–5). Entrenched as they were at the top of a hill, it was easy to pick off any enemy soldiers that approached. But they should not have been so complacent. David conquers Jebus, and from that point forward it is known better as the city of Jerusalem and will always be known as the City of David.

Critical Observation

Jebusites had inhabited the city of Jebus since before the Israelites had entered the promised land. If God's people had done as He instructed (Joshua 23:6–13) and driven out all their enemies before settling comfortably in the land, they could have avoided a lot of problems—including the one of a fortified city established on a hill that was thought to be impenetrable. But David accomplishes what all the Israelites before him failed to do.

David's victory at Jebus also allows someone else an opportunity to prove himself. As David steps into the role of king, his army is left without a commander-in-chief, so he promises the position to whoever leads the attack on the Jebusites. The challenge is accepted by one of David's nephews—a man named Joab. He is seen in scripture as a tough, though at times unethical, warrior.

Demystifying 1 Chronicles

Exactly how Joab is able to breach the defenses of Jebus when others could not is not fully explained. One possible scenario is that David knew of a 45-foot shaft from which the Jebusites brought water into the city, and Joab is able to climb up the shaft and open the doors for Israel's soldiers (see 2 Samuel 5:8).

11:10–12:40

DAVID'S FIGHTING MEN

David had a reputation as a great warrior, and he seemed to attract others who were also noteworthy in battle. He collects a small army of about six hundred men while on the run from King Saul (1 Samuel 27:2). Several of their names are recorded (1 Chronicles 11:26–47). A sampling of their exploits is also provided (11:10–25), although few details are given.

Slight variations in names and details occur between the Chronicles account and the one in 2 Samuel 23, but the list is overall quite consistent. One soldier kills three hundred (or perhaps eight hundred) enemy soldiers in a single encounter. A small group takes a stand in a barley field, turning a potential defeat into a great victory. One man goes into a pit on a snowy day to kill a lion and later slays a giant Egyptian soldier. And there are more great accomplishments briefly recorded.

In one touching story, David expresses a desire for a drink from a particular well in a location where the Philistines are encamped. He is simply stating a wish, but he is overheard. Three of his very best soldiers break through the Philistine ranks, acquire the water, and take it back to David. Realizing the extent of their faith and commitment, David doesn't even drink the water; instead he pours it out as an offering to God, the One who really deserves that kind of devotion.

Ziklag (12:1) is a Philistine city that had been given to David. After David had been on the run from the relentless pursuit of King Saul for almost ten years, he had decided he would be just as safe among the Philistines as in Israel. He approaches the Philistine king Achish, asking for a city where he and his six hundred men can reside. Achish wrongly perceives that David will be his ally against Saul and Israel. He gives David and his men Ziklag, where they live for about sixteen months.

David uses Achish's misperception to his advantage. He and his men go out and destroy cities of Israel's enemies, but Achish assumes they are fighting against Israel. The setup works well until one day when Achish enlists the help of David and his men to march against Israel. David cannot refuse without exposing his actual feelings, so he starts out with Achish. God steps in to give David an out. The other Philistine leaders refuse to fight with David, suspecting that he might turn on them in battle. They force Achish to reluctantly send David back (1 Samuel 27:6–7; 29:1–11). As it turns out, this is the very battle where Saul and his sons are killed.

When David and his men return to Ziklag, they discover the Amalekites have burned it and taken all their wives and possessions. At this point, David's men are ready to stone him. David seeks the Lord, who assures him that they will defeat the Amalekites and retrieve everything that had been taken, which is exactly what happens (1 Samuel 30).

The author of Samuel provides much information about David's experiences in Ziklag. The author of Chronicles adds that it is during all these events that various groups of warriors come to Ziklag to join David. The soldiers in the first group mentioned (1 Chronicles 12:1–7) are Benjamites—relatives of Saul. This group must have been valuable on the battlefield because they were ambidextrous: They could use various weapons with either hand. A second group, from Gad, had a remarkable reputation. The least of them was equal to one hundred regular soldiers; the greatest of them could face one thousand. They wouldn't be stopped by flooded rivers or any human opponent (12:8–15). Another group came from Manasseh, defecting from Saul's army during the time that David had marched out with the Philistines. When David is sent back to Ziklag, they go with him (12:19–21).

As each group comes to David, he goes out to receive them. He welcomes all who come in peace to support him, but he warns against any attempt to betray him (12:16–18). It is only natural for him to be a bit suspicious, but God is with David in Ziklag, just as He had been all along the way.

People are coming to him day by day, and David soon has a great army. By the time Saul dies and David moves on to Hebron, they are joining his ranks by the thousands, from all the tribes (12:23–37). After all that David had been through—dodging Saul, negotiating with the Philistines, and leading all those who came to him—this was a relaxing and joyous time. Volunteers had provided plentiful supplies of food, and David and his group spend three days eating and drinking (12:38–40). It is a well-deserved break for the new king of Israel.

Take It Home

Reviewing the early life of David should remind us of the importance of waiting for God to act in His timing. Our first look at David is as a shepherd, and he is the best shepherd he could be. When he is a soldier, he serves his king and country with all his heart and courage. Even as a fugitive, David remains faithful to God and accomplishes all he can. As a result, people are drawn to him. When the opportunity finally arrives for him to step into the official leadership role, he has the support of those who know him. While you are hoping for some big opportunity to come along, are you being faithful in little things? Can you identify one thing you can do to make your (or someone else's) life better in the meantime?

1 CHRONICLES 13:1–16:43

DAVID AND THE ARK OF THE COVENANT

Setting Up the Section

Once anointed the next king of Israel, David had already waited a decade or so until God had determined King Saul's reign should come to an end. Saul tried persistently to capture and kill David, but it was Saul who died on the battlefield after drifting away from God. David was initially the king of Judah alone, but he eventually won over all the Israelites and received their endorsement as king. This section describes some of his early acts in his official leadership role.

13:1–14

AN EARLY MISSTEP

Throughout his writing, the author of Chronicles assumes that his readers are familiar with Samuel and Kings. Many in the twenty-first century, however, are not so knowledgeable, so a review of what happened to the ark of the covenant is in order.

The ark's usual location is in the tabernacle, the portable center of worship used by the Israelites as they traveled. At times, however, Moses had taken the ark into battles because it reminded the people of God's presence and power. They had no king, so it was the Lord Himself who led them out of Egypt, around the walls of Jericho, and into the promised land.

But after being in the land for a while, the people fail to acknowledge God's leadership and everyone did as they wanted (Judges 21:25). Consequently, God allows Israel's enemies to overpower them so they will turn back to Him. In one such instance, when the Philistines are the opposing force, the Israelites decide to carry the ark into battle with them as Moses and Joshua had done previously. But God was not fighting for his disobedient people that day, and the ark was captured (1 Samuel 4:1–11).

However, the newly acquired ark is the source of nothing but trouble for the Philistines, and they soon decide to send it back to Israel (1 Samuel 5–6). Some of the Israelites unwisely decide to look inside it while they have the opportunity, and a plague breaks out that kills many of them. Afterward the ark is taken to a nearby house, and a person is consecrated to care for it. There it remained for twenty years (1 Samuel 6:21–7:1).

Saul had shown little if any interest in the ark (1 Chronicles 13:3), but David has the highest respect for this holy object that symbolized the presence of God. Having had just established Jerusalem as the capital city of the nation, David wants to bring the ark there to be in the heart of the land and the hearts of the people.

David anticipates that moving the ark will be a time of great celebration and joy. He assembles the Israelites for the procession (13:5–6). The ark is placed on a new cart, and the journey begins as the people celebrate in music and song (13:8).

But a tragic event brings the festivities to an abrupt end. Crossing a threshing floor, the oxen stumbles and it looks as if the ark might topple. One of the two people accompanying the ark, a man named Uzzah, instinctively reaches out to steady it. But as soon as he touches the ark, he is struck dead (13:9–10).

The ark of the covenant had been designed to be carried by the priests on poles, which were not to be detached (Exodus 25:10–16). The Philistines, in returning the ark to Israel, had transported it on a cart—the method adopted by those in David's processional. Had the Israelites used the intended mode of transportation, instability would not have been an issue.

David becomes angry toward God. The name of the place where Uzzah died becomes Perez Uzzah. The usual translation, "outbreak against Uzzah," is mild compared to the original Hebrew, which suggests an attack on someone by an enemy. David was indeed angry, but he was also afraid of God (1 Chronicles 13:12)—not the reverential "fear of the Lord" that scripture frequently refers to, but a more literal sense of terror. This incident revised his concept of God.

Rather than continue toward Jerusalem, David has the ark rerouted to a nearby house, the home of Obed-edom (13:13–14), where it remains for three months. While the ark is there, the blessings of God are evident on Obed-edom and his entire household. It is evident that God did not object to the moving of the ark to Jerusalem, but He had been very clear about the penalty for breaching the holiness of the ark, the symbol of His presence. When properly transported, not even those assigned to moving the ark would look at it or touch it (Numbers 4:15, 20). Uzzah's action, though spontaneous and apparently well-intentioned, was still an offense to God that proved fatal.

14:1–17

DAVID'S FAME BEGINS TO SPREAD

Before continuing the story of the ark, the Chronicler inserts a few interesting facts about David's early experiences as king. One of David's tasks was to build his living quarters. To help with the construction of the palace, David enlists the assistance of Hiram, king of Tyre (14:1). It is the beginning of an alliance that will carry on though the reign of Solomon.

Critical Observation

Some people use the example of David's association with Hiram as an illustration of how believers might benefit by going beyond Christian circles in their daily lives. By hiring the most qualified people to do the best possible work, God can be honored in a variety of ways.

At this point in his life, David is beginning to see things from God's perspective. He doesn't take for granted his position as king. Rather, he sees that God is using him for the good of the nation (14:2).

Still, this doesn't mean David is completely on track with God. The Chronicler notes that David continues to take more wives and have children by them (14:3–7). Because little, if any, editorial comment accompanies the statement, some people conclude that God must have endorsed David's behavior. This is not necessarily the case; however, the Mosaic Law does not prohibit polygamy. Instead, it regulates it (Exodus 21:7–11). God had specified, long before a king ever sat on a throne in Israel, that their king must not take many wives (Deuteronomy 17:17). God's model from creation had been to unite one man with one woman in a marriage relationship. The Chronicler is reporting the facts about David, but not necessarily endorsing them.

The Philistines continue to be a threat to Israel. Imagine the Philistines' surprise when David becomes Israel's king. It hadn't been so long before that David and his followers were living in a Philistine city and even going out to march (or pretending to) against Israel (1 Samuel 27:1–6; 29). Some had suspected his true convictions, while others had considered him a genuine ally. But they *all* knew his well-deserved reputation as a soldier and military leader, and now they are marching out to do battle against him.

David knew the Philistines and their tactics as well as anyone, but still he stops to consult God before deciding to fight. God gives him the go-ahead, and David and his men soundly defeat the Philistines (1 Chronicles 14:8–12). The Philistines had carried their gods into battle with them but left them behind when fleeing the Israelites, so David's men collect and burn them.

Later the Philistines regroup and attack again. David doesn't take anything for granted or make the assumption that he will again defeat them. He once more inquires of God. The Lord tells him to go ahead and fight, but He provides David with a completely different battle plan than before. David's army positions itself in an unexpected location, and God uses the sound of marching in the balsam trees in two ways: as a signal to attack and as a signal that God and His heavenly army are moving into the battle. David does just as God instructs and again wins a resounding victory. As a result, David's reputation spreads throughout the land—not just as a mighty warrior, but also as someone with a strong spiritual relationship with God.

15:1–16:6

THE ARK IS CARRIED TO JERUSALEM

Prior to its capture by the Philistines, the ark had been located in Shiloh, tended to by Eli the priest and his family (1 Samuel 4:4). But now that Jerusalem had been established as Israel's capital, David sets up a temporary tent there to house the ark. The tabernacle that Moses had used in the wilderness was also still in use, located in Gibeon (1 Chronicles 16:39–40), a town in Benjamin, northeast of Jerusalem.

David had apparently used the interval of time since his first attempt to move the ark to determine what he had done wrong. This time he allows no one but the Levites to handle the transportation of the ark (15:2), using God's guidelines rather than his own.

He isn't going to make the same mistake twice. He recruits Levites from various families to participate (15:3–11).

David's anger toward and fear of God seem to have abated by now. He makes no excuses for his previous failure. He appears ready to right his mistake and move forward (15:12–15).

Again, worship is an integral element planned for moving the ark toward Jerusalem. Singers are appointed to sing joyful songs with musical accompaniment. And this is no ad hoc group; everyone has specific assignments, and the leader is skilled at what he does (15:16–24).

In addition to the worship music is the aspect of sacrifice. As the priests methodically progress toward Jerusalem with the ark, every six steps they stop and two animals are offered to God (2 Samuel 6:13).

David isn't just watching the processional; he is actively participating. The account in 2 Samuel says that David "danced before the LORD with all his might" (2 Samuel 6:14), to the dismay of one of his wives. Michal finds his behavior inappropriate for a king (2 Samuel 6:20) and despises David in her heart (1 Chronicles 15:29).

Demystifying 1 Chronicles

Michal was the daughter of King Saul, and David's first wife. Saul had given Michal to David as his wife, although Saul actually hoped that David would be killed attempting to acquire the unusual dowry asked for Michal (1 Samuel 18:20–27). When David was forced to flee Saul and leave Michal behind, Saul gave her to a man named Palti as his wife. Palti loved Michal, probably more than David ever did. But when David eventually gained the throne after Saul's death, he sent for Michal. Palti followed her, weeping all the way, but was sent back home alone (2 Samuel 3:13–16). After Michal's scolding of David for dancing, she remained childless for the rest of her life (2 Samuel 6:20–23).

But David's joy could not be contained. When the ark arrived and was positioned in the tent that David had provided, more offerings were made as the people gathered (16:1-2). David realized that he had been blessed by God, and he wanted to share those blessings with the people around him; so he gave everyone a gift of bread, dates, and a raisin cake (16:3).

Levites were appointed for regular petition, thanksgiving, and praise of God (16:4–6). In essence, their job was to remember and commemorate what God had done. Music would continue to be an essential element of worship.

16:7–43

DAVID'S EXPRESSION OF THANKSGIVING

David is credited with at least half of the songs in the biblical book of Psalms. Much of his psalm of thanks recorded in 1 Chronicles is also found in Psalms 96, 105, and 106:

1 Chronicles 16:8–22	Psalm 105:1–15
1 Chronicles 16:23–33	Psalm 96:1–13
1 Chronicles 16:34–36	Psalm 106:1, 47–48

David's challenge to his listeners isn't merely to be content with making a personal acknowledgment of God in their lives. Although one's worship should certainly entail thanksgiving, petition, and praise, it should also include telling the nations what God has done (1 Chronicles 16:8). In other places, God's people are called to be a light unto the Gentiles, and David confirms that goal here. For believers to proclaim the name of God means to interact with other people and explain what they have discovered about God's character and what it means to know Him.

Critical Observation

Bible translators help readers distinguish the original intent of the writers when referring to God. When the publishers print *LORD* (in small capital letters), it signifies the *name* of God (Yahweh). When they print *Lord*, it refers to God's *title* as lord or master. God's name indicates action: *Yahweh* means "the becoming one." When combined with other words, a variety of names for God are formed. For example:

Yahweh-Jireh	"God will provide"
Yahweh-Rophe	"God heals"
Yahweh-Nissi	"God, my banner"
Yahweh-M'Kaddesh	"God who sanctifies"
Yahweh-Shalom	"God is peace"
Yahweh-Tsidkenu	"The Lord our righteousness"
Yahweh-Rohi	"God my shepherd"
Yahweh-Shammah	"God is there"
Yahweh-Yeshua	"The Lord has become our salvation"

David expresses thanks for a number of things. He acknowledges Israel's inheritance of the land of Canaan. In another psalm he attests that the earth is the Lord's (Psalm 24:1–2), and he is thankful that God had provided the Israelites with their homeland (1 Chronicles 16:11–18). David is also thankful for God's protection of His people. They had been frequently outnumbered and occasionally displaced, yet they were still around and going strong, thanks to the provisions of the Lord (16:19–22).

When David tells the people to give God glory and strength (16:23–29), he is speaking of serving Him with all their ability. The day would come when everyone—all the earth, the nations, and the land (16:30–33)—would acknowledge the sovereignty of God. When David finishes proclaiming his psalm, all the people can do is endorse everything he has said (16:36).

With the ark in its new and special location in Jerusalem, and the tabernacle still in operation in Gibeon, there are now two primary centers of worship. David ensures that both places are staffed with competent and attentive spiritual leaders (16:37–42). Consequently, this is a period when two high priests are designated: Zadok is the priest in charge of the tabernacle, and David appoints Abiathar to attend to the ark in Jerusalem (18:16).

This had been big day for Israel. The ark was not only back in their land, but it had finally been reestablished in a place of prominence. Their new king was showing spiritual strength that the former king had lacked. And David would continue to inspire his people throughout the early years of his reign.

Take It Home

How often do you hear of someone rejecting God or walking away from his or her faith after a spiritual setback? It's as if any little disappointment becomes a justification for blaming God and giving up. Even David—a man after God's own heart—had similar moments. After Uzzah died while transporting the ark, David was devastated, and it was three months before he returned to the task. But because he did, he brought great joy to all of Israel. His example of willingness to humble himself before God, and his determination to serve, should inspire more people to persevere whenever their spiritual journey gets a little bumpy.

1 CHRONICLES 17:1–20:8

DAVID THE WARRIOR

Setting Up the Section

David has become king, united the nation, moved the ark to Jerusalem, and built his palace. He is becoming a popular leader, respected by the people. Now he has a desire to provide a more permanent and fitting home for the ark. It sounds like a good idea at first, but God has other plans.

17:1–27

DAVID'S PLAN AND GOD'S RESPONSE

After David constructs a palace for himself and places the ark of the covenant in a special tent, he feels he needs to do more to honor God. He mentions his idea to Nathan the prophet, who thinks it is an admirable idea. In fact, it seems that Nathan automatically assumes God will endorse the idea, and he tells David to go ahead before he even consults the Lord (17:1–2).

That same night, however, God speaks to Nathan, telling him that David isn't the right person to build a temple to house the ark. Just because it appears to have been a good thing to do doesn't mean it is the will of God.

Later, as David recalls the story, he explains that God had declared that the one who builds His house should not be someone who had shed as much blood as David has (28:2–3). As a warrior, David had killed hundreds, if not thousands, of people (1 Samuel 18:27). Rather than having a temple constructed by those hands of violence, God reserves that right for a person of peace: David's son, Solomon. Keep in mind that this is not an ethical judgment on God's part. David is the one who completes the conquest at God's command, and it is only then that the temple which symbolizes stability can be built. Thus the son of the conquest completer, whose name means "Peace," should build it.

Besides, God shows little concern of having a house of cedar in which to live (1 Chronicles 17:4–6). The Lord had always been mobile, leading His people and living among them. He moved from one site to another as he led the Israelites. And just because they had settled in the promised land didn't mean that God would be any less active.

Critical Observation

The translation in some Bible versions may seem to suggest that God moved from one tent of worship to another, or from one tabernacle to another. That is not the intended interpretation. Rather, in the five hundred or more years that the tabernacle had been in existence, surely portions of it had worn out and had been replaced. But the Lord's presence with the Israelites had remained consistent.

In the first century, when John wrote that "the Word was made flesh, and dwelt among us" (John 1:14 KJV), his use of the word *dwelt* suggested a tabernacle or tent. So the presence of God has included, but has not been limited to, a tent in the wilderness, the temple that would replace the tabernacle, and the person of Jesus Christ. Today the residence of God is not in a building, but in believers (1 Corinthians 3:16).

Rather than expecting David to build Him a house, God said He would set David over a house (1 Chronicles 17:10–14). God had been with David all along, from shepherd to king (17:7–8). Under David's leadership, all of God's people were being blessed (17:9–10). And David's house would continue.

Like so many other prophetic passages, this promise of God has two intended fulfillments: one in the near future and a second that is more long-range. David's house will continue first through his son, Solomon, who will become the next king. In fact, the long series of kings of Judah will be from the Davidic line—an ongoing continuation of his "house." But beyond that, of course, is the anticipation of the Messiah who is to come from the lineage of David and who will sit on the throne and rule forever (17:14).

After Nathan delivers God's message (17:15), David is humbled. He realizes he has failed at times, and he feels unworthy to receive such abundant blessings from God. Yet David rightly acknowledges that the Lord is a God of grace who gives His people gifts, not because of their goodness, but because of *His* goodness (17:16–19).

God had chosen Israel to be His people, but not because they were more worthy than others. They were special only because the Lord chose to work through them. It had been clear from the beginning that the Israelites were a stiff-necked people (Deuteronomy 9:6) without adequate righteousness of their own, yet God graciously provided for them and lead them to the promised land.

If taken out of context, David's final response (1 Chronicles 17:23–27) might sound excessively bold. But David is only agreeing to the things that God has already promised him; he is affirming what God has said. It is because of his knowledge of God's will for his life that David can pray with such boldness.

18:1–17

DAVID'S MILITARY ACHIEVEMENTS

David's skill as a warrior is evident throughout his career. As king, he is a natural leader against Israel's enemies. One major accomplishment is his subjugation of the Philistines (18:1), who had been a recurring problem ever since Israel had entered the promised land.

The Moabites had also been an occasional enemy of Israel, even though their histories had frequently overlapped. The Moabites were descendants of Lot, originating from an incestuous relationship between Lot and his older daughter shortly after their narrow escape from the destruction of the city of Sodom (Genesis 19:36–37). David has strong ties to Moab: His great-grandmother is Ruth, who accompanied Naomi back from Moab. But since the Moabites continue to oppose Israel, David defeats them, and they offer tribute to him as his subjects (1 Chronicles 18:2).

The Edomites (18:12–13) are an opponent of Israel with a history going all the way back to the person of Israel (Jacob). The Edomites are Esau's descendants; the original tensions between Jacob and Esau continue between their offspring.

The Arameans are another adversary that keep afflicting the Israelites. David defeats them (again in great numbers) and erects garrisons in their territory (18:5–6), as he had done in Edom (18:13).

David was victorious over all these persistent foes of Israel because God was with him (18:6, 13). After conquering large numbers of enemy soldiers (18:3–4), David takes steps to minimize future conflict with the same groups. Establishing garrisons and demanding tribute kept such nations in line. He also hamstrung enemy horses—a practice that essentially eliminates their effectiveness in war yet allows them to live and serve a peaceful purpose.

David also begins to accumulate many valuable items from spoils of war, tributes received, and gifts from those who want to ally with him (18:7–11). He dedicates those assets to the Lord. Although David has not been allowed to build a temple for God, he is preparing for it. Solomon will later use the materials David is acquiring (18:8).

As the nation of Israel grows and prospers, the governmental structure begins to grow as well (18:14–17). David's nephew, Joab, is still over the army. Abishai's son, Ahimelech, has taken over as the high priest who attends to the ark; Zadok still serves at the tabernacle. The Cherethites (Kerethites) and Pelethites are David's royal bodyguards—the equivalent of a president's secret service personnel.

19:1–19

THE AMMONITE INCIDENT

David is a proven warrior, yet he doesn't see the need to fight when diplomacy will work just as well. He had formed an alliance with Nahash, the king of the Ammonites. When David hears of the death of Nahash, he sends a delegation of his men to express condolences to Nahash's son, Hanun.

Hanun's advisors, however, are suspicious and give Hanun some bad advice. They feel that the visit of David's men is only a ruse to allow Israel to spy on Ammon in preparation of overthrowing the country. The Ammonites treat David's men with the utmost disdain, utterly humiliating them by shaving off half of each man's beard and cutting off the bottoms of their garments so that the men's buttocks are exposed (2 Samuel 10:4; 1 Chronicles 19:4). A beard was a sign of masculinity at the time, which made the Ammonite insult intentional and personal.

David's delegation doesn't even want to return to Jerusalem out of shame. They send word to David about what has happened, and he sends back instructions for them to remain in Jericho until their beards have grown back (1 Chronicles 19:5). But David isn't going to ignore such an offense.

It doesn't take the Ammonites long to sense that they have riled David. They have become "a stench in David's nostrils" (19:6 NIV). They send immediately for Aramean (Syrian) mercenaries—thirty-two thousand additional chariots and charioteers to supplement their own large army. But David and his men are up to the challenge.

The Israelites divide into two forces: one led by Joab (the regular army commander) and a second commanded by his brother, Abishai. While Joab deals with the outer circle of Arameans, Abishai confronts the Ammonites. Each brother agrees to back up the other if the need arises (19:10–13).

As soon as the fighting starts, the Arameans quickly begin to flee, leaving the Ammonites on their own. The Ammonites immediately retreat into the safety of Rabbah, their capital city (19:14–15), while the Arameans recruit more of their countrymen to stand against the Israelites. The combined forces of the Arameans face off against David's army, and this time the entire Aramean army is defeated. They lose tens of thousands of their soldiers, including their army commander (19:16–19). As a result, they surrender and become David's subjects, effectively ending the Ammonite/Aramean alliance.

Meanwhile, the Ammonites remain within the protection of their city. They have weather on their side (for now) because fighting was usually suspended during the winter (rainy) season. (Chariots couldn't very well navigate in muddy terrain.)

But spring comes soon enough, and Joab begins a siege of Rabbah. The Chronicler provides a short note that David remains in Jerusalem (20:1), but this is an important fact in light of the account provided in 2 Samuel 11. It is during this time that David, while his men are all out on the battlefield, is passing time by walking on the palace roof and happens to see Bathsheba. And this is the battle where, after he unintentionally impregnates Bathsheba, David arranges to have her husband killed (2 Samuel 11:14–17).

Demystifying 1 Chronicles

Why does the Chronicler omit such a significant story as David's affair with Bathsheba? A couple of good reasons have been suggested. First, the focus of Chronicles is different than that of Samuel and Kings. And a second reason is simply that the people would have been well aware of David's story from the previous writings, and the repetition was not necessary. The Chronicler certainly isn't trying to gloss over or minimize the sins of David. He has already pointed out David's frustration while moving the ark (13:9–13) and his many wives (14:3–6), and he will soon detail an even more grievous sin (21:1–22:1).

David's sin has already been duly (and thoroughly) described in scripture. The Chronicler is not inspired to repeat it. Like a parent talking about a child, he chooses to dwell primarily on the positive qualities of his subject. David had sinned, repented, and confessed. God had forgiven him and no longer held his sin against him.

While David remained in Jerusalem, Joab had neutralized the threat of the Ammonite army. But when the city was ready to fall, Joab summoned David to come lead the final charge and receive credit for the victory. The Ammonite king had a magnificent (though hardly functional) crown made of gold and precious stones that weighed seventy-five pounds. The crown was removed from the Ammonite king and placed on David's head. David acquired much other plunder as well, and he put the conquered people to work doing common labor, thus adding the Ammonites to the list of peoples ruled by Israel.

20:1–8

SUBJUGATING THE PHILISTINES

The Chronicler has already said that in time David subdues the Philistines (18:1). Here he provides a few brief details of that process.

No physical heights are recorded for the Philistine warriors singled out in this passage, but it is reasonable to believe that Goliath is not the only giant among the Philistines. Giants are mentioned prior to the Flood (Genesis 6:4) and afterward (Genesis 14:4–5; Deuteronomy 3:11). The group of Philistines are identified as Rephaites (1 Chronicles 20:4) or descendants of Rapha (20:8)—a line of large people who continued through the time of the early Philistines. It is conceivable that the two lines intermarried and produced others like Goliath, who stood more than nine feet tall.

Goliath's brother is one of the specific Philistines mentioned (20:5). The shaft of Lahmi's spear is likened to a weaver's rod, which is the same description given for Goliath's spear (1 Samuel 17:7). Another huge man taunts the Israelites, and David's nephew kills him.

When Goliath first challenged the Israelites, it had taken six weeks or so before he could convince even a single Israelite soldier to confront him (1 Samuel 17:16). After David kills Goliath, David's faith and courage became legendary. But more than that, it was also inspirational and motivational. The soldiers are no longer sitting around waiting for David to act on their behalf. In this passage, at least three others become legendary giant-killers in their own right.

Take It Home

Not everyone will have the exceptional levels of faith and confidence in God that David had as he went out to fight Goliath. However, more people in today's church should be inspired by David's men who, once they saw God at work, stepped up and got personally involved. It's far too easy to sit back and watch others deal with the "giant" problems that confront the church when it would be much more productive to take a step of faith and act personally. Can you think of a situation or opportunity where your personal involvement might make a significant impact?

1 CHRONICLES 21:1–22:19

THE SIGNIFICANCE OF THE TEMPLE SITE

Setting Up the Section

With only a few exceptions, everything the Chronicler has said about David so far has been positive and uplifting. He chose to omit the story of David's affair with Bathsheba and subsequent murder of her husband—the sin that most people appear to be familiar with. But David has another serious breach of faith that puts his nation at risk, and that event is included in this section.

21:1–8

DAVID'S OFFENSE

When David first becomes king over all of Israel, it seems as if nothing can stand in his way. No enemy is too powerful for him, not even those who repeatedly defeated Israel in past battles. Under David's leadership, Israel's boundaries continue to expand and the people prosper. Yet even though David is stronger than any external enemy, he is still vulnerable internally. His affair with Bathsheba—not mentioned in Chronicles—is one example. The author chooses to record another as well.

At first it may be unclear as to what David has done wrong. As the leader of the nation, he takes a census of the people (21:1–2). Moses had previously numbered the people as they set out on their wanderings (Numbers 1:1–4) and again at the end of their journey (Numbers 26:1–4). Moses, however, was acting under a direct command of God. In contrast, the Chronicler attributes David's motive to the action of Satan (1 Chronicles 21:1). David is overseeing a time of unprecedented national security, and there is no real need to know the exact number of people. Joab's response to David's plan (21:3) confirms that it appears wrong. David's problem seems to be a matter of pride, of placing confidence in his military instead of in the Lord. Whatever David's inner motivation, it is clear that he later recognizes and acknowledges his sin (21:8).

Demystifying 1 Chronicles

Sometimes people point out the differences between the way this story is introduced in 2 Samuel to here in 1 Chronicles. The author of Samuel says that because God is angry with Israel (the reason was not provided), He tells David to take a census (2 Samuel 24:1). The Chronicler, however, writes that it is Satan who incites David's action (1 Chronicles 21:1). This is not actually a contradiction. Scripture clearly attests that God does not tempt anyone (James 1:13). But God can withdraw His control of a situation, allowing Satan to step in. In this case, David succumbs to temptation. As a result, God is then able to deal with David's pride as well as chasten the nation of Israel.

David had surrounded himself with good people, but in this case he does not take the advice of one of his closest counselors. It was against Joab's better judgment to go out to conduct the census. It is no small task, requiring almost ten months (2 Samuel 24:8). At last count, Joab has a total of 1,100,000 fighting men in the northern tribes of Israel and 470,000 men in Judah. (The numbers don't match exactly with the account in 2 Samuel 24:9, perhaps because they are rounded in one account, or because the count was never finalized.)

Yet even after all the time he devotes to the task, Joab does not complete it. He numbers most of the tribes, but does not count Levi or Benjamin. The Levites are omitted because their concerns are spiritual, not military (Numbers 1:47–53). And Joab apparently never got to the tribe of Benjamin because God confronted David before Joab finished (1 Chronicles 27:24). Besides, Joab never did feel quite right about conducting the census (21:6).

21:9–17

THE IMMEDIATE CONSEQUENCE OF DAVID'S OFFENSE

Joab's opinion proves correct. God is indeed angry with David. One impressive characteristic about David, however, is how quick he is to repent and confess after being chastened by God. King Saul had looked for excuses and tried to blame others for his shortcomings, but David takes responsibility for his actions and immediately seeks to make things right with God again.

Even though David is sincerely sorry, and even though God will forgive him completely, sin has consequences. In this case, God allows David to *choose* which of three options he prefers. David could (1) withstand three years of famine in the land, (2) endure three months of defeat at the hands of his enemies, or (3) experience the angel of the Lord bringing plague on the people for three days (21:9–12). God presents these options to

David through the prophet Gad, someone who had advised David well in times past (1 Samuel 22:3–5).

David reasons that putting his future in God's hands is better than any other option (1 Chronicles 21:13). Still, three days under the judgment of God is a terrible thing. As soon as the plague falls on Israel, seventy thousand people die. The angel of the Lord then stands between heaven and earth, with a sword drawn to destroy Jerusalem (21:16). It is at this point that David's insight into God's character proves valuable. God deems that enough suffering has taken place, and He relents.

Critical Observation

Scripture says that God is not a man, so He does not lie nor repent, and He does whatever He says He will do (Numbers 23:19). Yet in this instance, God does not complete the entire three days of plagues that He said would happen. While we can count on every *promise* of God to come to pass, David's experience is an ideal example of the mercy of God. The Lord does not inflict on humankind all that it deserves. Scripture also reminds us that, "Through the LORD's mercies we are not consumed, because his compassions fail not. They are new every morning; great is [His] faithfulness" (Lamentations 3:22–23 NKJV).

When David sees the angel about to destroy Jerusalem, he takes full responsibility for the sin that has been committed and pleads with God to punish him rather than the people (21:17). David, it seems, still has the heart of a shepherd. He does not back down when faced with danger, because his sheep depend on him. In this case, the shepherd is attempting to protect the people under his leadership.

21:18–22:1

THE LONG-RANGE RESULTS OF DAVID'S OFFENSE

God again communicates to David through the prophet Gad. This time the message is much better than the previous one. David is to build an altar on the spot where the angel had stopped (21:18). The trouble is that David doesn't own the land. The angel had been halted while standing on the threshing floor of a man named Ornan (or Araunah). In fact, Ornan and his four sons are in the process of threshing wheat when they see the angel, and the sons immediately run to hide (21:20).

When Ornan sees King David approaching, he quickly leaves the threshing floor and goes to meet him (21:21). David tries to buy the threshing floor, but Ornan offers it to him at no charge—not only the structure, but also oxen for the offering, equipment that can be burned for a fire, and wheat for an accompanying grain offering (21:22–23). David refuses, however, explaining that he will not offer God something that costs him nothing. So David arranges to pay Ornan for the site.

The amount that David pays is another discrepancy between the account in 2 Samuel (fifty shekels of silver) and the one in 1 Chronicles (six hundred shekels of gold). But it is reasonable to assume that, as specified in 2 Samuel 24:24, the lower amount only applies to the threshing floor and oxen. The greater total (1 Chronicles 21:25) is for the site, which likely included the surrounding land.

David builds an altar on the spot and makes offerings to God. When he calls on God, the Lord responds with fire from heaven falling on the altar (21:25–26). In conjunction with this miraculous sign, the angel returns his sword to its sheath (21:27–28).

David seems to realize that this is an appropriate place to worship God. Even though the tabernacle is still in Gibeon at this time, David is afraid to go there because of the judgment of God, so God tells him to make sacrifices right where he is. David continues to worship the Lord at the threshing floor of Ornan as he makes plans to construct a more permanent structure there (21:29–30).

22:2–19

PLANS FOR THE TEMPLE

David's isn't the first altar to be constructed in this location. As it happens, the threshing floor of Ornan is on the same spot where Abraham had traveled centuries earlier, intending to offer his son Isaac to God. It is the site where Solomon will soon build the temple (22:1). And roughly one thousand years later, Christ would be crucified approximately three blocks away at the location of Golgotha, in history's ultimate sacrifice.

David had been denied permission to build the temple for God. Some people might have taken that as a personal rejection and given up altogether, but David decides to do what he *could* do. He begins to gather the supplies he knows will be needed to construct the temple in order to give Solomon a head start. David's preparations are extensive (22:5). He collects enormous quantities of iron, bronze, and cedar logs, and he has stonecutters standing by, ready to go to work (22:2–4).

While the Chronicler continues to follow the life and exploits of David, from this point onward Solomon becomes a prominent figure as well. The building will come to be known as Solomon's Temple, but its construction was a team effort.

David is able to talk about his life's disappointments. Some people tend to dwell only on the things that have turned out well for them. But just as David is quick to confess his sins to God, he is apparently willing to also open up to others about his unfulfilled personal desires. His account to his son Solomon is one such example (22:6–10).

David is both supportive and encouraging as he charges Solomon to begin his task. He makes clear that as long as Solomon is careful to follow God's laws, he will find success in all he does.

Critical Observation

David's charge to Solomon (22:13) will not be the last challenge Solomon receives to be obedient. God Himself reminds Solomon of the importance of obedience on different occasions (1 Kings 3:14; 9:4–9; 2 Chronicles 7:17–22). But ultimately, Solomon will reject this wise advice, resulting in the deterioration of the kingdom that David worked so hard to establish and unite.

The quantities of precious metals that David gathers are overwhelming, translating roughly to be 3,750 tons of gold and 37,500 tons of silver. Other metals were so abundant they were not even measured (22:14–16).

David is a good leader. He doesn't just give Solomon the assignment of building the temple; he also enlists the support of all the people for his son's work. The people admire and support David, and he uses these good relationships to make things as smooth as possible for Solomon (22:17–19).

Take It Home

At this point it is a good idea to recall the opening lines of Psalm 127, a psalm attributed to Solomon: "Unless the Lord builds the house, its builders labor in vain. Unless the Lord watches over the city, the watchmen stand guard in vain" (NIV). Even though David and Solomon throw themselves wholeheartedly into the building of God's temple, they realize that God is the only one who deserves the credit. Can you think of things in your own life or ministry where you are actively involved, yet where the success cannot be explained other than the ongoing presence of God in what you are doing?

1 CHRONICLES 23:1–27:34

ORGANIZING PEOPLE TO SERVE IN THE KINGDOM

Organizing the Levites 23:1–32
Organizing the Priests 24:1–19
Organizing the Other, Non-Priestly Levites 24:20–31
Organizing the Singers 25:1–31
Organizing the Gatekeepers 26:1–19
Organizing the Other Temple Staff 26:20–32
Organizing the Soldiers 27:1–15
Organizing the Other National Leaders 27:16–34

Setting Up the Section

By this point in David's life, he is old and preparing to turn the kingdom over to Solomon. As plans for the temple construction are being completed, the human staffing is yet to be organized. In this section, David turns his attention to that job. While much of the content of 1 Chronicles has a corresponding version in Samuel or Kings, most of the content of this section is not found elsewhere.

23:1–32

ORGANIZING THE LEVITES

The amount of work required at a permanent, full-time temple took a much larger staff than many realize. David has already gathered many of the physical materials Solomon will need to construct the temple, but he doesn't stop there. He next turns his attention to the human element—the people who will oversee the worship and day-to-day operations of the temple.

Solomon's ascension to the throne (23:1) will be more detailed in 1 Chronicles 28–29, but it is briefly mentioned here to show that David is not acting independently. The closing chapters of 1 Chronicles are not strictly chronological, but are laid out in a way to show that God's promise to build a house for David (17:10–14) is being fulfilled. To this end, the attempts of other family members to usurp the throne—and the resulting bloodshed (1 Kings 1–2)—are omitted by the Chronicler.

It may appear a bit strange to see David once again counting the people, because that same action had caused problems previously (1 Chronicles 21:1–8). This time, however, his motive is entirely different. Rather than lining up his fighting men to determine his military strength, now he is seeing how many people will qualify to serve in the temple. The Levites are one of the two tribes that hadn't been included in the previous census (21:6), so they are counted at this time—apparently late in David's life (23:27).

Traditionally, a priest or Levite had to be thirty years old before he was allowed to minister before the Lord, and he retired from service at age fifty (Numbers 4:1–3). David's count finds thirty-eight thousand Levites in that category. David assigns twenty-four thousand of them to supervise temple work. Six thousand others will serve as officials and judges; six thousand will be gatekeepers; and the final four thousand will be musicians. David even provides the instruments that are needed (1 Chronicles 23:5).

The Levites are subdivided into three smaller groups: the Gershonites, the Kohathites, and the Merarites (23:7–23). The Chronicler has already provided a similar breakdown in 6:16–30 and will do so again in 24:20–30. Each subgroup has specific duties to perform. The official priests, however, all come from the Kohathites—specifically, the line of Aaron. The other Levites assist the priests (23:28, 32).

A previous list of their jobs included guarding the facilities, opening the temple each morning, keeping up with the inventory, baking, mixing spices, playing music, and so forth (9:22–33). Here the Chronicler adds their ongoing responsibilities for caring for the temple's courtyards and side rooms, purifying the sacred objects, and offering praise to God every morning, evening, and during Sabbaths and festivals (23:28–32). The extent of the work is so demanding that David enlists additional help by lowering the age requirement from thirty to twenty (23:24–27).

24:1–19

ORGANIZING THE PRIESTS

When the Chronicler begins to enumerate the line of people in the priesthood, beginning with Aaron (24:1–2), he briefly notes that Aaron's older sons, Nadab and Abihu, died before their father. Their deaths had been a tragic story from Israel's history, recounted numerous times in scripture. Nadab and Abihu had ministered in an inappropriate manner, and they were consumed by fire from the Lord (Leviticus 10:1–5). They had not yet had children of their own. Replacing Nadab and Abihu are two of Aaron's other sons, Eleazar and Ithamar (Leviticus 10:12; 1 Chronicles 24:2). Zadok, the priest who attends to the tabernacle, is a descendant of Eleazar. Ahimelech (son of David's other high priest, Abiathar) descended from Ithamar.

As it turns out, Eleazar has twice as many descendants as Ithamar, so lots are drawn to provide a fair and random assignment (24:3–5). A total of twenty-four families are available to serve (sixteen from Eleazar and eight from Ithamar). As the lots are cast, the assignments are duly recorded by Shemaiah, the scribe (24:6–19).

The priests' work is assigned in two-week shifts, so one full rotation lasts just about a year with each family serving once. (Later on, a shift is made to one-week commitments, with each family serving twice during the year.) The Chronicler provides no details as to the importance of the priesthood or the specific functions the priests perform, although his readers would have been familiar with such information.

Critical Observation

About half of the names of the family heads (24:6–19) are also names of priests who returned from the Babylonian exile or were active during the Maccabean era. The rest are found nowhere else in scripture. This observation, combined with the fact that the twenty-four-family division appears to be a later development of the Jewish priesthood (the date of its origin is uncertain), has given rise to the belief that Chronicles should have a date nearer the second century BC rather than during the time of Ezra (fifth century BC). There is no strong evidence for such an outlook, however.

24:20–31

ORGANIZING THE OTHER, NON-PRIESTLY LEVITES

This list of the other descendants of Levi (24:20) is quite similar to the list in 23:7–23. For some unexplained reason, the author again lists the Kohathites (24:20–25) and Merarites (24:26–30), but not the Gershonites, and he adds one extra generation. Since this list follows the list of priests, these may have been the Levites specifically involved as priestly assistants.

Just as they had done for the assignments of the priests, David and his two high priests oversee the casting of lots to determine the responsibilities of the Levites. Every family receives equal treatment with no favoritism (24:31).

25:1–31

ORGANIZING THE SINGERS

It's hard to miss the fact that music plays an integral part of Israelite worship. The Psalms (their hymnbook) are an extensive portion of scripture, centrally located in most Old Testaments. This portion of 1 Chronicles shows that such an emphasis on music is quite intentional. Much thought and planning went into the musical elements of Israel's worship life. The people weren't merely encouraged to sing; the music was modeled for them on a regular basis by gifted and well-trained Levites.

It might seem strange for David to work with the commanders of the army while assigning singing ministries (25:1). If indeed he did, it could indicate David's intent to combine the military and spiritual elements of his kingdom, with a goal of allowing each segment of his administration to influence and strengthen the other. However, a different usage of the Hebrew word would allow for a translation of "leaders of the Levites" rather than "commanders of the army"—a usage some scholars find more likely because of the preceding focus on the Levites.

Three key families are devoted to the music ministry: Asaph, Heman, and Jeduthun. The ministry of the singers/instrumentalists is clearly a musical one (25:1), yet their work is called *prophesying.* They are probably not foretelling the future as some of the prophets do, but rather forth-telling the mighty works of God through their music. Still, Heman is referred to as the king's *seer* (25:5), another word for *prophet.* (In other portions of scripture, the same title is applied to the other two: Asaph [2 Chronicles 29:30] and Jeduthun [2 Chronicles 35:15].)

Critical Observation

Of the three main families designated to serve as musicians, Heman appears to be the most prominent. In this section, only he is identified as a seer, and he has more than twice as many sons as either of the other two. Yet after the exile of Israel, references are found to the descendants of Asaph and Jeduthun, but there is no further mention of the descendants of Heman.

After being informed of the twenty-four divisions among the priestly families (24:7–18), it is interesting to note these three musical men have a total of twenty-four sons. Asaph has four sons (25:2); Jeduthun has six (25:3); and Heman has a whopping fourteen (25:4). Each of the twenty-four musical divisions is comprised of a twelve-person contingent (25:9–31), resulting in a total of 288 people (25:7). It appears likely that one group of musicians/singers is paired with one division of priests on each assignment at the temple.

Again, lots are cast to determine assignments. Perhaps singing didn't require as much training as some of the other areas of spiritual leadership. It is interesting to note that the musical positions are open to any qualified Levite—young or old, student or teacher (25:8).

26:1–19

ORGANIZING THE GATEKEEPERS

It is difficult to think of a contemporary job that compares to that of the temple gatekeepers. In one sense, they acted as ticket-takers at an amusement park or bouncers at a club. Entering the temple was a serious matter. There were sections where unauthorized people were prohibited from going, and the penalty for entering the forbidden areas was death (Numbers 3:10; 18:17). The gatekeepers not only served as security guards (9:22–27) but also as regular reminders to visitors and participants of the sanctity of the temple.

Compared to priests or the Levites who dealt with the holy items, the job of gatekeeper might not seem attractive, or even significant. But when viewed from a proper perspective, it is indeed a job that one might aspire to do (Psalm 84:10). The Chronicler never diminishes the roles of the gatekeepers in contrast to the groups he lists previously (1 Chronicles 26:12). He had already provided a list of the gatekeepers (9:17–27), and he reiterates their importance here.

Obed-edom (26:4) had been singled out in a previous story in scripture. After David first attempts to move the ark of the covenant to Jerusalem, and Uzzah dies trying to steady it on the shaky cart, David aborts his plans. The nearby home of Obed-edom had housed the ark for three months, during which time God blessed the people and possessions of the household (13:9–14). Obed-edom had also been blessed with many sons (26:4–5). Here Obed-edom heads up one of the three divisions of gatekeepers (26:4–8), the other two being overseen by Meshelemiah (26:1–3) and Hosah (26:10–11). As it works out, there are no representatives of the Gershonites involved in the temple gatekeeping, only Kohathites and Merarites (26:19).

Demystifying 1 Chronicles

Names that look odd to us may have been quite common in Old Testament times. Consequently, when we see a strange name that is used in different places, we may wrongly tend to presume that it is the same person, when instead it might be someone else with the same name. For example, the Asaph identified as one of the leaders of the singers in the previous chapter (25:1) *may* be the one mentioned in 26:1. Or the latter reference may be to a man named Ebiasaph, but using an abbreviation of his name. Similarly, some contend that one man named Obed-edom tended to the ark of the covenant (13:14), served as a musician (15:21), and was a part-time gatekeeper (15:18), while another man with the same name was a full-time gatekeeper (16:38; 26:4).

Casting lots is once more the method of determining which people will be assigned to each gate (26:13). The East Gate (26:14) is the primary entrance to the temple. It has two additional posts and requires more guards than the other sides (26:17). The Shalleketh Gate (26:16) is not mentioned anywhere else in scripture.

Only twenty-two jobs for gatekeepers are listed (26:17–18). However, these are probably the positions of the chief men (26:12). With four thousand gatekeepers available for service (23:5), each of the leaders probably had people who served *with* him.

26:20–32

ORGANIZING THE OTHER TEMPLE STAFF

Unlike the unfamiliar and antiquated function of gatekeeper, the job of treasurer is more understandable to most people today. The Chronicler writes of two different areas requiring treasurers (26:20). The treasuries of the house of God refer to the usual storehouse of wealth for the temple.

The treasuries for the dedicated things are a collection of spoils of war that have been set aside for God (26:27–28). In the days of Joshua, God had given specific instructions that everything from the defeat of Jericho should be devoted to Him (Joshua 6:17–19, 24). Other of God's military leaders had apparently continued this practice on a voluntary basis. However, none of the specific examples from 1 Chronicles 26:28 are found in scripture, with the possible exception of Saul (1 Samuel 15:21).

A couple of places in this section raise questions of interpretation. The original Hebrew in 26:20 is translated: "As for the Levites, Ahijah was [in charge of the treasuries]." The sudden appearance of a man named Ahijah, with no explanation, seems too abrupt for some translators. When the passage was translated into Greek for the Septuagint, it was rendered, "Their fellow Levites were [in charge of the treasuries]." Scholars are still divided as to which is correct.

Another concern arises in 26:27, where the Chronicler speaks of repair to the temple. The passage still refers to David's involvement in conjunction with Solomon (26:31–32), so the temple would not even have been built at the time, much less be in need of repair. Some people suggest this is a clue that portions of the passage may have been added at a later date or perhaps that the word for *repair* requires a broader interpretation. (Some translations interpret the word as *upkeep*, or *maintenance*.)

What does come through clearly in the passage, however, is the leaders of the treasuries. There had been no Gershonites involved as gatekeepers, but the first recorded overseers of the temple treasuries are the descendants of Ladan (sometimes spelled Libni [6:17]), a Gershonite (26:21–22). The treasury leaders in the following list (26:24–26) are Kohathites. (A review of the list is previously provided in 23:12, 15–20.)

Four specific subgroups of Levites are mentioned in 26:23. No details are provided pertaining to the duties of the Uzzielites. The Amramites are in charge of the official temple treasuries (26:24–28).

The Izharites had similar responsibilities in areas out and away from the temple, in other parts of the nation. Some of their duties involved roles as judges (26:29).

The Hebronites were spread throughout the land in significant numbers: seventeen hundred in the western tribes and twenty-seven hundred on the east side of the Jordan River (26:30–32). This is one of the few times when Israel's theocracy works as it should—when the work of the king and the work of God are one and the same (26:30). David's fortieth year (26:31) will be his last as king.

27:1–15

ORGANIZING THE SOLDIERS

Some people examine 1 Chronicles 27 with a critical eye and point out that suddenly the writer says nothing about the temple and, for that matter, hardly mentions God. But in the context of all the lists of chapters 23–27, the concluding section about the military organization actually fits quite well. First David organizes the spiritual aspects of his kingdom, and then he turns his attention to the military.

The Lord had blessed David with a strong army that had made possible the current peace and prosperity in Israel and allowed anticipation of the temple. The army had played its part, but it couldn't take credit for all the victories—that credit went to God. The Babylonians had had one of the best armies on earth, and they had gone down in defeat to the Persians.

David had suffered by conducting a census of his army, perhaps out of military pride, but he had repented (21; 27:24). Now he places a proper perspective on his fighting men. As he gets closer to finalizing the plans for the temple, all of his leaders will be involved, both spiritual and military (28:1).

Many of the people David names to head divisions of the army are previously listed among the mighty men who had fought alongside him (11:10–47): Jashobeam (11:11; 27:2), Dodai (11:12; 27:4), Benaiah (11:22–25; 27:5), and others. Asahel and Joab (11:26; 27:7) had been close to David from the beginning. Twelve divisions are established, one to be on duty each month (27:1).

Twelve divisions of twenty-four thousand men each yields an army of 288,000 soldiers. That total may have been a potential maximum number, however, rather than the actual count. Based on the original language, it is appropriate, and perhaps preferable, to understand that each army division had twenty-four *units*, with each unit comprised of *up to* one thousand soldiers.

27:16–34

ORGANIZING THE OTHER NATIONAL LEADERS

Leaders of tribes weren't normally referred to as *officers* (27:16), and the exact job description that goes with the title is unknown. These people may have been appointees of David, initiating a transition between the former system of individual tribes to a more unified and centralized system of government. Most of those on the list are not mentioned elsewhere in scripture.

The tribal divisions are not traditional. Asher and Gad are omitted for some reason. The total remains at twelve, however, with the inclusion of Levi (27:17) and with Manasseh designated twice (27:20–21): once for the half-tribe on the western side of the Jordan River and again for the Transjordanian portion.

No numbers are designated for this section as had been done for previous sections. The Chronicler again brings up the problem of David's census, the consequences of which had prevented completion of the head count. Another of his reminders, however, is more positive—the promise God had made to Abraham to make his descendants (the Israelites) as numerous as the stars in the sky (Genesis 15:5). The Chronicler also clarifies that the soldiers he had previously mentioned (1 Chronicles 21:5) are all males older than twenty years.

Numerous historic journals are mentioned in scripture that have been lost to us today (or not yet discovered). For example, 1 and 2 Kings refer to the annals of the kings of Israel and the annals of the kings of Judah. The Chronicler mentions the annals of King David (27:24), which would have preceded those other books.

Last on David's series of lists (27:25–34) are overseers of various aspects of the king's business: storehouses, field hands, vineyards, herds and flocks, olive and fig crops, and so forth. One of the last names on the list, Ahithophel, needed to be replaced as the king's counselor (27:33–34), but the reason isn't explained here. Ahithophel had been one of the wisest people in Israel, and his advice was usually trusted without question (2 Samuel 16:23). Ahithophel also happened to be Bathsheba's grandfather (2 Samuel 11:3; 23:34). Even though he was David's top advisor, perhaps he harbored hard feelings after the affair between David and his granddaughter. Whether or not that was his motive, he sided with Absalom when Absalom tried to take the kingdom away from David. But after Absalom decided not to take Ahithophel's advice on a crucial matter, Ahithophel realized it would only be a matter of time until David regained control, so he went home and hanged himself (2 Samuel 17:1–14, 23).

The final name on the list, Joab (1 Chronicles 27:34), will also desert David eventually. Joab has a strong will and an ability to come out on top of any situation, even if his success requires someone else's demise. Sometime after Absalom's thwarted attempt to take over the kingdom (which Joab had personally ended [2 Samuel 18:9–15]), another of David's sons attempted to take control. This time Joab sides with Adonijah rather than respect David's wishes to pass the kingdom on to Solomon. As a result, Joab is eventually put to death (1 Kings 2:5–6, 28–35).

Take It Home

This section of 1 Chronicles shows an intentional and well-conceived plan to strengthen God's kingdom. All jobs are deemed important, whether spiritual or secular, public or private, urban or rural. David realizes that once the temple is built and becomes a center of Israel's life, support systems would need to be in place to ensure its success. The concept of the New Testament church, functioning as each member identifies and applies his or her God-given gifts, is similar. How does your job have the potential to contribute to the community of faith? Are your skills offered joyfully to God? Do you offer a service to fellow believers? How might you better serve God and others through your regular job?

1 CHRONICLES 28:1–29:30

DAVID'S FINAL DAYS

Setting Up the Section

David has put much thought and work into his organization of labor for the temple. In this section he is approaching the end of his life, so he calls together all the leaders he has appointed to gather their support for his son and Israel's next king, Solomon.

28:1–21

CREATING SUPPORT FOR THE TEMPLE

As the Chronicler has shown, David is certainly not a perfect person. However, he is a person after God's own heart. He had made serious mistakes, but had repented and moved on with his life. His final words and actions in the closing chapters of 1 Chronicles show him to be, as always, someone with a desire to serve the Lord.

After all the appointments David had recently made (23–27), he gathers all the designated leaders (28:1) for a series of speeches. First he addresses the entire group (28:2–8). He was the greatest of Israel's kings, yet even at the close of his reign he considered the Israelites not his subjects, but rather, his brothers (28:2).

David had done much to prepare for the soon to-be-constructed temple of the Lord, but he takes no credit for it. He makes it clear that God directed him all along the way. He wisely realizes that God is never confined to a building. The temple in Jerusalem would not be like other temples of the time, perceived as a residence for the god to which it was dedicated. Instead, it is built to honor God's name (28:3). God's throne and residence are in heaven, but the temple will be His footstool (28:2).

David reiterates his personal desire to build the temple and God's veto of his plans due to all the blood David had shed (28:3). Yet David feels honored and humbled to be a part of God's plan. Judah had not been the oldest son of Israel, David had not been the oldest son of Jesse, and Solomon is not the oldest son of David (28:4–5). But in each case, God chose the person for the task He had in mind. Solomon is God's choice to be the next king and the builder of His temple. After that, no subsequent king of Israel or Judah will be referred to as *chosen*.

The Chronicler had previously recorded a similar speech by David (22:5–19). In both cases, David addresses both Solomon and the leaders of Israel. In the prior instance, however, more of the emphasis was on Solomon. Here he spends more time attempting to prepare the Israelites to support their new king and new temple.

Critical Observation

Compared to the account in 1 Kings, the Chronicler's version of the transition between David and Solomon is extraordinarily different. Nowhere does he mention the frailty of David in his old age, the revolt by Adonijah, the desertion of Joab and others, the retribution of Solomon (as instructed by David), or any other negative aspect. The Chronicles account focuses on the Lord's designated chain of succession without including the human struggling involved.

David's speech repeatedly highlights obedience as a crucial element of the ongoing success of the kingdom. God will perpetuate Solomon's kingdom as long as the young king remains faithful (28:7, 9). Yet the imperative of obedience extends to the entire nation. As long as the people maintain their strong relationship with the Lord, He will bless their lives in the land He has given them, and the land will be an inheritance to their descendants (28:8).

The king turns his attention from the assembled crowd to address Solomon alone (28:9–10). He challenges his son to consider more than merely his actions. Solomon's success will depend on his wholehearted devotion to God, including his thoughts and motives. It appears, however, that later in life Solomon needs to verify this fact for himself. The book of Ecclesiastes, usually attributed to Solomon, describes the author's search for fulfillment through building projects, books, studies, material possessions, pleasure seeking, and more. None of those pursuits bring the joy he desires. The author's final conclusion is, "Fear God and keep His commandments, because this applies to every person" (Ecclesiastes 12:13 NASB).

David also reminds Solomon that he has been chosen for the task of building the temple. He challenges Solomon to be strong and to devote himself to the work (1 Chronicles 28:10). David will soon repeat these crucial imperatives to his son (28:20).

The plans David had prepared for the temple are not some vague, general concept. Just as God had given Moses detailed instructions for how to construct the tabernacle in the wilderness, the Spirit of God had worked through David to provide specifics for the temple to be built. The temple is far more than a one-room sanctuary. The plans include porches, storerooms, inner rooms, altars, treasury storehouses, and more. David has already seen to the divisions of the priests and Levites for all the areas of temple work (28:11–13).

The temple plans are so complete that David even specifies the designated weights of various implements: gold and silver lampstands, tables, forks, bowls, pitchers, dishes, and such (28:14–18). Especially important is the design of the golden angels with outspread wings that are to sit atop the ark of the covenant to shelter it (28:18). And lest there be any confusion about what David says should be done, he assures Solomon that everything is written down for him (28:19).

Demystifying 1 Chronicles

David's mention of "writing from the hand of the LORD" (28:19 NLT) sometimes gives rise to speculation. Since David's plans for the temple so closely parallel the plans Moses received for the tabernacle, it is interesting to note that some of the communication between Moses and the Lord was "written by the finger of God" (Exodus 31:18 NLT). There is no clear evidence to surmise that the *handwriting* in David's possession is God's, but what is certain is that the *content* of David's plans was received from the Lord and was written down for Solomon's benefit (1 Chronicles 28:19).

The construction of the temple is an enormous project, and Solomon is a young and inexperienced king, so David repeats his challenge to be strong and to get the work done (28:20). This time, however, he adds much assurance and encouragement. Far from being alone in this project, the entire nation is aligned behind Solomon—every willing person skilled in any craft (28:21). Much more importantly, however, is the confidence that God will be overseeing the project and will neither fail nor forsake Solomon until the work is complete.

29:1–9

FUNDING THE TEMPLE

David again appeals to the entire assembled group, imploring them to support their new, young, inexperienced king. No one in Israel had faced the magnitude of the task ahead of Solomon. This is no ordinary structure, no stately palace for a regal human occupant. More than that, this will be the temple of their unseen, all-powerful, loving, and merciful God (29:1).

No one knows better than David the scope of the project ahead of Solomon. In addition to the detailed plans David is handing over, he has also been accumulating incredible quantities of materials that will be needed. The kingdom treasuries are capable of providing great quantities of gold, silver, bronze, iron, wood, stone, and precious gems (29:2). In addition to such an impressive amount of national treasure, David donates his vast personal wealth: 110 tons of gold and 260 tons of silver (29:3–5).

David also encourages the people to contribute, and their response reflects their enthusiasm. Inspired by the example of their leaders, they give freely and sincerely, resulting in a one-day commitment of 5,360 tons of valuable materials needed for the temple (29:6–9). This is in addition to the staggering 41,250 tons of gold and silver (and bronze too abundant to count) that David had previously provided (22:14). (A *daric* [29:7] was a gold coin of Persia, first used around the reign of Darius I [522–486 BC].)

Critical Observation

The people's willing and generous giving is another parallel between the temple and the Old Testament tabernacle. After Moses made known the needs for the construction of the tabernacle, the people had come day after day with contributions until Moses had to issue an order for them to stop bringing their gifts (Exodus 36:2–7). Similarly, the Israelites pour out abundant financial support for the temple.

29:10–20

DAVID'S RESPONSE

David is overjoyed to see such a response. He responds to all the giving with a prayer (29:10–19). Despite all David has done, and as important a project as the building of the temple, neither David nor the temple are prominent in the prayer. Indeed, David acknowledges his own insignificance (29:14) as he maintains a focus on the attributes of God. Certainly, without God's provision for His people, none of their gifts would have been possible (29:16).

David looks back with thankfulness to Abraham, Isaac, and Jacob (29:18) and at how God had established His people. Then David turns his vision to the future, asking for God's blessing on the reign of Solomon (29:19).

After leading the prayer, David instructs everyone assembled to join in praise to God. It has been a festive occasion, yet they all end the day's events by bowing low and offering their adoration to God (29:20).

29:21–25

THE CORONATION OF SOLOMON

The worship continues the next day with a long series of sacrifices offered to God: one thousand bulls, one thousand rams, one thousand male lambs, and numerous other offerings (29:21). The sacrifices are accompanied with feasting, and it is a day of great joy.

Such is the mood as Solomon is anointed and acknowledged as their new king. David's high priest, Zadok, continues to serve in the position and is again anointed to acknowledge his role under Solomon (29:22). We know from 1 Kings 1–2 that the transition from David to Solomon is not as smooth as they may have wished, but the Chronicler chooses to focus on the support that Solomon receives, not the opposition (29:24).

It is soon clearly evident that Solomon is indeed God's choice as king based on the prosperity throughout Israel during his reign (29:25).

29:26–30

THE DEATH OF DAVID

It is not known how long David continues to live after Solomon's coronation, but it probably isn't very long. His life is briefly summarized as 1 Chronicles concludes. He ruled a total of forty years, at first just as Judah's leader, but soon as the king of the united nation of Israel.

David had received three often-mentioned blessings of God: long life, wealth, and honor (29:28). And he lived to see Solomon begin to rule in his own right.

The sources cited by the Chronicler (the records of Samuel the seer, the records of Nathan the prophet, and the records of Gad the seer) most likely include the parallel account of 1 Samuel and possibly Kings. Samuel, Nathan, and Gad were all involved at various critical stages of David's life and rule as king.

The reign of Solomon will be impressive, but in the long line of kings until the fall of Jerusalem, no other leader will surpass David's lifelong reputation as a faithful king to his people and a devoted man of God.

Take It Home

David was a man who, during his lifetime, was guilty of sexual indiscretions, coped with intense family turmoil, and had his share of spiritual questions and dilemmas. Yet at the end of his life, those who had observed him had nothing but good to say about him. In spite of his shortcomings, David remained a person after God's own heart, quick to confess to the wrongs he had done and attempt to put them right. Too often people try to cover up the mistakes they have made and their transgressions against God and others. Can you think of any such instance in your own life, where an unresolved issue has resulted in guilt, embarrassment, or other undesirable emotions? If so, what steps can you take to deal with the problem and experience the freedom and joy that David came to know?

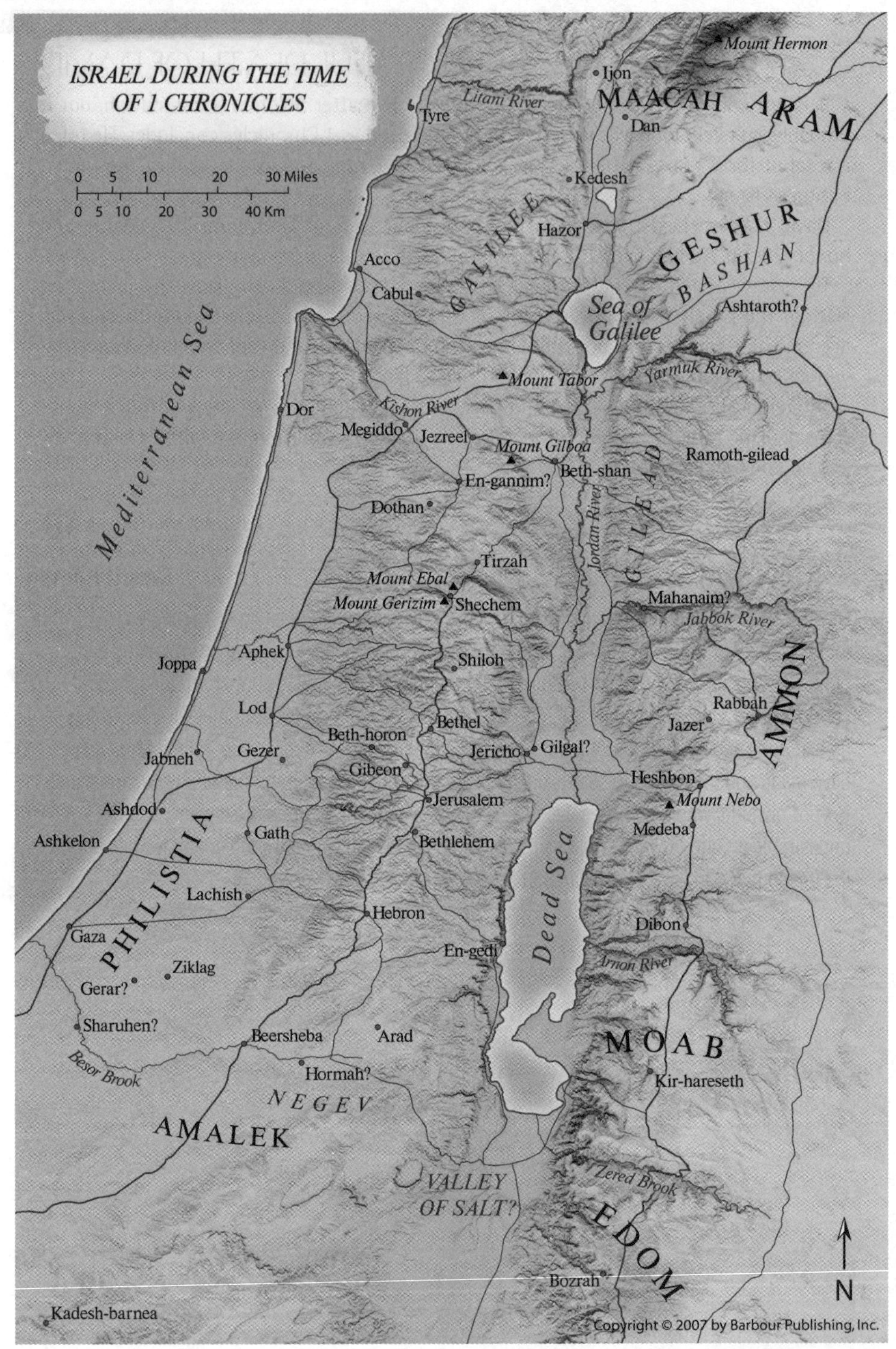
ISRAEL DURING THE TIME OF 1 CHRONICLES
0 5 10 20 30 Miles
0 5 10 20 30 40 Km
Mount Hermon
Ijon
Litani River
MAACAH
ARAM
Tyre
Dan
Kedesh
GALILEE
Hazor
GESHUR
BASHAN
Acco
Cabul
Sea of Galilee
Ashtaroth?
Mediterranean Sea
Mount Tabor
Yarmuk River
Dor
Kishon River
Megiddo
Jezreel
Mount Gilboa
Ramoth-gilead
Beth-shan
En-gannim?
GILEAD
Dothan
Jordan River
Tirzah
Mount Ebal
Mount Gerizim
Shechem
Mahanaim?
Jabbok River
Aphek
Joppa
Shiloh
AMMON
Lod
Rabbah
Bethel
Jazer
Beth-horon
Jericho
Gilgal?
Jabneh
Gezer
Gibeon
Heshbon
Jerusalem
Mount Nebo
Ashdod
PHILISTIA
Gath
Medeba
Ashkelon
Bethlehem
Dead Sea
Lachish
Hebron
Gaza
Dibon
En-gedi
Ziklag
Arnon River
Gerar?
Sharuhen?
Beersheba
Arad
MOAB
Besor Brook
Hormah?
Kir-hareseth
NEGEV
AMALEK
VALLEY OF SALT?
Zered Brook
EDOM
N
Bozrah
Kadesh-barnea
Copyright © 2007 by Barbour Publishing, Inc.

2 CHRONICLES

INTRODUCTION TO 2 CHRONICLES

The books of 1 and 2 Chronicles were originally written not as two books but as one continuous history. The majority of 2 Chronicles describes the history of Israel after Solomon's reign as the kingdom divided into northern Israel and southern Judah. This is not a history written as it was happening, however. Instead, it is a history written long after the fact to remind the people of Judah of the journey of their ancestors.

AUTHOR

The author of the books of 1 and 2 Chronicles is not explicitly stated in the text. Many scholars ascribe the work to Ezra, citing a unified authorship of the Chronicles and the books of Ezra and Nehemiah. However, there are parts of the book that are obvious additions and expansions on the original work, and it is difficult to date the entire book within Ezra's lifetime. The author was a wise and God-fearing person, writing with tremendous knowledge and insight into the significance of the community of God's people during this period.

PURPOSE

The book of 2 Chronicles is more of a commentary on a period of Israel's history than an exhaustive, chronological account of the events that took place during that time. The book is written to guide the remnant of God's people as they seek to reestablish their lives in the promised land.

OCCASION

While the accounts recorded in 2 Chronicles describe Israel's history during Solomon's reign and the fall of Israel afterward, the occasion of the writing is much later. It was written after the Jews had been exiled away from their homeland and had been given permission to return again. Therefore, it begins with Solomon, but it ends with Cyrus's decree that allowed the people passage back to Jerusalem.

THEMES

Beginning with the account of Solomon, and throughout this book, the Chronicler describes the dangers of religious compromise and demonstrates the vanity of seeking or serving anything besides God. He writes in order to help Jews returning to Jerusalem to know how they are connected to the past and how they should now live in light of their history. This is why negative stories about Israel are minimized here. The themes revolve around the temple, Judah, those who seek God, and a connection with past national history.

CONTRIBUTION TO THE BIBLE

This book is often considered one of the most unreadable of the Old Testament and therefore has been largely neglected and overlooked. Still, although at times the details seem mundane, the material supplements the stories told in Samuel and Kings and illuminates what was a very complicated and confusing period of Israel's history. From a broader biblical perspective, it emphasizes the continuance of the community of God and outlines how the Israelites are to interpret their history as a consistent reminder of God's faithfulness and love. The book also reminds them of the consequences of straying from the religious institutions God had established in order to help them honor Him and live well with one another.

OUTLINE

(SOLOMON'S KINGDOM)

WISDOM AND WEALTH 1:1–17

Solomon Seeks Wisdom 1:1–12
Solomon's Power 1:13–17

PREPARATIONS FOR THE TEMPLE 2:1–18

Solomon Requests Help 2:1–10
Foreign Aid 2:11–18

TEMPLE BUILDING BEGINS 3:1–4:22

The Temple Structure 3:1–17
The Temple Furnishings 4:1–22

THE ARK ARRIVES 5:1–14

Moving the Ark 5:1–10
The Coming of God's Glory 5:11–14

TEMPLE DEDICATION 6:1–42

Solomon Speaks to the People 6:1–11
Solomon Speaks to the Lord 6:12–42

TEMPLE DEDICATION CONTINUES 7:1–22

Solomon Dedicates the Temple 7:1–11
God Appears Again 7:12–22

FLEETING GLORY 8:1–9:31

Solomon's Additional Achievements 8:1–18
The Queen of Sheba's Praise 9:1–12
Solomon's Great Wealth 9:13–28
Solomon's Death 9:29–31

(THE DIVIDED KINGDOM)

2 CHRONICLES 1:1–17

WISDOM AND WEALTH

Setting Up the Section

Following the end of King David's reign over Israel, his son, Solomon, begins his reign seeking and receiving God's blessing with boldness.

1:1–12

SOLOMON SEEKS WISDOM

Solomon—who the text describes as exalted exceedingly by God—leads the assembled Israelites to Gibeon to visit the tabernacle of God. Historically, from other texts, we know that David had brought the ark up from Kiriath-jearim and placed it in a tent in Jerusalem (2 Samuel 6:2–17). But the tabernacle, the portable worship structure Moses had built some five hundred years earlier during their wilderness wanderings, was located in Gibeon.

With the tabernacle, besides the other temple articles, is the bronze altar in which the sacrifices were offered. Thus Solomon needs to go to Gibeon and offer his sacrifices to the Lord (Leviticus 17:11). It is only after that atonement is made that he can enter the presence of God, which the ark represents, and worship Him (2 Chronicles 1:1–5).

Demystifying 2 Chronicles

The burnt offering was given totally to the Lord, burned completely up, symbolizing the offerer's consecration to Him. On the other hand, the peace offering, also referred to in Leviticus 3 as the fellowship offering, was partly given to the Lord and partly eaten by those making the offering. It symbolized communion with the Lord. Historically, in this part of the world, when a person ate with someone, they formed an intimate relationship in a sense. Thus the connection between the names—peace and fellowship.

Solomon offers a thousand burnt offerings to the Lord before he approaches Him (1:6). When God speaks to Solomon, He is ready to grant him whatever he wants. Solomon's answer to this question reveals his heart (1:7).

Remember that Solomon is only fourteen years old at this time (David reminds him of his youth in 29:1). Solomon's prayers echo those of his father, David, who asked that God would give him wisdom and understanding to lead his people, for he rightly recognized he could not do it on his own. Solomon realizes that God had blessed his father, and at the outset of his own reign, he asks that God grant him wisdom and knowledge as well.

Critical Observation

Solomon's prayer can serve as a model prayer:

- He approaches God in a spirit of worship (1:6).
- He acknowledges God's history of kindness and leadership (1:8).
- He recognizes his own need for God's provision in order to obey and serve (1:10).
- He concerns himself with spiritual needs rather than material provision (1:10–11).

God honors the prayer of Solomon and gives him the desire of his heart, for it is what God wants for him. Solomon does not ask for his own personal gain, and since his heart is right, God blesses him abundantly (1:11–12). But unfortunately, Solomon does not apply all the wisdom God gives him to his own life.

1:13–17

SOLOMON'S POWER

As Solomon takes power in Jerusalem, he begins to amass wealth—and the seeds of destruction for the nation of Israel are being sown. Solomon is gathering chariots, horses, and riches. He becomes an arms merchant as he traffics in chariots, even going to Egypt to obtain them, and he also takes multiple wives. This is precisely what God had warned the Israelites against when He brought them into the promised land (Deuteronomy 17:14–17). God knew that these harbingers of military and economic power would distract His people from worshiping Him (2 Chronicles 1:13–17).

Take It Home

The same cleansing that Solomon had to observe is mirrored for the modern believer in the cleansing blood of Christ, which, like the blood of the sacrifice in the Old Testament, enables us to enter the presence of the Lord (Hebrews 10:19–20). Despite his best intentions, Solomon is corrupted by the military and economic power that God blesses him with. His love of money competes with his love for God. What do you trust more than God? What will tempt you to become distracted and turn away?

2 CHRONICLES 2:1–18

PREPARATIONS FOR THE TEMPLE

Setting Up the Section

Solomon almost immediately begins an elaborate and extensive building project constructing his own palace and the temple of the Lord.

2:1–10

SOLOMON REQUESTS HELP

Solomon gathers together a tremendous group of forced labor gangs—mostly foreigners, probably prisoners of war—to build his own palace and the temple of God, according to David's plans (2:1–2). Solomon requests manpower and materials from a nearby neighbor, Hiram of Tyre. His letter of request begins by emphasizing how magnificent and great the house of the Lord will be. Before a God this great, even the mighty and powerful King Solomon pales in comparison (2:3–5).

Solomon understands that no temple or building can contain God, for the universe can't even contain Him. The temple that Solomon is building is indeed a place for worship, but Solomon realizes that the presence of God fills the universe (2:6).

Solomon needs fine wood and skilled craftsmen to build the temple. He plans to send 160,000 bushels of wheat and barley and 150,000 gallons each of wine and oil as payment for the work he is commissioning on the temple (2:7–10).

2:11–18

FOREIGN AID

Hiram begins his reply to Solomon by praising God for His provision of a wise king to lead His people (2:11–12). The king replies that he will also send along a skilled craftsman to help oversee the work. Huram-Abi is the son of an Israelite mother (from the tribe of Dan) and a Gentile father (2:13). While Solomon has sought to enlist the world's most skilled people, God ultimately provides an Israelite to do the job. The fact that this craftsman is from the tribe of Dan creates a parallel with Moses' preparation of the tabernacle. In Moses' case, working in the wilderness, God appointed a Danite to oversee the work (Exodus 31:1–11).

Take It Home

God empowered these men to do the work by His Spirit. This is evidence that we can try to do the work of God in the flesh, but we will fail and come far short of what God intends to do. Or we can submit to God and be filled and lead by His Spirit, and God will do far above what we are able to do in the flesh. It is not by our might or by our strength but by God's Spirit working through us.

Hiram is going to send to Solomon the beautiful cedars of Lebanon. In order to do this, they have to tie logs together and float them down the Mediterranean Sea, some seventy miles, to the only seaport in the area, Joppa. From Joppa they are carried across land some twenty or thirty miles, to the city of Jerusalem, where they will be used in the construction of the temple (2:13–15). Solomon takes stock of the foreign labor force at his disposal and puts them to work according to the construction needs. Similar notes about aliens as laborers are made elsewhere in the Old Testament (1 Chronicles 22:2; 2 Chronicles 2:17–18; Isaiah 60:10–12).

2 CHRONICLES 3:1–4:22

TEMPLE BUILDING BEGINS

Setting Up the Section

Solomon begins construction on his temple at the site David had purchased for this very purpose (1 Chronicles 22:5).

3:1–17

THE TEMPLE STRUCTURE

Solomon began this construction project around 966 BC, about 480 years after the Exodus (according to 1 Kings 6:1, which many use to date the Exodus around 1446 BC). The temple is being built on the threshing floor of Ornan, which is located on Mount Moriah, the place where Abraham went to offer his son Isaac a thousand years earlier (Genesis 22:2–14).

The temple is ninety feet long by thirty feet wide, roughly twice the size of the tabernacle, which was forty-five feet long by thirty feet wide and fifteen feet high. All the beautiful wood they have brought from Lebanon is overlaid with pure gold (3:3–7). The Most Holy Place, or Holy of Holies, is thirty feet long by thirty feet wide. This is where the ark of God resides. The Holy Place is sixty feet long by thirty feet wide. But the whole temple area is much bigger—some fifty acres in all. Thus, this area has to be built up and secured with various structures to help support it. Today the temple area still exists, with some additions that Herod made, and is an area that is claimed as a holy site by Jews, Muslims, Christians, and Catholics (3:8).

Inside the Holy of Holies, standing above the ark of the covenant and the mercy seat, are two giant cherubim with a wing span of fifteen feet each. One of their wings touches the wing of the other, and their other wing touches the wall, thus filling the whole place (3:9–14).

The veil (3:14) separates the Holy Place from the Most Holy Place, for only the high priest is allowed to enter the Most Holy Place, and only once a year after a ceremonial cleansing. According to Jewish legend, even then the priest entered with a rope around his feet and bells on his robe; for if the bells stopped ringing, it meant God had struck him dead for being unclean.

Take It Home

In the New Testament, when Christ gives up His spirit and pays for our sins, the veil described here (3:14) is torn from top to bottom, signifying that God had opened the way into the Most Holy Place to all people (Mark 15:37–38). Now we can boldly come before God anytime we need to. There is no longer a priest who needs to intercede for us.

Two freestanding pillars flank the entrance of the temple. One pillar is named *Jachin*, to the south side, and the name means "He shall establish." The other is *Boaz*, to the north side, and the name means "In Him is strength." Thus, every time someone came to the temple, before he or she entered, they were reminded that God had established this nation, and it is only by His strength that this nation will stand. This would help the worshiper have the right perspective of things before entering the temple (3:15–17).

Critical Observation

It is unclear from the information here whether the pillars are load-bearing elements of the construction or if they are simply a part of the aesthetics. Some have imagined them as freestanding pillars with bowls at the top that could be filled with oil and thus used for lighting (much like large oil lamps).

4:1–22

THE TEMPLE FURNISHINGS

The bronze altar of sacrifice is thirty feet long by thirty feet wide and about seventeen feet high. It stands in the courtyard directly in front of the temple. The twelve bulls mentioned are probably symbolic of the twelve tribes of Israel but also demonstrate how Solomon had adopted the Phoenician symbol of fertility (the bull), representative of God's life-giving rain (4:1).

The sea of cast bronze, or the laver, is Solomon's version of the laver of bronze in Moses' tabernacle (Exodus 30:18). It is fifteen feet across, forty-five feet in circumference, and seven and a half feet deep. It can hold between twelve and fifteen thousand gallons of water. It is used by the priests for ceremonial cleansing and is located to the south side of the temple, or on the left as you walk in (2 Chronicles 4:2–5).

The ten portable lavers are used for washing. Each laver is able to hold some 230 gallons of water, and they are placed on carts for mobility. These are located on the sides of the temple, five on each side (4:6). The tabernacle only had one menorah and one table of showbread. Solomon makes ten of each, placing five on each side of the temple (4:7–8).

The court of the priests and the great courts are both mentioned in Kings (1 Kings 6:36; 7:12). The larger court is intended for the laity (2 Chronicles 4:9). The descriptions here are general.

Huram heads up the production of various articles for the temple. The casts for the temple articles are made of clay obtained in the plain of Jordan (4:10–17).

Note that they have so much bronze for use in the temple that they do not bother to weigh it (4:18). Solomon completes the work on the temple, a seven-year building project, and what a sight it must have been (4:19–22).

2 CHRONICLES 5:1–14

THE ARK ARRIVES

Setting Up the Section

With the help of a foreign king and a massive conscripted labor force, Solomon has completed the construction of the temple. Now it is time to bring the ark of the covenant into the new temple of the Lord.

5:1–10

MOVING THE ARK

The first verse of chapter 5 is a kind of transition. Once construction is complete, as described in chapter 4, Solomon moves the consecrated gifts of David to the treasuries (5:1).

The massive temple building project took seven years to complete. And now it is time to bring the ark of the covenant up from the city of David and place it in the temple. The city of David, also called Zion, was actually the easternmost hill in what we now know as Jerusalem. It was there that David had placed the ark in a tent (5:2). During the time of David, Zion was only about half of a city block wide and about two city blocks long, built upon the lower ridge of Mount Moriah.

The ark arrives at the area Solomon has built up as a site for the temple (among other structures). This area was previously known as Ornan's threshing floor. The account given here in 2 Chronicles follows almost verbatim the account given in 2 Kings 8:1–13.

The moving of the ark of the covenant takes place during the Feast of Tabernacles, which is on the fifteenth day of the seventh month (September–October), and lasts eight days. The festival proclaims God's kingship over His people and His world. The whole celebration ends with a seven-day feast as the temple is dedicated; thus, it is a fifteen-day celebration in all. As is the custom, the elders of Israel come, and the Levites take the ark according to strict rules established by God in the days of Moses (5:3–5).

Demystifying 2 Chronicles

The transportation of the ark was to be done by the Levites, the Kohathites specifically. When it was time for the children of Israel to move, the tabernacle was to be dismantled, and the Kohathites had the responsibility of caring for the ark and the other temple implements. They would walk into the Holy of Holies backwards, carrying a covering for the ark. Next they would place the covering over the ark and then lift the ark by two poles that were inserted through four rings located on the sides of the ark. The poles were then placed upon the shoulders of the Kohathites (see Exodus 25:10–16).

As the ark approaches, Solomon and the congregation of Israel assemble and make sacrifices—too numerous to count—to honor the arrival of the chariot-throne of God (5:6). The temple proper consists of two main rooms: The Holy Place is sixty feet long by thirty feet wide, and the Most Holy Place is thirty feet long by thirty feet wide. It is in the Most Holy Place, or the Holy of Holies, where the ark is to be placed (5:7). The wings of cherubim form a canopy for the ark within the Holy of Holies. Above the ark are two cherubs with their wings extending and filling the room. Each cherub has a wing span of fifteen feet (5:8).

Unlike David, whose first attempt at transporting the ark had gone awry because he failed to follow God's instructions (2 Samuel 6:6–11), Solomon transports the ark exactly as outlined in the Law of Moses. This is underscored in the events of the coming verses (2 Chronicles 5:9).

Earlier on, the ark contained the two tablets of stone in which the covenant was written, the rod of Aaron that had budded miraculously (Numbers 17:1–11), and the jar of manna (Exodus 25:16; Deuteronomy 10:2; Hebrews 9:4–5). Now only the two tablets of stone remain (2 Chronicles 5:10). The ark is relatively small: three feet nine inches long by two feet three inches wide by two feet three inches tall. The box is overlaid with gold, and the mercy seat covers the top of it. The ark contains the law of God, but God does not meet with us in the ark. Instead God meets with His children between the cherubim. This is symbolic of the fact that we cannot enter the presence of God by the law, only by His mercy. We deserve death, but God has offered us eternal life (Hebrews 9:22, 28).

5:11–14

THE COMING OF GOD'S GLORY

David had divided the priests into twenty-four divisions, each serving two weeks. After their work is done, they return to their city until the time of their next service. The priests have forty-eight Levitical cities spread throughout the land of Israel in which to live. Here, for the dedication of the temple, all who were present during this time of celebration to assist in the sacrifices (5:11).

Take It Home

As the people came together to worship the Lord, it was neither chaotic nor free-form. They sang in one accord, with one voice, and the focus was the Lord! God wants our full attention both in the silence of our own individual hearts and in the cacophony of the community. In a corporate setting, and in our own lives, worship is a reflection on God's faithfulness that refreshes us and fills us with His presence.

It is after this time of worship and praise that the Shekinah glory, the presence of God, fills the temple. In this tremendous moment for Israel, God inhabits the praises of His people (5:12–14).

The words of praise recorded in verse 13 are used at other times in the accounts of 2 Chronicles (7:3; 20:21).

2 CHRONICLES 6:1–42

TEMPLE DEDICATION

Setting Up the Section

The glory of the Lord has just filled the temple, and in response, Solomon speaks to the people and to the Lord. The account here parallels 2 Kings 8:14–21.

6:1–11

SOLOMON SPEAKS TO THE PEOPLE

Throughout the scriptures, the full glory of the Lord is shrouded from the people, because it would consume those unworthy (Exodus 33:20). The Bible says that God allows His children to see His presence through a veil, like looking through dark glasses, but one day we will see Him face-to-face, in all His glory, as we go to be with Him (1 Corinthians 13:12). Solomon explains this when he turns to address the people—that the Lord has said (see Leviticus 16:2; Psalm 97:2) He will dwell in the dark cloud (2 Chronicles 6:1–2).

When God chose David to be the first king of the Israelites, He also declared that Jerusalem would be the place for the temple. Solomon honors God by building the temple according to His instructions and choice (6:3–6). God does not allow David to build the temple because he is too busy with war. Yet God, and Solomon in this speech, honors David for having a desire to build a place that centers on the purpose of worship (6:7–8).

Take It Home

God rewards the desires of a person's heart, even those that are not realized. Jesus reminds His disciples that God will bless their hearts' desires, but He also cautions that the attitudes of their hearts will be judged. As the prophet Samuel declared when he anointed David as Israel's first king, "The Lord doesn't see things the way you see them. People judge by outward appearance, but the Lord looks at the heart" (1 Samuel 16:7 NLT).

God's faithfulness, Solomon declares, is demonstrated when He brings His promises to pass. God has honored His covenant with the children of Israel (6:9–11).

6:12–42

SOLOMON SPEAKS TO THE LORD

The picture of Solomon turning from the people to offer a prayer of dedication is striking—imagine the newly completed temple in all its beauty. Solomon takes confidence in God's future faithfulness by reflecting on His past provision (6:12–15).

Solomon asks for a conditional blessing. If Israel follows after the Lord, Solomon prays, God will bless Israel by maintaining the line of kings on the throne (6:16–17). Solomon understands that the heavens cannot contain God, and yet he asks that God look upon this city and this temple, that it will be a place where people can come together with God and repent of their sin; and when they do, God will forgive them (6:18–21).

God alone is a righteous judge—knowing the hearts and minds of people (6:22–23). Solomon considers the consequences of turning from the Lord: loss of His power and defeat by the enemy (6:24–25). Next Solomon considers how God often uses disasters to get His children's attention—such as a drought or famine, which forces people to awaken out of spiritual slumber and turn to God. Of course, in a fallen world, not all disasters are instances of God's judgment or results of sin. Sometimes the brokenness of this world reminds us of nothing else except our longing for the healing of the world to come. God is warning His people, through Solomon, that these things will come to pass if they fail to repent of their sins and cling to Him (6:26–31).

God opens the door for all to come to Him, not just the Israelites—an invitation not typically found in the Old Testament. Solomon asks the Lord to forgive all who come in repentance, even the foreigners (6:32–33). He prays that no matter where the people may be that God will hear their prayer and sustain them (6:34–35). Solomon's prayer is for mercy, because there is no one who does not sin, an idea that Paul repeats often in the New Testament (6:36).

Solomon not only foresees Israel's rebellion and exile but also hopes for her repentance. As Solomon closes his prayer, the priests are clothed in salvation and the people rejoice (6:40–42).

2 CHRONICLES 7:1–22

TEMPLE DEDICATION CONTINUES

Setting Up the Section

The Chronicler parallels 1 Kings 8:54, 62–66 in this section, but he changes the focus. Here, he emphasizes the glory of God rather than the people's blessing (the focus of the 1 Kings passage).

7:1–11

SOLOMON DEDICATES THE TEMPLE

In chapter 7, the glory of God fills the temple for a second time. The first time it is in response to worship, and this time it is in response to prayer (7:1–3). When God consumes the sacrifices, it is a sign of acceptance of those offerings. There are other examples in the Bible where this occurs. For instance, the same thing happened when the priests began their work in the tabernacle (Leviticus 9:23–24). Also, after David's unauthorized census described in 1 Chronicles, he offers sacrifices that are miraculously consumed (1 Chronicles 21:26).

The influence of David is clear in this passage. He invested heavily in the worship life of ancient Israel. He organized the worship leaders and the worship times, both day and night. He made the instruments used in worship and even wrote songs and psalms of praise to the Lord (2 Chronicles 7:6).

The bronze altar is the altar of sacrifice, which stands fifteen feet high by thirty feet long by thirty feet wide. Even so, it isn't big enough for all the sacrifices that are being offered. So Solomon sanctifies the entire outer court in order to offer all the sacrifices. The priests are in attendance for all the sacrifices and the work that needs to be done (7:7).

The feast lasts fifteen days, and as Solomon dismisses the people to their homes, they leave with joyful hearts. Even though the lessons have been difficult, God's children rejoice that God is working in them and among them (7:8–11).

7:12–22

GOD APPEARS AGAIN

Solomon's prayer is answered with a tremendous promise: God will hear His children's cry for repentance, forgive the people's sins, and heal their land (7:14). This promise is especially powerful considering that the original audience for whom the Chronicler was writing was the remnant of Jews who had returned home from their Babylonian exile. A promise of restoration would have given them great hope (7:12–14).

Demystifying 2 Chronicles

Why had these people, the original audience of the Chronicles, been exiled? Basically because of the very warning recorded here from Solomon—they had forsaken the God of their fathers and worshiped idols. In light of that, the city of Jerusalem and their temple, the very temple whose dedication this section describes, had been destroyed. Just as described in verse 20, the Israelites as a nation and a culture had become a byword to many of their neighbors. The journey of this ragtag group to reassemble as a nation is filled with hardships. In some cases, however, it is only because of these trials that God's people will turn to Him. When they do, He will protect and heal them (7:15–20).

The reason for the captivity is simple: The Israelites turned from the Lord. Solomon is warned against precisely that rebellion, and yet he and future kings do not heed this warning. May modern believers learn from their mistakes and heed the warnings of God. Solomon was praying for this very thing, and he still becomes distracted–and his fall is mighty and hard (7:21–22).

2 CHRONICLES 8:1–9:31

FLEETING GLORY

Setting Up the Section

Following God's conditional blessing of the work Solomon had accomplished, Solomon continues to build Israel's infrastructure, even receiving praise from the Queen of Sheba. And yet in the final analysis, despite his tremendous achievement and wealth, Solomon is destined to join his father in the grave.

8:1–18

SOLOMON'S ADDITIONAL ACHIEVEMENTS

Solomon spends seven years building the temple and thirteen years building his own house and administrative buildings. There is nothing wrong with building projects unless they become the focus of one's life, as with Solomon. Remember that when Solomon became king, he was just fourteen years old and dependent upon the Lord to guide him and give him wisdom to lead his people. Now twenty years have passed, and Solomon has become more self-reliant. He has placed his faith in himself instead of the Lord (8:1–8).

Critical Observation

The cities Solomon built up were located on the trade routes. Solomon used his God-given wisdom for his own personal and financial gain. Hamath Zobah was located 300 miles north of Jerusalem. Tadmor was a desert oasis located on the main highway from Mesopotamia, about 150 miles northeast of Damascus. Beth Horon was located about ten miles northwest of Jerusalem, on the border between Judah and the northern tribes. Baalath was located in the territory of Dan. These cities serve as places of prosperity and protection for the growing kingdom of Israel under Solomon's reign. Unfortunately, in many instances, the natives of the conquered cities remained and established a foothold within Israel. God had warned His people against not driving out the enemy—they posed a threat to Israel's faithfulness. But Solomon's heart was by this point focused on satisfying himself instead of obeying the Lord.

Verses 9–10 describe Solomon only using foreigners—and not his own brethren—as a forced labor force, as slaves. The children of Israel are placed in a higher position, overseeing the work (8:9–10). Later however, when the Israelites look back on Solomon's reign, they describe him as a harsh master (10:4).

Solomon recognizes that his marriage to Pharaoh's daughter is not pleasing to God. Although he is moving away from God and is aware of it, he continues going through the motions (offering sacrifices) without truly turning from his ways (8:11–15; see also 1 Samuel 15:22–23).

Take It Home

Many times God speaks to our hearts and warns us that what we are doing is wrong, and it is clear that He is not pleased with our actions. But instead of turning from what we are doing, we try to justify our actions and maybe make minor changes, as Solomon does, so that we can make ourselves look better and ease the conviction that God has placed upon our hearts. But that does not change how God feels about what we are doing. Be sensitive to His leading and then follow His direction.

The Israelites aren't a seafaring people, even though they sail and fish on the Sea of Galilee. So Solomon again hires Hiram, king of Tyre, to assist him in obtaining riches from other nations by his ships. The Phoenicians are truly a great seafaring people. These ships returned every three years full of riches and possessions from various nations. Solomon acquired 450 talents of gold from Ophir, which is quite small compared to the 3,000 talents of gold David acquired from Ophir during the same amount of time. Solomon is trying to do this by the works of his own hands rather than by the direction of the Lord. Solomon's focus is on obtaining wealth, but spiritually he is bankrupt (8:17–18; see Solomon's reflection on gold and silver in Ecclesiastes 5:10).

9:1–12

THE QUEEN OF SHEBA'S PRAISE

The Queen of Sheba travels some twelve hundred miles from Arabia to test Solomon's wisdom by asking him some tough questions. Tradition tells us that Solomon is tested with riddles. (This happens in the life of Samson as well [Judges 14].) Tradition also suggests that one of the riddles that the Queen of Sheba gives to Solomon has to do with two bouquets of flowers. One is real and the other fake. As she stands at a distance that makes it impossible to tell with the naked eye which is which, Solomon has bees released and they fly into the real flowers. Solomon solves the riddle (2 Chronicles 9:1–3).

The Queen of Sheba can't believe all she sees. Although she had been skeptical at first, the queen is now amazed at Solomon's wisdom and grandeur—so much so that she believes in God (9:4–8; Matthew 12:42).

When algum wood (or, as some translations say, juniper wood) is cut, it releases a sweet fragrance, which does not decrease in its intensity. Also, it does not rot like some wood. It is a marvelous gift (9:9–12).

9:13–28

SOLOMON'S GREAT WEALTH

Solomon places a heavy tax burden upon the people, but he does not need it any longer. The temple and the buildings are all completed, and he could have eased up on the taxation. His son, Rehoboam, is going to be asked to bring tax reform to the nation, but he refuses, and as a result, the nation is divided. Solomon's yearly income of 666 talents of gold is an interesting symbol of how wealth is often a tool used by the devil himself to corrupt even God's own servants (see Revelation 13:16–18). God is saying to Solomon and his future servants, "don't let the things of this world draw you away from serving me" (2 Chronicles 9:13–14).

The House of the Forest of Lebanon (9:16, 20) is one of Solomon's homes. This structure is 150 feet long by 75 feet wide and 45 feet tall. It is surrounded by forty-five cedar pillars, so as you look at the building, it looks like a forest. The richer the person, the more extravagant they are; they don't know what to do with their money. Solomon has his throne made of ivory, and then he goes and covers the ivory with gold. What a waste of God's money (9:15–17). Solomon's kingdom outshines any other. The people are hurting from the heavy burden of taxes, but even so Solomon is living a life of luxury (9:18–20).

Every three years ships returned from their voyages and brought back with them a huge cargo of merchandise. The common goods are no longer satisfying, and it is taking more to satisfy Solomon. The things he acquires seem to be getting more and more bizarre. This is true for anyone who turns from the Lord and tries to fill that void with other things (9:21).

Solomon is charging people to share this gift that God has given to him. God gave him this wisdom, and now he is making a profit off it. How sad when people prostitute the things that God has given to them. Greed is a terrible enemy to a relationship with God, and we see evidence of this within the church today (9:22–24). Solomon is doing everything that God told him *not* to do (Deuteronomy 17). Maybe Solomon thinks he is above the common people and that, because of his great wisdom, God no longer needs to speak to him. But he soon finds out how wrong he is and how prideful his attitude has become (2 Chronicles 9:25–28).

Critical Observation

The camel was domesticated and used for transportation by traders and merchants. They were perfectly suited to the region, because they could travel long distances through the desert without the need for water. Jerusalem was the hub between Egypt and Mesopotamia.

9:29–31

SOLOMON'S DEATH

Solomon's death marks a transition. Now his son Rehoboam is on the throne, and instead of following the spiritual influence of King David, Rehoboam continues riding the materialistic wave that began with his father, Solomon. The downward spiral that this creates in Israel will continue until their captivity.

2 CHRONICLES 10:1–11:23

POWER SHIFT

Setting Up the Section

Solomon has died, and his son Rehoboam reigns in his place. But the people are overburdened by taxes and stand ready to challenge their new leadership. The events described in this section propel Israel into a permanent state as a divided kingdom.

10:1–11:4

REVOLT AGAINST REHOBOAM

Note that Rehoboam travels to Shechem to be approved by the people as king, rather than Jerusalem where his father Solomon was anointed. Shechem was a significant place to several Jewish fathers. It was a strategic battle site as well as religious site. Abraham and Jacob built altars there (Genesis 12:6–7; 33:18–20). After the final conquest of Canaan, Joshua's covenant renewal happened there (Joshua 24).

Rehoboam, Israel's next king and the son of Solomon, reigns for seventeen years. In that amount of time, Israel deteriorates into a second-class nation. At one time, people from near and far came to see the glory of this kingdom, but that is going to change very quickly (10:1–2).

Jeroboam is a young and industrious man of whom Solomon had taken notice. Solomon placed him in charge of the labor force over the house of Joseph. It is after this that Ahijah the Shilonite, a prophet of God, meets with him in a field. Ahijah takes the garment of Jeroboam, tears it into twelve pieces, and tells him to take ten of those pieces (1 Kings 11:31–40). Solomon heard about this situation and tried to stop it by killing Jeroboam, who then fled to Egypt for safety. Now that Solomon is dead, Jeroboam returns from Egypt to Jerusalem (2 Chronicles 10:2).

Now that Rehoboam is king, the people want him to ease up on the taxation, for it is becoming a tremendous burden for them (10:3–4). Rehoboam, after hearing the requests of the people, takes three days to come to a decision—which shows his desire to make the right one. Rehoboam brings this matter first to the wise men, Solomon's counselors.

They tell the king to ease up on them and be kind to them—serve the people and they will serve the king. Often titles breed power and pride, and God is reminding His leadership to be humble and serve the people (10:5–7).

Rehoboam now consults young men to hear their counsel, for he rejects the counsel of the wise men. Although the text refers to these advisors as young men, they are no teenagers. Rehoboam has grown up with these men, and he is over forty years old himself. Nevertheless, due to inexperience, if not youth, their counsel is truly foolish (10:5–7). They tell Rehoboam to assert his authority and let the people know who is in charge (10:9–11).

The all-knowing God ordains what happens next (10:15). Rehoboam, in his pride and arrogance, thinks he is in total control, but he is completely unaware that he is going to fulfill what God had said would happen (10:12–15). The nation divides—the ten northern tribes separate from Judah and Benjamin in the south. This is a truly tragic chapter in Israel's history (10:12–16). Up to this point, both the northern and southern tribes are referred to as Israel. Here the conflicting groups are identified as the house of David and the house of Israel. Eventually, however, the northern tribes come to be known as Israel and the southern tribes come to be known as Judah, the largest of the territories there (10:16–17).

Hadoram (10:18) is sent to do the king's dirty work. But instead of paying their taxes, the northern tribes kill the messenger. Finally Rehoboam recognizes the trouble Israel is in and flees from Shechem, traveling about twenty-five miles south to Jerusalem (10:17–19).

Critical Observation

In verse 19, the term *Israel* refers to the northern tribes. The term *rebellion* is more than a description of the civil conflict. Here the northern tribes have rebelled against the covenant God had made with David, that his house would rule all of Israel.

God speaks to Rehoboam through the prophet Shemaiah and tells him to stay at home and not to fight (11:2–4). Rehoboam has developed a plan, but it is not God's plan, and he has to be redirected (Proverbs 16:9). Amazingly, he listens and obeys.

The division grieves God, and yet He allows it. The northern kingdom of Israel begins and ends in idolatry. They have no king who truly leads them in the ways of the Lord.

On the other hand, the southern kingdom of Judah is not perfect but at least has its share of godly kings who bring reform to the land. Thus, this division is healthy, in a sense, for the southern kingdom of Judah (2 Chronicles 11:1–4).

The references to Judah and Benjamin in verses 1 and 3 refer to tribes as well as locations.

11:5–23

FORTIFYING ISRAEL

In this section, Rehoboam is ready to buckle down and focus. He fortifies Judah's cities with military strength because he has legitimate concerns about his kingdom being overthrown (11:5–12).

Verses 13–17 describe the religious fallout of the civil rebellion. The Levites, who are spread throughout the land, side with Rehoboam. Jeroboam has cut them off from being priests anyway, and he sets up his own priesthood. Jeroboam is concerned that all the people might go to Jerusalem to worship God in the temple, and many won't return. So he makes two golden calves for them to worship. The priests—relieved of their duties by Jeroboam—head to Jerusalem to continue the work they are called to do. Not only do the priests begin to leave but some of the people do as well, in light of the idolatry that Jeroboam is bringing into the land (11:6–17).

The calf idols mentioned in verse 15 are reminiscent of the earlier act of rebellion in which the Israelites created and worshiped a golden calf after they left Egypt but were still on the way to Canaan (Exodus 32:1–10; Deuteronomy 9:16).

Rehoboam prepares his son Abijah to be the next king in the southern kingdom of Judah. But the king is also concerned that his sons might be murdered, so he spreads them out throughout the land to prevent them from being wiped out. Whereas Solomon's rule represents a time of great peace, the king is now afraid of rebellion from within and attack from outside. Israel has very little stability in her rebellion (2 Chronicles 11:18–22).

2 CHRONICLES 12:1–16

FURTHER TROUBLE

Setting Up the Section

In the first three years of his reign, Rehoboam walks in the way of David and Solomon, and the southern kingdom is strengthened.

12:1–12

EGYPT ATTACKS JUDAH

Rehoboam starts his regime looking to the Lord for help. He isn't a godly man, but as he takes over the kingdom, the nation is divided and he needs help. But he allows his success to deteriorate because of pride and self-reliance. The southern kingdom follows after their king, who forsakes the Lord. God brings judgment upon Rehoboam and the southern kingdom of Judah because they turned away from Him. When they looked to the Lord, the kingdom was strengthened, but now, because they have forsaken Him, the kingdom will be weak (12:1–4).

It is clear from verses 1 and 2 that Egypt's attack under Shishak is considered a judgment on the fall of Rehoboam and his people from faith. The reference to "all" of Israel in verse 1 is a reference to the southern kingdom. At this point, many of the faithful from the northern kingdom have immigrated southward. So this is a reference to all of Israel that remain in the southern kingdom of Judah.

Critical Observation

Keep in mind that the writer of Chronicles is not making a record at the time these events are happening. His audience, instead, is the last remnant of Jews who have experienced the complete fall of Judah, not just the division of the earlier kingdom. Here, as the writer recounts the beginnings of that fall, he is reminding the people of the price of disobedience.

God's prophet Shemaiah helps the king and his leaders recognize their failure and see the righteousness of God (12:5–6). God is waiting with His forgiveness, and as soon as they humble themselves before Him and repent of their sin, He forgives them (12:7). God is not going to allow Egypt to wipe Judah out, but He is going to allow them to oppress Judah. The contrast that is placed before Judah is clear: Serving a holy and merciful God is far more rewarding than serving a wicked and cruel earthly king (12:8).

Take It Home

When Shishak takes the gold shields, which may have been more a tribute paid by Rehoboam to Shishak than an actual theft, Rehoboam makes bronze shields to replace them. Bronze is worthless, but it can be polished so that from a distance it gives the appearance of gold. The king goes through all the motions, making it look like nothing has happened, and yet it is worthless. Our cover-ups cannot replace the reality of our faith lives (12:9–11).

12:13–16

THE END OF AN ERA

Rehoboam does not make it a priority to seek the Lord (12:14). God always sees the heart. Rehoboam's heart is not fixed on the Lord, and thus the fruit of his life is evil (12:12–14; see Matthew 6:21; 16:26). Moses prepared his heart before the Lord (Hebrews 11:24–26), because that was the only way to lead the nation in the right way. Rehoboam is preparing Abijah for the throne (1 Kings 15:1–8). Now he has replaced his father as king (2 Chronicles 12:15–16).

This account of Rehoboam's reign is much longer than the parallel account in 1 Kings. The extrabiblical documents listed in verse 15 may have supplied additional information. The mention of these documents reminds us that these writers were real-life people with records to keep and an interest in historical documentation.

2 CHRONICLES 13:1–14:15

CHANGING TIMES

Setting up the Section

Even as Israel experiences turmoil, power shifts, and civil war, God still works with them to restore the nation. This chapter tracks history in both the southern and the northern kingdoms of Israel.

13:1–14:1

THE REIGN OF ABIJAH

War breaks out between the northern and southern kingdoms of Israel. Abijah, king of the southern kingdom of Judah, is outnumbered two to one. Abijah tries to talk his way out of this battle, explaining that David and his descendants have the right to the throne and Jeroboam doesn't. He speaks boldly, because he knows that what he says is what God has already promised (13:1–3).

God has established the house of David to rule over the nation, and no other dynasty can rule. The covenant of salt speaks of preservation—the dynasty of David is not to end (13:4–5). Abijah blasts Jeroboam and his men for taking advantage of Rehoboam when he was young and inexperienced and leading the people into idolatry (13:6–8). The whole scene is a tragic moment for Israel as they struggle against their brothers from the northern kingdom in what is essentially a civil war.

Jeroboam has been defiant of God. He fires all the priests and makes for himself his own priesthood. To become a priest under Jeroboam, all one needs is a young bull and seven rams—Jeroboam treats it like an auction. Yet serving God is not for sale; it is a calling from God (13:9). Abijah declares that Judah has not forsaken God; their priests are of the Levite lineage, and they are doing what God has told them to do (13:10).

Abijah accused the northern kingdom of not serving God (13:10–12). As Abijah is giving this rebuke, the enemy encircles his men. They are outnumbered and surrounded. So they cry out to the Lord for help (13:13–14).

Critical Observation

Verse 12 provides a line drawn in the sand between the kingdoms as Abijah declares that God is on his side. To fight against Abijah's kingdom is to fight against God's purposes. This highlights the important of the covenant God made with David, that his house would rule forever. This covenant is Abijah's claim and his judgment against Jeroboam.

The smaller army of Judah kills over half of Jeroboam's men. God gives the southern kingdom of Judah the victory (13:15–17) and strengthens them (13:19–22). Verse 18 reveals the key to Judah's victory—they trusted God, the God of their ancestors. They were not relying on their own strength but on God's power. This statement would serve as a reminder to the original hearers of this document to return to the faith of their ancestors if they were to have any hope of reestablishing themselves as a nation.

In many ways, this period of turmoil and war with the north strengthens Judah, and when Abijah dies, his son Asa will reign over some of the most peaceful years during this era of Israel's history (14:1).

14:2–15

THE REIGN OF ASA

Asa is one of the few godly kings to rule the southern kingdom of Judah. He does what is good and right, meaning that he is not only going through the motions of serving the Lord, but his heart is in the right place as well (14:1–2). Asa brings spiritual reform to the southern kingdom of Judah, destroys the worship of foreign gods, and follows after the Lord. But, like many spiritual revivals, it does not go far enough (14:3–5).

Asa fortifies the cities of Judah and builds up Judah's army during this time of peace. When the enemy comes against them, they are prepared (14:6–7). Indeed, when Zerah the Ethiopian (or Cushite) comes, he brings an army of a million men. This far outnumbers Judah's forces (14:8–9), so Asa cries out to God for help—the key turn of events in this situation. He realizes that God does not need a whole army to win. Asa is at peace, because he trusts God (14:10–11).

Asa and the southern kingdom of Judah come home victorious in this battle against the Ethiopians. They must have been on a spiritual high. But sometimes this is when we need to be on guard, for after the victory we can easily take our eyes off the Lord. Judah has no more battles with Egypt until Josiah meets Pharaoh Neco in 609 BC (14:12–15).

Take It Home

Just as Judah, under Asa's godly leadership, prepares to meet the challenge of more invaders during a time of peace, we must practice daily the spiritual disciplines that strengthen us so that we can be ready when times of trial come. And when trials arrive, we must turn to the Lord for strength and trust that He will prevail—we will share in His victory if we are on His side.

Asa's prayer stands as a model still for us today. He acknowledges God's power, acknowledges his own helplessness and need, and then requests God's help, not on behalf of the convenience of the people but on behalf of God's glory and reputation.

2 CHRONICLES 15:1–17:19

JUDAH'S GODLY KINGS

Setting Up the Section

Asa, too, eventually becomes prideful and pursues his own desires. This does not go unnoticed by God. As the seer declares, "The eyes of the LORD run to and fro throughout the whole earth, to give strong support to those whose heart is blameless toward him" (16:9 ESV). Jehoshaphat picks up his father Asa's legacy and reigns in the fear of the Lord (17:3).

15:1–19

GODLY REFORMS

The prophet Azariah comes to Asa after this great victory and reminds him to continue walking with the Lord—warning that if he forgets to rely on the Lord for strength, God will forsake him (15:1–2).

Azariah is recounting Israel's history. Before there were priests, before there was the law, God was the one who was still faithful even though His people were not. It is as Jeremiah said, "It is of the LORD's mercies that we are not consumed, because his compassions fail not. They are new every morning: great is thy faithfulness" (Lamentations 3:22–23 KJV).

The *distress* referred to in verses 3–5 is not identified as a specific era or event in the history of Israel. Throughout the history, however, there were cycles of a falling away from the faith, the consequences that falling away incurred, and then God's deliverance of His people from the destruction faced in light of those consequences.

Azariah encourages Asa to continue in the work and to not give up. Even though the work may be difficult and seem unrewarding, the labor is not in vain, even though immediate results may not always be evident (2 Chronicles 15:3–7).

As word spreads to the northern kingdom about the spiritual reform in the southern kingdom of Judah, and how God is blessing Asa, many come down to Judah to reap some of those blessings (15:8–9). The nation comes together and they make a covenant to seek the Lord wholeheartedly. How awesome it would be if the nation did so (15:10–12).

The Israelites have good intentions, but they go too far when they put to death those who refuse to turn to God. You can't force love for God (15:13). The people come before the Lord in prayer and worship, not because they have to but because they have the desire to; it flows from their lives (15:14–15).

Asa removes Maacah, who is either his mother or his grandmother, from office because of her idolatry. His first loyalty is with the Lord; no one is given special treatment (15:16). The Asherah pole was a symbol of a Canaanite fertility god named Asherah. Moses clearly forbade the Israelites to set up any worship centers to Asherah (Deuteronomy 16:21).

Asa and the nation again enjoy a time of peace, a time to rebuild, to grow, and prepare for the coming battles. But just because he does right the first time doesn't mean he is going to continue down that path. But God is still working, molding, and shaping His servant into the leader He wants him to be (15:17–19).

16:1–14

THE EYES OF THE LORD

Baasha, king of the northern kingdom of Israel, builds up Ramah, which is located about five miles north of Jerusalem on the border between the two kingdoms and on an important trade route linking Egypt and Mesopotamia. This is to stop the migration of his people to Judah. In the process, Baasha brings his men and supplies to likely prepare for war against Judah (16:1).

Note the contrast in what Asa does here versus what he did when the Ethiopians had him outnumbered at the beginning of chapter 12. He is in trouble again, but instead of turning to God, he turns to a man. Asa takes the treasuries of God and gives them to Ben-hadad, king of Syria, to help him with his problems (16:2).

Ben-hadad has a treaty with Baasha, but he is bought out and comes to the aid of Asa. Now Baasha is down in Ramah, in the southern part of his kingdom, so Ben-hadad strikes Israel at its northern borders. The plan works. Asa is free of Baasha, but this success does not mean God is pleased (16:3–6).

God rebukes Asa through the prophet Hanani, a seer about whom we know nothing more than what is recorded here (except for a mention of his son, Jehu, in 2 Chronicles 19:2) Hanani reminds Asa that when the Ethiopians came upon him, he turned to the Lord for help. He did not place his faith in the arm of flesh (16:7–8).

Take It Home

God wants to use His people. There are three types of givers: the reluctant kind, the willing kind, and the proactive kind described in verse 9. God is not a reluctant giver—He is looking for people in whom He can invest. God is an aggressive giver. He gives to us abundantly for the work of the kingdom. But to know where He is leading means we must be in tune with Him, and we must be directed by His Spirit.

It is important to remember that 2 Chronicles 15:17 describes Asa as a person whose heart was fully committed to God. Perhaps his legacy can not be determined by any one downfall or disappointment (as is described in chapter 16). At his best moments, after all, his hope was in God's strength, not his own.

After Asa is told how God feels about what he has done, he angrily puts God's messenger in prison and oppresses those who oppose him. Let us never be so proud and arrogant that we never think we need correction (16:10).

God illustrates how trusting in the Lord as a last resort has become a pattern in Asa's life. Asa's walk with the Lord has been hampered. He no longer has an intimate relationship with the Lord, and his spiritual walk is hindered by his disease (16:11–12). Asa's life, like Solomon's, looks promising, and yet it has such low points of disappointment. At significant times he trusts more in mankind than he trusts in the Lord, particularly in the latter part of his life (16:13–14).

17:1–19

REIGNING IN GOD'S STRENGTH

Jehoshaphat does not seek Baals, (the nature gods) to make the land fertile, but instead he seeks the Lord. The Lord had told His people to not make graven images or idols for themselves (Leviticus 19:4). God is the only true God. The other gods are nothing more than demons (2 Chronicles 17:1–3).

At this time, the northern kingdom of Israel is ruled by wicked king Ahab and his wife, Jezebel. Ahab and Jezebel introduce Baal worship to the Israelites and even set up altars to worship this false god. Meanwhile, Jehoshaphat and the southern kingdom of Judah follow the Lord (17:4). Here is the difference between Solomon and Jehoshaphat: Solomon focused on riches and prosperity, while Jehoshaphat focuses on the Lord. He finds joy and peace in the ways of the Lord (17:5–6; see Genesis 15:1; Psalm 62:10; Matthew 6:33).

Critical Observation

The description of Jehoshaphat in verse 5 contains echoes of David's prayer as he dedicated the temple. He claimed God's kingdom all around with wealth (or riches) and honor. This may have been a way to affirm an answer to the prayer of David through the life of Jehoshaphat.

Jehoshaphat not only removes the idolatry from the land but he also recognizes that to successfully remove something from a person's life, you have to replace it with something else so that the person will not return to their old ways. So as he removes the false worship, he replaces it with the true worship of God. Jehoshaphat does not just condemn people for being wrong; he leads them in the ways they should go (17:7–9). Jehoshaphat enjoys times of peace and prosperity as a result of his faithfulness to God. Even the Philistines, who are a constant thorn in the side of Israel, are subdued during this time (17:10–11).

Jehoshaphat, like his father, brings spiritual reform to the southern kingdom of Judah. This brings the fear of the Lord to the kingdoms around Judah so that they do not seek war against Jehoshaphat (17:12–19).

Critical Observation

Asa's life parallels his great-grandfather Solomon's. Solomon started out young and inexperienced and asked God for wisdom to lead his people. He looked to the Lord for strength until he grew strong and wealthy. He then took his focus off the Lord as he grew confident in his own strength. Asa also takes his eyes off the Lord and places his confidence in his own strength toward the end of his life. His son, Jehoshaphat, manages to honor and seek God throughout his reign and enjoys God's blessing as a result—Judah experiences tremendous peace and prosperity once again. The eyes of the Lord are always searching for people whose hearts are loyal to use in His service, and He blesses them accordingly (16:9).

2 CHRONICLES 18:1–19:11

SEEK GOD

Setting Up the Section

Jehoshaphat allows his son Jehoram to marry the daughter of Ahab and Jezebel, the famously wicked duo of the Old Testament. As we read about the consequences of this and other choices made by Israel's leaders, we are reminded of how important it is to seek God in all our decisions.

18:1–27

A WARNING TO THE WICKED

Perhaps Jehoshaphat is trying to heal the wounds between the two kingdoms, but just as oil and water don't mix, neither do good and evil. An alliance between the two kingdoms, and between Jehoshaphat and Ahab, would be strange and unworkable (18:1).

As Jehoshaphat goes to visit Ahab, the king of Israel requests the help of Jehoshaphat in regaining Ramoth-gilead back from the Syrians (18:2). Jehoshaphat has only one request: Instead of rushing ahead, he wants to seek the Lord's will (18:3–4).

The false prophets described here are not the prophets of Baal, destroyed by Elijah at Mount Carmel prior to this time (1 Kings 18). These prophets are likely the false prophets of the calf worship that Jeroboam had established. Ahab has prophets, but not prophets of God. These men speak to please the king and use the name of God even though it is meaningless to them (2 Chronicles 18:5). Jehoshaphat recognizes that something is not right, for God has given him discernment as he looks for a true prophet of God (18:6).

Ahab is not interested in the truth. But Jehoshaphat rebukes Ahab for his harsh words against this man of God (18:7).

As both of these kings sit before the four hundred prophets, one of them, Zedekiah, grabs some horns, places them on his head, and starts charging all around the room. This is meant to show them that Ahab and his men are going to push back and defeat the Syrians. But these are not the words of God (18:8–10).

Take It Home

It is interesting that these false prophets know of Jehovah, but they do not follow after His commands (18:11; Matthew 7:23). Everyone knows that Micaiah speaks the truth of God, but they are not interested in the truth—they only want a positive message (2 Chroncles18:12). It is not always easy to speak the truth, but the heart of a true man or woman of God will always speak the truth. Our first responsibility must be to the Lord. We should not water down what we say or try to placate people. We must speak the truth in love (18:13).

The prophet says what the king wants to hear, but the king is not convinced the prophet is speaking the truth (18:14). The king picks up on the prophet's sarcasm. Ahab only wants Micaiah to speak in a convincing way (18:15). Eventually the prophet tells the king that he will be killed in the battle and that his men will be scattered. Clearly Ahab doesn't want to hear the truth, for once it is spoken, he shuns the words of the prophet and says to Jehoshaphat that he is a negative person (18:16–17).

Take It Home

Many theologians have difficulty with this passage—questioning how a holy and righteous God can send forth a lying spirit. Satan is not bound nor is his domain in hell alone (see Job 1:6). Satan and his demons will be cast from heaven, but that has not taken place yet (Revelation 12:7–9). God gives all of us a choice: If we reject the truth, then we open ourselves up to receive a lie, just as Ahab does. Ahab hears the truth, but he rejects it, and because of this he opens himself up to be deceived by the enemy (2 Chronicles 18:18–22). In this is a lesson for us all.

Zedekiah is a false prophet, and he contradicts what God has said (18:23). If someone is speaking for God, they will always speak according to His Word. And for those who speak of future events, time will tell if they speak the truth or not (18:24–27).

18:28–19:3

DEATH OF A KING

After hearing these words of Micaiah, Jehoshaphat follows after Ahab anyway, even though God tells him not to go (18:28). In this way, Jehoshaphat actually fulfills Micaiah's prophecy that he will be lured into destruction (18:20–22). Ahab, concerned that the prophecy of his death may come true, disguises himself as a regular soldier (18:29).

The king of Syria knows that if the king is killed, his army will be scattered. So he tells his men to focus on the king and destroy him. So Ahab is wise in disguising himself. Jehoshaphat works so hard to relate to Ahab, to unite the kingdom, that the enemy mistakes him for Ahab (18:30–32).

We know that nothing happens by chance, but all is ordained by God. As the archer releases his arrow, not trying for any particular target, it strikes Ahab between his armor with a mortal wound. You simply cannot escape the judgment of God no matter how hard you try (18:33–34).

As Jehoshaphat returns home, the prophet Jehu rebukes him for his actions. Jehu is the son of Hanani who rebuked King Asa of Judah when he entered into an alliance with a foreign king (16:1–9). In this case, Jehoshaphat was fellowshipping with Ahab, and it put him in a position to be led astray. But Jehu mentions the good that Jehoshaphat has done and the fact that he seeks after God, which tends to be a theme in Chronicles (19:1–3).

19:4–11

REFORMS OF JEHOSHAPHAT

During the king's absence, the people of Judah stray from the Lord. Jehoshaphat tries to get the people back on track, for without a shepherd the sheep are scattered (19:4).

As opposed to being merely representatives of the king, the judges appointed in this section represent God and His justice in the social order of Israel (19:5–7). It is crucial to have judges in office who are guided by God to deal with civil matters. Jehoshaphat seeks to restore godliness to the system in Israel since it is a nation guided by God. Note that he appoints two "attorney generals" of sorts, Amariah for religious matters and Zebadiah for civil matters (19:8–11).

2 CHRONICLES 20:1–37

THE BATTLE IS THE LORD'S

Setting Up the Section

This chapter describes how three nations rise up against the southern kingdom of Judah. This battle is not described in Kings, which parallels the same period of Israel's history. It is a powerful story distinctive to the Chronicles.

20:1–30

ENEMIES DEFEATED

Verse 1 mentions three people groups who come to make war. The third group, after the Moabites and Ammonites, is associated with the Edomites in this passage, but it is sometimes translated Menuites. While the Menuite territory was associated with Mt. Seir, a mountain range in Edom, they are a separate nation. In 2 Chronicles 26, this same people group brings a tribute to Hezekiah (26:7).

The Moabites and the Ammonites are all blood relatives of Israel. Both people groups descended from the daughters of Lot, Abraham's nephew. Their ancestors were the children of an incestuous relationship between Lot and his two daughters after the destruction of Sodom and Gomorrah (Genesis 19).

Verse 2 does mention specifically the Edomites. This nation was also related to Israel. Esau, the son of Isaac and the brother of Jacob (from whom the nation of Israel descended), is the ancestor of the Edomites (Genesis 36).

Jehoshaphat is fearful and seeks the Lord. Fear causes him to refocus on the Lord and look to Him for strength. Jehoshaphat sets out to seek the Lord and calls for a national fast (2 Chronicles 20:1–5).

Jehoshaphat brings his concerns before the Lord in a kind of prayer/speech. It is important to have a proper perspective on God, especially in the midst of battle. He is in total control; nothing happens without His knowledge and without His permission. Looking to God's history of faithfulness reminds us what He is capable of doing in our lives and gives us confidence for the situations we find ourselves in now (20:6–8).

When Solomon dedicated the temple, his prayer was that God would answer the cry of His people when they were in trouble. Jehoshaphat is echoing the prayer of Solomon here (20:9). When the Israelites had come out of Egypt, Ammon, Moab, and the Edomites had refused Israel passage through their land, and God had forbidden Israel from destroying them. Now this is how they are repaying them: They are joining forces to destroy Judah. (Edom: Numbers 20:18–20; Ammon: Deuteronomy 23:3–4; Moab: Judges 11:17–18).

Take It Home

Jehoshaphat recognizes that he cannot win on his own, and so his eyes are upon the Lord (see Psalm 46). It is when we lose the consciousness of God in our life that things get out of focus and we become anxious and terrified. Just like the Israelites, we often find ourselves surrounded by the enemy. We must remember what David said in Psalm 31:24. Cry out to God and He will remain faithful to answer your prayer (2 Chronicles 20:10–13).

God puts things in proper perspective: Through a man named Jahaziel, He reminds Israel that it's His battle (20:14–15). The battle plan is simple: Go into battle with praise and worship, and see the salvation that the Lord will bring. It seems like a foolish military plan, but God uses it to bring about a great victory (20:16–21).

Demystifying 2 Chronicles

Tekoa is located approximately twelve miles south of Jerusalem and about six miles southeast of Bethlehem. It is located on high ground between two watersheds. The area around it is referred to as the Desert of Tekoa.

As instructed, Jehoshaphat's army enters singing God's praises. The enemy, confused by the people's spirit of praise in the midst of difficulty, ends up killing one another (20:22–24). What was once the valley of the shadow of death God has now made the Valley of Beracah, or the valley of blessing (20:25–26).

When the other nations see what the Lord has done, how He fought for Judah, the fear of the Lord comes upon them. Now God gives the southern kingdom of Judah rest (20:27–30).

20:31–37

THE END OF AN ERA

Jehoshaphat is a godly king. Still he continues to make alliances with the ungodly kings of the northern kingdom in a misguided effort to bring unity between the two nations. Here he makes an alliance with Ahaziah, the son of Ahab. Treaties, however, are not going to smooth over the real differences that exist between the split nation (20:31–35).

Verse 33 reveals the continuing problem with the nation of Israel—they are still not wholehearted in their faith. Even after seeing God's provision, they had not set their hearts on God, clearing away the debris of idolatry around them (1 Kings 22:43).

God is not going to bless an endeavor with those who are rebelling against His law. Here Jehoshaphat makes an alliance with Ahaziah to gather some merchant ships, but before it even gets off the ground, God puts an end to it, refusing to bless the venture (20:36–37).

2 CHRONICLES 21:1–28:27

TURNING FROM GOD

Setting Up the Section

This section marks the end of two generations of spiritual reform in the southern kingdom of Judah under Asa and his son, Jehoshaphat, and the beginning of a period of turning from God.

21:1–20

JEHORAM'S WICKED LEGACY

The people and things you surround yourself with always affect your own walk of faith. Such was the case with Jehoram, the next king of Judah. In this section, the wickedness that flows from Ahab and Jezebel, rulers of Israel, not only affects their daughter, Athaliah, who becomes Jehoram's wife, but also the king himself.

Though Jehoram was preceded by a father and grandfather who led Judah to faith and prosperity, he instead begins his reign with the murder of his brothers (to remove competition for the throne) and leads the people of Judah into idolatry (21:1–6).

God could choose to destroy Jehoram, and thus the reign of a descendant of David, because of Jehoram's wickedness. Instead He honors His promise to David to establish his throne forever (2 Samuel 7:13; 1 Kings 15:4–5; 2 Kings 8:19; 1 Chronicles 17:4–14). Nevertheless, judgment does come upon the nation by various nations rising up against them (2 Chronicles 21:7–11).

Some have called into question the authorship of the letter attributed to Elijah in verses 12–15, since Elijah's death had been recorded in 2 Kings during Jehoshaphat's reign. Others point out, however, that Jehoram and Jehoshaphat ruled together for a time. Elijah would have been elderly but could have been alive long enough to be aware of Jehoram. The text does not say what affliction Jehoram is struck with, but it is serious enough to cause him a slow death (21:12–15).

Critical Observation

Just as Jehoram experienced God's judgment in the form of a physical ailment, so did Asa, the king of Judah who suffered from a foot disease but refused to ask for God's help (16:12–14), and Uzziah, the king of Judah who was cursed with a skin rash (26:16–19).

The reference in verse 13 to the people of Judah prostituting themselves is a reference to their idolatry. They were spiritually unfaithful to God because they mingled their religion with the Canaanite religions around them.

Jehoram only reigns for eight short years, and in his death there is no great burning of incense like they do for the other kings, the ones they loved. In fact, the scriptures say the people didn't care that he died, and they had no sorrow. A person living in sin is affected emotionally, spiritually, and even physically (21:16–20).

22:1–9

AHAZIAH'S FAMILY OF STRIFE

Families can be forces for good and supportive environments, or they can be sources of great strife, bad influences, and true tragedy. Athaliah greatly influences her son to rule wickedly. Ahaziah saturates himself with evil counselors, including his mother, and that is what flows from his life (22:3–4).

Demystifying 2 Chronicles

In 2 Kings 8:26, we are told that Ahaziah is twenty-two years old when he becomes king (not forty-two years old, as is stated here in 2 Chronicles). Scholars agree that it seems likely the copyediting error is here in 2 Chronicles (22:1–2).

This minor discrepancy is often cited as evidence that the Bible, especially the Old Testament, is unreliable. The earliest manuscripts of the Old Testament still in existence today are from the Dead Sea Scrolls, which date around 125 BC. In comparing those scrolls with a scroll of Isaiah from 900 AD, scholars find only 5 percent variation, consisting chiefly of spelling differences. No significant change in meaning is found. The scriptures have been one of the most highly analyzed books of antiquity and are found to be one of the most reliably and carefully transmitted works available today.

The relationships in the intermarriages between the rulers of Israel in the north and the rulers of Judah in the south are becoming increasingly messy. Acting to fulfill a prophecy that predicts he will become king, Jehu goes on a killing spree—he kills Joram, king of Israel; then he kills forty-two of Ahaziah's brothers; and finally he kills Ahaziah. This places Jehu on the throne in the northern kingdom of Israel, and in the southern kingdom of Judah the throne is vacant (22:6–9).

22:10–23:15

ATHALIAH'S LEGENDARY WICKEDNESS

Once Athaliah gets word that her son is dead, instead of mourning, she kills all the royal heirs and is now going to assume the role as king. This is a direct attack on God's promise to David that his descendants will rule forever. Note that with the other rulers, the Chronicler bookends their accounts with a kind of "stats" report. In Athaliah's case, however, no such stats appear. This provides a statement of a lack of credibility for her reign.

By God's grace, Athaliah has not been entirely successful in her campaign to wipe out the heirs to the throne, and the Davidic dynasty barely survives once again. This time the only surviving heir is one-year-old Joash. Joash is hidden by his aunt for six years in one of the chambers that surrounds the temple (22:10–12).

The Zodakite priest Jehoiada resists Athaliah even as he is raising the hidden heir to the throne. He raises support for reform both in the temple and politically, but it is still risky business to restore the throne to someone from the line of David. Extreme measures are taken to protect the young heir, who is the final link to the Messiah that God had promised (23:1–8).

Jehoiada influences Joash in a positive manner. As he is proclaimed king, he is given a copy of the Law of God, the first five books of Moses, so that he can read and apply them to his life. Joash is only seven years old at the time he takes the throne from Athaliah. Note the irony in verse 13 as Athaliah cries treason—she who usurped the throne and committed murder to attempt to ensure her power. While Jehoiada is credited with Joash's rise to the throne, it seems clear that the coup had both religious and political roots (23:9–15).

23:16–24:27

JOASH: YOUNG AND IMPRESSIONABLE

Jehoiada makes a covenant that Judah will once again be the Lord's people. The sacrificial system is brought back, as God is truly worshiped once again. Jehoiada is a positive influence on young King Joash and the entire kingdom of Judah (23:16–18).

The gatekeepers are needed not only to prevent anything that is unclean from entering and defiling the temple but also to allow those who belonged in the temple to freely enter (these people had not succeeded in protecting Israel from Athaliah). Now that the proper king, Joash, a descendant of David, is in place, peace returns to the land for a brief period (23:16–21).

At this point, high priest Jehoiada is truly the power behind the throne. He is a good role model for Joash, and the people of Judah are blessed by his actions (24:1–3). Joash wants to rebuild and repair the temple of God, and he sets the Levites in charge of this project. But they don't do it quickly and are dragging their feet, moving at a snail's pace. They have no heart to restore the worship of God (24:5–6). Athaliah and her sons plundered the house of God, and now it is time to restore and rebuild what she destroyed (24:6–7).

Demystifying 2 Chronicles

Verse 7 refers to Athaliah's sons, yet part of the history recorded is that Athaliah murdered any possible rivals to the throne. We don't know the exact use of this expression. It could be that her sons had a part in the plans for destroying the temple, or it could be that the term *sons* is used of Athaliah's followers.

Joash has a box placed outside the temple so that the people can give extra money to God for this restoration project. A half-shekel is already given each year, by every male over twenty years old, for the upkeep of the tabernacle and later the temple (Exodus 30). Now the people have a way to give more if they desire, and the people respond with a willing spirit by rejoicing in the opportunity to participate in the Lord's work (2 Chronicles 24:8–14).

Jehoiada dies once he has completed the work he was called to do (24:15–16). The description of his old age in verse 15 signifies honor and respect. He was a positive influence in the life of Joash, and the nation was blessed by God as a result. His burial is in sharp contrast to that of Jehoram. Jehoiada is buried with the kings because the people loved him for bringing spiritual reform to the nation and for putting God back on the throne (24:15–16).

Joash is like a spiritual chameleon, changing his behavior to fit those who are around him. Joash never really had a heart for the Lord—he is more influenced by others. God's desire is not to bring judgment and destroy Joash but to see him turn from his evil ways and live. In light of this, God sends prophets to warn him, but Joash refuses to heed their warnings (24:17–19).

Critical Observation

Asherah, the false god mentioned in verse 18, is a fertility goddess of the Canaanite religions and mythologies. Often associated with Baal, her shrines took the form of upright wooden poles. The tree was a symbol associated with Asherah worship.

Zechariah must have been like a brother to Joash, because they grew up together. Joash has a choice to heed the warnings from this close confidant, but instead he orders the death of Zechariah to be carried out at the very place he was anointed king by Jehoiada. It is a terrible sign of how quickly our hearts can forget. Oftentimes—even when we speak the truth in love—the truth is the opposite of what people want to hear (24:20–22).

Chronicles again equates the military defeat of Judah—at the hands of the Syrians—with the judgment of God against Joash's sin. This is meant to both remind and warn the remnant of Israel, who is the audience for the book. Just like with the other evil kings, no fanfare is given in Joash's death, which transpired at the hands of his own servants. He is not even buried with the other kings—a stark contrast to how his mentor was celebrated in his death (24:23–24).

25:1–28

AMAZIAH'S HARD HEART

Amaziah is not wholeheartedly devoted to the Lord, although he responds to the prophetic warning properly. This is an idea Jesus returns to when He speaks of those who honor God with their lips and yet their hearts are far from Him (Matthew 7:21–23). Amaziah executes those who murdered his father, which is considered a relatively mild reaction when compared to the customs of other kings at the time. He honors the laws of Moses by sparing the children, and in fact the Chronicler quotes the Mosaic Law in verse 4 (Deuteronomy 24:16; 2 Chronicles 25:1–5).

Amaziah hires 100,000 mercenaries from Israel to assist him in battle. But a prophet of God warns him not to receive help from Israel, for God is not with them. If he uses Israel to help him, they will be defeated. Amaziah is torn—he wants God's help, but he also wants the money (25:6–9).

God gives Amaziah and the children of Judah a great victory over the Edomites, even without the help of the dismissed mercenaries. These soldiers-for-hire lose the chance to add to their fee by taking spoils from the battle. On their way home to Israel, the mercenaries attack some of the cities and villages in Judah, getting back some of the spoil that they would have gained if they had been able to fight against the Edomites (25:10–13).

In response to Judah's God-granted victory, Amaziah immediately strays, gathers the gods of the people he has just defeated, and brings them home with him. In doing this, he is now worshiping these gods. God is gracious and sends a prophet to warn the king of his destructive ways. However, Amaziah has hardened himself so much to God that he is unwilling to heed the prophet's warning. Instead, he prepares to avenge what the mercenaries have done to his people by fighting the northern kingdom (25:14–17).

Demystifying 2 Chronicles

Amaziah's looting of the temple idols in verse 14 is not uncommon. At the time, these were considered war trophies. First Samuel, in fact, describes a time when the Israelite's ark of the covenant was captured and held on display by the Philistines (1 Samuel 5:1–2). Amaziah's worship of these gods, however, clearly disregarded God's commands and set him on a path of destruction.

The king of the northern kingdom of Israel is a different Joash than Amaziah's predecessor. The king of Israel cautions Amaziah against attacking them, reminding him that his victory against the Edomites was God's doing. As we watch yet another rebellious and wicked king lead the Israelites into trouble, we are struck by the Chronicler's explanation that Amaziah's hardness of heart is from God. As a result, Judah is defeated because of its sin (25:18–22). Not only is the house of God plundered, but so, too, is the king's house, and many are taken away captive as slaves (25:23–24).

Take It Home

Sin destroys your defenses, just as Israel destroyed six hundred feet of the wall of Jerusalem (25:23). The suffering of Judah reminds us of the consequences of sin—it affects our worship of God, destroys and robs us of our witness, and eventually enslaves us completely. Amaziah has led the people astray, and their anger burns into a murderous rage. His sin has pushed them over the edge and bred their own sinfulness (25:25–28).

26:1–23

UZZIAH: THE PROUD KING

People recognize that Amaziah's heart is far from the Lord, and during his reign, after only six years, his son Uzziah begins to co-reign with him. For twenty-three years they reign together. Then after his father's death, Uzziah is the sole king in the kingdom of Judah, reigning for another twenty-nine years. Uzziah is a good king and a strong leader, which is the reason the people place him on the throne at the age of sixteen (26:1).

After the death of his father, Uzziah begins to recapture cities that were lost to the enemy and restore them or build them up. The nation enjoys a time of prosperity, not because Uzziah is doing good works but because he places God before everything else in his life (26:2–5). God has begun to once again bless the southern kingdom of Judah with victory over their enemies. The Chronicler emphasizes this again and again: When the Israelites seek God, they become mighty (26:6–8). Under Uzziah's leadership, the people begin to honor God and also return to cultivating the land. As a result, it truly blossoms once again (26:9–10).

Uzziah is able to achieve success in three areas: victory in war, massive building projects, and making the land fruitful again. The strength of his army and his ability to develop weapons of war also help to put down the enemy (26:11–15). In fact, Uzziah becomes too self-important for his own good. He is a king, not a priest, and thus not allowed in the temple to offer incense to the Lord. But, because of his pride, he approaches God without humility. As a result, God strikes him with leprosy, and he is banished from the city, forced to co-reign with his son, Jotham (26:16–23).

Take It Home

Many today try and do what Uzziah did—approach God any way they desire. The story follows Uzziah from power to pride to his downfall. His strength is his weakness (Proverbs 16:18–19; 18:12). When we become proud, God always has a way to humble us and give us the right perspective again. We are strong when we look to the Lord for our strength in humility (2 Corinthians 12:10).

27:1–9

JOTHAM: A FORCE FOR GOOD

In contrast to the mixed records of his predecessors, Jotham is a good king. The Chronicler is almost completely positive about his reign. His only flaw is that he avoids the temple, most likely because he witnessed what happened to his father, Uzziah. Tragically, this kind of reluctance is common even today; children see what has happened to their parents in church and retreat or isolate themselves from any kind of Christian fellowship (27:1–2; see Hebrews 10:24–25).

Ophel is where the old city of David was located, farther down the slope of Mount Moriah (2 Chronicles 27:3). Jotham looks to the Lord for guidance, but he never really has a true heart of worship. Still, his victory over the Ammonites highlights God's approval of him (27:4–6).

As Ahaz, Jotham's son, takes the throne, Judah is at a relatively good place. Unfortunately, whatever strides were made toward the Lord are going to be pushed back by the new king. The kingdom of Judah will never fully recover from the influences of King Ahaz (27:7–9).

28:1–27

AHAZ: INFIDELITY AND DEFEAT

When God associates a king with the kings of Israel, it is a rebuke. Ahaz is just as wicked as the northern kings were. He is not at all like David, the standard for all kings to be judged by. Ahaz goes crazy and sets up places of false worship, offering sacrifices to pagan gods, and even offering his own children in the fire as a sacrifice to them (28:1–4).

Demystifying 2 Chronicles

The sacrifice of unwanted children was a pagan ritual mentioned elsewhere in scripture (Leviticus 18:21; Deuteronomy 12:31; 2 Kings 16:3). The place where they offer these children to the god Molech, by passing them through the fire, is located in the valley of Hinnom, which is just south and west of Jerusalem. In the New Testament, this area is used as a garbage dump, which continued to burn day and night. Jesus uses the valley of Hinnom as an illustration of hell, Gehenna (Matthew 10:28).

God now brings judgment upon Ahaz and Judah for their wickedness. He uses the Syrians and the northern kingdom of Israel to carry out His judgment. But Israel goes overboard and takes back home with them many slaves, which God forbids (28:5–8).

The prophet Oded rebukes Israel for thinking that they are better than Judah. The people in Samaria actually obey the prophet's warning (28:9–10). These leaders are wise in what they say. They recognize that they are not perfect, that the nation has many problems, and by continuing to disobey God's commands, they are fearful that they will just add to their sin and judgment (28:11–13).

It was a common practice to humiliate captives, and many times they took them away naked. But now they are given clothes and food, and the weak are even given donkeys to ride on so they can make their way home. The Israelites do the right thing in releasing their captives (28:14–15). Ahaz and the kingdom of Judah are being attacked from every side. You would think this would at least get Ahaz's attention, but the king's heart is so hard that he refuses to listen to the warnings. He shuts his eyes to the truth (28:16–21).

As the pressure from God increases, Ahaz hardens his heart even more and refuses to look to God. Ahaz is sincere in his walk with these other gods, just as many people are today (28:22–23). Because the king doesn't hear from the true and living God, he makes sure that no one else hears either, and he blocks the house of God so no one can enter.

In Ahaz's death, Hezekiah will now reign in Judah. Although he is truly a great king, he will not be able to overcome the spiritual darkness that was blanketed by his father, king Ahaz. The kingdom of Judah is only about 110 years away from the Babylonian invasion. Even one bad leader can affect the course of a nation for hundreds of years and generations to come (28:24–27).

2 CHRONICLES 29:1–32:33

HEZEKIAH: A GOOD KING

The Temple Restored	29:1–36
Passover Observed	30:1–27
The Reforms of Hezekiah	31:1–21
Humility Rewarded	32:1–33

Setting Up the Section

Judah never fully recovers from Ahaz's negative influence, and judgment in the form of the Babylonian captivity is looming a mere 110 years down the road. Even a good king, like Hezekiah, cannot reverse their path away from the Lord.

29:1–36

THE TEMPLE RESTORED

Hezekiah is probably the best king since the time of David. He brings spiritual reform to the nation, and he is also able to remove the idols that had crept into the people's practice of worship, including the bronze serpent that Moses had used to challenge the people to stop grumbling in the desert following their deliverance from captivity in Egypt (Numbers 21:4–8; 2 Kings 18:1–4). It's been about eight hundred years since their ancestors wandered in the wilderness, and the people are now worshiping this bronze serpent on a pole (2 Kings 18:4).

Hezekiah is sandwiched between his father, Ahaz, who was Judah's worst king up to that point, and his son, Manasseh, who also followed evil ways. Yet clearly God is the focus of Hezekiah's life. Isaiah the prophet influences his life in a positive manner

(Isaiah 36–39). Hezekiah wastes no time in bringing forth spiritual reform to the nation, beginning with the reopening of the house of worship, the temple. He begins immediately to cleanse, repair, and restore it to usher in an era of spiritual revival (2 Chronicles 29:3). Under his father, the temple had become a place to store junk—an appropriate metaphor for the clutter in the hearts of the people. Hezekiah is ready to de-clutter (29:4–5).

Hezekiah asserts that Judah is under judgment for its neglect of the temple—including the rituals that God had given the people to remember His faithfulness, such as lighting the menorah (29:6–9). Hezekiah is going to gather the religious leaders to see that they get right with God and to consecrate their hearts before the Lord (29:10–11; Hosea 4:6).

It takes sixteen days to clean the temple proper and to restore the house of God to a place of worship. Imagine the amount of garbage that needed to be hauled out. This is a major project of restoration (29:18–19). The ceremony of restoring the temple consists of three crucial parts: atonement sacrifices brought by the leaders, arrangement of music, and sacrifices of thanksgiving from the people. Hezekiah orders sacrifices to be offered for *all of Israel*—an expression that, from here on, the Chronicler uses to refer to Judah together with the refugees from the northern tribes. The entire process—propelled by God's Spirit and blessing—takes less than three weeks (29:20–36).

30:1–27

PASSOVER OBSERVED

The northern kingdom of Israel has been carried away captive by the Assyrians for their idolatry. Only a few people remain in the land, and Hezekiah reaches out to them and urges them to get right with God. Hezekiah began his reign the first month of the ecclesiastical (or religious) year, which was the month of Nisan, or March/April. Now the Passover was also celebrated in the month of Nisan. The problem was that the temple was not cleaned until the sixteenth of the month, and Passover began on the fourteenth of the month, followed by the Feast of Unleavened Bread. God made a provision to the people, through Moses, that if they could not celebrate Passover in the first month, they could celebrate it on the fourteenth day of the second month, so this is precisely what Hezekiah begins to institute (Numbers 9:9–11). The king also invites those who have escaped from the hands of the Assyrians in the northern kingdom, not only to join in the Passover celebration but to return to the Lord and restore unity to the kingdom (2 Chronicles 30:1–9).

Even after many have been carried away captive, some Israelites in the north still refuse to repent of their sin. They laugh in the face of God. Some do respond and go to Jerusalem to celebrate the Passover. In Judah, they experience unity in the Lord, which unites them as one nation (30:10–12).

Demystifying 2 Chronicles

During the feast of Passover you were to take your own lamb, without spot or blemish, and sacrifice it yourself (Deuteronomy 16:16–17). The problem was that many of the people had not ceremonially cleansed themselves, and so the Levites sacrificed the lambs for those who were unclean. These people were seeking God, and thus, they just came as they were. Hezekiah understood that it is not the religious ritual that makes one acceptable to God; it is a matter of the heart (2 Chronicles 30:13–20).

When true revival breaks out, God often gives new songs, as happens here. Studying the Word of God also becomes a focus again. The energy is so amazing that they extend their celebration, and Hezekiah gives out of his own possessions unto the Lord (30:21–24).

When your eyes are focused on the Lord, you can't help but rejoice. You have the right perspective on life (30:25–27).

31:1–21

THE REFORMS OF HEZEKIAH

The spiritual revival is leading now to social changes, as the false worship places are destroyed—and along with them all the sexual perversion and carnality that accompanies them. This is not only affecting the southern kingdom of Judah but has also spread northward, into Israel. Hezekiah is following the example that David laid out regarding temple service for the priests. Each division serves for two weeks out of the year in the temple, and the rest of the time they minister to those in their hometown. Remember that during the time of David, the priests were spread out throughout the land of Israel in forty-eight Levitical cities so that no one was more than a day's journey from a priest. Hezekiah leads by example. He gives to the work of God, and he is encouraging the people to do the same (31:1–4).

When people's hearts are touched by God, they willfully and joyfully give. For four months, the people keep bringing gifts to help support the priests and their families, so much so that it is in heaps. The priests and Levites are blessed beyond measure—they have more than they need (31:5–15; Ephesians 3:20).

Hezekiah makes sure everyone gets what is rightfully his or hers. Throughout the land, anyone who works in the temple receives a portion for every family member over three years old (31:16–19). (Children younger than three were still nursing, but once they were weaned from breast milk, they received their portion). Hezekiah and the nation prosper, because his heart is set on doing what is right before the Lord. His eyes are properly focused on God, and his priorities are right. He puts God first in his life (31:20–21).

32:1–33

HUMILITY REWARDED

King Ahaz, Hezekiah's father, had made a treaty with Tiglath-pileser, king of Assyria, for protection (2 Kings 16:7). Now that Hezekiah is on the throne, he breaks any treaties that his father had made (2 Kings 18:7). Jerusalem has two main sources of water, the spring of Gihon in the Kidron Valley and the spring of En-Rogel, which was two miles to the south. Hezekiah has two groups of workers—one group working from the spring of Gihon, digging a tunnel through solid rock toward the city, and another group digging from the pool of Siloam out of the city. His goal is to bring the water supply into the city. And this tunnel, which is some 1,777 feet long, is a constant source of fresh water. This tunnel Hezekiah builds exists in Israel to this day (32:1–4).

Hezekiah fortifies the city, builds what was broken, builds towers on the walls, and prepares weapons for war. Hezekiah does all that he can do, and then he commits the rest to God. Hezekiah not only strengthens himself but his people as well—by sharing with them the Word of God (32:5–8).

Lachish is about thirty miles southwest of Jerusalem. It's from this nearby location that Sennacherib, the king of Assyria, sends his representatives to Jerusalem to give the Israelites an ultimatum to surrender or die fighting. Intimidation plays a big role in what the Assyrians are doing. Rabshakeh, the field commander—not understanding why Hezekiah had removed the places of false worship—tells them that their God is not going to spare them when their own king has destroyed all the high places. Rabshakeh is comparing the God of Israel with other gods. However, this only reveals his ignorance of the God of Israel (32:9–15). As Rabshakeh speaks his threats in their native tongue, Hebrew (2 Kings 18:26), he is trying to also intimidate the crowd (2 Chronicles 32:16–19).

Hezekiah and Isaiah are prayer partners, lifting their concerns up to the Lord, the only one who can truly help them and give them peace in the middle of this storm. One angel wipes out 185,000 Assyrians in one night, so that when Israel wakes that morning, they see all the dead bodies of their enemy. Not bad for one night's work. Sennacherib, king of Assyria, heads home in retreat and goes into his temple to worship his god, and while he is there his two sons kill him (32:20–23).

With the southern kingdom of Judah victorious, Hezekiah is exalted, and this may be the spark that sends him on a downward trend. The account in Chronicles of Hezekiah's pride is fleshed out in more detail in 2 Kings 20 and Isaiah 38. First his pride begins to build, but Hezekiah recognizes it and repents of it. Because of that, God says judgment will not come in his days but in future generations. Again Hezekiah greatly prospers, which again leads to pride in his life. As these ambassadors from Babylon come, he opens all the storehouses and shows off his wealth. Isaiah tells him he acts foolishly and warns of the coming captivity (Isaiah 39:6–7). Hezekiah is truly a great king and comparable to king David in his actions. However, even his godly reforms are not enough to rescue the future of a rebellious people (2 Chronicles 32:24–33).

2 CHRONICLES 33:1–36:23

RAPID DECLINE

Setting Up the Section

The account of Manasseh in 2 Kings 21:1–18 is harsher than this one. The writer of Chronicles wants to emphasize to his audience that even the worst sinner can be forgiven and restored through repentance and faith. However, we also witness Israel's rapid decline before their eventual defeat at the hands of the Babylonians.

33:1–20

MANASSEH'S SINFUL REIGN

Manasseh was arguably the most wicked king in Judah's troubled history. Manasseh destroys the reforms of his father with remarkable speed. He even goes as far as setting up an idol in the Holy of Holies, sacrificing his children to the god Molech, and going after all the abominations that the nations who were driven from the land practiced (33:1–9).

God's mercy is unbelievable. Manasseh should have been wiped out, and yet God is calling to him, trying to get him to listen and gain the attention of the nation, but he refuses. Tradition tells us that during Manasseh's reign, he takes Isaiah the prophet captive, places him in a hollowed out log, and saws him in two pieces. He does not want to hear what the prophets have to say, for they go against what he is doing. Since he refuses to listen to the prophets, God tries to get his attention by taking him captive by the Assyrians. They place hooks in his nose and fetters on him, and carry him away to Babylon. This is exactly what Manasseh needs to turn to God. Manasseh's conversion is very similar to that of Nebuchadnezzar, king of Babylon. Nebuchadnezzar's pride brings him to a state of madness until he finally looks up to the true and living God (33:10–20).

33:21–35:27

FAITH IN THE FACE OF NEARING JUDGMENT

Amon, Manasseh's son, is also a wicked king, and he is spinning out of control. Amon does not repent of his sin but remains lost, moving in the opposite direction of God. The die is cast, and the nation sinks lower and lower, drowning in its wickedness. Amon is only king for two years before his own men assassinate him (33:21–25).

With Amon's death, Josiah becomes king and brings about the last revival before the southern kingdom of Judah is taken into captivity by the Babylonians. It is thirty-four years before Babylon's first invasion of Judah. Israel has already been in Assyrian captivity for eighty years. God brings judgment upon the northern kingdom of Israel via military defeat and enslavement, and Judah still does not repent. Since the split, Judah has had five good kings who try to steer the nation back toward God—Asa, Jehoshaphat, Joash, Hezekiah, and now Josiah.

Critical Observation

Josiah takes the throne in Judah when he is only eight years old. Then, when he turns sixteen, he begins to seek the Lord with all his heart. By the time he is twenty years old, he is purging the land of all the false worship that his grandfather, Manasseh, had started. Jeremiah's ministry begins in Josiah's thirteenth year as king, when Josiah is twenty-one years old, and continues some forty-one years—into the Babylonian captivity. Josiah is the fulfillment of a prophecy from three hundred years earlier (1 Kings 13:1–2), when God calls Josiah by name (2 Chronicles 34:1–7).

Shaphan goes throughout all Judah and Israel collecting money for the restoration of the temple, and when he is finished, he brings the offering to Hilkiah, the high priest. Now the massive temple restoration project begins. As they purge the temple of garbage, Hilkiah finds a copy of the books of Moses (34:8–15). Josiah tears his clothes because the Word of God pierces his heart. He understands why judgment has come upon God's people. Josiah rightly recognizes that not only he stands guilty before God but so does the entire nation (34:16–19).

Josiah wants Hilkiah and his men to go to Huldah, the prophetess, to inquire of God in what they should do next. Their sin is exposed and they need wisdom (34:20–22). Huldah tells them God will spare Josiah; however, judgment is still coming for the nation—God is not convinced that their hearts are sincere. Jeremiah describes Judah's reform as pretense rather than wholehearted repentance (Jeremiah 3:10). God rebukes Judah for her false loyalty (Jeremiah 7:8). The temple and the rituals of faith have become a false mask for the people's true convictions (2 Chronicles 34:23–28). Instead of giving up in the face of coming judgment, Josiah leads the people by giving them the Word of God and being an example to them (34:29–33). Just as his great-grandfather Hezekiah had done, Josiah reinstitutes the Passover celebration. Josiah also follows in his forefather's footsteps by properly organizing the priests (1 Chronicles 24; 2 Chronicles 8:14). He is generous with his own resources and models the heart of a shepherd caring for his flock (35:1–9).

The people celebrate the Passover with urgency, just as they did in Egypt during the first Passover (Exodus 12:11). The priests serve everyone, just as Christ will one day offer Himself for the salvation of the world (Mark 10:45). This Passover celebration is even bigger than Hezekiah's (35:10–19).

It is 610 BC, and the Assyrian Empire is on the decline. Nineveh has fallen to the Babylonians in 612 BC, forcing the Assyrians to concentrate their forces around Haran and Carchemish, in the area of the upper Euphrates River. Egypt also is weak and ineffective. So Pharaoh Neco is coming to Carchemish to make an alliance with Assyria to fight off the Babylonians. Pharaoh Neco warns Josiah not to get involved in this battle, but Josiah does not listen. It costs him his life. Josiah was truly a godly king, but he had his weaknesses as well (35:20–27).

36:1–23

INEVITABLE EXILE

The Chronicler quickly traces the reign and disobedience of Josiah's three sons (Jehoahaz, Johoiakim, and Zedekiah) and his grandson (Jehoiachin). The account is expanded on in Kings (2 Kings 23:31–24:20), but here it underscores how the Israelites are tumbling ever nearer to the inevitable exile from the promised land (36:1–14).

Critical Observation

The southern kingdom of Judah was in captivity for seventy years because of their idolatry and failure to follow God. God had lead them into the promised land and commanded them to work there for six years, allowing the land rest every seventh year—a year of sabbatical that was meant to purge and restore, and during which time all debts were forgiven. But the Israelites neglected to obey God's command for 490 years. Scholars note that God gave the land its seventy years of rest and taught His people about trusting in Him during their time in captivity.

The events of this chapter coincide with Jeremiah's prophecy. Often nicknamed "the wailing prophet," Jeremiah is crying out that it is all over and to not fight against the Babylonians, for this is of God (Jeremiah 21:3–10). The nation is sinking deeper and deeper into idolatry, becoming more wicked, even after the judgment of God has begun. God tries to warn them over and over again by sending them prophets, but they refuse to listen and mock the messengers of God. God's long-suffering has come to an end, and the people and the nation have come to the point of no return (Jeremiah 32:1–5). The time is now 586 BC, and the Babylonians make their final invasion into Jerusalem, destroying the city, the temple, and taking with them the rest of the people, killing many. Zedekiah and his sons are captured. Then the Babylonians put out the eyes of Zedekiah—the last thing he sees before being led away captive to Babylon is the death of his sons, who are executed before his eyes (2 Chronicles 36:15–21).

The Chronicler is careful to emphasize one final time the main theme of his account—the faithfulness of God. This passage is very similar to the opening of Ezra (Ezra 1:1–4), and Cyrus's release of Israel is intended to allow them to reenter the land that God has given them and rebuild the temple (2 Chronicles 36:22–23).

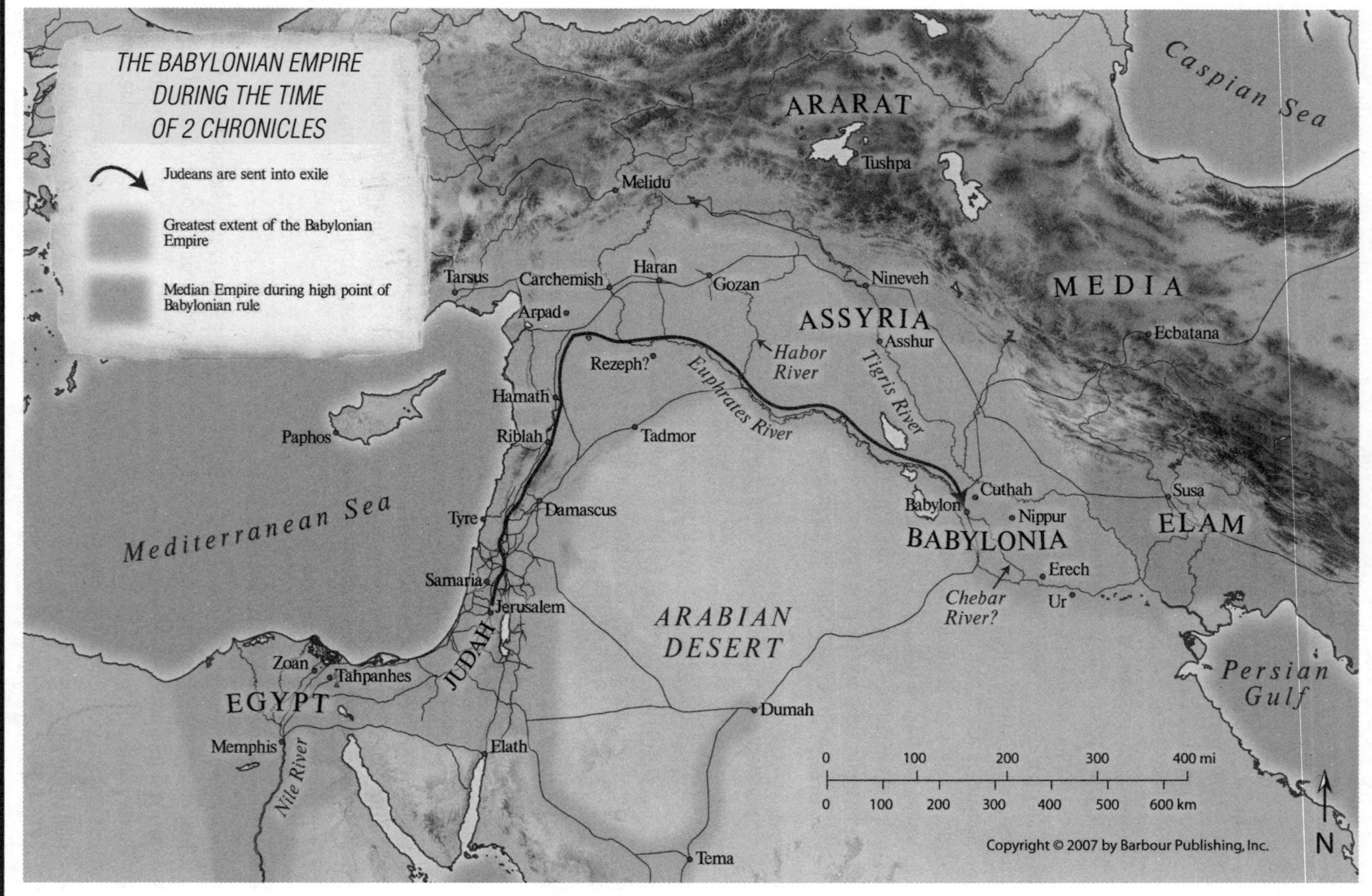

THE BABYLONIAN EMPIRE DURING THE TIME OF 2 CHRONICLES
Judeans are sent into exile
Greatest extent of the Babylonian Empire
Median Empire during high point of Babylonian rule
ARARAT
Caspian Sea
Tushpa
Melidu
Tarsus
Carchemish
Haran
Gozan
Nineveh
MEDIA
Arpad
ASSYRIA
Asshur
Ecbatana
Rezeph?
Habor River
Tigris River
Euphrates River
Hamath
Riblah
Tadmor
Paphos
Mediterranean Sea
Tyre
Damascus
Cuthah
Babylon
Nippur
Susa
BABYLONIA
ELAM
Samaria
Jerusalem
Erech
Ur
Chebar River?
ARABIAN DESERT
Zoan
Tahpanhes
JUDAH
EGYPT
Dumah
Persian Gulf
Memphis
Nile River
Elath
Tema
0 100 200 300 400 mi
0 100 200 300 400 500 600 km
N

EZRA

INTRODUCTION TO EZRA

The book of Ezra is a chronicle of hope and restoration. Originally, Ezra and Nehemiah were together as one book, recording the stories about a remnant of God's chosen people who had been taken captive by the Babylonians after the destruction of Jerusalem and who were returning to the promised land to rebuild their nation.

The dramatic narrative starts in 538 BC and revolves around three epic tales. First is the struggle to rebuild the temple in Jerusalem under Zerubbabel (chapters 1–6). Next is the second expedition from Babylon sixty years later, led by Ezra, a scribe and scholar, whose task it is to reestablish the Law of Moses (chapters 7–10). Third is the work of Nehemiah, the appointed governor leading the rebuilding of Jerusalem until around 433 BC.

AUTHOR

Bible experts have long suggested that the author of Ezra also wrote 1 and 2 Chronicles and Nehemiah, referring to the writer as "the Chronicler." But recent scholars question this assumption and conclude both Ezra and Nehemiah were not written by the Chronicler. As to who wrote Ezra and Nehemiah, there is support for the Jewish tradition that teaches Ezra was the writer of both books. It's interesting to note that the narration switches from third person to first person after Ezra appears in the story (chapter 7).

The book was likely written between 460 and 440 BC, but there are competing views regarding the date.

PURPOSE

Ezra, with Nehemiah, tells the story of God's faithfulness to His promises regarding His chosen people, restoring them to their land after seventy years of captivity.

OCCASION

Three views dominate regarding the date of Ezra's return to Jerusalem. If the Artaxerxes mentioned is Artaxerxes I, Ezra returned in 458 BC, in the seventh year of the king's reign. About thirteen years later, Nehemiah begins rebuilding the walls of Jerusalem. During the dozen years Nehemiah is building, Ezra returns again, and the two work together in shaping the nation. This view is the most plausible, but there are a few issues with it. For one, Nehemiah is not mentioned in Ezra. Also, Ezra is only mentioned once in Nehemiah, with nothing said of his reforms earlier in 458 BC.

Another view suggests Ezra actually returns to Jerusalem under Artaxerxes II, in 398 BC, after Nehemiah. This would fit better, for example, with the issue of marrying foreign wives. (Ezra battles the trend, so why would it still be a pervasive problem thirteen years later when Nehemiah arrives?) Yet Nehemiah 8:2 suggests Nehemiah and Ezra are contemporaries.

Third, Ezra may have returned in the thirty-seventh year of Artaxerxes I, during Nehemiah's second term (428 BC). This view is willing to say the text has been corrupted, with the seventh year actually meaning thirty-seventh. There is no evidence to support this position.

THEMES

Ezra, with Nehemiah, relates historical events that communicate the love and power of a God active in the world. Some themes include: God's sovereignty, God's covenant with His people, and God's grace.

HISTORICAL CONTEXT

Ezra covers the period following 539 BC, well into the time in biblical history called the post-exilic period. The exile of Judah occurred under Nebuchadnezzar, who deported the remnant of Israel to Babylon in 587 and 586 BC. But on October 29, 539 BC, Babylon surrendered to the Persians, and the policies of a new emperor, Cyrus II, came into place. This was good news for the Jews because Persians were known for being temperate in their treatment of captors. In general, they did not deport and relocate captive peoples. They also were ecumenical in their religious policy. They encouraged subject peoples to worship their own gods and goddesses. And, perhaps most importantly, they encouraged exiles to return to their homelands.

Demystifying Ezra

Here is a list of Persia's most prominent leaders, most of whom you'll meet in Ezra and its companion book, Nehemiah.

- Cyrus II, also known as Cyrus the Great (539–530 BC)
- Cambyses II (530–522 BC), son of Cyrus
- Darius I (521–486 BC)
- Xerxes I, also known in the Bible as Ahasuerus (486–464 BC), the king in the book of Esther
- Artaxerxes I (464–423 BC)
- Darius II (423–404 BC)
- Artaxerxes II (404–359 BC)

OUTLINE

GOD MOVES HISTORY 1:1–11

The Word That Drives History 1:1–4
The Secret That Explains Obedience 1:5–6
Signs That Encourage Believers 1:7–11

WHAT YOU CAN DISCOVER ON THE CHURCH ROLL 2:1–69

The Pilgrimage That Calls 2:1–35
The Passion That Rules 2:36–42
The Providence That Leads 2:43–58
The Uncertainty That Shadows 2:59–63
The Generosity That Shows 2:64–69

GOD'S PEOPLE IN GRAY TIMES 3:1–13

The Circumstances We Will Face 3:1–6
The Restoration We Can Expect 3:7–11
The Disappointment We Must Control 3:12–13

LET THE TROUBLES BEGIN 4:1–24

The World's Subtle Hostility 4:1–3
The World's Obvious Hostility 4:4–5
The World's Persistent Hostility 4:6–24

GOD IS THE RULER YET 5:1–6:22

The Stirring of the Word 5:1–5
The Surrounding Providence 5:6–6:5
An Extravagant Providence 6:6–12
An Encouraging Providence 6:13–15
The Seizing Joy 6:16–22

THE STRONG HAND OF GOD — 7:1–8:36

Ezra Arrives in Jerusalem	7:1–10
The Decree of the King	7:11–28
The Congregation of Israel	8:1–20
The Adventure of Faith	8:21–23
The Vindication of Faith	8:24–36

TROUBLE IN COVENANT CITY — 9:1–15

A Report of Faithlessness	9:1–4
A Prayer of Confession	9:5–15

MAKING CONFESSION — 10:1–44

A Word of Hope	10:1–4
A Process of Discipline	10:5–15
Careful Investigation	10:16–44

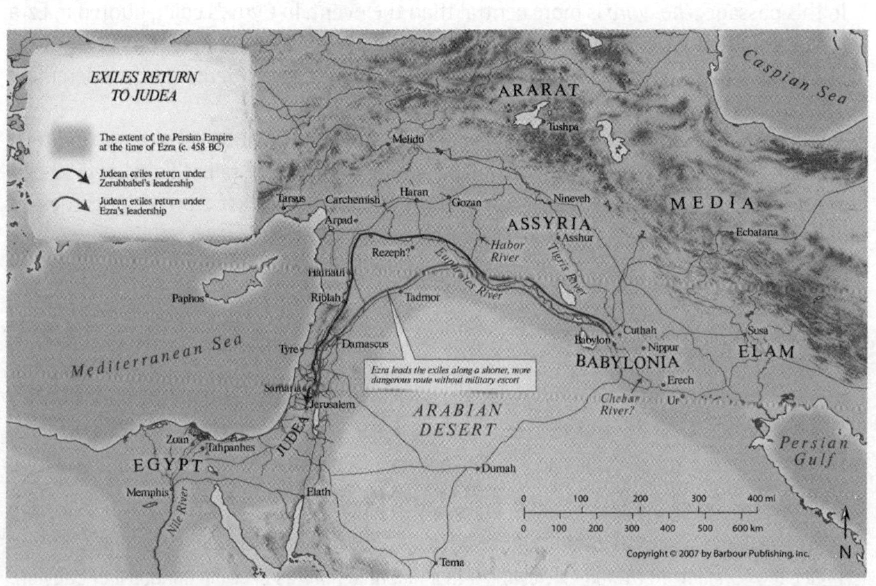

EZRA 1:1–11

GOD MOVES HISTORY

Setting Up the Section

Israel was not a major player in the days of Ezra and Nehemiah. The big powers were first Babylon, then Persia. No one cared about the postage-stamp size kingdom in the political backwater of the Ancient Near East or about the people who used to live there. But God did indeed still care about the Israelites. He had made promises to them and will see to it they are fulfilled.

1:1–4

THE WORD THAT DRIVES HISTORY

In this passage, *the word* is more central than the event. In Cyrus's edict, quoted in Ezra 1:2–4, the Jews are allowed to return to Judah and rebuild the temple. But behind this event is the word that Yahweh had spoken years previously to Jeremiah (see Jeremiah 25:12; 29:10–11).

Jeremiah had said there were seventy years for Babylon. The numeral is approximate. It was seventy-three years from the fall of Nineveh (612 BC) to the fall of Babylon (539 BC). From the accession of Nebuchadnezzar and the taking of the first crop of Judean exiles (605 BC) to the fall of Babylon, it was sixty-six years.

Critical Observation

The Jews' freedom came through Cyrus, the Persian conqueror. Note the prophecies about him in Isaiah 41:2–3; 44:24–28; and 45:1–6, especially verse 4. This text reveals the secret: It is the Lord who stirs the heart of Cyrus, king of Persia (Ezra 1:1), thus Cyrus's edict in Ezra 1:2–4.

Cyrus's permission for the Jews to return home and to rebuild Yahweh's house is consistent with his practices in Babylon toward conquered people. They are reflected in the famous Cyrus Cylinder, the cuneiform-covered clay cylinder that recounts his rule after the conquest of Babylon.

1:5–6

THE SECRET THAT EXPLAINS OBEDIENCE

God works not only in Cyrus's heart, but He also stirs the leaders of the Jewish remnant to leave what they have known and go home to rebuild the temple in Jerusalem (1:5).

Note the central focus: rebuilding the house of Yahweh (1:2–5, 7). Rebuilding the temple has to do with the restoration of public worship. Seeking God in public worship is the heart of the Jews' existence, and yet they have to be stirred up by God to do it.

Take It Home

This is the same thing that Paul teaches in Philippians 2:12–13. Why do Christians obey? Because "God is working in you, giving you the desire to obey him and the power to do what pleases him" (Philippians 2:13 NLT). We obey—we work out our salvation—because God enables us to do so.

1:7–11

SIGNS THAT ENCOURAGE BELIEVERS

Nebuchadnezzar originally takes the vessels mentioned in these passages to Babylon in 605 BC and places them in the "treasury of his god." Since Yahweh's furniture is pilfered, Yahweh is considered "weaker" than Babylon's gods (compare Ezra 1:7–8 to Daniel 1:1–2; 5:2–4, 22–23).

In Babylon they toast one another as they use the defeated god's table service (Daniel 5:4). (They don't know that in Daniel 1:2 we are told that the Lord gave these vessels to the Babylonians.)

But we see here in Ezra that the utensils that had been taken from Yahweh's house are being inventoried to Sheshbazzar, the leader of Judah (Ezra 1:8). The Jewish believer who saw this must have savored each vessel counted, each article tallied; each one was a token that defeat had been turned to victory.

Demystifying Ezra

The mundane inventory of this passage actually constitutes, item by item, signs that Yahweh is removing the stigma and taking away the shame. These are not dramatic signs. They are low-key signs that Yahweh is restoring His people and His worship. Although the Lord sometimes gives His people dramatic signs, those tend to be exceptional. He usually offers modest signs, like the bread and the wine at the Lord's Table.

EZRA 2:1–69

WHAT YOU CAN DISCOVER ON THE CHURCH ROLL

Setting Up the Section

Most of Ezra 2 is instructional more than entertaining. It shows what is—or should be—characteristic of the people of God.

Ezra 2 includes a list of returnees in 538 BC, the first group led by Zerubbabel—years before Ezra comes on the scene. There's a parallel passage in Nehemiah 7.

2:1–35

THE PILGRIMAGE THAT CALLS

In Ezra 2:1, we're reminded that this historical book is about *people*: the remnant of God's chosen ones, descendants of Nebuchadnezzar's captives who had not forgotten the promised land or God's promises—and who had not been forgotten by God.

The leaders are listed in 2:2. Zerubbabel is the grandson of King Jehoachin. There are ten others, eleven if Nahamani, listed in Nehemiah 7:7, is included

The lay people in Ezra 2:3–35 are listed either by a recognized family or clan, or by hometown. The totals do not exactly match Nehemiah 7, probably a result of copying errors as ancient manuscripts were copied by hand through the years.

2:36–42

THE PASSION THAT RULES

In verses 2–35 we have the tallies of the lay people; in verses 36–39 we have the tallies of four clans of priests. The total of almost 4,300 (actually 4,289) priests constitutes approximately 10 percent of the total found in Ezra 2:64.

One in ten of the returnees is a priest. Why so many? Because they long to serve at the altar in a restored temple and participate in public worship of God, serving where they are meant to serve.

Demystifying Ezra

Those mentioned in 2:40–42 probably are Levites, 341 in all. But some scholars think that only the seventy-four mentioned in verse 40 directly assisted the priests. That's one Levite to every fifty-eight priests: precious few to do the chores and the tasks connected with temple worship—a lot of work and little recognition. Not a big incentive for a Levite to move home, but nonetheless seventy-four of them do.

A good bit of Christian work is plain and basic, with not much flair involved. We are not called to gain recognition. Yet, an assisting role does not always appeal to our pride. These seventy-four Levites stand as an example of devoted assistants unscathed by pride.

2:43–58

THE PROVIDENCE THAT LEADS

This passage contains two sections of names: the temple servants (2:43–54) and the sons of Solomon's servants (2:55–57), totaling 392 people.

According to Ezra 8:20, David had given these temple servants to the Levites to assist them. Their work, therefore, consists of the most menial tasks around the temple complex.

Three quarters of the temple servants' names and more than a third of Solomon's servants' names are foreign, according to scholars. The speculation is that these people are descendants of prisoners of war (during David's time) or of the pagans that Solomon pressed into slavery (see 1 Kings 9:20–21). If so, now the descendants of these pagan ancestors are listed among the covenant people of God as they are restored to their land.

Take It Home

It seems a chance occurrence: an ancestor captured in war and taken to Israel to do grunt work around the first temple. But it places him or her in the very sanctuary of truth. Somewhere in the passing of generations, the truth takes hold so that these foreigners are later numbered among God's people.

Can you identify something similar in your life, or in the life of someone you know? A change of fortune, a circumstance altered—turning out to be a setting where God reveals Himself? That's the providence that leads us.

2:59–63

THE UNCERTAINTY THAT SHADOWS

This passage tells about three lay families and three priestly families that are unable to prove their ancestry. This is not to say they are not Israelites or priests, but they cannot *prove* it.

However, it does not keep them from coming up from Babylon, joining the pilgrim people, and returning to Jerusalem. They remain among the people of God even though this uncertainty hangs over them.

2:64–69

THE GENEROSITY THAT SHOWS

The gift of the heads of households consists of 61,000 darics (about 1,133 pounds of gold) and 5,000 minas (about 6,300 pounds of silver). The numbers in the Nehemiah 7 account differ somewhat. Note the number of slaves in light of the overall number (2:64–65), showing there to be about one slave to every six freemen. Therefore, some of the returnees must have substantial wealth, and though there is reason to hold it back in view of the uncertain times, they instead give generously.

EZRA 3:1–13

GOD'S PEOPLE IN GRAY TIMES

The Circumstances We Will Face	3:1–6
The Restoration We Can Expect	3:7–11
The Disappointment We Must Control	3:12–13

Setting Up the Section

A less-than-enthusiastic attitude toward life typifies the Jewish remnant around 538 BC. Life is hard and times are tough. But Ezra 3 shows that God's people can live through bleak times.

3:1–6

THE CIRCUMSTANCES WE WILL FACE

The focus in this passage is not on the temple but the altar. Observe how the text describes Israel and, by implication, all God's people.

1) *They are fearful.* In verse 3, we are told that the exiles set up the altar, for (note the causal connection) it is on account of dread upon them because of the peoples of the lands. The NIV obscures the connection (see the NASB). The *peoples* apparently mean not only the Samarians but also those of the surrounding territories.

2) *They are faithful.* In verses 2 and 4, Joshua and company join Zerubbabel and the others in building the altar to offer burnt offerings. Then they celebrate the Feast of Tabernacles (3:4). Their worship is inaugurated and carried out in accordance with what God requires of them (as it is written). Indeed, they establish a program of regular, ongoing worship (3:5–6).

Critical Observation

Verse 3 implies that fear drives the people to seek God and worship. Should we have higher motives than fear? Perhaps. But in our fears, what better recourse can we have than God? Together these two sub-points make a crucial point: You can be fearful and faithful at the same time.

3) *They are fragile.* Note the reference in verse 4 to observing the Feast of Booths, also known as the Feast of Tabernacles (see Leviticus 23:39–40, 42–43; Numbers 29:12–38). The seventh month indicates the time for this festival. The Feast of Tabernacles is meant to remind Israel of their wilderness experience post-Egypt. During this week, they live in huts (booths), which conjure up their precarious existence during the wilderness years. It is as though God is saying to Israel, "Don't forget that your life hangs by a mere thread."

3:7–11

THE RESTORATION WE CAN EXPECT

Now Israel looks beyond restoring the altar. The exiles start to plan to rebuild the temple. There is much preparation involved, including gathering materials, organization (3:8–9), and celebration (3:10–11).

Critical Observation

Verses 10–11 bring to mind the promise of Jeremiah 33:7, 10–11. Think what it must have been like when the Babylonians finally destroyed Jerusalem and the temple (the situation Jeremiah's word presupposes). In that heap of rubble and smoking destruction, who would have thought this day (Ezra 3:10–11) would come? Against all human likelihood, God's people see God's goodness again.

3:12–13

THE DISAPPOINTMENT WE MUST CONTROL

From the second part of verse 12, it seems as if the memory of the first temple clouds the day for some. The older individuals can still recall the magnificence of the original temple (see 1 Kings 5–7), and this projected temple will have none of the pizzazz of Solomon's. There is no problem here with the candor of their weeping, but there is a danger in the negativity of these people.

Take It Home

In our culture of materialism and immediate gratification, we tend to think that what is plain, simple, and quiet to be of less worth—even among God's people. Sometimes we can be so caught up in desiring revival and restoration that we forget it's possible, even preferable, to be faithful even when God has yet to send revival and restoration.

Ezra's account reminds us not to despise the little things (also see Zechariah 4:10). What matters is not whether the church is grand, but whether it is genuine.

EZRA 4:1–24

LET THE TROUBLES BEGIN

The World's Subtle Hostility	4:1–3
The World's Obvious Hostility	4:4–5
The World's Persistent Hostility	4:6–24

Setting Up the Section

The returnees from exile proceed to work on the rebuilding of the temple. But not everyone is excited about the project.

4:1–3

THE WORLD'S SUBTLE HOSTILITY

In this passage we see hatred under the guise of friendship. People in the area approach Zerubbabel to offer assistance in the rebuilding project (4:2). They seem trustworthy because they say they seek God.

But the Word of God has already labeled them for what they are: enemies of Judah and Benjamin. And Zerubbabel, Jeshua, and the leaders of Israel have the discernment to see them for what they really are (4:3).

Critical Observation

The people described in Ezra 4:1–2 refer to the Assyrian king Esarhaddon, which raises suspicions as to their intentions. This reference to the Assyrian kings reveals these people to be, to a large degree, pagan imports who probably have a religion that combines various deities (see 2 Kings 17:24–41, especially 17:33, 41).

The discoveries of fourth-century papyri at Wadi Daliyeh (located some distance above Jericho) seem to support this. A great number of skeletons were also found here, the remains of families of Samaria who had fled the advance of Alexander the Great in 331 BC. Their names include references to such false deities as the Canaanite Baal and the Babylonian Nebo.

The point? Sometimes the choice to stand separate, as the people do here, is crucial (Ezra 4:3). While we live in a world that values tolerance and inclusion, there are times when the task before us requires us to stand alone on behalf of our values.

4:4–5

THE WORLD'S OBVIOUS HOSTILITY

Now the enemies launch a withering campaign of hostility against the people of Judah. The Hebrew text stresses the ongoing, wearing effect of this opposition in that it has three participles, which indicates continuing action: They *kept on making* their hands drop; *kept frightening* them; *kept hiring* counselors against them.

Ezra 4:4 indicates that the intimidation must have occurred on site, with the hired professionals working the halls of power back in Persia (4:5). Apparently all this proves effective, as we will see in Ezra 4:24.

4:6–24

THE WORLD'S PERSISTENT HOSTILITY

To understand the flow of the intimidation, you need to know that 4:6–23 constitutes a sort of big bracket piece, breaking up the chronology of the entire chapter.

We've just seen, in verses 1–5, opposition in the time of Cyrus and into the beginning of the reign of Darius (522 BC). Then in verses 6–23, we read an ongoing description of opposition to Judah down through the years. But in verse 24, we are wrenched back to the early reign of Darius. If read in chronological order, one would read verses 1–5, then verse 24, then verses 6–23.

The opposition in 4:8–23, under Artaxerxes, is effective in bringing the project to a stop, as noted in verse 24.

It is as though the writer, who is relating the earlier days after the return from exile, begins telling about the opposition Judah experienced from the beginning and then decides that he will simply go on and pile up all the opposition that Judah has experienced through the years. But at 4:24, it is as if he says, "Now we need to go back to the time period that my record here in Ezra 4 really concerns; let's get back to about 520 BC, early in Darius's reign, when the work on the temple stopped because Judah seemed under so much duress."

The specific objects of construction help us detect the different situations. Note especially 4:12–13, where the people of Judah draw fire for rebuilding the city and its walls, not the temple, as in verses 1–5 and 24.

Demystifying Ezra

Ezra 4:6 contains an accusation against Judah in the reign of Xerxes (Ahasuerus). Scholars point out that when the emperor Darius dies at the end of 486 BC, Egypt rebels. His successor, Xerxes, has to march west to suppress the revolt. The Persians gain control by the end of 483 BC. If the accusation in verse 6 has to do with an innuendo alleging revolt by Judah during this time, one can imagine the Persians would be concerned, with Egypt already on their hands.

Verse 7 apparently deals with a second accusation (later than that of verse 6), this one leveled during the reign of Artaxerxes. Then verse 8 indicates a third accusation, also under Artaxerxes, of which we have a copy preserved in Ezra 4:11–16.

EZRA 5:1–6:22

GOD IS THE RULER YET

The Stirring of the Word	5:1–5
The Surrounding Providence	5:6–6:5
An Extravagant Providence	6:6–12
An Encouraging Providence	6:13–15
The Seizing Joy	6:16–22

Setting Up the Section

At the end of Ezra 4, the work on the temple had stopped. About fifteen years have passed. Chapters 5–6 consist of the inquiry of Tattenai and the favorable response of the Persian court.

5:1–5

THE STIRRING OF THE WORD

Note how verse 1 speaks of Haggai and Zechariah prophesying "in the name of the God of Israel, who was over them" (NIV). Ultimately, neither the king of Persia nor any other ruler is master. Only the God of Israel rules over the people.

Take It Home

In verse 1, we are told that Haggai and Zechariah prophesied, and in verse 2, Zerubbabel and Jeshua began to rebuild the temple. God's Word enables God's servants to do His will. The Word packs power that moves and sustains obedience. This is especially necessary in light of the fear and intimidation that the community had endured (4:24).

We see the same theology in 1 Thessalonians 2:13, where Paul alludes to the Word of God that is at work in believers.

No sooner do Judah's leaders obey God's Word than they run into renewed opposition (5:3–5). Tattenai, the governor, and Shethar-bozenai, his assistant, ask Judah for authorization for this project, but apparently theirs is not the blatant opposition related in Ezra 4.

Demystifying Ezra

In verse 5, the Aramaic verb *betel* is used (meaning "stop"; 4:21, 23–24). This is an example of negative providence: something God does not allow to happen (compare Psalms 124 and 129). Judah may be under investigation, and there is another potential frustration pending, but Judah is allowed to keep building in the meantime.

5:6–6:5

THE SURROUNDING PROVIDENCE

Ezra 5:6–17 records the letter written to King Darius by Tattenai and Shethar-bozenai. In it they lay out the background to their inquiry and ask Darius to verify the people of Judah's claims.

Note that in verses 11–16, Tattenai and Shethar-bozenai quote the response that the exiles gave them when they challenged them about their authority for rebuilding. In one sense these words are a response of praise. And yet they are also words of confession, as verse 12 makes clear. Judah admits that they are a people who have been under Yahweh's wrath, and He had taken the temple and land from them.

Critical Observation

The Persian Royal Road was a kingdom-wide communication network. Every fifteen miles or so sat a postal station where couriers could replace exhausted horses with fresh mounts. Scholars estimate that a courier could average 240 miles a day, in contrast with a caravan, which would average 19 miles. If Darius's road system was fully operational early in his reign, the correspondence noted in Ezra 5–6 could have been completed in a month or two at most.

6:6–12

AN EXTRAVAGANT PROVIDENCE

Darius finds a copy of Cyrus's original decree in the archives (see 6:1–5), confirming what the people of Judah had said. And not only is Judah granted freedom from interference from Tattenai and company (6:6–7), but the elders of Judah receive provision for the maintenance of the temple worship as well. Darius will underwrite the functioning of the temple with state funds and punish anyone who stands in his way (6:8–11).

Demystifying Ezra

The dimensions of the temple in Ezra 6:3 are sixty cubits high and broad, possibly indicating the limits of what the Persians would underwrite.

Take It Home

This occasion in Ezra 6 is very much like that in Exodus 2:1–10, where Moses' mother not only gets her baby back but raises him under state protection, and with a salary to boot. God delights to go far beyond all that we ask or think (Ephesians 3:20). Here also the Jews receive far more than mere permission to build. Providence strikes again.

6:13–15

AN ENCOURAGING PROVIDENCE

After Tattenai and Shethar-bozenai carry out Darius's decree, the elders of the Jews finish building according to God's decree.

The writer lets the timeline run down from Darius to Artaxerxes, omitting mention of Xerxes (Ahasuerus). Artaxerxes is king in Ezra's time (see 7:1). If Ezra is the one writing the historical account in chapters 5–6 (see 6:14), then he may have included Artaxerxes' name in his summary note because in his own time Artaxerxes had also supported the worship and life of the people of God (indeed, he did; see 7:11–26). It may be Ezra's little hint of acknowledgement that God is showing the same providence in Ezra's own time as He had shown to the previous generation about whom Ezra writes.

Demystifying Ezra

Adar, the last Babylonian month, is equivalent to our February–March. The temple is finished on March 12, 515 BC, a little over seventy years from the destruction of the first temple. Renewed work had begun on September 21, 520 BC (see Haggai 1:4–15), so a sustained effort continued for over four years to complete

6:16–22

THE SEIZING JOY

In Ezra 6:16–18, we see the people worshiping. The number of sacrifices on this occasion may be paltry compared to what Solomon had offered (see 1 Kings 8:63), but the sin offering is for all Israel, the entire twelve-tribe nation, even though most of those present are from Judah, Benjamin, and Levi.

The people in Ezra 6:19–20 are celebrating Passover. There is a diligence and eagerness about the ceremonial preparation of the priests and Levites. Would this post-exilic community have looked upon this Passover as commemorating a second Exodus, that is, from Babylon?

Verse 21 shows that the attitude of Ezra 4:3 is not narrow-minded nationalism. Here is a community open to others. Yet there is a price to pay: They must separate themselves from the impurity of the nations.

The last half of verse 22 explains the joy of their celebration: "Everyone was happy because the LORD God of Israel had made sure that the king of Assyria would be kind to them and help them build the temple" (CEV).

Demystifying Ezra

The king mentioned in 6:22 is Darius, king of Persia. Why is he called the king of Assyria here? Scholars note that there is evidence from the Ancient Near East that new rulers or foreign rulers were incorporated into the king lists of a particular country. Because Darius was also the sovereign of Assyria, he could easily have been called the king of Assyria.

EZRA 7:1–8:36

THE STRONG HAND OF GOD

Ezra Arrives in Jerusalem	7:1–10
The Decree of the King	7:11–28
The Congregation of Israel	8:1–20
The Adventure of Faith	8:21–23
The Vindication of Faith	8:24–36

Setting Up the Section

Ezra 7 introduces the scribe Ezra himself into the narrative. It's now 458 BC, decades after the first group of returnees returned from Babylonian captivity under Zerubbabel. Ezra 7 summarizes that King Artaxerxes authorizes Ezra to lead another, smaller group to Judea. Ezra 8 gives the details. A thematic element that binds these chapters together is the repeated reference to the hand of God.

7:1–10

EZRA ARRIVES IN JERUSALEM

The phrase *after these things* is a clue that what follows occurs a while later (7:1). In fact, Ezra 7 is set almost sixty years after the events narrated in Ezra 6. The writer is very selective as to what is included in the section. Not every detail is given, only what is significant for the people of God.

At this point the book is placing focus on different concerns: not only on restored worship (Ezra 1–6) but also on reformed life according to the law and the Word of God (Ezra 7–10).

In 7:1–5 we're shown Ezra's credentials by virtue of his ancestry (see 1 Chronicles 6:1–15). (See Ezra 2:59–63 on the importance of the documentation [see also Exodus 6:14–27]. Note the gaps in the genealogy.)

Demystifying Ezra

The date described in verses 7–9 can be interpreted several ways. Some scholars teach that Ezra departs April 8 and arrives August 4, 458 BC. Another proposal is based on amending the text of Ezra 7:7 to the thirty-seventh year (428 BC) as opposed to the seventh. Others have construed the seventh year as that of Artaxerxes II (which puts the date at 398 BC). Keep in mind, however, that the significance of the events is the same no matter the exact date.

In 7:6, Ezra is described with the term *mahir*, which means quick, speedy, and hence skilled. According to verse 6, the Law of Moses is a divine gift and apparently complete. Here is also the first "hand of God" clause. So here we have an assembly of realities: a completed revelation (the Torah of Moses) and an ongoing providence (the hand of God)—the latter operating in conjunction with human ingenuity and initiative.

Critical Observation

In Ezra 7:10 we're given a clue as to why the hand of God is on Ezra. The Hebrew text includes the initial *ki* ("because"). God prospers the venture because of Ezra's purpose. Ezra has set his heart to study the law, practice it, and teach it.

7:11–28

THE DECREE OF THE KING

This decree of Artaxerxes gives more people permission to return to Judah, but there are several other concerns and purposes. It is, in part, a fact-finding mission, as implied in verse 14.

The decree includes instructions having to do with the worship of the house of God, whether it is silver and gold—from royalty, from others in Babylon, or from the exiles themselves (7:15–16)—or the delivery of utensils to be used in the temple (7:19). Needs were to be met from the royal treasury (7:20–22), up to 3.75 tons of silver, 650 bushels of wheat, 600 gallons of wine, and 600 gallons of oil.

Note the royal concern in verse 23. Maybe the king is trying to cover all his religious bases. Still, according to Jeremiah 29:4–9, the exiles are to seek to benefit their captors and seek the welfare of the regime under which they exist.

Ezra 7:24 includes a cautionary note to Artaxerxes' regional IRS agents. The clergy (priests, Levites, singers, doorkeepers, and servants) are to be kept tax-free.

The people in Trans-Euphrates ("beyond the river"), mentioned in 7:26, are probably the Jews living there. Also note in verse 26 the law of Ezra's God is also the law of the king. Remember, Ezra's mission is to teach the people of God afresh the law and to discipline them to live according to it. Hence, the focus of Ezra 1–6 is the temple while that of Ezra 7–10 will be the Torah.

Ezra ends the account with a doxology in praise of Yahweh's covenant fidelity, sovereignty, goodness, and encouragement (7:27–28).

Take It Home

King Artaxerxes may make the decree and grant the permission, but why does he do so? Because there is another King behind Artaxerxes, one who turns the king's heart whichever way He desires (Ezra 7:27; Proverbs 21:1). Yet Yahweh's sovereignty is not always blatant—frequently it is hidden and subtle. Yahweh chooses to carry out His decrees through the decrees and decisions of the lesser kings and rulers of the earth.

Note in verse 28 the juxtaposition of the power heads of the Persian Empire (the king, his counselors, all the king's mighty princes) and Ezra's position. There is something astounding in how this miniscule Judean could command such favor from the bureaucracy of Persia! Ezra revels in the thought. Clearly God placed Ezra in a position of authority in Babylon for His purposes.

In verse 28, Ezra says he takes courage or strengthens himself. But he doesn't neglect to give credit to the hand of God, who is the anchor of his story.

8:1–20

THE CONGREGATION OF ISRAEL

The list of households in this section may provide a flicker of hope for the nation of Israel. In it is a descendant of the royal line of David, Hattush (8:2).

Those who came back under Ezra tend to be from families whose members also returned in 538 BC. Compare the list in Ezra 8:1–14 to that in Ezra 2.

Parosh	(2:3; 8:3)
Pahath-moab	(2:6; 8:4)
Zattu	(2:8; 8:5)
Adin	(2:15; 8:6)
Elam	(2:7; 8:7)
Shephatiah	(2:4; 8:8)
Bani	(2:10; 8:10)
Bebai	(2:11; 8:11)
Azgad	(2:12; 8:12)
Adonikam	(2:13; 8:13)
Bigvai	(2:14; 8:14)

Demystifying Ezra

See the listing of Davidic descendants in 1 Chronicles 3:17–24. If you scrutinize that list carefully, it seems that the main thread of the list goes from Jehoiachin, Pedaiah, Zerubbabel, Hananiah, Shecaniah, Shemaiah, to Hattush. Hattush is then the fourth generation after Zerubbabel. If Zerubbabel was born around 560 BC, and if one allots approximately twenty-five years per generation, then Hattush appears here about 458 BC, which fits the traditional date of Ezra's arrival in Jerusalem.

Ezra discovers a lack of Levites (8:15). So he sends ambassadors to a place called Casiphia (8:16–17). It's unclear where or what Casiphia is, but apparently it is a site near Babylon, perhaps a Judean study center. Note the acknowledgement of Yahweh's goodness in verse 18. The appeal nets a total of 38 Levites (8:18–19) and 220 temple servants (8:20).

There is likely a level of comfort, even prosperity, for the exiles in Babylon. If the Levites are to go with Ezra back to Judea, they will leave a life where they may have a good bit of autonomy from the strict routines of the temple. In Judea, life would be perhaps more about hardship and obedience, like the life the apostle Paul called Timothy to in 2 Timothy 2:3—to suffer hardship as a Christian.

8:21–23

THE ADVENTURE OF FAITH

In Ezra 8:21–23, we're reminded that the exiles are undertaking a nine hundred-mile journey. That is quite a peril to face. How fragile they seem. One can imagine the interest they might have kindled when word got out that a caravan was about to leave with goods (8:25–30). Could they afford to go without state-provided protection?

But Ezra's statement of faith sets the tone, especially in verse 22. There are times when faith must take priority over reason or fear, when what is professed must be expressed in concrete situations. So Ezra calls for fasting and a time of prayer (8:21, 23) to humble themselves before God (see Leviticus 16:29, 31). This pleading and confession does not contradict their professed confidence but is the expression of it.

8:24–36

THE VINDICATION OF FAITH

For a defenseless group of Jews exposed to daily danger for months, arriving safely in Jerusalem is proof of the strong protection of God. Their arrival is for them one of the outstanding miracle stories of life.

The inventory of Ezra 8:26–27 will come out a bit differently depending on the commentator. But the amounts on any scheme are substantial: 650 talents of silver equal 49,000 pounds, or about 25 tons of silver. One hundred gold talents equal 7,500 pounds, or 3.75 tons.

The twelve leading priests Ezra entrusts with oversight of this wealth (8:24) are called holy in verse 28, as are the utensils they guard. In the latter case, *holy* means, in part, "off limits." Note the vigilance that Ezra requires of these priests (8:29).

EZRA 9:1–15

TROUBLE IN COVENANT CITY

Setting Up the Section

Ezra and his group of exiles have been in Jerusalem about four and a half months when the problem of intermarrying, and therefore rejection of the law and its demand for spiritual purity, is brought to his attention.

9:1–4

A REPORT OF FAITHLESSNESS

The old problem of intermarriage with pagans, in violation of the Torah (Exodus 34:11–16; Deuteronomy 7:1–5) is a problem of sanctification. The people would be hard-pressed to stay true to their religious faith if they are mingling that faith with the idolatry of the cultures around them. Since the spiritual leaders such as the priests and the Levites are implicated as well, this is an extensive and serious issue.

Ezra visibly reacts by tearing his clothes, hair, and beard, and sitting down appalled (desolated, devastated). He seems simply beside himself in helpless frustration. Others share Ezra's essential reaction, even if theirs does not duplicate his exactly (Ezra 9:4).

Why is the news of intermingling with the people of the land such a shock? A possible answer comes from Ezra 8:36, namely that upon arrival Ezra did not stay in Jerusalem. He was taking his credentials from the Persian king to the high officials of the empire in the region.

Note two corollaries of this report of faithlessness in verses 1–4: 1) The professing people of God are disappointing. Never be surprised at how sinful covenant people can be. 2) We usually cannot understand a genuinely holy reaction to sin, as for example the violence and intensity of Ezra's response in verse 3. Don't demean the external as of no consequence (see Joel 2:12–13, where both the external and the internal are held together).

Critical Observation

Ezra says in 9:4, "Then everyone who trembled at the words of the God of Israel gathered around me" (NIV). This trembling is precisely what God wants in His people: "This is the one I esteem: he who is humble and contrite in spirit, and trembles at my word" (Isaiah 66:2 NIV). That is the paradigm for the church.

9:5–15

A PRAYER OF CONFESSION

Ezra's prayer of confession covers the immensity of guilt and the majesty of God's grace. Note how Ezra switches to the plural pronoun *our* in verse 6, in identification with the sins of his people.

The immensity of the guilt (9:6–7) involves quantity: Ezra tries to express the huge mass of guilt in these pictures. It also involves history: It goes back to their fathers, is longstanding, and has been experienced in judgments, the effects of which continue to the present time.

The majesty of God's grace (9:8–9) starts with a significant (brief) moment. It is the grace of survival (God left a remnant), security, encouragement, and consistency. Lastly, it is the grace of providence and protection. The wall (*gader*) is metaphorical for protection (9:9). It is not a literal city wall since it is in Judah and in Jerusalem.

Demystifying Ezra

The *peg* or *firm place* in Ezra 9:8 (NASB) could refer to a tent peg, driven into the ground as secure anchorage for a tent; or it could refer to, as in Isaiah 22:23, a peg or nail securely fastened in a wall so that items can be hung on it. Some theologians have taken the peg to refer to the rebuilt temple, as the following phrase "in his holy place" might suggest. In any case, the idea is that Israel has been given some degree of security in her otherwise tenuous post-exilic experience.

In 9:10–12, Ezra highlights the folly of such unfaithfulness and acknowledges that God's people have confronted the problem before. Hence, they are without excuse.

He goes on to note that God has punished the remnant of His rebellious people less than they deserve. How could they break His commandments? Will it mean God washes His hands of them?

Critical Observation

In Ezra 9:10–15 we see both suspense (in that there is no definite, particular plea that Ezra makes) and frustration (on Ezra's part, for what can he ask? He can only throw Israel upon the mercy of Yahweh).

The word *peletah* ("escaped remnant" NASB) occurs in verses 8, 13, 14, and 15. As we look back on the book of Ezra, we must say that it is a wonder there is an escaped remnant in light of their enemies (chapters 1–6) and sin (chapters 9–10).

EZRA 10:1–44

MAKING CONFESSION

Setting Up the Section

Ezra and his leaders respond to a large outpouring of exiles motivated by Ezra's lamentations to repent of their sin of intermarriage and make things right with God.

10:1–4

A WORD OF HOPE

Ezra may have been a highly respected leader, but he is willing to throw sophistication to the wind in his grief (10:1). The effect is to motivate his people to repent. Not just men, but women and children gather to weep and lament.

In verses 2–4 we see a minor character with a major role in the story. Shecaniah puts Israel's corporate unfaithfulness into words. The hope he refers to in verse 2 is based on a call to covenant with God, in which there is fruit that shows repentance. It is a repentance that takes the hard road: to send away the women and children.

Shecaniah also lays out a plan of repentance (10:3–4). He calls Ezra and the other leaders to courageous action and offers him the support of the people.

10:5–15

A PROCESS OF DISCIPLINE

In verse 5, Ezra succeeds first in getting the priests, Levites, and laity to enter into the covenantal proposal. He continues in his repentance in Jehohanan's private room (apparently in the temple; we are not told who Jehohanan is), refusing to eat food or drink water (10:6).

Critical Observation

Ezra's fasting has been called a reflection of Moses' fasting (see Exodus 34:28; Deuteronomy 9:18) after the golden bull-calf episode of Exodus 32. It would not be unreasonable to see Ezra as a kind of "second Moses."

In Ezra 10:7–14, the leaders call the assembly. The people generally live within fifty miles from Jerusalem. Non-participation means excommunication (10:8).

The leaders recognize that logistically it will be virtually impossible to have the entire assembly make confession out in the open because it's cold and it will take more than a few days (10:12–14). So they make a proposal that offenders appear to representatives by appointment. They should be accompanied by the elders and judges of their towns—an important element, supporting a fair investigation.

Demystifying Ezra

The date given in verse 9 (ninth month, twentieth day) is December 19, 458 BC. It is the rainy season, in which temperatures are in the forties.

The few who resist likely oppose the whole process, perhaps thinking it too harsh or wanting to protect relatives. The *Meshullam* of verse 15 may well be the same person named as son of Bani in verse 29, who himself had married a foreign wife.

10:16–44

CAREFUL INVESTIGATION

The hearings last from the first day of the tenth month until the first day of the first month (10:16–17). That's three months of work, finishing on March 27, 457 BC.

Offenders come from all levels: priests, Levites, and laity. According to the lists in 10:18–43, the offenders included seventeen priests, six Levites, one singer, three gatekeepers, and eighty-four laity. That makes a total of 111 (depending on the specific text). This indicates careful work. Assuming they take the Sabbath off, it takes abut seventy-five days to complete the investigations of 111 cases.

We're not told what happens to the divorced women and children. They probably went back to their extended families, but that is not the concern of this text.

Critical Observation

The marriage crisis here is on a par with the crisis faced by the earlier community (4:2), in which adversaries seek to help and then oppose the exiles' obedience.

The 536 BC community repulses the direct attack and avoids being diluted. The 458 BC community begins to succumb to a more subtle assault.

Yet, if the 111 names recorded in Ezra 10 is the total number of men who had taken a foreign wife, it's a very small percentage of the entire community. Estimates of its size at this point total 30,000 or maybe 50,000. Yet the purging must be done.

Take It Home

Is Ezra 9–10 a model for the Christian church to follow? There is debate about the matter, but most likely Ezra 9 and 10 are descriptive of a specific time, not prescriptive for all times.

What we see in Ezra 9–10 is Exodus 34:11–16 and Deuteronomy 7:1–5 applied in a new post-exile situation. Do those texts not still apply to the church? Do they incorporate Paul's stricture in 1 Corinthians 7:39, teaching that a Christian widow is free to marry only in the Lord? Ezra's action in these chapters could be viewed as a corporate application of Matthew 5:29–30.

But the situation Paul faces in 1 Corinthians 7:12 and following is different from that of Ezra 9–10. Paul is speaking of marriages that were originally between pagans but became mixed because one of the spouses was converted to Christ. In that situation, if the unbeliever is willing to continue the marriage, the Christian should not try to end the marriage.

The problem in Ezra involves covenant people contracting marriages with pagans. If this occurs in a new covenant context, such Christians should be—in accord with Matthew 18:15–20—admonished to repent of such deliberate sin.

Yet if there is repentance, would that require divorce? Wouldn't Ezra 9–10 point that way? Not necessarily. Ezra 9–10 was a unique situation. Remember what was at stake: the survival of a definable people of God in this world. Hence the drastic measures.

NEHEMIAH

INTRODUCTION TO NEHEMIAH

The book of Nehemiah is one of the Old Testament's historical books. Until the fifteenth century AD, Ezra and Nehemiah were considered to be one book, and we see evidence of this with Ezra's abrupt ending. The events of Nehemiah pick up naturally where Ezra leaves off, with the continual rebuilding of Jerusalem and the return of the final group of exiles from Babylon in 445 BC.

AUTHOR

Nehemiah is believed by some scholars to have written the majority of the text—much of the book of Nehemiah is written in the first person, and Nehemiah 1:1 identifies the speaker as Nehemiah, son of Hacaliah, an exiled Jew who served as the cupbearer to the Persian king, Artaxerxes I. Yet Jewish tradition holds that Ezra authored the books of Ezra and Nehemiah. Because Ezra and Nehemiah were one book, Nehemiah may have been edited by Ezra, or the two may have been combined by a historical chronicler. No one knows for certain.

PURPOSE

The book of Nehemiah has two primary purposes—to provide a historical account of the rebuilding of the wall of Jerusalem and to document the reformation of the post-exilic Israelites who returned to the city and renewed their covenant with Yahweh. Through these two main purposes, God's continuous provision for His chosen people is revealed.

OCCASION

The events recorded in the book of Nehemiah are dated from circa 445 to 431–432 BC. It begins with Nehemiah returning to Jerusalem in the twentieth year of the reign of King Artaxerxes I of Persia (1:1), approximately thirteen years after Ezra returned with the second group of exiled Jews. Nehemiah leaves Jerusalem for a brief period of time in the thirty-second year of the reign of Artaxerxes I and returns shortly thereafter (13:6–7), dating the events at the end of the book around 432 BC.

THEMES

Revival is one of the main themes of the book of Nehemiah. Nehemiah leads in the rebuilding of the wall, and he also makes sure the Jewish practices are reestablished so that temple worship is also revived.

This book also focuses heavily on the importance of godly leadership. Nehemiah seeks wisdom from the Lord.

Adversity is another theme evident throughout the book, as Nehemiah faces opposition to his rebuilding plan, conflict among the people working on the wall, and specific instances of the covenantal law being broken by the people. Despite the various adversities Nehemiah and the Israelites face, the wall is rebuilt and temple worship resumes, at least for a time.

HISTORICAL CONTEXT

While there were surely other groups of Jews returning from Babylon, those who return with Nehemiah to rebuild the wall mark the third group described specifically in the Old Testament. Of the specific accounts offered in Ezra and Nehemiah, Zerubbabel led the first group home in 538 BC (Ezra 1:1–6:22), and Ezra returns with the second group in 458 BC (Ezra 7:1–10:44). The first group is tasked with the rebuilding of the temple, a work that couldn't truly be celebrated until the wall that protected the city and the temple was also complete. Nehemiah brings closure to the events recorded in Ezra and the aftermath of the Babylonian exile.

CONTRIBUTION TO THE BIBLE

Nehemiah's memoir provides a genealogy of a third specific group of Israelites to return to Jerusalem. More than a history of the people and the rebuilding of the wall, Nehemiah also provides a historical account of the rejuvenation of the holy city. With the rebuilding of Jerusalem and its wall complete, it is once again the holy city of God.

OUTLINE

PRAYER IN THE PALACE	**1:1–11**
Background	1:1–4
Nehemiah's Prayer	1:5–11
FROM COURT TO CITY	**2:1–20**
A Day at Court	2:1–8
A Night at the Walls	2:9–16
An Hour of Decision	2:17–20
BLESSED BUILDERS	**3:1–32**
The Gate Workers	3:1–16
The Eastern Wall and the Final Gates	3:17–32
THREATS AGAINST GOD'S WORK	**4:1–23**
Ridicule	4:1–6
Intimidation	4:7–12
Organized Perseverance	4:13–23
FOLLY AMONG GOD'S PEOPLE	**5:1–19**
Nehemiah's Confrontation	5:1–11
The Response	5:12–19
STRATAGEMS AGAINST GOD'S SERVANT	**6:1–19**
God Gives Strength	6:1–9
God Gives Clarity	6:10–14
God Gives Tenacity	6:15–19
THE EXILES WHO RETURNED	**7:1–73**
The Registration	7:1–5
The Listing	7:6–73
THE FOUNDATION OF REFORMATION	**8:1–18**
Ezra Reads	8:1–12
The Festival	8:13–18

THE PREPARATION FOR REFORMATION 9:1–38

Prelude to Prayer 9:1–5
The Prayer 9:6–38

THE STRUCTURE FOR REFORMATION 10:1–39

The People Agree 10:1–29
The People Vow 10:30–39

THE ORDER OF THE PEOPLE OF THE LORD 11:1–36

Anchoring the City 11:1–24
Possessing the Land 11:25–36

THE CELEBRATION IN THE JOY OF THE LORD 12:1–43

Structuring the Worship 12:1–26
Dedicating the Wall 12:27–43

THE PERSEVERANCE IN THE WORSHIP OF THE LORD 12:44–13:3

Mundane Provisions 12:44–47
Essential Separation 13:1–3

THE ONGOING PERILS OF THE CHURCH 13:4–31

Compromise 13:4–9
Neglect/Indifference 13:10–14
Commercialism 13:15–22
Amalgamation 13:23–31

NEHEMIAH 1:1-11

PRAYER IN THE PALACE

Setting Up the Section

Nehemiah introduces himself and his times in Nehemiah 1:1–3. The reference to the twentieth year (1:1) is to the year of Artaxerxes I, or 445 BC. Comparing Ezra 7:7, we note that this is thirteen years after Ezra's coming. The month of Chislev is November–December. Susa was in what is now southwest Iran, in the alluvial plain 150 miles north of the Persian Gulf. It serves as a winter palace for the Persian kings.

1:1–4

BACKGROUND

Although Nehemiah lived most of his life in Babylon, his home was Jerusalem. Verse 2 reveals the concern and affection Nehemiah still has for his homeland and its people. His brother Hanani's news that the walls of Jerusalem remain in ruins causes Nehemiah much grief. Verse 4 indicates that Nehemiah's grief and distress are a continuing affair and that his fasts and prayers have been ongoing for some time. The prayer of verses 5–11, then, is a sample of what his prayers are like during this time.

Critical Observation

Ezra 6:6–12 includes an edict banning the reconstruction of Jerusalem's walls. The fact that the walls remained untouched reflected the oppression that crippled the Jewish people. Jerusalem was the holy city of the Jews, and a wall in ruin was a visible reminder of the city's prior destruction, the Jewish exile, and an overall loss of national identity and pride.

1:5–11

NEHEMIAH'S PRAYER

Nehemiah begins his prayer by identifying God as both awe-inspiring and faithful. Note how these two aspects of God's character complement one another: God is both frightening and dependable. Nehemiah goes on to state that God is approachable as well (1:6).

In verses 6–7, Nehemiah doesn't point an accusing finger at others but rather identifies with his people. The offenses, as noted in verse 7, are committed in violation of the revelation of God's law received through Moses. Verses 8–9 correspond with Deuteronomy 30:1–10, particularly verses 3–5. The language of Nehemiah 1:9 links up with the promise of help and restoration from judgment in Deuteronomy 30:3–5.

Nehemiah pleads to God on the basis of the identity Israel has because of redemption (Nehemiah 1:10). When Nehemiah uses the verb *redeemed*, he is likely referring to redemption from Egypt and the resulting covenant, not to redemption from Babylon after the exile. It's as if Nehemiah says, "Look at what you have made them. Look at what you have done for them. Do you mean all of that to go for nothing?"

Demystifying Nehemiah

Nehemiah's prayer is in reference to the contemporary need—the grave crisis of the people of Judah—as well as to the suspense over what the king's reaction might be. Nehemiah refers not merely to his own prayer but to the prayers of others (1:11). Nehemiah does not stand alone in prayer; there is a fellowship of intercession.

The text brings us up to the edge of when Nehemiah will broach the subject with the king. While most people do not have access to the king, Nehemiah reveals in verse 11 that he was the king's cupbearer, thus giving him access to approach the throne.

Critical Observation

The position of cupbearer was one of great responsibility and influence. Kings wanted a cupbearer they could trust. When Nehemiah makes his cupbearer remark, he is recognizing that Yahweh's providence has been at work long before this moment. He was high up in the civil service with access to the king, and therefore, in a favorable position to seek good for the people of Judah.

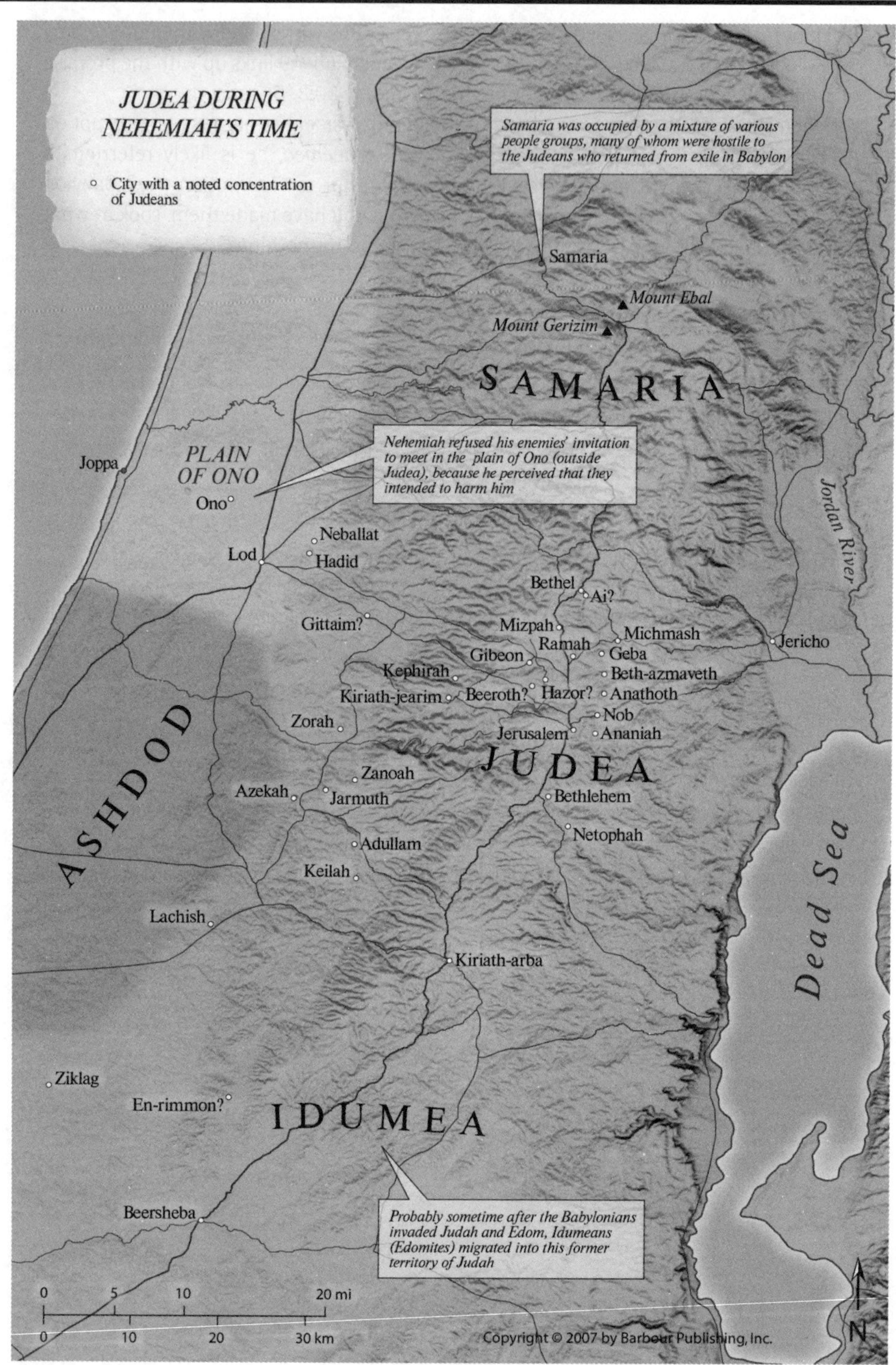
JUDEA DURING NEHEMIAH'S TIME
City with a noted concentration of Judeans
Samaria was occupied by a mixture of various people groups, many of whom were hostile to the Judeans who returned from exile in Babylon
Samaria
Mount Ebal
Mount Gerizim
SAMARIA
Nehemiah refused his enemies' invitation to meet in the plain of Ono (outside Judea), because he perceived that they intended to harm him
PLAIN OF ONO
Joppa
Ono
Jordan River
Neballat
Hadid
Lod
Bethel
Ai?
Gittaim?
Mizpah
Michmash
Ramah
Jericho
Gibeon
Geba
Kephirah
Beth-azmaveth
Kiriath-jearim
Beeroth?
Hazor?
Anathoth
Nob
Zorah
Jerusalem
Ananiah
ASHDOD
JUDEA
Zanoah
Azekah
Jarmuth
Bethlehem
Netophah
Adullam
Keilah
Dead Sea
Lachish
Kiriath-arba
Ziklag
En-rimmon?
IDUMEA
Probably sometime after the Babylonians invaded Judah and Edom, Idumeans (Edomites) migrated into this former territory of Judah
Beersheba
0 5 10 20 mi
0 10 20 30 km
N

NEHEMIAH 2:1–20

FROM COURT TO CITY

Setting Up the Section

Nehemiah doesn't act hastily on his desire to return to Jerusalem and lead in the rebuilding of the walls. Following his prayer in chapter 1, he waits four months before taking the first step toward returning—asking King Artaxerxes' permission to leave.

2:1–8

A DAY AT COURT

Nehemiah cannot keep his depression about the state of his homeland from showing—and this may have been a breach of royal court etiquette. Nehemiah's fear in verse 2 likely arises in light of the accurate diagnosis and the knowledge that this king has nullified precisely what Nehemiah seeks to do (see Ezra 4:7–23). Note that at this point Nehemiah does not explicitly mention Jerusalem.

Nehemiah 2:4 is the moment of opportunity—and of uncertainty—hence Nehemiah's resort to impromptu prayer. This is a reflection of Nehemiah's piety, but this prayer is also a balance between dependence and boldness (2:4–5). His request is presented and royal permission is given (2:5–6).

The care and planning and thought Nehemiah has given to this matter are reflected in his request for official letters and for obtaining materials (2:7–8). The explanation of Nehemiah's success comes not merely as information but as praise. The king gives provision, but it is by Yahweh's hand that he does so.

2:9–16

A NIGHT AT THE WALLS

Where Ezra rejects an armed escort as a matter of faith in Ezra 8:21–23, here we have Nehemiah's acceptance of an escort as a matter of wisdom (Nehemiah 2:9). It will add authority and support to his position and work.

Demystifying Nehemiah

Verse 10 introduces the opposition. They simply cannot endure a man who seeks good for the sons of Israel (2:10). This is not mere human animosity; this is the serpent's seed hating the seed of the woman. There is far more theology in this text and situation than is immediately apparent.

Nehemiah conducts a nighttime (2:12–13, 15) survey of the conditions of the wall. Nehemiah doesn't tell (2:12, 16) about his plans or his preliminary investigation. He needs direct knowledge of the condition of the wall, so if there are any objections, he will know on what basis to answer. Also, some of the Jews were in contact with neighboring peoples and may have leaked Nehemiah's plan.

If there is any incensed opposition, there is also a sense of divine calling on Nehemiah's part, as he points out in verse 12. This is not just Nehemiah's desire, but one spurred by God-given motivation.

2:17–20

AN HOUR OF DECISION

Nehemiah identifies with the people of Judah. His appeal is based on their current shame—they should rebuild so they will no longer be a mockery. He also intends for them to be moved by seeing how God has been at work in His providence as had been shown in the king's authorization for the project (2:18). In response to Nehemiah's motivation, the people agree to his plan to rebuild, and they begin the work. But the dissenters—Sanballat, Tobiah, and Geshem—make their voices heard. Notice that the enmity in verse 19 is expressed by both ridicule and innuendo. Nehemiah's response is typically abrupt and pointed (2:20):

God will give us success.
We, His servants, will build.
You have no part with us.

Take It Home

Chapter 2 marks the beginning of Nehemiah's leadership of the Jerusalem project, and already he has established himself as an effective leader, capable of both motivating the people in their rebuilding effort and handling the adversity that has already started to arise. Nehemiah's leadership will only be strengthened as the book continues. He is arguably one of the strongest examples of godly leadership in the Old Testament.

NEHEMIAH 3:1–32

BLESSED BUILDERS

Setting Up the Section

Chapter 3 is Nehemiah's detailed account of the rebuilding of Jerusalem's walls. The description starts at the Sheep Gate in the northeast corner and works its way counterclockwise.

3:1–16

THE GATE WORKERS

The account begins with an illustration of leadership by example (3:1). The high priest and other priests are the first people named as helpers in the rebuilding effort. They apparently do not have the idea that such work is for peons. Rather, those with sacred office take the lead in the restoring work. Many names are mentioned in this chapter as those who helped rebuild, evidencing that this was a task that demanded all hands on deck.

Because it is such a large city, Jerusalem is a necessary stop on many trade routes. Its size also requires many gates by which to enter the city, as mentioned in this chapter. The Fish Gate (3:3) is the entrance for one of the main roads, and it likely received its name because of the fish market that was just outside the gate (2 Chronicles 33:14).

Nehemiah 3:5 is puzzling, but it seems that there are some from the town of Tekoa, the nobles, who refuse to assist in the work. Perhaps they think it is beneath them to do this kind of work. By contrast, however, the chapter is full of others with social and political clout who avidly contribute their share to the work (3:9, 12, 15, 19). The men from Tekoa who do help evidently work on more than one section of the wall (3:5, 27). Meremoth, the son of Uriah, is mentioned in verse 4, and he, too, is named later as working on a second part (3:21). This taking on more than one's share speaks well for these workers.

The Jeshanah Gate (3:6) is also translated Old Gate, and it is repaired by a group of Jebusites, whose descendents were the original owners of the land on which the temple was built. The stretch of wall from the Old Gate to Broad Wall includes a wide range of people, from Jebusites to those from the Trans-Euphrates, to goldsmiths and perfume-makers (3:6–8). From the Broad Wall, the building continues around to the Tower of the Ovens, or Furnaces (3:11), which is located on the western wall of the city.

Critical Observation

There are some who seem marked by special zeal for the work. Shallum's zeal leads to making the rebuilding a family affair—even his daughters help in his section of repair (3:12).

The Valley Gate (3:13) is likely located near the southwest corner of the city. The Dung Gate, which received its name because it was the gate that led to Jerusalem's landfill, is next along the wall's repair route (3:14). The Fountain Gate and the Pool of Siloam (3:15) mark the southernmost point of Jerusalem. From there the wall route Nehemiah is tracing turns northeasterly along the valley of the Kidron.

3:17–32

THE EASTERN WALL AND THE FINAL GATES

Verses 17–27 continue with repetitious "next to him" statements, cataloguing the list of those who worked on the eastern portion of the wall between the Fountain Gate and the Horse Gate. The Horse Gate (3:28) is at the easternmost part of the wall. The Inspection Gate (3:31) is the last gate before returning back to the Sheep Gate, where Nehemiah begins his record. It marks the northern part of the eastern wall.

Take It Home

The names here constitute a roll of honor of Yahweh's workers, recorded for lasting remembrance. This is typical scriptural and divine practice, for Matthew 10:42 tells us that Christ sees and remembers all puny acts of love and devotion offered to and for Him (see also Mark 14:9; Hebrews 6:10).

NEHEMIAH 4:1-23

THREATS AGAINST GOD'S WORK

Ridicule	4:1–6
Intimidation	4:7–12
Organized Perseverance	4:13–23

Setting Up the Section

Having chronicled the building efforts in chapter 3, here, in chapter 4, we return to Nehemiah's memoirs. The last verse of chapter 2 reflects on the success God will grant to those in the rebuilding efforts (2:20), so it is not surprising that shortly thereafter an enemy's voice speaks out.

4:1–6

RIDICULE

Verse 1 suggests that ridicule proceeds out of helplessness. Note the presence of the army of Samaria (4:2), which indicates Sanballat has armed help at hand. And yet he can hardly benefit from it because Nehemiah has official permission from the king, which surely frustrates Sanballat to no end.

Not being able to use military force against God's people, Sanballat turns to mockery. Tobiah's fox remark is said in reference to walls that are undoubtedly thick and capable of withstanding strong military force (4:3). Note that Nehemiah does not let go with a retort to the mockers but has recourse to God (4:4–5).

Critical Observation

How are we to view Nehemiah's prayer? It is a prayer for justice against sin. As such, it is a prayer for God to act. Nehemiah is not presuming to take vengeance into his own hands; he commits that to God. These are not personal enemies but enemies of God's kingdom. There is no indication that Sanballat, Tobiah, and their men seek repentance. There is a high cost to mocking the people of God (implicit in Nehemiah's prayer in verses 4–5).

4:7–12

INTIMIDATION

Despite the resistance to their work, Nehemiah and the wall builders are persistent.

Verses 7–9 reveal that from all four directions the builders are surrounded. Sanballat has been angry, but now he and his cohorts are furious (4:7), so much so that there is a possibility of an armed assault (4:8).

Critical Observation

Since the time of the Assyrian conquest of Palestine, the Philistine territory had been a separate province called Ashdod. With Samaria to the north, Arabs to the south, Ammon to the east, and Ashdod to the west—Judah was surrounded.

The discouragement of the builders is evident in verses 10–12. Perhaps this is in light of the fresh threat in verses 7–9, and this is their despairing response. Not only does Judah speak but the enemy's threat and intimidation is also announced (4:11). It also sounds as though the Jews living in neighboring villages pick up the threats and propaganda from the enemies and repeat it to the workers (4:12). Perhaps the enemies leak word of the plans that are being made, then those Jews come to Jerusalem and repeat the rumors among the workers. It is all intended to demoralize.

4:13–23

ORGANIZED PERSEVERANCE

Nehemiah admits that people are placed in vulnerable positions to stand guard at the wall (4:13), but he charges them to remember the Lord (4:14). Note the effectiveness this immediate defense has on their attackers (4:15).

Demystifying Nehemiah

Nehemiah's speech in verses 14–15 is very much like Deuteronomy 20:1–4, and it serves to assuage the people's fear and remind them that they fight both in the name of God and in defense of their families. God's sovereignty is stirring (see Nehemiah 4:9) and moving the people.

In the revised building scheme there seems to be several groups. Some are permanent guards (4:16). Some serve as load haulers (4:17), who carry loads and their weapons at the same time. Then there are the builders (4:18), each with his sword strapped on. Finally, there is an alarm system in place (4:18–20).

Take It Home

In verse 20, Nehemiah says, "Our God [emphatic in Hebrew] will fight for us" (NIV), revealing the confidence that undergirds their toil. And with that reminder, the wall continues to go up. Commuting is done away with, and the people are constantly on guard. The unusually perilous circumstances call for uncommon measures for the immediate future.

NEHEMIAH 5:1–19

FOLLY AMONG GOD'S PEOPLE

Nehemiah's Confrontation	5:1–11
The Response	5:12–19

Setting Up the Section

While the threat of external assault is the fear in chapter 4, here in chapter 5, internal dissension begins to take place.

5:1–11

NEHEMIAH'S CONFRONTATION

Notice the outcry in verses 1–5. It seems there are three groups raising dissension in the midst of the building efforts. The first group consists of families who may have owned no land for food, and thus taking time to work on the wall diminished their ability to earn wages (5:2). The second group consists of those who are mortgaging their land, farms, and homes in order to get food, and these people will lose this security completely if they cannot pay their debts from the annual harvest (5:3). The third group consists of those having to borrow, with fields and vineyards as collateral, in order to pay the king's taxes (5:4–5). Some of their family members are in debt-slavery because of this hardship.

The crying shame in Nehemiah 5, however, is that the profiteers are fellow Jews (5:1, 7). The problem is probably not interest/usury but debt-slavery, with loan sharks possessing the pledge or the collateral that is put up. So Nehemiah turns prosecutor (5:8–9). Apparently, some Jews have been sold to surrounding peoples and redeemed, meaning that some of the loan sharks (5:8) must have sold their fellow Jews obtained by debt default to surrounding peoples.

Critical Observation

Nehemiah admits that he and his associates have also made loans of money and grain for collateral, but there is no reason to suppose that Nehemiah had pressed the claims and profiteered from the loans he'd made. In fact, he says that all claims are not to be pressed; they are to be abandoned. Hard-pressed people must be cut some slack.

5:12–19

THE RESPONSE

Nehemiah's order in verse 11 is for the profiteers to restore collateral they have sucked up as well as surcharges they have demanded. The moneylenders give their consent (5:12) to Nehemiah's directive. However, Nehemiah presses for even more clout and calls the priests to administer an oath, after which Nehemiah depicts the curse (5:13) that will overtake those who renege on their obligation.

Demystifying Nehemiah

Nehemiah 5:14–19 is something of an extract out of Nehemiah's diary. It interrupts the chronological flow of the matter at hand but is likely placed here to set forth a positive sample of Nehemiah's walking in the fear of God (5:15) over against the heartlessness of the profiteering Jews in verses 1–13.

Nehemiah has certain rights by virtue of his position as appointed governor—a food allowance, or a stipend—but he voluntarily relinquishes them. He also doesn't allow his staff to lord their stipends over the people as the underlings of past governors had (5:14–15). Apparently, Nehemiah pays for his stock and food supply (5:17–18). What motivates this kind of self-sacrificing, non-oppressive leadership? Why is Nehemiah different from his predecessors? Because he fears God (5:15). This is what should have—according to Nehemiah—motivated the wheelers and dealers in verse 9.

Take It Home

Here is the true basis for biblical ethics: the fear of God. The awe of God controls your treatment of others. The fear of God leads to compassion for people. Nehemiah not only demands the scoundrels of verses 1–13 change, but he himself has consistently set an example of proper servant leadership.

NEHEMIAH 6:1–19

STRATAGEMS AGAINST GOD'S SERVANT

God Gives Strength	6:1–9
God Gives Clarity	6:10–14
God Gives Tenacity	6:15–19

Setting Up the Section

The schemes recorded in this chapter are directed toward Nehemiah, either to eliminate him or at least to discredit him. Undoubtedly his enemies want to bring trouble to his exemplary leadership. Note the emphasis on fear throughout the chapter (6:9, 13–14, 19).

6:1–9

GOD GIVES STRENGTH

At this point there has been substantial progress on the wall. Now Sanballat and company want a consultation with Nehemiah (6:2). Verse 2 relates Nehemiah's perception, which is likely an accurate one: They intend to harm or do evil to him. Their persistence (6:4) shows their helplessness or weakness, since they can't think of any other approach except to repeat the last ploy. The fifth time (6:5–7) Sanballat sends an open letter. Note the interjected prayer in verse 9.

Critical Observation

There is an emphasis on fear throughout the chapter (6:9, 13–14, 19). However, Nehemiah remains perceptive (6:2), tenacious (6:4), and clear-headed (6:8), yet also weak. Otherwise, why pray this way? Here in the thick of it all he casts himself upon God's strength.

6:10–14

GOD GIVES CLARITY

Apparently Shemaiah wants an interview, so Nehemiah calls on him. Shemaiah's being behind closed doors could be a prophetic action reinforcing his word of seclusion for Nehemiah (6:10). The first part of Nehemiah's answer in verse 11 seems to mean, "I have more guts than that!" The second part of his answer seems to mean, "And it's wrong!" When he asks if one like himself (a layman and not a priest) can go into the temple, the expected answer is no. (He is referring to the temple itself, not merely its courtyards.) This is a privilege and right that is off limits to laymen (see Numbers 18:7; 2 Chronicles 26:16–20).

Shemaiah's intent is to get Nehemiah to commit a ritual transgression and thereby be discredited. But Nehemiah discerns (Nehemiah 6:12) that God has not sent Shemaiah, but that Tobiah and Sanballat have paid him off. It is all a plot to lead Nehemiah into sin (6:13). And Shemaiah is only a *part* of the problem; the prophetess Noadiah and other prophets are conspiring together (6:14), seeking to magnify Nehemiah's danger and send him into paranoia.

Demystifying Nehemiah

Verse 14 is a prayer for vengeance, a plea for God to remember and deal with the dastardly deeds and designs of the likes of Shemaiah. There is nothing wrong with such a prayer. What can be more wicked than placing one's office as bearer of God's Word up for hire, using the Lord's Word as a tool to manipulate people and gain power over them? This situation highlights the discernment God's servants need. This sort of ploy is so tricky because it involves a revelation claim, an alleged word from the Lord—and not just from one person but a plurality of people (6:14).

6:15–19

GOD GIVES TENACITY

The rebuilding of Jerusalem's wall is completed in just fifty-two days, on the twenty-fifth of Elul, which would've been late August or early September (6:15). All of the Jews' enemies are overcome with awe because there is no question that this building has been accomplished by the hand of God.

Verse 17 begins with the particle *gam*, translated *also*, as if to say, "This, too, is going on at that time." This is all taking place during the time Tobiah has steady correspondence with the more powerful people among the Jews. Likely, some of the important citizens of Jerusalem are against the isolation of Judah, perhaps for commercial reasons. Tobiah has many connections with the Jews, as many of them are under oath to him (6:18). Tobiah is also linked by marriage; his son is married into one of the families of the wall builders (3:4, 30).

Verse 19 highlights two items: intimidating letters from Tobiah and a constant stream of gossip, part of which is propaganda about the good deeds of Tobiah. This is continuous (as the Hebrew participles suggest). Some want to wear Nehemiah down to a reasonable solution of reconciliation and compromise.

Take It Home

There is no doubt that Tobiah is powerful, and his power combined with his desire to see Nehemiah's plans fail make for an intimidating combination. Whether Nehemiah is intimidated or not, Tobiah's threats don't stop him, and the wall is still completed in an extraordinary amount of time.

NEHEMIAH 7:1–73

THE EXILES WHO RETURNED

The Registration	7:1–5
The Listing	7:6–73

Setting Up the Section

The rebuilding of the wall, Nehemiah's original task, is now complete. But his work in rebuilding Jerusalem and the morale of the Israelites is far from over. This chapter begins the shift in focus from the wall to the securing and populating of the city.

7:1–5

THE REGISTRATION

In Nehemiah 7:1–5, Nehemiah makes a series of necessary arrangements after the completion of the wall. First Nehemiah appoints guards to the city's gates in order to ensure the city's safety (7:1). In charge of the guards, he appoints his brother, Hanani, and another man, Hananiah, based on their integrity (7:2). Second, he also establishes new security regulations that include the gates to the city only being open during the busiest parts of the day, and various people throughout the town stand guard over their neighborhoods (7:3). Third, Nehemiah notices the town's vacancy and the need for people to fill it (7:4). A city the size of Jerusalem is safer with more inhabitants.

Upon noticing the low number of inhabitants in the city, Nehemiah has all of the families in Jerusalem register (7:5). The list that follows is not a list compiled of the people who returned with Nehemiah to build the wall but rather is the genealogical record of those in the first post-exilic return in 537 BC. Nehemiah later uses this list of Israelite families as part of his plan in chapter 11.

7:6–73

THE LISTING

Nehemiah uses the same language following the genealogical parallel in 8:1 that Ezra uses following his in 3:1. But the gathering Nehemiah 8 describes is a wholly different gathering than that of Ezra 3:1. It occurs in the same month (seventh month), yet some ninety years later. Nevertheless, the editor of Nehemiah wants us to view the two assemblies side by side. He wants to draw a distinct parallel between the watershed beginning in Ezra 3 (when the returned exiles began to build the temple) and the contemporary gathering in Nehemiah's day after the temple had been rebuilt and the city restored. In this way, the editor emphasizes that the occasion of Nehemiah 8–10 is as central and seminal as its earlier counterpart, namely the initial restoration under Zerubbabel. That had been the critical commencement, and Nehemiah 8–10, in turn, is a kind of consummation.

Critical Observation

This list in Nehemiah 7:5–73 reproduces the record found in Ezra 2. The figure of 42,360 (in Ezra 2:64) appears as the total also found in Nehemiah 7:66, yet the individual items add up to three different totals. There is general agreement that the divergences are copying errors, arising from the special difficulty of understanding or reproducing numerical lists.

More than anything, the list shows God's faithfulness in preserving His chosen people. Genealogies are also important because Jews used them to prove their bloodline as descendents of Abraham. For this reason, two of the three Synoptic Gospels include genealogies that trace Jesus back to David and Abraham as well.

Demystifying Nehemiah

The covenant renewal of Nehemiah 8–10 can be seen on a plane with the temple restoration of Ezra 3. Ezra 3 stresses the people and temple, while Nehemiah 8 stresses the people and Torah. Or, to say it another way, one depicts worship restored and the other depicts the Word restored.

NEHEMIAH 8:1–18

THE FOUNDATION OF REFORMATION

Setting Up the Section

Now that the wall is rebuilt, Nehemiah moves on to the rebuilding of people's lives. The rest of the book of Nehemiah will deal with the reformation of the people, beginning with the reading of God's Law.

8:1–12

EZRA READS

Although Ezra had been in Jerusalem since before Nehemiah (Ezra 7:6–9), this is the first mention of him in the book of Nehemiah (Nehemiah 8:1). In addition to being the scribe, Ezra also serves as a priest. Nehemiah governs the people, but Ezra is in charge of their spiritual well-being. The Book of the Law mentioned in verse 1 is probably the Jewish Torah, or Genesis–Deuteronomy of the full canon.

The audience consists of men, women, and all who can listen with understanding (8:2). This hearing of the Word is marked by patience, attention, reverence, and worship (8:3–6). The Levites circulate among the people, perhaps doing exposition of the Word in small groups.

Critical Observation

Much ink has been spilt over the participle *mephorash* in verse 8, which qualifies the verb *read.* Some hold that it means "translating" (from Hebrew into Aramaic). Others hold that it means "making distinct," or as an adverb, "clearly." Still others take it as "paragraph by paragraph," breaking it down into manageable chunks. Probably the second or third option is preferable: breaking it down and explaining the meaning. The intent, in any case, is to make the Word of God clear, to highlight the insight it holds, and to make its applications obvious.

This assembly takes place on the first day of the seventh month (8:2), which is the Feast of Trumpets (Leviticus 23:23–25; Numbers 29:1–6). The weeping of the people (Nehemiah 8:9) may be over sin exposed through the reading of the Torah. The weeping and sadness of verse 9 are balanced by the joy and gladness of verse 12. They celebrate because they understand. But they have to be ordered by Nehemiah and company to be joyful (8:9–11). Note that this is a social joy, not a selfish joy (8:10).

Demystifying Nehemiah

Three times the people are told that the day is holy (8:9–11), and they are commanded to be joyful. The last line of verse 10 contains the primary argument against sadness: "For the joy of the LORD is your strength" (NIV). Perhaps there is the suggestion that ongoing sorrow and grief, while proper at times, can leave the people of God vulnerable. The text implies that joy and delight in Yahweh fulfill a protective function in believers' lives, keeping them, perhaps, from being swallowed in despair.

8:13–18

THE FESTIVAL

The heads of households meet for ongoing Bible study (8:13). They find written in the Torah the regulations about the Feast of Tabernacles (or Booths; see Leviticus 23:33–43; Deuteronomy 16:13–15, with the emphasis on joy in the latter passage). Nehemiah 8:16 indicates the various locations of their booths, while verse 17 emphasizes the uniqueness of the celebration.

Take It Home

The "celebration" of Tabernacles was an appropriate activity to post-exilic Judah, as it should be to the Lord's people in all ages. Tabernacles was meant to force Israel to recall their tenuous post-Egyptian existence in the wilderness journey. In the midst of Israel's settled life in the promised land, they need to remember their former hand-to-mouth existence. In the midst of what is also a harvest festival, they remember that life can be a wilderness, and their only sustainer is Yahweh. They must never forget their humiliation in the wilderness (Deuteronomy 8) or the God who sustained them through it.

NEHEMIAH 9:1–38

THE PREPARATION FOR REFORMATION

Setting Up the Section

The reading of the Word of God is a catalyst for the Israelites' reformation. Having been away from the temple and the daily worship practices, the scripture they hear reminds them that a change on their part is necessary.

9:1–5

PRELUDE TO PRAYER

After reading the Word of God, the people are now determined to get back to the business that had them so upset in Nehemiah 8:9. The term *seed* (*zara*) refers to the "seed of Israel" and implies the doctrine of the two humanities (in light of Genesis 3:15). Here Israel separates herself from amalgamating with the foreigners and from covenant compromise.

First comes the reading of the Torah and then confession and worship. The worship is built upon the Word (Nehemiah 9:3). The leaders on this occasion seem to be Levites. The Levites begin with a call to worship: "Arise, bless the Lord your God forever and ever!" (9:5 NASB).

9:6–38

THE PRAYER

Observe the historical moments the prayer covers: creation (9:6); Abraham (9:7–8); Exodus (9:9–12); Sinai (9:13–14); wilderness (9:15–21); conquest (9:22–25); the judges and following (9:26–37). The prayer can be divided into three sections based around what they reveal about God:

1) *The gifts of God's grace (9:6–15)*

   The majority of this section focuses on Yahweh as redeemer. However, verse 6 expresses homage to Yahweh as creator. Both verses 6 and 7 begin with the phrase *'attah hu,'* implying that the creator of verse 6 and the redeemer of verse 7 are one and the same. Verse 6 lauds Yahweh as not only creator of all things (heaven, earth, seas, and their contents), but as life-giver and sustainer as well. And for all this He receives worship from those conscious, invisible beings, the heavenly hosts. In the redemption section, the prayer highlights redemption and covenant (9:7–8). The root of covenant is election, as seen in the phrase "who chose Abram." The concern of covenant is place (the land) and people (his seed). The anchor of covenant is fidelity.

   Though the note of compassion is not lacking (9:9), verses 10–11 stress the judgment aspect of Yahweh's deliverance. Yahweh does not grant redemption while withholding direction. Note how positively the Sinai gifts are described: upright ordinances, true laws, good statutes and commandments, holy Sabbath (9:13–14). Sinai is the assurance that Yahweh does not redeem a people from bondage only to abandon them to ambiguity.

   Verse 15 reflects on the provision aspect of God's redemption. Episodes like those of Exodus 16–17 are in view here. This is not standard provision but the provision in extremity (hunger, thirst), provided in unpredictable ways: from heaven and from a rock.

2) *The tenacity of your goodness (Nehemiah 9:16–31)*

   After the second-person perspective in verses 9–15, highlighting all that Yahweh has done, there comes a third-person comment: "But they, our fathers, acted arrogantly" (NASB). Verses 16–17 use strong language. This is no momentary lapse on Israel's part. Everything speaks of deliberate, open-eyed resistance to God's will. Rebellion is absurd in light of all the preceding acts of grace (9:7–15), and God does not withhold His forgiveness (9:17).

Critical Observation

Here is the phenomenal character of Yahweh. As if this were insufficient, we find the amazing words of verse 17: "You never turned away from them" (CEV). This passage tells us that our hope is not in denying or explaining away our rebellion but simply in the character of God.

Verse 18 alludes to the golden calf episode of Exodus 32. While they commit these grave acts of contempt toward God, they receive the same grace and guidance and provision as before, as verse 21 testifies. The following verses celebrate the conquest of the land east of the Jordan (9:22–23) and west of it (9:24–25).

Demystifying Nehemiah

One must remember that all this provision comes in the wake of their stubborn disobedience (9:16–18). Remembering this context leads to an important observation: God's gifts are no sign of our righteousness.

The prayer next rehearses the behavior of Israel when settled in the promised land, during the period of the judges. As in a previous generation (9:18), Israel again commits great sin (9:26). For this Yahweh brings them into distress, but the wonder is that there is deliverance (9:27). But nothing changes. Israel is in a cycle of repeated infidelity (9:28–31).

3) *The rightness of your justice (9:32–37)*

The Levites and the assembly are ceasing their historical review to make their contemporary request. They ask the Lord not to look on all this history of troubles ("hardship, weariness") as trivial. They confess, however, that Yahweh has acted rightly in all the distress that He has brought upon them. They clearly admit the rightness of Yahweh's action and the persisting sin of Israel (9:33–35).

Verse 36 reveals their condition at the current moment: slaves (stated twice) in distress. Even though they are back in the promised land, they recognize that this is not a state of blessing, because they are ruled over and taxed by others.

The prayer of chapter 9 ends descriptively, as if to say, "This is our situation." There is no directive, no particular petition here. That, however, is an implied petition in light of the whole prayer. They are asking, "Have your great compassions altogether ceased? You will not now forsake us, will you?"

NEHEMIAH 10:1–39

THE STRUCTURE FOR REFORMATION

Setting Up the Section

Here we find the response to the prayer of chapter 9, or perhaps better stated, the consequence of the prayer. In light of the ongoing history of apostasy and infidelity, what can Judah do but repent? Covenant is the vehicle of repentance.

10:1–29

THE PEOPLE AGREE

The names in verses 1–27 include both the leadership and the laity. Nehemiah and Zedekiah seem to be by themselves, then the priests, listed mostly according to family names (10:2–8), followed by the Levites, listed as individuals rather than families (10:9–13), and then the leaders (10:14–27; verses 14–19 follow Ezra 2; these are mostly lay families).

Nehemiah 10:28–29 reiterates that the people are entering under a curse, calling down judgment on themselves if they do not keep their oath (see Jeremiah 34). Covenant renewal cannot thrive on generalities and vague resolutions. The promises included here are precise. Nehemiah 10:30 is the promise that they will not intermarry with the pagan people around them.

Critical Observation

The covenantal promise to not intermarry with foreigners does not imply that God looks negatively on those who are not Israelites simply because of their nationality. Rather, this insures that the Israelites maintain households that honor and serve Yahweh. The nations around the Israelites were pagan nations with a variety of deities and religious practices. It was this religious intermingling that was the concern. The Old Testament accounts of intermarrying with pagan nations never produce positive results (see 1 Kings 11:1–11).

10:30–39

THE PEOPLE VOW

Nehemiah 10:31 prohibits trade in Jerusalem on the Sabbath, maintaining that Yahweh, and not money, is the God of the Israelites. The promise that every seventh year individuals will stop working the land and cancel all debts is a reiteration of the Sabbath law as recorded in Exodus 23:10–11 and Deuteronomy 15:1–2.

Then in Nehemiah 10:32–33, the people make a promise that they will participate in the giving of funds for worship maintenance. Because the temple is now rebuilt, the people promised temple taxes and offerings will also be restored. The law is even so specific as to include the provision of firewood to ensure the sacrifices can be burned on the altar. The people's covenant includes a lots system for calendaring when families are in charge of providing the wood (10:34).

The people also assume responsibility for bringing a number of offerings to the temple each year, as noted in verses 35–39. These provisions deal with the maintenance of the temple worship itself, particularly the temple staff—the Levites who receive the tithe (10:38–39). Provisions include the firstfruits of their crops, firstborn sons, firstborn of all their animals, and a tithe of their crops.

Take It Home

The major concern in this chapter is found in verse 39: "We will not neglect the house of our God" (NIV). The people covenant, or promise, that they will keep worship priority in their lives.

The same matters here are still issues for Christians: marriage, Sabbath, and giving. While the cultural customs may work themselves out differently in modern culture, the call for God's people to prioritize their faith lives in practical ways is still the same.

NEHEMIAH 11:1–36

THE ORDER OF THE PEOPLE OF THE LORD

Setting Up the Section

Although Jerusalem had been a city with little structure and little to offer its residents, the completion of the wall and the city's increased morale make it a more appealing place to live. This section lays out Nehemiah's plan for encouraging the Jews to populate the city.

11:1–24

ANCHORING THE CITY

Remember this is the holy city (11:1, 18), and yet the present situation is a far cry from all nations streaming to it as depicted in Isaiah 2. The leaders already live in the city. Then there is the lot-casting scheme, and those who volunteer (Nehemiah 11:2) are those who have been selected by lot.

Critical Observation

Nehemiah proposes that with the casting of lots, one out of ten families living in the territory of Judah should relocate and reside in Jerusalem (11:1). In this way, it is not Nehemiah who forces them to live in Jerusalem, but it is the will of God. They cannot bear a grudge against Nehemiah; they have been drafted by the Lord. And yet those selected willingly go. Here is sovereign direction willingly accepted.

The move into the city for those whose lots were chosen is a sacrifice. They do not prefer to live in Jerusalem or they already would have settled there. So they face the trouble of uprooting themselves from homes and means of livelihood, leaving everything for the city.

The listing for Jerusalem (11:3–24) is part of a list of the population of the whole province of Judah in the times of Ezra and Nehemiah. The population of Jerusalem in verses 3–19 tallies both the newcomers (verses 1–2) and all others who were already in Jerusalem. If the tallies are followed (11:6, 8, 12–14, 18–19), there is 3,044, so after including wives and children, one could estimate a population between 10,000–12,000 people.

11:25–36

POSSESSING THE LAND

The next verses (11:25–36) record a list of villages outside of the city walls where some of the Levites were living. As citizens of one empire, these people are free to settle where they want if they keep the peace (11:36).

Demystifying Nehemiah

Though it is a small, mustard-seed sort of beginning, can we not see in these mundane verses a renewing (even in dark, hard times) of the place-element (land) of the Abrahamic covenant? Hence, there is a hint of the fidelity of God in the geography of Judah here.

NEHEMIAH 12:1–43

THE CELEBRATION IN THE JOY OF THE LORD

Setting Up the Section

This next section is the account of the dedication of the newly rebuilt wall of Jerusalem. We are not sure how long after the completion of the wall this dedication occurred. One has the impression that the dedication takes place after the events of Nehemiah 7–11. It is not something to be neglected, but there may have been other, more pressing concerns at the time when the wall was finished.

12:1–26

STRUCTURING THE WORSHIP

The list of names continues in Nehemiah 12:1–26, now with the names of the priests and Levites who return from exile. These verses break down as follows:

Verses 1–9 list the priestly families and Levites at the time of Zerubbabel and Jeshua in 536 BC (see 1 Chronicles 24:7–19; Ezra 2:40–42). Verses 10–11 list the high priests from Jeshua's line (see 1 Chronicles 6:3–15). Continuing in verses 12–21 is a list of the heads of twenty-one priestly families during Joiakim's time, the second generation. The notes and records from the book of annals, mentioned in verses 22–23, include the list of Levites that follows.

12:27–43

DEDICATING THE WALL

Now that the wall of Jerusalem is rebuilt, a celebration ensues for the people. Before the celebration began, verses 27–29 tell us that Levites, singers, and musicians from the region around Jerusalem were brought into the city to be a part of the dedication festivities.

The celebration begins with two large choirs circumnavigating the top of the wall, in opposite directions, singing songs of praise and thanksgiving (12:31–39). The choirs are accompanied by the Levites named in these verses. The first choir, which covers the wall from the Valley Gate counterclockwise, is led by Ezra (12:31–37), while the second group, covering the wall from the Valley Gate clockwise, is led by Nehemiah (12:38–39). The two groups meet at the temple where they continue to worship and offer sacrifices as they are joined by the women and children (12:40–43).

Take It Home

What is the significance of Nehemiah 12:1–26? Here are two historical generations of priests and Levites—people who are still serving in the worship of sacrifice and praise and vigilance as did an earlier generation. As God's people, we are part of a whole history of generations devoted to serving God. We cannot ignore the record of those who have served Yahweh before our own time.

NEHEMIAH 12:44–13:3

THE PERSEVERANCE IN THE WORSHIP OF THE LORD

Setting Up the Section

The dedication of the wall in Jerusalem marks a fully restored city, and as the holy city this means that the religious community is fully restored. Once again the temple functions as it once had, as the center of worship for a spiritually strong people. The Israelites have not had such a sense of security since before the exile, so to the very last detail they insure worship will resume as it once had.

11:44–47

MUNDANE PROVISIONS

The joy and delight in those who lead in worship insures the proper continuity of worship. Among this action is the appointing of a staff to keep up with the tithes that were received. The aforementioned tithes of firstfruits, crops, and so on will be a large accumulation, therefore it requires a staff to collect the offerings and redistribute them to the temple workers who receive portions of the tithe (12:44–45). See Numbers 18:21–32 for the portions referred to in verse 47.

Critical Observation

The repeated mention of David in Nehemiah's account of the temple organization leads one to perceive Nehemiah as doing for the post-exilic temple what David did for the original one. Because music had been such an important part of David's design for worshiping the Lord, Nehemiah guarantees provisions be made for the singers and musicians (12:46–47).

13:1–3

ESSENTIAL SEPARATION

The reference in 13:1 is to Deuteronomy 23:3–6. How do they interpret that passage? Do they infer from the mention of Ammonites and Moabites that the text intends the exclusion of all foreigners (13:3)? Observe how in 13:2 they recall not merely the threat of mankind but the protection of God.

There is a wonderful simplicity about this passage. There is something refreshing when the people of God order their lives out of the Word of God. Their practice simply flows out of what they had found.

Take It Home

Keep in mind Ezra 6:21 as you read this passage. The separation of Nehemiah 13:3 presupposes that such people clung to their paganism. After all, it was Israel's relationship with pagan nations that led to the exile that they were still recovering from. Converts to Yahweh were welcome. So, praise (12:44–47) and purity (13:1–3) must mark the ongoing life of God's people.

NEHEMIAH 13:4–31

THE ONGOING PERILS OF THE CHURCH

Compromise	13:4–9
Neglect/Indifference	13:10–14
Commercialism	13:15–22
Amalgamation	13:23–31

Setting Up the Section

The final chapter of the book of Nehemiah includes a closing series of reforms Nehemiah enacts among the people. Each reform covers an area of the covenantal law that the Israelites are guilty of breaking.

13:4–9

COMPROMISE

To highlight the reform of verses 1–3, Nehemiah describes a problem that he dealt with regarding too much intermingling with foreigners. The Tobiah of verse 4 is the same Tobiah who made himself an enemy of Nehemiah by opposing the rebuilding of the wall. Not only that, but he is also an Ammonite, and as such is prohibited to enter the temple. There is a note of defiance in this. The ease of compromise is clear in verse 4: Eliashib is close to Tobiah. This may mean he is closely associated with him, or it could mean he is related to him. There may have been a marriage tie (see 6:17–19), and if so, his behavior simply shows that blood is thicker than covenant. Eliashib believes pleasing people matters more than fidelity to God.

The opportunity for compromise is the absence of Nehemiah (13:6), but the cure for compromise is the arrival of Nehemiah (13:7–9). Eviction is the answer, so Nehemiah throws all of Tobiah's belongings out of the storehouse (13:8). The compromise of Eliashib is in clear opposition to the Word of God (13:1–3), and therefore it had to be dealt with harshly instead of gently.

13:10–14

NEGLECT/INDIFFERENCE

The Levites are to live on tithes that are given (Numbers 18:21), but they had not received them—the procedures of Nehemiah 12:44–47 having gone into eclipse. So, the Levites flee to the towns and to their fields to gather what living they can. Hence, the house of God is forsaken (13:11).

Verse 12 reports that obedience is reactivated. And to attempt to ensure the system from breakdown, Nehemiah appoints reliable men over this business (13:13).

Demystifying Nehemiah

Note Nehemiah's prayer in verse 14. This is not a works-merit prayer. It is a prayer in the spirit of Matthew 10:40–42, Mark 14:9, and Hebrews 6:10. It is the prayer of one who knows that God does not ignore the earnest service of unworthy servants. Nehemiah asks that God not wipe out his loyal deeds, those done out of a covenant commitment.

13:15–22

COMMERCIALISM

The issue of work on the Sabbath arises (13:15). The offense is twofold: The people of Judah are working on the Sabbath, bringing loads of food into Jerusalem and (apparently) selling them. Secondly is the issue of the foreigners, the Tyrians, who do their fish selling on the Sabbath as well (13:16).

Nehemiah's rebuke is a theological one (13:17–18): These Sabbath-breakers are placing Israel under the anger of Yahweh again. See this same argument pressed by the prophet Jeremiah in the pre-exilic period (Jeremiah 17:19–27).

To prevent further offense, Nehemiah closes and guards the gates. He places his own men there to prevent traders from entering the city (Nehemiah 13:19). Then he makes threats against the lollygaggers in verses 20–21. Perhaps these people tried to hang around outside the walls hoping to draw people outside the city to buy. But Nehemiah shuts this off as well. Then in verse 22 he institutes a more lasting provision to insure compliance.

Critical Observation

Exodus 31:12–17, especially verses 13 and 17, indicates that the Sabbath is a kind of sign. It marks out Israel as unique, for other peoples do not have the blessing of the Sabbath. The Sabbath is a gift for the people because they are able to cease working (Exodus 20:8–11; 34:21). In Egypt they wouldn't dare stop work! But when Yahweh frees them from bondage, He enables them to cease from work—every week. The Sabbath is a sign of grace and freedom, not of bondage.

13:23–31

AMALGAMATION

In Nehemiah 13:23, the issue of intermarriage resurfaces. Note the drift seen in the second generation (13:23–24). Intermarriage with pagans occurs, and one discovers that the cultural ties of the children are closer to the mother's roots (13:23–24). Eventually, this will prove true for religious ties as well. Note the action taken in verse 25. Nehemiah's cursing of the people means that they reap the negative consequences of the covenant they established with God. Nehemiah calls God's judgment into effect.

Then Nehemiah makes the people take an oath to not give their daughters in marriage to pagans or to take pagan women in marriage for their sons (this is what they have already sworn to do in 10:28–30). Nehemiah presses an argument upon them—a biblical, theological, and historical argument, based on Solomon's drift toward paganism (13:26–27). He enjoyed vast privileges but came to ruin because of this very offense. Marriages to pagans had occurred among the priestly circles of the community (13:28–29). A grandson of the high priest became son-in-law to Sanballat. A priest should have been an exemplar of piety and covenant fidelity (see Numbers 25:13).

ESTHER

INTRODUCTION TO ESTHER

The book of Esther is a good complement to the books of Ezra and Nehemiah. While those books describe the trials and challenges of the Jewish exiles who were finally allowed to return to their homeland, Esther shows the plight of the Jewish people in Persia during the same period of time. Some people uphold Esther and Mordecai as heroic figures, yet others question whether they were actually godly individuals. God is not once mentioned by name in this book, yet it is a testament to divine providence.

AUTHOR

The author is unknown yet certainly appears to be a Jewish individual who had remained in Persia after other Jews had departed.

PURPOSE

Esther and Mordecai have become role models for their courage and perseverance. Yet their success requires the reader to acknowledge God's work in post-exilic Persia (though God is never *specifically* acknowledged).

OCCASION

The account of Esther is a magnificent work purely on the grounds of literature: character, plot, conflict, and so on. But it was probably written to provide the background and setting for the creation of the Jewish holiday of Purim.

THEMES

Much of the action of Esther takes place during banquets. Many significant meals are mentioned in this short book (1:3, 5, 9; 2:18; 3:15; 5:4, 8; 7:1; 8:17; 9:17–18). But perhaps more significant are the themes that *aren't* mentioned: God, prayer, Jerusalem/Judah, and worship (other than fasting).

HISTORICAL CONTEXT

Esther would be near the end of the Old Testament if the books were positioned chronologically. As God had forewarned, His disobedient people had been carried off into captivity, many to Babylon. But by the time Esther was written, the Persians had already conquered the Babylonians.

CONTRIBUTION TO THE BIBLE

Along with Ezra and Nehemiah, Esther offers a look into Jewish life under the rule of the Persians. Esther's distinction is an insider's look from within the Persian Empire. The book also provides the only mention of Purim, a Jewish feast, in the Bible. More than anything, this book shows how God's providence preserves His people.

OUTLINE

ESTHER 1:1–2:18

A NEW QUEEN IN SUSA

Setting Up the Section

Due to their disobedience and pursuit of idols and other gods, the people of Israel and Judah have been carried into captivity by Assyria and Babylon. The Babylonians, in turn, are conquered by the Medes and Persians, so the group of Jews who originally went to Babylon is now under Persian rule. It is a trying time, but the story of Esther demonstrates how God's people obtain not only a voice but also an advocate in the king of Persia himself.

1:1–9

A LONG PARTY

The king in this passage is Xerxes, although many Bible translations use the Hebrew form of his name: *Ahasuerus*. He had been in power for three years after conflicts with Babylon and Egypt. His residence is in Susa, the capital of ancient Elam, which his father, Darius I, had rebuilt as a winter capital.

What had begun as an alliance between the Medes and the Persians (Daniel 5:28; 6:8, 12, 15) has by this time become the kingdom of Persia and Media (Esther 1:3, 14, 18–19), showing that Persia has become the dominant nation. Indeed, Ahasuerus is the great king of the Persians whom Daniel had prophesied would rise to power (Daniel 11:2).

The text does not provide the reason for Ahasuerus' elaborate six-month banquet, but history tells us that the following year he will (unwisely) wage war against the Greeks. This celebration may well have been an occasion for gathering support, rallying his group, and planning the military campaign. If so, Ahasuerus would have wanted everyone to see that he was richer and more powerful than anyone else.

After six months, the king's extravagance continues with a local weeklong banquet (Esther 1:5). Fine art is on display for the people of Susa—rich and poor—as they recline on expensive furniture, eat gourmet food, and drink fine wine. While the king entertains the men, the women have their own celebration, with Queen Vashti as their hostess.

1:10–22

THE FALL OF VASHTI

Much speculation is made about this section of the book of Esther. We know that at the end of the banquet, King Ahasuerus summons his wife, Vashti, to come wearing her crown to let everyone see how beautiful she is. But Vashti refuses to make an appearance. Was the king (who has indeed been enjoying wine) unreasonably asking his wife to appear before a crowd of drunken men, exposing her to potential embarrassment and shame? Or does Vashti coldly refuse a reasonable request to appear for the grand finale of the party? Opinions vary. But the result is clear: The king becomes furious (1:12).

Critical Observation

The Persian king had little regular interaction with his harem as a group. To ensure propriety, the women who associated with the king were attended to by eunuchs—men who had been castrated.

To his credit, Ahasuerus doesn't lose control and respond impulsively. He wisely calls his counselors and asks them how he should handle the situation. They know that as the most prominent woman in the Persian Empire, Vashti sets an example, and they fear that her actions will be influential on women throughout the kingdom. Consequently, they recommend that she be banned from ever again appearing with the king. Not only that, but they suggest she should be replaced by a woman more fit to be queen. Ahasuerus acts on their advice with an irreversible decree.

2:1–18

THE RISE OF ESTHER

After a number of years pass (1:3; 2:16), King Ahasuerus is again ready for a queen. If he hadn't passed an official ban against Vashti, perhaps he would have relented and taken her back. But instead, his advisors recommend a national search for young virgins from whom the king can select his next queen. Not surprisingly, Ahasuerus gladly agrees with their suggestion.

One eunuch (Hegai) is designated to prepare the contestants for their interview with the king. The young women will spend an entire year getting ready, and then each will spend one night with King Ahasuerus. Afterward, they are placed in his harem of concubines under the supervision of another eunuch (Shaashgaz). Unless the king requests one of them by name, these women will never meet with him again (2:14).

One of the Jews living in Susa at the time is Mordecai. He is raising his cousin Esther (*Hadassah* in Hebrew) as a daughter because her parents have died. She is very beautiful, and she is chosen to be among those contending for queen. She soon impresses Hegai, who gives her special attention and instruction (2:9, 15).

Everyone who sees Esther is impressed by her (2:15), and the king is no exception. He chooses Esther over all the other young women in the kingdom to become his new queen. He not only throws another great banquet to celebrate but he even proclaims a holiday to commemorate the wedding (2:18). But throughout the year-long process, Esther keeps her Jewish identity secret (2:10).

Demystifying Esther

The actions and direction of God are evident throughout the story of Esther, even though the name of God is never mentioned in the book. However, some hold the perspective that the book of Esther even more so reflects the struggles of Jewish exiles who became too attached to the land of their captivity, and thus dishonored God by not returning to their homeland when they were able to. From this perspective, God's providential care for the Jews in Persia was accomplished not because of their faithfulness but in spite of their unfaithfulness.

Take It Home

Esther was born as a captive in a foreign land where she had neither social status nor power. Yet she became queen over one of the greatest empires in the world. If nothing else, her story seems to demonstrate how God places the right person in the right place at the right time. Those who willingly allow Him to use them—where they are—may be surprised at what can be accomplished.

ESTHER 2:19–4:17

THE INFLUENCE OF MORDECAI

A Foiled Plot	2:19–23
Mordecai Makes an Enemy	3:1–15
Mordecai Enlists an Ally	4:1–17

Setting Up the Section

With Esther as queen, Mordecai has an ally at the highest level of government—and he will need it. He so alienates a villain named Haman that Haman determines to destroy not only Mordecai but all Jewish people. Because Esther has chosen not to reveal her ethnic identity, few people in Susa are aware that she is of Jewish descent. And that secret tends to complicate Esther's desire to help Mordecai.

2:19–23

A FOILED PLOT

The second group of virgins (2:19) may have been a regrouping of the first group (2:8) or yet another selection of beauties (2:12). Either way, the king would most likely have been preoccupied with them, and it would not have been the best time for Esther to approach him.

Yet Mordecai had overheard a plot to assassinate King Ahasuerus. (Mordecai's position in the city gate suggests he had a respectable degree of status.) Mordecai sends word to Esther, and she passes the information on to the king. Persian justice is swift; the two conspirators are immediately executed, and the details of their arrest and judgment are recorded.

The record of the event will be important later in the story. Also essential to the account is the fact that Esther never got around to telling her new husband that she had been among the Jewish people exiled to Persia.

3:1–15

MORDECAI MAKES AN ENEMY

The introduction of Haman to the story is sudden. Little is said about him or why Ahasuerus promotes him to second in command of the nation, but it soon becomes clear that Haman is a powerful and intolerant man. After he appears, we no longer read of the other princes who offered Ahasuerus wise counsel.

Critical Observation

One of the few things we are told about Haman is that he is the son of an Agagite (3:1). In contrast, Mordecai is a Benjamite (2:5)—the tribe of King Saul. By Persian times, the term *Agagite* might have been a reference to a geographic area rather than a specific person, yet Israelites and Amalekites had long been bitter enemies, which might help explain Haman's widespread resentment toward the Jewish people.

Before the Israelites had even crossed from Egypt to Canaan, they contended with the Amalekites, and God promised Moses their eventual destruction. (Exodus 17:8–16; Deuteronomy 25:17–19). Later, King Saul had been instructed to kill King Agag of the Amalekites (1 Samuel 15).

Understanding this history sheds light on Mordecai's attitude. Ahasuerus has commanded that everyone is to bow in Haman's presence, but Mordecai regularly refuses to do so. The king's servants are first to notice Mordecai's defiance. When they confront Haman, he becomes furious, and his rage is directed not just toward Mordecai but toward *all* Jews.

It is the first month of the year (April or May)—the Persian new year. Haman plans to annihilate the Jewish people, and he casts a lot (*pur*) to determine when it should be done (3:7). The lot designates the thirteenth day of the twelfth month.

Haman's appeal to the king is calculated and intentionally vague in that it never mentions the Jews specifically, and he mixes truths with half-truths and lies (3:8–9). For example, as a captive people, the Jews had been instructed to cooperate with their host nations (Jeremiah 29:7). Haman's charge that they disobey the king's laws is unfounded.

Haman gives Ahasuerus two incentives to grant his request: (1) a promised reduction of rebellion in the kingdom, and (2) a generous contribution to the national treasury. Although Ahasuerus appears to decline the monetary offer (Esther 3:11), his initial disinterest may be a customary oriental bargaining exercise. Perhaps the king expected to benefit both from Haman's initial payment and from later portions of the spoils that would be confiscated. The deal is struck, and letters are sent out throughout the kingdom to order the utter destruction of the Jews eleven months later (3:12–14).

Demystifying Esther

Due to the "pious bias" of many readers (the tendency to assume Bible characters are more righteous than average people), Mordecai is often presented as a hero in this story. Yet nowhere in the book of Esther is the reader told that he is a godly person, nor is he ever seen praying or making a declaration of his faith. The argument can be made that Mordecai represents the rebellious Jewish people of his day. Perhaps his refusal to bow to Haman is a conscious stand for God, although bowing does not necessarily indicate an act of worship. For most, it merely demonstrates submission to authority, which is not unreasonable. Mordecai's refusal could also reflect the longstanding hostility between the Jews and the Amalekites, of which Haman was one.

4:1–17

MORDECAI ENLISTS AN ALLY

The Persian king and his malevolent second-in-command have celebratory drinks after agreeing to the extinction of an entire people group (3:15), but the Jews across the Persian nation are soon fasting, weeping, and tearing their clothes. Although letters have gone out to all sections of the empire, the news still hasn't reached Esther. She finds out because she hears that Mordecai is just outside the city gate, mourning loudly and publicly. She sends new clothes to replace his sackcloth, but he will not be comforted. She then sends a messenger to see exactly why Mordecai is so distraught (4:4–5). Mordecai supplies all the details and sends the messenger back with a plea for Esther to intercede with the king.

Esther initially balks. She will be risking her life if she approaches Ahasuerus without being summoned, and she hasn't seen him in a month (4:11). But Mordecai presses her, appealing on both a personal and national level. Is it merely coincidence that she had been chosen as queen at just the time that her people are in dire danger? So Esther agrees to approach the king after a three-day fast of all the Jews in Susa.

Many people don't realize that Esther is certainly a reluctant heroine. Readers often presume that the fasting of her people also includes prayer and repentance, yet that is not necessarily the case. Fasting could be a ritual without real meaning (Isaiah 58:1–12). Even Esther's words, considered by some to be a statement of faith ("If I perish, I perish"), are actually a declaration of fatalism. Any nonbeliever can say as much, and often does when faced with similar circumstances.

Esther is certainly the heroine of the story, but she is not necessarily the godly heroine some people make her out to be. Otherwise, surely the writers would have included key observations such as prayer, repentance, and references to God. The absence of such things in the Esther account creates a deafening silence.

Take It Home

Many people find themselves in the position of Esther, to some degree. Life may be going quite smoothly for us even though we know of others who are fearful, endangered, or helpless. The need may arise to get outside of our comfort zones for the benefit of others, even if it involves a degree of risk. While Esther may have acted in response to Mordecai's coercion, our actions can be based on faith that God will see us through any situation. As a result, we might see God work in wonderful ways in our lives and in the lives of others.

ESTHER 5:1–7:10

TWO BANQUETS AND A HANGING

Setting Up the Section

Esther has been chosen to be queen by Ahasuerus, the king of Persia, but he still is not aware of her Jewish ties. Meanwhile, her cousin/stepfather Mordecai has made a powerful enemy of Haman, the king's second-in-command. Haman has secured the king's permission to annihilate all the Jews. Mordecai has enlisted Esther's help, but by approaching Ahasuerus without being summoned, she places her life at risk.

5:1–8

ESTHER'S FIRST BANQUET

After observing a three-day fast along with the other Jews in Susa, Esther approaches King Ahasuerus. Little is said about her state of mind, but she had numerous reasons to be fearful. To begin with, if she interrupts or interferes with the king at the wrong time, she might be put to death. And even if he welcomes her visit, she is going to have to confess to him that she is Jewish, convince him to reverse a law he has just instated (1:19; 3:10–11), and reveal that his closest companion (Haman) is a terrible villain. Most likely the king will feel deceived by Esther and/or Haman, and not many royal leaders like to admit to such poor judgment.

Still, Esther goes ahead with her plan. Dressed in her royal robes (5:1), she is graciously received by Ahasuerus. Yet when he asks what it is she wants, Esther only says she has prepared a banquet for him and Haman. The king sends for Haman right away, and as they are drinking after the meal, Ahasuerus again asks what Esther wants. She once more puts off her request by asking the two to attend yet another banquet the following day. At that time, she says, she will tell the king what she wants. The reasons for her delay are not explained, although during the interval God prepares the king to respond as He desires.

5:9–6:14

HAMAN'S HUMILIATION

Two special invitations for dinner—by the queen, no less—put Haman in a good mood, but it doesn't last long because Mordecai still shows him no respect. When he complains to his friends and family about Mordecai, they have a simple solution: Build a gallows and have him hanged. Haman need not wait for months until all the rest of the Jews are to be executed. Since he is so close to the king, he can get an edict to have Mordecai hanged right away. Haman is delighted with the idea and begins construction of the gallows immediately.

Critical Observation

In Persian culture, hanging was not the same as people today usually envision it. The execution was performed not with a rope around the neck, but by impaling the convicted person on a sharpened pole. The "hanging" is in reference to the impaled body displayed to public view.

While Haman plots with his kinfolk, the king is having trouble sleeping. To pass the sleepless hours, he has someone read to him from the chronicles of his reign, where he hears the account of how Mordecai had uncovered the plot on his life. He is disturbed that nothing has been done to reward Mordecai.

Enter Haman, rehearsing his request for Ahasuerus to grant him the right to kill Mordecai. But before he can even ask, the king has a question for him: "What should I do to honor a man who truly pleases me?" (6:6 NLT). Haman, of course, assumes the king is referring to him, so he gives a detailed and elaborate answer (6:7–9). What a bitter and shaming experience it must have been after Ahasuerus tells him to go out and do all those things for Mordecai. Haman rushes home in grief but receives no sympathy from his friends and family. They interpret it as a sign of bad things to come.

7:1–10

ESTHER'S SECOND BANQUET

Haman's dinner with the king will be no better this time. After the meal, when Ahasuerus asks Esther what her request is, she explains that her people are scheduled for annihilation. The king is incensed and wants to know who would do such a thing. She identifies the culprit as Haman (7:6).

After a big meal and plentiful wine, the enraged king goes into the palace garden. (Perhaps to get some fresh air or control his anger? To think of how to punish Haman? To give some thought to Esther's dilemma?) Haman senses that Ahasuerus has already passed judgment, and he wants to beg Esther for mercy. In approaching her, however, he falls onto the couch where she is reclining. At that moment the king returns and, in his anger, assumes the worst. He accuses Haman of molesting the queen and orders him to be led away.

Demystifying Esther

It was Persian tradition to recline while eating (7:8). The Greeks and Romans would do the same, and at some point the Jews adapted the habit. At the Last Supper, Jesus and His disciples reclined at the table (Luke 22:14), though some translations use the term *sat down*.

One of the king's servants was aware of the newly constructed gallows beside Haman's house. In a final irony, the king commands that Haman be executed on the gallows he had created for the murder of Mordecai.

Haman soon dies, but his dastardly plan is already set in motion. The order to kill all the Jews is still in effect. Addressing that threat is Esther and Mordecai's next priority.

Take It Home

Contemporary readers of the book of Esther should be encouraged by seeing what a difference a day can make. Life can appear to be desperate beyond all hope, yet God is able to turn things around in no time. He regularly saves and delivers those who turn to Him.

ESTHER 8:1–10:3

A NEW FEAST IS ESTABLISHED

Setting Up the Section

After discovering Haman's plot against all the Jews throughout the Persian Empire, Queen Esther has risked her life to approach the king for help. He is more than sympathetic to her request, to the point of having Haman immediately executed. Yet Haman's official message has already gone out, so Esther and Mordecai now turn their attention to preventing the potential damage that could be done.

8:1–17

MORDECAI'S PROMOTION AND DECREE

After Haman's death, King Ahasuerus gives everything Haman had owned to Esther and rewards Mordecai with the position that Haman had held, made official by the gift of the king's signet ring (8:2). The ring's seal would also provide authenticity for any missive sent out from the capital, Susa. After Esther pleads with Ahasuerus to rescind the order that Haman sent out, the king sends for his scribes. Mordecai dictates a new letter that is recorded and translated into the languages of the various peoples. The letter is written in the king's name and sealed with the king's ring. And lest anyone doubt where the king stood on this issue, the couriers ride the king's own horses (8:10). The previous order as written by Haman was supposed to be irreversible, but Ahasuerus makes it known that he now supports the Jews.

Critical Observation

Rather than a request based on the Word of God, the Abrahamic covenant, or some other spiritual basis, Esther appeals to the king solely on the basis of his affection for her and on what the destruction of the Jews would do to her (8:5–6). As for Mordecai, the king's order doesn't just provide *protection* for the Jewish people and give them permission to defend themselves; it authorizes them to *avenge* themselves (8:11–13).

Mordecai clearly has the king's favor. He leaves the palace attired in royal clothes, a distinctive purple robe, and a golden crown. The Jews in Susa are celebrating and feasting, as are those throughout the kingdom. And along with the sudden shift of power, many non-Jewish people are converting, perhaps more from fear of the Jews than genuine faith (8:17).

9:1–17

TWO DAYS OF VICTORY

Nearly nine months pass, but the mood among the Jews remains jubilant. The new law enacted by Mordecai gave them the right to fight back when attacked by their enemies on the thirteenth day of the twelfth month. They are ready. Mordecai has become a powerful man in the king's administration, and the people are terrified of him and his people. The Jews have no trouble killing and destroying their enemies (9:5). In a single day they kill five hundred opponents in Susa alone, including the ten sons of Haman (9:6–9).

Interestingly, although the Jews had been authorized to acquire the plunder of those they defeated (8:11), they choose not to do so (9:10, 15, 16). So the only Jewish person to profit from the exposure of Haman is Esther (8:1).

The king is still willing to accommodate a request by Esther, so she asks for a one-day extension for the Jews in Susa to continue eliminating their enemies, and she wants Haman's sons to be hanged (their bodies publicly displayed). So while the Jews in other territories have a day of celebration and rejoicing, those in Susa kill another three hundred men and do their celebrating the following day.

9:18–10:3

THE ORIGIN OF PURIM

Letters go out one more time to all the Jews in Persia. But this time they aren't forewarnings of death to come or a call to take up arms and fight their enemies. This time the news is to celebrate their victory over their enemies (9:20–22, 29–32).

The celebration becomes an annual event among the Jews that continues today. The name, *Purim*, is taken from the plural of *pur*, the die that Haman had cast to determine what day the Jews would be annihilated. The holiday is still celebrated on one day in most places, but one day later in walled cities (9:18–19).

Demystifying Esther

Purim is different from most other Old Testament feasts and celebrations. It was not established by God, but by people (9:27). It is a celebration of human achievement rather than God's deliverance (9:22). And rather than centering on worship as most other feasts do, Purim involves generosity and gift-giving that can border on self-indulgence. There is no element of sacrifice—just celebration.

The book of Esther concludes with two tributes. King Ahasuerus (Xerxes) is king of one of the greatest empires of all time, yet all that is said of him is that he taxed his kingdom. Mordecai, on the other hand, is given lavish praise (10:2–3). Ahasuerus will soon be assassinated, which presumably ends Mordecai's influence as well. About 150 years later, the glory of Persia will come to an end at the hands of Alexander the Great.

The book of Esther is a picture—not a very pretty one—of Jewish people who choose to stay in Persia rather than return to Jerusalem. It is a story of God's wonderful providence for people who don't seem to make Him a priority in their lives. As wonderfully as things turned out, there is no mention of Esther, Mordecai, or Purim elsewhere in the Bible.

Take It Home

God's providence is evident throughout the book of Esther, even though Esther and Mordecai didn't return to Jerusalem. The book challenges modern readers to consider God's care and guidance even when we are not in the ideal situation. His mercies do not depend on our location or even our own faithfulness. They are an outpouring of who He is in our lives.

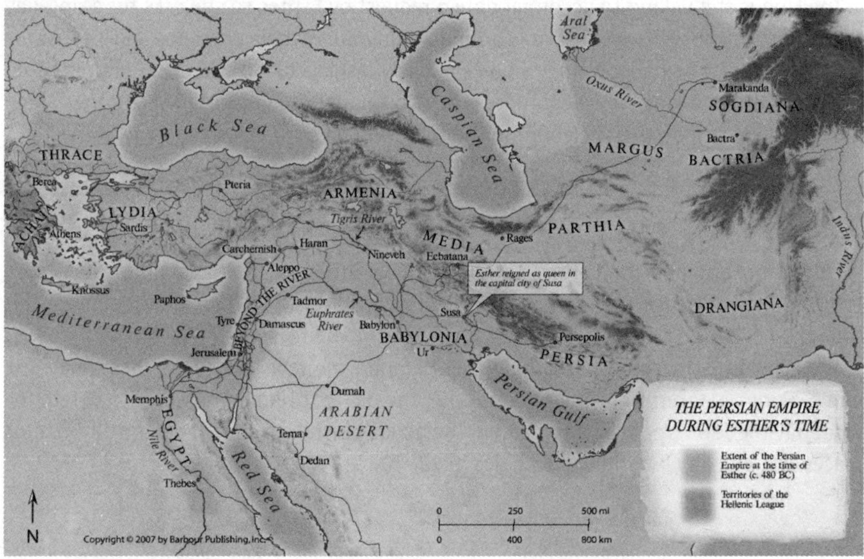

JOB

INTRODUCTION TO THE BOOK OF JOB

Many people who read the book of Job miss the God-centered message because they are focused on the man-centered problems. Why the righteous suffer is never really answered in this book. As God shows Job, knowing the answers to life's problems is not as important as knowing and understanding the awesomeness of God and how wise He is.

AUTHOR

The author of the book of Job is unknown. Most likely, he was an Israelite, because he uses the Israelite covenant name for God (*Yahweh*, or the *Lord*).

OCCASION

We do not know when Job was written, though the account describes history around the time of Abraham—that is, around 2000 BC. The first 11 chapters of Genesis pre-date the story of Job, but they were not written down in a book form until the time of Moses, around 1500 BC.

HISTORICAL CONTEXT

Job was likely a contemporary with Abraham, around three hundred years or so after the Flood. The reasons for placing Job in this period of time are as follows:

1) *Long life*: Job lives another 140 years after the events of this book (42:16), which makes him around 200 years old at his death. After the Flood, human life span progressively decreased. Terah, Abraham's father, was 205. Abraham was 175. Isaac, 180. Jacob, 147. So Job fits in nicely around the time of Abraham.
2) *No law*: There is no mention of the Ten Commandments or any of the Mosaic Laws in the book of Job.
3) *Sacrifices*: Before the Mosaic Law, the patriarchal head of each family would offer sacrifices, just as Job does (see 1:5).
4) *Wealth*: Job's wealth is listed in terms of livestock and not money, as was the practice during the time of Abraham (see Genesis 12:16).

CONTRIBUTION TO THE BIBLE

The book of Job is one of the five Wisdom Books, comprising Job, Psalms, Proverbs, Ecclesiastes, and Song of Solomon. Much of these books is poetic, but in the Hebrew sense. While much of western poetry is associated with rhyme and meter, Hebrew poetry is associated with contrasting thoughts or parallel thoughts set against each other.

OUTLINE

ELIPHAZ'S SECOND SPEECH 15:1–35

Calling Job a Fool 15:1–16
The Wicked Get What They Deserve 15:17–35

JOB'S SECOND RESPONSE TO ELIPHAZ 16:1–17:16

Attacked by God and Men 16:1–21
Harassed Till the Very End 16:22–17:16

BILDAD'S SECOND SPEECH 18:1–21

Calling Job to His Senses 18:1–4
Metaphors of Disaster 18:5–21

JOB'S SECOND RESPONSE TO BILDAD 19:1–29

A List of Complaints 19:1–20
A Plea for Pity 19:21–29

ZOPHAR'S SECOND SPEECH 20:1–29

Short-Lived Joy for the Wicked 20:1–19
More Punishment to Come 20:20–29

JOB'S SECOND RESPONSE TO ZOPHAR 21:1–34

Contradicting His Friends 21:1–16
Confused by God's Ways 21:17–34

ELIPHAZ'S THIRD SPEECH 22:1–30

Direct Accusation 22:1–20
A Call to Repentance 22:21–30

JOB'S THIRD RESPONSE TO ELIPHAZ 23:1–24:25

God's Omnipotence 23:1–17
The World's Injustice 24:1–25

JOB 1:1–22

THE STORY BEGINS

Setting Up the Section

The book of Job has been called a masterpiece that is unequaled in all literature. The meaning of the name *Job* is "enemy" or "to be hostile toward." While this does not seem to typify Job's character, it does reflect his experience. When we look at Job's circumstances, we see his faith lived out in his life—he practices what he believes.

1:1–5

PROLOGUE

In describing Job as blameless and upright (1:1), God is giving insight into the character of Job so that, as we read this story, we won't misinterpret what is going to happen to him. Job is a morally upright person—not perfect, but a good man who loves God. He fears God, meaning that he has a correct perspective of God as holy and righteous. Because he has this perspective, he shuns evil—literally meaning he turns away from it.

Demystifying Job

We are not entirely sure where the land of Uz (1:1) is located, but the Bible does give an interesting possibility. Lamentations 4:21 reads, "Rejoice and be glad, O daughter of Edom, who dwells in the land of Uz" (nasb). This seems to imply that the area of Uz was established before the Edomites came to dwell there. This area is located southeast of the Dead Sea.

Job is a wealthy man who is blessed with ten children (1:2). It is his number of animals that makes him wealthy (1:3). Money is not a part of his culture. The sheep are used for clothing and food, the donkeys and camels for transportation (the camels are the work horses of the desert. While donkeys are for short distances, the camels are used for cross country.) The oxen are for food, plowing, and milk.

It seems that Job's children like to party (1:4). With the wine flowing at these parties and clouding their judgment, Job fears that his children may have taken the name of the Lord a little too lightly (1:5). By their actions they are dishonoring God. So Job intercedes for his children, getting up early and offering ten sacrifices, one for each child.

1:6–22

JOB'S FIRST TEST

The interpretation of the Hebrew phrase *bene Elohim* is the cause of some controversy as to whether the phrase refers to angels or not. Some versions translate it as "sons of God," which can to some imply humanity. However, in Job 38:7, the phrase occurs in the context of creation, "when the morning stars sang together, and all the sons of God shouted for joy" (KJV). Angels were created before God created the heavens and the earth, and thus, they are the ones who shout for joy when the earth is created. So the "sons of God" reference is to angels and not mankind.

Critical Observation

The phrase *bene Elohim* is also found in Genesis 6, when we read of angels—sons of God—cohabitating with women and producing the Nephilim, or the fallen ones. Many suggest the ungodly men marry godly women and produce strange offspring. However, that is not what the scriptures say. Jude 1:6 tells us that "angels who did not keep their own domain, but abandoned their proper abode, He has kept in eternal bonds under darkness for the judgment of the great day" (NASB). These are the fallen angels, those who sided with Satan, whom God places in chains for the Day of Judgment. The rest of the fallen angels we call *demons*, and they are not locked up but are free to do the work of Satan.

Notice the restlessness of the accuser, going to and fro over the earth (1:7). Why? To see who he can destroy and what lives he can ruin. As 1 Peter 5:8 says, "Be on your guard and stay awake. Your enemy, the devil, is like a roaring lion, sneaking around to find someone to attack" (CEV). It's important to remember that Satan could *still* have access to the throne of God, the very presence of God, but he is *not* God, nor is he equal to God. Satan is not omnipotent, omnipresent, or omniscient, as God is.

God points out to Satan this man Job and his goodness (Job 1:8). The word *considered* is a military term that is used of a general who is studying a city before he attacks it so that he can develop a strategy to destroy it. So God is asking Satan if he has found any weakness in Job by which Satan might gain control or cause him to stumble. God's implication is that Satan can find nothing to cause Job to stumble.

Satan claims that the only reason Job loves God is because God is blessing him (1:9–11). Satan says the only reason Job (or anyone) serves God is because He pays well. The second indictment he makes is against God; he says God buys human love by giving blessings.

Satan can do nothing unless God allows it (1:12). Suddenly, over the course of a day, tragedies begin to fall upon Job's household (1:13–19). Verse 16 is interesting because the servant says that the fire of God fell from heaven. Yes God allows it, but Satan is behind it. The world likes to blame God for Satan's work.

After hearing all this bad news, Job begins to mourn (1:20), and who wouldn't? But then he begins to worship God (1:21). When things are going well, it is easy to worship God, but what if you lose everything? Could you still worship God as Job does?

Take It Home

When you have the right perspective of things, it is easy to worship God. Job realizes that all his material possessions, his wealth, and even his children are on loan to him from God. So when they are taken away, even though he is broken over it, he realizes he can't take them with him. Job does not understand why this happens to him, but he knows his God and thus, as we will see, he does not bring a foolish charge against God for what transpires.

Those who feel they are entitled to much are going to be angry and bitter toward God when their things are taken away. Nothing is ours to keep, for we are God's stewards, watching over that which He has entrusted to us.

Job passes the first test (1:22). Satan is wrong; it is not the material blessings that cause Job to worship God. But Satan is not going to give up easily, as we will soon see.

JOB 2:1–13

MORE TRIALS

Job's Second Test	2:1–10
Job's Three Friends	2:11–13

Setting Up the Section

Chapter 2 opens with another board meeting in heaven, as the angelic hosts come before the Lord, and Satan also comes to renew his charges against Job. Many people have a hard time understanding why God allows this to continue, but Satan is serving the purposes of God at this time.

2:1–10

JOB'S SECOND TEST

Job 2:1–3 are an exact echo of God's dialogue with Satan in Job 1:6–8, with the addition of the assertion that Job has remained faithful in the face of tragedy.

Critical Observation

The word translated *incited* in verse 3 means "to seduce, entice, persuade, provoke." Applied to God it seems confusing; we are trying to understand an infinite God with our finite minds and limited vocabulary. God is in control, and He is not pushed into situations by Satan.

Satan is looking for that Achilles' heel, that weakness in Job, so that he can get Job to turn from God. Surely when his health is gone, he will surrender to Satan (2:4).

What a pathetic picture we see here of a man who has everything and is now reduced to nothing; even his health has failed him now (2:6–8). We do not know for sure what disease Job has, but it is clear that it leaves him miserable and very ill.

Verse 9 gives us an indication as to why Satan does not kill Job's wife when he kills Job's children: She is more help to Satan alive than dead. Yet Job does not bring any foolish accusations against God. Job tells his wife that we are not only to accept good from God but also whatever else comes our way (2:10). Job is not giving up; he is placing his life in the hands of a sovereign God.

2:11–13

JOB'S THREE FRIENDS

Eliphaz, Bildad, and Zophar are true friends to Job, who come to comfort him during this difficult time (2:11). Job must have looked a mess, for at first his friends do not even recognize him (2:12). For seven days they cannot say anything; they just sit and mourn with him (2:13). As later passages will show, this is the best thing they do for him.

These first two chapters now set the stage for the rest of the book of Job, as he tries to understand why all these things have happened to him. Job's friends will quickly interject their opinions.

Take It Home

As tough as things are going to get for Job, and as tough as things may be for us at times, remember what Paul says in 1 Corinthians 10:13: "No temptation has overtaken you that is not common to man. God is faithful, and he will not let you be tempted beyond your ability, but with the temptation he will also provide the way of escape, that you may be able to endure it" (ESV). We give up far too easily many times, for God is right there with us.

JOB 3:1–26

JOB SPEAKS

Curses for the Day He Was Born	3:1–10
Wishing He Had Died at Birth	3:11–19
The Misery of Life	3:20–26

Setting Up the Section

The events of chapter 3 come on the heels of some tragic events in Job's life. In one day, Job, one of the wealthiest men in the area, loses all his material possessions. Not only that, but his ten children, who he loves very much, are all killed on the same day as well. And yet, in all this tragedy, Job is still able to worship God.

Some time after these events, Job's health is taken away. He develops boils from the top of his head to the tips of his toes. And yet in all this, Job does not charge God foolishly.

Job's friends Eliphaz, Bildad, and Zophar have gathered around him, mourning silently for seven days. And now Job is going to speak from his heart.

3:1–10

CURSES FOR THE DAY HE WAS BORN

When Job at last speaks, he curses the day of his birth, wishing it would be wiped off the calendar (3:1–6). He is not cursing God, but it does sound like he is questioning why he was even born if he was going to have to live a life like this (3:7–10). Job is not a stoic, and God is not allowing these things to come upon his life to see if Job can sit there unmoved, emotionless. God has a purpose for all this: to increase Job's faith.

Take It Home

Our common modern stereotype of Job is that of an incredibly patient man. As you read the scripture closely, however, Job is more characterized by his perseverance than his patience (James 5:10–11). His prayers reveal many of the same thoughts and feelings that we all experience when we face suffering.

It is important that we not miss God's mercy and compassion in the message of Job as well. We do suffer in this life, but we can trust God's purposes and His character. Remembering this helps us to persevere in our own suffering.

3:11–19

WISHING HE HAD DIED AT BIRTH

Job wishes he had been born dead, for it would be far better than the life he has (3:11–12, 18–19). He says that in death there is peace not only for the righteous (3:11–16) but also for the wicked (3:15–17).

Job is here speaking out of frustration and not out of revelation. God later says to Job, regarding this issue, "Have the gates of death been shown to you? Have you seen the gates of the shadow of death? Have you comprehended the vast expanses of the earth? Tell me, if you know all this" (38:17–18 NIV). Job does not understand what he is talking about regarding death, for he has never experienced it.

Critical Observation

Seventh-day Adventists and the Jehovah Witnesses formulate their doctrine for soul sleep and annihilation of the wicked from Job 3:11–17. They say that the righteous will be resurrected when the Lord returns, but until that time the soul is asleep. The wicked are also asleep in death until the Lord returns; then He will cause them to cease to exist, to be in a state of nothingness, with no punishment at all. This even goes for Satan.

However, in Revelation 20:10 we read, "Then the devil, who had deceived them, was thrown into the fiery lake of burning sulfur, joining the beast and the false prophet. There they will be tormented day and night forever and ever" (NLT). No soul sleep or annihilation there.

3:20–26

THE MISERY OF LIFE

Job is at the point where death itself seems more precious to him than all the treasures of the world (3:20–22). He closes his monologue by questioning the meaning of life (3:23) and contrasting its harshness to the presumed peace of the grave (3:24–26).

JOB 4:1–5:27

ELIPHAZ SPEAKS

Setting Up the Section

Job has broken a seven-day silence to wish he had never been born. Now, after all these words from Job, Eliphaz wants to interject some of his own thoughts regarding this situation.

4:1–5:7

BLAMING JOB FOR HIS TROUBLES

It seems that Job's friend Eliphaz can't hold back—he has to speak to Job about what Job has said and about what Job is experiencing (4:1–2). At first his words seem to affirm Job, as he reminds him of how Job has encouraged so many others in difficult times (4:3). But this affirmation turns to rebuke as he says, in effect, "Look, you have helped others through difficult times, but now you, the great counselor, can't even handle the difficult times you are going through. What's your problem Job?" (4:5–6).

Eliphaz says that the reason Job is going through these trials is that he is not innocent; only those who sin will go through times like this (4:6–7). This is a simplistic approach to Job's problem, but not a scriptural truth. But for the next thirty-six chapters, his friends are going to tell Job this very thing—that his sins have caused his suffering.

Critical Observation

The Bible has many examples of the righteous suffering, but the best, of course, is that of Jesus Himself. Peter says in 1 Peter 3:18, "For Christ also suffered once for sins, the just for the unjust, that He might bring us to God, being put to death in the flesh but made alive by the Spirit" (NKJV).

There is a measure of truth in that punishment will come for the wicked, but it is not always immediate. But this is not the only reason for suffering. Notice that Eliphaz comes across as being so spiritually insightful (4:8). Eliphaz's conclusion is that God will blast those who are evil just as He is doing to Job (4:9–11).

Eliphaz turns mystical as he builds up to the climax of his statement, claiming personal spiritual guidance (4:12–16), but his insight is less than profound. It doesn't take a mystic to recognize that God is more righteous than human beings (4:17). Eliphaz seems to suggest that Job ought to expect destruction because of his own wrongdoing (4:18–21).

Demystifying Job

Eliphaz bases his advice on this alleged vision. His advice does contain some truth, but ultimately God rebukes him for speaking untruth (see 42:7).

The holy ones to whom Eliphaz refers in 5:1 are angels, like those who gather in God's throne room (1:6; 2:1). Eliphaz's reference to those losing their homes and children (5:2–5) is a none-too-subtle parallel of Job's misfortunes which, Eliphaz contends, come to fools and simpletons—presumably like Job. After all, trouble doesn't spring out of nowhere (5:6), so clearly Job must have done something to bring it on himself.

Demystifying Job

The point of this book is that Job did not deserve the suffering he received. Thus, this book is associated with the question, "Why do bad things happen to good people?" While the Bible teaches that none of us is actually good (Romans 3:10–18), the question is still a relevant one. Keep in mind however that the book of Job does not carry the responsibility of answering that age old question. We can extrapolate our own reasoning about how Job's story reveals some purpose to suffering, but our best reasoning does not lead us to God's truth. Instead we need to understand what the scripture does teach—God's purposes continue even in our suffering. There is a bigger story happening outside of our own circumstances. And certainly elsewhere in scripture we find the truth that even in our suffering God's presence continues as well.

5:8–27

ELIPHAZ'S SOLUTION

Eliphaz turns holier-than-thou at this point, saying that if he were going through the things that Job is going through, he would repent before God (5:8–16).

It is true that God does chasten those He loves (5:17; see Hebrews 12:5–8). Eliphaz mixes truth with error, and that is always destructive. The problem here is that Eliphaz assumes Job is guilty of some sin and this is God's reason for chastening him. But we have already been told in chapter 1 that this is not the case. Eliphaz's glib assurances, that if Job repents all will again be well, only increase Job's pain (Job 5:18–27).

Take It Home

Here is an important lesson for us to learn from Eliphaz: When people are going through difficult times, it is not time to preach to them. In fact, the best thing to do is listen, comfort them, and simply show that you care. Giving pious platitudes is of no help to people in pain and will only bring them down.

JOB 6:1–7:21

JOB REPLIES

Setting Up the Section

After sitting with his friends in silence for seven days (4:11–13), Job pours out his anger and despair in a monologue (chapter 3), to which his friend Eliphaz feels compelled to reply (chapters 4–5). Eliphaz, after suggesting that Job has brought his troubles on himself through his own sin, suggests that Job plead his case (and presumably repent) before God. Chapters 6 and 7 contain Job's response.

6:1–30

JOB REPLIES TO ELIPHAZ

Job responds to Eliphaz by saying that his grief, if weighed against all the sand of the sea, would be far greater (6:1–3). He has allowed the situations of life, and maybe even some of the words of his friends, to cloud his picture of God, for he now thinks that God is his enemy (6:4). Job has never experienced anything like this in his life, and now God is exposing him to his weakness so that his faith may grow out of these circumstances.

Animals make noise when their stomachs are empty (6:5). Job feels he has a right to complain because his life has become empty—even the so-called comfort from his friends is tasteless and sickening (6:6–7). He is so miserable that he asks God to end his life before his misery leads him to deny God's goodness (6:8–10). He has nothing to live for and no hope for his future (6:11–13); even his friends have failed him. They are like flooding streams in the winter, when no one needs them, and vanish in the dry season when they might do some good (6:14–17). Just as desert caravans look in vain for an oasis, so Job looks in vain for comfort from his friends (6:19–20). Instead of supporting him at the only time he has needed it, they shrink back from his tragedy (6:21–23).

If his friends had anything to say that was worth hearing, Job would have been more than willing to listen, but they are not speaking the truth (6:23–24). Rather, they are implying that Job is the dishonest one for not admitting that his troubles are his own fault (6:25–30).

7:1–21

JOB REPLIES TO GOD

Job compares his life to what others face in their lifetime. One difference is that their problems last for days, and Job's problems last for months. He speaks of a military man, one who does hard service (7:1); he has a certain time to serve, and then it is over. There is an allotted time to serve even for the hired man (7:2). And yet for Job, the days turn into months, and still there is no relief (7:3). When night comes, there is still no comfort; he only tosses and turns with the pain and itching of his blisters and extreme loneliness (7:4). And as morning comes, it is another day of sorrow and pain.

Demystifying Job

Job compares death to the dissipating of a cloud (7:9), but the Bible does not teach that in death we enter a state of nothingness. Job's point is that, once dead, he is not coming back. There is no reincarnation, no recycling through life to become a better person, and no hope for a better earthly life next time (see Hebrews 9:27 and the Critical Observation at Job 3:11–19 on what happens after death).

You have one chance in this life, and if you reject Jesus Christ, you lose. God has done everything necessary for you to enter into abundant life, but if you don't accept it, you will suffer the fate of rejecting the truth.

As Job anticipates his life coming to a hopeless end (7:6), he addresses God directly. Not, however, in humble repentance as Eliphaz might wish (5:8–27), but rather in complaint (7:8–10). Job is going to pour his heart out, and he is not holding anything back (7:11).

Take It Home

Job is not the only person whose complaints against God are recorded in scripture. Many of the psalms express similar strong emotions. To be godly does not mean we express no negative emotion. God knows our complaints, whether we express them or not. We can bring our complaints to God and expect to hear honestly back from Him. In Job's case, we have examples of his heartfelt, honest prayers of complaint. But also later in the book (28–42:6), God takes exception with Job's complaints about his friends. When we come to God with our response to life, He is there to speak into our lives as well.

Job questions God, asking Him why He is watching over his life so closely, like a watchman standing guard on board a ship, watching out for sea serpents (7:12). Job sees God as an adversary, not only allowing physical and emotional pain, but also sending terrifying nightmares so that Job cannot find comfort even in sleep (7:13–14). When Job says he does not want to live forever (7:15–16), he is not making a theological statement about eternal life, but simply stating that his life on earth is not worth living.

Critical Observation

When Job asks, "What are people, that you should make so much of us, that you should think of us so often?" (7:17 NLT), he sees God's attention as a burden. David asks the same question, but in a positive light: "What are mere mortals that you should think about them, human beings that you should care for them?" (Psalm 8:4 NLT). Same words; two different perspectives of God.

Job feels that every step he takes, God is right there ready to strike out at him (7:17–19). He wonders why God has made him a target (7:20). Adversity can lead to a warped concept of God, and we see this happening with Job. He is unable to recognize God's forgiveness (17:21) because of the cultural assumptions Eliphaz has already expressed: If God loves you, you will prosper. Job even goes so far as to tell God that He will be sorry when Job is gone, because He will no longer have anyone to pick on.

JOB 8:1–22

BILDAD SPEAKS

Bildad's Shock	8:1–4
Bildad's Solution	8:5–19
Bildad's Summation	8:20–22

Setting Up the Section

Job has poured out his complaints to God, and his friend Bildad is shocked that Job dares to speak to God in this way. Here he takes Job to task.

8:1–4

BILDAD'S SHOCK

Bildad blasts Job and tells him to stop his pleas of innocence, for they are nothing more than a bunch of hot air (8:1–2). This, too, must have hurt Job. Bildad first tells Job that God is righteous and then says the reason for the death of Job's children is because of some sin in their lives (8:3–4). You see, it would be hard to refute Bildad without seeming to say that God is unrighteous. And yet we know that Bildad is wrong; he does not have the full picture. It is neither God's unrighteousness nor personal sin that brings tragedy on Job's children.

8:5–19

BILDAD'S SOLUTION

Like Eliphaz, Bildad has a simple solution to Job's problems: If Job will confess his sins, then God will make him healthy, wealthy, and prosperous (8:5–7).

Take It Home

Does Bildad's advice sound familiar? It is what many of the "health and wealth" teachers preach from their pulpits—and it is bad theology. Bildad is only speaking a half truth, and half truths are nothing more than lies. We again must understand that God does bless the just *and* the unjust. And we must also fall back on the sovereignty of God; He is in control.

Bildad points to history and the experience of former generations to bolster his point (8:8–10). He argues that the godless person will wither and die, just as the papyrus without the marsh, the reed without water (8:11–13). The implication, of course, is that since Job is experiencing all these troubles, he must be godless. The word translated *godless* in verse 13 means something like "hypocrite." To Bildad's way of thinking, Job is trusting his own (false, according to Bildad) reputation as a blameless man (see 1:1), but that trust is as misplaced as leaning on a spider's web or a rootless plant (8:14–19).

Demystifying Job

Job and his friends lived around the time of Abraham, which was only 250 to 300 years after the Flood. When Bildad refers to what previous generations learned, he is probably thinking of how God destroyed all the wicked by a flood. Now Job, presumably because of his sin, is being wiped out as if by a flood.

8:20–22

BILDAD'S SUMMATION

Bildad calls for Job to plead his case before God. If Job is innocent, he has nothing to worry about. If Job is not innocent, then God will deal with him appropriately (8:20–22).

JOB 9:1–10:22

JOB REPLIES TO BILDAD

Setting Up the Section

Job's friend Bildad has taken Job to task for questioning God. He has declared that God sends punishment to the wicked and brings blessing to the righteous, with the implication that Job will again be blessed if he lives righteously. This prompts Job to reflect on what it means to be righteous in God's sight.

9:1–35

HUMAN INNOCENCE VS. GOD'S POWER

Job tells Bildad that his words are empty because, even if Job could go before God, he can't win. All this righteousness that Eliphaz and Bildad are touting is out of reach for mere mortals (9:1–2), and even if one were innocent, who could beat God in an argument (9:3)? Not only is God wiser and more powerful than any human being (9:4–10), but He is spirit and, as such, can be difficult for the human mind to comprehend.

Demystifying Job

The name *Rahab* (9:13) means "to press or to assail" and refers to a mythical sea monster.

If God is not as good as we think He is, then His having all that power is scary (9:12–13). And Job isn't sure that God is good. Job is allowing his circumstances to cloud his picture of God. He doesn't stand a chance with God (9:14–16); he can't even catch his breath and defend himself (9:17–20).

Critical Observation

Job's despair over his status before God brings to mind Paul the apostle, who said, "I know that nothing good lives in me, that is, in my sinful nature. For I have the desire to do what is good, but I cannot carry it out" (Romans 7:18 NIV). But rather than fall into despair, as Job does, Paul finds the answer to his problem: "Therefore, there is now no condemnation for those who are in Christ Jesus" (Romans 8:1 NIV). Christ alone can help us by His Spirit to do those things that are pleasing to God. It is not by the will of the flesh but submission to the Holy Spirit that this is accomplished.

To Job, it doesn't seem to matter if you are good or evil, because God destroys both equally (9:21–22). In fact, it seems Job sees God getting a kind of perverse pleasure in destroying people, especially the innocent (9:22–24). Job clearly knows the greatness of God and His power, but Job is struggling with the goodness of God. He is struggling because he sees the innocent suffer, including himself, which he can't understand. And his friends are not helping one bit.

Notice Job's conclusion: If he is going to be punished regardless of his innocence or guilt, then why bother to repent (9:25–31)?

How can Job go into heaven, go before God, and plead his case (9:32)? He is a mere human, and there is no one who can bridge that gap, no mediator (9:33). Job sees God as a cruel taskmaster with His rod of discipline ready to strike anyone at His will, and Job is terrified of Him (9:34–35). Notice, as Job's picture of God gets more distorted, it is harder for him to truly love God.

Take It Home

Job knows his desperate need for a mediator (9:33) but despairs of finding one. How rich we are who know that "there is one God, and one mediator also between God and men, the man Christ Jesus" (1 Timothy 2:5 NASB). There is no one else that can bridge the gap—no priest, no man, not even Mary—but only Jesus Christ who, being God, made Himself flesh to die for our sins in order to bring us to God (1 Peter 3:18).

10:1–22

CHALLENGING GOD

Job is going to speak from his heart, and whatever comes out, let it be. He is not going to hold anything back (10:1). He knows that he is the work of God's hands, and yet it seems God despises him and loves the wicked (10:2–7).

Job now speaks of his own frailty, that God has created him out of the dust of the earth (10:8). Like a master potter, God has formed Job, and He has formed us, but these bodies of flesh will return to the dust of the earth (10:9).

Job sees himself trapped. No matter what he does before God, it won't be good enough and he will be judged (10:12–17). He asks why God allowed him to be born, if God is only going to torture him (10:18–19).

Job has had it; he can't take it any more. So he cries out to God, asking God to leave him alone, to give him a break, and let him try to enjoy the short time he has left (10:20–22).

JOB 11:1–20

ZOPHAR SPEAKS

Setting Up the Section

Eliphaz was eloquent with his words, but they were not encouraging, only judgmental. Bildad was brutal as he accused Job of not being as innocent as he tried to make others believe. And now Job's third friend, Zophar, comes on the scene and blasts Job with stinging sarcasm.

11:1–12

ZOPHAR'S QUESTIONS

Zophar begins with rhetorical questions that let Job know he is not going to be able to justify himself (11:1–2). Zophar is not going to let Job get away with his empty words, for the things that have come upon Job's life show that Job is not pure (11:3–4). Zophar does not believe in Job's innocence. In fact, he is calling to God to show Job all the evil that is in him, that secret sin that has brought this upon his life (11:5). And just to let Job know how spiritual he is, Zophar tells Job that God has spoken to Zophar and has shown him that Job has only received half of what he deserves (11:6).

Next Zophar takes Job to task for trying to understand God (11:7–9). Zophar says that Job will obtain wisdom when a man is born from a wild donkey (11:10–12).

Critical Observation

In the King James Version, verse 7 asks if we can find God by our searching. The answer to that question may surprise you. No, we can't find God by our searching because He is not lost; we are! God is the good shepherd who goes looking for His sheep. Jesus said in John 6:44 that no one can come to Him unless it is through the work of the Father. God is the initiator; we are only responding to what He has begun.

11:13–20

ZOPHAR'S ANSWERS

After all his rhetorical questions, Zophar offers his own simplistic answer: Get right with God, and the sun will once again shine on Job's life, a smile will return to his face, and he will be protected from his enemies just as a moat protects those living within the city walls (11:13–18). According to Zophar, Job's friends will also return if he gets right with God. But if he doesn't, his life will come to an end (11:19–20).

Take It Home

There is no way we can fully understand an infinite God with our finite minds (Isaiah 55:8–9). Things occur in our lives that we do not fully understand. Sometimes we can't intellectually understand what God is doing and why He is doing it. This is when we have to walk by faith and not by sight, trusting that God knows what is best.

JOB 12:1–14:22

JOB REPLIES TO ZOPHAR

Folly and Wisdom	12:1–25
Silence and Speech	13:1–28
Life and Death	14:1–22

Setting Up the Section

In response to Zophar's oration (chapter 11), Job again speaks.

12:1–25

FOLLY AND WISDOM

Now it is Job's turn to use sarcasm. He tells Zophar that undoubtedly, when Zophar dies, so too will die all the wisdom in the world (12:1–2). Job lashes out at his friends' pride as he tells them that he understands just as much as they do; that he has not heard anything earth-shattering from their speeches (12:3).

It seems hard for Job's friends to be compassionate when things are going well in their own lives. They are making themselves out to be righteous, for they are blessed. And they are making Job unrighteous, for he is cursed. Those who come to comfort him are only mocking him (12:4–5). Notice Job's argument against their counsel. They have their theological answers to Job's problems, but Job calls for them to apply that to the real world and see if it still holds water. And he shows them that it doesn't, for the robbers are still prospering and the unrighteous seem to live in comfort (12:6).

Demystifying Job

The meaning of the phrase "those who carry their god in their hands" (12:6 NIV) is uncertain. Since it is mentioned in the context of marauders, perhaps the "god in their hands" refers to their plunder, or possibly it refers to their swords, on which they depend for means to power in battle. It also may refer to those who try to bring God under their control or power, a common meaning of *hand* in this kind of context.

Job says creation itself knows that God is free to do whatever He wishes with His creatures (12:7–12). Every breath is a gift of God (12:10). Job is saying that God is sovereign over nature, over nations, and over the lives of humans (12:13–25).

13:1–28

SILENCE AND SPEECH

Job has had it with his friends' worthless counsel and does not want to hear their empty words any longer. He only wants to hear from God (13:1–4). He calls for his friends to be silent—that is the best counsel (13:5).

Job's friends think they are speaking for God, and yet their counsel is wrong (13:6–9). God will reprove them for their false counsel and their empty words, for they are meaningless, of no help, and most important, they are not of God (13:8–12).

Job now wants to speak his piece (13:13). He is still in his cave of despair, living in self pity, but then, seemingly out of nowhere, he makes a solid statement: "Though he slay me, yet will I hope in him" (13:15 NIV). Even though Job has no idea why all this has happened to him, and as unfair as it seems, he is now going to trust in God with his life. Job is learning to trust God more and his faith is growing. He sees God as his salvation (13:16–19).

Job wants to talk things over with God, but first he asks God to remove all the adversity that has come upon his life and let him rest for a while (13:20–22). Asking for God to show him his error, Job reflects on his youth and concludes that God is getting back at him for something done back then (13:20–28).

Take It Home

As we go through difficult times, we tend to look back and blame our present situation on what we have done in the past, just as Job does. But God brings us through trials to stretch our faith, not for the purpose of revenge or intimidation.

14:1–22

LIFE AND DEATH

The human life is short when compared with eternity (14:1–2). God knows the number of our days (14:3–5). Job here again sees God as his adversary and asks God to leave him alone (14:6).

Job concludes by bemoaning what he sees as the ultimate fate of every human being: death, which in his mind means the end of existence (14:7–12). He expresses a beautiful longing for renewal and forgiveness (14:13–17) but then concludes that there is no hope (14:18–22).

JOB 15:1–35

ELIPHAZ'S SECOND SPEECH

Setting Up the Section

Each of Job's three friends has had his say. Now Eliphaz begins round two with his second speech.

15:1–16

CALLING JOB A FOOL

Eliphaz questions Job's wisdom, saying that Job's words are nothing more than a lot of hot air (15:1–3). Eliphaz believes that Job is undermining people's piety by refusing to admit that his sins have brought his troubles on him (15:4–6).

Next Eliphaz attacks Job's credentials, asking Job if he is the oldest and wisest man around or if he has some private access to God's council that is denied to his friends (15:7–9). No, Eliphaz insists; the oldest and wisest men side with Eliphaz on this subject (15:10), and Job, far from being privy to God's wisdom, isn't satisfied with it (15:11). Eliphaz sees Job as a man who claims to be righteous but who is really entertaining sin (15:12). He sees Job's anger with God as another form of sin (15:13).

Take It Home

The Bible gives many examples of the anger and frustration that God's people feel when things go wrong. Anger itself is not the problem; the problem comes when that anger prompts people to do and say things they should not. For example, the prophet Jeremiah is angry when people do not respond to his preaching. He crosses the line into sin when he accuses God of deceiving him. God immediately calls him to account and repentance (Jeremiah 15:18–19).

Eliphaz is right to say that no one can attain righteousness on his or her own; even angels—holy ones—rebel against God (15:14–16).

15:17–35

THE WICKED GET WHAT THEY DESERVE

Eliphaz falls back on what he has seen and the worldview he has been taught (15:17–19): that the wicked suffer their whole lives (15:20). He assumes that the converse is also true: If a man is suffering, he must be wicked. All of Job's prosperity has been taken away, just as happens to the wicked (15:21). Job has met the same fate as the wicked (15:26).

Demystifying Job

In Job's time, weight was a sign of wealth (15:27), because the rich were able to enjoy much more food than the common people. Job probably looked well-fed before his troubles began, but by the time his friends arrived, he was probably skin and bones—so changed that at first they do not even recognize him (2:12).

His prosperity is gone; his life is dark and hopeless (15:29–30). In Eliphaz's eyes, Job is deceiving himself by claiming that he has done nothing to deserve his troubles (15:31). Eliphaz's metaphors of vines stripped of their grapes before they have matured, and trees dropping their flowers before they have had time to develop into fruit (15:32–33), must have fallen hard on the ears of a man whose children died untimely deaths. All Eliphaz predicts for Job now is barrenness; the only "children" Job will father are evil and deceit (15:34–35).

JOB 16:1–17:16

JOB'S SECOND RESPONSE TO ELIPHAZ

Attacked by God and Men	16:1–21
Harassed Till the Very End	16:22–17:16

Setting Up the Section

Eliphaz has enumerated the bad things that happen to wicked people—things that are now happening to Job. The implication is clear: Job is a wicked person. Now Job replies, addressing Bildad and Zophar as well as Eliphaz.

16:1–21

ATTACKED BY GOD AND MEN

Job blasts his friends for their insensitivity to his condition and calls them miserable comforters (16:1–2). He wants them to realize what they are doing by imagining they were in his shoes (16:3–4). Job tells them that if they were in a similar situation, he would comfort instead of condemn and encourage instead of discourage them (16:5).

Demystifying Job

To shake your head at someone (16:4) is to say that their words are empty—the very thing Job's friends have been doing.

Job is not finding any comfort in his own words or in the words of his friends (16:6). He sees himself being eaten alive, wasting away to nothing, and God continues to cause havoc with his life (16:7–9). Job complains that God has given him wicked friends who are continually coming against him (16:10–11).

Take It Home

The phrase *Job's comforters* has come to mean "people who don't comfort at all." We are not called to be that kind of friend (see 1 Thessalonians 5:14–15).

As a lion or tiger goes after its prey and grabs it by the neck to choke the life out of it, Job sees God doing this to him. In fact, Job sees himself as nothing more than a target on God's practice range; his suffering is tearing his guts out (16:12–14).

Job doesn't understand why this is happening to him; he feels that he does not deserve all of this (16:15–17). He wants to sit down and talk with God face-to-face (16:18–21).

16:22–17:16

HARASSED TILL THE VERY END

Again, Job sees his life coming to an end (16:22–17:1). His many friends have forsaken him, and no one will speak up for him (17:2–5).

Job had not only been wealthy but he had also been well respected. Others looked to him for help and direction (see 4:3–4). But now these same people look at him in disgust and begin to spit upon him (16:6). Job doesn't care what they say; he knows he is innocent, and he is not going to change his story (16:8–9). In fact, he gets a little sarcastic, telling his friends to come back and stick the knife in a little deeper (17:10).

Job wants to die. His children are gone, and now he claims death as his family, and he waits for them to come and take him away (17:11–16).

JOB 18:1–21

BILDAD'S SECOND SPEECH

Setting Up the Section

After hearing Job's complaint in chapters 16 and 17, Bildad steps up to the plate to have a second try at arguing Job into agreeing with his friends and their theology.

18:1–4

CALLING JOB TO HIS SENSES

Bildad sees Job as long-winded (18:1–2), and he is upset that Job is speaking so harshly to his friends (18:3)—despite the fact that Bildad and the others are equally harsh to Job. He tells Job that it is not God who is causing his pain, as Job claims (see 16:13), but rather it is Job inflicting pain on himself because of his sin (18:4).

Take It Home

Bildad and Job's other friends are very sincere in what they are doing; the only problem is that they are sincerely wrong. May we learn to stop and bring things before God, asking for His wisdom before we speak out of our own foolish hearts and cause more harm to others than good (see James 1:19–20).

18:5–21

METAPHORS OF DISASTER

Bildad now launches into a poetic speech intended to convince Job that he is wrong to believe that good things happen to evil people (see 10:3). He recites a litany of bad things that happen to wicked people—to all wicked people, according to Bildad.

Wicked people die, signified by the extinguishing of lamps and fires (18:5–6). This might seem rather obvious, since everyone dies, but the verb *snuffed out* suggests death at the hands of others. If that fate does not overtake a wicked man, perhaps his life will flicker out through weakness or illness, or even because his own schemes backfire (18:7).

Verses 8–10 enumerate the various ways that a wicked person can be "thrown down" (NIV), as verse 7 expresses it. He could wander into a net that is spread out on the ground (18:8)—maybe even a net that he has spread out to catch someone else but that he absentmindedly wanders into while plotting his next scheme. Even if he is alert to what lies on the ground in front of him, he could be caught from behind by a trap or snare (18:9). If his own schemes don't trip him up, then he may fall into a trap that someone else has set specifically to catch him (18:10).

Demystifying Job

The noose referred to in verse 10 is not a noose to hang a person by the neck. Rather, it is laid out on the ground as a trap. When the prey steps inside the noose, the noose tightens, the prey is caught by the ankle, and he is thrown off his feet. It is interesting that in all the ways described here that a wicked person might be thrown down, each trap catches the victim by the feet as he is walking. This calls to mind Psalm 1:1, "Blessed is the man who does not walk in the counsel of the wicked" (NIV).

Terror lies in wait everywhere for the wicked (18:11), and that terror is justified because calamity and disaster lurk around every corner (18:12). Job, with his blistered skin, must have identified with the wicked man whose skin is being eaten away (18:13) by "death's firstborn" (NIV)—probably a poetic name for a deadly disease.

There is no safety for the wicked man, even in his own home; he is torn from his home and delivered to death (18:14). Even if he were able to remain home, he would find it burning with sulfur—reminiscent of the destruction of Sodom and Gomorrah, those strongholds of evil (see Genesis 19:24).

Critical Observation

The king of terrors (18:14) is the frightening name for the Canaanite god that was death personified. Mot devoured his victims. Isaiah turns this imagery around and prophesies that the Lord will swallow death forever (Isaiah 25:8), and the apostle Paul explains that this prophecy is fulfilled in Jesus Christ's resurrection from the dead (1 Corinthians 15:54).

The wicked man's roots—his ancestors and his descendants—do not thrive (Job 18:16), and no one remembers him or his family once he is gone (18:17–18). He has no name, not only because his own name is forgotten, but also because his family name does not continue; none of his offspring or descendants survive (18:19). From east to west, a fate like this is viewed with horror (18:20). Quite possibly Bildad is thinking also of how appalled he and Job's other friends were when they first saw Job in his misery. It is easy for Bildad to see how many of these horrors reserved for wicked men have befallen Job, and he concludes that Job either does not know God or at least is on the way to becoming estranged by God because of his complaints against Him (18:21).

JOB 19:1–29

JOB'S SECOND RESPONSE TO BILDAD

Setting Up the Section

Job responds to Bildad's poetic discourse on the fate of the wicked—and by implication, the fate of Job—with some well-chosen words of his own.

19:1–20

A LIST OF COMPLAINTS

Words of hate and wrath that come from the heart of men and women are not of God and can hurt people. This is where Job is. He is broken, tormented by his friends' words (19:1–3). Job sees himself as innocent before God no matter what his friends say, no matter how much they make themselves out to be righteous. Job's conclusion is that God is wrong. He can't understand why all this trouble has come upon him (19:4–8).

In verse 9 Job is speaking of all that has been taken away from him. He has, in a sense, been laid out naked before all his friends and family.

Demystifying Job

Job speaks of his crown being removed (19:9). It may well be that Job was a king, and when this trouble came into his life, he lost his throne. Or the word *crown* might be a poetic way of referring to Job's honor, his wealth, or even his hair, which he had shaved off (see 1:20). No one knows for sure.

Again, Job perceives God as his enemy (19:13). He is about as low as a person can get. His friends and relatives have forgotten him and forsaken him (19:14). Even the few remaining servants have refused to listen to him anymore (19:15–16). No one is at his side any longer. Now even his own wife, who wasn't too supportive in the first place (see 2:9), is keeping her distance because of his offensive breath (19:17). All the children that used to gather around him, those that loved him, are now speaking against him and looking down on him (19:18).

Critical Observation

Job speaks of his own children ignoring him (19:17), which seems confusing when, in chapter 1, we are told that all his children were killed. The Amplified Bible helps clear this passage up. It says, "I am repulsive to my wife and loathsome to the children of my own mother." It could be that Job is speaking of his own brothers and sisters, who are ignoring him.

19:21–29

A PLEA FOR PITY

Job cries out to his friends to give him a break (19:21). He feels as if his friends are persecuting him just as God is doing (19:22). Feeling that no one is really listening to him, he longs for his words to be permanently recorded (19:23–24), possibly so that more unbiased readers might judge him less harshly than his friends do. And those words have indeed been recorded and passed down throughout the generations.

Take It Home

Job believed that God had brought this trouble on him. But that is not the case. Satan is the one responsible for Job's misfortunes, even though God does allow it—for Satan cannot do anything without God's permission. And remember that when the enemy does something it is not to build up, but to destroy (see John 10:10).

Now Job speaks of resurrection (19:25–27). In contrast to his earlier descriptions of nothingness after death, he now says that, even after he has died and his body has gone back to the dust of the earth, he will be raised up and in his body. Since this is the only time Job mentions the resurrection, it may be that we are incorrect to interpret his words through our New Testament understanding of the resurrection of the body. But certainly with our perspective, affected by New Testament teachings, we find hope in these verses.

Job also knows that no matter how much evil his friends speak against him, he is innocent. And as much as it hurts now, he knows that he will ultimately be vindicated. So he tells his friends to watch out because God will take vengeance; His wrath will come upon them for what they have done to him.

JOB 20:1–29

ZOPHAR'S SECOND SPEECH

Setting Up the Section

As we move into Job chapter 20, we are closing out round two of this verbal tongue-lashing that Job is receiving from his three friends. Zophar is going to respond to what Job has just said. Job accuses his friends of speaking lies and making up stories to prove their neatly packaged theology. They are accusing Job of hiding sin in his life and that is why all this calamity has come upon him. But Job tells them to be afraid of being judged themselves. He turns the tables on them now, and it is to this that Zophar is going to respond.

20:1–19

SHORT-LIVED JOY FOR THE WICKED

Even in the poetic style in which it is written, it is clear in Zophar's reply that he is very upset with what Job has said against him and his friends. Zophar is not going to take this lying down. He is not going to let Job walk all over him (20:1–2). Why is Zophar so upset? Because Job has insulted his character, just as Zophar has insulted him (20:3).

Zophar returns to the refrain Job has heard from all his friends: comparing what happens to the wicked to what is happening in Job's life. The wicked may prosper, but only for a short time (20:3–4). Eventually, even the highest-ranking among the wicked will be valued no more than human waste (20:7); nobody will even remember them (20:8–9). Their children will be poor and have to beg for food (20:10). One moment the wicked may be young and full of life, but the next moment they could be dead (20:11).

Critical Observation

The idea of not enjoying what one has worked for (20:18) is common in wisdom literature in the Bible. (See, for example, Ecclesiastes 2:18–23.)

The wicked savor evil the way a child might savor candy, but ultimately they will be left with a bad taste in their mouths (20:12–17). They may have every luxury, but they won't enjoy it (20:18). All their hard work won't bring them satisfaction (20:19).

Demystifying Job

Honey and cream (20:17) represent a prosperous life. The land of Canaan was said to be a land flowing with milk and honey (Exodus 13:5).

When Zophar talks of how the wicked treat the needy (20:19), he is implying that Job has oppressed the poor and repossessed homes by force. He has no proof of this. Maybe there were rumors to that effect, but more likely Zophar simply assumes Job's guilt to account for Job's current suffering.

Take It Home

Why do Job's friends go to such extremes to make Job appear guilty? Because to them, sin equals punishment—so Job must be a sinner. God will deal with the unrighteous according to His timetable and His ways. In this life we see the wicked prosper and suffer. We also see the righteous suffer and be blessed. God is sovereign; He is in control. Think about it this way: There are more than five billion people in the world today, and God is orchestrating each and every one of their lives. Most of us have a hard time taking care of ourselves. We don't always know the ways of God, but we do know the character of God, which is the same yesterday, today, and forever (Hebrews 13:8).

20:20–29

MORE PUNISHMENT TO COME

The fate of one who indulges his greed is to experience more greed—so much that he can never be satisfied (20:20). Ultimately, there will be nothing more to acquire (20:21). But the wicked are not going to get away with anything. Just when they think everything is okay, God will deal with them (20:22–26).

Zophar's summation of the fate of the wicked implicitly warns Job that if he continues to hide his sin, all these things that will happen to him—and there is worse yet to come on Judgment Day (20:27–29).

JOB 21:1–34

JOB'S SECOND RESPONSE TO ZOPHAR

Setting Up the Section

Not willing to let Zophar have the last word, Job responds to Zophar's speech.

21:1–16

CONTRADICTING HIS FRIENDS

In verse 1, Job is basically saying, "If your speech is supposed to comfort me, then mine will do the same for you" (21:1–2). Job is going to say what is on his heart, and then his friends can mock him more if they want (21:3).

Job must have looked awful. In fact, it seems that his friends have a hard time even looking at him. So Job calls them to take a good look at him, even though his appearance is shocking to those who see him (21:4–5).

Job contradicts Zophar's litany of what happens to the wicked by pointing to what really takes place in life. The wicked don't die young; they are profitable and powerful (21:6–7). They have many healthy children (21:8), their homes are safe (21:9), their livestock breed and are healthy (21:10), and they enjoy good times (21:12). Job's life seems to drag on in pain, while he sees the wicked not only living long, prosperous lives, but when they do die, they go quickly (21:13).

Demystifying Job

Just as Zophar goes to one extreme in saying that the wicked are always punished, Job goes to the other extreme and says that the wicked are always blessed. Neither is true (see Psalm 37:35–36). God is sovereign and He has a purpose for everything. We must be careful that when we speak, we are not speaking out of our emotions but according to the Word of God.

People who have everything they want see no need for God (21:14). They have it all; what more do they need? God is of no profit to them, or so they think (21:15–16). But when all is taken away, they tend to look up to God.

Critical Observation

Jesus makes the same point that Job makes here (21:14–15) when He says that it is easier for a camel to go through the eye of a needle than for a rich man to enter heaven (Matthew 19:23–24). The point is not that rich people won't go to heaven but that wealth can blind our eyes to our need for God.

21:17–34

CONFUSED BY GOD'S WAYS

Job's friends have been blaming Job and his hidden sin for the death of his children. Job argues that God should punish the wicked and not their children (21:17–21). But then Job seems to backtrack, acknowledging that it is presumptuous to try to teach God what to do (21:22). Still, God's ways are incomprehensible to Job. Why should one person live happily right up until his death, while another has nothing but misery in his life (21:23–26)?

Job is fully aware that his friends are trying to prove that his hardships are evidence of his wickedness (21:27–28). He challenges them to ask anybody, from any part of the world; anyone will agree that the wicked prosper (21:27–30). Even in death the wicked are honored; they are treated as heroes (21:31–33).

Job's friends are speaking nonsense, Job insists, and how can nonsense be of any comfort (21:34)?

JOB 22:1–30

ELIPHAZ'S THIRD SPEECH

Direct Accusation	22:1–20
A Call to Repentance	22:21–30

Setting Up the Section

The third round of this three-on-one conversation between Job's friends and Job now begins, with Eliphaz, as in the previous two rounds, taking the lead and speaking first.

22:1–20

DIRECT ACCUSATION

Eliphaz reminds Job that Job's actions do not benefit God at all (22:1–2). Job is not doing God a favor by being good (22:3). But the point is moot, Eliphaz implies, because obviously Job is not being good—God wouldn't allow all these troubles to happen to a good man, Eliphaz claims (22:4). Clearly, to Eliphaz's way of thinking, Job is unendingly sinful (22:5).

Take It Home

God desires us to do good because it is what is best for our lives, and we are blessed by it. But it doesn't add or take away from God at all. Yes, our unrighteousness grieves God, but it doesn't harm Him.

Up until this point, Eliphaz and the other friends have been satisfied to list the consequences of sin and let Job draw the conclusion that, since he is suffering those consequences, he is obviously a sinner. But Job hard-headedly refuses to draw that conclusion, so now Eliphaz comes out and accuses Job directly. Eliphaz has no proof that Job did any of the things Eliphaz is about to accuse him of, but he is trying to figure out the ways of God by applying life's situations to them. So he has come to the conclusion that Job has become wealthy by strong-arming the poor—taking their clothes, refusing to give them food and water, and disregarding the plight of the widowed and fatherless (22:6–9). That is why, Eliphaz says, everything is going wrong for Job now (22:10–11).

Eliphaz accuses Job of trying to get away with some kind of evil when God isn't looking (22:12–14). Ironically, God *has* been looking at what Job does and has decreed Job blameless and upright (1:8; 2:3). Eliphaz evokes the image of the Flood, as Bildad had done earlier (8:11). Just as God swept away the wicked with the Flood, so now He is deluging Job with judgment (22:15–16).

Demystifying Job

There was a belief that when clouds covered the earth people could do what they wanted because God, up in heaven, couldn't see through them (22:13–14).

Eliphaz now quotes Job's own plea for God to leave him alone (22:17; see also 7:20) and piously asserts that he, Eliphaz, has nothing to do with such wickedness (22:18). He goes on to say that the innocent rejoice in the suffering of the wicked (22:19–20). Since he has just identified Job as wicked and himself as innocent, the implication is that Eliphaz is happy about Job's downfall.

22:21–30

A CALL TO REPENTANCE

As the friends have done before, Eliphaz tells Job to get right with God and he will be blessed (22:21–28). He calls on Job to submit to God, lay up God's words in his heart, turn from wickedness to God, delight in God rather than in wealth, pray and obey, and be concerned for sinners. Perhaps Eliphaz sees himself in the role of the one through whom God will extend deliverance to Job (22:30).

JOB 23:1–24:25

JOB'S THIRD RESPONSE TO ELIPHAZ

Setting Up the Section

Eliphaz has exhorted Job to return to God (22:23). Job replies that that is just what he wants to do—not because he has wickedness to confess but because he wants to present his case to God.

23:1–17

GOD'S OMNIPOTENCE

Job wants to meet God face-to-face so that he can plead his case before Him. Job believes that if he can talk with God, he will be vindicated and God will relieve him of his troubles (23:1–8).

But search as he may, Job cannot find God (23:8–9). He is confident, however, that God can find him. And he is confident that he will not be found lacking. Job understands that trials are used to purify us, just as gold is refined in the refiner's fire so that it can become pure and all impurities removed (23:10). He maintains that he is innocent before God: He has followed God's ways (23:11) and treasured God's Word (23:12).

Critical Observation

When Job talks of testing (23:10), deep down he knows the truth about what God is doing, but it has been clouded at times by his recent experiences. The apostle Peter puts it this way: "In this you greatly rejoice, though now for a little while, if need be, you have been grieved by various trials, that the genuineness of your faith, being much more precious than gold that perishes, though it is tested by fire, may be found to praise, honor, and glory at the revelation of Jesus Christ, whom having not seen you love. Though now you do not see Him, yet believing, you rejoice with joy inexpressible and full of glory, receiving the end of your faith—the salvation of your souls" (1 Peter 1:6–9 NKJV).

Job speaks of the sovereignty of God (23:13). Unfortunately, this knowledge does not comfort Job; it makes him afraid (23:14–16). He is afraid because he thinks that this all-powerful God is out to get him (23:14–16). Job acknowledges God's sovereignty, but his circumstances have led him to forget God's love. Nevertheless, he will not be silent (23:17).

Take It Home

Job is right when he says that God does whatever He pleases (23:13). This does not negate our responsibility to pray, however, as some would have you believe. They say, "God is going to do whatever He wants, so why pray?" We pray because God tells us to pray. It is through prayer that God conforms our hearts to His.

God does answer our prayers, but we don't fully understand how it all works. When God was going to destroy unbelieving Israel, Moses stepped in and interceded for them, and God spared them. Did God change His will? Or was Moses' heart so conformed to God's that his request was in line with God's will? We don't understand these things, but we do know that God invites, even commands, our prayers.

24:1–25

THE WORLD'S INJUSTICE

Having affirmed God's knowledge and God's power, Job now questions why God doesn't provide, in essence, a court room in which people might urge God to use that knowledge and power to correct injustices (24:1). In short, why does a powerful God allow bad things to happen to good people? Job lists some of these injustices (24:2–9).

Demystifying Job

Moving boundary stones (24:2) was property theft. It effectively moved the lot lines to expand one person's property at the expense of his neighbor.

Job has seen the wicked do all these things. He has seen how the poor must work hard without getting the rewards of their labor (24:10–11). He hears their cries for help—surely God must hear them, too. But God does nothing (24:12).

Job continues to list charges against the wicked. The wicked run from the truth, the light, because it exposes their evil deeds. They love the dark because they can get away with murder (24:13–15). Darkness is the natural environment of the wicked, just as daylight is the natural environment of the innocent (24:16–17).

Strangely, Job seems to agree with his friends about the fate of the wicked. He lists many of the consequences that his friends have already described: early death, being forgotten after death, losing all that they have (24:19–24). Where Job differs from his friends is in turning the equation around. Job's friends say that because the wicked suffer, anyone who suffers is therefore wicked. Job disagrees; he persists in claiming innocence. Some suggest that these verses are not so much statements of fact as they are Job's desire for the wicked to receive their deserved punishment.

Job concludes with a challenge to his friends to prove him wrong, if they can (24:25).

JOB 25:1–6

BILDAD'S THIRD SPEECH

Setting Up the Section

We are in round three of the verbal tongue-lashing given to Job by his friends Eliphaz, Bildad, and Zophar. As Bildad begins to speak, he doesn't have a lot to say. It seems that he is running out of material with which to condemn Job. This may also be the reason that Zophar does not speak for a third time; we would expect him to take his turn after Bildad, but there is really nothing left to say; it has all been said before. Chapter 25 records the shortest speech in the book of Job, but it will lead to the longest speech in the book—from chapter 26 through chapter 31.

25:1–6

BILDAD'S THIRD SPEECH

Job has just concluded his previous speech with a challenge for his friends to disprove him if they can (24:25). Bildad does not take on this challenge, but instead he agrees with the first part of Job's previous speech: There is no one more powerful than God (25:1–2). Human kings may have large armies, but God's forces—the angels and heavenly armies—are too numerous to count. A wealthy man may illuminate his home with candles, but that is only a pale reflection of God's light, the sun (25:3).

If the contrast between divine and human armies and divine and human light is great, how much greater is the contrast between divine and human righteousness! In the face of God's righteousness, no mere human can measure up (25:4). In comparison with the brilliant moon and stars—which are infinitely less glorious than their Creator—human beings look like maggots.

Critical Observation

Bildad is right in what he has to say here in chapter 25. No one can be righteous before a holy God apart from Christ (see Romans 3:10–12). It is only because the penalty for our sin has been paid for by Christ that God can look on us with acceptance. It is only because the spotless Son of God, who chose to be born of a woman, has imputed his righteousness to us that others can stand before God as pure.

Take It Home

We don't much like to think of ourselves as worms (25:6). Some preachers have openly refuted this worm theology. The argument goes something like this: "You would only pay what something is worth; thus, because God gave His only begotten Son to die for us, we must be worth a lot! We must be valuable!" But Bildad's point here is not that people aren't valuable; his point is that we aren't, on our own, righteous material. There is no one God is not willing to save. God saves us by His grace and mercy alone, and not because we have some kind of redeeming quality in us. What God long ago said to Israel, we can easily apply to our own lives (see Deuteronomy 9:6).

JOB 26:1–31:40

JOB'S FINAL RESPONSE

On Power	26:1–14
On Justice	27:1–23
On Wisdom	28:1–28
On Former Happiness	29:1–25
On Loss	30:1–31
On Innocence	31:1–40

Setting Up the Section

Job's three friends seem to have run out of steam. After two or three rounds of arguing with Job, they have little left to say—as evidenced by how short Bildad's final speech is (chapter 25). Job, on the other hand, is just getting warmed up. What follows is his longest speech in the book.

26:1–14

ON POWER

Job's words drip with sarcasm as he responds to Bildad. (The *you* in verses 3 and 4 is singular, not plural. Apparently Eliphaz and Zophar have already been silenced.) What a comforting friend, wise and insightful, Bildad has been, Job says—meaning exactly the opposite (26:1–3). To speak so wisely must require inspiration—but from what spirit (26:4)? Clearly Job is not buying his friends' implication that they (and not Job) speak for God.

Perhaps in contrast to belittling Bildad, Job now exalts God. Nothing escapes God's notice and God's control. God created and still upholds (notice the present tense in verses 7–10) the skies; the earth stays where He put it, even though it seems to be suspended with nothing to hold it up (26:7). The water cycle is no less amazing: We take its transformation from liquid to vapor to liquid again (26:8) as a matter of course, but if a rock did the same thing, we would be amazed!

Demystifying Job

The Bible is not intended to be a scientific workbook, but it is remarkable how fitting verses 7–8 are to our current understanding of the cosmos. The science of Job's day up until the recent past includes some strange theories of how the earth is held. Some say it was on the back of an elephant, others on the back of the giant Atlas, and some even on the back of a turtle. But Job tells us that God hangs the earth on nothing. It is suspended in space.

The most commonplace of daily events are under God's control, Job says. When a cloud passes between earth and the moon, God is in control of it (26:9). When the sun rises over the eastern horizon and sets over the western horizon, God is in control (26:10). Storms that seem to shake the heavens (26:11) and churn the waters (26:12) are as nothing to God; He can blow them away with a single breath (25:13).

Demystifying Job

Rahab (26:12) is the name of a mythical sea monster—as is the "gliding serpent" (called Leviathan in Isaiah 27:1) mentioned in Job 26:13. In the Bible, these monsters are poetic representations of storms and other wild forces of nature.

All this evidence of God's power can be seen in creation, and yet it is only the tiniest fragment of what God is doing. What we know of God's power is like a whisper compared to thunder—far too great for us to comprehend (26:14).

27:1–23

ON JUSTICE

Although Job believes that God has denied him justice (27:2), he is committed to remaining truthful (27:3–4). A good part of that truthfulness, in Job's mind, is standing by his statement that he has done nothing to deserve the troubles that have come on him. To give in to these charges, Job says, *would* be wicked, because it would be a lie (27:5–7).

Demystifying Job

The breath of God that Job refers to (27:3) simply means life. At Creation, God breathed life into Adam (Genesis 2:7). Even while arguing that God has misjudged him, Job recognizes that life lasts only as long as God chooses to give it.

Job's friends have become his enemies through their false accusations, and now Job wishes they would be punished for their lies about him (27:7). He envisions Eliphaz, Bildad, and Zophar in the hopeless situation of begging God for help, as Job has, and getting no response (27:9–10). "I've listened to all your talk," he says in effect. "Now let *me* tell *you* a thing or two about how God works" (27:11–12).

Quoting what Zophar has said to him (20:29), Job begins a long litany of the things that a wicked person (in this case, perhaps his former friends) can expect from God (27:13). Their children will suffer (27:14), their wealth won't last, (27:16–18), and they will eventually vanish (27:20–23).

Critical Observation

When Job claims that the righteous will receive the wealth of the wicked, he is stating a principle of ideal justice. Ultimately, Job is convinced, God will punish evil and reward good. Although Job's experience at this point does not bear this happy thought out, Job knows enough of the character of God to cling to the conviction that justice will one day prevail.

28:1–28

ON WISDOM

Job now talks about those who go down into the earth to dig for precious stones and metals and bring them back up to the surface. It is dangerous work, but for those who are successful, the rewards outweigh the risks (28:1–11).

Wisdom is harder to find and harder for people to value, as well (28:12–13). One can't mine wisdom from the ground like silver or gold, nor gather it from the ocean depths, like pearls or coral (28:14). Nor can one buy wisdom with the riches that can be mined—with gold, silver, precious stones, coral, or topaz (28:15–19). As precious and valuable these stones and metals may be, they are worthless when compared to wisdom.

Take It Home

We live in a world that is vastly more intelligent than it was a hundred years ago. We have more information coming at us today than we know what to do with. And yet, for all that intelligence, we are unwise. Intelligence, in the Hebrew mind, is the accumulation of knowledge. Wisdom, on the other hand, is taking what we know and applying it to our lives—it is the application of knowledge.

Wisdom originates from God. Thus, as we apply the Word of God to our lives, we are exercising wisdom (see Proverbs 2:1–9). Do we as Christians dig into the Word of God as much as men dug into the earth looking for treasure? In the Word of God are riches that are more important than anything we can dig from the dirt.

Finding wisdom begins to seem hopeless (28:20). God alone knows the way to wisdom; He is the One who determines what wisdom is (28:23–27). And He defines it for human beings: The fear of the Lord is wisdom, and to shun evil is understanding (28:28).

Critical Observation

God Himself approved Job as a wise man when He described Job in exactly the terms used in verse 28 to define wisdom: Job is a man who fears God and shuns evil (1:8; 2:3).

29:1–25

ON FORMER HAPPINESS

Job now reminisces about his past, about the good times and joy he had before all this trouble came upon his life (29:1–2). Job walked in the light of God (29:3–4). His children, who are all dead now, used to run around his feet, and what joy their voices brought him (29:5). Luxuries like cream were as common as the dirt beneath his feet (29:6). Goodness at one time seemed to follow him wherever he went. But now that is all gone.

Job had been a respected man who sat at the gate of the city as part of the city council (29:7). The young deferred to him and the aged stood in respect of him (29:8). We get the idea that when Job talked it was so quiet you could hear a pin drop. Everyone wanted to hear what he had to say (29:9–10).

Earlier, Job's friends had accused him of oppressing the poor and taking advantage of the fatherless and widows. But Job contends that the opposite is true: He had a reputation as a good man (29:11) because he helped the poor and fatherless (29:12), comforted the dying, and brought joy to the widow's heart (29:13). When people looked at Job, they saw righteousness and justice (29:14). He helped the disabled (29:15), befriended strangers (29:16), and stood against the wicked (29:17). He was a good man who practiced what he believed.

At that time, Job had it all figured out. Since he was doing good, he expected to live to an old age, and his life would continue to be blessed (29:18). He would be like the righteous man described in Psalm 1, who is like a tree planted by streams of water (29:19). His reputation as the greatest man among all the peoples of the East (see 1:3) would be constant (29:20). But things are not working out as he has planned.

People used to gather and wait in line to hear the wisdom of Job (29:21). His words were refreshing to them; they stood drinking in his words (29:22–23). They were delighted when they won his approval (29:24). Job received a lot of respect from the multitudes of people that came to hear him (29:25). That is the way it was, but now things have changed dramatically.

30:1–31

ON LOSS

In Job's day there were people roaming the streets who were nothing more than thieves and troublemakers who no one wanted around. Now even these people mock Job. The lowest of society are putting Job down—a man who was at one time held in high esteem and highly respected (30:1).

These people live off the land and are not physically healthy. They basically take what they can find, even the garbage that people throw out (30:2–4). These people are hated by society and run out of town. No one wants them around, for they are troublemakers (30:5). These are the ones who now mock and spit upon Job. They make up songs to taunt him and treat him as if he is the outcast to be avoided (30:9–10).

Demystifying Job

Twice Job uses the imagery of a bow—in the good old days, his bow was always new (29:20), but now God has unstrung his bow (30:11). Bows and arrows were the main weapons for hunting in Job's time, and they represented a man's strength and status. A bow with no bowstring, however, was useless—a sign of weakness and humiliation.

Since God has taken away all Job's wealth, people no longer feel the need to show respect to him (30:11). While young men once stepped aside on the path to let Job pass (29:8), now they block his way (30:13–14). Where, before, people were eager to win Job's approval and feared his disapproval (29:21–24), now it is Job who is afraid and humiliated (30:15).

Previously, Job enjoyed the material luxuries of wealth and the blessing of God's friendship (29:4–6), but now he is in physical pain, and God's presence is like a straitjacket that chokes him and trips him up. Job's distress is so great that he feels he has become like dust and ashes, the symbols of remorse and grief (30:18–19).

It seems that God has closed His ears to Job's cry (30:20). Job is crying out for help, but things just seem to be getting worse and worse for him (30:21–22). He is certain now that he will be miserable for the rest of his life (30:23).

It seems unbelievable to Job that he, who has helped those in difficulty so often, should have no one to help him now (30:24–25). Yet this is the case; every hope for relief is disappointed (30:26), and his suffering goes on (30:27–30).

For Job, there are no more songs of joy; the only songs in his life are dirges (30:31).

31:1–40

ON INNOCENCE

Job contends that he has not looked with lust at any woman. Now this is not just by accident; Job made an intentional decision—a covenant with his eyes—not to look at a woman this way (31:1). This covenant, this conscious decision, affects all areas of Job's life, because he knows that God knows his every thought and action (31:2–4).

Take It Home

Job knew that resisting temptation took an act of will. This is true for us today, as well. Certainly, we can stand only in the righteousness that has been imputed to us by Jesus Christ. This is called *positional righteousness*—referring to our position or status before God—and many times that is as far as Christians go. But the New Testament abounds with instructions to make a conscious decision for holiness (see 1 Peter 1:13–16). This is *practical righteousness*—where we purpose in our hearts not to let lust (or anything that would incite temptation) enter our eyes and our minds, causing us to stumble in our relationship with God. We should have that desire to walk in righteousness. We need to make a conscious decision on our part to live as God wants us to live.

Job is willing to have his life actions be placed in the balances of God, and if it comes up short, he is willing to be judged accordingly. But Job feels that he has tried to do good and that his life has reflected that (31:5–8). He gives specific examples of his innocence, couching each in the same "if/then" structure: "If I have done this, then let me be judged for it."

"If I have been involved in an adulterous relationship," says Job, "then let me be punished by my wife's unfaithfulness" (31:9–10). Adultery is a shameful sin that brings destruction with it (31:11–12).

Job contends that he doesn't treat people differently because of their social status, the color of their skin, or their nationality (31:13). He acts this way because he acknowledges that God has created every human being in the same way, reflecting His own image (31:14–15).

Job says that he has never walked away from anyone in need but has come to their aid and given to them what they needed to live—be it food, clothing, even help against their enemies (31:16–22). Job does this because of his fear of the Lord. The "fear of God's splendor" speaks of reverence and respect for God (31:23).

Job does not worship his wealth or place his confidence in it (31:24–25), nor does he turn to horoscopes or other astrological enticements (31:26–27), because he recognizes that both are idolatry and unfaithfulness to God (31:28).

Demystifying Job

The worship of the heavens—the sun, moon, and constellations—was very popular and, of course, of pagan practice. That worship included kissing one's hand and throwing that kiss to the sun or moon.

Job claims that he has not gloated over his enemies' troubles (31:29) or cursed them (31:30), and he has offered hospitality to household staff and strangers alike (31:31–32).

He lived his life in the open for all to see. He is not a hypocrite, trying to hide his sin (32:33–34).

Job underscores the seriousness of his claims by putting his name to them—possibly literally signing a document, or perhaps symbolically. And he wishes that his accuser—God—would put His charges in writing as well, so that Job could refute the charges one by one (31:35–37). So confident is Job of his innocence that he again invites scrutiny of his behavior in another of his "if/then" statements (31:38–40).

With this, Job rests his case. In the remainder of the book of Job, we will hear only two brief statements from him (40:3–5; 42:2–6).

JOB 32:1–37:24

ELIHU SPEAKS

Compelled tw 36:1–37:24

Setting Up the Section

Job's three friends Eliphaz, Bildad, and Zophar have run out of gas. They have nothing left to say, for they have said more than enough to Job already. By this time a crowd has gathered to watch the confrontation—a confrontation that is loud and animated. And in this crowd is Elihu, a young man who has heard all these words and now has something to say.

32:1–22

COMPELLED TO SPEAK OUT

The three friends see the futility of arguing with Job more. Because Job will not admit that he has been wrong, that he has sinned, they see him as self-righteous (32:1). By now a large crowd has gathered to hear these encounters between Job and his friends, and within that crowd is a man named Elihu. Elihu is angered by Job's words (32:2), and he isn't too happy with Job's three friends, either, for they have condemned Job with no proof of sin. Elihu sees their reasoning as faulty (32:3). Out of respect for men older than himself, Elihu remained silent, but now that the three friends are giving up, Elihu can remain quiet no longer (33:4).

Demystifying Job

Abraham's brother, Nahor, had two sons, Huz and Buz (Genesis 22:21). Elihu was a descendant of the family of Buz, making him a Buzite (32:2).

Elihu begins respectfully enough, acknowledging the older men's right to speak first. But he points out that age does not always equal wisdom; wisdom is given by the Spirit (or breath) of God, and the young can receive that wisdom as well (32:8–9). Elihu is eager to share his wisdom (32:10).

Elihu has listened patiently to the words of the three friends, but they have come up short and not convinced Job of his error (32:11–13). All they have done is put Job on the defensive. Elihu hopes that Job will listen to him because he has not been part of the earlier arguments—and because he has something new to say (32:14). He doesn't see why he should be forced to remain silent just because the three friends have given up (32:15–16). Elihu has so much to say that he is ready to burst (32:18–20). He promises not to stoop to flattery or favoritism (32:21–22).

33:1–33

A VARIATION ON AN OLD THEME

Some time earlier, Job had expressed a desire for a mediator between him and God (9:33). Elihu says that he is that man who can stand in the gap and bring Job and God together. He claims to be righteous, sincere, and Spirit-filled (33:1–5)—in other words, someone God will listen to, but also someone Job doesn't need to be afraid of (33:6–7).

Critical Observation

Elihu is here describing the perfect mediator: truly righteous and truly human (see, for example, Hebrews 2:17; 7:26). What he gets wrong is the identity of this mediator, who is not Elihu, but Jesus Christ.

Elihu accuses Job of falsely claiming to be sinless (33:8–9). Here he is misrepresenting Job, who has readily admitted that he is a sinner (7:21; 13:26). Further, he regularly offers the appropriate sacrifices for sin (1:5). What Job has claimed is to be innocent of the kind of wickedness that deserves the punishment (as he perceives it to be) that he has received (33:10–11).

Elihu also accuses Job of claiming that God does not speak to humans (33:12–13). He lists many ways that God does in fact communicate: through dreams and visions (33:14–15), audibly or through the warnings of godly people (33:16–18), and even through pain, which can focus one's thoughts on God and on self-examination (33:19). What Elihu has to say is a little different than what Job's three friends were saying. Job's friends had maintained that the things happening to Job were a direct result of sin in his life. Elihu is saying that God has brought this upon Job because He is chastening him in order to confess his sin and get back on track (33:20–22).

Critical Observation

God does indeed sometimes use what C. S. Lewis calls "the megaphone of pain" to get our attention and lead us back to Him. But Elihu is wrong in assuming that Job's suffering is God's rebuke and call to repentance; Job 1 and 2 have already made clear that the reason is quite different. In the same way, we would be wrong to assume that suffering is always God's rebuke for wrongdoing. (See Luke 13:1–5 for Jesus' warning against that kind of judgment.)

Elihu tries to encourage Job with the possibility that one of the angels will intercede with God on Job's behalf (33:23–24). Ironically, Job's troubles result from exactly the opposite: Satan's accusations against him.

The appropriate response, Elihu instructs Job, is to confess first to God (33:26) and then to people that he has sinned (33:37) and that God has given him another chance (33:38). In fact, Elihu says, Job's suffering is actually evidence of God's love, as it gives Job a chance to repent and be restored (33:29–30).

Elihu pauses to ask whether Job needs any clarification before he continues with his instruction (33:31–33). Presumably Job does not, because Elihu continues his lecture.

34:1–37

REPENTANCE VS. REBELLION

Elihu now turns to address those around him, inviting them to be partners in the process of assessing Job's situation (34:1–4). He summarizes Job's claims of injustice (34:5–6) and then plays "good cop" to the three friends, saying Job has taken all their abuse, but Elihu is not going to do the same (34:7–8).

Despite what Elihu claims (34:10), Job knows that the wicked will be punished and there is a profit in doing good. Once again, Elihu is misrepresenting what Job has to say. Then Elihu begins to defend God, asserting that God does justice, not evil (34:10–12). No one supervises God (34:13); He holds us together and gives us the very breath we breathe (34:14–15).

Now Elihu turns back to speak directly to Job. The Hebrew for the verbs in verse 16 is singular. He accuses Job of condemning God as unjust in His dealings with Job (34:17). He contends that Job honors those in high positions, like kings, and yet he puts God down (34:18–20).

Evildoers can't get away with anything; God knows what they are doing (34:21–22), Elihu reminds Job. Although Job has been asking for a hearing before God, Elihu argues that hearings are unnecessary for a God who already knows everything (34:23). God will mete out justice, and that justice will be made public so that everyone can see what happens to people who reject God's laws (34:24–27) and mistreat the poor. Job has complained that God is silent when Job calls to Him. Elihu says that it's God's right to remain silent (34:28–29); God maintains justice over the nations even when He is silent (34:30).

Elihu sets out a model of behavior for Job to follow, first with a hypothetical situation (34:31–32), and then more directly with a rhetorical question about Job's apparent refusal to repent (34:33).

Elihu seems to be thinking aloud as he summarizes Job's position: Everyone knows (so Elihu believes) that Job is a fool (34:35). Job deserves even more troubles than he has already received, because not only is Job a sinner, but he refuses to confess that sin and thus rebels against God's chastisement (34:36–37).

35:1–16

GOD'S AUTONOMY

Elihu points out what he sees as an inconsistency in Job's complaint. Job claims that there is no benefit for not sinning, and yet he expects God to vindicate him for not sinning (35:1–3). Elihu points out that God is far above human beings (35:4–5). God does not owe Job anything. Nor is God affected by how good or how bad Job is (35:6–7). While Job can't hurt God by his actions, he can very much hurt or help himself and others by what he does and what he says (35:8).

Many cry out for help during difficult times, but they look for their help in all the wrong places (35:9). They don't look to God, who will put a song in their heart and give them hope and joy again (35:10).

Take It Home

We are not so different from the people Elihu refers to in verse 9. Like them, we look for help in all the wrong places. We look to drugs, alcohol, relationships, and so on—those only bring more difficulty in our lives. But during difficult times it is God who can put a song in our hearts and give us peace through the storms. Many of the great hymns were born out of these difficult times, and many of the psalms were also written from this vantage point. God gives us songs of hope and joy.

Many people speak boldly about things they don't know (35:11). But God does not respond to them, because they are arrogant (35:12–13). Job is equally arrogant, Elihu says, and that is why God doesn't answer him (35:14–16).

36:1–37:24

GOD'S POWER

Elihu has elevated himself to the position of spokesperson for God (36:1–2)—but God has not given him this position. Elihu claims he has obtained perfect knowledge through direct revelation from God, so Job had better listen (36:3–4). Because of His great power, God's justice will be fulfilled (36:5–6). Earlier, Job had complained that God would not leave him alone (7:17–19). Elihu considers it a comfort to know that God's eyes are continually upon His people (36:7). The righteous God exalts, but the arrogant He afflicts (36:8).

Job is angry because God has brought a clear charge against him (31:2), but Elihu argues that God does warn people of their sins (36:9) and brings trouble on them to get them to repent (36:10). If they do repent, they will prosper (36:11); if not, they will perish (36:12).

Elihu warns Job not to be like those who rebel against God's discipline (36:13–14) but instead to recognize it as God's loving way of bringing Job out of sin and misery and into joy and comfort (36:15–16). He sees Job in danger of choosing evil rather than submitting to God's discipline (36:17–21).

There is no one who teaches as God does (36:22). He is not wrong and He will never be wrong (36:23). We can know God because He has revealed Himself through scripture and through His creation (36:24–25). But we cannot understand God's thoughts and ways, nor can we fully grasp the truth that God is eternal. He has always existed (36:26).

Elihu points to the earth's atmosphere as an exhibit of God's wisdom, power, and provision. What follows is an accurate description of evaporation and distillation of water as rain (36:27), clouds (36:28; 37:11), and cyclones (37:12). Many feel that, as Elihu is speaking to Job, in the distance is a huge storm forming. As Elihu is trying to make his point, he sees this storm and begins to draw illustrations on the power of God and His awesomeness (36:30–27:13).

Elihu again asks rhetorical questions as he challenges Job to reflect on God's power and control over creation (37:14–20). Just as we find it difficult, almost impossible, to stare at the sun with our naked eyes, so, too, is it impossible to stand in the brightness of a holy and righteous God in our own righteousness (37:21–23). The only reasonable response is to revere Him (37:24).

JOB 38:1–42:6

THE LORD SPEAKS WITH JOB

God Speaks of His Power in Creation	38:1–40:2
Job Replies to God	40:3–5
God Speaks of His Justice	40:6–41:34
Job Confesses	42:1–6

Setting Up the Section

As Elihu is finishing his words against Job, a huge storm is forming in the distance. Elihu draws some illustrations from this storm and relates them to God. For some thirty-five chapters, Job and his friends have spoken, but now it is time for God to speak. For thirty-five chapters mankind has attempted to understand the how's and why's of God with finite minds—and no one has come to an understanding of these things. Now God is going to speak out.

What is interesting in this section is that God does not explain to Job—or us—exactly why He has done these things to Job. In fact, He asks Job a series of some seventy questions, and in the end, God's *answer* is far more important than an understanding of His *ways.* Simply speaking, God gives Himself as the answer.

38:1–40:2

GOD SPEAKS OF HIS POWER IN CREATION

Job has wanted to ask God questions, but God turns the tables and begins asking Job questions (38:1–3). This is probably to get Job refocused. Job has been looking and developing his ideas of God through life's situations instead of falling back on the truths of God. His picture of God has been clouded by life's circumstances, and God is going to clear things up.

God asks Job whether he was around when the earth was created (38:4). Today we do know the measurement of the earth (38:5). It is 24,901.55 miles in circumference at the equator, and its diameter is 7,926.41 miles at the equator. And yet we still know so little, as God is going to show us.

God is actively involved in creation and everything that has taken place since that time (38:6). The angels were present at earth's creation and shouted for joy at what God had done (38:7). But Job was not around. God set the boundaries for the waters without the help of Job (38:8–11). Job was not around when God created the days and the light (38:12–15). Again, God is trying to get Job to take his eyes off of the circumstances he finds himself in, and to look back to his Creator, where true help and hope come from.

The ancients were not aware of the fresh water springs that are on the ocean floor, nor the channels and pathways located in the depth of the oceans, but God knew (38:16).

Job had wanted death to come upon him, for he saw death as a place of nonexistence (3:11–17). But Job is wrong about that. God rebukes Job for speaking about something he knows nothing about (38:17–18).

What happens to the darkness when the lights go on? God knows (38:19–21). Who understands how God controls the weather to influence the outcome of battles (38:22–23)? We know today that light can be divided into the light spectrum (38:24), but how did they know this back then? God knew because He created the light.

Critical Observation

God uses the elements of nature to bring about His will. Remember in Judges 5, Barak defeats the army of Sisera when God causes a torrential rainfall, causing their chariots to be stuck in the mud so that they have to flee on foot. God causes hailstones to fall from the sky, destroying the Amorites in Joshua 10. And in 1 Samuel 7, God uses thunder to confuse the Philistines, giving Israel the victory.

God reminds Job that He waters the wilderness, causing the vegetation to grow (38:25–27). He did not just create life and sit back and watch what happens, as the deists believe (38:28–30); He is actively involved in sustaining His work.

The Pleiades and Orion (38:31) are winter constellations. The Great Bear (38:32), or Arcturus, is the fourth brightest star in the sky. Obviously, Job has no control over them (36:33), nor can Job make it rain (38:34–35, 37–38), but God can and He does.

Demystifying Job

Arcturas, the Bear of Job 38:32, is some thirty-six light years away from us. Now that sounds pretty close, but when you calculate out that light travels at 186,000 miles per second, and one year it would travel around six trillion miles, you realize that it is actually very far away. Our sun is 864,000 miles in diameter and contains 335 quadrillion cubic miles of violently hot gases with a core temperature of twenty-seven million degrees Fahrenheit. Arcturus is thirty times larger than the sun and eighty times brighter. It travels at 250,000 miles per hour.

God provides food for the various animals—even those Job will not go near (38:39–40). God points to nature and how the animals give birth without the knowledge of Job, but God is aware (39:1–4). The onager (39:5) is a wild donkey, and God is saying He cares for all of them (39:5–8; Psalm 50:10–11).

Demystifying Job

The mountain goat of Job 39:1 may be the Nubian Ibex, who does hide when it gives birth. Even today very few have seen the birth of an Ibex.

The wild ox (39:9) could be the Auroch, which became extinct in 1627. This creature refused to be domesticated. It was fierce and it was huge, just a little smaller than an elephant. And God is saying to Job, "If you can't stand before my creation, if you can't handle him, how can you stand before me?" (39:9–12).

The ostrich can stand seven to eight feet tall, weighing up to three hundred pounds. But they are flightless, unlike the stork (39:13). And they are without sense. But even though God did not give the ostrich wisdom, He gave it the ability to run (39:17–18).

It is God who made the horse for battle (39:19–25) and gave hawks the instinct for migration (39:26). God equipped the eagle to make its nest high up where it can see its prey from great distances (39:27–30).

Demystifying Job

The migration of birds, such as the hawk mentioned in Job 39:26, is an interesting subject. The Golden Plover travels some eight thousand miles from the Hudson Bay region and winters in Argentina. The Barn Swallow migrates a distance of nine thousand miles from northern Canada to Argentina. The Arctic Tern migrates a distance of fourteen thousand miles, traveling from pole to pole and back. And even in storms they can travel without getting lost. How do they know where to go? God has given them a way to know what they are doing.

God now calls on Job to respond to all these questions He has put to Job (40:1–2).

40:3–5

JOB REPLIES TO GOD

Job had much to say before, when his eyes were focused on his situation. But now that God has his attention, he has very little to say. He rightly recognizes his error and is ready to listen to God (40:3–5).

40:6–41:34

GOD SPEAKS OF HIS JUSTICE

Out of the storm, God again challenges Job to answer Him (40:6–7), using the same words He used earlier (38:3). This time, God addresses Job's primary complaint: that He has been unjust to Job (40:8; see 19:6). Job has claimed to be just, so now God challenges Job to demonstrate his power to administer that justice (40:9–13). If Job can do that, then Job can vindicate himself (40:14).

Verses 15–24 make up the first of two poems that God speaks to Job, returning to the themes of chapter 39 and God's control over nature. Here God describes the behemoth. This is an animal that God created (40:15), not a mythical being. It is one of the most powerful of all God's creatures, but God is even more powerful (40:16–19). The area described as its habitat (40:21–23) is probably the region north of the Sea of Galilee. The idea of any human capturing the behemoth is laughable (40:24), but God can certainly control it.

Demystifying Job

Scholars aren't certain exactly what kind of creature the behemoth (40:15–24) is. It is variously considered to be an elephant, a rhinoceros, a water buffalo, or a hippopotamus. It is a land animal that also lives in the water. It is also an herbivore—in other words, it eats grass. It is a massive creature that has a tail (or possibly a trunk) like a cedar tree. From the description that is given, it seems that the behemoth could be a dinosaur—possibly either a Brachiosaurus or an Apatosaurus.

Next God speaks a poem about the leviathan, asking Job if he would bring this creature home as a pet and play with it (41:1–5). The idea is obviously absurd; even professional fishermen armed with harpoons can't bring the leviathan down—one only needs to look at the creature to know the futility of such a task (41:6–9). If Job can't stand against this creature, God asks, then how can he stand against God who created this creature (41:10–11)? He can't!

God elaborates on the fearsomeness of the leviathan. It is powerful and untamable, with scary teeth—perhaps like a crocodile's (41:12–14). Apparently, it is a reptile with a scaly back that is like a protective shield (41:15–17). To get within breathing range of the leviathan is to court disaster (41:19–21). Its muscles are as hard as rocks (41:22–24), and it can take down ships with its thrashing (41:25). Swords and spears can't pierce its scales (41:26), and metal gives way under its biting (41:27). Even its underbelly—usually the most vulnerable part of an animal—is as hard and as sharp as broken pottery (41:30).

When the leviathan takes to the water, its thrashing can cause seas as rough as a storm would, complete with whitecaps (41:31–32). Nothing on earth—and certainly not Job—is its equal (41:33–34).

Critical Observation

The last verse of this poem about the leviathan (41:34) shifts from speaking of physical prowess to speaking of attitude and rank. It seems that the dragon that God is speaking of here is the same dragon found in the book of Revelation, Satan (see Revelation 12:3–4, 7–9).

42:1–6

JOB CONFESSES

Notice the perspective that Job now has of God and the situation he finds himself in. First of all, Job recognizes the sovereignty of God and that He is in control of everything (42:1–2). God shows Job that He not only created the heavens and the earth and all that dwells in it, but He sustains them also. Everything is subject to His sovereign rule.

Secondly, Job recognizes the foolishness of his words. Job has spoken about issues he knew nothing about (42:3), and yet he sounded so sure of himself. God redirects Job to fall back on the things he knows about God instead of coming up with foolish conclusions about life's situations.

It is one thing to hear God but quite another thing to *encounter* God (42:4–5). It is Job's encounter with God that causes him to see himself as a sinner, and he repents of his sin (42:6).

Take It Home

Many times, when we are hurting or we find ourselves in difficult situations, we take our eyes off God and what His Word has to say, and we come up with foolish words. If we will let God redirect us to fall back on the things we know about God through His Word, we, like Job, will find it is full of wonder, hope, and comfort.

JOB 42:7–17

EPILOGUE

Setting Up the Section

God's dialogue with Job is concluded, but God has two more things to do before the case is closed. First, He has a few things to say to Job's three friends. And second, He restores justice to Job.

42:7–17

EPILOGUE

God now turns from Job to Eliphaz and the other two friends. These men had not represented God correctly, and God held them accountable for their actions (42:7).

Critical Observation

God was angry with Job's three friends because they did not speak the truth about God. They had reduced God to a cause-and-effect God, and they assumed that they could both understand and predict all God's actions. In essence, they denied God's sovereignty by declaring that God must respond in a certain way to certain situations.

The three friends had spent much energy trying to convince Job of his sin and of his need to repent and offer sacrifices for that sin. How ironic it must have seemed when God told them that *they* were the ones who needed to offer sacrifices—and that God would accept those sacrifices for Job's sake and because of Job's righteousness (42:8–9).

When did God bless or restore Job? When he prayed for his friends who blasted him (42:10). Then all the friends and relatives who had abandoned Job (see 19:13–19) came rushing back, eager to comfort Job—and to eat his food (42:11).

Take It Home

Why did God wait to bless Job until after Job prayed for the friends who had attacked him? Job had some bitterness toward his friends, as his replies to them have shown. But to pray for them he had to let go of that bitterness.

God wants to bless us, but what are we holding onto? What bitterness, or anger, or whatever is keeping God's blessings from being bestowed upon us?

God blessed Job with even more wealth than Job had before—twice as many sheep, camels, oxen, and donkeys as before (compare the numbers listed in 42:12 with those listed in 1:3). It seems that Job had the same number of children (42:13), but the reality is he has twice as many, for seven sons and three daughters were with the Lord. Job treated his daughters with the same kindness as he treated his sons, even giving them an inheritance, which was unusual in those days (42:14–15).

Despite his friends' dire warnings that Job would die young (see 36:14) and leave no heirs (see 18:19), Job lived 140 more years and saw not only his grandchildren but his great-grandchildren and great-great-grandchildren as well (42:16). He died old and "full of years" (42:17).

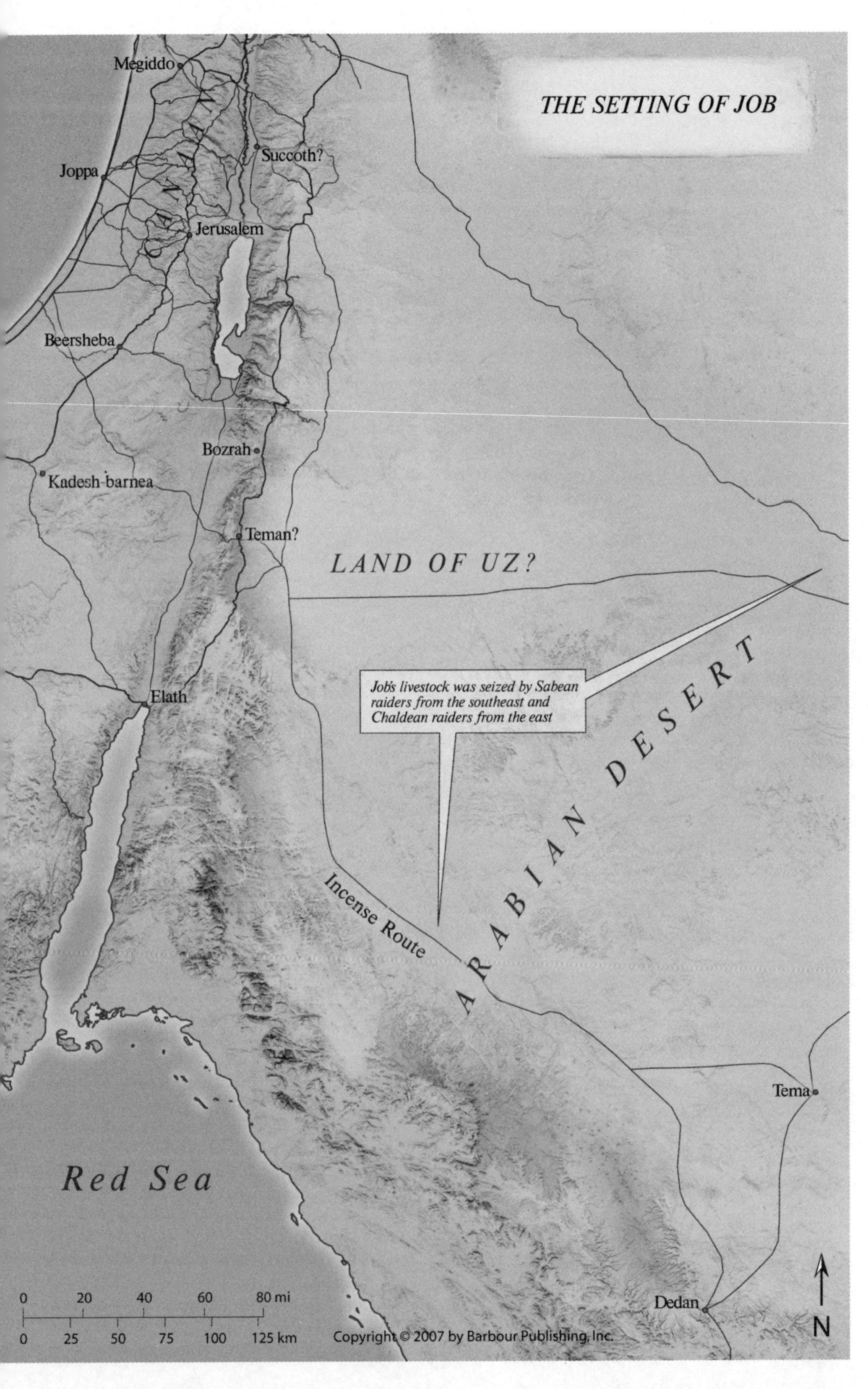
THE SETTING OF JOB
Megiddo
CANAAN
Succoth?
Joppa
Jerusalem
Beersheba
Bozrah
Kadesh-barnea
Teman?
LAND OF UZ?
Job's livestock was seized by Sabean raiders from the southeast and Chaldean raiders from the east
ARABIAN DESERT
Elath
Incense Route
Tema
Red Sea
Dedan
N
0 20 40 60 80 mi
0 25 50 75 100 125 km
Copyright © 2007 by Barbour Publishing, Inc.

PSALMS

INTRODUCTION TO PSALMS

The book of Psalms has been called the "hymnbook" of the Old Testament. Depending on one's perception of a hymnal, the title can be misleading, or it can be quite accurate. Sometimes the modern church approaches hymns lightly—singing one before the "real" worship service begins and another before going home. Or perhaps old hymns are disregarded altogether. But anyone who closely examines a traditional hymnal and reads the words of Martin Luther, Charles Wesley, Fanny Crosby, and others will find a wealth of biblical truth and weighty theological tenets. The fact that the words are rhymed and set to music may actually disguise their importance to modern ears.

This is the case with the book of Psalms as well. Its poetic format tends to diminish its importance for some people. They turn to Psalms for comfort or for light reading, yet many fail to approach the psalms with the same reverence as other portions of scripture. Yet for those who read closely, the psalms reveal much about God and the impact of His presence during the joys and struggles of human life.

And just as a modern hymnal may contain hymns with updated language in places, or perhaps a newer hymn set to an old familiar tune, so, too, the book of Psalms has revisions. It is believed that in certain instances, psalmists from the exile or later may have adapted much earlier psalms to apply to Israel's current situation.

AUTHOR

The psalms have a variety of authors. Some psalms identify the writer, and others don't. Yet even the people acknowledged as authors may not have actually written the psalm. A psalm attributed to David may have been written *by* David or possibly written *for* David. Or it could have been another psalmist's attempt to write in the style of David. One of the writers, Asaph, was a contemporary of David's, yet some of the psalms of Asaph refer to events of the exile that occurred long after his death. Therefore it is sometimes a challenge to verify authors. Other times the content of the psalm provides a clear indication of the author. In cases where the writer is uncertain (or not identified), it is traditional to refer to "the psalmist" as the author.

Almost half of the psalms (seventy-three) are attributed to David. Asaph (including his descendants, one of the clans of Levites assigned to oversee the music ministry of the temple) is credited with twelve psalms. Another music ministry clan, the sons of Korah, is identified with eleven psalms (although Psalm 43, which is unattributed, may have originally been an extension of Psalm 42 and therefore added to the total). Two psalms are assigned to Solomon. One each is assigned to Moses, Heman, and Ethan. That leaves forty-nine psalms with no designated author.

PURPOSE

The Hebrew title for the book means "praises." (The word *psalm* comes from the Greek translation rather than the original Hebrew.) Overall, the content of the book is intended for prayer and praise, although there is much variety within those broad categories. Some of the psalms were written as individual laments, some as community laments, some as thanksgiving hymns. Some are classified as penitential—confessional psalms asking God's forgiveness. Others were written as laments that cried for God's mercy on the psalmist and retribution on his enemies. Some were intended as regal celebrations when a new king was crowned.

OCCASION

Some psalms celebrate special occasions in the community, such as annual pilgrimages to Jerusalem, the coronation of a king, and liturgical ceremonies. Other psalms are written in regard to personal experiences. (Of David's seventy-three psalms, fourteen of the introductions refer to specific events in his life.) Yet the poetic nature of the psalms leads to their use on many occasions. Jesus and numerous New Testament writers naturally referred to the psalms to emphasize what they were trying to say. Jesus even quoted from the psalms as He hung on the cross (see Psalm 22:1 and Matthew 27:46; Psalm 31:5 and Luke 23:46).

THEMES

Unlike most of the biblical books that precede it, Psalms is not written in chronological order or any linear fashion. It is a collection of poetry written by numerous people over a long period of time. Yet regardless of the author, time period, or specific situation, the author invariably acknowledges the presence of—and humanity's total dependence on—God. Whether describing the wonders of creation, expressing a personal and painful trauma, recounting the history of the nation, bemoaning life in exile, or detailing any other experience, the psalmist's words are directed toward God. Some psalms express more faith than others, but they all appeal to God's strength, mercy, forgiveness, deliverance, and other qualities that are exclusively His.

HISTORICAL CONTEXT

With one psalm attributed to Moses and others to psalmists during and after the exile, the content of the psalms covers centuries of Israel's history. The scope of the psalms covers times when individuals and the nation were close to God and basking in His blessings as well as times when the people had drifted away from the will of God, and they were suffering as a result. In addition, some of the psalms have messianic applications, so the context is future as well as past and present.

CONTRIBUTION TO THE BIBLE

No collection of ancient lyrical poetry is more extensive than the book of Psalms. Hebrew poetry was not known for rhyme and meter but rather for repetition of thoughts and a style of parallelism that reemphasized or contrasted a concept in adjoining lines. The psalms also introduce some words that have never been clearly defined—words such as *sheminith* (Psalms 6, 12), *shiggaion*, (Psalm 7), *gittith* (Psalm 8, 81, 84), *alamoth* (Psalm 46), *mahalath* (Psalm 53), *mahalath leannoth* (Psalm 88), *miktam* and *maskil* (various psalms), and *selah* (found seventy-one times in thirty-nine psalms). Most are believed to be musical or perhaps historical references.

OUTLINE

The collection we know as the book of Psalms is actually a series of collections—five books in all. Books I and II are thought to be early collections, dating from the era of the kings. Book I may even have been compiled by David himself. The latter three books were probably compiled after the exile.

Book I	Psalms 1–41
Book II	Psalms 42–72
Book III	Psalms 73–89
Book IV	Psalms 90–106
Book V	Psalms 107–150

PSALMS: BOOK I

PSALMS 1–19

Setting Up the Section

The first "book" within Psalms is the earliest of the five compilations. It is widely associated with David's life and reign. This section contains the first nineteen (of forty-one) psalms from the first book.

PSALM 1

The placement of Psalm 1 does not appear to be coincidental. The work of editors seems clear from the fact that each book within the book of Psalms ends with a doxology. Similarly, Psalm 1 seems well chosen to emphasize a theme that will be ongoing. Throughout scripture God calls His people to set their standards higher than those of the world in general. People who commit themselves to God and are obedient to His clear instructions are promised rewards; those who reject Him can expect judgment. The first psalm reflects this ongoing biblical theme, as will others throughout the book.

In verse 1, the word *blessed* describes the status of someone who has placed trust in the Lord and lives according to His commands. This desirable state is one of inner joy more than financial prosperity, although the two are sometimes intertwined (1:3). Blessedness results from committing to certain activities while avoiding others (1:1–2).

Those desiring God's blessing must be careful of their worldly associations, according to the opening of this psalm. While being a light to the world, they must not allow themselves to linger too long around ungodly influences, lest they be seduced. They are not to walk among the wicked, and they are to remain focused at all times on God's Word (1:1–2).

According to verses 3–6, the reward for doing so is significant. The image of the wicked is that of chaff being blown away by a breeze (1:4). Those who devote themselves to righteousness, however, are portrayed as a fruitful tree, soundly rooted beside streams of water (1:3). No matter how great the thrill of various tantalizing sins might appear, it will not compare to being able to stand in (withstand) the judgment of God (1:5).

The wicked may appear to prosper, but their success is always temporary. Those who remain committed to the Lord and in His care will endure forever (1:6).

PSALM 2

Psalm 2:2 refers to the anointed one of God. The Hebrew for "anointed one" is the source of the English word *messiah*. New Testament references make it clear that the writers applied the psalm to Jesus (Acts 13:32–33). The original readers, however, would have considered it a reference to one of God's chosen kings in the Davidic line.

Critical Observation

Like Psalm 1, the author and date of Psalm 2 are not known. The leaders of the early New Testament church attributed Psalm 2 to David (Acts 4:25), although their intent may simply have been to give him credit as the primary author of Psalms.

The psalmist doesn't expect an answer to his opening question in verse 1. He is simply pointing out that by resisting the one anointed by God, the nations are resisting the authority of God Himself—a futile effort. The psalmist's original readers would have been familiar with the political turbulence that frequently took place surrounding the rise of a new leader. Perhaps they recalled that, in spite of David's credentials, the supporters of King Saul were still slow to accept him as their leader. Later, when Solomon's son (and successor) Rehoboam attempts to assert himself as a new king, the people strongly resist, and the kingdom is divided from that point onward (1 Kings 12:1–24).

The people whom the psalmist describes in Psalm 2:2–3 are not at all cooperative. They consider service to their king the equivalent of slavery. Such treason would have had harsh consequences from a human king, but this group is resisting God.

The Lord does not need these people or their cooperation. Their attempted resistance is laughable. He will carry out His plans, installing the one He has chosen to be the reigning king (2:4–6). How others respond does not impede His plans.

In verse 6, *Zion* is a term that often indicates Jerusalem in the Psalms. Zion appears to have originally been only one *section* of Jerusalem—a southern hill on which a Jebusite fortification was established until David conquered it (2 Samuel 5:6–7). In time, however, Zion became synonymous with Jerusalem.

The first-person comments in Psalm 2:7–9 are the affirmation of the one being anointed, directed to the sitting king. Today the psalm points out a clear messianic truth. Originally, however, it would not have been unusual for a king to be referred to in a fatherly position over other leaders who were subject to him. And in Israel, where it was understood that God was the king, any earthly figurehead was only a son in comparison. The great authority of the "father" king was therefore bestowed upon the "son."

In verses 10–11, the psalmist turns his attention back to the kings of the earth, who are gathered against the Lord's anointed one. Their arrogant and conspiratorial attitude is inappropriate. If they are wise they will acknowledge the Lord and devote themselves to Him in contrition. They will also honor the son to prevent incurring his wrath (2:12). The Lord and His anointed one are formidable enemies. But as allies, all who turn to Him for protection will be blessed.

PSALM 3

This is the first of the seventy-three psalms designated "of David." And in this case, the occasion of writing is included as well: when David fled from his son Absalom. The story of David fleeing from Absalom is told in 2 Samuel 15–18, but the sentiment expressed in the psalm is appropriate for anyone who has been betrayed or turned upon by a close friend or family member.

Demystifying Psalms

Psalms is divided into five books. Some people feel that each successive book is a compilation of songs assembled sometime after the previous collection. Book I may have been compiled during the time of David, so it isn't surprising to discover that all but four of the first forty-one psalms are attributed to him.

According to verses 1–2, David's numerous foes are not only rebellious and defiant but are also attempting to undermine his faith in God. But David realizes that God's presence in his life is the one thing that will enable him to endure. The Bible's frequent usage of a shield as an image of God (3:3) may not entirely register with today's readers. While being shielded from something harmful is understood, it's a different matter altogether to hold a shield in front of one's body for protection during hand-to-hand combat, feeling the shield absorb blows that might otherwise prove fatal. David's ongoing trust in God makes a very real difference in his life.

David's confidence in God is evident in his ability to sleep at night (3:4–6). Insomnia is one of the first side effects of worry. But rather than fretting and losing sleep, David talks to God, enabling him to have peace of mind and decent rest.

Throughout the psalms, the language of the writers will at times be quite harsh, as in verse 7. This is an expression of David's confidence in God, so it is in terms that a warrior might relate to. God will not merely defeat His enemies; He will utterly crush them.

But despite the indelicate language, David's intent is clear. God is always able to deliver His people (3:8). Even in the midst of persecution and troubled times, God's people can look to their Lord for help and hope.

Demystifying Psalms

The term *Selah* accompanies verses 2, 4, and 8, and will be used seventy-one times throughout the book of Psalms. The term may refer to "lifting up," but its precise significance is unclear. Most believe it is a musical cue of some sort, or perhaps a call for a congregational response. However, no one can be sure.

PSALM 4

Psalm 4 is another psalm of David, and scholars frequently detect a connection between this poem and the previous one. Perhaps David wrote them at approximately the same time. If so, this one may also pertain to David's feelings about Absalom's betrayal.

In verse 1, the psalmist again confesses a mindset of distress, yet he expresses the expectation of relief available only from a merciful God. According to the next verse, he is beset by other people who have not only turned away from him but also turned away from God to pursue delusions. David emphasizes that he has kept himself removed from such behavior, and he expects God to respond to him (4:3). Aside from a few well-known exceptions, David is usually faithful in consulting God during both the good and bad experiences of his life.

Another similarity between Psalms 3 and 4 is David's expression of how his faith in God allows him to sleep at night in spite of life's circumstances (3:5; 4:8). But one difference is David's attitude toward those who oppose him. He had previously prayed for God to "shatter the teeth of the wicked" (3:7 NLT). Here in Psalm 4, David's request is much warmer. He appeals to his opponents to not allow their anger to lead to sin, and he urges them to repent before God—to offer right sacrifices (4:4–5). Perhaps David's mind was indeed on Absalom as he wrote this, for it sounds like the plea of a parent worried that a grown child is in danger of harming himself.

In verse 7, David acknowledges that the joy God provides is greater than even the most festive times of regular life. He speaks from experience, but he hopes that others will discover the same truth.

Critical Observation

The superscript at the beginning of Psalm 4 explains that the song is to be accompanied by stringed instruments, which would have included lyres, harps, and similar traditional instruments of the time. Psalm 5 calls for flutes. The Hebrew word is used nowhere else in the Old Testament, so the exact nature of the instrument is unknown.

PSALM 5

Psalm 5 is apparently a morning prayer of David, perhaps to accompany a regular morning sacrifice (Exodus 29:38–39). David had learned that it is always a good idea to present one's requests to God in the morning and then wait in expectation—especially on days that begin with sighing and cries for help, as described in verses 1–3.

David can take consolation because he understands the character of God. The Lord cannot tolerate evil, so He does not respond to people who willingly participate in arrogance, lies, and deceit (5:4–6). Some people begin their mornings proud of what they feel they have achieved or scheming to acquire more through less-than-honorable methods. David, however, expresses his feelings to God and waits for a response.

David is a successful warrior and king, but he doesn't attempt to draw on his accomplishments to curry God's favor. As verse 7 indicates, he realizes it is only by God's mercy that anyone is able to approach the Lord, and he maintains an attitude of reverence and humility. Consequently, he acknowledges in verse 8 that even the assaults of his enemies make him stronger because they drive him to seek God's strength.

David's closeness to God allows him to see his enemies for what they are. They are corrupt throughout: their mouths, their hearts, their throats, and their tongues (5:9). They can expect a harsh downfall because of their rejection of God and their many offenses against others (5:10).

In contrast, verses 11–12 describe those who seek God and take refuge in Him. They experience God's protection, which allows them to be glad, sing, and rejoice. While on the run from King Saul, David had many times felt the surrounding protection of God. He knows for certain that the Lord's shield of favor is available to all who love and serve Him (5:11–12).

PSALM 6

The phrase in the opening superscription of Psalm 6, "according to sheminith," is not fully understood. The same phrase is used in association with Psalm 12 and in 1 Chronicles 15:21. It appears to be a musical term relating to the number *eight*—perhaps a reference to an octave or possibly an eight-stringed musical instrument.

Throughout scripture there are accounts of people who commit sin and, as a consequence, experience physical suffering as God's means of chastening (Miriam [Numbers 12]; Elisha's servant, Gehazi [2 Kings 5:26–27]; King Asa [2 Chronicles 16:10–12]; King Jehoram [2 Chronicles 21:18–19]; King Uzziah [2 Chronicles 26:16–21]; the sorcerer Bar-Jesus [Acts 13:6–12]). In this psalm David speaks of a similar instance, although it is unclear about what specific occurrence to which he refers.

Whatever David had done, he is penitent at this point. Psalm 6 is one of seven psalms that are sometimes classified as *penitential*. The others are Psalms 32, 38, 51, 102, 130, and 143.

Psalm 6 reflects travail on many fronts. On a spiritual level, David has done something that has resulted in God's anger (6:1). Physically, his whole body is afflicted with pain (6:2).

Demystifying Psalms

A common technique in psalm writing was to place the psalm's theme in the center. In this case, David's emphasis is expressed in verse 6.

David is sick of being sick—worn out from groaning and weeping. With his bones in agony and soul in anguish, his whole being is in pain and he knows that only God can heal him. His question in verse 3, "How long?" is asked frequently throughout the psalms.

To make things worse, verses 7–10 reveal that his enemies are taking advantage of his vulnerable position to taunt him. In light of such distress, he makes no effort to put up a brave front. His appeal to God is heartfelt and honest.

In verse 4, David expresses his hope for healing because of God's unfailing love. He appeals to God, reasoning that he can continue to acknowledge God as long as he is living, but death will put an end to any praise he might offer (6:5). He concludes the psalm with the confident expectation that God will indeed act on his behalf (6:9–10).

PSALM 7

The introduction to Psalm 7 includes more than one confusing reference. The term *shiggaion* is used only twice in the Bible, here and in Habakkuk 3:1. It appears to be a musical term but has an undetermined meaning. In addition, the man named *Cush*, to whom David refers, is not known elsewhere in scripture. However, the additional note that he is from the tribe of Benjamin makes it likely that he might have been an associate of Saul. This makes sense in light of the psalm's description of being pursued by relentless enemics.

In David's previous psalm, he is painfully enduring his enemies' nasty comments because he realizes he has done something to displease God. Here, however, his approach is entirely different. His enemies are again out to get him, but this time he is able to repeatedly affirm his innocence (7:3–5, 8, 10).

David has great confidence in the Lord, but that doesn't make the attacks of his enemies any less unsettling. According to verse 6, encountering the rage of one who has the capability of tearing someone to pieces like a lion requires no small amount of faith (7:1–2).

According to 1 Samuel, David twice had the opportunity to bring Saul's pursuit of him to an end (1 Samuel 24; 26), but both times he refused to kill Saul, whom he acknowledged as "the Lord's anointed." David chose not to act in vengeance, but rather left justice up to God, as he describes here in Psalm 7:6. By doing so, he allows God to examine his motives as he asks for divine help (7:3–9).

David has also witnessed the wrath of God. In verses 8–9, he realizes that God's wrath is in direct relation to his righteousness. Any conscientious judge, in the interest of justice, must occasionally pass harsh sentences when the guilty party shows neither concern nor remorse. David describes God as a warrior preparing for battle: sharpening His sword, stringing His bow, and lighting His arrows with fire (7:11–13).

According to verse 9, the targets of God's wrath are the wicked; righteous people are secure. Some people show blatant disregard for God and no desire for holy living. Such people are "pregnant with evil" (7:14 NIV), but their time will come. Those who choose such a life cannot prevent trouble in their own lives (7:14–16).

Despite the very real threat David is feeling from his enemies, in verse 17 he concludes this psalm, as psalmists so frequently do, with praise to God—and an advance acknowledgement of God's willingness to act on behalf of His faithful people.

PSALM 8

The introduction to Psalm 8 includes yet another ancient term: *gittith* (also found in the superscriptions of Psalms 81 and 84). The Hebrew word might be a reference to a winepress or to Gath, a Philistine city where David had spent some time (1 Samuel 21:10–15; 27:1–4). Its significance as a musical cue, however, is unknown.

Who hasn't stared into the heavens on a clear night and wondered about the nature of God, the origin of humanity, and other weighty questions? This psalm reflects David's musings about such things. David begins with an acknowledgment that the earth is God's. When God's presence is not considered, people come up with distorted answers to the question, "What is man?" (Psalm 8:4).

According to verse 1, those who are observant see the majesty of God. The expanse and the order of the solar system reflect the design of a Creator. And even the awe of small children as they encounter the wonders of the world gives praise to God (8:2).

When one ponders the vast extent of the universe, it is easy to feel small and insignificant. But verses 3–5 reveal that God has bestowed much significance on humankind. In fact, the word translated as *angels* or *heavenly beings* in verse 5 is *elohim*—one of the Hebrew names for God. It would be just as acceptable to translate the sentence, "You made him a little lower than God." Either way, human beings have certainly been crowned with glory and honor (8:5).

From the beginning, God had designated humankind to be the overseers of the earth (Genesis 1:28). People are privileged to rule over the other animals of the land, the sea, and the air. And this privilege is not to be taken lightly. It is still God's creation, and the people report to a higher master (Psalms 6–8).

The psalm begins and ends with the same verbatim statement (8:1, 9). "O Lord, our Lord" is not a repetition as it might appear to be when translated. The readers of the psalm would have realized that the first *Lord*—the one in small caps in most Bible translations—is a name for God (Jehovah). The second *Lord* is a different word that indicates a title for God. It's the equivalent of President George Washington or King Henry VIII, except the name and the title translate into the same English word.

Both the name and the title of God are majestic. Nothing on earth can compare. As David realizes, those observations are well worth repeating.

PSALM 9

Like several of the preceding psalms of David, Psalm 9 also deals with his struggles to endure the persecution of his enemies. In this case, however, David is eager to sing and rejoice because God has dealt with David's foes. They have not only been defeated but also rebuked, destroyed, and blotted out (9:3–5). Their ruin is endless, and soon there would not even be a memory of them (9:6).

So in verses 7–9, David begins to extol the character of God. He affirms that the Lord is an eternal king, a righteous judge, and a stronghold and refuge for those needing help. People who seek God can count on Him to come through for them (9:10).

Consequently, then, God deserves our praise (9:11–12). When God acts on our behalf, we should be quick to tell others what He has done. When people are afflicted, they cry out to Him (9:12). After God delivers them or administers justice, people should then voluntarily speak out in praise of Him.

Since, according to verse 12, God does not ignore the cries of the afflicted, David begins to voice his affliction (9:13). But rather than dwell on the current persecution he is facing, he quickly turns his attention to the future. He envisions himself already delivered, safe, and rejoicing once more in Jerusalem ("the gates of the Daughter of Zion").

As for the nations, they will reap what they have sown. What they plotted against others will be their own downfall (9:15–17). The justice of God will not allow them to prevail. God will remember and restore the needy, even as He humbles those who are filled with pride and power (9:18–20).

Critical Observation

A case can be made that Psalms 9 and 10 were originally a single psalm. Some dispute this possibility because the two divisions have quite different themes and each section holds up on its own. However, in the span of Psalms 3 to 32, Psalm 10 is the only one lacking a superscription. And if the two are combined, they create an acrostic poem (a poem where each unit begins with a successive letter of the Hebrew alphabet), albeit roughly. Perhaps they were two songs meant to relate to each other, or maybe a single psalm was divided at a point in church history to facilitate its use in worship.

PSALM 10

In Psalm 10, the psalmist (presumably David) goes into great detail about wicked people, describing both their attitudes and their actions. The people he writes about in verses 2–11 are arrogant, covetous, proud, self-centered, haughty, dishonest, and cruel. Their time is spent scheming, sneering, cursing, murdering innocent people, and otherwise preying on helpless victims. They scoff at God.

It looked as if the evil people were going to succeed in all their corrupt activities. So in verse 1 the psalmist questions God, wanting to know why He doesn't get more involved. Later he calls for God to arise and take action (10:12).

The psalmist knew cognitively that God saw what was going on; but speaking on behalf of the victims, he wants God to take immediate action (10:14–15). In brutal honesty, he wants those who regularly take advantage of innocent people to suffer. The broken arms mentioned in verse 15 would have brought an end to the dominance of the oppressors.

Like many other psalms, this one concludes with eager anticipation that God would indeed take action and would respond to the pleas of the writer. The psalmist verifies that God is in control and will continue to act on behalf of those who cannot help themselves (10:16–18).

PSALM 11

David is both a courageously faithful man and a practical one. He had been the one who matter-of-factly volunteered to go up against Goliath when every single soldier in Israel's army had been afraid to do so, even after forty days of opportunity (1 Samuel 17). But sometimes David also demonstrated that discretion is the better part of valor. After King Saul would not give up pursuit, David had negotiated with the Philistines to obtain a town of his own outside Israel's borders (1 Samuel 27:1–7). So David possesses a good understanding of when to flee and when to stand firm—the topic of Psalm 11.

If Psalm 11 is based on an actual event in David's life, we don't know exactly what it is. However, there are probably numerous times when he appeared to be in imminent danger and was urged by those around him to flee to the mountains for safety (11:1). Fear initiates panic, and at the first sign of potential danger, some people overreact and take drastic action. Soon an accompanying sense of hopelessness develops as well (11:3).

But David will have nothing to do with their negative thinking. The opening statement of Psalm 11 is his theme: "In the LORD I take refuge." Even though earthly events may seem to be more chaotic and turbulent than usual, one's spiritual condition is as reliable as ever. God is still on His throne (11:4). Nothing has changed. He sees what is going on, He will judge what He sees, and it won't be pleasant for those who have defied Him (11:5–6).

Psalm 11 ends with encouragement for the righteous—they may be shaken by the evil in the world, but they have nothing to fear from the Lord (11:7). Many believers comprehend that on a cognitive level. But what made David so special was that he truly believed it and acted in faith that his righteous Lord would always be there for him. In David's case, God is not just a vague presence but a refuge in the truest sense of the word.

PSALM 12

In Psalm 12 David describes the all-too-common feeling of looking around and seeing that one's world has deteriorated into a sorry state. The superscription comments for this psalm, "according to sheminith" are the same as for Psalm 6.

David is feeling somewhat alone in his commitment to God. The situation he describes in verses 1–2 is not unlike that of Elijah a few decades later (1 Kings 19:9–18)—a sense of loneliness sometimes experienced by those faithful to the Lord. It appears to David that all other righteous people have disappeared. Everywhere he looks he sees shallow people lying, boasting, and flattering one another (12:1–2).

In a short prayer inserted into the psalm, David asks God to deal with the widespread problem (12:3–4). He realizes the verbal outpourings are reflections of proud and callous hearts. People with any regard for God (or others, for that matter) would not speak in such a manner. Such people believe they are their own masters.

God's reply in verse 5 is immediate. He is preparing to arise, and He will certainly protect those who are being maligned. So although David's perception had been that the faithful and godly people had vanished, they are still around. It will not be the last time that the weak and needy appear to be invisible in society.

God's promise to take action in verse 5 is all that is needed. While the oppressing majority of people spout words that can't be trusted, God's words are never in doubt. According to verse 6, they are flawless and comparable to silver that had been refined and re-refined seven times (a number indicating perfection).

As the detestable people of earth "strut about" (12:8 NLT), it may seem that they are in control. But God will surely protect His faithful followers from such people forever (12:7–8).

PSALM 13

In Psalm 13, David expresses yet another complaint common to many people—the feeling that God has forgotten him. David cannot detect God's presence. He is distraught with sorrow and discomfiting thoughts. He is at the mercy of his enemies. So in verses 1–2, he repeatedly asks the haunting question: How long will this go on?

Perhaps David is seriously ill, which would have given his enemies an additional cause to celebrate. His words in verse 3, "Enlighten my eyes" (NASB) might have been a plea for healing, since references to failing eyesight were often indicative of a more widespread physical problem (see 6:7). If this is the case, the illness must have been quite severe because David is contemplating death (13:4). Then again, his words could have been a desire to acquire God's perspective on his situation rather than his own limited outlook.

Yet in spite of the somewhat bleak opening to the psalm, it concludes (like so many others) in verses 5–6 with the psalmist's expression of complete trust in God. The Lord may appear to be distant, but He isn't. David's enemies may have seemed triumphant, but they aren't. The fear of death may have been weighing on David's mind, but he is still alive and able to reach out in faith.

David's steadfast God is still the source of unfailing love, salvation, and goodness (13:5–6). The circumstances of life might change, but the grace and mercy of God never will.

PSALM 14

Psalm 14 builds on several of the themes from previous psalms, particularly the contrast between the holiness of God and the foolishness of wicked people. Psalm 14 places more emphasis on the fools who ignore God. In contrast will be Psalm 15, which focuses on the benefits of being among the righteous.

David begins in verse 1 with a perceptive observation: Foolish people assume that God does not exist. That inner presumption, although entirely wrong, then results in corrupt and even vile outward actions. As those who *do* believe in God look on, they are disturbed and even horrified by such behavior.

In Psalm 12, David wanted to call God's attention to the dearth of godly people. Here, in verses 2–3, God takes the initiative in seeking out anyone who might have any degree of spiritual sensitivity. Previously the godly had been far outnumbered by evildoers. But in this case, all are corrupt. Not even one can be found who is good.

The actions of the wicked people appear to be cold and calculated. They devour God's people like eating bread (14:4)—the modern equivalent might be "chewing someone up and spitting him out." And they never call on God.

However, in verse 5 such people are also portrayed as unsettled. While they won't personally acknowledge God, they can't help but see that He makes a significant difference in the lives of the righteous people. Consequently, the evildoers are left with a sinking sense of dread.

David struggles with the tension between the two groups of people. He hates to see poor and defenseless individuals taken advantage of by those who are powerful enough to do so. But in verse 6 he realizes that God will be there for those who are otherwise powerless. Still, David dreams of justice on a much larger scale. He longs for the day when God's salvation will influence the entire nation (14:7). When that time comes, God's people will truly be joyous.

PSALM 15

With so many of the previous psalms expressing the writer's confusion, despair, and outrage over the fact that ungodly people seem to be running rampant while believers in God struggle to get by, Psalm 15 is a simple but powerful reminder of what is really important. In verse 1, the psalmist (presumably David) opens with a simple question: What does it take to find favor with God? What kind of people may approach Him and spend time with Him?

The answer may have surprised early readers of the psalm. A specific list is provided, but nowhere on the list is the mandate to participate in tabernacle worship services or offer sacrifices. Several items on the list have to do with control of the tongue, which is always a challenge (James 3:2), and all the behaviors stand in bold contrast to the previously described actions of the wicked who oppress God's people.

The simple answer to the question is found in verse 2: "He whose walk is blameless and who does what is righteous" (NIV). Jesus later issues a similar challenge to His listeners in Matthew 5:48: "Be perfect. . .as your heavenly Father is perfect" (NIV).

The psalmist provides a breakdown of what blamelessness and righteousness entails:

- *Speaking truth from the heart* (15:2). Evildoers are easily identified by their lies. God's people should be known for their truthfulness.
- *Avoiding slander* (15:3). It's easy to bad-mouth someone else. Many people become so accustomed to it that they don't even realize what they are doing. But God hears and notices slanderous words.
- *Treating neighbors properly* (15:3). Sometimes it's easier to be kind to strangers than to be consistently decent to those we are closest to, yet believers are called to do both.
- *Refusing to cast slurs on other people* (15:3). For today's believers, this requirement would include issues such as ethnic jokes, road rage, gossip, and other verbal slurs.
- *Despising evil people while honoring those who fear God* (15:4). Believers are challenged to differentiate between evil people and those struggling to follow the Lord, and to treat each group accordingly.
- *Keeping oaths even when it hurts to do so* (15:4). The underlying assumption is that sometimes it will hurt to keep one's promises. The mark of a devoted follower of God is complete trustworthiness at all times.
- *Lending money without usury* (15:5). When able to help others financially, God's people should be willing to do so. Outright gifts are a preferable option when possible, but even loans should be offered without the expectation of extreme interest payments in return.
- *Refusal to take bribes* (15:5). People who use money and power to manipulate others are certainly not on the list of those who can dwell in God's sanctuary. But neither are those who accept money to look the other way when helpless people are being threatened.

It is no easy matter to do all these things consistently. Yet according to verse 5, those who do will stand firm forever.

PSALM 16

The superscription of Psalm 16 includes the first mention of a *miktam*, another presumed but undeterminable musical term. The word appears in later psalms (56–60) where David describes himself in personal peril. In this case, David may be experiencing a threat of some sort (16:1), although throughout most of the psalm he expresses overwhelming confidence and optimism.

In the opening verses of this psalm, David affirms God as his refuge, an image he frequently uses (2:12; 7:1; 9:9). God is his solitary source of comfort and safety. David also relishes the opportunity to see other believers throughout the land (16:3).

Idolatry was a persistent threat to Israel, and David had witnessed people in the land pursuing other gods (16:4). It is a sad sight to see fellow Israelites make sacrifices to false gods while turning their backs on the true Lord and Savior of Israel. The sorrows of such people will only increase.

This is a time in David's life when he feels particularly close to God. Using the imagery of what someone might be served at a meal (a portion and cup), in verse 5 David expresses satisfaction with the blessings God has given him. Then, shifting to a geographic image in verse 6, David expresses pleasure that his life is not a rocky wasteland or a dusty wilderness. Instead, his boundaries are pleasant and his inheritance delightful (16:5–6).

According to verse 7, David is receiving guidance from God throughout the day and into the night. With the ongoing sensation of God being so close, David's response is praise, and the result is that he is not shaken by the undesired circumstances of life (16:8). With his sense of security, David can rejoice and be glad.

David doesn't have the same perspective of resurrection and eternal life as modern believers. Even so, he is assured and positive as he thinks about death. David is expectant that his close connection with God will endure with ongoing joy and eternal pleasures (16:9–11).

Critical Observation

David's expression of faithful confidence in Psalm 16 is so powerful that the psalm is later quoted by both Peter (Acts 2:25–28) and Paul (Acts 13:35). After the life, death, and resurrection of Jesus, David's words about death take on a surprising new significance.

PSALM 17

Psalm 17 is sometimes compared to Psalm 16. Although David doesn't express his specific complaint for some time, he is again besieged by his enemies (17:9–12) and is beseeching God's help. He desperately wants God's attention: He opens the psalm by asking three different times for God to listen to him.

Verse 2 indicates David wants vindication in God's eyes. He affirms that his words come as a righteous request from honest lips (17:1). It takes a person of real integrity to be able to challenge God to probe and test him, convinced that God will find no charge against him (17:3). In particular, David's resolve to control his mouth is reflective of Psalm 15.

According to verse 5, David keeps on the narrow path to God and therefore feels comfortable calling on Him (17:6). David's situation may have been too much for him to handle on his own, but he knew he could turn to God for both love and deliverance (17:7).

David uses a couple of now-familiar poetic images to help describe his perception of how God has protected him. First he asks to be kept as "the apple of [God's] eye" (17:8 NIV). He likely knew the phrase from the Books of Law (Deuteronomy 32:10). *Apple* is apparently a reference to the eye's pupil, which destroys one's vision if damaged. Protecting it is a natural instinct.

David uses a second image in verse 8: the shadow of God's wings. Someone might rest from the summer heat by lingering in the shadow of a tree or building. Similarly, God is an ever-present source of protection to diminish (if not eliminate) the oppressive forces of life. Additionally, the image suggests a mother bird caring for her brood. It is a soft and tender portrayal of God's loving care—one that is missed by many who presume the Old Testament God to be consistently harsh and demanding.

The enemies surrounding David are serious threats: callous, arrogant, and compared to a lion crouching to spring at its prey (17:9–12). David is wise to turn to God for shelter in verse 8, but he also prays that God will confront and deal with his wicked oppressors (17:13–14). Such people live only for what they can accumulate in this world. The righteous, however, know that God provides more than enough (17:14).

The psalm's closing statement in verse 15 sounds almost like a New Testament affirmation of resurrection and eternal life, but David would not have had this perspective. His confidence is that God will eventually remove the problem with the evildoers, allowing David to awaken to a new day, able to fully enjoy his relationship with the Lord.

PSALM 18

This is another psalm about David's praise to God in gratitude for His help in dealing with aggressive enemies. Longer than any of the psalms that precede it, Psalm 18 opens with an introductory overture of praise containing a long string of terms to describe God: strength, rock, fortress, deliverer, shield, horn of salvation, and stronghold (18:1–2). These are all images of power, yet the God they describe is both accessible and personal (18:3).

In contrast, David is in a desperate situation, writing of distress, destruction, and the likelihood of death in verses 4–6. But rather than allow fear and panic to overwhelm him, David calls on God for help.

God hears David's cries. The description in verses 7–15 is vivid and includes imagery of God responding through the forces of nature, the intensity of an angry and powerful animal, and the accuracy of a soldier armed with arrows and bolts of lightning. The mention of cherubim (angels) in biblical texts is frequently an indication of the presence of God (18:10).

David's foes had been too much to handle on his own, but his faith in God is not in vain (18:17). According to verse 7, the Lord is angry and mighty; and He rescues David and delivers him to safety (18:16–19).

Based on the fearful description of God, one might think David would be afraid of Him. But David had a firm conviction that he had been living in obedience and faithfulness to God (18:20–24). The awesome power of God is directed against those who oppose Him, but it works in favor of those committed to living a righteous life.

David doesn't consider himself a special case to receive God's help and protection. In verses 15–27, he affirms that anyone who is faithful will witness God's faithfulness in return, and everyone who is blameless, pure, and humble stands to benefit from the righteous character of the Lord. But those who display deceit or arrogance will view God in a vastly different manner. God's presence provides David assistance and abilities he cannot get anywhere else: light in darkness, strength, courage, and more (18:28–29).

Critical Observation

Psalm 18 is also found in its entirety (with only slight changes in wording) in 2 Samuel 22 as David's song of praise after being delivered from his enemies, including King Saul.

Verses 30–50 are David's personal testimony to the difference God has made in his life. David acknowledges the perfection of God and the fact that the Lord is a unique entity who cannot be compared to anyone or anything else (18:30–31). It is God who empowered and sustained David to be victorious in battle (18:32–42). It is God who designated David to be king in spite of initial resistance he received from Saul and others (18:43–45). And in response, David enthusiastically praises his Lord as savior, avenger, and benefactor (18:46–50).

PSALM 19

God reveals Himself to humankind in numerous ways. In Psalm 19, David begins by giving attention to the natural world that reflects God's glory and then moves on to the revealed Word of God—the source of many various potential blessings.

Verse 1 says the heavens speak in their own way of the glory of God. Humankind has always had a fascination with looking into the skies for weather forecasts, for getting one's bearings, for observation, for warning signs, and simply out of a sense of wonder. The message of the heavens is heard throughout the world (19:3–4).

Verses 2–3 describe the simple repetition of day following night and the soothing sense of rhythm and regularity it provides, reflecting the concept that God is eternal, consistent, and can be relied on. In verses 4–6, the creative description of the sun is that of a bridegroom arriving at his wedding and of a gleeful runner on track across the sky. David's viewpoint would have stood out from most others during his time. He credits God as being in control of the sun, while many other pagan religions held that the sun *was* a god.

After looking into the heavens to witness the glory of God, David looks into the Word of God: its laws, statutes, precepts, commands, and ordinances (19:7–11). His experience is that an awareness of God's Word results both in practical help (wisdom, righteousness, and warning) and in positive, pleasant feelings (joy, enlightenment).

By regularly examining the wonders of nature, someone can come to a broad and general belief that a creator must have designed the world. But to stop there can lead to much speculation and potentially erroneous theology. The living God responsible for creation is revealed throughout the pages of scripture. David knew to consult both sources for an accurate and more complete understanding of God.

David's knowledge of God, in fact, inspires him to excel in his devotion to his Lord. In verses 12–13, David wants to rid his life of willful sins as well as hidden faults. In an often-quoted verse (19:14), David ends this psalm with a prayer that not only his words but his inner thoughts as well would be pleasing to God, whom he acknowledges as both rock and redeemer.

Take It Home

At almost halfway through the first book within the biblical book of Psalms, stop to consider the psalmists' honesty with God. In most cases, that honesty is accompanied by passionate feelings, both positive and negative. How do the psalmists' cries to God compare to your own prayers? What can you learn from the psalms (so far) that might strengthen your current relationship with God?

PSALMS: BOOK I, CONTINUED

PSALMS 20–41

Setting Up the Section

This section continues and completes Book I, the compilation that opens the biblical book of Psalms. Essentially all of the psalms in this section are attributed to David. It is the section that contains perhaps the most beloved and widely known psalm: Psalm 23.

PSALM 20

In the opening verses of Psalm 20, it may appear that the psalmist is offering blessings upon his readers, but in verse 5 it becomes evident that the voice is plural, and the message is being addressed to a singular subject. The psalm is actually written for an assembled group to join the king in prayer preceding a battle.

Significant spiritual preparation has already taken place. The king's prayers have been offered to God, along with sacrifices at the tabernacle (sanctuary) (20:1–3, 5). Battle plans have been made and David is mentally ready (20:4), but he wants to ensure that God is with him and that he has the support of the people. And indeed, the people are anticipating a joyous victory (20:5).

The singular voice in verse 6 may be that of David, the king. Or possibly it is a response assigned to a designated Levite participating in the worship ceremony. Even though the crowd is expecting victory, the credit goes to God even before the battle begins.

At this point, Israel's army stands out among the surrounding nations. Most kings strategize based on their number of chariots and horses (20:7). But faith in God frees one from depending on numbers. As Jonathan had wisely realized when opposing the Philistines, "Nothing can hinder the LORD from saving, whether by many or by few" (1 Samuel 14:6 NIV). Putting one's trust in the name of the Lord is to place faith in His character and known qualities. And doing so enables His people to stand up against trouble (Psalm 20:8).

Verse 9 concludes this psalm in the same way it began, with a united prayer of the people for God to answer and to save their king.

PSALM 21

Psalm 21 is similar in form and purpose to Psalm 20. Some people even feel it may be a follow-up psalm to the previous one, with Psalm 20 recited prior to a crucial battle and Psalm 21 used during the triumphant celebration of victory.

The first section of verses (21:1–6) is either a congregational recitation or the words of the king, expressed in third person. There is no suggestion of distress, as was evident in the previous psalm (20:1). Here is only rejoicing and thanksgiving offered for God's strength, victory in battle, answered prayer, and other blessings (21:1–3).

The crown of pure gold in verse 3 sounds like a metaphor for all of God's blessings. At least once, however, it is a literal truth. After a battle with the Ammonites, David wore the crown of their king—a 75-pound headpiece made of gold and set with precious stones (2 Samuel 12:29–31).

The wish for a king to live forever in verse 4 is a standard figure of speech (see Daniel 6:21). In David's case, however, he had received God's promise that one of his descendants would establish a kingdom and rule forever (1 Chronicles 17:11–14). Victory in battle, splendor, and majesty are three blessings David had already received, yet the expectation is for eternal blessings—an ongoing assurance of God's presence with him (Psalm 21:6).

The crucial theme of the psalm is located in verse 7, the center of Psalm 21: David's trust in God, in conjunction with God's love for David, creates a secure foundation for the psalmist. And his relationship with the Lord is the basis for all the other joy and blessings described throughout the psalm.

The second half of the psalm is a response by the assembled people in acknowledgment and gratitude of God's deliverance. In verse 9, the king is recognized for his strength and success, but ultimately it is God's wrath and judgment that is responsible for the fall of Israel's enemies. By destroying the descendants of enemy leaders, a leader greatly minimizes the likelihood of that opposing nation becoming a danger anytime soon (21:10). Their continued plots and threats would be in vain (21:11–12).

And yet again a psalm ends with an echo of its beginning, this time with an affirmation of God's strength and praise for His power (21:13).

PSALM 22

After two psalms that dwell on the strength of God and the victories experienced by David, Psalm 22 captures quite a different, more somber, mood. According to the superscription, the psalm is intended to be set to an already established tune: "The Doe of the Morning."

Psalm 22 opens with a familiar ring, because Jesus quotes its opening line while hanging on the cross. As will soon become evident, David's words in this psalm are surprisingly descriptive of Jesus' crucifixion.

In verses 3–5, David expresses a cognitive understanding that God is present, as He always had been, and that He had always come through for His people throughout their history. However, David also writes, in verse 1, of a personal experience of suffering during which his feelings did not mirror his cognitive faith. He felt abandoned by God and, like so many people throughout the ages, asked the question, "Why?" He cried out to God around the clock but could detect no response (22:2). He was a target of scorn and ridicule, forced to listen to his enemies mock his faith, yet he tenaciously held to what he knew to be true (22:6–11).

The next scene that David portrays sounds hauntingly like Jesus' crucifixion (22:12–18). According to verses 12–13, David was surrounded by strong bulls and roaring lions, two different symbols for powerful enemies. He describes complete exhaustion, disheartenment, weakness, and thirst (22:14–15). The picture is of someone surrounded by evil men who pierce his hands and feet and cast lots to see who gets his clothing (22:16–18). It's a scene we associate with Jesus, not David.

Jesus endured not only the physical agony of crucifixion but also the spiritual despair of taking on the sins of humankind. David, however, anticipates God's rescue from his own situation (22:19–21). Even before he detects God's deliverance, he is quick to praise God and affirm His faithfulness. Despite appearances, David knows God is fully aware of his situation and concerned about his safety (22:22, 24).

Consequently, in verse 23 David challenges his fellow Israelites to praise and revere God. He wants to set a good example (fulfill his vows) for them (22:25–26). Then he expands his scope to include the ends of the earth and the nations (22:27–29). David hopes the entire world will respond when they hear how God has helped him (22:30–31). And if David does indeed foretell the crucifixion of his most famous descendant in this psalm, the news of God's deliverance and salvation would be heard by the entire world as generation after generation continue to proclaim His righteousness. Of all the psalms, this one is quoted more than any other in the New Testament.

PSALM 23

In what is undoubtedly the best known of the psalms, David uses the imagery of a shepherd to highlight God's blessings and protection of His people. It was rather common for kings of the time to be compared to shepherds. Although King David had firsthand experience in the role (1 Samuel 16:11–13; 17:34–35), in this psalm he is only one of the sheep in the fold of God.

The prophets will later describe the distress of the people by using an absent-shepherd or bad-shepherd analogy (Isaiah 56:9–12; Jeremiah 25:34–38; Ezekiel 34:1–11; Zechariah 11:15–17). However, David's description of God is the epitome of a good shepherd—a title Jesus will later apply to Himself (John 10:11).

As a shepherd, God provides for every need of His sheep (Psalm 23:1). The green pastures and quiet waters are basic physical needs, but God also restores the soul, attending to the inner spiritual needs of humankind (23:2–3).

Guidance is another essential role of ancient shepherds. In a land where many of the paths were rocky and treacherous, the safety of the sheep reflected on the reputation of the shepherd. God keeps David on paths of righteousness (23:3).

David acknowledges God's calming companionship even as he walks through the valley of the shadow of death (23:4). David has had his share of potentially deadly situations: confronting fierce animals as a shepherd, facing off against Philistine giants, a long string of battles, and more. But God's presence dispels fear. The shepherd's rod and staff are comforting symbols to David.

Critical Observation

A shepherd used his staff for support. The rod is frequently perceived as a punishing tool, which it was at times. But that same rod of correction was also an instrument of protection when the sheep were threatened. And more often, it was used for gentle guidance: A tap on the side could prevent a wayward sheep from straying off the safe path. If the adage to "Spare the rod and spoil the child" (based on Proverbs 13:24) means to impose harsh punishment, it is unlikely that David (or anyone else) would have perceived the rod as a comfort.

Verse 5 reveals that even when surrounded by enemies, David is able to function normally and enjoy his life because he is under God's care. Spreading an abundant dinner table and anointing a guest with oil were common amenities of a gracious host. In response, David realizes that his life is overflowing with God's blessings.

In spite of life's other dangers, David has reached the point where God's goodness and love far outweigh those concerns (23:6). He is determined to continue his relationship with God at the tabernacle for the rest of his life.

PSALM 24

David's military victories had expanded the boundaries of Israel, and the spoils from his enemies had greatly added to Israel's treasury. But, as the opening verses of Psalm 24 reveal, David also realizes that his many successes are all the result of God's strength and direction. So from David's experience and perception, he can declare with certainty that the earth is the Lord's, as well as everything in it. The people are His also, although many times throughout their history they didn't seem to realize it.

A painter is acknowledged for the portraits she does, and a sculptor gets credit for the shapes he forms. Similarly, the Creator of the world is the rightful owner of what He has founded and established (24:2).

David's musings on the sovereignty of God lead him to a logical question in verse 3: Who is worthy to stand before such a Lord? The hill of the Lord is probably in reference to the mountain on which Jerusalem, and eventually the temple, was found.

David realizes that God welcomes people whose actions (hands) as well as thoughts (heart) are pure (24:4). Such people will avoid the ever-present opportunity to worship idols, and they will be truthful. In return, God will bless them (24:5–6).

Demystifying Psalms

Portions of Psalms 96, 105, and 106 were used in conjunction with the return of the ark of the covenant to Jerusalem (1 Chronicles 15:1–16:36). It is possible that Psalm 24 was also used on that occasion. If so, the personification of the gates and ancient doors could have been references to the structures of that ancient city.

Any king who approaches a city will receive a magnificent welcome; how much more should the nearness of the King of glory inspire a response (24:7). Even the gates and doors of the city are perceived as responding to the magnitude of the event.

Lest there be any doubt as to who the King of glory is, David repeats the fact for emphasis in verses 7–10. The Lord is strong and mighty in battle—impressive credentials for any king. God is indeed the King of glory.

PSALM 25

In Psalm 25, as in many of his others, David expresses a desire for greater closeness to God. In the original language, the psalm is an acrostic poem. The first verse begins with the first letter, and following verses continue with successive letters throughout the Hebrew alphabet.

Again it seems in verses 1–2 that David's desire is driven by the lurking of his enemies. If David's enemies are to triumph over him, they will interpret their victory as a failure of Israel's God. David wants to avoid that potential shame by all means. Instead, he prefers to put to shame those who cause trouble for no good reason (25:3).

In verses 4–5, David requests both knowledge and guidance from God. His understanding of God as Savior is just as accurate, though not quite as robust, as those referring to the New Testament concept of salvation. The Lord is David's *deliverer* and his sole source of confidence and hope.

As he recalls his imperfections in verse 7, David also calls upon God's mercy and love. He understands that God does not hold people forever responsible for their sins, but He both forgives them and forgets them. As a professed sinner, David needs God's instruction and guidance in order to discover God's way, which includes goodness, upright behavior, humility, love, and faithfulness (25:8–10). David doesn't attempt to hide or downplay his sin (25:11).

According to verses 12–14, God's forgiveness will open the door to numerous blessings, including clear instruction throughout life, prosperity, a decent inheritance for descendants, and awareness of God's covenant promises. David's afflictions and anguish have heightened his awareness of the need for God's direction (25:15–21). Again in verse 20, David uses one of his favorite symbols for God: his *refuge*. The forces of life are pressing in on him, but he can still feel secure and protected.

David's final thought in this psalm builds on his personal request and expands it to include all of Israel (25:22). His problems are Israel's problems. As David seeks God's presence in his own life, he also prays for God to redeem Israel from her troubles.

PSALM 26

Psalm 26 is David's prayer for vindication. In tone it is not unlike Paul's defense of his ministry in 2 Corinthians 11, when the apostle attempts to distance himself from unrighteous peers and their false accusations. He doesn't want it to sound like he is boasting (2 Corinthians 11:10, 16–18, 21), but he needs to state some truths about himself strongly and clearly. So, too, David feels it necessary to defend himself.

David's appeal in verse 1 is directed to God, so any misstatements or exaggerations will be quickly refuted. His claim to a blameless life doesn't suggest that he is sinless but rather that he has not intentionally taken advantage of others—one result of his unwavering faith in God. David invites God to examine his thoughts and feelings because he attempts to *continually* be aware of God's love and truth (26:2–3).

His actions also reflect his mindset. He states in verses 4–5 that he avoids contact with those who are deceitful, hypocritical, or otherwise wicked. Rather than lingering with such people, David cleanses himself externally as well as inwardly and goes to spend time in God's tabernacle. As he meets people along the way, he shares with them what he knows of God's wonders (26:6–8).

In verses 9–11, David declares he doesn't want to be lumped in with the host of unrepentant sinners. Such people tend to eventually suffer for their deeds, if not have their lives divinely abbreviated. Instead, David seeks redemption and mercy. He is on the "straight and narrow," so to speak, and he promises to continue to praise the Lord from whom he expects his vindication (26:12).

PSALM 27

Fear is a universal emotion that frequently triggers a "fight or flight" response in people. When afraid, some people muster all the courage they can and stand their ground, whether or not it's a wise choice. At the first sign of trouble, others flee so they can live to fight another day. David begins Psalm 27 with his own questions about fear and concludes it with another option for responding to fear that involves neither fighting nor fleeing.

David has given the matter of fear more thought than most people because he has already determined that God is his light, salvation, and stronghold (27:1). He will not stumble in the darkness, as many do. He has a deliverer and security, even during the times that are most alarming.

It isn't that David has nothing to be afraid of; if anything, as verses 2–3 point out, his troubles are worse than most. Enemies are approaching with evil intent, and he is at war against powerful armies; yet he is able to remain confident while his foes fall. (Some people suspect that this psalm was written with Absalom's revolt in mind. If so, David would have felt the added stress of being betrayed by a beloved son.)

When faced with fear, David keeps his priorities straight. Verse 4 reveals his priority—a lifetime relationship with God at the tabernacle. His eyes aren't directed toward the approaching enemy but rather toward the beauty of the Lord (27:4). Consequently, he has confidence that when trouble does come, God will protect and sustain him. Rather than panic, he can respond with songs and shouts of joy (27:5–6). He prays that God will continue to be merciful and available, and he believes that God will be there during the worst of times, when even those closest to him might forsake him (27:7–12).

With his steadfast trust in God's goodness, David expects to remain safe and alive. Even though his enemies are still numerous and powerful, he will not run. He will not hastily go into battle but will choose to do something that is often harder than either of those options: wait (27:13–14). His is no idle passing of time, however. To wait on the Lord when things are going badly takes both courage and inner strength. Yet during turbulent circumstances, it is always the best course of action.

PSALM 28

It is a powerful assurance to realize that God hears us when we pray. In the opening verse of Psalm 28, David begins by calling on God and entreating Him to listen. The *pit* is a synonym for the grave, so David is saying that he may as well be dead if God doesn't hear and respond to him. He emphasizes his desire by lifting his hands toward the Most Holy Place—the place in the tabernacle designed specifically to reflect the presence of God (28:2).

David makes a point not to associate with the wicked, and he purposefully attempts to distance himself from them in this prayer. He wants God to provide retribution for all the harm they have done. They seem particularly despicable because they will feign kindness toward others while they inwardly seethe with malice (28:3–4).

With little doubt that the actions of the wicked people will bring about their judgment, David begins to praise God (28:5–6). At this point David is convinced that God has indeed heard him.

In verse 7, David acknowledges his appreciation of God's strength and protection on a personal level. It is a source of joy and consolation for him, prompting songs of thanksgiving. Then David proclaims the benefits of God's strength on the nation as a whole. David is the anointed one who enjoys the fortress of salvation that God has provided. But God Himself is the shepherd over the people. Only He can deliver them from danger and ensure their future (28:8–9).

PSALM 29

Many of David's psalms to this point have been pleas for help, concerns about his enemies, responses to the accusations of the wicked, and so forth. In Psalm 29, however, David's focus begins and remains on the power of God. As the psalmist watches a powerful storm approach and roll through his location, he records his thoughts.

The power of the approaching storm reminds David of the power of the Lord. He begins in verses 1–2 by challenging the *mighty ones* to attribute glory and strength to God. Most likely this is a reference to the angels who attend to the Lord. Possibly the comment is directed toward people who consider themselves "high and mighty," and who need to humble themselves before God.

In verses 3–9, the storm is referred to as the voice of the Lord. First it thunders over the waters (29:3), which from David's perspective would have been the Mediterranean Sea. Then, in power and majesty, the storm blows into Lebanon, where it shatters mighty cedar trees (29:4–5). The earth appears to move beneath the fury of the storm. (Sirion is another name for Mount Hermon. Lebanon is also a mountain.) Meanwhile, lightning flashes overhead (29:7).

Deserts and forests are both affected by the storm (29:8–9). The Desert of Kadesh, approximately seventy-five miles north of Damascus, is shaken as the trees of the neighboring forests are stripped bare. This is a storm of impressive magnitude.

Demystifying Psalms

The original Hebrew of the initial phrase of Psalm 29:9 allows for two rather diverse translations. One likely option is that the oak trees were twisted as a result of the storm. Another possibility is that the deer gave birth (presumably prematurely) out of fright.

Greater still, however, is God whose power far exceeds any storm on earth. He is to be glorified (29:9). His ruling over the floodwaters in verse 10 may be a reference to how He oversaw the creation of the world, or perhaps a reference to the flood of Noah's day. Earthly weather conditions, no matter how severe, don't change the fact that God will always reign as King.

As a pleasant end to a somewhat frightening psalm, David assures his readers in verse 11 that the all-powerful God gives strength to His people. Realizing that God is omnipotent should cause believers to rest in a consoling assurance of peace.

PSALM 30

Even though the superscription of Psalm 30 indicates that it is for the dedication of the temple, it is difficult to target exactly when it was first used. Some people speculate that the superscription was added at some point after the psalm had been written, and that the psalm was used for dedications of later buildings (such as the reconstructed temple after the Babylonians destroyed the first one).

In verses 2–3, the psalmist (presumed to be David) mentions some kind of physical ailment and in verse 6 confesses to a temporary sense of arrogance. So one likely possibility, assuming that David is the author, is that he is referring to his census of fighting men, evidently conducted out of a sense of pride (1 Chronicles 21). God had given David some options for his punishment. David's choice had resulted in the deaths of seventy thousand people and, had it not been for God's mercy, would have included the divine destruction of Jerusalem. Immediately afterward, David provides great amounts of materials that were needed to build Solomon's temple (1 Chronicles 22:2–5). Perhaps this is the incident David has in mind as he writes Psalm 30.

Regardless of the origin of the psalm, it is a powerful reminder of the difference God can make in a person's life when things are going badly. The psalmist writes of being in the depths, of enemies eager to gloat over his vulnerable position, and perhaps even a near-death experience (30:1–3). Yet God had responded with deliverance, healing, and life.

David's experience had given him great insight into the character of God, which he shares with the people in verse 5. God's anger lasts but a moment, but His favor lasts for a lifetime. Consequently, people should be quick to offer songs and praise to Him (30:4).

David's confession in verses 6–10 is true for many people. When life is going well and we are feeling secure, we lose the pressing need to turn to God. Then, when we discover that we have lost touch with God, we become dismayed.

Yet God's mercy is abundant. David's wailing in sackcloth quickly turns to dancing for joy (30:11–12). He senses that God prefers songs and praise to the silence that accompanies mourning. And in response to the fresh start that God has allowed him, David will be forever thankful.

PSALM 31

This is yet another of David's psalms that describes his feelings of rejection and isolation, even though his emotions are offset by the actions of God to revive and restore him. Although David opens the psalm by asking for deliverance in verse 1, it takes a while to determine what is wrong. He requests rescue and speaks of a trap set for him (31:2, 4), but the source of these comments is not identified until verses 11–13, where we discover that David's persecution by his enemies has resulted in the desertion of all his friends.

Critical Observation

Psalm 31, along with Psalm 22, appears to have been on Jesus' mind as He hung on the cross. He quotes verse 5 as one of His final statements before dying.

In spite of his condition, David continues to turn to God, who is consistently his refuge, rock, and fortress (31:1–3). He is left with only God to turn to, and God is the only One who can alleviate his suffering at this point. David is a brilliant fighter and strategist, yet he realizes he can do no better in this situation than to commit himself into God's hands to avoid potential harm (31:4–5).

When in affliction and anguish, many turn to idols, whether the false gods of Canaan or more contemporary idols of wealth, reputation, and pleasure. But David will not be distracted from his pursuit of God, and he is rewarded for his efforts (31:6–8).

When David gets specific about his situation in verses 9–13, it is heart-wrenching to realize the depth of his suffering. He is distressed, in grief and anguish, weak, sick, hated by his enemies, avoided by his friends, broken off from any kind of human support system, and terrified. From time to time he can hear slander and conspiracies against him.

And yet his trust in God is not shaken. David realizes that if God delivers him, then it discredits his enemies. Their lies and contempt will be silenced (31:14–18).

In verses 19–24, David concludes his psalm, as he frequently does, with confidence in God's deliverance. He uses his personal experience as grounds to exhort all God's saints to be faithful as well. They will do well to follow David's example of strength (31:24).

PSALM 32

Psalm 32 is the first of thirteen psalms identified in the superscript as a *maskil.* (The others are 42, 44–45, 52–55, 74, 78, 88–89, and 142.) Like many of the other introductory terms, the meaning of the word has been lost. It is frequently assumed that a maskil is a poem intended for instruction or meditation.

Additional speculation about this psalm is that it was originally a follow-up to Psalm 51, David's confession of his adultery with Bathsheba. If true, Psalm 32 celebrates the relief that David feels after experiencing the forgiveness of God.

The apostle Paul will later make it clear that everyone has sinned (Romans 3:23), yet David here makes it just as clear that forgiveness is readily available, after which God no longer holds the person accountable for his or her sins (Psalm 32:1–2). In response to God's forgiveness, the pardoned sinner should have a renewed, pure spirit.

In verses 3–5, David points out that awareness of one's sin that has not yet been confessed to God can create miserable feelings. If this psalm is indeed a reference to David and Bathsheba, it is worthwhile to note that David allowed his unconfessed sexual indiscretion to escalate into deceit (attempts to fool Bathsheba's husband) and from there to premeditated murder (2 Samuel 11). Bathsheba's child was born before God sent a prophet to confront David, so many months passed before David confessed his actions to God.

Therefore, David writes from experience as he describes the terrible weight people can feel before finally confessing to God (Psalm 32:3–5). Fortunately, he also speaks from experience of the unfailing love of God that follows repentance and confession (32:10). It is far better to voluntarily turn to God during such times than to react like a horse or mule, stubbornly resisting until being forced to respond because of a bit and bridle (32:6–9).

Unrepentant wicked people are left with many woes, but God always provides a better option. After sin, repentance, and confession, God restores one's state of righteousness, enabling the person to once again be pure in heart. Because of God's mercy and forgiveness, the person is once again eager to rejoice (32:11).

PSALM 33

This is the first psalm since Psalm 10 that isn't specifically credited to David.

Psalm 33 is a beautiful acknowledgement of the sovereignty of God, who deserves worship and praise from His people because they can always count on His faithfulness, righteousness, justice, and love (33:1–5). He is the Creator, who spoke the stars and heavens into existence. In verse 7, the psalmist portrays God as placing the world's seas into jars, as a homeowner might keep jars of fruit or olives.

Just as God spoke to create the universe, His word continues to have power. As people begin to comprehend the unlimited power of God, they should respond with deep reverence (33:8–9).

People and nations have plans that don't always agree with those of the Lord. But God's plans will endure. When people are foolish and presumptuous enough to oppose God, He has no trouble countermanding their plans (33:10–11).

Rather than resisting God, it is far better to yield to Him and receive His blessing. God sees all. The Creator is aware of the actions and inner thoughts of those He created (33:13–15). Only God is capable of sure protection and safety, even though the people of the time looked to other things for security (33:16–17).

In a setting of frequent wars and famines, God is a constant hope for those who trust in Him. Because He sees all, He does not miss the faith and prayers of the righteous. For these He is a shield against calamity. They can learn to rejoice and receive His unfailing love, knowing they will receive His help whenever it is needed (33:18–22).

PSALM 34

The introduction to Psalm 34 explains that it is written with a specific incident in mind. When David was running from King Saul and hiding out in Philistine territory, he began to feel threatened. As a diversion, he pretended to be insane, doodling on the city gate and drooling. The Philistines insisted that he leave, but he apparently posed no threat, so his life was not threatened (1 Samuel 21:10–15). What isn't clear, however, is the name variation of the Philistine king. In the superscription of Psalm 34, he is called Abimelech; in the 1 Samuel account, his name is Achish. However, it isn't unusual for kings of the time to have various names and titles.

In verses 1–3, David opens the psalm with lavish praise to God. David had been afraid, but God had alleviated his fears (34:4). After David's personal expression of exaltation, he enlists others to join him in glorifying God.

Those with no other recourse can always call on God and be heard. And those who seek and receive God's help may even have a different look about them—they avoid the shame experienced by so many others, and their faces radiate with joy (34:5–6).

In verse 7, David affirms that the angel of the Lord will encircle and deliver those who trust God. It is interesting to note that in several stories of the Old Testament, the angel of the Lord turns out to be God Himself. But any of God's messengers are equipped to protect God's people.

Perhaps some people are on the verge of becoming more devoted to God. For them to go on about their lives without making that decision is like walking past an enormous feast without stopping to sample the food. In verse 8, David urges his readers to taste and see that the Lord is good. The lions of the world have no guarantee of success, but those who faithfully seek the Lord will find all they need and more (34:9–10).

In verses 11–18, David provides a number of specific exhortations, but his basic advice for success and long life is to avoid evil in all its forms and to devote oneself to God. A commitment to righteousness does not guarantee a problem-free life (34:19–21), but God responds to His people in their times of distress.

God's redemption and lack of condemnation of His people would have been emphasized for those hearing this psalm in the original Hebrew (34:22). The psalm is an acrostic. With one exception, the first letters of each stanza go through the Hebrew alphabet, a pattern that ends at verse 21. The additional final verse, then, would have drawn much attention to the psalmist's final statement in verse 22—a promise well worth remembering.

PSALM 35

Few experiences in life are as distressing as being in a vulnerable state and having other people take advantage of you while you're helpless. This is the position David finds himself in as he writes Psalm 35. Unable to personally retaliate or achieve justice, he calls out to God for help.

In verses 1–3, David enlists the power of God, speaking to the Lord as a heavenly warrior and asking Him to prepare to fight. Any good soldier would anticipate conflict by fitting himself with the appropriate uniform and weapons, so David appeals for God to dress for battle, so to speak.

David then identifies his problem in verse 4: People want him dead, or at the very least disgraced and ruined. He wants to see his enemies blown away like chaff in the wind, driven away by the angel of the Lord down a dark and slippery path (35:5–6). His is a prayer for a taste of their own medicine. When evil people go to the trouble to trap someone, it is sweet irony if they are to accidentally be caught in their own traps (35:7–8). David has done nothing wrong to evoke their actions, yet those actions reveal their corrupt intent.

His enemies had initiated conflict by ruthlessly repaying David's good with evil, which disheartened him. When *they* got sick, however, David fasted and mourned for them in all sincerity, as if for a close relative. Still, when David faced his next difficult situation, they again gathered to mock him, slander him, and make his life as difficult as possible (35:11–16). So to be rescued from such people would delight David, and he would be quick to rejoice and thank God (35:9–10).

David has had enough. In verse 17, he asks God to stop merely observing and do something. These people have no reason to detest him. And it isn't just David whom they bother; they create havoc for other peaceful people in the land (35:19–21).

Aware that he isn't telling God anything He doesn't already know, in verse 23 David asks Him to take action. David has remained faithful and righteous, and he wants God's public vindication. Not only will David then praise God and tell of what He has done but also others will see for themselves how God cares for those who love and serve Him (35:22–28).

PSALM 36

David is associated with a lot of psalms that feature a contrast between the behavior of the wicked (and the consequences of their actions) and the righteousness of those who seek the Lord (and the rewards for their faithfulness). In Psalm 36, however, David credits his insight on the matter to an oracle—a command or revelation from God. The prophets are usually associated with oracles, but in this case David had a clear epiphany on the subject that he had written so much about.

The crux of the matter is that wicked people have no fear of the Lord. In this case, the root word for *fear* is less suggestive of fright than of anxiety or trepidation. Some people commit grievous injustices that apparently don't trigger any sense of dread or accountability to God. Instead, such people couch the severity of their sin with flattering and deceitful speech. They detect no reason to stop their evil actions, and the problem intensifies to the point where they can lie in bed and dream up new offenses to commit (36:1–4).

In contrast, God has vast amounts of love and faithfulness. In David's imagery in verses 5–6, God has mountains of righteousness and oceans of justice. It's no wonder that self-centered, coldhearted wicked people cannot connect with Him.

Still, many people do indeed seek and find the Lord—people of all different statuses. Their relationship is like a feast, and God provides them both light and life (36:7–9).

In David's continued clarity, he sees that the evildoers will meet defeat (36:12). In the meantime, he prays in verse 11 that he will not be confronted by the proud and the wicked. His wish is for God to continue to love and uphold the righteous people who know Him (36:10).

PSALM 37

Psalm 37 is similar in theme to Psalm 36 in its comparisons between righteous and wicked segments of humanity. But as the psalm opens, David makes a crucial observation about wicked people that will make a critical difference in how people view them. Whatever seems to be in their favor now won't be true for long, because they will soon wither like grass (37:1–2).

In verse 3, David points out that those who trust in the Lord have the opportunity and privilege of a much more lasting result of their actions. And in the meantime, their relationship with God assures them of rewards that have real value. They have a good place to live, in secure surroundings. They have the desires of their heart because the source of their delight is God (37:4).

Critical Observation

Several times within Psalm 37 "the land" is mentioned as a reward for the faithful. After God delivered Israel from Egypt and slavery, He guided them to the land that had been promised to Abraham. Under David's rule, the boundaries of that land continued to expand. The people's homes and surroundings were the result of God's direct blessing. And God's previous faithfulness in escorting them to the land was an assurance of His ongoing presence and involvement among them.

In verse 6, God's righteousness and justice are compared to sunshine. When we consider life in a Middle Eastern locale centuries before the introduction of air conditioning, the noonday sun was something that would get everyone's attention.

In verse 7 it seems that wicked people are getting away with lies, cheating, and deceit. When witnessing such injustice, God's people have one of two choices: They can worry and respond with great anger (a natural response), but that will only lead to more evil; or they can realize that God is aware of the problem and wait for Him to act (37:7–8). Only then will true justice be ensured (37:9–11).

In verses 12–22, David lists a series of contrasts between righteous and wicked people. In each specific instance, given enough time, the apparent success of evildoers comes to a crashing end. The lasting effect of all that wickedness will never last (37:20). For the righteous, however, the blessings of God are both plentiful and eternal (38:18–19).

So, according to verses 23–40, it is far better to focus one's energies on living a righteous life than to fret over the wicked. It's easy to get distracted by personal offenses, but it is much more beneficial to watch blameless and upright people and learn from their example (37:37). Then, when looking back over one's life, the love and faithfulness of God is more readily apparent (37:25–26).

PSALM 38

Psalm 38 fits in the "penitential" category (along with 6, 32, 51, 102, 130, and 143) and recounts David's inner turbulence while dealing with God's disfavor. (The exact nature of David's offense is unknown.)

David quickly confesses to "foolish sins" in verse 5 (NLT). Still, the description of his physical and emotional misery is moving. The hand of God is heavy on him, and God's dealings with David are described in verse 2 as piercing arrows. He is overcome with both guilt and illness, including festering wounds and searing pain (38:5–8).

The situation might not have been quite as bad if it had been between only David and the Lord. But David's suffering leads to his friends deserting him and his enemies taking the offensive against him, both of which add to his agony (38:11–12).

Yet David does not respond to criticism. He may not have literally placed his hands over his ears, but he describes himself in verse 13 as deaf and silent, unwilling to hear or reply to the malicious chatter of his enemies. Even in his defenseless position, he realizes his best option is to wait for God to answer, forgive, and reestablish his physical and spiritual health (38:14–16).

David had sinned, but he confessed and is now dealing with the aftereffects of what he has done (38:17–18). His enemies have also sinned, yet they continue in their iniquity. Their sin is more disturbing because they are persecuting David as he strives to do what is right (38:19–20). So David continues to beseech the Lord, seeking help in the one place he knows he can find it (38:21–22).

PSALM 39

After David had established himself as king over Israel and many of his battles were behind him, he spent considerable time organizing the military and spiritual leadership of Israel. He assigned three clans to oversee the music ministry, one of which was Jeduthun, also known as Ethan (1 Chronicles 25:1), who is mentioned in the superscription of Psalm 39.

Similar to the previous psalm, David again confesses to sin in verse 8. Realizing that God has every right to judge and discipline him, David determines to keep silent (39:9). However, his self-imposed silence only causes additional inner turbulence (39:1–2). He continues to see wicked people around him, and he begins to burn with anger (39:1–3).

But in verses 4–5, David comes to the realization that life is short. The days pass quickly, which should challenge people to put the events of life into a proper context. David realizes that the annoyance and anger he feels toward the wicked is fleeting, so he determines to personally focus on what he can accomplish while he has time (39:6).

Turning his attention back to God, David affirms his hope in the Lord while asking to avoid being ridiculed by foolish people (39:7–8). Because each person's life is brief, David wants to restore his relationship with God as quickly as possible (39:10–11). From David's perspective, death is quickly approaching, so his desire is to rediscover the joy of the Lord as quickly as possible (39:12–13).

PSALM 40

In Psalm 40, David describes several of the same elements as in many previous psalms: his sin, the troubles he is facing, and numerous enemies (40:12–15). In Psalm 39, for example, he is struggling to make sense of his troubles and to regain God's favor. In this psalm, however, God has answered his prayer, and David's personal tribulations seem to pale in comparison to his joy.

In verses 1–3, we see that David's patience has been rewarded. God has heard him and responded. David's new song is one not of questioning and confusion but of faith and praise. He has regained his spiritual footing.

When people stop long enough to ponder what God has done for them, they discover it's impossible to think of everything. Therefore, to envy proud and irreligious people, or to pursue false gods, is all the more foolish (40:4–5).

God is not impressed by the outward practice of one's religion—sacrifices, offerings, and such. David realizes that the Lord far prefers a strong relationship where His Word motivates an ongoing desire to obey and respond to Him (40:6–8).

Demystifying Psalms

The reference to God's piercing of David's ears in verse 6 can be interpreted a couple of different ways. Some people believe it recalls the Israelite practice of piercing the ear of a willing servant with an awl to signify his desire for lifetime service (Exodus 21:2–6). But the word for *pierced* also allows for the possibility of God cleaning out David's ears (in a spiritual sense), permitting him to hear God more clearly and respond more quickly.

God's forgiveness and restoration don't stop with David. In response to what the Lord has done for him, the psalmist is motivated to speak up and tell others (40:9–10). He wants to continue to be surrounded with the love, truth, and mercy of God (40:11).

It isn't that David's problems are over, but quite the contrary: He faces too many troubles to number (40:12). They continue to have a negative effect on him. Among his problems is the ongoing persecution of his enemies who want to take his life, and in the meantime hound him verbally (40:13–15).

In verse 17, David counts himself among the poor and needy. Still, the renewed presence of God in his life makes all the difference. He is able to rejoice and encourage others as he waits for God to deliver him (40:16–17).

PSALM 41

Psalm 41 concludes the first section of the book of Psalms. In this section David is credited with thirty-seven of the forty-one psalms, but in following sections David's influence is less pronounced. This final psalm of the section opens as the first one had, with a definition of what makes a person blessed (1:1; 41:1).

David is again writing from personal experience. The psalm contains a personal confession of sin, the mention of an illness connected to the sin, the derision of enemies while David is physically impaired, and the faithful expectation of God to act.

From his sickbed, David expresses great confidence that God will heal him, deliver him from his enemies, and once again bless him (41:1–3). According to verses 4–6, David's enemies aren't all military foes. Some actually came to visit him while sick, offered insincere words of comfort, and then left to slander him and wish that he were dead. While David lay suffering, his enemies gather to fantasize about bad things happening to him (41:7–8). Their coldhearted attitudes must have been contagious; even those who had been David's trusted friends begin to forsake him (41:9).

Critical Observation

David's honest and uncensored description of being deserted and betrayed by so-called friends strikes a chord with many people. Indeed, as Jesus predicts His betrayal, He quotes David's words from Psalm 41:9 (see John 13:18).

Yet David continues to look to the future. He has confessed to God (41:4) and reestablished his spiritual integrity (41:12). He fully expects God to raise him back up and enable him to confront those who hope to take advantage of him (41:10–12).

This section of Psalms concludes in verse 13 with emphatic praise to the eternal Lord, the God of Israel. The other sections end with similar doxologies.

Take It Home

After perusing the first book within the book of Psalms, the reader gets a varied story of a life—ecstatic joys, traumatic struggles, and all points in between. In this case it is David's life, although untold numbers of people throughout the centuries have related to his genuine expressions. Not everyone is a poet, but anyone can express honest feelings. When you get a quiet moment, try composing a psalm of your own. If possible, try to do so on a regular basis. It won't take long before you, too, will be able to look back over the various events of your life and see how God has been present throughout good times and bad.

PSALMS: BOOK II

PSALMS 42–57

Setting Up the Section

As Book II of the biblical book of Psalms begins, new authors begin to be identified. In Book I, all but four of the psalms are attributed to David, and those four have no designated author. David will continue to contribute to the book of Psalms, but his name will be joined by several others from here on.

PSALM 42

What we know as Psalms 42 and 43 may have formed a single psalm in its original writing. They flow together well and even share a chorus (42:5, 11; 43:5). Psalm 42 is a *maskil*, as is Psalm 32 and others that will follow.

The sons of Korah mentioned in the superscription are one of three divisions of musicians in charge of leading music. One of the three leaders is Jeduthun, previously mentioned in the introduction to Psalm 39. Another is Asaph, whose first mention in Psalms will be in Psalm 50. The leader of the sons of Korah is a man named Heman (1 Chronicles 6:33; 25:1).

Demystifying Psalms

A psalm of Asaph, or psalm of the Sons of Korah, doesn't necessarily indicate that the designated person is the *author*. It is just as likely that the named individual was delegated to see to the performance of the psalm in the community worship ceremony. Therefore, the writers of these psalms are frequently referred to more generically as the psalmist.

In verses 1–2, the psalmist compares his thirst for God to that of a deer panting for water. Perhaps he envisions a deer desperate for a drink after being pursued by predators, because he immediately writes of a long procession of people insulting and making fun of him. No doubt he refers to a spiritual thirst, intensified by his recent diet of salty tears (42:3).

To make his situation worse, verse 4 points out that the psalmist has been prevented not only from attending worship services but also from taking part in his regular ministry there. Isolation and weeping have replaced fellowship, joy, and thanksgiving. Yet in the first of three identical choruses, he chides himself to overcome his negative mindset (some scholars accuse him of self-pity) and instead place his hope in God (42:5).

In verses 6–7, mountains and waters are the images used to portray the psalmist's feelings. He appears to be in a mountainous area, yet his desire is to be in the mountains around Jerusalem. That geographic region is also noted for waterfalls, so the psalmist uses the image to describe surging tides of trouble pouring over him (42:7).

He is lonely, sick, and filled with questions about why he is suffering (42:9–10). Yet he can still feel God's love, and he continues to pray, hope, and praise his Lord (42:8, 11).

PSALM 43

In what is likely an extension of the previous psalm, the psalmist continues to attempt to make sense of his depressing situation in Psalm 43. He has grown weary of the many accusations of his enemies (42:3, 10; 43:1), and he seeks vindication from God. He is holding to his conviction that God is his stronghold, yet he finds it difficult to comprehend why he continues to be rejected, mournful, and persecuted (43:2).

According to verses 3–4, the psalmist has been unable to travel to Jerusalem to worship as he had done in the past, and it is his ongoing desire to go there. He can pray to God wherever he is, of course, but the altar in Jerusalem is a place to worship publicly and enlist the participation of others in praise and music. His is not an unusual yearning. Regular pilgrimages to the temple in Jerusalem were expected from all those able to make the journey, and those trips were usually joyful times for the travelers.

The psalmist concludes in verse 5 with the refrain he has already used twice (42:5, 11). He continues to question his disturbed state of mind, but more importantly, he expresses his expectation that his hope in God will continue to result in praise as he waits for God to act.

PSALM 44

It is always difficult to try to understand why bad things happen, especially to people who don't seem to deserve it. But for the early Israelites, the issue was even more poignant. Their covenant relationship with God is based on His promise that if they follow His instruction they will be blessed. For them to think they are being obedient and yet still experience signs of God's displeasure is indeed a dilemma. The psalmist addresses the situation in Psalm 44.

The opening verse points out that the stories of God's provision and protection of His people have been passed from generation to generation as inspiration and encouragement. As Israel had been faithful, God had led them in driving away their enemies and establishing themselves in the promised land. They realize that their success isn't a result of their military skill but of God's power and love (44:2–3).

Notice the psalmist goes back and forth between singular and plural tense as he refers to Israel. Sometimes he uses *us* and *we* to indicate the collective voices; other times he uses *I* and *my* to portray a singular national identity. The people had acknowledged God and had offered Him praise. They realize He is solely responsible for their victories (44:4–8).

The fact that God is responsible for every victory is where the psalmist's confusion began. For some reason Israel's enemies have begun to be victorious. Israel has to retreat and is being plundered. The people feel that God has rejected them (44:9–10). It is a miserable feeling, like defenseless sheep being devoured by predators or worthless slaves being sold for almost nothing (44:11–12).

Verses 13–16 point out that surrounding nations have certainly taken notice, which is both embarrassing and potentially dangerous. For any neighboring countries out for revenge, Israel's vulnerable state is the ideal time to attack. It is easier to accept this vulnerable position if the people had been responsible for wrongdoing, but that is not the case. The psalmist affirms in verses 17–18 that Israel has not forgotten God or been unfaithful to Him. They realize God knows when they have strayed, and He cannot be fooled. So they would not attempt to do so (44:20–21).

The people are bewildered, crushed, depressed, and helpless (44:19, 22). In verses 23–26, they cry out to God, pleading with Him to show Himself and see their suffering. They still have confidence in His unfailing love, even during their times of sorrow and confusion.

PSALM 45

Psalm 45 was written to celebrate the wedding of a king. The kings of Judah came from the line of David, which seems to be the case in this instance. The psalm may have been used for numerous kings. In fact, the author of Hebrews later uses this psalm in reference to Christ (45:6–7; Hebrews 1:8–9).

The psalmist's praise for the king is profuse. He is moved by the event taking place, and he wants to put forth his best effort (45:1). In verses 2–5, he extols both the character of the king (grace, truth, humility, righteousness) and the impressive and valiant actions of the king (victory, conquest, splendor, majesty) (45:2–5).

Ideally, the king is anointed by God to rule over the land. Saul, David, and Solomon had all been designated by God to rule. Later, the line of kings included many who had no love for God and little, if any, spiritual awareness. Here, however, the king is not only acknowledged as blessed by God (45:2) but is even temporarily *addressed* as God (45:6). The very next verse, however, reestablishes the clear distinction between God and God's servant, the king (45:7). The reference to his throne lasting forever in verse 6 affirms God's own promise that a descendant of David will always be on the throne (1 Chronicles 17:11–14). A number of David's descendants will rule before the promise is ultimately fulfilled by Jesus Christ.

Critical Observation

Israel's God and Israel's king had similar roles in terms of overseeing the people, protecting the nation against its enemies, administering justice tempered with mercy, and so forth. The glory and majesty of the human king also reflected, to a much lesser degree, the throne of heaven. So to address the king as *God* (45:6) is, in a sense, a compliment that indicates he is doing the things he should.

The king's reputation for justice and righteousness sets him apart from others in similar positions—many of whom may have been attending the ceremony (45:7). A number of special fragrances are used on this wedding day, including myrrh, aloes, and cassia (an aromatic root), but the groom's joy has a prominent aroma because it is from God (45:7–8).

According to verse 9, the king stands beside his bride, dressed in gold. Ophir is thought to have been located in western Arabia. At this point the psalmist turns his attention to addressing the bride, advising her to shift her strongest loyalties from her family to her new husband. The king is stricken with her beauty, and she should honor him in return (45:10–11). The psalmist's description of the bridal court in verses 12–15 emphasizes not only its splendor but also the atmosphere of joy that prevails.

Turning back to the king in verse 16, the psalmist points out that his fathers had come before him and eventually his sons will succeed him in the royal line. And then the psalmist makes a bold promise to help people of all generations remember the king and his wedding (45:17). Since his tribute has been recorded in scripture for centuries, it seems he was true to his word.

PSALM 46

The introduction to this psalm contains an obscure term used only here and in 1 Chronicles 15:20: *according to alamoth*. Based on its usage, it is most likely a musical term. It may have to do with music in a higher register, such as high-pitched flutes, soprano voices, or young maidens with tambourines (68:25).

This psalm, with its focus on the power and sovereignty of God, is similar to some of the previous psalms of David. But where David's are frequently intensely personal, this one is written with the nation of Israel in mind (*our* [46:1, 11]; *us* [46:7, 11]).

Israel may have been facing some troublesome situations, but the psalmist envisions catastrophes to the extreme in verses 2–3. Even if the mountains are to fall and the oceans are to rise, God will be there with His people, and they need not fear. Therefore, the Lord will surely see them through lesser problems.

Nations may have been in turmoil, falling all around, but Israel can be secure in the knowledge of God's presence (46:4–7). Unlike many important cities, Jerusalem had no river. The river and streams mentioned by the psalmist in verse 4 are his poetic terminology to describe God's ever-present influence and blessing on His people.

The reference to the break of day in verse 5 could refer to a distressing time. For those coming out of a long, dark, troubling night, it is a time of insecurity and fatigue. And for a city it is when attacks tend to take place. But God is there to help His people at dawn and throughout the day. The city offers the people a certain degree of protection, but God is their true fortress (46:7).

The psalmist's final verses offer additional consolation. He invites the people to pay special attention to God's work in the world. God can bring peace, but it first requires the destruction of the nations that want to dominate others through force (46:8–9).

In the original language, the instruction to "Be still, and know that I am God" is less a suggestion than an emphatic command (46:10). The intent is not, "Quiet down and you'll discover God's presence," but rather, "Quit what you're doing right now and acknowledge who God is."

The last verse is a repetition of 46:7, likely a response by those in the worship ceremony. It is a closing reminder of God's ongoing presence and protection.

PSALM 47

Few ceremonies in the ancient world were as spectacular as the enthronement of a king. Each nation had its own traditions. A number of psalms are sometimes classified as enthronement psalms, which are those that acknowledge God as the great King. Most are found in a later section of the Psalms (scattered throughout Psalms 92 to 100). This one, however, seems to fit with the preceding and following psalms that highlight the sovereignty of Israel's God. Some people speculate that Israel may have used such psalms for the coronation of their own kings, but no proof yet exists.

While Psalm 46 focuses exclusively on Israel, Psalm 47 immediately makes clear in the opening verse that God is to be acknowledged by *all* the nations. Indeed, Israel's God is both the Lord Most High and the great King over all the earth (47:2). Both of these titles were at times bestowed on human kings of other nations, but those nations will rise and fall while God continues to be sovereign not only over Israel but over the entire world.

The subdued nations of Israel's history include some of the great powers of the world, not least among them the Egyptians and the Philistines (47:3). Israel's inheritance—the promised land—had been populated with many nations, some living in walled cities such as Jericho (47:4). Yet God overcame those peoples and fulfilled His promise to Israel.

Just as other nations celebrate the coronation of a new king, Israel should rejoice over the ascent of their God (47:5). The emphasis on joy is not to be missed: The command to sing praises is found four times in verse 6 alone.

Joy should continue with the awareness that God is King of all the earth (47:7). Israel still has enemies and will fight more battles, yet the truth remains that God is in control (47:8). The other nations might not be ready to concede that fact, but as long as Israel believes it they can look forward to a time when the truth of the statement will at last be realized.

PSALM 48

Psalm 48 is the third consecutive psalm to emphasize the sovereignty of God. In this case, however, God's power is demonstrated in the unequalled security of the city of Zion (Jerusalem).

Verses 1–2 point out that Jerusalem is both lofty and beautiful—appropriate for what is considered the dwelling place of God. Many times a mountain setting is associated with a nation's gods. Mount Olympus is perhaps the best-known example, where the Greek gods were believed to reside. The psalmist's mention of Zaphon in verse 2 might have been in reference to a Phoenician mountain where their primary god (Baal) supposedly lived. But Israel's God does not rely on the protection of the city of Jerusalem. Instead, Israel's God is the fortress that protects the city (48:3).

The city was thought to have been impregnable before it had belonged to Israel. But David had the faith and skill to conquer and claim it, and he made it the capital city of a united Judah and Israel in 2 Samuel 5:6–10. Now, with God's temple there and the blessings of God on the city, it is even more impenetrable. Nations can band together and make an assault, but God's protection will send them fleeing in terror (48:4–7).

Critical Observation

The ships of Tarshish in verse 7 were a noted fleet that sailed the Mediterranean Sea, transporting goods from faraway places. Occasionally one of the ships would encounter a gale and experience an untimely end. The psalmist compares the destruction of Israel's enemies to the shattering and sinking of one of these mighty ships.

God's reputation for protecting His people has long been part of Israel's oral tradition. But with the ability to visit Jerusalem, the people have a visual element to help increase their faith (48:8). The presence of God is even more personal within the temple (48:9). In such an intimate setting, the people are able to meditate on God's love and praise Him (48:9–10). The joy that results spreads from Jerusalem to surrounding villages (48:11).

In verse 12, the psalmist challenges the people to take a close look at the city of Jerusalem. As they do, they will see a well-constructed fortress of towers, ramparts, and citadels. Such defenses should remind them of their eternal God's protection, and they should be eager to share their confidence and enthusiasm with the generations to follow (48:13–14).

PSALM 49

Psalm 49 addresses a recurring theme: the apparent injustice of life as the rich dominate the poor. The psalmist will put things in perspective, however, by explaining that death is the great equalizer. No matter how rich or wise a person might be, there is no escaping the same inevitable end as the poor and the foolish.

The psalmist begins in verses 1–2 by summoning all to listen, both low (poor) and high (rich). What he has to say will be a warning to some and an encouragement to others. He will be pronouncing wisdom and understanding, yet his message will also be something of a riddle (49:3–4). The musical accompaniment adds an element of importance to his words.

In verses 5–6, he refers to people who count on their money to get by and boast of all they have. This is no small problem, because he describes being surrounded by such people. And then comes the brutal truth in verses 7–9: No redeemer has enough influence and no amount of money is ever enough to ransom one's life and avoid the grave.

What the psalmist is saying would have been evident to everyone. Upon death, riches are worthless. Accumulated wealth remains for the living. Some people may be remembered longer than others if they prearrange for elaborate tombs or spend some of their money on something (such as land) that will bear their name (49:10–11). Still, the donor is left with a tomb for a house. He will never know when others see his fancy grave or hear his name connected with land or other possessions.

The psalmist points out in verse 12 that people have no advantage over animals when it comes to life cycles. Human beings see beasts of burden live and die, thinking little about it, but then seek fruitless ways to avoid the same end (49:13–14). A common image of the time was of death (personified) devouring the living (49:14; see Job 18:13; 24:19). In some cultures the perception of death was that of a ravenous monster always on the prowl.

The point of this psalm is to challenge people to not allow themselves to become enamored by wealth and splendor. The privilege of the wealthy will not endure. Those who count on their riches have a common end (49:16–20). The upright, however, have a different outlook (49:15). Death is still a certainty, yet they can maintain the hope that God will not leave them in the grave.

PSALM 50

Psalm 50 is the first psalm attributed to Asaph, one of the three men from whose families the temple musicians were assigned (1 Chronicles 25:1). A few of the psalms have already been associated with the other two men: Heman (connected with the sons of Korah) and Jeduthun. Asaph may not have actually written this and other psalms that bear his name (73–83). The wording allows for the possibility that the psalm was written *for* him, or even for use by his descendants.

This psalm has a different tone than many of the others. Rather than portraying the psalmist crying out to God about a personal matter, in Psalm 50 God does most of the speaking about a spiritual matter. In fact, God summons the people of the earth for a judgment of sorts.

The gravity of what is to come is suggested in the opening phrase, where three separate titles for God are used to verify the unique qualifications of the heavenly judge. The description continues as the psalmist portrays God coming from His city, perfect and radiant, and surrounded by fire (50:2–3). The people over whom He will preside are supposed to be consecrated (devoted to God and obedient) and aware of the covenant between God and His people (50:4–6).

The initial pronouncement is not bad. In verse 8, God acknowledges the many offerings that have been made to Him. However, the people have the wrong idea about sacrifice. First, they aren't actually giving God anything because every creature on earth already belongs to Him (50:9–11). Second, their offerings are not like sacrifices made in other religions—attempts to satisfy the cravings of a god. Unlike those gods, Israel's God does not hunger or thirst; He is complete and perfect, without need for material things (50:12–13).

The people are encouraged to bring offering of thanks to God (50:14–15; see Leviticus 7:11–15). Burnt offerings were sometimes offered routinely, perhaps with little thought. But a thanks offering was made in response to something God had done (healing, consolation, deliverance). The offering of thanks requires acknowledgment of God's involvement in one's life and sincere gratitude in response.

After correcting the worship habits of those who conscientiously want to honor God, in verses 16–17 the Lord addresses those who aren't so genuine in their motives. Some people worship along with the rest, but have no regard for God's law. Their unrighteous acts are listed in verses 18–20 and include stealing, adultery, deceit, and slander. Because God has not yet taken action against them, this wicked bunch has the audacity to presume that silence gives consent. Not so, declares the Lord. This is the occasion for Him to refute their sinful actions personally and publicly (50:21).

Psalm 50 closes with an opportunity for those who have just heard God's pronouncement to consider what He has said and correct their attitudes and behavior. They have two options. Those who continue to oppose God will eventually face His judgment, and there will be no one able to rescue them. Far better off are those who choose to honor God and experience His salvation (50:22–23).

PSALM 51

This is the first of the psalms of David in the second book within Psalms (42–72) and is one of seven sometimes categorized as penitential. Its deeply personal and confessional tone is explained in the introduction. It was composed after David was confronted about his adultery with Bathsheba (2 Samuel 12:1–25). David has avoided God for many months (considering that the baby he had conceived was already born). But when faced with the severity of his sin, his confession is unabashed.

David makes no attempt to deny his sin or excuse his behavior. He readily admits in verses 1–3 that his actions were rebellious and sinful. Yet he is also confident that God is a source of mercy, unfailing love, compassion, and cleansing. David had gotten a married woman pregnant and then arranged to have her husband killed in battle, yet he realizes that his sin is against God (51:4). His propensity to sin reminds him of his sinful nature (51:5).

When he finally acknowledges his sin, David immediately wants to be forgiven. Realizing that inner truth and wisdom had ceased to influence his actions, David asks God for cleansing in verses 6–7. After God forgives him, David can again experience the joy and gladness that he has been missing (51:8). And after God has blotted out David's terrible offense, then David can renew his heart for God. David prays not only for a pure heart but also for a steadfast spirit and ongoing awareness of God's presence. After his grievous sin, he desires the joy of salvation and a renewal of his willingness to serve God (51:9–11).

Critical Observation

Hyssop (51:7) was a plant with a hairy stem. When immersed in water, the liquid clung well to the stem, so the plant was used in purification ceremonies. Hyssop was also used to apply blood to the doors of Hebrew homes just prior to the exodus from Egypt (Exodus 12:22) and to offer Jesus a drink while He was on the cross (John 19:29).

David wants to be a good example for God in both teaching others and demonstrating praise (51:13–15). He has good insight into what God wants from him. Rather than animal sacrifices, God much prefers the sacrifice of a submissive spirit and humbled heart (51:16–17).

David also seems to comprehend that the king's behavior and spiritual integrity (or lack of such) can affect God's perception of the nation as a whole. In verses 18–19, he closes his psalm with a prayer for the prosperity of Jerusalem and a time when the people's sacrifices will once again be righteous and pleasing to God. Some scholars have suggested that the last two verses may have been added to David's psalm at a later date, during Israel's exile. After a period away from home during which sacrifices were suspended, the desire to rebuild Jerusalem and reinstitute offerings would have been strong indeed.

PSALM 52

In many of David's psalms, it is difficult to match his comments with a specific biblical event. But beginning with Psalm 51, several of the superscriptions throughout this section describe what is taking place in David's life as he writes the psalm.

In the case of Psalm 52, David had been trying to hide from Saul and had sought shelter among a city of priests. He had been seen by one of Saul's shepherds named Doeg. Saul is irate to hear that the priests had assisted David and ordered them killed, but none of Israel's soldiers would respond. Doeg volunteered for the vile assignment and slaughtered not only eighty-five priests but also the entire population of the city where they lived—men, women, and children (1 Samuel 21:1–9; 22:6–19).

David may have had Doeg specifically in mind, but the opening description in verses 1–4 can apply to any number of people. Most believers attempting to live godly lives can identify with the type—oppressors who boast of evil, plot destruction, practice deceit, and love falsehood rather than speak the truth. They are good at what they do; unfortunately, what they do is evil.

Such people may appear to be securely entrenched in a community, and it may seem that no one is able to reason with them. But God is also affected by their actions, and righteous people can count on Him to act. According to verse 5, He will have no trouble uprooting the wicked, who aren't as entrenched as they think. Those who watch will have the last laugh (52:6). The observers will have renewed reverence for God after witnessing the end of those who get ahead by putting others down (52:7).

In the story of Doeg, David is the one on the run. Yet in contrast to the wicked, who will be uprooted, in verse 8 David compares himself to an olive tree—securely rooted, productive, and anticipating long life. (Olive trees can live for centuries.) More importantly, he is flourishing in his relationship with God. His trust in God makes all the difference, and he promises to continue to praise the Lord and place his hope in Him (52:8–9).

PSALM 53

The introduction of Psalm 53 contains a new distinctive term: *mahalath*. The word may pertain to illness or suffering, used here in the psalm in regard to hardship or persecution. A *maskil*, first noted in Psalm 32, may have been intended as an instructive writing.

If Psalm 53 sounds familiar, it may be because of its similarity to Psalm 14. Some scholars believe its (re)location between Psalms 52 and 54, both of which have introductions that tie them to events in David's life, suggests a similar (though unstated) association with David. It is possible that the reference to *fool* in verse 1 could recall David's frustrating experience with Nabal, the husband of Abigail (1 Samuel 25).

Demystifying Psalms

Throughout the first book within Psalms, the word used for God is almost always *Yahweh*. In the second book, however, the preferred word changes to *Elohim*. Despite all the similarities between Psalms 14 and 53, the word used to refer to God is changed.

Compared to Psalm 14, the only verse with significantly changed content is 53:5, replacing 14:5–6. Here David writes of foolish evildoers who are overcome with dread even though there is no good reason for it. Biblical examples abound of instances when God's people are threatened but where God delivers them by creating panic within the enemy camp (Judges 7:19–22; 1 Samuel 7:10–11; 14:13–15). Yet it seems that wicked people never learn (Psalm 53:4).

Another change from Psalm 14 includes the reference to the scattered bones of the ones who had attacked God's people (53:5). The image is one of the aftermath of a large battle that has left vast numbers of unburied dead as the result of an utter defeat—quite a grim outlook for those who oppose God and His people.

PSALM 54

The superscription of Psalm 54 mentions the Ziphites, inhabitants of the Desert of Zith, south of Hebron. David had hidden from Saul in that desert, but the Ziphites operated as Saul's spies, monitoring David's movements and reporting back to the king (1 Samuel 23:15–25). However, such specifics aren't included in the psalm, and it can be applied and appreciated by people in various situations.

As is typical of his psalms, David opens in verses 1–2 with a cry to God, asking for deliverance and vindication. Then in verse 3, he voices his complaint: Ruthless, ungodly, aggressive men are trying to kill him. The Ziphites were little more than informants, but by the time of David's encounter with them, he had been on the run from Saul for a long time. During those years he had undergone some periods of great faith and some other trying times, but God had sustained him through them all (54:4).

As usual, David asks God in verse 5 to address the problem of the evil people in pursuit of him. David had shown unusual patience and self-control in refusing to personally kill King Saul, even when he had ideal opportunities, opting rather to wait for God to act. Yet he had full confidence that God would eventually deliver him. He could speak as if his deliverance had already taken place, even as he continued to be oppressed (54:6–7).

PSALM 55

The introduction does not provide specifics about the event that inspired this psalm, but the psalm itself reveals a painful betrayal by someone who had been a close friend. The psalm may have been inspired by Absalom's revolt, during which several of David's trusted associates deserted him. One of note is Ahithophel (2 Samuel 15:12), perhaps the wisest advisor in the nation who, after Absalom fails to take his advice, realizes David will eventually regain the throne and commits suicide (2 Samuel 16:20–17:13, 23). However, no proof exists of this possibility, and scholars are left to speculate.

David's appeal to God in verses 1–5 includes an account of both the treatment he is receiving from others and the inner turmoil it is creating within him. He describes a progression from anguish, to fear and trembling, to horror. Given the opportunity, he would escape to the desert for some peace and solitude, leaving his tormentors behind him (55:6–7). The word translated *shelter* in verse 8 means "place of escape," and this is its sole appearance in the Old Testament. But apparently the option of escape is not available to him, and David will be forced to weather his emotional storm.

So again David turns the matter over to God. The offenses of the wicked people are mentioned in verses 9–11: violence, strife, malice, abuse, threats, and lies. The extent of their actions had reached the point where David not only prays for them to become confounded and confused but even that they would be surprised by their sudden deaths (55:15). What makes this situation particularly painful for David is the involvement of someone he had considered a close friend and had spent a lot of time with. They had even worshiped together (15:12–14).

In the wake of such emotional trauma, David cries out to God evening, morning, and midday (55:16–17). Without God's support, David would feel vastly outnumbered (55:18–19), yet he remains unharmed. He knows his enemies have no fear of God, and he is no doubt distraught as he realizes that his former friend is now included among them (55:19–21).

Critical Observation

David's regular prayer times, mentioned in verses 16–17, are reminiscent of Daniel's faithfulness and commitment to pray three times a day (Daniel 6:10). We might say, "Morning, noon, and night," but David cites "evening, morning, and noon" because the Jewish day started at sundown.

Yet David's response—and advice to others—is wise and appropriate (55:22). Those who cast their concerns on God will not be disappointed. God will simultaneously take care of the righteous while short-circuiting the work (if not the lives) of the wicked (55:23).

PSALM 56

Psalm 56 is another of David's psalms where the superscription provides a clue to the source of his emotions. Gath was a Philistine city where David went to hide while trying to keep from being captured by King Saul. Though he eventually made a tentative alliance with the King of Gath (1 Samuel 27:1–7), an earlier visit hadn't been so amiable. When the people identified him as the one who had killed Goliath and many more of their soldiers, he quickly became persona non grata and even began to fear for his life. To extricate himself from the situation, he feigned madness. The Philistines forced him out of the city but did not harm him (1 Samuel 21:10–22:1).

If this psalm is a true reflection of David's experience in Gath, then he would have been both pursued by Saul's army and slandered by his Philistine hosts (56:1–2). In addition, he would be running out of places to hide, so his fear is understandable (56:3). Still, he is able to maintain trust in God and realize that the Lord's protection is sufficient.

His enemies are insidious and aggressive. They watch him round the clock, looking for opportunities to harm him while conspiring with one another. If he attempts to defend himself or reason with them, they put words in his mouth to alter what he is really attempting to say (56:5–6).

But David wants to ensure that God hears him correctly. After asking God to not let his persecutors escape in verse 7, he wants God to keep track of his sorrows (56:8). In one interpretation of his request, he asks God to put his tears in wineskin. In other words, if God is well aware of David's situation, David trusts that the Lord will act to restrain the influence of his enemies (56:9).

Despite the ongoing onslaught of his persecutors, in verses 10–13 David reaffirms his trust in God. He expects God's deliverance to be certain, so he will move ahead in faith, continuing to praise his Lord.

PSALM 57

Psalm 57 has a number of similarities to Psalm 56. According to the introduction, this time David's mind is focused on the time he had hidden in a cave to escape the pursuit of King Saul. Ironically, it was the very same cave that Saul chose to enter and relieve himself. David and his men could easily have assassinated the king, although they would have been at the mercy of Saul's army (1 Samuel 24).

But as verse 1 shows, David counts on the mercy of God. A cave had turned out to be a less-than-reliable hiding place, but God is a constant refuge. Disasters will come and go, and during the worst of times the best place to be is in the shadow of God's wings (see Psalm 17:8 and commentary). Saul's army is pursuing David, but he is also being followed by God's love and faithfulness (57:3).

In verse 4, David describes his enemies as beasts, with weapons of war rather than sharpened teeth—just as threatening and just as potentially deadly. But unlike lions and other predators of the animal world, these beasts are cunning and set traps for David (57:6). As David continues to praise God, however, he is convinced that his oppressors will eventually fall into the nets and the pits they had constructed for him (57:5, 7).

He might be amongst beasts but, according to verses 7–8, David expects to awaken at dawn with a steadfast heart and a song on his lips. He is eager to praise God and declare to other nations and peoples what God has done for him. God's love and faithfulness are unlimited, reaching to the heavens (57:9–10).

This psalm concludes with a repeat of a previous refrain (57:5, 11). Because of God's character and concern for His people, He should be exalted over heaven and earth.

Take It Home

Perhaps you have begun to note the comments in the superscriptions of many of David's psalms. Most notably, Psalm 51 explains that it concerns David's adultery with Bathsheba, although others were written in regard to situations where David was displaying faith and courage. Can you think of events in your own recent life that might inspire a psalm? If so, express your heartfelt feelings to God, whether in repentance, praise, thankfulness, joy, or whatever motivation is most appropriate. You might want to write out your psalm, but the expression of your prayer is more important than its form.

PSALMS: BOOK II, CONTINUED

PSALMS 58–72

Setting Up the Section

This section continues and concludes the psalms found in Book II of the biblical book of Psalms. Most in this section are psalms of David. Some continue to have superscriptions that refer to specific events in the psalmist's life.

PSALM 58

In the opening verse of this psalm, David asks rhetorical questions. Are the rulers of the nation speaking justly and acting uprightly? Everyone already knew the answer is *no*.

In fact, the propensity for wickedness by such people could be traced back to the womb. So after a lifetime of practice, the injustice dispensed by such people is well orchestrated (58:2–3).

In verses 4–5, David compares the unjust leaders of the nation to snakes that are supposedly under the control of a snake charmer yet are no longer influenced by the music. The result is akin to having venomous cobras on the loose with little likelihood of rounding them up.

So David asks God, in verses 6–8, to do what people seem unable to accomplish: to rid the land of all those who are abusing their positions and meting out violence rather than justice. If they see themselves as lions, may their teeth be broken. If they perceive themselves as soldiers, may they discover their arrows dulled and useless. David wishes them the same end as water evaporating in desert heat, a slug that starts across a hot surface and doesn't make it, or as a stillborn child.

The original Hebrew of verse 9 defies clear interpretation. The underlying thought, however, appears to be that God's judgment on the people David has described will be sudden and swift—less time than it takes for a pot to feel heat when a flame is placed beneath it.

Critical Observation

Psalms such as this one are sometimes classified as *imprecatory*, meaning that the writer calls down curses or asks for utter defeat to come to the ungodly. Sometimes the requests are quite specific and graphic (104:35; 109:4–15; 137:8–9).

The thought of the righteous bathing their feet in the blood of the wicked (58:10) should not necessarily bring to mind a macabre scene like what might be portrayed in a horror film. However, the metaphor does suggest the aftermath of a battle, when the victor's sandals would certainly be splashed with some of the blood of his victims. In this case the battle is the means through which God has judged the earth, and the end result will be the long-awaited reward for those who have remained faithful (58:11).

PSALM 59

The introduction to Psalm 59 refers to the time when King Saul had ordered David's house watched so David could be killed while entering or leaving. But David's wife (Saul's daughter, Michal) warns him, and he escapes through a window during the dark of night (1 Samuel 19:11–18). However, the psalm itself doesn't appear to reflect such events. Some think, therefore, that a different psalmist updated the original psalm to apply to a later time in Israel's history.

Whoever the writer is, he cites a common complaint found in the psalms: persecution by his enemies. In verses 1–2, he opens with an appeal for deliverance from such people, whom he classifies as evildoers and bloodthirsty men. The psalmist proclaims his own innocence in the matter, yet his enemies continue to conspire against him, looking for opportunities to attack (59:3–4). In previous psalms, some of the psalmist's closest friends had joined in the treachery against him. In this case, however, the opposition seems to come from people outside of Israel (59:5).

In verses 6–7 and 14–15, the psalmist describes his enemies as a pack of snarling dogs, prowling around for food and howling when their appetites are not satisfied. It would have been a fright-inducing scene for most people, but not to the psalmist's God who would laugh and scoff at the pretension of such evildoers (59:8). And the knowledge that God feels no threat from the powers of the nations is assuring to the psalmist, who places his trust in God to minimize his fear.

The psalmist points out in verses 9–10 that as long as God goes before him as a fortress, he can remain impervious to the slander of others. He even has the presence of mind to realize that if God is to strike down the loudmouthed enemies all at once, the people of Israel might soon forget God's goodness and power (59:11). The psalmist wants them to suffer the consequences of their evil, to be sure, but far better to bide enough time to let them be "captured by their pride" (59:12 NLT). He doesn't merely want his enemies off his back; he wants God to be glorified as well.

Many gods of the time were praised for their strength, but the psalmist acknowledges both God's strength *and* His love (59:16–17). In spite of personal persecution and uncertainty, he will continue to sing praises to God.

PSALM 60

Of all the psalms with introductory superscriptions, Psalm 60 is the only one specifically designated for teaching. The historic reference in the introduction is to 2 Samuel 8:1–14; 10:14 and 1 Chronicles 18:1–13, passages that describe David's various victories, although there are minor discrepancies in some of the details. (Samuel and Chronicles cite the deaths of eighteen thousand Edomites rather than twelve thousand.)

This psalm expresses confusion in the wake of confidence. Israel had experienced a defeat in battle, usually a sign of God's disfavor. In this case, however, no explanation is given, and the people appear unaware of any reason God should have allowed them to fall to their enemies. Still, as verse 1 points out, they are aware of God's anger. Israel feels as if God has physically shaken the land to the point of fracture, and it is as if they have been given potent wine that causes them to stagger (60:2–3). They have lost all sense of security and are not themselves.

The intended meaning of verse 4 is uncertain. Troops gathered around banners and then followed those banners out into battle. Perhaps the psalmist is asking God to gather His people and lead them to victory. It is also possible, however, that he is expressing frustration that God led them to defeat instead of victory.

Yet from this point on, the psalm is nothing but confident and hopeful. Since God's anger has led to Israel's defeat, nothing but His favor will restore them. God continues to love His people, and in verse 5 the psalmist (presumably David) calls on God to help and deliver them. In response, God speaks and assures victory for His people.

A map would be helpful in comprehending the geographic references that follow in verses 6–8. The first series of places already belong to Israel. The cities of Shechem and Succoth roughly represent east and west, as do Gilead and Manasseh on a larger scale. The centrally located and well-defended Ephraim is like a protective helmet for the nation. Judah, the tribe from which David came, is portrayed as a royal scepter.

The remaining references (Moab, Edom, and Philistia) are all persistent enemies of Israel, yet they are under God's control just as surely as Israel (60:8). In response to God's pronouncement, the psalmist shows faith. He realizes that God will not only provide aid against, but also victory over, Israel's enemies (60:9–12).

Demystifying Psalms

The image of God tossing a shoe onto Edom in verse 8 is similar to a custom involving a legal transfer of property (as in Ruth 4:7–8, where a sandal is handed over to symbolize the official transfer of land). In this case, however, it is a sign of contempt

PSALM 61

Psalms 61–63 have the common theme of yearning for God during a time of trouble, and they all are written from the perspective of the king (presumed to be David). Psalm 61 appears to refer to specific events in David's life, but those specifics are not provided.

If indeed the psalmist is David, this might have been when he was driven from his throne during Absalom's attempted overthrow of the kingdom. In verse 2, David cries to God from "the ends of the earth"—a phrase that could refer to a sense of either geographical or spiritual distance. He is fainthearted and longs for the "towering rock of safety" (NLT). Perhaps this request is for a secure location that he cannot achieve without God's help, or the rock might be a reference to God Himself.

In verse 3, the psalmist is able to trust God during this crisis because God has always been faithful in previous times of trouble. He desires a more permanent sense of closeness to God with the protection of both the sanctuary of God and the Lord's personal presence (61:4). He has made promises to God, and he is counting on God's promises (heritage) to His people (61:5).

His prayer for long life in verse 6 is not a selfish one. With no anticipation of life after death, the psalmist's life on earth would have been his only opportunity to commune with God (61:7–8). He wants the experience to last as long as possible, committing to praise and obey God day after day. It is also a plea for his successors, not only for many generations but forever (see 1 Chronicles 17:11–12).

PSALM 62

The fact that this psalm is positioned between Psalm 61 and Psalm 63, coupled with the observation that opponents are attempting to topple the psalmist (62:4), suggests that it is authored by a king (again presumed to be David). A king has many resources at his disposal, yet David's sole source of help and comfort is God alone (62:1–2). God is his security (rock), deliverance (salvation), and protection (fortress).

Humanity, on the other hand, is a continual source of chaos. People have repeatedly attempted to undermine David. In verse 3, he compares himself to a weak and wobbly fence that could easily be pushed down. The assaults of others are verbal as well. They bless him to his face but curse him and tell lies about him behind his back (62:4). They do not rest from their efforts to put him down.

So again, David turns to God for rest and everything he needs (62:5–7). In verse 8, he challenges the people to do the same—to pour out their hearts and then trust God to take good care of them.

The psalmist's description of human beings in verse 9 is in direct contrast to his image of God. The Lord is a rock and fortress; people are nothing. Even those who perceive themselves as wealthy and entitled will soon be deflated and forgotten.

People tend to pursue riches, and many desperately turn to dishonest means (including stealing and extortion) to acquire wealth (62:10). Yet a person's accumulated possessions provide no long-range security. One's heart should remain on God, not any other substitute.

It is humbling to realize that God is not only strong but also loving. Devotion and obedience to Him will result in rewards that are both desirable and lasting (62:11–12).

PSALM 63

According to the introduction of Psalm 63, David writes it in connection with being in the desert of Judah. It is a vague reference. David had attempted to hide from Saul in the desert (1 Samuel 23:14), although the fact that the psalm is also written from the perspective of a king suggests a later time in David's life. This might be another psalm written during the period when Absalom had forced David to leave Jerusalem (2 Samuel 15:23).

The desert setting plays prominently in the psalm, however. In verse 1, David compares his longing for God to the thirst of a man wandering in a dry wilderness, desperate for water. For many people, the desire for God is a casual and occasional thing; for David, it is a matter of life and death.

David's desire for God is intensified because he knows what he is missing. He had worshiped God in the sanctuary in Jerusalem and knows what it's like to witness God's power and glory (63:2). It had been the spiritual equivalent of the fine foods he used to eat, but now he has to be content with more meager fare (63:3–5).

Still, he has fond memories of how God helped him in the past, and those memories fuel his faith for the future (63:6–8). He trusts God to sustain him now, just as He had done throughout the psalmist's lifetime.

As for the people who oppose David, their dominance will be temporary and short. They have positioned themselves against God's chosen king, so their end is certain. They will go down to the depths of the earth, being given over to the sword, and becoming food for jackals (63:9–10). They are liars who will be silenced once and for all (63:11).

In contrast, verse 11 says everyone who professes faith in God will offer praise, not least among them the king himself.

PSALM 64

As the opening verse points out, this is another psalm where David immediately turns to God after learning of a conspiracy against him. Those who oppose him use words as weapons. In verse 3, David compares their words to sharpened swords, and they aim them as one would point and shoot an arrow. Such people are also guerrilla fighters; they remain hidden as an unsuspecting person walks by and then attack without notice or provocation (64:4).

To make things worse, the evildoers serve as consultants for one another, encouraging each other and discussing their plans for future mayhem (64:5–6). David's observation in verse 6 that the human mind and heart are cunning is an understatement.

However, for all their many harsh and malicious words, these people will not have the last word. God will step in with arrows of His own, and the aggressors will be the ones struck down (64:7–8).

Those who observe God's judgment of the wicked will have two responses. At first they will experience a scornful satisfaction because the evil people have gotten what they deserve. More importantly, though, they will then turn their attention to God, giving much thought to His justice and proclaiming the good things He has done. After realizing that evil does exist, but only for a short time, righteous people can then satisfy themselves with God's protection and learn to rejoice in their relationship with Him (64:9–10).

PSALM 65

Psalms 65–68 have a similarity of thought and theme, as they focus on the gifts of God to His people. Praise and obedience are the appropriate responses to such a God. The vows to be fulfilled in verse 1 are probably promises made to God by people during prayer when seeking His presence and help.

The fact that God hears and responds to prayer draws people to Him (65:2). Foremost among His blessings is His great forgiveness in light of human sinfulness. And after forgiving them, God welcomes His people to come near to Him and spend time in His house (65:3–4). A renewed relationship with God makes temple worship a genuinely joyous and positive experience.

The psalmist also acknowledges God's power over creation. The Lord is Israel's hope, of course, but His works should have been apparent all around the world (65:5). God's control extends to the farthest seas and the mighty mountains of the world, as well as the chaos among the nations. Go far enough in one direction, the psalmist realizes, and the sun is coming up. Face the other direction and go far enough, and the sun is setting. Throughout that entire span, the people should notice and revere the works of God, and they should respond in joy (65:5–8).

The area of Canaan was heavily dependent on rain to sustain life. Drought could be a death sentence. So, in verses 9–11, the psalmist acknowledges God's part in abundantly providing the needed rains. The streams are filled with water, giving life to the land. Thankfulness for water naturally leads into thankfulness for crops and harvest.

Critical Observation

Some people think this psalm may have been used in conjunction with the barley harvest, during which the firstfruits were offered to God (Leviticus 23:9–14). It was an annual event that included both thanksgiving and celebration.

The all-too-rare greenness in the desert terrain is described as the hills being "clothed with gladness" (65:12 NIV). Just as the psalmist had challenged people throughout the world to sing for joy in their knowledge of the Lord, in verse 13 he calls creation itself to join the song.

PSALM 66

After fifteen straight psalms of David, Psalm 66 is not so designated, although the psalmist very well might have been a king. The psalm begins in verses 1–3 with a declaration of God's power and His works, along with a command to praise Him with shouts of joy. Nothing stands in God's presence: Enemies cower and all the earth acknowledges His sovereignty (66:4).

The invitation to "come and see" in verse 5 is to review what God has done for His people in the past. Perhaps the review is to be conducted at the temple (66:13–16). Centuries after the event, Israel is still recalling the power of God that led His people out of Egypt as the Red Sea was turned into dry land to provide them escape. God's great works in their past continue to inspire them. The stories are also reminders that God still rules and serve as warnings that any rebellion will be ultimately futile (66:6–7).

From the faithfulness of God in the distant past, the psalmist moves to the faithfulness of God in the recent past in verses 8–12. His people had been through some difficult times, including prison, defeat, and other trials. But rather than being brought down by such experiences, the psalmist realizes that they have merely been refined, as when precious metal is treated with intense heat in order to remove any impurities (66:10). God is to be praised because He preserved His people through the trying times and eventually led them to abundant land (66:12).

After challenging the people to praise God, in verses 13–15 the psalmist personally commits to sacrifice offerings to God at the temple and to fulfill the vows he had made. His example will motivate others to do the same. His prayer is sincere and confessional, and God responds with abundant love. Therefore, praise is the only appropriate response (66:16–20).

PSALM 67

Following the general theme of the previous two psalms, Psalm 67 also requests God's favor, in this instance as a group prayer. If the opening verses sound a bit like a familiar benediction, that's because they reflect the blessing taught to the priests in Numbers 6:24–26. As God blesses Israel, other nations will take notice and learn of salvation as well (67:1–2).

Ideally, praise will not be confined within Israel. In verses 3–4, the psalmist wants all the nations to praise God, who is a just ruler of people and a guide for all the countries. Those who acknowledge God's role in leading the nations can experience the joy that He provides. And if the psalmist's initial invitation isn't enough, he repeats it again in verse 5.

When the Israelite spies first searched out the promised land, they had been impressed with the produce that grew there (Numbers 13:23–27), and the abundance of the land continued to be of importance to them. In an agrarian society, the blessings of God were usually apparent in a bountiful harvest (Psalm 67:6–7). As God blesses the people and the crops grow, people from far away will revere the God of Israel.

PSALM 68

With an ongoing focus on God, Psalm 68 is a song of triumph. The first half of the psalm contains a number of references to Israel's exodus from Egypt and journey to the promised land. The song was probably used to commemorate Israel's victories throughout its history. Eventually the first-century church will adopt a portion of this psalm as a reference to the resurrection and ascension of Jesus Christ (68:18; Ephesians 4:8).

The psalmist points out in verses 1–3 that while those who love God are joyful as He rises to lead them, those who do not love God have no hope. No one can interfere with the progress of God. His opponents are blown away like a puff of smoke and melt like wax near a flame. The joy of God's people is for good reason because God responds to their needs and hurts. He is Father and defender, provider of fellowship for the lonely and the source of song among prisoners (68:4–6).

Verse 6 says those who rebel against God find themselves in a sun-scorched land. The righteous, however, can be in a wasteland and still experience God's provision through pouring rain and abundant showers (68:7–9). The mention of the shaking earth and Sinai in verse 8 would have reminded the psalmist's listeners of their people's journey through the wilderness. Settling in their inheritance is in reference to the promised land (68:9–10).

Continuing the review of Israel's journey, the next phase was the conquest of the land. Canaan was inhabited with various nations and their kings, but they all fled before Israel (68:11–14). This passage is difficult to interpret, but some believe Israel was God's dove and that the silver and gold probably represent the spoils of Israel's battles (68:13). Others think the dove might have been one of many valuable spoils of war, or that the dove and the colors could have referred to the colorful banners of the Canaanite kings. Either way, God's decisive victory is like white snow covering a dark mountain (the meaning of ZALMON).

The land contained many impressive and majestic mountains. In verses 15–16, the psalmist describes a feeling of jealousy the mountains felt toward Mount Zion because that was where God had established His dwelling place, the temple. In His grand entrance into His city, God is accompanied by a procession of thousands upon thousands of angels, portrayed as riding chariots (68:17). The captives and gifts in verse 18 are associated with victory in battle—submission and tribute even from those who had rebelled and lost.

Enthroned in His city, God is praised by the psalmist. In His sovereignty, God regularly bears the burdens of His people, saves them from death, and allows them to rejoice in the defeat of their enemies (68:19–23). God's procession to the temple was a festive occasion involving the whole nation. The singers and musicians established a celebratory atmosphere, and they were followed by the tribes of the nation. Only four tribes are mentioned by name, but they are representative of large and small, north and south (68:27).

Israel still had powerful enemies, so the psalmist asks God to continue to provide strength for the nation. Israel's enemies would be scattered and humbled (68:28–31). As God displays His sovereignty, the appropriate response of all nations—not just Israel—should be submission and praise (68:31–35).

PSALM 69

After the thrill and exultation of Psalm 68, Psalm 69 goes to the opposite extreme. David has sunk to a point where he can't get much lower. The psalm opens in verses 1–2 with a sequence of metaphors to describe his mood: waters up to his neck, sinking in mud with no foothold, swallowed up in deep waters. He can neither see God nor hear His voice; he receives no answer when he calls (69:3).

Meanwhile, David's enemies have taken full advantage of his desperate situation. He has done nothing to offend them, yet they are out to destroy him. He has to defend himself for things he has not done (69:4).

David admits he has sinned in verse 5, and he even acknowledges a wound from God (69:26). Perhaps he realizes his unenviable condition is God's discipline. Still, as verse 6 points out, he cares about how he carries himself as a believer in the Lord. He doesn't want to do anything that reflects badly on his Lord or impede someone else's spiritual progress. He has wept, fasted, and dressed in sackcloth, yet he continues to suffer painful indignities: scorn, mocking, shame, insults, and even taunting songs from drunkards on the street (69:7–12).

As a young person, already anointed to be the next king and on the run constantly from King Saul, David had learned to wait for God's timing. Here his patience is displayed during his spiritual crisis. He will attempt to stay above water until the time of God's favor (69:13–15). He trusts God and counts on His mercy and love, yet his struggle is severe. He hopes for a quick resolution, and he continues to detail his circumstances in his prayer (69:16–21).

David's persecutors are absolutely merciless, and in verse 22 he begins to pray more for retribution against them than deliverance for himself. Essentially, he wants them to experience the same things he is feeling: weakness, isolation, and despair. Even worse, he wants God to judge them harsher by blotting them out of His book of life (69:22–29).

Critical Observation

The book of life is mentioned from time to time throughout scripture. It appears to be an image that represents a record of those whom God has declared righteous. New Testament references to this book suggest that those whose names are listed can anticipate eternal life with God (see Philippians 4:3; Revelation 3:5; 13:8).

David is fully convinced that God hears those who are in need, and he is surely included in that category. Therefore he is able to glorify God in spite of his suffering. He could have offered sacrifices, yet he realizes God is more pleased with his heartfelt expressions of praise and thanksgiving. God will deliver David and all of His people (69:30–36).

The addition of verses 34–36 expands the usage of the psalm. It is not just one person's struggle to endure the taunts of his or her enemies but also a challenge for the entire nation to raise their voices to God.

PSALM 70

Although similar in theme to the previous psalm, Psalm 70 is more closely tied to Psalm 40. It appears to be a reworking of 40:13–17.

In verses 1–3, David again prays for God's hasty deliverance from a crowd of hostile enemies. They are mocking him while he is unable to retaliate, so David asks God to let them experience shame and confusion.

If David's deliverance is witnessed by others, they can then see for themselves that God is faithful and trustworthy (70:4). As a result, David's salvation might inspire the praise of many who believe in God.

David continues to be at the mercy of his enemies, but he has put his trust in a merciful God. He anticipates God's response soon—hopefully without further delay (70:5).

PSALM 71

Psalm 71 was written by someone who had the benefit, or perhaps the liability, of age. The psalmist looks back over his life and attests to his ongoing faith in God throughout the years. No introduction is provided. However, the next psalm is attributed to Solomon, which suggests to some scholars that this one may have been written from David's perspective as an older man. Psalms 71 and 72 close out Book II of the biblical book Psalms.

There is much to be said about an older person who continues to recognize his or her need for God. In verses 1–3, the psalmist expresses complete dependence on God. Surely the aggression of one's enemies seems even worse during old age (71:4), but God remains the psalmist's rock and refuge.

One advantage of the psalmist's age is his ability to look back over his life and see repeated proof of God's faithfulness. God had been involved in his life since birth, so he has no reason to think God will abandon him now (71:5–6).

Some people assume his problems are a sign that something is amiss in his spiritual life

(71:7). Others simply want to attack while he is weak and it seems God has deserted him (71:11). But the psalmist doesn't overly concern himself with what others say or do. He may have been older and weaker, but his God is as strong as ever (71:8–13).

Speaking with the wisdom of age, the psalmist continues to place his hope in God. He had not yet discovered the full extent of God's righteousness and salvation, but he had seen more than enough to proclaim God's goodness to others (71:14–16).

Thinking back to his childhood and to his current world as a gray-haired man, he can attest to God's power throughout his lifetime (71:17–18). With that knowledge, he is more eager than ever to have God near him. In his lifetime he has seen his share of problems, but he is confident that God will again restore him. Meanwhile, he will continue to acknowledge God's righteousness, praise His faithfulness, tell others of His steadfastness, and sing and shout with joy (71:19–24).

PSALM 72

Psalm 72 is one of two psalms attributed to Solomon, the other being Psalm 127. As with many of the superscriptions throughout Psalms, there is much debate as to whether the designated writer is actually the author. Many argue that rather than being written *by* Solomon, Psalm 72 may have been written *for* Solomon. John Calvin even suggests that this psalm is David's dying declaration, recorded by Solomon for posterity.

The content of Psalm 72 makes it an appropriate prayer or tribute for any king, and it is likely that it was used during various coronation ceremonies. The opening verses repeatedly emphasize a desire for justice and righteousness. Israel's king is in a position to help the poor and downtrodden as judge, provider, and protector (72:1–4, 12–14).

Verses 5–7 vary according to translation. Conceivably, the assurance of blessing and life beyond the sun and moon could apply to God. However, the poetic language may be intended to refer to the human king. In that case, the intent of the verses would be that the righteous reign of a good king continues to influence many generations to come.

The boundaries of Israel were never larger than during the reign of Solomon. The psalmist anticipates the king's widespread influence that includes the Euphrates, Tarshish (modern Spain), Sheba (the Arabian Peninsula), and Seba (northern Egypt). The specific sites are not named to detail the outer boundaries of the kingdom but rather to suggest that it will have no limits. The king's enemies will be submissive, and many kings from around the world will bring him tribute (72:8–11).

The psalmist then reiterates the concern of the king for the weak and oppressed in verses 12–14, followed by a wish for his long life and prosperity. He also calls on the people to support their king with prayers and blessings. The king's influence will extend to many nations (72:15–17).

The next verses apply to the entire second book of Psalms, not just Psalm 72. A doxology concludes each of the five sections (72:18–19).

Demystifying Psalms

The notation in verse 20 most likely referred at one time to a more limited collection of psalms that were all ascribed to David. The psalms of David do not end here, but they begin to be scarcer. Book III of Psalms begins with a long series of poems attributed to Asaph.

Take It Home

Book II within Psalms comes to an end at just about the midpoint of the biblical book. Based on what you've read so far, what recurring themes have you detected? Has any of the content surprised (or confused) you? What do you think about David's and others' frankness in their appeals to God?

PSALMS: BOOK III

PSALMS 73–89

Setting Up the Section

Book III of Psalms contains seventeen psalms, eleven of which are attributed to Asaph. However, several of the psalms contain references to events in Israel's history that would have been later than Asaph's lifetime, so there is good reason to believe that some of these psalms were penned by his descendants.

PSALM 73

According to their superscriptions, Psalms 73–83 are all credited to Asaph, one of the three men David had assigned to head Israel's choirs. The other two leaders are Heman and Ethan (Jeduthun [see 1 Chronicles 15:16–19]), who each are credited with one psalm in Book III of Psalms (Psalms 88 and 89).

Psalm 73 demonstrates the difference one's acknowledgment of God can make in his or her spiritual outlook. The psalmist is surprisingly honest in describing his envy of prosperous people. The fact that they are also arrogant and wicked only intensifies his confusion (73:3).

According to verses 4–9, the psalmist had paid close attention to such people. Based on his observations, they are healthy, strong, and worry-free. They have little in common with the average person, so they tend to be proud, insensitive, and self-centered. They have a sense of entitlement that surpasses earthly bounds and leads them to lay claim to heaven as well. Since it appears that the proud and selfish people aren't held accountable for their actions, others become enamored and even tempted to join their ranks (73:10–11).

From the psalmist's initial perspective in verse 12, such people seem to become ever wealthier and perpetually carefree. This distresses him. His thoughts even take a dark turn in verse 13, as he wonders if his commitment to righteousness and innocence has been for nothing. And with such a perspective, his sufferings make no sense (73:14).

Then, at exactly the midpoint of his psalm, the psalmist has an epiphany. He goes to the temple and realizes he is only seeing half the story. He is glad that he hasn't spoken his thoughts out loud (73:15–17). When he is able to see things from God's viewpoint, he realizes where the wealthy, arrogant people are headed. They are not on solid ground; they are traveling a road to ruin and destruction. Those who terrify others will be faced with terrors of their own (73:18–20).

After regaining his spiritual sight, the psalmist is contrite before God. According to verse 22, he feels like a "brute beast" (NIV)—senseless and ignorant. He has wasted time being bitter and hurt. He realizes that God has always been there for him and will continue to lead him. Nothing in heaven or earth can compare to that reality (73:21–26).

The psalmist closes in verses 27–28 with the comforting promise that God remains a refuge for all who remain near to Him. But in contrast, those who defy God will surely be destroyed.

PSALM 74

The temple in Jerusalem fell to the Babylonians in 586 BC, and the people of Judah were carried off in successive waves. Some of the psalms, such as Psalm 74, were written while they were in exile.

The loss of both God's temple and their beloved city was hard on the people of Jerusalem, even though they realized the judgment of God was well deserved. In this case, the psalmist never claims innocence but wonders how long God's anger will continue. The Israelites are still God's sheep, whom He had delivered in times past. God had indeed used the Babylonian army to impose His judgment on Judah, but the psalmist realizes that Judah's enemies are still enemies of God as well.

The Babylonians offended and insulted God. In verse 4, the psalmist points out their blatant disregard for God's dwelling place and His sanctuary. Their violent actions are bad enough, but their arrogance toward God is far worse (74:4–8), so the silence of God is mystifying. When Egypt had opposed God's people, God had responded with many miraculous signs to free His people. This time, however, there are no signs, and God's prophets appear to be absent (74:9).

Critical Observation

We know that prophets continued to minister throughout the exile. For example, Ezekiel went to Babylon (Ezekiel 1:1–3) and Jeremiah went to Egypt (Jeremiah 43:6–7). Conceivably the psalmist was with the remnant of people left in the Jerusalem area, who may have had no working prophet among them. Or his comment in Psalm 74:9 may mean that he isn't receiving the answers he is seeking.

Sadly, the silence of God is offset by the jeering of Israel's enemies (74:10). In verse 11, the psalmist boldly suggests that God is sitting with His hands in His lap, and he urges the Lord to retaliate. The psalmist certainly does not doubt the power of God, who is Israel's only source of salvation (74:12–13). The *Leviathan* mentioned in verse 14 represents the forces of chaos, which are no match for the power of the Lord. Creation itself is under God's control, including seasons and heavenly bodies. God can create springs of water where none exist and stop mighty rivers in their tracks (74:15–17).

Therefore, the psalmist has confidence that God will protect His people, even in their terrible situation. Adding to his confidence is the fact that God had established a covenant with Israel. For now, their enemies have the upper hand and demonstrate a continual uproar, but their clamor will not last forever. God will surely silence them as He protects and delivers Israel, His dove (74:18–23).

PSALM 75

Psalm 75 is an expression of confidence in God during a time when Israel is surrounded by arrogant and powerful nations. Verse 1 opens with the psalmist's thanksgiving for God's presence. The connection between the nearness of God's name and people telling of His deeds can be understood in two ways. Perhaps it means that those who worship the name of God naturally begin to talk about the great things He has done. Or it may be the other way around: As people recall the wonderful deeds of God, they can't help but give thanks that He remains so near.

In verses 2–3, the psalmist abruptly shifts to God's voice, and God speaks as a judge. God's judgment may shake the earth and its people, yet He continues to be a stabilizing force.

Verses 4–6 portray arrogant people as unruly animals with outstretched necks and raised horns, resisting any kind of control. God warns such people to humble themselves. No power on earth can overrule God's judgment, so it is the essence of wisdom to yield to God while there is still time.

When God's judgment is pronounced, it is like a potent wine the guilty are forced to drink, replacing their self-confidence and arrogance with an intoxicating stupor. The psalmist wants no part of such judgment and commits himself to praise God for as long as he lives (75:9). It appears that he returns to God's voice in verse 10. Almost certainly it is God who intends to lift up the righteous while cutting off the horns of the wicked—their source of power and pride.

PSALM 76

A victorious song celebrating the power of God, Psalm 76 focuses on what God has done for Judah. The psalmist writes of God's deliverance from Israel's enemies after an aggressive action toward Jerusalem. (Both Salem and Zion are references to Jerusalem [76:2].) Some scholars attempt to pinpoint the exact battle the psalmist refers to, and their opinions vary. Others believe his intent is more general—that God had delivered His people from any number of warring nations (76:3).

Demystifying Psalms

After God's people left Egypt, they soon became known as the nation of Israel, or the Israelites. After Solomon's reign, when the kingdom was divided, a distinction began to be made between Israel (the northern tribes) and Judah (the southern kingdom). But after both Israel and Judah had been defeated and their people exiled, the distinction was not as necessary. In many cases, as in verse 1, the two names are used interchangeably.

The description of God in verse 4 is magnificent. He is the essence of light and majesty. His rebuke of the wicked is a severe and perhaps final display of His wrath (76:5–6). For those who oppose God, His judgment is terrifying, producing silence across the land. But others will delight in the judgment of God because it means that at last they are free of those who regularly afflict them (76:7–9).

Verse 10 can be translated a couple of different ways. One option is to understand that God's wrath against people brings Him praise. In that case, the praise comes from those whom He delivers as well as from any who realize they might have been included in His judgment, yet were spared. A second option is to interpret the verse to read that the wrath of people brings praise to God. In that sense, when people stand defiantly against a sovereign Lord, God is always triumphant. Consequently, His sure and certain victories bring Him praise.

With such an understanding of God, it becomes incumbent on people to devote themselves to Him. Instead of fearful defiance, God wants people to submit to Him, honor their vows, and offer gifts to the sovereign Lord (76:11–12).

PSALM 77

Sometimes prayers begin with a focus on God and eventually work their way into the needs and desires of the individuals. Other times prayer starts with what is on the mind of the pray-er, and only after unloading one's concerns is the person able to shift to spiritual matters. Psalm 77 is in the latter category.

To the psalmist's credit, he has turned to God in his misery and unease. He is spiritually and emotionally fragile—in distress, unsettled, and faint of heart (77:1–3). But prayer doesn't seem to help at first. In the past he had been able to rejoice at nighttime and sing of the deliverance of God; now, because of his personal troubles, he is simply unable to sleep (77:4–6).

In verse 5, the thoughts of how God had helped him in the past, contrasted with God's seeming distance in the present, have the psalmist in a quandary. God doesn't appear to be responsive now. Would He ever respond again? The psalmist acknowledges God's unfailing love, so the thought that it might have failed is quite disconcerting (77:6–9).

Still, the psalmist can't stop thinking about God's power that had been displayed time after time to deliver previous generations of His people. There is simply too much evidence of God's involvement in Israel's history for the psalmist to give up hope at this point (77:11–12).

God is still holy, all-powerful, and a worker of miracles. No person, no force, no so-called god is greater. With renewed enthusiasm, the psalmist begins to recall one of God's greatest deliverances, the exodus of the Hebrew people from Egypt. To begin with, God's involvement was evident in the fact that the Israelites had made it safely away from Egypt and into the well-protected confines of the promised land. But more than that, God's presence had been dramatically displayed through the miraculous parting of the Red Sea, thunder and lightning atop Mount Sinai, earthquakes, and other means. Beyond a doubt, God had been with His people. Therefore, any doubts about God are unfounded. He is still a God of power and love who will deliver His people (77:13–20).

PSALM 78

Several of the psalms recall God's deliverance of His people from Egypt as evidence of His strength, love, and care for Israel. However, few are as extensive as Psalm 78.

The purpose of recalling God's previous faithfulness is to inspire and assure future generations. The stories are to be passed along. In one sense the teachings of God are parables and "hidden lessons" (78:2 NLT), yet not in any kind of mystical or secretive sense. They are clearly understandable (78:2–8). Jesus' parables are similar, as Matthew will later point out (Matthew 13:35) by quoting verse 2 of this psalm.

Hearing the facts about God's previous miracles is one thing; responding properly is another. Generations of Israelites had been stubborn and rebellious because they forgot the wonders of God (Psalm 78:8–12). Verse 7 points out the goal for future generations: to not forget and to place faith in God and keep His commands.

In the psalmist's recap of the Exodus, he points out the great contrast between God's faithfulness and the people's lack of faith. According to the image in verse 13, God had made the water of the Red Sea firm like a wall. When people complained of thirst in the wilderness, God had split rocks to create a source of flowing water (78:15–16). Such miracles that demonstrate God's unique power were performed purely for the benefit of His people.

Yet the Israelites were not long impressed with abundant water. They soon complained about the lack of food. Their utter disregard for the things God had done for them, and their instinct to immediately gripe about what they didn't have, made God angry. Still, God did not desert them. He provided food on a regular basis (78:23–25), as well as occasional feasts of quail (78:26–29). The manna was the "bread of angels" (78:25 NIV)—food dropped from heaven to feed thousands of people every day.

But the people continued to sin and rebel (78:17–18). God sent fire as a warning (Numbers 11:1–3; Psalm 78:21–22). Still, they didn't learn. Some of those who disregarded God's provision and continued to crave other food were stricken with a plague and died (Numbers 11:33–34; Psalm 78:30–31). God was attempting to lead them to a land flowing with milk and honey, yet the generation of those who began the journey died in futility and terror because they refused to acknowledge God's wondrous provision of food and water along the way (78:32–33).

The only thing that seemed to capture their attention was God's anger. When a group of people died as a result of their sinful actions and attitudes, the survivors eagerly turned to God again. But their repentance was short-lived. They would continue to say the right words, but they were not sincere. Again and again they provoked God, but in His mercy He had not ultimately destroyed them (78:34–41).

The Israelites *should* have learned from God's dealings with the Egyptians. They had seen the series of plagues fall on Egypt (78:42–51)—displays of God's anger, wrath, and hostility. And then He led His people like a shepherd leads sheep, through a path that took them right through a dried-up Red Sea to the promised land. Upon their arrival, He went before them to drive out the hostile nations and allow the Israelites to settle (78:52–55).

In spite of everything God had done for them, the people were no better in the promised land than they had been in the wilderness. During the era of the judges, the Israelites were quick to forsake God and turn to idols. By the time of Samuel, God had allowed the ark of the covenant to be lost, and many Israelites were killed in battle (78:56–64).

Demystifying Psalms

Ephraim was a large, prominent, and well-protected tribe in the northern kingdom. Judah was a much smaller tribe to the south. Yet it was from Judah that God chose David to rise up, confront, and defeat the many enemies of Israel. It seems that the people of Ephraim had an opportunity to prove themselves but had failed to do so (78:9–11, 67–68), although the specific occasion is not known.

If it seemed that God was sleeping as the Philistines ran roughshod over Israel, it wasn't long before He awoke to deliver His people yet again. In something of a surprise, the tribe of Judah rose to prominence with the exploits of David, who not only proved to be a great military figure but a spiritual leader as well. It was David who had established Jerusalem (Zion) and had brought the ark there (78:65–69).

In the observation of the psalmist, David had never stopped being a shepherd. God had simply moved him from tending his family's sheep to shepherding the Israelites. In contrast to so many kings who would come after him, David led his people with integrity and skill (78:70–72). The reign of David was a high point in the history of Israel being passed on for future generations to learn and repeat.

PSALM 79

Psalm 79 is one of the poems written during Israel's exile, recalling the tragic destruction of Jerusalem and the current helpless situation of the people. It was a perplexing state of affairs. Clearly, the fall of Judah and the exile had been God's judgment on His people, and He had used the Babylonians to carry it out. But now, from the psalmist's standpoint, a bigger problem is the attitude heathen nations show toward God.

Jerusalem was God's city, and the desecration of the temple was a particular insult. The Israelites had deserved punishment, and they had suffered for what they had done. But as verses 1–4 show, it seems that God's reputation is at stake. The mocking and scorn they continue to receive is also a derision of their God.

The question in verse 5 ("How long?") is a common query of the psalmists. The people had suffered personal pain and loss. Now their suffering is intensified as foreign nations laugh at the perceived impotence of their God. The psalmist requests mercy for Israel but judgment for the other nations that arrogantly assume that they are strong and in control (79:6–8). The sins of the fathers in verse 8 include generations of widespread idolatry and apostasy, with little concern for the things of God. But the people exiled in Babylon were contrite and repentant, so the psalmist feels emboldened to ask God to take action against Israel's enemies (79:9–11).

The Israelites are prisoners in the sense that they are imprisoned in another country. They are condemned to die away from the freedoms and blessings they had taken for granted. The psalmist's prayer is not simply for their release and return but also for God's retribution. *Seven* (79:12) is a number of completeness, in essence a request that God's action against the nations be total destruction.

The Israelites had strayed and had been reprimanded for it, but the psalmist still believes that they are God's people, the sheep of His pasture (79:13). And as he looks to the future, he envisions not a continuation of suffering and exile but many successive generations all offering their praise to God.

PSALM 80

Psalm 79 concludes with the concept of God as a Shepherd and the people as sheep, and Psalm 80 begins with similar imagery. Going further into the psalm, it becomes clear that the people *need* a shepherd—someone far more powerful than their enemies. In this case, the heavenly Shepherd is on a throne among angels, and His power is beyond question. So in his prayer for deliverance, the psalmist asks God to show His mighty power (80:1–2).

The three tribes mentioned in verse 2 suggest that the psalm is referring to the northern kingdom. When the nation divided after the reign of Solomon, his son Rehoboam was left with only the tribe of Judah. Geographically, portions of Benjamin were adjacent to Jerusalem—clearly as far south as Judah, but still considered at that point a northern tribe. If indeed the psalmist writes of the northern tribes here, then the aggressors would have been the Assyrians.

God is angry with His people, and as a consequence they have become a laughingstock for their enemies. Such mocking is difficult to endure. Tears had become both the food and drink of the Israelites (80:4–6). The psalmist's request for restoration is repeated throughout the psalm, in verses 3, 7, and 19.

The psalmist compares Israel to a vine that God had uprooted in Egypt and grafted into the promised land (80:8–10). At first its influence had been only positive, providing grapes and valuable shade to a large area. In verse 11, the sea is most likely the Mediterranean, and the river probably the Euphrates.

Eventually, however, God had withdrawn His protection. Without the security of walls, the vine is exposed to both passersby who take the grapes and wild animals that feed on it (80:12–13). In time the vine is cut down and burned (80:16). But the God who had grafted the vine to begin with is still more than capable of reviving it (80:14–15).

Demystifying Psalms

The terminology in this psalm may sound oddly familiar to those who have read the New Testament. The references to God's son (80:15) and son of man (80:17) are both commonly applied to Jesus. In the Old Testament world, however, "the son of God" was often a reference to the nation's king. And in this case, the reference might have been to Israel. (The word translated *son* can also mean "branch," and in the context of what the psalmist had written about the vine, this option would make sense.) Another possibility is that the son of man is a reference to Benjamin. This figure is also addressed as "the man at your right hand" (80:17 NIV), and the literal interpretation of *Benjamin* is "son of the right hand."

It is unclear exactly whom the psalmist refers to as the son of God, the son of man, and the man at God's right hand (80:15–17). What *is* clear, however, is the psalmist's desire for God's protection over that figure as well as the entire nation. In verse 19, the writer once again appeals for God's deliverance and restoration. And this time, as he says in verse 18, the people will stay committed and no longer turn away from God.

PSALM 81

The Day of Atonement was the most solemn and somber observance in the Hebrew year. But it was soon followed by the Feast of Tabernacles (Numbers 29:12–38; Deuteronomy 16:13–17), a weeklong joyful celebration of harvest and God's blessings. Psalm 81 is frequently thought to be a song used during the Feast. Some people prefer to associate the psalm with Passover because it mentions Israel's ordeal in Egypt and the wilderness, but the enthusiastic tone of the psalm makes it appropriate for a more festive celebration.

God had instructed people to be joyful at the Feast of Tabernacles (Deuteronomy 16:14), so the psalmist's opening instruction is to sing for joy and shout aloud. Harvest was a time when it was impossible to overlook what God was doing for His people. The jubilant mood is heightened with instrumental music to accompany the singing (Psalm 81:2). The ram's horn mentioned in verse 3 was probably used less as a musical instrument than to provide a ceremonial signal (Exodus 19:13, 16, 19).

Critical Observation

The Jewish year was established on a lunar cycle. The first day of the seventh month occurred with the new moon (Psalm 81:3), acknowledged by the ram's horn trumpet blast (Leviticus 23:24). This eventually became the Jewish New Year, because it wrapped up the harvest season and began a rainy, planting season. The Feast of Tabernacles did not begin until the full moon on the fifteenth of the month (Psalm 81:3), and the horn was sounded again.

Joseph, mentioned in verse 5, is a term for the northern kingdom (as opposed to Judah)—not a personal reference to the Old Testament patriarch. The reference to the language they don't understand is to the tongues of the various nations that Israel encounters.

The verses that follow (81:6–16) shift to a first-person address from God to the people. (This section would probably have been spoken by a designated Levite.) God had set His people free and had rescued them both from the Egyptians and the elements as they trekked through the wilderness. Meribah was the place where God had instructed Moses to strike the rock to provide water for the people (Exodus 17:1–7; Psalm 81:7). God had also provided ample food (81:10) and would have continued to do so, except the people had disobeyed His clear instructions to keep away from the gods of the alien nations (81:8–9, 11–12).

God had allowed the Israelites to go their own way, and they had suffered for it. Yet He is eager for the situation to improve. He promises immediate victory over their enemies if the people will listen and obey (81:13–14).

At this harvest celebration, the people would have certainly responded to the closing verses of being fed with the finest wheat (81:15–16) rather than finding themselves cringing before God. The honey from the rock mentioned in verse 16 is, in this case, a product of bees that had made their nests among the rocks. In many instances, however, when the Bible speaks of honey, it is a reference to a sweet concoction made from the fruit of the date palm.

PSALM 82

With the opening verse of Psalm 82, the reader is immediately faced with a question: Who are the gods the psalmist writes about? To the nations surrounding Israel, such a reference would make them think of their own pantheon of gods, much like the Greek deities thought to operate from atop Mount Olympus. Even the kings of many secular nations were often referred to as gods. The Israelites might have conceivably thought of angels among the great assembly of God.

In Israel, judges and kings are supposed to represent the Lord and model His concern and protection for people who might be taken advantage of. Yet those human rulers are included among those taking advantage of the poor, weak, and otherwise helpless (82:2–3). The description of such people in verse 5 is accurate, but truly bleak.

This psalm serves as a reminder of a ruler's job description. Rather than adding to the woes of the weak and poor, Israel's leaders are supposed to defend and rescue such people. But in order to save them from wicked people, those in authority first must stop being wicked themselves.

In the end, the only judge who matters is God. The human rulers may have a high position for a while, but they will meet the same end as everyone else. The more the psalmist thinks about the difference between God's rule and human leadership, the more he desires God's authority (82:6–8).

PSALM 83

David writes a number of psalms imploring God to intervene when he is being attacked by numerous personal enemies. This psalm is similar to those of David's, but here the threat is to the nation of Judah as a whole; the enemies are not individual people, but foreign nations.

The psalmist appeals to God to take action, and as he provides more details, the situation is indeed critical. Israel's enemies have formed a coalition with the goal of completely obliterating the nation (83:1–4). The list of enemies in verses 5–8 includes several nations that have regularly initiated conflict (Edomites, Moabites, Ammonites, Philistines, and Assyrians), along with some less familiar names. If the psalmist writes of a specific historic event, it is not recorded elsewhere in scripture. It may be that he lists a number of nations that have oppressed and corrupted Israel, intending for them to be representative of *all* of Israel's enemies.

In order to understand what the psalmist is asking of God in verses 9–12, some readers may need a history lesson to identify the names he recalls. Sisera and Jabin were the oppressors of Israel under the judgeship of Deborah and Barak (Judges 4–5). The four men named in verse 11 were defeated by Gideon (Judges 7–8). All the listed opponents of Israel had been strong and threatening, and Israel's victories had been clear signs of God's power and protection.

The psalmist asks God to respond the same way with Israel's new batch of enemies. The power of God has not diminished, so the psalmist wants to see his nation's enemies blown away like tumbleweeds. God's pursuit could be like fire spreading through a thicket or a deadly storm rolling in, resulting in both terror and shame (83:13–16). But the goal is not simply the removal of enemies; the desired result is that people will witness the power of God and turn to Him.

The list of nations represents much power in the ancient world. But the psalmist's closing reminder is that God alone is the Most High over all the powers on earth. And since those who oppose Him die in shame and confusion, perhaps others will acknowledge God and change their wicked ways (83:17–18).

PSALM 84

After someone has experienced a rich and rewarding relationship with God, it changes the person's perspective on life. Psalm 84 is an expression of longing by the psalmist to be closer to God and *remain* close. The opening verses appear to focus on the temple building with its courts, yet by the end of the psalm it becomes clear that it is the presence of God Himself that the writer desires.

Worshipers tend to feel closer to God at the temple. A person's approach to God is heightened through priestly intercession, and praise and worship take on a more public, communal feel. The psalmist is even jealous of the birds that nest in and around the temple, living among the priests (84:1–4).

But the writer appears to be one of many pilgrims who journeys only occasionally to Jerusalem (84:5). The Valley of Baca mentioned in verse 6 is not a known geographic location. *Baca* can refer to balsam trees or weeping, and the psalmist's phrase may be metaphorical, like David's "valley of the shadow of death" (23:4). A long journey to Jerusalem could be strenuous and even dangerous, but the psalmist thinks only about the positive aspects of the trip and the ultimate destination (84:6–7).

Verses 8–9 include a prayer for the king. The psalmist also tries to express the degree of his love for God's temple. He declares it a thousand times better than being anywhere else, and he would rather be a doorkeeper there than to live and thrive elsewhere (84:10).

Being in the presence of God at His temple is akin to standing in the brightness of the sun, yet being shielded and protected at the same time. For those who can stand before Him blameless, God will grant blessing and deny nothing good (84:11). Trust in God, however, is essential in receiving what He has to offer (84:12).

PSALM 85

Psalm 85 is another of the songs where the author acknowledges experiencing the wrath of God. Many such psalms have to do with the period of exile of the Israelites. Some people believe this particular psalm speaks of the situation that the people faced shortly afterward, when they returned to their homeland from Babylon, although no strong proof exists.

The psalmist takes hope as he looks to the past and reviews how God has previously shown His anger and yet forgiven the people and relented (85:1–3). The psalm contains no outright confession of wrongdoing, although the psalmist implies as much in verses 4–6 by asking God to suspend His anger and once again restore the nation.

God's love is unfailing, and His salvation is always available (85:7). He offers guidance that results in peace for those who listen and obey. But the pursuit of folly prevents people from benefiting from God's wisdom (85:8–9).

The psalmist emphasizes the gifts of God by describing them in pairs: love and faithfulness, righteousness and peace, faithfulness and righteousness. Even more than pairs, they appear to be married together in verses 9–11. Despite the current troubles of his nation, the psalmist maintains confidence that God will still provide good things for His people. The Lord's righteousness will prevail (85:12–13).

PSALM 86

Of all the psalms in Book III of the biblical book of Psalms (Psalms 73–89), this is the only one attributed to David. While many of the previous psalms are appeals to God on a national level, Psalm 86 is the prayer of an individual concerning his personal troubles.

Verse 1 provides David's general state of mind. He is poor and needy, but the specifics of his situation aren't revealed until later. First he wants to appeal to God for mercy and protection. David's trust is in God and he is quick to seek help, but his current situation has robbed him of joy (86:2–4). He is counting on God's love and forgiveness, fully expecting an answer (86:5–7).

David next acknowledges God's uniqueness. No other entity is like God in character or in accomplishments. God's "wondrous deeds" (86:10 NASB) single Him out from all other potential contenders. Consequently, David expects that all the nations will eventually worship and glorify God (86:8–9).

David desires instruction from God. He wants to know truth and to cultivate an undivided heart. God has loved him and delivered him, and he wants to praise and glorify the Lord as a result (86:11–13).

Only then does David get to the crux of the matter: He is being personally attacked by numerous unrighteous people who want his life. But his specific complaint doesn't matter; he has already entrusted himself to God, so the nature of the problem is inconsequential. God can handle it (86:13–14).

Demystifying Psalms

David's observation in verse 15 may have been based on his recollection of the law, specifically Exodus 34:6. If so, his recitation stops at a point that maintains a positive focus on his situation. As he prays for his enemies, he could have easily included the next phrase of the Exodus quote: the observation that God will punish the guilty (Exodus 34:7).

In addition, David acknowledges God's great grace and compassion. Since God has been slow to become angry with David in the past, perhaps the psalmist can understand why God doesn't immediately condemn others who are behaving sinfully. Therefore, rather than ask for his enemies' quick demise, David asks God to do something good for him that they will see—and perhaps shame them into repentance (86:16–17). In the meantime, David counts on God's strength, deliverance, help, and comfort.

PSALM 87

Psalm 87 is a distinctive and intriguing psalm that focuses on Zion as God's city and dwelling place. The date of the psalm is unclear—whether before, during, or after the exile of Israel.

Zion is certainly special because of the presence of God there. The earth is the Lord's (24:1), but of all the locations on earth, God has designated one particular mountaintop as a headquarters, of sorts. Even among the geography of Jacob (Israel), Zion is prominent in the eyes of God (87:1–2).

Psalm 87 stands out because of its inclusion of nations who are persistent enemies of Israel. The Babylonians and Philistines have been aggressive foes. *Rahab* is a name for the upper Nile region of Egypt (originating in mythological references). *Cush* is the area that is now southern Egypt, northern Ethiopia, and Sudan. And *Tyre* is the representative city of Phoenicia. These nations have created havoc and suffering for Israel. In other psalms, they are the nations the psalmists might ask God to destroy. Here, however, they are being granted citizenship into God's city and given privileges associated with birthright (87:4–6). The psalmist makes it clear in verse 4, however, that the reason these peoples are invited into the rolls of the city of God is because they acknowledge the Lord.

The fountains mentioned in verse 7 typify the blessings of God. Therefore, the music of the nations will acknowledge that God is the source of all good things.

PSALM 88

David is credited with several gloomy and dismal psalms, but Psalm 88 (by a different psalmist) is as grim as any that David ever wrote. It is similar to David's Psalm 22, which Jesus quotes while hanging on the cross.

The psalmist is clearly a person of faith, which makes his situation all the more excruciating. He steadfastly clings to his belief in God, but he can hardly come up with a single positive event in his life. The precise nature of his affliction is unknown, although it appears to be life threatening. In fact, he has already begun to associate himself with those already dead (88:3–5). And dead people, in the thinking of Old Testament believers, are no longer under God's care.

His suffering appears to be a consequence of God's anger. The psalmist is overcome with personal misery that is further complicated when his closest friends abandon him in his pain. It feels like being trapped in a deep and dark pit with no escape (88:6–8).

Still, day after day the afflicted psalmist cries out to God. His is not just an emotional plea; he uses reason as well. He is eager, almost desperate, to experience the wonders of God and to respond with praise. If he is pushed any further, to the point of death, he will regret being no longer able to worship (88:9–12).

The psalmist will not give up on God. His cry in verse 13 echoes those in verses 1 and 9. He continues to pray each morning, even as he keeps wondering why God seems so distant. His problems began during his youth, and he is still seeking relief. Yet despite all his efforts, nothing has resolved the problem.

The final verse is perhaps the bleakest of all. His despair from the ongoing terrors he has suffered is too much for his friends. His companions have deserted him, and his closest companion is darkness (88:18). Still, he will continue to cry out to God day and night, awaiting the Lord's intervention in his life (88:1).

Demystifying Psalms

Levi had three sons—Merari, Gershon, and Kohath (1 Chronicles 6:16)—who oversaw divisions of tabernacle musicians. In turn, Levi's three sons had descendants who assumed the same roles (1 Chronicles 25:1, 6) and who appear in the superscriptions of the psalms. Jeduthun (Ethan) was from Merari's family. Asaph was a descendant of Gershon. Heman, the leader mentioned in connection with Psalm 88, was from the family of Kohath. Both Heman and Ethan (the designated author of Psalm 89) are noted for their wisdom in 1 Kings 4:31.

PSALM 89

This final entry in Book III of the biblical book of Psalms is another that scholars find difficult to date or to link to a historic event. It begins as a bold and confident expression of praise to God, but it takes a sudden shift at verse 38 and concludes as a lament.

In verses 1–2, the psalmist begins with acknowledgement of God's great love and faithfulness, characteristics that are evident both in heaven and on earth and will be noticed by all generations of people. At verses 3–4, he introduces the covenant God had established with David—a theme the psalmist will soon return to.

God is to be praised for many reasons. His work in creation is evident throughout the heavens (89:5), the earth (89:11), and the seas (89:9). The mountains (Tabor and Hermon) sing for joy in response (89:12). No other being can compare to the Lord (89:6–8). His works are apparent everywhere. He had destroyed Egypt (Rahab)—just one example of His great power (89:10, 13). His character is unquestionable; He is surrounded by righteousness, justice, love, and faithfulness (89:14), and His qualities influence and inspire humanity (89:15–18).

In verses 17–18, the psalmist uses a couple of metaphors for Israel's king. The human ruler serves as both a *horn* (a symbol of power) and a *shield* (a symbol of protection). Then the psalmist reviews the covenant that had been established between God and David.

David receives the support and blessings of God. He is victorious in all his battles. He calls God *Father*, and the Lord bestows on him the entitlements of a firstborn son. No one will be more successful as king. As a result, God promises to establish David's line forever. As it turns out, David's descendants aren't as faithful as they should be, and some blatantly disregard God's commands. They will receive God's punishment for their disobedience, but even so, God will not break His covenant with David. Israel can count on God's promises to endure forever (89:19–37), or so the psalmist thinks.

The reality of life, however, does not seem to fit the promises God has made, and the psalmist begins to bemoan his nation's situation. The current king (anointed one) has not proven faithful to God, and therefore God has become angry and rejected him (89:38). God's relationship with this king is antithetical to His relationship with David, as described in verses 40–45. This king experiences not only defeat in battle but also the scorn of his enemies. The nation has been plundered. Its former splendor has disappeared, and the king is impotent to do anything about it. From all appearances, it looks as if God has gone back on His covenant (89:39).

And yet the psalmist continues to seek answers. He is tired of hearing the insults and mocking of others directed toward his king. He knows life is short, and he wants to again experience the love of God. He knows God has made promises to David that are still in effect, but he just can't understand his nation's state of despair. He ends the psalm on that unsettled note.

The positive message of verse 52 is not part of the psalm. This final verse is a doxology inserted as a conclusion for Book III. Following the lament that ends Psalm 89, it is a welcome addition.

PSALMS: BOOK IV

PSALMS 90–106

Setting Up the Section

This section contains the compilation of psalms comprising Book IV of the biblical book of Psalms. In this portion of Psalms, the introductory superscriptions are less specific than previous ones, and several psalms lack introductions altogether. Only three of the seventeen psalms in this section identify the writer, so there is more mystery and speculation as to authors and dates.

PSALM 90

This psalm is attributed to Moses, which makes it several centuries older than the other psalms. It begins in verses 1–2 with an acknowledgment of the eternal God—the Creator of the world and everlasting refuge for humanity. He is the source of everything people need. "From everlasting to everlasting" (90:2 NIV) is an expression to emphasize God's eternity.

But in contrast to the always-existing God is the impermanence of humanity. Human lives are transitory. The longest recorded life is Methuselah's—a 969-year span (Genesis 5:27). But to God, a thousand years go by like a single day (or a short segment of one night) for a human being. In the context of eternity, a human life is akin to grass that sprouts new in the morning but has withered away by day's end. In a short time, people return to dust (Psalm 90:3–6).

Critical Observation

For the Israelites, a "watch in the night" (90:4) was about four hours. The night was divided into three watches: (1) sunset until 10:00 PM; (2) 10:00 PM until 2:00 AM; and (3) 2.00 AM until sunrise. In the New Testament, references to watches in the night may not conform to this schedule because the Romans scheduled four watches of three hours each.

The holiness of God quickly becomes evident to sinful humans, so the shortness of their lives is spent in struggle. When people sin and offend God, they may experience God's wrath. Some people spend the entire span of their lives feeling that God is angry at them, and they try to keep their secret sins hidden, to no avail (90:7–9).

The lifespan of seventy or eighty years referred to in verse 10 is respectable. A study of Egyptian mummies has suggested that an Egyptian from the same approximate time period had an average life expectancy of forty to fifty years. However, if a person's years are filled with nothing but trouble and sorrow, then long life is nothing to cherish (90:10).

Sin will always be offensive to God, and people will continue to sin. But rather than attempting to hide sin and provoke God's anger, Moses entreats God both for instruction that will lead to accumulated wisdom (90:11–12) and for divine compassion (90:13). If human life is but a day in the time frame of God, then let the morning begin with God's unfailing love that results in lasting joy and gladness (90:14).

Verse 15 may refer to a specific traumatic time for the nation. The exact nature of the trouble mentioned is not known, although under Moses' rule, Israel offended God numerous times and suffered affliction as a result. So Moses' prayer is for God to replace their trouble with gladness. The people may have been unfaithful to God, yet God has not failed to show His favor to Israel. As the people remain aware of His actions on their behalf and teach their children about the splendor of God, life will take on new meaning as God blesses their work (90:16–17).

PSALM 91

In the opening verse of Psalm 91, the psalmist uses two of the most laudable names for God: *Most High* and *Almighty*. In doing so, the psalmist begins a reasoned argument for why people can feel secure even during times of trouble. Rather than use first-person to speak only of his own experiences, he uses third-person to indicate that the comforting protection of God is available to anyone willing to seek God's guidance.

Many psalmists write of God as shelter, refuge, and fortress. In verse 2, the psalmist uses those same images but then goes into more specific examples of God's protective presence. In verses 3–6, enemies are presented symbolically: bird hunters who have set traps, widespread plague and pestilence, night terrors, and incoming arrows. These are not theoretical dangers; indeed, such threats have the capability of killing tens of thousands (91:7).

That is why taking refuge in God is so important; it's what makes the difference between security and susceptibility to danger. God covers His people like a mother bird covers her chicks with her feathers (91:4). While in His protection, righteous people observe the demise of the wicked (91:8). Verse 9 is crucial to the understanding of the promises in this psalm. No ultimate harm will befall someone *if* he or she takes refuge in the mighty God.

According to verses 11–12, the Lord commissions angels to care for His people. However, this is the Old Testament's sole mention of angels in a guardian capacity. Again, in verse 13, the psalmist uses well-known dangers (great lions and deadly serpents) to symbolize human attackers.

God loves people, and some choose to return His love, prompting God's rescue and protection. When they call on God, He answers. When trouble strikes, He delivers them. And as a result, such people tend to experience longer, more satisfying lives (91:14–16).

Demystifying Psalms

It should be noted that the rewards in this psalm are *generally* true, but not in every case. A relationship with God is no guarantee of a long life, although those who adhere to His instructions will avoid much of the pain and struggles others are likely to face. In fact, a portion of this psalm is quoted in the New Testament by Satan himself. When tempting Jesus, Satan tries to convince Him to act irresponsibly and then count on the promise of angels rushing to His assistance. Jesus wisely replies that people should not test God in such a manner (Matthew 4:5–7).

PSALM 92

After the return from exile, the worship ceremonies of the Israelites included a weekly schedule of psalms sung to accompany the morning offerings. Psalm 92 is the song used each Sabbath morning. This psalm continues with some themes found in Psalms 90 and 91.

Praising God is not merely an obligation but a privilege—and not a privilege to be taken for granted. In verses 1–3, the psalmist reminds the people that it is good to praise God and to make music for Him. The poetic expression of the writer can be confusing to modern ears. The point of verse 2 is not to detach the love of God from His faithfulness and to set aside different times to acknowledge each one. Rather, God's love and faithfulness are intertwined, and people should proclaim them all the time (morning and night).

The psalmist has insight into the eternity of God and is inspired by God's actions (92:4). Those who don't have that perspective, he realizes, mistakenly think they are succeeding in life when in actuality they are wasting a woefully short lifetime (92:5–8). According to verse 9, if they continue to live for themselves and become enemies of God, they will surely perish and be destined for failure.

Speaking from personal experience, the psalmist attests to the positive results of God's presence in his life. Verses 10–11 sound as if they may have been written by a king. The word *horn* is a metaphor for power. *Oil* symbolizes joy and blessing. The writer's different senses (sight, hearing) detect the faithfulness of God all around him.

While evildoers spring up like weeds and quickly disappear (92:7), righteous people are deeply rooted and productive like palm or cedar trees. They continue to prosper even in old age, still praising God as they have throughout their long and happy lives (92:12–15).

PSALM 93

In one sense, Israel was a monarchy like the surrounding nations, under the rule of a king. But in reality, it was a theocracy—a nation subject to the rule of God. Some of the psalms, such as this one, were written to acknowledge God's rule over not just the nation but the entire world. Such writings are frequently called *enthronement* psalms, and they include Psalms 47, 93, and 95–99.

Regardless of the various forms of human government, the truth of the matter is found in verse 1: The Lord reigns. Human kings can be identified by their clothing; God's royal clothing is His majesty. He needs no weapon other than His own strength.

His kingdom (the world) is unshakable. His right to rule is established from eternity—it has always existed and always will (93:1–2).

The pounding waves of the sea form one of many voices of nature that rise up to God. The sea offers no threat to Him, and He is mightier than the strongest forces that human beings can envision (93:3–4). (Sometimes seas symbolize the nations of the earth, which may also be the case in this instance.)

Critical Observation

The oceans were frequently perceived as turbulent, chaotic, uncontrollable expanses. The followers of Baal believed that their god had risen to power by overpowering the god of the sea.

Human kings can issue orders on a whim and misuse power, but God doesn't. The Lord has established statutes to be followed, but they have proven to be beneficial to His people and will endure. The holiness that sets God above all other beings is both attractive and enduring. His rule will never end (93:5).

PSALM 94

Few things in life are as disturbing as seeing people commit intentional offenses against others, knowing that their actions are wrong, and then laugh because they continue to get away with their cruel behavior. The writer of Psalm 94 had such an experience, and his psalm is a plea for God to take vengeance on unrepentant evildoers.

The people the psalmist describes are not just wicked—according to verse 3 they gloat about what they are doing. The psalmist desires God's justice in the matter, and he details several of their many offenses. They are proud and boastful. They oppress God's people. In the case of the weak and helpless, their oppression has even led to death (94:4–6). They are convinced God either doesn't see or doesn't care, which implies that they know full well that their actions are wrong and that they are getting away with it (94:7).

Yet the psalmist realizes that God *is* aware of the situation. The One who created eyes and ears can surely see and hear what is going on in the lives of His creation. More than that, God knows every thought that passes through the human mind, no matter how futile those thoughts may be. Through the psalm, the writer issues a warning to the wicked people, exhorting them to become wise and avoid the punishing discipline of God (94:8–11).

God's discipline can be a wonderful gift that turns people from potential trouble and allows them to share everything God has to offer. Continued wickedness becomes a pit that consumes those who never change their behavior, but righteous people need not fear judgment. God will not allow faithful people to suffer forever at the hands of evildoers (94:12–15).

As troubling as it is to witness the evil around him, the psalmist finds help from God, who provides consolation for his anxiety and helps him maintain spiritual footing. Without God's intervention, he feels that his enemies might have been too much of a problem, possibly forcing him to his grave (94:16–19).

Retribution against the wicked people has not yet taken place, but the psalmist is certain it will occur. God will have nothing to do with a corrupt throne—those who create misery rather than administer justice. They band together for even greater power, but they are still no match for God. He is the fortress, the rock, and the refuge of the psalmist and other righteous people. God will destroy the wicked—the only adequate payment for all they have done (94:20–23).

PSALM 95

Psalm 95 is another *enthronement* psalm, as is Psalm 93, which glorifies God as far superior to all other gods. The psalm is intended for a group setting when the Israelites gather to worship. Not surprisingly, it opens in verse 1 with praise to God, the rock of salvation. God is the reliable, immovable support of the Israelites. He can be counted on to deliver them. The appropriate response, then, is praise, thanksgiving, music, and song.

For anyone with a monotheistic upbringing, verses 3–6 may sound like obvious statements: God rules the heights and depths, lands and seas of the entire world. However, this concept would have been perplexing for many of the nations surrounding Israel, who had gods of the mountains, gods of the seas, and so forth. Those polytheistic beliefs had frequently infiltrated into the thinking of the Israelites. So to make things perfectly clear, the psalmist states in verse 3 that God is not only the great God but also a great King above all gods. He is the creator, sustainer, and owner of the entire earth.

And yet that almighty God has established a personal relationship with humanity. The Israelites are under His care and provision (95:7). The psalmist calls the people to bow before God and worship Him.

However, an outward show of worship is not enough. The people are also to recall and take warning from the stories of their ancestors who had defied God along the way from Egypt to the promised land. The account of what happened at Meribah ("quarreling") and Massah ("testing") is found in Exodus 17:1–7. Those people had seen sign after sign that God was with them and leading them, yet they continued to complain and resist. As a result, an entire generation of people missed out on the peace and security that God offered them.

Psalm 95 ends on that stark note with verses 8–11, yet it is an appropriate ending. If indeed the Lord is the great King above all gods, He is due both outward worship and praise that wells up from a grateful heart. Hard hearts and stubborn wills will have severe consequences.

PSALM 96

God's rule over the earth has been a recurring theme in the previous three psalms, and it will continue in Psalm 96 and several that follow. In verse 1, the psalmist calls the people to sing a new song to the Lord. The occasion for a new song may well have been a new action of God to benefit His people, perhaps a recent act of salvation (deliverance) as mentioned in verse 2. Whatever the occasion, the psalmist exhorts the people to sing praise to God and to make sure other nations hear of all His glorious works among His people (96:3).

But the people shouldn't need a specific occasion to initiate their praise to God. According to verse 4, He is worthy of praise simply because of who He is. Anyone who puts trust in any other god should truly fear Israel's God, because in reality, all other gods are mere idols. The Lord is the authentic Creator who exhibits splendor, majesty, strength, and glory (96:5–6). Therefore, the nations should give God the glory that He is due.

The thrice-repeated phrase "ascribe to the LORD" in verses 7–8 echoes the three commands to sing to the Lord in the psalm's opening verses. The fact that the Lord reigns is cause for deepest reverence and trembling as well as exultant rejoicing (96:9–13). God will indeed judge the earth, and those devoted to His righteousness and truth have nothing to fear. Nature itself—heavens, seas, fields, and trees—will celebrate the justice of God.

The psalmist is dealing with his present time, yet he is looking forward to the coming of the Lord (96:13). The cause for celebration will only increase when the Lord arrives to enforce His justice, righteousness, and truth.

PSALM 97

In verse 1, the acknowledgement that the Lord reigns is a common reminder of the writers throughout this section of Psalms (93:1; 96:10; 99:1). Yet the Israelites may not have absorbed the full significance of that truth. They knew that God reigned over *them*, but the psalmists acknowledge God's rule over all other nations as well—in this case, expressed as "the distant shores" (NIV).

The psalmist's description of God gives evidence of His unchallenged authority. With a foundation of righteousness and justice, the Lord is surrounded by thick, dark clouds. He is also encircled with fire that destroys those who attempt to oppose Him. His presence is accompanied by lightning that strikes fear in all who see it. All nations witness His glory. Even the mountains and heavens are said to yield to the power and righteousness of God (97:2–6).

Critical Observation

The clouds that covered God would have shielded any observers from seeing His full glory. Even Moses, who was as close to God as anyone, was told that no one could see God and live (Exodus 33:20). In addition, dark clouds are signs of an impending storm and may have symbolized approaching judgment.

Anyone who gets a clear picture of God will be shamed to have ever worshiped anyone or anything else. Throughout their history, the Israelites were susceptible to the idolatry practiced by neighboring nations. In verse 7 the psalmist points out, with no small bit of sarcasm, that if other gods really exist, they will submit to and worship the true God.

The judgment of God will be a joyous time for His people (Zion and Judah) who remain faithful (97:8). For those who hate evil, the Lord is a guardian. Judgment will fall on the wicked, effectively freeing those who have been victimized by evil actions. The result, then, should be rejoicing and praise from the righteous followers of the Lord (97:9–12).

PSALM 98

Psalm 98 and Psalm 96 are quite similar, as they both celebrate the work of the Lord. The psalms may have been written in response to a particular act of deliverance, although they were probably used by groups of worshipers in expectation of God's *ongoing* involvement with His people.

The acts of God attract attention. The Israelites acknowledge His deliverance and attribute it to His faithful and loyal love. As the other nations look on and observe how God protects and provides for His people, they can't question His power or His righteousness (98:1–3).

Consequently, all the earth should respond with jubilant singing accompanied by harps, trumpets, and shouts of joy (98:4–6). If a human king was present among them, a great celebration would be expected. How much more, then, should they celebrate the presence of the Lord, the one true King?

Critical Observation

In most cases when a psalm refers to a *trumpet*, the word indicates an instrument made from a ram's horn. But verse 6 refers to the trumpets used at the temple—the only such mention in the book of Psalms. The official trumpets were long and straight, and made of hammered silver. They were used to assemble the community and to celebrate special feasts and festivals (Numbers 10:1–10).

People and nature alike are to respond with joy to the work of God. According to verse 1, He has already done incredible things, but His work is not finished. The whole world can look forward to the day when He will come as judge, bringing righteousness and justice. In anticipation of that day, joy and singing are quite appropriate (98:7–9).

PSALM 99

Following the theme of the series of preceding psalms, the writer again makes the observation that the Lord reigns (99:1; see also 93:1; 96:10; 97:1). Such knowledge makes nations tremble and the earth shake.

Demystifying Psalms

The observation in verse 1 that God is enthroned between the cherubim means more than angels attend to Him. When God provided instructions for building the ark of the covenant, He designed a covering (lid) on which two angels were sculpted, one at each end facing each other (Exodus 25:17–22). God agreed to meet with the high priest between the two cherubim (Exodus 25:22). With God's primary dwelling perceived to be heaven, the ark eventually came to be known as His footstool (1 Chronicles 28:2; Psalm 99:5). And in time, references to God's footstool eventually broadened to include the temple (Psalm 132:7) and even the city of Jerusalem (Lamentations 2:1).

God's reputation among His own people (Zion) causes other nations to exalt Him. As His holiness becomes apparent, people respond in praise (99:2–3).

When human kings become mighty, they sometimes lose touch with reality, becoming self-absorbed and using their power for their own pleasures or advancement. But the mighty, heavenly King has an undying commitment to justice and equity. A review of all He has done for Israel (Jacob) reveals His persistent righteousness. Therefore the psalmist calls for the people to worship their holy God at the temple, His footstool (99:4–5).

Throughout Israel's history, God had appointed individuals to oversee spiritual leadership and to intercede with Him on behalf of the people. Three such outstanding and well-respected leaders were Moses, Aaron, and Samuel—all of whom served during challenging and difficult times (99:6).

All of Israel had witnessed God's leadership as they followed Him in a pillar of cloud, and He had provided them with clear instructions for how to live (99:7). But the Israelites had frequently disobeyed God's statutes and decrees. When they did, they found themselves in trouble and called out to God, who never failed to respond. In His justice, God punished them. Yet in His mercy, He always forgave them and does not hold past sins against them (99:8).

The psalmist acknowledges God's holiness with a repeated exhortation for the people to exalt God and worship Him (99:5, 9). The footstool of God mentioned in verse 5 is later defined in verse 9 as God's holy mountain. Wherever one encounters the holiness of God, it is a location appropriate for worship.

PSALM 100

Psalm 100 concludes a series of psalms (93–100) that were all written to inspire people to praise God as Lord over all the earth. In verse 1, God's rule is the inspiration to shout for joy—or as the King James Version translates it, to "make a joyful noise." In verse 2, the psalmist challenges all the earth to participate in glad worship and songs of joy.

People have good reason to praise God. To begin with, He *is* God—the one and only sovereign Lord—a fact to be acknowledged. In addition, He is the Creator. Created humanity should identify with their Creator (100:3). Beyond that, God initiated a loving relationship with His people. They are not just created beings left to fend for themselves; they remain in God's care as the sheep of His pasture. These are all observations that should motivate people to be joyful.

Joy should be shared with others in communal worship. In verse 4, the gates and courts are references to the temple. Worshipers have to go through one of several gates in order to get to the inner courts. All along the way to worship, then, people are to express praise and thanksgiving to God. Praise and thanksgiving are often linked, and for good reason. Praise is grateful acknowledgment of who God is, and thanksgiving is appreciation for what He has done.

God is perfect in every way. The psalmist concludes this song in verse 5 by citing three strong reasons to praise and thank Him: His goodness, His enduring love, and His continual faithfulness.

PSALM 101

Psalm 101 is attributed to David, the first one so designated since Psalm 86. It is a royal psalm in which the king commits to be faithful in both his personal life and his rule over his house.

The Lord is a God of love and justice, and for that reason David opens his psalm with praise. But almost immediately, in verse 2, he responds to the justice of God. He wants to devote himself, both privately and publicly, to model a blameless life. And once his heart is blameless, he is determined not to get involved with things that might corrupt it (101:3).

Critical Observation

The word frequently translated *vile* (101:3) has the same root in Hebrew as the name *Belial*—a name regularly connected with evil (2 Corinthians 6:15). In many cases the phrase "sons of Belial" is translated simply as "wicked men."

David also intends to stay away from people who are involved with evil. Those with perverse hearts have no place around someone with a blameless heart (101:2–4). As king, David can do something about such people. He has the power to silence slanderers and humble the proud, and in verse 5 he commits to do so. Liars and deceivers will be banned from his presence (101:7).

Verse 6 makes clear that there are other faithful people in the kingdom, and the king will seek them out as his ministers and peers. Yet he will continue daily to address the problem of wickedness in his nation. Most likely this will be done in his role as judge, hearing cases brought before him. He will rule in favor of upright and honest people, regularly and relentlessly silencing evildoers (101:8).

In essence, David wants to rule much as God does, by recognizing and rewarding faithful people while confronting the regrettable problem of widespread evil.

PSALM 102

The introduction to Psalm 102 is like no other. It neither identifies the author nor provides a clue as to its usage or historical setting. Instead, it simply announces the travail of an individual pouring out his sorrows to God. Although normally classified as an individual lament, some people think the psalm could have been used in group assemblies because the reason for the author's troubles appears to be a national catastrophe that would have affected others as well. And some speculate that because the state of the nation was so closely tied to the king, one of the kings of the exile might have penned this lament.

The psalmist wastes no time expressing his distress and raising a plea for God to listen and respond. Days are going by with no substance and no purpose (102:3), and he fears that his life will soon end having had little effect (102:23). Meanwhile, his condition is appalling. Physically, he hurts all over. He has no appetite and has lost weight. He groans aloud. Emotionally, it feels like his heart has withered (102:4–5).

In his agony, he suffers alone. In verse 6, he shares the solitude of an owl in a desert wasteland. At night he feels vulnerable and exposed, unable to sleep. During the day he hears the insults of his (Israel's) enemies, using him as an example of how far someone can fall. He sits in ashes as he mourns and cries continually. To make things worse, he is convinced that God has brought about his desperate situation. God had been angry, resulting in the psalmist's being cast aside. The writer feels near death, like withered grass or the shadows of evening (102:7–11).

It isn't until readers get to verses 13–16 that they discover the source of the psalmist's dismay: The holy city has been destroyed. But he has not given up on God. He reminds himself that God is eternal—enthroned forever and always worthy of receiving honor (102:12). In addition, God has always been, and will always be, compassionate. Therefore, the psalmist has confidence that God will again show favor to Jerusalem (Zion). The city will be rebuilt and renewed to reflect God's glory. Many of the same enemies that are currently taunting the psalmist (and Israel) will eventually have a change of heart. Nations and kings will be humbled and show respect to God.

Considering himself to be among the destitute, the psalmist anticipates God's response to his prayer. He is so sure of it, in fact, that he wants it on the record that God will indeed hear His people and release them from their woeful situation (102:17–20). If God is to rebuild Zion (102:16), it is only a matter of time until people will again assemble there to worship and praise Him (102:21–22).

Even though the psalmist has confident hope in soon witnessing God's intervention in Israel's situation, for the time being he will continue to suffer (102:23–24). He asks the eternal God to allow him to live a while longer. People come and go, and the heavens and the earth will pass away also. But God remains unchanged, and those who choose to live in His presence will continue to experience His faithfulness (102:25–28).

Demystifying Psalms

The psalmist yearns for a more lasting relationship with God. It is interesting, then, that the author of Hebrews quotes Psalm 102:25–27 in connection with Jesus as the eternal Creator (Hebrews 1:10–12). Those who place their trust in Christ can experience what the psalmist so strongly desires—life forevermore in relationship with a loving Lord.

PSALM 103

Psalm 102 ends with the writer asking God for help and steadfastly hoping for a better future. Psalm 103 celebrates the work of God as He forgives and acts on behalf of His people. The two psalms weren't necessarily written at the same time, but the people who compiled the Psalms might have placed them together since 103 appears to complement 102.

Psalm 103 is attributed to David, who opens the song with personal praise. ("O my soul," the phrase found in verses 1, 2, and 22, was used as someone today might say, "Note to self.") The verbs used in verses 3–5 to describe acts of God are revealing: David has been forgiven, healed, redeemed, crowned, satisfied, and renewed. He has experienced the love, compassion, blessing, and infusion of strength that only God can provide.

After acknowledging God's work in his personal life, David writes of God's work among the nation of Israel. The people had experienced their share of oppression, and God had been with them all along. God had revealed to Moses His expectations for worship and for living, and He had provided other helpful guidelines. The people had seen His mighty deeds beginning in Egypt as they grew into a nation, and ever since (103:6–7).

David realizes that the Lord is a forgiving God. The iniquities of the people had at times resulted in His wrath, but it had been clear that God is slow to become angry and shows mercy to His people (103:7–10). God's wrath tends to get people's attention when nothing else does, but the psalmist points out that God's anger is just as evident as His compassion, grace, and love.

God receives no satisfaction from punishing human sin. Verses 11–12 are often quoted as a reminder that God's anger is not lasting because of His forgiveness. He desires for people to forsake their iniquities and turn to Him. When they do, He gladly removes sin as far as the east is from the west (103:12). Nothing is greater than the love of God.

It is difficult to comprehend such a degree of love, and the closest people can come is to consider the love they feel for their children. God, as the great Creator, is well aware of the weaknesses and impermanence of humanity—His children. People quickly come and go, but the love of God remains everlasting with those who know His commands and obey them. And ideally, as people model reverence to God and obedience to His laws, their children will notice and will continue the righteousness they have been shown (103:13–18).

Regardless of human response to the Lord, God's rule is total and unquestionable. He is praised and obeyed by the mighty angels of heaven. Creation itself speaks its praise. How much more, then, should people respond to the love and mercy of such a mighty God (103:20–22)?

PSALM 104

The greatness of God described in Psalm 103 is also affirmed in Psalm 104, although this psalm has no superscription to identify the author, and there is no reason to presume the same person wrote both. The previous psalm focuses more on God's relationship with humanity, while this one dwells on the evidence of His sovereignty in the realm of creation. It is difficult not to recall the creation story of Genesis 1 while reading through Psalm 104.

Beginning with a description of God Himself, the psalmist writes in verses 1–2 of the Lord's clothing, which includes splendor, majesty, and light. Then moving right away to the *works* of God, the writer envisions the creation of the heavens as if God were setting up a tent. It's as if heaven is an upstairs level of earth where God can dwell, built on beams that have been laid across the oceans as a foundation. God moves as if in a chariot borne on the winds (104:2–4). Wind and fire are often included in descriptions of God's presence.

In conjunction with creating the heavens, God established the earth (104:5). He separated the land from the waters, and the waters that had covered mountains receded (104:6–9). With the abundance of water throughout the lands, life of all kinds was sustained; springs in the ravines watered wild donkeys and other field animals, and trees were nourished, allowing birds to nest and sing beside the streams (104:10–13).

Grass and plants sprang up as well, providing food. God's people received not just basic nourishments of bread and oil but also wine. Whether in the mountain heights, the pine and cedar forests, or the rocky crags, God's creation is evident. He provides for all His creation wherever they are (104:14–18).

God also designed the cycles of day and night, and the rotating seasons. The lions and animals seek their food from God just as people do. Verses 19–23 are the psalmist's portrayal of nocturnal beasts hunting during the night and retiring at dawn, just as human beings are setting out for their day's work.

The assumption must be made that God has created certain creatures that human beings don't even know about. The earth is full of His creatures, and the sea contains too many creatures to count. Even the animals that are large and intimidating to people are small to God. The fearful leviathan, for example, is described as playing in the sea (104:24–26).

Critical Observation

The leviathan was a symbol of power in Canaan, although exactly what it was is uncertain. Its connection with the sea allows for numerous possibilities. In some cases the word seems synonymous with crocodiles. But in local mythology, the leviathan was represented by many heads, suggesting that it was more imposing than any known animal. Sperm whales have been sighted in the Mediterranean, fueling speculation of that possibility.

God's provision sustains the entire animal kingdom. His presence comforts; His absence terrifies. He supplies life and determines life spans, when it is time to return to the dust. And as impressive as His creation is, God is far greater (104:27–32).

Those who fail to connect with God in light of all He has done have no place in His world, and the psalmist prays that they will simply vanish from earth. He, on the other hand, commits to sing praise as long as he lives, rejoicing in all that God has done and attempting to please Him with worship (104:33–35).

PSALM 105

In Psalm 105 the writer praises God through a review of Israel's history, spanning the call of Abraham to the arrival of the Israelites in the promised land. No author is designated, although the first fifteen verses duplicate the content of 1 Chronicles 16:8–22, a passage that is associated with both David and Asaph.

In the opening verses, the psalmist challenges people to get involved with their relationships with God: to give thanks, call on God's name, tell other nations what He has done, sing, offer praise, recall His actions, take joy in Him, and continually turn to Him for strength and assurance (105:1–4).

The Lord is a God of wonders, miracles, and judgments. To prove his point, the psalmist recalls a series of stories from Israel's past. Addressing the people as both descendants of Abraham and sons of Jacob, he begins a concise, but systematic, review (105:5–6).

God hasn't simply interacted with Abraham for a bit; He has established an eternal covenant with the patriarch. God's promises to Abraham are passed on, in turn, to Isaac, Jacob (Israel), and Joseph. They all look ahead to the fulfillment of the promise of the land they are to inherit (105:8–11).

Verses 12–22 describe the period when Israel was only a family, prior to becoming a nation. According to verse 12, they were few in number, but God still watched over them. In the Genesis account of the story of Joseph (Genesis 37), it appears that Joseph's brothers had been in control when they sold their little brother into slavery. In retrospect, as the psalmist points out in verses 16–17, it became clear that God was sending Joseph ahead of the rest of the family to Egypt. What began as one person's imprisonment and anticipated life sentence turns out to be God's plan to honor His promise to Abraham to build a nation of his descendants.

Verses 23–36 review Israel's time in Egypt, during which a family of around seventy grew into a nation so sizable that it created military concerns for the Egyptian Empire. God's people became too numerous for their foes (Psalm 105:24). Four hundred years after Joseph, God's chosen leaders were Moses and Aaron (105:26). But it was the power of God displayed through the plagues that eventually secured the release of His people.

Then came the Exodus, described in verses 37–41. In verse 37, the silver and gold that Israel possessed was the result of gifts the Egyptians gave the people to induce them to hurry and leave, although God was behind the generous giving of Egypt (Exodus 12:33–36). All during Israel's time in the wilderness, God provided food, water, and a clear sign of His presence through a cloud and fire (Psalm 105:39).

This particular review highlights only the positive aspects of the journey; the psalmist mentions nothing of Israel's rebellion. His point is to show how God had followed through with what He promised Abraham. Israel inherited a wonderful land that other nations had worked hard to cultivate. Ideally, the Israelites should then have worshiped and obeyed God in the new land. It didn't turn out that way, but perhaps the people who used Psalm 105 in their worship would get the point and not make the same mistakes.

PSALM 106

Psalm 105 is a description of what God had done for His people throughout their history. As such, it is an overwhelmingly optimistic song. In contrast, Psalm 106 deals with many of the same events but looks at the actions and reactions of the people. Consequently, it is not nearly as positive.

Both psalms open with a command to give thanks to God, and the first five verses of Psalm 106 recall the faithfulness of God and the need to respond to His mighty acts. But verse 6 begins a confession of sin that continues throughout the psalm. God remained faithful to His people throughout their history, but they repeatedly disobey and rebel.

Verses 6–13 describe the Red Sea experience. The people panicked and wanted to turn back, but God miraculously led them through the sea and then drowned the Egyptian army behind them. In response they believed God and praised Him, but they quickly forgot what He had done for them (106:13).

The attitude of the Israelites went from bad to worse as they moved on into the wilderness (106:14–33). They tested God and questioned the leadership of Moses and Aaron. When Moses was absent for a few days, they had Aaron create a golden calf. When they finally got to the promised land, they lacked the faith to enter. They rebelled against God in order to follow the gods of other nations. Their grumbling was so persistent and unrelenting that they provoked foolish words from Moses that kept him from entering the promised land. In each of those instances, God responded with a disciplinary action, but to no lasting effect. The people felt sorry for a little while, but in a short matter of time they reverted to their whining and griping.

Demystifying Psalms

Psalm 106 lists a number of inglorious actions of the Israelites and the consequences they experienced because of their sin. Some of the original stories may be unfamiliar. If so, they are found in the passages listed below.

Crossing the Red Sea	Psalm 106:7–13	Exodus 13:17–14:31
Demands for food	Psalm 106:14–15	Numbers 11:4–34
Envy of Moses and Aaron	Psalm 106:16–18	Numbers 16
The golden calf	Psalm 106:19–23	Exodus 32
Despising the promised land	Psalm 106:24–27	Numbers 13–14
Idolatry, adultery, and Phinehas	Psalm 106:28–31	Numbers 25
Waters of Meribah/Moses' rash words	Psalm 106:32–33	Numbers 20:2–13

The people finally mustered enough faith to enter the promised land, but soon thereafter they again began to rebel against God. Verses 34–46 tell the sad story. They did not evict the inhabitants as God had instructed. Instead, they mingled with the Canaanites and soon began to worship their various gods, which sometimes included atrocious acts (106:37–38).

In response, God allowed Israel to be overpowered again and again, but the people would not make a permanent commitment to Him. Each time they cried out, He lovingly forgave them and sent help. But their faith never lasted long (106:40–46).

Apparently Israel has found itself in a similar situation in the present time because the psalmist asks God to "gather us back from among the nations" (106:47 NLT). After seeing their temple and the city of Jerusalem destroyed, Israel's exile in Babylon was certainly pitiable.

Verse 48 is an added doxology to conclude Book IV in the biblical book of Psalms. Each of the five books ends with such a note of praise.

Take It Home

Several of the psalms in this section describe the perfections and mighty acts of God. Sometimes such a perspective of God inspires confession and repentance. Other times the psalmist's intent is purely praise and thanksgiving. Do you acknowledge the good gifts of God on a regular basis, or do you tend to wait until you're in a situation when you miss them and only then begin to think about better times? What are some areas in your own life that might benefit from your intent concentration on who God is and what He has done?

PSALMS: BOOK V

PSALMS 107–134

Setting Up the Section

This section begins the last of the five books contained within the biblical book of Psalms. It is likely the final book compiled chronologically, so along with some additional psalms of David there are other songs that contain references to events later in Israel's history. This first half of the final book contains the shortest psalm, the longest psalm, and the series of fifteen psalms known as the Songs of Ascents.

PSALM 107

As Psalm 107 opens, verses 1–3 are a call to worship. The reference in verse 3 to people gathering suggests that the psalm was written during or after the exile. If so, the foe in verse 2 would have been the Assyrians and Babylonians.

The next section, verses 4–32, dwells on God's salvation (deliverance) of His people. Again and again, the psalmist describes people who find themselves in desperate situations. Then they cry out to God and He delivers them (107:6, 13, 19, 28). In response, the psalmist encourages the people to give thanks to the Lord, whose love is repeatedly described as unfailing (107:8, 15, 21, 31).

The situations described by the psalmist are varied: people wandering in desert wastelands needing food and water (107:4–5), shackled prisoners who have rebelled against God and find themselves subjected to hard labor (107:10–12), some who have rebelled and suffered physical near-death experiences as a result (107:17–18), and sailors who face frightening and turbulent storms at sea, battling waves the size of mountains (107:23–27). In each case, God is gracious and merciful as He forgives and delivers those who ask.

Clearly, these four cases are representative of God's ability and willingness to help anyone in any situation. In return, people should give much consideration to God's unfailing love and offer Him their thanks.

In addition to the regular and willing deliverance of God that should be received with thanksgiving, the closing section of Psalm 107 provides reasons to offer praise to the Lord. In God's sovereignty, He has power to change human situations. Rivers dry up and become deserts, or deserts are suddenly infused with water and become springs that sustain vineyards and human civilization (107:33–38).

Such examples are more than theoretical considerations for the Israelites who have experienced droughts—usually following times when they had forgotten the Lord. God had always forgiven them and restored life to their land. And yet the people eventually go too far in their rejection of God. He allows them to "wander in a trackless waste" (107:40 NIV). Many die, and the rest suffer (107:39). But again, God's discipline is temporary. He once more delivers His people, increasing the families of the upright and silencing the wicked. The psalmist's concluding challenge in verse 43 is for people to exhibit wisdom and give much thought to the tremendous love of God.

PSALM 108

If we think of the psalms as songs, then Psalm 108 is a medley of Psalms 57 and 60. Verses 1–5 of Psalm 108 echo Psalm 57:7–11. Verses 6–13 are a repetition of Psalm 60:5–12. The two previous psalms are credited to David, as is Psalm 108. Combined as they are here, the psalm is a song of victory to celebrate God's incomparable love and faithfulness as displayed in His deliverance of Israel from their enemies.

The first portion of the psalm, verses 1–5, expresses praise to God. David rejoices in having a steadfast heart, attributed to God's power and glory. His praise is followed by a prayer for continued triumph over the nation's enemies (108:6–13). God is sovereign over both Israel (Shechem, Succoth, Gilead, Manasseh, Ephraim, and Judah) and the enemies of Israel (Moab, Edom, and Philistia). Realizing that human power is worthless, David gives all credit to God (108:12–13).

PSALM 109

Attributed to David, Psalm 109 is sometimes placed in the category of *imprecatory* psalms (those that call for harm to come to the enemies of God and His people). Not all scholars agree, however, that such a category should exist. Several psalms contain sections of imprecations yet still are categorized as praise, lament, or so forth.

David wastes no time laying out his case before God. His enemies have been busy speaking lies and deceit, spouting hatred toward him. David has attempted to initiate friendship, but to no avail. He has given his opponents no cause to attack him, yet they do. Throughout it all, he continues to be a man of prayer (109:1–5).

The plural *men* and references to *they* in verses 1–5 are replaced in verses 6–19 with the singular *he*. Some scholars feel that verses 6–19 are the psalmist's recounting of his enemies' words toward him. More probably, David switches to singular because his many enemies have a ringleader who incites them, and it is that individual who warrants the most attention. Or perhaps criticism of David is so widespread that addressing one person effectively speaks to *all* his critics.

Demystifying Psalms

Psalm 109:6 can be interpreted different ways. The NIV translates the Hebrew as: "Appoint an evil man to oppose him; let an accuser stand at his right hand." But another equally valid translation is: "Appoint the evil one to oppose him; let Satan stand at his right hand." David clearly desires for his most outspoken critic to be confronted by a powerful accuser of his own.

David wishes the worst on the person who has caused him so much suffering and grief, and he uses strong words to express his feelings (109:7–15). But David also includes why he is so intent on seeing this person suffer. He explains his reasoning in verses 16–20. This person is an evil man who takes advantage of the weak and helpless. He never blesses people but is always quick to curse. Cursing others is his nature—not just an outer shell like clothing but steeped into his flesh and bones. So David prays that the man's heartless mentality be strapped around him forever, like a belt.

In contrast, David pours out his own condition to God. He is poor, needy, and heartsick. He has fasted until he became physically weak, and he is still an object of ridicule to his many accusers (109:21–25). Yet he continues to count on God to deliver him and leave his enemies in shame and disgrace. God will help the needy, and David is determined to continue to praise and honor Him (109:26–31).

This psalm, specifically verse 8, is cited in Acts 1:20 when the disciples choose a replacement for Judas.

PSALM 110

The third of a short series of Davidic psalms, Psalm 110 opens with a statement that immediately raises questions. The Lord God is the speaker, so who then does David have in mind as "*my* Lord" in verse 1? Clues in the rest of the psalm reveal that the figure is both king and priest, so that narrows the options.

Some people try to assign a late date to the psalm to match its contents with Jewish life during the Maccabean era, when the nation's priests sometimes held political power as well. However, Jesus acknowledges David as the author, confirming a much earlier date, and He also applies the psalm to Himself in Matthew 22:41–45. This psalm is quoted several times in the New Testament as proof that Jesus is the Messiah (Mark 12:35–37; Acts 2:34–35; Hebrews 1:13; 5:6; 7:17, 21).

Critical Observation

Some people question the messianic classification of this psalm. They argue that if David had received a revelation about Jesus, then his prophetic insight in this psalm predates other similar revelations of the prophets. Some prefer to believe that David possibly wrote the psalm to commemorate Solomon's coronation. By referring to his son as "my Lord," David would have acknowledged the transfer of power. Later generations would have applied the messianic references.

After a battle, the losing king would sometimes bow before the victor, and the winning king would ceremonially place his foot on the other's neck. The image in verse 1 of making an enemy one's footstool is probably derived from this ancient custom.

The Lord God invites this other lord to sit at His right hand (a position of great honor), and He promises to give him total victory over his enemies (110:1). In verse 2, extending the scepter is a way of promising an ever-increasing kingdom. The figure being addressed will have many supporters—willing volunteers to go with him into battle. Their comparison to dawn and dew in verse 3 implies freshness, youth, strength, and significant numbers.

More than a mighty warrior, this lord is also a priest in the order of Melchizedek (110:4). From the time of the Exodus onward, priests had to come from the tribe of Levi. But Melchizedek predates the Mosaic Law. He was the king/priest to whom Abraham paid tribute after a battle (Genesis 14:17–20). The Messiah will be both priest and king, holding a position higher than those who serve in the Aaronic priesthood. His priesthood will be forever (Psalm 110:4).

David, a warrior, describes God's Messiah in military terms. He will overcome all opposition and rule supreme, judging the nations. The reference to drinking from a brook in verse 7 suggests that he will be refreshed and will not fade during the rigorous demands of battle. Lifting up his head indicates victory and power.

PSALM 111

Scholars have long linked Psalms 111 and 112. Both are in the format of an acrostic poem, and the content is quite similar. It is possible that the same person wrote both psalms, probably after the exile. The two psalms are written in praise to God and with the intent of imparting wisdom among the worshiping community.

Verses 1–3 of Psalm 111 set the tone for extolling God. The setting is public, as verse 1 indicates. The reasons for praising God are many: His great works, His glorious and majestic deeds, and His enduring righteousness (111:2–3).

After these generalities, the psalmist gets more specific in verses 4–9. The Lord is a God of grace and compassion. He initiates a covenant with His people. He provides them with food, and He gives them victory over their enemies. He is powerful, faithful, and trustworthy. He has redeemed them. All such actions reflect the love of a God who is both holy and awesome (111:9). Popular usage may have diminished the intended definition of the word *awesome*. The meaning here is "awe-inspiring." When someone begins to comprehend the holiness of God, the result is a deep, fearful reverence.

Fear and awe are good things in this case, as the psalmist points out in verse 10. Such a response to God is wise. A reverential, submissive attitude initiates a better understanding of God and prompts praise from those who know Him.

PSALM 112

Continuing the theme of the previous song, Psalm 112 picks up where Psalm 111 leaves off. Those who fear God discover the joy of following Him, and therefore are eager to praise Him (112:1). The previous psalm focuses more on the work of God among His people, while this one enumerates some of the blessings that might be anticipated by those who acknowledge the sovereignty and holiness of God.

To begin with, a righteous upbringing is beneficial to children, helping them to thrive. And in the thinking of the time, the way in which an upright person would be remembered forever was through his line of descendants (112:6). Prosperity is also tied into righteousness. Verse 3 promises wealth and riches in the homes of godly people.

Everyone experiences dark times, but the darkness doesn't last for those who remain gracious and compassionate (112:4). Generosity and justice certainly benefit those who receive such gifts, but those who administer them are rewarded as well (112:5). God provides such people with stability and security. When bad news comes, they need not fear. Enemies may attack, but they will not prevail. As righteous people give to the poor to supply what they don't have, God supplies those righteous people with honor and power (symbolized by the horn in verse 9).

The psalmist ends this otherwise positive and uplifting psalm with a caveat for those who do not pursue righteousness. Wicked people will witness God's goodness to others and be vexed. Their longings will remain unfulfilled. Rather than praising God, they will grind their teeth and waste away (112:10).

Critical Observation

The similarity of Psalms 111 and 112 is noteworthy. The psalms that follow aren't as similar, although Psalms 113–118 will continue the theme of praise to God. Sometimes these praise-focused poems are called *Hallelujah* psalms. (Our word *hallelujah* is based on the original Hebrew that is frequently translated, "Praise the Lord.") In later Jewish tradition, this segment of the Psalter is used at Passover, with Psalms 113 and 114 sung prior to the meal and 115–118 afterward.

PSALM 113

The power, glory, and majesty of God are not reserved for the segment of humanity that considers itself powerful, glorious, and majestic. Just the opposite. Psalm 113 is a reminder of both the greatness of God and His love for those who have nothing to offer Him except their praise.

Indeed, the first two verses of the psalm open with repeated calls to praise the Lord. Praise is due God at all times and at all places (113:2–3). The reason God deserves the praise of humanity is because no one, no thing, no power is greater. Israel knew of many nations and many gods, but God was exalted over them all (113:4). The events of earth may appear overwhelming or traumatic to human beings, but God has to step down from His throne on high to see what is taking place.

When the Lord sees poor and needy people among the dust and ashes, He lifts them up. Israel's history contains no shortage of stories of barren women—a condition of utter humiliation and subsequent sorrow in their culture—who eventually conceive and rejoice at the powerful intervention of God. Abraham's wife, Sarah, is perhaps the best-known case in point (Genesis 18:9–15; 21:1–7). Other familiar examples include Rebekah

(Genesis 25:21–22), Rachel (Genesis 30:1, 22–24), and Hannah (1 Samuel 1:9–20). These are all examples of barren women who, in the psalmist's words in Psalm 113:9, settle into homes and become happy mothers of children.

In contrast with the high enthroned and mighty God, *all* humanity is poor, needy, and barren. So when people begin to comprehend that the great God of the universe has chosen to be actively involved in their lives, they should heed the psalmist's repeated exhortation to praise the Lord.

PSALM 114

The story of the Exodus was told and retold in Jewish songs and ceremonies. Numerous psalms refer to God's miraculous deliverance and protection of His people during that time. But Psalm 114 is one of the most unique, stylized portrayals on record of Israel's journey from Egypt to the promised land.

The psalmist is apparently reviewing Israel's past from a point beyond the reign of Solomon. His distinction between Judah and Israel in verse 2 suggests that he is writing during the period of the divided kingdom. But when the people first came out of Egypt, they were still the house of Jacob (114:1).

God performed many miracles during the Exodus. Only a few are mentioned in this short psalm, but they are creatively portrayed. In verse 3, two bodies of water are described as seeing God and fleeing before Him. The crossing of the Red Sea (Exodus 13:17–14:31) is well-known. Less familiar, but equally miraculous, is the sudden drying up of the Jordan River at flood stage while the people cross into the promised land (Joshua 3). In addition, God's presence was frequently associated with earthquakes—times when the mountains skipped like rams (Psalm 114:4).

It is as if the psalmist is interviewing various elements of creation to see what they think about the miracles God had performed (114:5–6). If rivers, seas, and mountains respond to the work of God, the implication is that people should notice and acknowledge the mighty deeds of the Lord as well. Comprehension of God's involvement among humanity results in reverential trembling (114:7).

Verse 8 concludes the psalm with one final miracle of God during the Exodus. A hard rock stood in the midst of an arid wilderness, and yet God turned that solid rock into flowing streams of water. With a mere sampling of the mighty works God had performed for His people, the psalmist makes his point and thus ends his song.

PSALM 115

Idolatry was a recurring temptation for the Israelites. They were surrounded by other nations with their various gods. And many times when some disaster or difficulty befell Israel, those nations would question the presence of Israel's God (115:2).

In the opening verse, the psalmist makes it clear that God deserves glory because of His love and faithfulness. He is an unseen God who rules from heaven, yet He is in complete control (115:3). This would have been a foreign concept to the polytheistic nations around Israel.

Critical Observation

The idols of this time period and location were usually carved of wood and then overlaid with thin sheets of gold or silver. They have been discovered in assorted shapes and sizes, including some that were life-sized. The carvings weren't believed to be actual gods, but the foreign deities were thought to use the idols to make known their desires. Some cultures took great care of their idols, going to the point of dressing and washing them each day, and even "feeding" them with sacrifices of food.

Almost all the surrounding nations worshiped visual, tactile idols that reminded them of their gods. They made them as lifelike as possible. The psalmist's description in verses 5–7 is detailed, with mention of idols with mouths, eyes, ears, noses, hands, feet, and throats. Yet as he makes clear in verse 4, the idols are carved by humans—totally inanimate and impotent.

On a more poignant note, the psalmist observes in verse 8 that those who put their trust in idols become like those idols—helpless and ineffective. In contrast, those who trust in Israel's powerful God are empowered, and those who put their faith in the compassionate God receive help (115:9–11).

Israel's God is unseen, but He is living and active. He has proven to be ever present with His people and will continue to respond to their needs (115:12–13). The psalmist includes a prayer that God will bless both those who are listening and their families. The maker of heaven and earth is the only One qualified to help them (115:14–15).

God is not only the Creator of heaven but also its owner. In His grace, He created the earth and then provided it as a dwelling for humanity. The dead no longer have voices with which to express appreciation, so in verses 16–18 the psalmist challenges people to offer their praise while they are able.

PSALM 116

There are many reasons to love God. The reason cited in this case is God's protection during a difficult time in the psalmist's life. The writer cried out for the mercy of God, and the Lord responded (116:1).

Whenever someone discovers that God answers, the wise and reasonable response is to continue to call on Him, as the psalmist commits to do in verse 2. He does not fully explain his situation, but it sounds quite severe. Overcome by problems made worse by emotional turmoil, he is afraid of dying (116:3). Yet it is at that low point of his life that he discovers God's grace, righteousness, and compassion. He doesn't attempt to feign strength or pretend that everything is all right. He depends on God to deliver him (116:4–6).

He has made a good choice. Who but God could have changed the psalmist's tears, stumbling, and nearness to death into a walk in the land of the living (116:8–9)? Apparently everyone else had lacked the faith that God would deliver him, creating great dismay. But the psalmist had believed, and God had restored him to health and safety (116:10–11).

Consequently, the psalmist is eager to repay the Lord for His goodness. He has been delivered, so he will worship God publicly and intently (116:12–14). The cup of salvation mentioned in verse 13 may have been a drink offering (Numbers 28:7, 10, 14, 31) to accompany the thank offering he later cites in verse 17. Even though he has been spared from death this time, he knows that God is well aware of the deaths of His faithful followers (116:15–16). After his recovery, the psalmist intends to gladly continue to fulfill his vows to God, setting a good example for everyone.

PSALM 117

There isn't much to say about Psalm 117, simply because the psalmist doesn't write much. At only two verses, it is both the shortest psalm and the shortest chapter in scripture.

The first verse exhorts everyone to praise the Lord—not only all peoples but also all nations. This psalm is another reminder that God's great love extends far beyond the Jewish states of Israel and Judah. The apostle Paul quotes this verse among a list of scripture references to make that very point in Romans 15:11.

In verse 2 the psalmist associates God's great love with His enduring faithfulness, which is a common pairing in the psalms. And he concludes with the phrase so frequently repeated in this section of Psalms: Praise the Lord (or Hallelujah).

PSALM 118

Psalm 118 is one of the more celebratory songs in the entire collection of Psalms, but the *reason* for the celebration is debated. It may be written by one of Israel's kings who rejoiced because God's people prevailed after a particularly difficult battle. Or the expression of thankful celebration may have been written after the Israelites returned from exile, with the psalm used to commemorate rebuilding the walls and temple at Jerusalem.

Critical Observation

Jewish traditions evolved to use particular psalms for specific festivals and events. Based on the knowledge of such traditions, it is possible that the hymn Jesus and His disciples sing as they leave the Last Supper for Gethsemane (Matthew 26:30) is Psalm 118.

The opening in verse 1 is a popular one in Psalms (106:1; 107:1), and verses 1–4 may have been written in a call-and-response format to get all the worshipers involved. Then, beginning with verse 5, the psalmist goes into a specific account of his situation. The point of view may have been that of the king at the time or one of the priests or Levites leading the worship. Regardless of the original author, the content of the psalm is applicable for worshipers of all generations.

In verses 5–7, the author describes a commonly expressed problem: being surrounded by enemies and experiencing anguish. But he had cried out to God and the Lord had freed him. He is victorious and no longer afraid, but he has not had a pleasant experience. His enemies have been numerous and they swarm like bees around him (118:10–12). But calling on the name of the Lord results in a quick response. Therefore, as the psalmist makes clear in verses 8–9, seeking refuge in God is far preferable to placing one's trust in people—even princes who have soldiers and wealth at their disposal.

God is never at a loss for strength. The symbol of His power, His right hand, is always there for support (118:15–16). It's never too late to call on Him for help. The psalmist feels as if he is about to fall (118:13), yet God delivers him. As a result, shouts of rejoicing are heard throughout the land (118:14–15).

In verse 18, the psalmist interprets his difficult times as God's chastening, yet he is thrilled to be alive and still able to testify to God's work in his life. God has delivered him, so he will go to the temple and give thanks (118:19–21).

Verse 22 may sound familiar because Jesus will later interpret it as a reference to Himself (Matthew 21:42). The original rejected stone, however, is probably the king of the time, looked down on by other leaders who thought themselves more powerful, yet who ultimately triumphed over them. Another possibility is that the stone is the nation of Israel, small and seemingly insignificant, yet continuing to persevere with the love and help of God.

Verse 24 is another frequently quoted verse, usually used to encourage rejoicing on any given day. Originally, however, it referred to a specific day of deliverance and victory.

The next section contains a prayer for God's continued protection (118:25), the recognition of those who value the name of the Lord (118:26), a public expression of the difference God's presence makes in life (118:27), and a commitment to exalt and thank God (118:28). When Jesus rides into Jerusalem on Palm Sunday, the crowds quote from verses 25–26, and they meet Him with boughs in hand (118:27; Mark 11:8–11).

Psalm 118 ends in verse 29 as it began in verse 1, with a call to give thanks to God for His goodness and everlasting love.

PSALM 119

Psalm 119 is the longest of the psalms (by far), and it is also a distinctive work of art. It stands out from other psalms in that it focuses primarily on the Word of God, rather than the works of God or the character of God. The psalmist constructs his observations as an acrostic poem, comprised of twenty-two stanzas of eight verses each. Other psalms are also written as acrostics (Psalms 111 and 112). But in this case, each of the first eight verses begins with the first Hebrew letter, the next eight verses start with the second Hebrew letter, and so on through the alphabet.

Almost every one of the 176 verses of Psalm 119 contains a reference to the Word of God. The psalmist uses eight different Hebrew terms for variety. The terms are used approximately the same number of times throughout the psalm (ranging from nineteen times to twenty-five times apiece). English translations vary, however, and the assortment of interpreted words include *word, law, decree, command(ment), statute, precept, promise, saying, judgment, testimony, way, path*, and perhaps others.

Verses 1–3 serve as an introduction: Those who keep God's laws are blessed. The psalmist immediately expresses a desire to be in that category of people (119:4–8). He wants a pure life. With God's Word as his internal guide, he can then recount God's laws to others. God's statutes are a source of joy for him as well as the subject of his meditations (119:9–16).

The psalmist is well aware of the influence of evil people. He mentions them several times in this psalm, first in verse 21. Rather than allowing their influence to affect him, he prays for God's enlightenment and protection (119:17–24). Even though he is weary with sorrow (119:25, 28), he chooses to cling to God's promises and continue to obey God's Word (119:25–32).

His understanding of God's Word results in delight. Ignorance or disobedience, on the other hand, leads to selfish gain, worthless pursuits, and disgrace (119:33–40). The laws of God also provide great confidence. The psalmist is prepared to stand before kings to declare the truth God has revealed to him (119:41–48).

Those who steadfastly follow God are subject to mocking, and perhaps even suffering at the hands of others. Yet the psalmist's comfort remains in God's laws. He feels indignation toward his tormentors, yet at night he focuses his thoughts on God and regains perspective on his life (119:49–64).

The psalmist writes from experience. He had previously gone astray and knew what it was like to be out of favor with God. It had ultimately become a positive experience for him, because after he returned to the Lord he realized what was really important. Afterward he wouldn't have traded his commitment to God's laws for silver and gold (119:65–72). He also acknowledges God as his Creator and wants to spend his life telling others about the Lord, offering them truth and hope (119:73–80).

Still, he admits to experiencing periods when he didn't feel the comfort and presence of God. His spiritual condition began to get dry and brittle like "a wineskin in the smoke" (119:83 NIV). But during such times he remained patient and persevering, faithfully looking and longing for the promises of God to return (119:81–88).

In spite of persistent attempts by his enemies to destroy him (119:95), the psalmist has nothing but good things to say about God's faithfulness. God had established the world, and He continues to sustain it by His Word. God's laws not only give the writer hope but also make him wiser than his opponents (119:98). With such wisdom, he is able to stay away from paths of evil (119:89–104).

The world can be a dark and imposing place, but according to verse 105 (a favorite of many people), God's Word provides a lamp to one's feet and a light to one's path. Thanks to God's precepts, the psalmist has so far evaded the traps that have been set for him. His determined commitment to the light of God's Word allows him to rebuke the evildoers who keep trying to trip him up (119:105–120).

Sometimes people who devote much time and effort to studying scripture develop a kind of spiritual arrogance, but that is not the case for the psalmist. He realizes he will always have more to learn about God, and he remains a humble servant to God (119:122, 124–125). He detests the arrogance of the evildoers, and he will have nothing to do with that attitude, leaving it to God to deal with the problem (119:121–128). In fact, he is so captivated by the Word of God that he weeps when he sees others disobey it (119:129–136).

The psalmist isn't committing to some set of randomly assembled rules. The Lord is a righteous God, and the laws He provides reflect His righteousness (119:137–138). According to verse 140, the writer has thoroughly tested God's promises and has seen them work, even in the worst of circumstances. Not only are they functional and effective—they are a delight (119:143–144). But the psalmist has no run-of-the-mill commitment. In seeking God's truth, he calls out with all his heart (119:145). He is up before dawn and awake through the night to meditate on God's promises. Wicked people are nearby, but as long as God is nearer with His commands, the psalmist knows he will persevere (119:145–152).

Appealing to God for deliverance, the psalmist continues to profess his great love for God's law. He realizes that the wicked people who pursue him have no hope for deliverance, which gives him a greater appreciation for God's compassion toward him (119:153–160). He is being persecuted by powerful people who have no cause to do so, yet what really gets to him is the power of God's Word. Each new insight is like discovering valuable treasure (119:161–162). The reference to "seven times a day" in verse 164 is a way of saying "all the time," because seven is a number that indicates completeness or perfection. His focus on God provides a sense of peace even in trying times (119:165–168).

The psalm's closing stanza, verses 169–176, looks to the future. The psalmist intends to keep crying out to God, asking for help, praising Him, and singing. He wants God to continue providing understanding, deliverance, teaching, help, and delight. In return for continued life, he will offer continued praise. And yet after all the writer has said about his devotion to God, he concludes with a confession that he has strayed (119:176). In the context of everything else he has written, this is probably not so much an admission of falling away as an expression of desire to be closer to his heavenly Shepherd.

Demystifying Psalms

Psalms 120–134 are identified as Songs of Degrees, or Songs of Ascents, a title that is not totally clear. The Jewish Mishna associates the fifteen psalms with the fifteen steps that led to the temple, where the Levites who led the music would sing the songs. More common is the belief that this group of songs was sung by people making pilgrimages to Jerusalem. Three such journeys for community-wide religious festivals were expected each year (Deuteronomy 16:16–17). (The pilgrims had to ascend to the high altitude of their capital city.) The psalms were likely not written for such a purpose but were later grouped together for special use. This seems clear from the fact that four are attributed to David and one to Solomon, while the remaining ten are anonymous.

PSALM 120

The first of the Songs of Ascents isn't one of the more positive ones. The unnamed psalmist opens with complaints of distress and being the target of lies and deceit, so he had called on God and God had heard him (120:1–2).

The question in verse 3 is directed to the wicked people and is not so much a query as a preface to the warning in verse 4. God's judgment is coming, and the wicked will be punished. The "broom tree" (NIV) mentioned in verse 4 is reference to a desert plant with a trunk of very hard wood that was a popular source of charcoal.

The psalmist writes that being surrounded by such negative people is like being in faraway places noted for their hostility (120:5). Meshech was far north, in Asia Minor. Kedar was in northern Arabia.

Verses 6–7 conclude with the writer's longing for peace. The wording suggests that he could have been a king. Most people might speak of conflict, disputes, arguments, or such. But in this case the alternative to peace is war.

PSALM 121

The protection of God is the theme of Psalm 121. Pilgrimages could be dangerous journeys with both geographical challenges and criminal elements to contend with. As the psalmist looks upward toward Jerusalem, his destination, he acknowledges that his help comes from God, who had created those mountains (121:1–2). Verses 3–4 offer additional assurance: God's protection is effective around the clock, because He does not sleep. (Gods of other nations were thought to need sleep, a frequent excuse for their being out of touch with people.)

Critical Observation

Psalms that are designated for public religious ceremonies might use different voices. Psalm 121 is a good example. One speaker probably began with verses 1 and 2. (Note the first-person *I*.) But verses 3–8 then shift to the second person: *you*. It is likely they were spoken by different people.

God's protection is like shade in the hot and sometimes hostile climate of the Middle East. It was also thought at the time that too much exposure to the moon could cause problems as well. (English words such as *moonstruck* and *lunatic* are examples of such a belief.) But God's protection works day and night (121:5–6). In addition, verses 7–8 affirm that God will watch the pilgrim for the round-trip—coming *and* going.

PSALM 122

Psalm 122 is the first of the Songs of Ascents attributed to David. He had conquered Jerusalem, taken it from the Jebusites, and established it as the capital city of Israel (2 Samuel 5:6–10). It is not surprising, then, that he takes great pleasure to stand in the gates of the city and consider how it had become a place to offer praise to God (Psalm 122:1–4). During a pilgrimage when hundreds of nonresidents gathered to worship and celebrate, the mood would have been festive and the city would appear to be compact (122:3).

Those in attendance had heeded the statute given Israel to go to Jerusalem three times a year for special occasions of worship (Deuteronomy 16:16–17; Psalm 122:4). Jerusalem was a place for both spiritual pursuits and political justice. Verse 5 highlights the thrones of judgment that were there.

Jerusalem means "city of peace," an appropriate title in the days of David and Solomon.

But those people who sang this psalm in the period following the exile of Israel would soon realize how turbulent the recent history of Jerusalem had been. The call to pray for the peace of Jerusalem (122:6) probably has more significance in later years.

After the psalmist calls for others to pray for the peace of Jerusalem, in verses 8–9 he offers his personal prayer for the city. The ongoing security and prosperity of Jerusalem will benefit all the pilgrims who continue to make the journey, seeking to restore their relationship with God there.

PSALM 123

It is not uncommon for those who are devoted to God to suffer ridicule or contempt from those who are not believers. Such is the case described in Psalm 123. As the psalm closes in verse 4, the writer finally identifies the problem. The source of the ridicule is not known, but the description is of one entire group of people being harassed by another large group.

In such cases, it is difficult to ignore the verbal jeers, yet the psalmist has been able to divert his attention and place his eyes on the Lord (123:1). With no thought of personal revenge or frontier justice, he leaves the matter in God's hands. He compares his status to that of a slave or handmaiden, looking to the master (or mistress) of the house for mercy.

According to verse 3, the people need mercy from God because their enemies have treated them with great contempt. In this case, no request is made for the persecutors to be silenced, but the people need strength from God during this difficult time.

PSALM 124

Psalm 124 is attributed to David, although there is more question about his authorship of this psalm than many others bearing his name. The theme appears to fit Israel's history after the exile rather than before. If so, the reference to David in the superscription would indicate a subsequent king in the line of David.

Regardless of the author, the placement of Psalm 124 fits nicely following Psalm 123. The awareness of God's involvement with His people is the only thing that consoles them. They have been attacked by angry men, who are described as a flood intent on swallowing Israel alive (124:1–5). But rather than being swept away by the rage of their enemies, the Israelites weathered the storm because of God's deliverance.

Critical Observation

The images used by the psalmist of exposure to raging waters and wild animals would have been appropriate descriptions of Israel's captivity. The escape from the flood and release from the fowler's snare suggest their eventual release. If that were the case, then David could not have authored the psalm.

Using examples from the animal kingdom, the psalmist offers praise to God. Verse 6 summons the image of a vicious animal baring its fangs, but the terrible teeth have done no damage. Verse 7 expresses the joy a bird must feel to be momentarily trapped in a hunter's snare but then escape to its freedom. And in this case, the snare is broken to be a threat no more.

The Israelites believed God had created the heavens and the earth. Therefore, He is more than able to deliver them from human powers and the problems they might present (124:8).

PSALM 125

Psalm 125 is yet another of the Songs of Ascents that celebrates the security that only God can offer. The psalmist differentiates between those who trust in the Lord and those who don't. The former group is compared to Mount Zion on which Jerusalem was built, protected all around by surrounding mountains. Similarly, God surrounds His people to prevent them from being shaken by their circumstances (125:1–2).

The *scepter* in verse 3 indicates foreign power. If God had not limited the foreign domination of Israel, in time even the righteous people might have become corrupted by the pervasive wickedness.

The psalmist doesn't take God's protection for granted. He prays that God will do good for those who are upright in their hearts (125:4). They need God's help to overcome the temptations that surround them. There is always danger that some will turn away, and those who do will come to the same end as the evildoers (125:5). The writer then closes with a short but emphatic prayer for peace upon Israel.

PSALM 126

The author of Psalm 124 compares God's people to a bird that has been released from a fowler's snare—an escape from captivity to freedom (124:7). The writer of Psalm 126 describes a more realistic account of that event. Imagine seeing (or hearing of) the destruction of God's temple and the cherished city of Jerusalem, and then being carried away to a foreign land (Babylon) for seventy years. Think of the sorrow and helplessness the people must have felt. But then, after the Persians defeat the Babylonians, imagine getting word that it is okay to return home.

It was like being sick and suddenly getting well again. Spontaneous laughter was heard instead of the wailing and the unsettling questions about whether or not God knew or cared about their situation. Joyful songs quickly replaced the sad songs of captivity. (See Psalm 137, for example.) Israel was certainly overjoyed at God's deliverance, but more than that, the other nations could clearly see that Israel's God was at work (126:1–3).

The release from captivity was just a start, however. In verse 4 the psalmist prays for a restoration of Israel's fortunes. He thinks of the wilderness of the Negev with its seasonal streams. In hot weather they either reduce to a trickle or dry up completely, but when the rainy season arrives they fill up again. The psalmist wants Israel to once again overflow with God's blessing.

The closing image in verses 5–6 may sound confusing for those who thoughtlessly proclaim, "You reap what you sow." The principle still holds true here, but with a slight twist. The sowing is done with tears and sorrow, *but it is done*. Perhaps the psalmist is describing the people's return to Jerusalem after seventy years to start over again with planting and building. No doubt many tears were shed when they saw the destruction that had been done to their homeland. However, as time passed between sowing and reaping, the attitude of the people gradually improved. The harvesting is accompanied by songs of joy. The seeds may have been sown with salty tears, but they will eventually produce an abundance of grain that will be reaped and stored amid much rejoicing.

PSALM 127

Any pilgrimage to Jerusalem held a sense of excitement and expectation for the travelers. For those who lived in agrarian communities or small towns, the regular visits to a large city were no doubt highly anticipated. Psalm 127, however, is an on-the-road reminder of the appropriate priorities in life.

A day-to-day life that doesn't rely on God is in vain. The pilgrims have left their various houses, and the psalmist wants them to realize the importance of allowing God to be the foundation in each home. Then, as the pilgrims begin to get glimpses of Jerusalem in the distance, the psalm reminds them that only God's watchfulness will effectively protect the city. Without God's presence, the watchmen are just wasting their time (127:1).

God is the provider for His people. Those who don't acknowledge that fact can lose a lot of sleep attempting to do things that God would willingly do *for* them. They get up early and stay up late, always fretting about little things. But trust in God allows people to sleep well (127:2).

Verses 3–5 follow the same line of thinking: People should acknowledge their children as blessings of God, not merely products of their own biological design. In the ancient culture, sons were especially valued. As male children grew, they provided help on the farms, protection against danger, and representation of the family. The more sons that parents produced, the more they felt that God had blessed them (127:5).

Whether the topic is domestic life, national security, or family trees, God should be acknowledged as the source of all success and contentment.

Critical Observation

Psalm 127 is attributed to Solomon. The content certainly appears to reflect the message of Ecclesiastes, that all pursuits in life are meaningless apart from a basic underlying relationship with God.

PSALM 128

In the thinking of ancient Israel, prosperity and happiness were signs of God's favor. As pilgrims made their way to Jerusalem for their festivals and worship ceremonies, they tended to dwell more consciously on the blessings of God, so Psalm 128 was especially appropriate during those times.

According to verse 1, it is the fear of the Lord that prompts His blessing because it motivates people to obey and persevere. God rewards their labor with plentiful harvests, prosperity, and fertility (128:2–4). Grapes (vines) and olives are key crops that symbolize both God's bounty and long life.

It is, of course, a blessing to arrive safely in Jerusalem for times of celebration. But in verses 5–6, the psalmist looks beyond those special times, asking for God's blessing all the days of their lives. And with God's blessing, those days are more likely to stretch out into long lives, enabling faithful followers to see several generations of descendants before they died.

The psalmist also prays for the prosperity of Jerusalem. The people would have understood that as long as Jerusalem remained well protected and under the rule of a righteous king, the entire nation had no need to fear. This thought is emphasized in the final phrase as the writer asks God for peace upon Israel.

PSALM 129

After a series of positive and celebratory psalms (124–128), Psalm 129 is quite a contrast. The psalmist reflects on how Israel has suffered in the past. Although the nation has a long history of outside oppression, it has never been ultimately defeated (129:1–2).

The imagery in verse 3 is harsh, with the nation personified as someone who has long furrows from foreign plows dug down his back. This is perhaps a reference to the recent Babylonian takeover of Jerusalem. But even as bad as that experience had been, God had eventually freed His people from their bondage (129:4).

The offenses of the wicked are not forgotten, however. The psalmist has no tolerance for those who oppress God's people (and thereby resist God). He wishes them nothing but shame and failure. They may have plowed the back of Israel, but Israel has roots (129:3). Evildoers are like grass seeds that have blown onto a rooftop, growing with no source of nutrition or fertilization, destined to quickly wither and die (129:6–7).

It was customary in those days for passersby to greet strangers by wishing them God's blessing. In the case of Israel's enemies, however, the psalmist will not extend that wish (129:8). Because they are unable to harvest even enough to fill a person's arms (129:7), it should be clear that God's blessing is *not* upon them.

PSALM 130

Psalm 130 is one of the seven psalms in the *penitential* classification (along with Psalms 6, 32, 38, 51, 102, and 143). The psalmist expresses remorse for the sins he has committed and anticipation that God will forgive him and redeem him.

Verses 1–2 reveal the writer's mental state. He is crying out from his emotional depths, asking God to hear and be merciful. He realizes that God is not a heavenly recorder of wrongs—no one would ever be able to please Him. God chose to forgive the sins of His people, which is an astounding fact. The response, then, should be reverential fear of God—not cowering in panic or horror but willfully submitting to Him in worship and obedience (130:4).

While awaiting full restoration to a faithful relationship with God, the psalmist remains hopeful and watchful. Like a night watchman longing for daylight, he waits. The new day will bring both light and the regular morning offerings to God, so the writer yearns for his spiritual darkness to come to an end.

Verses 7–8 expand the scope of his prayer. No longer limited to his own situation, the psalmist challenges *all* of Israel to place their hope in God, seeking complete forgiveness and redemption.

PSALM 131

Although Psalm 131 is ascribed to David, it is not surprising that it is included among the Songs of Ascents. Psalm 131 would have been particularly appropriate for pilgrims approaching Jerusalem to worship. It is a song of contentment and complete hope placed in God.

David begins by declaring that his heart is humbled and his eyes are not haughty. The latter part of verse 1 is a commitment not to seek grandiose adventures that draw attention to himself. If his hope is in God, as he is advising Israel in verse 3, then God should get credit for all the victories and achievements of his life and career.

Instead of seeking glory, David strives to quiet himself. (His *soul* is his very being.) He compares himself in verse 2 to a young child who takes great comfort in the nearness of his mother. Specifying a weaned child may suggest that in the same way a young child outgrows a dependence on something as desirable as mother's milk, David has gotten past the need to distinguish himself as a warrior and empire builder. His inner being has become stilled and content. All his hope—now and forevermore—is in God (131:3).

PSALM 132

This psalm is a request for God to favor the king, a descendant of David. It may have been written considerably earlier than many of the other psalms in this section. It may have originally commemorated the dedication of the temple (2 Chronicles 6:41–42; Psalm 132:8–10), or it possibly was used during coronations. (The use of the psalm after the exile would probably have raised questions as to how the restructuring of the government during Jerusalem's rebuilding would mesh with the promises God had made to David.) In its position among the Songs of Ascents, the psalm would have been a historical reminder of how special the place was to which the pilgrims were traveling.

David had many great achievements, but the one thing he was unable to fulfill was his desire to build a house for God (132:1–5). (The details are provided in 2 Samuel 7, although the oath, or vow, mentioned by the psalmist in 132:2 is not to be found.) God denies David's request and instead gives the task to Solomon, a man of peace. But David does much of the groundwork and collecting of materials.

Demystifying Psalms

Ephrathah, mentioned in verse 6, is a more ancient name for Bethlehem that eventually came to refer to an area *around* Bethlehem. The additional mention of the fields of Jaar points to the more specific location of Kiriath Jearim, the place where the ark of the covenant was housed for twenty years after it was returned by the Philistines (1 Samuel 6:21–7:2).

Part of David's preparation involved moving the ark of the covenant from Kiriath Jearim to Jerusalem. The location of the ark soon came to be known as God's dwelling place and His footstool (132:7–8). The temple was eventually built and priests were assigned to care for all aspects of community worship (132:9).

The first half of Psalm 132 deals with David's commitment to God; the second half addresses God's promise to David. One key element is that God said one of David's descendants would sit on the throne forever (132:11–12).

God also confirms David's choice of Jerusalem (Mount Zion) for His dwelling (132:13–14). Verses 15–16 relate God's promise to bless the city at all levels—the poor, the priests, and all the godly people (the saints).

Another promise of God closes the psalm in verses 17–18. With His previous covenant with David in mind, God promises to make a horn grow. The image is borrowed from the animal kingdom, where horns are symbols of power, so in this case it refers to the king, or the anointed one. God's king will rule in glory; his enemies will experience only shame and defeat.

In the original Hebrew, the word for *grow* is related to the word *branch*, which is a title often used for the prophesied Messiah. So the closing of the psalm hints of the ruler yet to come, who will be the ultimate fulfillment of God's promise to David.

PSALM 133

When Israel's priests are ordained, they are anointed with oil made from a special formula. It is sacred, not to be used for any other purpose (Exodus 30:30–33). The high priest, as in Aaron's case (Psalm 133:2), is dressed in his official priestly uniform, including a breastplate on which the names of the twelve tribes are found (Exodus 28:21, 29; Leviticus 8:1–13).

This would have been the image in David's mind as he wrote Psalm 133. The first time this special ceremony had been performed, the oil was poured on Aaron's head to consecrate him for service. David feels the same sense of wonder when he thinks of the unity of his people coming together to honor and serve their Lord (Psalm 133:1). Perhaps this psalm was written in response to the uniting of the kingdom after David had struggled for several years to bring together those who supported him with others who would rather have had a second king from Saul's family.

The thought of oil flowing down Aaron's beard is reinforced by the image of dew on Mount Hermon. At an altitude of more than 9,000 feet, Mount Hermon was often the only splash of green on an otherwise dry and brown landscape. The refreshing difference that unity made for the people of Israel was no less striking than the effect that water had on an arid land. These thoughts would have been especially appropriate for pilgrims making their way to Jerusalem to worship with their brothers.

PSALM 134

In this last of the series of Songs of Ascents, the servants of the Lord are acknowledged in verse 1. These servants are the priests who minister in the temple, both day and night (1 Chronicles 9:33; 23:28–31). In this case, perhaps the evening ceremonies are wrapping up and the participants, as they leave, are encouraging the priests who remained behind on the night shift. Verse 2 reflects the image in Psalm 28:2 of priests lifting their hands toward the sanctuary (the Most Holy Place that contains the ark of the covenant and signifies God's presence).

The closing verse of the psalm, and therefore the concluding thought of the series of Songs of Ascents, is a prayer for God's blessing. It may have been the prayer of the pilgrims directed to the priests. Or perhaps Psalm 134 was used as a dialog, where the community would recite the first two verses and a designated priest would respond with the blessing in verse 3.

Take It Home

As a group, the Songs of Ascents covers a wide variety of thoughts and emotions, all appropriate for people journeying toward Jerusalem to worship. As they sang the same songs along the same route year after year, the songs surely took on special significance. Can you think of songs that do the same thing for you—that highlight certain places or seasons when you feel especially close to God?

PSALMS: BOOK V, CONTINUED

PSALMS 135–150

Setting Up the Section

This section finishes up Book V, and therefore the biblical book of Psalms as well. Of the sixteen psalms that remain, half of them comprise a series attributed to David. The remaining ones are anonymous.

PSALM 135

Although not designated as one of the Songs of Ascents, Psalm 135 appears to have been used for special occasions in the temple worship ceremonies. It begins and ends with the familiar cry to praise the Lord, and the psalm contains many specific reasons to do so. The first challenge to praise God goes out to the temple servants—the priests and Levites.

God is deserving of praise from His people. To begin with, He is good (135:3). In addition, He has reached out to people. He chose Jacob (Israel) and all Jacob's descendants (the Israelites) to be His treasured possession (135:4).

The people of the surrounding nations cannot make the same claims about their gods. God is sovereign and able to do whatever He wishes (135:5–7), yet He chooses to create, sustain, and bless His people.

Verses 6–7 are reminders that God's power is seen in all of nature—earth, skies, and seas. Clouds, wind, rain, and lightning are all part of His wonderful design. Rain was a particularly appreciated blessing of God in the climate and geography of the Middle East.

But God is not limited to working through nature. He is a God of miracles that defy the laws of nature. In verses 8–9, the psalmist recalls the plagues sent upon Egypt—perhaps the best known of God's miracles. But Egypt's Pharaoh was only one of many leaders who caused problems for Israel. As God continued to lead the Israelites toward the promised land, there were other kings who tried to stop them. Each time, God delivered His people (135:10–12).

Demystifying Psalms

The Israelites had encountered Og and Sihon (135:11) in the wilderness on the way from Egypt to Canaan (Numbers 21:21–35). And when they finally entered the promised land, they were immediately confronted with a series of other powerful forces they had to defeat before they could settle in the land (Joshua 6–12). But God was with them all along the way and gave them the land as an inheritance, just as He had promised Abraham.

Those events had taken place long ago, yet God is still a reliable source of protection and compassion (135:13–14). Other nations had tried to overthrow Israel, and Israel had even turned to the gods of those nations from time to time, but God had never forsaken His fickle people. The psalmist points out the impotence of idols in verses 15–17. They may be designed to *look* like people or gods, yet they remain handmade lumps of wood and metal unable to speak, see, hear, or breathe. The tragic effect of idol worship is that the people who worship idols become like the idols—spiritually impotent with no hope of real life or positive change (135:18).

So the psalmist again calls all who will listen to praise the Lord—both those who are responsible for spiritual leadership and the laypeople who are assembled to worship (135:19–21).

PSALM 136

It seems pretty clear from the structure of Psalm 136 that it was used for public worship, with a designated Levite reciting the first portion of each statement as a temple choir, or perhaps the worshipers in attendance, responded with, "His love endures forever." The format of the psalm makes it unique, but its content is similar to that of Psalm 135. Both psalms begin with the affirmation that God is good (135:3; 136:1) and then detail ways to indicate that He is also great.

God is good (136:1). He is God of gods and Lord of lords (136:2–3). With these initial observations, the accompanying triple command to give thanks in the first three verses is an emphatic opening.

Verses 4–9 provide a short synopsis of the creation story using language similar to that found in Genesis 1. In verse 4, the list of great wonders of God begins with His creation of heaven and earth, sun and moon.

From Creation, the psalmist moves to the Exodus in verses 10–15. God had done what the people assumed was impossible at the time: freed them from the power of the mighty Egyptians. The plagues are summarized with only the last, most effective one (136:10). Israel had been powerless, so they had to depend solely on God's power and sovereignty (136:12). When Pharaoh changed his mind and gave pursuit, God remained in complete control even though deliverance included having His people walk through the midst of a divided Red Sea, pursued by the Egyptian army that ended up drowing (136:13–15).

After escape came the challenge of the wilderness wanderings. Again, the people made it harder than it should have been, yet God's love endured. God dispensed with the opposing kings both in the desert and after the Israelites crossed the Jordan into the promised land. (For information on Sihon and Og, see comments on Psalm 135.)

Verses 23–26 summarize the ongoing work of God. He never forgot His people when they were suffering. He had always delivered them from their enemies. He provided food and necessities, and His provision went beyond Israel. God had been Creator of the world, and His gifts were available to every living thing (136:25).

There are many reasons to give thanks to God. But at the top of the list, as the psalmist reminds his listeners twenty-six times during this song, God should be thanked because His love endures forever.

PSALM 137

Psalm 137 begins as a mournful recollection of Israel's time spent in Babylon, and it ends with a brutal imprecation against those responsible for the destruction of Jerusalem. The request of Israel's captors in verse 3 adds insult to injury. The Israelites were in great distress over the fall of their city and temple. They experienced the end of life as they had known it. They were powerless in a foreign land, and then the people there started asking to hear some of their native music, which heightened their despair. So they hung up their harps and opted for silence (137:1–3).

Critical Observation

The prophet Jeremiah had encouraged the Israelites to make the most of a bad situation—to settle down in Babylon, increase in number, and pray for the people there. He told them their stay would be limited and that God would then return them to their homeland (Jeremiah 29:4–14). Clearly it wasn't a terrible place to be because the people were dwelling beside rivers with poplar trees (Psalm 137:1–2). Still, the losses they had incurred were painful to them.

Verses 4–6 attest to the people's great love for Jerusalem. They were far away from home, but they weren't about to forget what it had meant to them. They had taken much for granted in the final years of the monarchy, and they had suffered the consequences.

But memories of Jerusalem—the setting of their temple, worship, feasts, celebrations, and more—had become their greatest source of joy. They even called down curses on themselves if they dared to forget their home city.

Finally, in verses 7–9, the Israelites wish the worst possible retribution upon the people who had been responsible for the terrible treatment of Jerusalem. The Edomites had been longstanding enemies of Israel and Judah, and they had taken cruel pleasure in seeing the Babylonians invade and conquer Jerusalem. The Israelites wish the same end to come to Edom—an end that is, in fact, later prophesied (Isaiah 63:1–6; Lamentations 4:21).

Worse than the Edomites, however, are the Babylonians. Even after the Medes and Persians conquered the Babylonian Empire, Babylon remained a symbol for everything opposed to God. The wish of Israel was that Babylon would become the victim of the same atrocities that they had inflicted on others.

Psalm 137:8–9 contains the most severe of the imprecations in Psalms. It is interesting to note, however, that while Israel was a rocky country, Babylon was not. The desire for infants to be dashed against rocks may well have been a general cry for God's justice rather than a specific, literal request.

PSALM 138

Psalm 138 begins a series of the final eight psalms of David that have been recorded. In this song, David offers his praise to God for a number of reasons, and his praise is unrestrained.

The gods he mentions in verse 1 may be foreign kings (men with a seriously inflated sense of importance), or they may be the actual worshiped deities. Either way, David is comfortable worshiping the Lord in front of these other gods. And as with other psalms attributed to David, his use of the term *temple* in verse 2 is presumed to mean the temporary housing he established for the ark of the covenant before it eventually took its more familiar position in the Most Holy Place of Solomon's temple (2 Samuel 6:17).

David gives God credit for making him "bold and stouthearted" (Psalm 138:3 NIV). He had called out to God, and God had answered him, resulting in his praise for God's love and faithfulness. He knows that God's name and God's Word are above all things (138:2).

David's prayer is that *all* kings will hear the words of God and respond with praise, acknowledging His glory (138:4–5). Much will depend on their individual attitudes. God is highly exalted, yet He is always willing to respond to the lowly—those who humble themselves and seek His help. Those who attempt to exalt themselves in pride, however, miss out on God's compassionate help and support (138:6).

David is among those who had humbled themselves. He had frequently found himself threatened, and God had always delivered him (138:7). In verse 8, David first states his belief that God will accomplish His will. Then he affirms his faith that God's love will endure forever. And finally, even in light of the confident faith he had expressed, he asks God yet again to continue to work in his life.

PSALM 139

Psalm 139 is an amazing expression of God's loving familiarity of David, and David's unrelenting devotion in return. David's description of God's awareness of his life might be off-putting for many people. God is watching when the psalmist wakes up, goes to bed, sits down, and gets up. He knows every word David says and thinks (139:1–4).

How does David feel about the close scrutiny of God? It depends on how one interprets his comments. When he writes in verse 5 of being hemmed in, both in front and behind, and of having the hand of God upon him, does he feel restricted? Protected? In verses 7–12, is he describing futile attempts to carve out a little personal time and space for himself? Or is he speculating about the unlimited ability of God to watch over him wherever he might find himself—heights or depths, day or night, one side of the sea or the other? Either way, his musings have shown him that the omnipresence of God is both too lofty and too wonderful for him to absorb (139:6).

Demystifying Psalms

Throughout Psalm 139, David's use of the term *wonderful* (139:6, 14) is not what modern English speakers might assume. David uses this word in the sense of *wondrous* or *miraculous*—beyond human comprehension.

David acknowledges God's involvement in his life from conception (139:13–16). The word *for*, that opens verse 13, connects this thought with the previous sections. Since God creates a person's inmost being and knits him or her within the mother's womb, doesn't it only make sense that He would also have an acute awareness of everything that person does as an adult? David surmises that God had his life span and accomplishments in mind before David was born.

Such deep thinking fascinates David. Verses 17–18 describe his thoughts as precious, vast, and innumerable. Every morning brings new wonder that God is still available and accessible to him.

Even though God knows David intimately, there is still much about God that David does not understand. He expresses confusion over why God allows wicked people to continue in their bloodthirsty pursuits, apparently unimpeded (139:19–22). They have no regard for God and even less for righteous people, so David declares any enemy of God an enemy of his. Yet as David was wont to do, he leaves vengeance up to God (139:19).

Finally, verses 23–24 offer one of the most fascinating challenges of scripture. David had certainly committed some grievous sins against God on occasion. But at this point in his life, he is able to ask God to examine both his actions and his thoughts to attempt to detect anything offensive or improper. Few people get to a point in their spiritual lives where they will consider making such an invitation.

PSALM 140

Much of David's life was spent on the run from people who wanted to see him dead. Psalm 140 recounts one such time when he cried out to God for help. David's adversaries are both evil and violent (140:1–2). In verse 3 he compares them to snakes, with sharp tongues like serpents and poison like vipers. They are cunning and devious, setting snares and traps (140:5).

David prays for both rescue and protection (140:1, 4). He feels threatened and vulnerable, yet he is confident that God is strong and merciful (140:6–7).

In verses 8–11, David's prayer takes an imprecatory turn as he asks God to allow his wicked adversaries to suffer. However, David's desire is essentially an eye-for-an-eye request for justice. His persecutors had troubled others with their words, so David asks that their lips cause *them* trouble. They have stalked innocent victims and set traps like hunters, so David wants them to become the prey, hunted down by some kind of divine disaster. The ultimate result, he hopes, will be a permanent end to their slander and violence.

On a more positive note, David concludes in verses 12–13 with an affirmation of God's justice and His care for the poor and needy. Righteous and upright people ultimately have nothing to fear.

PSALM 141

One of the insidious consequences of wickedness is that people are prone to instinctively return evil for evil. In Psalm 141, however, David prays that God will prevent him from responding in such a way to people who provoke him. In the opening verses, he compares his prayer to the worship ceremony that took place in the tabernacle, including the smoke of incense rising to God as a prayer and the lifting of his hands as might be done during an evening sacrifice.

David is aware of the actions and intentions of wicked people. They have gotten away with their evil behavior and are enjoying fine foods and an elegant lifestyle as a result. It is tempting to want to join them in their opulence, yet he wants nothing to do with them. He asks God to guard both his lips and his heart (141:3–4).

Verse 5 makes clear that David is by no means opposed to discipline or rebuke. He welcomes constructive criticism from righteous people, even if it is frank and harsh. He considers such help refreshing, like oil on his head. David has no tolerance for the words of the wicked, however. He wishes them to be thrown down from cliffs, realizing in their final moments that he has used only well-spoken words in his dealings with them. Verse 7 is not clear in its intent, but it seems to be a desire for the bones of the wicked to be dispersed like clods of dirt in a farmer's field, indicating the lack of a proper burial.

Much clearer is David's next declaration of trust in God (141:8). God, as always, is his refuge. He will keep his eyes on God and trust Him for deliverance from death. He knows the snares of the wicked are still out there (141:9–10). With God in control, however, David will be able to travel in safety while the evildoers become entangled in their own traps.

PSALM 142

The fifth of the eight psalms of David in this section, Psalm 142 has common themes with others in the set. This is the only one of the series, however, that provides a clue in its introduction as to David's situation. As David writes this psalm (as well as Psalm 57), he appears to be thinking about the time when King Saul unexpectedly went into the cave where he was hiding (1 Samuel 24).

When strong and powerful enemies threatened David, he turned to God for help. Not only did God hear David's cry, but He also responded with mercy and protection. God was a consistent guide and supporter even when David grew weak and found himself in danger (142:1–3).

To this day, people speak of a right-hand man, meaning much the same that David does in verse 4. The position to one's right is where a bodyguard, advocate, or loyal friend would have stood. David points out that he has no one there. He is alone.

With no other source of support, David turns to God as his sole refuge. Even in his desperation, he is counting on God to deliver him. Without God, David's enemies are too strong for him. But after God's intervention, David fully expects to gather with other righteous people in the land of the living to praise the name of God and thank Him for His goodness (142:5–7).

PSALM 143

This prayer of David is classified among the *penitential* psalms, the final one of this category in the book of Psalms (along with 6, 32, 38, 51, 102, and 130). Although similar in content to many of David's other psalms, this one contains the acknowledgment that he is among the unrighteous people worthy of judgment, and he asks to be spared (143:1–2).

Critical Observation

The author's content within the psalm is only part of the reason the song might be classified as penitential. Another criterion is how the psalm is later used by the early Christian church.

As was his habit, David turns to God when his enemies begin to threaten him. His situation is certainly unenviable. Verse 3 describes how his pursuers crush his spirit and create a deathlike darkness. He is fainthearted and dismayed, but he takes comfort in recalling better days (143:4–5). He knows of God's faithfulness in the past, and he continues to count on it. He thirsts for God, realizing his need is like parched land needing water for any life to continue (143:6).

David's condition leads to his request for God to answer *quickly* in verse 7. Those who go down to the pit, who are mentioned in verse 7, are people who die. The darkness in David's life is severe. He needs light, so he asks God for relief by the morning. His trust remains in God, and he is eager for God to act (143:8).

David doesn't just ask for deliverance from his enemies. He is also eager for God to teach him and provide a solid foundation for his life (143:9–10). When God delivers David, it will reflect His righteousness and power.

According to verses 2 and 12, David considers himself God's servant throughout this whole ordeal. From beginning to end of this psalm, he remains humble. The psalm doesn't reveal if his prayer is answered, but David's willingness to allow God to handle the situation is a likely indication that it is.

PSALM 144

Another psalm attributed to David, Psalm 144 combines the psalmist's praise for God with a request for deliverance. Verses 1–2 begin immediately to list reasons God should be praised. Ever the military man, David notices the strong and powerful aspects of God. The Lord is a rock, fortress, stronghold, shield, and refuge. He can be counted on for training and skill in battle, delivering His people, and subduing enemy nations. Yet David doesn't miss the point that the Lord is also a loving God.

Verses 3–4 touch on the almighty God's concern for weak and temporal humanity—the same themes as David's Psalm 8, where they are a bit more fully developed. David then asks to witness the strength of his mighty God in the form of rescue from his enemies. David's foes are liars and deceivers (144:7–8, 11), so he wants God to scatter them with lightning and power (144:5–6). In return, David will play and sing a new song to acknowledge God's victory (144:9–10).

David is looking to the future, to a time when Israel's enemies will no longer be an influence and God will rule supreme. Children will be strong and productive. The country will be prosperous. The city will be safe. And above all, God's blessing will be felt by the people, who will be loyal to Him in return (144:12–15).

PSALM 145

Psalm 145 is a psalm of praise—the only one in the entire book of Psalms so designated in its introduction. It makes a satisfying finale for the series of eight psalms attributed to David, who asks for nothing for himself, but rather keeps his focus on God throughout this song. It is also a fitting transition into the final five songs in the Psalter. From this point onward, much emphasis will be placed on the importance of praising God. And while the psalmist is communicating his many reasons to praise the Lord, he structures this song as an alphabetic acrostic.

First and foremost in verses 1–2 is David's commitment to praise God—every day, for ever and ever. Next he describes *why* God deserves praise. To begin with, the greatness of God is incomprehensible (145:3). His mighty actions and splendor are topics of teaching and conversation between generations (145:4–5).

David makes sure to include himself among the worshipers. In verses 5–6 he uses both third-person and first-person references: "*They* will speak. . .and *I* will meditate." "*They* will tell. . .and *I* will proclaim." In doing so, he notes God's splendor, His wonderful (awe-inspiring) works, His goodness, and His righteousness.

Verses 8–9 continue the list. God is gracious, compassionate, slow to anger, and rich in love. His goodness and compassion are evident from everything He has created. People who identify and appreciate the work of God will not only praise Him for His works but will also tell other people. God's kingdom is enduring and everlasting (145:10–13).

People in need will especially be glad for the gifts of God. He is loving, He honors His promises, He uplifts the fallen, He provides food, and He is the source that can satisfy all desires (145:13–16).

For all these reasons and more, David concludes this psalm in verses 17–21 with his final expression of praise to God, inviting every living thing to join him. Those who call on God will discover that He is near. Those who love God will be protected. But those who reject Him to continue to live in wickedness will eventually be destroyed.

PSALM 146

When people need help, they have a choice. They can depend on other people or they can turn to God. This psalm offers praise to God because He is always dependable.

Critical Observation

Psalms 146–150 focus on praising God. Each of these songs that close out the Psalter both begin and end with the phrase, "Praise the Lord" (or "Hallelujah").

According to verses 3–4, putting one's trust in people eventually leads to disappointment. All people, even those with power and influence, are mortal. Their ability to help is limited in both time and degree. Situations will arise where their power is insufficient. And their influence ends with death.

So the psalmist offers praise to God, who is not limited in any way (146:1–2). God is the Creator of all things, and He remains faithful (146:5–6). The people who need help most can always count on Him: the oppressed, the hungry, the prisoners, the blind, those who are bowed down, the alien, the fatherless, and the widows (146:7–9).

God's love and help extend to all who are righteous, the psalmist declares in verse 8. Those who are wicked, however, will find themselves frustrated. God should be praised regularly because His reign will last forever (146:9–10).

PSALM 147

This psalm of praise is in regard to God's faithfulness to Israel after their exile. Immediately after the opening call to praise, the psalmist begins to recount the events after the people's release from captivity. Verses 2–3 recall the gathering of the exiles and the building (actually, the rebuilding) of Jerusalem. The people were brokenhearted to see what had been done to the city and how much repair needed to be done, but God was there to heal their wounded spirits.

The psalmist reminds everyone that the same God who helped them is the One who had created, numbered, and named the stars. The rain He provides supplies life-supporting water for both domestic and wild animals. His understanding and His power are unlimited. And while His power will be used to subdue the wicked, it will always provide support for the humble (147:4–9).

People tend to be impressed by strong animals and athletic feats, but God delights in those who fear Him and respond to His unfailing love (147:10–11). The psalmist challenges His people to praise the Lord because God will strengthen Jerusalem and bless those within the city with peace and prosperity (147:12–14). God's care for the earth can be seen in the seasons—some with frost, ice, and hail, and others with warm breezes and flowing water (147:15–18). But the people of Israel have an additional reason to praise God that no one else has. Verses 19–20 conclude with the reminder that God has revealed His Word to the Israelites. No other nation knows His laws and has the same privilege of responding and relating to the great God of creation and redemption.

PSALM 148

Psalm 148 is a call for everyone and everything to praise God. Verses 1–6 exhort those in the heavens to praise Him: angels and heavenly hosts, sun, moon, stars, clouds and waters above the skies. All have been created and established by God, and He deserves their praise.

Verses 7–12 bring the praise more down to earth as the psalmist beckons the great creatures of the sea, the elements (lightning, hail, snow, clouds, and winds), mountains, trees, wild and domestic animals, human rulers (kings and princes), and *all* people—young and old, male and female. Of everything the psalmist lists, nothing is worthy of praise except the name of the Lord. People have limited knowledge of heaven and earth, but God's splendor is unbounded (148:13).

The horn mentioned in verse 14 is a symbol for power that frequently represents the king. But sometimes, and this may be one such case, the horn is symbolic of the glory God has provided for His people. God's people are close to His heart, and for that reason (among many others) He should be praised.

PSALM 149

Psalm 149 is a call for the entire community of Israel to offer praise to God. As God continues to act on behalf of His people, the appropriate response is to sing a new song of praise to Him (149:1).

The people should praise God for their salvation (149:4). According to verses 2–5, their praise should take various enthusiastic forms: dancing, tambourine and harp music, songs during the night, and an overall attitude of gladness and rejoicing.

In addition, the people should praise God because He has empowered them to be victorious. They have not sat idly waiting for God to remove their problems; they have taken up swords to protect their nation. The victory will always be God's, but His people are involved and faithfully committed to Him, which entails occasional struggles and conflicts with other nations.

Critical Observation

The double-edged sword mentioned in verse 6 was a relatively new invention at this time. Earlier mentions of a sword in scripture, such as the time period of Joshua and the judges, frequently refer to a curved instrument with the outside edge sharpened. By this time, though, the sword had evolved into a straight weapon with both sides of the blade sharpened and able to inflict blows.

With God providing victory and safety for His people, they should always be prepared to praise Him.

PSALM 150

Psalm 1 appears to be positioned intentionally to introduce the book of Psalms. Similarly, this concluding psalm may have been written to close the book with a final emphasis on the importance of praise. Each book within the biblical book of Psalms ends with a short doxology. In this case, the final psalm serves as the doxology for Book V.

The Israelites perceive that God has a temple in heaven as well as the one they are familiar with in Jerusalem, and verse 1 calls for God to be praised in both locations. God is to be praised for the feats He had performed for Israel in His power and for His greatness that surpasses all others.

The long series of instruments listed in verses 3–5 includes strings, wind instruments, and percussion. When united, the result will be an enthusiastic accompaniment to praise, along with dancing (150:4). God, the Creator of all things, should be praised by everything that has breath (150:6). The psalm (and the book of Psalms) concludes with one final "Praise the Lord."

Take It Home

Many of the psalms in this section reflect life in Israel after the Babylonian invasion and the captivity of God's people. A few of the psalms focus on the negative aspects of the experience. Some look back to review the blessings the people had before they were conquered. Several dwell almost exclusively on praise for a new beginning. When things have gone badly in your life, do you tend to dwell on the past, or are you quick to attempt to learn from your mistakes and move on in faith and praise to God?

PROVERBS

INTRODUCTION TO PROVERBS

As the preface to the book states, Proverbs is about wisdom. On one level, wisdom is a skill of living, a practical knowledge. Wise people know how to say the right thing at the right time and to do the right thing at the right time. They live in a way that maximizes blessing for themselves and others in the world that God created.

But at a deeper level, wisdom is more profound than an ability to navigate life well. Indeed, it begins with a proper attitude toward God characterized by "fear." This is not the type of fear that makes someone run away, but it is more than respect. It is the awe that a person should feel when in the presence of the sovereign Creator of the universe.

Proverbs is a book about wisdom, and it intends to make its reader wise.

AUTHOR

The book of Proverbs is associated with Solomon, Israel's wisest king. His writings—or his teachings put into writing by a scribe—form most of the book. It was revealed in 1 Kings 4:32 that Solomon spoke three thousand proverbs, and it is good to have the book of Proverbs to see what he was teaching. A few additional short sections come from other contributors: anonymous writers (22:17–24:22), Agur (chapter 30), and Lemuel (chapter 31).

PURPOSE

The purpose of the book of Proverbs is stated in 1:2–3: to provide wisdom that, when applied, will lead to a godly life. Solomon seemed especially eager for his son to learn and apply the principles in this book, but they are general enough (and simple enough) for everyone to benefit from.

THEMES

The theme that runs throughout Proverbs is the value of wisdom, particularly in contrast to folly in its various forms. Wisdom should permeate one's life in personal attitudes and behaviors, family relationships, business dealings, worship, and every other aspect of the human experience. The fact that such teachings are associated with the wealthiest king in Israel's history gives them added weight.

CONTRIBUTION TO THE BIBLE

Proverbs belongs to the collection of Old Testament books called Wisdom Literature, which comprises the books of Job, Psalms, Proverbs, Ecclesiastes, and Song of Songs (also known as Song of Solomon). These books are all concerned with ordinary life and how to live it well.

The book of Proverbs has two major parts. In chapters 1–9, the reader encounters speeches. Mostly, they are the speeches of a father to a son (see 1:8–19), but occasionally a figure named Wisdom speaks to all the young men (1:20–33).

The second part of the book is filled with proverbs, short observations, warnings, and encouragements that are typically very practical.

A proverb is a very important literary device that played a prominent role in Israel and also the Middle East. A proverb is a short saying that combines knowledge with action. It is a truth that is applied to real life.

Look at Proverbs 13:3: *Whoever guards his mouth preserves his life; he who opens wide his lips comes to ruin.* (ESV)

There is a truth being put into real life. A person who speaks without thinking, and thus speaks things that are hurtful or harmful, will in the end hurt himself. A person who takes responsibility for his thoughts, guards his heart, and thus watches what he says, will not suffer the fate of the careless.

This proverb deals with the issue of a person's heart (there is the lofty principle)—what we are thinking about and what we are focusing on—and offers a practical application of how to guard the heart.

OUTLINE

PROVERBS 1:1–9:18

FATHERLY WISDOM

Setting Up the Section

The book of Proverbs is not just a grouping of pithy sayings but rather the application of the knowledge of God to real life. This is true wisdom. When we acquire such wisdom, we have more than just good advice; we have the key that unlocks the door to instruction, moral discernment, guidance, and spiritual insight.

The book of Proverbs does not begin with a long set of instructions as to how we are to live our lives. It begins by telling us the great value of wisdom and that the first step in gaining wisdom is to fear God.

1:1–7

TOWARD A PURSUIT OF WISDOM

Verse 1 establishes the credibility of the proverbs in this book by identifying them with Solomon, the wisest man (except for Jesus Christ) who ever lived. When Solomon took the throne, God gave him "a wise and discerning heart, so that there will never have been anyone like you, nor will there ever be" (1 Kings 3:12 NIV).

Verses 2–6 outline several purposes of the book of Proverbs, all having to do with wisdom and understanding. The Hebrew word translated *knowledge* in verse 7 is a synonym for *wisdom*. This type of knowledge is not just possessing information; it is the ability to apply that information in real life. Many people are what could be called *practical* fools. A practical fool might mentally acknowledge the presence of God, but God plays no part in the way this person lives his or her life.

Critical Observation

The NLT Study Bible defines "fear of the Lord" this way:

Fear implies respect, awe, and (at times) knee-knocking terror. It also acknowledges that everything, including knowledge and wisdom, comes from total dependence on God. The fear of the Lord leads people toward humility and away from pride (3:7; 15:33). With such an attitude, readers of Proverbs are more apt to listen to God than to their own independent judgment. (*New Living Translation Study Bible.* Carol Stream, IL: Tyndale House, 2008, page 1030)

1:8–19

FROM GENFRATION TO GENERATION

According to verse 8, wisdom begins when a child listens to his father and mother. The word *listen* in this text carries the idea of listening with the intent to obey. The implication here is that the parents are themselves wise and godly people.

The articles in verse 9 (variously translated as crown, pendant, garland, etc.) are signs of success and blessing.

The greatest threat any young person faces is that of being deceived into falling with a group of people who do not love what God loves (1:10–12). The enticement of sin is to acquire things that God has not given (1:13–14).

The warning in verse 15 is clear: The goal is not to get as close to a sinful lifestyle and see how much of your Christian virtues you can keep. The goal is to stay off the path altogether.

It is foolish to try to trap a bird by setting a trap while the bird is watching (1:17). It is just as foolish to try to profit illegally (1:18). If you follow this path, you will self-destruct (1:19).

1:20–33

THE CALL OF WISDOM

Wisdom is personified as a woman in Proverbs (1:20). Wisdom is not waiting for people to come to her. Instead, she is going into the streets to meet people (1:21). God does not wait in some passive manner for His people to come to Him; He goes to them.

The simple ones mentioned in verse 22 are immature or ignorant, and they are perfectly content in this situation. The scoffers, or mockers, hear the wisdom of God but make fun of it.

They have a condescending spirit toward the truth. The fools reject the very notion that God exists. They do not simply avoid wisdom as the simple do, or make fun of it as the scoffers; they oppose it and reject it outright.

Yet to these three groups wisdom continues to speak with a strong message of mercy: If you seek wisdom, wisdom will not run from you (1:23).

Verses 24–25 are transition verses, telling what is going to happen because the simple, scoffers, and fools do not listen: disaster. Wisdom has four responses to the calamity that comes upon those who have rejected her. She laughs, mocks, refuses to answer, and hides (1:26–28).

Take It Home

The responses outlined in verses 26–28 might seem callous. Is God really so hardened that when human folly leads to disaster He will not respond? The reality is that before God responds this way, He reaches out over and over again. This response is not the first response of God but the last.

Yet it is a merciful response. Only when we see the fullness of the folly of our ways will we be able to walk away from our folly. God's consequences are the means and the tools God uses to break us of our foolishness.

Those who have chosen folly do not do so out of ignorance; they have made a conscious decision to do things their own way rather than doing things God's way (1:29–31). They will experience the pain and misery that comes from doing things their own way, while the wise will enjoy security and freedom from fear (1:32–33).

2:1–22

THE PURSUIT OF WISDOM

In chapter 2, the father again speaks. He lays out three conditions for true knowledge, using *if* statements. One must receive wise advice with respect and with the intention of taking it to heart (2:1–2). One must not only accept wise guidance when it is offered but seek it out (2:3). In fact, one must value wisdom so much as to make the pursuit of wisdom a high priority (2:4). Then he or she will gain the fear of the Lord (2:5). (See the Critical Observation at 1:7 for a definition.)

The father is not talking about just listening to his own words with this gusto but rather to the wisdom of God. The Lord loves to give wisdom to people, and He does so with generosity (2:6).

Take It Home

The role of teaching in the home is not simply teaching a trade, or even all our personal ideas about life. The role of the parent is to point children to the wisdom of God.

There is a moral dimension to gaining wisdom; those who are upright will find that God will go before them, protecting them in this world (2:7–8).

Verse 9 begins with the word *then*, which shows that this is a result of what has just been said. If a person seeks wisdom from God, many things will happen. He will understand what is right—how the holiness of God is meant to express itself in time and space. He will be a person who is fair, good, and noble. He will know what path to take and what decisions to make (2:9).

Knowledge will become pleasant to the seeker (2:10). He will develop such a taste for it that he will pursue it more and more. The wisdom and discretion he gains will protect him from the folly that comes when one does not operate as a wise person in this world (2:11).

Verses 12–19 outline two specific forms of protection. First, a wise person will be protected from falling in with a bad crowd (2:12–15). Only wisdom will keep a person from falling into this path. Second, a wise person will be protected from sexually immoral people (2:16–19). This protection does not come from living an ascetic lifestyle. The true solution comes from fearing the Lord and living for God's glory and seeking after wisdom as a way of life.

Demystifying Proverbs

The book of Proverbs identifies two main categories of temptation. The first is that of being tempted to run with a crowd of people who pursue sin. The second is to be pulled into an immoral relationship with a woman. Wisdom protects against both, as 2:12–19 promises.

In verse 20, the end result is that the wise person will walk in a manner that pleases God. Those who do walk in this manner will have the promised blessing that all Israelites seek (2:21). But those who do not walk in this way will have the pain and misery that comes from folly (2:20).

3:1–35

TRUSTING IN THE LORD

Since a young person does not have as much experience, he should heed the wisdom of his parents (3:1). The fruit of this obedience is a life that escapes the pain associated with foolishness (3:2).

What one has around the neck—close to the throat—influences one's words, and words reflect character. The heart refers to the core of what motivates all that one does. Thus, the whole person is to be influenced by love and faithfulness (3:3).

Such a person will be respected by both God and people (3:4). Those who are at odds with God and others will have difficult lives. Those who are in favor with God and others have true success.

Verse 5 is not setting the mind in opposition to the heart but rather teaching that humanistic reasoning will not lead to wisdom. Only when a person's heart is fixed on God can a person begin to think properly. Walking according to God's will puts someone in the position to have God lead the way and open the doors to the life that He desires (3:6).

Trusting in one's own wisdom is nothing more than pride, and this, in the eyes of God, is pure evil (3:7). A life lived in this way is a life in which the body feels the weight of sin. A life that is in accordance with wisdom is one that finds peace and refreshment with God (3:8).

Demystifying Proverbs

Living against the will of God invites physical trials into that life. A life lived in the will of God has rescue from the consequences of sin. This does not mean that a person living for the glory of God in the wisdom of God will never get sick. Every human being lives life on this side of heaven in a fallen body. What the promise in 3:7–8 refers to is the reality that walking in the wisdom of God means the person will be spared from adding to the depravity of godless living. The will of God is a true healing balm—which is what the Hebrew literally says—for the body. Wisdom has both a spiritual and physical benefit for the one who follows it.

The focal point in verses 9–10 is not the offering as much as it is the heart behind the offering. We give to God because we acknowledge Him as our provider. This giving from a heart of trust does have an apparent blessing associated with it– God will continue to abundantly provide. This principle is meant to establish a basic assumption, not an automatic response.

Verses 11–12 are also cited in Hebrews 12:5–6. The child of God should not despise God's discipline. God's discipline is the way that God corrects and makes the child better.

Verses 13–18 constitute a song of praise, book-ended with the promise of blessing, or joy. Wisdom is a better investment than silver or gold (3:14–15) because it never fails to increase in value for the one who possesses it. Wisdom is depicted as a woman holding blessings in her hands and as the tree of life (3:16–18).

Critical Observation

The tree of life in verse 18 first appears in Genesis 2:9. Separation from the tree of life was a consequence of the fall (Genesis 3:24). By using this image, God is making an important point: The life that is coming to the one who partakes of wisdom is not just a good physical life; it is an eternal spiritual life.

The earth is a place where the very wisdom of God became the logic and the order by which the world was created (3:19–20). Those who abandon wisdom run against the very structure by which the world was made.

Even when problems come to the wise, they know how to handle them. This is what wisdom brings to people—not escape from the sin of the world, but the ability to handle problems as they come (3:21–26).

The irreducible heart of wisdom is true and genuine love for others. The wise are called to live in true kindness and love toward others (3:27–30).

Those living in this way have no need to envy those who pursue easy prosperity by violence and crime (3:31). Such people miss out on God's friendship, blessing, grace, and honor (3:32–35). To envy the wicked is to envy those who are on a path to destruction.

4:1–27

MORE FATHERLY WISDOM

The home is the primary place of education, especially moral education (4:1–4). The affectionate and pleading tone of these verses shows that parents who love their children make the best teachers.

The short discourse in praise of wisdom in verses 5–9 maintains the personification of wisdom as a woman who rewards those who embrace her.

Critical Observation

In some Bible versions, the Hebrew of verse 7 has been translated, "Wisdom is supreme." The better translation, "The beginning of wisdom is 'Get wisdom,' " is difficult in that it is both redundant and uses an imperative phrase as a predicate. But this can be a deliberate anacoluthon (violation of syntax) meant to drive home the idea that the first step in the pursuit of wisdom is to determine to obtain her. Wisdom is the greatest possession anyone can have, and the young man should make winning her the primary goal of his life.

The appeal in verses 10–19 has the normal structure of a paternal exhortation: an opening appeal to listen (4:10–13) followed by an exhortation in a specific area (4:14–19). In this case, the exhortation warns the reader to avoid one of the two tempters, the criminal. But the relative length of the appeal to listen implies that the family bond is a major concern of this text. If the young man should go wrong, he not only hurts himself but also his parents.

The passage also presents in vivid colors the depravity of the wicked. They live for crime. It is their food, drink, and sleep (4:16–17). They do not commit crimes in order to live but live to commit crimes. Even so, their punishment will be appropriate. Their greatest satisfaction is in making others fall, but they, too, shall fall and not know how or why.

In the closing appeal in verses 20–27, the father does not concern himself with specific moral issues. Instead, his focus is to encourage the son to stay true to wisdom. The imagery of body parts floods this text. The eyes are to stay fixed on right teaching (4:21, 25), and the feet are to stay on the right path (4:26–27). The mouth and lips must shun using crooked words (4:24). Above all, the heart must be guarded by sound doctrine (4:21, 23). If the son listens to his father, the whole body will be healthy (4:22).

Demystifying Proverbs

When Proverbs refers to the *heart*, it is not referring to the physical organ but to the mind, the whole personality of the individual. It is the wellspring of life in that the capacity to live in this world in peace comes ultimately from within and not from circumstances. The corrupt heart brings one down to the grave, but wisdom protects the heart from being brought down to the abyss. Thus, if the heart is protected from folly, then life, joy, and peace become available.

The fourth exhortation, in verses 25–27, closes with a return to the image of the path. The warning to move neither to the right nor to the left (4:27) is also found in Deuteronomy 5:32; 17:11; 28:14; and Joshua 23:6. The idea is that one should not be distracted from the way of wisdom. The way of wisdom should not be ignored, added to, or subtracted from. Wisdom provides the way of life, and everything around it is the way of destruction.

5:1–23

MORAL FIDELITY

In verse 1, the father again appeals to the young man to pay attention to his teaching. Morality is always an issue of the heart. If one's heart remains pure, then one can maintain a life of integrity (5:2). Current history is littered with those who have failed to live with integrity and have lost their voice in the world.

In verse 3, the immoral woman uses flattery to draw the young man in. Her lips are filled with words that appeal to the pride of the man and pull him into an inappropriate relationship with her. Verses 4–6 describe the bitter outcome of this relationship: torment, disappointment, emotional suffering, and even death. In other words, there is no upside to this relationship; all it does is harm people. To join this woman on her path to destruction is to join with death (5:6).

Demystifying Proverbs

The writer of Proverbs is not exaggerating when he says that consorting with an immoral woman can lead to death. In ancient Israel, sexual sin was punishable by death (see Leviticus 20:10).

In verse 7, the father warns his sons not to stray from his warning. A contemporary image is that of a man guiding his sons through a minefield. The goal is not to get as close to danger as possible but rather to stay far away (5:8). Then the sons will not have to worry about their reputations, losing their money in fast living, or sexually transmitted diseases (5:9–11). The use of the plural in this passage has led many to believe that this woman could be a prostitute or someone who is involved with a whole immoral system that will draw this young man in and destroy him.

Even when the sons are older, they will still feel the impact of an immoral relationship. They will regret the day until they are old (5:12–14).

In contrast to the dire consequences of sexual immorality, the father now extols the joys of sex within marriage in verses 16–17. He makes the point that one's body is meant to be shared with a spouse and no one else. Men and women who hold to this view will have the blessing of a great life of intimacy together (5:18). God-pleasing sexuality is intended to be joyous and satisfying. In such a relationship there is no need to look elsewhere (5:19–20).

The Lord knows not only what everyone does but also everyone's thoughts. A secret rendezvous is no secret; God will know (5:21). Those who abandon God's plan for marriage will suffer the pain that is associated with this lifestyle (5:22). There is no moral neutral ground—to consider this immoral action is a step toward death. Such a person will die for lack of discipline. In short, the man will sow the seeds of his own destruction if he follows this path.

6:1–35

LIFE SKILLS

At face value, verses 1–5 seem to say that one should not cosign a loan. The heart of this text, however, is that no one should get into legal entanglements and debts that are out of their control.

The ants are models of diligence. They have a work ethic that drives them to work hard and prepare for winter (6:6–8). In contrast, laziness leads to certain poverty and ruin (6:9–11). The lazy person places rest and sleep as the non-negotiable in life. Sleep is meant to give the body energy for work; it was never intended to be a way of life. Laziness will siphon off resources until the slothful have nothing left.

The people referred to in verses 12–14 can best be described as hucksters. A huckster is someone who pretends to be a friend; they tell people all the things they want to hear. But they do this to get something in return. A huckster takes advantage of people. This person will use every deceit in the book to get his or her way. This lifestyle is one that God will not bless. Because they sow destruction in the lives of others, they will reap destruction (6:15).

Verses 16–19 enumerate things that God hates, in a clear, numerical manner for easy memorization. The first five things mentioned in this list are body parts. These body parts are set in a sequence that moves from the head to the feet (6:17–18). These five items concern general moral characteristics: pride, dishonesty, and a violent or manipulative character. The last two are types of people that specifically belong to a court or governmental system (6:19).

The final section of Proverbs 6 contains another warning about sexual immorality. The exhortation begins in verse 20 with the now-familiar appeal for the son to heed his father's words. The father's teachings function as a guide, guardian, and companion (6:22). They are meant to accompany the son wherever he goes. The father's teaching is to shed light on the moral decisions of life and to help the young man recognize when a woman seeks to pull him into her web of sin through seductive words (6:23–24).

Such a woman is alluring and even beautiful to the young man (6:25). Yet she is deadly. To embrace her is to embrace destruction and death. A prostitute can impoverish a man, and the consequences of messing around with a married woman are even worse: The outraged husband will bring all his fury down upon the adulterer (6:26, 29). A person can't play with fire and not get burned (6:27–28).

In verses 30–31, the writer makes a comparison between adultery and theft. Even a thief who steals out of hunger must repay his victim seven times over. How much more will adultery bring down a harsh verdict on an adulterer—for this is the worst of all of actions. The marriage bed is to be held in high honor, and those who violate this will be punished to the worst degree. The young man must understand this, for it will serve him well as he enters the world where this kind of behavior goes on.

7:1–27

BEWARE OF THE ADULTERESS

As this section opens, the father urges the son to keep his commands (7:1–3). This is said with the same force that is often used of God's commands. In other words, what is about to be said has to be heeded and treated with the utmost respect.

In verse 4, *sister* is a term of endearment for a girlfriend or wife. The young man is to love wisdom rather than the immoral woman. He is to love what God loves and not offer his heart to immorality (7:4–5).

In order to make his point in the most powerful manner, the father tells of an occasion when he actually observed a young man being seduced by an adulteress. When the father looked out his window, he saw a young man walking toward the house of an immoral woman at twilight. It is not clear whether he was intentionally going there or just passing by. The woman's loud, seductive, and inappropriate behavior shows that she is the type of woman that he should run away from (7:6–13).

The woman has either paid her vows or needs to do so (7:14). If she has paid her vows, her sins are atoned for, and she apparently feels free to start accumulating a load of sin again. Or perhaps she is suggesting exchanging her favors for the animal she needs to sacrifice. Her husband is gone with all the money (7:19–20), so she is turning to prostitution to pay her vow. This might be a deceptive ploy to get the man to agree with her. Because of the serious nature of vows, he might seek to help her with this promise.

Demystifying Proverbs

Deuteronomy 23:17–18 warns against using money earned by prostitution for paying vows. Apparently this was one of the ways that people sought to raise the money to pay their vows.

Now, having dealt with the young man's moral qualms, she devotes the rest of her seduction to a promise of a night of passion (7:15–18). In his acquiescence, the young man is both passive, like the ox going to slaughter, and dim-witted, like a deer or bird going into a trap (7:21–23). He is about to pay the full price for this sin—his life.

When the son comes across a woman like this, he is to run from her as far and as fast as he can. Her heart and her house are the way of death; there is no upside to following her (7:24–27).

8:1–36

A SECOND MESSAGE FROM WISDOM

In verses 1–3, wisdom calls for an audience at the places where people need her message: from the heights by the road, at crossroads, and at entrances to the city. Her message is not just for the elite but is brought for all people to hear.

While claiming that her gifts are for everyone, wisdom especially offers understanding to the foolish and simple (8:4–5). Nonetheless, her words are profitable for everyone because they are right, honest, and wholesome, without anything twisted or perverse (8:6–8). The wise as well as the foolish will benefit from wisdom's instruction because God's wisdom is worth more than all the riches in the world (8:9–11).

Critical Observation

The placement of wisdom's second message here in chapter 8 is significant. The previous chapter highlights the dangers of ignoring wisdom. Now, to make sure that we get the point, wisdom calls out for everyone to listen to her message.

Even though wisdom is accessible to everyone, it is still the most deep and profound reality in the world. This is first seen by the way it deals with the world. Observe that wisdom claims to possess prudence, knowledge, and discretion (8:12). The word *prudence* carries the idea of sensible behavior (1:4; 8:5). The word *discretion* refers to careful behavior that arises from clear and wise thinking. Wisdom teaches how to live a balanced and careful life as opposed to a reckless life that leads to suffering the pain of folly.

This prudence is attained by fearing the Lord. According to verse 13, those who fear the Lord will hate what God hates and love what God loves. Wisdom also gives direction to life as well as strength to endure whatever the world brings (8:14).

Take It Home

The prudence that comes from fearing the Lord implies one strong and important point: If a person fears the Lord, then evil behavior, pride, and wicked speech are all rejected (8:13). Those who practice such foolish behavior, however intelligent they may be by earthly measures, are fools because they have rejected the wisdom of God.

The reach of wisdom is not just for independent followers of God. Wisdom is also meant to be used by the leaders of the world. Wisdom is essential for those who have been given the responsibility to lead in government (8:15–16).

God has not made His wisdom inaccessible; His wisdom is available to all those who seek it (8:17). When wisdom arrives, she will bestow blessings and treasures on those who love and seek her (8:18–21). But improper motives with the pursuit of wisdom do not mix. In other words, we cannot try to pursue wisdom for the sake of gain. Rather, the pursuit of wisdom is the pursuit of the things that God loves for the purpose of the glory of God.

Verses 22–31 describe wisdom's role in creation. It is an important part because it sets the stage for the relationship between wisdom and the world. This passage could be divided into three parts: the birth of wisdom (8:22–26), wisdom's part in creation (8:27–29), and the joy of wisdom (8:30–31).

Wisdom is claiming to be the first principle of the world ever created and the pattern by which the world was created (8:22–26). The point here is that wisdom is the oldest of all principles in the world. As such, she holds to a superior position in the world and should be valued higher than creation itself.

Critical Observation

It is important to note the fact that wisdom existed before the dust of the ground (8:26). Mankind came from the dust of the ground. Therefore, humans, as dust, are part of the created world and cannot live contrary to the order by which the world was created. People who reject wisdom, therefore, reject something that is more powerful and wiser than they could ever hope to become. This is why every human needs to order his life by the wisdom of God.

Wisdom was present at two very significant points in creation, namely, the making of the heavens and the placing of restraints over the power of the sea (8:27–29). This is a powerful statement with direct implications. These two moments shaped creation. If humans are to live in this world in harmony with the world, then they must live according to the wisdom that shaped this world.

In the development of the world, wisdom found great joy (8:30–31). The creation of the world was in harmony with the logic of wisdom. Wisdom is an artisan, and the principles of wisdom are woven into the fabric of the created order. Thus, to truly understand the world around us, we need the wisdom of God.

Verses 8:32–36 are a fitting ending to this chapter. Since the whole world is embedded with wisdom, then it is very important to listen to wisdom. Those who listen become wise, but those who neglect to listen will suffer. In short, to have the blessing of God is to seek His wisdom. To fail to seek wisdom means that we will end up hurting ourselves and gaining destruction and death.

9:1–18

TWO WAYS TO LIVE

The first major section of the book of Proverbs closes with a simple appeal: Will we walk in the way of wisdom or the way of folly?

Demystifying Proverbs

Proverbs 9 strongly emphasizes the notion of the two ways, a concept developed most completely in Proverbs and Deuteronomy. Either a person is with God and has life or rejects God and His ways and gets death. There is no neutrality—one is either on the side of life or death, and that is it.

The simple point of the passage is that if we enter wisdom's house, we will have life. Yet this point is made in some complex ways. The nature of wisdom's house of seven pillars is uncertain (9:1).

Wisdom has sent out a servant to invite everyone to her banquet (9:2–6). What this means is that the message of wisdom has been shouted around the entire world. The feast wisdom provides is illustrative of life, health, and celebration. It contrasts with the banquet of the dead behind folly's door (9:18).

The warning against trying to instruct mockers in verses 7–9 is common in Proverbs. Even though the call goes out to everyone, it always recognizes that there are some who will never listen. This reality appears even in 1:7, the theme verse of Proverbs.

Fear of the Lord is at the heart of being wise (9:10). To fear the Lord is to love what God loves and to hate what God hates. It is to have a heart of reverence for God that seeks glory to Him and Him alone.

The promise of life and statement of individual responsibility in verses 11–12 are a fitting conclusion to the call of wisdom. The joy and blessing that she offers is for the taking. Yet if someone rejects this message, he will bear the consequences of his folly all by himself, without help.

Verses 13–16 outline the way of folly. Like the adulteress (7:11), folly is loud, careless, and seductive. The parallel of verses 14–16 to verses 3–4 is obvious, but folly sits and accosts those who pass by as would a prostitute or a criminal in ambush.

Folly's promise of stolen water and food eaten in secret (9:17) is important to understand. Stolen water looks back to 5:15–18, where sexual relations are described as the drinking of water. Food eaten in secret is literally "bread of secrecy." It refers to the criminal conspiracies that tempt the young man to easy money, as in 1:11–14; 4:14–17; and 6:12–15. Folly entices one to sexual sin and to easy gain through immoral and illegal means. This is what folly appeals to—the basic instincts of our sin nature.

Verse 18 looks back to the two tempters—the man who draws the youth into a life of crime and the woman who draws him into promiscuity. Both are in the house of folly, and both draw more victims to the banquet of the dead. In short, everyone that joins in this way is dead spiritually. We cannot have life in this context. The only way to have life and blessing is to walk according to wisdom. We either walk in life by seeking the wisdom of God, or we walk in death seeking our own folly and walking and living among the spiritually dead.

PROVERBS 10:1–15:33

SOLOMON'S WISDOM, PART I

Setting Up the Section

This chapter marks a change in the way the book of Proverbs is written. Chapter 10 begins the part of Proverbs that most people think of when they encounter this book: short pithy statements of wisdom.

10:1–32

CONTRASTING WISDOM AND FOOLISHNESS

In verses 1–5, the first theme emerges: that of the wise son versus the foolish son. The theme of these first verses is that a family will flourish if the children are diligent in their work but will fall apart if they are lazy or resort to crime.

A simple point emerges in verse 1: The behavior of children helps shape the happiness of the parents. If children are wise, parents find joy; if they are foolish, parents are grieved. This is a warning both to parents, to instill wisdom in their children, and to children, to recognize that their actions have a direct impact on their parents' hearts.

Verse 2 contrasts two possible paths for a young adult. If he gains wealth through immoral means, that wealth will be limited to this life only. If he gains success through the right means, he will have more than just earthly prosperity; he will have eternal life.

Demystifying Proverbs

Material wealth was often seen as a sign of divine blessing in Solomon's culture, and Proverbs 10:4 holds up wealth as a reward for hard work. But Proverbs 10:2 makes it clear that wealth by itself has no redeeming value. To pursue wealth through immoral means is to do nothing but find emptiness in life, and death in the end. For this reason, it is important to pursue righteousness rather than wealth.

Verse 3 unfolds the security that comes to the righteous. God cares for His children. He is their provider and thus there is no need to lie, cheat, and steal to get money. At the same time, God works against the wicked. If they think that fame, success, money, freedom, and material things are going to make them happy, they are chasing a shadow. God will not allow them to have the happiness they think those things will give them.

The focal point in verse 4 is work ethic. The person who does not work hard will be sowing the seeds of poverty in his or her life. Many people turn to God for a quick path to riches, but God has made it clear that work is to be the primary means through which one acquires possessions and resources.

Critical Observation

Verse 3 says that God promises to care for His children, but verse 4 says that a lazy person will sow the seeds of poverty. Does this seem contradictory? The reality is that the one who seeks to serve God and trusts in God has the heart and the desire to do the work God has provided. A heart for God causes people to love what God loves, and one of the things that God loves is when His children work diligently. It is the means that God uses to provide.

Verse 5 points out that a person who works when he is supposed to work will bring honor to his parents and ultimately bring glory to God. A lazy person will bring shame to his family.

The contrast between a righteous person and a wicked person is common in Proverbs. Solomon wants his son to understand this difference, so here he sets out to explain it using six contrasts.

First, wicked people can be identified by their deceitful speaking; they try to hide what is truly in their hearts. The righteous, however, are known by the evidence of God's favor upon their lives (10:6). This blessing does not necessarily mean monetary blessing. In fact, when God blesses people, usually money is not the central piece. Usually blessings encompass a whole life that is touched by God.

Demystifying Proverbs

In the book of Proverbs, *righteousness* means the holiness of God carried out in life. It is the justice of God, the goodness of God, the equity of God put in action in the world. Thus the righteous one is the one who puts into practice the very character of God.

The second contrast deals with the legacy of a person (10:7). When God works in and through a person, he is remembered for what God did and thus has a great legacy—a legacy that continues to bless. When a wicked person dies, his name will not just be forgotten, but it will be run through the mud and he will be remembered for who he really was—a wicked man.

Demystifying Proverbs

Whenever the notion of a person's name is mentioned in the Old Testament, it refers to more than just a person's title. It refers to one's character, the way that a person is understood. The simple point in Proverbs 10:7 is that the character of a person will be made known for generations to come.

The third contrast is in how a person receives wisdom (10:8). A righteous person is humble and is able to learn from anyone; he is teachable. The wicked person here is called a babbling fool. The idea is that of a person who does all the talking and is not able to learn from anyone. The inevitable result is to fall flat on one's face.

The fourth contrast in verse 9 has to do with integrity—being the same on the inside as on the outside. A person with integrity walks in this world secure because he has nothing to hide and is free from the fear of being caught. In contrast, the wicked have no real security in this life because their sin and depravity will eventually come to the forefront, and all will see it.

In verse 10, the fifth contrast highlights the trouble that comes from the deceptiveness (winking the eye) of wicked people. Righteous people, in contrast, are peacemakers.

Critical Observation

Proverbs 10:10 has been translated in two different ways. Some follow the Hebrew text: "Whoever winks the eye causes trouble, but a babbling fool will come to ruin" (ESV). Others follow the Greek version of the Old Testament: "People who wink at wrong cause trouble, but a bold reproof promotes peace" (NLT). Those following the Greek version argue that a copyist accidentally recopied verse 8 instead of verse 10—a mistake that was corrected in the Greek version.

The sixth comparison (10:11) contrasts the speech of the righteous and the wicked. In the Hebrew culture, the mouth was considered the window to the heart of a person. What a righteous person says reflects a heart that has been refreshed by the righteousness of God. With words of encouragement, rebuke, and so on, a righteous person passes that refreshment on to others. In contrast, the purpose of wicked people's speech is largely to cover up the wickedness that is in their hearts.

Critical Observation

Jesus confirms that one's words reflect one's heart in Luke 6:45.

The proverbs in verses 12–17 outline how righteousness would look lived out in contrast to wickedness lived out. If wickedness is the driving motivation in life, then strife will be the fruit; the one who is righteous will not attack an offense but will cover that offense with love (10:12). The wise use their tongues carefully, but fools bring suffering on themselves by their words (10:14). Verse 13 gives a graphic example of that suffering.

In general, life is easier for the rich than for the poor, but wealth that is wrongfully gained will bring a person to ruin and death (10:15–16). A sinful person who is seeking righteousness will listen to correction, while the one who rebels against wisdom leads others down the road to destruction (10:17).

Proverbs 10:18–32 is set up in what is called *chiastic* fashion. A topic is introduced—in this case the tongue, which is destructive in a wicked person and positive in a godly person (10:18–21). Then a second topic is talked about—in this case the stability of the righteous over the wicked (10:22–25). Then a third topic is introduced—in this case laziness (10:26). Then the second topic is revisited—the stability of the righteous (10:27–30). Finally the first topic is revisited—the tongue (10:31–32).

Demystifying Proverbs

The *chiastic* pattern used here and in other places in Proverbs sets parallel ideas in mirror image to each other. If one thinks of the first topic as labeled A, the second as B, and the third as C, the chiastic structure would arrange the topics ABC CBA.

11:1–31

WHAT THE LORD HATES

God hates fraud, pride, and dishonesty (11:1–3). Riches gained by the unrighteous will not help them on the Day of Judgment (11:4). Their dishonesty and ambition will be their downfall, while the godly will be rescued—to the delight of those watching, because they know that godly people make good fellow citizens, while a bad neighbor goes around gossiping (11:5–13).

A nation will flourish when its leader pays attention to trustworthy advisors (11:14). But because so many people are untrustworthy, it's foolish to cosign a loan with a stranger (11:15).

Ruthless people may get rich, but they can't buy the respect that is due to someone gracious and kind (11:16–18). Ultimately, all that their ill-gotten gain can buy them is eternal death, because God hates people with crooked hearts (11:19–20, 13), but He rewards the godly with eternal life (11:19–20). According to verse 21, even the children of the godly benefit.

Tucked in almost as a sidenote is a warning that beauty is no more a guarantee of a good life than is wealth. Beauty without character is like fancy jewelry on a pig (11:22).

Verses 25–28 elaborate further on the role of material wealth: It is to be shared with the needy. When money becomes too important to a person to share, it will trip the person up (11:28).

People's wickedness doesn't affect only the people themselves; it affects family and friends (11:29–30). If that is apparent already in earthly relationships, think how significant it will be in eternity (11:31).

12:1–4

A GOOD MAN

Proverbs defines a good man as one who loves discipline, obtains favor from the Lord, is steady in the righteousness of the Lord, and has an excellent wife.

The man who loves the discipline of the Lord (12:1) is the man who loves knowledge, because he understands that, on his own, his thinking is depraved. Thus, when God reproves him and instructs him in the way he should go, he is excited because he can walk in this world the right and proper way. The one who hates reproof is the one whom the Bible calls stupid. Any person who wants his own folly over the wisdom of the Lord is not thinking right.

The good man is the one who obtains the favor of the Lord (12:2). He will obtain this favor because he seeks God's wisdom. God blesses the one who lives for Him and condemns the one who pursues evil. God does not show His favor to those who spurn Him.

The good man also does not seek to establish himself by wickedness (12:3). This means he will not seek to find his way in the world by manipulation. Instead, he seeks to establish himself in the righteousness of God. By doing this, he gives his life a sure and steady root upon which to grow.

Finally, the good man is the man whose wife becomes his crown (12:4). What this means is that the wife who is truly righteous has such an impact on a man that it makes him better and more respected in the world. The wife who is not righteous not only has to contend with her own wickedness but she is equated as rottenness in his bones.

12:5–8

STABILITY AND RESPECT

The next three proverbs flow together in a way that makes a significant point. Observe the progression: The righteous make plans that are just, but the wicked scheme with deceitful counsel (12:5); the wicked attempt to ambush the righteous with their lies, but the righteous are delivered by their integrity (12:6); the wicked are totally destroyed, but the righteous stand secure (12:7). The heart of this passage is that the righteous will stand secure in this world because they are established in the righteousness of God. Whatever comes against them will not uproot the security that they have in God.

With this stability comes respect. Solomon wants his son to understand that respect is not given by accomplishments alone; respect is gained by wisdom. If a person has the good sense to walk according to the wisdom of God, he will earn respect from those around him. On the other hand, to follow his own sense of twisted wisdom will lead to not only his own destruction but to being ridiculed by the world (12:8). The key to being respected is to walk in the wisdom of the Lord.

12:9–15

A HUMBLE WORK ETHIC

This section opens with a reminder that a lifestyle of moderate comforts is far more desirable than the pretense of wealth (12:9). Verse 10 builds on this by saying that a good man cares for those who provide for him, even if they are only animals. The wicked take advantage of everyone and everything. This builds to a key point in verse 11: True success comes by hard work rather than by looking for the get-rich-quick scheme.

Solomon now broadens the topic of work and payment to make a powerful point about the wages that come to the wicked and those that come to the righteous. Wicked people are not repulsed by the wickedness of others but actually covet the spoils that others have managed to steal for themselves. They are never satisfied and are constantly wanting more. In contrast to this is the righteous man, who continues to prosper without stealing or defrauding people (12:12).

The evil man who walks down this road becomes ensnared by his lips. The lies that he tells will catch up to him, and he will be brought down by his own depravity. The righteous do not need to fear this kind of trouble because they walk in integrity, and integrity will not allow a man to become ensnared (12:13).

Verse 14 sums this up by saying that words are like labor. A person who uses his words with integrity will enjoy the fruit of that integrity. For what comes from the mouth reflects what is in the heart, and a righteous heart is satisfied with good words. The wise person is also ready to listen to words spoken with integrity, while fools are so sure of themselves that they never seek advice (12:15).

12:16–22

THE RECKLESSNESS OF LYING AND THE VALUE OF TRUTH

The characteristics of fools described in this text are:

1) They react thoughtlessly to everything they hear and hurt others with thoughtless words (12:16–18).
2) They are liars and will incur the wrath of God (12:17, 19, 22).
3) They plot and scheme but in the end only bring trouble on themselves (12:20–21).

In contrast, characteristics of the wise are:

1) They respond with patience in the face of trials and insults (12:16, 18).
2) They bring healing with their words (12:16, 18).
3) They are honest and gain long life and divine favor (12:17, 19, 22).
4) They seek the well-being of others while gaining it for themselves (12:20–21).

The tongue of the wicked brings destruction, while the tongue of the righteous brings healing.

Critical Observation

Verses 16–22 use a form of repetition to make a point about the value of truth and the recklessness of lying. The issue of reckless words emerges two times (verses 16 and 18). The issue of honesty and lying emerges three times (verses 17, 19, and 22). Two times the issue of trouble for the wicked and peace for the righteous are addressed (verses 20 and 21). The parallels are not exact parallels, but instead they are loosely connected themes expressing similar ideas from slightly different points of view.

12:23–28

A LIFE OF WISDOM

The final six proverbs of chapter 12 describe the characteristics of a life of wisdom.

According to verse 23, wise people are slow to speak and slow to share what they know. In addition, they seek to help their friends and be a source of assistance rather than leading them astray (12:26). In contrast, foolish people talk a lot and thereby proclaim their folly (12:23). In their talking, they also lead their friends astray rather than help their friends along (12:16).

Wise people know the value of hard work. Again we see how much God values hard work and blesses the diligent (12:24, 27). Slothful people, however, will be forced into work against their will and will not be able to feed themselves (12:24).

Wise people also know the value of good words. Correctly used, words can build up a person weighted down by the stress of life (12:25).

The culmination of all of these dictums is that there is true life in righteousness (12:28). To walk in the righteousness of God means to find true life.

Take It Home

The only way to walk in the righteousness of God is to exchange your sin for God's righteousness. This occurs through bringing your sin to Jesus Christ (2 Corinthians 5:21). Once a person is walking in the righteousness of God, death will have no sting. In the righteousness of God there is life in abundance.

13:1–11

WORDS AND ACTIONS

The theme of the mouth reemerges in chapter 13. The wise son listens to what his father says, while the wicked son does not listen but instead uses his mouth to mock his father's instruction (13:1). When a person uses good words, it is like eating a good meal (13:2). Good words nourish a person and cause a person to become healthy and strong. Those who guard their mouths avoid trouble. Those who do all the talking come to ruin (13:3). The talker is symbolic of those who do not listen to rebuke and speak out of their own arrogance. People like this will find themselves coming to ruin because of their pride.

Again the issue of a work ethic emerges—a common topic in Proverbs. The point to be drawn here is that, as a principle, lazy people will not get what they desire, because what they desire is gain without effort. Diligent people, on the other hand, want to reap the results of hard work, and generally they do (13:4).

Solomon wants his son to understand that the person who walks in integrity is protected by that integrity. Problems emerge for those who do not love righteousness and truth. Yet those who love righteousness and truth have the great privilege of finding protection from the consequences that befall those who hate righteousness (13:5–6).

Verses 7–11 deal with wealth and its deceptive nature. There is more to verse 7 than just pretending to be rich or poor. The bigger point is that things are not always what they seem. One person may appear to be rich but in fact is not, and on a more fundamental level has nothing. This is illustrated in verse 8: The rich may be able to pay a ransom, but the poor don't have to worry about being kidnapped in the first place. Verses 9–11 reiterate one of the central issues of Proverbs: A person who pursues wisdom will gain a reward far more lasting than the person who pursues money at all cost.

13:12–19

HOPE AND DISAPPOINTMENT

Verses 12–19 follow the chiastic pattern of parallels that is used in 10:18–21. Outlined, it would look like this:

A. Hope fulfilled or deferred (13:12)
B. Advice received or rejected (13:13)
C. Reliable vs. unreliable instruction (13:14)
D. Good sense vs. foolishness (13:15)
D. Good sense vs. foolishness (13:16)
C. Reliable vs. unreliable instruction (13:17)
B. Advice received or rejected (13:18)
A. Hope fulfilled or deferred (13:19)

To receive the tree of life is to have an abundant life that cannot be taken away. To gain that abundant life, one must practice obedience, learn from people worthy of respect, and not act rashly (13:13–16).

Critical Observation

The tree of life is first mentioned in Genesis 2:9. Adam and Eve's sin puts the tree of life out of reach; they are banished from the garden where it grows. The book of Revelation tells of regaining the right to eat from the tree of life (Revelation 2:7; 22:14). Proverbs is the only other book of the Bible in which the tree of life is mentioned (Proverbs 3:18; 11:30; 13:12; 15:4).

A messenger is an example of a person charged with a serious responsibility (13:17). Just as an envoy is charged with representing someone and speaking the words of the one he represents, so too the faithful child of God must represent the wisdom of God and take it seriously. There are consequences for not being faithful.

13:20–25

RELATIONSHIPS

Verses 20–21 speak of choosing friends wisely. Just as good friends have good influences, a friend who gets into trouble generally gets his friends in trouble with him.

Verses 22–25 present a worldview of the family. A wise family provides for the next generation in both physical and spiritual ways. God sets the pattern for this provision. Ultimately, God will use the wealth of the wicked for His children (13:22). A truly righteous person is satisfied. He is not seeking to get more and feeling the sting of consumerism. But a wicked person is never satisfied; he wants more and more (13:25).

Take It Home

The underlying point of this verse is that parents who spoil their children aren't providing a strong foundation of character for their children's future. They are taking the easy way out. It's more work—and wins fewer popularity votes—to consistently pay attention to your child's behavior, encouraging positive actions and disciplining negative actions. It is also the way a loving parent behaves.

14:1–17

FOOLS

The book of Proverbs continues to make the point that there are two paths in life: the path of those who fear the Lord (in other words, the wise, since according to Proverbs 1:7 the fear of the Lord is the beginning of wisdom) and the path of the foolish, who despise the Lord (14:2). The following verses give examples of this principle.

If a woman is wise, her home grows and gets better and better, but a woman who is foolish will bring pain and destruction upon her home (14:1).

Foolish bragging leads to painful consequences in a man's life, whereas the wise will speak the words that bring healing and hope to their lives (14:3).

Some people seek the ease of avoiding work (illustrated by the clean and empty stable), but a wise person knows that those who take the burden of work (here illustrated by caring for an ox) also get the reward that comes from the work (14:4).

Yet again the mouth is brought into the conversation. The way that a person speaks reflects the condition of his or her heart. It is wise to avoid liars and mockers, because their language reveals the foolishness of a heart that does not fear the Lord (14:5–7).

Those who fear God understand what they are doing and why they are doing it. In contrast, foolish people will be seeking to hide the true intentions of their hearts (14:8).

A foolish person will sin and find no need to make things right before God, but a wise person seeks the path that God established to deal with guilt, and thus enjoys the forgiveness and acceptance that comes from having guilt wiped away (14:9). Everyone knows the real state of his or her own heart, so when the wicked deny their need for forgiveness, they lie to themselves and to God (14:10).

Even though wicked people may amass things on this earth, destruction will come. Even though righteous people might not gain as much, in the end they will know the security of being right with God (14:11). The way that seems right to wicked people is not really right at all. They might look at the world around them and feel as if they have everything, but in the end they will have nothing but destruction (14:12). They may seem to have fun, but the reality is those who live without God do not have the fun and excitement that they appear to have (14:13). When they leave the charade of fun and acknowledge their real condition, they will find that they chose the wrong path (14:14).

Critical Observation

The idea of the backslider in verse 14 is not the contemporary one of a Christian who progressively falls away from God. In this passage, the idea is that of people who eventually cannot keep up the external face of everything going well and begin to walk in their sin without a facade of goodness.

Wise people will think about what they hear and weigh what they are being asked to participate in, while foolish people jump at everything (14:15–16). Wise people understand that they must follow God. Foolish people think of nothing because God means nothing to them. Those who are quick to anger will make one foolish decision after another (14:17).

14:18–27

THE REWARDS OF THE HEART

Solomon wants his son to understand what will happen to the wicked and the righteous on this side of heaven. Those who do not pursue wisdom will inherit folly; they will have to deal with the fruit of their wickedness. Eventually foolish people will bow down before the wise. They will not have honor in this world. The only way to have honor is to seek to honor God (14:18–19).

Verses 20–22 acknowledge that no one wants to be poor, and the poor do not garner the respect in the world that the rich do. But those who show kindness toward others, regardless of their social and economic standing, are blessed by God.

While it is true that many people are poor despite their best efforts, verses 23–24 make clear that this is no excuse for not working. The principle remains that the fruit of real work is reward, but people who hate work and only talk a good game get nothing.

The proverb in verse 25 appears to have the notion of legal proceedings as its theme. Honesty in court is not a mere fine point of law; people's lives depend upon it. This is why many legal systems have a moment where those giving testimony are called to give an oath that they are telling the truth.

Verses 26–28 give more examples of the benefits that accrue to those who fear the Lord. Fearing the Lord provides security from the storms of life and a kind of early warning system against the moral traps that wait. Thus, fearing the Lord is not just a religious or ceremonial act but a path of security in the world.

14:28–35

WISDOM AND THE NATION

The health and well-being of a nation depends upon both the ruler and the governed. A ruler must be fair and, above all, must respect the rights of his people. The people, on the other hand, must have virtue in their lives or they will bring society into chaos. No government can succeed without the people, and no people can thrive if corruption and evil abound.

Without people there is no nation to govern (14:28). Thus, every leader must realize that the people he leads are also the people he needs. He must honor and serve those whom he has been entrusted to rule.

Verse 29 stresses the importance of patience. In this context, an impatient king may lose his people (14:28), and a headstrong servant of the king may lose his place before the king (14:35). Thus, patience must be a ruling virtue for both king and subject. Patience is essential for a healthy life as well (14:30).

Verse 31 stands as a warning to rulers not to trample upon the rights of the poor. The king who ignores this advice will soon find himself without a nation. God takes it personally when people disrespect the needy and hurt them for the purpose of personal gain. To honor God is to care for those who cannot care for themselves.

Wicked people will be overthrown, not by their enemies, but by their own evildoings. Yet those who pursue righteousness have hope, even on their deathbeds (14:32). This hope does not come from power; it comes from walking in the fear of the Lord—true wisdom (14:33).

Wisdom is not just for personal gain—there is a national aspect to it as well. A nation's political health depends to a great degree on the moral integrity of its people (14:34). For this reason, political leaders are better served by people of integrity (14:35).

15:1–17

THE TONGUE AND THE HEART

The ability to avert quarreling and to live in harmony with others is a virtue of wisdom. A wise person knows how to speak gently, appealingly, and truthfully (15:1–4). He both listens to and gives good advice, and the prayers he speaks are pleasing to God (15:5–8). But God hates the religious practices of the wicked. What pleases God the most is not religious ceremony but a heart that pursues righteousness all the time (15:9).

God will allow a fool to have the complete consequences for all of his actions. And those who do not repent under this discipline and continue to reject it will die (15:10–11). This death could refer to spiritual death alone, but Proverbs makes it clear that both physical and spiritual death are included in the consequences. How foolish it is to reject correction (15:12)!

Demystifying Proverbs

Some versions of the Bible use the words *Sheol* and *abaddon* in verse 11, while others use the words *death* and *destruction*. *Sheol* refers to the place of the dead. *Abaddon* refers to the experience of destruction for the wicked. The point is that God has the power to bring death and destruction to those whose hearts are set against Him.

Verse 13 reminds the reader that the focal point should always be the heart and nothing else. A person cannot control his experience with this world from the outside in; it has to be from the inside out. A wise person seeks to understand the world from God's point of view, which brings joy to the heart (15:14). A happy heart has a continual feast (15:15). In fact, to have a heart feasting on the joy, fear, and love of the Lord is better than a literal feast (15:16–17).

15:18–33

TWO ROADS

The remainder of chapter 15 outlines a series of contrasts between the wicked person and the righteous person in relation to anger (15:18), laziness (15:19), relationships with parents (15:20), joy (15:21, 30), taking advice (15:22, 31–32), speech (15:23, 28), prudence (15:24), protection (15:25), intentions (15:26), greed (15:27), and prayer (15:29).

The summation of all these contrasts is that the ultimate starting point of wisdom is the fear of the Lord (15:33).

Take It Home

These proverbs were written with the intent of helping the king's son become a better leader. While you might not have a kingdom to oversee, you may have equally important areas of responsibility as a parent, household provider, office manager, committee chairman, or so forth. What advice from these proverbs can you apply to your own "domains"?

PROVERBS 16:1–22:16

SOLOMON'S WISDOM, PART II

Setting Up the Section

In this ongoing segment of the proverbs of Solomon (10:1–22:16), this particular section begins a minor shift. Chapters 10 through 15 made a lot of contrasts between righteous and unrighteous behavior. Chapters 16 through 22:16 contain fewer contrasts and instead begin to focus more on the value of righteous behavior.

16:1–15

THE HEAVENLY KING AND EARTHLY KINGS

Chapter 16 begins with a reminder that God is sovereign. If Solomon's son were to truly rule in peace, he must first acknowledge that he did not have ultimate control over the world. Everything he did must be submitted to the ultimate will of God.

Verses 1 through 3 are a reminder that *all* human plans are subject to the will of God, who will have the final say as to what will actually happen. This is not meant to discourage people from planning, the importance of which is emphasized in other parts of scripture (see Luke 14:28–33), yet it is important to remember that God's will is the ultimate trajectory of life. The Lord knows people's hearts and understands why they desire what they do. If He overrides someone's plans, it is because He knows what drives those plans. The more a person fears the Lord, the more his or her plans will be in accordance with the will of God.

God is intimately involved in this world and has made everything for His purposes (Proverbs 16:4). Even nonbelievers, as they eventually suffer the consequences of their actions, reveal God's righteous judgments. Verse 5 affirms that wicked people will certainly not go unpunished. People can live entire lifetimes being prideful and powerful, appearing to be in charge and getting their way. But in the end, they will be humbled in the judgment of God.

Avoiding the problem of pride is a simple matter of fearing the Lord (16:6). God is a God of mercy and truth who has made atonement for the sin of the proud (Isaiah 53:5). People can be forgiven of their sin and learn to walk right with God if they submit to Him in fearful reverence. Not only will they begin to avoid evil, but they will also see positive changes in the everyday circumstances of life (Proverbs 16:7).

Critical Observation

The promise in Proverbs 16:7 is a general principle. The writer does not mean that a godly person will not have enemies. However, when God's favor shines on a person, he or she is much less likely to experience opposition from others.

After someone develops a fear of the Lord, his or her perspective shifts (16:8). The person begins to understand that it is more preferable to have only a little in this world while remaining righteous than to acquire much without justice. Verse 9 echoes verse 1: People make their plans, but God ultimately directs their steps.

While these insights are valuable for anyone, they are especially relevant for human leaders. Solomon's son would be next in line for royal leadership, so it was important for him to understand how a king was to act.

To begin with, a king should remember that his words are not just for himself, but that he speaks decrees for the entire nation (16:10). He is not to use the role of "oracle" for his own personal purposes. The word metaphorically describes the king as having deep spiritual wisdom allowing him to become the channel for the plan of God.

Justice is another crucial criterion for a godly king. While verse 11 does not directly mention the king, it is in the context of kingly instructions. Justice is derived from God, and human leaders do not have the authority to suspend or violate the principles of fairness. King and subjects alike should honor honesty and justice.

If a king uses his position for personal profit, he ignores the justice of God and commits an utter abomination. Kings should acknowledge and reward those who speak the truth (16:12–13). In return, people should show proper respect for their king. The king controls the power of the nation, and the sword may fall on anyone who incites his wrath. It is far wiser to appease the king than to antagonize him (16:14–15).

16:16–33

A DISCIPLINED LIFESTYLE

Life is a series of choices, which is why Solomon yet again emphasizes the importance of wisdom (16:16–17). People see the value of tangible things like gold and silver, yet wisdom and understanding are far more valuable. Choosing positive but intangible qualities over the riches of the world requires humility, as Solomon explains in verses 18 and 19. Those who take pride in their riches are destined for destruction.

A person's words reflect his or her inner motives. Wise words are instructive (16:20), pleasant (16:21), and life-giving (16:22). A wise heart guides one's speech. Wise words are as exciting and pleasurable as candy to a child (16:24).

The choice of "ways" in life is the issue of verse 25. Imagine a person committing to a particular road that looks just fine, yet when he comes to the end he discovers that death lies before him no matter which way he turns. The image suggests that anyone left to his own natural thoughts will end up pursuing a path to destruction.

Honest people work in order to eat (16:26). In contrast, some people seek easier, less demanding ways to make money. They create evil schemes to acquire wealth unethically. Verses 27 through 30 expose the motives of the crook, the wicked person, and the violent person. Such people bring nothing but pain and misery on themselves and others.

Making good life choices can be difficult, but it is ultimately rewarding. A person who lives a righteous life is more likely to live longer (16:31). Controlling one's temper reflects great inner power—more than that of a victorious military leader (16:32).

Verse 33 concludes the chapter as it had begun, with a reminder that the sovereignty of God directs all human activity. People have a number of ways to decide how to proceed in life, but they should be thankful that God is the One whose will is ultimately accomplished.

Demystifying Proverbs

A *lot* (16:33) was like a die or dice thrown to help leaders ascertain God's direction (see, for instance, the Urim and Thummim of Exodus 28:30). God would control the piece(s) and make His will known. The casting of lots is found throughout the Old Testament and the Gospels, culminating with the selection of a disciple to replace Judas Iscariot (Acts 1:23–26). But after the coming of the Holy Spirit, the casting of lots was not mentioned again in scripture.

17:1–28

THE PAIN OF FOLLY

Proverbs repeatedly makes it clear that peace resulting from the blessing of God is far preferable to acquired wealth that creates problems and suffering. Solomon had untold riches at his disposal, yet he understood that the simple essentials of life with "peace and quiet" were better than great wealth accompanied by strife (17:1).

Verse 2 was a profound point for the son of a king to consider. Wisdom would allow one's ability and character to overcome any disadvantages of birth, and those born to advantage could forfeit their position through immorality and sloth. Choosing wisdom is not always as simple as it might seem. God will sometimes "test the heart" (17:3), bringing out the true nature of a person.

People often have little choice of whether or not they *hear* gossip and slander, but they can always choose whether or not to *believe* it. Those who thrive on taking gossip seriously are malevolent and hate the truth (17:4). Similarly, those who mock or celebrate the sufferings of others display a cruelty that will certainly be punished. The offense is not only against their fellow human beings but also against God (17:5).

Some people like to revel in their individuality, but they are not as independent of others as they might like to think. Verse 6 puts things in perspective. Older adults derive a sense of honor from their descendants, while children depend on their parents for a sense of self-worth.

People's words should reflect their true natures. It quickly becomes evident when a foolish person attempts to be arrogant or when the leader of the nation is telling lies (17:7).

Demystifying Proverbs

Proverbs 17:8 is what some scholars call an observational proverb. Its intent is not to promote offering bribes. The point, rather, is to show that those who give gifts often receive special favors and are treated differently from those who hoard their wealth.

The section that follows shows the pain and destruction that come from foolishness and why it is of extreme importance that people of God not associate with fools. To begin with, the foolish people who keep harping on the offenses of others are unable to establish lasting friendships (17:9). "Covering" an offense includes not only forgiving the wrongdoing but also refusing to bring it up again. Fools, however, keep dwelling on the mistakes of their peers.

However, that doesn't mean people are always to "look the other way" when someone sins. Verse 10 continues the thought and clarifies that the wise person's pursuit of truth will include a willing acceptance of well-intentioned rebukes for things he or she has done wrong.

Fools, on the other hand, tend not to be swayed no matter what happens. One hundred lashes would not turn foolish people from their corrupt ways (17:10). Such obstinacy makes it dangerous to be near fools (17:12). People who refuse to accept constructive criticism create chaos for all of society.

The rebellion of foolish hearts has consequences, according to verse 11. Rebellious people are repeatedly sought out to receive imposed justice. They will never escape problems in their lives. And those who repay good with evil will soon find themselves plagued with evil (17:13).

Conflicts cannot always be avoided, yet they can be controlled. Starting a quarrel is more dangerous than it may seem. . .not unlike breaching a dam. It's much easier to keep the water from overflowing to begin with than to try to stop it once it begins to gush. Wise people are quick to respond to contention with kindness, directness, and forgiveness (17:14).

With no desire for wisdom, foolish people acquit the guilty and condemn the innocent (17:15). They can collect money for schooling, but without a genuine desire for wisdom, the money goes to waste (17:16). No one wants such people around during difficult times. That's when people seek the help of true friends (17:17). A real friend is more than just someone who vouches for another (17:18); a genuine friend is there around the clock. But those who never resist the tendency to sin are quick to quarrel, and they will eventually fall hard, like an oversized gate in a city wall (17:19).

Folly is particularly painful within households, yet people with perverse hearts and deceitful tongues (17:20) affect those close to them as well as outsiders. Verses 20–22 imply that the greatest source of a crushed spirit is trouble in the family. Foolish children create much pain for righteous parents (17:21, 25). Such foolish behavior circumvents the happy hearts that are key to full and healthy lives (17:22).

It seems that some people literally "lose sight" of wisdom (17:24). They accept bribes to punish the innocent and/or allow the guilty to go free (17:23, 26).

A wise person uses few words (17:27). According to verse 28, even fools can appear wise if they keep their mouths shut. By paying attention over time to what (and how much) a person says, one can determine whether that person is wise or foolish. Words are the fruit that reflect the quality of the heart.

18:1–24

WISE AND FOOLISH WORDS

The selfish pursuits of foolish people result in the frequent expression of their personal opinions (18:1–2). In the absence of wisdom, they are drawn to vanity and narcissism.

The contempt and shame associated with foolish and wicked people are usually accompanied by verbal insults. In contrast to such shallowness, wise people are described in verse 4 as a fountain—not only deep, but refreshing and life-restoring as well.

Foolish words can be harmful to others when innocent people are deprived of justice and wicked people get away with their corrupt behavior (18:5). But those same words are also harmful to the people who speak them, resulting in potential physical violence and spiritual defeat (18:6–7). Similarly, gossip may be considered "tasty" by some (18:8), yet consumption of those morsels of gossip results in conflict and eventual destruction.

Gossip and inappropriate speech are not the only problems among wicked people, of course. Laziness is another common factor (18:9). Such people also tend to depend on their wealth for security, while wise people know that God is the only reliable refuge (18:10–11). Lessons of humility come too late for the wicked, who learn only after a disaster that their self-reliance is insufficient.

People who "answer before listening" (18:13) reflect an arrogant spirit not concerned with truth. They reject instruction and are unwilling to hear others' opinions, which is both a folly and a shame. Their words can have powerful effects, even to the extent of crushing a person's spirit (18:14).

While many people adopt the behavior of the wicked, others see its limitations and commit to seeking wisdom instead (18:15). The gift that opens the way for the giver, mentioned in verse 16, may be a reference to the gifts God gives people that allow them to help others, or its meaning may be along the lines of 17:8, suggesting that bribes are an effective means to prompt people to respond as one wishes.

Wise people do not respond too hastily to the words of others. Someone presenting his case may make quite a persuasive argument, but it is always valuable to hear the other side of the issue before reaching a final decision (18:17). When disputes arise, it is wise to seek God's mind in the matter—which was the purpose of casting lots. If the nation were to continue to function smoothly, it would be important for the people to settle their controversies quickly and justly (18:18–19).

While words can be misused in any number of ways (18:21), when used properly they can edify others. Verse 20 suggests that just as food satisfies one's hunger, well-chosen words can be an equally pleasurable source of contentment. Wise people take their words seriously.

From words, Solomon turns to relationships. The book of Proverbs has much to say about the importance of avoiding the wrong women and forming relationships with spiritually strong females. In this case, the emphasis is on the favor God will bestow on the husband of a good wife (18:22).

A person's financial status can affect his or her attitudes toward justice. The poor have no other recourse than to plead for mercy. Those who are rich, however, may tend to rely more on their status and respond harshly—to dictate terms rather than beg for forgiveness (18:23).

Finally, the choice of one's friends is a matter of wisdom versus folly as well (18:24). Those with many friends have little time for intimacy with any of them, and such people may be led astray by some of their many acquaintances. True friendships, however, can be much closer than family relations.

19:1–29

PRIORITIES FOR THE BEST POSSIBLE LIFE

This section concludes the extensive "Proverbs of Solomon" that began in 10:1. What Solomon has been doing, and continues to do, is to help his son think through some important priorities for life. Many people try to get ahead by lying, cheating, and stealing, but there is a better way.

Honesty and integrity are crucial ingredients of the best possible life (19:1). Impulsiveness should be avoided. Hard work in itself is not enough because people should have an awareness of what they are doing and why (19:2). A respect for wisdom should underlie one's pursuits. Too often people go through life doing whatever they want to do, and then when things don't work out they are quick to blame God (19:3).

The proverb in verse 4 may say more than it appears to at first reading. Of course, wealth attracts friends more than poverty does, but what does that say about those "friends"? Genuine friendship should be the same between poor people as between rich ones. Wealth, then, seems to attract gold diggers and fortune hunters in the guise of "friends." The other side of this issue is reinforced in verse 7. The brutal truth is that many people don't necessarily like to associate with their poor friends and relatives, so what kind of "friendship" is that? In order for poorer people to have the best possible life, they need to find satisfaction in God. And wealthy people who truly love God will reach out to the poor.

Honesty is important at all times—not just when it is convenient. Witnesses need to speak the truth, even if they might profit in some way from a lie or half-truth (19:5). Similarly, in trying to impress rulers or people in power, the tendency is to tell them what they want to hear when truthfulness would serve a better purpose (19:6).

Rather than attempting to curry favor with influential people, it is far better to seek wisdom and find satisfaction with one's own life (19:8). The sense of satisfaction should be enough in itself, but it also prevents eventually being judged and punished for lying (19:9).

Verse 10 makes a simple, but astute, observation. People who seek wisdom and work hard to accomplish something of their lives can truly appreciate blessings and rewards when they come. But foolish people who somehow are plunged into luxury are no more able to enjoy life than a slave who somehow is promoted to rule. Neither is ready to appreciate the position that a wise person would be grateful for.

Those who walk in wisdom learn to control their emotions. Patience and slowness to anger are frequent challenges throughout Proverbs as well as the rest of scripture

(19:11). This is particularly true for leaders (19:12). The power that kings hold can easily be misused if they do not control their anger, but leaders set memorable examples when they are gracious and forgiving.

Contentment within the home must be a cooperative effort. One person can create misery for all the others, such as a foolish child or quarrelsome spouse (19:13). One aspect of wisdom is seeking God's direction in choosing one's lifetime mate (19:14).

One person's laziness has an effect on others as well, whether those others are family members or a wider community (19:15). It is difficult to effectively relate to people who would rather sleep than work or eat.

Two themes reoccur throughout Proverbs: obeying parental instructions and keeping the commandments of God. According to verse 16, such obedience is actually a matter of life or death more than people may realize. Children are not naturally wise and need to be trained in wisdom. Parents who love their children will discipline them lovingly and properly (19:18).

Verse 17 explains that the kindness shown toward other people is not only noticed by God but is also counted as if He were the recipient of such actions. Poor people may not be able to repay loans, but God certainly can. . .and will.

Critical Observation

Jesus would later make the same point as Solomon (19:17; Matthew 25:31–46). Whatever people do to "the least" of humanity is perceived as their attitude toward God.

The reason discipline is important at an early age (19:18) is to prevent problems such as the one described in Proverbs 19:19. When people fail to control their emotions, anger issues are not easily resolved. It can become a full-time job for someone to repeatedly "rescue" an angry friend or family member.

Wisdom comes from acknowledging and obeying God's instructions. A person's plans eventually come into alignment with God's plans for him or her. Poverty becomes less troublesome than loss of integrity in the search for unfailing love. With an ongoing, unyielding focus on obeying God, the rewards of life are great, including contentment and freedom from trouble (19:20–23).

As parents pass along God's instructions to their children, they may need to address common problems such as sloth, mocking, blatant dishonesty, and even violence. Discipline can turn children from such problems and teach them prudence and knowledge. Failure to address the problems, however, is likely to result in shame and disgrace for the entire family (19:24–26).

Sometimes parents do all they can do, and the children still don't respond. So Solomon follows with some specific warnings for those who ignore what they have been taught, beginning with his own son. An ongoing refusal to respond to the teachings of God and one's parents will surely result in evil, penalties, and punishments (19:27–29).

20:1–30

PRIORITIES FOR BECOMING THE BEST POSSIBLE HUMAN BEING

It is difficult enough to avoid conflicts in life under the best of conditions, so it is the essence of wisdom to minimize problems whenever and however possible. One way is to avoid intoxication that might otherwise lead to brawling. Another is to keep from provoking those in power. People who avoid conflict are seen in a positive light because any fool can pick a fight (20:1–3).

A wise person knows when to take action. In Israel's agricultural society, the seasons for planting and reaping were determined by the weather. Someone who refused to plant in the proper season would not be able to do so later, and such sluggards would be empty-handed at harvest time (20:4).

Solomon realized that many people claimed to be wise and righteous but never actually demonstrated it. Most people have deep feelings, but only a truly wise person will sort through those feelings and "draw out" significant truths about himself or herself. Once someone is able to learn to live in righteousness, however, his or her children receive the positive effects as well (20:5–7).

Verse 8 is another reminder that Solomon's mind is on the role of the nation's king. It is easy for those with much power to become corrupt, but a king with integrity has the power to "winnow out all evil." He just needs the determination to do so. Integrity is a challenge for everyone, from kings down to the children in the kingdom (20:8–11).

Demystifying Proverbs

The challenge of personal integrity is greater when society as a whole is corrupt. Solomon provided a number of clues as to the widespread problem of fraud in his nation. In 20:10 he cites "differing" weights and measures—tools used by unscrupulous merchants to cheat their customers. But lest we feel too sorry for the customers, they are shown in verse 14 loudly complaining about poor quality (no doubt to secure a lower price) and later boasting of the great deal they got.

Just as children are taught to look *and* listen before crossing a street, Solomon challenges his son not only to listen to a person's claims of wisdom and righteousness but also to see for himself if the person lives up to what he says (20:12). Remember, many people claim things that are not necessarily true (20:6). Sometimes all it takes is for a slothful person to stop lazing and stay awake. Before long he will see the results of his work (20:13).

One problem is that people don't tend to acknowledge the real value of wisdom. Solomon reminds his son that wisdom is a precious commodity even rarer than gold and rubies (20:15).

Wisdom involves doing certain things and *not* doing other things. Vouching for someone's debt, particularly that of a stranger, is usually not smart. Defrauding someone in order to eat ends up leaving a bad taste in a person's mouth. Rushing into major commitments without the advice of others is foolhardy. Talking too much and revealing sensitive information will lose friends. Cursing one's parents is a direct violation of God's law. Quickly squandering an inheritance will prevent enjoying it. Hasty revenge is not as satisfying as waiting for God to act. Dishonesty in business dealings both offends one's associates and angers God. Vows made without adequate thought can become problematic (20:16–25). Although many of these actions seem commonplace and natural, the wise person will exhibit patience and see better results.

Critical Observation

Clothing served as a sort of IOU for debts in the ancient world (Deuteronomy 24:10–14). Solomon warned to be careful whose debt one assumed (Proverbs 20:16).

God created human beings. They belong to Him and He has their best interests at heart. Yet even when He leads them where He wants them, it can still be confusing. People make plans, and many times those plans coincide with God's will for them. When the plans don't mesh, however, wisdom dictates that people follow God's path rather than their own (20:24).

When wickedness is rampant, a wise leader will use insight and understanding to discern the problem and mete out appropriate consequences. The image of the threshing wheel rolling over the wicked in verse 26 referred to separating the valuable seeds of grain from the worthless chaff. Winnowing, then, involved tossing up the product of threshing so the seeds would fall back to the ground while the chaff blew away. Yet even as kings address problems of wickedness, they should display love toward others and faithfulness to God (20:28).

Verse 27 suggests that people owe everything to God. He is the source of light and life. He knows everything about every person, and no one can hide anything from Him. Consequently, those with wisdom realize the importance of living before God in openness and honesty.

People are blessed with different gifts at different phases of life. Many bemoan losing the strength of youth when, in fact, they should rejoice at the accumulation of wisdom that comes only with age (20:29). Wisdom helps people understand and endure the painful experiences of life. In time they see how their sufferings work to keep evil at bay and make them stronger individuals (20:30).

21:1–31

ASSORTED PROVERBS FOR LIVING

The proverbs in this section reinforce many great themes that were established in previous chapters—themes such as righteousness, hard work, self-control, and the sovereignty of God.

The sovereignty of God becomes evident from the beginning. Even Solomon, with all his wealth and power, realized that a king was like water that God could direct anywhere

He wished. Indeed, *all people* need to weigh their feelings and understanding of the world in light of God's wisdom. It is not enough to do as one wishes and offer God the occasional sacrifice; what God desires from people is consistent righteousness and justice (21:1–3).

Verse 4 recalls 6:16–19, but the language there was even stronger. God *hates* haughty eyes and a wicked heart. Pride and arrogance are at the root of any number of other sins.

There are right ways and wrong ways to accomplish most things. In seeking to make a living, for instance, planning and diligence are usually rewarded with success. Getting in too big of a hurry is detrimental, lying to get ahead is downright deadly, and unprovoked violence is never the right course of action (21:5–7). Sometimes it appears that wicked people are prospering, and others are tempted to emulate them. But that path always has an abrupt and destructive end. Upright conduct will yield much greater rewards (21:8).

In home situations, an argumentative spouse is a continual source of tension. It is better to withdraw than to argue endlessly or to be an ongoing target of verbal abuse (21:9). If a corner of the roof doesn't provide enough distance, another option is to move to the desert (21:19). Wicked neighbors are no better than contentious spouses. Such neighbors quickly lose the respect of others and find themselves alone after pushing away everyone they encounter (21:10).

Demystifying Proverbs

Homes in ancient Israel had flat roofs that could provide additional housing if needed. The image of Proverbs 21:9 is not as awkward (or comic) as it might appear in a modern neighborhood of steep, sloped roofs.

Verse 11 restates 19:25. Seeing a wicked person punished is an encouragement to faithful people. Wise people need not get to the point of punishment. They will learn from positive instruction and/or an occasional rebuke that keeps them on the right track.

The identity of "The Righteous One" in verse 12 is debated. Some people believe the term refers to righteous people in general. More common, however, is the belief that the phrase refers to God. Proverbs repeatedly makes clear that God will oppose and judge the wicked.

Everyone is in need from time to time. People who ignore the needs of others usually discover in their own time of despair that no one responds (21:13). Appeasing someone with a gift can help minimize potential anger. The "bribe" issue arises again in verse 14, as it did in 17:8 and 18:16. In this case, the focus is on the importance of peacemaking and justice; the passage does not endorse the use of bribes to circumvent fairness (21:15).

The choices of life do not include a "neutral" path. People must choose either the road of understanding and life or the path of wickedness and death (21:16). Many of the habits of the wicked and foolish are evident: living only for pleasure, overindulgence in alcohol and fine food, gluttony, and more (21:17–20). Equally apparent are the behaviors of the righteous and godly: disciplined accumulation of life's necessities, long life, prosperity, honor, success in the struggles of life, control of one's words, and so forth (21:20–23).

Negative emotions and behaviors, left unchecked, lead to even more problems. Pride and arrogance result in mocking. Sloth results in craving for more and more things that working could easily provide. Attempting to appear godly (offer sacrifices) with a wicked heart is a spiritually detestable act. Lying can result in offering false testimony, which is harmful in a number of ways. Perhaps one of the worst resulting sins is hypocrisy. A wicked person usually doesn't want to *appear* wicked to others, so he or she puts up a "bold front" (21:24–29).

How much better (and more effective) it is to acknowledge and seek the superiority of the wisdom of God. No other "wisdom" can approach God's wisdom (21:30). It is fine to plan and prepare for success, yet no one succeeds without God's help. No matter what kind of battles people fight, "victory rests with the LORD" (21:31).

22:1–16

WHAT GOD VALUES

This closing section of the proverbs of Solomon provides some critical observations about what God values and what He hates. Verse 1 underscores a key theme in Proverbs: the fact that integrity is integral to being a child of God. Given the choice of a good name or great wealth, people should always choose the former. Sadly, many are quite willing to sacrifice their reputation for financial gain. People make distinctions based on wealth, but God doesn't (22:2). He created all people, and He does not prorate His love according to personal bank accounts.

Sometimes wisdom is displayed in simple common sense. When danger approaches, prudent people use their heads and seek protection, while naïve people plunge ahead and suffer the consequences. The "danger" (22:3) may be a physical threat, but it is just as likely a spiritual temptation that wise people avoid while foolish ones get caught up and trapped. This seems clear from verse 5, which describes the "thorns and snares" on the path of the wicked. More than merely avoiding danger, those who humbly fear the Lord receive wealth, honor, and life (22:4).

Verse 6 is probably one of the most quoted from the book of Proverbs. Like many others, this proverb is true in a general (not an absolute) sense. When parents fear God, seek wisdom, get their priorities straight, and attempt to instill the same things in their children, those children have a much better likelihood of learning to make good decisions on their own. Still, many will stumble and fall. Some will rebel and succumb to various temptations. But most will appreciate the solid training they received and carry it with them into their adulthood.

Verses 7 through 9 are a series of general observations rather than insights. Most people can look around and confirm that the rich rule over the poor, that borrowing money makes the borrower beholden to the lender, that those who act wickedly are in for trouble, and that those who are generous to others will be blessed with satisfaction.

Those who suffer because of quarrels and insults need to eliminate the source. Conversely, gracious speech has a positive effect, even attracting the ear of the king. God values truth, and those who attempt to distort truth will ultimately be frustrated (22:10–12).

People who dogmatically resist seeking wisdom come across looking pretty foolish at times. The sluggard of verse 13 is a master of lame excuses to avoid going to work. The men who fall prey to the lure of the adulteress in verse 14 are certain to suffer consequences later on. And those who attempt to impress the rich with gifts until they spend themselves into a level of poverty are perhaps the most pathetic of all (22:16).

Critical Observation

The "rod" mentioned in 22:15 referred to a shepherd's tool used to guide the sheep away from a dangerous direction. It was not used in a harsh manner. Any discipline conducted in anger is improper.

In his conclusion of this section, Solomon once again emphasizes the importance of disciplining children. Acting foolishly is not only potentially embarrassing but frequently harmful as well. Loving parents will dedicate themselves to helping their children get beyond the allure of folly to discover the true joy of godly wisdom (22:15).

Take It Home

In your own circle of acquaintances, can you differentiate between people who display genuine godly wisdom and those who can only attempt to emulate that wisdom with a "bold front" (21:29)? How are their lives different? Do you relate to the two groups in the same way, or is there a difference? Can you think of any ways to ensure that your own wisdom is genuine and godly, and not merely the product of human training and techniques?

PROVERBS 22:17–24:34

SAYINGS OF THE WISE

Setting Up the Section

Proverbs 10:1–22:16 contains proverbs of Solomon, and more follow in 25–29. But this section is made up of "Sayings of the Wise." The unknown writer lets his readers know that he has provided thirty sayings of counsel and knowledge. Like Solomon, he is focused on the perfect wisdom of God that brings nothing but the best results for those who find it.

22:17–24:22

THIRTY SAYINGS OF COUNSEL AND KNOWLEDGE

Verses 17 through 21 are an introduction to this segment of Proverbs. The writer attests that his words are true and reliable, yet he wants his readers to respond not to him but rather to the wisdom of God. He begins with a series of warnings, most of which are clear. The poor and needy already have trouble enough, so we must not add to it by exploiting or pressuring them. We are to avoid relationships with easily angered people, or risk becoming one ourselves. And we are not to be too hasty to cosign loans for others, or we may soon find ourselves impoverished (22:22–27).

The warning in verse 28 is a bit more obscure. Land in Israel was very important for survival. The ancient landmarks established boundary lines, and moving them was a subtle method of stealing property that belonged to someone else.

The proverb in 22:29 shifts to a positive example. People who are skilled at what they do, and who do their work without complaining, will succeed. Soon they will be recruited to serve before kings.

It's important to understand the context of 23:1–3. Eating before a king required tact and proper etiquette. A visitor would want to acknowledge the honor and show appreciation for the splendid meal, yet to overeat and appear to be gluttonous was likely to incur the king's wrath. It was a delicate situation, to be sure.

Verses 4 and 5 reinforce a point that runs throughout Proverbs (and the New Testament as well): Although God can use money and although money can bring some temporal benefits, it should never be a primary pursuit of one's life. Wealth is a temporal entity.

The warning in verses 6–8 is about avoiding a stingy person. God loves a generous heart that sacrificially cares for others. Stingy people can't enjoy personal relationships because they are always focused on the cost. Wise people will not waste their time and expose themselves to such pain.

Verse 9 stands on its own as a proverb yet echoes a frequent theme of this book—the actions of a fool. There is no reason to try to argue or reason with a fool because he wants nothing to do with wisdom.

Verses 10 and 11 begin the same way as 22:28, but the proverb here is more specific. Moving ancient landmarks literally changed the boundaries of a piece of land. Here the intent was not just to expand one's own land; in doing so the person intentionally wanted to steal the land of widows and orphans, the socially powerless and vulnerable.

Critical Observation

The reference to a *redeemer* or *defender* in verse 11 carries a double meaning. Certainly God is the Redeemer of the disenfranchised. In addition, a custom in the ancient Israelite world allowed a family member to redeem the land a widow or orphan might lose after the death of the family patriarch. In either case, the warning in 23:11 is that while one might perceive a widow or an orphan as defenseless, a defender might actually be nearby.

Verse 12 encourages a posture of learning. This challenge leads well into the admonition of verses 13 and 14 regarding parental discipline. Training and instructing a child are essential in helping that child differentiate between wisdom and foolishness. Parents who fulfill the role of training preserve the lives of their children. Those who neglect it bring harm upon their children. Verses 15 and 16 reflect the joy that comes from seeing a child who values wisdom.

Sometimes it is easy to envy someone who seems to get away with wrongdoing. Verses 17 and 18 are a reminder to continue to obey God. Walking in the fear of the Lord brings true and lasting hope, life, and peace.

Verses 19–21 are a call for a son to wisely avoid a life of excess—specifically regarding food and drink. The call continues in verses 22–25, this time as a reminder that the way the son lives affects the joy of the parents.

Critical Observation

The concept of *buying the truth* in verse 23 means that the truth is so important that it is worth any sacrifice to acquire and keep.

And in verses 26–28, the warning shifts to the illusive allure of a prostitute or wayward wife. Such women are outwardly attractive to young men, yet they will draw the man into a trap from which he cannot easily escape.

The final verses of Proverbs 23 are a warning to stay away from the seduction of wine (23:29–35). The painful symptoms of overindulgence are listed in detail. Alcoholism affects one's body, causing the person to become disoriented, lose control, and disregard wisdom.

Those who are involved in various sins may seem to get what they want and are sometimes even objects of envy. Yet it is wrong to be jealous of wickedness. Behind the facade of success is a heart devoted to violence and troublemaking (24:1–2).

Just as a house is constructed and then filled with goods that make it livable, a commitment to wisdom builds up people, and ongoing knowledge edifies them and allows them to function together (24:3–4). Wisdom also makes people powerful because knowledge provides strength that goes beyond the physical. A group of wise people can achieve victory in whatever they do (24:5–6). Foolish people find that they cannot attain wisdom. Without it, they attempt public discourse and discussion yet have nothing of substance to offer. Instead, they exhibit only a desire to scoff and hurt others. The folly of such people alienates them from the community (24:7–9).

Endurance is essential when trials and problems arise. Being strong allows someone to pursue justice and rescue others who are treated unfairly or even being led to their death. God, who knows what is in each heart, will judge those who neglect to stand up for what is right (24:10–12).

Wisdom's effect on the soul is comparable to honey's sweetness in one's mouth. Those who feast on wisdom will never lose their hope for the future (24:13–14).

Verses 15 and 16 serve a twofold purpose: to both warn the wicked and encourage the righteous. It is foolish for the wicked to try to overpower the righteous because godly people have the strength and wisdom to endure difficult times. The wicked, lacking strength in God, will be worn down by trials. It is important to remain humble even when one's enemies suffer the consequences of their sin (24:17–18). Another person's judgment is no occasion to gloat or rejoice.

The righteous should not desire to be like evildoers, who have no future (24:19–20). Sin and wickedness lead to death, so it is foolish to envy people involved in such things. Verses 21 and 22 issue a call to fear both God and the king—to respect those in leadership, both divine and human. Associating with people who rebel against authority is wrong and dangerous.

24:23–34

A FEW ADDITIONAL SAYINGS

A series of final instructions—additional sayings of the wise—begins in verse 23. First is an admonition to be fair in judgment. People see how others respond to evildoers, and they judge those actions and attitudes accordingly (24:23–25).

The one who tells the truth does something that is right and pleasurable (24:26).

One should first commit to his "outdoor work" (source of income) before starting to build his house. In other words, all things should be done in the wise and proper order (24:27).

Verses 28 and 29 caution against creating trouble for one's neighbor without a reason and add a warning against deception. When one is offended by another, it is wrong to automatically respond with an equally offensive action. Forgiveness is far preferable to retribution.

The final caution is against laziness, a problem more severe than it might appear at first (24:30–34). The writer realizes that the eventual outcome of laziness is poverty, although it comes so gradually that the person is caught unaware. It might seem a small matter to value sleep over work, but laziness is as effective as a bandit in stealing everything a person has. Sloth leads to destruction.

Take It Home

This section of Proverbs warns of many things that can prevent or impede success in life: greed, drinking too much, cheating others, callous attitudes, laziness, and more. Looking back over your own life, which of these (or other) problems have you struggled with? How can you prevent such things from robbing you of the wisdom and contentment that are available?

PROVERBS 25:1–29:27

SOLOMON'S WISDOM, PART III

Proverbs Fit for a King	25:1–28
Characteristics of the Foolish	26:1–28
An Attitude Adjustment	27:1–27
Practical Righteousness	28:1–29:27

Setting Up the Section

Chapter 25 begins a new section of the book of Proverbs. Chapters 1–9 provide a more narrative approach to the value of wisdom and the importance of shunning evil. Chapters 10–22:16 present the first collection of the words of Solomon. Chapter 22:17 through chapter 24 contain another section of Proverbs that was probably added later. Chapters 25–29 return to the wisdom of Solomon with a series of unrelated proverbs.

25:1–28

PROVERBS FIT FOR A KING

The collection of proverbs contained in chapters 25 through 27 was either compiled or rediscovered by King Hezekiah (25:1). The collection begins with a series of proverbs about kings. While the king needs to search things out to understand them, God does not (25:2). Similarly, a king's subjects cannot fully understand the king (25:3).

Demystifying Proverbs

The proverbs in chapters 25 through 29 may have been locked away some two hundred years after Solomon's reign, when King Ahaz closed the temple (see 2 Chronicles 28). When Hezekiah succeeded Ahaz as king, he reopened the temple and recovered many of the temple objects (2 Chronicles 29). Quite possibly these proverbs were among them (see Proverbs 25:1).

Just as the dross needs to be taken away from silver before it can be used to create something, so too wickedness needs to be removed from the kingdom in order for it to be justly established (25:4–5).

It is foolish to try to exalt ourselves to make us known before the king (25:6). If the king does not feel the same way, we will be publicly humiliated and cast down to a lower position than where we started (25:7).

Verses 7–8 warn against bringing people too hastily into court. If we respond out of emotion, we may be made a fool of in front of all. The best thing to do is to bring our problems to our neighbors directly (25:9). There is a pragmatic reason for this: In the course of a trial, our own sins and failings will be brought to light (25:10).

Words spoken at the right time have extreme value (25:11). The focal point of this proverb is that saying the right thing at the right time is what is important. The comparison with a golden apple is a bit difficult to understand. The most likely meaning is that it refers to some type of a precious stone. When the stone is in the right setting, its beauty is seen. So, too, the right setting for words enhances the beauty of the words. Even reproof needs to be done at the right time to benefit the one hearing it (25:12).

Take It Home

One of the critical lessons that Proverbs teaches is that not only should we say the right thing but we must say the right thing at the right time. Understanding our environment is of critical importance when we speak. Just as an apple of gold by itself is enhanced by the right setting, so too are words spoken in the right setting.

We could restate verses 13 and 25 this way: A faithful messenger brings comfort to his boss in the same way an air-conditioned tractor refreshes a farmer on a hot summer day. The person who over-promises and under-delivers frustrates many people (25:14).

Tough leaders are won over not by a show of force but through patience. All a fight does is embolden the ruler (25:15).

The proverbs in verses 16–17 and 27–28 deal with having too much of a good thing. Too much of any of the pleasures of life is a bad thing.

The one who would sell out his neighbor for his own personal gain is a deadly person to be around (25:18), and placing faith in such a person will only bring pain and complications (25:19).

Blithely overlooking someone's grief produces a reaction in that person in the same way that vinegar and soda react (25:20).

In ancient Middle Eastern cultures, revenge was a way of life. The proverbs in verses 21 and 22 offer another way of dealing with the enemy—serve him and meet his needs. The point of pouring burning coals on the enemy's head is not to wreak vengeance but to shock him with this response.

A person with a loose tongue is a storm of problems (25:23).

Verse 24 repeats the proverb found in 19:13 and 21:9.

26:1–28

CHARACTERISTICS OF THE FOOLISH

Chapter 26 focuses on the characteristics of four kinds of people who do not pursue wisdom: the fool (26:1–12), the lazy person (26:13–16), the maddening person (26:17–22), and the hypocrite (26:23–28).

A fool never deserves honor (26:1–3) and should never be encouraged to think his ideas are valid (26:4–5). Putting confidence in a fool is suicide (26:6). Wisdom is useless to a fool—he cannot use it (26:7–9); it would be pointless to expect anything from him (26:10). Despite consequences, a fool will do the same foolish thing over and over again (26:11).

Yet, the worst thing in the world is not to be a fool—it is actually to be a prideful person. Pride is so destructive that there is more hope for a fool than the prideful man (26:12).

The lazy person is condemned just like the fool. The lazy person is worthless for a variety of reasons: He makes excuses (26:13), he loves sleep over work (25:14), he is too lazy even to feed himself (26:15), and he is extremely prideful (26:16).

Critical Observation

The fact that *seven* wise people are mentioned in 26:16 is no doubt symbolic; seven is the number representing perfection. In other words, when a lazy person is presented with perfect wisdom, he will pick his lazy attitude every time.

Some people are simply maddening. They meddle in problems that they have no reason to be involved in (26:17). They cover their lies by saying they were only joking (26:18–19). They start quarrels and keep them going with their gossip (26:20–21), savoring the rumors they spread (26:22).

The final verses expose the deception of hypocrites. Like a glazed ceramic, the words of the hypocrites seem good at face value, but in reality they mask malice (26:23). These people use their lips to hide their hearts (26:24–25), but in the end they will be exposed for the liars that they are (26:26). This is why the warnings of verses 27–28 are important: Any harm we plan for others will come back to hurt us in the end. God knows that the lying tongue is out to hurt others (26:28); people who utter lies will face their own self-inflicted destruction because hypocrisy cannot stand before God.

27:1–27

AN ATTITUDE ADJUSTMENT

Chapter 27 deals with right and wrong attitudes. One's attitude determines how one will respond to everything in this world.

A boastful attitude is a foolish attitude, whether one is boasting about himself or what he will do in the future (27:1–2). Resentment and envy are two attitudes that foster dangerous conflict (27:3–4).

Critical Observation

Proverbs 27:1 provides the foundation for the warning found in James 4:13–16.

A real friend is willing to tell the truth and say the tough things. Those who receive a rebuke should receive it as a sign of love, not of hate (27:5–6). But the context of a person's life—whether he is "full" or "hungry"—determines *how* he hears what he hears (27:7). When tough things have to be said, it is more dangerous to leave and ignore those tough words than to stay and endure them (27:8). Through friendship people are challenged, changed, refreshed, and supported (27:9). Friendships already established in the family are worth trusting in and ministering to (27:10).

Solomon wants to know the joy of his child's obedience and the honor that comes from wise children in the community (27:11). Some marks of that kind of wisdom include anticipating and avoiding trouble (27:12), not being an easy target for swindlers (27:13), and saying the right thing at the right time (27:14). If Solomon's son marries a contentious woman, it will be a great annoyance in the home (27:15–16).

Godly friendships, as earlier proverbs have said, exhort and motivate people to be godly (27:17). In a similar way, mutual respect between boss and worker benefits both (27:18).

The last set of proverbs in this chapter deals with issues of the heart. The heart of someone is who that person really is (27:19). The desires that are in the heart are never satisfied (27:20). Verse 21 can be understood to mean that what people say about a person reveals his character, or that how a person responds to praise and flattery reveals his character. In either case, if foolishness has taken over the heart of someone, then that foolishness will be impossible to remove (27:22).

This chapter ends on a practical appeal: to have a shepherd's heart for the resources that God has entrusted to us (27:23–28).

28:1–29:27

PRACTICAL RIGHTEOUSNESS

In chapters 28 and 29, we see righteousness played out in practical terms for both the king and his subjects.

The boldness of the righteous is equated to the boldness of a lion—which is a courage that stands up against any foe. What one gets when walking in the righteousness of God is the ability to stand up for what is right regardless of the foe (28:1).

If a leader takes advantage of his people and operates in an unfair manner, then they will rise up and there will be a conflict between leaders in the nation. The ruler who realizes this and pursues a righteous approach to leadership will rule over a stable land for a long time (28:2). Under a bad leader, poverty becomes so widespread that the poor even prey on one another (28:3).

Individuals, as well as leaders, contribute to how society functions. A person who breaks the law is in essence endorsing all lawbreakers, while obeying the law is a blow for justice (28:4–5).

In most cultures around the world, being rich seems to be the best of all possible achievements. But if being rich causes someone to lose integrity, then it is much better to remain poor and maintain a good reputation (28:6). Similarly, overindulgence is a shame to be avoided (28:7), as is charging excessive interest (28:8).

Demystifying Proverbs

The law of God forbade one Israelite to charge a poor Jew interest (Exodus 22:25). They were to show kindness to those in need and not to make a profit off of them.

Practical righteousness involves joining prayer with obedience (28:9), setting a good example (28:10), and having the right perspective on success (28:11–12). It means taking responsibility for one's actions (28:13) and consciously choosing right over wrong (28:14). For a ruler, it includes governing with integrity and compassion (28:15–16). The consequences of unrighteousness—whether it be disregard for human life (28:17) or any other crookedness—are fatal (28:18).

As a general rule, the trustworthy, hardworking person does better than the person chasing a get-rich-quick scheme—especially at the expense of others (28:19–22). Without honest accountability (28:23), it is far too easy for greed to lead to conflict within the family and beyond (28:23–25). It is wiser to abandon a self-centered perspective and use what one has to help others (28:26–27). That way of life is better for everyone (28:28–29:2).

Again Solomon returns to some key themes: the impact children's behavior has on their parents (29:3), the importance of just rulers for a stable society (29:4), and the dangers of flattery (29:5). He again emphasizes the consequences of actions (29:6), the importance of caring for the poor (29:7), and the trouble a loose tongue can cause (29:8).

He repeats his warning about the futility of taking a fool to court (29:9), how differently good and bad people react to the innocent (29:10), and the wisdom of keeping one's temper (29:11). Rulers are again warned against listening to bad counsel and reminded that rich and poor are equal in the Lord's eyes (29:12–14).

Solomon concludes his proverbs with a review of how children's behavior reflects on parents (29:15, 17); the impact of those in authority (29:16, 19, 21); the importance of taking correction (29:18); the dangers of thoughtless speech, temper, and pride (29:20, 22, 23); and the foolishness of aligning oneself with lawbreakers (29:24).

This final section of Solomon's wisdom ends by affirming that ultimately God's judgment trumps any judgment human beings may offer (29:25–27).

Take It Home

You may notice that Solomon keeps coming back to the same themes he feels are important. Sometimes parents, church leaders, business managers, and so forth may feel they are "harping" on an issue if they feel a need to repeat it more than once or twice. Yet essential issues may bear repeating. Think through the things in life you feel are absolutely the most important, in any areas over which you have influence, and try to formulate some ways to restate them so that others might respond more readily to your passion and enthusiasm.

PROVERBS 30:1–31:31

WISDOM FROM THE MASSAITES

People in Relationship to God	30:1–17
People in Relationship to Earth	30:18–33
The Warning	31:1–9
Wisdom Personified	31:10–31

Setting Up the Section

Chapter 30 marks the beginning of the final section of the book of Proverbs: the sayings of the Massaites. Massa was a clan from the line of Ishmael that lived in north Arabia. The two men whose wisdom is recorded here were contemporaries of either Solomon or Hezekiah and probably were influenced greatly by the theology of Israel. Some have speculated that Agur (chapter 30) was a leader of the Massaites and that Lemuel (chapter 31) was probably the king of that region.

30:1–17

PEOPLE IN RELATIONSHIP TO GOD

Agur, whose words are recorded in chapter 30, begins by acknowledging the frailty of humanity. He is weary. He feels stupid. He doesn't understand life. He lacks wisdom. All this is for one simple reason: He does not know God (30:1–3).

To highlight how little he knows, he asks a series of rhetorical questions (30:4):

Who has ascended to heaven or come down from heaven?
Who has gathered the wind in His fists?
Who has wrapped up the waters in a garment?
What is His name—and His Son's name?

Take It Home

The great news is that there is an answer to Agur's questions in 30:4: Jesus Christ—the very wisdom of God.

Agur is in awe of the complete trustworthiness of the Word of God and the total danger that would be involved if someone added or subtracted from it (30:5–6). He then makes two requests of God: (1) that God would remove falsehood and lying from his life, and (2) that God would give him neither poverty nor riches (30:7–8). He wants enough food to eat so that he will not profane God for not having enough, but he does not want so much that he forgets about God and lives only for himself (30:9).

It is important to Agur that truth be held high. He describes ways that deceit and falsehood are expressed in the world: by slandering a worker to his employer (30:10); by dishonoring parents (30:11, 17); by self-righteousness (30:12); by arrogance (30:13); and by cruelty (30:14).

The reason there is such deceitfulness and falsehood is that the human heart is wicked and never satisfied. It is like a leech that continually sucks the blood of its victim and is never satisfied (30:15). To describe this even further, Agur lists four more things that are never satisfied (30:16):

1) Sheol—or death. Every moment of every day someone dies, and this will never end on this side of eternity.
2) The barren woman—nothing will satisfy a woman who wants a baby and cannot have one.
3) Dry land—when a place is very dry, it seems that no matter how much it rains it is never enough.
4) Fire—fire keeps burning as long as there is fuel to keep it going.

30:18–33

PEOPLE IN RELATIONSHIP TO EARTH

Next Agur sets forth a series of wonders about the world around us: an eagle in flight, a serpent slithering on a rock, a ship on the high sea, and a couple in love (30:18–19). Agur responds to each of these with a sense of awe. He wonders how anyone who sees what God has made can act as if God's laws have no validity (30:20).

Agur next outlines a series of things that would throw his world into disarray: political, moral, marital, and domestic chaos (30:21–23). The point here is that certain structures are essential for society to function. There is a need for order, and this drives us to our need for God.

Agur next extols the great virtues of wisdom by picking some of the smallest and most vulnerable creatures from the animal world to illustrate the great power of wisdom (30:24): hardworking ants (30:25), small rock-dwelling mammals (30:26), hordes of locusts (30:27), and lizards that live even in the richest homes (30:38).

Four more examples identify creatures that demonstrate a certain authority (30:29): the head of a pride of lions, the rooster that dominates the henhouse, the nimble male goat, and the commander-in-chief of an army (30:30–31).

Agur's point is that fools who have tried to present an impressive image or do harm need to stand quiet before God (30:32). To persist in their foolishness will inevitably cause problems (30:33).

31:1–9

THE WARNING

Chapter 31 contains lessons that King Lemuel's mother taught him (31:1). A king must hold himself to a high standard. Playing around with adulterous women brings nothing but pain and misery to a king and his kingdom (31:2–3). Nor is a partying lifestyle appropriate for a king (31:4). Drunkenness is a dangerous thing. It can lead a king to make decrees he knows nothing about and do things to hurt people and not act out of justice and righteousness (31:5). Strong drink should be provided for people who are dying so that they can have some comfort and forget their pain (31:6–7). Rather than opening his mouth for debauchery, a king should speak up for those who cannot do so for themselves (31:8–9).

31:10–31

WISDOM PERSONIFIED

This final section of Proverbs is an acrostic poem. Each of the twenty-two verses begins with a consecutive letter of the Hebrew alphabet.

Critical Observation

At one level, the poem in Proverbs 31:10–31 appears to be about a godly wife. On another level, when this chapter is taken in the context of the book of Proverbs, it could also be seen as a personification of wisdom. It is probably not intended to be a checklist for a woman to evaluate her worth. Instead, this is no doubt the expression of how wisdom would act if wisdom were a wife. All of the virtues adorned in the book of Proverbs are mentioned in this chapter: work, wise use of money, wise use of time, caring for the poor, planning ahead, respect for one's spouse, wise counsel, and fearing God. Both men and women can learn from Proverbs 31:10–31.

The wife of noble character is a rare jewel (31:10). This echoes the description of wisdom in Proverbs 8:11. The question, "Who can find such a woman?" does not suggest that such women are nonexistent but that they should be admired, and the husband who finds such a woman should be ecstatic.

The noble wife's husband has confidence in her. He trusts her completely because she is wise (31:11). Her careful management of the home enhances their family's living. He lacks nothing of value within his home because of her hard work (31:12).

This kind of woman is an asset, not a liability, because her motives are to do good to her husband and her family. She is not defined by what she gets but by what she gives (31:13–15). She works hard and with gusto and energy. Her wise business dealings are profitable (31:16–18).

Critical Observation

Because women were not permitted to buy land at the time Proverbs was written, some have concluded that verse 16 shows that the poem is not about a woman but about the personification of wisdom. However, a wife, even though she might not be the one actually buying and selling, could just as easily give the instructions for the purchase.

The noble wife is also selfless and generous. She understands that it is the desire of God to care for the poor, and therefore she does it with all of her heart. At the heart of wisdom is a love for the poor (31:19–20).

Her preparedness has provided her entire family with all that they need (31:21). She even makes her family's bed coverings so that they can sleep in comfort. She also takes care of herself and her appearance (31:22).

A noble woman enhances her husband's standing among those who transact legal and judicial affairs at the city gate among the elders. Though she is obviously proactive and competent, she functions in a way that honors her husband's position in the community (31:23–24).

At the end of the day, when people look at this woman it will not be how she is dressed that will matter; it will be her strength and dignity. She can face the future confident that she is walking in integrity and that, no matter what happens, she will respond with faith in God and faithfulness to her family (31:25).

The book of Proverbs speaks a lot about controlling one's tongue. This woman has such self-control. She is praised for her wisdom and faithful instruction. She speaks with the intention of being wise and building others up (31:26).

Her children honor her for her hard work and loving care for them and call her blessed. Her husband praises her. He realizes that there are others who have done much, but he tells her that she has surpassed all other women in the world. (31:27–29).

At the heart of this woman is godly character. Even though she might be physically charming and beautiful, those qualities do not last. The key to her godly wisdom is the fact that she fears the Lord (31:30). This is the key application of the entire book of Proverbs (see 1:7).

The writer urges his readers to recognize and praise the faithful work and kindness of this woman. She deserves public recognition for her fear of God and faithfulness to her family (31:31).

Take It Home

As you review this section of Proverbs—and the book as a whole—consider what goals you might want to set for yourself in the future. For example, have you ever prayed (like Agur in 30:8) for neither poverty nor riches? Or how would your personal demonstration of wisdom-in-action compare to the woman described in 31:10–31? The book of Proverbs holds up some lofty goals, all of which should inspire us to be better people.

ECCLESIASTES

INTRODUCTION TO ECCLESIASTES

The book of Ecclesiastes is considered part of the Wisdom Literature of the Old Testament. Contained within its verses are proverbs, teachings, stories, reflections, and warnings about a myriad of topics. But the underlying pursuit of the book as a whole is the meaning of life. The author explores the purpose of life and, more importantly, asks what humanity's purpose is as a creation of a sovereign God. Verse by verse through the book of Ecclesiastes, the author answers that question. The purpose of life, meaningless though it may feel, is to fear God and obey His commands.

AUTHOR

The question of authorship of Ecclesiastes is a debated subject. The author does not directly identify himself, but he does state that he is the son of David and king in Jerusalem. Traditional scholarly opinion is that Solomon is the writer of the book, and early church testimony supports this view. A few passages that support this view internally include 1:1, 12; 2:4–9; and 12:9. Solomon was known for his wisdom and dedicated most of his life to its pursuit. He also wrote most of the books of Proverbs and Song of Songs. With Solomon in mind as the author, many of the teachings of the book seem to have a direct correlation to the events of his life.

It wasn't until the 1700s that Solomon's authorship came into question. The chief argument against Solomonic authorship is rooted largely in debates over the original Hebrew, which is a different dialect than that of Solomon's other writings and seems to reflect a later version of Hebrew. Furthermore, the writer refers to himself as *Qohelet*, or *the teacher*, a pseudonym that scholars argue would be unnecessary for the king. As far as internal evidence against Solomon's authorship is concerned, in 1:12 the writer seems to allude to a time when Solomon was alive following his reign, but no such time exists. It should also be noted that after chapter 3, the references to Solomon taper off, and many of the proverbs and teachings that follow seem to contradict those in Proverbs.

Within this commentary are included some of the opposing views and relevant points that support each view, and the author will be referred to by the generic title *Qohelet*. It should also be noted that there is an unmistakable narrator present in 1:1–11 and 12:8–13, who is likely the author of the book. For those who favor Solomonic authorship, this is an elder Solomon reflecting back on the pursuits and teachings of much of his life—the body of the work within the frame. Those who take a non-Solomonic view, however, believe this to be the voice of the author. The switch to first-person in 1:12, then, begins the quotation of the unidentified Qohelet.

PURPOSE

The main purpose of the book of Ecclesiastes is threefold. First, it paints a picture of a sovereign God who controls everything in the world. Second, Qohelet's teachings highlight the meaninglessness of life apart from fearing and obeying the sovereign God. And lastly, the book provides wisdom and counsel for future generations rooted in the things Qohelet learned throughout his life's pursuit of meaning.

OCCASION

The date of Ecclesiastes depends heavily on which view of authorship one holds. Most scholars who deny Solomonic authorship agree that Ecclesiastes should have a date in Israel's late history, anywhere from 450–250 BC. Because the book doesn't contain any direct internal evidence that helps date it, the date is based largely on the style of the Hebrew it is written in, which most agree is similar to a later Hebrew style. On the other hand, for those scholars who hold to Solomon's writing, the book must have been written during his reign, which covers a span anywhere from 971 BC to 931 BC.

THEMES

Ecclesiastes contains several proverbs and teachings, but they all center on just a few main themes. These themes include: wisdom, the sovereignty of God, the limitations of humanity, and death. Throughout the author's quest for meaning in life, he returns again and again to the meaninglessness of everything, a reality based on humanity's smallness in the face of God's great sovereignty and control.

CONTRIBUTION TO THE BIBLE

Many of Qohelet's teachings seem to contradict teachings in other parts of the Bible. However, one cannot deny that Qohelet's reflections on life paint one of the most realistic pictures of the fallen world in which we live and humanity's purpose within that world. As God's sovereignty is acknowledged again and again throughout the book, one can't help but look forward to the coming of Jesus Christ and His redemptive work on the cross. Ecclesiastes paints a picture of a fallen world and the impact of sin, but knowing the promises that have been fulfilled post-Christ make the realities of this world bearable. Christ is the meaning to all the meaningless Qohelet observes, and the death that he fears takes on a new hope for all who believe in Christ.

OUTLINE

QOHELET'S OPENING THOUGHTS	1:1–11
EVERYTHING IS FUTILE	1:12–2:23
The Futility of Wisdom	1:12–18
The Futility of Pleasure	2:1–11
In the End Wisdom and Folly Are Futile	2:12–16
The Futility of Work	2:17–23
GOD'S PURPOSE AND TIMING	2:24–3:22
The Small Pleasures of Life	2:24–26
A Time for Everything	3:1–8
God Determines the Time for Everything	3:9–22
THE BURDENS OF LIFE	4:1–12
Oppression	4:1–3
Labor	4:4–6
Friendlessness	4:7–12
EVERYTHING IS FUTILE	4:13–6:9
Political Power Is Futile	4:13–16
God's Holiness *Is Not* Futile	5:1–7
The Futility of Wealth	5:8–6:9
QOHELET'S WISE COUNSEL	6:10–12:7
The Smallness of Humanity	6:10–12
A List of Proverbs	7:1–8:1
Miscellaneous Counsels	8:2–9:16
A Second List of Proverbs	9:17–11:6
Reflections on Youth, Old Age, and Death	11:7–12:7
EPILOGUE	12:8–14

ECCLESIASTES 1:1–11

QOHELET'S OPENING THOUGHTS

As is common with many books of the Bible, Ecclesiastes begins with a superscription introducing what will follow as the words of Qohelet, son of David as scribed by the unknown narrator. It is this opening line that draws the initial correlation between the speaker and King Solomon.

Verse 2 sets the tone for everything to follow. The declaration that everything is meaningless is repeated in 12:8, forming the bookends for everything that will be read in between. With the critical understanding of the book riding on this single phrase, it is important to understand what the author means by the use of the Hebrew *hebel*. The concrete meaning of hebel is "breath" or "vapor," and it can either be understood metaphorically as "meaningless" or "transient." *Vanity* is an old English word that means the same as meaningless.

Having stated the mantra for the book, in verse 3 the author poses a rhetorical question to engage the reader and further emphasize the meaninglessness of life. If everything is meaningless, then the obvious answer to the question posed is that people do not profit from their hard work.

Critical Observation

It is interesting to note that the Hebrew word *yitron*, translated here as *profit*, occurs nine times in the book of Ecclesiastes, but it does not occur anywhere else in the Bible (2:11, 13; 3:9; 5:9, 16; 7:12; 10:10–11).

Verses 4–11 illustrate the meaninglessness of humanity's toil by appealing to the cyclical, unchanging world in which we live. Although time is progressing and generations come and go, nothing else is changing (1:4). Verses 5–7 provide specific examples from nature of these repetitive patterns of the world. When viewing the cycles of nature in such a way, it's no doubt that the writer's tone is one of pessimism and weariness—his life exists within this repetitious cycle, where there is always more to see and hear (1:8).

From nature the narrator now turns to history as another example of the futility of everything. Although time passes and generations change, history seems to be on the same cyclical pattern as nature (1:9–10). The human condition remains the same—meaningless. The narrator closes the prologue by noting that not only has history proven to repeat itself but the pattern will not be broken in the future.

Take It Home

Reading through Ecclesiastes, it is repeated time and again that everything about life is meaningless. This can be overwhelming and may illicit a variety of responses, but above all it should encourage us to fear God and seek to live in obedience to Him.

ECCLESIASTES 1:12–2:23

EVERYTHING IS FUTILE

Setting Up the Section

Verse 12 notes the shift from the narrator's voice to the voice of Qohelet, who will be the speaker through 12:7. While the narrator (or the elder Solomon) establishes the tone and theme in the prologue, it is Qohelet's first-person reflections that form the bulk of the book.

1:12–18

THE FUTILITY OF WISDOM

Qohelet briefly introduces himself in verse 12 and then moves into his initial reflection on his quest for wisdom. Qohelet points out that he isn't just trying to gain some additional insight into the world around him but that he has been tasked with trying to gain all the wisdom under heaven. In verse 13, he describes this as a burdensome task given him by God.

Having searched for all the wisdom in the world and studied everything under the sun, Qohelet came to his conclusion: It's all meaningless (1:14). Qohelet quotes a proverb in verse 15, supporting his idea that what is wrong with the world cannot be righted by mankind. The crooked imagery attests to the perversity of the human condition. Because of the fallen world and sin's presence, the human heart knows only evil unless affected by God. It is interesting to note that the prophet Isaiah uses this same imagery when he talks about the coming Messiah (Isaiah 40:4). The reflection in verses 13–15 is repeated in verses 16–18, with verse 16 reemphasizing Qohelet's quest, verse 17 again noting the meaninglessness—here of folly in addition to wisdom—his quest uncovers, and verse 18 including a second proverb that supports his frustration.

Demystifying Ecclesiastes

This passage in the opening chapter of Ecclesiastes is one of the key texts used to argue Solomonic authorship (1:1; 3:1–8; 8:2–6; 12:9–12). Whether Solomon is the author or not, the comparison is important because it raises the question, if the most wise person in the world finds everything meaningless, what hope does anyone else have to reach a different conclusion?

2:1–11

THE FUTILITY OF PLEASURE

Qohelet's pursuit moves from wisdom to a selfish pursuit of pleasure, but he doesn't leave the reader guessing of his quest's findings—this also proves to be meaningless (2:1). Among the ways he pursues meaning in pleasure are drinking and folly (2:3); building mansions and expansive grounds (2:4–6); employing servants and amassing animals, treasures, singers, and concubines (2:7–8).

Verses 9–11 summarize Qohelet's reflection on the endless pleasures he pursued. While his pursuits were greater than those of anyone around him, he was able to maintain his wisdom throughout, since the pleasures were a part of his greater quest for the meaning of life (2:9). In his pursuit of worldly pleasures, he didn't hold back from anything he desired, but it was all in vain, because he reached the same conclusion that his pursuit of pleasure was meaningless with no profit (2:10–11).

2:12–16

IN THE END WISDOM AND FOLLY ARE FUTILE

This section of Qohelet's thoughts is set apart from the reflections on wisdom in 1:12–18 by the emphasis on death being what renders both wisdom and folly futile. It seems to be Qohelet's impending death that is forcing him to reflect on his life's pursuits and draw the conclusion that they have been meaningless. Qohelet makes this comparison personal in verse 15, when he refers to himself as a wise man who will encounter the same fate as any fool. Not only do both the wise and the fool face the same fate but their deaths render them one in the same—forgotten (2:16). Such futile thoughts leave the writer hating all he has worked for in his life, and he again closes with the mantra that everything under the sun is futile (2:17).

Critical Observation

Contrasting wisdom and folly is not unique to the writer of Ecclesiastes, as it is a common characteristic of proverbial writings. What stands out in Qohelet's comparison, however, is that he concludes that the lives of both the wise and the fool result in the same fate (death), thus nullifying the importance of wisdom.

2:17–23

THE FUTILITY OF WORK

Verse 17 leads Qohelet from wisdom and folly into a reflection on the meaning of work. But again, the thought that work might provide some semblance of meaning is negated by the fact that in death his life's work will be passed on to someone else, and he'll have no control over who receives it (2:18–19). However, Qohelet doesn't simply stop with the conclusion that work is rendered futile in death. Because one's work holds no long-lasting value, all the present pain, toil, and sleepless nights it creates are futile as well (2:20–23). In Qohelet's observation, these two factors—the present and future futility of work—support his conclusion that work, also, is meaningless.

Take It Home

A single refrain is heard echoing throughout the early sections of Ecclesiastes: Everything is futile. Qohelet has searched for meaning in wisdom, selfish pleasures, and work, only to maintain the same sense of defeat at the end of each pursuit. With a foreboding sense of his life's finiteness, Qohelet's quest has left him empty-handed thus far.

ECCLESIASTES 2:24–3:22

GOD'S PURPOSE AND TIMING

Setting Up the Section

Having presented his initial observations of life and its futility, Qohelet now shifts gears—be it ever so slightly—from reflection to instruction. In the following verses, Qohelet presents the reader with advice gleaned from his life's pursuit.

2:24–26

THE SMALL PLEASURES OF LIFE

This section, which marks a notable shift in Qohelet's tone, is the first of several passages that give advice on how to find fulfillment in one's day-to-day life amid the foreboding sense of meaninglessness. Qohelet's advice? Find a way to enjoy the small pleasures in life—namely to eat, drink, and enjoy one's work. What is critical to this advice, however, is the understanding that apart from God, enjoyment of daily pleasures is impossible (2:24). God enables a person to enjoy these things because they are not looking for ultimate satisfaction in them; that satisfaction is found in God alone (2:25).

Verse 26 points out that there are two different types of people—those who please God and those who offend Him. Qohelet observes that it is up to God to determine who will have the ability to enjoy these small pleasures. But Qohelet finds even these pleasures of God to be meaningless in the grand scheme of things (2:26).

3:1–8

A TIME FOR EVERYTHING

Ecclesiastes 3:1–8 contains several verses that support the line of thought that Solomon is the author of this book and is speaking out of personal experience. The overarching theme in this passage is the sovereignty of God, whose hand controls everything. Humanity's limitations and futility are made most evident in comparison to God's sovereignty. Part of what frustrates Qohelet about the futility of life is that everything is out of his control. In this passage, he employs the literary device of a poem to further this idea that there is a time and a season for everything (3:1).

Critical Observation

Included in Qohelet's poetic verses are several stylistic elements. Among these literary devices are rhyme (lost on us in the translation but present in the Hebrew), repetition of the phrase "a time to" that begins each line, and antithetical parallelism in which each verse contains a pair of opposites that illustrate a parallel meaning.

Included in the body of this poem are fourteen different pairs of opposites, each supporting the idea that everything on earth functions within its predetermined time frame (3:2–8). The poem breaks down as follows: Verses 2–3 illustrate that everything has an already established beginning and end time, whether it be life and death or construction and destruction. In verse 4, Qohelet observes that we experience our varying emotions at their predetermined times. The time when things will be excluded and included has already been set (3:5), as has the time for obtaining and ridding oneself of possessions (3:6). Even experiencing strong personal emotions, and the way those emotions manifest themselves in relation to others, is out of one's control (3:7–8).

3:9–22

GOD DETERMINES THE TIME FOR EVERYTHING

In verse 9, Qohelet returns to the rhetorical question of what profit might be gained from work in such a structured world. Qohelet establishes in 2:24–26 that it is in God alone that someone can find purpose in daily life, even in the simple things like food, drink, and work. He mentions God again here in response to his rhetorical question (3:10). In a statement almost identical to 1:13, Qohelet observes that searching for meaning in such a structured world is a burden.

Demystifying Ecclesiastes

Verse 11 seems to stand in opposition to the burdened feeling of verse 10. The first line of the verse reflects on the beauty of God's timing and the eternal perspective He brings. However, the second part of the verse, as well as the context of the verses surrounding it, attests to the frustration Qohelet feels at being unable to understand God's plans and His timing.

In verses 12–13, Qohelet returns again to the conclusion that because everything is orchestrated in God's timing, humanity is resigned to settle with enjoying those lesser pleasures of daily life mentioned in 2:24. Furthermore, Qohelet concludes that the timeline God has set in motion cannot be altered, a testimony to why God is worthy of being revered (3:14).

But Qohelet doesn't stop there with reasons why God is to be feared. At this point in his observations of the world, he brings up the idea of God's justice, which has been established within the ordered world He has created (3:15–22). When he observes the world around him, Qohelet can't find any justice—only wickedness and injustice (3:16). So he adds justice to the list of things that God will bring to pass in His timing, at which point He will bring justice to both the wicked and the righteous. This idea of future judgment directs Qohelet's thoughts toward death, which as noted previously is a terrifying concept to him. Chief among God's sovereignty is that in His time He will bring glory to His name and enact His judgment on the world.

Verses 18–21 include his reflection that in death there is no difference between humanity and the animals, because both eventually end up dead.

Take It Home

Qohelet's lack of understanding regarding the afterlife is made evident by verses 20–21, wherein he questions the shared fate of humans and animals. If there is no afterlife, when will God right all of the world's wrongs? Once again Qohelet concludes that finding pleasure in the small things, namely work, is all humanity can count on (3:22).

ECCLESIASTES 4:1–12

THE BURDENS OF LIFE

Setting Up the Section

Qohelet's search for purpose moves from the role of justice in the world to the heavily burdened people he has seen around him, including the oppressed, those who labor in vain, and the friendless. For each he concludes the same thing—this, too, is meaningless.

4:1–3

OPPRESSION

In the same vein of the injustices in the world and the reign of wickedness, Qohelet now laments the oppression he sees everywhere he looks. The chief problem he observes in regard to oppression is the powerlessness of those being oppressed (4:1). But like many of his other observations, he simply resigns to that powerlessness and concludes that in lieu of such oppression it would be better to be dead (4:2). And beyond that, it would be better still to have never been born and never exposed to the wicked world (4:3). Qohelet feels crippled in the face of oppression and hopeless to bring about any change.

Critical Observation

Verse 2 contains the first in a series of "better than" statements that Qohelet will make over the succeeding verses (4:3, 6, 9, 13; 5:5; 6:3). In each instance, Qohelet emphasizes the negativity of something by comparing it favorably to something else.

4:4–6

LABOR

Having already spent some time on the meaninglessness of work, Qohelet returns to that observation in verses 4–6. Here he draws an additional conclusion—both toil and success come from the envy of one's neighbor (4:4). It is Qohelet's conclusion that humanity is motivated by jealousy, which is yet another reason that all of humanity's toil is futile. To support this conclusion, he then states two proverbs that present three differing types of workers. The first is the lazy person who doesn't work at all, who the proverb deems a fool (4:5). The second is the person who works some as needed but also knows how to rest, while the third is the person who knows only work and no rest (4:6).

Of the three, the only one Qohelet seems to approve of is the second, whose combination of rest and work is better than the other two, if for no other reason than their life isn't dominated by something Qohelet has already concluded to be futile.

 **4:7–12**

FRIENDLESSNESS

If a life spent toiling away in vain isn't meaningless enough, Qohelet goes on to state in verses 7–8 that the one who labors away *alone* is even worse off. Thinking about loneliness leads Qohelet to form another "better than" conclusion in verse 9: Having a friend is better than being alone. He then lists four practical reasons why the one who has a companion lives a less-burdened life than a lonely person (4:9–12). The final image of the passage—that of a three-strand cord—summarizes why companionship is better than loneliness: There is strength in numbers (4:12).

Take It Home

While all three of the aforementioned situations—those who are oppressed, whose labor is motivated by jealousy, and the lonely—seem very different, the unifying theme is that all are living lives that seem to be utterly meaningless.

ECCLESIASTES 4:13–6:9

EVERYTHING IS FUTILE

Setting Up the Section

Having paused to voice his thoughts on the predetermined structure of time and those who live burdened lives, Qohelet returns once again to his subject of futility. While the meaninglessness remains the foundation for his conclusions, verse 13 picks up where 2:23 ends.

4:13–16

POLITICAL POWER IS FUTILE

The themes of wisdom and folly return in this passage, as Qohelet ponders the meaninglessness of political power. To illustrate this, he compares two very different characters in verse 13. One is poor, young, and wise; the other is king, old, and foolish. It is also pointed out that the king is foolish because he ignores the advice of others. Wisdom is better than foolishness, regardless of the circumstances (4:14). The tone in verses 15–16 is reminiscent of 2:12–17, and again wisdom is no better than folly and power is no better than being powerless. Furthermore, because each share the human condition of imperfection, it is highly likely that the young ruler will become like the older one in time.

5:1–7

GOD'S HOLINESS *IS NOT* FUTILE

Amid his discourse on futilities, Qohelet includes a word of caution. God's holiness is not among the meaningless; therefore enter into the place of worship with caution. In this passage, wisdom most certainly trumps folly, and Qohelet gives three examples of worship wherein caution is key: sacrifice (5:1), prayer (5:2–3), and vows (5:4–6).

Critical Observation

The speaker includes another "better than" statement in verse 5, as it relates to taking vows. Because vows are not a mandatory part of worship, Qohelet warns that he who never makes a vow is better off than he who cannot keep the vows he makes. Jesus makes a similar warning in Matthew 23:16–22. Vow-making is no longer a part of our worship today because the ultimate vow was made—and kept—on our behalf when Christ died on the cross.

Verse 7 reiterates the point made in verse 2, that in worship one is to speak little and listen much. Qohelet then gives a command that will be reiterated throughout the rest of the book: Fear God. The point has already been made that God, who is in heaven and separate from mankind on earth, controls the timing of everything. Mankind is dependent and powerless, therefore God is worthy of humanity's fear and awe.

5:8–6:9

THE FUTILITY OF WEALTH

Next Qohelet enters into a discourse on the meaninglessness of wealth. But he begins by warning that while God's divine authority is to be feared, human authority is by nature corrupt and therefore worthy of caution (5:8–9). The drive for profit controls one's desire for power, the perfect segue into Qohelet's observation on the futility of wealth.

It is not surprising that Qohelet finds the accumulation of, and attempt to enjoy, wealth utterly meaningless. To present his observations, Qohelet begins with three proverbs that illustrate the inability to find pleasure in money. Qohelet determines wealth meaningless because one never has enough of it (5:10); the more you have the more others are collecting (5:11); and having much leads to many sleepless nights—whether from worry or a lack of hard work (5:12). However, the implications of these verses reach beyond just wealth and shine a light on the insatiable nature of lusting after things.

In verses 13–17, Qohelet presents two scenarios that illustrate his conclusion that wealth leads to evil. The first scenario is the evil of hoarding all of one's wealth (5:13). No pleasure can come from money that is hoarded. The same can be said of losing one's money (5:14). If a person depends on money for happiness, then when it is lost the person has nothing and can pass on nothing to his offspring. Just as death renders wisdom and folly futile, it does the same for wealth (5:15–16). Whether one's riches are hoarded or stolen, in the end it makes no difference.

Demystifying Ecclesiastes

Earlier in his writing, Qohelet observes that because all of life is meaningless, one must seek pleasure in the simple things such as eating, drinking, and enjoying one's work (2:24–26; 3:12–13, 22). When wealth is involved, however, even those small pleasures aren't possible. The blind pursuit of wealth nullifies even the simplest of pleasures.

The only exception to the futility of wealth is when it is a gift from God. Just as some are able to find pleasure in their work because God allows it (2:24–26), so a special few are able to find pleasure in their wealth (5:19–20). Qohelet considers these people to be a fortunate few, especially in consideration of the fact that to others God gives wealth and does not let them enjoy it (6:1–2).

Verses 3–6 contain another "better than" statement, in this case that a stillborn baby who has never known anything of the unfairness of the world is better off than the rich man who can't enjoy his wealth. And, as he has concluded several times before, isn't the fate of the stillborn baby and the rich man the same?

Take It Home

Qohelet closes his section on the futility of wealth with a final series of proverbs that conclude that neither the desire for wealth nor the attainment of it lead to any real satisfaction (6:7–9). In the end, the pursuit of riches for pleasure is meaningless, too.

ECCLESIASTES 6:10–12:7

QOHELET'S WISE COUNSEL

Setting Up the Section

These three brief verses (6:10–12) are a pivotal point in Ecclesiastes. Now, halfway through his discourse, Qohelet turns his attention from his observations to wise counsel for how others should live.

6:10–12

THE SMALLNESS OF HUMANITY

In verse 10, Qohelet reiterates his "there is nothing new under the sun" mantra with a reminder that humans are dependent on One who is stronger, presumably God. In such a world, mankind can only understand so much, so an increase in words is an increase in meaninglessness. The two rhetorical questions that close this section focus on two thoughts that plague the writer: the uncertainty of the future and of death (6:12). Only God knows the certainty of such things, and coming to this conclusion has been the long, arduous journey of pursuits Qohelet has relayed in prior verses.

7:1–8:1

A LIST OF PROVERBS

Qohelet begins his section of wise counsel with several pieces of advice written in the form of proverbs. This pattern will continue throughout most of the verses that follow. The use of the literary style of a proverb is just one of the elements of Ecclesiastes that attest to Solomonic authorship.

Verses 1–14 function as Qohelet's response to the rhetorical question of 6:12: "Who knows how our days can best be spent?" (NLT). Qohelet includes a series of proverbs—many in the "better than" structure—to present some of the values he has found in an otherwise meaningless life. Two dominant themes are prevalent in verses 1–12, and neither theme is new to Ecclesiastes: death (7:1–2, 4, 8) and the wisdom/folly relationship (7:4–7, 9–12).

Verses 13–14 conclude the preceding list of proverbs with the counsel to consider what God has done. In verse 14, Qohelet advises that they should make the most of their days, whether good or bad.

The second section of proverbs, verses 15–22, focuses on the limitations of humanity as established in the two preceding verses. Qohelet warns against the extremities of life, especially when it comes to pursuing righteousness and wisdom (7:16) or wickedness and folly (7:17). It is Qohelet's advice that people should search for balance in life.

Righteousness and wisdom don't guarantee a longer life than the wicked or the foolish. And furthermore, no one is perfect, so the endless pursuit of perfection will leave one empty-handed (7:20). Qohelet's final point, the fact that no one can escape sin, is demonstrated in verses 21–22.

Critical Observation

Verses 23–24 are an interlude in which Qohelet reminds the reader of the pursuit of meaning he has been on for much of his life. These two verses also serve to set up the counsel that will follow, in which the action of seeking and finding, or more often *not* finding, is of utmost importance.

The final portion of this set of proverbs centers on the sub-par view of humanity Qohelet develops during his quest for meaning (7:25–8:1). While we know from the previous six chapters that Qohelet's quest does not lead to the answers he had hoped for, he does learn at least three things about humanity. First, a manipulative woman is more bitter than death (7:26). Second, a virtuous man is rarely found, and no woman is upright (7:27–28). And lastly, God may have created humanity pure and sinless, but humanity has strayed from that state (7:29). Qohelet wraps up this initial list of proverbial reflections with rhetorical reminders to the reader that his quest for wisdom has proven that indeed no person can attain it (8:1).

8:2–9:16

MISCELLANEOUS COUNSELS

At this point in his discourse, Qohelet shifts his focus to several points of counsel that seem unrelated. However, each point, from how to act in the presence of the king to the shared fate of all, further supports the aforementioned conclusion of Qohelet's pursuit: God alone is in control of everything that happens in the world.

Qohelet has repeatedly noted that God alone controls everything that happens in the world, from the timing of everything to the administration of justice. However, that does not negate the power the king has been given. Just as a person is expected to obey God, the same expectation goes for obeying the king (8:2–3). In verse 4, Qohelet gives the impression that people should be obedient to the king because, regardless of his demands, he has the power to do as he wishes. Generally speaking, those who act in obedience to the king will avoid the trouble that opposing him will bring about—this is an example of acting wisely (8:5–6). However, Qohelet gives the caveat that because of the corruption of the world, there is no guarantee that obeying the king will keep someone out of trouble, again pointing out the limitations of wisdom in the grand scheme of things (8:7–9).

Demystifying Ecclesiastes

One's view of the authorship of Ecclesiastes determines how Qohelet's insight in this passage is to be interpreted. If Qohelet is not Solomon and not a king, then he is speaking from one subject of the court to another. However if Solomon is the author, then his advice stems from his personal experience as king and how he expects a king to be treated.

Qohelet returns to the concept of justice for the wicked, which he previously mentions in 3:16–22. It seems evident from his quest that the wicked are not receiving the punishment they are due (8:10). And even worse than that, Qohelet concludes that the lack of justice is simply encouraging people to continue acting in evil ways (8:11). The only hope one has is that in the end God will enact His justice (8:12–13). Even though Qohelet includes this statement, it is difficult to be convinced he believes it based on his tone throughout the book. Again he looks around and only sees meaninglessness and a lack of justice (8:14). It seems that the best advice Qohelet can give is to trust that in the end divine retribution will make up for the lack of justice in the world. Verse 15 repeats the now familiar refrain that all one can do is take pleasure in the small things of eating, drinking, and working.

Pondering such things leads Qohelet to once again summarize the quest for wisdom and meaning he has been on (8:16). But again Qohelet concludes that the work of God in the world is beyond human comprehension (8:17). We will never be able to fully grasp God's sovereignty.

Critical Observation

It has now become evident that mankind's inability to understand God and the way He chooses to work in the world is one of the main themes of Qohelet's discourse. For the other instances when he makes this point, see 3:11; 7:25–29; 9:12; and 11:5.

Chapter 9 elaborates on a point Qohelet has made several times prior: In death everyone and everything is rendered meaningless. Piggybacking on the point he makes in 8:10–15, Qohelet reiterates that being righteous and wise doesn't mean one is in control of his or her fate (9:1). To support this point, he lists five pairs of opposites in verse 2, all of whom share the same fate—death (9:3). Verses 4–5 include a slight note of hope that life may be a little better than death, and then in verse 6, Qohelet reveals that the ability to have strong emotions is something to be missed in death. Inasmuch as the wicked and righteous share the inevitability of death, God's sovereign judgment is still pending, and it is in that judgment that the difference between the wicked and the righteous will be seen in the end.

In light of this unavoidable death, Qohelet's advice in verses 7–10 is to seek pleasure in the little things of life, like eating and drinking, being pampered, and enjoying one's wife. Qohelet encourages his audience to do each of these things, because they will all be impossible after death. While he reminds them that in these things they won't find ultimate purpose, he implies that some pleasure will be gained from enjoying them. And the enjoyment of such things is necessary, since no one knows when hard times might come (9:11–12).

Take It Home

Qohelet closes this section of miscellaneous advice with a short story demonstrating that in the end everything is futile (9:13–16). The subject of the story is a poor man, but he is wise. He saves an entire city of people, only to be forgotten, along with the wisdom he shared. This story sums up Qohelet's underlying point that in the end everything, including wisdom, is meaningless.

9:17–11:6

A SECOND LIST OF PROVERBS

To bring his discourse to a close, Qohelet dedicates the final chapters of his work to a series of proverbs that cover a wide range of topics. Though these proverbs may seem random, they center on the same few themes: wisdom versus folly, dealing with the king, seeking pleasure in the small things, uncertainty of the future, and impending death.

Verses 9:17–10:3 include five different proverbial examples of why wisdom is superior to folly. Present in these verses, however, is Qohelet's undeniable skepticism that folly carries some weight because of its ability to taint wisdom. The proverb of verse 4 is Qohelet's counsel on how to handle an angry superior, presumably the king. His answer? Stay calm.

The following verses (10:5–7) make up a story that demonstrates what Qohelet means in the proverb of verse 4. Just as folly wreaks havoc among wisdom, so a foolish decision in leadership leads to a messed up world.

The next set of proverbs addresses seemingly unrelated illustrations, each of which proves an argument Qohelet has been making throughout his teaching: Life is unfair, even for the wise. But if there is any doubt that wisdom has some value, the next proverbs erase it. Verses 12–15 provide several illustrations that support the undeniable truth that wisdom must trump folly, even if just barely.

Critical Observation

If the proverbs of 10:12–15 sound familiar, it may be because they are more closely related to those in the book of Proverbs than to Qohelet's other sayings. See Proverbs 10:8, 21; 15:2; and 18:7 for these comparisons.

Again Qohelet mentions the king, this time making a statement about how contagious leadership is, regardless if it is foolish or wise (10:16–17). The king sets the standard that others follow, which is why it is all the more important he rules with wisdom. Qohelet will readdress the king in verse 20, but he pauses momentarily to offer two bits of seemingly random advice: Don't be lazy (10:18), and sometimes money leads to happiness by paying for the things that bring enjoyment (10:9). The latter seems a contradiction to the earlier section on the meaninglessness of wealth. The final piece of advice Qohelet has in dealing with the king, and any superior for that matter, is to always be wise and cautious in dealing with them (10:20).

Verses 1–2 of chapter 11 return to Qohelet's previous teaching that with the future comes uncertainty. While it is uncertainty that earlier frustrates Qohelet in his pursuit of wisdom, he does not use it as an excuse for inactivity, as is seen in the following verses. He uses several images from nature to support the idea that the future is out of human control and in the control of God (11:3–6).

11:7–12:7

REFLECTIONS ON YOUTH, OLD AGE, AND DEATH

The reflections of 11:7–12:7 build from the enjoyment of youth (11:7–8) to the inevitability of death (12:7). Ecclesiastes 11:7–8 includes the most hopeful tone Qohelet displays in regard to youth, but he quickly brings the reality of youth's fleeting nature to view. The pattern of verses 7–8 (enjoy your youth, but death is coming) is repeated in verse 9, with the addition of judgment accompanying death.

Demystifying Ecclesiastes

Verse 10 is a frustrating verse in true Qohelet fashion. He seems to have been praising youthfulness and encouraging his readers to enjoy it because of its carefree state. But then in the same breath he calls youth meaningless. These discontinuities in the text are not unusual to Qohelet's thoughts and further the notion that Ecclesiastes covers more questions than answers, as the writer wrestles with the meaning of life and God's sovereign work in the world.

For his closing reflection in 12:1–7, Qohelet turns to rich symbolism to illustrate old age and the destruction of the body it brings, all culminating in death. God is in view as the main subject of these verses, because He is the controller of time.

Take It Home

The metaphors end with the symbolism of man returning to his state as dust in the ground—a reversal of man's beginning as described in Genesis 2:7 and 3:19. Thus concludes Qohelet: Death is the end.

ECCLESIASTES 12:8–14

EPILOGUE

Qohelet's message is summarized in verse 8: Everything is meaningless. While this conclusion dominates the text of Ecclesiastes, it is verses 13–14 that summarize the overarching message of the book: Fear God and keep His commandments. This is the punch line of the whole book. Even in light of the futile elements of human life, we are to live in the reality of God's presence and judgment. We will give account to Him for what we do with our journey, though disillusionment may be inevitable. While we may call something "meaningless," we will not truly understand what matters and what doesn't until God reveals that in His judgment of life. He has the final word.

Demystifying Ecclesiastes

The switch to the third-person narrative voice in verse 8 marks the end of Qohelet's discourse and the beginning of the conclusion. For those who hold to the Solomonic authorship, these closing verses are from present-day Solomon, wise and repentant in his old age and reflecting back on the pursuits that dominated his youth. Those who do not hold to a Solomonic authorship argue that this shift in perspective closes Qohelet's discourse and returns to the voice of the narrator.

SONG OF SONGS

INTRODUCTION TO SONG OF SONGS

Song of Songs (or Song of Solomon), for the most part, is a book of poems about romantic love.

AUTHOR

The title "Song of Songs" suggests that it is the greatest of all songs. There is disagreement among scholars as to whether Solomon wrote Song of Songs, but he is mentioned in the book and many credit him with part of its authorship, if not all.

PURPOSE

The Song celebrates sexuality in its proper context. While some apply it as an allegory of spiritual truths (for example, the relationship of God and Israel or of Christ and the church), here it is treated as poetry that describes a love relationship between two people.

OCCASION

The Song of Songs represents the courtship of a man and a woman, both young, probably just coming to maturity. In ancient Israel, marriage took place in the early or mid teen years. Many define the major sections of the book as courtship (1:2–3:5), wedding and honeymoon (3:6–5:1), and lasting marriage (5:2–8:4). Others, however, consider this book a collection of love poems that don't occur in any chronological kind of order.

OUTLINE

THE TRANSFORMATIONS OF LOVE 1:1–2:17

The Beginning of Love 1:1–17
The Difficulties of Love 2:1–17

THE JOY OF LOVE 3:1–5:1

The Celebration of Love 3:1–11
The Intimacy of Love 4:1–5:1

THE ENDURANCE OF LOVE 5:2–8:14

Love's Antidote 5:2–16
The Leisure of Love 6:1–13
The Depth of Love 7:1–13
The Power of Love 8:1–14

SONG OF SONGS 1:1–2:17

THE TRANSFORMATIONS OF LOVE

Setting Up the Section

In this first section of the Song of Songs, we learn about the joys and difficulties of love.

1:1–17

THE BEGINNING OF LOVE

While the majority of Song of Songs is love poetry, verse 1 serves as a superscription, describing the contents of the book. This verse mentions Solomon, who is mentioned seven other times in the book. While there is disagreement as to Solomon's authorship, this may indicate that he wrote some of the poems included here.

The poetry begins with verse 2, when the woman takes the initiative to ask for a kiss (1:2–4). The woman also invites the man to get away with her to a private place; the words used in this case refer to an inner chamber. While this is the first entreaty of this kind, it is a theme that appears again.

Demystifying Song of Songs

In verses 5–6, the woman addresses not the man but the daughters of Jerusalem. Throughout the rest of the book, the poems will go back and forth between the perspectives of the man, the woman, and this chorus of women. This chorus is sometimes the audience of the man and the woman who affirm their relationship, and sometimes they are the disciples of the woman.

In verse 5, the woman complains that the sun has made her dark, which she considers unattractive. This has nothing to do with race, but social class. She attributes her dark complexion to the vineyards she is forced to work in. She also uses the word *vineyard* in a more allegorical sense, perhaps meaning that she hasn't tended to herself or her own beauty.

Addressed once again to the man, verses 7–8 open with a kind of tease, or a request for a location where the woman can meet him.

Critical Observation

The mention of a veil in verse 7 highlights the fact that the Israelite women didn't always wear veils. They were for special occasions, such as weddings. Some attribute the veil to the clothing of a prostitute, but there is nothing else here that points to any kind of impropriety. If anything, she may not wish to be mistaken as a prostitute.

Verses 9–11 reveal the man's admiration of the woman's physical beauty. He refers to her as a mare among chariots. This relates to a military strategy. Stallions, not mares, pulled chariots. When chariots were bearing down on their enemy, one could defend oneself by loosing a mare in heat as a red herring. The stallions would then change their target and chase the mare instead. Likewise, the beloved is a distraction with her stunning beauty.

In verse 10, the man admires only the parts of her body that are visible. This reflects the stage of their relationship. In verse 11 the use of *we* doesn't indicate that the man will have a hand in creating the jewelry, but rather that he will only enhance her beauty with these gifts of jewelry.

Verses 12–14 constitute a responding poem of admiration toward the man, but in verses 15–17 the two have a back-and-forth dialogue. The beloved's eyes are compared to doves. While it is obvious that this is a flattering statement, we can't be sure what trait of an ancient dove relates to a woman's eyes, whether it is the color, the softness, or the fact that doves are known for faithfulness to their mates. The trees mentioned—cedar and fir—were known for their fragrance.

2:1–17

THE DIFFICULTIES OF LOVE

Verse 1 begins a poem building on the symbols of flowers and trees. The following verses, while continuing this theme, are also good examples of poetic parallels. In verses 2–3, a simile opens the verse and is interpreted in the second part.

The thorns, mentioned in verse 2, are unattractive and invite anything but intimacy. So in this description, the man is clearly raising his beloved above her peers.

Whereas in chapter 1 the woman is described as having been forced to work in the direct sunlight, which damaged her skin, here in verse 3 she is privileged to rest in the shade of her beloved. The banner she describes in verse 4 is a public declaration that she belongs to him.

Demystifying Song of Songs

The raisin cakes and apples mentioned in verses 5–6 were used in pagan fertility rites and were viewed by some as aphrodisiacs. Because both fruits have many seeds, they were associated with fertility.

Verse 6 is a description of an embrace, while verse 7 is a strong warning to the woman's peers to not rush their journey to love (repeated in 8:3–4).

In verses 8–17, the woman describes her beloved in his eagerness. The description in verse 9 (repeated in verse 17) of the man as a buck or gazelle implies someone swift, powerful, and beautiful.

Critical Observation

Winter in Palestine runs from October to April, the only time rain falls. Since these rains end in April, the timing for the occasion of this poem is probably around May. The woman notes the end of winter and the beginning of springtime in many ways: The rains have ended, the flowers have blossomed, singing has begun, and the turtledove (known to return to Palestine in April) is cooing (2:10–13).

Verses 14–15 are probably a continuation of the woman quoting the man rather than a switch of voices. Lacking confidence, she hides metaphorically in rocks to make herself feel secure. The foxes in that part of the world were notoriously cunning and destructive. When they were small, they were even more undetectable. Here, they represent obstacles to new love.

Verse 16 is repeated in 6:3 and 7:11. Verses 16–17 are full of images which can be interpreted a variety of ways. Lilies somehow seem to represent the woman herself or some element of her womanhood. The stag and gazelle are mentioned again, but differently. The mountains are seen by some to symbolize her breasts. These images are clearly meant to be expressions of desire.

SONG OF SONGS 3:1–5:1

THE JOY OF LOVE

Setting Up the Section

The opening of chapter 3 is a poem about yearning. Absence and longing always lead to search and discovery in the Song.

3:1–11

THE CELEBRATION OF LOVE

The scene changes throughout verses 1–5. What is described here may be more like a dream sequence rather than an experience unfolding in a chronological way. Verse 2 begins the woman's search for her love—something that happens again in chapter 5.

While in some of the previous poems it is left to interpretation where a poem ends or begins and how much connection exists between them, verses 6–11 are clearly a section unto themselves. The only other marriage poem in the Bible is recorded in Psalm 45.

Critical Observation

Solomon's name appears several times in this passage (3:7, 9, 11). Some believe that Solomon is the author of this whole book and is in fact the man, and later groom, mentioned throughout. Others hold that this reference to Solomon is a poetic way of painting a picture of opulence and luxury—often considered a young woman's ideal marriage scenario.

The images and fragrance in verse 6 emphasize wealth. In verse 7, Solomon's portable couch is a *palanquin*, which was an enclosed couch carried on the shoulders of men by poles.

It is noteworthy that sixty warriors surround the couch. This is double the number that accompanied Solomon's father David during his ceremonial travels (2 Samuel 23:18–19, 23). These sixty warriors are friends of the groom who will provide safety for the wedding party (Song of Songs 3:8).

According to verse 9, the carriage is made from timber from Lebanon, known to be the highest quality. It was probably aromatic cedar and represented beauty, luxury, and excellence. Silver, gold, and purple wool or cloth all indicate royalty (3:10). The incense and the couch were very expensive—weddings, as they still are now, are a time to show off one's worth.

The *daughters of Zion* (3:11) is a unique phrase to this book, but it is clearly an alternate for the often used *daughters of Jerusalem.* It is not clear, however, whether the crown mentioned in verse 11 pertains to a coronation crown or if it is a special wedding crown reserved for this occasion.

4:1–5:1

THE INTIMACY OF LOVE

The words in verses 1–7 are affectionate: *Beautiful* appears several times as the groom describes his bride's hair, teeth, lips, neck, and breasts.

The man undresses his new bride, beginning with her head and working his way down to her breasts. This differs from his earlier description in 1:15, which is repeated in the first half of 4:1. Here, he comments on everything he sees.

Chapter 4 can be divided into several poems, but thematically they are tied closely together. In verses 1–7, the man declares the woman beautiful. In verses 8–9, he draws her to him, proclaiming his love. Then from verse 10 through the first verse of chapter 5, the poetry focuses on the image of a garden.

Demystifying Song of Songs

Verse 8 mentions several mountains. Hermon is perhaps the most well-known. It lies in the northern region of Israel. Amana and Senir are part of the Lebanon range that connects to Hebron in northern Israel. The groom is inviting his bride closer. He wants her close to him and safe from threats, here described as lions and leopards (or panthers).

In verses 10–11, the groom calls his love his *sister.* In the ancient Near East, *sister* was at times an affectionate term for one's wife.

In verses 12–15, the man continues working his way down her body as she undresses for him. She is a virgin—a locked garden, inaccessible (4:12)—and he is praising her for it. And in her garden are the choicest exotic spices. This exaggeration in number and variety of spices is a form of flattery. Verse 15, while confirming the man's satisfaction with his wife, introduces a new image associated with her body—a well or fountain.

Verse 16 is the woman's invitation for her groom to enjoy her virginity. She invites him in, using symbolic language with openly sexual overtones. Though the language here is sometimes used in modern culture to imply oral sex, that is not the intent here. These words refer to the satisfaction of one's sexual appetite.

The first verse of chapter 5 documents the man's satisfaction after the couple's first sexual experience. He claims with highly sexual overtones to have entered his bride. The last part of this verse is attributed to the daughters of Jerusalem. It is an invitation for the couple to enjoy their sexual partnership with gusto, drinking their fill of love even to the point of intoxication.

SONG OF SONGS 5:2–8:14

THE ENDURANCE OF LOVE

Setting Up the Section

The remainder of chapter 5 makes up a poem that actually spans through verse 3 of chapter 6. Rather than the symbolic language as in the poems of chapter 4, the woman seems to be telling the women of Jerusalem about an actual experience.

5:2–16

LOVE'S ANTIDOTE

The woman is awakened by the abrupt knocking at the door by her lover. He calls her four terms of affection: *sister, darling, dove, flawless one*. While getting ready for bed was more involved in the ancient world (dirt floors, less sophisticated door locks), the woman's hesitation to answer the door costs her the opportunity to be with her lover.

The mistreatment she experiences in verse 7 doesn't even seem to faze her. In contrast, she had previously been assisted in her search by the watchmen (3:3). In this case, it is likely that the watchmen represent the social difficulties which the woman works her way through in order to get to the object of her desire.

In the first part of this chapter, her focus is exclusively on herself and her own comfort, but in verses 8–16 her focus is exclusively on the man. He had earlier described the woman as he addressed her; here the woman describes the man, but she is addressing the daughters of Jerusalem. In ancient Near Eastern literature, such physical descriptions of one's lover were almost exclusively male descriptions of females.

The comparison to gold in verse 11 implies great value, especially since gold had to be imported to Palestine. Verse 13 indicates that his cheeks smell of cologne. In verse 15, his legs are described as marble, signifying strength.

It was common to describe another's physical characteristics from top to bottom, but after working her way down, she goes back up to his lips once more. This, along with 1:2, suggests that she is particularly attracted to his mouth—both with his kisses and his sweet words. She concludes by calling him her friend (5:16).

6:1–13

THE LEISURE OF LOVE

While chapter 6 continues the poem begun in 5:2, in verse 1 the daughters of Jerusalem respond to the woman, offering to help her find her missing groom. Then, in verse 2, the bride seems to know where her groom is. Keep in mind that this is poetry, not to be understood as a linear story line.

Note that verse 3 is the same as 2:16 but in reverse order.

Verses 4–9 are written from the man's perspective; then he is joined by the chorus in verse 10. He compares his bride's beauty to two famous cities in Israel—Tirzah and Jerusalem (6:4). Tirzah was captured by Joshua and, following the split of the nation, was named the capital of the northern kingdom (1 Kings 16:8–9, 15). The compliments offered in verses 5–7 are similar to those offered to the bride on her wedding night in 4:1–3.

Critical Observation

Verse 8 mentions three categories of women in a royal harem: queens, concubines, and young women. These form concentric circles of relationship to the king—which especially pertain to how their offspring might or might not be considered in line for the throne. The sons of queens are in direct succession to the throne. The sons of concubines are not, unless the king specifically appoints them. Young women have either not yet been presented to the king or not borne children—in which case theirs is a temporary label, and they will become either queens or concubines. The mention of these women here makes the point that this one woman is worth more to the king than all the others.

Some disagree as to who is speaking in verses 11–12. Most likely the woman is talking, and the man invites her to turn to him in verse 13. Verse 12 may be the most confusing verse in the book. The wording varies widely among the different Bible translations. There are two things that most commentators agree on, however. First, the difficulty of the text. And second, that it reflects passion so powerful that someone gets carried away with it.

7:1–13

THE DEPTH OF LOVE

In verses 1–10, the man expresses his admiration for his bride (4:1–15; 6:4–8; 7:1–9). This passage in chapter 7 is considered even more intimate than that of their honeymoon (4:1–15).

He begins with her feet, perhaps because she is dancing. While his comparison of her navel to a mixing bowl and her belly as a mound of wheat does not sound flattering from a modern perspective, these descriptions show how his wife satisfies him (7:2).

In verses 4–10, the man comments once again on his wife's eyes, comparing them to Heshbon, which is a beautiful area to the east of the Dead Sea. He also compares her to a palm tree. In verse 8, his desire to climb the tree and take hold of its fruit indicates his desire to be intimate with her and enjoy her breasts.

In verses 11–13, the woman initiates physical intimacy with her husband, speaking *to* him rather than about him (as she does in 1:2; 2:6; 4:16). She invites him to be with her in the vineyards.

8:1–14

THE POWER OF LOVE

The first four verses of chapter 8 describe a yearning for love. In the ancient Near East, public displays of affection were culturally frowned upon unless the person was a relative. This is the reason the woman wishes that her husband was her brother—so she could dote on him without receiving stares. This also speaks to why she constantly invites him away from public view to isolation and intimacy—she isn't even supposed to kiss him in public. This section ends with the same warning that appears, at least similarly, in 2:7 and 3:5.

Verses 5–7 provide comment on the very nature of love. The first part of verse 5 is attributed to the women of Jerusalem, but the remainder is credited to the woman. Verse 6 may be the most powerful in the book. The seal and signet indicate ownership and personal identification. The first seal—the cylinder—was more common in Mesopotamia, and it was rolled across clay to leave an impression. The second seal—the signet—was more common in Palestine, and it was simply pressed into clay to make an impression.

While there is some disagreement about this, verses 8–9 are attributed to the woman's brothers, mentioned earlier as having forced her to work in the fields, thus darkening her skin. They represent her as the little sister they remember—undeveloped. In verse 10, however, the woman clarifies the reality—she is a fully grown woman.

While Solomon appears in chapter 3 in a positive light, in verses 11–12 he appears in a negative light. Baal Haman, the site of his vineyard, is an unknown location. Earlier, the *vineyard* is used as an image for the woman's beauty or for a place of intimacy. While this poem is puzzling, it is clear that the woman is claiming herself, someone whose love cannot be purchased, perhaps comparing the significance of her relationship with her beloved with the anonymity of Solomon's harem.

Verses 13–14 make up the final poem of the book, one last interaction between the man and woman. After the man calls out to the woman, her words are reminiscent of earlier images—the gazelle or stag (see 2:9, 17). And she finishes the book in a familiar way—by calling him away to solitude and intimacy.

Take It Home

The book ends abruptly in mid-story, open-ended. In these poems, however, God does more than endorse marriage; He endorses physical love within the context of marriage.

In verses 6–10, the man compliments once again his wife's eyes, comparing them to Tirzah, which is a beautiful area, to [illegible] of the [illegible]. He also compares her to a palm tree. In verse 8, his desire to climb the tree and take hold of its fruit indicates his desire to be intimate with her and enjoy her breasts.

In verses 11–13, the woman initiates physical intimacy with her husband, speaking to him rather than about him [illegible] she does in 1:2; 2:6; 4:16). She invites him to be with her in the vineyards.

THE POWER OF LOVE

The last [illegible] verses of chapter 8 [illegible] the power of love. In the ancient Near East [illegible] also speaks to wife [illegible] 2:7 and 3:5.

Verses 6–7 provide a comment on the very nature of love. [illegible] [illegible] [illegible] [illegible] [illegible] [illegible] [illegible] [illegible] [illegible] of Jerusalem, but the [illegible] is credited to the woman. Verse 6 [illegible] the most powerful in the book. [illegible] The second seal [illegible] [illegible] [illegible] [illegible] [illegible] [illegible] [illegible] [illegible] [illegible] [illegible] [illegible] [illegible] [illegible] [illegible]

While [illegible]

[illegible] [illegible] [illegible] in Chapter 8 [illegible] [illegible] [illegible] [illegible] [illegible] [illegible] [illegible] Baal-hamon, the site of his vineyard [illegible] [illegible] [illegible] [illegible] [illegible] [illegible] used as [illegible] [illegible] for the woman [illegible] Solomon's harem.

[illegible] [illegible] [illegible] [illegible] [illegible] [illegible] point of the book [illegible] [illegible] between the man and woman [illegible]

The [illegible] ends [illegible]

ISAIAH

INTRODUCTION TO ISAIAH

The book of Isaiah is a potentially intimidating challenge for novice Bible readers, but it is a rich and rewarding pursuit for those willing to delve into it. Its sixty-six chapters comprise the fifth longest book of the Bible in terms of word count. But even more daunting than its sheer length is the prophetic nature of the writing. The author (or perhaps authors) writes of events that cover centuries, and it can be difficult in places to tell if he speaks of the present, the near future, or the long-range future. Yet while the prophet's narrative can be a bit confusing in places, large portions are quite clear in presenting a merciful God who does not give up on His people even though they have been repeatedly rebellious and wayward.

AUTHOR

The name *Isaiah*, "Salvation of Yahweh," is closely related to that of *Joshua* ("Yahweh is salvation"), which is the Old Testament equivalent of *Jesus*. However, not much is known about the prophet other than what he reveals in his book. He is identified as "the son of Amoz" thirteen times. He also writes that he has a wife and two children (7:3; 8:3). Little more is known about his personal life. Justin Martyr recorded the tradition that Isaiah died a martyr's death at the hands of King Manasseh, sawed in two (possibly the source of the reference in Hebrews 11:37).

A debate has raged for more than a century now as to whether the book of Isaiah was written by a single person or more than one author. Most scholars agree the book has distinctive sections. Chapters 1–39 comprise one unit and chapters 40–66 another. (Many purport that 40–55 should be a second unit and 56–66 a third, and that a different Isaiah wrote each section. Still others suggest the existence of an Isaiah "school," where disciples carried on the work of the original Isaiah.) If a single author wrote the entire book, he was given extremely precise insight into Judah's future, including the name of the ruler who would release the people after their captivity (44:28–45:1). Yet Cyrus wouldn't come to power for more than a century, after the Medes conquered Babylon, which was the rise of Babylon and fall of Assyria. However, the oldest available scrolls have no breaks between the different sections, recording Isaiah as a single book. And numerous New Testament figures, including Jesus Himself, quote from various portions of Isaiah as if the writing is from a single author. So the debate will continue, but for purposes of this commentary, references to the author throughout the entire book will be, simply, "Isaiah."

PURPOSE

Isaiah's purpose in writing is described during a vision in which he receives his calling from God (6:6–10). He is instructed to speak to his people, even though most are spiritually rebellious and disobedient and will not listen to him. (Jesus later quotes this very passage to explain why He uses parables to teach the people [Matthew 13:13–15].) Isaiah faithfully brings God's word to the people, warning anyone who will listen of what is to come.

THEMES

God's sovereignty is evident throughout Isaiah. The Lord maneuvers great empires to accomplish His will, including the chastisement of His people, and then brings those "powers" to nothing in judgment of their arrogance and sin. He allows His people to be dispersed throughout the world but then promises to call them back to Jerusalem, bringing their captors with them to worship together. Even in the turbulence and violence of the ancient world, the supremacy of God was always certain.

The book of Isaiah repeatedly emphasizes the sinfulness of humanity as well as the holiness, mercy, and grace of God, creating an overarching theme of redemption. In one section are four "Servant Songs" that describe a special servant God will provide to suffer for and deliver His people.

HISTORICAL CONTEXT

During Isaiah's lifetime in the eighth century BC, the Near East was already a political miasma. Nations continually struggled for dominance. Egypt was still a major power, yet she could no longer hold her own against a more recent contender: Assyria. As the surrounding nations grew in power, thus jostling to control more and more territory, the small nation of Judah was caught in a crossfire. Assyria conquered the northern kingdom of Israel in 721 BC. It appeared that Judah would follow quickly, but Isaiah assured the people that Assyria would not, in fact, take Judah. Jerusalem and the southern kingdom stand until 586 BC, when Nebuchadnezzar's Babylonian forces destroy the city and carry away most of the productive population. The people remain in Babylon for seventy years until the empire falls to the Persians, who allow the Jewish people to return to their homeland. Isaiah covers this entire span of history in his writing.

CONTRIBUTION TO THE BIBLE

Isaiah is sometimes called the evangelist of the Old Testament (or even "the Paul of the Old Testament"). The influence of his writing is reflected by its frequent citations in the New Testament. (Isaiah is quoted more than all the other prophets combined.) The prophet is identified by name twenty-one times and is cited in numerous other places without direct attribution.

OUTLINE

AN OMINOUS INTRODUCTION 1:1–5:30

ISAIAH'S CALL, GOD'S SIGN, AND ISRAEL'S FAILURE 6:1–12:6

PROPHECIES AGAINST OTHER NATIONS 13:1–23:18

THE WORLD STRUGGLES, BUT GOD REIGNS SUPREME 24:1–35:10

A HISTORICAL VERIFICATION 36:1–39:8

GOOD NEWS IN BAD TIMES — 40:1–44:23

Anticipation of Comfort	40:1–31
Israel amid the Nations	41:1–29
God's Servant	42:1–25
God's Great Promise	43:1–28
Life-Giving Water and Lifeless Idols	44:1–23

ISRAEL, BABYLON, AND CYRUS — 44:24–48:22

Help from an Unexpected Source	44:24–45:25
The Demise of Babylon	46:1–47:15
Israel's Obstinacy	48:1–22

THE WORK OF GOD'S SERVANT — 49:1–55:13

An Introduction to the Servant	49:1–26
A Submissive Servant	50:1–11
A Historic Reminder	51:1–16
Wrath, Then Assurance	51:17–52:12
The Fourth and Final Servant Song	52:13–53:12
A New Opportunity	54:1–55:13

PROMISE FOR (AND PREVIOUS FAILURES OF) GOD'S PEOPLE — 56:1–59:21

Broadening the Invitation	56:1–8
Israel's Inglorious History	56:9–57:21
A Call for Genuine Worship	58:1–14
Accusations and Confession	59:1–21

THE GLORY OF THE LORD — 60:1–62:12

The City of the Lord	60:1–22
The Favor of the Lord	61:1–11
The Lord's New Relationship with Zion	62:1–12

LOOKING AHEAD WITH HOPE — 63:1–66:24

God Is Mighty to Save	63:1–64:12
The Futures of the Righteous and the Wicked	65:1–66:24

ISAIAH 1:1–5:30

AN OMINOUS INTRODUCTION

Setting Up the Section

It can be disheartening to read the opening of Isaiah without context, yet even providing the historical background doesn't help much. Israel and Judah, having deserted God for the gods and customs of surrounding nations, find themselves powerless pawns in an international struggle. Assyria, Babylon, and Egypt are all attempting to establish and/or maintain empires. Israel's and Judah's loyalties, which should have been to God, have been bouncing from one power to another in an attempt to persevere. But Israel will soon fall to Assyria, followed more than a century later by Judah's overthrow at the hands of Babylon.

1:1–31

AN OPENING WARNING

In verse 1, Isaiah's vision is primarily in regard to the southern kingdom of Judah because the kings he lists are all from the south. Most of the other Old Testament prophets spoke of bringing *the word* of the Lord to the people. Isaiah is unusual in stating that what he is presenting is a *vision*, although there are a few other exceptions (see Obadiah 1:1). Isaiah's father, Amoz (who is not the same person as the prophet Amos), is mentioned several times.

Isaiah doesn't pull any punches as he begins his writing. His presentation is essentially an arraignment, a legal accusation argued before the judges of heaven and earth (Isaiah 1:2). Immediately he compares the people of God (unfavorably) to a dumb ox or donkey that would at least have the sense to recognize its master (1:3). Soon he will be comparing them to the iconic cities best known for wickedness: Sodom and Gomorrah (1:9–10).

Critical Observation

Isaiah receives his calling in the year that King Uzziah [Azariah] died (6:1), which was 740 or 739 BC. King Hezekiah took the throne no later than 716 BC and ruled until 686 BC. Therefore, based on Isaiah 1:1, the prophet's ministry could have been no less than twenty-three years and may well have lasted fifty years or longer.

The accusations against Judah continue: sin, guilt, evil, rebellion, rejection of God, defeat, and desolation (1:4–8). Although the people have a pretense of religious commitment, their prayers and offerings are devoid of meaning, and God is not pleased with them (1:11–15).

Jerusalem (the faithful city) has become corrupt, along with the values of its inhabitants. The rulers take bribes and do not defend the helpless (1:21–23). Still, there is hope for the people as Isaiah presents God's exhortation to start doing right and to repent (1:16–18). If the people choose to submit to God in obedience, they can prosper. If not, they will not survive the coming judgment (1:16–20). Jerusalem will again be faithful, but it will come after a purging from God (1:24–31).

2:1–22

THE DAY OF THE LORD

Isaiah can see plainly what has gone wrong with Judah and Jerusalem, even though the people appear oblivious to their sinful actions and attitudes. In addition, Isaiah is given great insight into what will happen later. In verse 2, he writes of the last days. Some debate the time frame of the last days with much speculation, but all that can be safely presumed is that the reference is to a period of time after Jesus' incarnation (when some believe the "last days" began) that will culminate with His second coming.

More important than *when* this will occur is *what* the people of God can expect. Isaiah describes an elevation of the mountain of the Lord's temple (2:2). The temple of Solomon had been built on the spot where Abraham had attempted to offer Isaac. The entire area was later known as Zion, a designation Isaiah uses many times throughout his prophecy.

In the Bible, *mountain* often symbolizes stability and is often associated with divinity. Isaiah's description indicates that one day the kingdom of the Messiah will be preeminent over all the kingdoms of the earth. The nations (Gentiles) will desire to know God's truth and will stream to the house of God, resulting in an unprecedented time of peace (2:3–4). Although the Messiah is not named in this passage, later portions of Isaiah (chapters 7, 9, 11, 53) will be quite specific about His character and the role He will play. In this instance, He fulfills the role of judge. In light of what God will eventually accomplish in the Gentile world, Isaiah challenges the house of Jacob (Judah and Jerusalem) to walk in the light of the Lord (2:5).

Demystifying Isaiah

This portion of Isaiah (2:2–4) regarding the Messiah's future kingdom is repeated almost verbatim in Micah 4:1–3. We don't know if one writer borrowed from the other or if they both drew from the same source.

The existing situation in Judah, however, is bleak. Isaiah's account of God's people might have described any of the surrounding unbelieving nations. In fact, they have adopted various superstitions, idolatry, and occult practices from numerous places.

Isaiah's reference to the East in verse 6 could be to the Assyrians or Syrians. The Philistines were in the southwest. Their practice of divination could be either an attempt to foretell the future or to maneuver people and situations to their advantage. In their pursuit of the futile practices of other nations, God's people have turned away from the only One who knows the future and is in complete control. They have wealth and resources, but rather than seeing such things as blessings, those assets further turn the hearts of the people away from God (2:6–10).

But Judah is about to be humbled. The people's arrogance will be destroyed along with their dependence on wealth and idols, and it will be a turbulent transition. Isaiah warns that people will flee to caves and hide among the rocks. They will again acknowledge God, but their change of attitude will begin with a sense of great dread. The result, however, will be the disappearance of all idols and their exaltation of God alone (2:11–22).

3:1–4:1

A CHANGE IN GOVERNMENT

God alone is good. God alone cares for His creation. God alone is beneficent. Yet God's people reject the government of their good, caring, beneficent God, so He removes all supply and support from Judah and Jerusalem through a series of foreign invasions (3:1–3). Included in their losses will be food, water, all leadership of any consequence, honor, skill, and respect. Within a hundred years of the death of Isaiah, this prophecy is fulfilled when Babylon breaches the walls of Jerusalem, destroys the city, and carries off most of the people.

In place of qualified leadership, Judah will get leaders who are boys and mere children (3:4). The reference is usually less in regard to physical age than the person's maturity level. *Boys* refers to those without wisdom and experience. However, this prophecy comes true literally when Manasseh succeeds his father Hezekiah as king at age twelve. During Manasseh's fifty-five-year rule, he acquires the designation of the most wicked ruler in the history of Judah.

Isaiah describes a terrible breakdown of social order: young against old, crude against honorable, neighbor against neighbor, and individual against individual. People will be desperate for leadership, but no one will be qualified (3:5–7). Yet even in their confusion and disarray, the people will remain arrogant, plundering the poor and continuing to parade their sin (3:8–9, 11–14).

The problem will be widespread, but there will be exceptions. Isaiah assures righteous people that things will end well for them (3:10). God certainly does not fail to see what is happening, and He will soon expose the arrogant population for what they really are. The description in 3:15–4:1 is brutal in its honesty. As the men of Judah fall in battle, the women will lose every pretense of arrogance and symbol of finery, reduced to desperation and groveling.

God's warning that He is about to remove supply and support from Judah (3:1) is initially confirmed by the Assyrian invasion but is demonstrated even more emphatically by the subsequent Babylonian domination.

4:2–5:7

A BRANCH AND A VINEYARD

At this point, Isaiah's writing takes a sudden shift. He moves abruptly from talking about the nation of God as ruins (3:6) to a section where every phrase seems to insist on a meaning that moves the reader toward the future fulfillment of the kingdom of God. Something has happened. There is a new day beyond the disgrace of the people of the old covenant, and Isaiah is serving as a herald of that coming day.

The difference is the appearance of the branch of the Lord—Israel's Messiah. Those who come to the kingdom by His name are holy in Him. Their names have been duly recorded. God has washed away their filth (4:2–4). It is not the trappings of wealth that ensure survival (3:18–23) but the purifying fire of God in the judgment poured out on His Messiah (4:4). Eventually the day will come when God's divine presence will be evident to the senses. God will be the ever-present light, with no need for artificial lighting (4:5–6). Believers know this in their best moments, but someday they will recognize God's presence clearly and continually.

Demystifying Isaiah

Some people believe that in this case the *branch* of the Lord signifies believers—the remnant of humanity who repent and are therefore beautiful and glorious (4:2). However, in chapter 11 Isaiah will use a branch analogy where the indication is clearly in reference to God's Messiah, Jesus.

Vineyards were important commodities in ancient Judah. When someone went to the trouble of planting a vineyard, he expected to eventually reap fruit from his labor. So the song of the vineyard in Isaiah 5:1–7 is a prophetic parable, and there is no doubt as to its meaning.

Verse 7 clarifies that the vineyard of the Lord represents the house of Israel. God has taken great care of His vineyard. He has done all He can, but still the vineyard does not yield fruit as it should. God looks for the fruit of justice but finds bloodshed. He desires righteousness but hears instead an outcry from the oppressed, poor, and powerless. Therefore, God will remove His protection, and what had once been a beautiful vineyard will be trampled and destroyed. With no further blessing (rains) or cultivation, it will become a wasteland.

Critical Observation

Throughout Isaiah are instances (as in 5:7) where *Israel* refers to the southern kingdom (rather than the more traditional *Judah*). After the northern kingdom's fall to the Assyrians, Israel continued to refer to the people of God wherever they were.

5:8–30

AN INDICTMENT OF JUDAH

From the parable, Isaiah moves into a more direct pronouncement of woe upon his people. They have ignored God in many ways, including failure to acknowledge that He owns their land and established laws to protect the poor throughout the generations. Families could legally lease their land to others for income, but it was supposed to eventually revert to the original family. The people of Judah, however, disregarded God's instructions and joined house to house and field to field. People live in large homes with extensive vineyards, but the land will become unproductive and the homes will soon be empty (5:8–10).

With no regard for the concerns of God, the people are devoting themselves to late-night drinking and feasting. They are content with falsehood and darkness and are quite proud of themselves. Meanwhile, guilty people are being acquitted by paying bribes, while innocent people are deprived of their rights (5:11–12, 18–23).

Since so many refuse to exercise justice and righteousness, God Himself will enact those standards—beginning with His people! His righteous judgment will include exile, hunger and thirst, the death of many, and the humbling of the rest (5:13–15). And through His demonstration of justice, God will be exalted (5:16–17).

God is the one who pronounces judgment, but the means of affliction will be nations that are far away. Isaiah is clear on the matter: God is angry, and His anger is not easily diffused (5:24–25). The Lord is portrayed as whistling for distant nations to come, and when they do they roar as lions, growling as they seize their prey. The once-prosperous land of Judah will be a site of darkness and distress (5:26–30).

Yet in the wake of God's anger is His great mercy. If God only wanted to demonstrate His justice, He could have destroyed the world immediately after the sin of Adam. He is able to also show His mercy without sacrificing His great holiness and justice.

Take It Home

Have you ever given serious thought to how God can exact justice and still show mercy on those who are guilty? Justice demands that wicked people be punished, and *all* people are lawbreakers in the sight of God (Romans 3:23). Mercy allows those people to be forgiven and blessed. How can God possibly accomplish both justice and mercy without negating one or the other? Isaiah will later speak to this conundrum, foretelling an eternal substitute who will bring mercy to those who deserve God's judgment. Today God's people can give thanks for the assurance of their eternal security. Still, they should quake at the discipline of the Lord in this world of sorrow.

ISAIAH 6:1–12:6

ISAIAH'S CALL, GOD'S SIGN, AND ISRAEL'S FAILURE

Setting Up the Section

In this section Isaiah describes his distinct calling and begins to provide some hope-inspiring prophecies about Immanuel. The people certainly need hope because of conflict with the Assyrians that is devastating their nation. It is a desperate and miserable time, so the anticipation of God's Messiah is especially welcome.

6:1–13

ISAIAH ANSWERS GOD'S CALL

When Old Testament priests and kings were invested with the authority of their offices, it was traditional for them to have oil poured onto their heads. The anointing was symbolic of the Holy Spirit's designating and empowering the person for a specific job. Kings were often referred to as "the Lord's anointed."

Prophets, however, tended to bypass human ceremony. They were anointed by God's Spirit as they were commissioned for service. The work of a prophet was not an easy calling. Isaiah records his own experience as God calls him and speaks to him about the difficult ministry before him.

During a vision, Isaiah is shown the throne room of God (6:1–4). He sees the Lord on the throne, surrounded by mysterious fiery angelic creatures. (This is the only biblical mention of seraphs ["burning ones"], or seraphim, although some of the heavenly beings mentioned in Revelation have a similar description [Revelation 4:6–8].) Some consider the seraphim to be the angels closest to God since that is how they are described here.

Critical Observation

Many people seem to have a fascination with angels, but where angels appear in the Bible they almost always insist that people focus on God. The interest of heaven is the Lord God Almighty, as it should be for God's people on earth.

As soon as Isaiah witnesses the glory of God, he senses that he is in mortal danger. Even Moses, when he had asked to see God, had been told that no one could see God's face and live (Exodus 33:20). Isaiah immediately acknowledges his sin and the sin of the community in which he lives (Isaiah 6:5). In response, one of the angels takes a burning coal from the altar and touches it to the prophet's mouth (6:6–7).

The coal is a symbol. When God established the Day of Atonement ceremony, one duty of the high priest was to take coals from the altar into the Most Holy Place and burn incense there (Leviticus 16:11–14). The altar was where sacrificial animals were slaughtered, and their blood ceremonially took away guilt and atoned for sin. But Isaiah is witnessing the actual heavenly temple.

Isaiah must have experienced an immediate inner change. When he hears the invitation of God, he volunteers at once to go and serve (6:8). God's response is also immediate. God does not provide many specifics, but the severity of Isaiah's mission is clear. He is being sent to people who will not listen or respond to him, yet he is to continue his work until their nation is destroyed (6:8–13). Israel and Judah have been like a mighty oak, but eventually they will fall and only a stump will remain. Still, the stump will be the holy seed—the remnant of believers from which the tree will grow again (6:13). All is not lost, but the near future will not be pleasant.

Demystifying Isaiah

Though it may seem that Isaiah's calling comes after he had already started to prophesy, since it is placed in chapter 6, it is doubtful that Isaiah worked as a prophet for a time prior to receiving his heavenly calling. He probably simply waited until this point in his narrative to relate the events of his call. The despair of the first five chapters is somewhat offset by this unmistakable experience with the Lord God Almighty, still on the throne and enlisting people to do His work, even during times of national peril and failure.

7:1–25

AN UNMISTAKABLE SIGN

Ahaz is not one of Judah's better kings. He brings much trouble on the nation by encouraging false worship. In this section he is shown as weak and frightened (7:1–2), and for good reason. The northern kingdom of Israel has formed an alliance with the Syrians (Arameans), and they are bearing down on Jerusalem.

Sometimes the nation of Israel was called *Ephraim*, because that particular tribe was large and centrally located among the others. Consequently, the battle described in this section came to be known as the Syro-Ephraimite War. The alliance of Syria and Ephraim had been formed to defend against the expanding empire of Assyria—a useless action since Assyria will be God's instrument in executing His judgment.

God speaks to Ahaz through Isaiah, telling him not to fear. Israel and Syria are only "burned-out embers" (7:4 NLT). In fact, both of these nations are facing impending disaster and will fall. God draws attention to the head of Israel and the head of Syria. The implication is that Ahaz may be the king of Judah, but God is ultimately the head of the house of David in Jerusalem.

God emphasizes the certainty of His message in two ways. First, He encourages Ahaz to strengthen his spiritual commitment—he must stand firm in faith or not at all (7:9). Then He gives Ahaz permission to ask for a sign to confirm that the word of Isaiah is the true promise of God. Ahaz expresses reluctance to make such a request, claiming that he does not want to test the Lord. Actually, it is his lack of commitment that is testing God's patience, so God chooses a sign: A virgin will conceive and bear a son named *Immanuel* ("God with us" [7:10–16]).

Demystifying Isaiah

Many modern believers are familiar with Isaiah's prophecy in 7:14 because of its long-range application to the birth of Jesus, cited in Matthew 1:22–23. This is the first of several messianic prophecies in Isaiah. However, most Old Testament prophecies also have a more immediate fulfillment, as is evident from Isaiah 7:15–16. While opinions vary, a likely explanation is that Isaiah refers to a young unmarried woman—a virgin at the time—who will marry and raise a child. The time frame for the initial fulfillment of the prophecy, then, will require a minimum of nine months for the pregnancy and another couple of years or so until the young child is eating solid food and beginning to make moral decisions. Centuries will then pass before Isaiah's words will be understood to also apply to the Virgin Mary and her son, Jesus.

Although Judah will not fall to the Assyrians, they will suffer from the presence of such a powerful enemy (7:17). The Assyrians will arrive like swarms of flies and bees. The Assyrian king will humiliate Judah like a razor shaving off a warrior's hair and beard (7:18–20). The glut of milk and honey (7:21–22) might sound promising at first, but it actually predicts a shortage of young animals to nurse and flowers being pollinated in fields that should have been growing crops. This less flattering scenario is confirmed by the prediction of briers and thorns in verses 23–25.

8:1–22

RIGHT AND WRONG REASONS TO FEAR

Next Isaiah receives an interesting assignment from God. He is to father a son and give the child a Hebrew name that designates the coming of an invading army (8:1–2). It is an intriguing name and the longest personal name in the Bible: *Maher-shalal-hash-baz*. The name is a battle cry, meaning "quick to the plunder, swift to the spoil." Some people try to make the case that this child of Isaiah's is the child predicted in 7:14, but the name is a far cry from Immanuel. And unless Isaiah has a second wife, the child-of-a-virgin requirement is out of the question because the prophet already had one child (7:3).

Before this new child of Isaiah can develop any significant speech patterns, the Assyrians will have defeated both the armies that are threatening Judah: Aram and Israel. Judah will not be unscathed; Assyria is portrayed as a large devouring bird of prey. But God will be with Judah, and Assyria will not prevail (8:5–10).

Unbridled fear can lead to various problems. But such problems can be prevented if one's source of fear is properly placed. Those who fear God—who regard Him as holy and live to do His will—can be spared many other fears (8:11–17). Even the powerful Assyrian Empire is no threat for those who place their trust in God. But those without God exhibit a pathetic existence. Without the genuine source of truth, they seek advice from mediums. When they get distressed and hungry, they curse their leaders and their God. And still, they perceive only distress, darkness, and gloom (8:18–22).

9:1–7

A COMING RULER

Isaiah, like other Old Testament prophets, has two major roles that are very different. One of his responsibilities is corrective in nature, as he prosecutes God's case against the Lord's own people for their unfaithfulness. His other major function is celebratory: to herald a coming day of blessing and connect the people with the approaching new covenant era. These two aspects of prophetic ministry do not conflict with each other, yet the alternating sections of disciplinary and celebratory messages can seem quite jarring to the reader.

For example, the gloom Isaiah warns of in 8:22 is temporarily offset in 9:1–2 by his foretelling of a great light to come. This great light will accompany the birth of a child (9:6), and the reader immediately recalls Isaiah's recent promise of Immanuel (7:14).

This is another case where, in retrospect, it becomes clear what Isaiah means in these prophecies. Yet for his original audience, Isaiah's words in verses 6–7 must have sounded almost too good to be true, and most likely confusing as well. The Wonderful Counselor is to be a descendant of Adam, yet He is also Mighty God and Everlasting Father. And His other title, Prince of Peace, must have been puzzling in light of the war and destruction Isaiah had been predicting. Clearly Isaiah is bringing good news, yet it must have been a bit mystifying to his generation.

9:8–10:34

THE SAD STATE OF ISRAEL

After a short passage about this person who will reign on David's throne, Isaiah goes right back to why God's anger against Israel has not relented. The people have simply refused to turn to the Lord (9:13). The nation is beginning to deteriorate, but in their pride they presume they will rebuild it even better than before (9:8–12). Wickedness is pervasive among young and old, rich and poor (9:16–18). So God is about to deal with both the head (elders and the well-to-do) and tail (false prophets) of Israel (9:14–15).

The land is about to be scorched by God's wrath, and the people will begin to turn on one another (9:18–21). Those who have been preying on others will be brought to justice. Their options are limited: be taken captive or be included among those who will be killed (10:1–4).

Israel has a false sense of strength that is exposed when a mightier adversary (Assyria) threatens. But Israel's greatest adversary is God Himself. Isaiah makes it clear that in this case God's anger is not quickly turned away (9:12, 17, 21; 10:4). Assyria only *appears* to be the threat to Israel; that powerful nation is actually the hand of God (10:4).

Yet even though God chooses to use Sennacherib and the formidable military might of the Assyrians, Assyria will also be judged. They have no respect for the things of God, and they take it for granted that Jerusalem will be next on their list of easy conquests (10:6–11). God will allow them to trouble Judah, but only to a point. When God completes His work of judgment against His own people, Assyria will find itself powerless against Him (10:12–19).

Critical Observation

The intensity and proximity of the Assyrian threat is better detailed in 2 Kings 19. Isaiah's assurances to King Hezekiah are confirmed when an angel of the Lord puts to death 185,000 Assyrian soldiers overnight, followed by the withdrawal of Sennacherib. Perhaps the deaths are connected to the disease mentioned in Isaiah 10:16.

The Assyrians will do ample damage to Judah before being miraculously repelled by the power of God. They barrel through many of the cities but only get close enough to Jerusalem to shake their fist before being cut down like a lofty tree (10:26–34). The remnant of God's people who survive and endure will have the opportunity to witness the end of God's anger and again learn to rely on Him alone (10:20–25).

11:1–12:6

NEW GROWTH FROM A STUMP

During Isaiah's vision of his calling from God, he had been told that the nation will be destroyed like a large tree cut down, leaving only a stump (6:11–13). In 11:1 he again writes of a stump, but the imagery is a little different. In this case, the stump is of Jesse. The series of kings of Judah had all descended from Jesse's son, David, yet the time will come when it seems that the line has ended. But from that stump a branch will one day spring up. It is a marvelous fact that God's Son will be born from the line of the kings of Judah.

This prophetic section of Isaiah provides insight into the character of Christ as king. He will be filled with the Spirit of God (11:2–3). This most powerful of all kings will have no hint of corruption that seems to permeate human positions of power. Instead, the qualities of righteousness and faithfulness will be so clearly attributed to Him that they are called His belt. One day His righteousness will result in the frightening vengeance of God against the wicked (11:4–5).

The person and purpose of this Prince of Peace (9:6) are described in idyllic terms. Under His influence, fierce predators and their prey will become happy inhabitants of the kingdom. Children can safely play around cobra nests. All who are ruled by the king will have perfect security. This blessing is not just restricted to Judah and Israel: The whole earth will be full of the knowledge of the Lord (11:10). Through the knowledge of this ruler from the root of Jesse, peace will be extended far beyond the borders of Israel.

God's people will be called out of captivity, and all their adversaries will be overwhelmed (11:10–16). In response, people will offer widespread and unbridled praise to God (12:1–6). Praise seems especially meaningful after God's people have been delivered from a particularly difficult experience. Praise had been abundant after the Lord delivered the Israelites from Egypt and when David united the kingdom after the civil war between Israel and Judah. Later generations will praise God during the days of Ezra and Nehemiah, when they return to their homeland after several decades in captivity. How much more should today's believers praise God when they realize His Prince of Peace has removed all obstacles that previously stood in the way of complete and eternal fellowship with Him!

Take It Home

Israel had a harmful tendency to become lax in their praise and worship when things were going well. They would slide spiritually to a point where God would need to discipline them. Then only when they began to lose the blessings they had taken for granted did they turn back to God. Contemporary believers have the advantage of the incarnation of Jesus and the coming of the Holy Spirit, yet they may follow the same pattern. We're still a long way from the blissful state described by Isaiah. But as we wait for that day, how might you improve your worship and praise to become more devoted to God and grounded in your faith?

ISAIAH 13:1–23:18

PROPHECIES AGAINST OTHER NATIONS

Setting Up the Section

For the next several chapters, Isaiah presents a number of judgments concerning the nations around Israel and Judah. He has already been writing about Assyria and the crown jewel of its empire: Babylon. Eventually Babylon overtakes Assyria to form an empire of its own. In this section, Isaiah addresses Babylon and a number of other countries, delivering messages from God.

13:1–14:27

A MESSAGE FOR BABYLON AND ASSYRIA

One of the challenges of great might, wisdom, or beauty is the danger of pride forming as a result. People quickly forget that God, the one in whom they live and move and have their being, is continually above them. If human pride is not resisted, it will lead to destruction. At times an entire society may be swimming in arrogance with the danger of God's wrath so near that it would seem that there is no way out.

Babylon is first on Isaiah's list. Ruthless and arrogant, Babylon is considered the "jewel of kingdoms" (13:19 NIV). But the might of Babylon at its pinnacle is no match for the power of the Lord God Almighty. Isaiah declares its certain destruction. He describes an army that God Himself is forming (13:1–6). The haughtiness and ruthlessness so prevalent in Babylon will be replaced by terror and anguish. Some of the actions taken against Babylon will be horrendous (13:7–16).

Demystifying Isaiah

The superpowers of Isaiah's day were the Assyrians and the Persians. There was not always a clear succession of one empire falling and being replaced by the next. Rather, various nations coexisted for periods and had numerous coalitions and conflicts. For example, there was an alliance between the Medes and Babylonians in the late 600s BC, but about fifty years later the Medes were absorbed by the Persians, who then conquered Babylon. Various opinions exist, but it is likely that Isaiah's reference in 13:17 is to an early conquest of Babylon by the Assyrians in 689 BC rather than its more notable defeat by the Persians in 539 BC.

There is general agreement that the *Babylon* in verse 19 refers to the city rather than the empire. The people's arrogance and sense of immortality will be shattered. After centuries of existence and influence, Babylon will come to an inglorious end. History confirms that Babylon does indeed become a ghost town by the seventh century AD, confirming Isaiah's prophecy in 13:19–22.

Yet for the time being, Babylon is one of the biggest threats to Israel and Judah. What a surprise and comfort it must have been to hear Isaiah's prediction that one day, thanks to God's great compassion, He will reestablish Israel and people will flock there from all nations (14:1–2). Israel will have the last word with Babylon. God will lift up His people even as their enemies are falling (14:3–23).

Critical Observation

Isaiah 14:12–17 is sometimes said to be a biblical account of Lucifer's pride that caused him to be cast out of heaven, but there is no basis for this in the text. This poetic description of the king of Babylon (14:4) stands as a warning for anyone who allows ambition to override commitment to the service of others.

Assyria is right up there with Babylon on the power scale. Yet they, too, are going to be crushed. God has planned it, so it is certain to happen (14:24–27).

14:28–32

A MESSAGE FOR THE PHILISTINES

The Philistines had long been oppressors of Israel. The Israelites occasionally came out victorious, most notably during the rise and reign of David. But the Philistines had frequently been the victors, and when they were, they could be quite cruel.

Isaiah's oracle warns the Philistines against rejoicing so quickly at the demise of their enemies. Perhaps the reference in verse 29 is to Assyria. The fall of one enemy leader might be cause for celebration, but victory is tentative because others will arise to replace the fallen leader. The Philistines won't even have the honor of dying in battle. Instead they will be afflicted with famine (14:28–32).

15:1–16:14

A MESSAGE FOR MOAB

The Moabites were frequently at odds with the Israelites. During Israel's exodus from Egypt, Moabite King Balak had hired Balaam to curse the Israelites, but God didn't allow him to do so (Numbers 22). Moabite women had attempted to seduce the Israelites (Numbers 25:1–9). During the era of the judges, Moab had oppressed and financially burdened Israel until Ehud assassinated Moabite King Eglon (Judges 3:12–30). Saul and David had both defeated Moab, but Solomon had been persuaded by one of his wives to worship the Moabite god Chemosh (1 Kings 11:1, 7).

The origin of Moab can be traced back to the child conceived as a result of the incestuous relationship between Lot and his older daughter (Genesis 19:30–38). Moab is going to be destroyed, but not because of its ethnic heritage. The Lord despises the Moabites' false gods and high places of idolatry. He hates the way they have repeatedly turned against His people with violence. Yet Isaiah appears to demonstrate a heart of sympathy for Moab in distress (15:5). Entire cities (Ar and Kir) will fall in a single night. Even armed men trained for danger will be filled with fear in the face of a far more powerful enemy (15:1–4).

This is not the first time God's sympathy has been recorded for Moab. Israel had not been permitted to destroy Moab on the way to the promised land (Deuteronomy 2:9), nor was Moab among the nations that were to be dispossessed by Joshua and his generation during the conquest of Canaan. Ruth had been from Moab, returning to Israel with Naomi to eventually become the great-grandmother of David and be included in the genealogy of Christ (Ruth 4:13–22). It is clear that God's mercy extends beyond the borders of Israel.

Yet Moab remains a proud nation (Isaiah 16:6). They would have done well to unite with Judah (send lambs) because Judah will escape the conquest of the Assyrians (10:24–25). Instead, they will experience great suffering (15:6–9; 16:7–12). They have only three years remaining as a nation (16:13–14).

17:1–14

A MESSAGE FOR SYRIA

Syria was one of the great ancient nations. It was common for an entire nation to be referred to by the name of its leading city, so in Isaiah 17 Syria is called *Damascus*. (Similarly, Israel is called *Ephraim* [17:3] after its prominent tribe.) And when a key city falls, the entire nation feels the humiliation of the defeat.

At one time Israel and Syria (Aram) had been impressive nations. But here Isaiah compares them to a human body wasting away, a field that has already been harvested, and an olive tree picked clean except for a few remaining olives that can't be reached (17:4–6). Their devastation will be horrendous, but not total.

Demystifying Isaiah

Damascus is captured by Tiglath-pileser, a king of ancient Assyria, in 732 BC. Shortly afterward, the kingdom of Israel and her capital city of Samaria will also be subdued. All that will be left of Syria is just a small percentage of the fruitfulness that she once enjoyed, proving the accuracy of Isaiah's prophecies.

After trouble arrives, the people will forsake their idols and turn to God—something they could have done all along, but refused to do (17:7–14). Their once-popular fertility cults will no longer be a pleasant diversion. In such a time of great trouble, God alone is a rock of refuge.

18:1–20:6

A MESSAGE FOR EGYPT AND CUSH

As Isaiah turns his attention to nations farther away from Israel, his description becomes more exotic: whirring wings (strange insects?), papyrus boats, tall and smooth-skinned (clean-shaven?) people, and strange-sounding dialects (18:1–2). The land of Cush, south of Egypt, was essentially the most remote portion of known geography for those living in the Near East.

Perhaps Cush had sent their envoys to Israel to broach the idea of forming an alliance against Assyria. No evidence of any such proposal exists, although they were, after all, described as an aggressive nation (18:2). The Cushites are not alone in their desire to resist Assyria, so Isaiah's message is directed to all people (18:3). The fall of Assyria is up to God's timing, and when it happens, everyone will be sure to hear of it. Indeed, judgment of all the nations is in the hands of God (18:4–6). In time, however, the people of Cush will be among those who stream to Mount Zion to offer their gifts to God.

Egypt has much more of a history with Israel. God had long ago removed His people from the idolatrous nation, but their idolatry had continued (19:1–4). Egypt remained a formidable power largely because of the Nile River that provides constant water in a land where such a resource is rare. The Nile allows Egypt to produce grain for much of the world, and Egypt takes great pride in the Nile.

But Isaiah warns that the Nile will one day dry up (19:5), causing many previously stubborn people to humble themselves before God in the midst of their great suffering. None of Egypt's leaders or presumed powerful idols can keep the mighty river flowing to deliver the nation from disaster (19:5–18). Yet, like Cush, the long-range prediction for Egypt is positive. God has a wonderful plan of grace that includes the Egyptians. It must have been quite shocking to hear that Assyria and Egypt will someday be embraced by God like Israel (19:18–25). They will all know and fear the Lord, and somehow they will all worship together.

But first Egypt and Cush must endure the wrath of Assyria. As the Assyrians move into Philistine territory, capturing the city of Ashdod, God gives Isaiah an unusual assignment: The prophet is to remove his clothing and sandals and minister three years this way (20:1–6). His actions are symbolic of what will happen to Egypt and

Cush. Their people will be led away to Assyria, naked and humiliated. Anyone who had looked to Egypt for support against Assyria (as Judah had been tempted to do) will be disappointed and frustrated.

Critical Observation

It is debated whether or not Isaiah was completely naked for this three-year period. The word used can certainly be interpreted that way. Still, some people presume a sense of propriety would be necessary and believe that the prophet was expected to remove his *outer* clothing. Either way, whether Isaiah was totally nude or only in his loincloth undergarment, it would have been both disconcerting for the prophet and attention-getting for those who saw him. For anyone who may have presumed him to be among the lunatics who run about scantily dressed, the fulfillment of his prophecy would be especially emphatic.

21:1–10

ANOTHER MESSAGE FOR BABYLON

Isaiah's prophecies in chapters 13–20 may be difficult for modern readers to properly interpret and understand, yet they are reasonably clear and to the point. Chapters 21–23, however, are not as straightforward and can be even more difficult to comprehend.

In this section, for example, Babylon isn't mentioned by name until verse 9, which then helps explain the "desert by the sea" reference in verse 1. Babylon referred to their southern region as "the land of the sea," so Isaiah seems to indicate their impending defeat by the Assyrians. Babylon will eventually rise against Assyria and rule in glory for a short time, but then the Medes and Persians will rise to power.

Isaiah describes his vision of Babylon's destruction as a source of anguish, making him bowed over, dismayed, and appalled (21:2–4). What a contrast with the way others, oblivious to the coming destruction, live around him (21:5). But soon enough a messenger will arrive bearing the terrible news (21:6–9). Isaiah leaves no doubt that God is the source of his vision (21:10).

21:11–17

A MESSAGE FOR EDOM AND ARABIA

Brief words of coming difficulties are addressed to Edom and to Arabia. Although Edom is not mentioned by name, its identity is known because of *Seir*, the residence of Esau's descendants and another name for Edom.

Perhaps one of Edom's citizens had approached Isaiah looking for a positive word, displaying the optimistic expectation of Scarlett O'Hara that, "tomorrow is another day." Isaiah agrees that another morning is coming but adds that another night will follow immediately afterward. In other words, their circumstances are not likely to improve (21:11–12).

The people of Arabia are also in a dire situation. They can expect harsh defeat within a year at the hands of the Assyrians. The people will attempt to flee, but only a few will survive (21:13–17).

22:1–25

A MESSAGE FOR JERUSALEM

In this list of God's pronouncements directed at Assyria, Babylon, Edom, and other nations, it is unsettling to see one against Jerusalem as well. Jerusalem is literally a city on a hill, intended to be a place of great spiritual value. It is supposed to be a light to the surrounding Gentile world. But the people have rejected God, their source of spiritual strength and insight. Consequently, Isaiah addresses the city as a valley (rather than a hill [22:1]).

Because Jerusalem has persistently committed evil, their people will face discipline from the Lord. The leaders will attempt to flee the city to save themselves rather than stand firm in faith, but they will be captured (22:1–4).

Demystifying Isaiah

Isaiah is not speaking symbolically; his words in 22:3 are literally fulfilled. When the Babylonians siege Jerusalem, King Zedekiah and his entire army try to sneak out of the city, but they are pursued and captured. The Babylonians make Zedekiah watch as they kill his sons, and then they blind him (2 Kings 25:1–7).

God had long ago decreed a day of destruction, and it will soon arrive. God instructs His people to weep, mourn, put on sackcloth, and humble themselves. And although He is the one who will bring the day of disaster, the people will not respond to Him. They attempt to prepare for conflict but refuse to acknowledge God or repent (22:5–13).

Shebna (22:15) is a high-ranking official who was involved in dealing with the Assyrians when they threatened Jerusalem (2 Kings 18:17–19:37). But instead of a godly humility, Jerusalem's leaders appear to have a strange arrogance and even a hedonistic fatalism. Shebna attempts to establish the glory of his name in a potential day of disaster for the people of God. As a result, he is replaced by another man, Eliakim (Isaiah 22:20), who has more concern for the good of those who are looking for responsible leadership. Eliakim is an honorable and successful leader for a while, but even *his* time of influence will be limited (22:20–25).

23:1–18

A MESSAGE FOR TYRE

Tyre was a location known for its ships and merchants at a time when many nations counted on trade with the Phoenicians. If Tyre was to fall, numerous other powers would suffer as well. Isaiah lists Tarshish (very likely located in Spain), Cyprus, and Egypt among those who will feel the effect of Tyre's destruction. Even the seas are personified as mourning the loss (23:1–5).

Tyre will face a generation or more of trouble, and its fall will create more than economic concerns for its allies. The description is similar to that of the death of a loved one. Egypt will be in anguish (23:5). Tarshish will wail (23:6). And for those seeking an explanation, Isaiah makes clear that God has planned the change of Tyre's fortune in response to the great pride that had resulted from their success (23:9). No matter how respected a person or nation may be in the opinion of humanity, a refusal to acknowledge God will result in failure and dishonor. No nation's security is assured. Even the Babylonians have been bested by the Assyrians (23:13).

Yet Babylon will again become a world power, and Tyre will also revive after seventy years (23:15). In the meantime, however, Tyre is portrayed as a forgotten prostitute in a pitiful journey through the cities of the world, singing songs of better days. And when Tyre *is* eventually reestablished, it will be to benefit the people of the Lord. Even this proud city will be used to accomplish God's purpose (23:16–18).

Take It Home

It is possible to read through this series of grim judgments on various nations and give little thought to the person who is called to deliver them. But put yourself in Isaiah's place for a moment. How would you like to confront influential people all around you with the severity and inevitable consequences of their sin? And what if God wanted you to do so in a hyper-conspicuous manner, as He did by having Isaiah remove his clothes? To what extent would you be willing to face personal embarrassment to take a stand for God and His truth?

ISAIAH 24:1–35:10

THE WORLD STRUGGLES, BUT GOD REIGNS SUPREME

Setting Up the Section

After delivering a series of judgments against numerous nations (chapters 13–23), Isaiah expands his focus to the world as a whole. Isaiah 24–27 is frequently called Isaiah's Apocalypse, although many argue that the term is a bit strong. The remaining chapters in this section (28–35) are more specific and develop a historical perspective for the reader, although they do so with a series of woes.

24:1–23

THE EARTH DEFILED, THEN DEVASTATED

From the opening verse of the Bible, it is clear that the rule of the God of Israel is not limited to the area around Palestine. God formed the heavens and the earth and created humanity in His own image. No power on earth or heaven is a threat to Him. Kings must answer to Him, and His salvation can reach the most humble sinner.

It might be supposed by some that only people who have been given God's law in written form will be judged by God's commandments. However, all the lands of the earth are aware of God and His majesty. Everyone has been given a conscience that is more or less informed concerning the ways of God (Romans 2:15). All should seek to further understand and experience God's presence because all are guilty before the Lord and without excuse for breaking the relationship with the Almighty Father. Eventually people in every territory will face the Lord's righteous wrath in judgment (24:1–4).

It is important to understand why God would do such a thing—completely lay waste and plunder the earth (24:3). It is because people have totally defiled the earth through disobedience and utter disregard for His laws. God established a covenant with His people, and they have broken it (24:5).

As a curse consumes the earth, the time for partying comes to an end. Wine loses its appeal, and the tambourines are put away. The singers, dancers, and merry-hearted people return to their homes as joy turns to gloom for those who do not know the Lord (24:6–13). There will be exceptions, although very few (24:6). However, those few who escape God's judgment on the wicked will respond with shouts of joy and praise (24:14–16).

People who remain disobedient will be so furious that the very pit of destruction will seem to swallow up all the inhabitants of the earth. Terror results from the earth splitting apart and being violently shaken. Once-powerful authorities and rulers in high places will be called to account. At long last the wicked oppressors, both in heaven and on earth, will be shut away for eternity as the Lord Almighty reigns on Mount Zion and in Jerusalem (24:16–23). It will be a day of great vindication for those who trust in the Lord's unfailing righteousness.

25:1–26:21

AN INTERLUDE OF PRAISE

It is always assuring to see the violent plans of a powerful force thwarted as it attempts to destroy a weak and vulnerable opponent. Some adversaries seem simply too strong to defend against, and what could be more demoralizing to the desperately weak guardians of Israel than the victory song of an overpowering enemy? But the Lord is capable of silencing that victory song in a moment and stopping the onslaught of the mightiest power. And when His people see such powerful demonstrations of God's protection, the result is spontaneous praise (25:1).

The destroyed city in 25:2 is probably representative of all the cities/nations that have defied God throughout the ages. Israel's victory is not just another instance of "the little guy" able to survive another day with a massive military force arrayed against him. This time those ruthless powers are facing utter defeat. God's victory will be world-changing and life-giving. The veil of misery and confusion will be lifted. Death will be defeated, and tears will all be wiped dry (25:3–8). The powerful enemies of God who want to see His plans thwarted will not succeed. They will be most soundly defeated in the hour of the Lord's choosing (25:9–12).

Isaiah records a song to the glory of the city of God (26:1), thus directing the reader's attention to the kingdom of heaven. Isaiah 26 provides a lens through which present-day believers can anticipate the ultimate victory of God on behalf of His people in the coming Day of the Lord. Believers need to live in the light of that event every day of their lives. As they become more steadfast, God provides perfect peace (26:3).

God *will* deliver His people (26:7–21). Someday the song of deliverance will be sung in earnest. Until then, God's people seek and find Him every day. Through His grace they follow in the journey of the righteous. The reality of sin may load their pathways with spiritual and physical land mines, but the Lord is their safety and His promises are sure. Not only shall the remnant of Israel and Judah be saved but also the inhabitants of the world will love the judgments of God and learn the way of righteousness. Even the righteous dead shall live, and their bodies shall rise because of the conquering Lord (26:19).

27:1–13

THE POWER OF THE LORD

In this section, Isaiah describes the Lord's ability to protect His people by portraying Him as holding a powerful sword with which He slays Leviathan (27:1). Many of the nations surrounding Israel had legends and mythologies that included their gods doing battle with sea monsters, of which Leviathan was one of the best known. But Isaiah uses the image of the great sea monster to symbolize the powerful nations that show more regard for such mythologies than for the God of Israel. When it comes down to a matter of conflict, no other power can rival the power of the Lord.

Critical Observation

From the opening chapters of the Bible, serpents have represented evil and opposition to God. Sin entered the world as Adam and Eve were deceived by the serpent and disobeyed God (Genesis 3). But no sooner did that take place than God announced that the seed of the woman would eventually crush the serpent's head. The slaying of Leviathan (Isaiah 27:1) is another portrayal of God's triumph over an evil serpent.

By slaying the serpent, God protects His kingdom, which is symbolized by a vineyard to which God devotes much personal attention (27:2–5; see 5:1–7). In that day of the Lord's deliverance, Israel's influence will be greatly expanded. Jacob will take root, growing to eventually fill the world with fruit (27:6).

The guilt of God's elect will be atoned for. People of God can be identified by their refusal to be involved with idols. However, that atoning will first involve war and exile. In 27:8, the fierce blast of the east wind may be a reference to the Babylonians. For a while, Jerusalem will be desolate and forsaken (27:10–11). But the day will come when the people of Israel will be again gathered one by one and return to worship God in Jerusalem (27:12–13).

28:1–31:9

A SERIES OF WARNINGS

As Isaiah begins a series of pronouncements of woe to various places, the first is directed to *Ephraim*, another name to indicate Israel (the northern kingdom). The nation is portrayed both as a drunkard and a fading flower (28:1). It is a proud nation yet is past its prime and soon to be humbled by the Lord's hailstorm, destructive wind, and flooding downpour (28:2–4).

Demystifying Isaiah

Many of Isaiah's prophecies concerning Israel will be fulfilled with the invasion by Assyria in 722 BC, after which most of the population is carried away into captivity.

Yet even Israel will have a remnant of people who are protected by God. That holy remnant will turn to the Lord Almighty and find Him to be beautiful and glorious. In contrast, the drunken priest and prophet will find no help from the God they are supposed to represent (28:5–8). They will still claim to bring a prophetic vision, but since their own lives are covered with filth, who will believe them?

Verse 10 reflects the people's mocking of what Isaiah is trying to teach them. Perhaps the misguided priests and prophets feel they are being talked down to and respond with taunting. If so, Isaiah is not fazed. He acknowledges that they don't have to listen to him, but they will soon be forced to learn their lesson from foreign oppressors—the Assyrians (28:11). Instead of growing little by little in the way of righteousness, they will little by little fall away and eventually be utterly broken.

So Israel—the northern kingdom—does not learn the message of God. Lest the southern kingdom of Judah and capital city of Jerusalem presume the way will be smoother for them, Isaiah reveals that they will be scoffers. Their leaders will be grave disappointments, with false confidence in the religious practices they have learned from pagan nations. The covenant to cheat death (28:15) is something that they (mistakenly) imagine will protect them from the grave, but the truth is that their covenant with death will be annulled (28:18–19). No other gods or religions can save them. Consequently, it is appropriate for them to stop mocking Israel and realize their own peril (28:20–22).

Demystifying Isaiah

The *cornerstone* that Isaiah mentions (28:16) is a term that frequently applies to the Messiah, Jesus Christ (Zechariah 10:3–4; Acts 4:9–11; Ephesians 2:19–20; 1 Peter 2:4–8). It is unclear whether Isaiah intends this particular reference to be messianic. Perhaps he is simply affirming that God will ensure justice and righteousness in Judah.

However, Isaiah uses a number of analogies to assure his listeners that their coming troubles will only be temporary. Just as planting requires first breaking up the soil to be effective, and just as certain seeds must be beaten or ground to break the outer shell, God's people need to be broken in order for them to become useful and productive. Hard times will be necessary to effect positive change, but the difficulties will not be permanent (28:23–29).

After addressing Israel (28:1–13) and then Judah (28:14–29), Isaiah's narrative narrows to the city of Jerusalem, addressed here by the name *Ariel*. The name can mean either "lion of God" or "altar hearth" (29:2). In the context of Isaiah's message, perhaps the latter definition is more appropriate. Just as Jerusalem had been the place where people brought their animal offerings to be burned in sacrifice, the city itself will soon be a site of bloodshed and burning.

God is going to bring judgment on faraway nations and on the northern kingdom of Israel, and then He is going to judge the very center of His presence on earth during the days of the kings—the city of Jerusalem. Isaiah describes God as the one encamped and constructing siege works for the destruction of the holy city (29:3–4). His people have become haughty, and He is going to humble them.

God's people will suffer a period of disgrace, but their enemies will eventually be even more humiliated. When the Assyrians approach, it may seem that disaster is imminent for Jerusalem, but God will provide divine protection. The invaders will become like a bad dream that vanishes with the dawn of a new morning (29:5–8).

Experiencing such a miraculous delivery should capture the attention of God's people, yet it won't be long until they return to a spiritual daze. The prophets are a disgrace to their titles. Worship is not sincere but rather confused and hypocritical. What passes for wisdom is neither genuine nor lasting. It is a ludicrous situation: People who reject the leadership of God are like lumps of clay questioning the work of the potter (29:9–16).

Still, Isaiah again interjects a reminder that better days are ahead, when Zion will experience real joy. It will be a time of widespread divine healing. The deaf will hear and the blind will see. Even the land will have a vast increase in yield. Those previously subdued by the powerful will be vindicated, and the poor will celebrate their deliverance. All of the redeemed will glorify God. Even those who have gone astray in spirit will be brought back to an understanding and receptivity to spiritual instruction. This exciting announcement of hope stands out for the faithful remnant of God's people (29:17–24).

But Isaiah then immediately returns to his series of woes, now directed to rebellious children (30:1). God has a long history of delivering His people in times of trouble, but the Israelites are like children who never seem to learn to trust Him. This time Assyria is the outside threat—mighty, to be sure, but no match for the power of God.

Still, rather than turn to God for deliverance, the people of Judah seek help from Egypt (30:1–2). Egypt has tangible assets: chariots, horses, and soldiers. God is all-powerful, but invisible, and human beings frequently make the same mistake of trusting what can be seen. The people have a plan, but it isn't God's plan, so it will surely fail. Isaiah sees clearly that Egypt will be no help to Judah against the Assyrians (30:3–7).

Judah is like a child who will not listen to wise advice. The people resent the seers and prophets who pass along the message of God to them. So God instructs Isaiah to write down their words as a witness against them (30:8–14). Their only hope is in God. The wise course of action is to repent and wait quietly and faithfully for Him to act, but they are unwilling to hear. Instead, they run toward the clamor of Egyptian power, forgetting the God who created them and who had, on a previous occasion, rescued them from the hand of Egyptian oppressors (30:15–17).

The sad fact of the people's actions is that all the time they are seeking help from foreign human powers, God yearns to show them grace and compassion (30:18). The very reason for their adversity and affliction is to help them recognize truth. He wants them to acknowledge their prophets (teachers) again. He wants them to hear His voice and dispose of their idols. He wants to bless them with rain and food. He wants to bind up their injuries and heal their wounds (30:19–26).

It will be a while before the people experience such a significant turnaround. First, God will give them a reason to rejoice by delivering them from Assyria (30:27–33). The people will not need the help of Egypt.

Demystifying Isaiah

Topheth (30:33) was a location south of Jerusalem associated with fire and burning. It was where, on occasion, children were sacrificed to Molech, a god of the Ammonites. The Assyrians will be disposed of like a load of wood readily consumed by fire, except the source of heat in their case is the breath of the Lord.

Turning to Egypt is an offense to God (31:1–3). In Israel's history, Egypt was a place of bondage, a nation of idolatry, a symbol of commitment to the things of this world. God had done things through Moses that were far beyond the capabilities of just a man with a staff in his hand. Great waters had parted. Water had come from a rock. And a nation of God's people had been liberated from a great oppressor. Now those people are attempting to go back voluntarily rather than recall what God had done and trust Him to continue to deliver them.

God is not intimidated by any adversary. He will come down to fight on Mount Zion and shield Jerusalem from harm. Just as the angel of death had passed over homes in Egypt with the sign of blood on the doorposts, God will see that danger passes over Jerusalem in the days to come. Assyria certainly appears to be the stronger power by far, yet they will fall as Jerusalem stands (31:4–9).

32:1–35:10

RIGHTEOUSNESS, JUDGMENT, AND JOY

In his writing, Isaiah moves back and forth between his present time and the messianic age ("that day"). Israel and Judah had recently known very few good kings, so Isaiah again looks to the future to describe a different kind of leader yet to come. Much good can come from an excellent king. A ruler who leads in righteousness provides stability and protection even during a time of shifting circumstances. And God's future king does more than that. He gives sight and hearing. He helps people discern what really matters. He showers them with gifts from heaven. When such a leader arrives, it will become clear how incompetent previous leaders have been (32:1–8).

One danger of poor leadership is complacency among the people. Isaiah singles out the women of Jerusalem who use drinking to foster a false sense of security (32:9–15). He offers people a happiness that does not turn to panic when the grape harvest fails. No amount of wine can produce fruit among God's people that is available from the Spirit of God (32:15). Once people get beyond complacency in their lives, they open themselves to the possibilities of justice, righteousness, peace, and other blessings (32:16–20).

At this point Isaiah comes to his sixth and final woe in this section (28:1; 29:1; 29:15; 30:1; 31:1; 33:1), this time directed toward the destroyers (this is probably speaking of Assyria). The destroyer will eventually be destroyed, and the betrayer will be betrayed. According to the sovereign plan of the Lord, Assyria will have its day, but like all the powers that have come before, it will then fall.

The righteous remnant of people realizes that the God of Israel controls all their affairs with His mighty hand. They can be happy as they wait for the Lord and His grace to be their salvation in times of trouble (33:2–6).

But the sinners in Zion will have a completely different experience. The nearness of destruction will terrify them. Brave men will weep. Highways will be empty as people fear to travel. Once-plush areas of land will become like deserts. The people who have made plans apart from God will be subject to burning and consumption (33:7–13).

As always, God will see to the welfare of righteous people. Those who continue to place their faith in God will behold His great beauty in a land that stretches to the horizon. The humble servant of the Lord will find refuge, but the proud can not dwell there. The Lord Himself will be king, judge, and lawgiver. For the time being, however, Jerusalem is like a ship in disrepair, nowhere near ready to go to war. Its future might be glorious and secure, but it will first experience additional strain and conflict (33:14–24).

One day all the nations of the world will face the judgment of God. The destruction described in this section is massive and vivid. The coming of the Lord's mighty vengeance will go beyond the destruction of the peoples of the earth and will include the very heavens being rolled up like a scroll as stars seem to fall from the sky (34:1–4).

Edom is singled out in this passage as representative of all the nations who will face the sword of the Lord on that day (34:5–17). Why Edom? One likely possibility is that Edom took great joy at the harsh discipline of God against His covenant people. Those descendants of Esau had long shown disdain for the chosen status of God's people who descended from Jacob.

Critical Observation

The Lord God has a jealous love for His people (Exodus 20:5; 34:14). He may discipline them and even use unbelieving nations to do so. But those nations dare not celebrate the shame of the people of God. The Lord will not stand for their pride, their boasting in their idols, their unbelief, and their immorality. They will discover that He is an enemy who knows how to rescue His own beloved ones when they call out to Him for aid. They are likely to end up as Edom does in this passage: destroyed, desolate, deserted, and never to rise again.

Then, in abrupt juxtaposition, Isaiah brings marvelous news. A day is coming when people will be able to see what they now know only by faith. Land that is currently parched and dry shall be fruitful, with refreshing streams of clear water for thirsty lips. People will be strengthened, encouraged, and healed. A road—the Highway of Holiness—will be made available for the redeemed and those the Lord has ransomed who travel to Jerusalem. Dangers will be removed, and the general atmosphere will be one of gladness and joy (35:1–10).

Take It Home

It is important to note in this section how intent God is that His people not rely on the strength of the world for their survival. The world He created contains not only many things that are visible but also a number of invisible spiritual realities. Preeminent among those realities is God Himself. Yet most people can relate to the insecurities (and perhaps even desperation) of the Israelites. What are some of the things you tend to rely on in threatening situations? How can you prepare to more readily reach out to God in faith the next time those situations arise?

ISAIAH 36:1–39:8

A HISTORICAL VERIFICATION

Setting Up the Section

This section of Isaiah is quite different from what precedes and follows it. For a few chapters, Isaiah provides a historical narrative with specific dates, names, and events.

36:1–37:38

JERUSALEM IN PERIL

Prior to this point, Isaiah has been prophesying that God is going to use the Assyrians to serve both as a means of punishing Judah's sins and as a motivation for the people to once more turn to the Lord in faith. Yet Isaiah has also said that Jerusalem will not fall to the mighty Assyrians. Just as God will certainly discipline His own people, He will also punish the Assyrians for their arrogance.

As the events in this section begin to unfold, the king in Judah is Hezekiah—definitely one of the better kings of the southern kingdom. The nation has watched the Assyrians get nearer and nearer in their conquests—seemingly unstoppable. Now these powerful enemies are at the threshold. The northern kingdom of Israel has fallen, and much of Judah already suffered from Assyrian domination. It looks as if Hezekiah and Jerusalem will be next.

Critical Observation

Another description of these events is found in 2 Kings 18–20. Isaiah's account was written first and may have been the source for the author of 2 Kings. It is also possible that both writers drew from yet another (unknown) source.

The king of Assyria at the time is named Sennacherib. After he captures a number of Judah's well-defended cities, he sends a message to Hezekiah by way of his field commander. The Assyrian official goes to a public place where the leaders of Jerusalem and the populace as a whole can hear his message (36:1–3). Speaking in the language of the common people (36:11–12), he delivers a frightening warning that contains much truth interlaced with lies and half-truths, all designed to inspire fear among the Judahites and make them less likely to support Hezekiah in resisting the Assyrians.

Sennacherib has a well-deserved reputation as a powerful leader in Assyria. He will not be stopped by the empty words of an enemy attempting to negotiate out of a confrontation (36:4–6). The people of Judah had a tendency to place their trust in foreign alliances and considered going to Egypt for help against Assyria, but Sennacherib knows that not even Egypt can stand up to Assyria. (God had told Isaiah as much.) The Assyrians greatly outnumber those in Jerusalem, and the people might even feel more insecure than usual because Hezekiah has removed many of the idolatrous high places and altars where they tended to go instead of worshiping God at the temple (36:6–7). If the people cannot depend on Egypt, or their God, or even the other gods they seek out, then what hope do they have against the Assyrians?

Another realistic consideration is what was likely to occur if the Assyrians conducted a lengthy siege against Jerusalem. It wouldn't be just the leaders who suffered, but everyone within the city. The Assyrian field commander makes sure the people of Judah are aware that they might soon be forced to consume their own body wastes for lack of other options (36:12).

To an extent, what the Assyrian field commander says is the truth. But as he continues, he adds some lies as he tries to dissuade the people from counting on the faith of King Hezekiah (36:13–20). He says that trusting in their Lord will not work for the people of Judah, which is a wicked falsehood. To even attempt to compare Judah's God to the idols of other nations is a horrible deception. An earnest and humble request for God's help will not be wasted breath. God hears the pleas of His people, as will be clear in the chapters that follow.

The field commander finishes his speech, and the people remain silent as Hezekiah had instructed them—probably not the response the Assyrians had hoped for. The underlying theme of the message has been, "Fear Assyria and her king, and surrender now." And indeed, the people are shaken. Three palace officials with torn clothing (a sign of mourning) deliver the message to King Hezekiah (36:21–22).

Hezekiah shows great wisdom in responding to this crisis situation. He, too, tears his clothes and puts on sackcloth in a demonstration of repentance. He goes to the temple and sends for Isaiah, realizing that the words of the Assyrian messenger have been deeply offensive to God (37:1–4). When Isaiah receives God's reply for King Hezekiah, the first instruction is to not be afraid (37:5). Assyria will be soundly defeated, not due to any military competence on the part of Judah, but because God will intervene in those international affairs. God informs Isaiah that Sennacherib will return to Assyria, where he will be killed.

Just as God had promised, the King of Assyria makes a hasty retreat. Before he leaves, however, he receives word that Egypt is sending troops to help Judah, and he sends another threatening message to Hezekiah. Sennacherib is quite confident that Judah's God poses no more threat to him than all the other gods he had confronted in other nations. Sennacherib's plan is to deal with his immediate problem and then return to lay waste to Jerusalem (37:8–13).

Hezekiah reads the second letter, returns to the temple to lay his problem (literally) before God, and then prays. He recognizes the great power of Assyria but also acknowledges that the power of his God is much greater still, and he asks for God's deliverance (37:14–20).

In response, God sends another message to Hezekiah through Isaiah. God is pleased with Hezekiah's prayer, and He despises those who mock His name and threaten Judah. He has allowed Assyria to have power over Judah for a while, but He will remove them before they cause any further trouble (37:21–29). The people of Judah will have additional years of peace (37:30–32).

Furthermore, as Isaiah affirms for Hezekiah, Sennacherib's threats will never be carried out. He will not so much as shoot the first arrow or build a siege ramp (37:33–35). In a single night, an angel of the Lord kills 185,000 Assyrian soldiers. With his army decimated, the next morning Sennacherib returns to Assyria the way he had come. Eventually he is assassinated by two of his own sons (37:36–38).

38:1–22

HEZEKIAH'S ILLNESS AND PRAYER

On another occasion, Hezekiah receives a message from Isaiah that he will not recover from a life-threatening boil (38:1, 21). God is giving Hezekiah advance notice of his death so he can put his house in order (38:1).

Demystifying Isaiah

Evidently, Isaiah's historical accounts concerning Hezekiah are not in chronological order. Hezekiah's near-death illness (38:1–22) must have occurred prior to his encounter with Sennacherib (36–37). For one thing, God's decision to extend Hezekiah's life is accompanied by His promise to deliver Hezekiah and Jerusalem from the Assyrians (38:6), so they must have still been a threat to Judah. Also, history tells us that Merodach-baladan, the Babylonian leader mentioned in connection with Hezekiah's illness (39:1), ruled *prior to* Sennacherib's invasion of Judah. It seems likely that Isaiah positioned the accounts as he did because Hezekiah's encounter with the Babylonian leaders segues into the prophet's next chapters foretelling a Babylonian captivity to follow.

Hezekiah turns to God with a plea for deliverance from this trouble. He attests to his own faithfulness as he weeps bitterly (38:2–3). The fact that Hezekiah can stand before God and point to his devotion is a good indication that he is indeed attempting to live a righteous life. Many kings of Judah are remembered primarily for doing evil in the sight of the Lord, but Hezekiah is a positive exception (although he is far from perfect, as Isaiah will record in chapter 39).

In answer to Hezekiah's heartfelt prayer, God sends Isaiah back to the king to tell him he will have another fifteen years of life. A poultice of figs applied to the boil will clear it up (38:21). The reversal of the prophet's message is so rapid (see 2 Kings 20:1–11) that perhaps Hezekiah is a bit reluctant to accept the good news at face value, so Isaiah gives him a sign from God. The sign is fascinating: A shadow that has just come down the steps of a stairway is reversed and goes back *up* (38:7–8).

Critical Observation

When Isaiah leaves Hezekiah after delivering his first message, he hasn't even gotten out of the palace before God turns him around to tell Hezekiah that he has fifteen more years to live (2 Kings 20:1–11).

Anyone who has been unexpectedly freed from an immediate death sentence is likely to be dumbfounded. Hezekiah expresses his emotions in a psalm-like work with the first stanza (38:10–14) describing his initial feelings of despair and the second stanza (38:15–20) focusing on praise and elation.

39:1–8

VISITORS FROM BABYLON

Had Hezekiah's story ended with the account of his healing, he would be remembered more fondly. But Isaiah's final story provides a different tone. After hearing of Hezekiah's illness and recovery, a group of officials from Babylon visit him (39:1).

Critical Observation

At this time, Assyria is definitely the dominant nation in their part of the world. Babylon is not yet a great world power, but not for lack of trying. Merodach-baladan (39:1) has already led a few attempts to break free of Assyria and has actively sought to ally with other nations. So the appearance of his envoys in Judah merely to visit a sick king might be perceived as suspicious.

Hezekiah welcomes his visitors and hides nothing from them. He naively shows them everything about Jerusalem that might make it attractive to the invading force of a foreign power (39:2). After the Babylonians leave, Isaiah asks Hezekiah what they had said and where they were from. Hezekiah explains that they were from Babylon and that he had shown them all the treasures of Judah (39:3–4).

Speaking through Isaiah, God declares that the time will come when everything of worth in Jerusalem will be taken by Babylon. Even descendants of the king will be carried off, and nothing will be left (39:5–7). This was likely a surprising prophecy to Hezekiah. The predominance of Assyria made them the likely candidate to conquer smaller nations. But from this point onward through the writing of Isaiah, the Babylonian captivity is in view.

Hezekiah's response to Isaiah's prophecy is most troubling (39:8). Instead of repentance or regret, the king seems genuinely happy. His reasoning is that there will at least be peace and security in *his* day. Perhaps Hezekiah takes it as a foregone conclusion that the Lord will eventually fulfill His word and send His people into exile. He may have presumed that no amount of tears will change the situation. So, in a sense, it would have been good news that the day of reckoning for Jerusalem would not come during his lifetime. Still, his response to the foreboding warning concerning his nation appears insensitive and inappropriate, marring what is otherwise a respectable report by Isaiah.

Take It Home

The various accounts of Hezekiah may raise questions about prayer. It is amazing to read of Isaiah's declaration that Hezekiah will not recover from his illness (38:1) and then see that Hezekiah's prayer appears to change God's mind. Yet upon hearing the shocking news that his nation is destined to be conquered and destroyed by the Babylonians, Hezekiah hardly flinches (39:5–8). Which response is most like your own approach to prayer? Do you attempt to stoically accept the situations of life as they occur, or do you plead with God to change things for the better? Or does it depend on the situation?

ISAIAH 40:1–44:23

GOOD NEWS IN BAD TIMES

Setting Up the Section

This section begins a shift in tone and focus in the book of Isaiah, so much so that many believe it must have been written by someone other than the author of Isaiah 1–39. The regularity of judgmental pronouncements diminishes, as much more is written about salvation and restoration. The previous chapters present Assyria as the dominant threat; the following ones jump ahead to anticipate the end of the *Babylonian* captivity. (After the fall of Israel to Assyria, Judah remains as a nation for more than a century, and their exile in Babylon lasts another seventy years before they are able to return to their homeland.) But regardless of one's opinion of whether or not a second "Isaiah" takes up the writing of the original prophet at this point, this section contains some of the more optimistic looks toward the future in all the Old Testament.

40:1–31

ANTICIPATION OF COMFORT

The fortieth chapter begins a new section of Isaiah. While God will continue to correct His people, His word from this point forward is filled with much comfort. Yet this is not a comfort defined by the spiritual equivalent of a plush sofa, but rather a deeper sensation that demands careful attention because it comes at a great cost.

In the opening verses it is interesting to note that God provides His prophet with not only a *message* to deliver to the people but also clear instructions as to the *emotions* to accompany the message. Isaiah is to speak tenderly to the people as he brings them an uplifting prophecy of comfort (40:1–2).

Yet despite the optimism of the message, Jerusalem will continue to face great difficulties for decades to come after Isaiah. When will this good news arrive for the people of God? It will first be announced by a special prophet who will be a voice crying out for the people to prepare the way of the Lord. In the style of many Old Testament prophecies, this voice is probably that of Isaiah for a short-term fulfillment of prophecy. But centuries later, this figure will be identified as John the Baptist for an entirely different generation of God's people (40:3–5; Matthew 3:1–3).

God is eternal and everlasting, as opposed to humanity that is like grass in its fleeting existence. This is a world of the perishing. People come and go in the blinking of an eye.

But God provides permanence through His Word, which stands forever (Isaiah 40:6–8). The omnipotent God creates worlds and fashions mountains, islands, and waters. Compared to Him, the most powerful nations of the earth are but dust on the scales (40:12–17). And yet that Almighty God gently leads those who are His and gathers them in His arms like a shepherd (40:9–11).

When people begin to comprehend the reality of God, all idolatry seems foolish. God is the eternal Creator, Savior, and Deliverer. Idols, in contrast, must be man made. Care must be taken that they don't too quickly rot or fall over. Any glory of the idol comes from gold overlay and silver adornment (40:18–20). Yet God's people have repeatedly forsaken His leading and turned to such idols.

Isaiah attempts to renew the people's understanding of God. The Lord made all things, visible and invisible. The most impressive rulers do not faze Him. He can bring the high and mighty to nothing, and He can raise up the poorest slave to sit among princes. He is familiar with each individual star throughout the universe, so it should be no surprise that He is just as knowledgeable of each human being He has created (40:21–27).

God is not only *aware* of the struggles of His people but He also is actively *involved.* The affairs of life are demanding and tiring. But God is consistently present to provide strength to the weary and power to the weak. With the renewed energy He provides, God's people can soar on wings like eagles and run without wearing down. They can rest in the assurance that He has not forgotten them (40:28–31).

41:1–29

ISRAEL AMID THE NATIONS

As Isaiah continues, he affirms that God is the one who was at work behind all of the power struggles and international events in the Near East in the eighth century BC. The people of Judah may have seen only a powerful king with an unstoppable army bearing down on them from the East, but Isaiah is trying to make them aware that God was behind the situation. The Lord takes no pleasure in disaster, but He works all things according to the perfection of His holy will.

Demystifying Isaiah

The observation that the threat from the East moved on unfamiliar ground (41:3) suggests that Isaiah is no longer talking about Assyria. The new power in the East is most likely Cyrus, the Persian leader whom the prophet will soon identify by name (44:28–45:1). In addition, Isaiah has already said that the Medes will conquer Babylon (13:17–19). A later reference to Cyrus speaks of him coming from the north (41:25) because that is the site of his Babylonian conquests. Worldly powers will continue to shift, but God remains in control of them all.

As trouble approaches, people will respond in different ways to the power of God. Those who don't know Him will be fearful, forming alliances and turning to the worship of other gods (41:5–7). But God's people can respond differently. God tells them not to panic. He will not only be with them but He will also strengthen and help them (41:10).

God's plan for His nation Israel is no insignificant part of His overall design for the glory of His name and the redemption of the elect. It will be from Israel that one special servant will come as the only Redeemer of His people. God had called Israel into being for a purpose, and He had never abandoned that purpose for His chosen ones. He was always with them and will continue to help them (41:8–16).

Strong enemies will continue to try to destroy God's people and undermine His plan. But God is able to defeat all such enemies, seen and unseen, and even demonstrate His strength through the weakness of His people. Through Isaiah, God foretells all that will happen. Then He challenges the nations and their idols to do the same, proving that their gods are worth nothing (41:17–24).

God will allow the Babylonians to conquer His people and carry them from Judah into exile, but God's people will then see Babylon defeated by Cyrus and the Medes (41:25–29). And one day the Lord will send a herald of good news—a servant who will bring good news of redemptive love to God's people.

42:1–25

GOD'S SERVANT

As Isaiah continues, he begins to describe the character and responsibilities of God's servant. He describes a specially designated representative of God on whom God will bestow His Spirit. God's servant will faithfully promote justice until it is achieved throughout the earth. In the meantime, he will not add to the burdens of the weak, who are described as weak reeds and flickering candles. God will delight in this figure (42:1–4).

Demystifying Isaiah

Isaiah provides four servant songs: the first being found in 42:1–17, with three others to follow. Sometimes, as in this case, the servant he refers to will be the coming Messiah. On other occasions, he writes of Israel as the servant of God. His intended meaning is usually clear based on the descriptions he provides and the context of what he is saying.

This is definitely good news that should result in praise among all the nations. Kedar (42:11) was an Arabian area noted for its nomadic peoples and their flocks. Sela was an Edomite capital south of the Dead Sea. Edom, like Judah, had previously received Isaiah's words of warning (34:5–17), yet here they are invited to sing a new song to the Lord (42:10–12). God will take action to turn darkness into light, make rough places smooth, and guide the blind through unfamiliar territory (42:13–17).

Israel and Judah *should* have been a light for the Gentiles (42:5–9), but as it turned out, they were the ones who were actually blind and in desperate need of a savior. They had seen and heard God working among them, yet they paid no attention. As a result, God responded in anger (42:18–25).

43:1–28

GOD'S GREAT PROMISE

In their condition, the only effective savior for Judah will be the Lord Himself (43:3, 11), and in this section God promises them the best thing He can—that He will be with them as they go through the challenges they face. Yes, they will still have to deal with deep waters and flames, but the floods will not overwhelm them and the fires will not consume them. Even when Egypt and Cush fall, God will save Israel. With words filled with love and commitment, God tells His people not to be afraid (43:1–5).

God's people will be carried away to faraway nations, but God will gather them when their exile is over. It will be an act of redemption, salvation, and love. It will also be a demonstration of God's great power (43:6–13).

Critical Observation

This great promise of God to summon His people (43:1) will be fulfilled at several levels. First, Isaiah is prophesying an exile to Babylon, after which many of God's people will eventually be restored to the land under the leadership of Ezra, Nehemiah, and others. Second, after the coming of Jesus Christ and the outpouring of the Holy Spirit upon the church, people of faith will be gathered to the Lord in an amazing way. Finally, at the second return of Christ, the Lord will gather His people and take them home for good in His eternal kingdom.

Even before the people go into Babylonian captivity, God assures them of their release. The Israelites have always seen their exodus from Egypt as a historical high point, but God tells them to stop focusing on the past so they can see the new thing He is doing that will be even better (43:14–19).

Some people are likely to ask the question, if God is going to gather His people eventually, why would He go to the trouble of having them experience the pain of being conquered and forcibly leaving their land? Isaiah has already pointed out several times that the people are stubborn and unrepentant. Here God compares them (unfavorably) to wild animals. God is receiving more acknowledgment from jackals and owls than from the people who supposedly worship Him (43:20–28). After their exile, they will be much more receptive to the love and commitment He continually shows them.

44:1–23

LIFE-GIVING WATER AND LIFELESS IDOLS

It is common knowledge that people need water to live, but those dwelling in the ancient Near East were more regularly reminded of that fact than modern people who take water for granted. Without water, there is no life. And God uses this fact to teach that without His Spirit, there can be no spiritual life (44:1–5). Without the Spirit of God, people are first bone dry in a spiritual sense, and eventually dead in their sins.

The Lord is the provider of both needs: the water that sustains physical life and the Holy Spirit who bestows blessings to those who know God. Isaiah foretells the day when large numbers of people (springing up like grass and poplar trees) will turn to God. Not only that, but their reluctance will disappear and they will again *desire* to be known as believers in the Lord (44:4–5).

There is only one God, but the world has never had a shortage of false gods. Isaiah has already noted the futility of idol worship in a number of places (see 40:18–20; 41:7, 21–24), but this section (44:6–20) is one of the longer and more explicit descriptions. The images are truly ridiculous and pitiable.

The book of Genesis describes the wonder of God creating people, but Isaiah writes of people creating their gods. As they do so, the people get hungry, thirsty, and faint. Or someone gathers wood to cook a meal (food and fuel being two blessings of God), but the person sets aside part of a log with which he makes an idol, and then he prays to that god for salvation. People's minds were so spiritually cloudy that no one questioned the logic of praying to a block of wood (44:12–20).

Rather than being deluded by the practices of idolatrous nations, God challenges His people to return to Him for forgiveness, redemption, and renewed joy (44:21–23).

Take It Home

Isaiah has begun an emphasis on the comfort available for God's people, although there are going to be challenging situations they must face before experiencing such a degree of comfort. What are some situations you face that tend to prevent you from feeling the comfort you might like to sense in your life? What criteria do you use to determine whether or not you are at an appropriate spiritual comfort level?

ISAIAH 44:24–48:22

ISRAEL, BABYLON, AND CYRUS

Setting Up the Section

Isaiah has been attempting to help his people understand that they will certainly be conquered by Babylon and taken into exile. Here, however, he moves ahead to write of the fall of Babylon and the end of their captivity, predicting a benefactor that Israel might not have counted on: a foreign leader named Cyrus.

44:24–45:25

HELP FROM AN UNEXPECTED SOURCE

In previous chapters, Isaiah has written that the Medes will bring the rule of the Babylonians to an end (13:17–22). More details are provided in 41:2–4, 25. But here Isaiah provides the name of the Persian leader: Cyrus (44:28; 45:1). Not only is Cyrus specifically named but he is also identified as the Lord's anointed—the same title used for Israel's kings and that will be given to the Messiah.

Critical Observation

Isaiah ministered during the eighth century BC, long before the birth of Cyrus, which leads some people to question this particular account. Those who aren't convinced of the reliability of predictive prophecy believe that the specific mentions of Cyrus must have been added to the narrative at a later date—perhaps even after the release of the exiled people of Israel. Some believe the omniscience of God was at work in Isaiah's writing and that the prophet's ability to be so exact only proves that he spoke for the Lord. Others have varying opinions (a second Isaiah, etc.).

An *anointed one* is someone chosen by God for a special task of deliverance and salvation for God's people. It is highly unusual to see the title applied to a non-Israelite emperor, yet God is able to use a wide variety of resources to accomplish His will. He will bring Cyrus to power by removing the obstacles that stand in his way (including the Babylonian Empire). God is more than capable of calling such a person for the benefit of His people Israel, even though the individual may not personally acknowledge God.

After defeating the Medes in 549 BC and Babylon in 539 BC, Cyrus is well-established as the leader of the Persian Empire. History may give Cyrus the credit for his accomplishments, but Isaiah declares that it was God who went before Cyrus to level mountains, break down strong gates, and accumulate wealth (45:1–3).

What wasn't evident at first was that whatever benefited Cyrus in his rise to power would eventually benefit Israel. To question God's methods was as useless as a lump of clay challenging the skill of the potter. As Creator of heaven and earth, surely God was a more than competent architect of plans to deliver His people (45:4–13).

God remains unseen (hidden), yet His will is accomplished among the nations, and He puts to shame those who seek the wisdom and help of idols (45:14–20). One of the end results of God's will is the deliverance of His people. But in addition, the population reaching to the ends of the earth can also turn to Him to be saved (45:21–22). Every knee will bow and every tongue will attest to the strength and righteousness of Israel's God (45:23–25).

46:1–47:15

THE DEMISE OF BABYLON

Idol worship is a lot of work for the participants. People have to provide the gold and silver for the image, as well as pay a craftsman to create it. Then they have to transport the finished product with some difficulty, either carrying it on their shoulders or transferring it to a beast of burden. When they get it to the desired location, they then have to be sure to anchor it. Finally, they pray to it—all to no avail. It is just a hunk of metal that cannot answer (46:1–2, 6–7).

Demystifying Isaiah

The gods mentioned in Isaiah 46:1 were Babylonian. *Bel* is not synonymous with *Baal* of the Canaanites, although the two were similar in influence in their respective cultures because they were the prominent deities. Bel is also known as Marduk. Nebo was the son of Bel and the god of wisdom.

Idols had to be carried from one place to another—a difficult job left to people because the gods themselves were unable to help in any way (46:2). But Israel's God had carried His people from cradle to grave. He is always available to sustain and rescue them. There is no comparison between God and other gods (46:3–5).

The Babylonian leaders will fare no better than their gods. God's purpose will soon be revealed and accomplished. He will summon a bird of prey from the east (Cyrus). As a result, the Babylonian rebels will be defeated and salvation will come to the people of God (46:8–15).

God portrays the nation of Babylon as a young virgin girl. Things appear to be good. Babylon is recognized as a queen of the kingdoms (47:5) and has no inkling that anything will change their privileged status (47:7). Babylon will take God's people captive for a while, but the day will arrive when Babylon will be on the other end of the power scale.

The virgin daughter will find herself sitting in the dust, having lost not only her throne but also everything that had made her attractive. Forced to work and to roam, she will be subject to nakedness and shame (47:1–3). Sitting in darkness and silence, Babylon will have time to contemplate how it had arrived at such a state. God makes that point clear: He has allowed His people to be overpowered by Babylon, but the Babylonians had shown them no mercy. Soon it will be Babylon who will seek the mercy of other stronger powers (47:5–6).

Babylon is a proud nation, thinking itself invincible. The people practice magic and sorcery, and they feel their secret knowledge gives them an advantage. They are wicked at heart, even though they think no one is aware of their evil actions (47:8–10). The arrogance of Babylon is undercut as the taunts of God through the prophet Isaiah tell them to continue with their dark magic (to prevent their demise). Maybe they will scare someone. Maybe their famed astrologers and stargazers can come up with a plan (47:11–13).

Demystifying Isaiah

It can be a bit disappointing, if not downright frustrating, that Isaiah provides so few details regarding the transition between Babylonian rule and the conquest of Cyrus of Persia. The same event is noted in Daniel 5, with little more said between the feast of Babylonian leader Belshazzar with the writing on the wall one night and his replacement by Darius the Mede the next day. (Darius may be another name for Cyrus, or perhaps a different leader appointed by Cyrus.) Bible scholars who believe Isaiah was written by a single person point to the absence of details as evidence, suggesting that a second Isaiah, who would have written after the events, would not have omitted so much.

But no, God is going to bring certain disaster on Babylon, and when He does, their people will find themselves helpless (47:11). Those they had always counted on will not even be able to save themselves, much less the nation (47:14–15).

48:1–22

ISRAEL'S OBSTINACY

When it comes to arrogance and stubbornness, Babylon is no worse than God's people. God observes that the muscles in His people's necks are iron, and their foreheads are bronze (48:4). They pride themselves in being associated with God and having a long, magnificent spiritual history. But in reality, they have strayed from God's truth and righteousness (48:1–2).

Of course, God sees through their pretense. His understanding of Israel's sin influences His revelation (or withholding of it). Recognizing their sinful tendencies, He had revealed certain things long ago so this generation of people cannot claim that their idols brought about those events. At other times He withholds sharing His plans so that His people cannot claim to know the hidden things of God (48:5–7).

Despite repeated rebellion among His people, God remains committed to them, ultimately for the glory of His own name. In the meantime, He continues to love them as He attempts to test and refine them through their struggles (48:8–11). Much of that refining process will be accomplished through the approaching Babylonian captivity, but Israel's testing will have limits. They can count on being released from their future captivity, although it is still tragic that such an action is necessary. If Israel had been obedient, they could have had peace, righteousness, fertility, prosperity, and more. Because of their lack of faithfulness, however, they will suffer much. Yet they will ultimately experience the great joy of freedom (48:12–22).

Take It Home

The sovereignty of God keeps coming through in Isaiah's writing. How do you feel when you read that God allows His people to be tested through captivity/suffering before returning to Him in joy? How about the fact that God uses a cruel enemy to dominate His people as part of their restoration? How about the haste of God's people to turn to idols rather than submitting to God in obedience? Do you see such things as exclusively historic events, or do you detect any similarities with how God and His people relate to one another in modern times?

ISAIAH 49:1–55:13

THE WORK OF GOD'S SERVANT

Setting Up the Section

The first of four songs for God's servant is found in Isaiah 42:1–4 (or possibly 42:1–7 or 42:1–9). The other three songs are found in this section: 49:1–6 (possibly 49:1–7 or 49:1–13); 50:4–9 (possibly 50:4–11); and 52:13–53:12. These songs and the surrounding material foretell a servant of God who will be a deliverer not just of Israel but of all the nations as well. In fact, the emphasis of Isaiah's writing shifts to the point that neither Babylon nor Cyrus is mentioned again. The people of God are still in a captivity of sorts, but it is less the harsh physical captivity of specific nations and more of a spiritual bondage that only a special agent of God can remedy.

49:1–26

AN INTRODUCTION TO THE SERVANT

The servant songs of Isaiah are among the most exciting features of this impressive book of prophecy. The second of the four songs begins in chapter 49 and, depending on which scholars one consults, comprises the first six, seven, or thirteen verses of the chapter.

The figure at the center of these songs is the personification of the faithful Israel. As the songs progress from first to fourth, it becomes clearer that this perfection of Israel will actually come as a person with an appeal that extends far beyond the nation of Israel. His initial address is to the distant nations (49:1)—Gentile territory. He was born for the role he is to play. His words are powerful, like a sharp sword. God will use him and protect him from danger (49:1–4).

At first it will appear that his mission has yielded nothing. However, the Lord will reassure His servant, who will not only restore the Jews to God but also become a light to the Gentiles. The work of the servant will result in salvation reaching the ends of the earth. Nevertheless, he will first be deeply despised—a theme that will be further developed in the remaining songs. Despite the fact that some people will hate the servant, God will encourage him until someday many powerful rulers will bow before him. He will serve others in suffering and humility, but they will eventually prostrate themselves before him (49:5–7).

Additionally, the land will be restored and firmly established. Prisoners of sin and death will receive their liberty. The hungry will be fed and satisfied. Streams of living water will be available for those who thirst. Those brought to God's city from afar can expect protection and provision (49:8–13).

Critical Observation

In retrospect, it is easy for modern believers to see that many of Isaiah's prophecies describe the life and ministry of Jesus Christ. For the original hearers, however, those promises must have seemed wonderful, yet also mysterious and possibly confusing.

Such promises may have been hard to believe. When times get difficult, it is more challenging to see with eyes of faith. People might think that God has turned away from them and ceased to love them, but the Lord is like a tender parent. He might discipline His children, but He will never forget or fail them. Indeed, it is as if their names are engraved on His palms (49:14–16).

Israel will undergo a period of bereavement, yet when times improve she will discover great numbers of descendants she was not aware of prior. She will even be a strong and positive influence on Gentile nations. Normally captives are not expected to ever be rescued, but God will certainly deliver His people from the hands of their captors (49:17–26).

Demystifying Isaiah

This section may be an instance where both short-term and long-term fulfillments occur in regard to the same prophecy. When Israel was released from Babylonian captivity and returned to their homeland, it might have seemed that Isaiah's prophecy was coming true. Yet at that time they were weak and disorganized, and they demonstrated no influence on other nations. It would seem that Isaiah, then, was also referring to a future event.

50:1–11

A SUBMISSIVE SERVANT

A shift of address is made between Isaiah 49 and 50. In Isaiah 49, Israel is addressed as a mother. But as chapter 50 begins, God is addressing children—perhaps the faithful remnant among His people—and explaining that He has allowed their mother to be sent away for a while because of her sins. It is not unlike a husband declaring a divorce, which was accepted at this time of Israel's history (Deuteronomy 24:1–4). But in the case of God and His people, the divorce is only temporary (see Isaiah 54:5–7; Jeremiah 3:6–13). God could easily have protected His people, but they had repeatedly refused to call on Him (Isaiah 50:1–3).

The narrative now shifts to the perspective of God's servant once again in the third of the four servant songs (50:4–9 or possibly 50:4–11). Israel is in a desperate state, yet they are not helpless. The wonder of the gospel is that God, in His justice, comes again as God in His mercy. Unlike the other people of Israel, the servant of God welcomes instruction and is never rebellious. His words bring life. His ear listens to the voice of the Lord morning by morning. He stands on the side of the covenant people and never turns back from his mission to love God.

Consequently, he must be willing to suffer according to the need. He will give his back to those who strike him. He will turn his face toward those who spit on him. He is the only hope for the people, yet he receives their hatred (50:4–6).

What will be different about the servant to enable him to remain strong while others falter? He knows where to turn for strength. His help will come from God. As long as God is his vindication, he will never be overcome or put to shame (50:7–9).

The Lord and His servant provide the people an option that is otherwise unavailable. Some are likely to insist on providing their own sources of "light," but God declares that such people will lie down in torment. Everyone will fare far better if they will willingly fear the Lord and obey the word of His servant (50:10–11).

51:1–16

A HISTORIC REMINDER

God has a long, reliable record of proving that He can deliver His people even when things seem hopeless. Citing one such instance, He tells the people to recall the story of Abraham. Sarah and Abraham had wanted a child throughout their entire lifetimes, but Sarah had been unable to conceive. God waited until Sarah was well past childbearing age, so that when she got pregnant there could be no doubt that God was the one responsible for the miraculous event. Through Isaac, and then Jacob (Israel), comes a nation that inherited the promises God had initially made to the faithful Abraham.

In time that nation turns away from the Lord. But God's point is that just as He had been able to create a great number of people from the aged Abraham and barren Sarah, so, too, can He restore them even when all they see are ruins and wastelands (51:1–3).

The world and all it contains will pass away, but the salvation that God makes available to humanity—not just to Israel, but to all the nations—will be eternal. They who insult and persecute God's people have no future, but God will be available to His people forever (51:4–8).

Without the love and power of God, humanity has no chance of life, even for a moment. But by the strength of the Lord, His redeemed will be forever kept alive. They will come to Zion with joyful singing. The return under Cyrus will be only temporary, but one day a heavenly Zion will be made available to them forever (51:9–11).

Demystifying Isaiah

Rahab (51:9) is a reference to Egypt, and other references to Israel's exodus from Egypt are found in the passage: "days of old" (51:9 NLT), "dried up the sea" (51:10 NLT), and "making a path of escape through the depths so that your people could cross over" (51:10 NLT). Egypt's association with the monster (51:9) is similar to the link between Leviathan (27:1) and some of the Canaanite nations.

God is the only guarantee for the people to gain for themselves what they cannot acquire by their own strength. He is the Creator who set the heavens in place, laid the foundations of the earth, and controls the raging sea. He can surely remake His people and secure for them blessings that will never be taken away (51:12–16).

51:17–52:12

WRATH, THEN ASSURANCE

The people of Judah are hearing both good news and bad news from God through the lips of Isaiah. They will certainly experience the wrath of God, symbolized by potent wine that causes them to stagger. Alcoholic intoxication can be a deadly thing, but even more devastating is to be drunk on one's pride and false delusions of safety. For a while the people of Judah will be inconsolable as they undergo famine, violence, and ruin. They have sinned, and they will suffer the consequences (51:17–20).

But God's wrath will not last. After a time, He will deliver Israel as He passes the cup of wrath to her enemies (51:21–23). For God's people it will be like waking from a fitful sleep to greet the day with a message of truly wonderful news. Their enemies will threaten them no more. The people can dress in beautiful garments again, feeling anew the thrill of freedom and redemption. Shaking off the dust of the past, they will arise as a glorified city of God. They had previously been at the mercy of Egypt, and more recently Assyria had been a major threat. But God has demonstrated His sovereignty by delivering them from both worldly superpowers. Babylon will be next, but the Babylonian Empire will be no more a problem for God than any previous threat (52:1–6).

Not surprisingly, messengers bearing good news from far away were well received in ancient times. Watchmen were stationed to hear and report updates. But the best news that Judah could hear is a simple message: The God of Israel reigns (52:7–8).

Critical Observation

Naturally, any good news is reason for celebrating. Judah's release from Babylon is one such example. But the emphasis on peace and salvation (52:7) suggests that here, too, Isaiah is looking beyond his own times to the coming of the Messiah and His kingdom. At that time people can see the Lord return to Zion with their own eyes (52:8).

God's deliverance of Judah will get the attention of all nations (52:9–10). His people will burst into song in response to God's comfort, redemption, and salvation. He will call them out of unclean places, personally escorting them both before and behind (52:11–12).

52:13–53:12

THE FOURTH AND FINAL SERVANT SONG

Any lasting positive change among God's people must come about through the work of God's servant. This section is the last (and longest) of the four servant songs in Isaiah. It is also probably the best known because various portions of it are frequently cited throughout the New Testament.

God's servant will not look like a specially designated leader of humanity. In fact, his appearance will be appalling and disfigured (52:14). Perhaps this is a reference to Jesus' disfigurement on the cross. Or the point might be simply that the Messiah will not be a physically striking figure. Still, the servant's ministry will be effective. World leaders will acknowledge the truth of his message, and ultimately he will be raised up and highly exalted (52:13, 15).

The news Isaiah is revealing is almost too good to be believed (53:1), although it may not appear that way at first. The servant is nothing to look at. He is despised. He is a man of sorrows. People do not esteem him. He will suffer to the point that people have to look away (53:2–3). Yet the actions of the servant are for the benefit of humanity. He is standing in the place of weak and sinful people. He carries the grief they should feel. He receives the wounds they should receive as a result of their transgressions. He takes the weight of the Lord's crushing justice in response to human iniquity. He endures the punishment so people can have peace. People have wandered away from God, but the servant pays the penalty for their iniquity (53:4–6).

Critical Observation

It is evident in Isaiah's writing, and becomes even clearer in the New Testament, that humanity's penalty is not owed to any person or spiritual force other than God the Father. From the beginning, God made it clear that justice demanded consequences for sin. But through a plan between the heavenly Father and His Son (the servant in Isaiah), the death penalty fully deserved by sinful humanity was paid by Jesus Christ. Because of the great mercy of God, believers have the gift of freedom and eternal life.

Amazingly, the servant will face God's terrible wrath in silence. He will go to his death with complete awareness of what will happen to him. But he also knows what his action will accomplish, so he approaches death like a lamb about to be slaughtered. It will not be his own will to do so, but the servant submits to the Father's will in silent willingness (53:7–8).

He has done nothing wrong, yet he will face oppression, the corrupt judgment of his human peers, physical death, and finally, the grave. If this all seems unjust for the servant, it must be emphasized that he is acting to ensure God's justice. Isaiah makes it clear: It is the Lord's will for him to suffer (53:9–10).

But God's plan does not end there. Beyond the grave awaits the greatest exaltation for the righteous servant. God's plan involves the suffering of His Son, but also great honor to follow. The servant's selfless act of obedience will yield blessing upon blessing and grace upon grace as the centuries move forward (53:11–12).

Demystifying Isaiah

Isaiah's final song about God's servant speaks with precision about the final days and moments of the life of Jesus Christ. Among other things, Jesus was:

- Pierced (Isaiah 53:5; John 19:33–34)
- Wounded (Isaiah 53:5; Matthew 26:67–68; 27:26–31)
- Silent (Isaiah 53:7; Matthew 27:12–14)
- With the rich in His death (Isaiah 53:9; Matthew 27:57–60)
- Numbered among transgressors (Isaiah 53:12; Luke 23:32–43)

54:1–55:13

A NEW OPPORTUNITY

The willing submission of God's servant will yield a number of lasting results, beginning in Israel but soon spreading to affect the entire world. God's elect has become like a barren woman longing to be a mother. Indeed, the situation is familiar to those who know the stories of Sarah (Genesis 18:9–15; 21:1–7) and Hannah (1 Samuel 1). Few things are more disheartening than infertile women who long to have children, and a similar feeling will permeate the nation during their time of exile. But just as God eventually rewarded Sarah and Hannah with a cherished child, so too will He end the barrenness of His people.

Indeed, the barren woman is commanded to shout for joy because she will bear children in abundance (Isaiah 54:1). In fact, God tells His people to prepare to expand. As a fertile mother, they will produce descendants that will not be restricted to the promised land in Palestine. They will spread out to many nations and provide an international scope from that point onward. Israel will no longer suffer the shame of its youthful sins or the temporary widowhood of exile and captivity (54:2–4).

In addition to being a fruitful mother, the nation will also become a beloved bride with God as her Husband, Creator, and Redeemer. The international aspect is again seen in this promise because the Lord is the God of all the earth (54:5).

God seems to have abandoned His people for a short time, but after hiding His face for a moment, He extends His great compassion and kindness as He renews His relationship with them (54:5–8). God has been angry with His sinful and unrepentant people, but He recalls His previous promise to Noah (Genesis 9:12–17) and determines not to take action that will destroy them (Isaiah 54:9–10).

God's people will be like a fruitful mother. They will be like a beloved bride. They will also be like a beautiful building, adorned with precious gems (54:11–12). The turbulence of the past will be forgotten as the future looms bright. Clearly, the riches of the city refer to people rather than literal precious stones. As the passage continues, the promise is made that God will teach the children, providing peace and righteousness. What other treasure can approach the value of being continually in the presence of God?

Finally, God promises that His people will be safe from all enemies. Tyranny and terror will be far removed (54:13–14). This promise has never been perfectly fulfilled because God's people throughout the ages have had to contend against ungodly people and forces. Yet no weapon directed against the church can ultimately prosper. One day the perfect peace of God will be realized (54:15–17).

Until then, people will struggle with temptations to pursue things other than the Lord, but God extends an open invitation for all to come to Him (54:1). This invitation begins, in a very literal sense, with a call extended to the people of Judah after their captivity in Babylon. On a broader level, however, it is an appeal for them to return to God. Those who come to the Lord need no money because the servant of God has paid the price necessary for sinful people to approach a holy Lord (53:4–6).

Still, people tend to invest in other things that are far less rewarding. Idolatry is like a spiritual diet of junk food when God is offering fresh bread. No matter how hard people may work, they are not likely to be satisfied if their efforts have no lasting purpose (55:2). God's spiritual food and drink is His Word. It costs nothing, but it does require a listening ear (55:3).

God reminds His people of the covenant He had made with David (55:3). God had promised David that one of his descendants would be on the throne of an everlasting kingdom (2 Samuel 7:8–9, 16). It appears for a while that the dynasty of David had come to an end when Judah falls to Babylon and the people are carried away as captives. But Paul will later quote this verse from Isaiah as proof that Jesus is the one from the line of David who will fulfill God's former promise (Acts 13:34).

In light of this leader who will eventually arrive, the previous invitation to come is extended to everyone. God's people will become a beacon that will attract other nations (Isaiah 55:4–5). So it is especially important for Israel to turn to God while they have the opportunity. He will show mercy and pardon them freely (55:6).

People don't have to understand the mind of God. In fact, it is impossible to do so. God's thoughts and ways are far beyond human capacity to comprehend. Yet God's Word and works never fail. Isaiah compares them to rain. Water falls from the sky as rain and snow and evaporates back into the atmosphere. Yet as it follows that simple cycle, it waters the earth, causes seed to sprout in the soil, and provides food for everyone on earth. Similarly, God's Word falls on people and returns, and as it does, it accomplishes all that God intends it to do (55:10–11).

These are indeed assuring words for people coming out of exile. After decades of captivity and dejection, they can expect joy and peace, with even nature seeming to burst into song around them. It will be a historic event that will stand as an everlasting sign of God's power and love for His people (55:12–13).

Take It Home

The people who first heard the prophecies in this section were most likely confused. God is promising to send a servant who will make life much more rewarding. Yet the people are also being told to expect Babylonian conquest and captivity. Similarly, modern believers have many promises of God, the assurance of Jesus Christ, and the empowering of the Holy Spirit. Still, most of them face times when they cannot see beyond the harsh realities of daily life. To what extent do the promises of God lift you above undesirable circumstances and mundane responsibilities?

ISAIAH 56:1–59:21

PROMISE FOR (AND PREVIOUS FAILURES OF) GOD'S PEOPLE

Broadening the Invitation	56:1–8
Israel's Inglorious History	56:9–57:21
A Call for Genuine Worship	58:1–14
Accusations and Confession	59:1–21

Setting Up the Section

Isaiah has been writing about a rather optimistic future for the people of God. But the spiritual strength of their future will be largely dependent on their willingness to take action in the present and correct the things they are doing wrong. The invitation of salvation is being extended to those outside of Israel, and God's people need to start taking an honest look at their own spiritual actions and attitudes.

56:1–8

BROADENING THE INVITATION

The Lord's instructions to His people through Isaiah are nothing new. He isn't asking great things of them. He simply expects them to maintain a sense of justice in the land, to do what is right—keep the Sabbath, stay away from evil. Those who do such things will see God's righteousness revealed (56:1–2).

The people of Israel and Judah have developed a sense of special status in their relationship with the Lord. God's intentions to rescue His elect will broaden to include foreigners and eunuchs, two groups that have never before had full privileges in Israel. Among other restrictions, foreigners and eunuchs have not automatically been allowed to worship with the Israelites (Deuteronomy 23:1–3), but that is about to change.

God is appealing to His covenant people for a greater level of obedience. At the same time, others outside the nation are invited to demonstrate the same spiritual commitment and receive the blessings of God. Eunuchs can never bear children, but God promises them something even better. Foreigners who choose to worship God will find great joy and satisfaction and will no longer be treated as aliens (Isaiah 56:3–7).

Sincere worshipers from all nations will be welcomed at the altar of God. All will be encouraged to pray there. Israelites returning from exile will be joined by many others in a renewed devotion to the Lord (56:7–8).

56:9–57:21

ISRAEL'S INGLORIOUS HISTORY

God's plan reflects His love and mercy toward all people. Unfortunately, Israel's leaders have not yet developed the same attitude toward others. Like the prophet Jonah, they do not want to witness the fullness of God's mercy if it means that people who have long been their enemies will also be able to find peace with God and receive His greatest blessings. The leaders have drifted away from a real understanding of the plan of God and have turned instead to furthering their own private interests. They make no effort to help the weak and confused but rather plan great things for themselves while focusing on sleeping and drinking. The result will be an invasion of beasts that, here again, symbolize foreign nations (56:9–12).

Critical Observation

In Isaiah's day, as in every generation, there are those who desire the outward label of covenant-keeper, yet they actually prefer false gods. But in this case, the corruption will be so pervasive that righteous people will feel completely out of place. It will get to a point where upright people will be taken away by God through death, not as a punishment but as a reward (57:1).

Only in death can peace be found (57:1–2). Even so, God is not willing to ignore the widespread sin and idolatry among those who claim to be His people. In a culture that should have known purity and faithfulness to the Lord, the people are linked to sorceresses, adulterers, and prostitutes (57:3). Their pursuit of idolatrous practices has exposed them to numerous habits that God had prohibited in their law. While they mock other people, they participate in magic, rebellion, lying, lust, and even child sacrifice (57:4–5).

The irony is that the people are faithful to their false gods while ignoring the living Lord. The imagery is graphic. The people of Israel are depicted as shamefully leaving a marriage bed to partake of affairs with various other lovers, among them the Ammonite god Molech, to whom parents sometimes offer their own children. Even though such a lifestyle becomes quite wearisome after a while, the people will not give it up (57:6–10).

God's promises are still sound. Those who turn to Him for strength and deliverance will inherit the land and find refuge (57:13). Those who don't, however, will be left on their own. Since the people insist on worshiping false gods, the Lord will direct them back to those useless forms of wood and stone when trouble comes. They will discover too late that the power of idols disappears with a mere wisp of wind (57:11–13).

God's plan for people is always substantially better than what they tend to choose for themselves. Those who choose to pursue idolatry have to remain in good standing with those gods by providing regular gifts and offerings. God is in need of nothing, yet rather than remaining in His holy place, He willingly reaches out to provide help, strength, and fellowship for those who are contrite and lowly in spirit (57:14–15).

God holds His people accountable and is displeased with sin, but He never loses control. He has seen His people's sinful greed, and He has punished those who are guilty. Yet His accusations and anger are short-lived. Rather than enforcing lingering and lasting punishment, God instead offers healing, guidance, and comfort. Those who respond to Him discover peace and restoration. But those who remain unrelenting in their wickedness are unable to find peace and will continue to suffer (57:16–21).

58:1–14

A CALL FOR GENUINE WORSHIP

People can be far away from God yet still consider themselves to be in His good favor. While maintaining a form of godliness, they lack the power to break free from the prisons of laziness, self-centeredness, and addiction. Such is the case with Israel.

Isaiah is being told to shout out the truth of the people's rebellion, to broadcast it with the volume and intensity of a trumpet fanfare. The people are apparently oblivious to the extent of their spiritual lethargy. They claim to seek God's will, proclaiming eagerness to hear what He has to say. They even go to the point of blaming God for not noticing their faithfulness, their fasting, and their humility (58:1–3).

But God has indeed noticed. The purpose of fasting is to focus on the things of God rather than the usual comforts of life. Yet on days of fasting, the Israelites ended up quarreling with one another and fighting. They are self-centered and violent, with their minds remaining far from disciplines such as humility and repentance. Yet they still expect God to respond to their requests (58:3–5).

Had they truly been listening for God's voice, they would have known what they should be doing: fighting injustice (rather than each other), freeing the oppressed, feeding the hungry, sheltering the homeless, clothing those in need, and taking care of their own family members (58:6–7). God cares about how people deal with those created in His image.

Critical Observation

True humility before God must involve more than tears and sadness over the misery of one's life and disappointment in what may appear to be unanswered prayer. Genuine submission allows humble people to see the beauty of God's perfect law and, in response, creates a sense of abhorrence when confronted with their sin.

If the people had offered heartfelt worship to God, it would have included ministry to those around them, and they would have noticed an immediate difference: light in their darkness, healing, righteousness, and clear responses from God to their cries for help (58:8–10).

With a genuine concern for worship and the welfare of others, God's people will discover the ongoing strength and guidance of the Lord. Even in a desert setting, they will be like lush gardens. The ruins of their city will be rebuilt. Rather than having a reputation for quarreling and exploitation (58:3–4), they will be known as rebuilding and restoring their city. Keeping the Sabbath will not be a joyless obligation but a time of true delight. Instead of dry and tasteless religion, the people will be blessed with joy and feasting. All their holiest desires will be satisfied, and a new day will come for following generations (58:8–14).

59:1–21

ACCUSATIONS AND CONFESSION

Many people acknowledge the problems created by sin, but few describe it as precisely as God does in this section of Isaiah. Sin is sometimes defined as "separation from God," which is an accurate description according to 59:2. But that is just the starting point of this depiction.

When the Lord speaks about the sin of His beloved people, He does not ignore the depth and ugliness of it. Here He speaks of bloodstained hands, lying lips, and discomfiting involvement with spiders and snakes (59:3–5). Sin results in an empty and meaningless life, and attempting to hide behind one's sinful lifestyle without being exposed is no more successful than attempting to make clothing from cobwebs (59:6). Actions, thoughts, and direction in life are all affected by sin. Whatever the person seeks remains hidden. Those who wallow in their sin find neither contentment nor peace (59:6–8).

Demystifying Isaiah

At this point in Isaiah's narrative (59:9), he shifts from God's observations to the people's response. The prophet joins his people in confession and repentance.

The spiritual state of God's people is not good, and they begin to admit the truth. They describe seeking light but not finding it. As a result, they are attempting to feel their way in the dark, stumbling like blind people as they do. Justice and deliverance seem unattainable.

They are both angry and mournful, yet for all they are able to accomplish on their own, they may as well have been dead (59:9–11).

To their credit, the people acknowledge that their sin is against God. Their offenses are numerous and include rebellion, treachery, rejection of the Lord, instilling oppression, and lying. The standards by which their society had been founded—justice, righteousness, and truth—are now nowhere to be found (59:12–15).

It is a distressing situation, but not a hopeless one. The people may not realize it, but the Lord knows that they lack the power to solve their problems. Because no one else is capable of intervening and dealing with the lack of righteousness, God will solve the problem Himself (59:15–16). In fact, righteousness and salvation are so integral to the Lord that they are described as His breastplate and helmet. For those who repent of their sin, God will be a certain redeemer (59:17, 20). But those who continue to resist Him will discover that the Lord's garments also include vengeance and zeal. They will face His wrath and retribution (59:17–19).

Eventually the relationship between the Lord and His redeemed people will become permanent, thanks to the power of God's Word and His Spirit (59:21).

Take It Home

In this section of Isaiah, God reveals a direct connection between the sincerity of one's worship and the response the worshiper can expect. God wants His people to notice the needs of the people around them and, where possible, attempt to make a positive difference among those who are prisoners, homeless, hungry, family members, and so forth. As you think of these categories, do any ministry opportunities spring to mind? If so, what can you do this week to help in one or more of those situations? If nothing immediately comes to mind, spend time during the next few weeks asking God to provide opportunities for you to supplement your worship by helping others.

ISAIAH 60:1–62:12

THE GLORY OF THE LORD

Setting Up the Section

This section is a bright respite coming after a number of dark and sometimes even disturbing passages. Israel's recent past has been one of drifting away from God. Their immediate future will involve God's judgment on them as well as on numerous other nations. But their long-range future is something to look forward to. Isaiah has already written of God's servant who will make possible such a future. In this section he describes a number of wonderful outcomes that result from the work of the servant.

60:1–22

THE CITY OF THE LORD

The Old Testament describes a clear distinction between the Israelite people and everyone else. The Israelites are God's chosen people; the other nations are without God and in spiritual darkness. However, Isaiah has already explained that God will be close to His people so that they will be a light to the Gentiles (42:6–7).

Just as the Israelites are special to God, so is the area of Zion, near Jerusalem and the temple. In this section, Israel is instructed to prepare for a great influx of people from other nations to stream into Zion (60:1–3). The hostility between Israelite and Gentile will come to an end, and the grace of God can be embraced by those who had once been strangers to Zion. They, too, can count God's city as their city.

This must have been a difficult concept for the Israelite people to comprehend. Never before had Gentiles been considered to be in right relation with God without first becoming circumcised Israelites. But the image portrayed by the prophet is by no means threatening. God's fulfillment of His promises will somehow bring something much bigger than His people had previously known.

Not only are people coming to *visit* Zion; they are coming to contribute and to get involved with the good of the area. The wealth of other countries will flow into Zion. The mighty ships of Tarshish will bring back people and riches. Herds and flocks will be commonplace. Foreigners will willingly rebuild walls and make repairs. The anger that God felt toward His people at one time will be gone, replaced by His great compassion (60:4–10).

Critical Observation

In Isaiah's time, seeing camel caravans in the area (60:6) was the equivalent of someone today seeing a UPS truck in the neighborhood. It was a sign that something good was being delivered from a great distance.

It is likely that Isaiah is describing the church age or beyond, using the knowledge and worship idiom of his day. If so, think how challenging it would have been for a prophet from the eighth century BC to adequately describe a worship experience where Christ is head of a body of believers and the Holy Spirit is active in involving and empowering all believers, whether Israelite or Gentile.

Other indications suggest this scene comes from beyond the church age, after Christ has returned again. All the kings will either be supportive of Zion or destroyed (60:11–14). It will be a time of pride, joy, and great prosperity (60:15–17). Violence will be ended and peace will rule (60:17–18). In addition, there will be no more need of sun or moon because God Himself will provide everlasting light and glory (60:18–20).

This time, the people of God will never again lose the land. It might take centuries for this change to take place, but when the time comes, God will see it done quickly (60:21–22).

61:1–11

THE FAVOR OF THE LORD

Some of the prophecies in these chapters seem to apply to a still-future time, but others are fulfilled with the first advent of Jesus. The opening verse of Isaiah 61 would have been good news at any time, of course. Most likely the *me* was first thought to be Isaiah, or it might have been believed to be the servant of the Lord that Isaiah had foretold. But centuries later all doubt is removed. This is the passage that Jesus reads in a Nazareth synagogue very early in His ministry. After reading the passage, He sits down and tells those in attendance: "Today this scripture is fulfilled in your hearing" (Luke 4:16–21 NIV).

Demystifying Isaiah

Isaiah's readers were probably a bit in the dark, being unable to fully understand his promises involving the coming of the Messiah. Similarly, when Jesus arrived on earth, He promised to return. Consequently, today's believers still remain a bit in the dark as to their expectations involving His second coming. In retrospect it appears that Isaiah addresses both events: the initial incarnation of Jesus and His subsequent return to earth. In places it is debatable as to which occasion the prophet is referring to.

As the kingdom of God is coming near, it will be Jesus who is appointed to preach good news to the poor, to nurture the brokenhearted, and to free those who are captive to darkness and sin. It will be a time of the Lord's favor, when the garments of mourning and the ashes of grief will be exchanged for a beautiful wardrobe of celebration to the praise of the great God.

This is the announcement of something solid—something strong, like a mighty oak of righteousness. Ancient ruins will have new life. Strangers and foreigners will find their place in the drama of bountiful blessing. Faithful people will serve as priests of the true and living God, supported by the wealth of many nations. Shame and dishonor will be replaced by sounds of everlasting joy that cannot be contained (61:2–7).

This period of rejoicing will not come about due to God's mere excusing of human wrongdoing. Human sin cannot be overlooked. God's day of vengeance, as Isaiah had previously noted, will still be very real (61:2). God's justice will not be preempted. The demands of God's law must be satisfied; to do less is unjust. The penalty for disobedience requires a just and holy atoning sacrifice. Jesus will be not only the prophet who announces the coming good news but also the sacrifice that satisfies divine justice and reconciles people to God.

God is clear that He not only loves justice but also hates iniquity. Yet after sin is atoned for, God will reward faithfulness and bless the people and their descendants (61:8–9). Those who respond to His forgiveness will experience great delight at a level best compared to a bride or groom preparing for a formal wedding ceremony. The Lord will continue to cause praise and righteousness to spring up like shoots in a fertile garden (61:10–11).

62:1–12

THE LORD'S NEW RELATIONSHIP WITH ZION

God will not keep silent. Jerusalem and Zion had once displayed His glory but in time had fallen away and earned the nicknames such as "The Forsaken City" and "The Desolate Land" (62:4 NLT). God is not content for His cherished land to bear that reputation, so He will act to restore and rename Zion. The new names associated with the area will be *Hephzibah* ("My delight is in her") and *Beulah* ("Married"). The surrounding nations will no longer see Jerusalem as a wasteland but as a crown of splendor and a royal diadem. The land is portrayed as a bride, thrilled to approach her wedding, with God as the bridegroom (62:1–5).

In an interesting challenge, God exhorts the people not to rest until Jerusalem is again recognized as the pride of the earth. But more than that, God urges them to give *Him* no rest until that day. They are supposed to keep praying until He establishes Jerusalem in full. Like watchmen, they are supposed to be ever vigilant in their watchfulness and expectation (62:6–7).

Critical Observation

The prophets serve as a type of spiritual watchmen (see, for instance, Ezekiel 3:16–21; 33:1–9). They receive messages from the Lord and try to move the people in the actions of faith. But whether or not the people respond, the prophets are expected to proclaim the truth revealed by God.

Israel's history has involved many cycles of oppression by their enemies with periods of freedom interspersed. Foreigners had eaten their grain, drunk their wine, and killed their loved ones. But here is the promise that the day will come when the enemies of Jerusalem will never again take control of the city (62:8–9).

The people are to anticipate the arrival of their Savior. Their preparation will involve both work (clearing a pathway and building the road) and celebration (raising a banner). The nations (Gentiles) will be involved, too—not just the Jewish people. *All* believers will be deemed holy people and redeemed ones. Together they will give Zion new names (62:10–12).

Take It Home

It will be centuries before many of the prophecies of Isaiah are fully realized with the coming of Jesus Christ. And it has been additional centuries of waiting for Jesus' return for the fulfillment of even more of the promises in Isaiah. But it is as important as ever for God's people to act as watchmen, looking in anticipation for good news of sure deliverance. In the meantime, the evil one continues to prowl like a roaring lion, seeking someone to devour (1 Peter 5:8). On a scale of one (least) to ten (most), how good are you at patiently waiting for something to happen? How can you be more faithful in your watchful waiting, as you continue to anticipate the eventual return of the Savior?

ISAIAH 63:1–66:24

LOOKING AHEAD WITH HOPE

Setting Up the Section

As the book of Isaiah concludes with this section, the prophet reviews several of his ongoing themes, including God's vengeance, judgment, salvation, and redemption. But throughout it all is the assurance that Israel's future will be much better than its recent past, or even its present state. The Lord is in control of everything that is taking place, and His ultimate plan is to restore His people and renew close fellowship with them.

63:1–64:12

GOD IS MIGHTY TO SAVE

The final section of Isaiah (60–66) is largely positive and optimistic as the prophet describes God's glory and the future redemption and restoration of Israel. But throughout his writing, he has included occasional references to God's vengeance (see 61:2), and this section opens with yet another such passage.

A figure is described coming from Edom, one of Israel's regular enemies to the south. (Bozrah [63:1] was one of Edom's key cities.) The figure identifies himself as the Lord. He is a solo warrior, stained with the blood of His vanquished enemies. His blood-spattered clothing is reminiscent of those who trod on grapes in a winepress. The Lord goes into battle alone because no one else can accomplish the victory. When no one else is capable, God is mighty to save (63:1–3). And the result of the battle is significant: It prepares the arrival of the year of God's redemption (63:4–6).

Critical Observation

The Lord's solo battle against Israel's enemies is symbolic of what His servant (the Messiah, Jesus Christ) will do later on the cross. One of the consequences of Jesus' atoning for the sins of humanity is the ultimate defeat of their spiritual enemies. It is a painful but victorious battle He endures alone.

Although the imagery is violent, the response is one of prayer and praise. It is the power of God that effects salvation and deliverance, as Isaiah (speaking for the nation) recalls in 63:7–64:12. God had repeatedly proven His faithfulness to Israel in the past. Their distress is His distress, so He had lifted them up and carried them for many centuries. Though they had rebelled against Him, He remains committed to them. His people had always needed Him, although sometimes they realized it more than others, as in the days of Moses when mighty waters parted before them and each day's food fell from heaven. On later occasions, they would remember such times and realize how far away they had drifted from God, causing them to cry out for Him (63:7–14).

This is another such occasion. The prophet asks God to look down from heaven and renew His zeal, power, tenderness, and compassion among His people. He also confesses the problem is that the people's hearts have become hardened. Those who had once lived in peace and joy will see their enemies trample down the temple. The appeal is to God's reputation: If the people who were called by His name are permanently overthrown by other powers, it will seem that God is helpless (63:15–19).

So as the praise/prayer continues, Isaiah asks God to deal with their enemies. God had always been in control, of course (64:4–5), but many times His government of all things had appeared to be subtler than His people would have preferred. By His continual providence, He works through countless ways to achieve His holy will, rarely drawing enough attention to Himself to be noticed. Isaiah prays for a clearer manifestation of God's presence. He wants God to come down from the heavens—much like a football team bursting through a paper banner to take the field. He wants mountains to tremble and nations to quiver (64:1–3).

Isaiah makes no attempt to downplay the sin of the people (64:5–7), yet he boldly continues and asks for God's forgiveness. Only God is the Father. Only God is the Potter who can make things right amid the broken lives of His clay vessels. Only God can change the land that has become a desert back into the flourishing garden it had been before. Only God can rebuild a city that has been left in ruins (64:8–12).

Although the people had sinned, they had not been utterly consumed. They have faith that God will still act. Although God may usually appear silent to human senses, the fact remains that He is still almighty and will speak clearly to those with ears to hear.

65:1–66:24

THE FUTURES OF THE RIGHTEOUS AND THE WICKED

When God responds to Isaiah's prayer, He explains that He has not been as silent as the people think. He has revealed Himself, but the people weren't seeking Him. He had said, "Here I am," but the people had made no attempt to listen. He had extended His hands many times, but the people remained obstinate (65:1–2).

God knows why they had not heard Him. They had been too busily involved with pagan practices while defiantly disregarding their own laws. And while doing so, they had developed a smugly superior attitude. They were certainly religious, but they had completely lost touch with the one true God (65:3–5).

Demystifying Isaiah

Sitting among the graves (65:4) was often connected with practices of ancestor worship. People who tried to contact the dead would frequently spend time where the person was buried in the belief that the message would be clearer.

Theirs was not a spiritual slipup from giving in to temptation or being cleverly misled. No, they were provoking God to His face continually (65:3). So God will no longer be silent. However, when He breaks His silence, it will be in judgment (65:6–7).

But not everyone had defied God. A remnant of people continued to seek Him, so He will show mercy to them. Israel is compared to a cluster of grapes that is going bad. But before tossing out the entire bunch, the good ones will be picked and kept. The people had not valued God's prior promises to Abraham (63:16), but those assurances are still in effect. The line of Abraham's descendants through Jacob (Israel) will continue. Those who seek the Lord will continue to be blessed (65:8–11). The locations mentioned in 65:10 (Sharon and Achor) were both fertile and geographically pleasing areas. But the unrepentant people who had forsaken God will not share in the blessing. Because they followed pagan gods (Fortune and Destiny), they will be destined for destruction (65:11–12).

So one group of people will eat, drink, rejoice, and sing. Another group will go hungry and thirsty, experience shame, and wail in anguish (65:13–14). But after that separation is made, God's people begin to experience entirely new things. They get a new name, with their previous sins forgiven and forgotten (65:15–16). God will even create new heavens and a new earth. Jerusalem will be renewed, with no more weeping or early death (65:17–20).

Homes will be established with fruitful vineyards. The blessings of God will be so effective that work and child rearing are completely fulfilling pursuits. Even before a prayer leaves the people's lips, God will answer it. The dangers of nature are suspended as wolves and lambs, lions and oxen mingle together. The protection of the Lord will ensure complete security and satisfaction (65:21–25).

Throughout his entire writing, Isaiah has been faithfully relating what God has told and shown him, and he makes that point clear again as he closes. A prophet is nothing at all unless he is an authoritative spokesperson for God. So the Lord—the speaker in this section—has heaven for a throne and earth as a footstool. He has no need for people to build Him a house (temple). He does not go hungry, whether or not animals are burned on altars (66:1–3).

Worship ceremonies should have inspired the people to keep their hearts and minds focused on the Lord, but the Israelites had gradually lost their love for God. Yet they had continued to pray and sacrifice as mere rituals, and their actions became blatantly offensive to the Lord. What God desires from His people is not a thoughtless sacrifice but rather a contrite spirit and a sense of humility (66:2–3).

Demystifying Isaiah

In graphic terms, God points out that the people have lost any sense of distinguishing the holy from the unholy (66:3). Dogs and pigs are unclean animals, and the very thought of using them in a sacrifice should have been horrific. The people's sacrifices have become little more than animal abuse, and God deems their so-called devotion to Him the equivalent of idol worship.

Throughout Isaiah, God has made clear distinctions between the righteous and the wicked, and the prophet's writing concludes with yet another instance. Those who choose their own ways and delight in abominations will experience great dread as the judgment of God comes upon them. He has spoken, but they neither listen nor respond (66:3–4).

The Lord will be coming with fire and sword in His judgment. His fury and judgment will be widespread (66:15–16). Isaiah never attempts to downplay the severity of this horrible news. Yet the reality of God's furious judgment is offset by another reality.

Judgment is for those who reject God. But others will hear His Word and respond in fearful reverence. The obedient have been hated, mocked, and scorned by the wicked. Yet God has seen and heard it all, and He will mete out terrible punishment for the evil that has been done (66:5–6).

As for the faithful, they are in for a surprise. God will renew His land and His people, and it will be both sudden and delightful. It will be like the joy of having a child, but without the discomfort of labor pains. Zion will give birth to her children, and a new nation will be born in a day. The people will have Jerusalem as a mother (66:11–12). In addition, God Himself will provide the comfort that a mother offers her child (66:13). The righteous will be rewarded with new life and joyful hearts (66:14). The previous injustices of life are brought to an end with God's just and fair judgments.

When Jerusalem is reestablished, God's grace and mercy will extend to all nations (66:18). The righteous will be sent out to faraway lands, where people will hear of God's love and travel to Jerusalem to worship Him, bringing back with them others from Israel who have been relocated. Some of those from other nations will even become priests and temple workers (66:18–21).

Critical Observation

In His original call for Abraham to leave Ur and go to an as-yet-unrevealed land, God had promised that all peoples on earth will be blessed through the great nation that Abraham would become (Genesis 12:1–3). This final image in Isaiah describes the fulfillment of that promise.

God will establish new heavens, a new earth, and an enduring kingdom. With the unrighteous removed in the judgment of God, the righteous remnant of all humankind will bow down to worship the Lord in joy and peace (66:22–24).

Take It Home

The problem described in this section of Isaiah is one that has continued for centuries: Righteous people are mocked, manipulated, and abused by wicked people who wield power. Can you think of any similar examples in your own life and your associations with others? How can the words of Isaiah help inspire faith and perseverance (and maybe even peace) the next time you personally encounter such a problem?

JEREMIAH

INTRODUCTION TO JEREMIAH

The Old Testament book of Jeremiah is considered one of the canon's major prophets and is named after the book's author, the prophet Jeremiah. By word count, Jeremiah is actually the longest book of the Bible, with even more words than Psalms, making it the lengthiest prophetic work in the canon. It follows the work of another major prophet, the book of Isaiah, and precedes the short poetic work Lamentations.

AUTHOR

The book of Jeremiah is highly autobiographical, and more can be learned about the prophet from his work than from any other historical source. Jeremiah was a Judean, from the town of Anathoth, located about three miles outside of Judah's capital city, Jerusalem. We don't know when he was born, but he probably died in Egypt after the exile of 586 BC. His call to prophecy came around 627 BC. Jeremiah was assisted in compiling the book of Jeremiah by his scribe, Baruch, who is referenced several times in the work and accompanies Jeremiah on many of his journeys.

Jeremiah's writing is permeated with his personal feelings and the emotional turmoil he experiences as he ministers to the people of Judah. These are his fellow countrymen, and he is deeply burdened for their spiritual state. It is from the emotional overtones and many recorded laments that Jeremiah receives the nickname "the weeping prophet." The prophet is chosen by God to speak judgment to a people who have turned their backs on Him. For his troubles, Jeremiah is beaten, thrown in pits, placed in stocks, and publicly ridiculed. His own townspeople put out a contract on his life. Even his family members become his enemies. God had instructed Jeremiah to not take a wife—his ministry was to be too difficult to sustain a marriage and the coming judgment so severe as to preclude having a family. Jeremiah lives a life of loneliness and depression, and he certainly earns his nickname of "weeping prophet."

PURPOSE

As a prophet of God, Jeremiah is tasked with communicating God's message of coming judgment to the people of Judah, the southern kingdom, and more specifically the city of Jerusalem. The people had fallen into a pattern of idolatry, and it was going to destroy the nation if they did not soon repent of their sins and turn back to God. Jeremiah preaches a message of hope and repentance until it becomes evident that the people have no intention of repenting. Then his message becomes one of warning about God's coming judgment as he prophesies the invasion by a nation from the north that will destroy Jerusalem. Jeremiah's prophecies target all people groups in Judah: kings, priests, prophets, and ordinary townspeople. The book also includes a series of oracles to foreign nations, in which God voices judgment on them for their sins as well. It should be noted, however, that Jeremiah saw beyond the judgment to the restoration after the judgment. Chapters 30–33, in particular, reveal this restoration as a part of Jeremiah's task.

OCCASION

The book of Jeremiah is composed of writings and preachings throughout Jeremiah's ministry, which began in approximately 627 BC. The precise date the final work was compiled is unknown, but it can be estimated to be sometime after the last historical reference in the book, which extends beyond the release of King Jehoiachin from Babylonian captivity in 561 BC (52:31–34) and into the return of the Jewish exiles to Jerusalem after 586 BC in chapters 40–44. It is important to note that the events recorded in the book of Jeremiah do not unfold in chronological order. Jeremiah's prophecy takes place during the reigns of Judah's last five kings: Josiah, Jehoahaz, Jehoiakim, Jehoiachin, and Zedekiah. This is the time leading up to the Babylonian invasion of 586 BC, when Jerusalem falls. The historical events surrounding Jeremiah's prophecies are recorded in 2 Kings 21–25 and 2 Chronicles 33–36.

THEMES

A few main themes make up the bulk of Jeremiah's prophetic work. Chief among these is God's personal involvement with His people. Jeremiah's role as prophet is to communicate God's words to His people on His behalf. The reason such communication was necessary was because of the sin of idolatry the people had made a habit in their lives, the second main theme of the book. By sinning in such a manner, the people are guilty of breaking their covenant with God, established just after the Exodus. Another theme in Jeremiah's prophecies is the nation's repentance, or turning from idolatry back to God. Many of Jeremiah's prophecies also cover the theme of God's judgment, which was what the people could expect if they failed to repent and continued down the path of idolatry away from God. Ultimately, Jeremiah includes the theme of God's restoration of His people.

HISTORICAL CONTEXT

The superscription to the book of Jeremiah dates his prophecies from 627 BC (the thirteenth year of Josiah's reign) to 586 BC (the eleventh year of Zedekiah's reign), with chapters 39–44 extending beyond this time frame into the exilic period. Jeremiah's contemporary prophets were Ezekiel, Daniel, Zephaniah, and Habakkuk. The two national superpowers at that time were Egypt to the south and Assyria to the north. The northern kingdom, Israel, had been infiltrated and dispersed about one hundred years earlier, but Judah had survived through the faith of Hezekiah and Isaiah.

In 640 BC, Josiah becomes king of Judah at the age of eight and eventually begins to purge his country of idolatry, about the time that Jeremiah begins his ministry. In 622 BC, Josiah finds part of the Mosaic Law in the temple. These writings had not been seen or read for many years. Assyria was too distracted with her enemies, the Babylonians and the Medes, to control Josiah's reform. Later, in 609 BC, Josiah is defeated and killed when he tries to stop the Egyptians at Megiddo. He is succeeded by Jehoiakim and Zedekiah, his sons, and Zedekiah rules until the fall of Jerusalem in 586 BC.

Much of the prophecy of Jeremiah has to do with this political and spiritual climate. Judah was like a pawn in this major political upheaval, a mere buffer between Egypt and Assyria, and later between Egypt and Babylon. A major part of this book deals with Judah making unwise treaties with these nations to gain protection and deliverance. In the midst of this tumultuous time, God announces judgment, but He is still reaching out to save His people. During the ministry of Jeremiah, Babylon to the east begins its ascent and is on its way to becoming the next world power, replacing Assyria. Babylon becomes the invader from the north, mentioned several times in Jeremiah's prophecy. In 586 BC, Jeremiah's prophecy of Judah's downfall and the people's exile comes true when Babylon, under the reign of King Nebuchadnezzar, destroys Jerusalem.

CONTRIBUTION TO THE BIBLE

As part of the biblical canon, Jeremiah is considered one of the three major prophetic books. Although it is largely a prophetic work, the book of Jeremiah contains a wide variety of literary elements in addition to prophecy, including history, poetry, and narrative. The presence of all of these elements makes Jeremiah's work arguably one of the most compelling books of the canon. The book of Jeremiah has also been referred to as an anthology of Jeremiah's prophecies and an autobiographical account of the prophet's life.

OUTLINE

JEREMIAH'S CALL AND PURPOSE — 1:1–6:30

- Jeremiah's Call and Confirmation — 1:1–19
- God's Message to Israel — 2:1–4:31
- God's Justice — 5:1–6:30

HYPOCRISY AND WRONG RELIGION — 7:1–10:25

- The People's Sins — 7:1–8:3
- Responses to the Message — 8:4–10:25

JUDAH'S BREAKING OF GOD'S COVENANT — 11:1–13:27

- Jeremiah Dialogues with God — 11:1–12:17
- The Warnings Begin — 13:1–27

GOD'S WARNINGS — 14:1–20:18

- Warnings and Response — 14:1–15:9
- God Dialogues with Jeremiah — 15:10–17:27
- Metaphors — 18:1–19:15
- Persecution of Jeremiah — 20:1–18

MESSAGES ABOUT LEADERS AND CAPTIVITY — 21:1–25:38

Kings	21:1–23:8
Prophets	23:9–40
Captivity	24:1–25:38

JEREMIAH AND JUDAH DIALOGUE — 26:1–29:32

Judah Responds to Jeremiah	26:1–24
Jeremiah Responds to Judah	27:1–28:17
Jeremiah's Letter to the Captives	29:1–32

THE BOOK OF CONSOLATION — 30:1–33:26

Some Restored and Saved	30:1–31:26
The Future	31:27–33:26

INCIDENTS SURROUNDING THE FALL OF JERUSALEM — 34:1–45:5

Before the Fall	34:1–35:19
Jeremiah and the Scrolls	36:1–38:28
The Fall and Aftermath	39:1–41:18
Egypt	42:1–44:30
Baruch	45:1–5

PROPHECIES AND THE NATIONS — 46:1–51:64

Egypt	46:1–28
Philistines	47:1–7
Moab	48:1–47
Ammon	49:1–6
Edom	49:7–22
Damascus	49:23–27
Arab Tribes	49:28–33
Elam	49:34–39
Babylon	50:1–51:58
Seraiah	51:59–64

CONCLUSION OF THE BOOK OF JEREMIAH — 52:1–34

Jerusalem Fallen	52:1–11
The Temple Sacked	52:12–23
To Babylon	52:24–30
Jehoiachin Released	52:31–34

JEREMIAH 1:1–6:30

JEREMIAH'S CALL AND PURPOSE

Setting Up the Section

The book of Jeremiah begins with an introduction of the prophet and his call to prophesy to his own people as well as all nations. In the first section, which includes chapters 1–6, God sends His prophet to the people with a warning of impending judgment and punishment because of their lifestyle of sin. This judgment is based on the covenant God made with this nation and the consequences that would come to them if they failed to follow God's laws.

1:1–19

JEREMIAH'S CALL AND CONFIRMATION

As is customary for the prophetic books of the Bible, the book of Jeremiah begins with a brief biographical introduction to the prophet (1:1–3). Jeremiah, for whom the book is named, was called to be a prophet of the Lord as a teenager in 627 BC, and ministered in that capacity for forty years. He grew up in Anathoth, a city about three miles northeast of Jerusalem. Anathoth was one of the Levitical cities, but there is no evidence that Jeremiah functioned as a priest. His name means "Yahweh loosens" (referring to the womb), or "Yahweh exalts."

Verses 4–19 detail Jeremiah's call to prophecy and the two initial visions he receives from the Lord, the first being evidence of his calling and the second a preview of the message the Lord will deliver to the Israelites through him. Verse 5 specifies God's personal involvement in Jeremiah's life. The verb *formed* means "to create or craft," like a potter (see chapter 18). God carefully designed and crafted Jeremiah in the belly of his mother. *Consecrated* means "to make holy, sanctify, set apart." Before Jeremiah came out of the womb, he was chosen to be on God's side, but he still has to be obedient. *Appoint* here is actually the word meaning "gave." Jeremiah was designed and set apart by God so that God could give his life away.

Jeremiah responds to God's call with reluctance in the same way that Moses answers God's call in Exodus 4 (1:6). Jeremiah feels inadequate because of his young age. He claims he doesn't know how to speak. But God encourages him with a series of promises, instructions, and signs (1:7–10).

Critical Observation

Deliver means to rescue, save, snatch away, or free from the firm grip of distress. God's promise of deliverance in verse 8 is one that is tested repeatedly throughout the book of Jeremiah. However, God never removes Jeremiah from the tough situations he finds himself in; rather God meets him in these situations and delivers him by bringing him into His company and under His hedge of protection.

Touch is important to God; He is not a distant being. God touches Jeremiah in order to put His words on his lips (1:9). He is very specific with Jeremiah about this message that he is to speak to Judah, Egypt, Assyria, and Babylon. God uses six verbs related to agricultural and architectural processes as images (1:10). Four of the verbs speak of demolition: to pluck up, to break down, to destroy, to overthrow. Two speak of renewal: to build and to plant (see Jeremiah 31:28). These images sum up the message Jeremiah is to deliver to the people of Israel—a message of great judgment, followed by renewal.

To confirm his calling, God reveals two visions to Jeremiah. The first sign is an almond branch (1:11). In the original language, the word *almond* sounds like the word that means *watch* in verse 12. The almond is the first tree to greet the spring. Everything seems dormant, but God is watching, waiting to open. When Jeremiah sees the blossom, he will anticipate the fulfillment of God's Word.

The second vision, a boiling, seething pot, is a sign that judgment will come from the north, from Babylon (1:13–15). A flash flood will engulf the land and burn everything it touches, and the armies of Babylon will use the old invasion route of the Assyrians to invade Judah. Although this vision is tied to Israel's political future, God's judgment is deeply theological. Judah commits the gravest of sins by burning sacrifices to other gods and bowing down to them (1:16).

God warns Jeremiah that because of his prophecies, all of Judah will fight him. But God also promises that he will prevail as long as he stands firm in God's message (1:17–19). God contrasts the fate of Jeremiah with the future of Jerusalem. The people will not be able to save Jerusalem, but Jeremiah will be as strong as a fortified city (see 1:8). God calls Jeremiah to ministry, but with it comes the reality that his life will be largely filled with pain, doubt, anxiety, depression, fear, anger, and hopelessness. He will be rejected, persecuted, mistreated, and misunderstood.

2:1–4:31

GOD'S MESSAGE TO ISRAEL

Jeremiah uses metaphors to remind Israel of their former relationship with God, a literary trend that will continue throughout his prophetic work. The first is marriage (2:2). From God's perspective, the honeymoon phase was during the wilderness wandering, a time when Israel depended heavily on God. Another of Jeremiah's metaphors is harvest (2:3). Israel is the firstfruit of God's labor. Other fruit will come as other nations become God's people, but Israel was the first.

God brings a series of charges against Israel as if in a courtroom (2:4–13). The word *contend* means to bring a case against someone (2:9). The defendants are the house of Jacob and all the families of the house of Israel (2:4). The witnesses are heaven and earth (2:12).

Among the charges, God names two crimes: forgetting the Lord and walking after idols (2:5). God specifically mentions land (2:6–7) because He brought Israel out of Egypt through a land of desolation into a land of promise, but Israel defiled that land through their worship of Baal. The leaders and priests are just as guilty (2:8), which causes a breakdown in public life and collapse in public institutions.

Israel follows after things from which they cannot profit: the idols of the Canaanites (2:8, 11). God expresses the absurdity of idolatry. He questions why Israel would leave her faithful husband (2:5), notes that never before has a nation traded gods (2:10–11), and asks even the heavens to be appalled and shocked (2:12). Israel's choosing idols over God is like working tirelessly for dirty water instead of letting fresh water flow to her (2:13).

In verses 14–28, Jeremiah uses more metaphors to describe Israel's behavior. Slavery is the first. God had freed Israel to never enter slavery again (2:14), but Israel became slaves again because they were continually drawn into compromising and dangerous alliances with Egypt and Assyria. Memphis and Tahpanhes were cities in Egypt (2:16). The reference to the Nile (also called Shihor in some translations) and the Euphrates in verse 18 connects back to verse 13. Israel left her true protector to trust in changeable political alliances (2:19).

The second metaphor of a harlot, an unfaithful wife (2:20, 23, 32–33), is familiar in the Old Testament. Israel was God's adored bride, but she was unfaithful. She was a Baal worshipper, a cult preoccupied with fertility whose worship practices included prostitution. Within these same verses, God also compares Israel to a choice vine that becomes degenerate and wild (2:21). Israel's salvation could not be done by her own means, and God claims she is even in denial of her sin (2:22–23).

The she-camel (2:23–24) was known to be unreliable and easily disturbed, and even violent when in heat. She sniffs out the scent of the male and chases him instead of vice versa. Likewise, Israel is so intent on pursuing her lusts that the idols do not have to seek her—she finds them. God portrays Israel as having given up on trying to resist such behavior (2:25).

The metaphor of the thief who is exposed (2:26) applies not just to the common people of Israel but also its leaders, the kings, princes, priests, and prophets who also worship Baal. Ironically Israel can't even get its idolatry right. Trees represent female Canaanite deities; stone pillars represent male Canaanite deities. Israel should be ashamed, humiliated, and embarrassed (2:27–28).

Despite God's efforts to discipline Israel, she continues to misbehave (2:30). God describes her as a bride who forgot her wedding attire—the jewelry and sash that marked her as being married (2:32–33). Israel has become so accomplished at her harlotry that she teaches the wicked women her ways. The people's sins even include taking the lives of innocent people who have done no wrong (2:34).

Because Israel will not accept guilt (2:35), even though God has tried repeatedly to restore her (2:30), God responds the only way His justice allows: by promising judgment.

Israel will be put to shame by Egypt and Assyria (2:36–37).

In chapter 3, God continues to expose Judah's idolatry and sin (3:1–11) but invites both Israel and Judah to return to Him (3:12–25). God leads with a rhetorical question about the law of marriage and divorce to continue the imagery of unfaithful Judah (3:1–2). The law prohibits the return of the first husband to his wife because, socially, the woman is considered defiled and rendered unacceptable. According to the law, then, God does not have to accept Judah if she chooses to turn back from her unfaithful ways. In other words, there is no provision in the law for God and Judah to be reconciled. As a result of her harlotry, Judah defiles and pollutes the land (3:3). Ironically, the people of Judah join the fertility cult so as to invoke blessing on their crops, but God withholds the spring rain. Judah's harlotry is more brazen than the Israelites'; they speak admiringly of God and continue to turn to Him even in the midst of their idolatry (3:4–5).

Jeremiah recounts the history of faithless Israel, the northern kingdom, in contrast to Judah, the southern kingdom (3:6–25). God judges Israel, and Assyria takes the northern kingdom into exile; God sends Israel away with a writ of divorce (3:6–8). Not only does Judah follow Israel's example, but they also feign allegiance to Yahweh (3:8–11). In this way, Judah's treachery is worse than Israel's.

But God assures hope to unfaithful Israel through an extraordinary invitation that goes against the earthly law (3:12–14). Israel's opportunity to return to God is not based on their becoming acceptable, but on God accepting them. The one condition, however, is that Israel has to acknowledge their guilt and sin (3:13).

Critical Observation

Return is the word used most often in the Old Testament to picture repentance. God extends His invitation to return several times in the following verses. The first invitation is to Israel, the northern tribes that have already been scattered by Assyria (3:12). (The assumption is that both north and south will return from exile.) The words *return* and *faithless* come from the same root word. They speak of moving in opposing directions, either toward or away from something. Literally, the text is saying, "turn to me, turning-away Israel" (3:12, 14, 22).

The word *master* (3:14) is a wordplay with Judah's idol, Baal. It is actually the same word. God is saying that He is the true *Baal.* Among the things God promises the people if they will return to Him are that leaders and rulers will not be unjust but will feed the people knowledge and understanding (3:15); the people will be cleansed from all idolatry; God's throne will no longer be an ark but a city (3:16–17); He will bring a remnant of Israel and Judah home to Zion (3:18); the sons of Abraham will be joined by all the nations; and they will inherit the most beautiful of all the nations (3:19).

The weeping heard in verse 21 is characteristic of Baal worship. Perhaps the hills were bare because Josiah destroyed their idols as part of his reform. Perhaps the people are weeping because they are saddened by the consequences of their sin. The people have loved wrongly and badly, and have done so from their youth (3:23–25).

The next part of God's invitation through His prophet Jeremiah highlights three more characteristics of repentance: remove all idols and cast off all other loyalties (4:1); swear obedience to the true, living God (4:2); and make hearts receptive to God's Word (4:3–4). The images of breaking up fallow ground and circumcising hearts are akin to the idea of confession and exposing one's sins before God. Fallow ground is unplowed, hard land. The crusty earth has to be ploughed so that the seed will germinate. Breaking up the ground is equivalent to not planting among thorns, since one function of plowing is the removal of noxious weeds that inhibit a fruitful harvest. Jeremiah warns that if such repentance does not occur, God will judge.

The next section (4:5–18) describes an invader from the north (Babylon) coming to destroy Judah and bringing God's judgment (4:5–6). The prophecy includes metaphor sprinkled with an exhortation for the people to repent and reminders of the reasons for the situation (4:7–9). Verse 10 includes one of several pictures of Jeremiah's anguish at this message.

Another metaphor emerges in verse 11 of a scorching wind. This wind is not the gentle breeze that aids the winnower at harvest time; rather it is a blast that will strike down everything in its path. The next verse reminds listeners why the judgment is certain (4:12), and another metaphor of threatening clouds foretells impending darkness and devastation (4:13). This section closes with another exhortation to repent and a reminder that this invasion is God's justice (4:15–18).

The final verses of this chapter (4:19–31) reflect Jeremiah's anguish and include descriptions that convey the utter devastation of the Lord's coming judgment. Verses 19–21 are an intercession from Jeremiah as he reflects on the gravity of the message he is delivering and the details of God's pending judgment.

Demystifying Jeremiah

Jeremiah's prayer of lament in verses 19–21 gives evidence as to why Jeremiah received the nickname "the weeping prophet." Jeremiah is intensely troubled. He is anxious and convulsing over what will happen to Jerusalem. Jeremiah's agony reflects God's agony. God lives with great heartache and turmoil. He doesn't like the idea of judgment, but He is committed to making a holy people. He is anxious for His people to obey Him, and He can't overlook their sin.

God resumes speaking in verse 22, when He claims His people no longer know Him. The next verses remind listeners of the condition of the universe before God formed creation out of chaos (4:23–26). The connection between these verses and Genesis 1 is unavoidable. Four times in the text God looks and sees the conditions of the universe prior to creation—the earth is formless and void; there is no light in the heavens; there is neither man nor bird. All that exists is barrenness and wilderness—the murky conditions of the beginning. The destruction of Jerusalem is likened to the creation coming undone and returning to a state of chaos. That which was proclaimed good by God is now evil. All of creation will pay the price for Judah's sin. God's comments also remind listeners of His actions in Noah's time, when He took disciplinary action but chose not to completely destroy creation (4:27–28). Some people try like harlots to allure the invaders, but neither sweet-talking nor cries of agony will ward off the attackers or change God's mind (4:30–31).

5:1–6:30

GOD'S JUSTICE

As with Abraham at Sodom (Genesis 18), Jeremiah unsuccessfully tries to find one righteous person to persuade God to spare Judah (5:1–2). The prophet comments on the truth of God's only remaining option: judgment in the face of Judah's refusal to repent (5:3–6). But God continues to argue that His people are following false gods and committing adultery against Him (5:7), and He uses the stallion metaphor to illustrate His point (5:8). In the Old Testament, horses were often associated with the powerful that assert their might and seize the initiative. Here the metaphor illustrates shameless self-assertion. Then in verse 9, God restates His need for justice: "Should I not punish them for this?" (NIV).

In verse 10, God again applies the image of Judah as a good vine that turns bad (see 2:21) and has to be dealt with. Regardless of how God's justice will be enacted, however, God reminds again (see 4:27) that He will not destroy the nation completely (5:10). He also restates the reasons for the discipline: idolatry and refusal, even among the prophets, to recognize sinful actions (5:11–13).

Critical Observation

The people's sins against God aren't limited to Judah. Israel has been treating God with irreverence and apathy for some time. As verse 12 notes, one of the lies spread by people from both the northern and southern kingdoms is that God won't judge them, even though He has proven otherwise in the lives of their ancestors. And as if that isn't bad enough, some of God's own prophets had taken on the same complacent spirit and no longer feared Him (5:13). But Jeremiah, a prophet who continues to speak God's truth, is quick to remind them that no one can escape God's judgment.

God has chosen Jeremiah to speak this harsh truth to the people (5:14). His judgment will come in the form of an invasion from a foreign nation (see Deuteronomy 28:49) that will overpower Judah, bring unfamiliar language and customs, and take everything Judah has for their own (5:15–17). It will be the nation of Babylon that fulfills this prophecy. Again, though, God reiterates through His prophet that He will not completely destroy Judah, only discipline them for their sins (5:18–19).

The final verses of this section (5:20–31) restate God's case for His discipline and judgment. God reminds His people, who have stopped listening to Him, of His nature and power: He is the Creator (5:20–22). Unlike the sea, God's people have stopped responding to His law, yet they still continue to enjoy the fruits of creation until God chooses to withhold them (5:22–25). The nation's sin is so bad that it entraps others (5:26). It leads to corruption that causes the innocent and powerless to suffer, and God responds with punishment (5:27–29). Kings, princes, prophets, and priests—all of them are out for their own gain, proclaiming peace where none exists. The final verse of this chapter blames Judah's leaders for turning away from God, allowing sin to affect the entire community and nation, and doing nothing to repent and restore justice (5:30–31).

It is interesting to note in the first verse of chapter 6 that Jeremiah belongs to the tribe of Benjamin, so he sends this particular warning of God's approaching justice to his own tribe. Again the warning is that God's justice is coming from the north to God's people (6:2–3). This appears to be a well-planned, premeditated attack on a nation that continues to defy God (6:4–7). God likens His power and ability to completely destroy them to a good harvester who picks all the grapes off a vine (6:8–9).

Demystifying Jeremiah

Jeremiah's role as prophet to God's people looks a lot like God's vinedresser metaphor. God uses Jeremiah to examine the state of the vine—the people of Israel—and attempt to glean whatever vines he can by spreading God's message of approaching justice. Before God brings His judgment down on the people, He is certain to make sure everyone has been warned and given a chance to repent and escape judgment. The state of the Israelites' souls is placed in the hands of God's vinedresser, Jeremiah (6:9).

The next section (6:10–21) both condemns Judah for not heeding Jeremiah's warnings and extends the reasons for God's judgment. The people are accused of not hearing the word of their Creator, and the Lord has had enough (6:10–11). Jeremiah prophesies specific details of what can be expected from the Babylonian invasion, and again God blames each of the citizens of Judea for the nation's collective sin (6:12–13). His accusations toward the religious leaders are telling: They perform rituals and chant words, but their spirits are not pure (6:14–15).

The Judeans had the chance to listen to the priests and prophets who spoke truth and return to the true God, but they refused and chose to continue sacrificing to God while living in a way that did not bring Him glory (6:16–20). God doesn't tolerate their hypocrisy, and Jeremiah proclaims that God's correction will have devastating consequences (6:21). Again, in effective oration, the invaders from the north are predicted and their actions detailed (6:22–23). Peace and normal life for the nation is quickly coming to an end (6:24–26).

Jeremiah's final metaphor of this chapter likens his search for people who do not deserve God's judgment to a metalworker searching for good, strong metal among weaker metal. The process includes hot fires stoked with bellows, and yet the metalworker burns and burns without finding any good metal (6:27–30).

Take It Home

The first six chapters of Jeremiah are filled with warnings about coming judgment, but the warnings are laced with opportunities for repentance. Jeremiah's message to the people of Judah starts out hopeful, but as will be seen as the book progresses, this hope and the opportunities for repentance begin to dwindle.

JEREMIAH 7:1–10:25

HYPOCRISY AND WRONG RELIGION

Setting Up the Section

This section of the book of Jeremiah continues with the prophet's warnings to the nation. In this portion of prophecies, the warnings are more specifically geared toward the sins of hypocrisy and practicing false religion, and the consequences of those sins.

7:1–8:3

THE PEOPLE'S SINS

Chapter 7 is from a sermon God instructs Jeremiah to deliver at the gate of the temple in Jerusalem (7:1–2). Chapter 26 refers to the same occasion or a similar one. This event could have been at the beginning of Jehoiakim's reign, when, despite Josiah's restoration of the temple and true worship, cultic practice was again the norm. The temple gate was the most sacred and public place in Jerusalem. Jeremiah's message would have been very upsetting to the establishment, but the nation's leaders were clearly at fault for leading the people down a path of such disobedience.

The first two commands of this chapter are designed to get the attention of the people of Judah (7:3–4). They are repeated twice, the second repetition filling out the first. To amend one's ways means make good, do well, do right, do what is pleasing. It is concerned with practical elements of everyday life: practicing justice, loving one's neighbor, caring for orphans and widows, and not walking after false gods (7:5–7). The people of Judah are failing to do what is right, and they are worshiping the wrong god to their own ruin. They are being selfish, exploiting people for their own gain. *Deceptive* means to deal falsely, or to lie, which is the opposite of being faithful and true. This word is used 113 times in the scriptures, one-third of which are found in the prophecy of Jeremiah (7:8).

The deception that the people are trusting in is the notion that they can do anything they want and then find safety in God's temple (7:9–11). God uses Jeremiah to remind the people that the presence of the Lord's temple didn't save the people of Shiloh, so they shouldn't expect it to save them either (7:12–14). Just as God exiled the Israelites in the northern kingdom, the people of Judah can expect the same fate if they don't repent and turn back to Him (7:15).

In verse 16, God speaks directly to Jeremiah, telling the prophet not to waste his time praying for God to forgive the sinful people of Judah because it is too late. Their doom is certain, and they have definitively rejected the possibility of repentance. This can seem confusing, because in this part of Jeremiah the oracles are not in chronological order. Some are from the period when repentance was possible, but others are from the period when repentance was no longer an option.

Demystifying Jeremiah

The Queen of Heaven in verse 18 is a reference to the worship of any number of Babylonian goddesses (see 44:17; see also 2 Kings 21; 23:4–14; Amos 5:26). This worship of these goddesses often appealed more to women, and one of the customs involved making cakes in the goddess's image (Jeremiah 7:18). The fact that people are making cakes in the privacy of their homes as a form of worship to a false god and then showing up at the temple in public to worship Yahweh was the ultimate form of hypocrisy.

Because of the people's attempts at worshiping more than one God, Jeremiah includes a warning emphasizing the importance of obedience instead of empty sacrifices (7:21–29). God knows the offerings are futile if the people's hearts aren't engaged in worshiping Him (7:21–22). What He cares about is obedience, as He told their ancestors when He led them out of slavery in Egypt (7:23–24). A key word in the text is the Hebrew word *shema.* It appears eight times in chapter 7 and is translated as both "listen" and "obey." God desires a simple obedience from a heart devoted to Him. But no matter how often God sends this message to His people, they reject Him and His messenger (7:25–28). God urges Jeremiah to mourn (including the act of cutting off his hair) because of Judah's grave sins (7:29).

Among Judah's sins is the practice of child sacrifice (7:30–31). The valley of Topheth, or Hinnom, was just outside the city of Jerusalem to the south. This was a garden of the Canaanites and later a center of Baal worship. Jeremiah says that the valley of Topheth will become the valley of slaughter and will be a dumping ground for all the bodies of people who die in the coming invasion (7:32). The word *topheth* rhymes with the Hebrew word for shame. The valley of the son of Hinnom will become Jerusalem's garbage dump, and the ruined land will be devoid of all joy (7:33–34).

Verses 1–3 of chapter 8 close out the sermon at the temple gate. Jeremiah prophesies that when the city is invaded, the intruders will dig up the graves of everyone from kings to laypeople. Proper burial is highly valued in the Jewish culture, and this is a further example of the disgrace and ruin that will come upon the land. Their disgraced remains will be exposed to those aspects of creation (sun, moon, stars) they worshiped. The final word leaves no comfort—death will be better than life for those who survive the Babylonian invasion (8:3).

8:4–10:25

RESPONSES TO THE MESSAGE

True wisdom involves being aware of the health of one's spiritual life and, if necessary, course correcting immediately. Judah hasn't been doing that (8:4–6). The metaphor of the birds knowing their migratory patterns implies again that people—who have much more intimate relationships with God—should know their role with God but do not (8:7).

Not even the ability to literally write down the law of the Lord is immune from corruption (8:8–9). The scribes take out their red markers and trim God's Word to what is acceptable to them. Their pen has changed truth into lies. Others reject God's Word completely. The people are caught in their own trap.

The wives and fields being gone is a reference to the coming exile, when the invaders will take what matters most to the leaders of the nation (8:10). The spiritual leaders are guilty of lying to the people about the gravity of their sins, a lie that should have brought about feelings of guilt and shame (8:11–12). However, the priests and prophets feel no guilt about their misleadings, and it is because of this lack of a repentant heart that God will punish them (8:12).

No harvest is available for the people, which means there are no resources for them (8:13). Being inside a city means protection inside the city walls, but once resources run out or spoil, the people will suffer from starvation and likely die (8:14). Peace is no longer an option, and the invaders from the north are coming as Jeremiah prophesied (8:15–16). In verse 17, God compares the coming destruction to poisonous snakes that can't be charmed—there is no way to resist the fatal strike.

Critical Observation

Chapters 8–10 of Jeremiah include a miscellany of prophecies in no chronological sequence. The key word linking all of the prophecies is *hokma*, which is translated "wisdom." The word *wisdom*, or *wise*, appears nine times in this portion of the text. It refers to the idea of being skilled in an activity. In the context of the kingdom of God, wisdom is the skill of living life rightly and beautifully. The opposite of wisdom is *foolishness*. This word occurs three times in chapter 10. It means brutish, dull-hearted, and unreceptive. Sin and idolatry are the context for this study of wisdom in contrast to foolishness.

In the closing section of chapter 8, Jeremiah grieves over Jerusalem's fate (8:18). Jeremiah laments that his people question God's presence and recalls God's warning about worshiping other gods (8:19). Because of their failure to repent, the people now face inevitable judgment (8:20). Jeremiah believes the people's salvation is within reach, that all they have to do is repent, but they are acting like salvation isn't possible. The metaphor he uses is "balm in Gilead," a reference to medicine from a neighboring town that the people were unable to get (8:21–22). This section closes with a picture of how much pain Jeremiah is in for his people: The weeping prophet wants his eyes to become never-ending streams of tears for their suffering (9:1).

Chapter 9 begins with several verses describing just how depraved Judah has become. Disgusted at the spiritually adulterous people around him, Jeremiah wishes for reprieve from his situation and his people (9:2). God describes His people as so treacherous that no one can rely on anyone, making trust and true community impossible (9:3–6). The only recourse God has is to refine (see 6:27–30) the people because of their deceitfulness and their actions toward one another (9:7–9). The punishment will be so thorough that even nature will mourn, and only jackals—animals that thrive in the wasteland—will be left (9:10–11).

The people of Judah find themselves in this situation because they did not choose wisely. Verses 12–16 highlight characteristics of what would have been the wiser choice for them. The people should have chosen to keep to God's law and listen to His voice instead of worshiping the idols of other nations (9:13–14). Because they chose poorly, they are subjected to bad food and water (9:15; 23:15) and will be destroyed as a community (9:16).

God tells the people to prepare not only the current generation for mourning but also the following generation, because the losses will be so great and continuous (9:17–21). The massiveness of the destruction is seen in the prophecy that corpses will not even be buried, an indicator of how completely incapacitated and humiliated Judah will be—they won't even be able to bury their own dead (9:22).

The theme of wisdom appears again: True wisdom means not trusting in human and earthly resources (9:23). Evidence of following the true God will not be seen in earthly treasures but in loving-kindness, justice, and righteousness (9:24).

Verses 25–26 emphasize God's thoughts about religious actions versus true righteousness; even people who think they are of the true religion (the circumcised) are no better than those who are not, and all will be punished equally (9:25–26).

Critical Observation

The first sixteen verses of chapter 10 are a satirical contrast of God and idols. Such writing is not uncommon to the Old Testament, and the prophet Isaiah often employs similar rhetoric in his writing (Isaiah 44:9–20). Later in the book of Jeremiah, the prophet reiterates verses 12–16 (51:15–19).

True wisdom recognizes the difference between the impotence of idols and the majesty of God (10:1–16). The first part of this section emphasizes how idols are made by people (10:3–5, 8–9, 11, 14–15), but the true God is like no other (10:6–7, 10, 12–13, 16). The words *delusion* (10:3, 8) and *worthless* (10:15) are the same word that is used in 2:5. The word means vanity, emptiness, vapor, nothingness.

Chapter 10 closes with a lament about the coming destruction of Jerusalem. The prophecy describes the people as having bundles, warning them to be prepared to leave because the exile is at hand (10:17). The last four verses in this chapter show Jeremiah's distress, but he uses the language of nomadic shepherds to indicate that he speaks of the pain of loss of civilization and community for all the people of Judah (10:19–21).

The judgment is coming from the north as prophesied (10:22), and the judgment is a necessary action from God to restore righteousness to His people (10:23–25).

Take It Home

Chapter 10 closes with Jeremiah's prayer that God will pour out His wrath on all of the people of Judah. Jeremiah no longer seeks God's mercy and forgiveness for the people, because the prophet knows that the people have regressed so far into their sin that they deserve the punishment of God's justice.

JEREMIAH 11:1–13:27

JUDAH'S BREAKING OF GOD'S COVENANT

Setting Up the Section

Chapters 11–13 of Jeremiah detail the consequences in store for Judah as a result of having broken God's covenant. The covenant being referred to is the Mosaic Covenant, in which God promised to bless the Israelites if they obeyed Him. Their idolatry is a severe disobedience and breach of the covenant. This section also includes two of Jeremiah's laments about the gravity of the nation's sin and God's pending judgment.

11:1–12:17

JEREMIAH DIALOGUES WITH GOD

Jeremiah communicates to the people that they have broken the covenant between them and God that was made with Moses on Mount Sinai. This covenant was to be foundational to the people and dependent upon them hearing and obeying the words of the true God (11:1–8). Instead, they have chosen to follow other gods, and their punishment is now inescapable (11:9–11). God predicts that the people will not find refuge from this destruction in Him and will thus turn to the idols for help (11:12). Verse 13 helps the listener understand how pervasive this idol worship had become (11:13; see 3:24). God insists that the people are so far gone in their sin that having Jeremiah pray for them or performing rituals in the temple will not restore the people's hearts (11:14–15). Jeremiah had previously likened Judah's state to a diseased or wide vine that emerged from a healthy or chosen vine, and that image is revisited here. In this case, the formerly productive tree will be burned down in judgment (11:16–17).

Critical Observation

In verse 16, Jeremiah reminds the people that God had called Judah to be "a thriving olive tree with fruit beautiful in form" (NIV). The psalmist also likens God's chosen people to an olive tree (Psalm 52:8–9). For the psalmist, such imagery describes total trust in and worship of God, which is what God desires from His people.

Throughout the book of Jeremiah thus far, the listener has heard Jeremiah's emotional and spiritual anguish over the condition of his people, but this is the first time the listener understands the physical danger Jeremiah is in because of his prophecies. Jeremiah knows of this danger because God reveals it to him (11:18). The tree in verse 19 refers to Jeremiah, and the fruit is the prophetic message he delivers. The people want Jeremiah dead so that they don't have to listen to his warnings any longer. Jeremiah asks God for justice, since he is working on God's behalf (11:20). God reassures Jeremiah, but not before it is revealed that these plotters are from Jeremiah's own hometown, which means that the plotters are possibly family members or priests (11:21–23).

Demystifying Jeremiah

God responds to Jeremiah's plea for protection from his enemies by declaring that He (God) will punish them. The punishment God declares is death by the sword to the young men and famine to the harassers' children (11:22). By killing their descendents, God makes sure no one will remember Jeremiah's enemies, just as the enemies want to make sure no one remembers the prophet.

Jeremiah hears God's reassurance, but he has more to say to God and more questions for Him. Through prayer, the prophet enters God's metaphorical courtroom, carrying a complaint against God. Desiring to plead his case and discuss matters of justice, he appeals to God's righteous and just character (12:1). Jeremiah's statements here capture age-old feelings and questions: Why do good things happen to bad people (12:2)? *Prosper* means to succeed, to be able to accomplish what is intended. *At ease* means to be secure, unconcerned, undisturbed, carefree, and at rest. It is disturbing to Jeremiah that these people are wicked and yet successful. And because God withholds any sense of justice, they are allowed to grow and even produce fruit. Jeremiah argues that their success is no accident.

But there is also an implied corollary complaint. Why is God allowing this to happen to people who love Him? Not only is Jeremiah outraged that the wicked prosper, but he can't understand why righteous people like him are suffering. He argues that God's name is on the lips of the wicked but is far from their minds. The wicked believe God is indifferent, meaning they can get away with their evil ways because He will not see what they actually do. Jeremiah reminds God that he is doing everything that is expected of him and that God knows and sees that this is true. The prophet wonders why there are not more signs of blessing in his life. It seems the scales of justice are out of balance (12:3–4).

God's first response indicates that things will get worse for Jeremiah before they get better (12:5–6). Second, God says to consider His grief (12:7–13). God laments over His people, His inheritance. Judah roared at God like a lion (12:8). She became like a speckled bird of prey whose plumage attracted the jealousy of other nations (12:9). The shepherds of Judah—the invading army—ruined God's vineyard (12:10). God's gift of a land flowing with milk and honey became desolate, and no one cared (12:11). So God has no choice. He forsakes and abandons Judah in the same way that she has forsaken Him (12:7). God gives His people over to their enemy (12:12–13; 46:6–7). In the midst of Jeremiah's confusion and anger, God is saying, "Have you ever thought about how I feel?" The words *my* and *me* are repeated a dozen times. Jeremiah's tragedy is God's tragedy in miniature. Jeremiah's rejection by his family parallels the nation's rejection of God.

Third, God tells Jeremiah to consider the extended view (12:14–17). *Uproot* is the key word (used five times) in these verses (12:14–15, 17). The word describes a plant being pulled out of the ground. It takes us back to God's mission statement to Jeremiah (1:10). God says that He will take care of every nation in its turn (12:16–17). He will uproot Judah and all of her enemies—Syria, Ammon, Moab, even Babylon. Then God will show compassion and bring Judah back. Not only will He have compassion on Judah, but He will have compassion on all the other nations and bring back each to His inheritance and to His land. If these former enemies who led Judah into idolatry learn the ways of God, then God will build them up. But if they do not listen, they will be destroyed. Every nation will be treated just like Judah.

13:1–27

THE WARNINGS BEGIN

First, Jeremiah is commanded to buy a belt—or waistcloth, waistband (13:1). The linen belt was an intimate piece of apparel that clung closely to the body of the wearer and served as a thigh-length underskirt. Jeremiah obeys and puts the article of clothing around his waist (13:2). Second, Jeremiah is commanded to go to the Euphrates and hide the belt in the crevice of a rock (13:3–4). This would have meant a very long journey for Jeremiah, and the people of Judah may have been aware of his actions. In any case, Jeremiah obeys the Word of God (13:5). Third, Jeremiah is commanded to retrieve the belt (13:6). Once again he obeys, only to find that the belt is ruined (13:7). It is totally worthless and useless and no longer fits to accomplish its intended purpose.

Critical Observation

The *linen belt* in verses 1–11 is the first of several symbols and acts Jeremiah uses as a tangible way to portray God's message. There is a loose structure to the description of Jeremiah's symbolic act. The Lord issues three commands to Jeremiah, and after each command Jeremiah acts in obedience to what he is told. Following the three commands, there are three statements from God, which match the three commands, in reverse order.

The belt is a spiritual symbol of Judah's relationship to God. God gives a word that matches each action in reverse order. First, God says He will destroy the pride of Judah and Jerusalem in the same way the belt was destroyed.

The words *ruin* and *destroy* (13:7, 9) are the same. Second, God points out the reason for Judah's destruction: She refuses to listen to His Word. The people "follow the stubbornness of their hearts" (13:10 NIV). This is a favorite phrase of Jeremiah to describe the sin of Judah—he uses it eight times in this book. The people had ignored and neglected their relationship with God in the same way that Jeremiah had neglected the belt, and the people of Judah had hidden themselves from God in the same way that Jeremiah had hidden the belt. Third, God says that His original intent for Judah is that His people cling to Him in the same way that a belt clings to a man's waist (13:11). This last statement in verse 11 matches Jeremiah's first action in verse 2. The word *cling*, meaning to adhere or be glued together, describes the kind of dependent relationship that God intends His people to have with Him (see Genesis 2:24).

Verses 12–14 tell a parable of wine jars. There are several references to wine in the book of Jeremiah. The wine jar (or wineskin) referred to here is a large earthenware container, and it symbolizes the people of Judah (13:12). These jars are to be filled with wine, but God adds a twist: The inhabitants of Judah will be filled not with wine, but with drunkenness, which is symbolic of their addiction to idolatry (13:13). In the coming time of crisis, the inhabitants of Judah will be so inebriated by their sin that they will destroy one another like wine jars that collide and break, and God will not intervene to stop them (13:14).

Verses 15–17 are a warning against arrogance. It is impossible to miss the imagery of verse 16: darkness, dusk, deep darkness, and gloom. The figure of dusky mountains can refer to either twilight or dawn and of travelers on a mountain path overtaken by the gathering gloom before reaching their destination. *Deep darkness* refers to overwhelming darkness or grief. *Gloom* speaks of heavy clouds or thick darkness. The increasing darkness is a metaphor for the judgment coming upon Judah for her pride and haughtiness. The exhortation is that the light is fading, but there is still hope if Judah will listen to God. Exalting God and giving Him glory will dispel the darkness. Notice the agony of the poet in 13:17. If Judah doesn't listen, Jeremiah will be overcome with grief.

Demystifying Jeremiah

The king of verse 18 is King Jehoiachin of Judah, mentioned several times elsewhere in conjunction with the queen mother Nehushta. Jeremiah prophesies events in the year 597 BC, when Jehoiachin and Nehushta are banished into Babylonian exile with the first group of Jews.

The king and queen mother are commanded to take a low seat because their beautiful crown has been removed (13:18). They are used to privilege, but will become exiles. They might seek refuge, but Jeremiah warns that all the cities of the Negev, the area to the south of Jerusalem, are barricaded so that fleeing fugitives will not be able to find a place to hide (13:19). Dethroned kingship is a metaphor for judgment. God opposes the proud: Those who exalt themselves will be brought down. No one is exempt from the Lord's hand of judgment and discipline, which is coming from the north as prophesied (13:20).

The final picture is a lament over the disgrace to come upon Jerusalem (13:21–27). The judgment will come by the hands of the Babylonians, the very people whom Judah courted as companions, and it will be painful, like the pains of labor (13:21). In the midst of their sin, the people have forgotten God and resorted to falsehood (13:22). And worst of all, they have no hope of change. Judah can no more change its evil ways than the Ethiopian the color of his skin or the leopard its spots (13:23). Babylon will scatter the people like straw in the wind, a reference to exile, because of their behavior (13:24, 26–27).

Take It Home

Not even Jeremiah's warnings of captivity by an intruder and exile to a foreign nation can motivate the people of Judah to repent of their sins and return to worshiping Yahweh alone. Even though verse 23 records God's words that the people are beyond hope to change, the fact that Jeremiah continues to prophesy, in this case, means they still have the opportunity to repent. As the book continues, however, it becomes increasingly evident that the people do not intend to change.

JEREMIAH 14:1–20:18

GOD'S WARNINGS

Setting Up the Section

The next section of Jeremiah begins with a detailed prophecy of the drought and famine that will accompany the coming invasions. From there, it moves into a series of confessions from Jeremiah about his personal hardships as they relate to his ministry among the people of Judah, followed by another section of metaphors symbolizing the nation's relationship with God. This section ends with an example of the persecution Jeremiah faces because of the message he delivers. Interspersed throughout are additional warnings against Judah's idolatry and their need to repent to avoid the coming judgment.

14:1–15:9

WARNINGS AND RESPONSE

A drought will come over Judah that is so powerful that all classes of people, all animals, and even the earth will be affected and cry out in anguish (14:1–6). Jeremiah connects this drought to God's judgment and intercedes with God on behalf of the people, appealing to his own sense of justice despite the nation's sinful ways, asking God not to forsake them (14:7–9). God rejects Jeremiah's plea, citing the people's consequences for their own wandering feet. Although they may be feeling pain and remorse now, based on their history it is likely they will wander away again (14:10).

God tells Jeremiah to stop interceding for the people, because by this point no amount of intercession or sacrifice will change God's mind about the judgment due the nation (14:11–12). Jeremiah points out that other prophets are testifying to the people about peace and being spared, but God calls them false and insists that both the false prophets and the people listening to them will face His justice (14:13–16).

God and Jeremiah continue to dialogue for several verses about Judah's situation. Jeremiah again weeps over the physical and spiritual state of the nation (14:17). His tears represent the hopelessness of the people of Judah if they don't repent of their sins. Death is all around Jeremiah, both in cities and in the country as a result of the famine and the diseases that accompany it (14:18). Seeing the death and destruction around him, Jeremiah questions God's rejection of the nation (14:19). Jeremiah confesses the sins of the nation and pleads with God that He not forget the covenant He made with their ancestors (14:20–21). In the midst of pleading with God, Jeremiah admits that God alone controls creation and has the power to make it rain; the false idols the people worship can do nothing to remedy the situation (14:22).

God's wrath continues to burn against the nation of Judah. Even though Jeremiah's generation attempts to repent, God's justice requires that the flagrant sins of past generations be vindicated. Perhaps Moses, who interceded for the nation at the giving of the law—can appeal to God for mercy. Or Samuel, who interceded for Israel as they cried for a king. But God knew that the repentant words from Jeremiah were no match for the hearts of the people, and He says neither Moses nor Samuel can make Him change His mind (15:1). Verse 2 describes the four different judgments that people will face: death, the sword, famine, and captivity. Then verse 3 lists the four different destroyers that will bring about this judgment: the sword, dogs, birds, and beasts. Judah will not avoid God's discipline and will become an object of horror and a symbol of God's wrath among the nations (15:4). Though God holds us all accountable for our actions, the Bible consistently claims that teachers and leaders are to be more accountable. In the case of Manasseh, the son of King Hezekiah, his evil exceeds even that of the nations that God appointed to destroy (15:4–6).

Critical Observation

The reign of King Manasseh, and the evilness he orchestrates and allows, is described in 2 Kings 21:1–16. Manasseh is described as being the most corrupt king of Judah, which is ironic considering he was the son of one of the most righteous—King Hezekiah. Verse 4 implies that the nation continues to follow in Manasseh's evil ways long after his reign. As the perpetrator of the people's wickedness, Manasseh is responsible for God's coming judgment.

The winnowing fork (15:7) was a primitive pitchfork used to scoop up the harvest and pitch it into the air, allowing the wind to blow away the lighter chaff while the heavier wheat remained. In this case, the winnowing fork has a dual purpose of separating the ungodly and inflicting death. God threatens to make widows as numerous as the sands of the sea (15:8). The reference to a widow of seven sons is likely a symbolic reference to the city of Jerusalem itself, a proud reference to the past glory of the nation of Israel (15:9). The glory of the nation is soon to be destroyed, as God does not relent in His quest to punish His beloved.

15:10–17:27

GOD DIALOGUES WITH JEREMIAH

Jeremiah is perplexed by Israel's condemnation of him. In spite of the fact that he is not a lender or a borrower, he is deemed to be a contentious leader; he pities his own mother for giving birth to one who has become such a curse upon the name of Israel (15:10). But God speaks words of comfort (15:11). God's reference to iron and bronze from the north is symbolic of the prophetic sweep of force by Nebuchadnezzar's armies as they converged upon Jerusalem to steal away Israel's dreams of glory (15:12). As with any domination of one nation over another, the buildings are leveled and the temple is destroyed. The people are humiliated and carried off to Babylon to serve their new king and his many pagan gods (15:13–14).

Verses 15–21 of Jeremiah's lament can be divided into four parts: address, petition, statement of innocence, and complaint. Jeremiah begins with an address to God (15:15). Although his words can seem to be words of trust, given his distress at his current situation it is more likely that they are a statement of reproach. Jeremiah claims that God knows what is happening to him but isn't doing anything about it. The prophet cannot believe that God is allowing him to suffer even though he is innocent.

Jeremiah's petition consists of four imperatives: remember, take notice, take vengeance, and do not take away (15:15). He is not asking for revenge but for justice and lawfulness. Expressing his anxiety about death, he fears being taken away. He tells God not to be too patient, too slow to anger. He wants God to unleash His judgment against Judah right away. Second, Jeremiah reminds God that he has filled his stomach with God's words (15:16). He is probably referring to the discovery of the law in the temple during Josiah's reign. When God's Word was found, Jeremiah devoured it. He is satisfied with God's Word in the same way we are satisfied by a delicious meal. But now, being called by God's name is like swallowing a bitter pill.

Third, Jeremiah reminds God that he has not gone the way of the crowd (15:17). Literally, he doesn't sit in the secret counsel of the partygoers. He sits alone because God's hand is upon him. He is filled with anger at the sin of Judah and perhaps his own afflictions. Finally the prophet issues his complaint and voices the deepest emotions of his soul (15:18). The prophet's pain is without end. Similar statements are often used in conjunction with sin and ensuing judgment. Sickness follows sin. But Jeremiah's pain prompts him to ask another penetrating question: "Will you be to me like a deceptive brook, like a spring that fails?" (15:18 NIV). Jeremiah paints a picture of a dried-up creek that fills with water only when it rains. In chapter 2, Jeremiah says that God is a fountain of living water, but that living water seems to have quit flowing. God no longer seems reliable to Jeremiah, whose focus has shifted off of the wicked nation and onto his own suffering. Jeremiah wonders if God has lied to him when He promised to be with him during his ministry. He is claiming that God is the cause of his misery.

What does God have to say to Jeremiah? Before He gives an encouraging word, He gives a bracing word (15:19). The first part of God's reply is a condition. God tells Jeremiah that he must repent of his attitude. In effect, God asks Jeremiah to do the same thing that Jeremiah is urging upon the people of Judah. The prophet is pouring out his heart to God, but his words are tinged with self-pity and blame. God tells him to turn away from that. God wants Jeremiah to be faithful to his calling. To "extract the precious from the worthless" (15:19 NASB) refers back to chapter 6, when God tells the prophet to be an assayer and remove the dross of idolatry from the precious metals. The second part of God's response is more reassuring (15:20–21). These words reiterate what God tells Jeremiah in chapter 1, when Jeremiah was a young boy. God reaffirms that He is with him. Three powerful verbs—save, deliver, and redeem—describe God's presence. God is reliable and will stand by His messenger.

Demystifying Jeremiah

Verses 16:1–9 include another object lesson in which Jeremiah's life situation mimics the state of the nation. God uses Jeremiah's call to celibacy and bachelorhood as a picture of the relationship that is ending between God and the people, and the sorrow and loneliness that the people will soon experience.

Chapter 16 opens with the instructions that Jeremiah is not to marry or have children (16:1–2). Not only has God promised to sentence the people to lives of captivity in another land, but He also prophesies horrible deaths that many will face (16:3–5). Those who die, both great and small, will be left in the streets to be scavenged by the vultures in the air and the roaming beasts on the ground (16:6).

Families will not be allowed to honor the dead. The days of children playing and villages celebrating are long gone. In God's judgment, He is going to take from Israel its voice of gladness (16:8–9). By obeying God's instruction to avoid participating in mourning or in celebratory events, Jeremiah's life is a model for the people of how God feels toward them.

God prepares Jeremiah for the questions he will field in response to the gravity of his message (16:10). His answer is to be that Israel's forefathers forsook Him and turned to wooden idols. But the idolatry didn't stop with their ancestors; the people are also guilty of their own sins (16:11–12). God prophesies to them that they will be cast out of their sacred promised land, a land they have now inhabited for almost a thousand years (16:13). At each Passover meal, they speak of how God delivered them from Egypt into the land of milk and honey. Now, their history will be modified to say that God also delivered them from the lands of the north (16:14–15). Despite their sins, He will once again show them mercy. But that is in the distant future. First, they must pay the price for their wickedness, and the price has doubled: They now must pay the penalty for their forefathers and for their own iniquities (16:16–18).

The coming judgment is again offset by the promise of hope, restoration, and future blessing. Jeremiah prophesies a season when people from all nations will return to God, realize the absurdity of their idolatrous practices, and recognize God's power and might (16:19–21).

The next section, 17:1–18, is a continuation of the theme of Judah's sin and guilt as recounted in chapter 16. In Jeremiah 17, readers encounter the word *heart* four times, beginning in 17:1, when God insists Judah's sins are written clearly and permanently on their hearts. This sin is also written on items of their idolatrous worship (17:1–3). Again it is prophesied that punishment through exile and slavery is forthcoming (17:4).

Verses 5–8 set out a remarkable contrast between the person who places his or her trust in people and the person who trusts in God. Those who trust in human flesh and human strength are cursed (17:5–6). These words are addressed primarily to the people of the covenant. At the time, the nation was surrounded by superpowers—Egypt, Assyria, and the rising Babylon. Judah kept trying to make alliances with these nations, especially Egypt, to achieve national security. But God warns that the person who trusts in the strength and power of mankind and whose heart turns away from God will be cursed.

Such an individual will lead a dry, lonely, isolated, withered life. This is revealed in the three metaphors in verse 6: a bush in the desert, stony wastes in the wilderness, and a land of salt without inhabitants.

On the contrary, the one who trusts in God is wise and will see benefit from that trust. People who trust in the Lord turn their hearts toward Him. They not only trust *in* the Lord; their trust *is* the Lord. The curse of verse 5 is contrasted with blessing (17:7). The person who trusts in the Lord and turns his heart toward God will be like a tree that will always have a supply of water (17:8). He will not fear when the heat comes; he will not be anxious in times of drought. The leaves of this tree will be green and healthy. It will bear fruit and yield a blessing to others.

Critical Observation

The tree of verse 8 is in contrast to the desert shrub of verse 6. One is destined for life, the other for death. One has a root system that brings nourishment, the other does not. One has adequate water, the other does not. One sees the good, the other does not. One has no fear or anxiety, the other is always desperate. Those who place their trust in mankind to find security will find their source of comfort lacking. The only way to avoid these things is to trust completely in the Lord.

Misplaced trust is symptomatic of a deeper problem, the source of which God reveals in the next verses. The human heart is naturally bent toward sin, and it is the root of not only misplaced trust but every other way in which people sin against God (17:9). While people may not be able to discern why their hearts produce the type of deceit they do, God can discern and will judge according to the state of one's heart (17:10). The proverb of verse 11 is a reminder to all who hear it that coming upon wealth by unjust means does not earn the favor or blessing of God.

In 17:12–13 we are reminded of Jeremiah 2:13. God's throne is His place of honor. In the sanctuary, people worship and draw near to Him. He is the source of blessing, hope, and life. He alone has living water. But the people of Judah are deceitful. They turn away from God to place their trust in human resources, forsaking the fountain of living water. Their hearts therefore become dry and hard.

Jeremiah reflects on the condition of his own heart and makes his petition to God (17:14–18). He realizes that he needs God's help to cure his heart and deliver him from his sins (17:14). The people of Judah are coming to Jeremiah with questions about why the things he has prophesied have yet to come true (17:15). But Jeremiah knows that his prophecies are valid because they are not self-serving, and he has not shied away from proclaiming the Word of God (17:16). Although Jeremiah's trust in God wavers at times, in these verses he displays complete trust that God will not turn away from him (17:17). He also prays that God will act justly on his persecutors but keep him from harm (17:18).

In 17:19–27, Jeremiah delivers a sermon about the importance of keeping the Sabbath. Notice the repeated mention of the word *gate* in this passage. The public gate is the entryway into the city (17:19–20). It is from one of the gates to the city that Jeremiah preaches against breaking the Sabbath. The people have forgotten the Sabbath and are carrying on with their daily and weekly activities (17:21–23).

Notice the essence of God's instruction: If the people obey the Sabbath and cease their activities in order to honor God, then He will continue the Davidic reign and Jerusalem's strength as a city (17:24–26). But if the people refuse to obey this command and continue working on the Sabbath, then God will kindle a fire at the very gates of the city, and the palaces of Jerusalem will be destroyed (17:24–27). God uses the Babylonians to fulfill this promise to Jeremiah's generation.

18:1–19:15

METAPHORS

God takes Jeremiah to the potter's house for His next message (18:1–2). Jeremiah observes the potter spinning a pot on the wheel, but then the craftsman takes the clay and crushes it and begins again (18:3–4). It is obvious that something isn't right with the pot; it has a design defect of some kind. However, the potter doesn't throw out the clay; he makes it into another vessel, working the lump until it meets his specifications. Most pots require several attempts before the potter is pleased. The meaning behind this scene at the potter's house is obvious to Jeremiah: God is the potter, and the house of Israel is the clay, but the clay has become spoiled through idolatry and sin (18:5–6). The people of Judah have forsaken God to pursue worthless and empty idols. As a result, the pot is not turning out the way God had intended. It has spiritual flaws and character defects. So He will crush the clay and begin again, remolding and reshaping His people.

God speaks a word of judgment on Judah in verses 7–12. God informs the people of Judah that their response is very important in determining His actions. While He may plan to destroy a nation, if that nation repents, He will relent or possibly change His mind (18:7–8). Likewise, if God plans on doing good to a nation but that nation does evil, then God will send judgment instead of blessing (18:9–10).

God informs Judah that He is planning on calamity, but His exhortation is to repent—it is not too late to change God's course of action (18:11). Sadly, the people of Judah have no intention of changing their evil ways (18:12). They want to follow their own plans and are unwilling to turn from the stubbornness of their evil hearts.

God continues speaking through Jeremiah, asking the people rhetorical questions and making statements reminiscent of chapter 2. God asks how His people could have forgotten their true identity, but He also laments that they have done so by worshiping idols and other gods (18:13–15). He will leave them to endure His absence during their judgment (18:16–17).

The people attempt to discredit Jeremiah's message from God and plot to kill him (18:18). Although the threat is only verbal, Jeremiah has had enough. The lament that ends this chapter is different from the previous ones (see 11:18–23; 15:10–21; 17:14–18). Jeremiah had interceded for the people before, but this time he asks God to do justice, honor His loyalty, and punish the people (18:19–23).

The metaphor of the potter and the clay resumes with God having Jeremiah buy a piece of pottery (19:1). The first several verses of chapter 19 again illustrate the people's idolatrous sins against God and the judgment that God will enact as punishment (19:2–9). After these reminders of the message God has sent through Jeremiah, God has

Jeremiah go out in front of the elders and some senior priests and break the pottery he purchased (19:10). Judah has become so hardened there is nothing left for God to do but to break the pot (19:11–15). A spoiled vessel can be reshaped on the potter's wheel (18:1–6), but once it becomes hardened it is beyond reconstruction and is fit only for breaking. Jeremiah's act is a sign proclaiming that just as he broke the pot, so God will destroy Jerusalem and its inhabitants.

20:1–18

PERSECUTION OF JEREMIAH

Jeremiah's prophecy in 19:1–15 foretells a grave future for the people of Judah. When one of the religious leaders, Pashhur, hears what Jeremiah has said, he has Jeremiah physically abused (20:1–2). Upon his release, Jeremiah renames Pashhur *Magor-missabib*, which means "terror on every side," an indicator of how Judah will soon be surrounded by Babylonian invaders (20:3–6). Jeremiah's message from God is clear: Because the religious leaders no longer recognize the words of the true God, judgment will come harshly and completely.

Verses 7–18 of chapter 20 include another of Jeremiah's laments to God. The cost to Jeremiah for his boldness is great, and his confidence gives way to despair.

Verses 7–10 set out Jeremiah's complaint. On one level, he complains about his unjust treatment. He is the object of public ridicule, a laughingstock. He is mocked, and his obedience has resulted in reproach and derision all day long (20:7–8).

Jeremiah trusts God, but in these verses he admits feeling like God has taken advantage of him. The prophet feels he is in a no-win situation. If he speaks God's word of judgment, he is the object of mockery, ridicule, and hostility. If he doesn't speak, then God's Word is like a burning fire in his body that he is unable to contain (20:9).

The remainder of this chapter includes an assertion of trust, a petition, and a doxology (20:11–18), though it ends with a surprising twist. Jeremiah feels God's presence, its meaning for his survival, and the success of God's mission through him (20:11–12). Verses 11–12 are a genuine assertion of trust, but they are also an attempt to motivate God. Jeremiah asks God to be God and be just (20:12). In asking God to take care of his enemies, Jeremiah seeks from God the very vengeance his enemies seek for him. He feels that he has proven his case and that God should act accordingly.

Critical Observation

The key word in verses 7–12 (used four times) is *prevail*, which means "to overcome." In verse 7, God prevails over Jeremiah. In verse 9, Jeremiah cannot prevail in holding in God's Word. In verse 10, Jeremiah's enemies are looking to prevail. But in verse 11, it is determined that Jeremiah's enemies will *not* be able to prevail.

Jeremiah's lamenting is broken for a moment by a doxology (20:13). The prophet gives way to praise and breaks into song. How can Jeremiah sing in the midst of his afflictions? Jeremiah states that he sings because God delivers the soul of the *needy* one. This word is used to describe the destitute, the day laborers of the ancient world who were completely dependent on others for their survival. What is delivered is the needy soul, not the needy body. In the midst of afflictions people must depend on God.

The odd juxtaposition of texts is intriguing. One would expect the lament to end with the doxology, but it continues and intensifies in 20:14–18. This represents the tension of the life of faith. The themes of lament and praise do not cancel each other out; both are honest emotions. Jeremiah had previously complained about his unjust treatment from people and his unfair treatment from God. But here, in a cry of hopelessness and futility, he complains about his very existence. He wishes he had never been born. He begins verse 14 with a curse, which is not addressed to God or to anyone in particular. It is a curse for the day he was born and the man who brought the news of his birth (20:15). He wishes there had been no announcement and no celebration. As he has been rejected as a messenger of God's Word, so he would reject this messenger (20:16). He wishes that this messenger would suffer the agony of God's wrath, like the inhabitants of Sodom and Gomorrah, because he did not kill Jeremiah in the womb (20:17). He wishes that the womb had been his grave (20:18).

Take It Home

The reason Jeremiah laments so deeply lies in the question of verse 18: Why was I ever born if all I experience is trouble and sorrow? What a contrast to God's statement to Jeremiah in his youth, when He promised He knew Jeremiah in his mother's womb (1:5). At one time Jeremiah had hope, purpose, and direction, but his life has become a series of afflictions. Sorrow is the only thing he knows.

JEREMIAH 21:1–25:38

MESSAGES ABOUT LEADERS AND CAPTIVITY

Kings	21:1–23:8
Prophets	23:9–40
Captivity	24:1–25:38

Setting Up the Section

Previously in the book of Jeremiah, the prophet delivered a series of prophecies detailing the future judgment by God on the nation of Judah. In chapter 21, Jeremiah transitions into more specific prophecies directed at Judah's kings and spiritual leaders. This section of prophecies culminates in the prophecy of the seventy years of Babylonian captivity (Jeremiah 25).

21:1–23:8

KINGS

Chapters 21 through the beginning of 23 address the corrupt kings of Judah and pronounce the judgment that all will suffer because of their ungodly rule. These oracles detail some of God's qualities necessary for right leadership.

Critical Observation

The following is a brief review of Judah's kings during Jeremiah's prophetic reign. King Josiah began his reign over Judah in 640 BC, when he was only eight years old. His rule ended in 609 BC, following his death in a battle with the Egyptians. During this great king's reign, a part of the law was found in the temple, and Josiah led a reform movement to encourage his people to turn back to God. Josiah and Jeremiah, partners in this endeavor, sought to restore true worship in Judah. Following the death of Josiah, things quickly deteriorated. Prior to the fall of Jerusalem, Josiah was succeeded by four kings: Jehoahaz, Jehoiakim, Jehoiachin, and Zedekiah. However, none of these kings sought the Lord with all their heart. Zedekiah was installed as a puppet king by Nebuchadnezzar, king of Babylon, in 597 BC. Zedekiah continually tried to overthrow the rule of Babylon, leading to the destruction of Jerusalem in 587 BC.

With Babylon threatening, Zedekiah sends a messenger to Jeremiah in hopes of a word from the Lord that will give him assurance and confidence against Nebuchadnezzar (21:1–2). Instead, he receives a word of judgment: The God who did wonderful things for Israel in the Exodus will now stand against the nation (21:3–6). Furthermore, Nebuchadnezzar will kill Zedekiah and the rest of the war's survivors (21:7). It will be up to the people whether they stay in the city and die or are exiled to Babylon to live (21:8–9). God makes

His plan for Jerusalem and its inhabitants clear—it will be overtaken by the enemy and burned (21:10). Following the word of judgment there is an exhortation for the king (21:11–14). The king is supposed to uphold justice and righteousness and the rights of the poor, the needy, and the afflicted. He is to uphold the integrity of the court system so that innocent blood will not be shed.

God sends Jeremiah directly to the palace to deliver clear directions to the nation's leaders: dispense justice and righteousness and care for the socially weak and powerless (22:1–3). The king's conduct is decisive for the wealth or woe of the entire social system. If he acts according to God's command, then his royal power will be guaranteed (22:4). If he fails to do so, the house of David will be terminated (22:5).

God contrasts two images to explain the result of both following His instructions and choosing to disobey them. The kingdom will be plush and fertile if the leaders obey, or it will be like a desert if they do not (22:6–7). The result depends on what the leaders choose to do (22:8–9). But the royal house forsakes God's covenant, and a description of the judgment to come follows in the text.

The first king to succeed Josiah is his son Jehoahaz, but his reign lasts only three short months before he is exiled to Egypt (22:10–12). The second king to follow Josiah is Jehoiakim, another of his sons (22:13–19). Jehoiakim fights against Babylon and enters into a dangerous political exploitation that evokes the anger of that nation. His chief sin is conducting his business without justice and righteousness (22:13, 17). He uses people and exploits the poor to surround himself with comfort and luxury (22:14). Jeremiah contrasts him with his father Josiah, who was just and righteous (22:15–16). After his death, Jehoiakim will be treated like a donkey because of his sin (22:18–19). There will be no funeral and no expression of grief or lament (22:19).

The next verses remind listeners of how God has continually tried to reach out to leaders, but they refuse to listen. They prosper and live in comfort (the mention of "cedar" refers to houses made of the finest timber available), but their judgment is forthcoming (22:20–23).

The third king to follow Josiah is Jehoiachin (also called Coniah and Jeconiah), the son of Jehoiakim and grandson of Josiah (22:24–30). Jehoiachin begins his rule in 598 BC, but he is exiled to Babylon in 597, reaping the curse of his father's corrupt politics. God claims that if Jehoiachin was a ring on His hand, He would pull it off, ending the relationship between the two of them and, consequently, the house of David (22:24). Ultimately this separation happens when Jehoiachin is exiled (22:25–26). With his exile, the royal line comes to an end and the land is forfeited (22:26–29). Although Jehoiachin has several sons, he might as well have been childless since none of his descendants will succeed him as king (22:30). These four kings not only forsake the Lord; they are also guilty of not doing the things they were supposed to do according to the law and the Word of God. These leaders of Judah exalted themselves and exploited their people for their own personal gain.

The leaders of Judah are supposed to care for their people, as a shepherd cares for his flock. However, the kings and other leaders of Jeremiah's day were not good shepherds. Rather, they destroyed and scattered the sheep of God's pasture (10:21; 23:1–2). Their leadership falls to such inappropriate levels that God Himself has to intervene (23:3–4).

Verses 5–6 are a word of hope in the midst of great sorrow: Jeremiah prophesies that God will bring a leader who will exemplify godly leadership and rule in stark contrast to the four kings previously mentioned (23:5–6). In the midst of failure, the Lord makes a promise to Judah: One is coming who will sit on the throne of David and rule with wisdom, justice, and righteousness (23:5). The phrase "a righteous branch" is one that in the Old Testament signals the idea of a Messiah who will fulfill the salvation God intended for His people. The name of this coming king will be *The Lord Our Righteousness*, and under his rule, both the northern and southern kingdoms will prosper in peace and safety (23:6). Future generations will not celebrate God as the One who brought His people out of Egypt—the way God was described previously in Jeremiah—but as the God who restored His people after their destruction by the northern invaders (23:7–8).

23:9–40

PROPHETS

In verse 9 of chapter 23, the focus shifts from the kings to the prophets of Judah, the nation's spiritual leaders. These men occupy a very important position in Israel. They speak in the name of the Lord. As seen in 18:18, Judah's prophets are proclaiming one thing about the spiritual state of the nation, but it conflicts with the words of the Lord that Jeremiah delivered. Jeremiah will be vindicated in time, but in these verses he has a painful message for the brothers who share his vocation: Their bad leadership has fostered immorality in the nation (23:9–10). Both prophet and priest are polluted, literally twisted and defiled, and the holy temple has become the site of sexually oriented fertility rites (23:11). Following other patterns throughout Jeremiah, at the end of this statement of sin, God assures He will judge the false prophets (23:12).

False prophets strengthen the hands of evildoers rather than turn people back from sin (23:13–14). They are more concerned about aligning themselves with people than they are with proclaiming God's truth. The comparison with Samaria in verse 13 is designed to shame the southern prophets. Judah is worse than Samaria because the idolatry of Jerusalem is more shameful than the Baal worship of Samaria. In fact, the evil so repulses God that in His eyes Judah is no different than Sodom and Gomorrah (23:14). God must punish the prophets the same way He said He would in 9:15 (23:15). The sin of the false prophets is so severe because they use God's name to speak a message that is not His (23:16, 25, 30). False prophets draw their messages from their own imaginations, literally, their own hearts. The content of their message is filled with lies and false assurances (23:17).

How are the people to respond to the false prophets? God commands the people to simply not listen to them (23:16). (He also provides criteria for judging the veracity of a prophet in Deuteronomy 13 and 18.) Counterfeit spiritual leaders lead people into futility, into things that are worthless and profitless. They claim authority from God, but they have no authority (23:18–22). The scene in verses 18–22 describes a council meeting that takes place behind closed doors. The false prophet is like a journalist who speculates over some matter of government which is discussed in private. The true prophet is the government spokesman who emerges from the meeting to speak with the ruler's authority. Had the false prophets sat in the council, they would have preached repentance and sought to turn people from their evil ways. Therefore these false prophets have no mission, no message, and no authority. Contrary to what the false prophets teach, God is capable of being both active in the midst of the people to save and protect them, and holy and just in His dealing with sin (23:23–24).

God's response to the false prophets in Judah is clear: He is against all false prophets and anyone who misrepresents what He has said in His Word (23:25). One characteristic of false prophets God points out is that they simply repeat what they hear each other say (23:26–27). False prophets contrast to the Word of the Lord like straw to grain (23:28). The idle dreams and self-induced visions of the false prophets are like straw—they lack substance. But the Word of God is like grain: it has a nourishing quality. The Word of God is powerful, like a refining fire that burns within us. It is also like a sledgehammer that shatters selfish dreams and stubborn hearts (23:29). God wants His people to know His rejection of those who speak falsely in His name (23:30–32).

In the closing verses of chapter 23, God addresses the false prophets' telling of oracles. He reiterates that anyone proclaiming a message in God's name that isn't from God will face His punishment (23:34). With so many people claiming to be delivering oracles from God, no one is able to discern His true message, so God tells Jeremiah to stop using the common phrase, "the oracle of the LORD," in order to discern the true prophets from the false (23:35–37). God's word to Jeremiah concerning the false prophets closes with the assurance that all false prophets will be cast from God's presence in exile and shame (23:38–40).

24:1–25:38

CAPTIVITY

The opening verses of chapter 24 reveal that some captivity has taken place. Sources show that this captivity refers to Nebuchadnezzar taking captives in 597 BC (24:1). Jeremiah sees a new image that serves as a message from God to His people: a basket with good and bad figs (24:2–3). The good figs are the people who have been promised restoration, and the bad figs are the ones who have not (24:4–10). The frightening message the fig image symbolizes is that for some people, even exile and imprisonment will not return them to God.

The fourth year of Jehoiakim is 605 BC (25:1). By this time, Jeremiah has been a prophet for twenty-three years, so many people have had the opportunity to hear him (25:2–3). Jeremiah has been consistent in the prophecies he has delivered against the people's bad behaviors and their worship of false gods, but they still refused to listen (25:4–7). Because of their disobedience, God will send Babylonian forces, led by King Nebuchadnezzar, to invade Jerusalem from the north (25:9). This event is the fulfillment of the invasion Jeremiah has been prophesying about repeatedly throughout the book of Jeremiah. The destruction to the city will be so bad that significant life events, such as marriages and harvests, will cease (25:10).

Verse 11 contains the prophecy that the exile will last for seventy years. After the seventy years of punishment, God will also punish the captors and other nations for the same sins for which Judah is guilty (25:12). Conquering another nation and exploiting their citizens for labor is not just treatment, so even though God uses the invading nations for His purpose, their actions will not go unpunished (25:13–14).

In verses 15–38, God invokes another image to symbolize His judgment of nations other than Judah—a cup filled with God's wrath (25:15). God instructs Jeremiah to take the cup to a list of nations for them to consume (25:15–26). Unlike the clay pots Jeremiah broke in front of Judah's leaders (19:10), this vision most likely symbolizes the message God wants to send the sinful nations. The message of drinking to excess is interesting, almost as if there is a connection between the leaders being unable to control themselves and the punishment that they have brought upon themselves (25:16, 27). God makes it clear, though, that the choice to drink is no longer theirs; because of their past actions, God will force them to drink so that they will face the fullness of His wrath (25:28–29). The next verses depict God roaring and stomping people like grapes and expanding His judgment to all humankind (25:30–32). Again, the destruction will be so great that it will be impossible to bury the dead, much less mourn for them (25:33). This judgment appears to be particularly centered on leaders, those who are shepherding their followers (25:34–36).

Demystifying Jeremiah

In Jeremiah 3:15, God endows Judah with a special gift when He says, "I will give you shepherds after my own heart, who will lead you with knowledge and understanding" (NIV). The shepherds of Jeremiah 25, however, are not the same. These shepherds are the leaders of the offending nations. Beginning with the Egyptian empire and then the Assyrian empire and then the Babylonian empire, these nations surrounded Judah and sought her destruction. God invites humiliation upon these proud, arrogant leaders. Their penalty is watching the Lord destroy the shepherd's pasture—the land, agriculture, and prosperity they sought.

The final two verses of chapter 25 remind people of how dependent they are on God: It is His decision when people experience peace or horror (25:37–38).

Take It Home

Chapter 25 marks the end of Jeremiah's prophetic warnings of God's judgment against the people of Judah, which began in chapter 2. By this point, the Babylonian invasion has taken place, and God's judgment is being poured out on the nation.

JEREMIAH 26:1–29:32

JEREMIAH AND JUDAH DIALOGUE

Setting Up the Section

The central theme of chapters 26–29 is dealing with the false prophets who continue to speak lies in the name of God. The focus shifts from what Jeremiah is proclaiming to how the people react to his prophecies. Jeremiah represents the genuine prophet, and the false prophets are contrasted to him and his message.

26:1–24

JUDAH RESPONDS TO JEREMIAH

God has Jeremiah again take His message to the public and the religious leaders by returning to preach in the temple courtyard (26:1–2). God wants the people to hear and repent and avoid the judgment He will impose if they do not turn away from their sin (26:3). God repeats all the ways He has tried to communicate with His people: through His own voice, through His law, and through prophets He sent again and again (26:4–5). The message here is clear: God wants peace and a relationship with His people, and He will wait until the last resort to punish them back into obedience. If they refuse to listen, then they will endure a fate like a city before them: Shiloh (26:6).

Critical Observation

Shiloh was the first place of worship in the land. This was where the tent of meeting was set up and the inheritance divided. The yearly feast was held there, and the ark of the covenant resided there. Shiloh was where Hannah went to pray for a son and where Eli and his two evil sons, Hophni and Phinehas, were priests. Because of the evil of Hophni and Phinehas and the people who followed them, the Philistines defeated the Israelites, captured the ark, and God's glory departed from Israel. Shiloh lost its significance when the ark of the covenant was captured by the Philistines; and later, the temple there was destroyed (1 Samuel 4:18; Psalm 78:60).

Jeremiah prophesies the same fate for Jerusalem (26:6). Judah possessed the temple, God's dwelling place. But this very temple is destroyed in 587 BC. The second temple is destroyed in AD 70. God's message to His people again and again is that their protection is not bought through religious activity. God will destroy even His most holy places—Shiloh, Jerusalem, Eden—in order to discipline His people and restore His relationship with them.

Verse 7 is powerful in its specificity. The message Jeremiah delivers to them is, in their minds, sacrilegious and insulting, and demands his death (26:8). All who gather—leaders included—agree that Jeremiah should die for his message (26:9–11). Jeremiah responds by saying that their salvation from this prophecy depends on their choice to repent and behave differently, a repeated theme throughout Jeremiah's sermons (26:12–13). But regardless of their choice, Jeremiah insists that the message he speaks is God's, not his own (26:14–15). With this perspective, the people change their minds—leaders included—and acknowledge that Jeremiah does speak on behalf of God (26:16). The elders remind the people of similar prophecies in the past when God demanded they repent or face judgment. Sometimes the people listened and repented (26:17–19), and sometimes they killed the prophet (26:20–23). In this case, the wisdom of the elders prevails. They choose to look at the history of how God has acted in the past, and they decide that repentance is God's wish and message to His people. Jeremiah's life is spared (26:24).

27:1–28:17

JEREMIAH RESPONDS TO JUDAH

In chapter 27, Jeremiah receives another word from the Lord, this time instructing him to speak out against the nations that are planning to fight back against Nebuchadnezzar's invading forces (27:1). Jeremiah's message to the people is this: Get ready to put yourselves into submission. God has Jeremiah use yet another visual aid to symbolize His message, this time, a yoke (27:2). The prophet is commanded to wear a yoke around his neck, similar to the wooden yokes worn by oxen. Jeremiah becomes a walking illustration of the bondage the nations will endure by coming under the yoke of Nebuchadnezzar.

The audience for this message is a group of kings from surrounding nations who are trying to come up with a way to respond to Nebuchadnezzar (27:3). Despite their desire to resist the invasion, God makes it clear that He has orchestrated Nebuchadnezzar's attack and is delivering His people over to Babylon (27:4–8). God again warns against false prophets. Anyone who proclaims the nations will avoid Nebuchadnezzar's rule is lying, and any leader who believes those falsehoods will be completely destroyed (27:9–10). Those who obediently submit to Babylon's yoke will serve Nebuchadnezzar for a time but will survive the period of servitude (27:11).

Jeremiah reiterates God's message to Judah's king Zedekiah, because it is imperative that he hears the true message over the false prophets (27:12). Verses 13–15 repeat the distinction between the messages both sets of prophets are preaching. Jeremiah has the same warning against false prophets for the priests to hear (27:16). Some have been saying that items from the temple seized by the invaders will quickly be restored to the people (27:16–18). These items are valuable—not to mention sacred—and will be scattered in the chaos of invasion and enslavement. However, God declares that even the remaining temple relics will not join the people where they are in exile (27:19–20). Perhaps this separation of the people from their objects associated with God, their holy relics, is part of their discipline and chastisement. The true prophets, God says, will not be worried about what is left behind and where those relics end up; eventually all will be restored to Jerusalem (27:21–22).

Chapter 28 breaks from the prophecies to recount a specific confrontation Jeremiah has with a false prophet by the name of Hananiah (28:1). Hananiah claims to hear God saying the captivity will last only two years instead of seventy, and he speaks specifically about the same two things in Jeremiah's last prophecy: yokes and vessels (28:2–4). However, Hananiah's prophecy directly contradicts Jeremiah's, and Hananiah is sharing it publicly with all the religious leaders (28:1, 5). Jeremiah supports Hananiah graciously, saying he wishes Hananiah's words were true, but they aren't. Jeremiah restates the prophecy he received from God (28:6–9). Hananiah reacts fiercely, taking the yoke off Jeremiah's neck and breaking it (28:10). He is not backing off his false prophecy (28:11). Notice that Jeremiah does not resist, protest, or make a scene. But later, he receives a rebuke from God to pass on to Hananiah. He may have broken the yokes of wood, but his angry outburst has severe consequences: yokes of iron (28:12–13). God insists that Judah's captivity will continue (28:14). Jeremiah condemns Hananiah's prophecy as lies (28:15). He also predicts that Hananiah will die, and his word is fulfilled later that year (28:16–17).

29:1–32

JEREMIAH'S LETTER TO THE CAPTIVES

This segment of the book of Jeremiah ends with what is commonly called "The Letter to the Exiles." The text is a letter Jeremiah composed in Jerusalem and sent to the leaders and the people in exile in Babylon (29:1–3). These are, again, God's words to His people through Jeremiah (29:4). Some have explained this is how Jeremiah instructed the exiled Judeans to live in the midst of their captivity.

God wants His people to make families and become members of their communities, seeking God's will for the city of Babylon and its welfare (29:5–7). Apparently, Babylon has its own fair share of false prophets who claim to speak for God. Like other false prophets, they, too, claim that the exile will not last long, and this perspective causes discontent among the Israelites (29:8–9). Those who believe the captivity will only last two years instead of seventy are only living from day to day and are not making commitments or plans. They don't plant and they don't build.

God's message for them is clear and powerful: The exile will be seventy years, but He has plans to be with them during that time (29.10–11). Although their exile and captivity is a result of their own sinful ways, they still belong to God, and He sends them this word of hope through His prophet. The Israelites will survive their situation, and their relationship with God will be restored, allowing them to once again communicate with Him and hear His voice (29:12–13).

Demystifying Jeremiah

Repeatedly in Jeremiah's earlier sermons, God voices His frustrations that the people of Judah no longer hear their Creator and that they turn to false gods and prophets for guidance and worship. God now tells the people that eventually they will again hear and respond to Him, and He will restore to them everything they lost (29:14). In the midst of God's judgment and punishment, the mercy and redemption He planned for His people is slowly coming into view.

In Babylon, the people are susceptible to false prophets promising them quicker relief from the seventy-year punishment God promised (29:15). God reminds them again not to listen to them. Further, God explains that the people who remain in Judea, who were not taken captive, will still face punishment (29:16–19). The punishment declared for them is familiar: sword, famine, and plague (see 14:12). God names two particular false prophets who are misleading the exiles in Babylon: Zedekiah and Ahab. Jeremiah prophesies that both will die, and the memories of their fate will live on in the lives of the exiles as a reminder of their blasphemy and sin (29:20–23).

Jeremiah writes a letter to the false prophet Shemaiah, as recorded in verses 24–28. Shemaiah had written letters to the people still in Jerusalem and to Zephaniah the priest (29:25). As part of his letter to Zephaniah, he reminded the priest that part of his role included taking prisoner every madman who acts like a prophet (29:26). At the root of Shemaiah's question to the priest is why the prophet Jeremiah has not yet been taken prisoner, since he is continuing to deliver God's messages to the exiles—messages that contradict those of Shemaiah and other false prophets (29:27–28). Zephaniah reads this letter to Jeremiah (29:29).

After he hears Shemaiah's letter, Jeremiah writes to the exiles again, this time delivering God's message of condemnation against Shemaiah for his attack on God's prophet (29:30–31). As punishment for his false prophecies against God, neither Shemaiah nor any of his descendants will live to experience God's mercy and the return from the exile (29:32).

Take It Home

As is evident from chapters 26–29, speaking falsely in the name of the Lord has dire consequences. As part of his role as one of God's true prophets, Jeremiah is tasked with delivering messages of warning not just to the people who sin against God but also to those who lead the people awry.

JEREMIAH 30:1–33:26

THE BOOK OF CONSOLATION

Setting Up the Section

Hundreds of years after enslavement in Egypt, the children of God are once again experiencing captivity in another land. As Judah braces itself for seventy years of anguish, the God of comfort wants His children to know that there is hope. Chapters 30–33 include text that reiterates the hope of a coming day when normal life will return for God's people—Judah and Israel—and they will return to activities like building and planting. While in exile, Judah can read these words and find comfort in the midst of barrenness. This is why Jeremiah 30–33 is often referred to as the Book of Comfort.

30:1–31:26

SOME RESTORED AND SAVED

Two phrases in chapters 29–33 merit close examination. The first is "days are coming" (30:3; 31:27, 31, 38; 33:14–15), and the second is "restore the fortunes" (repeated eight times: 29:14; 30:3, 18; 31:23; 32:44; 33:7, 11, 26). God announces that days are coming and with them the promise of restoration. To restore the fortunes literally means, "to turn the turning." The implication is that everything will be reversed. Restoration is certain. Sin, exile, barrenness, and even the exiles' desire to turn away from God will be reversed. God wants His people to know this is coming and instructs Jeremiah not only to tell the people but also to write the message down (30:1–3).

Immediately following God's proclamation of a coming day when fortunes will be restored, there is a word of judgment (30:4–7). The coming Day of the Lord is a day of both salvation and judgment. It is going to be a day of glory for some but one of dire judgment for others. This is what Jeremiah means by the "time of trouble for Jacob" (30:7 NIV): There will be intense pain, pictured here by a strong man buckled over like a woman in childbirth (30:6). But God's people will be saved; exile in Babylon is not the final chapter of their story. For God's people, judgment precedes salvation.

Several images describe this salvation for Judah. There will be a new freedom from captivity and slavery. The God who put the yoke of Babylon on Judah's neck will remove it (30:8). Instead of worshiping Baal, Judah will serve the Lord her God (30:9). Notice that she will serve David her king as well. Instead of the unrest described in verse 5, there will be a new peace (30:10). A new security will replace the fear and dread of verse 5—the presence and protection of the Lord (30:11). *Discipline* means "to chasten or correct, instilling values and norms of conduct by verbal means or, after the fact, by rebuke or even physical chastisement." God chastens Judah while they are in Babylon, a necessary punishment to cleanse them from their sins.

In verses 12–17, God's character and will for His people is amplified through the metaphor of sickness and healing. Judah's condition is portrayed as an incurable wound or injury (30:12). *Incurable* is the same word that is used to describe the desperately sick heart in 17:9. The prognosis is not good. In human terms, there is no chance of healing and no recovery; no human physician can help cure or even ease the pain (30:13, 15). Judah's lovers have forgotten them, and they have no friends who care (30:14). This is a reference to Egypt, whom Judah sought as an ally to help save them when they should have turned to God. God is the source of the nation's sickness. The reason for His judgment, repeated twice, is clear: Her guilt is great and her sins are numerous (30:15).

God asks the question, "Why do you cry out?" (30:15). By now, God emphasizes, His judgment should not come as a surprise. Judah should have expected to pay a penalty for their sins. But God says He will judge Judah's enemies (30:16). Instead of benefitting from their attack on God's people, they can expect a similar fate. All who devour, enslave, plunder, and prey upon others will be devoured, enslaved, plundered, and given as prey. God's people will be miraculously healed and restored (30:17).

Sickness and healing are metaphors for what happens to God's people in exile. The restoration comes and a miracle occurs—a terminal condition is reversed. Why does God do this? He restores and heals because His name is at stake. In many ways, verses 12–17 parallel verses 4–11. The same principles are reiterated. Judgment and discipline are necessary in the sanctifying process. Sickness is not the end; there will be complete healing. God's goal is salvation, even though it is completely unmerited and undeserved.

Demystifying Jeremiah

Interestingly, the incurable wound inflicted by God in verse 12 is described with the same language Jeremiah uses in his personal lament in chapter 15, when he cries out to God, "Why has my pain been perpetual and my wound incurable, refusing to be healed?" (15:18 NASB). The same words are used to describe the pain of suffering and the horror of judgment. In other words, it doesn't matter whether we are unfaithful like Judah or obedient like Jeremiah; both the experience and the results of what God does in our lives can be exactly the same. He uses our sin or our suffering to draw us to Himself, to show us His deep compassion and commitment, to mold and shape us into what He desires us to be.

The final verses of this chapter reiterate God's power and character. He specifies how He will bring healing. In addition to health, God will also restore community, including civil life and religion (30:17–18). The people, knowing their help comes from the Lord, will express thanksgiving and increase their numbers (30:19). These offspring will serve the true God, and God will protect them (30:20). Instead of being oppressed or invaded, they will be led by one of their own, someone humble enough to be called by God—exactly the opposite of the false prophets God calls out in previous chapters (30:21). Verse 22 references God's original covenant with Abraham (as does the promise of offspring in verse 20). The fulfillment of God's covenant is possible because of the cleansing, refining work God has done for His people. The future tense of the verse is a reminder that God can bring about the same restoration again (30:22). God's people will come to understand that He acts as needed until His purpose is fulfilled (30:24).

The words of hope continue in chapter 31, as God specifies what restoration will look like for the Israelites. Some commentators emphasize the phrasing of this language as signifying a future time. As stated in chapter 30, the people will again know the true God as their God. With God stating that He will be the God of all the families of Israel comes the hope of restoration of all the remnants—both the northern and southern kingdoms—and all those who are scattered in exile. They will be reunited as one family under God (31:1). The first half of this chapter (31:1–22) refers specifically to the northern kingdom, Israel; the next part (31:23–26) refers to the southern kingdom, Judah; and the final verses refer to both (31:27–40).

For Israel, those who survive the Egyptian captivity find God (31:2). His love for them, described in verse 3, is the same as the marriage kind of love He mentions in 2:2. God again describes Israel in marriage terms and promises that she will be returned to a state of celebration and happiness (31:4; see 18:13). Before too long they will again farm and harvest their own land, and regular worship of the true God by all in the community will be restored for the first time since the division of the northern and southern kingdoms (31:5–6).

Verses 7–9 describe a time of great joy. Whereas earlier in the book of Jeremiah God commands people to repent, He now tells them to sing, shout, proclaim, and give praise. After all the messages of woe and punishment, the time for rejoicing has come. The object of that joy and praise is God, and the reason is for the salvation of the remnant of Israel, or Jacob, another name for Israel (31:7). The active, present tense in which Jeremiah speaks God's words is exciting for the people who had suffered for so long. God is bringing Israel back; they will return from every place they have landed during the ravages and consequences of war and exile. And they will be reunited with their brethren, healed, and will bear children together (31:8). Although they were persuaded through their trials, God will nurture and support them with every step toward restoration (31:9).

The restoration will be so whole and permanent that Israel will be able to share the truth of it with other nations as evidence of God's choice to restore His people (31:10). Ultimately, God is the one who controls Israel's fate, not leaders of other nations (31:11). The restoration will last long enough for harvest and bounty (31:12). Civil and family life will return—a powerful indication of healing after the complete collapse of such things earlier in the book (31:13). And remember the religious leaders who lost their way and were specific objects of God's wrath? Even they will be infused with the Spirit of God again (31:14). The healing and restoration will be so complete that the people will be satisfied and have no need to look beyond the true God (31:14).

Critical Observation

Ramah was a town north of Jerusalem, where many of the Israelites saw home for the last time before being deported. The crying of the mother for her children signifies both weeping over lost exiles and the northern kingdom weeping over the loss of some of its tribes (31:15). All those who heard Jeremiah's prophecies—whether they actually lived them out or not—could imagine the torment one would feel in these circumstances.

God has a word for those who weep in despair: Their toil and pain is not in vain. The ones who are lost will return (31:16). Reality seems dire, and truly it is, but God's Word promises restoration and hope (31:17).

The voice shifts in verse 18 to focus on the specific tribe of Ephraim. In these verses, Ephraim acknowledges its former arrogance and present humility (31:18–19). God asks a rhetorical question in 31:20: Does Ephraim still belong to me? This is reminiscent of God's earlier question about Judah: Is she still my wife even though she acts like a harlot? The answer is an emphatic *yes*. God still knows, owns, and yearns for His children, and He will act with mercy toward them (31:20).

The final verses of chapter 31 relate to the northern kingdom, Israel. God is offering wisdom and guidance to His people, encouraging them to remember their journey away from God (31:21). By doing so, Israel can remind both herself and future generations of this critical experience of sin, exile, repentance, and restoration.

Demystifying Jeremiah

Verse 22 generates much conversation among scholars and commentators. One opinion is that "a female will shelter a man" (HCSB) is a prophecy of the coming of Christ's birth to the Virgin Mary. Another understanding is that it is simply a metaphor for the coming time when things are so peaceful that women can protect men—an uncommon view at that time. More likely, however, is the opinion that the image describes a repentant Israel (often described in the feminine) returning to God (the male imagery).

The next four verses (31:23–26) refer to the southern kingdom of Judah, the recipient of the bulk of Jeremiah's prophetic messages. Like Israel, Judah will again worship God in truth in the same place their ancestors did (31:23–24). They will once again be a city of righteousness, and the community of God will be together again. The trials they just endured will not be forgotten, but God will refresh them (31:25). Jeremiah includes a personal note in verse 26: Upon waking from this latest vision, he reports that his sleep is pleasant. This must have been refreshing for the prophet, who had conveyed many heartbreaking messages from God to his own community and endured the harsh responses from the people upon being faced with God's truths.

THE FUTURE

Chapter 31:27–40 records a new message from God to the Israelites concerning their relationship with Him. These verses have since been labeled The New Covenant. Previously in Jeremiah, the prophet explained to the people that keeping religious rituals and attending temple services didn't matter to God if their hearts were disengaged. Relationship and faithfulness—which Jeremiah often describes with marriage language—is what God wants from His people, not sacrifices of animals and burning of incense. The new covenant described in these verses will accomplish what the old covenant could not.

Verse 27 opens with a reminder that just as God allowed calamity to come to Israel and Judah, He will also allow restoration (31:27–28). Furthermore, God does not punish people for the sins of their ancestors; people are only responsible for their own actions (31:29). Generations won't suffer because of what their ancestors have done, but they will suffer for their own sins (31:30).

God established a covenant with the Israelites' ancestors, but He has plans to establish a new one with them (31:31–32). The old covenant centers on the people's obedience to the Mosaic Law. But Jeremiah reveals that God intends to have an even more intimate relationship with the people He brought back from exile. He wants His wisdom and His ways to be a part of the people themselves, so much so that He will write it on their hearts, making it a part of their very being (31:33). The consequence of this new, more intimate way of knowing God is that people will no longer have to rely solely on the intercession of priests, leaders, and prophets to call them to God. All Israelites—regardless of rank or class—can enter into relationship with God on their own volition (31:34).

Critical Observation

Even though the notion of the new covenant is woven throughout the Old Testament, the only time the actual words are stated is here in Jeremiah 31:31. The next time this phrase is used, it comes from the mouth of Jesus, when He speaks to His disciples in the upper room: "And in the same way He took the cup after they had eaten, saying, 'This cup which is poured out for you is the new covenant in My blood' " (Luke 22:20 NASB). The writer of Hebrews further explains how the new covenant accomplishes what the old covenant could not (Hebrews 9).

The first characteristic of the new covenant is a new heart, and thus a new obedience (31:33). The people did not obey the old covenant, and thus their hearts were not changed. With the new covenant, God writes His character on the hearts of His people, using the pen, or influence, of the Holy Spirit. Then, once hearts are transformed, actions follow—God Himself lives through His people.

The second characteristic of the new covenant is the often-repeated promise of God: "I will be their God, and they will be my people" (31:33). The new covenant creates a new community, a restored humanity, and a new way of relating. This is a unique relationship between God and His chosen people, the Israelites. The third characteristic of the new covenant is a new intimacy and access to God (31:34). Under the old covenant, the life of God was mediated through the offices of priests and prophets. This verse will see its fulfillment in Christ's death, when the veil is removed from the entrance to the Holy of Holies (Matthew 27:50–51), giving all who believe a direct relationship with God through Jesus, the Mediator.

The fourth characteristic of the new covenant is a new sense of acceptance and freedom (31:34). Under the old covenant, the sacrificial system provided the means for confession and forgiveness for sins. In the new covenant, however, true forgiveness is achieved through God's promise to not remember the sins of His people. This forgiveness is later achieved through the atoning death of Jesus, the Son of God.

Verses 35–37 echo the new covenant poetically and remind readers of God's character. God, the Author of both the old and new covenants, is Creator and Sustainer of all creation, upon whom all creation is dependent (31:35). Verses 36–37 emphasize the security of God's people by expressing the impossible—God cannot stop being the Creator and Sustainer, and His creation cannot fully be measured. Because of who God is, His people are eternally secure in Him (31:36–37).

Chapter 31 closes with a final pronouncement. The city of Jerusalem will be rebuilt, and it will be larger than before (31:38–39). The ground upon which such suffering and destruction had occurred at the will of God will remain sacred to Him and to His people (31:40).

Demystifying Jeremiah

Chapter 32 slows down Jeremiah's rapid-fire prophecies to tell about a single event in the life of the prophet—his purchase of a plot of land in Anathoth. At the time of Jeremiah's purchase, the land was already under Babylonian control, meaning he bought land that he couldn't live on. But God instructed Jeremiah to buy the land as a prophetic message to the people that one day they would return to Judah, and the land they once owned would again be theirs.

The joy and hope of the future depicted in the previous chapter quickly returns to the harsh reality of punishment in chapter 32. In the years 587–586 BC, the city of Jerusalem is close to defeat by the Babylonians (32:1). Jeremiah is under arrest for proclaiming God's message of judgment regarding Judah and its king, Zedekiah, who doesn't take kindly to Jeremiah's predictions (32:2–5). Jeremiah, falsely charged with collaborating with the enemy, is shut up in the court of the guard, but he is permitted certain freedoms, one of which is receiving visitors.

God informs Jeremiah that his cousin Hanamel is going to offer to sell him a field in Anathoth, Jeremiah's hometown, just outside of Jerusalem (32:6–7). God's prediction is fulfilled, and Hanamel approaches Jeremiah because, as a family member, the prophet has the right to buy the field and keep it in the family (32:8). Because Jerusalem is under siege, the value of the land is dubious due to the military occupation. However, Jeremiah is instructed by God to purchase the land. So despite the uncertainties surrounding the deal, he makes the purchase (32:9). The text records the entire transaction with great specificity: The purchase price is seventeen shekels of silver (roughly seven ounces), and witnesses are called in to verify the signing of the deed and the exchange of money. Then the deed is given to Baruch for safe storage (32:10–14).

Buying a field in Anathoth in the middle of an invasion seems foolish, and yet Jeremiah's response is one of obedience and confidence in the Lord. He is confident that houses, fields, and vineyards, the most common elements of economic life, will again be bought and sold in the land of Judah (32:15). He makes a long-term investment based upon a future hope. Furthermore, his purchase shows the people that God's prophet believes there will be life after the exile in Babylon.

Verses 16–25 record Jeremiah's prayer following his purchase of the land. The prayer begins with praise and a doxology to God's character and name (32:16–17). God created the heavens and the earth with His outstretched arm. Nothing is too difficult for this great and mighty God. The prophet recognizes God's fidelity and justice, which Jeremiah has been witness to time and time again (32:18–19). Jeremiah goes to speak of God's great power in the exodus and the conquest of the land (32:20–22). But God's people do not obey him, so the outstretched arm that saves Judah will judge her (32:23). The prophet concludes by conveying what is happening to Judah at that time: The land is being invaded, and in the midst of it God has Jeremiah purchase land in front of witnesses (32:24–25).

Jeremiah hints at an unasked question underlying his prayer: I know that you are a great and powerful God, but are you sure you have this right? Buy a field in Anathoth (32:25)? God answers Jeremiah by asking a rhetorical question: "Is anything too difficult for Me" (32:27 NASB)? The word *difficult* is often translated "wonderful." In the Old Testament it is always used to refer to the great and miraculous deeds of God (see Genesis 18:13–14; Joshua 3:5). God reminds Jeremiah that He is the God of wonderful things in the past and the God of wonderful things in the future.

God goes on to outline the terrible judgment that will come upon Judah and Jerusalem as a result of their aforementioned idolatry and Baal worship (32:28–35). Judah's guilt is certain, and her discipline must be severe. But again, God promises to not completely destroy His people and to eventually bring restoration and healing. The Babylonian invasion is not a random act of violence. It is the will of God, again described by the trilogy of sword, famine, and plague (32:36). But this time God also reassures Jeremiah with a familiar phrase: "They will be my people, and I will be their God" (32:37–38; see 31:33). Their restoration will include the renewal of their hearts and will be so powerful that it will last for several generations (32:39). God also guarantees a continued relationship between Him and His people (32:40–41). The coming renewal is as much a part of God's plan for the Israelites as the current punishment He is inflicting on them (32:42). God's response is His way of reassuring Jeremiah that buying land is exactly the right thing to do, both as God's prophet sending a message of faith to his people and as a member of a nation that will endure and eventually be restored to full civic life (32:43–44).

Chapter 33 opens with Jeremiah still imprisoned and still communicating with God (33:1). God again speaks to Jeremiah, reminding the prophet of His true character as Creator and Sustainer of all and inviting Jeremiah to an ongoing relationship with Him (33:2–3). God lets Jeremiah know He is aware of the destruction happening to the people of Judah (33:4). Reflecting on the pain of invasion and war, God reiterates that He allowed the Babylonian invasion to happen as a way of cleansing Judah of its wickedness (33:5).

Verses 6–13 comprise another message of hope for the future: God will restore both His people and their holy city, Jerusalem. God's specificity about restoration matches His specificity about destruction. He will bring both health, which can refer to one's physical condition, as well as healing, which can refer to one's emotional and spiritual condition (33:6). The injuries of war last longer than war itself and significantly alter the mindsets of those who have experienced them. God speaks to this reality, saying He will reveal an abundance of peace and truth to the people (33:6). God's message is that He will heal their bodies and their spirits. Furthermore, He will heal their civic life. War inevitably affects commerce and infrastructure, leading to significant economic hardship. But God promises that He will restore the fortunes of both Israel and Judah (33:7). He will do this not simply for the sake of civic life but in conjunction with the whole point of this punishment in the first place: They will be cleansed and forgiven, making them an example to other nations (33:8–9). The city of God that was destroyed and desolate will again be a place where people thrive and live abundantly, all because of the hand of God (33:10–11). God sends this message in the midst of destruction, implanting a vision of hope in the nation's future (33:12–13).

Verses 14–26 close the chapter with a reminder of the Davidic covenant, God's promise that all of Israel will be restored through a descendant of the line of David, foreshadowing the coming Messiah. God reiterates that He will restore both Israel and Judah (33:14). During that restoration, He will choose a particular familial line, the branch of David, from which the Messiah will emerge to bring justice and righteousness to the earth (33:15).

Critical Observation

In just three chapters, God's plan has unfolded from His relationship with the Israelites through the old covenant of the law to a coming new covenant first for the Israelites and then all nations to a new leader who will bring justice and righteousness to all the earth.

Judah and Jerusalem will know a new level of salvation and safety (33:16). Under this new reign, Israel will always have a leader, and access to God will be assured (33:17–18). God emphasizes His point in the same way He does in 31:36–37, by the unrealistic *if/then* statement. Since God is the Creator and Sustainer of all creation, and will be for all eternity, the promises He makes with His people are also eternal (33:20–21). Again, hearkening back to the original covenant between Abraham and God, God reiterates that His people will multiply (33:22).

Finally, God closes by addressing a claim that foreign nations were making about Israel and Judah—that God abandoned them (33:23–24). God explains that His attachment to His people is as certain and predictable as day and night and the turning of the seasons (33:25–26).

Take It Home

Repeatedly throughout the book of Jeremiah, God asserts Himself as Creator and Sustainer of the earth and all that is in it. By doing so, God not only reminds His people of His faithfulness to them and His inability to abandon them despite their sins, but it is also a means of contrasting His character with the false gods His people had experimented with.

JEREMIAH 34:1–45:5

INCIDENTS SURROUNDING THE FALL OF JERUSALEM

Setting Up the Section

Chapters 30–33, referred to previously as the Book of Consolation, provide a series of hope-centered prophecies for the nations of Judah and Israel in the midst of much suffering and struggle. The four chapters also serve as an intermission from Jeremiah's prophetic messages of God's judgment against His sinful people. Chapter 34, however, resumes where 29 leaves off—with a description of Jerusalem just prior to its captivity and fall.

34:1–35:19

BEFORE THE FALL

Chapter 34 begins with God's message for His prophet Jeremiah at the time King Nebuchadnezzar invades Jerusalem (34:1). His message for Zedekiah, the Judean king at that time, is that the invasion he is experiencing is the work of God. Jeremiah prophesies that Zedekiah will be captured, come face-to-face with Nebuchadnezzar, die a peaceful death, and be buried with dignity (34:2–7). Given how God had warned the people of countless corpses they wouldn't be able to bury, much less with formal rites and rituals of mourning, this message must have come as a comfort to Zedekiah.

Verses 8–22 tell a story that highlights a significant broken promise (34:8–11). King Zedekiah had made a covenant to release the slaves, who were those Jews unable to pay their debts and therefore put into slavery (34:8–10).

Demystifying Jeremiah

Zedekiah's initial action in verses 8–10 is consistent with the requirements of the law to cancel a slave's debt after six years of service (Exodus 21:1–6; Deuteronomy 15:1–11). Although the reason behind his benevolent action is unclear, it may have been motivated by economics. Jerusalem is under siege from Babylon (Jeremiah 34:21–22), and masters probably don't have enough food to feed their slaves, so they release them rather than starve them. Regardless of the motive for the release, it is an act of kindness consistent with God's Word.

Slaveholders obey the king's command, but their initial action of loyalty is soon followed by a reversal, when leadership reneges and takes back the slaves (34:11). God responds by reminding Jeremiah's listeners of their agreement regarding slaves (34:12–14). God released the people of Israel from slavery. He was faithful to His covenant and did not turn back. Zedekiah, too, released slaves, but he was not faithful to his covenant (34:15–16). The words *turn around* and *took back* come from the same Hebrew word *to return.* These words have emerged multiple times in the book of Jeremiah. The double turning indicates fickleness and inconsistency. A promise is given and a promise is broken.

God does not take kindly to this breach of covenant, and Zedekiah and his officials will suffer a harsh judgment. God again refers to the triad of destruction He has promised—sword, plague, and famine—throughout Jeremiah's oracles (34:17). The implication is that God holds back the floodwaters of judgment, but there comes a point when He opens the gates. The consequences will be brutal, and to express how brutal, God refers to the ritual of confirming an agreement (or covenant) by cutting a calf in two and walking between the pieces (34:18). The ritual signifies that anyone who breaks the covenant should become like the calf that is split in two. All those involved in breaking the agreement about the freeing of the slaves—the officials of Judah, the officials of Jerusalem, the court officers, the priests, and all the people—are guilty (34:19). Their punishment will be as severe as indicated in the message of the halved calf (34:20–22).

Chapter 35 records another instance when God has His prophet make a point by acting something out. The story of Zedekiah from 34:8–22 is contrasted with the story of the Recabites. The context changes from the days of Zedekiah to the time of King Jehoiakim, his brother (35:1–2). Most of the accounts in Jeremiah 30–39 take place during Zedekiah's reign, but for the insertion of this story, the chronology is unimportant. This account, which occurred at least ten years earlier, is placed here to establish a contrast with chapter 34.

In chapter 34, the main characters are Zedekiah and the other leaders of Judah, public and well-known figures. But in chapter 35, the main characters are the Recabites, an obscure family clan (35:2). Jeremiah is instructed by God to call the Recabites to the temple and give them wine to drink, a beverage that will be in direct contrast to the Recabites' way of life. Jeremiah brings the entire family into the temple of the Lord, a very holy and public place (35:3–4). The entire family fits into one chamber, so this incident is witnessed by important leaders. There in this public setting, the prophet sets before this family pitchers of wine and tells them to drink (35:5). The Recabites refuse to drink (35:6–11). Even though Jeremiah gives them permission to do so, and even though they have already compromised a bit by moving into the city for fear of the Babylonians, the Recabites remain faithful to the covenant vow of Jonadab.

Demystifying Jeremiah

The Recabites are mentioned in more detail in 2 Kings 10, where we read that Jonadab (or Jehonadab), the son of Recab, joins himself to Jehu when Jehu ruthlessly slaughters the worshipers of Baal. Jonadab, who is zealous for the Lord much like Jehu, institutes strict disciplines for his family. They are nomads living in tents, not houses, and they do not raise crops. They do not plant vineyards, and they do not drink any wine. The Recabites are metal workers, but we don't have enough additional information to know exactly why they took the vows of Jonadab.

The key words in the next four verses are *listen* and *obey*. Both of these words come from the same Hebrew word, *shema*. This term means more than merely hearing; it means to hear and then put into practice what one has heard. God interprets the story of the Recabites (35:12–16). In verse 13, the words *receive instruction* (or *learn a lesson*) mean to listen and act on what is heard. God is about to reveal the lesson by contrasting the Recabites and Zedekiah. The Recabites listened; Zedekiah does not. The Recabites made a promise and remained faithful; Zedekiah made a promise and broke it (35:14–16). The specific details of the Recabite way of life shouldn't be the focus of the story. What is important is the fact that the Recabites lived in obedience and integrity. God repeatedly spoke to Judah and sent His prophets to them with the message of repentance, but Judah did not listen. The Recabites, on the other hand, listened and continued to obey even after 240 years.

Not only is there a contrast in fidelity, but there also is a contrast in results (35:17–19). Here we observe two different destinies. For Judah, the result of failing to listen will be judgment and disaster (35:17). They will lose their land and cities and be carried off into exile. But the Recabites will never lack a man to stand before God (35:18–19). The Davidic line was cut off with Zedekiah, but the line of the Recabites will continue. Two different stories of covenant loyalty end in two different destinies.

36:1–38:28

JEREMIAH AND THE SCROLLS

Chapters 36–38 include another remarkable story from Jeremiah's life, clues to the development of the writing of the book of Jeremiah, and accounts of more of the prophet's imprisonments. Chapter 36 opens in 605 BC, during the reign of the selfish, perverse King Jehoiakim. Under this man's leadership, life in Judah is unsettled and disordered socially, politically, and religiously. Despite Jeremiah's plea, however, the people of Judah do not turn from their idolatrous ways.

The story begins with God coming to Jeremiah during the time of Johoiakim's reign (36:1). God tells Jeremiah to record everything He says to him concerning Israel, Judah, and all the nations on a scroll (36:2). Scholars think these writings, as a result of God's commandment, comprise all of Jeremiah's preachings from 627 to 605 BC (chapters 1–25 of the book of Jeremiah). Behind the assignment is the hope that the people might hear God's Word and repent of their sins (36:3). This is not the first time in the book of Jeremiah that God encourages His people to think back on His history with them or reflect on His past words and actions toward them.

Jeremiah appoints Baruch, the son of Neriah, to be his scribe and deliver the final product to the temple (36:4–5). It is likely that Jeremiah's past messages in the temple made him unwelcome there (see chapters 7 and 26). But God wants the prophecies to be shared with the people in their religious setting in hopes that they will repent (36:6–7). Jeremiah and Baruch obey God's command: The text records three readings of the scroll that are dictated by Jeremiah, including one near the New Gate, the same gate mentioned in chapter 26 (36:8–10). Verse 9 states that the people are fasting, which likely indicates the Babylonian invaders have already made progress in overtaking the city. The particular chamber mentioned in verse 10 is associated with a powerful political family. Even though a large crowd is present, it is obvious that God is targeting the leadership of the nation.

Critical Observation

Baruch is mentioned first in chapter 32, when Jeremiah buys his cousin's field in Anathoth. Baruch, a political figure, is from a distinguished family. Associating with Jeremiah meant that Baruch was risking his life. Chapters 36–45 are framed with the mention of his name. This section of the text is frequently referred to as Baruch's document.

When Micaiah, son of Gemariah, hears the Word of the Lord being recited in the temple, he takes it seriously. He goes back to the king's house and tells all the officials, one of whom is his father. The officials listen to Micaiah (36:11–13). Wanting to investigate the matter further, they send for Baruch himself (36:14–15). Upon actually hearing Baruch read the prophecies, the officials react with fear and a sense of urgency, and they immediately want to report the words to the king (36:16). Perhaps the texts read by Baruch voiced their own concerns or gave words to feelings they had been having and observations they had been making.

Critical Observation

Jeremiah faces much trouble in his lifetime, but there are times when God sends people to rescue him. The officials mentioned in this passage may well have been the very ones who rescued Jeremiah in chapter 26. Gemariah and Micaiah are instrumental in protecting Jeremiah and Baruch when King Jehoiakim burns the scroll and seeks to kill Jeremiah. Then, after the fall of Jerusalem in 587 BC, Nebuchadnezzar himself gives word to the captain of the bodyguard to protect Jeremiah from harm. When the choice is given to Jeremiah to go to Babylon or stay in the land, he attaches himself to Gedaliah, the son of Ahikam.

The officials validate the document by putting questions to Baruch concerning its origin, authenticity, and credibility, and Baruch explains its origin (36:17–18). Then they instruct Baruch and Jeremiah to hide (36:19). By doing this, the officials become protectors of the subversive voice of Jeremiah, who is tasked with reporting God's Word. Knowing the king, these leaders and powerful people are aware his reaction will be harsh. But they want to remove any connection between themselves and the informants so they cannot be implicated as being responsible for the message itself (36:20).

After hearing the message, the king sends for the scroll and has it read to him (36:21). Verse 22 gives the reader a few additional details of time and place. A *brazier* (36:22 NASB) is a metal container for burning coal or charcoal, either for cooking or heating. Jehoiakim is likely sitting in the comfort of his home, warming himself before a fire in the wintertime, when he hears the words of God contained in Jeremiah chapters 1–25. God is specific about the failures of civic and religious leaders in those passages of scripture. Jehoiakim is convicted by the words read to him, specifically of sin against God. In response, Jehoiakim throws out God's Word (36:23). He yields nothing of himself to the claims of the scroll. He shuts it out and refuses to let it touch his life. Likewise, the people of Jehoiakim's household who also hear the words let them pass over them without conviction. The men who had brought the message and the scroll to the king try to persuade him to respond differently, but to no avail (36:25). After destroying the words of God, the king calls for the arrest of Baruch and Jeremiah, but the Lord hid them (36:26).

Critical Observation

Jehoiakim's response contrasts with the response of the earlier officials in this chapter. They hear the words of God and fear Him (36:16), but the king hears the same words but does not fear (36:24). His response also contrasts with the response of his father, Josiah, seventeen years earlier. Josiah had been presented by Shaphan (Josiah's secretary) with the scroll of Deuteronomy, rediscovered in the temple. Hearing the Word of God, Josiah tears his clothes (2 Kings 22:11). A generation later, the scenario is repeated between the sons. Josiah's son, Jehoiakim, is presented with a scroll by Shaphan's son, Gemariah. His response is completely different. Jehoiakim does not tear his garments. Instead he tears the pages of the scroll, and the text specifically notes his servants do not tear their garments (36:24).

In response to Jehoiakim's actions, God tells Jeremiah to take another scroll, rewrite the words that were burned by Jehoiakim, and then confront Jehoiakim about his actions (36:27–29). God has a new message for Jeremiah to deliver to Jehoiakim: Destroying the scroll did not destroy the message of God. Because Jehoiakim did not listen, he is going to die, and his family will suffer the effects of the Babylonian invasion (36:30–31). The final verse of the chapter describes Baruch and Jeremiah recreating and elaborating on the original scroll (36:32).

Chapter 37 returns to the reign of Zedekiah, the king who breaks the promise of the slaves' freedom. Verse 1 reveals that Zedekiah is made king by the invading king of Babylon, Nebuchadnezzar. The text also reveals that Zedekiah continues to ignore the way of the Lord, even after being reminded of God's words through Jeremiah (37:2). Despite the continued sin of Zedekiah and his people, he still asks Jeremiah to intercede for them (37:3). At this point in the story, Jeremiah is still a free man, and reinforcements are coming for Judah to help fight the Babylonians (37:4–5). God takes this opportunity to respond to Zedekiah's request for intercession: The reinforcements are not going to help, and Jerusalem is still going to fall to the Babylonians (37:7–9). Reinforcements cannot thwart the will of God (37:10).

The supporting army from Egypt helps for a time, and during that brief period Jeremiah goes out to take possession of the land he had purchased from his cousin (37:11–12). But as he is leaving, a member of the army thinks Jeremiah is deserting Jerusalem and going to join the Chaldeans (Babylonians) (37:13). Despite Jeremiah's protests, he is arrested and thrown in a jail in the house of a man named Jonathan, where he is mistreated (37:14–15). Jeremiah's harsh treatment might have been because he was suspected of being a deserter, but there is also the possibility that it is because of his role as God's prophet and the message of judgment he had been preaching for years. Eventually Jeremiah is moved to a dungeon, possibly a cistern (37:16).

King Zedekiah sends for Jeremiah and secretly asks him if there is a word from the Lord, to which Jeremiah answers yes, defeat is certain (37:17). Jeremiah continues, asking Zedekiah to justify his imprisonment (37:18). Why is he imprisoned, Jeremiah asks Zedekiah, while the so-called prophets who prophesy peace and contradict Jeremiah are free, even though the current circumstances in Judah prove the false prophets lied (37:19)? Jeremiah asks the king to not return him to the jail at Jonathan's house where he is treated badly (37:20). Zedekiah agrees and, although he keeps Jeremiah captive, he is imprisoned in better conditions as long as the siege in Jerusalem allows (37:21).

Chapter 38 provides further detail regarding the prophet's imprisonments. Scholars question if the events in chapters 37 and 38 are the same, or if they represent separate occasions. Regardless, the message for the contemporary reader is the same—participating in God's work can mean having to endure suffering and injustice. The chapter opens with a list of men who hear Jeremiah prophesying about the coming justice of God by sword, famine, and pestilence (38:1–2). According to his prophecy, joining the Chaldeans (the largest tribe of Babylonians at this time) is a way to keep one's life. Since Jerusalem is going to fall to Babylon, if the people go ahead and surrender, they may be allowed to continue to live in their homes rather than be exiled when they are defeated (38:2–3). The leaders ask the king to kill Jeremiah, reasoning that his latest message is hurting troop morale, which will increase the likelihood of Babylonian victory (38:4). King Zedekiah dismisses himself from the situation and leaves Jeremiah to the mob (38:5). The men imprison Jeremiah in a cistern, a muddy place with only fetid water (38:6; see chapter 2).

It is likely that many people knew of Jeremiah's situation. But the text is specific about the one person who acts to ease his suffering: Ebed-melech the Ethiopian, a palace official (38:7). *Ebed-melech* means "servant of a king." This man is a foreigner from Ethiopia and a government official with no legal rights in Judah. None of Jeremiah's own people care enough about him or his message to fight for him, but Ebed-melech goes against popular opinion and asks the king to pardon Jeremiah's life (38:8–9). When he is granted permission, he pulls Jeremiah out of the pit (38:10–13).

At the close of chapter 38, Jeremiah again finds himself face-to-face with King Zedekiah (38:14). Jeremiah uses the opportunity to bargain for his life, pointing out to Zedekiah that in the past, even when Jeremiah told the truth about God's prophecy, Zedekiah didn't take actions to repent or change his behavior (38:15). Zedekiah promises, in the name of the true creator God, to neither order Jeremiah's death nor leave him to the whims of the mob like he did previously (38:16). Apparently satisfied, Jeremiah reveals God's latest word (38:17).

Jeremiah informs Zedekiah that if he turns himself over to the officers of the invading army, he and his family will live and the city's destruction will not be as vast as it has the potential to be (38:17). However, if Zedekiah continues to resist, the Chaldeans (Babylonians) will destroy the city completely and even kill Zedekiah (38:18). Zedekiah confesses his distrust of the alliances that formed in war and indicates that he doesn't trust his fellow countrymen to deliver him to Nebuchadnezzar safely (38:19). Regardless, Jeremiah assures the king that he must follow God's direction or face specific consequences: The remaining harem in Judah—Zedekiah's wife and daughters—will be brought to the officers of the invading Babylonian army (including the largest tribe of Chaldeans), where they will be raped, forced into marriage, and possibly killed (38:20–22). Furthermore, Zedekiah will be killed, and the city will be completely destroyed by fire (38:22–23). Zedekiah instructs Jeremiah to keep this message to himself, because this information can be used against the king (38:24). The king does not want his court to know that he truly trusts Jeremiah's prophecy, so he asks Jeremiah to lie about the purpose of their meeting (38:25–26). Jeremiah seems to support the king's secrecy and ultimately survives this event (38:27–28). However, as the next chapters reveal, Zedekiah does not heed God's Word, and the city of Jerusalem does fall to the Babylonian forces.

39:1–41:18

THE FALL AND AFTERMATH

Chapters 39–41 detail what happens to the exiles in Babylon and Egypt and gives the fates of specific people: Zedekiah, Jeremiah, Ebed-melech, and Gedaliah. The continuing theme is that God's judgment falls on both those who obey Him as well as those who do not.

The Babylonians storm the city of Jerusalem for thirty months before finally breaking through the city walls in July of 586 BC, marking the fall of the city (39:1–3). With the fall of Jerusalem, both nations of divided Israel have been conquered: Israel, the northern kingdom, is conquered by the Assyrians in 722 BC; and Judah, the southern kingdom, is conquered with this event in 586 BC. The king of Judah at the time of captivity is Zedekiah, who has been warned by Jeremiah of the coming calamity (39:4). Zedekiah, his sons, and the nobles of Judah flee into the desert, only to be captured and returned to Nebuchadnezzar, the great king himself (39:5). Conquering kings believed it served no good purpose to keep the conquered king and his family alive. Sooner or later, any vestige of leadership or family was likely to attempt to retaliate. For this reason, Nebuchadnezzar disposes of Judah's leaders and Zedekiah's sons, burns the palaces to the ground, and gouges out the eyes of Zedekiah before presenting him as a trophy before the Babylonians (39:6–7). The Chaldeans, the largest of the Babylonian tribes, destroy the city of Jerusalem (39:8). The strongest of the people who are still in the city after its destruction are captured as exiles and begin their thousand-mile journey on foot to the great city of Babylon in the modern-day country of Iraq (39:9). The poorest and weakest citizens of Judah are left behind in the destroyed city, where they are given what remains of the vineyards and fields (39:10). The next four verses provide readers with Jeremiah's whereabouts during the attack. Jeremiah is taken from his prison by a captain named Nebuzaradan (39:11). Nebuchadnezzar ordered that Jeremiah be kept safe and obeyed (39:12). Jeremiah's reputation as a prophet and a man of power among Judah's leaders—albeit an unpopular man—was likely known by Nebuchadnezzar, and Nebuchadnezzar probably considered Jeremiah's message helpful to his own cause. Ultimately, Jeremiah ends up in the care of a man named Gedaliah, who is the son of the man who saves Jeremiah in 26:24 (39:14). Gedaliah seems to be of a godly heritage and believes Jeremiah speaks the words of the true God. Jeremiah 40:5 states that he remains in Jerusalem after the exile, where eventually Jeremiah joins him.

Before Jeremiah leaves his guardhouse prison, God speaks to him (39:15). He instructs him to take a reassuring word to Ebed-melech. Even though an entire city went up in flames by God's hand, He wants this one individual, a foreigner who does not belong to the people of Judah, to know he will be spared (39:16–17). Ebed-melech is rewarded for recognizing and believing the prophet of the true God (39:18).

Nebuchadnezzar's bodyguard, Nebuzaradan, knows that Jeremiah is a prophet from the Lord who has spoken an advanced warning of calamity for Jerusalem (40:1–2). He takes Jeremiah to a place north of Jerusalem, where exiles are taken and assessed for their worth, and speaks with him there. Nebuzaradan acknowledges the work of God in the invasion and conquering that has just occurred (40:3). He then offers Jeremiah a choice: come to Babylon or stay behind with Gedaliah, the new leader of the land formerly known as Judah (40:4). Jeremiah chooses to return to Mizpah, near Jerusalem, to be with Gedaliah, whose name means "watchtower" or "lookout" (40:5–6).

The forces in the field, mentioned in verse 7, are groups of Jewish troops who have not yet been captured (40:7). When they learn that Gedaliah has been appointed governor of the land by Nebuchadnezzar, they go to him in the city of Mizpah (40:8). In verse 9 Gedaliah tells the Judeans not to fear the Chaldeans (the largest Babylonian tribe). Further, he instructs them to stay and raise crops (40:10). It seems that the people can resume their lives under Nebuchadnezzar's reign. When other people from Judah, who are neither displaced by the war nor exiled, hear of Gedaliah's community, they join them, remembering that Gedaliah is the son and grandson of godly men who had served Josiah (40:11). These people also begin raising crops (40:12).

While stability and community seem to be returning to the land, a threat is brewing. Some of the forces in the field come to Gedaliah and tell him of a threat against him by a man of royal descent (and a former member of Zedekiah's army) named Ishmael (40:13–14). Gedaliah dismisses the charge and actually calls the accuser a liar (40:15–16). Gedaliah must have been willing to trust that Ishmael did not wish him ill. It is an unfortunate trust that will lead to disaster.

Three months after Jerusalem's capture and Gedaliah's appointment as leader of the Jewish community, Ishmael brings ten men to Mizpah and kills Gedaliah and all the people who are with him (41:1–3). Ishmael kills Gedaliah during a hospitality meal, while eating bread together. The inclusion of this fact in the text reveals what a cowardly and unjust act Ishmael committed. But it only gets worse. On the day after the first murders, eighty men from Shechem (in Samaria) come to visit Gedaliah and to worship (41:4–5). Ishmael greets them, acting as if he is mourning Gedaliah's death. He lures the men into the city, where he kills them and dumped their bodies into a local cistern (41:6–7). Ten are spared because they bribe Ishmael, further evidence that Ishmael is nothing but a self-motivated killer (41:8). Verse 9 describes the cistern as being a particular one made by King Asa (41:9; see 1 Kings 15:22; 2 Chronicles 16:6).

Ishmael's atrocities continue. He captures all the Jews who are under Gedaliah's protection with the intention of carrying them across the Jordan River into the area known as Jordan (41:10). Ishmael plans to take them to the sons of Ammon, a reference to the ancient residents of the modern city of Amman, Jordan. To the rescue, however, is Johanan, the leader of what is left of a small Jewish army allowed to protect the city from further assault and one of the men who had tried to warn Gedaliah of Ishmael's threat (41:11, 13). He puts together a group and rescues the kidnapped (41:12–14). Verse 13 notes that the people are glad when they see Johanan coming, further indicating his status as a good community member. After he rescues the Jews from Ishmael, Johanan goes after him (41:15). Johanan and the other army officers lead the rescued Jews to a place called Geruth Kimham, near Bethlehem, as a place to stop on their escape to Egypt (41:16–17). Their plan is to escape to Egyptian land to avoid any punishment that might come from Gedaliah's death (41:17–18).

42:1–44:30

EGYPT

The remnant of people from Jerusalem has been through one traumatic experience after another, and all they want is security. Faced with the absence of the only leader they have had since the invasion, destruction, and exile of their fellow citizens and family members, they turn to Jeremiah. They want him to intercede to God on their behalf because there are so few of them remaining and they need God's guidance (42:1–3). They know they can no longer trust Jerusalem to protect them—the city's walls have been torn down in the war. Jeremiah, who for many years acted as an obedient prophet to these people, also shows the leadership of a priest by ministering to them in this way. He assures them that he will pray to God for them, and he will not hold back a word of God's answer (42:4). The people's response to Jeremiah seems to indicate that at least this remnant has learned to be responsive to the Word of the Lord received through Jeremiah. They promise to obey the message no matter what it is (42:5–6).

After ten days, Jeremiah has an answer, and he calls all the people back together (42:7–8). Jeremiah opens his statement by qualifying that it is from the God of Israel, who Jeremiah petitioned on behalf of this remnant of people (42:9). God's message is consistent with what He has said all along: The worst is over, and God will nurture them as they restore and rebuild their city (42:10). Nebuchadnezzar is no longer a threat, and because of God's will for His people, He will work through Nebuchadnezzar to support the people in their restoration efforts (42:11–12).

However, this restoration is dependent on the people staying where they are in the midst of the destroyed remains of Judah and Jerusalem. God knows the people are considering leaving the land and moving to Egypt for an easier life (42:13–14). And though God said the people have a choice to remain or flee, He implies that their minds are already made up, and predicts the same three kinds of destruction present throughout the book of Jeremiah. They can expect to face swords, famine, and plague if they flee (42:15–18). God's message is clear: Don't go to Egypt (42:19). Jeremiah also seems to know that despite the promises the people make in verses 5–6 to obey God's message no matter what, they might as well have already left. Disobedience to Jeremiah's messages has become a pattern (42:20–22).

Demystifying Jeremiah

The people cannot let go of their old thoughts about God. Just as they thought rituals would save them no matter what the condition of their hearts (see 7:21–29), they think that because Jerusalem has been destroyed, God is no longer with them. They need to understand that Jerusalem is merely a symbol of God's protection. They look at their reality—the large majority of Jews in exile and their new leader, Gedaliah, murdered—and logic tells them it is time to give up on the promised land. In their immediate struggle, they fail to understand that God wants them to stay in Jerusalem to remain the faithful remnant, that He has not deserted them, and that He will not remove His hand of protection.

Jeremiah speaks words of truth and warning to the remnant of people from Jerusalem, and yet they do the exact opposite of God's command. Azariah and Johanan are the first to voice resistance to the Word of the Lord, calling Jeremiah a liar (43:1–2). They even accuse Jeremiah of letting Baruch talk him into delivering the small remnant to the Chaldeans (43:3). Despite Jeremiah's words of hope, the people flee to Egypt (43:4–7). Those who flee include all the leaders (even Johanan, who had acted so honorably in previous situations), everyone who had been rescued after Gedaliah's murder, and Jeremiah and Baruch (43:4–7).

Demystifying Jeremiah

Prophets were stoned if their prophecies did not come to pass. The very idea that Jeremiah has survived all these years is a testimony that his prophecies are true. This fact should have been proof enough for the people to listen to him. But instead, the Judean remnant retreats back to the land God had miraculously led them out of a thousand years earlier. They journey back to the Red Sea to the place called Tahpanhes, the modern-day Suez Canal. Pharaoh had a palace at this juncture of the Mediterranean and the Red Sea.

God sends Jeremiah with the people on this journey and has him perform another symbolic act once they reach Tahpanhes (43:8). Jeremiah places stones in the patio of the government building to mark the spot where Nebuchadnezzar will soon set up his own palace as his conquests continue (43:8–11). This prophecy is fulfilled in 568–567 BC. God promised to tear down the temples of Egypt and burn their pagan deities (43:12). He also promised to shatter the obelisks of Heliopolis (43:13). *Heliopolis* is another name for "sun city," a place dedicated to worshiping the sun as a god. In honor of the sun god, the people erect tall, slender stone monuments which become known as fingers of god.

Chapter 44 begins with two major players: Jeremiah and God. Even in Egypt, God continues to be with the people and with Jeremiah (44:1). But this chapter also begins the last message Jeremiah delivers to the people. In this message, we see the same elements that have been present throughout the book of Jeremiah. God summarizes where they have been: He punished His people in many ways because of their persistent sin, and He sent prophets again and again (44:2–4). But the result is the same: The people turn away from God and His Word, and follow their own ideas about safety and prosperity in other places with other gods (44:5). Because of this behavior, Judah and Jerusalem are in ruins (44:6).

Critical Observation

God says to the unrepentant remnant of Judah, "Again and again I sent my servants the prophets" (44:4 NIV). Over a period of three hundred years, God sent the following prophets: Elijah, Elisha, Jonah, Joel, Amos, Obadiah, Hosea, Micah, and Isaiah. And now Jeremiah stands before the people with words of conviction, warning them of impending doom if they do not turn from their idolatry. God's indictment to the people is very clear: They burn sacrifices to other gods. Through the ages people continue to defy God by finding new and different ways to create idols and worship those idols at creative new altars. We are not immune from the perennial sins that weave their way through every generation.

In verses 7–9, God expresses His anger with His people by asking a series of rhetorical questions about their actions up to this point. The people did not get God's message, did not realize their sin, and did not learn to commit themselves to Him (44:10).

In the same pattern seen throughout the book of Jeremiah, God follows the statement of reality with the consequences. This time, even though only a remnant of Judah remains, God abandons them to the consequences of their decisions (44:11). They will die in Egypt by sword, famine, and plague (44:12–13). None who went to Egypt will return to Judah, except for a few refugees (44:14).

The people respond to Jeremiah by telling him they are going to ignore him (44:15–16). At this point, one would expect deep and mournful repentance. But instead, they tell Jeremiah they will no longer listen to him. Their defiance has become an open act of rebellion, and they justify it by saying when they used to worship the other gods they did not suffer (44:17–18). They admit to preparing flat bread images of Ishtar (the "Queen of Heaven"), the Egyptian goddess of love and fertility (44:19). Their baked goods became a creative new act of burnt offering, and they topped off their bread by hosting wine parties dedicated to their favorite deities.

Jeremiah responds to the people's latest argument by saying God was watching the entire time (44:20–21). He endured their behavior as long as He chose to, and when He decided to teach the people their sins were unacceptable to Him, He allowed them to be punished (44:22–23).

Once again the people sin against God by worshiping the gods of a foreign land. "Go ahead then, do what you promised! Keep your vows!" Jeremiah yells (44:25 NIV). God proclaims that never again will the sacred name of Yahweh be used by the remnant in Egypt (44:26). In a reversal of the hopeful promise of 29:11, God assures the people He is watching over them for harm and not for good (44:27). The few who will emerge from Egypt will have no doubt about God's power (44:28). In his final words of prophecy, Jeremiah speaks of a sign. Egypt's Pharaoh Hophra will also fall under the growing dominion of King Nebuchadnezzar, which comes to fruition in 569 BC (44:29–30).

45:1–5

BARUCH

Jeremiah's message to Baruch, recorded at the start of chapter 45, was written in the fourth year of Jehoiakim's reign (see Jeremiah 36), almost twenty years before Baruch went to Egypt with Jeremiah. The letter addresses some of the complaints Baruch is having about his role in Jeremiah's ministry (45:1–3). Verse 4 echoes the phrasing of 1:10, with language of overthrowing, building, uprooting, and planting. The fact that these themes sustained themselves through all these years is evidence of the consistent message of God and the loyal obedience of Jeremiah. It is not surprising that, given Jeremiah's enemies and his own honest times of frustration with God, Baruch would also have such struggles. Jeremiah encourages his assistant by asking him a question to gauge Baruch's perspective: Are you seeking great things for yourself? Jeremiah then reminds him that flesh is temporary and life with God is the real reward, a lesson Jeremiah learns through enduring much (45:5).

Take It Home

The name *Baruch* means "blessing," and this is what Baruch is to Jeremiah. He came from a distinguished family. He might have had a moment where he sought great things for himself and questioned his role in Jeremiah's ministry, but he counted the cost and gave it all up in order to bless Jeremiah. Baruch's work ensured that Jeremiah's prophecies and story would survive for generations. Chapter 45 marks the close of the narrative regarding the fate of the remnant that fled from Jerusalem. The narrative will not resume again until chapter 52.

JEREMIAH 46:1–51:64

PROPHECIES AND THE NATIONS

Egypt	46:1–28
Philistines	47:1–7
Moab	48:1–47
Ammon	49:1–6
Edom	49:7–22
Damascus	49:23–27
Arab Tribes	49:28–33
Elam	49:34–39
Babylon	50:1–51:58
Seraiah	51:59–64

Setting Up the Section

Chapters 46–51 chronicle Jeremiah's prophecies concerning the nations (46:1). Such prophecies are not unique to Jeremiah. All of the prophetical books of the Bible contain a similar collection of prophecies, with the exception of the book of Hosea. The themes of this section include God's judgment for idol worship and misplaced trust; the punishment that comes as a consequence of such sins; and the continuing theme that God either won't destroy completely or will destroy now but restore later, which can be seen as evidence of God's amazing mercy. The geographical catalog of nations moves from west to east.

46:1–28

EGYPT

During Jehoiakim's reign, Jeremiah receives a word from God concerning Egypt. The first two verses reference the battle of Carchemish, fought in 605 BC by Egypt and Assyria against the growing power of Babylon and King Nebuchadnezzar (46:1–2). God instructs the people to continue preparing for war by readying their horses, weapons, and armor (46:3–4), and He indicates that the mighty Egyptians will lose terribly (46:2, 5–6). The rivers are referenced for their benefits but also for their uncontrolled power, and the leaders are encouraged in their futile battle (46:6–9). But ultimately God is in control, and because of His justice, He allows Egypt to be defeated at Babylon's hands (46:10). As in Jeremiah 8, God references a possible balm available for healing but calls any attempt at healing vain (46:11). Egypt's desire for power overcomes the nation, and it must fail (46:12).

God goes on to explain that Nebuchadnezzar is the king who will lead the Babylonians in Egypt's destruction (46:13). Egypt can prepare itself, but the invasion is going to come, and Egypt will suffer as the Lord decreed (46:14–15). As in 46:12, the warriors won't even be able to put up a unified front and will retreat (46:16). As is common in defeat, the defeated leader will be questioned (46:17). Just as God warned Judah many times that an invader was coming from the north, He warns Egypt that one is coming to destroy them just as others have been destroyed by invaders from Tabor and Carmel (46:18). The ones who survive will be taken prisoner and marched away from their homelands, which will be destroyed (46:19).

In this passage, Egypt is described as a beautiful heifer, symbolizing the nation's size, strength, and importance as a world power that had dominated the nations even before 1800 BC, until the rise of Assyria in 722 BC. God's description of Egypt is of one that prospered for a while, with the invasion beginning as simply an annoyance (46:20). A horsefly (or gadfly), a pesky little insect (compared to the heifer) is symbolized as the threat of Babylon. Horseflies, unlike other insects, have the ability to tear flesh, suck large amounts of blood, and infect the target with disease and parasites. When the invasion becomes serious, Egypt will not be able to defend themselves (46:21). The Babylonian army marches 550 miles, like a swarm of horseflies, attacking everything in sight, until they achieve the coveted title of world dominator. Destruction will be real, and Egypt will be subjugated to Babylon (46:22–24). The gods of the Egyptians will be punished, as will the Pharaoh, and then everyone will be turned over to Babylon. The destruction will not be complete or permanent, though; Egypt will rise again (46:25–26).

Despite this chronicle of devastation, the chapter closes with God's simple, yet sustaining assurance that the sons of Jacob will not be consumed during the ravage of war. God will continue to discipline, correct, and punish them, but He will not remove them from their coveted position as God's chosen people (46:27–28).

47:1–7

PHILISTINES

Chapter 47 contains the prophetic oracle for the Philistines. The area of Philistia was located geographically near Egypt (47:1). God's message to them is similar in that the invader is also Babylon (47:2). The image of a flood indicates that the invasion will be severe and widespread. The prophet Jeremiah describes the onslaught of Babylonian siege as a mighty torrent of water, sweeping through the land and consuming everything in its path. Philistia will be so overpowered that parents won't be able to save their children (47:3). Neighboring nations—allies—won't be able to help save Philistia, because this invasion and destruction is the will of the Lord (47:4). Those who survive will become captives of the Babylonians and will be shaved bald as part of their enslavement. Likewise, cutting is an act of mourning for some pagans (47:5). It is unclear who is asking God to sheathe His sword—it could be the Philistines themselves wondering if such harsh justice is necessary, to which God responds *yes* (47:6–7). Or it could be Jeremiah, wondering how God could allow such devastation to take place. When will God step in to restore order and peace?

48:1–47

MOAB

As is similar to each of the prophecies for the nations, Moab's coming destruction is described in chapter 48 as if it has already happened. The oracle to Moab is lengthy because of Israel and Judah's long history with the country. The judgment begins with the word *woe*, indicating a time of mourning has come (48:1). All of the cities mentioned early in this chapter—Nebo, Kiriathaim, Heshbon, Madmen, Horonaim, and Luhith—would have been well known to the original hearers of this prophecy (48:1–4). The cities that have already been invaded warn others to flee (48:6). Similar to accusations against Judah and Egypt, God specifies that Moab trusts too much in its own achievements; and consequently, its false god Chemosh, priests, and princes will suffer (48:7). No city in the entire country will survive the invasion, and all the citizens of Moab will either die or be captured (48:8–9). God is so intent on fulfilling the nation's judgment that He takes a break from detailing their sins to motivate His instrument, the Babylonians, to act swiftly (48:10).

Critical Observation

The territory of Moab was a mountainous plateau on the eastern side of the Dead Sea, in modern-day Jordan. The Moabites were descendants of Lot, Abraham's nephew, who reportedly fathered Moab by his oldest daughter (Genesis 19:30–38). Perhaps the best-known resident of Moab was Ruth, who left her home country to embrace the land and culture of Israel. The Moabites received protection from the Egyptians in return for their allegiance to pagan gods.

Verse 11 uses the imagery of wine, one of Moab's resources, to compare the Moabites to wine that is left alone instead of separated into containers. Nothing changes for the wine—it is the same for a long time. God likens this to the Moabites themselves, who have been left alone and never separated among nations. But this is about to change (48:12). Like Judah, Moab is about to see the futility of its faith in false gods (48:13).

The idea that Moab's warriors will be able to defend against God's justice is laughable (48:14). When God decrees His judgment for Moab, it is time for the people to begin their mourning for the nation and expect to see examples of its destruction (48:15–17).

Cities on hills are often the safest and manage to avoid destruction, but God calls those in Dibon, who survived the initial destruction, to come down from the hill and experience it for themselves. God links the destruction of the country to that of the individual citizens (48:18). Word begins to spread that Moab is destroyed and the people disgraced (48:19–20). Verses 21–24 list all the communities in Moab that are destroyed. The imagery in verse 25 is that of a mature stag that loses its horns or a person whose arm is broken. Such will be the crippled state of Moab.

As in Jeremiah 25, God describes Moab as drinking uncontrollably from a cup. Their gluttony leads to their illness and destruction (48:26). When Israel was weak, Moab took advantage of that weakness (48:27). Now, God instructs them to flee their cities and take up refuge in hiding places like animals (48:28).

In addition to being idol worshipers and opportunists, the Moabites are also arrogant and prideful (48:29). But God observes that this pride is misplaced and futile (48:30). Consequently, the mourning for Moab will be thorough, as seen by the specific groups God is mourning for, and the mourning will be even more intense than others known in history (48:31–32). The winepresses that once kept Moab in economic prosperity will quit working, and no income will be produced (48:33). The destruction will be far-reaching (48:34). Jeremiah prophesies that Moab will be destroyed as a people because of their idolatry (48:35). God mourns as if at a funeral for a nation that once prospered but now is destroyed (48:36). The survivors wear the markings and the behaviors of slaves horrified at their state (48:37–39).

Verses 40–47 open with the image of an eagle, an often-seen image of destruction in biblical texts (48:40). The invasion brings great pain, and the country of Moab will be destroyed because of its arrogance (48:41–42). Anyone who lives there will experience punishment, and escape is impossible (48:43–44). The destruction moves from city to city throughout the country, and the destruction and harm is intense (48:45). The god that the Moabites had worshiped fails them, and the Moabite children are taken captive by the invading nation, a method of destroying an entire culture (48:46). History shows that the people of Moab will assimilate into other cultures and cease to have a genetic identity. Yet God promises to restore the fortunes of Moab in the latter days (48:47).

49:1–6

AMMON

In chapter 49, God opens the judgment against Ammon in an oracle directed toward Ammonites who have occupied Gad's ancestral land. The oracle begins with a question about how His people's families teach their children and others about the true faith. Because the people have begun worshiping yet another foreign god, Malcam (or Molech), God wonders if Israel has any sons or heirs who have learned about the covenant with the true God and kept the true religion alive in its community (49:1).

Mourning has begun for Ammon, indicated by wailing and people dressed in sackcloth rushing inside the city walls (49:3). The false god Malcam is said to be in exile along with his priests and princes, similar to Moab's false god Chemosh (49:3; see 48:7). The people once boasted in the beauty of their lands, but Jeremiah prophesies that those lands will be destroyed. God points out the futility of that misplaced boasting, pride, and arrogance (49:4). Punishment for this country is certain, God says, and it will come from all sides and result in masses of exiles (49:5). But in a recurring theme of divine mercy, God says He will eventually restore the fortunes of the people of Ammon as He does with Moab (49:6).

Critical Observation

The sons of Ammon lived to the east of the Jordan River in a town called Rabbah. Today that town is called Amman, the capital city of Jordan, which neighbors Israel. Ammon, like Moab, was born to Abraham's nephew Lot. And the Ammonites, like the Moabites, had angered God with their pagan worship.

49:7–22

EDOM

The second oracle in chapter 49 is against Edom. Apparently this nation used to act with wisdom, but that has ceased, and God asks if the wisdom is gone (49:7). As with Moab and Egypt, Edom's residents are urged to flee, perhaps even into nooks and crannies (depths or caves) like animals (49:8). Jeremiah mentions Teman and Dedan in 25:23, specific areas within Edom. The reference to Esau in verse 8 is because Edomites are descendants of Esau.

Verse 9 refers to the common practice of leaving part of the harvest behind, called *gleaning*, which is a way for the poor to come behind and get some harvest for themselves. God says that even thieves only take until they have enough. But what God will do to Edom is strip it completely bare, leaving nothing behind, not even what people try to hide (49:10). But, as with Moab and Ammon, God promises to save a few, namely, the most vulnerable: orphans and widows (49:11).

God references His own righteous character to assert His next pronouncement, and He seems to be continuing with the theme of those who are responsible versus those who are innocent. The cup of wrath (25:15–38; 48:26–28) will be drunk by those who deserve God's wrath. But God says the orphans and widows will be safe. God then rhetorically asks the listener, are you innocent? Will you be acquitted? And the answer is an emphatic *no* (49:12). God again references His own righteous character in that Bozrah, another city in Edom, will become an example of God's wrath and punishment (49:13).

In the next five verses, Jeremiah inserts his voice again, saying he has heard a message from the Lord and that all the nations should gather together and prepare for battle (49:14). The voice switches back to God's, and God reminds the listeners of His power and hand in their success or failure. God has made them small and taken away the might that the nations once had (49:15). The people who experienced the benefits of the nation's might and power—which will be the same people who lived highest off the ground—will now be brought down by God (49:16). God again states that Edom will become an example of God's punishment and be so destroyed that no one will return to live there (49:17–18).

God lets listeners know that His wrath is coming like a lion approaching a well-tended pasture. In biblical times, this pasture would house vulnerable sheep. Upon God's approach, all will run and leave the sheep untended. Again, in biblical times, as in any agrarian society, anyone or anything attacking livestock would be dealt with. But no one can dispute or stand up against God's just wrath (49:19). Because of this, God urges all to listen to what is coming: Edom will be conquered, and people will be taken captive (49:20). The fall of the mighty city will not go unnoticed (49:21). At the end of this segment, the eagle image that appeared in the Moab prophecy appears again. The people will feel much pain (49:22).

49:23–27

DAMASCUS

The third nation prophesied against in chapter 49 is Damascus. The cities mentioned here, Hamath and Arpad, are both cities in the Damascus region. Shame and anxiety have come to these people because they have heard of the Lord's coming judgment (49:23). Even those who want to flee are paralyzed with fear, and fleeing is no longer an option, just as a woman who is in labor must stop until she has delivered the child (49:24). Because of this, people have not left the city, and they will die where they stand (49:25–26). Afterward, the Lord will completely destroy Damascus (49:27).

49:28–33

ARAB TRIBES

The fourth group of prophecies in this chapter is against two nomadic communities in Arabia, Kedar and Hazor. Verse 28 conveys that both tribes will come under Nebuchadnezzar's control. Where in other areas of Jeremiah destruction of cities includes tearing down walls, to destroy nomadic communities means taking their tents and their flocks (49:29). As with Edom and Moab, the people are told to flee to caves because Babylonian troops are coming (49:30). Again, nomadic tribes move from place to place simply by moving their poles and tents, so God points out that they are an easy target, with no gates or bars for protection (49:31). These people depend upon their flocks for travel, food, and trade. God warns that these flocks will be destroyed or taken by the invaders, and the people left will be dispersed (49:32). The area where these nomads used to congregate will be so devastated that only scavenging animals like jackals will be there (49:33).

49:34–39

ELAM

The final set of prophecies in this chapter is against Elam. Verse 34 indicates that this is one of the prophecies that Jeremiah shared when Zedekiah was still king of Judah (49:34). As with Moab, God's wrath is specific to the skill Elam is known for: archery. God describes His judgment as breaking Elam's bow and finest archers (49:35). The metaphor of four winds indicates how complete the destruction will be and how far flung the Elamites will be (49:36). God indicates no hope for anyone trying to survive (49:37). Rather than others being worshiped in Elam, God will be restored as the rightful leader and king, and eventually God will restore Elam itself (49:38–39).

Critical Observation

Elam is mentioned in Genesis as one of the sons of Shem, who is Noah's son (Genesis 10:1, 22). The Elamites were known as a warring people, constantly at odds with the Hebrews. The Assyrians claimed to have wiped out all the Elamites during the Assyrian's reign of terror, but there was still a remnant during the later time of the Babylonians. God promises to break their mighty men and scatter them to the four winds. But God's mercy prevails, and He promises to restore their fortune in the last days.

50:1–51:58

BABYLON

Chapters 50–51 contain multiple pronouncements against Babylon, the instrument of God's wrath against Judah and other nations. As horrifying as Jeremiah's specific predictions of destruction against Judah and the other nations have been, the pronouncements against Babylon are going to be even worse. How is this possible, since this nation is applying God's justice? Remember that in pronouncing punishments, God also pronounces reasons. These reasons will be detailed in the next two chapters. The chapter opens with a clear statement that the Lord is speaking against Babylon. Some translations identify Babylon by its largest tribe at this time, the Chaldeans (50:1).

God pronounces to all the nations, probably through Jeremiah, that Babylon will cease to be the invader and will itself be conquered. Babylon's god, Marduk, has been destroyed (50:2). Just as Judah was invaded from the north, so Babylon will be invaded by the Persians (50:3). Just like the other nations prophesied about in the book of Jeremiah, Babylon will become a wasteland and no one will remain (50:3).

The destruction of Babylon will be endured by the citizens of Israel and Judah, who survived Babylon's invasion and are now living in Babylon as exiles. These people are now looking to restore their relationship with Yahweh (50:4). Their original shepherds had let them down back in Judah. As their invaders are now conquered, they long more than ever for their home religion and its covenant with the true God (50:5). God laments for them and what they are forced to endure: The ones who had become their leaders are now under siege themselves, and in the chaos of war, the Judeans are left to fend for themselves (50:6–7). In this chaos, God allows them to leave Babylon while He plans His wrath against that country (50:8–9). The Chaldeans, again, are linked with Babylon; they will not escape punishment (50:10).

In the next section, it becomes evident why God intends to punish the people who He had used to be His punishers. God has established throughout the book of Jeremiah that nations prosper when He allows them to prosper. When a nation forgets God as the source of blessing, peace, safety, and prosperity, and begins to look to themselves, their allies, and false gods as sources of those things, God must intervene. God is angry that Babylon enjoyed the role He gave them in refining His people (50:11). After God's action, anyone affiliated with Babylon will be ashamed and humiliated at what Babylon has become

(50:12). God's anger will result in the destruction and desertion of Babylon (50:13). Because of God's wrath, Babylon is now an easy target for anyone who wants to conquer the nation (50:14). The city's civic life no longer exists, and its defenses are literally gone (50:15–16).

Attention now turns back to God's people within this chaos. Again referring to His people as sheep, God reminds the listener that His flock has been conquered before (50:17). God will punish this last invader, just as He did the first one (50:19). As this happens, Israel and Judah can rest easy; the cleansing God wants for them has occurred, and God is pardoning those who have survived (50:20).

In verse 21, God uses two sarcastic names for areas of Babylon: *Merathaim*, which means "double rebellion," and *Pekod*, which means "visitation" (50:21). It is no surprise, then, that God uses such names in ordering their destruction. Consequently, war breaks out against Babylon just as God intended (50:22–24). God speaks as if He personally is outfitting the invading Persian army and inviting it to do whatever it wants to Babylon and Chaldea (50:25–27). The consequences of war have come to Babylon: Its own citizens are now fugitives and refugees. This is the justice of God (50:28).

The next four verses reiterate what God is allowing to happen to Babylon. Now is the time to conquer this nation that has been so destructive to so many (50:29). Invading armies will succeed, and Babylon's people will suffer (50:30). This harsh justice is specifically because of the arrogance with which Babylon conducts its affairs (50:31–32).

In verses 33–34, God reminds the listener of His work on behalf of His people. God needs to perform a work on His people, and He does so through Babylon's armies. But those soldiers themselves are also subject to the will and the work of God (50:33–34). In verses 35–38, God again asserts the destruction that will come against the Chaldeans and the Babylonians, but this time He is specific about who will suffer: officials, wise men, priests, horses, chariots, and foreigners. God even states that drought will come. God adds here that this punishment is coming also because of Babylon's love of idols. Consequently, only scavenging animals will remain where Babylon used to be (50:39–40).

God states again that the instruments of His wrath against the Babylonians will come from the north (50:41). The people who work against Babylon will do so with gusto (50:42). Nebuchadnezzar is now reaping what he has sown for many years (50:43). The same image God uses for Himself in 49:19 appears again here in verse 44. God has spoken: The people of Babylon will be destroyed, and those who survive will become captives (50:45). The entire world will see the humiliation and suffering of the nation that has been so mighty for so long (50:46).

Critical Observation

The Chaldeans lived in the southwest corner of the Babylonian Empire. Abraham left Ur of the Chaldeans (or Chaldees) to journey westward, as God directed him toward the land of the Canaanites, later to become the land of Israel (Genesis 11:26, 31). The chronicles of Jeremiah have focused on the time leading up to the siege of Nebuchadnezzar. Chapter 50 looks forward to the execution of God's judgment on Babylon as the new empire, the Persians (power from the east), now inflicts their own version of terror and domination. The national god Marduk will soon be replaced by the national god of the Persians. The empire of Babylon that sowed destruction will now reap that same destruction as another ego seeks to replace the splendor and majesty of the Babylonian empire. Babylon has become arrogant before the Lord, and God promises to punish them by cutting down the young men in the streets and silencing the men of war. Terror is on every side.

God promises to raise up a spirit of destruction against rebellious Babylon and those who are called in the Hebrew *Leb Kamai*, which means "the heart of those against me" (51:1). God promises to raise up the tribal groups ("foreigners") of Ashkenaz (Germanic/ Slavic), Minni (Iran), and Ararat (Turkey), all parts of the Medo-Persian Empire which will soon crush the regime of Nebuchadnezzar (51:2; see 51:27)). Verse 3 begins with God talking to the Babylonians and then instructing the invading Persians. As stated before, Babylon will be destroyed (51:4), and any injustices that occurred to God's people while they were being refined by God are now avenged (51:5).

Again, God instructs some people to flee Babylon because the wrath of God is coming. But why are some instructed to flee as if they are innocent? God is speaking to His people from Judah and Israel who have been captured and kept as slaves in Babylon. The destruction of Babylon is certain, and He doesn't want them to endure such wrath twice (51:6). In the next few verses we again see the cup of God's wrath, which, when drunk to excess, renders the drinker arrogant and sinful (25:15–38; 51:7–8). Any attempt at recovering from God's actions toward them will be futile (see 10:19; 15:18; 30:12–13), because it is God's will that they be destroyed beyond healing (51:9). The remnant of Israel and Judah see this as vindication for injustices they endured from the Babylonians during their own punishment from God (51:10).

Even more forces are awakened against Babylon to perform the Lord's work, and this particular people, the Medes, fulfill an earlier prophecy that they will participate in Babylon's fall (51:11–12). Babylon's placement near rivers has allowed it to amass great fortune, but the end has come by the hand of the Lord (51:13–14).

In the next two verses, God again reminds the listener of His work as Creator and Sustainer of all creation. This section is highly reminiscent of not only Genesis but also of earlier passages in Jeremiah, where God contrasts His nature as true God against the false, created gods Judah has turned to (51:15–16). God is the Creator, and people are the created; when human beings try to create as God creates, they reveal their foolishness (51:17). The idols and gods they create from their own limited minds are worthless, and those who do such things will be punished (51:18). God is the one true God (51:19).

God uses anyone He wishes to do His work (51:20–23). In this case, He must punish those Babylonians and Chaldeans who let themselves act of their own wills instead of the will of God (51:24). Verses 25–26 reveal that the ones who have been so mighty are now at the mercy of God and will not survive their punishment.

In this version of the war party against Babylon, three new groups are recruited: Ararat, Minni, and Ashkenaz (51:27). Their task on behalf of the Lord is as clear as the others have been: Destroy Babylon in the name of the Lord (51:28–29). The warring is taking its toll on the Babylonians (51:30–32). God notes that it is almost over (51:33).

The voice here shifts to that of a survivor of Judah, detailing what has happened at the hands of Nebuchadnezzar (51:34). God willed and allowed Judah to be invaded by Babylon, but chapters 50–51 have shown that Babylon acted as much out of its own arrogance and greed as it did out of respect for God's will. For the injustices that occurred in the midst of God's punishment, the survivors want retribution (51:35–36). Their desire is fulfilled; Babylon will be utterly destroyed (51:37–40). The next four verses detail how the mighty, fearsome Babylon has been brought down (51:41–44). Many of the same phrases of destruction that have been applied to other nations in the book of Jeremiah now apply to Babylon.

Similar to earlier in this chapter, God instructs the Judeans and Israelites who are living in Babylon as exiles that He is about to punish Babylon (51:45). He has prophesied this so word will get to His people in the coming years (51:46). The fact that God is speaking to His people personally and trying to comfort them with these details indicates that, as seen earlier in Jeremiah, the prophet and priest function still exist even after war and exile (51:47). God wants His people to know that the coming wrath is targeted toward Babylon (51:48).

The reason for God's punishment of Babylon is restated: They were excessive in their treatment of Judah (51:49). Now, vengeance must be had for the Judeans who were killed. Those Judeans who survived must now flee and remember the Lord and Jerusalem (51:50). In the meantime, Babylon's punishment is coming because of its arrogance and its worship of false idols. Her former power cannot save her (51:52–53).

The prophecy against Babylon closes with verses about the impact God's wrath is having on the Babylonians (51:54). They now know God's intent is real, and everything they've done to others will now be done to them (51:55–56). The leaders become drunk with arrogance and power, so much so that they will not survive (51:57). The city itself will not survive either; its walls will be destroyed, and its remains will be burned down (51:58).

51:59–64

SERAIAH

This chapter closes with a specific message from Jeremiah to a man named Seraiah (Baruch's brother). Chapters 50–51 detail Jeremiah's delivery of the prophecies regarding Babylon. He is communicating to the Babylonians while traveling with the exiled Judeans (51:59). Jeremiah writes all these messages on a single scroll and instructs Seraiah to read every bit of it as soon as they got to Babylon (51:60–61). Jeremiah, fulfilling his role as prophet, wants God's message to get to the people (51:62). And just as he has so often done as a prophet, he creates one final visual image: He instructs Seraiah to tie a stone to the scroll and, when he is finished reading God's message, throw the scroll in the Euphrates so it will sink to the bottom. Babylon's fate is the same as the scroll's (51:63–64).

JEREMIAH 52:1–34

CONCLUSION OF THE BOOK OF JEREMIAH

Setting Up the Section

In this section, the reader gets an overview of how all of Jeremiah's prophecies look from a historical perspective. This section is almost exactly like 2 Kings 24:18–25:21. Most importantly, though, is the inclusion of the fall of Jerusalem as the final chapter of this book of Jeremiah's prophecies, revealing that the city's destruction happens just as Jeremiah said it would—validating Jeremiah's prophecies.

52:1–11

JERUSALEM FALLEN

The reader is taken back to a time when the king who ended up accompanying Judah into Babylonian exile, and who was brutally killed as a prisoner of war, is just coming to the throne at age twenty-one (52:1). Despite Jeremiah's prophecies about God's anger and coming wrath, Zedekiah, like his predecessor, Jehoiakim, continues to lead the nation in sin (52:2). God then punishes Judah as He promised. Apparently, for a time, Zedekiah rebels unsuccessfully against Nebuchadnezzar (52:3).

The next verses explain in detail how Jerusalem falls to the Babylonians. In the ninth year of Zedekiah's eleven years as king, Nebuchadnezzar arranges his army around Jerusalem, cutting off traffic in and out of the city (52:4–5). After six months, the people are out of food, and the Babylonian troops break through the city walls (52:6–7). Babylonian troops are supported by the Chaldeans, who capture Zedekiah and bring him to Nebuchadnezzar for sentencing (52:8–9). In a brutal fashion not uncommon in war, Zedekiah is forced to watch as all his sons are killed. He is then blinded and imprisoned in Babylon, remaining there until he dies (52:10–11).

52:12–23

THE TEMPLE SACKED

About a month later, Nebuchadnezzar sends his chief into Jerusalem to burn not only the temple but also all the large houses he can find, including Zedekiah's (52:13). This is the culmination of progressive actions Nebuchadnezzar has been taking to conquer Judah. This is the end. The Chaldeans destroy the city walls (52:14). As seen earlier in Jeremiah's prophecies, huge numbers of people who haven't already been captured are taken prisoner (52:15). But also mentioned before, the poorest and the weakest are left behind (52:16). The next seven verses list in detail items that are taken from the temple. These are the items the exiles are longing for in 27:16–22.

52:24–30

TO BABYLON

Verses 24–30 give additional information about some of the people who are captured: They are of religious and civic importance—leaders of the people who have just been conquered (52:24–25). Like Zedekiah, they are taken to Nebuchadnezzar and killed (52:26–27). With these leaders dead, the exile can begin (52:27). At least three waves of exile are listed here (52:28–30).

52:31–34

JEHOIACHIN RELEASED

The final verses of the book of Jeremiah show that despite the destruction of Jerusalem and its temple, and the death and exile of so many of its citizens, a king of Judah remains alive. This king (though in name only) is Jehoiachin, and Nebuchadnezzar's son Evil-Merodach takes him out of prison (52:31). Probably as a gesture of good will, Evil-Merodach improves Jehoiachin's living situation by giving him new clothes, allowing him to share meals, and providing him an allowance. Even amongst prisoners there is hierarchy, and the improvement in Jehoiachin's situation is an indication of hopefulness that closes this powerful book.

Take It Home

The closing words of the book of Jeremiah disclose that 4,600 of Jerusalem's finest are bound into slavery to serve out their lives in subservience to King Nebuchadnezzar. Little do they know that God will use them as an object lesson to the world, to prove His uncompromising mandate for sovereignty in their lives, and to prove the severe and widespread consequences of bowing in worship to false gods. In every generation, we disappoint God with new ways of disobeying Him. Yet in new ways every generation, He proves His faithfulness to us and proves that His loving-kindness is everlasting.

LAMENTATIONS

INTRODUCTION TO LAMENTATIONS

Wedged between two of the major prophet works—the books of Jeremiah and Ezekiel—is the short, five-chapter poem titled Lamentations. The book's name reveals what it is—a poem of lament. It records in grave detail and sorrow the aftermath of one of the lowest points in the history of the Israelites. But it also provides one of the greatest testimonies of God's justice and mercy.

AUTHOR

There is a tradition that the prophet Jeremiah wrote this book, and thus it has its place in the Bible following the book of Jeremiah. However, no author is named in this specific book itself, and there is no place in the rest of the Bible where this writing is attributed to Jeremiah.

PURPOSE

Lamentations is a poem that reflects on the nation of Judah's suffering. The author witnessed the fall of Jerusalem and the exile of many Israelites, and in this work he is grieving the nation's fall and the demise of his people. God punished His people for their unfaithfulness to Him and His covenant, and the author and poet who wrote this poem wrote it from that place of suffering as both a reflection on the people's sins and its consequences and a prayer to God for His mercy and redemption.

OCCASION

Lamentations was most likely written soon after 586 BC, shortly after the fall of Jerusalem at the hands of the Babylonians. The author is reflecting on what he sees around him, making it most likely that the city's fall was recent at the time the book was written. In this work he alludes to the future redemption God promised His people, but that redemption has not happened yet, and the wounds of their sins and consequences are still fresh.

THEMES

The themes of the book include the following: sorrow and grief, as evidenced by the book's title; the consequences of sin; and God's judgment, mercy, and sovereignty. However, the strongest theme, which is largely unexpected based on the historical context of the book and its genre, is that of hope. Hope in God and His mercy is the foundation on which the author's lamenting takes place.

HISTORICAL CONTEXT

In 586 BC, the Babylonian army under the command of King Nebuchadnezzar attacked the city of Jerusalem, Judah's capital and the holy city that housed the temple of God. The city and temple were destroyed, and the people who weren't killed were exiled to Babylon. These events are recorded in 2 Kings 25 and 2 Chronicles 36. The people would remain in exile for almost fifty years. The author witnessed the city's fall and wrote this book shortly thereafter.

CONTRIBUTION TO THE BIBLE

Lamentations is one of the poetic books of the Bible. Chapters 1–4 are written in the very specific literary structure of an acrostic, with each verse beginning with progressive letters of the twenty-two letter Hebrew alphabet. Chapters 1, 2, 4, and 5 have twenty-two verses, and chapter 3 has sixty-six. Each Hebrew letter is used in three verses in chapter 3.

OUTLINE

THE ELEMENTS OF GODLY GRIEF 1:1–22

- The Author's Loneliness 1:1–7
- The Causes of Judah's Grief 1:8–11
- The Purposes of Judah's Grief 1:12–17
- Judah's Confession 1:18–22

JERUSALEM'S SUFFERING 2:1–22

- God's Righteous Anger 2:1–10
- The Author's Response 2:11–13
- False Prophets Revealed 2:14–17
- The Need for God 2:18–22

HOPE 3:1–66

- God's Love and Mercy 3:1–24
- God's Goodness and Control 3:25–39
- God's Forgiveness 3:40–66

EVIDENCE OF JERUSALEM'S DESTRUCTION 4:1–22

- The Costs 4:1–12
- The Causes 4:13–20
- The Conclusion 4:21–22

THE POET'S PRAYER 5:1–22

- Relief from Physical Suffering 5:1–13
- Relief from Emotional Suffering 5:14–18
- Plea for Redemption 5:19–22

LAMENTATIONS 1:1–22

THE ELEMENTS OF GODLY GRIEF

Setting Up the Section

The introductory chapter to the book of Lamentations focuses on the depth of the author's grief over Jerusalem's destruction. The fall of the city marked the fulfillment of what had been prophesied for years—that eventually the people's idolatry would be their downfall.

1:1–7

THE AUTHOR'S LONELINESS

Chief among the grievous feelings the author has is loneliness—the first observation he makes is how deserted the city is. The loneliness he feels when observing his fallen city is compounded by all of the losses he notices. Verses 1–7 catalog some of these losses. Among them are abundance, allies, a home, worship, prestige, courage, and prosperity. But despite all the tragedy the author notes, he quickly acknowledges that the destruction isn't undeserved (1:5). Rather, in the poet's own words, "The LORD has brought her grief because of her many sins" (1:5 NIV).

1:8–11

THE CAUSES OF JUDAH'S GRIEF

Judah's sin has devastating consequences, not just for the state of the nation, but in the lives of its inhabitants. The author's grief is rooted largely in how much he cares for Judah's people and the sorrow he feels regarding their downfall. In verse 8, he notes the shame the people feel after their idolatry is exposed. The people's sin also leaves them defiled (1:9), and the unclean aren't allowed to enter the presence of God. Because of their sin, their worship is tainted. One of the worst consequences of the Babylonian invasion for the city of Jerusalem as a whole is the desecration of the temple. The most holy place on earth has been invaded by a group of pagans who would never have even been allowed in it (1:10). Verse 11 notes that another devastating consequence of the nation's sin, probably one of the most strongly felt by the people of Judah, is the famine caused by how long the city was held captive before being overtaken.

Demystifying Lamentations

The cause of Judah's grief and destruction isn't a mystery—it is a direct effect of the sin in which they had been living for many years. God was gracious to the nation by sending prophets to speak truth into the people's lives, but they repeatedly refused to listen. Even the most holy places of the temple were corrupted by priests practicing idolatry. This is the ultimate example of disloyalty to the one true God.

1:12–17

THE PURPOSES OF JUDAH'S GRIEF

While the suffering of the nation is undoubtedly deserved, and long overdue because of their sin toward God, God doesn't exact suffering on them for punishment's sake alone. At this time idolatry was rampant, and God had to remind the people who their true God was. The severity of their punishment is to get their attention and turn them back to Him (1:12–13). Their suffering also serves the purpose of making them slaves to their sin (1:14). God gave His people the freedom to make their own choices, but they became slaves to their sins' consequences. But no matter how much one suffers inwardly as a result of sin, nothing is as humbling and serves as adequate a wake-up call as being crushed in the presence of one's enemy. And that is exactly what Judah experiences when its capital city is destroyed (1:15).

1:18–22

JUDAH'S CONFESSION

The nation comes face-to-face with the consequences of their sin, and this stark reality leads them to some confessions: God is righteous and acts rightly, and we were wrong to rebel against His Word (1:18–19). Having confessed the foundation of their sins and their recognition of God's holiness, the people appeal to God to hear their cries of sorrow and act mercifully toward them (1:20–21).

LAMENTATIONS 2:1–22

JERUSALEM'S SUFFERING

Setting Up the Section

The second chapter of Lamentations describes God's anger at the sin of His people. For too long, the people of Judah have lived in a state of continual sin through the idolatry they both practiced and tolerated.

2:1–10

GOD'S RIGHTEOUS ANGER

The results of God's righteous and just anger are described in a series of powerfully descriptive verbs that capture the severity of God's anger against Jerusalem (2:1–8). Verses 9–10 describe the reaction of the city and its people to this outpouring of God's wrath. The gates and walls of the city literally crumble, mimicking what happened to the people as well.

Critical Observation

Lamentations 2:1–10 mentions more than forty times how God was personally involved in Jerusalem's downfall and what happened to the people within its walls. This repeated mentioning of God's control reiterates that although King Nebuchadnezzar may have commanded the attack on the city, it was ultimately God's judgment that orchestrated the events.

2:11–13

THE AUTHOR'S RESPONSE

Having just described the response of the city and its people to God's anger, the author describes his own reaction—one of both torment and a sorrowful understanding of the justice of God. He understands that God's discipline is appropriate for the sin of the people of Jerusalem, but that doesn't make it any easier for him to stomach the city's destruction (2:11). He is admittedly without words of comfort in the face of the people's suffering (2:13).

2:14–17

FALSE PROPHETS REVEALED

There were many false prophets who were telling the people that they had nothing to fear (see Jeremiah 27–28). In the wake of the city's destruction, however, it becomes evident that these prophecies were false (2:14). Although Jerusalem's enemies gloat in the face of its downfall, the enemy's involvement in Jerusalem's destruction is secondary to God's (2:15–17).

2:18–22

THE NEED FOR GOD

Verses 18–19 include a command to the people to let their grief overtake them. They are encouraged to wail and mourn at the consequences of their sin, the worst of which is the suffering of the innocent, especially their children (see 1:5, 16; 2:11–12). In the aftermath of Jerusalem's destruction, horrific atrocities occurred such as women eating their children, priests slain in God's sanctuary, and both young and old people dead in the streets (2:20–21).

Take It Home

The author admits that God's actions are a direct consequence of His Word (2:17). Deuteronomy 28 warns the Israelites of the consequences of disobeying God's commands and prophesies a time when they will be taken captive to a foreign land. God proves that His character is steadfast and that His Word is true.

LAMENTATIONS 3:1–66

HOPE

Setting Up the Section

Because of the faithlessness of the people of Jerusalem, this holy city has been destroyed. The people who survived the attack were taken off into Babylonian captivity. Their situation is one of complete hopelessness. But God is a faithful God. It is in this truth that hope for the nation of Judah rests.

3:1–24

GOD'S LOVE AND MERCY

Lamentations 3:1–24 reveals the measure of God's love and mercy to His people. Verses 2:1–18 paint a picture of just how desperate the situation in Jerusalem has become.

The chapter opens with an identification of a man who is afflicted (3:1). Most scholars see this man as a personification of the city of Jerusalem, much like the widow mentioned at the opening of the book. Others think, however, that the author is simply referring to himself and his own desperation.

Throughout the first part of chapter 3, the author uses a variety of analogies to build a picture of hopelessness. But it is from this place of suffering that he voices a profound word of hope. Verse 21 begins with the word *yet,* which marks the powerful transition from the desperation all around to the hope of God. This hope is rooted in the fact that God didn't destroy everyone, therefore He hasn't completely abandoned His people (3:22). Verses 23–24 attest to God's faithfulness. Just as He was faithful to bring the judgment and destruction He had promised, He will also be faithful in the mercy and renewal He promised.

3:25–39

GOD'S GOODNESS AND CONTROL

Despite the suffering the author has witnessed, the goodness of God is still evident (3:25–26). The people's suffering doesn't change this aspect of God's character. Being able to recognize the characteristic of God's goodness doesn't happen overnight, but it is rather a testimony to living continually under God's instruction and discipline, so that when in the midst of affliction, one cannot deny that God is good (3:27–30). Verses 31–39 are a reminder that God is in control, even during times of grief.

3:40–66

GOD'S FORGIVENESS

Judah rebelled against God, and they have been punished for their repeated sins of idolatry. However, their punishment produces repentance, and they find themselves pleading for God's forgiveness (3:40–42). In verses 43–49, there is a catalog of a series of sufferings, but they now seem out of place following the author's statements of hope in God's goodness, faithfulness, and control. This suffering is still the reality, but the author trusts that the characteristics of God he knows to be true will soon return and bring relief to those who seek God's forgiveness (3:48–50).

Critical Observation

For those who consider Jeremiah the author of this book, verses 52–58 seem to be an obvious description of an event from Jeremiah's life when he was attacked, thrown into an empty water tank (or cistern), and left to die (Jeremiah 38:6–13). Just as God rescued him from that situation, he prays that God will rescue the nation from its suffering.

As if the sufferings of the nation aren't enough, the author once again finds himself being attacked and persecuted by his enemies (3:59–63). He knows the Lord is capable of delivering him, and he prays that God will rescue him and punish his attackers (3:64–66).

Take It Home

God's mercy and forgiveness are limitless to those who believe in Him and repent of their sins. The book of Lamentations serves to encourage the people of God to repent so they, too, can experience God's forgiving grace.

LAMENTATIONS 4:1–22

EVIDENCE OF JERUSALEM'S DESTRUCTION

The Costs	4:1–12
The Causes	4:13–20
The Conclusion	4:21–22

Setting Up the Section

Lamentations reaches its climax in chapter 3, when the author responds to God's unwavering mercy, goodness, faithfulness, and control. In chapter 4, he looks more closely at what caused God to judge Judah in this manner by comparing the state of the city of Jerusalem before and after the Babylonian attack.

4:1–12

THE COSTS

The fourth chapter opens with a description of the costs of the people's rebellion against God in imagery they would understand. Although their lives had once been as valuable as gold, they are now as dispensable as everyday pottery (4:1–2). Their rebellion has physical costs as well. The children are starving, and people who were once considered royalty are sleeping in ash heaps on the streets (4:3–5). In verse 6 there is a comparison of the situation in Jerusalem to that of Sodom, but in this case the author says Jerusalem is worse off in that her suffering lingers (see Genesis 18–19).

Verses 7–12 paint a picture for the reader of what the suffering in Jerusalem is like following the Babylonian siege. Bejeweled princes are sickly and roam the streets unrecognizable and covered in filth (4:7–8). People are constantly dying of starvation due to famine (4:9), and the author again notes the horrific scene of women cooking their children to survive (4:10). All of this is a result of what is referred to in verse 11 as God's fierce wrath.

4:13–20

THE CAUSES

Having detailed some of the results of God's judgment, this section gives more specifics about its causes. The first is in verse 13: Those who were supposed to be the example of holiness and the mediators between the people and God were leading the people astray with lies and corrupt practices. The priests who survive the Babylonian attack are left to wander the streets and are shown no honor (4:14–16). But unfortunately, the priests' damage had been done, and the nation paid for their sins.

Not only do the people of Judah follow their religious leaders in idolatrous practices; they also falsely trust the hope of a political leader and ally nation to save them from Babylon when they should have been trusting in God (4:17). They put misplaced hope in their king, Zedekiah, who was heavily influenced by the false prophets and even tries to escape from Jerusalem after its fall (4:20; see 2 Kings 25:3–7).

Demystifying Lamentations

Jeremiah 37:5–7 records how the people of Jerusalem look to Egypt and Pharaoh Hophra to ally with them against Babylon. In Lamentations 4:17, the author notes that this prophecy has come true. Even after the attack, some of the people who survived and weren't taken into captivity sought refuge in Egypt, where they would be free to continue their idolatrous practices (Jeremiah 44:7–30).

4:21–22

THE CONCLUSION

But for the people of Judah, there is good news, and the author wants to make sure they hear it. Their enemies, the Edomites, who took delight in what happened to Jerusalem, will face their own day of judgment from the Lord (4:21–22). Even better, though, is the prophecy that the Israelites' punishment will end (4:22).

Take It Home

Although the aftermath of the fall of Jerusalem is horrific, God still proves faithful to His promise of forgiveness and mercy. For those who maintained hope, how great these words must have sounded: "O beautiful Jerusalem, your punishment will end; you will soon return from exile" (4:22 NLT).

LAMENTATIONS 5:1–22

THE POET'S PRAYER

Setting Up the Section

Having grieved for the suffering of the nation, cataloged the related tragedies, voiced words of hope and a reminder of God's mercy, and prophesied an end to the suffering and the downfall of the enemy, Lamentations closes with a prayer for God's swift mercy.

5:1–13

RELIEF FROM PHYSICAL SUFFERING

The prayer opening chapter 5 is a petition to God to remember the suffering His people are experiencing (5:1). The suffering is deserved, but many are repentant and God will not turn away from them forever. Verses 2–10 describe the people's condition at the time of the prayer. Their property (inheritance) is gone, they are exiled to a foreign land, and they are impoverished and at the mercy of their enemies. Everyone has suffered in some way. Verses 11–13 mention six different people groups, all of whom have experienced extreme suffering. The entire nation feels God's punishment on an individual level.

5:14–18

RELIEF FROM EMOTIONAL SUFFERING

Verses 2–13 focus on the nation's physical suffering, but in verses 14–18, the prayer shifts to the topic of emotional suffering. There is no joy among the people, and their hearts are faint because of what they have endured (5:17). More importantly than physical healing, the people's spirits need to be restored to the joy of the Lord they once knew.

Critical Observation

Prior to the fall of Jerusalem, the nation was ruled by the line of David in fulfillment of the Davidic covenant (2 Samuel 7). But the fall of the city marks the end of Davidic rule. The covenant is ultimately fulfilled in Jesus Christ's reign, but the reign of Davidic earthly kings is finished (see 5:16).

5:19–22

PLEA FOR REDEMPTION

Verse 19 is the crux of this prayer and reveals the foundation of the author's hope. God is the only One with power to right the people's punishment and bring physical and emotional healing to the nation. The author prays for restoration and for God, in His mercy, to turn the people's hearts back to Him if mercy is in His plan (5:21–22). He admits that God, in His sovereignty, may not choose to lift the punishment and show mercy, but it is his prayer that that is not the case.

Take It Home

The underlying theme in Lamentations is that of hope. God had promised restoration, just as He had promised the punishment the people suffered, and it was this promise of salvation that the author clung to. He knew God's character to be good and merciful, and he hoped that with repentant hearts, God would soon lift His punishment from them and return them to Himself.

EZEKIEL

INTRODUCTION TO EZEKIEL

Ezekiel was a prophet caught up in the turmoil of his time. He was among ten thousand exiles carried off to Babylon in the second of three deportations from Judea (2 Kings 24:14). He and his wife settled in a Judean community established near Nippur, on the Kebar Canal. God's people needed a prophet in Babylon because, with some wonderful exceptions, they carried all the spiritual baggage from the years of idolatry and apostasy that began their ruin.

AUTHOR

Ezekiel was a priest, and his priestly orientation comes through in his prophecies. More than any other prophet, he depicts the consummation of the kingdom of God in terms of a new temple and revitalized worship. His prophetic call came at age thirty, which would have made him a young eyewitness to the spiritual reforms during the reign of King Josiah. Unable to serve as priest in a traditional capacity due to his relocation (and subsequent destruction of Jerusalem's temple), his spiritual preparations are still put to use as God calls him to be a prophet during a crucial time of Israel's history.

PURPOSE

Ezekiel has a clear voice from God during a difficult time. He prophesies several years in Babylon before the Babylonians actually destroy the temple and the city of Jerusalem, warning his people of what will happen. He then continues to minister several years afterward to assure them of God's continued sovereignty throughout their bleak circumstances.

OCCASION

God's people were caught in the maw of conflict between world powers Egypt and Babylon. International tensions overshadowed the circumstances of many smaller states and turned the lives of countless individuals and families upside down. Ezekiel's world was turbulent, which makes his message surprisingly relevant for today.

THEMES

Ezekiel's book contains a number of themes:

- *Visions.* No other Old Testament prophet is given as many visions as Ezekiel, and no other Old Testament book devotes so much space to visions.
- *"Then you will know that I am the Lord."* This phrase is found again and again throughout Ezekiel's writing. Israel has forgotten the Lord her God. Ezekiel repeatedly passes along God's reminder to assure the people that God is still at work to put Israel's culpable ignorance right.
- *Individual Responsibility.* The people tended to blame their problems on their ancestors or circumstances beyond their control. Ezekiel stresses the importance of one's individual relationship with the Lord.
- *God using Ezekiel as a sign.* Many other prophets were orators, and Ezekiel did his share of preaching. Yet he is distinctive in how frequently God uses the prophet himself as a sign. Much like Jeremiah, Ezekiel acts out or symbolizes what he is saying on several occasions.

HISTORICAL CONTEXT

When Ezekiel began his prophetic work, Babylon had gained the upper hand and was holding sway over the entire ancient Near East. Judah's King Jehoiakim had first submitted to Babylon, but later rebelled (with the encouragement of the Egyptians, but against the advice of Jeremiah). As a result the Babylonian leader, King Nebuchadnezzar, dragged him to Babylon in shackles where he was apparently executed. Jehoiakim's eighteen-year-old son, Jehoiachin, succeeded him as the Babylonian appointee, but he, too, was summoned to Babylon a few months later.

CONTRIBUTION TO THE BIBLE

Much of what Ezekiel teaches is similar to the writings of Jeremiah or other prophets. But unique to his writing is the fascinating vision of the valley of dry bones (37:1–14) and his vision of a temple unlike anything that has yet been constructed (chapters 40–48).

OUTLINE

THE CALL OF A PROPHET 1:1–3:27

- Ezekiel's Vision 1:1–28
- Ezekiel's Call 2:1–3:11
- Ezekiel's (Possible) Reluctance 3:12–27

LESSONS IN DIVINE JUDGMENT 4:1–7:27

- Ezekiel's Symbolic Actions 4:1–5:17
- A Prophecy for the Mountains of Israel 6:1–14
- A Prophecy Concerning "the Day" 7:1–27

A VISION OF JERUSALEM'S TEMPLE 8:1–11:25

- Wickedness within the Temple 8:1–18
- God's Response to Israel's Wickedness 9:1–11:25

EZEKIEL SPEAKS OUT 12:1–14:23

- A Visible Lesson 12:1–28
- Confronting False Prophets 13:1–23
- Confronting the Elders of the People 14:1–23

THREE ALLEGORIES TO DESCRIBE ISRAEL 15:1–17:24

- Allegory #1: Israel Is the Wood, Not the Fruit, of the Vine 15:1–8
- Allegory #2: Jerusalem as an Unfaithful Wife 16:1–63
- Allegory #3: A Vine and Two Eagles 17:1–24

A RETIRED PROVERB, A LAMENT, AND MORE WARNINGS 18:1–21:32

- Clarifying a Proverb 18:1–32
- A Lament while Reviewing Israel's Past 19:1–14
- The Problem of Ongoing Idolatry 20:1–44
- Prepare for Babylon 20:45–21:32

SOME FINAL WORDS FOR JUDAH 22:1–24:27

- Jerusalem on Trial 22:1–31
- A Tale of Two Prostitutes 23:1–49
- Judgment and Mourning to Come 24:1–27

EZEKIEL 1:1–3:27

THE CALL OF A PROPHET

Setting Up the Section

The first section of Ezekiel (chapters 1–24) is devoted to prophecies of judgment and divine wrath to befall the citizens still remaining in Judea and Jerusalem. The first subsection of this large division concerns the call of Ezekiel.

1:1–28

EZEKIEL'S VISION

Ezekiel is among a group of expatriate Jews living in Babylon along the Kebar River at Tel Abib (1:3; 3:15). It is his thirtieth year (1:1), the age at which a priest should be beginning his official service to God (Numbers 4:3). He is far away from the temple in Jerusalem, but God has not forgotten him.

Critical Observation

Verses 2–3 shift from first person to third person, likely the insertion of an editor to provide objective dating for Ezekiel's call and/or to make the opening more consistent with other prophetic books. The date would have been July 31, 593 BC. It may seem strange that this account is dated according to the reign of Jehoiachin (1:2), a king who ruled only three months and accomplished nothing. Yet Jehoiachin is perceived as the last of the kings in the Davidic line.

There in the land of Israel's enemies, while God's people are in captivity, Ezekiel receives a magnificent vision. A sudden storm blows in, accompanied by wind, lightning, and fire. In the center of the fire are four creatures, each with four faces (Ezekiel 1:4–6). They will be identified later (10:2) as *cherubim*, a specific rank of angels.

Each of the four faces of the creatures is significant: The lion is chief of the wild animals, the ox chief of domestic animals, the eagle the primary bird, and human beings chief of all animals (1:10). The four faces orient the beings in all directions, so they therefore have no need to turn while navigating (1:9, 12). They move, literally, like lightning: They are both brilliant and quick (1:13–14).

Demystifying Ezekiel

The description of these cherubim may have appeared less bizarre to Ezekiel's original audience than to modern ears. The iconography of the ancient Near East included figures that had more than one head, multiple sets of wings, human bodies with animal heads, etc. However, no symbols have been discovered that exactly match Ezekiel's depiction.

Just as fascinating and puzzling is the prophet's portrayal of the wheels by which these creatures move from place to place (1:15–21). The beings could move in any direction, including leaving the ground. In Hebrew and Greek, the same word can be used for wind and spirit, so the *windstorm* (1:4) is associated with the movement of God's Spirit. No prophet writes of the Spirit as much as Ezekiel. This energizing power of God directs him from place to place, at least in his visions. And the movement of the four creatures is in response to the Spirit (1:20).

We shouldn't be surprised if Ezekiel's description leaves us unsatisfied. He is attempting to describe something that is beyond his power to understand, much less communicate to others. He uses a great number of analogies to try to explain what he is seeing, but it is still difficult to make sense of his account.

After the creatures and the wheels, Ezekiel describes a gem-like firmament—an expanse or platform above the creatures upon which the throne of God will rest (1:22–28). The throne of sapphire (1:26) is reminiscent of Moses' description of seeing God on Mount Sinai (Exodus 24:9–11). Even describing the sound the creatures made is a challenge for Ezekiel. He likens it to three different things: the roar of a great torrent, the voice of the Almighty, and the tramp of a great army on the march (Ezekiel 1:24).

Yet these amazing sights are only a prelude for what is to come. Ezekiel's attention is arrested first by a voice from above and then by a figure like that of a man, sitting on a dazzling throne. The shining brilliance of the figure prevents Ezekiel from seeing anything other than a general shape, yet the prophet leaves no doubt that he is witnessing the terrible majesty of Yahweh. In response, he falls facedown before the Lord God (1:28).

2:1–3:11

EZEKIEL'S CALL

Throughout the entire book of Ezekiel, God never addresses the prophet by name. Instead, He uses the term *Son of man*, which highlights Ezekiel's humanity in contrast to the Lord's divine glory.

God is sending Ezekiel to speak to his own people, the Israelites. But at this point in their history, they are rebellious, obstinate, and stubborn (2:3–4). They are subjects revolting against their King and children rebelling against their Father. But according to verse 5, they are about to discover a real prophet among them. The problem with false prophecy is that it is invariably rosy and frequently proven false by real-life events. Ezekiel, on the other hand, will provide stark promises of divine wrath, and the people will see his prophecies come to pass.

Demystifying Ezekiel

References to *Israel* can be confusing. The name originated with Jacob (Genesis 32:27–28). By the end of Genesis, phrases such as "the tribes of Israel" (Genesis 49:16) or "the children of Israel" (Genesis 50:25) indicate the people of God. Centuries later, after Solomon's death, the tribes divided. The ten northern tribes continued to be known as *Israel* while the southern tribes comprised *Judah*. Technically, the Jews exiled to Babylon were from Judah, but they were the only ones to return to their homeland after captivity. From that point, biblical writers again use *Israel* to refer to them, as Ezekiel does (Ezekiel 2:3; 3:5, 7). And while the term *Jew* is by definition someone from the kingdom of Judah, the term soon broadens to include any of the citizens of the remnant of Israel after the exile.

Ezekiel has a challenging assignment. Not only is he being sent to his own people, which is difficult enough, but there are many exiled priests in Babylon. Why should the people pay special attention to *him*? In addition, the people's rebellious attitude toward God will make Ezekiel's message especially hard for them to hear. No patriot wants to prophesy the doom of the nation he loves. But Ezekiel is up to the task.

In fact, God warns Ezekiel of the danger of getting caught up in the rebellious attitude of his people (2:8). He offers him something to eat, and Ezekiel no doubt expects some kind of food. Instead, he is handed a scroll. Jeremiah had written of eating the words of God (Jeremiah 15:16), but Ezekiel goes beyond metaphor into a more concrete (and most likely unpleasant) experience, as he is instructed to fill his stomach (Ezekiel 3:3). The message he is digesting is summed up by lament, mourning, and woe (2:10).

The message certainly isn't appealing, yet the taste of the scroll is sweet (3:3). The sweetness must have come from the prophet's encounter with the Word of the Lord itself. Opening one's life to God's Word and God's will is humanity's highest privilege and the greatest conceivable satisfaction.

Had Ezekiel been sent to some other people, they might be expected to respond, as the Assyrians had listened to Jonah. But the people of Israel had a long habit of rejecting God, so Ezekiel should expect the same response (3:4–7) and not take it personally.

Critical Observation

A soldier on the battlefield doesn't wring his hands or ask the enemy soldiers firing at him, "What did I do to you?" Rather, he understands that the opposition is the result of a deeper and larger cause. He is a target only because he is serving the cause of his government or nation. Ezekiel was to have a similar outlook in his ministry.

God promises to help toughen up His prophet. (The name *Ezekiel* means "God strengthens.") We speak in terms of "facing" difficult situations, so it is Ezekiel's face that is hardened to help the prophet cope with his listeners (3:8–9). And it is at this point revealed that Ezekiel's assignment is to preach to the community of exiled Hebrews (3:11).

EZEKIEL'S (POSSIBLE) RELUCTANCE

So how does Ezekiel feel about his call from God? We see no overt resistance, and we hear no objections from his mouth. Many assume, then, that he readily accepts the call to become God's prophet. But a close examination of the text and a combination of several observations suggest that Ezekiel may have responded much like Moses, Gideon, and Jeremiah in initially resisting God's invitation.

Much of scripture—especially in regard to the experiences of the life of faith—is communicated indirectly and subtly. The reader is expected to pay close attention with his or her imagination fully awake to the personal dimension. When reading this section of Ezekiel in such a way, the impression is that the prophet does not want to do what the Lord is calling him to do and has to be cajoled and persuaded, if not compelled, to undertake the assignment.

Following is some of the evidence to support such a viewpoint:

- The length and detail of Ezekiel's call narrative is almost 50 percent longer than that of Moses, who is clearly disinclined to respond to God at first.
- The power and scope of the vision preceding Ezekiel's call.
- In 2:8, Ezekiel is personally commanded not to rebel like the rest of the people. A similar warning is not necessary with Moses, Isaiah, or Jeremiah.
- He is told three times to eat the scroll before actually doing so (2:8–3:3).
- God gives Ezekiel two commissioning speeches (2:3–8; 3:4–11), with considerable repetition in the second.
- Ezekiel's first response that we know of is bitterness and anger (3:14).
- When Ezekiel returns from his encounter with the Lord to sit among his people, he is in a state of shock and spiritual desperation until God finally breaks the silence with a strong and uncompromising warning to get to work (3:15–17).
- It appears that God attempts to forestall any effort on Ezekiel's part to plead for or defend Israel.

Regardless of his other mental disposition at the time, Ezekiel is angry as he makes the transition from witnessing the glory of God to returning to his home and assignment (3:14). He has been forced to take a difficult assignment. He has suddenly moved from at least a measure of tranquility among his fellow exiles to the prospect of living with their rejection and hostility. His personal future has quickly become dark and foreboding. The Lord's hand is upon him to see him through the assignment, but he isn't happy about it (3:12–15). He did not volunteer; he was drafted.

But Ezekiel will not be evaluated based on the *results* of his prophecies—just his faithfulness in speaking for God. The image of the watchman in verses 16–21 will be repeated again in 33:1–6. Ezekiel's role as a prophet is like that of a watchman for a city. It is his job to sound an alarm after being made aware of an approaching threat. All Ezekiel has to do is pass along God's message to the people. They might respond and be spared a tragedy, or they might ignore the message and suffer the consequences. God's truth is a fragrance of life to those who are being saved and an odor of death to the defiant. The results are not under Ezekiel's control, but the prophet *will* be held responsible for speaking the truth clearly.

Ezekiel had previously been carried by the Spirit (3:14–15), but he later moves under his own power in response to God's command (3:23) before the Spirit again comes into him, lifts him up, and speaks to him (2:1–4; 3:24). But what the Lord tells Ezekiel in verses 24–27 has created no small degree of confusion among those reading and trying to interpret the text. We are left wondering how to understand Ezekiel's confinement and speechlessness. It is likely that this is the first of several instances throughout the book of Ezekiel where the prophet himself is used as a sign from God. Later examples will be more apparent as to their intent. In this case, the symbolic action may be primarily applicable to Ezekiel rather than the entire nation because the prophet has been stubbornly unhappy about receiving his assignment from the Lord.

Critical Observation

Ezekiel has already been told repeatedly and emphatically that he is to deliver a message to Israel, so he is clearly not being *totally* silenced (3:24–26). Nor is he being bound *entirely*, because he will soon be given specific assignments. Perhaps the reason for his being bound and muted is singularly in response to his initial unwillingness to undertake the assignment God gave him.

Ezekiel will not be allowed to plead for Israel, to argue the case for her escaping God's judgment. He will not be allowed to soften his message or shape it in a way that will make him less unpopular with the Israelites. He will speak what the Lord tells him to—that and nothing else! Ezekiel's binding and muteness are also demonstrations of the withdrawal of God's favor from His people that will last until the destruction of Jerusalem seven years later.

The final statement in the narrative of Ezekiel's call (3:27) seems to clarify, once again, that Israel's spiritual condition is fixed. Israel is once more characterized as hardened in rebellion and no longer eligible for appeal. This is the heavy burden of Ezekiel's assignment, to proclaim judgment and doom against Israel without offering hope of pardon or deliverance. While this may sound cruel or unreasonable in light of what we like to think about God's mercy and grace, the Israelites had long had faithful prophets warning them of God's wrath if they did not repent. The people of Judah had already witnessed the devastation of the northern kingdom, just as the prophets had warned. They had seen the dark clouds gather on the horizon as Babylon made her way westward. Yet they were so hardened, so spiritually dead, that they didn't get it, still refusing to acknowledge their own fault or God's perfect justice.

Yes, God is gracious and merciful, but the Israelites of this day indifferently rejected His repeated offers of mercy. Ezekiel is letting them know that the Lord has departed from them. When it becomes obvious that they will not be able to withstand the Babylonians, they cry out to God in a panic, but He is unwilling to listen.

Ezekiel is called to address Israel's distressing spiritual condition—that of settled rebellion, defiant unbelief, and the inability to interpret their situation correctly. It is evident that God anticipated that some of the rebellious Israelites would repent and return to a life of faithfulness (3:21).

Take It Home

Ezekiel opens with some big surprises. To begin with, in Near Eastern thinking, gods ruled over specific territories. It would have been totally unexpected—and significant beyond our understanding—for Israel's God to make a glorious appearance to Ezekiel *in Babylon*. Is there an equivalent to Babylon in your life, where you don't normally expect to experience God, yet where He could make a meaningful difference? Then, in a second surprise, God's opening statements focus not on hope and comfort but on doom and judgment. How do you think most believers today compare to the Israelites in regard to expecting primarily good news from God, even when they are slow to respond to His leading and reluctant to repent?

EZEKIEL 4:1–7:27

LESSONS IN DIVINE JUDGMENT

Setting Up the Section

The people of Judah are being taken in large groups to Babylon where they will live in captivity. Ezekiel was among one of the earlier groups, and while in Babylon, God called him to a prophetic ministry. He appeared to be initially reluctant, but in this section he begins to respond to God's instructions, even though many of his actions must have seemed quite strange to onlookers.

4:1–5:17

EZEKIEL'S SYMBOLIC ACTIONS

Ezekiel received his call to be a prophet in 593 BC. The Babylonians would destroy the city of Jerusalem in 586 BC. Many of Ezekiel's first assignments were to predict the fall of Israel's beloved city. If the previous section (chapters 2–3) seems repetitive in its depiction of the Jews as hard of heart and obstinate in their refusal to humble themselves before the Lord, this section will prove equally repetitive in describing God's determination to punish Jerusalem for the Jews' betrayal of His covenant.

God first tells Ezekiel to construct a model of the city of Jerusalem (4:1–2). The prophet would have drawn a map of the city on soft clay and then allowed it to harden under the Middle Eastern sun. Jerusalem was on a hill, so any attempt to overtake the city would require ramps to transport battering rams and other weapons to the walls. Conquering a walled city was no easy task, so enemy armies would usually lay siege to the city first in order to weaken its resistance. Ezekiel's model of the city includes the ramps, weapons, and surrounding armies.

Iron was the hardest metal available at the time (4:3). God tells Ezekiel to use an iron pan, normally used to bake flat cakes over an open fire, as an impenetrable wall between the prophet's face and the model of the city. The message is clear: While Jerusalem is surrounded and suffering, anticipating defeat, God is hiding His face from the people.

Critical Observation

The text doesn't elaborate about Ezekiel's enactment of God's instructions, although it isn't likely that the prophet is doing these things in private. The object lessons are designed to be public and to incite first curiosity, and then a reaction. As people walked by Ezekiel's home, they saw the map of Jerusalem and the prophet's mock siege. It wouldn't be long before everyone in the community was talking about it.

Next Ezekiel is told to symbolically bear the sin of his people. He is to lie on his left side for 390 days, most likely representing the 390 years or so between the building of the temple in Jerusalem to its destruction (4:4–5). Presumably, his face would have been turned toward his model city. We are not to suppose his is a round-the-clock vigil. Just as someone might say that it took three weeks to read a book, never intending to infer that he or she read continuously for twenty-one straight twenty-four-hour days, Ezekiel probably assumes his position for only a segment of each day, perhaps during times when many people will observe him.

After spending 390 days turned toward the northern kingdom, Ezekiel reverses sides to deal with the sin of Judah—a forty-day commitment this time. The number in this case may have been symbolic of the generation that would suffer the consequences of exile on account of Israel's sin. Adding the 390 with 40 yields 430—the number of years of Israel's previous sojourn in Egypt (Exodus 12:40). And if the forty years is considered symbolic, it is close enough to harmonize with Jeremiah's prophecy of seventy years of exile (Jeremiah 25:11–12; 29:10).

Ezekiel's bare arm would have symbolized Yahweh's power and determination to act (Ezekiel 4:7). We aren't told exactly how Ezekiel is bound with ropes (4:8), although the purpose is to demonstrate the unalterable character of the prophecy of Jerusalem's destruction and Judah's punishment.

Ezekiel's next sign involves baking bread using an unusual combination of ingredients: grain and vegetables (4:9). The intent is to simulate a siege diet, much like those remaining in Jerusalem would be forced to eat (4:16–17). The shortage of available grain required making bread out of whatever could be found. The daily allotment is only eight ounces (4:10). Water is rationed as well, with Ezekiel only allowed about two-thirds of a quart each day.

Ezekiel doesn't balk at any of God's instructions until he is told to cook his meals using human excrement for fuel (4:12). This distasteful practice would also be part of life under siege. But Ezekiel had always striven to uphold his principles as a priest, so

God is sympathetic to his request and grants the prophet a concession. Ezekiel's symbolic actions in Babylon are to reflect the horrific conditions of life in Jerusalem. It is important not to overlook the qualifying phrase in verse 17. The people are certainly suffering, but their situation is because of their sin. Ezekiel's symbolic demonstration continues with a severe haircut. In 5:1, he is instructed to remove his hair and beard. Normally, priests were forbidden to shave their heads (Leviticus 21:5), so the action would have drawn attention. But the haircut is just the beginning. More significant is what Ezekiel is told to do with the hair; he is to weigh it and divide it into thirds.

After his observation of the siege periods, he is to burn one-third of the hair inside the city (his clay representation). Another third is to be stricken with a sword and placed around the city. The final third is to be tossed into the wind (Ezekiel 5:2). But Ezekiel is to hold back a few strands (5:3). The explanation for these curious acts are provided in verse 12. No one in Jerusalem is going to weather the siege well. The people will either die from plague or famine inside the city, be killed outside the city, or be scattered by God to faraway places. Any survivors who may have remained complacent are represented by the few strands of hair first held back by Ezekiel but eventually added to the fire (5:3–4).

God's frustration with Israel is evident, and for good reason. The Israelites are supposed to be a light to the Gentiles, an example of higher standards. Yet they have degenerated to the point where they don't even meet the standards of the nations around them (5:5–7). Even after thousands of people have been carried away in two large deportations, the remaining Israelites continue to offer sacrifices to Canaanite gods (5:8–9). As one awful consequence, they are going to be driven to cannibalism as Jerusalem is besieged and their food supplies dwindle to nothing (5:10–11). Although the Babylonians are the instrument of their fall, God makes it clear that He is the one responsible for what is happening (5:8–17).

The events described should have come as no surprise to the Israelites. They are the very punishments described in the Law for those who broke their covenant with God (Leviticus 26:23–39; Deuteronomy 28:15–68). However, since God remains in control of the situation, the terrible circumstances will not last forever. He will see His people through, even in their desperate situation (Ezekiel 5:13).

6:1–14

A PROPHECY FOR THE MOUNTAINS OF ISRAEL

After being told to make models of Jerusalem, lie on his side for weeks at a time, and cut his hair, Ezekiel is instructed to simply prophesy (6:1–2). He is told to address the mountains of Israel. (The phrase *mountains of Israel* occurs seventeen times in Ezekiel but nowhere else in the Bible.)

The phrase is significant for a couple of reasons. First is a topographical observation. The Israelites had been deported out of the mountainous region of Jerusalem and Judea and reestablished on the plains of Babylon. When they thought of home, they thought of mountains. Second is a spiritual concern. Ezekiel would be addressing Israel's embrace of pagan idolatry. Such idolatrous worship commonly took place in high places—usually on hilltops and mountaintops (6:13), although elevated sites could be constructed within cities as well.

So Ezekiel's oracle to the mountains of Israel begins with God's pronouncement of judgment on the high places around Jerusalem. While the people in Jerusalem will eventually hear what Ezekiel is preaching in Babylon, the Hebrews already exiled in Babylon realize they are implicated in Jerusalem's sins and have already suffered punishment for them. The Lord does not speak abstractly about judgment but rather talks about the punishment of real people in specific times and places. It is common for people to read biblical prophecies of judgment and assume the dire predictions apply only to people in other times and places. But by linking His wrath to real events in human history, God forces people of all eras to reckon with prophecy's meaning for them.

Other than the object of worship, idol worship in the high places is not dissimilar to worship at the temple. People burn sacrificial animals on an altar of dirt, stone, or wood that is usually overlaid with bronze. This offering for the benefit of the particular god at that site is accompanied by incense burned in incense altars, creating a pleasing aroma for the god (6:4).

But Yahweh is about to thoroughly devastate such idolatrous worship (6:4–7). The exposure of corpses as punishment is among the curses spelled out for those who betray God's covenant (Deuteronomy 28:26). Yet God will spare some of the people to bring them to a right mind and restore them to a life of faith. There is a terrible irony in that those who are restored first have to be cast out of the land the Lord has given them and stripped of all the privileges that have been theirs as His people (Ezekiel 6:8–10). But that's what it will take for some people to know that He is Lord (6:7, 10, 13–14).

Demystifying Ezekiel

Ezekiel is told to clap his hands, stamp his feet, and cry out in response to the wickedness of Israel and their subsequent fall, but the underlying emotion is unclear. Some have suggested the intended attitude is one of anger for what is happening. Others believe it is appropriate in this instance to express joyful delight in the misery of another—although God does not tolerate this attitude among Israel's enemies (25:6–7). Either way, Ezekiel acts in the Lord's place to express disgust over what Israel has become.

7:1–27

A PROPHECY CONCERNING "THE DAY"

The next prophecy Ezekiel receives from God is no more optimistic than the previous one. Indeed, he is foretelling "the end" for the entire nation. "The four corners of the land" in verse 2 is an all-encompassing reference much like "mountains and hills, ravines and valleys" in 6:3. Disaster will befall the entire nation of Israel, but God's judgment is no more than God's justice. Israel has committed detestable acts and will receive only what is deserved (7:3–9).

When Ezekiel speaks of "the day," his listeners would have known what he is talking about (7:7). Other prophets (Amos, Isaiah, Joel, Zephaniah, and others) had already spoken and written of the Day of the Lord. Ezekiel's prophetic ministry falls squarely in line with these other prophets who warned of God's terrible judgment if His people did not repent and return to Him.

The rest of this passage describes the appalling effects of that day. However, the reader needs to be aware of the examples of hyperbole—the use of exaggeration for effect (the way we might say, "She lost a ton of weight"). For instance, Ezekiel says that no one will be left after God's judgment (7:11), yet he will soon speak of the survivors (7:16).

Ezekiel does not explain what he means about the rod that has budded (7:10). Perhaps it is a reference to Nebuchadnezzar or other oppressive rulers who will soon dominate Israel. What is clear, however, is that the economic consequences of God's judgment will be catastrophic. All the normality of daily life—buying and selling, for example (7:12–13)—will be forgotten as Judah is driven from their land.

Critical Observation

We should note that although Ezekiel speaks of "the day" in present tense (7:10, 12), it will still be about six years before his prophecy is fulfilled. Yet the likelihood of the event taking place in the future is just as certain as if it had already happened.

Sword, plague, and famine have been recurring themes in Ezekiel so far (5:12; 6:12; 7:15) as the three forms of death associated with siege warfare. And the few who escape death won't be able to rejoice. They carry with them their own guilt and God's anger toward them on account of their rebellion. They will be overwhelmed, powerless, and psychologically devastated (7:16–18).

Wealth will no longer provide comfort. Without food to buy or people to influence, money will have no purpose. Not only will personal assets become plunder for the enemy but also the temple in Jerusalem will be robbed and desecrated (7:19–22).

The city of Jerusalem has been spared for some time, and even under Babylonian control life is not particularly unpleasant at first. But Jerusalem will eventually be destroyed and associated with bloodshed. Those who don't die will be subject to chains—captivity and exile (7:23–25).

It will be a time of "calamity upon calamity" (7:26 NIV). Their prophets will have no visions. The priests will offer no teachings. The elders will provide no wise counsel. Not even the king will be spared indignity and despair. The people will have nowhere to turn as they realize that they are bereft of help (7:26–27). Jerusalem had been Israel's pride and joy. Its destruction will be their most agonizing memory.

Take It Home

Ezekiel chapters 4–24 are largely devoted to the same theme, affording readers the opportunity to develop a theory of divine wrath. The prophet presents the Lord as a God of vengeance as surely as He is a God of love. Humans tend to want to soften their image of God, yet God's wrath is not only a feature of divine nature and character but also the exercise of His justice. God is never shown as capricious, ill-willed, arbitrary, or unstable. Very much the contrary! God's wrath is His holy justice in operation. Think about your own beliefs in this area: Do you agree with Ezekiel's image of God? Is the wrath of God difficult for you to comprehend? Does the image of a wrathful God in any way affect how you live?

EZEKIEL 8:1–11:25

A VISION OF JERUSALEM'S TEMPLE

Wickedness within the Temple	8:1–18
God's Response to Israel's Wickedness	9:1–11:25

Setting Up the Section

Ezekiel has been delivering some hard-to-hear messages to the Israelites who have already been deported to Babylon. The city of Jerusalem will soon be conquered and the temple destroyed. In this section, Ezekiel is given a vision that makes evident the source of God's displeasure in regard to the temple.

8:1–18

WICKEDNESS WITHIN THE TEMPLE

This vision takes place some fourteen months after Ezekiel's initial vision (1:1). The date is September 18, 592 BC, still several years prior to the fall of Jerusalem at the hands of Babylon. The fact that the elders are gathered at Ezekiel's home indicates that they recognize his prophetic authority.

As in his first vision, Ezekiel sees a general shape of a man, fiery and bright (1:26–27; 8:2)—another manifestation of Yahweh Himself. The details of this vision continue through 11:24, so one must wonder what the elders observed as Ezekiel witnessed what God was showing him.

The Lord assumes a form Ezekiel is familiar with (a hand) to lift him up. While remaining bodily in Tel Abib with the elders, Ezekiel is taken to Jerusalem *in visions* (8:3).

Ezekiel first sees the north gate of Jerusalem's temple. Three gates lead from the outer court to the inner court, the north gate being the one used by the king and likely the most prominent. An idol stands in full view. The pathetic sight of an idol in the temple is soon contrasted with the glory of God Himself in the fullness that Ezekiel had previously witnessed (1:26–28; 8:4). The Lord tells Ezekiel that he will see things even more detestable (8:6).

The prophet is instructed to look north, where he sees a curious hole in the wall. He is instructed to enlarge it sufficiently to pass through it. He discovers a doorway, and behind it he sees Israel's leadership participating in full-blown pantheistic idolatry, surrounded by all kinds of images.

Jaazaniah (8:11) is from a prominent family and probably known to Ezekiel before his removal to Babylon. His father had served under Josiah, the last of Judah's righteous kings (2 Kings 22:3), and one of his brothers had been a defender of Jeremiah (Jeremiah 26:24). How sad, then, that Jaazaniah is leading Israel astray in the worship of animals. His involvement, along with that of the other elders, indicates that the spiritual rot has thoroughly penetrated the highest reaches of Israelite society.

Critical Observation

Pantheism, the belief that everything is a god (or part of one) and that the gods are part of everything, was rife in the ancient world. With a belief that all life is divine, the practice had even reached the point where the Egyptians worshiped dung beetles.

The elders of Israel are attempting to appeal to the spirits of various animals, represented by images on a wall (Ezekiel 8:9–11). Incense is burned to appeal to the selfish and sensual natures of such gods. Worship of the Lord also included the burning of incense, but as an emblem of prayer—an act of personal confidence in a God of love who cares for His people.

The irony in this scene is almost too much to fathom. The elders, clustered in one of the temple's inner rooms (Nehemiah 13:4–9), wrongly assume that Yahweh has been defeated by the gods of Babylon and is no longer able to help them. They look for help wherever they can find it. But the accusations they make are not about God but rather about the very images in which they place their faith. Yet Ezekiel has still not seen the worst (Ezekiel 8:12–13).

Tammuz (8:14) is a Babylonian fertility god who is particularly appealing to women. They are mourning because tradition held that Tammuz had been banished to the underworld. Then, moving from the inner room to the entrance of the temple, Ezekiel sees about twenty-five men worshiping the sun. Sun worship is nothing new in Judah (2 Kings 23:5, 11), but it has never been more brazen than in this temple setting. The temple faced the east; so, logistically, to bow to the sun in the east one had to turn his back to the temple. Yahweh is being displaced in His own sanctuary!

Corrupted worship of God and crimes against other humans go hand in hand, so it is not surprising that Ezekiel notes the violence that fills the land in verse 17. The phrase "the branch to the nose" is not used elsewhere in scripture, and its meaning is uncertain. It may be a reference to some pagan ritual or perhaps a disrespectful (obscene?) gesture.

EZEKIEL 9:1–11:25

GOD'S RESPONSE TO ISRAEL'S WICKEDNESS

The men who are summoned (9:1–2) are most likely angels sent to execute God's sentence. Six have weapons, the seventh a writing kit. The six executioners will accomplish their work through the Babylonian army. The seventh is assigned to mark the people of the city who lament the detestable acts taking place throughout Jerusalem. The mark (9:4) is the *taw*, the last letter of the Hebrew alphabet. Jeremiah would have been one of the inhabitants of Jerusalem at this time, so he and a minority of other citizens would not have been complicit in Jerusalem's apostasy. God's judgment will therefore make appropriate distinctions between those who participate in idolatry and sin and those who are grieved by such things.

Those with the mark are to be spared, but no one else. The widespread destruction, including women and children (9:6), is a feature of the holy war—a divine war against a wicked people. There is no mention of adult men because they will have been killed in combat.

Ezekiel fears that this judgment of God might do away with Israel altogether (9:8). Galilee and Transjordan had been lost in 733 BC. Samaria and what was left of the northern kingdom fell, and its people were carried off in 721 BC. Little territory was left around Jerusalem. But the section concludes with the reminder that every true believer has been marked—a remnant will be spared.

Israel has defied God in the most brazen and disgusting ways by forsaking Him for the ridiculous mythologies of other cultures. Their spiritual apostasy has led to a culture of violence and injustice. As severe as their judgment will be, it will be nothing they don't deserve.

The angel who had been given the task of marking the righteous is next assigned to bring the fire of Yahweh's judgment upon Jerusalem (10:2). It is at this point that Ezekiel identifies the creatures he had seen in his initial vision (chapter 1) as cherubim (10:20–22).

Demystifying Ezekiel

The Bible maintains a close connection between cherubim and the presence of God. Large images of cherubim stood above the ark of the covenant, the physical sign of God's enthroned presence in the temple (Exodus 25:18–22), and the temple was filled with carvings of cherubim (1 Kings 6:29, 35). In the Old Testament, Yahweh is routinely portrayed as borne by cherubim. Ancient Israelites expected that wherever cherubim were found, God would also be present (Psalms 18:10; 80:1).

The cherubim seemed to accompany the Lord's chariot (Ezekiel 10:9–14), which was parked to the south of the temple (10:3)—perhaps because of the idol that stood in the north gate. God is planning to depart from the temple. The cloud, representing the glory of the Lord, first moves from its established position in the Holy of Holies to the threshold of the temple (10:3–4). Soon it moves from the threshold to the place where the cherubim are assembled outside. It is significant that the temple is called the Lord's house at precisely the moment He is leaving it (10:19).

More evidence of the wickedness within the temple is seen as Ezekiel is shown another group of men. (The Jaazaniah in 11:1 is not the same as in 8:11.) They are arrogant and self-confident, presuming that, as meat in the pot (11:3), they are secure and protected in Jerusalem—unlike the exiles in Babylon. The repeated command to prophesy indicates urgency (11:4). Not much time remains.

As always, the Lord's gaze penetrates human motives. The group of men is placing confidence in Jerusalem, but the city will provide no safe haven. They will be driven out to suffer either death or captivity (11:5–12). In fact, the city's leadership will become the target of mass executions after the Babylonians overrun the city (2 Kings 25:18–21). The people *will* know that Yahweh is the Lord eventually (Ezekiel 11:12).

The death of Pelatiah, one of the men Ezekiel had witnessed in the temple (11:1, 13), is intriguing. It seems that he actually dies, not in the vision that Ezekiel is having, but *while* Ezekiel is prophesying. If so, his death would have symbolized what would soon come to pass for the rest of his peers. Ezekiel acknowledges the significance of Pelatiah's death and expresses fear that God will completely destroy the remnant of Israel (11:13).

But the people with Ezekiel in Babylon are a remnant, and God will eventually return them to Israel. Those who remained in Jerusalem had somehow come to believe that *they* were the favored few, even with their inferior leadership established by the Babylonians after two previous deportations of Israel's principal citizens. God contradicts their assertion. A new exodus will take place, this time comprised of the exiles returning to Israel (11:14–17).

As God had promised previous generations of Israelites (Exodus 6:7), He again affirms that they will be His people and He will be their God (Ezekiel 11:20). Ezekiel will have more to say about the renewed covenant later on. For now, however, judgment remains his primary theme (11:21).

The glory of God continues its progress out of the temple, ascending to a place above the Mount of Olives, east of Jerusalem (11:22–23). The vision concludes and Ezekiel is again set down in Babylon, where he reports to the exiles what he has seen and heard.

Take It Home

Humanly speaking, it was easy for the people in Jerusalem to believe that Yahweh had favored them and rejected those in exile. But Ezekiel's vision demonstrates that the situation, in fact, is precisely the reverse. God is departing His temple and leaving behind those who give Him no thought. Instead, He will restore those in exile who had a humble and submissive mind toward Him. Can you think of contemporary examples where people wrongly presume to have God's blessings simply because nothing bad is happening to them at the moment? Or instances where suffering people think God has given up on them, when in fact He is closer than they realize?

EZEKIEL 12:1–14:23

EZEKIEL SPEAKS OUT

Setting Up the Section

Having been shown the deplorable spiritual condition of Jerusalem in a vision, Ezekiel is now told to enact the exile of all those remaining there—or more accurately, the exile of the few who will survive the destruction of the city. He is also told to confront other so-called prophets who are telling the exiles only what they want to hear.

12:1–28

A VISIBLE LESSON

Ezekiel has just related a detailed vision to the exiles (11:24–25). But God knows the people remain resistant and rebellious, so He has Ezekiel act out what those in Jerusalem will soon undergo. As the exiles watch, the prophet packs his belongings, digs through the wall of his house to retrieve them, puts them on his shoulder, and carries them off (12:3–7). When people ask what he is doing, Ezekiel is to explain that it is a sign of what will soon take place in Jerusalem: Babylonians will break through the walls of the city, and most of the remaining survivors will be exiled.

Evidently, the exiles in Babylon still believe fervently in the security of Jerusalem, as do those who remained there. They do not accept that their exile has been divine punishment for their sins. The complete destruction of Jerusalem will not directly affect the circumstances of the exiles already in Babylon, but it will dash their hopes of a speedy return home.

Babylon will be the instrument of the fall of Jerusalem, but Yahweh is the Judge (12:12–16). The reason the prince (King Zedekiah) will not see is because he will be blinded by the Babylonians (2 Kings 25:7). Eventually, the remnant of people who survive will acknowledge their sin and God's hand in the matter (Ezekiel 12:16).

Continuing his symbolism of the situation at home, Ezekiel is to publicly eat and drink while trembling (12:17–20). His actions symbolize the anxiety and despair of the people not just in Jerusalem but in its surrounding towns as well.

Yet people are slow to acknowledge harsh truths. The prevailing attitude among the exiles is that Ezekiel's prophecies are not coming true and that he must certainly be talking about a distant time in the future (12:22, 27). God's response is that every vision (of His true prophets) will indeed be fulfilled, and there will be no further delay (12:23, 28).

13:1–23

CONFRONTING FALSE PROPHETS

True prophets of God receive a message from the Lord and repeat to the people what they have been told or shown. False prophets have no such message, so they must make one up. False prophets had long been by-products of Israel's deteriorating spiritual condition, but at this point Yahweh charges Ezekiel to confront his professional competition head-on.

Critical Observation

Although Ezekiel may appear to be singled out as a solitary spokesperson for God surrounded by false prophets, there are a number of other true prophets who are his contemporaries, including Daniel, Habakkuk, Obadiah, and Jeremiah.

The false prophets are portrayed as "jackals among ruins" (13:4 NIV), an image of destruction. They prophesy what people want to hear—peace and safety—so no one feels motivated to repent or to expect the coming judgment of the Lord. Ezekiel is trying to repair and rebuild Israel; other prophets are merely capitalizing on its spiritual ruin (13:5).

Divination (13:7) was a widespread practice posing as a science, by which the practitioner presumed to learn what the gods intended in the future by studying animal livers, the stars, or some other symbol. The practice was forbidden in Israel because the Israelites were supposed to maintain godly character and faithfulness to God's covenant, leaving their future in His hands.

The consequences of prophesying falsely are severe indeed. The false prophets will face loss of membership in the assembly, have their names stricken from the census register, and lose their right to the land, since they will not participate in the return of the exiles to Judah and Jerusalem (13:8–9). Theirs will be permanent excommunication.

It is characteristic of Israel's and Judah's false prophets to proclaim peace. Their income depends on contributions, and people are far less likely to pay to hear about gloom and doom. Such false preaching encourages lazy complacency. If the people never acknowledge their sins, naturally they don't anticipate judgment. Yet pretending that all is well when their nation is on the brink of catastrophe doesn't change reality. God compares the false prophets to builders who whitewash a flimsy wall and make it look good, but it can't withstand the violent wind, torrents of rain, and hailstones God will send (13:13). The wall will fall, and the facade of the false prophets will be exposed for what it is—nothing but lies. No matter how regularly or boldly they declare "peace," there will be no peace (13:10, 15–16).

Israel had female prophetesses as well as male prophets, so it stands to reason that there would be a number of female false prophets. It is surprising, therefore, that Ezekiel provides one of the very few judgments against women found in the Old Testament prophets (13:17–23).

The language Ezekiel uses is clear enough to verify that Israel's magic and divination practices are wrong and offensive to God, but obscure enough to prevent stating exactly what those methods are. It seems likely that some of the exiles had adopted Babylonian magical ideas. *Magic* is a negative term in a biblical sense, as it broadly refers to all efforts to influence events by manipulating unseen powers. It is utterly foreign to the teaching of scripture that emphasizes a person's character and his or her fidelity to the Lord.

Adherence to practitioners of magic can be alluring and addictive. In this instance, God is preparing to take strong action against those who are involved in order to set free people who have been ensnared and save their lives (13:20, 22–23). If the magicians had literally killed people, it is unclear. But they had profaned Yahweh by reducing Him to the level of Babylon's petty deities, so they had definitely killed people spiritually by undermining their faith in God.

14:1–23

CONFRONTING THE ELDERS OF THE PEOPLE

Having faced the false prophets, Ezekiel's next communication from God concerns the elders and the people themselves. They have come to Ezekiel to get some direction from God. Perhaps they are worried about something Ezekiel has said and they want more information, but God speaks to the prophet before they can.

God knows that the elders of Israel in Babylon are still involved in idolatry, although it is perhaps more covert than before (in their hearts; 14:4). They found Babylon to be far more wealthy, prosperous, and powerful than their own nation, and they have been tempted to imitate Babylonian ways. But attempting to combine recognition of Yahweh's lordship with recourse to other gods is a bad idea.

Demystifying Ezekiel

Idolatry was the standard form of religion and religious practice in Babylon and surrounding areas at the time. People believed that any depiction of a god, however crude, partook of the essence of the god himself or herself. Anything offered to the image was thus offered to the god. It was also believed that the gods appreciated gifts and would respond in kind. They were relatively easily pleased; and the more generous the worshiper, the more prosperity he or she would receive from the gods.

The gods of the Babylonians could tolerate other loyalties, but not the one, living, and true God of Israel. The Ten Commandments lead off with, "Thou shalt have no other gods before me" (Exodus 20:3 KJV). The reason, of course, is because other gods are foolishness: false and unreal. The Babylonians had so many gods that it's difficult to know which particular ones might have been most appealing in Israel at this time. Excavations in Canaan have uncovered large numbers of small statuettes of Babylonian and Egyptian deities.

So the elders of Israel have come to Ezekiel, not planning to submit their lives to the Lord in true faith, but to consult the prophet as if he were merely a fortune-teller. They want an answer to a question, and then they fully intend to return to the lives they have been living. They aren't looking for their covenant God to speak His truth to them.

Considering their spiritual state, one might not expect God to reveal *anything* to them. In this instance, however, He promises to answer their inquiry directly, although it will not be the kind of answer they are hoping for. God's response (14:4–11) is made for the sake of the larger people of God and not for this particular generation.

This is the first of very few calls to repentance in Ezekiel that may seem to contradict the earlier statement that the prophet will not be preaching for repentance (3:26). Indeed, the die has been cast for Israel: This generation will be judged, and there is no hope left for it. Still, repentance remains God's desire for His people.

God will not tolerate an idolater continuing to pose as a member of His covenant people. His judgment of such a person will be designed precisely to disabuse the rest of God's people from committing the same sin (14:7–8). Any prophet who is complicit in such hypocrisy will also suffer accordingly, because his power to influence people is not to be misused. As a result of God's judgment, the people will learn not to take seriously the messages of prophets who do not remain faithful to the Word of God. The intent is for people to stop straying and again find satisfaction in belonging to God (14:11).

Beginning with verse 14, God assures Ezekiel in four successive paragraphs of the inexorable and merciless judgment that awaits those who rebel against Him. Although the Lord speaks generally, it is Israel who is being addressed here. (His judgments for other nations will come later.) The particular judgments listed are the typical curses of the covenant for those who prove unfaithful to God: famine, wild beasts, sword, and plague (Leviticus 26; Deuteronomy 32).

Noah, Daniel, and Job (Ezekiel 14:20) are all conspicuously godly men who live outside of Israel. The Israelites seem to presume that because there are heroically good people among them, they will be exempt from judgment. God had agreed to spare Sodom if only ten righteous people could be found (Genesis 18:26–32), but He did not intend to establish some kind of divine law or principle that would be observed in every case.

Demystifying Ezekiel

The Daniel mentioned in verse 20 may not be the prophet with whom readers of scripture are familiar. The Daniel of the lions' den was a contemporary of Ezekiel, and a young one at the time of this writing—too young, some think, to be listed with such ancient and venerated names as Noah and Job. In addition, Ezekiel spells his name differently than it is spelled elsewhere.

The sad fact that God addresses *Jerusalem's* great sin makes the judgment even worse. The people had known His truth and had His light shine upon them, so their judgment will be heavier (14:21). The one consoling consequence will be that the exiles in Babylon will see the new exiles come from Jerusalem (14:22–23). When they realize how faithless and wicked they were, they will also acknowledge that God is entirely just in destroying the city. The impiety of the newcomers will be evident to the entire Israelite community in Babylon.

Take It Home

Ezekiel is proven right in 586 BC, when Jerusalem is destroyed. The false prophets are exposed as charlatans and fakes, and the people of God feel the Lord's wrath. They had believed a message that was too good to be true. So do many people today. Consider the false prophets of Ezekiel's time and of ours. Why do people go to phonies and pay them for their advice? Why do you think fortune-telling is such big business today, as sophisticated as our culture imagines itself to be? On a personal level, do you tend to be more attuned to preachers of peace or to those who proclaim the reality of God's judgment?

EZEKIEL 15:1–17:24

THREE ALLEGORIES TO DESCRIBE ISRAEL

Setting Up the Section

As Ezekiel continues to address the spiritually defiant exiles in Babylon, passing along God's judgment for their recurring rejection of the Lord and pursuit of idolatry, he is given three allegories that illustrate Israel's condition. In each case the meaning is clear because the interpretation is provided.

15:1–8

ALLEGORY #1: ISRAEL IS THE WOOD, NOT THE FRUIT, OF THE VINE

Grapevines have a single purpose: to grow grapes. The vine itself is woody, but the wood is virtually useless. It is too soft even to use for making pegs (15:2–3). At least it burns, even if it doesn't make particularly good firewood.

It is the fruit of the grapevine that makes it important, which was especially true in the agricultural life of ancient Canaan. Wine was a staple of life, and Israel no doubt had a flattering estimation of herself as the fruit of the vine. But in reality, the nation had ceased to bear fruit. As a vine, it then became good for nothing except fuel for the fire.

What the Israelites don't realize is that they are already in the fire. The nation has been burned at both ends and charred in the middle by the first two Babylonian incursions into the Holy Land (15:4). It was customary at the time for invading armies to burn the cities they captured, so this allegory merges into a literal account of Jerusalem's future. Nothing is left but to cast the remaining wood into the fire to be consumed.

16:1–63

ALLEGORY #2: JERUSALEM AS AN UNFAITHFUL WIFE

At about 830 words (depending on the translation), this single chapter of Ezekiel is longer than six of the twelve books of the Minor Prophets. It is certainly the longest allegory in the Bible. Like the previous example, its meaning is obvious, yet it is more elaborate and says much more about *how* Israel got into her present situation. It is also quite sexually explicit, employing the metaphor of prostitution to describe Israel's spiritual infidelity.

But the first image of Jerusalem is that of a baby, abandoned by Canaanite parents. Indeed, Jerusalem was originally a Canaanite city steeped in pagan roots. Abandoning a child has never been the norm at any point in human history, yet it is not unheard of for poverty and other considerations to drive desperate parents to abandon a newborn—especially a daughter.

This allegorical "child" has not even been washed or rubbed with salt (16:4), a custom still practiced by some Arab mothers to this day. The origin of the custom has been lost, although it may have been for hygienic reasons.

Yahweh is depicted as a passerby who spies the abandoned girl in an open field, helpless and near death, and chooses to make her live (16:5–6). The girl grows up to become a beautiful young woman. She is mature but still naked, creating a completely different situation. Yahweh preserves the young woman's purity and marries her.

The custom of spreading a corner of a garment over one's intended (16:8) is mentioned in Ruth 3:9. The Lord's relationship with Israel had long before been described as a marriage, and Ezekiel's hearers would have known he was speaking about Yahweh's covenant to be Israel's God. The allegory and the theology merge at the end of 16:8.

Yahweh dresses His bride and bedecks her in fine jewelry. The blood washing from her suggests virginal bleeding, the effect of the first lovemaking (16:9). At this point, Israel is an innocent maiden. As His wife, the Lord lavishes luxuries upon her. The previously abandoned baby girl is now a queen, and fed and clothed as one (16:10–14). Her beauty, status, and fame are all Yahweh's doing. She owes everything to Him.

Critical Observation

Some of the language of this section, such as *embroidered cloth* and *fine linen*, is also found in previous descriptions of the tabernacle, its curtains, and the priestly robes. The fine leather of her sandals (16:10) is mentioned elsewhere in the Bible only in regard to the tabernacle and temple. Even the special food can be compared to the Israelites' sacred offerings.

Yet despite His great generosity and love for His bride, Yahweh begins to speak as a betrayed husband (16:15–19). His wife has begun to use her beauty for purposes other than for the pleasure of her husband. The verb meaning "to act as a prostitute," or some derivative, occurs twenty-two times in this chapter and may be regarded as the key word of the passage.

As if prostitution weren't bad enough in itself, the bride of Yahweh also participates in child sacrifice, the ultimate cultic crime. Involvement in such a barbaric act requires both a pagan mindset and the most extreme repudiation of Yahweh's covenant. The practice seems to have first been introduced to Israel in the eighth century BC, in the northern kingdom (2 Kings 17:17), spreading to Judah during the reign of Ahaz (2 Kings 16:3) and becoming rampant during the reign of Manasseh (2 Chronicles 33:6). Josiah took steps to eliminate Israel's participation (2 Kings 23:10), but after his death the practice returned (Jeremiah 32:35). Israel, who had been rescued as an unloved and abandoned baby, is killing her children with her own hands (Ezekiel 16:21–22).

The details of Israel's promiscuous actions continue in verses 23–34. If the first portion of the description reflects her religious betrayal of the Lord, the second part deals with the political betrayal of her status as the people of God. Israel trusts her welfare to everyone but Yahweh.

Here prostitution is a metaphor for military and political alliances with other nations, each of which represents a failure to trust the Lord. The order in which other nations are mentioned—Egypt, Philistia, Assyria, and Babylon—reflects Israel's history. Each of these political relationships proved harmful, yet Israel moved from one such affair to another.

In the original language, Ezekiel's description is more explicit than what is interpreted in most Bible translations. Israel's effort to attract other lovers is brazen. Even the pagan nations around her are shocked by such behavior (16:27).

In spite of her repeated conscientious efforts, Israel doesn't make a good prostitute. The point of prostitution is to make money, yet Israel paid others to be involved (16:32–34). The money is a reference to the bribes and tribute Israel gave to foreign powers over the years. Israel would not have *wanted* to make those imposed payments, but Ezekiel sees it all as the result of her philandering.

After the husband's case is made and Israel's betrayal has been exposed, the sentence is pronounced (16:35–43). In an ironic twist, the wayward wife, who bared her nakedness without shame to entice her various lovers, will be stripped and shamed before them. Her fortune has come full circle. She who began naked and abandoned by her parents will find herself naked and abandoned by the Lord.

Adultery is a capital offense in the Mosaic Law. In this case, the sentence would be carried out by Israel's paramours (16:38–41). Yet once the punishment has been inflicted, God's holy wrath will be satisfied (16:42). Ezekiel often reminds his readers that God's judgment is not a fit of divine temper but rather the exercise of His holy justice.

Ezekiel can't seem to emphasize enough, throughout his writing, that what is happening to Israel is a result of her own actions. He makes the point again that Israel has ignored and forgotten the grace of God, His covenant, and His kindness to her (16:43).

God then compares Jerusalem to other notable cities in history. Samaria (16:46) had been the capital of the northern kingdom of Israel until the Assyrians conquered it during the previous century. What compounded Judah's sin was that the people had witnessed the fall of Samaria—punishment for the betrayal of Yahweh's covenant—and still did not repent (16:51).

Perhaps more surprising is the comparison between Jerusalem and the city of Sodom (16:48). God did not dwell on the rampant homosexuality in Sodom; perhaps it would have been too easy for Israel to deny such a comparison. But equally heinous were Sodom's sins of arrogance, self-centeredness, and lack of concern for the poor and weak (16:49–50). The noted city of sin had nothing on Jerusalem in those regards. It is hard to know what is meant by the restoration of Sodom in 16:53–55, although it is meant as a backhanded rebuke of Jerusalem. The point is that since Jerusalem's wickedness is greater than Sodom's or Samaria's, those cities should be restored if Jerusalem is.

Yet as is so common in the prophetic books, the Lord looks beyond judgment day to the new work of grace He will perform among His people (16:59–63). The restoration of Jerusalem will be a humbling experience. Sodom and Samaria are portrayed as being united with Jerusalem—a picture of universal salvation also common to prophetic books. The original covenant God made was with Israel, not with other nations, but the nations will not be left out in the end.

17:1–24

ALLEGORY #3: A VINE AND TWO EAGLES

Ezekiel's third allegory approaches the style of a fable where animals and inanimate objects talk and act with human characteristics. And although its meaning is not as clearly evident as the first two, the explanation is eventually provided.

Demystifying Ezekiel

This allegory is much more like a riddle. In fact, the word used in 17:2, commonly translated as *allegory*, is the same word used to describe Samson's riddle to the men in his wedding party (Judges 14:12). The literary style would have had an impact on Ezekiel's listeners because they would not have been able to figure it out until he provided them with the meaning.

The allegory begins with a precise description of an eagle that breaks off the top of a cedar tree and carries it away (17:3–4). Babylon had long gone to Lebanon for wood, so the tree in Ezekiel's allegory represents Israel. The top of the tree (the leadership of the nation) had been carried away (deported to Babylon in 598 BC).

The seed in verse 5 is Zedekiah, the member of the royal family that the Babylonians placed on the throne as their puppet king in Jerusalem. For a time, Zedekiah was loyal to Babylon, indicated by the branches turned toward the eagle (17:6). But then a second eagle appeared, also powerful, yet not described quite as impressively as the first one (17:7). If the vine then sent its roots out toward the second eagle rather than the first, would it survive? Ezekiel's question is confusing, so he provides the answer first and then the explanation.

The vine will *not* thrive; it will wither (17:9–10). The second eagle represents Egypt. After a while, the galling yoke of subjection to Babylon begins to provoke thoughts of rebellion from Zedekiah. Egypt is nearby—a longstanding enemy of Babylon. As far as we know, Egypt never actually provided assistance to Judah other than selling them some warhorses (17:15). In this context, the east wind is the siroccos that heat Palestine from the desert (17:10).

Zedekiah had sworn an oath of loyalty to Nebuchadnezzar, and a treaty had been written spelling out his obligations. He knew that if he betrayed the treaty, he would invoke a curse upon himself (17:13). Yet Zedekiah violates his oath and breaks the treaty. His change of disposition toward Babylon seems to coincide with the accession of a new pharaoh in Egypt, although it is not known if the new Egyptian leader encouraged the revolt. Depending on the date of Ezekiel's prophecy, the Israelites in Babylon may have already heard of Zedekiah's overtures to the Egyptians. They may have entertained the hope that he would succeed in delivering Judah from Babylonian control.

But when Babylon returns to reassert its control over Judah, the Egyptians stand by and watch as Jerusalem is destroyed. Zedekiah's betrayal of the treaty is not just an offense to Nebuchadnezzar; it is an affront to God as well. God would have regarded such an action as the act of a traitor, even though Babylon had imposed the treaty on Israel. The offense is made clearer by the account in 2 Chronicles 36:13, where it is shown that Zedekiah had sworn loyalty *in Yahweh's name*. Zedekiah's enemy, the one that counts, is not Babylon. It is Yahweh Himself (Ezekiel 17:19).

Zedekiah's loyalty to the wrong eagle results in the Babylonian army bearing down on Jerusalem in 586 BC. After being forced to watch the execution of his sons, Zedekiah is blinded and taken captive to Babylon. His army, seeking to escape, is caught and destroyed (17:21). The rest of the population, with the exception of a few poor people left to tend the fields, is sent into exile. The details are found in 2 Kings 25.

But this third allegory has a surprise ending (17:22–24), as the Lord promises the eventual restoration of the remnant of Israel. He will choose and plant another shoot from the top of a cedar tree (provide another king). The positive influence of this new king will be felt around the world. The Lord will eventually cause Babylon to fall and restore life to the nation of Israel.

Take It Home

Jesus' New Testament command to love one's enemies is a novel concept, yet it has some precedent here in Ezekiel. God's people are to show integrity, even to their enemies. When Zedekiah broke an oath—even though the oath was to a pagan king and his intentions were to preserve his nation—the action was an offense to God. Do you tend to make distinctions on how you deal with others based on whether or not they share your faith?

EZEKIEL 18:1–21:32

A RETIRED PROVERB, A LAMENT, AND MORE WARNINGS

Setting Up the Section

Ezekiel 18 is one of the better-known sections of this mostly unfamiliar book. In this section, the prophet clarifies God's attitude toward sin and who is responsible. Afterward, Ezekiel returns to his message of judgment on Judah and Jerusalem.

18:1–32

CLARIFYING A PROVERB

Ezekiel begins this section by illustrating that someone cannot begin to really understand human existence until he or she acknowledges that each life belongs to God. The emphasis throughout the chapter will be on the *individual* life.

The proverb in verse 2 suggests a world of fatalism, which is by no means true. Every single person will one day stand before a personal God, and He will judge each one accordingly. Jeremiah had cited the same proverb (Jeremiah 31:29), but both he and Ezekiel foretell an end to its popularity. The belief that God will hold future generations accountable for the sin of an ancestor is not accurate.

"As I live" (18:3) means that the Lord charged the nation by an oath taken symbolically upon His own life. God judges each person according to his or her holiness. It is evident that the use of *die* in this context is a reference to spiritual death—death that continues in the world to come (18:4).

God provides Ezekiel with some illustrations to help his listeners clarify their thinking. The first describes a righteous man who has an unrighteous son (18:5–13). The father not only avoids actions that are clearly sinful but he also chooses to act honorably in everything he does. The son, however, is violent and disregards both civil and spiritual laws. The unrighteous son will answer for his own sins; his father's righteousness will be of no help to him.

Critical Observation

The biblical language used in verse 9 and other places is often questioned. God isn't saying, through Ezekiel, that a person deserves life rather than death because he or she follows God's laws. Works of faith do not accumulate points for anyone. Rather, such actions are the proper response of anyone whom God has already delivered from the fear of death. It is due only to God's deliverance, not a person's actions, that he or she will live.

The second illustration is a reverse of the first one: The father is the sinful party, but the son refuses to follow in his father's offensive footsteps (18:14–18). The father will be judged for his wrongdoings, but the son will certainly not be punished for the father's sins. He will be treated by God as the righteous man that he is.

The Lord expects objections to what Ezekiel is proclaiming and prepares the prophet with a good response: "The soul who sins is the one who will die" (18:20 NIV). If a wicked person turns away from sin and starts obeying God, the Lord will show forgiveness and acceptance of the person (18:21–22).

The same principle applies in reverse (18:24). If someone repudiates a life of covenant faithfulness to God, his or her past "righteousness" will be no more a help than another person's past sins will be a hindrance. There is neither a treasury of merits nor of demerits. One generation cannot build up merits for another to trade, nor can the individual. And there is no measure of sin that reaches a point where the individual stands beyond hope of forgiveness and new life.

Demystifying Ezekiel

God isn't saying that children *never* suffer as a result of the sins of their parents and previous generations. The very reason the Israelites are in Babylon is because of the sins of Manasseh, several kings earlier (2 Kings 24:1–4). And modern statistics show, for example, that children of abusive parents tend to become abusers themselves. Children *can* suffer from the sins of parents, but Ezekiel clarifies that such suffering is not *inevitable*. Each person has the opportunity to answer the Lord's summons in faith, find forgiveness, and walk in the ways of righteousness. Repentance can mend anyone's past. Faith can open to anyone a new and bright future.

Still, the people are accusing God of being unfair (18:25–29). Ezekiel ends this particular oracle with a plea for his audience to accept responsibility for their own destiny. What may be true for the generation as a whole need not be true for any specific individual. His call for them to receive a new heart and spirit refers to the seat of thoughts, attitudes, and desires (18:31). God will have to make the change, but the individual must initiate the desire. Faith, repentance, and obedience are at one and the same time divine gifts and human duties.

Again, the references to death throughout this passage are in regard to *spiritual* death. Ezekiel is manifestly not talking about a longer life on earth (18:32). The exiles had dodged a fatal bullet when they were carried to Babylon instead of being killed on the spot in Jerusalem. They might, in fact, lead long lives, yet they will still *die* if they do not repent and turn to God.

19:1–14

A LAMENT WHILE REVIEWING ISRAEL'S PAST

Several laments can be found throughout the Old Testament—dirges composed and sung at the death of an individual or over the destruction of a nation. (The book of Lamentations is a series of five laments.) One of the general features of a Hebrew lament is the "once. . .now" pattern that contrasts the glories of the past with the misery, indignity, and shame of the present. Such is the pattern of Ezekiel 19.

In addition to using the term *Israel* rather than the more accurate *Judah* in this passage, Ezekiel also uses *princes* to indicate their kings. The plural indicates that Ezekiel has in view not just Zedekiah but probably the whole series of unrighteous rulers who have led Judah to its final catastrophe.

The lion imagery in verses 2–3 refers to Judah, which had been true since the days of the patriarchs (Genesis 49:8–9). The lion was a symbol of rule, and Judah was the tribe that would rule over the other tribes of Israel, so Ezekiel's reference is to the kings of Judah.

The reference in Ezekiel 19:4 is to King Jehoahaz, the only one of Judah's last kings to be taken to Egypt (2 Kings 23:34). As to whom Ezekiel is describing in 19:5–9, a case can be made for any of three kings: Jehoiakim, Jehoiachin, or Zedekiah. Perhaps Jehoiachin is the most likely candidate because Ezekiel seemed to consider him the last legitimate king of Israel, and he had been taken to Babylon at the same time as Ezekiel, so the past-tense setting of the lament would have made sense. If Ezekiel has Zedekiah in mind, the passage is a *prediction* of the leader's downfall and exile.

In verses 10–14, Ezekiel's shift of imagery from lion to vine is yet another tie-in to Genesis. In Jacob's prophecy concerning his son Judah (more than fifteen hundred years before Ezekiel), the boy's future is portrayed in terms both of the power of a lion and the fruitfulness of the vine (Genesis 49:8–11). After God's subsequent covenant with David, Judah had seen twenty-two kings from David to Zedekiah. But during that time, the kings of the house of Judah and David had become arrogant. They ruled Judah without regard to their obligations to God or the people of Israel. Consequently, the line of royalty came to an end (temporarily) because there was no strong branch left on the vine "fit for a ruler's scepter" (Ezekiel 19:14 NIV).

It is important to note that this lament is for the people of Israel, not just the kings. It is *about* the kings, but it will be sung *by and for* the people (19:14).

20:1–44

THE PROBLEM OF ONGOING IDOLATRY

After his lament, Ezekiel returns to the central theme of his writing: condemnation of the people of Israel for their betrayal of God's covenant, the anticipation of God's judgment about to befall them, and beyond that, the eventual restoration of Israel. However, in this section he emphasizes that the reason for the problem is Judah's idolatry.

According to verse 1, the date is August 14, 591 BC, almost a year after Ezekiel's most recent dated prophecy. Again, some elders of the nation have come to consult with the prophet about something, but Ezekiel doesn't bother to say what the group wants to know. God is unwilling to respond to their agenda, but He has a message for them nevertheless.

Critical Observation

Just because Ezekiel is obedient in passing along God's message to his peers in Babylon doesn't mean he isn't fazed by his duty. It would have been no easier for him to deliver a message of woe to his friends and neighbors than for anyone to announce to his or her loved ones that they are doomed and about to suffer the judgment of God. In addition, such people are typically objects of ridicule and scorn.

Ezekiel's contemporaries have a romantic recollection of their history. They take pride in their past accomplishments. It is a common assignment of God's prophets to review the past with a critical eye. Just as Stephen will later do before Israel's spiritual leaders (Acts 7), Ezekiel here begins to recall the history of Yahweh's relationship with the nation, underscoring the long pattern of Israel's unbelief and infidelity to God. By the time he finishes, it is evident that the current generation is committing the same offenses that their ancestors had made throughout their history.

God reveals information through Ezekiel that had not been provided earlier in the scriptural account. In making a covenant with Israel, God had made it absolutely clear that there could be no compromise with idolatry. Any such practice is a denial of the one, true, and living God and a repudiation of the revelation God had provided about Himself. However, Israel in Egypt was hardly a devoted and faithful people, waiting patiently for the promises of God to be fulfilled. Rather, they were idolaters who had adopted the religious practices of the Egyptians (20:5–8).

Yet Yahweh does not punish Israel as she deserves (20:9–10). Her idolatry notwithstanding, He is gracious and brings her out of Egypt. The Sabbath is a sign in that it is a regular weekly reminder of God's covenant (20:12). As it is confirmed in weekly worship, it became a perpetual reminder of Yahweh's goodness of delivering His people from the seven-day workweek by which slaves were exploited in the ancient world.

Demystifying Ezekiel

It is frequently proposed that the commandment to keep the Sabbath originated at Sinai, along with most of the other laws. By this way of thinking, God's people would have been under no obligation to keep one day holy prior to their wilderness experience. Yet Ezekiel clarifies that God gave *all His laws* to Israel in the wilderness (20:11–12)—that is, they were all formally codified at that time. Israel had already abided by certain civil laws (prohibitions to kill, lie, steal, etc.) and religious regulations (offering sacrifices, prohibitions to worship idols, etc). It is reasonable to believe, therefore, that observing the Sabbath was also among their already established practices, even though it is not mentioned specifically until Exodus 16:21–30.

Yet the observation of the Sabbath was soon regarded by Israel as a burden more than a boon, so even in the wilderness they failed to keep the Sabbath holy. The rebellion mentioned in 20:13 is most likely a reference to the incident with the golden calf at the foot of Sinai. At any rate, the first generation of Israelites to escape Egypt rejected God's laws, disobeyed His clear instructions, and desecrated the Sabbaths. In spite of everything God was doing in taking them from slavery to a promised land, they continued to put more faith in idols than in Him (20:13–17). Still, God does not destroy them, both out of His mercy and to prevent surrounding nations from profaning His name (20:14, 17). He gives their children (the next generation) another chance to follow Him more faithfully. That generation enters the promised land, but they prove to be hardly more faithful than their parents had been (20:18–26). Reading through the passage, it is impossible to miss the repetition Ezekiel uses as a literary device to emphasize God's patience in light of Israel's persistent denial of God's covenant, their disobedience to His commandments, and their ongoing profanation of the Sabbath.

At this point, Ezekiel begins to make a transition from the history of Israel to their current state. One might think that the one place where Israel would have been faithful to God was the promised land itself—a beautiful place God gave them in spite of the fact that they did not deserve such a gift. Yet they quickly adopted Canaanite idolatry as they had practiced Egyptian idolatry previously. Ezekiel's point is that the people of his time are descended from blasphemers, and idolatry is in their national DNA.

Now they are in Babylon, surrounded by yet another pantheon of idols. English speakers miss the relevance of the question in 20:29. *Bamah*, the word meaning "high place," is sounded several times in Ezekiel's phrasing. The implication is that the current generation of Israelites is still seeking out high places to worship other gods, even in Babylon, as their ancestors had repeatedly done.

Even more offensive than anything their forefathers had done, this group of Israelites has become involved in idolatry to the point of child sacrifice—a monstrous outrage against the holiness of God (20:31). Yet they have the audacity to come to Ezekiel hoping to get some specific answer from the Lord! Rather than serving God, they expect God to serve them.

The people are out calling on idols, and God is going to judge them (20:34–35). The Babylonian exile is, in a way, a repetition of Israel's history of slavery in the wilderness.

But in Babylon, the people will be purified and then restored to the promised land in a second exodus—a return from exile and new beginning (20:37–44). Their restoration will have nothing to do with their achievement or performance. As always, it will be entirely due to God's grace, mercy, and faithfulness to His Word.

20:45–21:32

PREPARE FOR BABYLON

As God continues to speak to the people through Ezekiel's oracles (20:45–48), it isn't certain that even Ezekiel is aware of the meanings at first. Clearly his listeners aren't making sense of the imagery because they accuse him of just telling stories (20:49). But God will soon supply the proper interpretations: Fire represents war; the south is Judah; the green tree symbolizes righteous people; the dry tree stands for the wicked people.

The Babylonian armies will be the sword God uses (21:2–5). The route they take from Babylon will result in Judah/Jerusalem being to the south (20:46). Consequently, there will be much reason to groan (21:6–7). Ezekiel's symbolic groaning will pique their curiosity and make a point, but the time is coming when they and all of Israel will groan for real. And a fact of war and other circumstances is that sometimes righteous people suffer in the punishment visited upon a wicked nation (21:4).

The proper interpretation of 21:10 is unclear. Perhaps the people first imagined that the image of Yahweh brandishing His sword would have been good news. In this case, however, He is not preparing to defend and avenge Israel. Just the opposite: God is preparing to destroy Jerusalem. The sword will soon be handed to Nebuchadnezzar (21:11). In response, Ezekiel's groaning escalates into wailing and beating his breast, for good reason (21:12–17).

Nebuchadnezzar will arrive at a crossroad and seek direction through divination, beseeching his gods, and other signs. Then he will choose the route that takes him to Jerusalem for conquest (21:19–23). But since God is telling Ezekiel exactly what will happen, it is clear that the choice is not Nebuchadnezzar's at all, but God's.

Critical Observation

Usually divination methods were used in cases where one of two choices needed to be made: go to war or not, attack this way or that, and so forth. Examining the liver of animals (hepatoscopy) was one standard technique of divination that was very popular with the Babylonians. Also, arrows would be marked with various symbols and drawn from a bag, not unlike drawing straws (21:21). And it was around this time that astrology—the effort to discover the future in the stars—was being developed in Babylon. The ancients were fascinated with attempting to know the future. But God's people were forbidden from such practices. The future was to be left to God; people were to concern themselves with faith and obedience in the present.

The Jews might have thought themselves safe from Babylonian attack because they had sworn loyalty to Nebuchadnezzar. But after the oath of loyalty was broken by Zedekiah (2 Chronicles 36:13), they should have had no expectation of security. Zedekiah was the profane and wicked prince (Ezekiel 21:25–27). The threefold repetition of *ruin/rubble* in verse 27 is the ultimate Hebrew superlative. The outcome will definitely not be pleasant.

Ezekiel's prophecies of judgment against other countries (besides Israel/Judah) will begin in earnest in chapter 25. But Ammon is the only one mentioned in chapters 1–24 (21:28–32). Perhaps it is the single exception for the contrast that could be made. Ammon had joined Israel in rebellion against Babylon, and their people must have heaved a sigh of relief when the Babylonian army attacked Jerusalem rather than their town of Rabbah (21:20). The diviners in Ammon were forecasting good news for their nation (21:29). But the truth of the matter is that the sword will soon strike them as well. And while Israel will eventually recover from their tragedy to receive a future that includes the blessings of God, Ammon is to disappear, never to rise again (21:31–32).

Take It Home

Review Ezekiel's lament in chapter 19. In today's religious culture that focuses heavily on God's promises and blessings, do you feel that people give adequate attention to lamentable things that aren't as they should be? Do you think God ever laments over the condition of His church?

EZEKIEL 22:1–24:27

SOME FINAL WORDS FOR JUDAH

Setting Up the Section

With this section, Ezekiel completes the first of three major sections of his book. He will finish his message of judgment directed to Judah/Jerusalem, after which he will begin to address other nations. But as he concludes this portion, his words will be punctuated with symbolic actions, even in regard to the death of his wife.

22:1–31

JERUSALEM ON TRIAL

This section has the overtones of a courtroom scene where a defendant is found guilty by a judge. It first appears that Ezekiel is the judge, but it quickly becomes clear that he is only Yahweh's spokesperson. And although Ezekiel addresses Jerusalem, the city clearly represents the nation as a whole.

The prophet, like any good prosecutor, begins by indicting the people for their betrayal of God's covenant, and then he amasses the evidence of their crimes. He doesn't cite chapter and verse because he has repeatedly addressed this topic, but every violation he lists is clearly an act of disobedience to the law of God as it had been revealed to Israel. The result is that the great empire of David and Solomon declines into nothing, and other nations make jokes about it (22:4–5). Had Israel been faithful to the covenant God had established with her, the nation would have been exalted above all the other nations of the earth. Instead, their sins create the opposite situation, where they are humiliated before all the other nations.

A reference to blood, or bloodshed, occurs seven times in the first sixteen verses. The terms are not limited to literal physical violence committed against another person, but they also include, by extension, *any* harm done to another. Ezekiel begins his case with the sins of the leaders of the nation (22:6), but the problem isn't limited to them. The leaders only represent the more widespread problems that permeate the nation.

The list of specific accusations is only a sampling that represents a cross section of violations of God's law (22:7–12). Taken together as Israel's way of life, they reveal that the people have forgotten Yahweh. So the sins are not presented simply as specific violations of God's covenant but rather as evidence that the people have lost all interest in honoring the God who had brought them into covenant with Himself.

Still, this is among the longest lists of sins found anywhere in the Bible. The offenses cover a broad spectrum: religious idolatry, taking bribes, demanding sex from menstruating women, incest, and more. They are listed with no sense of one sin being more or less harmful than another, not an arrangement on a continuum of evil. They are all sins, so all are offensive to God. And sin *will* be punished.

Ezekiel, still speaking for the divine Judge, moves from the list of charges to the pronounced punishment. The image of Yahweh striking His hands together in verse 13 is a gesture to indicate both His anger and His order to put an end to all such behavior. Israel may have forgotten God, but He has not forgotten her (22:16).

All proper punishment has three purposes. First is *retribution*, paying back what is deserved and balancing the scales of justice. Human beings have a sense of retributive justice because they are created in the image of a just and holy God, who will by no means clear the guilty. The second aspect of punishment is *correction*, by which a person learns not to commit the same sin again. A driver who has just received a ticket is much more likely to slow down the next time he or she is on the same stretch of highway. And the third purpose of punishment is *purification*. God doesn't simply want His people to correct their errant behavior; He wants to create in them a new heart, a new mind, and a new attitude. Yet punishment is not pleasant. Here, as in other places, it is compared to a refiner's fire that will burn away the dross and leave what is valuable (22:17–22).

Although most of the people in Israel are guilty of the various sins cited, their leaders continue to be addressed. Ezekiel mentions five different groups of leadership: kings, priests, government officials, prophets, and wealthy landowners (the people of the land) (22:23–29). These are the cultural elite, the opinion shapers, the people with clout. They influence the beliefs and ethics of the people, so they carry the greatest responsibility for the society that forms under their leadership. Too few leaders realize that leadership is a call to responsibility, not a call to privilege.

Critical Observation

Israel was a land that had precious few sources of water other than rainfall, and rain was scarce. Therefore, drought was almost always interpreted as a judgment from God or a curse (22:24).

The priests are indifferent to the Word of God. Government officials take advantage of people rather than protect them. False prophets outnumber faithful ones. God doesn't want to pour out His wrath on the people, but it has gotten to the point where He cannot find a single person committed to making a difference (22:30–31). The Judge has declared His people guilty and pronounced His sentence on them.

23:1–49

A TALE OF TWO PROSTITUTES

It is not uncommon to find instances of Israel or Judah compared to a prostitute, in that the people reject a loving God to pursue false gods and the idols of other nations. But nowhere is the imagery as stark as in this portion of Ezekiel. He uses some of the coarsest and crudest language in the Bible. In Jewish tradition, this chapter of Ezekiel was among the last to be taught to young men because of its potential to offend. But, of course, that is exactly the point.

Ezekiel describes two sisters, Oholah and Oholibah, who represent Samaria and Jerusalem (the capital cities of Israel and Judah). Both women engaged in prostitution from a young age, beginning while they were in Egypt. More recently, however, Oholah (Samaria) had become enamored with the Assyrians. At that time the Assyrian Empire was among the greatest powers in the world. Israel (the northern kingdom) wants to emulate Assyria and copies both their cultural and religious practices.

This instance of prostitution is, in fact, adultery. Assyria turns out to be a cruel lover. The Assyrians destroy Israel in 721 BC, depopulating the land and scattering the population across the great empire (23:9–10).

Ezekiel's audience had come from the southern kingdom of Judah. They had probably heard of Israel's demise; after all, the northern kingdom had virtually disappeared from the face of the earth. It was not hard for the people of Judah to assume that Israel had done something to offend God and that He had dealt with them. But Judah wrongly assumes that since Jerusalem is still standing and they are still around, God is not as angry with them.

Ezekiel declares that God is in fact even angrier with Judah than He had been with the north. Their spiritual lust and prostitution had continued more intensely than ever, even after they witnessed the Lord's furious response to the behavior of the northern "sister." Judah has no excuse for continuing infidelity, but their attitude is portrayed as the lust and fascination of a young woman for a dashing, handsome lover (23:11–21).

Yahweh has finally turned away from His wife in disgust, proclaiming that Judah will face the same end as her northern sister. The lovers to whom she had given herself will be the instruments of her destruction (23:22–35). She will undergo the same foreign invasion and conquest that Israel had suffered a century and a half prior. The bond between Judah and the surrounding nations had never been a satisfying one, yet the severing of that bond will be horrific. Ezekiel's depiction of foreign armies stripping off clothes and fine jewelry of their victims is more literal than symbolic (23:26). In certain chronicles written by conquering nations during this time, the brutality of the treatment of prisoners was a source of pride.

The numerous accusations against Oholah and Oholibah appear all the more heinous in the context of promiscuous seduction (23:36–45). The picture is of women who can't get enough, losing all standards as their loyalties shift from one foreign country to another. Judah's adultery is shameless, and in the Law of Moses the punishment for adultery was death. Unrepentant actions are about to have consequences (23:46–48).

24:1–27

JUDGMENT AND MOURNING TO COME

As Ezekiel completes the section of his writing having to do with the judgment of Judah, he provides yet another date (24:1). The siege on Jerusalem will begin on January 5, 587 BC, but the city won't fall until August 14, 586 BC, so the people there are in for more than a year and a half of turmoil.

Ezekiel had previously cited a proverb indicating that the inhabitants of Jerusalem viewed the city as a cooking pot and themselves as the meat, worthwhile and protected (11:3). God's message in this passage is that, yes, the city might be a cooking pot, but it is a place where the people will be confined and consumed (24:3–12). In this case, the pot is encrusted due to heat applied so long and at such a high temperature that only a scummy residue remains (24:6). Emptying the pot "piece by piece" seems to suggest the depopulation of the city. And no lot is cast, because the casting of lots presumes the Lord's active involvement in the people's lives. Yahweh is no longer accommodating the people's presumption that they have special status before Him.

Based on Ezekiel's earlier personal involvement with his prophecies, it is likely that he acts this one out as well: filling a cooking pot with water, placing choice pieces of meat in it, setting fire beneath it, and so on. The pot would have been heated until the meat burned away and only bones were left (24:5). The visible blood is a witness to Jerusalem's crimes (24:7–8). And like a modern self-cleaning oven, great heat is used to char the remnants on the sides and bottom of the pot until they can be brushed away (24:11–12).

After Ezekiel's parable ends, God abandons the metaphor and makes His point clearly (24:13–14). The Lord's people had failed to become cleansed, but after undergoing this traumatic experience they will be clean again. God's wrath is not an unreasonable response to their persistently lewd conduct.

Ezekiel had acted out a number of his prophecies, including lying on his side for a portion of each day for weeks at a time (4:4–8) and shaving his head (5:1–4). But nothing he had done so far compares to the personal toll the next object lesson requires of him. God tells him his wife will die (24:15–17).

Although not certain, the circumstances appear to be that his wife has died suddenly and unexpectedly. What *is* clear is that her death is Yahweh's doing, despite the fact that Ezekiel loved her very much (24:16). Five traditional (though not biblically mandated) acts of mourning are mentioned: sighing, removing one's turban (normal wear for a priest), going barefoot, covering one's mouth, and eating special (less flavorful) food (24:17). Ezekiel is denied several of these outward traditions. He is permitted his grief, but not the public demonstration of it.

Demystifying Ezekiel

Ezekiel's comment in verse 18 appears to suggest that Ezekiel told his hearers one morning that his wife would die that day, and then she died that evening. But the wording also allows for the possibility that Ezekiel preached that morning as usual, as if nothing were amiss, even though he was aware that his wife would die. Nothing is said of any conversations between husband and wife after receiving the news, or whether Ezekiel may have pleaded for the life of his wife as David had pled for his son after being told that he would die (2 Samuel 12:15–17).

Naturally, Ezekiel's atypical behavior would have aroused curiosity. It would have been not only surprising but also disturbing and insulting for a man to fail to mourn the wife who he delighted in. The prophet's peers sense that the issue has something to do with them, and they finally ask him what it is (24:19). Their question provides the opportunity for him to tell them what God wants them to hear in a context that is bound to arrest their attention.

Jerusalem was the delight of Israel's eyes and God's as well (24:21). The popular theology of the time was that as long as the temple stood, the nation was safe. But when it fell, the people would be too affected to even mourn properly. While Ezekiel has every right to mourn his wife's death, the exiles have little justification to mourn the downfall of Jerusalem. The destruction of their prized city is fair punishment for their horrific crimes against God (24:20–24).

With the fall of Jerusalem, God's judgment is executed. Ezekiel's duty in preparing his people for the event is fulfilled. Therefore, his period of imposed silence comes to an end (3:26–27). Now the prophet, after a six-year ministry of preaching the doom of Jerusalem, is free to speak again and resume a normal life. He will next turn his attention to God's judgment concerning other nations.

Take It Home

It becomes evident from the repeated enumeration of Judah's problems that patterns of sin are hard to break. Their idolatry started in Egypt. They were delivered and led to the promised land, but the sinful habits continued. The easiest bad habits to break are those that are never formed, especially in matters of faith and obedience to God. Can you identify any potentially damaging patterns beginning to form in your life? If so, what can you do at this early stage to prevent even worse problems later in life?

EZEKIEL 25:1–32:32

IMPENDING JUDGMENT AGAINST THE NATIONS

Setting Up the Section

After completing his six-year ministry of preparing the exiles for the fall of Jerusalem, Ezekiel next turns his attention to God's judgment on a number of surrounding nations. Babylon is not included because, at this time, Babylon is the *instrument* of God's judgment. In fact, this section provides a wider sense of the impact of Babylon's imperial designs on the nations of the ancient world.

25:1–7

JUDGMENT AGAINST AMMON

Ezekiel has shown so far that Judah certainly deserves God's judgment, but the surrounding nations are just as guilty of wrongdoings and atrocities. Were they to escape any kind of divine retribution? Certainly not, as Ezekiel will now go on to describe. Many of Israel's enemies watched with smug satisfaction as Jerusalem fell, but God was by no means finished.

The common bond of the nations Ezekiel will next address is that they are all enemies of Israel. The prophesied judgment of these nations would have therefore provided some hope for the people of God.

Ammon is first on the list. It is the lone nation designated for judgment, other than Judah, in the first twenty-four chapters of Ezekiel (21:28–32). Ammon was located east of Israel, across the Jordan River on the fringe of the Arabian Desert. Israel had a longstanding history of conflict with Ammon, beginning when the Israelites were in the wilderness on the way to the promised land. Saul and David both fought the Ammonites.

When Nebuchadnezzar had come into Palestine, it was essentially the flip of a coin that decided whether he conquered Ammon's capital city of Rabbah or Jerusalem (21:21–23). Since God had ordained Judah's punishment, Nebuchadnezzar chose Jerusalem. But rather than heaving a sigh of relief or giving thanks, the Ammonites took joy in seeing the destruction of Judah. *Aha* is the equivalent of a cheer (25:3). They were sure that their ancient foe had been destroyed and would never rise again.

But although Yahweh had acted in judgment against His people, He had not ceased to be their defender. He will punish those who rejoice at the punishment of Israel, no matter how just that punishment is.

The people of the east are Arabs from the desert who will overpower Ammon (25:4). Yahweh is not like the territorial gods they know, conquered when its people are. Ammon will still have to deal with Israel's God, as will every other nation and every other people.

25:8–11

JUDGMENT AGAINST MOAB

Moab, a territory located east of the Dead Sea, between Edom and Ammon, had also been delighted to see Jerusalem fall. Their response was a bit more understandable because they had been dominated politically and militarily by Israel throughout much of their history. Still, they had been aware that God had intervened on Israel's behalf in times past. Their sin was to deny Israel's election, to suppose that Yahweh was unable or unwilling to act on behalf of His people. It isn't surprising, though, that they failed to acknowledge that Israel was unlike any of the other nations. Israel had come to have the same view of herself, motivated by a great desire to be just like those other nations (20:32). Moab, too, will fall to the desert tribes, beginning with its key cities (25:10).

25:12–14

JUDGMENT AGAINST EDOM

Ezekiel does not enumerate the sins of Edom, but other biblical passages provide reasonable clues. Edom's territory was to the east of the Dead Sea near Moab. Israel (descended from Jacob) and Edom (descended from Esau) had been at odds since Genesis 25. The Edomites had refused Moses' appeal to pass through their territory as the Israelites were leaving Egypt (Numbers 20:14–21), and there had been little camaraderie between the two groups in the years and centuries that followed.

It appears that as soon as Judah became preoccupied with Babylon's army, Edomite raiders took advantage of Judah's unprotected southern borders, attacking towns there as well as Jews who were fleeing south to escape the Babylonians. Not enough is known of history between the sixth century BC and the third century BC to determine exactly how Israel was used as the instrument of the Lord's vengeance on Edom (25:14), although the same result was foretold in Obadiah. But we do know that by the fourth century BC, Edom had ceased to exist as a political entity, and its people were no longer a distinguishable population.

Demystifying Ezekiel

In verse 13, the phrase "from Teman to Dedan" is a sweeping geographical term to indicate the entire nation of Edom from the very south to the very north. The Israelite equivalent was "from Dan to Beersheba," although this reference is from north to south.

25:15–17

JUDGMENT AGAINST PHILISTIA

The Philistines had given their name to the entire region: *Palestine* is derived from *Philistine*. They lived along the Mediterranean coast (in what is now the Gaza Strip). During Israel's era of the judges and early monarchy, the Philistines repeatedly threatened to dislodge the Israelites as rulers of the promised land. David finally subdued them (2 Samuel 5:17–25). Perhaps as a result of that defeat, their hostility toward Israel never abated. When the Babylonian invasion provided the opportunity to get back at Israel, they took malicious advantage of it (25:15). But they, too, experience the divine vengeance of God. No record exists of Philistine civilization after the second century BC.

Critical Observation

We must remember that Ezekiel is telling these prophecies to Israelites exiled in Babylon, and there is no indication that the messages are ever actually delivered to the peoples addressed by Ezekiel. So it is evident that the Israelites are actually the intended audience. Ezekiel's listeners, and his readers today, can take comfort in knowing that even though persecution borne out of the malevolence of others is an unfortunate reality of life, God is aware of all injustice and will settle the score in His own timing.

26:1–28:19

JUDGMENT AGAINST TYRE

Tyre was only one hundred miles from Jerusalem, originally situated on an island in the Mediterranean Sea about six hundred yards off the coast, connected by what was then a narrow man-made causeway. (It has since expanded due to winds and tides to create a peninsula.)

The date of Ezekiel's pronouncement against Tyre (February 3, 585 BC) came several months after the fall of Jerusalem, which would have been approximately the time that Ezekiel and the exiles were hearing the news. At the same time, Nebuchadnezzar was initiating a siege of Tyre. The many nations that will oppose Tyre in 26:3 include the various ethnic groups within the Babylonian army because imperial armies were comprised of soldiers from various conquered peoples.

Tyre's mainland settlements, unprotected by the sea, will naturally be the first to suffer attack (26:7–14). Still, the protective walls require a siege—in this case, a siege of thirteen years. The final destruction of Tyre will not occur until the time of Alexander the Great.

The word *coastlands* refers to other maritime peoples who will identify with a seafaring and trading city like Tyre (26:15). It is dreadful to consider that if the powerful Tyre can fall, the same can happen to them. The Babylonian appetite for new lands is voracious. Also, Tyrian control of the seas had provided stability. Now there is uncertainty.

As had been true with the fall of Jerusalem, the Babylonian army is the implement of destruction, but Nebuchadnezzar is only fulfilling the will and action of the Lord. Yahweh uses first-person language (26:19–21), and He speaks of more than mere physical death. The Israelites had a doctrine of the world to come. They would have identified a number of phrases as references to judgment and the next life: "down to the pit," "to the netherworld," "never to return to the land of the living," "a horrible end" (26:19–21).

The city itself will never entirely cease to be. It exists today. But it never recovers significance or becomes the great nation-state it once was.

At this point Ezekiel begins a lament for Tyre. In describing the glories of the past, Tyre is likened to a magnificent ship (27:1–11). The description is poetic in its mention of many of the very best products that Tyre shipped throughout the Mediterranean: Lebanon cedars, cypress wood, ivory, and so on. An actual ship would not, for example, have had linen sails (27:7). Tyre's glory is accented by the geographic breadth of its servants (27:10–11) and trade associations (27:12–24). This list is a historic review rather than a current list of allies. Israel, for example (27:17), had been destroyed about a century and a half earlier.

Yet the glory of Tyre will soon come to an end. If Tyre is a ship, she is going to wreck at sea and sink, and her demise will be hard to watch (27:27).

It is interesting to note that the reason for Tyre's fall is not described much in terms of her various sins, although it is clear that the city is guilty of slave trading and pagan practices (27:13). However, Ezekiel's accusations have more to do with a location that is simply wealthy, fat, and sassy. Tyre's prosperity rests on the sea trade that she has come to dominate (27:25–36). She is accustomed to the luxuries of life. And worse than that, she is proud of herself—a theme that Ezekiel will continue to develop.

At this point Ezekiel's prophecy gets a little more personal. He turns his attention to the king of Tyre, although, in an absolute monarchy of the ancient world, the fates of the king and the kingdom were so intertwined as to be virtually indistinguishable. The people tended to admire and support a king who was responsible for the nation's prosperity and greatness, and they would consider an oracle against such a leader to be directed at themselves as well.

In Ezekiel's day, the king of Tyre was Ethbaal II ("Baal is with him"), a clever man who amassed power and wealth as a result (28:4–5). Many people use such worldly wisdom to great advantage, but he isn't as wise as he *thinks* he is (28:1–3). Normally, the Mesopotamian-Syrian states believed a king was *appointed* by the gods but not actually a god himself. Perhaps Ethbaal II is attempting to elevate his status among the people. Or it could be that Ezekiel uses such language to indicate that the king has a far too high opinion of himself—that he is "playing God," so to speak.

Critical Observation

Daniel gets another mention here (28:3; see 14:14). This is not likely the Daniel whose prophecy is recorded in the Old Testament.

The glory of Tyre and the presumed wisdom of its leader will both disappear with the coming of "the terror of the nations" (28:7 NLT)—Babylon. The king, in his arrogance, has now reckoned with Yahweh.

The Phoenicians, like the Israelites, also practiced circumcision, though for different reasons and at a different time of life. For one of their leaders to die at the hands of uncircumcised foreigners was the ultimate indignity (28:8–10). No historical record has been found detailing the fall of Tyre, but it is not unreasonable to assume that after a thirteen-year siege, the king of Tyre would have been executed, if not tortured first, for creating so much trouble for Babylon.

Ezekiel has already related a lament for Tyre (chapter 27) and at this point is directed to shift from a prophecy against the king of Tyre to a lament for him as well (28:11–12). Few biblical laments are as extreme as this one. The king of Tyre is likened to the first angel in the Garden of Eden, magnificently clothed (unlike Adam) in gold and precious stones (28:11–15).

Ezekiel has twice described cherubim (chapters 1 and 10). Here he compares the king of Tyre to those glorious angelic beings. Cherubim were not unfamiliar to the people of Tyre; a number of their ivory carvings of cherubim have been found.

In the ancient Near East, the dwelling of God was often likened to a mountain. The Genesis account of Eden never suggests it is a mountain, but it is so designated by Ezekiel because of God's presence there (28:14). It was there this cherub walked as a creature of power and privilege.

Then, due to his wickedness, he changes. His great position, status, wealth, and power corrupt him and lead to his fall (28:15–19). The Eden imagery continues as the guardian cherub is driven out, and then the language becomes more general—more relevant to Tyre than Eden.

Critical Observation

Many Christians from the third century until this day believe that Ezekiel 28:11–19, in addition to applying to the king of Tyre, is also a reference to the fall of Satan. We know that God created Satan as good, because everything God creates is good. We presume Satan falls into sin prior to the fall of humans because he approaches Adam and Eve as a tempter and a liar. Scripture never provides the reason for his fall or additional details. It is certainly striking that Ezekiel describes the king of Tyre not simply as a glorious human but as a guardian cherub. Others of his descriptions also seem to allow for this interpretation. Whether or not the passage is intended to apply to Satan, it is clear that Ezekiel's theme is an illustration of pride going before a fall.

28:20–23

JUDGMENT AGAINST SIDON

Sidon was the second city to Tyre in Phoenicia. In fact, this is the only place in the Old Testament where the city is mentioned without its tie-in to Tyre, so it seems logical that it would be a partner in this oracle of doom (28:20–23). Sidon would not be spared the same destruction that was in store for Tyre.

28:24–26

A BRIGHT SPOT AMID THE PROPHECIES OF DOOM

This short section of Ezekiel 28 is almost exactly halfway through the portion of his prophecies that concern the grim futures of Israel's enemies (chapters 25–32). It is also the pivot around which the entire section turns. God is dealing with Israel, but these other nations are also being judged so Israel will be freed from their influence, both spiritually and politically. This section paves the way for the third section of Ezekiel (chapters 33–48): Israel's return from exile and the renewal of the life of the people of God in the promised land.

The Israelites in Babylon understood the difficult, and usually permanent, fate of captives. But the Lord will not be prevented from delivering His people and blessing them again in the land, even if it means the destruction of entire nations.

29:1–32:32

JUDGMENT AGAINST EGYPT

Ezekiel's oracles of judgment against Egypt comprise the final and longest segment of the second section of his book. Of all of Israel's enemies, the Egyptians are by far the most powerful. From the perspective of both Jeremiah and Ezekiel, the Babylonians are working as an instrument to accomplish the Lord's will. Egypt, on the other hand, has resisted Babylon's incursion into Palestine—an action viewed as resistance to God's will. When the Jews remaining in Jerusalem turn to Egypt in hopes of help and deliverance from the Babylonians, it is one further demonstration of their intransigent unwillingness to repent and honor the Lord.

Ezekiel's various oracles against Egypt are stretched across a considerable period of time. Most are dated, but they are not necessarily presented in chronological order. For example, the one beginning in 29:17 is the last of the prophecies (dated 571 BC). The one that follows it (beginning in 31:1) is dated fifteen years *earlier*. Some of the prophecies were spoken prior to the fall of Jerusalem, and others long after.

The first of Ezekiel's prophecies against Egypt is dated January 7, 587 BC. As was true of the king of Tyre, Egypt's Pharaoh had delusions of grandeur and would suffer for them along with his kingdom. It would be difficult to overestimate Egypt's dependence on the Nile. Due to the scarcity of rainfall, all agriculture and plant life depended on the water brought north from the highlands of central Africa by the great river. But Pharaoh, who was so proud of his control of the Nile, is portrayed as a great fish caught in the river and thrown onto the land to serve as food for animals (29:1–5).

Through the centuries, Israel had occasionally sought help from Egypt against her enemies, always in defiance of the warnings of Yahweh. Beseeching Egypt had not helped against the Assyrians, and it will do no good against the Babylonians either. Ezekiel's image is that of a person leaning on a staff, but the staff is a weak reed that quickly gives way under weight (29:6–7).

As a result, God will humble Egypt. The nation won't cease to exist as some of Israel's other enemies, although it will become a small, insignificant kingdom (29:8–16).

Critical Observation

In 29:10, "from Migdol to Aswan" is another usage of locations at extreme ends of a nation to indicate totality (in this case from north to south). Migdol is a delta city. Aswan, the site of the famous modern dam, is in the south, not far from Egypt's border with Ethiopia.

In the next of Ezekiel's dated prophecies concerning Egypt (29:17–21), Babylon is shown as doing the Lord's work, though hardly by her own intention. Still, the reward for her pains is the wealth of Egypt. Not much of the historical record exists for this portion of Egyptian history, but it appears that the Pharaoh had to contribute large amounts of money to Babylon to help fund their siege of Tyre. Meanwhile, Israel begins to regain strength (29:21).

Just as Ezekiel had given a lament for Tyre, so also he relates one for Egypt, a nation that had never before suffered a catastrophic invasion (30:1–26). The Assyrians, at the height of their power, had managed to render Egypt a client state for a time, but Egypt had weathered that storm. However, the Day of the Lord is approaching (30:3). Babylon will invade in 568 BC, crushing the might of Egypt while devastating all her allies (30:4–26). Even after the fall of Babylon, Egypt will remain a Persian colony until 404 BC, and after that she will fall to Alexander the Great in 332 BC.

In a lengthy metaphor, Ezekiel likens Egypt to a great cedar tree of Lebanon (31:1–18). But then, Assyria had also been a great tree, a wonder to behold and without equal. It had then been cut down, never to recover. Egypt, too, will fall and fare only slightly better in the aftermath.

Ezekiel concludes this section with a lament for Egypt's Pharaoh, describing Egypt's fall in the most sweeping terms (32:1–32). Egypt has been a dominant power, but God will soon dominate Pharaoh (32:1–16). The final scene is one of a number of fallen powers, Egypt among them, buried together in the pit in various stages of ignominy and shame (32:17–32).

Take It Home

Ezekiel shows that in a powerful and successful country, it is easy to put one's trust in the wrong things: military might, reputation, wealth, and so on. After Israel and Judah had forsaken God, they longed for help from what seemed to be indestructible nations (Assyria, Babylon, Egypt, etc.). But all those mighty forces came to the same end. As contemporary Christians, it is easy to make the same mistake. Any person or nation who commits the same sins, in defiance of the lessons of human history, will pay dearly. What steps can you take today and in the weeks to come to ensure that your trust and hope are in God alone?

EZEKIEL 33:1–36:38

AFTER GOD'S JUDGMENT OF JUDAH

Setting Up the Section

This section begins the third and final segment of Ezekiel's writings. Most of what he has said so far has been somber. The first section (chapters 1–24) dealt with God's judgment on Judah. The second section (chapters 25–32) covered the judgment of Judah's enemies. With those matters behind, however, his look to the future is hopeful and positive. In the final chapters of his book, he foresees Israel's restoration and prosperity as they again receive the blessings of God.

33:1–33

AN APPROPRIATE RESPONSE

Ezekiel has already explained that God designated him a watchman (3:16–21), but he reiterates the concept. The logic is clear and unassailable: If a watchman warns of impending catastrophe but the people ignore his warning, they have no one to blame but themselves for the disaster that overtakes them (33:1–9). The watchman is to blame only if he detects the danger but fails to sound the warning.

Ezekiel has been a conscientious watchman. He sounded the warning. In response, the people see that their suffering is a result of their sins, and they are depressed and discouraged about their situation (33:10). Their pessimism is understandable. After all, they had been exiled from their homeland, and Ezekiel had for years been forecasting Jerusalem's catastrophic devastation. But was theirs a state of repentance or simply sorrow?

Under such circumstances it is easy to lose sight of the power of God and His willingness to bless those who trust Him. The Israelites have a hard time believing their lives can become dramatically different, but Ezekiel keeps challenging them to repent and reestablish their hope (33:11). A person's (or a people's) past does not necessarily determine the future. Someone who has lived a righteous life by all appearances will not be excused if later he or she turns away from righteousness to sin. Likewise, a person who has lived a wicked life is not prevented by his or her past from becoming righteous at once by turning away from sin to the Lord (33:12–20).

For a number of years, Ezekiel has faithfully spoken for God, predicting the fall of Jerusalem. In the twelfth year of exile, word arrives that the dreaded event has finally come to pass (33:21–22). Judah, the remainder state of Israel, exists no more. The date of the fall of the city is August, 586 BC, but it would have taken months for the news to travel to Babylon. When Ezra later travels from Babylon to Jerusalem, it takes him more than four months, and that is with an escort along well-maintained roads during a time of peace. A fugitive attempting to remain hidden from Babylonian soldiers might have taken much longer to go the same distance.

Critical Observation

Apparently the second section of Ezekiel (chapters 25–32) interrupts the chronological flow of the book. The Lord had imposed a symbolic silence on Ezekiel (3:26), but the restriction was to be lifted when a fugitive informed the prophet of the fall of Jerusalem (24:25–27). The arrival of that fugitive is announced in 33:21–22, and Ezekiel is finally free to resume ordinary day-to-day speech with other people.

It appears significant that Ezekiel does not use the names of Jerusalem or Judah throughout this section. It is as if the city and the land no longer deserve their names. Indeed, neither the exiles in Babylon nor the people who remained in Judah had a proper perspective on the situation.

Some of the Israelites remained in the area of Jerusalem, even though the city was in ruins. These are the poorest of the Israelites that the Babylonians had three times left behind (2 Kings 25:12), yet they have the mindset that they have managed to outlast the others. They even compare themselves to Abraham: If God had given the patriarch—one man—the land, then certainly a group of them had the right to it. But comparing themselves to the righteous Abraham isn't appropriate. Ezekiel quickly lists a number of their ongoing sins and what the consequences of those sins will be (33:23–29). Jeremiah's account confirms Ezekiel's prophecy: The lives of the people left behind go from bad to worse. An abortive rebellion leads to the flight of many to Egypt and an increase in poverty. When the exiles eventually return from Babylon, the people who had remained in Judah are found eking out a hardscrabble existence.

The exiled Israelites in Babylon don't fare much better. They come to recognize Ezekiel as an authentic prophet of God. He enjoys a newfound popularity as people come to him to hear what God has to say. But God sees through their spiritual facade. The recognition of truth is not always coupled with the willingness to obey. Ezekiel faithfully proclaimed God's truth, but the people saw him as no more than an entertainer and responded in the same way they might to a singer or musician (33:30–32). Eventually, however, they see God's Word come to pass and acknowledge that when Ezekiel spoke they were hearing the words of the Almighty Himself (33:33).

34:1–31

SHEEP AND SHEPHERDS

Ezekiel had previously placed responsibility for Israel's pathetic spiritual condition on its leaders (22:6–12). Here God has him prophesy against the nation's *shepherds*. When contemporary believers hear the word, they tend to think of pastors or ministers, but Ezekiel's hearers would have immediately thought of their *kings*, not prophets or priests. The likening of kings to shepherds was commonplace in the ancient Near East.

The kings of Israel and Judah are compared to shepherds who are glad to benefit from the food and wool available to them yet refuse to take care of the flock that provides those assets (34:1–6). Of the forty-two kings who ruled from Saul to Zedekiah (about 1030 BC until 586 BC), very few were consistently faithful to their responsibility as overseers of the people of God. Another handful were moderately faithful, but most were completely insensitive to the needs of the people as they used the position only to aggrandize themselves. Israel's exile is the direct result of the malfeasance of her kings.

Yahweh is about to take matters into His own hands. He will hold the incompetent shepherds accountable for their unfaithfulness. His primary interest, however, is not to punish the rulers but rather to rescue His sheep from them (34:7–16). Utterly unlike the selfish reigns of Israel's kings, Yahweh will attend to the needs of His people and provide for them. (Ezekiel 34:16 is the mirror opposite of 34:4.)

Yet the problems will continue for a while (34:17–22). Those who are wealthy and powerful—"the sleek and the strong" (34:16 NIV)—will continue to take advantage of the poor and weak people. In fact, the matter will not be ultimately resolved until God provides a new shepherd, one akin to His servant David (34:23–24). This will be a single person who perfectly embodies the kingly ideal.

It may have seemed that the collapse of Judah, the capture of her kings, and the exile of her people to Babylon had signaled the end of God's covenant with the house of David. However, Ezekiel's pronouncement of God's promise reveals that the covenant with David has by no means been revoked. The promise is still in force. David's descendant will again sit on his throne.

With the appointment of this new king, the Lord will establish a covenant of peace with Israel. Ezekiel lists a number of images of blessing and prosperity that the covenant will bestow upon the people of God (34:25–31; see Leviticus 26; Deuteronomy 28). Everything God had promised Israel will eventually be realized.

35:1–36:38

ISRAEL AND EDOM

Israel and Edom were two mountainous nations that shared a long history of animosity and conflict (Israel tracing its roots to Jacob and Edom going back to Esau). This section of Ezekiel contrasts their respective destinies.

After the fall of Jerusalem, Judah is left with an economy in shambles and a lack of effective government or military. Edom, encouraged by the Babylonians, takes advantage of Judah's vulnerability and invades at that time, taking whatever the Babylonians haven't already removed and annexing portions of the land. It might seem that this particular passage should have accompanied the previous section of judgments against foreign nations (chapters 25–34). However, the promise of Edom's destruction, coming immediately after the destruction of Jerusalem, serves as the background for a prophecy of Israel's restoration.

Mount Seir (35:2) is symbolic of the entire nation of Edom (35:15). The two nations Edom has in its sights are Israel and Judah (35:10). The Edomites are celebrating the desolation of Jerusalem; even worse, they slaughter the Jews they catch fleeing from the Babylonians (35:5–6).

But soon Edom's punishment will fit their crime as they experience similar desolation (35:10–15). Those who use their strength to take advantage of others are rarely popular. When Edom eventually faces the same crisis for which they had ridiculed Israel, the rest of the world takes a perverse delight in their misery.

Demystifying Ezekiel

The entire book of Obadiah (short though it is) is devoted to a similar prophecy against Edom. Obadiah also foretells that the violence of the Edomites will bring God's wrath upon them.

Edom declines steadily under Babylonian, then Persian, then Greek, and finally Roman rule. Its former mountain strongholds are now only tourist stops in southern Jordan.

Just as Mount Seir represents Edom, the mountains of Israel stand for the entire nation (36:1). Ezekiel does not provide a date for this prophecy, but it is clear that it is given after the destruction of Jerusalem while Judah is at the mercy of her enemies. God's message to Israel is just the opposite of the accompanying prophecy to Edom (and other nations). In fact, it was probably hard for many people to believe such a promise, considering Israel's current circumstances: nation and temple in ruins, people in exile, kings dead or imprisoned. So throughout this section, Ezekiel repeatedly punctuates his message with, "This is what the Sovereign Lord says."

Indeed, the news is good. God is renewing the blessings previously spelled out in His covenant with Israel, including increased fertility of the land and the people (36:8–12). The people have done nothing to deserve it. They had defiled Israel, and when God removed them from that defiled land, their continued inappropriate conduct caused other nations to profane God's name (36:16–18). The assumption of Israel's enemies is that Israel's God must not be very powerful if He can't save His people from such indignities.

Yet the Lord loves His people and will deliver them even though Israel has done nothing to deserve His mercy. Ezekiel makes it clear that Yahweh is not rewarding the people for their goodness, because they haven't been good or faithful for a long time. Rather, God is acting to show the holiness of His own name, His faithfulness to His own Word (36:19–23).

God's faithfulness to His Word is seen in the promises of 36:25–27, which are another form of the same promises previously given in Deuteronomy 30:6–8. And as the Spirit of God works among the people, many will respond with deep contrition (Ezekiel 36:31).

Take It Home

The problem Ezekiel is confronting on a national level can also be problematic at a personal level. God's judgment of His people is somber and at times tragic. As other nations witness it, the appropriate response is repentance for their own wrongdoings, but instead they rejoice and celebrate. Do you think people today—even believers—sometimes take joy in the ignominious downfall of their enemies (either nationally or individually)? How might you avoid feeling that same inappropriate satisfaction when a personal enemy has a bad or embarrassing experience?

EZEKIEL 37:1–39:29

DRY BONES AND NEW LIFE

Life Restored to Dry Bones	37:1–14
Restoration and Unification	37:15–28
Judgment against Gog	38:1–39:29

Setting Up the Section

This section contains one of the few passages from the long book of Ezekiel that might be somewhat familiar to the average person. As Ezekiel continues his message of God's redemption of Israel, he is shown in a most emphatic way God's immense power to restore His people. Ezekiel also alerts the people of a king to come who will unite them again, and he delivers a prophecy against the land of Gog.

37:1–14

LIFE RESTORED TO DRY BONES

Although Ezekiel has been prophesying with great regularity, this is the first *vision* he records since chapter 11. The message of chapter 37 essentially repeats what Ezekiel had proclaimed in chapter 36, but in a different way that makes the same point and drives home the message.

God shows Ezekiel a valley with a great many dry bones (37:1–2). The fact that the bones are unburied and baking in the sun suggests a curse concerning those who break the Lord's covenant: "Your carcasses will be food to all birds of the sky and to the beasts of the earth, and there will be no one to frighten them away" (Deuteronomy 28:26 NASB). It is a reminder that Israel has suffered precisely the fate the Lord long ago warned about if she was not faithful to His covenant.

Ezekiel is instructed to walk among the bones, perhaps to see for himself how brittle they are. These bones have had all the skin, flesh, and sinews removed by decomposition and/or scavengers, and they have been bleached in the hot Middle Eastern sun.

Critical Observation

Ancient burial customs tended to require interment twice. The body was first placed in a family tomb on a shelf cut out of the rock for that purpose. Later, when the shelf was needed for another body, the family would place the desiccated bones in an *ossuary*, literally a "bone box." The skeleton would have to be broken up with the bones packed individually. Sometimes many sets of bones were stored in the same ossuary.

The Lord's question to Ezekiel in verse 3 is intended to start the prophet thinking about life after death. Next Ezekiel is instructed to address the long-dried-up bones, to prophesy to them (37:4–6). More specifically, he is told to tell the bones that God is planning to make them live again. The word for *preaching* in this section, often translated as "prophesy" (literally, "to speak for God"), occurs seven times throughout the passage.

The obvious question is: What possible good is it to make such an effort? So much time has passed, and the bones are so dry that they are not even connected to one another. They are loose bones, not intact skeletons. Yet Ezekiel does as he is told (37:7).

Demystifying Ezekiel

In Ezekiel 37:1–14, the prophet writes of *breath, wind,* and *spirit* in various contexts. We miss the significance, but his listeners could not have overlooked the clever wordplay because in Hebrew (and later in New Testament Greek) the same word is used to define each of those terms. Ezekiel uses the word ten times in these fourteen verses to emphasize how the breath of God's Spirit allows us to become living spirits and how God's sovereignty is highlighted by the fact that He controls the four winds.

In response to Ezekiel's preaching, the bones not only come together to form complete skeletons but also grow tendons, flesh, and skin (37:7–8). However, they still have no breath until God instructs Ezekiel to prophesy once more, after which the former pile of bones rises to form a vast army (37:8–10).

This vision, as it turns out, is Yahweh's response to the hopelessness and despair of His people. A saying has begun to circulate among the dispirited Jews in Babylon: "Our bones are dried up and our hope is gone; we are cut off" (37:11 NIV). Ezekiel's vision demonstrates that for God's people, hope is never gone.

To reinforce the positive message of the vision, God speaks of opening the graves of His people to restore them to Israel (37:12–14). The image of resurrection and anticipation of a new exodus are brought together to describe what the Lord is going to do for Israel: Israel will be made alive spiritually, and she will be brought back as a people to the promised land. Yet nothing in the world would have appeared less likely when Ezekiel saw this vision and reported it to his fellow exiles in Babylon.

37:15–28

RESTORATION AND UNIFICATION

After the vision of the valley of dry bones, God provides Ezekiel with yet another depiction of Israel's restoration. God instructs him to take two sticks (representing Israel and Judah) and join them together. It is not clear exactly how he does this, but the result is the appearance of a single stick, demonstrating that the nations will again be one.

Demystifying Ezekiel

Israel had previously been the name of the northern ten tribes. Sometimes *Ephraim* was used as a synonym because it was the principal tribe (from which all the northern kings had come) and it covered the geographical area of Samaria, the capital of the northern kingdom. But Israel had been conquered and absorbed into surrounding nations more than a century ago. Judah was all that was left of the original nation of Israel. In the view of all the prophets, including Ezekiel, Judah had inherited the title of *Israel* and remained a divinely chosen people in covenant with Yahweh.

Like the meaning of the valley of the dry bones, this too would have been hard for Ezekiel's audience to understand (37:18–19) and almost too good to believe. God is promising not only a political/social restoration but also spiritual renewal (37:20–24). The phrase, "They will be my people, and I will be their God" (37:23 NIV), reflects God's covenants with Abraham and Moses, and some say it is a succinct way to describe New Testament salvation.

God's people will be united under a single king. He is called David because he will be a leader from the house of David (37:24). Modern believers may recall David's adultery, fall, and the miserable second half of his reign. But David was a man after God's own heart. It was under his reign alone in the history of Israel that the nation was free of idolatry and polytheism—a remarkable achievement in a world where the great number of gods made religion without idols seem a contradiction in terms.

The closing reference to God's dwelling place among the people anticipates a major theme that Ezekiel will develop in chapters 40–46 (37:27–28).

38:1–39:29

JUDGMENT AGAINST GOG

The nature of biblical prophecy is such that sometimes people can examine the same passages and come up with quite diverse interpretations. This particular section of Ezekiel is one such complicated and potentially confusing section. For example, there was no real political restoration for the Jewish nation as Ezekiel describes in the second half of chapter 37. The exiles return to Judah, to be sure, but never gain true independence again. After Babylonian exile, they remained a tiny client state of a succession of powers: Persia, Greece, the Seleucids, Rome, and the Turkish Empire.

From there Ezekiel moves on to the Gog/Magog section (chapters 38–39) and then the elaborate account of building a new temple (chapters 40–48). Some people approach these passages as unfulfilled prophecies of Israel's eventual restoration as a great nation in the promised land. However, that is not the way the Bible itself treats these prophetic texts.

Ezekiel and numerous other prophets wrote of the future of God's people as a whole—Jews and Gentiles alike. The promised land, never limited to a piece of Canaanite real estate, was ultimately a promise of heaven and eternity.

Demystifying Ezekiel

Continuing through the rest of Ezekiel, a number of presumptions will influence how his visions and prophecies will be interpreted:

1) The covenant that God made with Abraham and renewed with Israel at Sinai is the theological/spiritual arrangement by which modern Christians live today. There has always been, and will always be, but one people of God.
2) The Bible is a single book with a single message about a single people and their single Savior. A failure to see Gentile believers as the object of so much of biblical prophecy inevitably leads people to think that the Old Testament has to do with another people and their situation, not with us and ours. The whole Bible comes alive as we realize it is our family history, our story, and not someone else's.
3) Modern Christians are in the same situation as our ancestors were in the days of Ezekiel: We are awaiting the consolation of Israel and the fulfillment of the new covenant.
4) We have been given a number of anticipations of this ultimate consummation: the return of the Jews from Babylon, the incarnation of the Son of God and His resurrection from the dead, the Lord's changing of individual hearts, the survival of the Jews through the last twenty-five hundred years and the rebirth of their national identity in 1948, and so forth.

Magog, Meshech, and Tubal are three grandsons of Noah (38:1–3; see Genesis 10:2), and the peoples who descended from them were still known to Ezekiel's contemporaries. Magog is thought to have been a land in western Asia Minor, though that is not certain. Meshech and Tubal are two relatively small nations of Cappadocia (present-day Turkey). Ezekiel has already mentioned the latter two locations in passing (27:13; 32:26). Meshech had a warlike reputation due to frequent conflicts with the Assyrians (Psalm 120:5–7). The name *Gog* seems to have been derived from the name of a powerful king of Lydia (western Asia Minor) in the first half of the seventh century BC. So Ezekiel refers to two separate nations with the king from a third—a great force gathering to invade the south sometime in the future.

Gog's great army will be enlarged by mercenary troops from a variety of other nations that span the furthest reaches of the known world, all united to invade the promised land where Israel lives in safety (Ezekiel 38:5–6). Ironically, Gog and his legions will be following Yahweh's orders (38:7–16). Sheba and Dedan are caravan trading nations, one to the east and one to the west, hoping to profit at Israel's expense by buying plundered goods to resell to their trading partners (38:13).

This assault on Israel will be the fulfillment of other predictions made by Old Testament prophets. The description of the Lord putting an end to Gog's aggression is universal and cosmic. The entire earth is involved; all creatures tremble. The account of warfare in Revelation reflects many of the same events as Ezekiel 38:17–23: earthquake (Revelation 11:13), fire and hail raining down from heaven (Revelation 8:7; 20:9), and birds eating the flesh of the enemies of God (Revelation 19:17–21). There is evidence that the beast of Revelation is to be understood as Gog.

Ezekiel 39 is a repeat of Ezekiel 38, but with more emphasis on Gog's destruction than the attack on Israel. It will be total annihilation, with no survivors to bury the dead and even the homelands of the invading armies lay to waste (39:1–6). Ezekiel's reference to "the day" in 39:8 ties in to other biblical prophecies about the Day of the Lord. On that day, God will reverse which side does the plundering and looting (39:9–10). The burial of enemy soldiers will take seven months, but the ritual purification of the land (including removing all bones) will take much longer (39:11–16).

With such an image of the victory God will give His people, it should have been abundantly clear that it isn't for any want of power on Yahweh's part that Israel falls prey to the Babylonians. He is judging His people, but the long-range result will be a restored house of Israel—a transformed and spiritually renewed people living in communion with God and in willing obedience to Him (39:17–29).

Take It Home

Israel's promised turnaround from exiled captives to those being renewed and restored to fellowship with God in their own land is almost too much to believe. Put yourself in Ezekiel's place as he was chosen to deliver such news. Do you think he even comprehended the significance of his message? And note especially his willingness to preach to a valley filled with dry, disconnected bones. Can you relate to trying to encourage someone who perpetually seems unable or unwilling to listen? If so, reread Ezekiel 37:1–14 as a reminder that God's Spirit is powerful enough to reach *anyone*. God's people need to continue to speak faithfully for Him, even in situations where a positive outcome seems unlikely.

EZEKIEL 40:1–46:24

A NEW TEMPLE

Setting Up the Section

The final nine chapters of the book of Ezekiel, beginning with this section, are a great vision of the future of Jerusalem and Israel presented in terms of an idealized temple and promised land.

40:1–4

A DIFFERENT KIND OF VISION

Ezekiel has been given some very specific visions to proclaim to the people of God exiled in Babylon, not least among them the fall of Jerusalem and the confident expectation of being freed to return to their homeland. Other visions of his were much more symbolic than specific, such as the valley where a pile of dry bones sprang to life. His vision of a future temple has been interpreted both ways.

Some people consider the closing chapters of Ezekiel a description of an actual temple to be built in Jerusalem at some point in the future. (Its description and measurements do not match any previous temple.) But a number of reasons arise from the biblical text to discourage such a viewpoint. The high mountain position (40:2) suggests the dwelling of God, and we may assume that Ezekiel intends for us to understand that he is looking southward toward Jerusalem (although the city is not specifically mentioned). However, there is no high mountain north of Jerusalem, or anywhere in Israel for that matter.

In addition, the design of the temple is highly stylized or idealized: Its dimensions are dominated by multiples of five, with twenty-five a common number and everything exactly proportioned. It is not unlike the description of the heavenly Jerusalem found in Revelation 21—a description so fabulous it is impossible to visualize.

Demystifying Ezekiel

The date would have been April 28, 573 BC, but of equal significance is the *way* Ezekiel's vision is dated. The fact that it is twenty-five years after Ezekiel's exile may be a subtle reference to the year of Jubilee (40:1). Every fifty years all enslaved Israelites were to be freed (Leviticus 25:8–13). The twenty-fifth year would mark the turning point when people no longer looked back to the catastrophe of the exile but forward to their restoration. The vision also occurs at the first of the year, which invites comparison to Israel's deliverance from bondage in Egypt (Exodus 12:2).

40:5–42:20

MEASURING THE TEMPLE

One other thing to keep in mind is that Ezekiel's descriptions were not illustrated. His audience had only his words. Modern readers may find the temple section of his writing repetitive or overly detailed, but that was the only way the prophet could attempt to describe the splendor he witnessed. He needed to provide lots of details to help his listeners/readers form appropriate pictures in their minds.

As his celestial host proceeds to measure the temple, Ezekiel records not only the measurements but also a number of observations (40:3–4). Starting at the east gate (40:5–16), they move into the outer court (40:17–19) and its north (40:20–23) and south (40:24–27) gates before continuing to the inner court with its gates and special rooms (40:28–47). Ezekiel, as a priest, is able to enter the Holy Place, but he remains there as the angel goes alone into the Most Holy Place (40:48–41:4). Additional side rooms surround the temple in three layers (41:5–7). The cherubim carved into this temple have only two faces rather than the four that Ezekiel had previously seen firsthand (41:5–26; see 1:10). Finally, Ezekiel is shown the priests' rooms (42:1–20).

This must surely have been an inspiring vision for the people of Israel. As they will eventually discover, the temple they had known is completely gone. When it is reconstructed after the exile, even the foundation has to be rebuilt. Impressive buildings are still a measure of the greatness of a city. The reputation of Paris would be diminished without its Eiffel tower, Notre Dame, and Arc de Triumph. Rome is enhanced by the Coliseum, St. Peter's, the Trevi Fountain, the Spanish steps, and the Pantheon. Jerusalem without the temple was just not the city it should be, and Ezekiel envisioned a marvelous temple indeed.

43:1–12

GOD'S GLORY RETURNS

As Ezekiel's vision continues, he discovers that another attribute of this new temple is its permanence (43:6–7). Israel is still in shock over the loss of their first temple—the one Solomon had built. It will soon be reconstructed by Zerubbabel, but it will also fall. Later Herod enlarges and restores the temple during the time of Jesus. This permutation has the shortest existence of all, destroyed by the Romans only a few years after its completion. The temple Ezekiel describes, however, would be the dwelling place of God forever (43:7).

This is a powerful vision. Ezekiel had previously described the glowing, fiery radiance that indicated the presence of God, and he had heard angels' wings that sounded like the movement of a great army (1:24–28; 43:3).

It is significant that the glory of the Lord enters this new temple through the east gate, for it was from the east gate that His glory had departed in Ezekiel's former vision (10:18–19). A great reversal is taking place as the complete manifestation of God's divine majesty returns to take its place among His people. The filling of the temple with the glory of the Lord (43:5) is a phenomenon previously seen in the days of Solomon (1 Kings 8:10–11) and in one of Isaiah's visions (Isaiah 6:4).

Critical Observation

The noun *tabernacle* derives from a verb sometimes translated "I will live" (43:7). The word has a biblical history that recalls the place of the tabernacle and the temple as an embodiment of God's presence among His people. It is just as applicable for the present and future as well. When John writes that the Word became flesh and *dwelt* among us (John 1:14), he is conveying the same idea that, in Jesus Christ, God was present among humanity.

The presence of Yahweh is further confirmed by His voice (Ezekiel 43:6). The reference to the temple as the place for the soles of His feet (43:7) recalls the ark of the covenant in earlier passages as the Lord's footstool (1 Chronicles 28:2). While the ark is the embodiment of the Lord's presence in the old temple and viewed as Yahweh's throne, it is not prominent in this new visionary temple. The temple itself is God's throne and dwelling place. The shift of emphasis away from the ark to God's more widespread presence is also reflected in Jeremiah's writing (Jeremiah 3:16–17).

The nature of the defilement mentioned in Ezekiel 43:7–8 is unclear. Various sources have speculated that the problem might involve the tombs of kings being placed too near the temple (although no evidence of such a practice exists), some kind of cult that worshiped the dead, or memorials being built nearby that detracted from a single-minded focus on Yahweh. Whatever the specific problem had been, it was yet another way Israel had betrayed God's covenant and shown indifference to His holiness.

In this visionary description of the future consummation of salvation, the people of God are still summoned to live in holiness. Even when all is complete, obedience and loyalty to the Lord are expected. The end of history is connected to the responsible actions of the Lord's people.

Ezekiel is challenged to keep the description of the new temple before the people, who are still mourning the fall of Jerusalem's temple (43:10–11). It is the next best thing possible to snapping a photo of what he had seen and showing the snapshot to encourage and strengthen those who saw it. Ezekiel's regular descriptions also remind the people that they had strayed away from God in the first place, creating the problems they eventually faced. However, they are now able to again enjoy God's presence, thanks to His forgiving grace.

43:13–46:24

THE FUNCTION OF THE TEMPLE

Unlike the gods of the surrounding territories, Yahweh has no interest in a temple where He can enjoy basking in the glory of His surroundings. Israel's temple had an ongoing function to be the place where people worship the Lord and He fosters holiness among them. Yahweh desires fellowship with His people, which necessitates their purity and righteousness.

Ezekiel next makes a transition from describing the incredible temple to providing regulations that will govern worship. The altar needs to be properly dedicated (43:13–27), and this time the priests will serve faithfully (44:1–31). Interestingly, there is no mention of a high priest in this section, although the prince who abides in the temple with God is mentioned frequently in the material that follows, beginning in 44:3. The priests will not only attend to the temple but also serve as preachers, teachers, and rulers of the people (44:24).

The division of land is summarized in 45:1–8; it will be covered in greater detail in 48:1–22. Great emphasis is placed on justice in the land. The king will rule justly and for the sake of the people, not himself, and private land will be protected from royal confiscation (45:8–12).

The next section (45:13–46:24) specifies the offerings to be made and the feasts to be celebrated in the new temple. They are similar to, but not identical with, the regulations in the Law of Moses. In addition are guidelines for other public services and daily offerings.

Ezekiel's vision is, in a sense, a map of holiness. Every detail serves to emphasize an ideal worship depicted in forms that are understandable and meaningful to his contemporaries. The Lord draws near and invites His people to come near to Him, but He does not cease to be the God of terrible holiness. His people must revere Him accordingly.

Take It Home

It is a common problem for people and/or churches to disregard or minimize the holiness of God. Certainly, God does invite His people to draw near to Him (Hebrews 4:16; 10:22; James 4:8). He is abundant in grace and mercy. Yet as we approach God and come to see Him more clearly, there should be times when, like Ezekiel, we are floored by His glory (Ezekiel 1:28). How would you rate your own awareness and respect for the holiness of God? What experiences have you had when the Lord's holiness was most evident to you?

EZEKIEL 47:1–48:35

THE RIVER MEASURED AND THE TERRITORY DIVIDED

Setting Up the Section

As Ezekiel finishes describing his vision of a future temple, he also concludes his lengthy book. In this section he depicts the river flowing out of the temple and explains how the land is to be divided among the tribes.

47:1–12

THE RIVER THAT FLOWS FROM THE TEMPLE

Numerous references to a river of life are found throughout the Bible. The theme begins in Genesis as four rivers flow through the Garden of Eden and continues to the final chapter of scripture that describes a river, clear as crystal, flowing from the throne of God. The latter example, written by John, appears to derive in a substantial way from Ezekiel's description in this passage. All ancient Near Eastern temples faced east, and Israel's was no exception (47:1). The worship was conducted according to completely different principles, of course, but the sanctuary would have looked familiar to that culture. As Ezekiel returns from the kitchens in the outer court of the temple to the sanctuary itself in the inner court, he sees a small stream of water gushing out from beneath the slab of stone at the base of the main doorway.

The east gate had been closed (44:1–2), so the flow of water is diverted to the south side of the gate structure. Ezekiel exits through the north gate (47:1–2). As he watches, his angelic escort does periodic depth checks. After walking about 1000 cubits (a standard Hebrew cubit was 17.5 inches), the water is ankle deep. Another 1000 cubits, and it has become knee deep. Another stretch, and it is waist deep. At the fourth measurement (by that time, well over a mile away from the temple), the water has become an impassable stream—both too deep and too wide to cross (47:3–5). No mention is made of tributaries, so the stream appears to become larger through miraculous effect.

Critical Observation

The physical topography of Israel would have required that a literal river cross valleys and ascend and descend mountain ranges before it could drop several thousand feet to the basin of the Dead Sea. What Ezekiel sees is a miraculous river in a vision.

During Ezekiel's time, as is true today, little life could be found in the Dead Sea. It has no exits, and the water that gathers there is filled with various toxic materials, including salts. But Ezekiel witnesses flowing water that will freshen the sea and soon have it teeming with life. In fact, the Dead Sea will rival the Mediterranean as a popular fishing spot (47:8–10).

Ezekiel begins and ends this section with an emphasis on where the water originated (47:1, 12). He sees fishermen standing on lush lakeshores and casting nets in spots that have for millennia been barren desert wastes. En-gedi and En-eglaim (47:10) were a significant distance apart, emphasizing that the entire lake is fresh and full of fish. Yet the surrounding swamps and marshlands remained salty because salt was a prized commodity. The various kinds of fresh fish would be preserved in the salt. In addition, the water creates a lush habitat for fruit trees (47:12). Ezekiel paints a verbal picture of unlimited abundance.

47:13–48:35

THE DIVIDING OF THE LAND

The division of the territory as viewed by Ezekiel is considerably different from the boundaries that God had given Joshua centuries before. The boundaries described are essentially those that Israel possessed during the time of David and Solomon, except that the land east of the Jordan is not included in Ezekiel's vision (47:15–20). This time the division is to be equitable, where originally some tribes had considerably more land than others (47:14).

Another variation is a broadening of who will be entitled to a stake in the land. Under the Law of Moses, aliens could become circumcised and gain membership in the community, yet they were banned from owning land, which relegated them to something of an outsider status. But with the ability for outsiders to join the community *and* possess land, the distinctions between them and the native Israelites are entirely eliminated (47:22–23).

Ezekiel's description of the allotment of the land is so idealized that it ignores the topography of Canaan. Each tribe's designated segment runs east and west, from one side of the promised land to the other. Near the center of those bands is one strip reserved for the city, the sanctuary, the priests, and the prince (48:8–22). Seven tribes will be situated north of that strip (48:1–7), and five tribes south (48:23–28).

A number of intriguing details come to light in Ezekiel's depiction. For one, the sons of Jacob's two wives (Rachel and Leah) are positioned nearest the central reserve and the sanctuary. The children by handmaidens Bilhah and Zilpah are further removed. Another change is the location of Judah, now in the northern section rather than the south.

Demystifying Ezekiel

Judah's move from a southern tribe to a position farther north (48:7) is perhaps a symbol of the overcoming of longstanding animosities between Israel and Judah existing since the kingdom had been divided. Nevertheless, Judah remained closest to the central reserve on the north, and Benjamin on the south.

Still another surprise is that the names of the tribes connected with the twelve gates of the city (48:30–35) do not match the names in the land allotment. The land division is as before, with Joseph being replaced by his two sons (Manasseh and Ephraim) and with Levi omitted (because the Levites were distributed for ministry among the other tribes). But the *gates* include a gate for Joseph and one for Levi, reverting to the twelve original sons of Jacob (Israel).

Finally, we find a great ending to a great book (48:35). The continuing story of the kingdom of God is a story of the presence of the Lord. Because of Israel's unbelief and disobedience, she had forfeited the presence of God. But the new epoch would herald the arrival of Immanuel—God with us—and it would eventually result in His coming to be with His people forever.

Take It Home

The prophetic books have a reputation for proclaiming "gloom and doom," and certainly Ezekiel has much to say about God's judgment. Yet the final chapters of his book are actually quite encouraging. His message to Israel is that the God who had judged them will also restore them to fellowship with Him. What can you learn from Ezekiel that will help you develop a broader understanding of who God is and how He relates to His people?

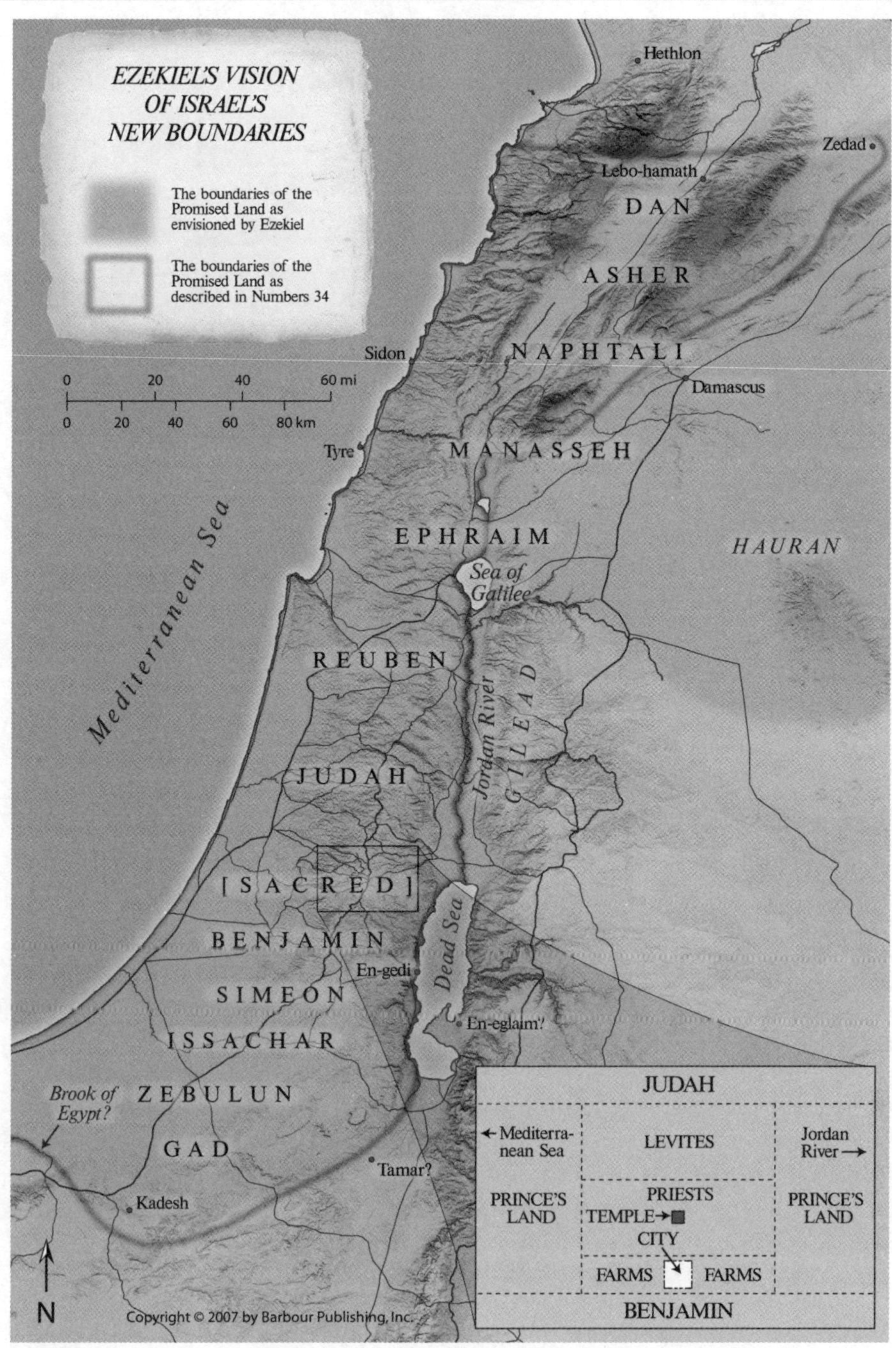

EZEKIEL'S VISION OF ISRAEL'S NEW BOUNDARIES
The boundaries of the Promised Land as envisioned by Ezekiel
The boundaries of the Promised Land as described in Numbers 34
0 20 40 60 mi
0 20 40 60 80 km
Hethlon
Zedad
Lebo-hamath
DAN
ASHER
NAPHTALI
Sidon
Damascus
Tyre
MANASSEH
EPHRAIM
HAURAN
Mediterranean Sea
Sea of Galilee
REUBEN
Jordan River
GILEAD
JUDAH
[SACRED]
Dead Sea
BENJAMIN
En-gedi
SIMEON
En-eglaim?
ISSACHAR
Brook of Egypt?
ZEBULUN
GAD
Tamar?
Kadesh
N
JUDAH
← Mediterra-nean Sea
LEVITES
Jordan River →
PRINCE'S LAND
PRIESTS
TEMPLE→
CITY
PRINCE'S LAND
FARMS
FARMS
BENJAMIN

DANIEL

INTRODUCTION TO DANIEL

The book of Daniel contains some of the best-known stories in the Bible, but it also provides some of the most challenging and intriguing passages to attempt to comprehend. Some of the prophets had sent warning of a judgment of God's people to come; others are present at the end of the captivity to help encourage and empower the beleaguered exiles. But Daniel goes into exile along with his countrymen and provides an insider's view of Judah's experiences in the faraway land of Babylon.

AUTHOR

Daniel came from a royal family. He is compared with Noah and Job in terms of faithfulness to God and righteousness (see Ezekiel 14:14). Daniel also demonstrates great wisdom, always giving God complete credit. Unlike Solomon, who started life strong as a young man but strayed from God as an adult, Daniel's faith and wisdom are consistent and evident throughout his long lifetime.

OCCASION

Daniel describes events that occur during one of the worst situations the people of God ever experienced. The nation of Israel had fallen to the Assyrians more than one hundred years earlier, but Judah survived. Yet Judah continues to refuse to heed God's warning and soon faces humiliating defeat themselves. The Babylonians breach the walls of Jerusalem, ransack the temple, and carry off most of the population in a series of deportations. Daniel is among the first group taken. His writing offers much assurance in that even though circumstances are bad, God is still with His people.

THEMES

From start to finish, the theme of the book of Daniel is the sovereignty of God. This theme is detected in the way the Lord interacts with individuals, controls nations, and shares with Daniel plans for the long-range future of His people.

HISTORICAL CONTEXT

Babylon was considered to be one of the most glorious and powerful kingdoms of the world at the time that Daniel was written. The palace and gardens are listed among the seven wonders of the ancient world. God uses Babylon's strong armies to conquer Judah after the people refuse to serve Him. In the process, the Babylonians kill many Judeans and take many into captivity. Yet by the end of Daniel, the Babylonian Empire has already fallen to Cyrus, leader of the Medes and Persians.

CONTRIBUTION TO THE BIBLE

In addition to some of the Bible's most beloved stories (including the fiery furnace and the lions' den), the book of Daniel is an invaluable source of information concerning various events of future history. Coupled with John's writing in Revelation, many of the symbols of the apocalyptic literature begin to cohere and make sense. Certainly, there are numerous ways to interpret the same information, and it can be difficult to do more than speculate in many places. However, Jesus quotes Daniel as a source for what to look for in the future (see Matthew 24:15–16), giving the prophet's writing the highest degree of credibility.

OUTLINE

DANIEL TAKEN TO BABYLON 1:1–21

A Distressing Beginning 1:1–2
The Best in a Bad Situation 1:3–7
Passing the First Test 1:8–21

DANIEL INTERPRETS NEBUCHADNEZZAR'S DREAM 2:1–49

Nebuchadnezzar's Challenge 2:1–13
Daniel's Response 2:14–23
Daniel's Interpretation 2:24–43
The Final Kingdom 2:44–49

THE FIERY FURNACE AND GOD'S DELIVERANCE 3:1–30

Nebuchadnezzar's Statue 3:1–7
The Hebrews' Dilemma 3:8–18
Nebuchadnezzar's Lesson 3:19–30

NEBUCHADNEZZAR'S HUMBLING EXPERIENCE 4:1–37

Nebuchadnezzar's Second Dream 4:1–18
The Dream's Interpretation and Fulfillment 4:19–37

DANIEL AND BELSHAZZAR 5:1–31

Belshazzar's Banquet 5:1–4
The Writing on the Wall 5:5–12
The Writing's Interpretation 5:13–31

DANIEL AND DARIUS 6:1–28

Daniel's Exemplary Character 6:1–4
The Conspiracy against Daniel 6:5–12
Daniel Survives the Lions' Den 6:13–28

DANIEL 1:1–21

DANIEL TAKEN TO BABYLON

Setting Up the Section

The book of Daniel describes some of the same era as 2 Kings and 2 Chronicles, yet Daniel describes this era from within the Babylonian exile. Due to persistent disregard for God's laws and other sins throughout Judah, the Lord had allowed His people to be conquered. The Babylonian armies had shown little mercy as they marched into Judah, laid siege to Jerusalem, and eventually left the city and the surrounding territory in ruins. Many people died while fighting; many others starved to death. Most of those who survived were deported to Babylon—Daniel among them. The people feel as though God has deserted them. However, Daniel repeatedly attests to the power of the one true God at work, even while His people are exiled in the idolatrous land of Babylon.

1:1–2

A DISTRESSING BEGINNING

Daniel has one of the bleakest openings of any book of scripture. Within the first two verses, the beloved city of Jerusalem falls into the hands of one of the most terrifying empires on earth. The temple's holy items are carted away and placed among the idols of Babylon. To make things worse, it is the Lord who has given Jerusalem over to her enemies. The captivity that results is a God-designed plan to chastise His people for their ongoing rebellion. The year is 605 BC. Judah's king at the time is Jehoiakim.

This is one of the worst experiences in the history of Judah. (The northern kingdom of Israel had faced a similar end more than a century earlier at the hands of the Assyrians.) Yet despite this potentially depressing beginning, Daniel never ceases to be encouraging and optimistic. Right from the start, the theme of his book is the sovereignty of God. The Lord is in control of the nations and is working out His plan in this world. He is absolutely in control.

Critical Observation

The prophet Habakkuk confirms that God permitted the brutal Babylonian invasion as a result of the wickedness of His people (Habakkuk 1:5–11). In fact, Habakkuk tries to talk God out of impending disaster (Habakkuk 1:12–2:1). He learns, however, that the plans of God are God's alone, and that the best he can do is walk by faith, no matter what happens.

Other sources describe various horrific events associated with the fall of Jerusalem, so it is interesting to notice what Daniel focuses on in his record. Of all the dreadful and repulsive things taking place around him, he singles out the degradation of the temple (1:2). Israel's worship had become ritualistic rather than genuine, so God took worship away from them. He allowed all of the gold previously used in temple worship to be used to mock Him in the presence of false gods. It is humiliating to Judah and to the Lord.

Israel's mind-set and practice of worship as ritual had no effect on their day-to-day lives. Placing their so-called holy objects among the idols of other nations is God's way of giving them a picture of what is in their hearts. Their "worship" is no different than that of the Babylonians.

God wants to see His people redeemed. He wants Judah to repent and fall before Him in complete devotion. Therefore, He allows them to endure much heartache and lose their temple temporarily so that ultimately they might be saved.

1:3–7

THE BEST IN A BAD SITUATION

After Jerusalem falls, Babylonian King Nebuchadnezzar conducts a search for some of Judah's top young people—a common practice of the time by victorious rulers. By indoctrinating the up-and-coming leaders of the defeated nation, Nebuchadnezzar hopes to ensure that new generations will settle into the Babylonian way of life rather than attempting escape or revolt.

Daniel is one of four young men from Judah mentioned by name who are taken (1:6). At the time, they are probably about fifteen or sixteen years old. Nothing is said of their parents, but the Babylonians wouldn't have thought twice about breaking up families to carry off anyone they wished.

Being handsome and without defect (1:4), Daniel and his three peers clearly have genetics working for them. But they also are noted for their quickness to learn and their aptitude for accumulating wisdom. They are expected to quickly assimilate into Babylonian culture by absorbing the language and literature of their new home. They are also given Babylonians names.

Demystifying Daniel

A change in names had spiritual as well as cultural significance. The Hebrew names all acknowledged characteristics of the awesome God of Judah:

Daniel meant, "God is my Judge."

Hananiah meant, "Yahweh is gracious."

Mishael meant, "Who is like God?"

Azariah meant, "Yahweh is my helper."

The newly assigned names, in contrast (Belteshazzar, Shadrach, Meshach, and Abednego), acknowledged various Babylonian deities: Bel, Aku, and Nego/Nebo.

Theirs was a demanding, three-year program (1:5). Nebuchadnezzar changed their names, clothes, language, home, and culture, yet he was not successful in changing their hearts.

1:8–21

PASSING THE FIRST TEST

However, there are benefits in addition to the demands for these men. The young trainees are entitled to a daily allotment of food from the king's own table—the best of the best (1:5). This is intended to be a privilege, but Daniel and his friends do not see it that way. Daniel is probably well aware of the numerous dietary restrictions in Jewish law, and the gourmet food of Babylon did not meet those standards. Also, the Babylonian food was associated with their idols.

Regardless of his motivation, Daniel determines not to defile himself with Nebuchadnezzar's choice food or fine wine (1:8). This verse is key in understanding who Daniel truly is. He is a young man, away from home and family, plunged into a new and potentially mesmerizing culture, and offered the best of everything. Many young people would quickly succumb to exotic opportunities and temptations, especially in a setting where it appears that righteous behavior does not matter. Yet Daniel never loses his resolve to live a holy life for the Lord.

He acts on his belief, and the way he does so also attests to his character. He doesn't make a big scene, attempt to manipulate anyone, or tell little white lies. He realizes this is a delicate situation—one that can get his supervisor killed if things go badly (1:10). So Daniel goes behind the scenes and makes an agreement with the delivery boy, suggesting a ten-day test period.

Daniel acts wisely, yet the text makes it clear that it is God who is at work to resolve the problem (1:9). Even as God's people are being disciplined, the Lord is at work among them, still preserving and protecting them. All the other trainees in Nebuchadnezzar's program are given the rich foods, while Daniel and his three friends stick to a vegetable and water diet (1:11–14).

After ten days, Daniel and his three friends are noticeably healthier and better nourished than their peers. Their supervisor breaths a sigh of relief and continues their vegetable diet, and they feel no more pressure to defy their religious convictions in order to fit in (1:15–16).

But the diet test is just a beginning. God gives Daniel, Hananiah (Shadrach), Mishael (Meshach), and Azariah (Abednego) great understanding and wisdom in all areas of learning and philosophy (1:17). Daniel is given a special ability to understand dreams and visions. Daniel and his friends aren't actively seeking special favor from God, yet the Lord responds to their devotion and obedience.

Critical Observation

In the midst of destruction and misery for Judah, God is still blessing His people. And through them, others will be blessed. In this case, Daniel's supervisor comes out looking good. Before long, the young men of Judah will be influencing kings.

At the end of the three-year training period, Nebuchadnezzar interviews each of the young men who have gone through his program. Again, Daniel and his three friends are clearly exceptional. The king deems them ten times better in terms of wisdom and understanding than any of the magicians and enchanters from whom he seeks advice (1:20).

Ten times better (1:20) is not a quantitative term. Just as people today think in terms of "a perfect 10" at an Olympic event, or judge an extremely attractive person as "a 10," the number had similar meaning in ancient times. *Ten* was a number that represented fullness or completeness.

Considering their young age and circumstances, the faithfulness of Daniel and his friends is particularly amazing. And yet, both Daniel and his three friends will face far greater challenges (and successes) ahead.

Take It Home

Daniel demonstrates that the battle for holiness is either won or lost in the small areas of life. Instead of attempting to change circumstances that are beyond his control, he shifts his focus to simply obeying God. In fact, sometimes the desire to maintain control is the polar opposite of faith. Can you think of any areas in your life where you might need to relinquish control in order to let God act on your behalf instead?

DANIEL 2:1–49

DANIEL INTERPRETS NEBUCHADNEZZAR'S DREAM

Nebuchadnezzar's Challenge	2:1–13
Daniel's Response	2:14–23
Daniel's Interpretation	2:24–43
The Final Kingdom	2:44–49

Setting Up the Section

After going through Nebuchadnezzar's three-year training period and excelling among his fellow participants (1:3–5, 18–20), Daniel is soon put to the test. In an account that demonstrates how eccentric and brutal Babylonian leadership could be at times, the king makes a demand of his advisors that seems impossible, yet their failure will result in their deaths. As the Lord had done previously, He again provides a way out for Daniel—an act that delivers not only Daniel but also spares the entire group of Nebuchadnezzar's advisors.

2:1–13

NEBUCHADNEZZAR'S CHALLENGE

Before delving into the crux of the passage, a matter of interpretation needs to be addressed. Daniel 2:1 records that this account occurs during the second year of the reign of Nebuchadnezzar, yet Daniel and his friends are put into the king's service after three years of training (1:5, 18). Because of this apparent discrepancy, some people have actually sought to dismiss the book of Daniel as unauthentic or even fictional.

However, in the Babylonian system, a king's years of service are counted the same way people today number birthdays. Even though Nebuchadnezzar might have been well into his third year chronologically, the record would have shown it as his second. This observation should be coupled with another one that explains why Daniel uses the Babylonian counting system. At this point in his narrative (from 2:4–7:28), Daniel shifts from Hebrew to Aramaic in his writing. Aramaic was a widespread language, understood by many diverse peoples. (Nebuchadnezzar's advisors, for example, were probably from different nations, and according to 2:4, they spoke in Aramaic.) Daniel reverts to Hebrew for chapters 8–12.

So in a common language, Daniel writes of a dream that had troubled Nebuchadnezzar. It is a divine dream that creates a divine disturbance, driving Nebuchadnezzar to reconcile the disturbance that he feels. He needs to make sure that the dream is interpreted correctly, so he sets forth a challenge that rattles his entire staff. Not only does Nebuchadnezzar demand an interpretation to his dream; first he wants his magicians and astrologers to tell him what he has dreamed! If they do, he will reward them handsomely with wealth and honor. But if they don't, he will have them cut into pieces and their houses destroyed (2:5–6). They attempt to negotiate a better deal, but Nebuchadnezzar will not back down from his ultimatum, and he accuses them of stalling (2:7–9).

Critical Observation

At first, Nebuchadnezzar's demand to have someone else tell him what he (Nebuchadnezzar) had dreamed was an unusual request. He wanted a proper interpretation for his disturbing dream that he believed may have been sent by God and thought that he could completely trust the interpretation of anyone able to first relate to him his dream. It would turn out that his instinct was correct, but this was not the Babylonian way. According to Babylonian custom, the king would have related his dream and then the wise men would interpret its significance.

When Nebuchadnezzar remains adamant, his usual counselors attempt to plead and reason with him. They tell him that in the known history of the world, no one has ever expected such a thing. It is an impossible task. They say only the gods can do such a thing, and that the gods do not dwell with people (2:10–11).

The response of Nebuchadnezzar's magicians reveals their worldview. They perceive a distinct separation between gods and people. From their perspective, gods stay in their world, and it is the responsibility of humans to reach out to them. The magicians' statement sets the stage for the rest of the book of Daniel, which explains the gospel message in terms that can be understood by the Gentile world of the Babylonian culture. Daniel will go on to describe how God enters the world of humanity to rescue people. Every story told from this point forward demonstrates how God interacts with this world. The second half of Daniel's book describes more specifically how and when God will come to the world in the person of the Messiah.

The court magicians' pleas to Nebuchadnezzar are to no avail. The infuriated king immediately gives the order to have all the wise men of Babylon put to death—an order that includes Daniel, Shadrach, Meshach, and Abednego (2:12–13). This apparent crisis is divinely orchestrated to create a supposedly impossible situation through which God's plan for the world will be revealed.

2:14–23

DANIEL'S RESPONSE

The captain of the king's guard is sent to inform Daniel of the grim news. Daniel, however, responds with discretion and discernment. He asks for a bit more time so that he might do what the king has asked (2:14–16). Even though Nebuchadnezzar had just accused his court magicians and sorcerers of attempting to stall for time (2:8), it seems that he respects Daniel's request (2:16).

Daniel gathers his three Hebrew friends, and the four of them pray (2:17–18). They realize this is a divine challenge that they face, so they turn to God for clarity. They appeal to Him for mercy and wisdom, and He provides the solution.

Daniel has a vision during the night in which God gives him the answer that Nebuchadnezzar desires (2:19). But after receiving the solution, Daniel doesn't immediately go running to the king. First he takes time to praise God, appropriately ascribing all wisdom and power to the Lord.

It appears that Daniel's prayer is also influenced by the content of the dream God reveals (a dream not yet revealed in scripture). It is God who determines times and seasons, who sets up and deposes kings as he sees fit (2:21)—all in anticipation of a Messiah to come. Daniel acknowledges God's sovereign hand in the world. Unlike the gods of the Babylonians, the Lord *does* interact with this world. Not only does He interact, but He also controls the world.

The Lord is a God of light, who exposes the things of darkness. He also reveals hidden things. God enables Daniel to be wise and discerning, and Daniel uses his wisdom to seek God's help. In return, God makes known to Daniel something that Daniel couldn't possibly discern on his own. Daniel's knowledge of Nebuchadnezzar's dream will allow many people to live who otherwise would have been put to death. So Daniel also praises God for revealing Nebuchadnezzar's dream to him (2:22–23).

2:24–43

DANIEL'S INTERPRETATION

Daniel's praise to God is not limited to the privacy of prayer. When he is called back in to speak to Nebuchadnezzar, he gives God full credit before the king. Daniel makes it patently clear that no human—not wise men, enchanters, magicians, or diviners—could have given Nebuchadnezzar the answer he sought. Yet his God is in heaven and can reveal mysteries (2:26–28). Daniel elevates the focus from humanity to God.

Only a revelation from God could enable anyone to understand Nebuchadnezzar's dream. Through Daniel, God is letting Nebuchadnezzar know that God is at work in the world, revealing His glory. This is the Lord's world, the future is in the Lord's control, and even the ability to see and understand what the Lord is saying requires divinely inspired insight.

Demystifying Daniel

The entire book of Daniel is a revelation of the gospel. God has just demonstrated to Nebuchadnezzar the seed plot to the teaching of justification by faith. To interact with the wisdom of God and understand what He is doing, one must go to God and seek His kingdom, wisdom, and righteousness. Later portions of Daniel will reveal even more about God's plan.

Then Daniel begins to relate the specifics of what Nebuchadnezzar had dreamed. The king had seen a great statue (2:31). Even though Nebuchadnezzar is the mightiest king in the world, who had conquered every nation in his path, he is not the center of the dream; the statue is. Nor is he in control of the events in his dream; he is merely an observer. Perhaps it is the sense that someone or something is more powerful than he is that had created all the fear and anxiety behind his threats toward those who serve him.

The statue is made of different kinds of metal. The head is gold, the chest and arms are silver, the middle portions are bronze, the legs are iron, and the feet are iron mixed with baked clay (2:31–33). As Nebuchadnezzar continues to observe, he sees a rock that is cut out, but not by human hands (2:34). The rock smashes into the statue. The statue topples over and breaks into pieces, which are quickly swept away by the wind like chaff at threshing time. The rock, however, grows into a huge mountain that fills the whole earth (2:34–35).

This dream both humbled and frightened Nebuchadnezzar. This was no mere nightmare that resulted from indigestion or an active imagination. Daniel will soon make it clear that this is a divine revelation that Nebuchadnezzar had received (2:45). God is allowing Nebuchadnezzar to come face-to-face with a future not under his control, but the Lord's. As Daniel goes on to interpret the dream, Nebuchadnezzar will receive the first of several lessons concerning the sovereignty of God.

Daniel's explanation foretells four world empires. Each section of the statue represents a different nation. He starts with Nebuchadnezzar and Babylon.

For modern readers with New Testament awareness, it may sound peculiar to read that Daniel refers to Nebuchadnezzar as "king of kings" (2:36–37). Literally, the phrase refers to a king that all other kings are subject to, which is why it becomes such a meaningful messianic title for Jesus. But Daniel uses the term to affirm that Nebuchadnezzar is a dominant figure. From Babylon's inception (Genesis 10:8–12), it had always stood for defiance of God. In time, the kingdom of Nebuchadnezzar came to symbolize the kingdom of this world. So in a literal sense, Nebuchadnezzar is indeed king of kings over those who are opposed to God.

Critical Observation

During the decline of the Roman Empire, Augustine wrote a monumental work called *City of God*. His observation was that there are really only two kingdoms: the kingdom of man and the kingdom of God. Those in the kingdom of man live to serve themselves, while those in the kingdom of God live to serve the Lord.

The head of gold on the statue in Nebuchadnezzar's dream (2:32, 36–38) symbolizes Babylon. Nebuchadnezzar is the leader of the most glorious of all the kingdoms in the world. Yet it will not be a lasting kingdom.

Next on the statue are the chest and arms of silver (2:32, 39). The nations that conquer Babylon (the Medes and Persians) will be inferior to Babylon. They will be stronger, but not as glorious. Daniel is letting Nebuchadnezzar know that his days are numbered. The kingdom he has established will fall to another.

But then a third kingdom will arise after the second. The statue's belly and thighs of bronze (2:32, 39) represent Greece. Just as bronze is stronger than silver, Alexander the Great will dominate the leaders of the Medes and Persians. Yet the Greek Empire will be less glorious than the Persian Empire had been.

Stronger still will be the Roman Empire, the statue's legs of iron (2:33, 40). At a point in the future, the Romans will arise and conquer all the surrounding kingdoms. Yet again there will be a diminishing of the glory of the kingdom. In addition, this fourth kingdom will be divided. Portions will be as strong as iron, but other parts will be like clay—and iron and clay certainly don't mix well (2:43). The imagery is most appropriate. As it turns out, the mighty Roman Empire will lack unity as it is plagued by civil wars, social unrest, and moral relativism.

Demystifying Daniel

Daniel speaks only of a series of specific kingdoms to come and doesn't identify them by name. Yet history shows that the series of Babylonian, Medo-Persian, Greek, and Roman world domination provide a fitting fulfillment of Daniel's prophecy. The rock (the establishment of the kingdom of God) also seems to fit the historic scenario very well with the birth of Jesus Christ during the time of the Roman Empire.

2:44–49

THE FINAL KINGDOM

The imagery in Nebuchadnezzar's divinely inspired dream is important. Even though four great nations are mentioned in Daniel's interpretation, they comprise a single statue. The series of nations, even though distinct from one another, represent one world system.

As Daniel continues to interpret the dream for Nebuchadnezzar, he explains that the cut rock (2:34) represents the kingdom of God (2:44). The stone smashed into the feet of the image (the Roman Empire) and the entire statue (the human world system) come crashing down. God's kingdom, ruled by Jesus, will destroy the kingdom of the world. All the combined glory and strength of humanity will not be able to stand before the kingdom of God.

Modern readers need to remember that Daniel wrote this account to remind the Jews that God is sovereign, and therefore nothing is beyond His control. Specifically, even Judah's domination by the Babylonians is part of God's plan. Nations that rise do so because God allows it. Nations that fall do so because God brings them to an end. All nations are temporary until the final kingdom of God. The rock in Nebuchadnezzar's dream produces a mountain that fills the whole earth (2:35), and it will last forever. In demonstrating to Judah that God is still in full control of their future, Daniel is also warning Babylon that they are not eternal and will see their kingdom fall one day.

Daniel's accurate recall of Nebuchadnezzar's dream, and his insightful interpretation of what it means, impresses the king. Nebuchadnezzar becomes very appreciative and accommodating. He even acknowledges the superiority of Daniel's God above all other gods and kings (2:46–47). However, Nebuchadnezzar's contrition will be short-lived. In the following section, his ego will be back in full bloom, and God will humble him again. In fact, Nebuchadnezzar will have numerous encounters with the humbling arm of God.

Meanwhile, Daniel is rewarded with many gifts and elevated to a position of power above all the other wise men of the court. At Daniel's request, Nebuchadnezzar also promotes Shadrach, Meshach, and Abednego (2:48–49). God is at work to place His people in positions of influence over the entire Babylonian world at that time.

Take It Home

Throughout this section, Daniel refers to God as a *revealer of mysteries* (2:19, 22, 28–29, 47). Certainly, there may be mysteries of life that people will not or cannot understand in this world. Other deep truths, however, are available to those who seek God's wisdom as Daniel did. Sometimes you might find yourself in Daniel's position, providing valid answers for someone else. Other times you may find yourself like Nebuchadnezzar—confused and seeking help. What are some of the mysteries that persistently pique your curiosity? What are some sources you might consult (people, reference materials, etc.) to help gather information as you continue to seek God's answers for your hardest questions?

DANIEL 3:1–30

THE FIERY FURNACE AND GOD'S DELIVERANCE

Nebuchadnezzar's Statue	3:1–7
The Hebrews' Dilemma	3:8–18
Nebuchadnezzar's Lesson	3:19–30

Setting Up the Section

Four men of Judah are mentioned by name as being taken from Judah to Babylon to be trained to serve King Nebuchadnezzar (1:6–7). The primary focus so far has been on Daniel. In this section, however, the attention is placed on his three friends, better known by their Babylonian names: Shadrach, Meshach, and Abednego.

3:1–7

NEBUCHADNEZZAR'S STATUE

To get a proper perspective on this account, one must relate it to the events of Daniel 2. In chapter 2, King Nebuchadnezzar dreams of a great statue and is eventually told that he is the head. So when Nebuchadnezzar subsequently has a huge statue built of his image, there can be little doubt that the statue expresses his desire to see his dream not only fulfilled but surpassed.

Nebuchadnezzar has been told that he is the king of kings—the head of gold (2:37–38). It is commonly thought that the king's pride leads him to then make a statue of himself in complete gold. Perhaps he is so prideful that he misses the point of the dream and hears only that he is the king of kings. The statue, then, communicates that his kingdom is beautiful and will last forever.

It is not only an ambitious project but also a huge expense. The golden figure is ninety feet high and nine feet wide (3:1). It is the ultimate expression of human ego; Nebuchadnezzar is so enthralled with himself that he brings his entire staff together and has them listen to a new decree (3:2–6). A close reading reveals that the unveiling of Nebuchadnezzar's statue is shrouded in religious overtones. He is not just introducing the image as a token of remembrance; he is presenting a new religion.

The unveiling ceremony involves much religious symbolism: a dedication (3:2); music and a desire to create a worship ritual (3:5); and the act of bowing down in honor, reverence, and worship (3:5). It seems safe to presume that the image is of Nebuchadnezzar. If so, then the people are required to bow down to worship his image every time the music is played. Apparently the king believes that he is the sovereign lord of the earth and the leader of the world, and therefore he deserves worship. But in order to think in such a manner, he has to disregard the interpretation of his dream that Daniel provided—that Nebuchadnezzar's kingdom is a gift of the true God.

Demystifying Daniel

This section of Daniel introduces some obscure words. But since translations vary, it is enough to say for our purposes that the list of terms in 3:3 (*satraps*, *prefects*, and so forth) is of government leaders at various levels. And the list in 3:5 is an assortment of musical instruments of the era.

It is easy to be critical of Nebuchadnezzar's haughty attitude, but it is far more common than many might like to admit. It is a temptation for all humankind to take credit for the things with which God has blessed them. People tend to never be satisfied with what God provides and feel that they deserve more. Then, when they get more, they lose sight of the fact that every blessing is a result of the kindness and mercy of God. Nebuchadnezzar is only one example.

It seems that most people have no problem with Nebuchadnezzar's new ruling. When the music plays, they bow as they have been ordered (3:7). This naturally exposes anyone who doesn't bow, as is the case with Shadrach, Meshach, and Abednego.

Demystifying Daniel

The question that usually comes up at this point is, "Where is Daniel while all this is going on?" His three friends are left to themselves to deal with a high-pressure situation. It seems likely that Daniel would have been required to travel in his position as Nebuchadnezzar's top assistant. He might well have been in another part of the kingdom. One should also note that considerable time has probably passed between Daniel 2 and Daniel 3. Ninety-foot-tall gold statues are not quickly constructed.

3:8–18

THE HEBREWS' DILEMMA

It takes little time for a group of Babylonians to go running to Nebuchadnezzar and tell him that certain Jews have not bowed down like everyone else. Their specific accusations bear close attention. They accuse Shadrach, Meshach, and Abednego of: (1) disregarding

Nebuchadnezzar; (2) not serving his gods; and (3) not worshiping the golden image he has set up. Nowhere in Nebuchadnezzar's decree did he stipulate that everyone had to serve his gods, but these men add it to their list of charges.

It is likely that the accusers are jealous of the prior success of Shadrach, Meshach, and Abednego, because the charges are certainly exaggerated. In reality, the three Hebrews have not disregarded the king or defied his position. They are three of Nebuchadnezzar's greatest assets and more than willing to serve on his staff. But in that culture, no king could afford to easily dismiss accusations of treason against those close to him.

Nebuchadnezzar's response to the news is immediate rage. He sends for Shadrach, Meshach, and Abednego. He personally repeats for them the mandate that had previously been announced publicly. Then he gives them an ultimatum: Either bow down and worship him now or be thrown into the fiery furnace and die (3:13–15).

Nebuchadnezzar's final comment during this brief conversation is telling. If they refuse to bow to the image, he wants to know, "What god will be able to rescue you from my hand?" (3:15 NIV).

The king has dismissed everything Daniel told him. He has established himself as a god again. He presumes his form of torture is the maximum punishment in both this world and the heavenly world. And in the greatest offense of all, he believes that the Hebrew God is impotent in comparison to him.

Critical Observation

It is always awkward for a well-meaning person to encounter a dominant superior who is angry to the point of ranting. How much more intense it must have been when the furious person was the leader of a ruthless empire who was accustomed to getting his way.

Despite the unreasonable hostility of Nebuchadnezzar, the response of Shadrach, Meshach, and Abednego remain fearless and well-reasoned. They don't feel compelled to answer him because his threats are empty in light of the power of their God. Still, they *choose* to respond and explain themselves. In doing so, they reveal four important points.

First, they fully trust God's sovereignty. Even in this difficult and threatening situation, they do not consider it foolish to trust God. Nebuchadnezzar's power pales in comparison to God's. Second, they remain true to the scriptures. This isn't just a difference of opinion between them and the king. They only disobeyed Nebuchadnezzar because they were following a higher law by refusing to bow down to any image or idol (Exodus 20:3–6). Third, they are willing to die for their faith. They know God is powerful enough to rescue them, whether or not He chooses to do so. And fourth, they remain completely submissive to God's will. Their faith is not conditional, based on a prescribed outcome. At issue is not their comfort; it is their obedience to God.

3:19–30

NEBUCHADNEZZAR'S LESSON

The response of Shadrach, Meshach, and Abednego is not what Nebuchadnezzar wants to hear. His very countenance changes (3:19). He had trusted these men and placed them on his elite team. Now he feels betrayed and wants to see nothing less than their total destruction. In his great fury, he orders the furnace to be heated to seven times its usual temperature—most likely, to its maximum heat (3:19–20). He has the three traitors bound (3:20), which serves no good purpose other than the psychological strategy of removing control from them, preventing them from even minimally shielding themselves from the heat. Doing his work for him are his strongest soldiers.

Critical Observation

Nebuchadnezzar is parading his strength for all to see. He wants the totality of his power to be made known so that the three young men and everyone observing will know that he is the most powerful man on earth.

The punishment for Shadrach, Meshach, and Abednego is intended to be most cruel, as is proven when a number of their captors die just from tossing the three into the flames (3:22–23). The judgment intended for the Hebrews falls instead on some of Nebuchadnezzar's most valiant warriors. As for the three who have so deeply angered the king, they are about to astonish him.

Peering into the furnace, Nebuchadnezzar sees the men walking around, but there are four figures instead of three (3:24–25). He asks his advisors for confirmation, and they assure him that only three people had gone into the furnace. But the king can clearly see four men walking around unbound and unharmed.

Not only does God preserve Shadrach, Meshach, and Abednego; He joins them in the furnace. Some people think the fourth figure may be the preincarnate Christ. Nebuchadnezzar can only speculate as to the fourth figure, calling him a son of the gods, but he definitely wants to know more.

He approaches the furnace and calls for the three to come out (3:26–27). As they do, all the Babylonian leaders gather around to inspect them. No one would even suspect the men had been near fire. Not only is their skin, clothes, and hair unaffected, but they don't even smell of smoke! Apparently all the flames had done was burn off the ropes with which they had been bound.

As a result, Nebuchadnezzar has a complete change of heart (3:28–30). At this point, he is both impressed that they have defied him and overwhelmed that their faithfulness to their God is stronger than their physical security. He correctly reaches the conclusion that no other god can deliver someone in the manner that their God has just done. Moreover, Nebuchadnezzar amends his previous mandate. From now on, he says, anyone who speaks out against the God of Shadrach, Meshach, and Abednego will receive the worst punishment conceivable.

As for the three young Hebrew men, they are again promoted (2:49; 3:30). Even though they haven't sought any tangible result from their display of faith, God allows them to prosper. Their steadfastness during great crisis is rewarded.

Take It Home

People of faith can expect occasional debates, disagreements, or conflicts with people who don't believe in God, and they can learn much from Shadrach, Meshach, and Abednego. Even at risk of their lives, the Hebrew trio refuses to compromise their beliefs. Although under great pressure, they remain remarkably calm and even understated. They don't attempt to overpower or outshout Nebuchadnezzar, or maneuver their way out of a tricky situation. They simply explain what they believe to be true and leave the outcome to God. Can you think of current examples where Christians and nonbelievers are at odds over important issues? In each instance, how well do you think the believers involved represent their God and their faith? On a personal level, what can you learn from this narrative that will help you be a better spokesperson for God?

DANIEL 4:1–37

NEBUCHADNEZZAR'S HUMBLING EXPERIENCE

Nebuchadnezzar's Second Dream	4:1–18
The Dream's Interpretation and Fulfillment	4:19–37

Setting Up the Section

The previous two chapters of Daniel have shown how God is dealing with the pride of King Nebuchadnezzar, first through Daniel and then through Shadrach, Meshach, and Abednego. This section is the final segment concerning Nebuchadnezzar, as the king recounts what he has learned. Even Nebuchadnezzar has come to realize that God is the Lord of the universe, and he opens and closes the section with a declaration about the sovereign power and glory of God.

4:1–18

NEBUCHADNEZZAR'S SECOND DREAM

Daniel 4 is a letter to the nations that Nebuchadnezzar composes after he is finally convinced of the sovereignty of God. Coming from the pen of a Gentile king, this chapter provides some incredible transforming insights about the Lord.

The positive opening temporarily shields the fact that Nebuchadnezzar has been through a horrendous experience. However, the experience has taught him about his own sin and the nature of God, so he records the lesson for all the governors in his kingdom so they will not make the same mistake he has (4:1–2).

Nebuchadnezzar opens by acknowledging four aspects of God that he has discovered (4:3). First are the great *signs* he has observed. The Lord has communicated with the king through dreams and then provided Daniel to interpret the dreams. God even enabled Daniel to know what Nebuchadnezzar had dreamed without being told (2:5–6, 19). God had specifically communicated with Nebuchadnezzar, and the king praises Him for such an extraordinary experience.

Next Nebuchadnezzar praises God for His mighty *wonders*—God's intervention in this world. God literally changes the course of life for Nebuchadnezzar, as the king will soon explain. The story he tells will confirm the great wonders God can perform. As previously noted, the Babylonian gods were not known to step into the world of humanity, but Judah's God is undoubtedly active among His people.

Third, Nebuchadnezzar praises God's *eternal kingdom*. For the first time, the reader sees the Babylonian leader acknowledge a greater kingdom. Babylon will not be a lasting empire, but God's kingdom will have no end. Such acknowledgment reflects a significant change in Nebuchadnezzar, demonstrating the extent of his humility.

Finally, the king concedes God's *rule* over the earth. The Lord's dominion extends throughout all generations. God is the only authentic ruler of the world because no kingdom, past or present, is beyond His control.

Nebuchadnezzar begins his story by explaining that everything in his life and kingdom was going well—or so he thought (4:4). He was prosperous, contented, and happy. And then he has another dream.

The previous dream of Nebuchadnezzar's—the image made of different metal (2:31–35)—had no small effect on the king. But this one is apparently even more influential. This dream terrifies him, and he can't get it out of his mind (4:5).

Seeking some kind of clarity or insight, Nebuchadnezzar calls for his staff of wise men and describes his dream to them. But they are no more helpful in this case than they had been before (2:10–11). When they fail to understand and interpret the dream, the king calls for Daniel, who again comes through for him. Why Nebuchadnezzar always waits to ask Daniel is unknown, although his tendency to do so repeatedly proves that the Lord enlightens Daniel in ways that none of the other magicians, enchanters, astrologers, and diviners (4:6–7) can come close to matching.

Critical Observation

The Hebrew captives who had been drafted into Nebuchadnezzar's service have been given Babylonian names. Daniel's three friends—Hananiah, Mishael, and Azariah—are better known by their new names: Shadrach, Meshach, and Abednego. Daniel's name is also changed. Since Daniel 4 is from Nebuchadnezzar's perspective, Daniel's Babylonian name (Belteshazzar) is used (4:8–9, 18–19). However, in most other cases, Daniel's Hebrew name is used, and that is the name by which he is best known.

Nebuchadnezzar has made two key observations about Daniel. First, he realizes that "the spirit of the holy gods" is in him (4:9). It is not likely that Nebuchadnezzar is giving the one true God full credit here, although some translations use the upper case *G* for *gods*. This passage is within the portion of Daniel that is written in Aramaic (2:4–7:28), and translators face some difficulty putting the original language into English. Yet at the heart of the king's expression is his certainty that Daniel has been given insight by some divine source.

The second observation about Daniel is that no mystery baffles the young man. Daniel has already proven himself beyond doubt, and the king has great confidence that Daniel can interpret any dream—even one that has stumped all his peers on Nebuchadnezzar's court.

So Nebuchadnezzar lays out his dream for Daniel to hear (4:10–18). It is indeed a strange account of a great tree that flourishes for a time until a heavenly voice commands it to be chopped down. The stump and roots are left in the field, bound with iron and bronze. Then the tree appears to become a beast, sentenced to live in the field for a period of time. Finally, a declaration is made about a person being removed from power so that everyone will know that the One speaking is the Most High Lord of the universe.

It is likely that Nebuchadnezzar has a sense of what the dream means, which is probably why it troubles him so much. He may even have enjoyed the first part of the dream as he saw himself as the great tree that touched the sky and provided shelter and sustenance for so many. If so, he is surely unsettled as the dream unfolds and strange events begin to occur.

4:19–37

THE DREAM'S INTERPRETATION AND FULFILLMENT

After Daniel hears the dream, he is unsettled himself—not because he doesn't understand the meaning, but because he *does*. He is reluctant to look the king in the eye and deliver bad news, yet Nebuchadnezzar encourages him to speak truthfully.

The last time the king had dreamed about the future, Daniel identified Nebuchadnezzar as king of kings (2:37) and the head of gold (2:38). Shortly afterward, Nebuchadnezzar built a ninety-foot statue in honor of himself (3:1). This time, however, Daniel has the responsibility of telling Nebuchadnezzar that God is going to take his kingdom away, and the king will suffer in even worse ways as well.

Daniel confirms that the tree in the dream is indeed a symbol for Nebuchadnezzar (4:20–22). He has become the most powerful man in the world, and the rest of the world is subject to him. More than being merely strong and mighty, Babylon is known for its glory. Yet as dominant as Nebuchadnezzar has become, he is still merely a human. Heavenly forces are at work over which he has no control. At a single command by a holy messenger, the great tree is cut down.

The future of the king is grim. He is going to go mad and then be driven from Babylon. God's action will be the result of the king's refusal to recognize that it is the Lord who rules. Nebuchadnezzar has acknowledged that Daniel's God is a strong God, and he notes that Daniel and his friends benefited from serving their God. But Nebuchadnezzar has always stopped short of *submitting* to Daniel's God.

Demystifying Daniel

When Daniel tells Nebuchadnezzar that the king needs to acknowledge that "heaven rules" (4:26), he is using a figure of speech that substitutes a place for a person. Similarly, someone today might say that an action made by the president is made by Washington, or the White House. Daniel isn't attempting to soften what he is saying. Indeed, he has been quite bold when speaking about God to King Nebuchadnezzar (2:27–28).

Daniel exhorts Nebuchadnezzar to cease his sin and start practicing righteousness (4:27), supposing that he might be able to avoid the judgment predicted by the dream. Daniel's approach is tactful and humble. He still respects the office of Nebuchadnezzar. He doesn't leap right to accusations and judgment; he starts with the opportunity of repentance. He lays out the option for the king to start right away to cease his wickedness and serve God by showing mercy to the weak. In that case, maybe the king's prosperity will continue.

Perhaps Nebuchadnezzar takes Daniel's words to heart for a while, but not for the long run. A year later, the king is walking on a royal rooftop and starts looking out over his kingdom. With Daniel's warning forgotten, in a moment of unrestricted pride and arrogance, Nebuchadnezzar boasts of how he is responsible for the success of Babylon (4:28–30). The words aren't completely out of his mouth before a heavenly voice decrees the removal of his royal authority. In addition, the voice says Nebuchadnezzar will spend a length of time (probably seven years) with beasts, living as an animal (4:31–32).

His sentence begins immediately. The once-arrogant king is driven away from people. He eats grass like cattle. He stays outside in the dew as his hair grows long (like the feathers of an eagle) and his nails become like bird claws (4:33).

Critical Observation

A fragmentary cuneiform tablet in the British Museum refers to Nebuchadnezzar, apparently during this part of his life. It states that "life appeared of no value to" Nebuchadnezzar, that "he does not show love to son and daughter," and that "family and clan does not exist" for him any longer.

Animals don't reason as humans do, and perhaps Nebuchadnezzar suffers in that respect as well. But eventually he raises his eyes toward heaven. In that action, he evidently submits to God, and his sanity is restored (4:34).

When he is able, he praises, honors, and glorifies God. He acknowledges God's eternal dominion and kingdom, as well as God's complete sovereignty over both the powers of heaven and the people of earth (4:34–35).

Afterward, God does indeed allow Nebuchadnezzar to prosper again. In fact, the king says he becomes even greater than before (4:36). And this time he doesn't make any attempt to take credit for his fame. Instead, he exalts and glorifies the King of heaven (4:37). Had he done so earlier, in response to Daniel's advice, he might have avoided a lot of misery.

Take It Home

Perhaps one reason that Nebuchadnezzar's strange experiences were recorded for posterity as well as for his peers at that time is to caution everyone of the importance of fully submitting to God as the Lord of the universe. It's rather easy to verbally acknowledge God, to claim to know God, or even to express love for God. However, such actions mean nothing if not accompanied by complete and humble submission to Him. On a scale of 1 (least) to 10 (most), how would you rate your submission to God in recent days? Can you tell a difference in your life when your obedience begins to lessen a bit?

DANIEL 5:1–31

DANIEL AND BELSHAZZAR

Belshazzar's Banquet	5:1–4
The Writing on the Wall	5:5–12
The Writing's Interpretation	5:13–31

Setting Up the Section

At least six years have passed between the previous section and this one. In that time, King Nebuchadnezzar has been replaced by Belshazzar. It appears that Daniel's high-profile position in the king's court has also come to an end. Although the previous section highlights a public letter from Nebuchadnezzar warning his fellow Babylonian leaders what can happen if they defy the God of Judah, Belshazzar is either oblivious or defiant. Either way, he will suffer for it.

5:1–4

BELSHAZZAR'S BANQUET

After the death of Nebuchadnezzar, his successor is his son Evil-Merodach. This son rules for two years until he is assassinated by Labashi-Marduk and replaced by Neriglissar. After Neriglissar, Evil-Merodach's brother-in-law, an Assyrian named Nabonidus takes control of the kingdom. As new king, Nabonidus establishes a home in the oasis that is now the location of Saudi Arabia. He appoints his son Belshazzar to reign as vice-regent and handle the business of Babylon.

The first thing the Bible records about Belshazzar is that he throws a banquet. It is no small affair, attended by a thousand of the leaders of Babylon along with their wives and concubines (5:1–3). This event may have been a kind of preparation for war, since Babylon was already under the attack of the Persians.

The banquet became the backdrop for a major misstep on the part of Belshazzar—his callous disregard for the holy Jewish objects stored in his treasury. When he sees that his wine is of a good vintage, he sends for the golden goblets that had been taken from the Jerusalem temple. They were originally set aside to be used exclusively for the worship of God. Even after Nebuchadnezzar seized Jerusalem and took the temple furnishings, he had several encounters with the God of Daniel and eventually came to have a respect for the King of heaven (4:37), decreeing that the Lord should not be mocked under penalty of death (3:29).

As Daniel will eventually make clear, Belshazzar cannot plead ignorance. He knew about Nebuchadnezzar's decrees and the holiness attached to the Jewish goblets (5:22–23). He just doesn't care. In the ultimate mockery of God, he uses the temple's sacred vessels for his party, passing out wine to impress his nobles as well as their female companions. Even worse, as they drink they praise their gods (5:4).

5:5–12

THE WRITING ON THE WALL

Belshazzar considers Judah's God a trivial matter, but his casual and carefree attitude changes in an instant when a disembodied hand suddenly appears and begins to write on the palace wall. The king's defiance of God has been public; so, too, is God's condemnation of Belshazzar. In front of all his guests, the king turns pale, goes limp, and is gripped by fear to the point of terror. Then, after the experience of seeing the hand come and go, Belshazzar is left with a message he can't comprehend (5:5–6).

Critical Observation

Clearly, Belshazzar doesn't know what (who) he is dealing with. Yet his response of such intense fear indicates that he acknowledges something more powerful than he is. His initial fears will soon be confirmed.

He brings together all of the spiritual leaders of his cabinet to attempt to interpret the words left on the wall, promising to promote anyone who can do so to third place in the entire kingdom. (Belshazzar is responsible to Nabonidus, so the top two places are already filled.) It is a magnificent offer, yet no one is able to decipher the message (5:7–9). The sum total of the religious wisdom of the day is unable to read or understand the words, and the king has no peace.

Belshazzar thinks he is out of options. God has spoken to him, yet the leaders of Babylon can't determine what God has said. God has extended Belshazzar beyond his limits, just as he had for Nebuchadnezzar. And the answers will come from the same source: God's servant, Daniel.

The queen at the time may well have been the queen mother—possibly the widow of Nebuchadnezzar, or perhaps his daughter (5:10). In any case, she is well aware of the recent goings on within the palace. In particular, she knows of Daniel and his reputation of divine knowledge and understanding, and also his ability to interpret dreams, explain riddles, and solve difficult problems (5:12). It is the exact job description Belshazzar needs, so he takes the queen's advice and summons Daniel.

Demystifying Daniel

In addressing Belshazzar, the queen refers to "your father the king" (5:11). The usage of *father* cannot be assumed to mean a biological relationship or even a relationship in terms of one generation to the next. The word was sometimes used in referring to a person's lineage. The Jews often spoke of Abraham as their father. Similarly, Nebuchadnezzar could be considered a father by any number of offspring, not merely his biological children.

5:13–31

THE WRITING'S INTERPRETATION

Daniel had risen to the top of Nebuchadnezzar's group of advisors (2:48–49), yet he must have been sidelined when the new king came into power. Clearly, Belshazzar doesn't even know who Daniel is. Ironically, Belshazzar will get to know him the same way Nebuchadnezzar had—by bringing him in only after every other option has failed.

Belshazzar goes through the proper protocol of flattering Daniel, briefly summarizing the situation for him and offering him great rewards for his much-needed help (5:13–16). Daniel agrees to help, but not because of the proffered rewards. He is more confrontational with Belshazzar than he had been with Nebuchadnezzar, and for good reason. Nebuchadnezzar had left the world a letter outlining his sin of pride and the ultimate result. He had learned that God—not the leader of Babylon—deserved the glory for whatever good happened in the world. But Belshazzar had ignored the lesson of the past and in a matter of a few years openly defied God. Daniel will do as the king asks, but he has no desire to work for this new regime (5:17). (Of course, it will turn out that in interpreting God's message, Daniel is foretelling the fall of the existing king anyway.)

Daniel begins with a short history lesson that will put God's message into context. Nebuchadnezzar had been bestowed with the most powerful and glorious kingdom of the world—not because of anything special he had done, but because it was part of God's plan. When pride became an issue, God had removed the kingdom from Nebuchadnezzar and had driven the king out to live like an animal. Eventually, after Nebuchadnezzar lifted his eyes to heaven and acceded that God was the sovereign ruler of the world, he was reinstated into his position as king with a much clearer understanding of who God is (5:18–21).

And here is Daniel's point: He isn't telling Belshazzar anything the king doesn't already know (5:22). A mighty ruler who leaves the throne for a while to live in the fields, eat grass, and grow animal-like hair and nails is not quickly forgotten. Belshazzar knows the story, but he hasn't heeded the lesson of Nebuchadnezzar. Because Belshazzar refuses to honor God, his defiant party is the last one he will ever have.

The words the hand had written on the wall—*Mene, Mene, Tekel, Parsin* (5:25)—essentially mean, "Number," "Weigh," and "Divide." The message that no one else could determine is quite clear to Daniel: The days of Belshazzar are numbered, his life has been weighed (evaluated) by God, and because he is found deficient, his kingdom will be divided as the Medes and Persians take over. Simply put, the end is at hand for the king.

Belshazzar's response is telling. He certainly must have believed Daniel, because he restores the authority and prosperity that had been taken away from him (5:29). Yet this appears to be his *only* response. He hears a disturbing message that has been divinely delivered in an astounding manner, and he does nothing. He shows no hint of remorse, repentance, confession, or desire to change. Perhaps this is why God's punishment is much swifter than it had been with Nebuchadnezzar. It is this very night that the Medes breach the walls, take over the city, and put Belshazzar to death (5:30).

The new ruler of the kingdom is Darius the Mede. In the next section, he, too, will learn a lesson about God because of his experience with Daniel.

Take It Home

The fall of Belshazzar is particularly brutal because he failed to learn from the experience of Nebuchadnezzar who had come before him. Can you think of any spiritual lessons, either positive or negative, that you have observed in the lives of other people? To what extent do those lessons influence your personal faith? What lessons do you hope to pass on to others who might be observing the way you live?

DANIEL 6:1–28

DANIEL AND DARIUS

Setting Up the Section

The previous section ends with the demise of Babylonian King Belshazzar and his replacement by Darius the Mede. This section continues with the establishment of Darius as king and how he comes to experience the power of Daniel's God.

6:1–4

DANIEL'S EXEMPLARY CHARACTER

Throughout the book of Daniel so far, kings have come and gone while Daniel's service to God, as well as to his human rulers, has remained consistent. It seems clear that the godly wisdom demonstrated by Daniel in his youth has carried into his senior years as well. He serves as one of three key leaders to whom another 120 officials report. This leadership structure is used by Darius so that he can protect his interests (6:2). In other words, Darius is wisely attempting to avoid losing his kingdom to a rebel group or having the wealth of his kingdom pilfered by an unscrupulous, unsupervised overseer. He is aware of the temptations inherent with power and control.

It is in this environment that Daniel's character shines. In a competitive setting with little regard for righteousness, Daniel continues to faithfully follow God. Before long, Darius has plans to reward Daniel's exceptional qualities and promote him to the top position over the entire kingdom (6:3).

Critical Observation

Daniel's integrity becomes evident in a close comparison between verses 2 and 3. At first King Darius is cautious about placing too much power in the hands of any one person (6:2). But when he sees how Daniel lives and works, he trusts him to have even more power without fear that he will misuse it (6:3).

Not surprisingly, there is a good deal of resentment when the other leaders hear that Daniel is in line to become their boss. They decide to work together, watch him closely, and get some dirt on him that they can take to Darius. But the closer they monitor his behavior, the more evident it becomes that he isn't doing anything he shouldn't do, nor is he neglecting to do anything he should be doing (6:4).

6:5–12

THE CONSPIRACY AGAINST DANIEL

When Daniel's jealous peers can't find a single problem with his integrity, they change their strategy. When they closely examine his life, they see his bold faith in God and realize his spiritual consistency is all they can use against him (6:5).

Apparently *they* have no problem operating without integrity. They devise a plan to present Darius with a proposal for a law requiring his subjects to pray to no one but him for a thirty-day period. Furthermore, the law will make it clear that anyone who disobeys the injunction will be thrown into the lions' den (6:6–8). Scripture doesn't say that Darius is flattered at their proposal, but he doesn't appear to need much coaxing. It is said simply that he puts the decree into writing, which makes it an unalterable law (6:9). Not even Darius can revoke it.

Although it is a despicable attempt to get rid of Daniel, the plan is an intelligent one. Darius had structured his leadership team to protect the kingdom from disloyal people, and at face value it appears that this proposal will support the king in his desire.

Daniel is well aware of the king's signing of the decree. He understands the consequences of breaking it. He goes to pray to God in his usual place at his usual time (6:10). He has other options, such as waiting thirty days or praying in a more private location. But Daniel truly believes what he has been communicating to Nebuchadnezzar and Belshazzar: God is sovereign and in control. God's kingdom is a priority for him, and if death is a result of his commitment, so be it.

Evidently the conspirators have Daniel's home staked out. It takes little time for them to witness him in prayer and go running to Darius. First they clarify the essence of the decree that has been passed and ensure that it cannot be revoked. *Then* they inform the king that Daniel has defied the law.

Note how expertly they pervert the truth (6:11–13). They had found nothing wicked or illicit for which they could accuse Daniel. So they manipulate the legal system to pass a binding, unrighteous law. When Daniel maintains his integrity and ignores the law, his accusers present him as a wicked person, disloyal to the king.

6:13–28

DANIEL SURVIVES THE LIONS' DEN

It appears that Darius is not fooled by their manipulation, but there is nothing he can do about it. He searches for legal loopholes but can find no way to avoid sentencing Daniel to the punishment as set forth in the decree (6:14). So when Daniel's accusers return as a group, the king has little recourse but to order Daniel thrown into the lions' den (6:15). Yet in that moment it becomes clear how much Daniel's faithfulness to his God has influenced Darius. It is admirable that Daniel displays faith that God will deliver him, whether in life or in death. But as a result of his consistent faith, even *Darius* suggests that Daniel's God might deliver him (6:16).

The lions' den is an enclosure with no visual access. Daniel is apparently lowered into it, a stone is laid over the top, and the king seals it with his signet ring. It is a fretful night for Darius. He can't sleep, won't eat, and refuses any kind of entertainment (6:17–18). He is up at dawn to return to the lions' den, and he is surprisingly optimistic. He doesn't just call out to Daniel; he asks a question that demands a response (6:19–20). And Daniel's voice assures him that, yes, God has indeed delivered him from the lions. He also sets the record straight by averring, "I have not wronged you, Your Majesty" (6:21–22 NLT).

Demystifying Daniel

Daniel has defied a Persian law and submitted to what was intended to be the Persian death penalty. So God's deliverance of Daniel is more than simply a reward for his steady faith. It is also God's divine declaration of Daniel's innocence based on the law of the Lord and an emphatic demonstration that God's law is to be feared over any human law.

Daniel is freed from the den unharmed. He has no bite marks and no scratches (6:23). God's rule of the world includes both corrupt political systems and the animal kingdom.

The people who had attempted to destroy Daniel are then rounded up and thrown to the lions, along with their wives and children (6:24). Their scheme is revealed for what it is: a malicious attempt to murder an innocent man. Historians have learned that Persian law dictated the destruction of entire families of people who were harmful to the kingdom. It may be that in a culture of violence and vengeance, it was believed that the children of an offender might attempt vengeance when they grew up.

For whatever reason the men and their families are condemned, their deaths make a certain point: The lions are hungry. Before the wicked conspirators even hit the bottom of the den, the lions overpower them and crush them (6:24). It becomes clear that Daniel had not escaped death because the animals had been overfed or drugged the night before. The king's seal is affixed to the only entrance/exit to the den. Any attempt to explain away a divine solution to Daniel's dilemma is met with a biblical counterargument.

The section concludes with a new decree, written by King Darius and sent throughout the land to people of all languages (6:26–27). The king mandates that everyone in his kingdom must show reverence to Daniel's God. Just as the Lord made Himself known to Nebuchadnezzar and Belshazzar in phenomenal ways, so, too, He persuades Darius of His unequalled power.

Critical Observation

The decree that had been designed to entrap Daniel supposedly could not be repealed (6:12, 15) and was supposed to be in effect for thirty days (6:7, 12). Perhaps King Darius waited a month before issuing his new order, although it appears to have been sent out immediately after Daniel's release. It might have been that Darius came to the conclusion that God's law effectively superseded any contradictory human law, and he repealed the first decree after all.

After his return trip from the lions' den, Daniel does quite well throughout the reign of Darius (6:28). In fact, his service continues into the rule of the next king, Cyrus.

Take It Home

In previous situations, Daniel had wisely used compromise to keep from doing something that would have gone against his beliefs (1:11–16). In this case, he wisely trusts God to see him through, and he refuses to alter his prayer habits in any way. It can be difficult to know when to yield a bit and when to stand firm. What do you think determined how Daniel decided to respond in various circumstances? Can you think of similar examples from your own life? How do you decide when it is appropriate to seek compromise and when you need to be completely unwavering in the exercise of your beliefs?

DANIEL 7:1–28

DANIEL'S FIRST VISION

Setting Up the Section

The first half of the book of Daniel (chapters 1–6) is a mostly chronological narrative of Daniel's service to various kings of Babylon and Medo-Persia. The second half (chapters 7–12) contains more personal accounts of some of Daniel's dreams and visions.

7:1–14

DANIEL'S DREAM OF FOUR STRANGE CREATURES

The book of Daniel was written during a time when the Jews had just been conquered, their temple destroyed, and most of the potential leaders taken captive and carried away. It appears that aggressive human forces are in control and that God either no longer cares or is unable to do anything to deliver His people.

But Daniel has repeatedly highlighted the ongoing sovereignty of God throughout the first half of his book. God makes it clear that even though human kingdoms are being allowed some temporary successes, they will not reign forever. The kingdom of God will arrive, it will succeed, and God will be the eternal King.

Beginning in chapter 7, Daniel shares a series of revelations to explain how God plans to bring about the end of the human kingdoms. The prophecies deal with the destruction of arrogant human rulers and the coming of the Messiah, who will sit on the throne to rule forever. Chapter 7 provides an overview of what is going to happen in the world, setting up the prophecies that follow.

The chronological progression of Daniel is interrupted at this point as the author returns to the reign of Belshazzar (7:1). In Daniel 5, the observation is made that Daniel appears to be sidelined when Belshazzar replaces Nebuchadnezzar. Perhaps Belshazzar didn't make use of Daniel during that time, but here it is evident that God did. It also appears that Daniel saw more than he recorded but only wrote down all the high points.

His vision begins with an image of the great sea (the Mediterranean) being greatly disturbed by "the four winds of heaven" (7:2). Those who sail for a living pay close attention to wind direction, partly because the direction helps determine what kind of storm to expect. In Daniel's vision, God stirs up the waters to bring about various storms of discord and confusion.

Critical Observation

For those living in the Middle East, the only great sea they knew was the Mediterranean Sea. It was the territory that all the kingdoms of the world sought to control. The Mediterranean provided a path for international shipping, sustenance for living, and protection from invading forces. It was both literally and figuratively a "great sea."

As Daniel continues to observe, four different types of "great beasts" come out of the sea (7:3). He will later be told that the beasts represent kingdoms (7:17), so his description is more to differentiate their qualities and characteristics than to detail their specific physical appearances.

The first creature is like a lion with wings like an eagle—both powerful and swift (7:4). But then its wings are plucked, and it is placed on the ground with two feet instead of four, with a human's power to reason. The implication is that the figure began as a wicked being, fell from earthly glory, and was restored to normal. Nebuchadnezzar immediately comes to mind after his account provided in Daniel 5, although some people believe this will be a king yet to come. At this point, more information is needed.

The second creature is compared to a bear—powerful and vicious, but with a tendency to be slow and lazy (7:5). It is raised up on one of its sides, perhaps indicating a walking position. And it has been feeding on another animal, having been given permission to conquer.

The third beast is described as a four-headed, four-winged leopard, meaning it is swift, fierce, and has the ability to cover a lot of territory quickly (7:6). The biblical concept of multiple heads frequently symbolizes different kingdoms or regions, so the creature is perhaps a single kingdom with four regions.

Comparisons fail Daniel while he attempts to describe the fourth creature (7:7). He can only say it is dreadful, powerful, and frightening. Its large iron teeth crush and devour its victims. It is different from any of the others in that it has ten horns. Animal horns are symbols of power, and ten is a number of completeness, so this final creature appears to have all rule and power.

This fourth beast is captivating. Daniel continues to watch it as yet another horn emerges, uprooting three of the existing ones. This new horn is different from the others. For one thing, it is smaller. Even stranger, however, is that it has eyes and a mouth, and the mouth is boasting (7:8).

Yet as fascinating as this bragging, multi-horned beast is, Daniel's eyes are drawn to an even more intriguing sight. He sees God (the "Ancient of Days") taking His seat among a number of thrones. His garments are white, symbolizing purity, as is His hair. His throne is ablaze. Fire flows from Him like a river, representing God's judgment poured out over all the earth (7:9–10). His is the throne of a judge; the other thrones are set up for those who will be watching the proceedings. (The book of Revelation speaks of great multitudes who will witness God's final judgment [Revelation 7:9–10; 19:1–3].)

Demystifying Daniel

The books that Daniel sees opened in 7:10 may be the same books mentioned in Revelation 20:11–15. God's judgment is based on the deeds recorded in these books. God notices the injustices done in this world, and they will not go unpunished.

Despite the presence of the Ancient of Days, the little horn continues its boasting. As Daniel watches, the fourth beast is killed as it speaks, and its body is thrown into a roaring fire. The other beasts are still around, but all their authority has been removed (7:11–12).

Then, in stark contrast to the boasting beast, Daniel sees another figure, whom he describes "like a son of man" (7:13–14). All the previous rulers of the world have been described as various animals (symbols of strength and power). It is clear from the text that this new figure is a special ruler, and he is somehow related to the Ancient of Days, yet he is perceived in human form. The concept of God ruling the earth in the form of a man is a profound thought, and would have been especially so to the religious leaders of Babylon and Persia.

The new ruler is given authority and power over all nations and peoples. The scope of his rule is unlimited, as is its length. His position as ruler is everlasting (7:13–14).

7:15–28

THE INTERPRETATION OF THE DREAM

Even within his dream, Daniel is troubled. It must have been overwhelming to realize he was seeing what is in the future yet not fully understanding his visions. So he asks for clarification, and one of the heavenly figures (angels) helps him interpret the symbols and meaning (7:15–16).

The various beasts are kingdoms. Four of them will arise from the natural order of the earth. They will threaten and persecute the people of God, but God's kingdom will never be in doubt.

Critical Observation

The word interpreted *saints* in 7:18 can mean a couple of different things. It may be instinctive to see the word and think of people who are devoted to the lordship of God and who willingly submit to Him. However, Daniel is still writing in Aramaic throughout this section, and in that language *saints* could also mean "angels." This possibility is bolstered by later sections of Daniel that indicate an intense heavenly conflict taking place beyond what is visible on earth.

Not surprisingly, Daniel is particularly eager to learn more about the fourth beast (7:19–22). It is the most vicious and terrifying. The numerous horns, of shifting number, are mysterious. Even as he continues to watch, the boastful, outspoken horn is warring against the saints and is actually winning until the Ancient of Days puts an end to the matter by pronouncing judgment in favor of His saints.

The angel's response to Daniel reveals that the fourth creature is a cruel beast that will control ten kingdoms and conquer the world (7:23–27). Another king would arise after the others, displacing three of the existing kingdoms and supporting the beast in speaking out against God and His followers. He will even work through the legal system to change laws in his oppression of God's people. His reign of terror will last for "a time, times, and half a time" (7:25). In Aramaic, the use of the word *time* refers to the passing of one year (4:16). A common interpretation of the phrase, then, is to consider *a time* as one year, *times* as two years, and *half a time* as half a year, yielding a total of three and a half years.

Demystifying Daniel

The four beasts in Daniel's dream appear to correspond with the four sections of the great statue of Nebuchadnezzar's first dream (2:31–35). The descriptions of the four creatures lend credence to their representation of Babylon, Medo-Persia, Greece, and Rome. Much debate takes place as to the significance of the ten horns and the final, boastful horn. Many people connect this section of Daniel with John's writing in Revelation and believe that Daniel's dream describes the end-times Antichrist (called the "beast" in Revelation) and the false prophet who serves as a type of prime minister for him.

After the violent reign of this figure, God's heavenly court will assemble to strip him of power and destroy him once and for all. The people of God will then be given control of all the kingdoms of the world. God will be acknowledged as the true King, ensuring everlasting peace and contentment (7:26–27).

It is a satisfying ending, to be sure, yet the dream completely overwhelms Daniel. It is quite a burden to not only be informed of the end of the world as he knows it but to witness and experience it to a certain extent. He is deeply troubled, but he doesn't say anything about it to anyone.

Take It Home

Sometimes people feel they have witnessed the worst that humanity has to offer. In Daniel's case, he could make that claim with confidence, and he was physically shaken by the experience. Yet every time a prophet confronts his readers/listeners with bad news, it is coupled with the assurance that beyond the bad times, God will step in to restore and reward those who are faithful to Him. What are some distressing events you have recently experienced? If you could be absolutely sure that God is in control of those events, how would your perception of them change? What can you do to strengthen your awareness of God's sovereignty?

DANIEL 8:1–27

DANIEL'S SECOND VISION

Setting Up the Section

This section follows the previous one as another account from the private life of Daniel, in contrast to his interactions with various kings in chapters 1–6. This vision of Daniel's is also filled with symbols, as is his dream in chapter 7.

8:1–14

A RAM AND A GOAT

In this chapter, Daniel returns to writing in Hebrew. The section between 2:4 and 7:28 was written in Aramaic and was a message of God's sovereignty over all nations. In chapter 8, the focus of Daniel's writing shifts to what God is planning to do *to* and *through* the nation of Israel.

Another notable observation of Daniel 8 is that it is a description of rage. The nations rage as they seek control of the world. One figure in particular rages in his attempt to take over the world. And, ultimately, the rage of God is witnessed as He punishes those who have rejected Him to embrace the world. The chapter should be approached as a description of events that are difficult to accept. However, an interpretation is provided for the vision that is specific and helpful for properly understanding its meaning.

This vision occurs during the third year of Belshazzar's reign (8:1), which is about two years after the dream Daniel previously described (7:1). The location in the vision is Susa, a city in the heart of the Medo-Persian Empire that will later become a common vacation spot for King Darius. So during the final years of the Babylonian Empire, Daniel is shown a vision of the destruction of the Persian Empire that will follow (8:1–2).

The citadel in Susa is synonymous with the success of the Persians, and the ram in the vision (8:3–4) is later identified as the Medo-Persian Empire (8:20). The ram dominates all other animals in every direction. The variance in the size of its two horns is most likely a prediction that the Medes will be the stronger of the two allied nations at first, although the Persians later gained power.

The land acquisitions of the Medo-Persians were not typically peaceful. They frequently resulted in war, death, destruction, pain, and misery. A raging ram is an appropriate symbol to represent their approach to surrounding nations.

Critical Observation

The geographic spread of the Medo-Persian Empire was one step in preparation for the Roman Empire to eventually unite diverse areas in language and customs. In the first century AD, the gospel will be taken throughout the world with great efficiency. In this way, the unity formed (forced) by the Persians could be seen as laying the foundation for the early church.

But the ram finally meets its match in the form of a goat that shatters its two horns (8:5–7). Daniel will soon be informed that the goat represents Greece (8:21). It has a single prominent horn between its eyes (a single leader) and moves across the earth without touching the ground (indicating great speed).

The goat strikes the ram and quickly overpowers it. And when Persia comes up against Alexander the Great, it falls hard and fast. Alexander will go on to conquer most of the populated world before he is thirty. His combination of strength, speed of conquest, and youth will stand out in history. Napoleon and George Patton are two of many military leaders who studied the strategies of Alexander in designing their own battle plans.

Daniel's vision continues as he sees the goat grow in fame, but it suddenly has its large horn broken off. In place of the severed horn grows four other horns (8:8). History confirms that Alexander became quite proud and exalted himself. Yet by the age of thirty-three, he had died (the cause of which is widely disputed). After his death, the Greek nation is split into four states, each with a different leader.

God is not revealing these events to Daniel simply to give him preview of what will occur in history. These events will have a direct impact on the Jewish people. One of the four horns from the goat (Greece) starts small but quickly becomes great. Among the territories to which he turns his attention is *the Beautiful Land*—the name the Jews use for Jerusalem (8:9; Psalm 48:2).

The language that follows (Daniel 8:10–12) includes war imagery. "The host of heaven" is the army of heaven, a term sometimes applied to angels. Stars can represent large numbers of people. The horn strives to set himself up as an equal to God ("Prince of the host") by eliminating other religious ceremonies. He is associated with rebellion and a disregard for truth.

Again, history sheds light on this prophetic vision. One of the leaders who rises to power after Alexander the Great is a man named Antiochus Epiphanes. He has an intense dislike of the Jews, persecuting them, killing their high priest, and entering their temple to have pigs sacrificed to him because he believes he is the Messiah. In the ultimate insult, he corrupts and twists the entire religious system of the Jews so that it serves him.

Critical Observation

The religious corruption initiated by Antiochus Epiphanes will actually turn out to be a worse experience for the Jews than their exile. In Babylon, they mourned because they knew their temple and city were being neglected. But later, when they see their religion perverted and a false Messiah desecrating their temple, it is heart-wrenching.

Daniel overhears a heavenly conversation taking place regarding the length of time the rebellious horn will be allowed to trouble God's people (8:13–14). The answer has created a bit of confusion. It seems reasonable that 2,300 evenings and mornings should be 2,300 days, or almost six and a half years. Another possibility is that it means 2,300 *sacrifices*, with one each morning and one each evening for a total time of only half as long. But since the daily sacrifices are suspended during this time, this option doesn't seem as likely.

8:15–27

THE INTERPRETATION OF THE VISION

Modern readers who are confused by passages such as this may be comforted to realize that Daniel also struggled to understand what he was seeing (8:15–16). First he is confused. As the angel Gabriel begins to explain the vision to him, he becomes terrified. Then when he discovers that the vision concerns a time of the end, he is so physically afflicted—almost comatose—that he needs help standing (8:17–18).

Gabriel's reference to the "time of the end" (8:19 NIV) should be interpreted from Daniel's perspective, not a modern one. The Jewish people are undergoing a time of God's discipline. They are currently exiled in Babylon, and Daniel is discovering that this won't be the worst of it. It is a couple of centuries before the horrors of Antiochus Epiphanes falls on them, but soon thereafter the consequences for the sins of Israel will come to an end.

Demystifying Daniel

When Daniel is addressed as *son of man* (8:17), it is not intended as a special title, as when it is applied to the Messiah. Rather, Daniel is among heavenly beings, so it is only logical that he would be singled out as the human in the group.

However, it is also fair to say that Antiochus Epiphanes is a picture of the end-times Antichrist (the beast in Revelation). The description in 8:23–25 is applicable to both figures: "completely wicked," "master of intrigue," and "very strong" (NIV). Both feel superior and spread deceit. Both are especially destructive because they establish their power while people feel secure. Only later do they reveal their true natures. And eventually, both will be destroyed, but not by human power (8:25). (Antiochus isn't killed; he eventually dies of tuberculosis.)

The wrath that Gabriel speaks of is God's response after God's people allow themselves to be fooled by the false religion of Antiochus (8:19). After they agree to the Greek leader's twisted religion, God will allow them to suffer the consequences. But as Daniel is about to be shown (in chapter 9), shortly afterward will come a Messiah to rescue God's people.

Daniel is assured that what he has seen is true (8:26). But then he is asked to seal the vision—not to discuss it with anyone. The reason, he will discover, is that he is about to receive another vision that will take precedence. Daniel can see some of the behind-the-scenes operations of God's kingdom, but the Lord doesn't want people motivated to come to Him out of fear. The next vision will reveal the coming of an anointed one, a Messiah, who acts out of compassion and offers salvation.

The knowledge of what is ahead for God's people overwhelms Daniel for a period of time. He is physically sick for several days. Even when he recovers and goes back to work, the vision continues to weigh on him. He will continue to struggle with what he has seen until God reveals more to him and puts his mind to rest.

Take It Home

Brazen leaders have defied God throughout history. Antiochus Epiphanes is certainly one of the worst, but there are many others. In fact, John warns God's people to watch out for antichrists who have already come (1 John 2:18). Such people need not have widespread influence. Anyone who persistently opposes God and attempts to sway others to that belief is, by definition, an antichrist. Do you know anyone whom you would place in that category? How do you tend to respond/interact with such people?

DANIEL 9:1–27

DANIEL'S THIRD VISION

Setting Up the Section

Continuing his record of various divine revelations he has received, Daniel describes a prayer for which he is given a most emphatic response. During his prayer, he is visited by the angel Gabriel, who tells Daniel what to expect in the future, although the symbolism used is challenging and difficult to properly interpret and understand.

9:1–19

DANIEL'S PRAYER

The date that Daniel provides in 9:1 reveals that fourteen years have passed between his previous recorded vision (chapter 8) and this prayer. At the end of the previous section, Daniel is left exhausted, sick, and confused about what he has witnessed. He has been shown that God is going to bring the kingdoms of humanity to an end and that He is going to discipline the Jewish people. Seemingly, those fourteen years have been a time of searching for Daniel. He has not questioned that both discipline and judgment are deserved, yet God has promised that they will not last forever. So Daniel is seeking to discover when God will restore His glory.

Critical Observation

Jerusalem was an integral part of worship for the Jewish people. It symbolized the land God had given to His people, and the temple represented the presence of God amongst them. With the temple destroyed and the people scattered, Jerusalem was desolate at the time of Daniel's writing.

He has searched the scriptures available to him and found Jeremiah's prophecies, written prior to the invasion of Babylon, warning the people of what will come (Jeremiah 25:11–12). But along with the bad news of the coming captivity is the announcement that after seventy years the people will be allowed to return to Jerusalem.

This is encouraging news to Daniel, so he begins to pursue God in prayer. He realizes that the reason the Jews have fallen out of fellowship with God to begin with is because of their sin. So Daniel approaches God in prayer and petition, fasting, and sackcloth and ashes (9:3). His mind-set, habits, and dress are all designed to place his full focus on the Lord.

Daniel's prayer begins with confession, which is followed by a request for mercy (9:4–19). He first acknowledges the character of God (9:4). God is great and awe-inspiring because He can be counted on to keep His promises and care for His people.

God's people, however, have sinned in many ways (9:5–6). They have been wicked and rebellious, ignoring God's commandments. When God sent prophets to confront them about their sin, the people had rejected them. They had persistently lived for themselves, not for God.

Their rejection of God leads to their being scattered to various countries and their leaders driven from positions of responsibility. Daniel acknowledges that they deserve everything that has happened to them. However, in spite of the sins of the people, Daniel realizes that God remains merciful and forgiving (9:7–10).

The people have no excuse for their sinful rejection of God. The consequences of such sin are clearly spelled out in the Law of Moses (Leviticus 26:14–20). They had ignored Moses and a long series of prophets, and God had done what He said He would do (Daniel 9:11–14). The Lord's action in response to their sin is only proof of His righteousness.

Daniel then moves on to his request: He asks God to turn away His anger from Jerusalem (9:15–16). This is not a personal request. Rather, Daniel is asking God to reestablish His glory in the world. Ever since God allowed the Babylonians to conquer Jerusalem and take away the people, there has been no specific physical location where God is acknowledged and worshiped. Daniel's request is not just to get "home" but rather to see the glory of Jerusalem restored and an end to God's name being mocked by pagan nations.

Critical Observation

When Daniel (or any other Jewish person, for that matter) states that his God is more powerful than any other god, it appears to be a foolish statement to anyone outside of Judah. The Jews had been brutally defeated and were still living as captives. From all appearances, their God either doesn't care or is unable to do anything to improve the situation. Daniel's prayer is to correct such misperceptions about God.

9:20–27

GOD'S RESPONSE TO DANIEL'S PRAYER

Daniel is still in prayer in the evening, when the angel Gabriel appears to him in swift flight. Daniel recognizes the angel from his previous vision (9:20–21). Ever since then, for fourteen years, Daniel must have wondered about the future. Gabriel had shared with him a description of punishment the Jews could expect in those days, but he had said nothing at the time about their salvation/deliverance (8:15–26). Finally, Gabriel has been instructed to provide Daniel with additional insight and understanding (9:22–23).

Still, what Daniel is about to hear has since been described as one of the most difficult passages in the Bible. Gabriel begins to depict a unit of time comprised of seventy sets of sevens, during which God will bring about redemption for His people (9:24). Numerous theories abound as to what this message really means. Some consider each "seven" to be a seven-year period. If so, much of what Gabriel says begins to fit a historic time line starting when a decree is passed to rebuild Jerusalem (which is described in Ezra 7:12–26) and carrying through to Jesus' ministry.

What is known for certain—what Gabriel tells Daniel—is that a ruler will appear who will again destroy the temple and the city of Jerusalem (Daniel 9:26). It will be a time of war. The destructive ruler to come will establish a covenant with the people for that final "seven" (9:27), but halfway through that period he will abolish all sacrifices and offerings, desecrating the temple with something called *an abomination that causes desolation* (NIV). But the ruler's end, already decreed, will occur shortly thereafter.

Demystifying Daniel

The *abomination that causes desolation* (NIV) means "the abomination that desolates or appalls" (9:27). It is a reference to something so detestable and repugnant that no decent, ethical, religious person will have anything to do with it. Such people will be nowhere near it, leaving that area desolate.

One understanding of this passage is that the destruction and desolation described in Daniel takes place in 70 AD, when the Romans overthrow a Jewish uprising by completely demolishing the temple. The ruler at the time is Titus. Those events fit a portion of what Daniel is told to expect, but not all.

More likely, the final "seven" is a still-future period of time. It seems logical to relate this new information that Daniel receives from Gabriel with the prophet's previous vision of the beast with the ten horns (7:19–27). If the ruler of 9:26–27 is the same as the boastful horn (7:20–22), the final "seven" will begin with the contract made by this malicious leader. He will break his covenant midway through, and great suffering will ensue for God's people. But after a period of time, God will remove him from leadership and make all things right.

Daniel's response to this new information is not recorded. However, it must have been encouraging to be assured that the predicted punishments he learned of in his previous vision will indeed come to an end and that God will make atonement for the sin of the people and provide everlasting righteousness (9:24).

Take It Home

Although the specific interpretation of future events as presented in this section may be confusing and debatable, one clear observation is that God has a plan. Events are moving toward the dates that He has specified. Even in the worst of times—especially in the worst of times—believers need to remain faithfully committed to Him. When are some recent times when your faith may not have been as strong as you wished? What are some specific truths about God that you might want to recall the next time you face similar situations?

DANIEL 10:1–12:13

DANIEL'S FOURTH VISION

Setting Up the Section

Daniel has recorded three visions so far: one of the destruction of human kingdoms and establishment of the kingdom of God (chapter 7), one of the punishment that will be inflicted on God's people because of their sin and rejection of God (chapter 8), and one of the coming Messiah who will conquer sin and provide a way of everlasting righteousness (chapter 9). In the rest of his book, Daniel records one final vision that encompasses, integrates, and further explains much of what he has already witnessed.

10:1–11:1

THE FRAMEWORK FOR THE VISION

Daniel regularly dates his visions based on the reign of the leader at the time (7:1; 8:1; 9:1). This one is last chronologically. Darius (9:1) and Cyrus (10:1) rule Persia at the same time. Cyrus was the great king over the entire Persian Empire, which at this time included Israel. Darius may have been a subking under him as emperor. During Cyrus's first year, he passes a decree allowing the Jews to return to Judah and rebuild Jerusalem (Ezra 1:1–4). This final vision of Daniel's is two years later.

Critical Observation

Some people question why Daniel doesn't return to his homeland when he had the opportunity. No reason is given, although a couple of possibilities seem logical. First, he would have been at least in his mid-eighties, and a long journey could be difficult. Second, God had used Daniel as a consistently faithful voice in the midst of a people who had no knowledge of the Lord. Daniel had already demonstrated that he lived for the kingdom of God and not for his own well-being, advancement, or success. Perhaps his was a conscious decision to remain and serve where God had placed him.

Daniel's vision is nothing new, but it is more developed than his previous ones. As he begins to comprehend more clearly, he grows very troubled and goes into mourning, setting aside all the pleasantries of life such as wine, choice food, and lotions used to minimize the effects of the hot, arid climate (10:1–3). He is still troubled over the sin of God's people and the approaching punishment that will be the consequence. His emotions are probably heightened by the date as well, which would have coincided with the annual Passover to celebrate God's deliverance of His people in the past (10:4). Daniel is passionate about both the will of God and the people he loves on earth.

A biblical reference to the "great river" usually means the Euphrates, but Daniel clarifies that he is beside the Tigris (10:4). There he sees a heavenly figure whose description is similar to that of Jesus in Revelation 1:12–16. Some people have suggested that it is indeed a preincarnate appearance of Jesus, but the difficulty this figure faces in spiritual warfare would not have been true of the Lord (10:13). Daniel witnesses the splendor of one of God's angels, but not Jesus.

The figure is bedecked in linen (a sign of purity) and a gold belt (worn by royal leaders). His body is like beryl, a shiny and transparent gold-colored stone. His face is like lightning, his eyes like flaming torches. His arms and feet have a gleam like polished bronze. His voice is unusually powerful (10:5–6).

As impressive as this figure is, only Daniel is enabled to see him. Those with Daniel only realize something unexplainable is happening, and they run to hide (10:7). Daniel, too, is affected; he goes pale, feels entirely weak and helpless, and soon falls into a deep sleep (10:8–9). A touch of the angel helps him up, first to his hands and knees, and then to a standing position, although he is still quite wobbly (10:10–11).

The angel addresses Daniel as a man who is "highly esteemed" (10:11 NIV). God honors Daniel because his heart is not callous. The Lord values the pain that Daniel feels as a result of the people's sin.

Daniel has been fasting and praying for three weeks, and the angel had been quickly dispatched to respond to his prayers and desires. Daniel's prayers are heeded because he has set his heart on understanding and because he has humbled himself before God (10:12). Yet there has been a long delay between Daniel's petition and the angel's response, because the messenger sent to Daniel became involved in a fight with the prince of the Persian kingdom that lasted three weeks (10:12–13). Clearly this is a hostile and aggressive spiritual being, perhaps working to affect the kingdom of Persia for evil. Eventually the messenger of God, still struggling against the evil force, summons the help of Michael the archangel, the most powerful of the angels, and is able to continue on his way to Daniel.

Demystifying Daniel

This passage (10:12–14) alerts the reader to some of the truths about the unseen spiritual world. It is evident that angels are real, and both good angels and bad angels (demons) can influence the affairs of human beings.

Daniel has already heard what to expect for the Jews in the latter days, but he is about to receive another summary. Again, Daniel feels weak and unworthy to be part of such a divine moment (10:14–17). And again, he is touched by the heavenly messenger and encouraged to remain courageous and strong. As he listens, Daniel begins to regain his strength (10:18–19).

The angel is preparing to return and reengage in spiritual warfare, but first he wants to share with Daniel what is written in the Book of Truth (10:20–21). The messenger angel and the angel Michael stand opposed to the evil in the land, both in Persia and Greece. God had allowed those nations to thrive for a time, and His people had suffered. But here it is seen that God's protection is always in place. The sovereign Lord controls everything—including limiting the evil that occurs.

Demystifying Daniel

The Babylonians thought their gods had a Tablet of Destiny that supposedly foretold their history. Gabriel's reference to the Book of Truth in 10:21 may have suggested Daniel's awareness of such a Tablet, and it could have been the angel's way of assuring Daniel that God is sovereign and has the future in His hand. In any event, Gabriel is about to reveal some truth about the future to Daniel (11:2).

11:2–35

THE VISION UNFOLDS

At this point, Gabriel begins to relate to Daniel a rather complex explanation of future events. It is helpful to keep in mind that as God orchestrates the events of the world, it is toward the purification of Israel and all of His followers. Some degree of purifying the nation will include punishment and persecution. God's plan includes the temporary emergence and dominance of various nations along with individual world leaders who exert a certain amount of control. Afterward, God's people will be purged and ready to serve Him.

Daniel has already been assured that no matter what takes place in world events, and as bad as things will become, God is always in control and permits evil to continue only for a limited time (9:24). With that in mind, he is then told that four more kings will arise in Persia, the fourth creating conflict against Greece (11:2). The three Persian leaders who follow Darius are Cambyses (530–522 BC), Smerdis (522 BC), and Darius I (522–486 BC). However, the Persian Empire had a total of thirteen leaders, and opinions vary as to whether the three referred to in Daniel 11:2 are the consecutive kings after Darius or the three most prominent leaders who succeed him.

Also debated is the identity of the fourth Persian king, although much evidence points to Xerxes I (486–465 BC). He is a strong king whose empire and wealth grow to large proportions. Eventually he seeks to attack Greece and incorporate the nation into his empire, but he fails miserably. His antagonism may have been the primary catalyst for the fall of Persia to Greece more than a century later.

However, almost everyone agrees that the "mighty king" who will appear and do as he pleases is Alexander the Great (11:3). The description in 11:4 fits Alexander precisely. His few family members are assassinated shortly after his death, and none of them inherit the great empire he had conquered and organized. Instead, rule goes to his four primary generals ("the four winds of heaven"), essentially segmenting the large empire into four separate kingdoms.

Two of those four kingdoms become prominent: Syria (the kingdom of the north) and Egypt (the kingdom of the south). The king of the south (Ptolemy I) and the king of the north (Seleucus I) begin as allies. Seleucus spends time with Ptolemy in Egypt while avoiding conflict with another power in the north. They fight together to defeat that opponent, and Seleucus returns to the north, settling in Babylon.

Tension forms between these two powers over the land in between them—the area of Palestine. It technically belongs to Seleucus, but Ptolemy occupies it. This tension appears to have continued to their successors, who attempt to resolve it with a marriage to unite the two kingdoms.

Ptolemy II (the successor of Ptolemy I) offers his daughter Berenice to Antiochus II Theos (the grandson of Seleucus). Antiochus agrees to the marriage, although he has to divorce his first wife, Laodice, to do so. Laodice had a son with him (Seleucus II). Antiochus and Berenice then have a son who appears to be next in line for the throne. In time, Antiochus reconciles with Laodice, which proves to be a mistake. She evidently doesn't like seeing another woman's son being groomed for leadership because she poisons Antiochus, Berenice, and their son. Laodice then occupies the throne until her son, Seleucus II, is ready to rule.

Needless to say, Laodice's actions are not well received in Egypt. Not long after the brother of Berenice (Ptolemy III Euergetes) takes the throne, he marches north to do battle against Seleucus II. He is initially successful and carries off the images of the northern gods, but subsequent battles continue between the two forces (11:5–8).

Critical Observation

This may sound like a complicated ancient history lesson. However, the details are important in demonstrating how accurate and succinct Daniel's account is, who recorded his prophecies two to four hundred years prior to the occurrence of the events.

Daniel's descriptions in 11:9–19 are pretty much self-explanatory, except for the names that are later provided for the participants. Laodice's son rules for twenty years before he dies and is replaced by his two sons, Seleucus III and Antiochus III. During the war described in 11:10, Seleucus III is murdered, leaving Antiochus III as sole leader of the northern kingdom. In the next battle that ensues, Antiochus assembles 62,000 infantry, 6,000 cavalry, and 102 elephants. He sends his army to Egypt, where they confront an opposing force of 70,000 infantry, 5,000 cavalry, and 73 elephants. The Egyptian army of Ptolemy IV Philopator is victorious, enacting a wholesale execution of the north and taking much land (including Palestine). Fifteen years later, Antiochus assembles an even larger army and begins to reacquire much of the territory he had lost (again, including Palestine). He presses on until he has gained control of Egypt. But for many years, the balance of power continues to go back and forth between the two nations.

The king of the north in Daniel 11:14–19 is still Antiochus III. The marriage of his daughter (Cleopatra I) to the king of the south (Ptolemy V) doesn't work as anticipated. Antiochus was hoping to win Ptolemy's favor. Instead, his daughter sides with her new husband rather than her father.

Stalled in his efforts against Egypt, Antiochus begins to tangle with the Roman army that is beginning to make some serious advancements in the area. The Romans first defeat Antiochus and then require him to pay heavy fines for his attacks, which place an economic strain on his country. When Antiochus returns home, he is killed by an angry mob who resents paying so much to Rome (11:18–19).

Demystifying Daniel

All the names and conflicts of this section definitely correlate with history. However, they serve the primary purpose of explaining the rise of one figure in particular: Antiochus IV Epiphanes. He is the ruler who most directly affects the people of God in their homeland.

After the death of Antiochus III, his son Seleucus IV takes over. He is the one who sends out a tax collector in an attempt to pay Rome the taxes they demanded (11:20). That tax collector, however, kills Seleucus in an attempted coup. He is unsuccessful, yet his actions leave the throne open to other contenders. The person who comes out on top is Antiochus IV Epiphanes. The rightful heir to the throne, a man named Demetrius, is being held hostage in Rome until his nation's taxes are paid. So Antiochus seizes the leadership role; he is not *given* the honor (11:21).

Still, Antiochus IV uses political savvy and false promises to gain and maintain power. When Egypt launches an unsuccessful attack attempting to regain Palestine, Antiochus takes their king captive. The brother of Egypt's king uses that opportunity to secure Egypt's throne for himself. The former king then proposes to Antiochus that they can work together to regain the Egyptian throne and rule the entire region together. Antiochus likes the idea. He signs an agreement and gives the Egyptian leader the title "prince of the covenant." But no sooner has the former Egyptian king been released than he breaks the covenant with Antiochus and forms an alliance with his brother to attempt to drive Antiochus out of Palestine. The forces of Antiochus are too strong, however, and the Egyptian attack fails (11:22–23).

In the peaceful interlude that follows, Antiochus begins to show his true colors. He begins to plunder the wealth of his own land, including the riches from the temple in Jerusalem. And when some of the Egyptians later betray their king, Antiochus is able to overpower that country as well, at the cost of many lives (11:24–26).

Yet another attempted alliance between Antiochus IV and the king of Egypt fails to work out. Antiochus returns home but then marches against Egypt again. However, this time ships from Rome are in the Mediterranean Sea with support for Egypt, and Antiochus is turned away (11:27–30).

He is not in a good mood as he returns home through Palestine, and he takes his anger out on the Jews. He not only kills Jewish people, but he seeks to destroy Judaism as well. (This is perhaps the time that Daniel had previously written about, when a figure would arrive under the pretense of peace and gain support, but would then break his promises, turn on the Jews, and sacrifice a pig to himself in their temple [9:27].)

Some Jews will be deceived and side with him. Some will be betrayed, but they will choose to remain silent rather than be confrontational. A few will resist Antiochus and fight back, many of whom will die as a result (11:31–34). This will be the beginning of the purging to purify God's people, although more is to come (11:35).

Critical Observation

One of the most notable opponents to the aggression of Antiochus IV Epiphanes is a man named Judas Maccabeus, who stands for God. He forms an army of dedicated fighters. They are unable to rid their land of Greek influence, but they do regain the temple.

11:36–12:13

FURTHER INTO THE FUTURE

Up until this point in the vision, the events described appear to have been fulfilled by very specific events in history between Daniel's time and the modern day. In fact, the amazing accuracy has led some scholars to believe that Daniel must have lived in the second century BC and backdated his prophecy. The literary technique was not unusual at the time, but a close study of numerous additional aspects of Daniel's writing has convinced other scholars of its much earlier date, its reliability, and the reliability of his predictive prophecy. As Daniel repeatedly tells King Nebuchadnezzar, God is a revealer of mysteries (2:22, 28, 29). The precision of Daniel's visions only confirms this fact.

Beginning with 11:36, however, Daniel's prophecy makes an almost imperceptible shift. He continues to write about the king of the north and the king of the south, but the events no longer correlate to what has been recorded about Antiochus Epiphanes. In addition, his language adopts a grander scale than previously, and he begins to speak of end times.

It is difficult to state with certainty exactly what Daniel knew at the time and intended to communicate, but several scholars believe he must be writing of the last-days Antichrist, a figure who certainly can be compared with Antiochus Epiphanes in terms of deceit, hatred of God's people, and self-importance. The following comments will be based on that presumption. However, according to one school of thought, Daniel may not even have realized that his prophecy was jumping from a future Greek Empire to an even more distant future.

Many times people study the events concerning the end of the world and become scared when it seems that God cannot or will not stop the evil that is so strong and prevalent. Yet it is clear that God is always in control. In fact, He uses the events of the last days to bring about the cleansing and purging of evil that is necessary so He can establish His eternal kingdom. Just as He allowed the persecution of Israel during the reign of Antiochus IV Epiphanes, He will allow a similar purging during the final period of "seven" under the rule of the Antichrist (9:27).

The first thing revealed about this end-times figure is that he does as he pleases (11:36). He is able to carry out every notion and plan that comes to his mind. Antiochus had assumed the role of Messiah, but this figure goes one step further to position himself above *all* other gods, even the one true God (11:36–37). He will be successful, but only because God allows it.

Demystifying Daniel

Translations of 11:37 vary. Some say that the figure described has no desire for women, which would indicate that he is so consumed with himself that no other relationships matter. Other translations say that he has he has no desire for the god loved by women. In this case, the reference might be to a Babylonian fertility god named Tammuz. (The only overt biblical mention of this god is in Ezekiel 8:14.) His following was much like the one that would follow for the Greek god Adonis.

The only god that appeals to this individual is power (11:38–39). His religion is based on his ability to conquer. As he accumulates more and more power, it confirms his misassumption that he is the one and only god.

Sill, nations see the harm this figure can do, and they attempt to resist, even though they are not successful. He will go wherever he wishes. He will have strength like no king before him (11:40). Yet as he nears the land of Israel, for some reason he is unable to overtake the southeastern portions that include Edom, Moab, and Ammon. Why these areas are spared is not known. But other than the areas that God deems off-limits, the destructive leader will be allowed widespread conquest. Along with his territorial acquisitions comes economic strength as well (11:41–43). When he hears of threats, his intent is to annihilate (not merely stop) his opponents (11:44).

One observation that must have greatly disturbed Daniel's original readers is the location of this individual's headquarters. He sets up "between the glorious holy mountain and the sea" (11:45 NLT)—right in the heart of Israel. But as soon as this fact is revealed, it also confirms that his success will be limited. His time of conquest will quickly be concluded. When God finally takes action against him, his end is inevitable.

The period designated *at that time* in 12:1 is "the time of the end" (11:40). When the beast takes up residence in Israel, the great archangel Michael will depart. His presence has been to provide protection, and once that is removed, a time of unprecedented distress will occur. By this time, the Jewish people have already suffered through the rage of Antiochus IV Epiphanes and have been brutally murdered in great numbers by Hitler. But Daniel warns that what is yet to come will be even worse.

Critical Observation

It should not be presumed that Daniel is seeing *all* the events to take place in future times. More likely, he is shown the highlights in some semblance of order. Therefore, translators and interpreters have differing opinions as to many of the specifics involved.

However, God is aware of which people have placed their faith in Him, and He will deliver the believers (12:1). A resurrection will take place as well, one that includes both righteous people and those who died as unbelievers. The righteous will receive rewards, including everlasting life (12:2). Those who are rewarded are identified as wise, or insightful (12:3). They are the people who understand that the world is God's and through Him are saved and find their purpose. They also share with others what they have discovered about God. Such people live forever, shining like stars in a clear night sky (12:3).

In ancient times, an official document was concealed or put in a safe place after being sealed. Gabriel instructs Daniel to close and seal what he has seen and heard (12:4). When later generations are ready to increase their knowledge, this book will be available to them.

Daniel is still on the bank of the river (10:5). At this point, he overhears two angels, one on either bank of the Tigris. One asks how long it will take to fulfill these astonishing things and is told it will be a period of three and a half years (12:5–8). Furthermore, it will be a time when the power of the holy people has finally been shattered (12:7).

Since the inception of Israel as a nation, the people had not learned to steadfastly serve God, so the Lord is going to deal with their rebellion through this persecution. The result will be a final end to the people's rebellion.

Even after seeing and hearing so much, Daniel can't help but ask what the outcome will be of all these events (12:8). What will be the result of the separating and shattering of the people?

Most people are intrigued with what will happen in the future and end-of-the-world events. Daniel is no exception. Yet even Daniel, with all his wisdom and devotion, is told to go (12:9, 13). God will see to everything in His own way and His own timing. It is not always for people to try to figure out everything He will do and when it will be done.

However, wisdom will provide understanding for the things the Lord *does* want people to know (12:10). His people can be purified and acquire greater spiritual knowledge, but intentionally wicked people will never comprehend the plan of God.

Wisdom requires patience, and Daniel's patience results in a final bit of information: The evil end-times ruler will openly persecute God's people for 1,290 days (three and a half years), beginning with his cessation of Jewish temple rites and his desecration of the temple. This is a long time for people to remain faithful to God. And even beyond the 1,290 days is another forty-five-day period during which people are to patiently persevere (12:11–12).

Demystifying Daniel

No explanation is provided for the different lengths of time mentioned in Daniel 12:11–12 (1,290 days vs. 1,335 days). Conceivably, a forty-five-day period might pass between the time God puts an end to the suffering of His people and His ultimate destruction of the person responsible for it.

The best Daniel can do in response to all he has seen is to continue on until the end (12:13). He has faithfully served his God throughout his long life. In return, he is promised rest and eventual resurrection, after which he will receive everything God has in store for him.

Take It Home

Many times people are reluctant to discuss spiritual matters with others because there is so much they don't fully understand. It should be somewhat comforting, then, to see that even Daniel doesn't completely comprehend the things of God. Still, he is expected to continue serving and speaking out faithfully. Indeed, God's people have a challenge before them to lead many to righteousness (12:3). What is your opinion of evangelism? Do you feel it is everyone's responsibility, or is it best left to the experts (pastors, teachers, scholars, etc.)? When believers don't have all the answers to life's mysteries, do you think their testimony to others is adversely affected?

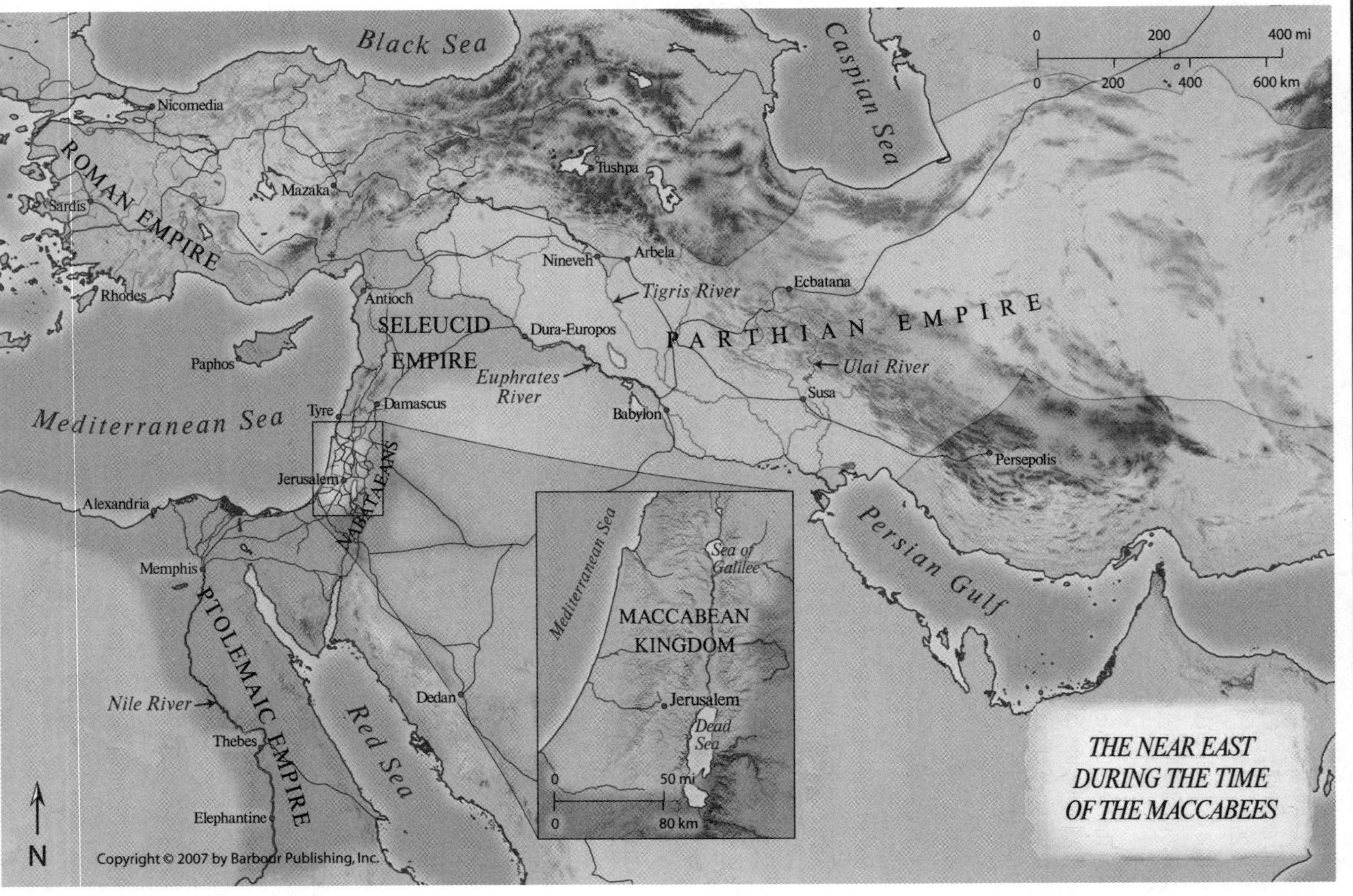
THE NEAR EAST
DURING THE TIME
OF THE MACCABEES
Black Sea
Caspian Sea
Mediterranean Sea
Persian Gulf
Red Sea
ROMAN EMPIRE
SELEUCID
EMPIRE
PARTHIAN EMPIRE
PTOLEMAIC EMPIRE
NABATAEANS
Nicomedia
Sardis
Mazaka
Rhodes
Paphos
Antioch
Tyre
Damascus
Jerusalem
Alexandria
Memphis
Nile River
Thebes
Elephantine
Dedan
Tushpa
Nineveh
Arbela
Tigris River
Dura-Europos
Euphrates
River
Babylon
Ecbatana
Ulai River
Susa
Persepolis
Mediterranean Sea
Sea of
Galilee
MACCABEAN
KINGDOM
Jerusalem
Dead
Sea
0
50 mi
0
80 km
0
200
400 mi
0
200
400
600 km
N
Copyright © 2007 by Barbour Publishing, Inc.

HOSEA

INTRODUCTION TO HOSEA

In our present age, fixed truths, moral absolutes, divine imperatives, sure hope, and life-transforming power often seem to be overshadowed by uncertainty, insecurity, and subjectivism. Yet in the story of Hosea, we are confronted with the truth about God's persistent and unlikely love for an unfaithful people, the Israelites, even as we marvel at the tragic and remarkable beauty of one prophet's unconditional love for his faithless wife that exemplifies the love story between God and humanity.

AUTHOR

Hosea's prophecy may have existed first simply in spoken form, then later it may have been gathered together in written form by disciples or scribes. Still, this work is traditionally attributed to Hosea, the son of Beeri (1:1). We don't know much about the prophet's life except for the little that we learn from chapters 1 and 3.

PURPOSE

The purpose of the book of Hosea is to remind God's people of their unfaithfulness and of the judgment that will come because of that unfaithfulness. Hosea teaches that, in spite of their unfaithfulness, it is impossible to escape the love of God, who is ultimately their only hope of salvation from themselves.

OCCASION

When Hosea is called to serve as God's prophet, the nation of Israel is in a state of rebellion. Based on the kings reigning during his prophecy (1:1), we know that the nation of Israel has been split by civil war (1 Kings 12) and that Hosea is sent to the northern kingdom of Israel, which is characterized by corrupt kings, crime, and compromised morality (Hosea 4:1–2).

THEMES

Both themes of love and judgment run through Hosea's prophecy. God's saving love is faithful even in the face of unfaithfulness. Yet, the consequence of that unfaithfulness will be faced. Hosea's ministry is meant to awaken the Israelites to their own unfaithfulness to God and to call their adulterous hearts back to Him.

HISTORICAL CONTEXT

God called Hosea to the northern kingdom, or Israel, at a time when the nation was in a position of strength and wealth, probably during the later years of Jeroboam II's reign. Hosea was a contemporary of other Old Testament prophets: Amos, Isaiah, Jonah, and Micah. Already on the horizon was the Assyrian menace, and within thirty years, Israel had fallen in defeat.

OUTLINE

HOSEA 1:1–2:1

AN UNUSUAL CALLING

Called by God 1:1
Hosea's Family 1:2–2:1

Setting Up the Section

God calls Hosea to an unlikely method of ministry: Hosea becomes an example of God's message to a rebellious and unfaithful people.

1:1

CALLED BY GOD

The book of Hosea provides its reader with some important facts that ground the story in its historical context. God calls Hosea during the reigns of Uzziah, Jotham, Ahaz, and Hezekiah, kings of Judah, and during the reign of Jeroboam II, king of Israel. Israel has split from civil war (2 Kings 13:12–13), and the people are pursuing nearly everything except God. Even their kings are often quite corrupt. Hosea is a contemporary of Amos, Isaiah, Jonah, and Micah—other Old Testament prophets charged with declaring God's love and faithfulness in the face of Israel's wayward rebellion. Yet Hosea is given a unique charge (as we will see).

1:2–2:1

HOSEA'S FAMILY

What the Lord requires of Hosea is shocking indeed: to forsake the natural hopes he may have for a happy marriage and instead consign himself to endure the emotional anguish and dishonor of a wife who will be persistently unfaithful. Hosea fulfills God's calling in his marriage to Gomer (1:2–3).

The names that the Lord requires Hosea and Gomer to give to their children express the Lord's intention in the most decisive and unmistakable way. The name *Jezreel* declares God's intention to punish Israel for her unfaithfulness to Him. *Lo-ruhamah* means "not loved," as the Lord is prepared to not love Israel anymore because she has broken His covenant. *Lo-ammi* means "not my people." This harsh denial of their place as God's nation is ultimately what the Lord is warning this generation of Israelites about: Their fate is based on their unfaithfulness (1:4–9).

Critical Observation

The Lord's instruction to Hosea has been widely taken to mean that the Lord commands Hosea to marry a woman of ill repute, perhaps a prostitute. Some scholars maintain that the whole account of Hosea and Gomer is only a parable and not a description of what actually happened. It is a story to make a point. Another view suggests that perhaps Gomer is not a prostitute, but instead the term *adulterous wife* is used metaphorically, as *prostitution* is used metaphorically to refer to Israel's spiritual adultery. Since the most natural reading is to take the story literally, that is how it is approached here.

God uses revelation by action throughout the Bible—most obviously in the ultimate revelation of His love in the incarnate person of Jesus Christ. Jeremiah remains a bachelor his entire life, against all social expectations and his own desire, as an enacted prophecy against the people of God (Jeremiah 16:2). The death of Ezekiel's wife and the odd behavior God commands His prophet to display in connection with it are made symbolic of God's purpose and plan for His people (Ezekiel 24:15–27). Abraham was asked to sacrifice his son, Isaac (Genesis 22:1–18), as a demonstration of his faith and also to picture the future sacrifice God makes by sending His own Son to die on the cross for the salvation of all His children.

Ultimately, after God has judged and punished this generation of His people, He will return to them and restore them to Himself and renew His covenant with them. God's promise to restore His people unto relationship with Himself is fulfilled, at least in large part, in the gathering of the Gentiles into the church after Pentecost (Romans 9:22–26). It is this promise of restoration that is prophetically enacted in Hosea's relationship with Gomer (Hosea 1:10–2:1).

Take It Home

Throughout all generations, God's people are called to examine themselves and their faith—to make their calling and election sure, to strive to be certain that they belong to the people of God, not only in an outward way, but essentially and eternally.

HOSEA 2:2–23

PUNISHMENT AND RESTORATION

Setting Up the Section

Hosea describes God's coming punishment of Israel for her sin, telling of God's wrath and anger and, ultimately, His saving love that brings about the restoration of His people.

2:2–13

HOSEA'S ANGRY GOD

The Old Testament prophets devote an immense amount of their preaching to what the modern church has neglected almost altogether: the judgment and the wrath of God. The centerpiece of the prophetical preaching is God's divine wrath against sin and the impending doom of those who betray His covenant and do not believe His Word. Hosea describes the punishment that God intends to put upon Israel in stark uncompromising terms: God will make Israel like a desert, blocking her path with thorn bushes; strip her naked; slay her with thirst; and ruin her vines and fig trees (2:2–13).

God wants His people to know the reality of His judgment and wrath and to attend to many false prophets in their thinking and living. The prophets of the Old Testament, like Christians today, had to contend with many whose messages were all sweet and lighthearted (Micah 2:11). Recognizing the reality of God's wrath toward sin helps make sense of a broken world, and accepting it spurs God's children to take their own lives more soberly. The suffering we experience in this world is the curse of God upon humanity because of rebellion against Him. The curses Hosea describes are the very curses God promised to visit upon His people if they betray His covenant with Israel in the days of Moses (Leviticus 26; Deuteronomy 28).

2:14–23

THE PROMISE OF RESTORATION

God promises a new and tender courtship of Israel and holds forth the possibility of bringing new life in their relationship through a return to the wilderness—a place where Israel had previously experienced both judgment and cleansing. This is intended to give hope that the coming punishment is not intended to ultimately hurt the nation but instead help them and restore them to a right relationship with God (2:14–15).

Like other prophets, Hosea foretells that the eventual consequence of God's wrath will be a restoration in which a new covenant will be written on the hearts of wayward Israel (Jeremiah 31:31–34; Ezekiel 36:26–27). The Valley of Achor (or Valley of Trouble) points back to Achan's sin of taking riches God had said were off-limits when the Israelites first took the promised land (Joshua 7:26). The Israel of Hosea's day has chased after the "gifts" of her lovers. But the grace of God will reverse the curse so that what was once a marker for sin becomes a door of hope (Hosea 2:15).

Israel's hope is found in what God is going to do in their hearts. They will forever banish the name Baal from their religious life. The term *Baal* literally means "master," and it was the term used for the false gods that the Canaanites worshiped. The Israelites' acceptance of this name for God began the process of compromise and the nation's fall.

What comes out of one's mouth is a representation of what is in the heart (Proverbs 13:3; 16:23). Thus by calling God *Baal*, they are in essence showing that they have given their hearts to false worship. Yet God will cleanse them, and they will address God in terms of a deep love relationship rather then abandoning Him in false worship. Israel will call God *husband*—a term of endearment and relationship. Thus the restoration will be great (Hosea 2:16–17).

Instead of the wilderness being a place where the wild animals are a threat and a danger to mankind, it now becomes a place where the animals themselves are brought into covenant relation with the redeemed people. What Hosea describes is a restoration of the creation order in which God is going to make all things new again (2:18). It is a vision of the new heavens and the new earth (Isaiah 11:6–7; Revelations 21:1).

Despite Israel's unfaithfulness, God is going to pursue her again, and this time the marriage covenant will be stronger—one that will bring an eternal relationship. This new covenant will be one in which love will rule. It is the beginning of an unprecedented relationship of love between God and His people. It is a new covenant.

God gives righteousness, justice, love, and compassion as the means by which He obtains His bride (2:19). It is God's righteousness and justice, not Israel's, that redeems her. God is the One who pays the price to make us His own. Faithfulness becomes the summary of the other four qualities in a single word (2:20). The unfailing goodness of God is the basis for Israel's salvation.

The goal of God's wooing of the people is that they will know Him. To know God implies the deepest relationship with Him. To know God is to love Him, to be one of His people, to abandon all other gods, and to be eternally committed to Him. What God is promising here is that Israel will be bound in an unbreakable covenant, and all the people from least to greatest will know Him.

God promises to reverse the famine of 2:9 by making what has become a wilderness a land that meets the needs of His people. God is going to respond to the people's call for help by providing for them. Jezreel, the name of Hosea's firstborn, had been a warning of brokenness for Israel (1:4–5), but now it implies salvation and prosperity. The name *Jezreel* literally means "God sows" (2:21–23).

Hosea concludes this promise with a final reversal: the reversal of the names Lo-ruhamah and Lo-ammi. God will have compassion on those who have not had compassion, and He will call those who are not His people to be His. The people's response ("You are my God") fulfills the prophecy of 2:20, that they will know the Lord, and reverses the rejection described in 1:9 ("I am not your God"). God will resolve all of the self-inflicted consequences for our sins. Rather than eternally punishing mankind, God has offered a way of salvation (2:23).

Take It Home

We are reminded by passages such as Hosea's that the stakes are high—heaven or hell (the love and favor of God or His wrath and curse; eternal life or everlasting doom). An understanding of the immensity of the issues of life or death should drive each of us to live a serious and self-examined life. In the end, our hope is in the Lord, who will renew our faith even in the midst of our own unfaithfulness.

HOSEA 3:1–5

RECONCILIATION

Love Covers a Multitude of Sins 3:1–5

Setting Up the Section

Hosea is called to reconcile with his wife despite her adultery. God draws a parallel between the story of Hosea's love for his wife and God's love for unfaithful Israel.

3:1–5

LOVE COVERS A MULTITUDE OF SINS

God requires Hosea to reclaim his wife, Gomer, though she is an adulteress (3:1). This command is extraordinary considering how seriously God takes faithfulness, but He gives Hosea a model in His own love for the unfaithful Israelites. The general view of this passage is that Hosea must purchase his wife, who is on sale as a slave, perhaps for debt. God describes how the Israelites were unfaithful to Him by loving sacred raisin cakes, which were used in the worship of false deities (Jeremiah 7:18). The Lord's love cannot be extinguished even by the people's outright apostasy (Hosea 3:1).

Hosea purchases Gomer with an assortment of items—fifteen shekels of silver and five bushels of barley—which demonstrates how he had to tap all of his resources to recover his unfaithful bride. Hosea initiates a period of discipline during which his wife will live with him for many days before the resumption of full marital relations (3:3). This interim is meant to signify the exile Israel has to undergo before the restoration in the last days (3:5). The word *return* is used repeatedly throughout Hosea's prophecy—a total of twenty-two times—and is a significant theme of the message. Like Gomer's return to Hosea, Israel's return to the Lord does not come without a cost and a period of purification and exile. Israel, like Hosea's wife, is ultimately restored to her true happiness with her rightful God through a miracle of God's grace.

HOSEA 4:1–19

THE CASE AGAINST ISRAEL

Setting Up the Section

Hosea lays out God's charges against Israel, describing the people's sinfulness and God's holiness.

4:1–3

THE WORD OF THE LORD

In this passage, Hosea is laying out a prophet lawsuit—a charge from the Lord that comes with evidence and judgment (4:1).

The charges are fairly straightforward and damning. "There is no faithfulness, no kindness, no knowledge of God in your land" (4:1 NLT; see Proverbs 24:2). There is instead plenty of transgression—cursing, lying, murder, stealing, adultery—that is already bringing about negative consequences for the people and even the land (Isaiah 33:9; Jeremiah 4:28). The land mourning is likely a reference to a drought (Hosea 4:3), and the death of the animals is mentioned in other Old Testament prophecies (see Jeremiah 4:25; 9:10).

4:4–19

THE PRIESTS' CULPABILITY

As it had been in 2:2, God's main point in this lawsuit against Israel is that the priests have forsaken their true calling and responsibility, and they are responsible for the spiritual defection of the people and the debacle that God is about to bring upon them for their breech of the covenant (4:4).

So far as it is possible to assign particular blame for Israel's apostasy, Hosea is willing to say it is the ministers' fault that the people will perish under God's judgment. The priests have led them astray, kept them from a true knowledge of God and His covenant, and have encouraged unbelief and disobedience. But God, in His holy vengeance, now intends to bring justice.

Hosea explicitly says that the priests have perverted the law of God. In fact, under their false teaching, Israel is perishing for lack of knowledge. No doubt that teaching included a great deal of paganism (drawn from the surrounding culture), a radical undermining of the authority of God's law, and a relaxing take on the standards of holiness God requires (4:5–6).

Hosea blames the priests because they bore the greatest responsibility for the spiritual life of the people of God. Their ministry of the Word and worship, or lack thereof, had a far greater influence upon the people—for good or for ill—than the ministry of any other. Sin multiplied under and among these false teachers (4:7–8).

Demystifying Hosea

Malachi provides what may be the Old Testament's most succinct description of the calling of a priest or a minister in the Lord's reminiscence of the priestly ministry of Aaron: "True instruction was in his mouth and nothing false was found on his lips. He walked with me in peace and uprightness, and turned many from sin" (Malachi 2:6 NIV). The priests of the northern kingdom in Hosea's day are the perfect antithesis of that description and therefore are the subject of God's stern rebuke and judgment.

This greater responsibility and consequent accountability does not absolve the rest of the Israelites. God will punish both the priests and the people for their wickedness (4:9). Like Gomer, the Israelites will give themselves over to prostitution. This part of the prophecy describes how God will punish the Israelites for their persistent unfaithfulness—through depriving them of prosperity and joy and by launching a full-scale attack on the Baal cult (4:10–14).

Hosea warns Judah (Israel's southern sister) not to follow Israel in the path to destruction (4:15–19). The use of the name *Ephraim*—in reference to Israel—signifies that because of their lack of allegiance to David, the northern kingdom does not even deserve to be called Israel (4:17). Themes of drunkenness and prostitution continue as Hosea presents God's case against His people (4:18).

Take It Home

Hosea teaches us that the spiritual health of the priests and ministers of God's message is a matter of great importance and bears directly on the spiritual health and well-being of the larger community. As a body of believers, we must support, encourage, and hold our leadership accountable to the Word of God. We must pray for our leaders, knowing that our spiritual journeys are intertwined, just as Moses prayed for Levi (Deuteronomy 33:11).

HOSEA 5:1–15

THE JUDGMENT

The Point of No Return 5:1–15

Setting Up the Section

One of the solemn messages Hosea and other Old Testament prophets are called to deliver is the terrible seriousness of rebellion against God. Not only will God's people someday have to give an account for their unfaithfulness, but there will also be immediate consequences for their rebellion.

5:1–15

THE POINT OF NO RETURN

Hosea calls again to get the people to listen—there is judgment against them, and God wants their full attention. These opening verses renew the fact that God is making a direct charge against Israel's leaders, the priests, and even the royal family (5:1–2). Tabor and Mizpah are places associated with worship of Baal. Legal imagery continues as well in the use of words like *judgment* and *testifies* (5:1, 5).

God sees everything and declares that Israel is corrupt, or unclean. This image points back to Hosea's unclean wife, whom God calls Hosea to love in spite of her unfaithfulness. The speaker in this verse can either be Hosea or Yahweh (5:3). Israel's sin is so tremendous that it prevents them from returning to God even if they want to, a concept that resurfaces in the New Testament (5:4; see Mark 3:29; 1 John 5:16).

God has even withdrawn from receiving the people's sacrifices. This is another of the curses that God long ago promised to visit upon those unfaithful to His covenant (Deuteronomy 31:18). The New Moon festivals that will devour the people and their fields (Hosea 5:7) likely refers to pagan rituals that are mentioned elsewhere (Isaiah 1:14).

Ephraim is reduced to waste, and Judah acquires a territory of Benjamin by military force (5:8–9). This action violates the sacred tribal land allotments which God's covenant had fixed and is what Hosea is probably talking about when he says Judah's leaders move boundary markers (5:10). These actions of violation provoke God's wrath (Proverbs 22:28).

God identifies Himself as the real threat to a sinful people floundering about in unfaithfulness (5:14). Not even their allegiances with Assyria will cause them as much oppression as their allegiance to idols (5:11). God is their judge and the only One who can save them from themselves (5:12–13). The consequences of the people's rebellion do not stop with destruction and despair. God withdraws Himself until they are able to repent of their sins (5:14–15).

Take It Home

The sins of Israel take hold because they are permitted to take hold. It becomes so much the habit of life as to make these people beyond the reach of even prophecies about their own destruction. These words call each of us to seriously examine our lives, to deal with sin as soon as we recognize it, and remember not to underestimate how far-reaching its affects can be. The psalmist reminds God's children: "We are the people he watches over, the flock under his care. If only you would listen to his voice today!" (Psalm 95:7 NLT).

HOSEA 6:1–11

ISRAEL REFUSES TO REPENT

Setting Up the Section

Most of Hosea's prophecy focuses on proving how Israel betrayed the Lord and His covenant and enumerating the curses which God is about to visit upon His people for their faithlessness and apostasy. Hosea also proclaims that after God is finished with His judgment, He will return to bless a future generation of His chosen people.

6:1–3

THE LORD PROMISES FORGIVENESS

Finally, in the midst of the despair of God withdrawing His life-giving presence from His people, there is a glimmer of hope and forgiveness. God will return to bless His people. Hosea has been hammering away at Israel with his message of doom and the grim promise that she is about to fall under God's unrelenting judgment. And now, in the next breath, Hosea proclaims the compassion and mercy of God and His willingness to forgive His people in defiance of the wrongs they have committed against Him.

Hosea does not contemplate that his contemporaries will dodge God's wrath—they will be judged. But at some point in the future, God will return to His people with grace. The *us* (6:1–3) refers not to Hosea's contemporaries but to people in a distant time in the future. Similarly, when God said to Israel in the wilderness in Deuteronomy 4 that He will send them into exile, He isn't referring to that very group of people but to people in a distant time.

God is a God of great mercy, and He will forgive and restore human beings to fellowship with Himself, even when they are guilty of every manner of sin against Him—if they will repent (6:1). Even when they have defied His grace, spurned His commandments, and abused His gifts, His grace reaches the heights and the depths. Just as Christ was raised on the third day, so the image of Israel's revival and restoration to live in God's presence is described (6:2). If there is anything that Israel can hope in—even in the midst of God's judgment—it is God's own merciful return (6:3).

Take It Home

In the midst of judgment, God's love shines like a beacon of hope. As great as Israel's sins are—and as great as our own—the mercy of the Almighty God will sweep them away like the coming of dawn if only they repent. God is a holy God who demands justice but who also delights in mercy and freely offers grace to His people. "Who is a God like you, who pardons sin and forgives the transgression of the remnant of his inheritance? You do not stay angry forever but delight to show mercy" (Micah 7:18 NIV). "May your unfailing love rest upon us, O LORD, even as we put our hope in you" (Psalm 33:22 NIV).

6:4–11

WORSHIP GONE WRONG

The tone shifts noticeably in verse 4 as Hosea returns to the main idea at hand for the Israelites—God's sorrow at their sin. God is suspicious of the people's love and desire to return to Him—their love is as ephemeral as the morning mist (6:4). God reminds them of what He has proclaimed through earlier prophets—that He requires more than empty promises and He desires acknowledgement of Himself (6:6). The word *mercy* in 6:6 is the same word rendered *love* in 6:4. In reference to God, this word translates to "grace" and "loving-kindness." But with reference to Israel, it refers to that love and loyalty that is their part of the covenant with God. Hosea's great point is that Israel has been disloyal to God and the covenant; she has failed to do her part.

Israel has come to think about her God, the living and true God who created all things and knows the hearts of His people, in the same way that the pagans around her think of their false gods and idols. The Israelites had come to believe that by offering sacrifices and performing rituals, they could ingratiate themselves with God and get Him to do good things for them, allowing them to live however they please. To worship God as Hosea's contemporaries worshiped God, with outward rituals but no inward devotion, is to be false to God. God is not interested in that kind of worship at all (6:6).

Just as God judged and banished Adam from the garden for breaking the covenant, God is banishing His people from the benefits of the covenant they have broken (6:7; see Joshua 23:16). Hosea provides a powerful image of a city "stained with footprints of blood" (6:8 NIV).

Israel has lost a sense of what worship is intended to be. Her worship had first become a true hypocrisy before it became naked paganism. Israel does not love God and does not care about what pleases Him. They leave their worship of God, do exactly as they please, commit whatever sins they desire to commit, and live between their trips to offer sacrifices a life of unrelieved disobedience and rebellion against God (6:9–10).

Take It Home

Worship is the true test of where a church, or any churchgoer, really stands before God. Worship is the test. Israel's worship had clearly gone far wrong (4:12–14). God demands more from us in our worship than just lip service. Israel's sin is the same one the Pharisees committed in Matthew 9:13. Outward rituals and religious formalities do not please God unless one's heart and life are aligned to His will.

HOSEA 7:1–16

ISRAEL'S GREAT CHALLENGE

Setting Up the Section

Hosea dwells on Israel's complete, final, and irreversible failure of faith. The people continue to be religious and call upon the Lord, but all the while they do not really put their trust completely in Him. God longs to redeem His people, but they persist in their sin. The great challenge for Israel is to admit that she has lost her faith and to return to God's truth.

7:1–8

LIVING BY SIGHT

Israel, on account of her disobedience and disloyalty to the Lord, is teetering on the brink of extinction. God's desire to "restore the fortunes" is a reference to the same healing and restoration of the covenant relationship described in 6:1 (6:11–7:2). It is the recovery anticipated in the New Year festival. Israel's real hope lies in the Sovereign God who knows how to deliver His people, as He has so often in the past. But instead of trusting in this, the people are putting faith in the sort of diplomatic maneuvering that never brings true success (7:1–2).

Israel's failure, Hosea says, is a failure of faith, and all of her terrible disobedience is evidence of the fact that she does not really believe in the Lord or trust in Him. Because their faith is weak, the Israelites continue to regularly and instinctively count more upon that which they can see and hear and touch than upon an unseen God. This faithlessness leads to a time of tumultuous political uncertainty (7:3–7).

7:9–16

BLIND TO THE TRUTH

Israel has for so long beckoned to the world of sight and ignored the unseen realities of the life of faith and of God's covenant, that she now has become totally blind and deaf to those realities. Her faith is so feeble that she is completely cut off from understanding what faith in God alone gives. No amount of evidence can make Israel realize what total folly she has chosen for herself (7:9–10).

Critical Observation

Israel persists in making terrible decisions that only further her destruction. Hosea pictures Ephraim in her clumsy waywardness like a dove flapping every which way (7:11). The context for what Hosea is referencing is the foreign policy decisions that Israel made to play off Egypt and Assyria (2 Kings 15:19–20; 17:3–6). Israel thinks she can find a way out of her mess, but God will see to it that all her plans are frustrated and that she gets what she deserves. He will not be mocked! Israel had hoped that Assyria or Egypt would be her savior, but lurching between the one and the other, she became hateful to both of them. Assyria will become her conqueror, and Egypt will make sport of her when she is destroyed.

The simple evidence is that Israel continues to maintain the pretence of faith in God without actually being sincere. The people do not think they are faithless—they pray and worship God. Yet Hosea says these actions are meaningless because of the intentions of their hearts to continue harboring sin. Everything we do is abundantly clear to God; He is not deceived by our calculations to look good. Just as God said to Samuel when He was anointing David king, "The Lord doesn't see things the way you see them. People judge by outward appearance, but the Lord looks at the heart" (1 Samuel 16:7 NLT).

God's revelation through Hosea concludes with another warning of final disaster and an implication that the nation will return to Egypt and God will no longer choose them to be His people (7:13–16). God is tired of the way He has been misrepresented—through lies, turning away, and evil plots (7:13–15). The wailing is a reference to the worship of Baal (see 1 Kings 18:28), and God calls them out on the duplicity of their cry for help, implying that the people are actually calling for Baal (7:14–15). Israel's arrogance and failure to call on the one true God makes them a laughingstock even among their enemies in Egypt (7:16).

Take It Home

Israel has become interested in pleasing people more than drawing near to the One who actually, and finally, holds their fortunes in His hands. They know that God is the only true deliverer, and yet they fail to practice daily on this knowledge. Their faith is so weak that they are more inclined to trust themselves and others than God. Like the Israelites of Hosea's day, our faith is weak. The greatest way for us to grow in grace is to seek God by practicing, nurturing, and exercising our faith in community, Bible study, and prayer.

HOSEA 8:1–14

REAP THE WHIRLWIND

Inevitable Judgment 8:1–14

Setting Up the Section

Hosea's prophecy continues to describe how Israel is about to reap the whirlwind of God's judgment for their unfaithfulness. His manner is serious and somber and sets the tone for the punishment to come in the chapters ahead.

8:1–14

INEVITABLE JUDGMENT

The theme of this chapter is to prepare Israel for the punishment that she is about to receive. The trumpet signals the approaching danger. The eagle is more accurately translated as a *griffon vulture*, which signifies that death is already settling over Israel and the birds of scavenging are taking their places (8:1). Israel's cries of acknowledgment in the midst of her unfaithfulness only serve to further arouse and inflame God's anger and judgment. The people refuse to turn to God; they have "rejected what is good" (8:2–3).

God reviews Israel's rebellious ways. She has set up kings and princes He does not approve of (8:4) and uses the treasures of the land to fashion idols of gold and silver that violate the covenant and bring destruction (8:5). Jeroboam I, the first king God had not appointed or anointed, also initiated the idolatrous cult. This example is a reality that both Hosea and the people know. The reference to the monarchy also signifies Israel's attempt to do without God.

The calf-idol of Samaria refers to the two calves at Bethel and Dan (1 Kings 12:28–30), and these man-made imposters will be destroyed just as they have brought about the destruction of Israel (8:5–6). The next set of verses is a return to Israel's political misdeeds, particularly their alliances with foreigners. Hosea quotes two proverbs—"sow the wind and reap the whirlwind" and "the stalk has no head, it will produce no flour" (8:7 NIV). These proverbs seem to underscore the inevitable judgment that Hosea is prophesying—events have been set in motion by Israel's disobedience (8:7).

Hosea continues to hammer home the punishment that awaits Israel for her unfaithfulness. She will be "swallowed up" by those she believes to be potential allies, and she is now considered worthless, for she has failed in her divine purpose (8:8). The image of Israel as a wild donkey underscores her aimlessness and isolation. The reference to selling herself to her lovers returns to the themes of prostitution from Hosea's early prophecy and further illuminates how desperate she has become (8:9). The result of Israel's unfaithfulness and sin is no longer something she can deny or avoid—she is no longer a nation and certainly not a nation worthy of being claimed as God's people. She has lost herself (8:10).

In the conclusion of this chapter, Hosea returns to enumerating Israel's religious misdeeds by describing how she has turned to other gods. Altars that were intended to cleanse the people from sin became, ironically, places where their sin increased as they misused them for Baal (8:11). Even God's guidebook to the people became indecipherable to their sinful hearts—seeming like a foreign thing (8:12). God gave His law to the people, but they came to think of it as strange and far removed from the real interests and issues of their lives. Israel has lost all true regard for the law of God and all true interest in keeping God's commandments. She has made a life's work of rebelling against that law and defying it at every turn.

Hosea promises doom to Israel for her disobedience, though all along she has claimed to believe in God. No one can ever save themselves by keeping the commandments of God; but it is just as true that everyone who is truly saved by the grace of God will practice obedience to His commandments. Jesus saves us in order to sanctify us, to make us holy—being obedient to God's law. He saves us to make us zealous for good works, and by *good works* He means all that we do in obedience to His commandments.

Hosea puts it bluntly: Israel has chosen for herself the path of disobedience to God's law, and God is now preparing her doom (8:13). Throughout the Bible, it is proclaimed from the rooftops that those who are truly the people of God will love and obey His law. Those who do not, whatever they may protest to the contrary—and Israel does protest her faith in God to the bitter end—will not be numbered among God's children and will not be spared His wrath in the Day of Judgment.

Again and again, Hosea says this: Israel calls upon the Lord to save her, but she will have God only on her own terms. She has no intention of living according to the commandments of God. She wants His forgiveness and His help, but she does not want to be ruled by Him and by His law. The name *Maker* for God refers to His election of Israel from among the nations, not their physical creation (8:14; see Psalm 100:3; Malachi 2:10).

God will not listen to the prayers nor will He accept the sacrifices of people who will not do what He says. He instead promises to send fire to consume their fortresses. God's judgment will include both Judah and Israel (8:14–15).

Take It Home

One idea that sometimes gets lost in Hosea's sobering prophecy of inevitable judgment is the truth that Israel has forgotten—that obedience to God leads to blessings in this life and the life to come. Hosea is full of this simple and happy truth. Hosea is here to remind the transgressors of what their choices are really reaping and also to remind them that the way of the Lord leads to great reward. God gives us His commandments because He loves us and knows what is best for us. The only absolutely reliable plan for the achievement of happiness and self-fulfillment is the plan for living by the law of God.

HOSEA 9:1–10:15

PUNISHMENT TO ARRIVE

Setting Up the Section

Israel tried to be like other nations by seeking to become wealthy by the same means that the nations used: the fertility cult. But Israel isn't like the other nations; Israelites are God's children, and God will not bless them to operate with this level of harlotry. When Israel embraces these pagan religious practices, they are acting in a way that is inconsistent with their own identity and calling.

9:1–17

NO REASON TO REJOICE

Israel's harvest has failed, and God commands them to stop rejoicing. Their harvest has failed because of their prostitution against God. When Hosea refers to "the wages of a prostitute at every threshing floor" (NIV), he is talking about the immoral acts that often accompany the party atmosphere at harvest in which sexual license is considered to encourage agricultural prosperity (9:1). The harvest they seek from this harlotry will not produce prosperity for the nation. In fact, their produce will not sustain them at all. God will keep the product of their harlotry from feeding the nation (9:2).

Not only is God going to prevent the harvest from sustaining the nation, but He will also drive Israel from the land. Because they have defiled themselves, they will be unfit for residence in the holy land and will instead eat defiled food in a foreign land (9:3).

They have no offerings to give that are suitable for use in worship. Because of their harlotry and the consequence that is coming, there is no sacrifice that will be acceptable to God (9:4). The "bread of mourners" refers to the fact that those who are in mourning, and who must deal with the burial of a dead body, contaminate the food they touch. Therefore, such bread is unfit for offering to God (see Deuteronomy 26:12–14).

Israel has embraced false worship and rejected God. Though they have maintained a form of ceremonial worship, they have nothing to recommend themselves to God. No matter how much they adhere to the proper forms, it is not a worship that brings glory to God (9:5). The people are suffering from the plight of famine—the food is unfit to offer to God because of its poor quality and because it comes from an environment where death and contact with the dead are common. The people, devastated, will go down to Egypt, just as Abraham did, to find relief. The famine-ravaged Israelites will seek deliverance in Egypt and will not find it (9:6).

Critical Observation

Memphis (9:6) is the Greek name for the Egyptian Mamphta, which is the capital of Egypt at this time (Isaiah 19:13; Jeremiah 2:16; 44:1; 46:14; Ezekiel 30:13). Its name means "the dwelling of Phta," the Greek Vulcan. In it is the well-known court of Apis. There, in the home of the idol to whom the rebellious Israelites look for refuge, they will be gathered to be buried. This place is a favorite burial place of the Egyptians. Hence the place of their refuge is the place of their destruction.

The false prophets had continually deceived the people, promising them that days of destruction will never come. They have escaped this day of judgment for only so long, but now it is upon them. In God's purpose, the days of judgment are inevitable. Hosea gives to the false prophets the title which they claim for themselves: "the prophet" and "the man of the spirit" (ESV). Yet, these prophets are not God's men, and they do not have the Spirit of God in them. They are mad and crazy prophets who speak destructive lies to the people. They lead the people astray (9:7–8).

The reference to Gibeah brings us back to Judges 19–21, in which a Levite's concubine is raped and murdered at Gibeah. The Levite, to obtain vengeance, cuts her body into twelve pieces and sends the pieces to the tribes of Israel to provoke their outrage. This begins a civil war and a series of grotesque atrocities. Hosea declares that the people of his day have fallen to the level of this most corrupt generation of Israel's history. They are just as judged by God (9:9).

One does not expect to find edible grapes in the desert, and such a discovery would make a real feast for a traveler. Similarly, the firstfruits of a fig tree in spring would be especially delicious to people in the ancient world. The point of both metaphors is that Israel in her youth was a special source of delight to God, yet something happened. The people went to Baal Peor and consecrated themselves to shame. Just like fruit going bad, the people, upon arrival in Israel, gave themselves over to Baal and became a stench to the One who loves them (9:10).

Demystifying Hosea

Baal Peor was the location of a shrine to Baal in the plains of Moab, some twelve miles northeast of the Dead Sea (Numbers 25:1–9). After Balaam failed to bring a curse down on Israel, the Israelites brought one down on themselves by yielding to the temptation to have sexual relations with Moabite women. A plague began in Israel, and the plague did not come to a stop until the priest Phinehas took a spear and ran it through the bodies of an Israelite man and a Moabite woman. By calling the attention of Israel to this, the people will see that their apostasy to Baal began before they entered the promised land.

Ephraim's glory will depart. As a sign of judgment, they will not be able to have children. Since children are a sign of God's blessing, God will remove the ability to be fertile. Instead of the blessing of children, Israel will bear the consequence of their sin (9:11–12).

God formed this nation to be strong and glorious, planted in a great meadow. Yet, instead of growing and becoming strong, they are leading their children out to slaughter. Rather than growing, they are acting like those who worship Baal and thus killing their children. Just as those who worship Baal sacrifice their children to him, Israel is now doing the same (9:13).

Israel had attributed their fertility to Baal, and now barrenness is the only appropriate judgment. Since they turned to Baal for life, the only logical consequence is for God to give them over to death. Thus, God will remove the fertility of the land (9:14).

Gilgal is the prototypical city of Israel—it contains every evil that the book of Hosea condemns. Gilgal is the city that prompts Yahweh to declare Israel His enemy. Gilgal is described as a cult center in 4:15 and 12:11. The rebellion that is here is so hated by God that He is going to drive the people out of the land and punish all the leaders who have led Israel into such apostasy (9:15).

Israel is so cursed that life will not be given to them. God will show them how cursed they are as a nation. They will be wanderers among the nations—exiled and forced to live as aliens and strangers in the world. They will lose their blessing, their home, and their fertility. In short, they will live cursed because they have rejected God and turned to Baal (9:16–17).

10:1–15

THE CONSEQUENCES OF SIN

Israel and her reach are compared to a spreading vine (10:1), a metaphor that Jesus Himself used when describing the life of God's children. The message from Hosea is that in the midst of their prosperity, Israel grew unfaithful to her God and thus "must bear their guilt" (10:2). Hosea predicts the destruction of both the kings and the cults that have failed Israel so miserably (10:3–7). And Israel will be so distraught and desperate that, in the absence of both their false saviors, they will cry out to the mountains to cover them up and for the earth itself to consume them (10:8).

God is in control and will give Israel what she deserves—divine judgment. It is not what God wants to do, but it is what Israel has sown with her wicked ways. The Bible is full of conditional statements like the ones here in 10:12–13. The prophet says that if Israel will trust and obey the Lord, the nation will prosper; but because she has disobeyed Him and His covenant, she is suffering and faces destruction.

Long before, when God made His covenant with Israel during the days of Moses, He had promised them that if they fully obey Him, they will be set high above all the nations and all manner of blessing will be poured out upon them. But, at the same time, the Lord promised Israel that if she betrays His covenant and proves disloyal to Him, then He will curse her and deprive her of all of those blessings (10:10–13).

The Bible is full of declarations having to do with sowing and reaping (10:12). The book of Proverbs is devoted to the theme that godly living brings blessing and prosperity and that sinful living brings ruin. In this chapter, Hosea is reminding Israel that her suffering is a result of her disobedience to God.

Critical Observation

Hosea does not say, nor does the rest of the Bible, that all of these consequences are to be visited upon the Israelites immediately. God brings the fruits of faith or unbelief to light in His own timing. Hosea's own ministry stretched over twenty or thirty years, and when he began to preach Israel's doom, she remained for some time a nation at peace and enjoyed an almost unprecedented prosperity. Only slowly, during the course of Hosea's life and work, did the judgment he prophesied begin to appear. And, of course, Israel had been in deep rebellion against the Lord for two centuries prior to Hosea's ministry.

Scripture measures blessedness and punishment in different ways than mankind is accustomed to measuring these things. To be holy and near to God, and to have one's life blessed by salvation, are the markers of true life (1 Timothy 6:19). And these joys are so strong and so great that they can lift even a much-afflicted life right out of the sorrows and pains of this world.

Hosea prophesies doom for Israel on account of her betrayal of the covenant, but the doom she suffers at the hands of Assyrian armies is but a foretaste of the judgment that awaits. The blessing that God promises to lavish on those who love and serve Him, though rich beyond words in this world, is rich beyond thought in the world to come. You will never take the measure of what faith brings or what unbelief brings until you see the full issue of each in the next world (10:14–15).

Take It Home

Does God really mean that if we are faithful we will prosper and if we are not we will suffer? If it is for the nation of Israel, is it true for all of God's children? We must trust that the ways of the Lord bring blessing (Psalm 1). Yet we also know that in this life we will encounter trials of many kinds, just as Jesus Christ did (James 1:1–3), and we should not assume that trials or suffering are consequences of our own sin (consider Job; Psalm 73; Matthew 5). Even in the midst of a suffering world and our own suffering, the joy of the Lord and His banner of love over His children preserve and protect in this world and in the world to come (Revelation 22:1–7). This is the reason for the hope that is within us (1 Peter 3:15).

HOSEA 11:1–12

GOD'S DISPLEASURE

Setting Up the Section

This chapter draws heavily on two components of Israel's history: the Exodus and the destruction of Sodom and Gomorrah.

11:1–5

REVISITING THE EXODUS

Hosea warns that God will undo Israel's exodus and send His people to a new Egypt (Assyria) and into servitude to a new pharaoh (the Assyrian king). The childhood of Israel refers to the occasion when Israel was first in Egypt (11:1; see Exodus 4:22). The metaphor of Israel as God's son is distinct from the earlier terminology (Hosea 1:10) that describes the people as God's children and the corporate nation as God's adulterous wife (1:2). By calling Israel a son, God is making the point that He trained them and gave them what they needed to serve Him and do His work. This description highlights the rebellion of Israel. Another reason the reference works is because this text is used to refer to Jesus' move from Egypt back to Israel (Matthew 2:15). The uniqueness of referring to Israel as a son here is God's way of doing two things in this text: highlighting Israel's sin and foreshadowing a picture of the Messiah.

Critical Observation

Many scholars have observed that Jesus' fulfillment of Hosea 11:1 corresponds to the typology that one finds throughout Matthew, in which Jesus recapitulates the story of Israel in the way that He lived His life. Jesus spends forty days in the wilderness, just as Israel is there forty years. Jesus gives His law on a mountain, just as God gives the law at Mount Sinai. Jesus miraculously feeds His followers in the wilderness, just as Moses gives the people manna. Jesus has to walk in the path of Israel without sin so that He can be proven worthy to take the penalty for mankind.

If you look at the history of Israel, you see how through the centuries the people disregarded the prophets' messages. The more God spoke, the more they rebelled. The more God revealed Himself, the more they ran from Him. From the moment they left Egypt, they were fighting against the will and plan of God, seeking to do things their own way. The text continues to reflect upon what God did for Israel to care for the people. God cared for the needs of the nation—describing Israel as His child and His animal. Yahweh fed Israel throughout the Exodus (11:2–4). Hosea warns that the Exodus will be undone and Israel will return to its former condition of slavery. Yet this time the captivity will not be in Egypt but in Assyria (11:5).

11:6–12

LESSONS FROM THE PAST

Hosea turns to another example from Israel's past—one of judgment and not redemption: the story of God's destruction of Sodom and Gomorrah. Under Assyrian domination, Israel will become like the cities that were eternally annihilated because of their rebellion against God. The image of the sword slashing through the bars probably means that when the Assyrians come, they will put an end to the boasting of the Israelites and destroy all of their vain attempts at securing their own future. All the things that they once trusted in, and all their self-focused wisdom, do nothing for them. They cannot protect themselves from what is coming (11:6).

The Israelites are deepening their rebellion against God. The reality is that the more they deepen their rebellion, the more they depend upon false religious practices to get them through. Therefore, there will not be the type of deliverance that God had provided in the past. They will feel the sting of this rebellion (11:7).

The mood of the text changes abruptly when God reveals His heart. Like a father who is facing the rebellion of a strong-willed child, God puts on the table the conflicting feelings of His love and His anger. In verse 8, He is seeking to resolve His compassion for Israel and the punishment demanded by their sin. This text is metaphorical, as God shows His love in terms that human minds can understand. God has very real feelings about the horrendous nature of sin. Zeboiim and Admah, together with Bela, are the other cities of the plain in the same region as Sodom and Gomorrah (Genesis 14:2). These cities represent the depravity that God destroyed (Genesis 19; Deuteronomy 29:23). God mentions them as a way to get the attention of the Israelites.

Hosea presents Israel as a city in danger of repeating the history of Sodom, Gomorrah, and the cities of the plain. When God says He will not unleash His anger, it does not mean that Ephraim is going to escape punishment. Rather, it means that God will not give full vent to His fury, as He did in the case of Sodom. In other words, Israel will not suffer the total, irreversible annihilation that Sodom experienced (11:9).

Hosea uses an intense image to talk of the restoration of Israel—he describes God as a lion with a mighty roar. Yet, this roar will not be to destroy Israel but to restore it. The image, like many in the prophets, is disorienting: A lion roars and the birds come to it rather than flee (11:10–11; see Numbers 24:8–9). Hosea's point here is that there is to be a new exodus in which God will again play the part of the lion and deliver His people from their enemies and into a new land. This call will bring them back. Israel will no longer be a silly dove wandering to and fro (7:11). This foretells of the day when the people will return not only from Egypt and Assyria but also from the west, the regions around the Mediterranean (11:10–11).

HOSEA 12:1–13:16

LESSONS FROM HISTORY

Setting Up the Section

Hosea continues his meditation on the history of Israel's relationship to God—tracing the nation's sin and how it has provoked God's judgment.

12:1–14

ISRAEL'S SIN

Hosea persists in employing legal language to describe God's case against Israel—laying out God's charge against Israel (12:2). Hosea brings up examples from Israel's past, as well as Judah's, in which Jacob rebelled and wrestled to get his way (12:3–5). Hosea returns again to his crucial themes of love, justice, and patience, commanding Israel to return to the Lord in repentance as Jacob did (12:6).

The Lord unmasks Israel's pride through Hosea and warns His children never to imitate Israel in her fundamental and tragic blasphemy. God shows through Israel what pride can do and, by recording it in scripture, warns His children to stand against it. Israel's spiritual pride is plain dishonesty. It is the big lie of Israel's life. Pride is false security. Ephraim has boasted and taken credit for her economic prosperity, luxurious lifestyle, and success, when in fact it is God's favor she has enjoyed (12:8).

God shifts the focus of His complaints from the Exodus and pre-exodus to the message of the prophets. Hosea will pick up this shift in the opening of his next complaint (12:12–13). Once again, God declares that He will undo the Exodus and return Israel to the status of no longer being a nation. God speaks of a return to wilderness rather than a return to slavery. God asserts His sovereignty over them. The feast referred to in this text is the Feast of Tabernacles, or Booths (Leviticus 23:33–44). This verse looks ahead to the time when Israel's people will be scattered from their homeland (Hosea 12:9).

God's complaint has shifted to how Israel is presently ignoring His warnings—even the ones His prophet Hosea is speaking. God is warning the people, albeit sometimes in puzzling forms (visions and parables), but they are too rebellious to listen to the warnings (12:10). The obvious answer to God's rhetorical question (12:11) is that there is nothing besides sin in Gilead. *Gilead* represents all the country east of the Jordan, and *Gilgal* represents the land west of the Jordan. They both have sinned and sacrificed to Baal. And in both, God has shown forth His mercies.

Critical Observation

Hosea returns to the story of Jacob by citing incidents from Jacob's life in order to make a comparison between the patriarch and his descendants. Hosea compares Jacob's experience to the Exodus and to the ministry of the prophets. First, both Haran and Egypt are foreign lands that serve as places of refuge. Second, Jacob works like a slave for a ruthless master. In the same way, the Israelites are enslaved by Pharaoh. Just as God creates a situation in which Laban is eager to have Jacob leave (Genesis 31:1–14), God delivers Israel from the Egyptians, who are also ready to be rid of Israel after God afflicts Egypt with plagues. In both cases, the Israelites depart with the wealth of their hosts. The prophet who brings Israel out of Egypt and guards them through the wilderness is no doubt Moses (Hosea 12:12–13).

Yet, Ephraim has continually rebelled against the Lord. Hosea asserts that Ephraim has *provoked* God, a term that implies exasperating God through worshiping idols and placing one's heart away from God. These crimes are worthy of capital punishment. They will have to pay the penalty for this rebellion. Idol worship is the worst offense to God. God wants to be worshiped solely. Anything less is a provocation toward Him (12:14).

13:1–16

GOD'S ANGER AGAINST ISRAEL

God continues to describe His people's unfaithfulness in terms of their idolatry. He recognizes that despite the consequences of their sin, they persist in it by making even more idols. He compares them to the morning mist, suggesting that rather than preserving them and making them a great nation as He promised to Abraham, they will surely pass away (13:1–3).

Israel is too proud to be saved, and the wrath of God is surely coming upon them. This is the culmination of Hosea's message of doom—and it describes the destruction of Israel in no uncertain and seemingly final terms. God recounts the many ways that He has been faithful in providing for and working out the Israelites' salvation—bringing them out of Egypt, caring for them in the desert, and feeding them (13:4–5).

Yet the Israelites grow proud and forget God. This is their deadly sin. Israel's chief problem is not idolatry—that is only an aftereffect. The people worship idols because they make no room for a God who deserves their loyalty and devotion. But the God of Abraham, Isaac, and Jacob demands that Israel acknowledge no one (not even Israel herself) but Him. For the nation to worship God, she would have to stop worshiping herself, and this she could not do (13:6).

God will not be mocked. The Lord had warned Israel that this would happen if she broke the covenant (Deuteronomy 6:10–12; 8:17–18). If we forget to be grateful to God for the blessings of our lives, He will take what He has given us "like a bear robbed of her cubs" (13:7–8).

The Lord solemnly makes the point and swears that Israel's boasting will be overturned, her cities in ruins, and her security gone. This is the tragedy of pride (13:9–16).

The God who gives can take away, and the God who gives and is not properly acknowledged promises to take away as part of His judgment upon dishonesty and ingratitude. This, then, is the Lord's warning through Hosea, His prophet: Pride is a hopeless illusion that will certainly be shattered (13:10–13).

Scholars disagree over the precise meaning of the ransom described by God. Some suggest that it points ahead to Christ paying the ransom for His people (13:14; see 1 Corinthians 15:55). However, in Hosea's context, those factors are in the future. Ultimately the Lord decides against paying the ransom, declaring that He will have no compassion. The images in the final verses of Hosea are truly ghastly—the people will bear their guilt, and even little ones and pregnant women will be subject to the violence (13:16).

HOSEA 14:1–9

BLESSING FROM REPENTANCE

Setting Up the Section

Following the total disaster and judgment described in the previous chapter, Hosea ends with the blessing and hope that his own story—of loving restoration of his unfaithful wife Gomer—parallels. Hosea's vision of Israel's restoration is partial.

14:1–3

RETURN TO GOD

Hosea is still desperate to have Israel hear God's plea to return to Him. He reiterates the theme of the book—that their sins have been their downfall—and encourages them to turn to God in repentance (14:1–2). Hosea's last chapter is a reprise of a main theme of his preaching from the very beginning of the book: It is a call to repentance, an invitation to Israel to repent of her sins (14:2–3).

As Hosea has already declared, God demands sincerity of heart. Repentance is not merely the recognition of one's own sin. It will not be enough for Israel to recognize that she has disobeyed the Lord and betrayed His covenant. Even Pharaoh confessed that he had sinned in not letting Israel go from Egypt after the plague of hail. But he did not really repent. Repentance, as God requires it, is not merely sorrow and remorse for sin. Judas was so overcome by sorrow when the enormity of his betrayal of the Lord Jesus came home to him that he committed suicide, but he had no repentance.

Critical Observation

Repentance begins with a change of mind and heart about sin. Sin becomes not a thing to be loved but a thing to be abominated. In Psalm 51, David expresses the mind of every man or woman whom the Spirit of God has brought to a true repentance. Repentance wants nothing so much as to be right with God and to walk with God. Repentance is a turning away from sin to God for pardon and forgiveness. True repentance is always the fruit of a genuine faith in Christ, and it is called into being by the wonderful discovery that there is forgiveness with God. Indeed, there is no real repentance ever in the heart of a person who does not think that his sin can be removed and forgiven. Israel must believe that nothing besides God can save her (14:3). Repentance is a change of will and behavior—just as Israel denounces her sin, she also draws near to God, in whom the fatherless find compassion.

14:4–9

GOD'S RESPONSE

Hosea declares that repentance is just the beginning of a great new adventure with God. God will heal Israel's waywardness and love them freely, and Israel will blossom like a flower (14:4–5). It is a beautiful picture to end a serious and solemn prophecy (14:6–8).

The final verse of Hosea is an editorial note, reminding the reader to take careful heed of the message of the book and repeating that message succinctly (14:9). The Lord Himself echoes Hosea's last word in John 15:5 when He says "Those who remain in me, and I in them, will produce much fruit" (NLT).

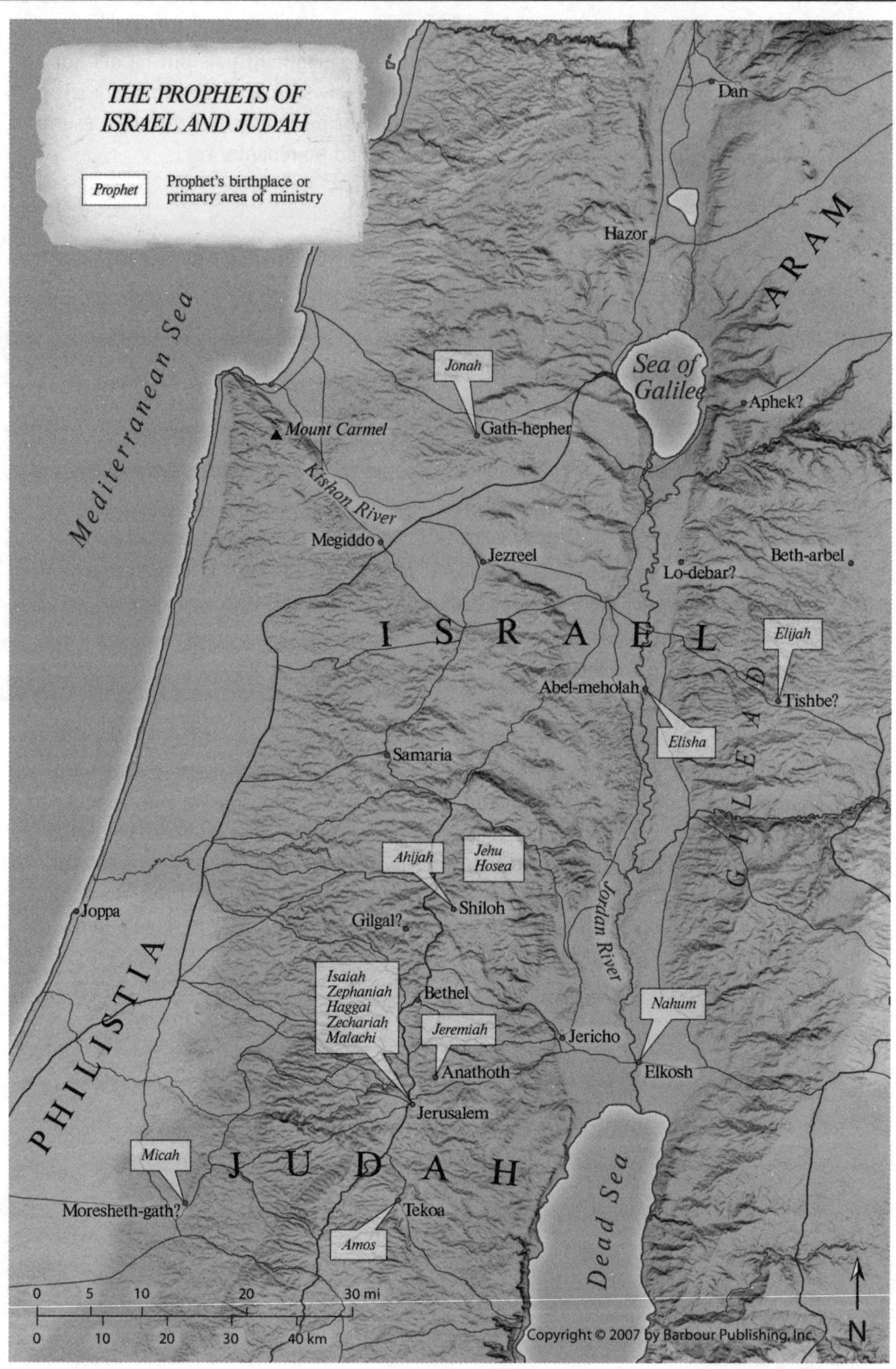
THE PROPHETS OF ISRAEL AND JUDAH
Prophet
Prophet's birthplace or primary area of ministry
Mediterranean Sea
Dan
Hazor
ARAM
Sea of Galilee
Aphek?
Jonah
Mount Carmel
Gath-hepher
Kishon River
Megiddo
Jezreel
Lo-debar?
Beth-arbel
ISRAEL
Elijah
Abel-meholah
Tishbe?
Elisha
GILEAD
Samaria
Ahijah
Jehu
Hosea
Shiloh
Joppa
Gilgal?
Jordan River
Isaiah
Zephaniah
Haggai
Zechariah
Malachi
Bethel
Jeremiah
Jericho
Nahum
PHILISTIA
Anathoth
Elkosh
Jerusalem
Micah
JUDAH
Dead Sea
Moresheth-gath?
Tekoa
Amos
0 5 10 20 30 mi
0 10 20 30 40 km
N
Copyright © 2007 by Barbour Publishing, Inc.

JOEL

INTRODUCTION TO JOEL

The book of Joel is an intriguing book, beginning with the fact that we know little about the author, his historical time frame, or even whether he was writing to the northern kingdom of Israel or the southern kingdom of Judah. We are left, then, with the words themselves—the brute force of the message of the divine author.

We may be unaware of the specifics of Joel's personal information or the audience to whom he writes, yet he delivers the message of God with boldness and clarity.

AUTHOR

Joel (meaning "Jehovah is God") is a popular name in the Old Testament, with a dozen other men bearing the same name. However, little is known about the prophet Joel.

PURPOSE

Joel writes in response to a devastating attack by locusts. But the destructive insects are described as an invading army, symbolizing the potentially greater destruction awaiting those who do not heed the words of the prophet and repent. Then, beyond the immediate situation in the land, Joel writes of the Day of the Lord, when judgment will come to the enemies of God's people and Israel will eventually be restored.

THEMES

The Day of the Lord—a time, known only to God, when He will exact judgment on the nations—is a key theme throughout Joel. The concept encompasses other related themes, including the need for repentance, the certainty of coming judgment, and eventual redemption and restoration for the people of God.

HISTORICAL CONTEXT

Without any references to specific events, it is difficult to put Joel's message into a specific historical context. Some people cite the enemies of Judah that are listed (Egypt, Edom, Philistia, and Phoenicia [3:4, 19]) and suggest an early, pre-exilic date for the book. But with no mention of the northern kingdom and a specific reference to Greece (3:6), others feel the book must have been written much later—and was perhaps the last of all the Old Testament prophetic books. So, proposed dates of writing can vary by as much as six or seven centuries.

CONTRIBUTION TO THE BIBLE

Perhaps the most well-known use of Joel's prophecies is on Peter's lips on the Day of Pentecost, when the Holy Spirit comes upon the church. Joel's insight into the fresh manner in which God's Spirit will interact with human beings is a tremendous contribution to scripture (2:28–32; Acts 2:14–21).

OUTLINE

JOEL 1:1–2:11

DESTRUCTION: PRESENT AND FUTURE

Setting Up the Section

The terrible arrival of a swarm of locusts is the catalyst for Joel's writing. In his opening section, he responds to the great destruction, calling on the people to mourn. Such a sobering event should also remind them that an even worse time of suffering is in store for those who refuse to humble themselves before God.

1:1–12

THE PRESENT DESTRUCTION

It may seem slightly disconcerting that the exact nature of the problem taking place in Joel is unclear, but the terrible situation is only going to get worse. Wave after wave of locusts have overrun the nation's crops (1:4), and that is in addition to a drought (1:10–12).

For a nation characterized as drunkards (1:5), the loss of the grape harvest is particularly disheartening. Along with the failure of all the other crops (wheat, barley, fig, pomegranate, apple, and so forth), the situation is indeed dire. A disaster of this magnitude had not been witnessed by recent generations (1:2–3). The locusts are described as a lion-like nation with such numbers that they cannot be counted, invading without mercy (1:6–7)

Demystifying Joel

It is rather common in scripture (as well as in other ancient literature) to read of invading armies described as swarms of locusts. In Joel's case, it appears he has reversed the imagery. He describes a literal invasion of locusts in terms of a human army attacking (1:6–7). As far as the effects on an agrarian society, locusts could be every bit as merciless and cruel as enemy soldiers.

Joel addresses the elders of the nation (1:2) because they should have borne a special responsibility to clothe themselves with humility before God and seek His mercy on behalf of the people. Yet they are the ones who have allowed the spiritual state of the nation to decline, so they probably feel the effects of the crisis just as much as anyone. All the priests can do is mourn; the daily grain and drink offerings have been suspended during the crop failure and drought (1:8–9). All previous sources of joy have withered away (1:12).

1:13–2:11

THE FUTURE DESTRUCTION

Joel exhorts the priests to demonstrate appropriate behavior, considering the situation they are in. They are to dress for mourning—in dark, rough sackcloth rather than their usual clothing. Instead of offering their usual prayers, they are to wail (1:13). Then they are to prepare the people: Declare a fast and call an assembly. The nation as a whole is to cry out to God together (1:14). Joel will soon clarify that it isn't the actions being taken that will appease the wrath of God but rather the proper attitudes by the people (2:12–13).

He describes a future destruction that he identifies as "the day of the LORD" (1:15), which he says is approaching. Joel will use this phrase several times in his short book, as do numerous other prophets. It refers to a time, known only to God, when He will exact judgment on the nations. The event will trigger much great suffering, although the end result will be the deliverance and restoration of those who remain faithful. The precise timing of that day remains a mystery. But as the people begin to attempt to cope with the devastation resulting from the locusts, their fear and confusion should put them in a somber state to ponder the severity of the Day of the Lord.

Critical Observation

The Hebrew words for *almighty* and *destruction* sound quite similar, so Joel's statement in verse 15 has added impact. Specific historic events are associated with the Day of the Lord, including Israel's fall to Assyria and Babylon's subsequent conquest of Judah.

This is a time for the people of God to come before Him with the truth. It is a time to speak to Him about their trials and to acknowledge Him as the only One who can ever provide food, shelter, safety, and joy. Such an acknowledgment should occur *before* disaster strikes, but even in the depths of their despair, God's people can call on Him for help. No such help can be found from any other source (1:16–20).

When Joel writes of *fire* (1:19–20), it is probably used as a metaphor. Perhaps the locusts are portrayed as a fire that devours all the nation's crops. Or maybe he intends to acknowledge the accompanying drought. In the heat of the Middle East, when water is short, it doesn't take long for the land to dry out and become unable to sustain plant growth—essentially the same result as fire.

Scholars are divided as to what Joel really means when he warns about the Day of the Lord and the invading army. Some believe that he continues using the army metaphor to describe actual locusts. Others think that as he begins to say more about the Day of the Lord, he speaks of a conflict involving human armies. If that is the case, the shift is subtle as his description of insect devastation in chapter 1 sets up the image of an even worse catastrophe to follow.

Either way, the coming event is in relation to the Day of the Lord. It will be a day of darkness, gloom, clouds, and blackness, and it will involve the encroachment of the largest army ever seen. At first it will be the sheer size that is noticeable: The army will appear "like dawn spreading across the mountains" (2:1–2 NIV). Only later will people realize, as Joel reveals, that this is the Lord's army with forces "beyond number" (2:11 NIV).

Demystifying Joel

Even for those who want to understand this army as a continuation of Joel's description of literal locusts, it is fair to consider it the Lord's army. Just as other prophets explain that the Assyrian and Babylonian armies had acted to fulfill the will of God, so, too, will this army of locusts.

The analogy to locusts is a fitting one. The land will lie beautiful and plush, so much so that it is compared to the Garden of Eden, but by the time the army has passed through, all that will be left is a desert wasteland. Again, a comparison to fire is appropriate to describe utter loss (2:3).

The appearance of this army will stun those who see it. The noise and destruction will dishearten all observers. Nothing can be done to stop its progress. It is described as marching straight ahead, plunging through defenses, scaling walls, and even entering private homes. The impact of the aggression will shake the earth. In response, entire nations will be in anguish and become pale with fear (2:4–11).

In this sense, the Day of the Lord will indeed be "dreadful" (2:11 NIV). And Joel's question ("Who can endure it?") must have seemed unanswerable to those hearing his description of things to come. Thankfully, Joel doesn't stop here. He provides an answer in the following section.

JOEL 2:12–32

SURVIVING THE DESTRUCTION

A Call to Return to the Lord	2:12–17
The Short-Term Result	2:18–27
The Long-Range Result	2:28–32

Setting Up the Section

After a rather distressing section pertaining to a current plague of locusts and an even worse similar scourge to come, in this section Joel at last offers some hope to the readers and listeners. Yes, the coming Day of the Lord will be dreadful, but there are things the people can do to avoid its potentially terrifying consequences.

2:12–17

A CALL TO RETURN TO THE LORD

When the Day of the Lord arrives, there is nothing people can do to stop God's judgment. However, it is never too late for *God* to act. Speaking through His prophet, God provides a note of hope for those remaining in a situation that appears completely hopeless. He invites the wayward people to return to Him "even now" (2:12). However, such a return will accomplish nothing if it is based on hypocrisy or empty ceremony. God knows the hearts of people and sees through insincerity.

The people are called to return to God with all their hearts—weeping, fasting, and mourning. However, God cares little for their outward expressions of sorrow, per se. He is more intent on seeing humbled hearts than torn clothing. And God reminds His people that He is gracious, compassionate, slow to anger, and abounding in love. He doesn't *want* to send calamity on those who claim to be His people. Perhaps He will put off their impending doom (2:12–14).

In addition, the people are told to gather in a sacred assembly that should take priority over everything else. Nursing children are to attend, as are newlyweds. The priests can then intercede for the people (as should have been their role all along). The people will be reminded that their prior refusal to act as if they belonged to God has left surrounding nations with the wrong impression. When God disciplines His people for their defiant behavior, outside observers will see the consequences and perceive the Lord's corrective judgment as His absence. They will doubt the power and the concern of Israel's God, and they will scoff at His people (2:15–17).

2:18–27

THE SHORT-TERM RESULT

Joel calls the people to repent—young and old, priest and populace. In return, the Lord promises to respond dramatically and bountifully. He will hear their cries and take pity on His people who have no other recourse than His mercy. He will bless their land far beyond their expectations, including ample new grain, wine, and oil. He will protect them from foreign threats. Rather than Israel being an object of scorn, it will be the other nations who falter and fall (2:18–20).

Critical Observation

The locust invasion previously described by Joel gives more impact to what he writes here about the smell arising from a retreating army (2:20). Historic accounts tell of enormous locust swarms that flew out to sea, drowned, washed up on shore, and created a terrible stench.

God will replace His people's fear with gladness and rejoicing. He will send rain and make the ground fruitful again. He will restore what the locust horde had destroyed, promising that the people will eat plentifully and be satisfied. Here, as in other places throughout scripture, rain is perceived as the blessing of God (2:21–24).

As terrible as the losses had been that resulted from the locusts, the land will recover and the people will be able to eat their fill. In return, they will praise the Lord and have a greater awareness that only He is truly God (2:25–27).

In spite of the people's previous sins, God will temper His judgment with mercy and compassion. His people will not be destroyed. It is terrific news for those who appeared to be doomed. Yet even better news is promised for the future.

2:28–32

THE LONG-RANGE RESULT

The date of these future events is left a mystery. God's promise of the future will come "afterward" (2:28). As it turns out, some of Joel's prophecy from this section will be remembered and applied in connection with the arrival of the Holy Spirit on Jesus' followers shortly after the Lord's death and resurrection (Acts 2:14–21).

God speaks through His prophet of a great day to come, when His Spirit will pour out—not just upon Israel but also on all faithful believers (Joel 2:28). The power of God will be felt by young and old, men and women. God's plan will be known through dreams, visions, and prophecies (2:28–29). When that day arrives, the effect will be so dramatic that onlookers will presume the recipients of God's Spirit are drunk (Acts 2:13).

Demystifying Joel

When Joel 2 is quoted by Peter (Acts 2:17–21) and Paul (Romans 10:13), it becomes clear that the ultimate fulfillment of the prophecy will be a *heavenly* Jerusalem and Mount Zion. And from the New Testament perspective, another important detail is drawn out of the shadows and brought into clear light: The Lord Jesus Christ is the Son of God who died on the cross for sinners and rose again. He is the Lord of the resurrection. It is His name people must own in order to receive the fullness of salvation that comes by the grace of their merciful God.

Yet that time will also include a sense of foreboding of the coming judgment. The Day of the Lord will include the greatest of blessings for some, but it will also involve an unspeakably frightening curse for others. It will be reminiscent of the destruction of Pharaoh and his armies during the time of the exodus of God's people from Egypt. Joel provides few specifics, yet he includes hints of blood, fire, and billows of smoke (2:30). The light of the sun and moon will be affected, perhaps from the great conflict to take place. The coming of the Day of the Lord will be great for some and dreadful for others (2:31).

Yet God will ensure that those who call on His name are delivered. It will be a terrible time, but there will certainly be survivors. God is both Judge and Savior, and His justice will prevail (2:32).

Take It Home

Joel looks ahead to the Day of the Lord. How do you feel as you contemplate a day that will involve dread and judgment for some? If you remained more aware of a coming day when God will deliver those who remain faithful to Him, how might it affect your day-to-day life?

JOEL 3:1–21

THE COMING JUDGMENT

Gathering the Nations	3:1–16
Jerusalem Restored	3:17–21

Setting Up the Section

Up to this point, Joel has primarily dealt with God's message to His own people. In this section, after God has just promised redemption and restoration of Israel, the Lord turns His attention to the judgment of other nations that have treated His people badly throughout history. Their relentless cruelty has not been overlooked. Their judgment will be harsh indeed, and although Israel had been guilty of much wrongdoing in the past, they will experience God's great forgiveness.

3:1–16

GATHERING THE NATIONS

Joel continues to peer into the future as he relates God's message. The still-to-come Day of the Lord looms ahead, and God continues to describe what will happen in those days (3:1). It will include a restoration of Judah, Jerusalem, and Israel (3:1–2), and the prophet will soon go into detail about what such a recovery will entail (3:17–21). But first God will address the offenses of other nations.

The nations are to be *gathered* in a sense that sounds much like a summons to appear in court. The charges against them are quite severe. For one thing, they have ransacked the wealth of Israel (3:5). They are also guilty of scattering God's people throughout the various lands of the time. And while it is true that they were acting under the auspices of God's control, they treated their captives horribly. The remaining specific charges that are included in the narrative are some of the worst imaginable offenses, with human trafficking and child prostitution among them (3:3).

The Valley of Jehoshaphat (3:2, 12) has never been identified as a specific geographic location, in the past or present. However, the precise location is not as important as the name itself. *Jehoshaphat* means "the Lord judges." It matters little where the judging is taking place; what matters is that the time has come for justice to be exacted against those who had long persecuted God's people.

Demystifying Joel

The specific nations and offenses listed (3:4–6) present some challenges to determining the time of Joel's writing. The Philistines are among the earlier enemies of Israel, yet the reference to scattering the people points some scholars to the Babylonian captivity (3:2, 4). At that time, the temple treasury was plundered (2 Kings 25:8–17), although neither the Philistines nor Phoenicians (Tyre and Sidon) were involved. Some believe that this is a case where perhaps a number of Israel's persistent enemies are listed to represent *all* of the persecutors of God's people throughout their history.

The various nations committed numerous offenses against Israel and Judah during times when God's people had forsaken the Lord and were vulnerable. Israel's enemies presume they have gotten away with their despicable behavior, but God continues to hold them responsible for what had been done. The insulting treatment of God's people is a transgression against God. It had been God's silver and gold that was stolen. It had been God's people who were sold for wine and thrust into prostitution (3:2–6).

It will appear for a time that Israel and Judah are no more, with their populations removed and deported to faraway countries. But God will then reverse the harm that had been done. He will recall His people from the various places to which they have been sold, and He will return on them what they had done to Israel and Judah. Judah's enemies will see how it feels to witness their children sold to distant lands (3:7–8). (This prophecy comes true soon thereafter, as the Greek Empire begins to spread and various countries find themselves subjugated and/or enslaved.)

Just as God had promised to rouse His people from among the nations, Joel tells the nations to rouse their warriors. If they are going to be foolish enough to oppose the Lord of Israel, they may as well prepare for it. Their tools for everyday living ("plowshares" and "pruning hooks") should be converted into weapons of war ("swords" and "spears"). They should join forces and assemble (3:9–11).

But they will be marching toward their judgment. The gathering place will be the Valley of Jehoshaphat, where God will sit and judge their great wickedness. They will come forth in all their pride and power, but they will be approaching their own destruction.

Those who defiantly oppose God will not long stand. They will meet utter defeat. The comparisons are made to swinging a sickle and trampling grapes—two common actions the people of that time are familiar with. Just as wheat falls before a reaper's scythe, so will the enemies of Israel fall. Just as grapes are trodden on to fill the winepress with juice, so will flow the blood of those hostile peoples (3:12–13).

Critical Observation

The apostle John uses similar imagery in his apocalyptic vision recorded in Revelation. There, too, God's judgment is compared to both reaping and trampling on grapes (Revelation 14:14–20).

God's judgment of the nations is connected with the Day of the Lord, and afterward the Valley of Jehoshaphat [God's judgment] will become the "valley of decision" (3:14). Again, this event is said to be accompanied by great signs in the skies—a darkening of the sun, moon, and stars (2:10; 3:15)—and a shaking of the earth (2:10; 3:16).

As terrible as the Day of the Lord will appear to those who oppose God, people who turn to Him will find surprising security. God will be a refuge and stronghold for those who remain faithful (3:16).

3:17–21

JERUSALEM RESTORED

Numerous prophets had made it clear that because of the persistent sins of the people, God will allow Jerusalem to fall to the Babylonians. Yet here, even after the city had fallen and the people had been dispersed to various lands, God will still rule from Jerusalem and Zion. The earth is still the Lord's. Nothing has been ultimately lost (3:16–17).

Joel's closing description portrays such a positive outlook for Jerusalem that it must be a reference to a yet-future time. Certainly, Jerusalem has not yet experienced a period where it could be said that foreigners will never again invade her (3:17). But someday the city will truly be holy—set apart for the glory of God. Joel's description anticipates Revelation 21–22 and the description of the New Jerusalem.

The surrounding land will also undergo a wonderful transformation. In a lush contrast to the opening description of the territory in the wake of the locust infestation, Joel foresees a time when "mountains will drip with sweet wine, and the hills will flow with milk" (3:18 NLT). While other sources refer to Canaan as a land of milk and honey, Joel provides a distinctive descriptive pairing of wine and milk. Vineyards were frequently planted on hillsides, so the description is appropriate. The addition of milk suggests abundant herds, readily sustained by the water that will never again be in short supply (3:18). In fact, the water will be associated with the presence of God—a fountain flows out of the temple to water the land.

Critical Observation

Acacias (3:18) tend to grow in arid desert areas where not much else survives. The picture of their being well watered suggests a wilderness being refreshed and capable of sustaining new life.

In contrast, those who remain hostile toward God and His people (symbolized by Israel's persistent enemies, Egypt and Edom) will lack water and life. They who had shed innocent blood will be left a desolate, desert wasteland (3:19). But Judah will be forgiven of their past sins, and God's presence will be with His people forever (3:20–21).

When the Day of the Lord arrives, one age will end and another, eternal one will begin. The Lord's coming will overwhelm the current created order and, by the plan and power of God, there will be a new heaven and a new earth fit for a renewed population of resurrected bodies. For the new Israel, the age of discipline will finally yield to the age of perfect delight.

Take It Home

In the New Testament, Paul teaches that, "in [God] we live and move and exist" (Acts 17:28 NLT). People have spent centuries attempting to understand the biology, chemistry, astronomy, and physics of creation. Yet God is bigger than everything the scientists, astronomers, and cartographers can comprehend. When people complete their lives, they still have an existence in God. God's sovereignty is not limited by what people understand to be physical realities. As you reflect on Joel's prophecies, how do you respond to the fact that no matter how grave the judgment of God will be upon the sins of some, those who place their faith in Him can count on full pardon and eternal life?

AMOS

INTRODUCTION TO AMOS

The prophet Amos was a contemporary of Old Testament prophets Hosea and Isaiah. He stood for justice in an era of Israel's history in which the nation was politically strong but spiritually weak.

AUTHOR

The first verse of this book attributes the writing to a man named Amos. Though his prophecy is directed to Israel, the northern kingdom, Amos himself is from Tekoa, a town in Judah, five miles south of Bethlehem. His work as a shepherd and gardener implies he belongs to the working class until the Lord commissions him to be one of His prophets.

PURPOSE

Amos's prophecy condemns the powerful, self-satisfied, wealthy upper class that had developed in Samaria, the capital of Israel.

OCCASION

Amos's ministry falls in the first half of the eighth century BC, during the last half of the reign of Jeroboam II (793–753 BC). Israel is enjoying a measure of domestic affluence and international power that she has not known since the reign of Solomon. Israel and Judah have expanded to the point that they nearly encompass all the land that David and Solomon controlled two centuries before. It is a time of military conquest and economic prosperity. It is also a time of moral darkness.

THEMES

Themes in the prophecy of Amos include God's sovereign power, the covenant agreement between God and Israel, and the day of the Lord's judgment.

OUTLINE

AMOS 1:1–2:3

THE COMING LION

Setting Up the Section

The opening section of Amos is a series of oracles of judgment pronounced against Israel's neighbors: Syria (Aram), Philistia, Tyre (a city in Phoenicia), and so on. In each case, these nations are condemned not for their false religion and worship but for their various crimes against humanity. They have violated principles of morality that are universally recognized by human beings. But Amos does not preach these oracles to these nations themselves. They are rather part of Amos's sermon against Israel—Israel being, as we learn in 1:1, the focus of Amos's preaching and prophecy. The point of these oracles of judgment is that if these foreign nations cannot escape God's wrath on account of their sins, Israel most assuredly will not escape it for her similar sins.

The six nations listed in the first two chapters are the principal nations bordering on Israel, and they are the world as Israel encountered it. Syria (Aram, see 1:3–5), Philistia (1:6–8), and Tyre (1:9–10) are simply Israel's neighbors; Edom (1:11–12), Ammon (1:13–15), and Moab (2:1–3) share ancestry with Israel; and Judah (2:4–5) was once one nation with Israel.

Demystifying Amos

Uzziah was king of Judah between 791 and 740 BC. Jeroboam II (not the first Jeroboam, who was the very first king of Israel after the division of the kingdom after the death of Solomon) was king of Israel from 793–753 BC. Jeroboam II is also known as Jeroboam the Great. Apparently what we have in the book of Amos is the preaching of the prophet over a comparatively short period of time, hence the "two years before the earthquake" (1:1). That earthquake must have been very powerful, for it left its mark on Israel's history. There is mention of it again hundreds of years later in Zechariah 14:5.

Amos 1:1 reveals that even though Israel is in a time of prosperity, God's prophet knows Jeroboam's kingdom is not far from total extinction after his death. Verse 2 mentions a roar thundering from Jerusalem. This roar from Jerusalem is probably of a lion about to pounce, ready to lunge at its victim, Israel. Israel has voluntarily cut herself off from the temple in Jerusalem and its worship, but that is where the Lord's presence is represented. Part of what the Lord holds against Samaria, the capital of Israel, is the sanctuaries they have built rather than attending the temple in Jerusalem.

The recurring phrase regarding not just three sins but four is a reminder of the Lord's mercy and patience. Punishment does not happen because of the first sin, or the second, or the third. There are multiple opportunities for repentance before judgment falls (1:3).

Notice that God condemns the nations not for their false worship or religious practices but for their violations of the obligations they owe to other human beings—in Syria's case, her barbarity and inhumanity in war.

Demystifying Amos

Gaza, mentioned in verse 6, is representative of Philistia. Gaza is one of Philistia's chief cities and is accused of brutality.

In verse 9, Tyre is accused of slave trading, but the sin for which she is to be destroyed is her violation of covenant she made with another nation, apparently Israel. This is significant because it reveals a second similarity with Edom, who is also condemned for violations of brotherhood (1:11).

Edom has already been implicated in slave trading (1:6, 9), but the fourth sin for which God is angry is like Tyre's: a violation of family bonds. Edom is indeed Israel's brother, descended from Esau as Israel is from Jacob, and Isaac is the grandfather of both. But Edom has long harbored animosity toward Israel. The cities of Edom (1:12)—Teman to the south and Bozrah to the north—are mentioned to make the point that the entire country will suffer God's wrath, from top to bottom.

The last two nations, Ammon and Moab, are condemned for atrocities committed against the most vulnerable, fragile, and helpless of human beings: pregnant women and their unborn children in the first case and dead bodies in the second. And the Ammonites did this for temporal advantage, to enlarge their borders. They stepped on the weak to advantage themselves (1:13–2:3). In verse 14, Rabbah, Ammon's only significant city, receives the threat of destruction at the hand of Assyria.

The first three verses of chapter 2 complete Amos's prophecy against the surrounding nations. Moab and Edom hate each other, and evidence of this is the disrespect for dead bodies described in 2:1. The idea may have been to prevent the king's body from being resurrected.

The harsh, brutal reality of human sin that results in these kinds of cruelty—slavery, war, desecration of bodies—lies at the base of Amos's charge against these nations and the threat of divine wrath.

AMOS 2:4–16

THE PATH TO APOSTASY

Setting Up the Section

The two oracles of judgment in chapter 2—against Judah and Israel—show the progress of apostasy. Things are not as bad in Judah during Amos's ministry as they are in Israel, but eventually Judah will be guilty of all the sins that Amos accuses Israel of in verses 6–12.

At best, relations between the divided kingdoms—Israel to the north and Judah to the south—took the form of a peaceful coexistence. But more often, the two kingdoms interacted with outright hostility and sometimes war. Amos's Israelite audience would have enjoyed his message thus far. They would have been glad to hear of the Lord's judgments to befall their surrounding enemies and glad to learn that Judah is going to suffer.

While the six nations in the first section are condemned for crimes against humanity, Judah is condemned for a failure to obey God's law as revealed by Moses and the prophets. The *law*, as it is used here, means much more than simply commandments or rules—it means instruction from God about the life He has called His people to live (2:4).

The remaining verses of chapter 2 describe Israel as guilty of the same crimes against humanity that the pagan nations around her have been accused of.

Israel has blatantly disobeyed the commandments of God's Word, involving herself in incestuous and promiscuous sexual relations, especially, no doubt, in regard to fertility rites at the temples and shrines. Amos represents Israel as deliberately throwing off the claims of the Lord.

In verse 8, the garments "taken in pledge" (or as collateral for a debt), according to God's law, are to be returned at night to the debtor (Exodus 22:26–27). According to this description, however, the Israelites do not return these garments but instead use them at altars, making their religious life the context for their disobedience. Moreover, fines are to be according to the Law of Moses, a vehicle for making restitution, not for enriching the wealthy, who are drinking them up in orgies at their sanctuaries.

The Amorites, mentioned in verse 9, are inhabitants of the region before it became known as Canaan.

In verses 10–12, Israel's sins are against God's goodness. He has done so much for them, and they are repaying Him with selfish indifference to His will. God has spoken to His people through His prophets and used the plight of Nazirites, who consecrated themselves only to God.

Verse 12 twists the oracle from what God has done for His people to the way in which they have repaid His goodness. That which God has provided, Israel has ignored or disobeyed. Nazirites vow not to drink wine, yet the Israelites force them to do it in an act of cruel blasphemy. Or perhaps, more likely, this statement is to be taken metaphorically to describe Israel's utter indifference to the spiritual challenge and example of such godly people.

Critical Observation

In both Judah and Israel, the mistreatment of God's revelation is the first cause of the disaster that is about to befall them both. Judah receives the truth from God but chooses instead the traditions of culture. And what is true to a degree in Judah is entirely true in Israel.

Verses 13–16 describe God's wrath as inescapable, regardless of anyone's earthly wealth, power, or talent. As before, with the other nations, God's judgment will come in the form of an attack by a stronger nation. This will prove to be Assyria, of course, just a few decades later. The Assyrian's theory of conquest is the complete devastation of a nation, the depopulation of its territory, and the terrorization of its remnants.

Take It Home

Amos's prophecy raises the issue of how much the people of God incorporate the practices of the culture around them. This issue is still relevant for the church today, with people of faith landing on both sides of the balance. How much is our faith affected by the cultural customs we incorporate?

AMOS 3:1–15

WITHIN BUT WITHOUT

Setting Up the Section

In this section, the indictment that Amos has drawn up against Israel in 2:6–16 is expanded, clarified, and proved. Israel believes she, as Yahweh's people, was delivered from bondage in Egypt on eagles' wings, but her rebellion, disobedience, and unbelief render her the object of God's wrath, not His care and protection.

The opening words of chapter 3 are repeated in 4:1, 5:1, and 8:4. Amos speaks to Israel as one nation, though the nation has long ago been divided and its people have been addressed separately already in this prophecy. The verses following will make it clear, however, that Israel, the northern kingdom, is chiefly in Amos's view.

In some translations of verse 2, God claims that Israel is the only nation He has *known*. In others, the word *chosen* is used. Either word points out the covenant relationship God has with these people.

The questions in verses 3–6 make a point. In verses 4–5, the coming of God's judgment is certain. Just as nature moves when it has purpose and need, so will God's justice move on His people. Verse 6 refers to the blowing of a trumpet, a ram's horn, which would have been familiar to the people of Amos's day. While the preceding questions rhetorically point to a "no" answer, the questions in verse 6 point to a "yes" answer. Perhaps the last question makes the main point—these people are not expecting disaster and do not see themselves in Amos's question.

With verse 7, Amos switches from rhetorical questions to direct statements. Yahweh not only does bring disaster upon the unrighteous, but He communicates His intention to do so through His prophets. Just as one pays attention when a lion roars, so the Lord's prophet cannot ignore or fail to deliver His Word (3:8).

The pagan nations around Israel, mentioned in chapter 1, are invited to observe Israel's life to see whether the sins of Samaria deserve God's judgment (3:9–10). The point here is that Israel's sins are so egregious that even the wicked nations around her will stand in judgment of her.

The picture painted in verse 11 is that Israel's strongholds and fortresses—the things she has trusted for protection—will prove little obstacle to the Assyrians. Neither will Israel's wealth be her protection. According to verse 12, the wealthy in Samaria, who indulge themselves on fine and comfortable furniture, will be swept away. Only a few will survive.

Demystifying Amos

Verse 13 introduces a new oracle. It is directed to Israel, referring to the nation as the *house of Jacob*. Jacob was the son of Isaac, grandson of Abraham. He had twelve sons, and the tribes of Israel were tracked according to each son. In referring to Israel this way, the heritage of the nation is brought to mind, including their covenant of obedience to God.

Verses 14–15 combine the image of Bethel, a name which means "house of God," with a variety of other houses. When the house of God falls, no house remains. Israel's great houses are monuments to her corruption and her ill-gotten wealth.

AMOS 4:1–13

THE POINT OF NO RETURN

Setting Up the Section

Chapter 4 begins a new indictment against Israel that opens with a call to the upper-class women.

Bashan was known for the size and quality of its livestock (Deuteronomy 32:14; Psalm 22:12). In Amos 4:1, the women are likened to animals fattening themselves on rich pasture. They live their lives for pleasure, yet the poor remain oppressed. They make demands of their husbands for the household service they should be providing.

There are a variety of opinions about the meaning of the hooks in verse 2. What is certain is that the reference is to the women of Israel being humiliated by their enemies.

We do not know the location of Harmon, mentioned in verse 3. Some have supposed it to be a dump where the women's bodies will be thrown after their deaths. Other translations simply refer to it as a fortress or palace. In either case, the breaks in the walls are an important element of the description. What should have protected these women becomes simply a portal through which they are undone.

In verse 4, Amos taunts the Israelites by saying that all they are accomplishing with their worship is the multiplying of their sins and the deepening of their judgment. He exaggerates their practices as if they are doing almost nothing but making pilgrimages to Bethel and Gilgal. The implicit question becomes: What good is all of this doing?

The description in verse 5 reveals the unbelief and self-absorption of these people. Their inappropriate worship—freewill offerings are to be private, yet they brag about them—makes matters worse, not better. This theme of inauthentic ritual is strong with Old Testament prophets.

Verse 6 begins a new section that continues through verse 11, marked by the first-person pronoun *I* and the refrain that the people have not returned to God even with all He has done to draw them back. There is a deliberate contrast between what Yahweh has done and what Israel is doing. Israel has been busy rebelling against the Lord; the Lord has been busy seeking to bring her to repentance.

All of the catastrophes listed in this section have been signs of God's wrath, and Israel has ignored them all. According to verses 12–13, the God whose justice and judgment Israel must now face is the sovereign Lord who controls nature. She cannot withstand the Lord when He comes against her in judgment.

Take It Home

Amos is particularly difficult for the modern reader. Like Israel in the eighth century BC, we are a prosperous people. Also, in our scientific age, we are much less likely to connect events in the world with the action of the Almighty. But every Bible reader, sooner or later, has to decide how to understand that God is both merciful and wrathful.

AMOS 5:1–27

REPENTANCE AND THE DAY OF THE LORD

Setting Up the Section

This book begins by condemning the nations that surround Israel for their sins and with a promise of God's judgment. If these other nations will not escape God's wrath, how much more judgment must Israel face, a nation who has sinned against God's grace? Chapter 5 is an eloquent plea addressed to the nation of Israel, in hopes that at least some of her people will hear it and respond.

The poetry of verses 1–3 follows the form of a Hebrew funeral dirge. At this time, Israel is at the height of her prosperity under Jeroboam II. Like the virgin mentioned in verse 2, it seems that Israel's best days are ahead. But verse 3 reveals that her military strength will be wrecked and her soldiers slaughtered in battle.

Instead of empty rituals, God wants His people to seek Him (5:4–5). Bethel, Gilgal, and Beersheba are important sites in Israel's history. Apparently all three cities held shrines to which Israelites made faithful pilgrimages—even Beersheba, which lay at the southernmost end of Judah. But the people had been commanded to go to Jerusalem to worship. Amos is once again pointing out the futility of Israel's religious practices. Her people worship, but instead of following God's guidelines, they make their own rules. They offer worship that offends the Lord rather than pleases Him.

The "house of Joseph," mentioned in verse 6, is a reference to the northern kingdom of Israel. Regions were often identified by their principal tribe. In this case, that tribe is Ephraim, made up of the descendants of one of Joseph's sons.

Verses 7–11 have a unique structure. Verse 7 characterizes Israelite life as unjust and unrighteous, something that Amos has already established. Verses 8–9 function as a kind of doxology. The verses describe God in terms of His power and majesty. He alone can save Israel from the disaster that looms. Then, the characterization that began in verse 7 continues in verses 10–11. By the middle of verse 11, the announcement of judgment begins.

Verses 12–13 reveal that, in essence, the religion of the Israelites does not touch their lifestyles; they are heedless of the claims of justice and God's law. Verses 14–15 state what the people need to do if they indeed want to be the people of God they claim to be. The last half of verse 14 reveals the state of mind of the Israelite people—they mistakenly believe God to be on their side, even while they are disconnected from their true spiritual state.

Take It Home

Amos 5:14–15 has great application for us in that it offers a clear account of what God requires of His people.

If the people do not turn back to their God, the destruction will be so great that farmers will have to be summoned to wail because there will not be enough professional mourners to go around (5:16). Yahweh will pass through Israel as her destroyer, reminiscent of the angel of death passing through Egypt long before (5:17).

Verses 18–20 include the earliest recorded use of the expression *Day of the Lord*. It will occur many more times in the prophets of the Old Testament and again in the New Testament. But clearly, it is already a familiar phrase by this time as a religious figure of speech. Because of their disconnection from God's view of their spiritual state, the Israelites think that the Day of the Lord will bring happiness and triumph to them when, in fact, it will bring disaster.

Amos has already said that the Lord won't accept Israel's sacrifices. However, in verses 21–24, he says the Lord won't accept Israel's praise, either. This continues the theme in Amos that God is looking for meaningful relationships with His people, not empty worship. Because the people have refused to hear this message, God indicates that it is time for His justice to flow as naturally, strongly, and completely as water flows down a mountain.

Verse 25 can be seen as a rhetorical question, in which case the assumed answer is no. We don't know if the people neglect to offer sacrifices on their journey because they are disobedient or because the rituals of sacrifice are not implemented yet.

The prophet continues making the point that Israel's sacrifices are disconnected from her faith relationship with God (5:25–26). The people of Israel seem to think that as long as they offer Yahweh sacrifices, all will be well, no matter their obedience in other areas of life. Amos is reminding them that their own history is the disproof of that idea.

Verse 27 refers to a place beyond Damascus, which is Assyria. Assyria does eventually defeat the northern kingdom of Israel.

AMOS 6:1–14

A HARD TRUTH

Setting Up the Section

Amos continues to focus on the northern kingdom in this section. The influential and the rich who live and work in the capital cities are the target of Amos's condemnation. Both their complacency and their coming judgment are described.

As he has done before, Amos, at the opening of chapter 6, presents Israel as serenely confident of God's approval without good reason to be so confident. Zion, a synonym for the capital city of Judah, seems to be a reference to the whole southern kingdom. Samaria, capital city of the northern kingdom, is used in the same way to represent the whole kingdom of Israel.

The cities mentioned in verse 2 may have fallen during Amos's lifetime or before. Either way, he lifts these cities up as a reality check to Israel, that trusting in her own supremacy may be a futile effort. Amos accuses his nation of bringing a "reign of terror" by its disobedience (6:3 NIV).

Verses 4–8 describe the affluence of the wealthy in Israel. The average Israelite may have eaten meat only three times a year, the poor even less. Only the rich can afford to spend time playing and listening to music. The reference to David suggests that the people think of themselves and live as if they are kings. And they drink so much wine that they don't bother to pour it first into cups; they take it straight from the bottle. The anointing of the body was common in the ancient Near East, especially after bathing. It soothed the skin and served as a protection against both heat and lice. The rich added expensive spices and perfumes to the oil. The wealthy who have prospered the most in their rebellion against the Lord will be the first to suffer the Assyrian wrath. That is always the conqueror's way, of course: Cut off the head, and the body will fall easily enough. What God wants His people to also notice, though, is how the body—the innocent and the poor—suffers the consequences of the head's actions and choices.

Israel's military self-confidence will be turned into a cruel joke. The picture in verses 9–10 is that of ten men who have survived the terrors of the siege so far and are found taking refuge together in a single home—probably a large home. This is a picture of the wealthy of Samaria, but even these will die, probably of disease, a feature of siege warfare, as suggested in verse 10. The few remaining survivors hope that Yahweh will consider the judgment sufficient and, if they keep a low profile, perhaps He will not bring upon them any further punishment. But according to verse 11, their defeat is certain.

Two supremely unnatural and absurd activities—running horses up cliffs or plowing the rocks (or the sea; either reading is possible) with oxen—serve as analogies to point out how preposterous and unreasonable Israel's behavior has been (6:12–13). Defying the Lord successfully is just that impossible. To deal with it, God sends brutal conquest by another power (6:14). At this moment, during Jeroboam's reign, the other nations of the region are relatively impotent, including Egypt and Assyria. In that vacuum, Israel's power seems impressive. All of that will change quickly. Lebo Hamath, mentioned in verse 14, is Israel's northernmost boundary and Arabah her southernmost. So the description is one of total defeat.

Take It Home

What honest Christian cannot find himself or herself in Amos's words? How many times have we found ceremony replacing godliness in our own lives? How many times have we caught ourselves going through motions in respect to our faith and the things of God?

AMOS 7:1–17

THE CONTEST FOR THE TRUTH IN THE CHURCH

Setting Up the Section

While the prophecy thus far has included accusations and condemnations, this chapter marks a change. Here, Amos begins to describe a series of visions. Much of the rest of his prophecy will follow this same form.

Each of Amos's visions opens in the same way—attributing his vision to the Lord. Locusts represent an unstoppable agricultural disaster in the ancient world. In this first vision, this swarm of locusts is to fall at a difficult time in harvest, destroying the fruit of the second planting (7:1). This is the part of the harvest that is reserved for the farmers themselves. Without it, neither they nor their livestock will have food to carry them over to the next harvest.

In verses 2–3, God is described as relenting. This is not the first time in scripture the picture is painted of God desisting from a planned course of events in response to human appeal. Moses interceded for Israel when Yahweh threatened to destroy His people (Exodus 32:9–14). Here Amos is the intercessor, and as a result of his intercession, there will be no swarm of locusts (Amos 7:2–3).

Critical Observation

Repeatedly throughout this section, Amos refers to the nation of Israel as *Jacob*. This is a common custom in the writings of the Old Testament. Nations are sometimes identified by the name of their ancestors. Jacob is the forebear of the twelve tribes of Israel.

The vision described in verses 4–6 is of fire sweeping over the land. Amos again appeals to the Lord, and the Lord, even in His wrath, again relents.

In the third vision, a plumb line illustrates the deviation of Israel from the true path (7:7–8). A plumb line is a string with a weight tied to one end. A person holds it upright vertically, and the weight drops the string straight down toward the ground. Anything that isn't straight will look crooked next to the plumb line. God will set a straight line beside Israel, and her crookedness will be evident to all. This time Amos is given no opportunity to intercede. The Lord has determined to punish Israel as Amos has described throughout this prophecy.

The objects of God's divine wrath are mentioned in verse 9—the false places of worship and the royal families who have abandoned God's covenant and forsaken their responsibilities to lead God's people in the ways of righteousness.

Amos's message in verse 9 is the last straw for the priest Amaziah. Amaziah not only wants to punish Amos, but he wants to discredit him and get rid of him (7:10). The quickest path to this goal is creating trouble for Amos with the current government. For Amaziah to say that the land cannot bear Amos's words is simply to say that these words should not be tolerated.

Demystifying Amos

Amaziah is the chief priest at the sanctuary at Bethel, one of the major sanctuaries set up in the northern kingdom in opposition to Jerusalem. Amaziah is not a descendant of Aaron, and therefore, under Mosaic Law, he should not have held that position. No doubt he takes personally Amos's condemnation of Israelite life and worship. The accusation that Amaziah brings against Amos is suited to provoke the maximum response from the king. Jeroboam had reigned for a long time, and almost certainly there was opposition to him abroad in the land. Upon Jeroboam's death a few years later, his son is assassinated, further suggesting that there had been political intrigue already during the later years of Jeroboam's reign, so he would have been alert to any threat to his throne. Amos is certainly no political conspirator. He has not spoken treasonously against the king, he has taken no action against the king himself, and he has not conspired with anyone else to do so. But the Lord's public condemnations of the king and of the nation through His prophet could easily be taken in that way, and so they provide Amaziah with a pretext for his charge.

In verse 11, Amaziah exaggerates, as do most people who wish to cast someone else in a bad light. Amos never predicts that Jeroboam will die by the sword (in fact, he died of natural causes), but Amos had said enough about the nation's sins and God's impending judgment by military conquest that it was only a small step to saying that Amos predicted Jeroboam's death.

The treatment that Amos receives reveals animosity and superiority on the part of Amaziah (7:12–13). The insinuation is that Amos is preaching in Israel because the money is better in the wealthy north. Amaziah is judging Amos by his own standards. He thinks of his own work as simply a job, and he imagines it to be the same for Amos. In verses 14–15, however, Amos clarifies the issue. He is not a prophet for hire; he is called by God. This sets him apart from Amaziah, a bureaucrat doing the king's bidding.

Demystifying Amos

The temple in Jerusalem is the only authorized center of Israel's worship. But to keep Israelites loyal to the northern kingdom and to prevent them from advertising Israel's illegitimacy by traveling to Jerusalem three times a year for worship, sanctuaries were set up at Bethel and elsewhere (1 Kings 12:25–33). Most of the old Mosaic ritual is still visible in Bethel, but the *yahweh* who is worshiped at Bethel is a god of Amaziah's devising, not the living God who revealed Himself to Israel at the Red Sea and gave His law to her at Mount Sinai.

While Amaziah wants Amos to stop prophesying against Israel, he receives not only a prophecy against Israel but also against his own family (7:16–17). Verse 17 is a ferocious judgment pronounced against Amaziah for his false ministry. His wife will become a prostitute to survive, his children will be killed, his property will be despoiled, and the nation to which he purported to provide spiritual leadership to will be destroyed. The last line of the curse is the explanation of the previous four: Israel will be conquered and its people sent into exile. The other punishments can all be explained as typical effects of military conquest and exile. In any case, events will prove which of the two men has been speaking the truth and is a servant of the true living God.

AMOS 8:1–14

TOO LATE

Setting Up the Section

Chapter 8 opens with a basket of ripe fruit. While Amos may be seeing a physical bowl of fruit, he is likely seeing a vision. Significant to this scene is that the fruit is ripe. In this way, the fruit is an image of Israel.

In describing the basket he sees, Amos says it includes ripe fruit. Typical fruit for Amos's region and era included figs, olives, and grapes.

Amos has already referred to music in Israel's temple worship (5:23), but when the Lord's judgment falls, the only music to be heard at Israel's sanctuaries will be wailing. Dead bodies will be scattered everywhere (8:3).

Verse 4 begins with a call to listen. This is the formula that Amos uses repeatedly to begin new sections of his prophecy (see 3:1; 4:1; 5:1).

We are again given a description of Israel as religiously scrupulous, at least outwardly—the people observe the Sabbath and the other festival days punctiliously—but they are morally bankrupt (8:5–6). They don't do business on the Sabbath, but they can't wait for it to be over so they can resume their acts of greed. They were able to buy off the poor, because the poor people were reduced to pennilessness after paying high prices for food and, in turn, became desperate for money.

Critical Observation

From the beginning of His covenant with Israel, Yahweh reminds His people that He will be a protector of the poor and will hold anyone accountable who misuses them. Twice before in Amos, we have heard the Lord use the word *swear*. In 4:2 He swears by His holiness, and in 6:8 He swears by Himself. Here, in 8:7, He swears by the "Pride of Jacob." Earlier in verse 6:8, God states that He abhors the pride of Jacob. In this earlier instance (noted in some translations by a lowercase *p* in pride), the reference is to the haughtiness of Israel trusting in her own strength. Here (noted by some translations by an uppercase *P* in Pride), it is a reference to God Himself.

The Nile River, mentioned in verse 8, rose and fell every year and often caused great damage by its flooding. It is a useful illustration of the convulsion to come in the land of Israel. An enemy will sweep over Israel like floodwaters and leave nothing but devastation behind. The same expression is used again in 9:5.

In verse 10 we read of the Israelites mourning, wearing sackcloth, and shaving their heads. Amos compares their mourning to that found at the funeral of an only son, which would have been understood by Amos's listeners to be an ultimate and bitter loss.

According to verse 12, the Israelites will stagger from one sea to another. This reference implies the Dead Sea to the Mediterranean, which is a way of saying that this will affect all of Israel. The famine will be so severe that it will consume not only the old and weak but also the young and strong (8:13).

In verse 14, Samaria's shame is a contrast to the mention of Jacob's pride in verse 7. It refers to the false gods who have been added to Yahweh's worship at Israel's shrines. To swear by a god is to commit themselves to the reality of those gods and their power to help them. Yahweh is saying, "You chose those gods over me, let them save you now." They can't! Israel's lack of true repentance shows that in that same day, they will still be found calling on other gods and looking to their idols as well as to Yahweh.

AMOS 9:1–15

FUTURE BLESSING

Setting Up the Section

The theme of this conclusion is that no one can escape God's wrath. God punishes unfaithfulness, and no person can get in His way.

Verses 1–4 contain the fifth and last of the visions that God gives Amos—this one of the destruction of the temple. (The first four visions are recorded in chapters 7–8.) The pillars of the temple support the roof, and the cut stone thresholds are at the bottom of the great doors. The picture here is of the complete collapse of the temple from top to bottom. One of Israel's sanctuaries is in view, probably the principal one at Bethel. The picture of the building collapsing on the worshipers indicates that Israelite worship is conducted in some significant measure inside the sanctuary, in the Canaanite fashion, not outside in the court in the orthodox fashion prescribed in the Law of Moses.

The structure of verse 2 is a common biblical figure of speech that uses two extreme parts together. In this case, heaven and hell are extremes that communicate that all of God's creation is included. There is nowhere to hide. The mountain mentioned in verse 3, Mount Carmel, was known for its thickly wooded mountainside honeycombed with caves. For Amos's contemporaries, this image would serve to reinforce the pervasiveness of God's judgment, as would the reference to *exile* (or *captivity*) in verse 4. Even an enemy nation will not be powerful enough to keep God's judgment at bay.

The Nile's rising and falling is used as an image of destruction in 8:8. Here, in 9:5, the Nile serves as another image of the totality of the Lord's judgment—like a flood that covers the land before it recedes, it leaves nothing but destruction behind.

Verses 5–6 have a hymnlike quality in their mention of God's power and their images of water and the heavens.

With verse 7, the Lord begins to speak in the first person, asking two rhetorical questions that place Israel, spiritually speaking, on equal ground with all others. First, Israel is no more exempt from God's judgment than the people of Cush, a reference to Ethiopia. Israel, by her lack of faith and her betrayal of God's covenant, has become just like these other people instead of the people of God she was called to be. Since the Philistines and the Arameans (NIV) (or Syrians, KJV) were hated enemies of Israel, the comparison would have been particularly galling to Amos's audience.

There is a hopeful element to verses 8–10. The kernels of grain that fall through the sieve to the ground represent the believing remnant of Israel. The pebbles—those who don't believe—will be caught in the sieve and thrown out. They will die by the sword—Amos's last reminder that the Lord's wrath will come upon Israel in the form of military conquest.

In verse 11, Amos first sees David's kingdom (his "tent" NIV) as destroyed but then as renewed and rebuilt. The restoration of David's dynasty is another way of speaking about the Messiah and His kingdom, as the Messiah is, in all biblical prophecy, the future of David's dynasty and the hope of his kingdom.

Edom was a particularly bitter enemy of Israel. Here it represents the nations of the world that, in the last days, will be subject to the kingdom of God (9:12). David was the only king of Israel who not only conquered Edom but held it. So Edom makes a particularly good representative for the nations of the world that will become subject to David's descendant, the Messiah.

Verses 13–14 describe a time of unprecedented bounty. The picture is of fields so fertile and harvests so large that the reapers will still be gathering the grain as the soil is being turned over for the next planting. And the image of wine flowing downward from the hills where the grapes are grown is, again, a picture of unimaginable plenty.

Critical Observation

We have this picture very often in the prophets and as early as Jacob's blessing of Judah in Genesis 49:10–12: The Messiah will restore the world to its pure state, as it was in Eden before the fall. Additionally, there will be peace, enabling the people of God to pursue their life's work without fear.

Amos closes with a promise that when the people of God are restored and resettled in the promised land to enjoy the blessings and benefits of God's favor, they will never be judged again. The judgment of the nation is upon them. This has been Amos's primary theme from the beginning of the book, but when the Day of Judgment is passed and Israel is restored, it will be for good.

Take It Home

Amos's prophecy concerns all the people of God, Jews and Gentiles alike. The living, faithful church—whether Jewish or Gentile—is the true Israel of God, as we are often told in the New Testament. Also, the promise here is primarily a promise of eternal salvation, of the life of heaven, and of the complete fulfillment of human life as it will be experienced at the consummation of all things. Amos's description of the future here is simply another version of that description of heaven that John gives us at the end of the book of Revelation. Amos ends with a promise of a wonderful day, a day of fulfillment, joy, and perfect satisfaction for every human being who is numbered among the true people of God when history comes to its close.

OBADIAH

INTRODUCTION TO OBADIAH

The book of Obadiah is the shortest of the Old Testament, yet its brief message has numerous applications far beyond its relevance to Edom. Obadiah provides a warning to anyone who mistakenly believes that sin will go unnoticed (and unpunished), but he also offers confidence that for those who continue to seek God, the Lord is able to both forgive and deliver.

AUTHOR

Personal facts are scarce concerning the prophet Obadiah. He provides no family references or pertinent locations that enlighten the reader as to his biography. Even his name (meaning "worshiper of the Lord") was a common one in his day. At least a dozen Old Testament men are named Obadiah.

PURPOSE

Obadiah has a single purpose in writing: to bring God's message of judgment to the people of Edom. The nation's deeply rooted sense of pride will result in its certain downfall.

THEMES

Obadiah highlights the problems that arise from unbridled arrogance and self-centeredness. Edom (the descendants of Esau) has family ties to Israel (the descendants of Jacob), so Edom's sadistic glee in response to the previous troubles of the Israelites does not go unnoticed; they will be judged for their actions.

HISTORICAL CONTEXT

With so few clues provided, it is difficult to determine a precise date for the writing of Obadiah. But the conflict between Edom and Israel was ongoing and had existed throughout their entire histories. If the event referred to in verses 11–14 is the Babylonian destruction of Jerusalem (586 BC), then Obadiah was most likely written during the exile.

CONTRIBUTION TO THE BIBLE

Obadiah is a seldom-quoted book. Even the New Testament writers, who cited many of the Old Testament prophetic writings, are silent in regard to Obadiah. Yet the message of this short writing has practical applications that make it a significant contribution to scripture.

OUTLINE

BOOK OF OBADIAH

THE PROBLEM WITH TAKING JOY IN THE SUFFERING OF ONE'S ENEMIES

Judgment in Store for Edom 1–14
Deliverance in Store for Jacob 15–21

Setting Up the Section

The concise writing of Obadiah is a pointed accusation against the nation of Edom, whose people had survived while they saw Judah fall to powerful enemies. More than that, Edom had taken perverse pleasure in seeing their enemies suffer and had even acted aggressively against Judah during a vulnerable time. What Edom didn't realize, however, was that Judah's fall was a result of God's judgment on His people. Obadiah now reveals that God will certainly judge Edom as well and that judgment will be severe.

1–14

JUDGMENT IN STORE FOR EDOM

Israel and Edom had a long and interwoven history. Sometimes they had joined as allies against a common enemy. More often, however, the original rivalry between Jacob (Israel's forefather) and Esau (Edom's forefather) created ongoing conflicts between the two nations.

The timing of Obadiah's writing is debated, but it is clear that Judah has experienced a bitter defeat at the hands of enemies (verse 11). The Edomites foolishly believe they are exempt from a similar outcome. Edom was located along a span of wilderness that stretched from the southern tip of the Dead Sea to the northern portion of the Red Sea. It was mountainous territory where the inhabitants lived among rocky cliffs, confident of their security and the impenetrability of their cities. It is as if they feel untouchable, high among the stars (verses 3–4).

But from their heights of arrogance, they are about to fall and become small among the nations (verse 2). They may dwell above much of the world, but God is higher still and will bring them down (verse 4).

Demystifying Obadiah

Israel had requested permission to travel through Edom during their exodus from Egypt, but the Edomites had marched out with a large and powerful army to deny them passage (Numbers 20:14–21). Later, when Israel was an established nation of its own, the Edomites waited until other people attacked Israel and then invaded and took prisoners (2 Chronicles 28:16–21). And when Jerusalem eventually fell to the Babylonians, the Edomites cheered and celebrated (Psalm 137:7–8).

During a typical theft, the robber(s) will leave behind some of the person's belongings, but Edom's loss will be total. Even worse, those whom Edom considers their close friends and allies will prove deceitful. The very people whom they trust enough to sit around the table and share a meal with will destroy them with alarming treachery. The wisdom and power of the most accomplished descendants of Esau will not be adequate to anticipate this trouble nor deliver their countrymen from a horrifying slaughter (verses 5–9).

God disciplines those He loves, which is a difficult concept for outsiders to understand. When nonbelievers observe God's people undergoing a period of corrective discipline, they tend to presume that God has no abiding love for those who worship Him. Some even take a perverse pleasure in celebrating the suffering of God's people, but it is never wise to gloat over those whom the Lord has called His special possession. He will stand up for them in the day when He comes to judge and will bring upon the heads of their enemies the very vengeance those people had sought for them. Edom will learn this lesson too late, as they find themselves covered with shame and destroyed (verses 10–14).

15–21

DELIVERANCE IN STORE FOR JACOB

Jesus will later teach that, "So in everything, do to others what you would have them do to you," saying that this so-called Golden Rule "sums up the Law and the Prophets" (Matthew 7:12 NIV). The prophet Obadiah records how the Edomites have treated God's people despicably, and God's pronouncement of their judgment is, "As you have done to Israel, so it will be done to you" (Obadiah 15 NLT).

After contributing to the (temporary) defeat of Jerusalem, the Edomites had apparently celebrated with strong drink. But the cup of God's wrath (see Isaiah 51:17) is in store for them to drink. Edom represents all the nations who have opposed God—they all will one day completely disappear from existence, while Jerusalem is restored. The house of Esau will have no survivors (Obadiah 16–18).

Critical Observation

While Obadiah's prophecy focuses on Edom, other Old Testament prophetic books include prophecies against these people (Jeremiah 49:7–39; Ezekiel 35:1–15; Malachi 1:1–4).

Mount Zion (Jerusalem) will be delivered, once again holy and home to the house of Jacob (Israel). Surrounding land that had been ceded to other nations will be reclaimed and restored. People will be called out of exile to resettle in their homelands. Deliverers will be assigned to help govern, but the kingdom will be the Lord's (verses 19–21).

The short book of Obadiah confirms what many other prophets teach in greater detail. The Day of the Lord will one day bring judgment on all who persistently defy God and live in disobedience, while bringing deliverance and restoration to those who repent and seek God's mercy. What appears to be injustice is only temporary. God is aware of every deed and attitude of every person, and He will punish or reward accordingly.

Take It Home

Obadiah's message to Edom is a relevant lesson for many people today. Even though Edom and Israel were ongoing enemies, it becomes clear that God was displeased for one side to take delight in the suffering and downfall of the other. Can you think of times when you have taken pleasure in seeing someone "get what was coming to him or her"? The command to "love your enemies" (Matthew 5:44) begins by being more sensitive to others' pains and problems. What can you do in the weeks to come to develop a stronger empathy with those you don't normally get along with?

JONAH

INTRODUCTION TO JONAH

Jonah is the only prophet who is recorded as having run away from God. In this way, Jonah is not known for his piety but for his prodigality. Jonah, in his rebellion, disobedience, and hardness of heart, is a man who typifies the rebellion of Israel as described by other prophets. Ironically, the name *Jonah* means "dove," a bird often associated with peace.

AUTHOR

Very little is said of the prophet Jonah outside of the book of Jonah itself. It does seem safe to conclude that the Jonah in 2 Kings 14:25 is the same person who is the subject of the book of Jonah, especially since both are identified as the son of Amittai.

The book of Jonah does not name its author. While it is about Jonah, there is no specific claim as to whether Jonah actually wrote it.

PURPOSE

The book stood to reveal to Israel the possibility of repentance, even for those whom Israel would have considered the most wicked. The point was, if repentance is a possibility for the most wicked, then repentance is a real possibility for Israel herself as well.

OCCASION

Jonah is a prophet in the northern kingdom of Israel during the first half of the eighth century BC. His predecessors are Elijah and Elisha. The ministries of Hosea and Amos immediately follow that of Jonah.

THEMES

Throughout the book of Jonah runs the theme of second chances, worked out through opportunities for repentance, some taken and some wasted. Hand in hand runs the theme of those who choose to obey God and those who don't.

HISTORICAL CONTEXT

Jonah is associated in 2 Kings 14:25 with the reign of King Jeroboam, a time of prosperity for Israel. Assyria, whose capital city is Jonah's target of Nineveh, has already begun to exercise her dominance in the Near East, but for a time her control will wane, allowing Israel to expand her borders. Israel's empowerment at this time may have been a factor in her lack of repentance. This makes the story of Jonah all the more pointed, in that a nation Israel considered to be wicked repents before God when His own people won't.

CONTRIBUTION TO THE BIBLE

In the New Testament, Jesus mentions Jonah (Matthew 12:39–41; 16:4; Luke 11:29–32). When asked for a sign, Jesus refers the religious leaders to the sign of Jonah that already exists. He points out the parallel of Jonah's three days in the fish and the Son of man's three days in the heart of the earth.

OUTLINE OF JONAH

JONAH 1:1–17

JONAH AND THE SAILORS

Setting Up the Section

At the opening of Jonah's story, he is given a divine commission to go to the great city of Nineveh, capital city of Assyria and a potential threat to Israel (see Genesis 10:8–11).

1:1–3

RUNNING FROM GOD

The description of Nineveh as *great* in verse 2 probably refers to its size and its influence, but its sins were great as well. Its wickedness has come to God's attention, and Jonah is to be God's messenger. But instead of doing what God instructs him to do, Jonah catches a ship heading in the opposite direction (1:1–3).

The city of Nineveh is located on the Tigris River, more than five hundred miles to the northeast of Israel. But Jonah goes west toward Tarshish, which seems to have been located on the western coast of Spain. Jonah flees from God's presence, a truth repeated twice in verse 3. Jonah is not trying to flee the literal presence of God, but he is attempting to avoid his role as a prophet.

1:4–11

A POWERFUL STORM

But God does not let Jonah flee. He hurls a storm in Jonah's path—a storm so great that it terrifies veteran sailors and threatens the ship (1:4–5). The sailors begin casting the cargo overboard in an effort to save the ship and their own lives. At the same time, each sailor is praying to his gods for deliverance. These pagan sailors would have worshiped gods they thought influenced the seas on which they traveled.

As the sailors gather the cargo to throw overboard, they find Jonah deep in sleep (1:5). The ship's captain is irritated to find Jonah sleeping while the rest of the crew members work to stay alive during the storm. He doesn't ask Jonah to help cast the cargo overboard, but he does command Jonah to pray to his God (1:6). The text does not reveal if Jonah obeys the captain's orders.

The captain and the sailors understand the storm to be a religious matter. When praying doesn't stop the storm, they try another religious technique: casting lots to find the person whose sin has caused the problem (1:7). The lots land on Jonah and identify him as the culprit.

The sailors are in fear for their lives, but in spite of the imminent danger, and the likely urge to throw him overboard, they interrogate Jonah, asking about his origin, purpose, and heritage (1:8). In his answer, Jonah separates himself religiously from the sailors but apparently reveals insight into his mission. From his responses, the sailors immediately know that Jonah has indeed caused the storm and that his sin has endangered the entire ship's crew (1:9–10).

The response of the sailors—appalled at Jonah's disobedience—shows that even the pagans are shocked at how this man has chosen to defy God. They, too, are experiencing the consequences of Jonah's actions, so they ask Jonah what to do to appease the wrath of his God (1:11).

1:12–17

GOD'S PROVISION

Jonah tells the sailors to throw him overboard and the sea will calm (1:12). Given the intensity of the storm, this request would have made his death seem a certainty. Some believe this shows repentance on Jonah's part, but others feel that Jonah wants to die to avoid God's command to confront Nineveh. The sailors could have responded quickly to Jonah's instructions, yet because they are reluctant to cause his death, they make one more risky attempt to save him by rowing for the rocky shore (1:13). When they conclude that Jonah's solution is their only alternative, they pray once more before casting him into the sea (1:14). Many scholars agree that at this point the sailors are praying to Jonah's God. Having prayed, they pick up the prophet and cast him into the sea (1:15).

As Jonah sinks beneath the waves, the winds cease and the sea calms down. This confirms for the sailors that Jonah's God is the only true God. Thus, at the end of the chapter, we see the sailors worshiping by sacrificing and declaring their faith in God (1:16). In trying to avoid preaching to the Ninevites, Jonah has unwillingly preached to the sailors, and they have come to faith in his God.

The fish that God provides for Jonah has become the focus of this story, yet it is simply a provision of the Lord (1:17). The miracle is not the fish itself or in the details of how the fish swallows Jonah; the miracle is God's grace toward Jonah, saving him from almost certain death in order that Jonah may receive all that God's call on his life has to offer.

Critical Observation

Jesus refers back to Jonah's plight in the belly of the fish in Matthew 12:39–41, comparing Jonah's three days and nights to the three days and nights the Son of man spends in the earth. This is called the sign of the prophet Jonah.

JONAH 2:1–10

JONAH AND HIS PSALM

Setting Up the Section

Jonah 2:1 picks up the story from under the sea. Verses 2–9 present Jonah's prayer in psalm format.

2:1–9

JONAH'S PETITION

Jonah's descriptions of what is happening to him in the water affirm that he knows God is in control and responsible (2:2–3). The word *Sheol* typically means "grave" but sometimes has connotations of the underworld. Nevertheless, Jonah's words reveal that he acknowledges death as an imminent threat.

Jonah mentions seeing the temple, most likely the temple in Jerusalem (2:4).

In verses 5–7, Jonah describes his situation with graphic detail. He acknowledges God's rescue. In verses 8–9, he appears to contrast Gentile pagans with his own belief in God. This sense of separateness, and even at times superiority, speaks to the core of Jonah's dilemma. God called him to preach to a wicked place, to those who were enemies to his own people. His unwillingness reveals his inability to see how much God values even those who have not yet come to know Him.

2:10

JONAH'S DELIVERANCE

There is little emphasis on the actual fish itself here, perhaps because the fish is obedient to his commission. Jonah's prayer is answered, and he is not only expelled from the fish but also returns to dry land (2:10).

Take It Home

In chapters 1 and 2, the pagan sailors are the ones who seem to act with pure hearts, acknowledging the true God and worshiping with sacrifices and declarations of faith. Jonah, on the other hand, acts rebelliously by disobeying God, and in doing so he endangers many people. It is easy for those of us who consider ourselves to be on God's side to assume that our attitudes will be right. We must always be vigilant, however, that we are acting as servants of the Lord.

JONAH 3:1–10

JONAH AND THE CITY

A Second Chance	3:1–3
Nineveh's Repentance	3:4–10

Setting Up the Section

In chapters 1 and 2, Jonah's sin is apparent yet still somewhat subtle and passive. But this changes in chapters 3 and 4, for Jonah's preaching and the repentance of Nineveh reveal his sinfulness in its ugliest dimensions. In the following chapters, all appearances of piety vanish in the account of the prodigal prophet.

3:1–3

A SECOND CHANCE

God commands Jonah for the second time to deliver His message to the Ninevites (3:1–2). It is almost a repetition of the command given to him in 1:2. This time Jonah obeys the Lord. Verse 3 describes Nineveh, perhaps including its suburbs, as large; the mention of a three-day journey refers to how long it will take to walk around it.

3:4–10

NINEVEH'S REPENTANCE

Jonah's message is simple, to the point, and frightening: In forty days, Nineveh will fall (3:4). Just like the sailors in chapter one, the people of Nineveh take Jonah's words of imminent divine judgment seriously—they believe. The faith of the Ninevites is not simply a fear of judgment. They call a fast and put on sackcloth—a sign of helplessness and despair (3:5). The text specifies that the belief and repentance starts with the common people and rises upward to Nineveh's leadership (3:6).

Because the king also believes Jonah's warning, he makes every effort to assure total compliance to the citywide repentance. He begins by personally repenting. The king then makes a proclamation which requires all of Nineveh to fast and to abstain from drinking water (3:6–7). Both men and animals are to be covered with sackcloth, and all the people are to call upon God and stop their wicked ways and violence (3:8).

The wicked ways of the Ninevites are not detailed, except for use of the word *violence* (3:8). Nineveh's motivation is that God may change His mind (3:9). God had instructed Jonah to deliver not a promise of things to come but a warning. The Ninevites understand God's message correctly. God takes note of Nineveh's repentance because it involves more than mere words or token gestures. The Ninevites have changed more than outward appearances; they have changed their evil ways (3:10).

Critical Observation

Jesus' reference to the repentance of the Ninevites is particularly informative (Matthew 12:38–41). If the Ninevites can repent with so little evidence, then surely the problem with the Jewish leaders, scribes, and Pharisees was not a lack of evidence. Like Jonah, the Jewish leaders, scribes, and Pharisees did have evidence but refused to believe that God would act in a way unexpected by them—and thus no evidence was enough to change their willful rejection.

JONAH 4:1–11

JONAH AND THE SHADE

Setting Up the Section

Had Jonah been any other prophet in the history of Israel, he would have been overjoyed with the results of his ministry—the repentance of the great city of Nineveh. In chapter 4, Jonah blurts out his reasons for rebelling against the command of the Lord. The events in this chapter reveal Jonah's sin.

4:1–3

JONAH'S ANGER AGAINST GOD

In spite of the repentance of Nineveh, Jonah is angry with God (4:1). Jonah is not hesitant to explain, and he protests to the Lord in prayer (4:2). Jonah is angry with God because He shows grace toward the Ninevites, who are enemies of Israel. Instead of learning this lesson about God's loving and merciful character, he complains that he would rather die than live (4:3).

4:4–11

THE PLANT AND THE PRODIGAL

God acknowledges Jonah's anger toward Him (4:4) and presses on with another experience: the giving and the taking away of a plant.

Jonah goes outside the city, where he makes a shady booth from which he can watch the spectacle of the destruction of Nineveh (4:5). God causes a plant to grow, and for the first time in the narrative, Jonah is described as being happy (4:6). With the advent of the worm that eats the plant, and with the arrival of the scorching wind, Jonah loses his comfort and his happiness (4:7–8). Jonah could have chosen to walk away from his suffering and join the Ninevites in their worship of God, but he allows his anger to keep him in discomfort and isolation. He once again begs God to let him die.

For the second time in this chapter, God offers the opportunity for Jonah to examine his anger; and again, Jonah chooses anger over any other emotion (4:9). He is so adamant about his anger that he insists upon keeping it and wishes to die.

God has the final word in the book of Jonah, and His last words press to the heart of the matter. He wants Jonah to see that just as Jonah had compassion on the plant, God had compassion on the people (4:10). God wants Jonah to examine his feelings for the plant—they were strong, even though Jonah had nothing to do with the plant's growth or existence.

The book of Jonah does not end nicely and neatly. We are left somewhat suspended by God's final words of rebuke. We are never told if Jonah repents.

Take It Home

Jonah had rejected the principle of grace. Resisting and rejecting the grace of God is just as great and just as common a sin today as it was in Jonah's time. God's grace takes unexpected forms. He was gracious to Jonah, saving him by means of the great fish. God is gracious to His children by using even pain and adversity in their lives. May we today embrace God's grace however it is bestowed upon us.

MICAH

INTRODUCTION TO MICAH

Sometimes called the prophet of the poor, Micah is a contemporary of Isaiah and speaks a similar message, though, as recorded in the Bible, shorter. King Hezekiah initiates sweeping spiritual and moral reforms in Judah in response to the preaching of Micah and Isaiah, but unfortunately these reforms are short-lived.

AUTHOR

The first verse of this book ascribes the authorship to Micah, a prophet about whom we know very little outside of what is revealed through this prophecy. The prophet is mentioned in only one other place in the Bible, in Jeremiah 26:17–19. In this account, Micah is described as a prophet during the reign of King Hezekiah. When Micah prophesied a bad end for Jerusalem, the king repented, saving Jerusalem from the destruction Micah had prophesied.

PURPOSE

Micah prophesies to stir his readers to action. His writing takes the form of three oracles of judgment. This judgment falls on his countrymen, who act as oppressors, as well as on his society in general, which is filled with corruption. Micah also reminds his people of God's restoration (as do other Old Testament prophets), which awaits them in the future.

OCCASION

The first verse of this prophecy identifies the monarchies under which Micah prophesies—Jotham, Ahaz, and Hezekiah. This places Micah in the eighth century BC. The prophecy references the destruction of Samaria and the invasion of Sennacherib in 701 BC, which would agree with that chronology.

THEMES

While Micah's prophecy is not a theological treatise, running through it are the themes of God's sovereignty, His consistency of nature, and the destiny of the remnant of the faithful.

OUTLINE

MICAH 1:1–16

THE JUDGMENT TO COME

Setting Up the Section

Micah begins with the announcement of judgment because of sins against God and unfaithfulness to God's covenant. This is a major theme of the prophets, leading up to the destruction of the northern kingdom in 722 BC and the devastation and exile of the southern kingdom some 150 years later. This lesson also reveals the nature of God's divine justice, the ferocity of divine wrath, and the final and conclusive judgment of all people at the end of the world.

The kings listed in 1:1 reign from 742 BC to 686 BC. It is widely thought that Micah mentions only the southern kings—though he mentions the northern kingdom (Samaria) as well as the southern (Jerusalem)—because he did not regard the northern kings as legitimate and did not want to dignify them by mentioning them by name.

The call goes out to the entire earth, even though the message concerns Samaria primarily and Jerusalem to a lesser degree. They are all being summoned to a trial to face the Judge of all the earth (1:2). In verse 3, the Lord appears from heaven as an avenging judge.

The specific sins will be enumerated in chapters 2 and 3 and again in chapter 6. But here the case is put generally as rebellion (1:5). The capital cities are mentioned both to represent the entire nation and because it is where the living embodiment of the corruption that has destroyed the nation originated. The punishment on Samaria and Jerusalem foreshadows punishment for all people who worship idols (1:6–7). The meaning of the second half of verse 7 could be that, because idols are bought with the revenues of the cult prostitutes, the conquerors whom God will use to punish Israel will break them up not only for their precious metals but also for spending the money earned from them on the same prostitutes.

The description in verse 8 of the prophet stripped of clothes is not a picture of penitence but of exile. Exiles, barefoot and naked, tramp miserably away from home in long lines under the supervision of enemy soldiers. The same idea is expressed with the howling of the jackal. Jackals howl in the waste places, in the wilderness, and that is what Judah will be reduced to. The gate is the place in the community where announcements are publicly made (1:9).

The following verses (1:10–16) mention several Judean towns, all of them within fourteen kilometers of Micah's hometown of Moresheth. All of the names are omens—they are given some special significance by means of a play on the name, either on the meaning or the associations of the name, or on its sound.

The first name, Gath, is significant because the city does not exist at this time, having been destroyed by Sargon (1:10). The idea, as any Israelite would immediately realize, is that the house of David is now falling, just as the house of Saul had done before. Dust is a symbol of abject humiliation and defeat (1:10; see Genesis 3:14). Verse 11 continues the name-play. The idea in verses 11–12 is that the towns of Judah are hoping for help from the capital, but it is under siege. Lachish is apparently the place where idolatry got its foothold in Judah, spreading outward from there (1:13). With the loss of Lachish, which is a key defensive point and, in fact, holds out longer in 701 BC than the other towns and villages of Judah, the nation must expect to pay tribute. The idea of verse 14 is that towns that belong to Judah and contribute to her must now be paid for instead, as they are in enemy hands. Again in the name-play of the verses above, the allusion in verse 15 is literary, not literal. As David had to flee from Saul to the cave of Adullam (see 1 Samuel 22:1), so the sons of David—the kings and the nobles (the glory of Israel)—will be driven out.

Micah sees the future destruction of Judah on account of her sins, and he considers that the appropriate response is to mourn with true sincerity (1:16). But in this culture, there were professional mourners, so it wasn't always done with as great a depth of feeling. An official mourner does not grieve the loss of a husband as a loving wife does, or of a child as her parents do.

MICAH 2:1–13

FROM OPPRESSION TO HOPE

Setting Up the Section

This next oracle is a pronouncement of judgment against the leadership of Judah. But it goes beyond simply promising judgment against the northern kingdom (1:6–7) and the southern kingdom (1:8–16). This oracle specifically identifies one of the sins for which Israel will be judged.

The reference to the light of morning alludes to the time of day when the courts meet (2:1). The indication here is that the people in power are controlling the courts, which should be a place of justice for all, not just the powerful. But the first part of verse 2 explains how the powerful are taking others' physical property and taking advantage of the people. In this culture, if you take away a person's land, you take away that person's livelihood. Consequences include becoming a day laborer at best and potentially a slave.

Those in power are gaining possession of people's fields by lending money to the landowners and then foreclosing. The result of this is the evacuation of the middle class—most people in prosperous Israel are in the middle class in these days—and the creation of a large poor class serving a smaller, but much wealthier, ruling class. The violation here is in coveting others' property instead of recognizing their ownership and ignoring the fact that, regardless of what one might own and what others might own, all things belong to God and are to be used in His service and for the accomplishment of His will.

The people mentioned in verse 3 indicate a group acting with corporate solidarity. The people who are being ruined by these wealthy land barons are not completely innocent themselves, though. The entire social and religious fabric is rotten, not just the leaders and people in power. Because of this, the Assyrians will come and take the land itself, the very possession the Lord had promised to Israel (2:4). The sacred land of Israel will be distributed to infidels, people who had curried the favor of the Assyrians. This section clearly indicates that this takeover will be done with the help of God.

Critical Observation

God's judgment, as described in chapter 1, is an example of "an eye for an eye and a tooth for a tooth." While this kind of judgment can sound brutal, at the heart of it is the principle that a punishment should fit the specific crime. An eye for an eye is harsh. But it is more equitable than a life for an eye. Here are other examples of punishments that specifically fit the transgressions: Esther 7:9–10; Psalm 7:15–16; Ezekiel 36:6–7; Matthew 26:52.

Micah 2:6 launches an oracle against the false prophets and against the leadership of the people who favor these prophets and approve of their teaching. In its original writing, the imperative not to prophesy is directed to more than one person. This suggests that Micah is not the only one preaching against the sins of the day. We know that Isaiah and Hosea were contemporaries of Micah. There is also a remnant of faithful people who would have repeated the teaching of these faithful men.

The first half of verse 7 shows what the false prophets are teaching, and the second half reveals Micah's response to that teaching. The message of the false prophets amounts to an assurance that because God is love, Israel has nothing to fear. But Micah explains that while God is gracious, He is also a God of judgment to those who do not believe in or obey Him. And because Micah's generation is such an unbelieving and disobedient people, He is going to be a God of judgment to them, not a God of grace and mercy. He will reach out to them if they cry out to Him for mercy and forsake their evil ways, but they will not.

Micah includes some specifics. When men return from battle, as in verse 8, they are confident, assured, at peace, and not expecting trouble. But the leadership pillages them. In other words, the leadership treats the people just like the enemy does. Women are being evicted from their homes, and the descriptions of those homes indicate the people of Judah are, at this time, prosperous and comfortable (2:9). The listeners are instructed to leave, to flee what is coming as a result of sin (2:10). Unfortunately, that means they must go away into exile.

Micah mocks the message preached by the false teachers as simply another version of what people want to hear (2:11). He is being properly cynical of the base motives of the false teachers.

Historically there have been two different interpretations of verses 12–13. Some see the verses as a further prophecy of woe and judgment. Most, though, take the verses to be a message of hope and consolation, a promise of at least a temporary deliverance—a direct prophecy of the deliverance of Jerusalem from Sennacherib's invading army in 701 BC. The sheep pen, or fold, is Jerusalem (2:12). The Shepherd of Israel is gathering His flock to protect it from marauders.

Demystifying Micah

The force of verse 13 lies in the description of the Lord as breaking open the way. Micah's contemporary listeners would have noticed a similarity to David's reference to the Lord breaking out against His enemies (the Philistines) in 2 Samuel 5:20, 24. In other areas of scripture, God is the One who breaks open a way to save His people. The second half of verse 13 is a spiritual picture of this procession out of the city; the Lord at the head of His people (eventually not the human king, but the King Shepherd of Israel, the Christ).

MICAH 3:1–12

JUDGMENT ON THE LEADERSHIP

Setting Up the Section

Chapter 3 contains three oracles of judgment of equal length and identical in form, with the same theme in every case—corrupt leadership.

Micah is the person speaking in verse 1. He uses imagery to show that the leaders are, in effect, consuming people for their own gain (3:2–3). (We've seen already in chapter 2 how they steal people's houses and render them destitute.) There is a startling new development in this oracle—the fact that the Lord will punish these false teachers in keeping with their crimes (3:4). The oppressed cry out to these leaders, and they do not answer or help them. So, when the leaders cry out to God for help, He will not answer them. This indicates a point of no return.

In verse 5, the prophet speaks for the Lord rather than on his own behalf, with the following verses addressing the false prophets. Verse 6 specifically mentions divination, or fortune-telling, something that is forbidden to people of God (Deuteronomy 18:10). It is considered a betrayal of the sufficiency of God's revelation and a serious mistaking of the way to live a life pleasing to God.

In Micah's day, these false prophets held equal status with God's prophets, if not higher because of the popularity of their message. Yet, one hundred years later, these same false prophets will be walking through the ruins of Jerusalem like unclean lepers (3:7). But Micah is filled with God's Spirit and with the power to speak on His behalf to the people (3:8).

Verses 9–12 make up the third oracle against the corrupt leadership of the people. This last oracle speaks to the leadership in general, adding the priests, by name, to the leaders and false prophets.

Micah continues railing against the leaders for their unjust ways (3:9–10). Both the civic leaders and the religious leaders are accused of taking bribes instead of following God for justice (3:11). Verse 12 is the only verse in the Old Testament that is cited word for word somewhere else in the Old Testament (Jeremiah 26:18), some one hundred years later. The Lord relents because of Hezekiah's faithfulness, and this prophecy does not come to pass.

MICAH 4:1–13

ZION'S FUTURE

Setting Up the Section

While Jerusalem is still being addressed in chapter 4, the mood of the message changes. Micah 4–5 contains the first of the oracles of salvation. These are oracles of an eventual deliverance, unlike the apparent near-terms deliverance described in 2:12–13. These oracles describe a new epoch that lies beyond the judgment that Micah is prophesying for Israel and Judah in the near future.

The prediction that opens chapter 4 is similar to other instances in the Old Testament prophets such as Isaiah 2:2–4 and Hosea 3:5. The opening mention of the last days is used in the New Testament also to refer to the future when God will bring all prophecies to fruition (1 Timothy 4:1; 2 Timothy 3:1; 1 Peter 1:5; Jude 18). There is debate about whether these days refer to a time before Christ comes again or the time after Christ actually has returned.

In the opening verses of this fourth chapter, Micah overhears the nations and reflects on what he has seen and heard and what will come of it: The law of God will be embraced by the nations and the result will be peace, to the point that weapons will be retooled for growing food. This is a refreshing contrast to the forms of justice Micah has just condemned. The final verse of this segment has been described as a liturgical response on the part of the righteous: Until this vision is a reality, God's people will participate by faith.

Demystifying Micah

Almost every ancient Near Eastern religion and deity had a mountain dedicated to it, and most often a temple stood on that mountain (or hill, as the case may be). In this era, the mountain symbolizes God's bringing of order over chaos, access to heaven, and His presence on earth. All of this is the context for Micah's prophecy in verses 1–5: The Lord's mountain rising above the others means that Yahweh will reign supreme as the nations come to recognize and honor Him as the true God.

The opening phrase of verse 6—*in that day*—refers to the events of 4:1–5. The prophet is anticipating the reality of the exile that has already been prophesied. God's remnant will be made up of the weakest ones of society, and He will use those people to rebuild His strong nation (4:6–7). This can be seen as a foreshadowing image of what God will do through Christ—born in a stable yet God in human flesh. In fact, in the next verse, God directly addresses Jerusalem as He will later address Bethlehem (5:2). Eventually, the depleted people of God will become the nucleus of something far greater, stronger, and more permanent in the future. Judgment will come first; deliverance, salvation, and triumph later. Indeed, much later—far beyond the horizon of the people to whom Micah is preaching this message.

Take It Home

The response of the faithful in verse 5 reminds Christians of all eras that we are to bear witness to Micah's vision of the peace that comes from God's sovereignty. We can participate in it in advance, by living according to this same law in our lives today. We can whet our appetite—and that of the culture around us—for what is to come by living by faith in the reality we believe for the future.

Verses 9–13 contain two parallel sections: Each refers to *now* (4:9, 11), moving from the present distress of God's people to a future deliverance; each has a command (4:10, 13); each has a promise that is the rationale for obedience (4:10, 13); and each takes a similar view of present circumstances as being the outworking of a plan that people do not understand.

The suffering of the people in the coming captivity is foreshadowed in verses 9–10. Some Bible translations interpret *king* and *counselor* as a reference to human figures and thus interpret the question in verse 9 as sarcasm. But if verse 9 parallels verse 11, it suggests that these words are a reference to God. In this understanding, the question is rhetorical. Has God perished? Of course not.

There is a twist in verses 11–13. While these nations think they are destroying Israel on their own, in reality God is using them to punish and purify His people. While their actions are being used by Him at this time, eventually He will punish these nations for both their actions and their intentions.

God's plan and purpose is to bring eventual salvation out of the present distress and judgment. He will eventually order Israel to take action instead of simply writhing in agony (4:9, 13). But for now, Israel must pass through judgment until these nations—which, in their hubris, seek to destroy God's people and God Himself—will be destroyed. The commands of verses 10 and 13 are a summons that, in the meantime, those who belong to the faithful remnant are to step out in faith and endure the judgments of the Lord, knowing that vindication is in His hands.

MICAH 5:1–15

THE COMING CHAMPION

Setting Up the Section

The first verse of chapter 5 actually completes the closing thought from chapter 4. With verse 2, then, Micah begins a hopeful oracle regarding a champion who will come from Bethlehem. Verses 2–4 discuss the rule and triumph of the Messiah Himself, and verses 5–6 describe those who rule in His name. The ideal king of the ancient Near East is a shepherd king, one who provides for and cares for his people. The Messiah will be such a king.

The idea in verse 1 of Israel's leader being stricken on the cheek is an image of Hezekiah's total humiliation. He is so defenseless that he cannot even protect his face. He cannot defend his people—it's as if they have no king at all. It is in this context of Israel's humiliation and the demonstration of her powerlessness against a mighty foreign army that the great messianic prophecy is given. Once again, Micah is moving from the present distress of Israel—in this case, the Assyrian invasion of 701 BC—to a future deliverance.

Demystifying Micah

The Assyrian invasion in 701 BC is the context of this oracle. This is demonstrated by several things: 1) In verses 5–6, Nimrod, that is Babylon, is an inferior power, so this must be when Babylon is subject to Assyria, not later when it rules over the former Assyrian Empire; 2) in the verses following verse 5, Assyria is used as the representative of the forces of hostility to the kingdom of God, which makes sense if it is the great enemy of the people of God in the day of this prophecy; and 3) the term *leaders*, or *principle men*, at the end of verse 5 is rarely used, but it is one the Assyrian king Sargon used for his leaders.

Beginning with verse 2, Micah addresses the city of Bethlehem. With the advantage of hindsight, we know that Micah is about to share words related to the coming of Christ. The mention of old or ancient times seems to be a reference to the Messiah's bloodline—the ancestry of Jesse and David. It will be a new start from the original root.

The idea of verse 3 is that Israel's distress will continue until the Messiah comes. The *remnant*, or the *rest*, is the same idea as in Isaiah 11:11–12 and Zechariah 10:10, the gathering of those who have been dispersed because of exile or defeat.

In verse 4, the Messiah is called a shepherd, and this shepherd will protect His people from the *Assyrian*, as if describing an individual (5:5–6), but the name represents the enemies of the kingdom of God. The use of the number seven is a depiction of the idea of perfection (5:5). Then, the number eight offers the idea of even more than perfect. The Messiah's kingdom will have all the necessary leaders and the very best of them; the enemy will be no match for them. The golden age will be a messianic age. The consummation of the kingdom of God in the world will be brought to pass by the rule of this coming king.

The previous oracle links the earlier prophecies with the coming of the Messiah. In the oracle beginning in verse 7, the Messiah will expand His kingdom through the nations of the world by means of the remnant.

Dew is life-giving water that comes from God—humans are powerless to create or control it (5:7). This water comes from the Lord to and for people, and when it comes, it covers everything. This sets up the promise that comes next. As before in Micah, a parallel structure appears in verses 7–8. Each verse has as its subject the remnant among the nations, and each has a description in simile form of what the remnant will be—like dew and like showers in the first case; like a lion and like a young lion in the second. Each concludes with an explanation of the descriptions—in the first case, an image of salvation; and in the second, judgment and destruction.

The promise for the remnant includes a new strength for the group (5:9). But this eventual blessing can come only when God punishes His own people in order to purify them (5:10–14). The destruction in Micah's own day comes by means of the Assyrian invasion, and it will continue with the exile to Babylon (which has already been foretold by Micah). The specific details of the destruction highlight God's anger at Israel's worship of false gods. The word translated *destroy* or *demolish* in verse 14 is the same word used in Leviticus concerning the punishment of sin in the camp in order to maintain a holy people (Leviticus 17:10; 20:3).

MICAH 6:1–16

MORE ACCUSATIONS

Setting Up the Section

The first oracle in chapter 6 is a kind of lawsuit God brings against the people. Then the chapter closes with a pronouncement of Israel's sentence.

The opening phrase of the chapter highlights that these are the Lord's words spoken through Micah. The following case or lawsuit against the people is a common theme in the Prophets. The Lord is the plaintiff, witnesses are called, the evidence is presented, and a judgment is rendered.

The mountains in verse 2 are personalized and called upon as witnesses for several reasons: First, they are the original witnesses of the covenant God made with His people when they entered the promised land (Deuteronomy 27:12–13). Also, Micah indicates that they are enduring and unchanging, outlasting a thousand generations of God's people, and can therefore bear witness to the everlasting validity of God's covenant with His people.

God defends Himself against the complaint of His people, as they essentially blame Him instead of themselves for the present calamity (6:3). This extends the metaphor of God trying His people before a court, and here He is making His case. In the next two verses (6:6–7), Israel replies, saying it will perform rituals and sacrifices. But as seen often in the Prophets, God responds strongly, saying He doesn't want such things. Instead, we read one of the most well-known verses in Christian history, because it succinctly states God's desires for His people (6:8). It is a magnificent account of what true covenantal life involves and requires, and what God's gracious salvation must and will bring to pass in the lives of those who trust in Him. This idea expressed in verse 8 represents one of Micah's chief emphases. The failure of Israel's faith is demonstrated in the people's indifference to justice and mercy toward others, especially toward those who are poorer or weaker than themselves.

Critical Observation

In the Old Testament, a call to remember carries the idea of participation (6:5). In remembering, the people are reliving and reclaiming events of the past. This is very much the same thing that is involved, or is to be involved, in the Lord's Supper when we are told to "do this in memory of the Lord." We are to bring what He did into our present experience.

Verse 9 is a summons to the city to listen to what the Lord has decided. In the legal analogy, this is the sentencing phase of the oracle. The rod mentioned in this verse is a picture of the Assyrians, who will attack and who will function as God's chastisement of His people.

Demystifying Micah

An *ephah* (6:10) equals twenty-two liters or about a half-bushel. Lack of technological expertise made the manufacture of precise weights and measures impossible. All you needed to make an unfair profit was an ephah that actually held less than it should, so then you would get the price for a full ephah while giving less than an ephah to your customer. There was little a customer could do in the day before weights and measures inspectors. Besides, as Micah says in chapter 2, the authorities were in the pocket of the cheating merchants.

Verses 10–13 catalog Israel's sins, beginning with cheating in business practices. The wealthy who are called out in verse 12 are the royal family, the land barons, and the military elite. We have already heard of their unjust treatment of the middle class in 2:2, 8–9 and 3:11. What comes next is the righteous sentence of the Judge they have ignored (6:13). The actions to avoid God's punishment will be futile; verses 14–15 show how normal activities for sustenance and comfort will no longer suffice.

In the final verse of this chapter, we see the only mention of kings by name in a prophetic message. It suggests that the sins of Omri and Ahab, more than a century before Micah's time, had by this time served as a paradigm for falling away from faith and engaging in injustice (6:16; see 1 Kings 16:23–30).

The judgments pronounced in verses 13–16 are the very curses that God long before (all the way back to Deuteronomy and Leviticus) promised to visit upon His people if they proved unfaithful to His covenant with them.

MICAH 7:1–20

EVENTUAL HOPE

Setting Up the Section

While Micah's prophecy is full of solemn accusations and bleak acknowledgments, it ends with a sense of triumph. It is Micah's statement of faith.

Chapter 7 opens with an image that anyone in Micah's agricultural society would understand—a vinedresser and orchard manager who, after long and patient labor, finds his vineyard stripped by vandals. God feels the same way when He comes to delight in His people and finds, instead, so much sin. The last part of verse 2 can sound like a manhunt, but it is actually a reference to the way in which fellow countrymen are mistreating each other (7:1–2).

Micah again specifically calls out the leaders and judges for their sins (7:3). In verse 4, he calls the best of them a briar, and a group of them like a hedge of briars, again an agricultural reality for the original audience. Briars only keep people or animals from harvesting ripe fruit—they leave painful digs and scratches on those who try. In this case, the briars are obstructing justice.

The watchmen in verse 4 won't help protect anyone, and this repeats the idea that one should not trust in his own protection, because God is the only source of protection, safety, and peace. Further, even the most intimate human relations snap under the strain of the terror of enemies, and each one looks out for oneself, as is happening to these people (7:6). This is a fitting sentence for a nation that preys upon its brothers (7:5–6).

Micah watches in hope for the Lord and waits for God his Savior (7:7). The appropriate response to such a moral and spiritual catastrophe is just so: to wait upon the Lord.

Take It Home

The instruction to wait on the Lord is found in a great many other such passages: Psalms 37:7; 38:15; Lamentations 3:26; and many more. People must humbly submit and wait upon the Lord's outcome. It is not ours to worry or fret, or to take matters in our own hands by doing what the Lord forbids. We must simply wait upon the moving of God. In the meantime, a proper spiritual posture for the believer is to always look to God to redress wickedness and, in the meantime, serve Him faithfully. Micah watches in hope for the Lord, and he waits for God his Savior. This is the most appropriate response in the midst of a moral and spiritual catastrophe.

The next section of verses (7:8–13) opens almost like a psalm, with Jerusalem telling her enemy not to gloat. She is being punished justly for her sins; but precisely because the Lord always does what is right, the remnant within Israel who acknowledges their sin and repents will once again enjoy the Lord's favor. Though she sits in darkness now, she will again sit in the light. And, then, those who were the instrument of her downfall will reap their just punishment.

In verse 11, the prophet speaks to Jerusalem, but the idea of walls here is not to imply defensive fortifications. These walls are more like the wall that surrounds a vineyard. Their mention speaks to Jerusalem's prosperity, not her self-defense.

Verse 12 indicates the universal reach of Yahweh's salvation—not just to one people, but all people. This is the fulfillment of God's ancient promise to Abram (Genesis 15:18) in a new and still more glorious form—the promise extends not just to the area but to the people in that area. God's justice will see to it that nations that leave Israel desolate will suffer a compensatory desolation (Micah 7:13). This last judgment is described in highly figurative language, just as it is everywhere else in the Bible.

With verse 14, the prophet turns from representing the Lord to Jerusalem and begins to represent the people in prayer to God. Addressing God as Shepherd is appropriate in several ways. In the ancient Near East, a king's role was to resemble that of a shepherd, caring for and protecting his people.

Bashan and Gilead are both known for their rich pastures, and thus they build upon the image of a shepherd (7:14). They are places fit for a king's sheep to graze. Israel doesn't possess these places anymore; they have been lost to her because of her infidelity to God. But Micah is asking that Israel be restored. It is not a presumptuous request, because God has already promised that Israel's former dominion will be restored to her (4:8). Micah's prayer is that God's Word, His promise, will come true.

The Lord interrupts and speaks in verse 15, promising to show His people in the future wonders of His grace and power such as He showed Israel when He brought them out of Egypt and through the wilderness. The stories of the Exodus are faith affirming for the people of Israel. They remember God's mighty acts as He freed His people and miraculously led them toward the land He had promised them.

After the brief interlude in which God speaks, Micah takes over again in verses 16–17. In these verses, the images of nations with deaf ears and hands on mouths represent a sense of awe and even a sense of being put in one's place. In fact, all the images in these verses are of people who recognize the greatness of Israel's God.

The final three verses of Micah's prophecy include three terms for sin (*sin*, *transgression*, and *iniquities*) and six descriptions of God's character: His pardons, His forgiveness, His ability to let go of anger, His delight in showing mercy, His compassion, and His faithfulness. These terms are reminiscent of the Exodus account in which God identifies Himself to Moses (Exodus 34:6). Micah sings the praises of the true God while educating his listeners and readers about the character of God.

Take It Home

An unworthy, undeserving, but repentant people can hope in a glorious future precisely because of God's unchanging mercy and because of His fidelity to His promise. Micah's prophecy reminds us all that while we will experience God's chastisement, there is hope for every heart that has the ability and the willingness to repent.

NAHUM

INTRODUCTION TO NAHUM

Nahum is a book that calls into reckoning Judah's enemy, Nineveh. A careful reading of this book reveals that the author has a high view of God and His Word; he preaches against idolatry, immorality, injustice, and all manner of sin.

AUTHOR

We don't know many facts about Nahum, but there is no reason to doubt he is the primary author of the material that bears his name. From his writing style we can assume he was born into a family with enough means to provide him literary training.

OCCASION

Nahum witnessed the reduction of his nation to vassalage during the early campaigns of Assyria. These events, a prelude and a means to the judgment of both Judah and Nineveh, are part of the process that accomplishes the restoration of God's people.

PURPOSE

Nahum writes his short prophecy (1) to announce the doom of Nineveh and the demise of the mighty Assyrian Empire and (2) to bring a message of consolation to an oppressed Judah.

THEMES

The most basic theological perspective of Nahum is that of God's sovereignty. God is seen as supreme over nature and nations. He moves in just judgment against His foes but with saving concern for those who put their trust in Him. God is shown to be jealous and to abhor sin, but He is also long-suffering and has distinct purposes for His redeemed people.

HISTORICAL CONTEXT

The origin and setting of Nahum's prophecy can be deduced from the earliest and latest events mentioned: the fall of Thebes (663 BC) in Nahum 3:8 and the fall of Nineveh (612 BC), an event that is predicted throughout the book. The book of Nahum is intimately bound up with this period of dramatic change.

OUTLINE

NAHUM 1:1–15

THE DOOM OF NINEVEH DECLARED

A Hymn to the Sovereign God 1:1–10
God's Justice for Nineveh and Judah 1:11–15

Setting Up the Section

Nahum begins his prophecy with a notice of its central focus—Nineveh (1:1)—and then turns his attention to a description of Nineveh's certain doom (1:2–15). Throughout the book, Nahum's prophecies deal with Nineveh's doom, its eventual defeat, and its destruction. In the opening section, doom is declared to be certain, because it has been decreed by the sovereign and just Judge of the world, who deals equitably with all.

1:1–10

A HYMN TO THE SOVEREIGN GOD

Nahum begins his prophecy with a two-part hymn that sets forth the theme of the section and depicts selected key elements of God's nature. The hymn emphasizes that God is a God of justice, who will punish the wicked and avenge His own (1:2). Further, He is a sovereign and mighty God who, although He is long-suffering, will defeat His guilty foes (1:3–6) and, though He is beneficent, will destroy those who plot against Him (1:7–10). The rehearsal of these general truths concerning the character and work of God provides a foundation for their application to the world situation of Nahum's day.

Nineveh, having plotted against God's people and afflicted God's people, will experience His judgment, while a previously punished Judah will know relief from affliction and be restored to peace and joy (1:12–15).

In the majestic hymn to Yahweh in verses 2–10, critical scholars have recognized the skeleton of an acrostic based on the Hebrew alphabet. The acrostic is difficult to trace in that the prescribed letter of the alphabet may occur within the line rather than as the first letter. However, the hymnic nature of verses 2–10 is undeniable.

By calling his prophecy a vision, Nahum underscores the fact that what he says is not of his own invention but is that which God has specially revealed to him. At the outset, then, Nahum makes clear that his words are not his own insights based upon his observations of the events of his time. Rather, they are nothing less than the message given to him by the sovereign God, whose word he must deliver however difficult it might be.

Nahum's prophecy is directed at Nineveh, as is made clear at the start. It begins with an indication of its theme: God is a God of justice who will punish the wicked and avenge His own (1:2).

Critical Observation

Nahum's employment of the idea of jealousy is in harmony with the familiar scriptural motif of the husband and the wife. This motif is often applied in the Bible to God's relationship to Israel. Israel had been the object of God's eternal love. She had been brought into the family of God in the exodus from Egypt. He had cared for her and nourished her in the testing of the wilderness and had brought her safely into the land of inheritance.

Thus vengeance becomes a key to understanding Nahum's prophecy. Because God is holy, He cannot let sin go unpunished. Because only God is perfectly holy, just, and wise, only He can exact the proper punishment (see Psalm 94). The last line of Nahum 1:2 is important for understanding the process of God's vengeance: It is not always immediate. At times He holds in reserve His wrath against His foes until the proper occasion.

Having drawn the reader's attention to a sovereign and just God who deals in judgment with the ungodly (1:2), Nahum further develops this theme as his hymn to Yahweh continues. The first part of the hymn (1:2–6) is drawn largely from traditional Exodus themes underscoring God's wrath against an unbelieving enemy. The second part (1:7–10) comes from a wider spectrum of praises to God for His defense of His own while defeating the enemy.

In all this, Nahum gives a graphic picture of the limitless and invincible power of God. Having painted such a poignant portrait, Nahum returns to the subject of the destruction of God's foes (1:8–10). God, in His judicial wrath, will come against them like a victorious commander pursuing his foes to the farthest recesses of the earth. Indeed, God's enemies will come to understand that He will overturn their insolent plotting against Him so thoroughly that, like men entangled in thorns or overcome with their own drunkenness, they will be easily overthrown. God's fiery wrath will consume them like fire. They will not devise their devious plot a second time.

The ruins of Nineveh show abundant evidence of the intensity of the conflagration that consumed the fallen city. Whatever application these verses have to God's enemies in general, it is obvious that Nahum's prophetic pronouncements have a particular relevance for Nineveh.

1:11–15

GOD'S JUSTICE FOR NINEVEH AND JUDAH

With the completion of the hymn, Nahum turns to the two nations and their capitals that are the subject of his prophecies. The latter half of his hymn has been directed against those who plot against God. Keying in on that term, Nahum turns to the supreme example of such activity: Assyria and its capital city of Nineveh. In four short verses, Nahum brings God's charges against Nineveh—it will be judged regardless of its seemingly limitless strength (1:11–12, 14). This judgment will result in a respite for Judah in its affliction (1:12–13). The section closes with a stirring message of good news: Because wicked Nineveh has been judged, a repentant Judah may once again worship God in peace (1:15).

This short section is distinct from the previous hymn in 1:2–10. In a dramatic structural shift from hymnic to narrative style, Nahum turns to Nineveh in application of the teaching of his hymn. Nineveh/Assyria is identified as a plotter, an identification that seems obvious in the light of the military exploits of its most prominent kings. The word translated in verse 11 as *wickedness* (NIV) is often translated *worthlessness.* It speaks of a character of life so totally reprobate that the term came ultimately to apply to Satan himself (2 Corinthians 6:14–15).

The initial phase of Nahum's messages against Nineveh follows in Nahum 1:12–14. For Nineveh, there is the solemn affirmation that her long night of cruel domination is soon to end. Nahum's use of the word *name* is particularly appropriate, as it here connotes *existence* (1:14). Nineveh/Assyria is to be destroyed and left without descendant.

So hopeless is Nineveh's case and so devastating will be her demise that she will not even have a memorial left to her greatness, nor will anyone erect a monument to her memory. Because of her debased activity, she has gained such contempt for herself that her demise will bring to the lips of the observers of her fall a sigh of relief and a song of rejoicing (1:15).

With the pronouncement of the irreversible decision of divine judgment, there is a good word for Judah (1:13). Nahum's prophecy is a near-historical realization of Isaiah's. Isaiah foresees the day when an oppressed Israel will be freed at last from oppressors and invaders, and its people will not only hear the message of the Lord's salvation but also experience the everlasting serenity that comes with His presence in royal power in their midst (Isaiah 52:1–10).

Critical Observation

The emphasis of Isaiah and Nahum on God's good news becomes an important motif for the New Testament revelation. Jesus' birth is announced as an occasion of glad tidings (Luke 2:10), and Christ announces that His ministry is in initial fulfillment of the message of salvation and joy that Isaiah prophesied (compare Luke 4:16–21 with Isaiah 61:1–2). Peter makes clear to Jew and Gentile alike that Christ has effected their full salvation, with the result that God's full peace can be enjoyed by all (Acts 10:34–43), a message of good news that Paul likewise affirms (Ephesians 2:14–18). It is no wonder, then, that Paul later builds on the theme of the message of good news and peace that Christ has provided both as scriptural evidence for the Jew and as a challenge to all believers to bear the gospel to a needy mankind (Romans 10:9–15; see Isaiah 52:7; Nahum 1:15).

NAHUM 2:1–13

THE DOOM OF NINEVEH DESCRIBED

God Will Punish Wicked Nineveh and Restore His Own	2:1–2
First Description of Nineveh's Demise	2:3–10
The Discredited City	2:11–13

Setting Up the Section

Having declared Nineveh's certain doom and Judah's sure relief, Nahum turns to the chief consideration of his prophecy: the fall of Nineveh. The whole section is filled with the book's basic thesis: God will punish wicked Nineveh and restore His own people. This theme is developed with regard to Nineveh by means of a long narrative section (2:3–10) and a woe oracle (3:1–7).

2:1–2

GOD WILL PUNISH WICKED NINEVEH AND RESTORE HIS OWN

The fate of Nineveh is carried forward in the announcement of the arrival of its attacker. In the light of the critical announcement, Nahum issues a fourfold command. Each of the imperatives in verse 1 produces a staccato effect and lends urgency and dramatic appeal to the scene. Nahum's admonitions are probably to be understood as irony, perhaps with a touch of sarcasm. Because Nineveh's doom has already been announced (chapter 1), all such efforts are obviously destined for failure as God restores His own (2:2).

2:3–10

FIRST DESCRIPTION OF NINEVEH'S DEMISE

Nahum now turns from his introductory theme to the first of two descriptions of Nineveh's certain destruction. The section contains two parts: (1) a description of the attackers (2:3–6) and (2) the consequences of the attack (2:7–10). It is marked by several distinctive literary features by which the poet makes skillful plays on words.

Nahum's description of the attack against Nineveh begins with a consideration of its attackers (2:3–6). In these verses, there is a clear pattern describing the siege: the enemy's assembling of his forces (2:3), the initial advance (2:4), the all-out attack (2:5–6), and its aftermath (2:7–10). The scene progresses from one of preparation and advance to one of conflict.

As the account unfolds, the attackers have gained entrance to the city, for the Assyrians are seen as being captured and led away into exile, while the women, pleading for mercy and bewailing their fate, are led away moaning.

The inevitable consequences that follow the city's capture are then detailed in verses 8–10. The fate of the fallen city is in view. Conquered Nineveh is said to be like a pool of water. The simile is effective and appropriate. Mighty Nineveh lay in a favorable location that has blessed her with an adequate water supply. But now the blessing has turned into a curse at the hands of the enemy, whose siege has left Nineveh a "leaking water reservoir" (2:8 NLT). The panicked masses flee from the waters and the crumbling city.

Demystifying Nahum

In remarkable agreement with Nahum's prophecy that there is no end to Nineveh's treasures is the factual account in the Babylonian Chronicle that the spoil taken at Nineveh's capture is "a quantity beyond counting." The city is completely sacked.

2:11–13

THE DISCREDITED CITY

Contemplating the demise of arrogant Nineveh, Nahum utilizes a taunt song, a literary form common in the ancient Near East. Using an extended metaphor (or allegory), Nineveh is ironically compared to a lion's den, now no longer the lair of an invincible predator or a den of refuge for its cubs but reduced to ashes. Nineveh will be judged for its selfishness, rapacity, and cruelty.

Nahum can now ask, "Where?" The mighty lion of the nations (Assyria) used to proceed at will from its impenetrable lair (Nineveh) to return its prey to its pride (the citizens of Nineveh). Where is all of that now?

Like Nahum's first oracle (chapter 1), this section ends with a pronouncement of judgment for Nineveh/Assyria, but it includes a message of hope for Judah (2:12–13). Nahum's second oracle is not yet through, however, and before he adds a further note of good news (3:19), he will again consider the defeat and demise of Nineveh, detailing the reasons for the divine sentence (3:1–7).

NAHUM 3:1–19

THE DOOM OF NINEVEH DETAILED

Setting Up the Section

With the completion of the first description of Nineveh's doom, capped by a taunt song castigating the discredited city (2:3–13), the demise of Nineveh is rehearsed again, this time underlining the reasons for the devastation (3:1–7). Nahum will build upon that description with another taunt song, which will occupy the greater portion of the third chapter (3:8–19).

3:1–7

SECOND DESCRIPTION OF NINEVEH'S DEMISE

Nahum writes his second description of Nineveh's certain doom in the form of a woe oracle. The initial *woe* is a word drawn from a lamentation liturgy for the dead. As utilized by the prophet, while containing a prophetic declaration and description of the coming judgment, it also constitutes a formal denunciation of the doomed city. Woe oracles normally contain three elements: invective (3:1, 7), threat (3:2–3, 5–6), criticism (3:4).

In verses 2–3, Nahum moves to a vivid description of the coming battle. Whether reporting what he has seen in a vision or merely envisioning the future scene, his portrayal is done with picturesque brevity using vivid images.

This nation who had brought havoc and ruin to so much of the ancient Near East will now face death and destruction. Here again a notable crux occurs. Does the statement relative to Nineveh's harlotry (3:4) explain the death and destruction described in the previous verses, or does it initiate the following declaration of God's judgment against the city?

Further, Nineveh will be pelted with filth (3:6). The word translated *filth* denotes that which is detested. A strong word, it is usually reserved for contexts dealing with aberrations connected with pagan worship. The word carries with it the idea of the loathing that all such detestable practices produce; the thought is that despoiled Nineveh will be treated as a detested and abominable thing.

The woe reaches its climax with a sarcastic appraisal of Nineveh's hopeless plight: Nineveh is destroyed, destitute, and devoid of mourners (3:7).

3:8–13

A COMPARISON OF NINEVEH AND THEBES

Before Ashurbanipal's victory, Thebes seemed unconquerable. As described in verse 8, Thebes was surrounded by a strong defensive wall and a water system that included lakes, moats, canals, and the Nile. Thebes had been able to boast of the help of not only all Egypt but also its seventh-century allies: Sudanese Cush, Put (perhaps the fabled land of Punt in coastal Somaliland), and Libya. None of these, however, supplied strength and protection for Thebes at all.

Verses 12–13 depict the hopelessness of Nineveh's defensive measures. Nahum says the city's massive fortifications will crumble as readily before the eager attackers as first-ripe figs fall into the mouths of those who shake the trees. Further, its famed defenders will prove to be no more successful in protecting the city than untrained and weak women.

3:14–19

A CONCLUDING CONDEMNATION OF NINEVEH

With verse 14, Nahum approaches the end of his prophecy. The verses that follow form the second portion of an extended taunt song that functions as satire. This short section contains two short commands given in irony—verse 14 through the first part of verse 15, then the last part of verse 15 through verse 17. Verses 18–19 are a final gibe that forms both a concluding denunciation and a doleful dirge.

Nahum's sarcasm is evident throughout. He prophesies that Nineveh will know the besieger's fiery torch and sword as the enemy sweeps through the city like a horde of devouring locusts. Nineveh's merchants and officials flee and leave her alone, leaderless, and ill-equipped to meet the advance of the army that is about to surround her.

As Nahum approaches the end of his prophecy, Nineveh's leaders are compared to shepherds who have nodded off to sleep and allowed the sheep (the Ninevites) to be scattered (in flight or in exile) and subjected to harm. Even worse, no one comes to gather them. The choice of this motif as the final one for the book may suggest, as many commentators have observed, that the "sleep" of the shepherds/officials is death (3:18).

Critical Observation

Nahum's words have been dramatically precise in their fulfillment. They find corroboration in the findings of archaeologists who note the hasty strengthening of the walls at strategic defensive positions.

The fall of the city due to water (1:8; 2:8) has been attested both by archaeologists and ancient historians. Unusually heavy rains were known to have given difficulty to Nineveh, which was served by three rivers: the Tigris, the Khosr, and the Tebiltu. A high-water season and a sudden storm, accompanied by the swelling of any or all three rivers, would account for the fulfillment of Nahum's prophecy.

Nahum also predicts the burning of the city (1:10; 2:13; 3:15), a fact confirmed by archaeological excavation. Nahum's emphasis on the destruction of Nineveh's temples (1:14) is also confirmed by the excavations at Nineveh. Minute details concerning the events of the final days before Nineveh's fall—such as the drunkenness (1:10; 3:11), cowardice, degeneracy (3:4), and the desertion (2:8; 3:17) of the city by its leadership—are also abundantly recorded in the ancient traditions. Nahum's prophecies concerning the final slaughter of Nineveh's citizens (3:3) and the looting of the city (2:9–10), its utter destruction (2:10; 3:7), and the virtual disappearance of its people (3:17–19) are facts confirmed in the ancient records.

Nahum once more utilizes a rhetorical question to conclude the section, here with sobering effect. Had anyone escaped Nineveh's cruelty? The implied negative answer guarantees the universal rejoicing over Nineveh's demise. This last use of a rhetorical question (a double one, in the light of verse 18) is one of five such instances that have been woven into the book's fabric. Twice, rhetorical questions introduce the poet's satirical taunt song (2:11; 3:8). Three times a rhetorical question closes a unit with striking effect: underscoring God's irresistible judgment of sin (1:6) and emphasizing Nineveh's much-deserved destruction (3:7, 19).

Take It Home

Israel no doubt joined in the exultation and took comfort in the good news (3:19). Her dreaded enemy has faced God's judgment, a reminder of God's promise concerning His judgment of all Israel's foes. May Nahum's words, as well as those of God's prophets, teach all God's people to trust fully in Him, the Shepherd and overseer of souls.

HABAKKUK

INTRODUCTION TO HABAKKUK

Like Nahum, Habakkuk begins by referring to his message as an *oracle*, or a message placed upon his heart by God. Like Nahum, Habakkuk assures his readers that what he is about to relate is not from his own ingenuity but is from God. Unlike Nahum, however, Habakkuk does not state that his message is specifically directed at any one individual or group of people, though he will devote a great deal of space to a denunciation of the Chaldeans, which is a representation of the Babylonians.

AUTHOR

We don't know anything more about Habakkuk than what can be gleaned from this book. We do know, however, that his authorship of this message was accepted from very early on.

PURPOSE

The book of Habakkuk is less of a prophet preaching to his people and more of a prophet speaking to his God. Habakkuk asks probing questions which lead from the current state of Judah to the eventual future of the kingdom.

OCCASION

While Habakkuk may differ from the other prophets in terms of whom he addresses in his message, he is similar in that he is troubled by the disobedience of his people. In Habakkuk's case, however, rather than pleading with God for more time or with the people for more attention, he questions why God's judgment hasn't already fallen on his nation.

THEMES

While judgment and the eventual vindication of Israel is a part of Habakkuk's message, as with other Old Testament prophets, he also addresses themes such as faith in God's sovereignty.

OUTLINE

HABAKKUK 1:1–17

THE PROPHET'S PERPLEXITIES

Setting Up the Section

Habakkuk plunges into a rehearsal of his spiritual wrestling with God. In so doing, he tells his readers of his perplexities as to the divine working and of God's answers to his questions (1:2–2:20). This chapter will consider Habakkuk's superscription, his two questions, and God's answer to the first.

1:1–4

HOW CAN GOD DISREGARD JUDAH'S SIN?

Immediately after the notice of the source of his prophecy (1:1), Habakkuk at once plunges into a dramatic rehearsal of a time when the impact of Judah's unchecked sin overwhelmed him. His questioning of God forms the backdrop for the examination of the relation of God's holy standards to the operation of the divine providence that follows later.

The nature of Habakkuk's complaint to God, begun in the invocation (1:2) and elaborated in the statement of the problem (1:3–4), can be better appreciated when one examines the words he uses to describe his perception of Judahite society. They depict a society characterized by the general spiritual and ethical havoc that exists where such sin abounds.

Habakkuk is disturbed by God's silence with regard to his country's injustice and his own cries for help and intervention. His questions and doubts have an extra emotional and spiritual dimension. He is an unhappy, perplexed, and frustrated prophet.

1:5–11

GOD WILL JUDGE JUDAH

To the emotional and dramatic cry of the prophet, God gives a dramatic, amazing answer—God is already at work on the problem. He will send the Chaldeans (Babylonians) to chastise Judah (1:5–6). God then supplies some additional details as to the martial abilities of the violent Chaldeans (1:7–11).

Critical Observation

The term *Chaldea* is used in reference to the tribes that lived in southernmost Mesopotamia. They made up the biggest part of Babylonia. By at least 705 BC, Chaldean king Merodach-Baladan took the title "King of Babylon," with the result that the terms *Chaldean* and *Babylonian* became used interchangeably in the Old Testament.

God's reply mirrors the words Habakkuk had used. God tells Habakkuk to look at the nations (1:5). God is already at work in and behind the scenes of earth's history to set in motion events that will change the whole situation. And when Habakkuk learns what is to happen, he will be utterly amazed. In fact, he probably will not be able to believe it.

The reason for Habakkuk's astonishment becomes apparent in verse 6: God will raise up the Chaldeans. Verses 5–6, revealing Habakkuk's astonishment at God's sending the Chaldeans to judge His people, are crucial to understanding the setting of the book.

By telling Habakkuk of the Chaldeans' future prominence, the Lord reassures him of His sovereign control of the details of history. Since God's prophet will be surprised at the announcement about the Chaldeans, God goes on to supply a brief résumé of their character and potentially devastating power (1:6–11).

Contrary to Habakkuk's complaint, God assures His prophet that He sees all that comes to pass and hears the prayers and complaints of His people. Habakkuk's own word is sent back to him. Has Judah done violence? It shall in turn suffer violence at the hands of a violent nation whose well-trained and battle-seasoned army will move forward with such precision that the whole striking force will march as one to achieve its objectives, at the same time taking many captives (1:9).

Although the language is hyperbolic throughout verses 6–11, in light of the ancient records it is not inappropriate. Many texts could be cited concerning the Chaldeans' successful campaigning. The picture of Chaldean armed might is of one who holds all his foes in contempt and mocks them. Such a nation knows no god but strength (1:10).

Habakkuk is informed, however, that God's avenging host is not without responsibility. The Chaldeans will be held guilty for their actions. Had Habakkuk listened as carefully to the last line of God's answer as he did to the extended description of Judah's chastiser, he might have avoided the second perplexity that gripped his soul, the report of which is contained in the verses that follow (1:12–17).

1:12–17

HOW CAN GOD EMPLOY THE WICKED?

God's answer and extended description of his agent of judgment against Judah puzzles His prophet. Habakkuk simply cannot reconcile God's use of the Chaldeans, a people more corrupt than those they are to judge, to punish His people. He begins his second perplexity with an invocation in which he expresses his consternation (1:12). Faced with the prospect of destructive judgment, perhaps even the death of the nation itself, Habakkuk cries out to Israel's God, the Holy One of her salvation, who alone is her refuge in such times.

The precise understanding of Habakkuk's impassioned words, "we will not die" (1:12), is difficult to grasp, but most see it as a statement of confidence in God.

Despite that confidence in God, Habakkuk has reservations concerning the situation. His reservations are detailed in verses 13–17. While he understands the necessity of Judah's judgment and the Chaldeans' role, he cannot comprehend why a holy God plans to use a nation more wicked than the nation He desires to punish. Not only does God's announcement seem out of character for a holy God, but also the use of the Chaldeans provokes another thought. Once this plan is put into operation, will not a helpless mankind always be at the mercy of these God-commissioned agents of chastisement (1:13–17)?

Adopting fishing imagery, Habakkuk portrays the scenario that God has set in motion as one of fishermen (Chaldeans) who use their powerful hooks and nets (military might and methods) to catch helpless fish and creatures of the sea (the various conquered peoples). The success of these fishermen will only cause them to rejoice and have their appetites whetted for still greater pleasures.

Habakkuk's fears are not unfounded, for the Chaldean war machine was effective enough to gain for them political dominance across the northern part of the Fertile Crescent and through the Levant to the borders of Egypt.

Critical Observation

Habakkuk takes his place beside many others—such as Job, the psalmist Asaph (Psalm 73), Jeremiah, and Malachi—who question God as to His fairness in handling the problems of evil and injustice. Like these other questioners, Habakkuk will be shown the necessity of fully trusting in God.

HABAKKUK 2:1–20

GOD'S SOVEREIGNTY

Setting Up the Section

Habakkuk offers God's reply to his complaint, communicates an essential and timeless message about faith for all people, provides insight into the operations of divine government, and reveals the ultimate fate that will befall the wicked Chaldeans.

2:1–4

INSTRUCTIONS

Habakkuk ends his complaint with a renewed statement of his confidence in God (2:1). He also reports his intention to assume the role of a watchman. As the city watchman mans his post atop the walls to look for the approach of danger or a messenger, or to keep watch over current events, Habakkuk will assume the role of a prophetic watchman, taking his post to watch for the Lord's reply.

Before God's specific points of reply are given to Habakkuk, He has preliminary instructions for His prophet. The Lord's commands are intended to prepare Habakkuk for the revelation of crucial issues relative to the operations of divine government that will introduce the discussion of the whole matter of Habakkuk's concern: the disposition of the voracious Chaldeans (2:5–20).

Critical Observation

The place of Habakkuk 2:4 in the history of biblical interpretation can hardly be overestimated. Its threefold citation in the New Testament (Romans 1:17; Galatians 3:11; Hebrews 10:38) attests to its basic importance to the Christian revelation.

Accordingly, verse 4 is best taken with what follows. Though it forms the essence of the divine revelation that is to be heralded to all, it is woven into the structure of verse 5, both verses thus serving as the basis for the woes that follow.

Habakkuk is told in verse 2 to write the issue of the divine reply upon tablets. He is to communicate a message of lasting importance. Everyone who reads or hears these words is to consider themselves a herald of a significant communication intended for all people everywhere. Probably the precise words are to be found in verse 4, the latter part of which is of crucial significance. The message is to be written plainly so those who pass by might be able to understand it and bear the news to others.

Habakkuk now is told the basic guiding principles upon which the operation of divine government unalterably proceeds until the coming of that final appointed time (2:3). The revelation of these truths will make clear the culpability of the Chaldeans (2:5), whose woe is pronounced in the rest of the chapter (2:6–20).

2:5–20

THE CHALDEANS

Beginning with verse 5, God's answer takes the form of a logical argument: If it is true that the arrogant have ungodly desires and never come to enjoy the blessings of God, how much more certain is it that the qualities accompanying such an attitude will ultimately betray them? The underlying implication is clear: The Chaldeans' selfishness and success will be their undoing.

The first woe: The plundering Chaldean will be despoiled (2:6–8).

Each of the five woes, beginning in verse 6, pertains to one or more of the Chaldeans' sins. The first woe centers on the Chaldeans' rapacity. The language recalls their multiplying of wealth at the expense of others. The depth of the Chaldeans' insensitivity toward others may be seen in that they add to their riches by extorting pledges from their debtors, something condemned in the Torah and a violation against all mankind. The charge, only an example of the Chaldeans' unjust activities, provides entrée into the following metaphor taken from the world of finance.

Verse 7 reveals that those who had been so oppressed will arise suddenly and send collectors who will press their claims for back payment with a force equal to that of the Chaldeans' former violence. The chief point is that the plundering Chaldean will eventually know the effects of plunder himself. He who has so misused others—conquering, looting, and enslaving many—will himself experience the conqueror's heel and learn the sorrow of those whose people and possessions have been carried off as booty.

The second woe: The plotting Chaldean will be denounced (2:9–11).

The second woe underscores the Chaldeans' capacity for cunning schemes against mankind. Building upon the imagery in the first woe, the Chaldean is portrayed as one who achieves wealth through violence and evil means. Verse 11, with its stone walls and beams, is a reference to the Chaldeans' building projects. In the end, the Chaldeans will have no lasting empire.

The third woe: The pillaging Chaldean will be destroyed (2:12–14).

The image of construction found in the second woe is continued in the third. The chief materials used in constructing the city are seen for what they are: bloodshed and injustice. Such conduct is an affront to a holy and righteous God. It marks the Chaldeans as those who, unlike the righteous who reflect God's standards, are arrogant and presumptuous.

Babylon (and all such wicked people) will be judged, not only for her unbridled arrogance, but also because God's purposes include a universal experiencing of His own glory. The words of verse 14 are adapted from Isaiah 11:9. Isaiah's prophecy looks ahead to the great messianic era in all its fullness and perfection; Habakkuk uses it to validate the pronouncement of the destruction of the Neo-Babylonian Empire.

The fourth woe: The perverting Chaldean will be disgraced (2:15–17).

The tie between the third and fourth woes is not as pronounced as between the first and second or the second and third. However, they do have in common a reference to a city or town (2:12, 17).

The fourth woe begins with an invective formed with a strong allegory. The Chaldean is a man who gives his neighbor a drink in seeming hospitality. The apparently innocent cup contains a draught of wrath, for it is designed to get its partaker drunk. The allegory depicts the giver of the drink as one who is forced to imbibe of his own drink and suffer the disgrace of exposure. Several familiar biblical motifs and expressions are contained in verses 15–16. The cup as a motif of judgment is well attested elsewhere. Particularly enlightening for the understanding of Habakkuk's fourth woe is Jeremiah's use of the cup to portray God's relation with Babylon (Jeremiah 51:6–8).

Habakkuk makes the same point, although the image is slightly different. The Chaldean now knows the shame he has brought on others. Therefore, he is given a sarcastic command: "Go on! Drink and expose yourself!" (2:16). The last imperative is graphic. It means to show oneself as uncircumcised. Not even in the marks of his body can the Chaldean claim covenant relationship with Yahweh.

The reason the Chaldean must drink the cup follows in verse 17. His will be a wanton disregard of the value of the natural world, the animal kingdom, and civilized humanity.

The scene shifts to the animal kingdom. It, too, will suffer violence at the hands of the Chaldeans. The natural and animal worlds are often made unwilling participants in mankind's sin and greed. It is a crime that has increasingly plagued human society. Such thoughtless conduct by the Chaldeans indicates again their godless arrogance and selfish presumption for which punishment must come.

The fourth woe is closed with a reiteration of the charge made against the Chaldean in the first. He will have a callous disregard even for the sanctity of human life. In his quest for power, he will destroy everything that stands in his way, be it lands, cities, or those who dwell in them.

The fifth woe: The polytheistic Chaldean will be deserted by his idols (2:18–20).

In drawing the woe oracles to a close, Habakkuk deliberately changes the order he has previously employed by beginning with the reason for the threatened judgment (2:18).

The religious orientation of the Chaldean is now examined and shown to be without foundation. His idolatrous polytheism is seen to be worthless. Since idols are only mankind's creation, to put one's trust in them is to trust one's own creation rather than the Creator.

Before going on to give the most crucial reason for the doom of the polytheistic Chaldean, Habakkuk delivers an invective and a threat (2:19).

The fifth woe ends with a pronouncement that displays the vast difference between Israel's God and the gods of Babylon. Unlike those gods, who have neither life nor word of guidance for their followers, Yahweh is a living God. The gods of Babylon (and their devotees) can only remain silent before Him.

The invective and threat against Babylon (2:19) thus have more than sufficient cause. Since the Chaldeans worship gods of their own creation (2:18) rather than the Creator, controller, and consummator of history, their condemnation is certain. This is their most besetting sin. The verdict is final. Habakkuk can be assured that the Chaldeans will be judged, for they will violate the standards of God.

Verse 20 has another application. Because the idolatry that leads to the neglect and rejection of God is a universal problem, all the earth is to be silent before the living God.

HABAKKUK 3:1–19

THE PROPHET'S PRAYER AND GOD'S EXALTATION

The Prophet's Prayer	3:1–2
The Redeemer	3:3–15
The Prophet's Pledge to the Redeemer's Purposes	3:16–19

Setting Up the Section

A perplexed prophet had awaited and received God's instructions in chapter 2. In humble response, Habakkuk turns in prayer and praise to God.

3:1–2

THE PROPHET'S PRAYER

Having heard and understood God's principles of judgment and their application, Habakkuk returns to the matter of Judah's judgment. What follows is his prayer psalm, a composition to be set to music for use in worship.

In verse 2, Habakkuk begins his prayer with a cry and a statement of praise that reflect his fear of God. The choice of the word *Lord* (Yahweh) rather than a more general term probably emphasizes the fact that Habakkuk addresses his words to Israel's covenant God. He has heard of Yahweh's past mighty deeds. Habakkuk has in mind the Exodus, the subject of verses 3–15.

In accordance with God's message of the near chastisement of Judah, Habakkuk prays for God's miraculous intervention. He asks that (as in the past) God will renew His deeds and thus again make known His work of redemption. With an aching heart, he urges God to be compassionate in the coming turmoil.

3:3–15

THE REDEEMER

Habakkuk has prayed for God's mercy in the midst of judgment. He does so on the basis of his consideration of God's past redemptive acts for His people, some of which he now rehearses for all to contemplate. The prayer-psalm-poem consists of two distinct works (3:3–7 and 3:8–15). The first poem deals with Israel's movement up from the Sinai Peninsula, on the way to the Jordan River crossing.

In a graphic simile, the brilliance of God's glory is detailed. The association of the glory of the Lord with Sinai is unmistakable; the point here, however, may be that the same glory that was seen at Mount Sinai and traveled with the people on their journeys (Exodus 40:34–38) now moves in surpassing brilliance ahead of them. This first poem closes with a consideration of God's initial strikes against the enemy (Habakkuk 3:6–7). The land of the Midianites is identified primarily with the southern part of Transjordan, and evidence now exists that Cushan was also located there.

The second poem is a victory ode that sings of the mighty strength of Israel's Redeemer. His power is displayed at the waters of testing (3:8–9), unleashed in the natural world (3:9–11), and viewed by the enemy (3:12–15). Whereas the first two sections deal in a general way with the entire Exodus event, the final section fixes its attention on the initial stage of the Exodus.

Addressing God personally, Habakkuk asks whether His actions against the waters are out of anger. All three words for wrath here characterize God's judicial activity against anything that opposes His will. Yahweh is portrayed metaphorically as Israel's mighty warrior who appears in His battle chariot, armed with bow, club, arrows, and spear (3:8–11). This is no cosmic battle between deities; Yahweh comes as Israel's champion against human opponents.

The reference to waters here probably refers to God's activities in the entire Exodus event. The theme of water is prominent not only in the triumph at the Red Sea (Exodus 14) but also in passing through the Jordan (Joshua 3–4).

The scene changes from preparation to engagement in battle. The predominant image in this description of nature's response is the agitation of cosmic waters. The description in verses 9–10 fits well with the details of the crossing of the Jordan. The drama of warfare continues in verse 11 with a hyperbolic description.

Habakkuk had begun his prophecy with a perplexity as to why God tolerates injustice (1:2–3). When he is informed of God's intention to use the godless Chaldeans to bring judgment to His people (1:5–11), the prophet is all the more perplexed (1:12–2:1). The words of the ancient epic poem that he now considers remind him of the just nature of God.

The poem closes with details that provide a follow-up to the previous scene (3:14–15). The enemy's warriors storm out against the people of God like brigands coming upon the helpless. If, as suggested above, verse 8 deals primarily with the events toward the end of the Exodus experience, verse 15 produces the basis for the whole chain of events: the great deliverance from Egypt. The double psalm thus ends on a note of redemption. Israel's God, who brought them through the waters of testing with a mighty power that left all nature in convulsion, and who led His people in triumph, is the One who has been with them since the deliverance out of Egypt.

3:16–19

THE PROPHET'S PLEDGE TO THE REDEEMER'S PURPOSES

Habakkuk ends his prophecy with affirmations of personal commitment and praise. Having been dramatically reminded of the past exploits of God against the wicked and His saving intervention on behalf of His people, the prophet is overwhelmed. Now that he understands who God is and the principles and methods of His activities, it is enough for Habakkuk. He will trust Him through the coming hour of judgment and rejoice no matter what may happen (3:16–18). The words for *rejoicing* here represent strong emotions; Habakkuk used them previously to express his anxiety over the unbridled avarice of the Chaldeans (1:14–15). Here he underscores his repentant heart and triumphant faith. Together these words express his resolve not merely to rest in the Lord's will through everything that will come to pass but to rejoice fully in his saving God.

Borrowing phraseology from the repertoire of ancient Hebrew poetry, he closes the account of his spiritual odyssey on a high note of praise (3:19). The order is significant. Whatever strength he has he owes to the One who is his strength; but basic to everything is the fact that Yahweh is his Lord and his Master, the center of his life.

Habakkuk 3:8–15 constitutes a victory song commemorating the conquest itself and points to the basis of that success in the Exodus event, particularly in the victory at the Red Sea. After Habakkuk pleads for mercy in the midst of wrath (3:2) and reviews God's past record (3:3–15), his reverential trust in God is renewed. Israel's great Redeemer is his also. He will trust in the Lord no matter what happens (3:16–19). He who had acted both in judgment and deliverance for Israel in the past can be counted on to do so once again, both for Israel and His prophet. Thus Habakkuk's final prayer of praise to Israel's Redeemer stands not only as a unified composition but also as the climax to the whole prophecy.

ZEPHANIAH

INTRODUCTION TO ZEPHANIAH

Zephaniah denounced the materialism and greed that exploited the poor. He was aware of world conditions and announced God's judgment on the nations for their sins. Above all, God's prophet had a deep concern for God's reputation and for the well-being of all who humbly trust in Him.

AUTHOR

Although some concern has been raised with regard to many passages in the book that bears his name, Zephaniah has generally been accepted as the author of most of this book. Zephaniah traces his patrilineage four generations to a certain Hezekiah. Jewish and Christian commentators alike have commonly identified this Hezekiah with the king by that name, though this is not conclusive.

PURPOSE

Zephaniah speaks out for God and against wickedness. He writes to inform and warn his people of God's coming judgment, not only against all the world, but also against Judah and Jerusalem. Zephaniah also writes to give the people details of the fearsome events of the Day of the Lord that must come because of sin and because of the Lord's undying concern for His people who have humble and contrite hearts.

OCCASION

The occasion for Zephaniah's prophecy lies in the deplorable spiritual and moral condition of Judah in the early days of Josiah's reign. Taking the throne as an eight-year-old, Josiah finds himself the head of an immoral society. As Zephaniah writes, he is cognizant of the conditions that will surely spell the end of Judah itself (2 Kings 23:26–27).

THEMES

Zephaniah is best remembered for his presentation of God as the sovereign and just judge of all. It is He who punishes the wickedness of people and nations, particularly those who have opposed His people.

HISTORICAL CONTEXT

Few scholars have failed to accept that this book's author, as the first verse states, prophesied during the reign of Josiah (640–609 BC). Most discussions about the setting of the book of Zephaniah concern which period of Josiah's reign provides the backdrop, though many favor Josiah's early reign, because many of the problems that Zephaniah describes in his nation would have been corrected in Josiah's reforms.

OUTLINE

ZEPHANIAH 1:1–18

THE ANNOUNCEMENT OF THE DAY OF THE LORD

Setting Up the Section

Zephaniah begins his prophecy with notices of his reception of the word of the Lord, his ancestry, and the time of his ministry (1:1). He then announces the coming of God's worldwide judgment and supplies important details concerning the devastation of that coming Day of the Lord (1:14–18).

1:1–6

PRONOUNCEMENTS OF JUDGMENT

God's prophet warns of a universal judgment that will one day descend upon the earth and all that is on it. The pronouncement is solemn; its phraseology is at first reminiscent of the flood (Genesis 6:17; 7:21–23). The disaster envisioned here, however, is more cataclysmic, for every living thing that dwells on the land, air, and sea dies. Man's sin is weighty, involving not only himself but his total environment (1:2–3).

Zephaniah alludes also to the Creation. His catalog of death is arranged in inverse order to God's creative work: mankind, beast, the creatures of the air, and those of the sea (see Genesis 1:20–27). The coming destruction will begin with humanity, who has denied the Creator and involved in his sin all that is under his domain (1:6). Because of their idolatry and apostasy, Judah and Jerusalem will find God's hand of chastisement stretched out against them (1:4–6).

Demystifying Zephaniah

Baal is a god associated with the storm and fertility; his veneration, together with licentious worship rites, is a constant source of temptation to Israel. Fascination with Baal had been a prime reason for the fall of the northern kingdom and will prove to be so for Judah as well. Although Zephaniah's denunciation of those who worship the hosts of heaven on the rooftops is a further indication of the turn that the worship of Baal often took, the adoration of Baal and the stars was a besetting sin in Judah when Josiah came to the throne.

1:7–13

EXHORTATIONS BASED ON JUDGMENT

In the light of the pronouncements of judgment, Zephaniah issues exhortations to Judah. Since the coming of judgment is certain, it is time for them to examine their spiritual condition. The unit is made up of two sections, each introduced by an imperative (1:7, 11) followed by additional details (1:8–9, 12–13). Accordingly, verse 10 is a hinge verse that proceeds on the basis of the time framework of verses 8–9 and predicts the lamentation of the merchants upon which the call for wailing is issued (1:11).

In view of the certainty and severity of coming judgment, Zephaniah advises silence and submission, fear and consecration. The motive for his call for silence follows in verse 7—the Day of the Lord. Although Zephaniah delays his description of the terrors of the Day of the Lord until the next section (1:14–18), the seriousness of that time is underscored in a dramatic metaphor of a sacrificial banquet. The sacrifice itself is Judah and Jerusalem.

Critical Observation

The metaphor of the sacrificial banquet provides a ray of hope in the clouds of doom. Although judgment is coming, there is still time. By acknowledging God as their Master and by responding in fear to the prospect of judgment in repentance from sin and repudiation of idolatry, God's people can join a believing remnant in coming to the feast as guests acceptable to Him. There is hope after all.

But there is also caution. Guests who remain unrepentant, and hence unclean, will be disqualified and will discover that they are not only invited guests but also victims. God has summoned others (the Chaldeans or Babylonians) who will destroy Judah, Jerusalem, and the unrepentant people who inhabit them (1:8–13).

In verse 8, Zephaniah gives a further message with regard to that coming day. Israel's leadership has adopted a foreign lifestyle, including its dress. There could be a veiled threat here. Do they prefer foreign attire? They will soon see the specter of foreign uniforms throughout the land. The threat is literally carried out (for examples, see 2 Kings 23:31–35; 24:10–16; 25:1–21).

Additional charges follow in verse 9, this time leveled against all the citizens of Judah and Jerusalem who have adopted pagan customs in their worship. In this case, the custom involves avoiding contact with the threshold of the temple by leaping over it. The practice had originated among the priests of the god Dagon, during the incident of the collapse of his statue before the ark of the Lord (1 Samuel 5:1–4). The verse goes on to report that the citizenry had perpetrated deeds of violence and deceit against the less fortunate in order to achieve their ambitions.

Further information concerning the sacrifice on the Day of the Lord is in Zephaniah 1:10. Although lamentation will come from all parts of the city, Jerusalem's greedy merchants will particularly be affected. From the Fish Gate through areas of commercial activity will come a great cry. Zephaniah tells the merchants to wail over their lost wealth (1:11).

Zephaniah concludes by reporting that God's judgment will be thorough. God's instruments of invasion will seek out every corner of Jerusalem in carrying away its treasures. If not in theory, at least in practice, the people of Judah behave like full-fledged pagans.

Take It Home

Whereas today's believers may applaud Zephaniah's warning to his fellow countrymen as well given due to the apostasy, immorality, and injustice of that time, we must apply Zephaniah's words to ourselves. A far more insidious danger lurks today: Apathy and inactivity will ultimately take their toll. Those who sit back and do nothing are just as culpable as those who engage in evil.

1:14–18

TEACHINGS CONCERNING THE DAY OF THE LORD

Zephaniah's exhortations based on the surety of the coming judgment are amplified with further information concerning the Day of the Lord (1:14–18). In language bordering on the later apocalyptic genre, he tells of frightful conditions in the natural world and terrible destruction throughout the earth.

Zephaniah declares that the Day of the Lord is near. He previously used that fact to provide grounds for submission to the Lord (1:7). Now he supplies added details to provide a further reason for the citizens of Judah and Jerusalem to repent and submit to God. He describes conditions that will exist primarily in the final stages of the Day of the Lord. But the prophecy must be viewed as one vast event. Some matters that he mentions will soon take place during Jerusalem's fall in 586 BC; others will be repeated in various historical epochs (AD 70), until the whole prophecy finds its ultimate fulfillment in the end times. Keeping such distinctions in mind enables one to keep a clear perspective as to both the meaning of the text and the effect the prophecy must have had upon Zephaniah's hearers. However much the events detailed here may have full reference only to the final phase of the Day of the Lord, they are an integral part of the prophecy and can occur anywhere along the series.

For this section of describing the Day of the Lord, Zephaniah has drawn upon the works of Isaiah, Jeremiah, Ezekiel, and Joel, but he is particularly indebted to Joel (see Joel 2:1–11).

Because of wrath against sin, the earth will experience great distress and anguish. Other prophets report that so severe will be the testing of the eschatological day that it will be called "the time of Jacob's trouble" (Jeremiah 30:7). Zephaniah makes a similar prediction and adds that the day will bring great anguish to all who experience it (Zephaniah 1:15).

Zephaniah goes on to describe conditions in the land and in nature (1:15). Destruction will dot the landscape; everything will be a desolate waste. Once again, Zephaniah draws upon phraseology employed by Job in describing a wasteland (Job 38:27). From the physical world, Zephaniah turns to the socio-political realm in verse 16. That day will be a time of great warfare. Zephaniah concludes by observing the tragic cost in human life and experience that all this will effect (1:17–18).

There is a play on words and ideas in verse 17. Because it is a day of distress and anguish, God will cause distress to mankind. So intense will be the conditions, that people will grope like blind men. How appropriate the punishment, since the charge against them is that they are spiritually blind (Exodus 23:8; Matthew 15:14; Romans 2:19; 11:25; Ephesians 4:18; 1 John 2:11). The effect of these tragic conditions is that human life (flesh and blood) is reduced to a thing of no value, with even corpses being treated as despicable refuse (Jeremiah 9:20–22; 16:1–4; 25:32–33).

The chapter closes with a reiteration of two prominent themes: (1) the self-indulgent greed of the godless wealthy and (2) the certain judgment of all men and nations (1:18).

ZEPHANIAH 2:1–15

DETAILS CONCERNING THE DAY OF THE LORD

Instructions in Light of That Day 2:1–3
Pronouncements of Judgment 2:4–15

Setting Up the Section

In light of the horrifying spectacle of the judgment of the Day of the Lord, Zephaniah presses his fellow countrymen to gather in repentance and humility before God. Utilizing images drawn from the process of separating straw from chaff, Zephaniah gives them a spiritual message designed to achieve the safety and deliverance of those who repent and put their trust in the Lord.

2:1–3

INSTRUCTIONS IN LIGHT OF THAT DAY

In the opening of this section, Zephaniah uses straw and its collection to symbolize the assembling of people (2:1–2). He employs the concept of threshing to point to the necessity of being broken before God. He uses the idea of chaff in connection with the speed and ease with which it is blown away: Like chaff, the Day of Judgment is rapidly approaching; like chaff, wayward sinners will be destroyed in the Day of the Lord.

To *gather together* (2:1) means to come together in genuine repentance and submission to the will of God. Zephaniah's plea is urgent, for God's decree is settled and will soon be put into effect.

The second portion of Zephaniah's prophecies (2:4–3:20) is made up of pronouncements (2:4–3:7), an exhortation (3:8), and teachings (3:9–20). After his preoccupation primarily with the fate of his people in the first part of the book, Zephaniah turns his attention to the foreign nations (2:4–15). He began the first major portion of his prophecy by similarly considering all nations (1:2–3). Here he deals with specific nations that are tied to Judah's situation geographically and politically—Philistia (west), Moab and Ammon (east), Cush (south), and Assyria (north). Some translations refer to Cush as Ethiopia. The Cushites do eventually settle in that area, but for Zephaniah, Cush would have more likely referred to Ethiopia.

2:4–15

PRONOUNCEMENTS OF JUDGMENT

Philistia

Philistine presence in Canaan had been reported since the days of the early patriarchs. The region was made up of city-states—Gaza, Ashkelon, Ashdod, Ekron, and Gath—four of which are mentioned in verse 4.

Zephaniah calls these Philistine settlers *Kerethites*, a name associated with the Philistines (perhaps an early tribe or a branch of the Philistines). According to Zephaniah, the prosperous seacoast district will become pastureland dotted with caves for Israelite shepherds and folds for their flocks. It will belong to the remnant of Judah (2:5–7).

Moab and Ammon

Zephaniah's pronouncements of judgment turn to Judah's eastern neighbors across the Jordan River, the nations of Moab and Ammon. Like the Philistines, these nations are numbered among Israel's traditional foes. Zephaniah's is not the first curse against this people.

Demystifying Zephaniah

According to Genesis 19:30–38, both Moab and Ammon are descendants of Lot, Abraham's nephew. They are conceived incestuously with Lot's daughters through a scheme set by the young women. Later in Israel's history, the Ammonites join the Moabites in hiring Baalam to curse the Israelites. Both nations harass the Israelites in the days of the judges, and Saul and David fight against them.

Zephaniah condemns both nations for their pride and their blasphemous insults against God and His people. He predicts that both nations, who have often worked together, will be treated like Sodom and Gomorrah—the whole area will be turned into a perpetual wasteland, overrun with weeds and pocked by salt pits (2:9).

Cush

Building on the concept of universal judgment in the preceding verse, Zephaniah tacks on the notice that the judgment of Cush, too, is part of the punishment that will overtake all peoples (2:12). Zephaniah's use of the term *Cushites* refers to Ethiopia, a part of Egypt. As the Cushite dynasty had passed, so also will Egypt and, one day, all earthly powers that stand in opposition to the Lord.

Assyria

In verses 13–15, Zephaniah's fourth message against the foreign powers swings around to the north—Assyria's capital city, Nineveh, will be rendered desolate, fit only for animals. Assyria's rapacity, pride, and cruelty demand her destruction. The reason for the demise of Assyria in general and of Nineveh in particular is given in verse 15—haughtiness. Centuries later, the city's ruins are unrecognizable.

ZEPHANIAH 3:1–20

FINAL WORDS

Setting Up the Section

Although the judgments in Zephaniah's prophecy and the pronouncement of woe upon Jerusalem at the opening of this chapter are not encouraging, the prophet's message is not yet complete. Before the final word has been said, his readers will come to understand that the day of the Lord's judgment, however dark, is but the path to a brighter day.

3:1–7

JUDGMENT FOR JERUSALEM

Zephaniah concludes his messages on judgment by turning to his own nation and to the holy city in particular. In delivering his pronouncement against Jerusalem, Zephaniah utilizes the form of the woe oracle, including invective (3:1), reason (criticism) for Judah's punishment (3:2–4), and implied threat (3:5–7).

The judgment begins with a woe in which Zephaniah calls Judah's capital a rebellious and defiled city where oppression is the order of the day. These words describe a lifestyle and social structure at variance with God's character and laws. Zephaniah charges God's people with refusing to obey God's commandments and with unwillingness to learn from chastisement (3:2). They have neither concern nor time for God and His standards.

Even the priests of Jerusalem are defiled. They who were charged with the purity of God's house and the sanctity of His law have violated both. With bold metaphors, Zephaniah exposes Jerusalem's leaders for what they are (3:3).

Zephaniah reminds his hearers of Judah's ultimate leader (3:5–7). In contrast to Jerusalem's corrupt leadership, the Lord is righteous. Unlike the wicked who know no shame, He does no iniquity. With the light of each new day, He brings evidence of His unfailing justice.

Take It Home

God's righteousness may also be seen in His merciful dealings with His people in attempting to woo them back to Himself (3:6–7). Yet rather than demonstrating a desire for repentance, Judah and Jerusalem display only an increased bent for shameless corruption. How do we respond today when God calls us back to Himself? In particular, how do we respond if returning to the Lord requires us to leave a life that is comfortable and profitable for us?

3:8–13

ADDITIONAL TEACHINGS CONCERNING THE DAY OF THE LORD

Beginning with verse 9, Zephaniah turns from judgment to its outcome—God's blessing of the people of the world. In a vivid and varied metaphor, the prophet portrays a courtroom scene in which God rises first as witness on His own behalf and before the assemblage, and then presides as judge to deliver His righteous sentence. The double emphasis on judgment and hope is prominent in 3:9–20. Rather than being irreconcilable themes, judgment and hope are two aspects of one divine perspective.

Structurally, verses 9–13 provide a further reason for the exhortation to wait for the Lord (3:8). The first reason has to do with God's determination to gather the nations for the long-awaited judgment. The second deals with God's promises to a humble and purified future remnant. This section thus carries the author's thoughts to information concerning a future day that will provide the grounds for the closing admonitions of the book (3:14–20).

3:14–20

HOPE IN LIGHT OF THAT DAY

Verses 14–20 form a closing unit of instructions concerning the Day of the Lord. For Jerusalem, faced with the divine sentence against her, Zephaniah has words of instruction that will doubtless be carried out: Sing for joy, shout out loud, be glad, and rejoice. The commands are happy ones, heaped up to underscore the great expectation of the joyous times that lay beyond the immediate punishment. Although the command is aimed at the future Jerusalem, the message will not be lost on the godly worshipers of Zephaniah's own day.

The promise of release from fear is accompanied by words of encouragement not to let either fright or anxiety grip their hearts (3:16–17). Such assurances form a striking contrast with Zephaniah's earlier prophecy that the Day of the Lord will be filled with such horror that even the bravest of warriors will cry out bitterly (1:14).

In a climactic finish to all that he has prophesied, Zephaniah reveals the personal promises of Israel's Redeemer. Though from a literary standpoint verses 18–20 provide a further reason for the commands concerning rejoicing in verse 14, their force must not be missed: God Himself is speaking. The Lord's opening assurance here stands in stark contrast to His pronouncements at the beginning of the book (3:18). Unlike the earlier announcement of God's gathering of the nations together so as to sweep them from the face of the earth (1:2–4), the Lord will gather up those who have been driven away from Jerusalem and, therefore, from the opportunity to partake of Israel's periods of festivity. In God's providence, His sinning people had been punished by being carried away into exile as booty to their conquerors. Now judgment has given way to hope. God will regather His chastised and cleansed people in order to lead them home.

A threefold promise follows in verse 19, part of which is repeated in verse 20, emphasizing Israel's own festive future. The certainty of Israel's newly acquired felicity is assured.

Zephaniah closes his prophecy on the highest of notes. Not only is that which he has just recorded (3:18–20) the word of the Lord, but the whole prophecy is as well. God Himself has spoken.

HAGGAI

INTRODUCTION TO HAGGAI

Haggai's message, so effective in shaking the Jews of 520 BC from their lethargy, has an abiding relevance for all who fail to seek first the kingdom of God and His righteousness. The book of Haggai consists of four addresses.

AUTHOR

We know very little about Haggai outside of the four months of ministry described in this writing. He is mentioned in the book of Ezra.

PURPOSE

Haggai's purpose is clear. The exiles who returned to Jerusalem after their captivity in Babylonia have failed to complete the temple. Haggai calls these citizens to repentance and to action.

OCCASION

Haggai dates his first recorded revelation to the first day of the sixth month of the second year of the Persian king Darius Hystaspes (522–486 BC). Haggai's ministry falls between the sixth and eleventh months of Darius's second year. After years of exile in what was first Babylonia and then Persia, some of the Jewish exiles are allowed to return home. Their city is in ruins as is the temple, their center for worship. Throughout their history, the spiritual well-being of these people has been typified by the state of their place of worship. There is much in need of repair.

THEMES

Themes in Haggai include those familiar to other prophets—repentance, obedience, and worship. In Haggai's writings, however, these themes are built around the temple and all it means to the community of Jews.

HISTORICAL CONTEXT

In a day of profound discouragement and misplaced priorities after the Jews' return from Babylonian exile, the prophet Haggai sounds a call of rebuke, exhortation, and encouragement to his contemporaries. They have begun to rebuild their homes and businesses and to establish their statehood as a Jewish community but have been derelict in tending to the construction of the temple and making the Lord the central focus of all their hopes and dreams.

The prophets Haggai and Zechariah were contemporaries in Jerusalem at the end of the sixth century BC. This setting can be precisely identified; no other biblical author, with the exception of Ezekiel, ties his ministries and messages more closely to a chronological framework.

OUTLINE OF HAGGAI

HAGGAI 1:1–15

REBUILDING THE TEMPLE

Setting Up the section

The opening superscription provides the setting for the first oracle of the prophet (1:2–11) and identifies him and the immediate recipients of his message.

Haggai, whose name means something like "festive" or "festival," appears (apart from self-references in this treatise) only in Ezra 5:1 and 6:14. Since the oracle is transmitted on the first day of the month, a festival day (Numbers 10:10; 28:11), the prophet's name itself is revelatory of the occasion.

1:1–11

THE EXHORTATION TO REBUILD

Zerubbabel son of Shealtiel, named in verse 1, is the second in a line of Jewish governors. According to Jeremiah, Gedaliah was the first governor (Jeremiah 40:7). The last mentioned in the Bible was Nehemiah (Nehemiah 8:9). The term *governor* suggests an overseer. Joshua the son of Jehozadak is here designated the high priest.

Verses 2–6 highlight the indifference of the people. The prophet chides the returned exiles and their fellow countrymen for putting their own interests ahead of the Lord and the temple. The result has been calamitous, for the more they seek self-satisfaction, the less they achieve it.

In verse 2, God's reference to the Jews as *these* (or *this*) people (rather than *my* people) implies alienation from God. The real issue is clear: The Jews who have returned from exile in Persia are more concerned for their own well-being than for honoring God by building His dwelling place among them (2:4–9). Throughout their history, establishing

God's dwelling had been an essential religious touchstone.

In verses 3–5, God, speaking through the prophet, shifts His attention from Zerubbabel and Joshua to the people at large, asking if it is appropriate for them to build their own houses even though they have protested building Yahweh's house. He challenges them so they might understand the connection between their negligence of God's house and their lack of success in everyday life (1:6).

Haggai gives four examples of the futility of selfish effort. There may be metaphorical overtones to this statement, but it also has literal meaning. Evidently the crops have failed, and now, when the fall harvest should be underway, prospects are grim.

Critical Observation

In verse 2—and elsewhere in 1:5, 7, 9, 14; 2:4, 6–9, 11, 23—Haggai refers to God in a way that describes His almighty power. This description is particularly important to the prophets, such as Zechariah and Malachi, who minister after the exiles' return and must encourage tiny, defenseless Judah in the face of imperial Persia's enormous might.

The exhortation in verse 5 is repeated in verse 7. In light of the preceding indictment (1:2–6), the people need to reflect on their ways. Their indifference leads to instruction so that the impasse might be resolved and the temple construction begun. The prophet points out that the people have sown much but harvested little and looked for much but received little (1:6, 9). Furthermore, they suffer from a lack of food, drink, clothing, and resources–a condition attributed to the drought the Lord brought upon the land, the effects of which are again listed in the same order: food, drink, protection, and productivity (1:10–11).

The cause of this disastrous condition, hinted at in verse 4, is articulated in verse 9: God's house is in ruins. The command to rebuild (1:8) is in strong antithesis to those who, in verse 2, insist that the time for rebuilding Yahweh's house has not yet come.

In verse 7, after the normal introductory formula, Haggai once more urges Zerubbabel, Joshua, and presumably the people to remember with seriousness their past failures and the remedy about to be announced.

Demystifying Haggai

Lack of any reference to stone or other materials does not mean the temple is a wooden structure, for clearly there is abundant stone from the demolished temple of Solomon lying all about. Ezra records a letter from Tattenai, governor of Trans-Euphrates (western Asia), containing a complaint to King Darius that the Jews, thanks to Haggai and Zechariah, are already rebuilding the temple with stones and timber (Ezra 5:8).

As though to reinforce His point that the promised glory has been frustrated by Judah's indolence and self-centeredness, Yahweh reiterates that the people have sought much for themselves but with meager results (1:9). As long as the temple remains unfinished, the people can continue to expect poverty and lack of fulfillment (1:10–11).

1:12–15

THE RESPONSE OF GOD'S PEOPLE

The first oracle, which ends with this section, consists of an address (1:2–11) and a response (1:12–14), bracketed by an introductory and concluding date formula (1:1, 15).

Haggai's stern rebuke and urgent appeal to the leaders and citizens has the desired effect, for they immediately resume construction on the temple, which had been set aside for sixteen years. Though fear is a factor, more important is Yahweh's pledge to be with them, and the supernatural stirring of their spirits to carry out His mandate (1:12–14). Within a month, they organize themselves, make their plans, marshal their labor force, and begin the work (1:15).

The people here are referred to as a remnant. The notion of a remaining few who will survive both apostasy and judgment to become the nucleus of a restored nation is pervasive in the Old Testament.

Verse 13 is an assurance of God's presence among the people. This assurance finds expression in His supernatural movement among them. Governor, priest, and people alike respond to the kindling of their dormant spirits by setting to work.

The date here reveals a twenty-three day interval between the time the message to rebuild is first proclaimed (1:1) and the time of its execution (1:14). We can't know with certainty the reason for the delay, but it may have been as simple as tending to harvest (1:11).

HAGGAI 2:1–23

LOOKING AHEAD

Setting Up the Section

In this chapter comes the message that the unpromising beginning of a second temple will someday give way to one whose magnificence and glory far transcends that of Solomon's. Yahweh is with His people and will, in line with His ancient covenant promises, reenact the Exodus and restoration to such a degree that the temple will become a place of pilgrimage from all nations. Yahweh will bring in the day of peace.

2:1–9

THE GLORY TO COME

Virtually all students of Haggai agree that 2:1–9 (or 1:15–2:9) constitutes a single and undivided oracle, though opinions differ on its placement in the book. The oracle as a whole contains language that is markedly concerned with end times, especially in verses 6–9.

Critical Observation

Significantly, this word of Yahweh comes on the twenty-first of Tishri (October 17), which is precisely the seventh day of the Feast of Tabernacles. Exactly 440 years earlier (Tishri, 960 BC), Solomon had finished and dedicated his temple (1 Kings 6:38; 8:2), to which the prophet is about to compare the one under present construction. Twenty-six days have passed since construction began, and already the differences are becoming painfully evident.

No one will be more aware of the contrast between Solomon's temple and the structure under construction than those old enough to have experienced the Solomonic temple so ruthlessly destroyed by the Babylonians sixty-six years earlier. To these people, Haggai addresses his question. He concludes that they view the new building as inconsequential compared with the old.

In verses 4–5, Haggai speaks one more word of encouragement to the leaders and the people, urging them to be strong in boldness and confidence. The somewhat veiled allusion to Moses and Joshua in verse 4 (most appropriate in view of the name of the present high priest) becomes more transparent in verse 5, with its reference to the Exodus. Just as Yahweh had been with His people in the ancient days, so He will be with them now. Haggai thus harks back to the past but also anticipates future redemption and glory. This provides an entry into the end-times message of verses 6–9.

In this first extended apocalyptic vision of the book, Haggai describes the tremendous upheavals that will attend the epiphany of Yahweh in the last days.

In verse 6, the objects of the shaking—heavens, earth, sea, and land—draw attention to Yahweh's violent intervention in the past and suggest that He will do so once more, and in just a little while.

These phenomena will accompany the new exodus and new covenant as well, as both Haggai (2:6–7) and other prophets attest. There will be a shaking of the natural structures and of men and nations. These cataclysmic events will cause the peoples to bring their precious belongings to the holy city and temple. Once this has come to pass, Yahweh will fill the temple with His glory. The house's glory will be greater than before (2:9).

The real glory of the final temple will not consist of material things. This may, in fact, be the primary thrust of verse 8. Haggai affirms that its glory will consist not of silver and gold but of God's presence (2:4–5) in the temple and among His people (2:7).

2:10–19

THE PROMISED BLESSING

Many scholars divide the third oracle (2:10–19) into two sections—2:10–14 and 2:15–19. They do this because of the assumption that "this people" of verse 14 refers not to Judah but to Judah's enemies in the land. However, "this people" is a perfectly appropriate description of the Jews, especially since Haggai has already used this description (1:2).

The third oracle is dated on the twenty-fourth of Kislev (or December 18, 520 BC), about three months after the work on the temple had begun again in earnest (1:15) and two months after its pitifully modest prospect begins to become apparent (2:1, 3). The people have deluded themselves into thinking that holiness is gained merely by association with holy things (2:11–12) and have failed to consider that unholy associations render one unclean (2:13–14).

The specific occasion for the oracle is unclear, but it could well have been delivered as a warning against cooperation with the Samaritans and others in the work of the temple, and the religious influence the non-Jews wielded.

If so, it is clear why the hypothetical set of questions posed by Yahweh are targeted to the priests, the religious leaders. Verse 12 asks if a person can make unholy things into holy things simply by touching them with holy hands. The meats mentioned here, if profane because they are gifts from pagan kings, will remain profane no matter who touches them. The gifts of pagan kings, no matter the spirit in which they are given, cannot become clean and acceptable to Yahweh just because they come in contact with the sacred sites and rituals of the covenant people. Such gifts should, therefore, be politely refused. To fail to do so is to render oneself unclean (2:14).

Verses 13–14 represent a converse case. Granted, unclean things don't become clean by virtue of their association with the clean. However, will things that are clean become contaminated by the unclean? The answer is an unqualified *yes*. The example is the corruption caused by contact with a corpse. The dead body mentioned here isn't linked with something in the immediate context of this passage. The point is that God's people can pollute, and have polluted, themselves because of their ungodly associations (2:14).

Take It Home

While it is impossible to know precisely what calls forth these words of denunciation, the context of the book suggests that it is the people's self-centeredness and inverted priorities (1:2–4, 9), and their tolerance and acceptance of assistance of their pagan neighbors—assistance that involves even the presentation of sacrificial animals. Haggai's prophecy speaks to us today, not so much in terms of the food we eat, but in terms of the priority we place on our faith and the spiritual practices that sustain that faith.

The community's moral and spiritual defilement described in the previous passage calls for divine discipline (2:10–14). From the very beginning of their postexilic life, before the foundations of the temple were laid some sixteen years earlier, the people had suffered Yahweh's wrath because of their self-service (2:16–17). This chastening marks their whole life until Haggai, called by God, urges them to forsake their shortsighted materialism and resume the work of building a house for Yahweh.

The language of failed expectation here is like that of Haggai 1. Yahweh visited the people with drought, a generic term fleshed out in the blight, mildew, and hail of the present passage (1:11; 2:17).

In verses 18–19, Haggai refers back not to the initial groundbreaking for the temple in 536 BC (2:15) but to the renewal of construction exactly three months earlier. This reference provides a backward glance focused on the refounding of the temple and subsequent events. In spite of this backward glance, however, verses 18–19 relate to the present and future. The date of the laying of the foundation is the date of the oracle, the twenty-fourth day of the ninth month (2:18). The seed has already been sown, and the fruit trees promise rich production in the season to come, but the growing season is a future event. In the midst of December, there is little on which to subsist. Verse 19 contains a promise of better days ahead. Even though the vestiges of the people's previous disobedience remain to make their existence most uncomfortable, all this will change. God will begin a new age of prosperity.

2:20–23

ZERUBBABEL THE CHOSEN ONE

This fourth and final message of Haggai is received and delivered on the very same day as the third, but to Zerubbabel alone. The apocalyptic language focuses on the destruction of all things hostile to the rule of Yahweh, a destruction that cannot be separated from the last clause of 2:19. In verse 19, the promise to bless from that very day finds its expression in the end-times hope outlined in verses 20–23. In terms reminiscent of his second oracle, the prophet speaks of a shaking of heaven and earth and the overthrow and shattering of human kingdoms (2:6–7).

The difference in the two addresses is the results of the shaking. In 2:7 it results in tribute to Yahweh in His temple. Here, it is a defeat of the nations so severe in its results that no one and nothing remains but Yahweh and His own sovereign ruler.

Continuing with His focus on the future, the prophet introduces the climax of his message by relating it to "that day" (2:23). Since the context indisputably is apocalyptic in nature, the Zerubbabel to whom the oracle is directed cannot be the governor whom Haggai has so frequently addressed. Rather, one must see Zerubbabel as a prototype of one to come who will be Yahweh's servant and chosen vessel.

Demystifying Haggai

Zerubbabel the governor is a descendant of Jehoiachin, most likely his grandson (1 Chronicles 3:17–19; Matthew 1:12). Because of this, using his name in this oracle has prophetic significance. Zerubbabel is a link in the Davidic monarchy. It is to this monarchy that God promises eternal reign. When someone of that bloodline became governor of Judah, it must have seemed to the restored community that God's ancient covenant promise—that there would never fail to be a son of David on the throne (2 Samuel 7:16; Psalm 89:24–37)—had come to pass.

ZECHARIAH

INTRODUCTION TO ZECHARIAH

The books of Haggai, Zechariah, and Malachi were composed in the postexilic period of Israel's history to offer hope to a people whose national and personal lives had been shattered by the Babylonian destruction of Jerusalem and captivity of the people. Zechariah goes beyond Haggai's burden for the immediate, earthly situation of the postexilic community and sees, through a vision and dream, the unfolding of divine purpose for all of God's people and for all the ages to come.

AUTHOR

At least thirty people mentioned in the Bible bear the name *Zechariah*, which means "the Lord remembers." The prophet and author of this book, however, is further identified as being the son of Berekiah and grandson of Iddo (1:1). He was born during Judah's captivity in Babylon and returned to Jerusalem with a group led by Zerubbabel. Iddo was a priest during that time (Nehemiah 12:1–7), and Zechariah eventually succeeds his grandfather in that role.

Some people propose that the latter portion of Zechariah (chapters 9–14) likely has a different author. They cite a variation in writing style and the author's inclusion of historical events that span beyond a single lifetime. Yet those variations are not evidence enough to sway the beliefs of other scholars, who continue to maintain that the book has a single author.

PURPOSE

After about seventy years of exile in a foreign land, God's people are released to return to their homeland, only to discover that the walls and temple of Jerusalem have been demolished. Projects are planned for reconstruction, but the people need much encouragement and faith during this period. As both prophet and priest, Zechariah brings assurance of God's faithfulness and hope for the future of His people.

THEMES

Zechariah adopts an already existent apocalyptic tradition of writing from which he draws heavily and to which he makes a significant contribution. The apocalyptic format receives immeasurable momentum from the trauma of the exile, a calamity that not only shook the social and political structures of Judah but also threatened to undermine the covenant faith itself. So Zechariah shifts the focus from the present to the future, from the local to the universal, and from the earthly to the cosmic and heavenly.

HISTORICAL CONTEXT

The release of the people of Judah was in conjunction with the overthrow of the Babylonians by the Medes and Persians. Zechariah begins his ministry in the eighth month of the second year of the Persian king Darius (1:1)—520 BC. Zechariah's final chronological reference (7:1) is to the ninth month of the fourth year of Darius (518 BC).

If one accepts that Zechariah is the sole author of the book, the latter date presumably marks the occasion for all the oracles and other messages of chapters 7–14.

The opposition to the rebuilding projects in Judah occurs prior to Darius, and serious antagonism of the Jewish people does not arise again until Xerxes (486 BC). It is safe to assume, therefore, that work on restoring the temple goes unimpeded during the two years of Zechariah's ministry.

CONTRIBUTION TO THE BIBLE

Rich in apocalyptic imagery and packed with messianic prediction and allusion, Zechariah's writings become a favorite of the New Testament evangelists and apostles. No minor prophet excels Zechariah in the clarity and triumph by which he looks to the fulfillment of God's program of redemption.

OUTLINE

ZECHARIAH'S NIGHT VISIONS, PART I 1:1–3:10

Introduction 1:1–6
Vision One: The Four Horsemen 1:7–17
Vision Two: The Four Horns 1:18–21
Vision Three: The Surveyor 2:1–13
Vision Four: The Priest 3:1–10

ZECHARIAH'S NIGHT VISIONS, PART II 4:1–6:15

Vision Five: A Gold Lampstand and Two Olive Trees 4:1–14
Vision Six: The Flying Scroll 5:1–4
Vision Seven: The Ephah 5:5–11
Vision Eight: The Chariots 6:1–8
A Concluding Oracle 6:9–15

ZECHARIAH'S ORACLES 7:1–14:21

Oracles Concerning Hypocritical Fasting 7:1–8:23
An Oracle Concerning the Lord's Sovereignty 9:1–11:17
An Oracle Concerning Israel 12:1–14:21

ZECHARIAH 1:1–3:10

ZECHARIAH'S NIGHT VISIONS, PART I

Setting Up the Section

The overall message of Zechariah, though occasionally obscure, is largely clear and plain. The prophet seeks to comfort his discouraged and pessimistic compatriots, who are in the process of rebuilding their temple and restructuring their community, yet who view their efforts as making little difference in the present and offering no hope for the future. Zechariah challenges members of the restored remnant to work confidently and to fully expect that what they do will be crowned with success when God, true to His Word, will bring to pass the fulfillment of His ancient promises to their forefathers. This section introduces the book and covers the first four of eight visions the prophet sees in a single night.

1:1–6

INTRODUCTION

The rather lengthy introduction to the book of Zechariah is clearly intended as a preface to all the night visions that follow (chapters 1–6), if not the entire book. This is evident from the fact that 1:7 is also an introduction, perhaps for the first vision only, but more likely for all eight visions that follow.

Zechariah, here identified as the son of Berekiah and grandson of Iddo (1:1), is also mentioned in Ezra (5:1; 6:14) and Nehemiah (12:16). However, both of those citations imply that the prophet is the son of Iddo, and neither mentions Berekiah. It is likely that Zechariah's father died young and Zechariah was raised by his grandfather. This would also explain why Zechariah succeeds Iddo as priest (Nehemiah 12:10–16).

"The second year of Darius" refers to 520 BC, and the "eighth month" is October/November, so Zechariah's visions are only a month prior to Haggai's final vision, which would have been December 18, 520 BC (Haggai 2:10, 20). Zechariah is likely quite young, and his ministry may have extended well beyond his people's return from exile.

Zechariah begins his book with a solemn exhortation to learn from history. God had been extremely displeased with the generations past (1:2) because they had stubbornly refused to heed the appeal of their prophets to turn to the Lord (1:3–4). *Ways* and *practices* (deeds) refer not to incidental sins but to a whole pattern of rebellion and disloyalty.

Zechariah next turns his attention to the calamity that overcame their ancestors because of their failure to heed the prophets' warnings. Both they and the prophets who had warned them had long since passed away (1:5), but God's Word had come to pass. The wicked nation had been overthrown according to the terms of the covenant, and those who lived to see it had been forced to admit that God brought to pass everything He had threatened (1:6).

The message of Zechariah will be precisely the same as that of his prophetic predecessors. His people must turn to the Lord in covenant affirmation if they expect God to reciprocate (1:3).

Critical Observation

Zechariah's use of *the Lord Almighty* (NIV) as a title for God (three times in 1:3) is most striking. In this book, the prophet uses the title fifty-three times. Yet such usage coincides with other prophets at work at the same time. Malachi uses the title twenty-four times, and Haggai uses it fourteen times in only thirty-eight verses. In light of the emergence of universal empires at the time, Judah needs to be reminded that the Lord is indeed almighty. He is the Lord of hosts—Lord even of those mighty worldly powers.

1:7–17

VISION ONE: THE FOUR HORSEMEN

The second introduction to the book of Zechariah (1:7) embraces all the visions to follow (1:8–6:16). The next introductory passage does not appear until chapter 7. The date equates to February 15, 519 BC, in the modern calendar—approximately three months after the initial call of Zechariah (1:1) and two months after Haggai's last revelation (Haggai 2:10, 20). Significant events around this time that may have bearing on elements of Zechariah's first vision are (1) the return of Darius to Persia from Egypt (through Palestine) and (2) the approaching of New Year's day, a time when Zerubbabel will be crowned as Judah's king, restoring a Davidic successor to the throne (Haggai 2:20–23).

It appears that Zechariah is recounting a series of dream-visions from a single night. These dreams are not random or from his own imagination because they are presented in a historical and chronological sequence on one hand, and in an interlocking literary pattern on the other. Similarities are found between visions #1 and #8, #2 and #7, #3 and #6, and #4 and #5.

Both Zechariah's first and eighth (1:8; 6:1–8) visions feature four kinds of horses. Much effort has been made to connect the two visions, but the colors of the horses are not the same, and there is no reason to assume that the horses in both visions must match. In the first vision, either the man on the red horse dismounts and stands in the ravine, or the horse itself stands there with the rider still on him. Hebrew grammar favors the former, as does the description in 1:10. As for the three horses in the background, it is not certain whether or not they have riders. Presumably they do, because verse 11 indicates more than one speaker.

Critical Observation

The myrtle is a particularly appropriate element of this vision. A fragrant, decorative shrub that sometimes reaches the size of a tree, it is used in connection with the Feast of Tabernacles and in postbiblical times in betrothal celebrations. Its perpetual greenness and aromatic qualities provide a suitable setting for the inauguration of the Lord's domain, which is everlasting and pleasant in every way.

It seems that Zechariah stands with an interpreting messenger-angel and that both of them hear the answer to Zechariah's question as given by the man among the myrtles (the angel of the Lord). His response is confirmed by the riders of the horses. Overwhelmed by his own response, the angel of the Lord addresses the Lord Himself to ask about the conclusion of the seventy years of discipline. The Lord's answer is directed to the messenger/interpreter beside Zechariah, for it is the prophet who had raised the inquiries about the vision he had seen. That messenger in turn speaks to Zechariah, commanding him to deliver the Word of God to his people (1:14).

The mission of the rider of the red horse (and presumably all four horsemen) is to walk across the whole earth (1:10). To walk about on the earth is to assert sovereignty over it (see Genesis 13:17; Job 1:7; Ezekiel 28:14). Here the Lord, through the symbolism of four cavalry charges, announces that He is Lord of all.

The result of the horsemen's roaming the earth is that the land is at rest and quiet (1:11). It is therefore a suitable time for the Lord to end the judgment of the seventy-year exile by displaying His compassion for His elect people (1:12). His jealousy for Judah (1:14) is, after all, an expression of His singular interest in her and His determination to restore His people. The mention of Zion reflects the Davidic reign as part of the messianic program of redemption.

The nations, on the other hand, have become the object of the Lord's judgment. God had indeed been a little angry at His people (1:15), but the enemies of God's people brought about a measure of retribution beyond what God would have imposed.

This vision has clear implications for the end times, but it also relates to the historical circumstances of the late sixth century BC. The peace established by Cyrus strengthened and expanded under Darius, who put down rebellions associated with his ascension to the throne. Cyrus and Darius did not realize, however, that their universal peace was brought about by the Lord, God of Israel. The horses of Darius are, in fact, the horses of the Lord.

Still, the conditions are suitable for the seventy-year exile to be over. Jeremiah first refers to a seventy-year period, dating its end with the demise of the Babylonian (Chaldean) kingdom (Jeremiah 25:11–12). It is clearly understood, however, that the seventy years have a flexible starting and concluding date because their termination is also connected to the completion of the second temple (Zechariah 1:16). It may also be noted that the completion of Jerusalem's second temple takes place in 516 BC, exactly seventy years after the destruction of Solomon's temple in 586 BC.

Demystifying Zechariah

Many of Zechariah's visions, including this first one, are accompanied by oracles. The primary purposes of these oracles are (1) to confirm the message of the vision; (2) to provide further understanding of its meaning; and (3) to exhort the audience to carry out its commands.

Zechariah records in 1:13 that the Lord had spoken "kind and comforting" words to the interpreting angel. Those words are revealed in the oracle that follows the vision (1:16–17). God promises to either *turn* or *return* to Jerusalem (the intended translation is uncertain, as is whether the tense is present or future. But either interpretation would have been good news for the people of God).

We know from Haggai that God promises to bless His people, beginning with the ceremony of laying the temple foundation (Haggai 2:18–19). The work of reconstructing the temple began about five months prior to Zechariah's night visions (Haggai 1:15), but it is far from finished. The good news given to Zechariah is that what had been started will now be brought to fruition. Indeed, not only will the temple be rebuilt, but also the reconstruction will include outlying cities in addition to Jerusalem. They will become abundantly prosperous (1:16–17).

1:18–21

VISION TWO: THE FOUR HORNS

Just as Zechariah's first and eighth visions complement each other with similar themes and perspective, so, too, his second and seventh visions are a matched pair. They each have two parts, and both are concerned with the nations. This second vision has no accompanying oracle.

The connections between this vision and the first one are also striking. The fact that the first vision is of four horses and this one describes four horns and four craftsmen is significant. The horses of the first vision are God's instruments of dominion over all the earth (1:10–11); the four craftsmen will reduce the nations to defeat.

Critical Observation

Symbolizing political and military power by the horn of an animal is common not only in the Old Testament but also in other ancient Near Eastern literature. A horn represents power, authority, prestige, and influence. For example, David describes the Lord as his rock, fortress, deliverer, shield, tower, and horn (Psalm 18:2). Other prophets make similar references to horns (Jeremiah 48:25; Daniel 7–8; Micah 4:13).

Zechariah's second vision contains two elements (four horns and four craftsmen), so the interpretation is divided into two parts. In response to the query about the horns (1:19), the angelic interpreter first asserts that they are scatterers of Judah, Israel, and Jerusalem. Under further interrogation, he adds that the horns are associated with the nations. The nations had used their horns (military might) to effect the dispersion of God's people (1:21).

As for the craftsmen, the messenger reports that their task is to bring down those nations, to nullify the effect of their great power (1:21). The ultimate result will presumably reverse the scattering so that the dispersed can return again to their land.

The listed order of those attacked is somewhat puzzling: Judah, Israel, and Jerusalem (1:19). Later, only Judah is mentioned (1:21). If Judah is seen as central, then Israel may denote the nation in its broadest sense and Jerusalem in its narrowest. The order indicates, then, that the scattering is total.

Some people attempt to identify four specific nations or events to associate with the horns. But what is suggested here (and elsewhere) by the number four is the universal character of the persecution of God's people by the nations. Israel's struggle against the nations had persisted from their settlement in Canaan until the fall of Jerusalem to the Babylonians. But the final destruction had been so climactic and irreversible that it stands out in Zechariah's text.

There is no reason to attempt to identify any particular forces to associate with the craftsmen. The word *craftsmen* used can apply to any skilled artisan regardless of his medium. But in this case, the way the word is used in the original language suggests that these four particular craftsmen are also destroyers, or devastators. They have come forth to throw down the arrogant nations that had scattered God's elect. After the Babylonian horn is cut off by the instruments of Darius, the rebuilding promised in Zechariah's first vision can take place.

2:1–13

VISION THREE: THE SURVEYOR

Zechariah's third and sixth visions both have to do with measuring and/or dimensions, with a focus narrowed down from international interests to Jerusalem itself. In this vision, only Zechariah and one other unidentified man are participants.

It was necessary to reestablish the ancient boundary lines of Jerusalem preparatory to the city's full reoccupation. Zechariah witnesses a form of surveying, as the properties are measured out for redistribution.

Critical Observation

Before the fall of Jerusalem, Jeremiah had been told to anticipate the day when houses, fields, and vineyards would once more be bought there (Jeremiah 32:6–15). It had always been God's intent for His people to reclaim the land. Ezekiel, too, had been shown a similar scene, but the surveyor in his vision measured out the land with a reed (rod) rather than a cord (Ezekiel 40:3).

The task of the man in this third vision is to measure Jerusalem by breadth and length (2:2). The reason breadth comes first in this instance may be due to the orientation of the city. In fact, only here and in Ezekiel 40–48 are "breadth and length" designated rather than "length and breadth."

The interpreting messenger-angel appears again, this time to provide further information to Zechariah ("young man") than he had already obtained from the surveyor (2:4). This secondary messenger appears only in the first and third visions. In a sense, he is an interpreter for the interpreter. In this case, he urgently commands the first angel to go to Zechariah and provide the meaning of the vision. What is about to happen is imminent, and those who hear the message cannot be slow to act upon the news.

Zechariah is informed that the surveyor is in the process of laying out allotments in and around Jerusalem in preparation for the burgeoning population that will live there. In the absence of the walls that formerly stood, the old boundary lines will need to be redrawn. Jerusalem will be reoccupied by such a vast population that the walls that once enclosed it will be inadequate (2:4).

This prophecy has definite end-times significance, but it is also relevant for Zechariah's own circumstances. It is impossible to know a great deal about the construction and configuration of the walls about Jerusalem in the postexilic period. For the greater period of time, there were no walls—none sufficient, at least, to provide protection.

Demystifying Zechariah

It should not be assumed that Jerusalem had been continually without walls between the Babylonian conquest (586 BC) and the restoration work overseen by Nehemiah (completed in 445 BC). Ezra refers to walls existing during the time of King Artaxerxes (464–424 BC) that were most likely constructed during the earlier reign of Xerxes (Ezra 4:12). And Nehemiah's appeal to Artaxerxes was that the walls of Jerusalem had been destroyed and needed to be rebuilt (Nehemiah 1:3; 2:4–5). Everyone knew that the Babylonians had leveled the walls of Jerusalem, so Nehemiah's surprise at hearing that the walls were missing suggests that the walls had been replaced for a time and destroyed yet again.

Early Jerusalem housed only six thousand to eight thousand inhabitants. One estimate of the city's population in 700 BC is twenty-four thousand. And it is unlikely that preexilic Jerusalem ever contained as many as forty thousand people. Yet the people who returned from exile in 538 BC numbered 42,360 Jewish citizens, 7,337 slaves, and 200 singers (Ezra 2:64–65). Add to that crowd of people a group of animals exceeding eight thousand (Ezra 2:66–67). Admittedly, not all of them would have settled within the city limits of Jerusalem, but it seems that many did (Ezra 2:70; 4:4).

Eighty years later, Ezra himself leads about five thousand more individuals back to Judah (Ezra 8:1–14), most of whom apparently settle in or about Jerusalem (Ezra 8:31–32). Yet when Nehemiah arrives thirteen years after that, he finds that any former walls have been reduced to rubble. With the ruin of the walls, the population of the city had evidently evacuated (Nehemiah 7:4). After Nehemiah sees to the repairs, he conducts a lottery to repopulate Jerusalem (Nehemiah 11:1–2).

But regardless of the shifting population and varying conditions of the walls of Jerusalem during ancient times, Zechariah learns of a future when there will be no need of walls to protect the great population of the city. The Lord Himself will be a wall of fire and a source of glory for all the inhabitants (2:5).

The oracle following Zechariah's third vision (2:6–13) is a summation of the first three visions as a whole. It serves as both a warning to Babylon (2:6–9) and a promise of blessing to Judah (2:10–13).

The land of the north (2:6) is soon clearly identified as Babylon (2:7). Yet by Zechariah's time, the Babylonian exiles have already returned, so it appears that Zechariah is describing a future, more widespread regathering of God's people. In the language of the prophets, *Zion* (2:7, 10) is a key term used to refer to the end-times kingdom. And *the four winds* (2:6) suggest that exiles will be returning from all directions, not only from the north.

The *apple of God's eye* (2:8) is a reference to either the opening of the eye or the pupil. Either way, the eye is one of the most important and vulnerable parts of the body. This bold metaphor warns that to strike a blow at Zion is equivalent to striking at the Lord, attempting to wound Him in a most sensitive area. God will surely respond to such aggression. Long ago God had told Abraham, "I will bless those who bless you and curse those who treat you with contempt" (Genesis 12:3 NLT). That pledge is never abrogated and proves to be in force even with respect to the postexilic community of Judah.

The warning directed toward Babylon is closely associated with the blessing of Judah. The blessing of God's people can ultimately occur only after all hostile powers have been put down. The two parts of the oracle are also connected by the literary themes of "daughter of Babylon" versus "daughter of Zion" (2:7, 10). The personification of Zion suggests not only the corporate nature of Judah's existence as one people of the Lord but also the tenderness that God feels toward them as their Father. The names *Zion* and *Jerusalem* are frequently used synonymously.

Zion's response to the promised redemption in 2:6–9 is a ringing cry of joy. The reason for such unmitigated joy is that the Lord is coming and will live in Zion's midst (2:10). Both Haggai and Zechariah share this theology of divine presence, a note that was especially meaningful in the days of the regathered community struggling to build a temple worthy of God's dwelling place. But Zechariah is particularly concerned with orienting this theological truth to the age to come, when all nations (not just Israel and Judah) will join themselves to the Lord and be His people (2:11). In addition, God will take the land of Judah as His special allotment in all the created universe. Zechariah's reference to "the holy land" (2:12) is unique to this verse in scripture.

Demystifying Zechariah

One of the major tenets of ancient Israel's faith that distinguishes the nation from the paganism of the ancient world is her concept of the nearness of her God as opposed to the aloofness of the gods of the nations. The Lord is utterly transcendent, but the revolutionary contribution of Israel's theology is the awareness that God also lives among His people, even if invisible. Adam and Eve in the garden, Moses leading the Israelites, the psalmists, and the prophets all recognized the Lord as One who dwelled in their midst. The same message continues in the New Testament. Early in his Gospel, John identifies God's Word as One who becomes flesh and makes His dwelling among us (John 1:14).

Of interest here is the increasingly narrow parameter of the Lord's inheritance, from the whole earth to the Jerusalem temple. This narrowing of compass runs parallel, however, to an increasing broadness of His saving activity. He becomes not just the God of Abraham, Isaac, and Jacob, but the God of the nations.

3:1–10

VISION FOUR: THE PRIEST

Zechariah's fourth vision is quite different from most of the others in a number of ways. Only it and the following one (4:1–4) deal with actual identifiable human beings. The usual introduction formula that precedes a vision is lacking. There is no interpreting messenger in this case. And there appears to be an absence of standard formulaic language in the vision.

The person identified in the vision is Jeshua (3:1), a high priest with whom Zechariah is personally acquainted. The same figure appears later in Zechariah (6:11), in Haggai (Haggai 1:1), and frequently in Ezra (2:2; 3:2, 8; 4:3; 5:2; 10:18) and Nehemiah (7:7; 12:1, 7, 10, 26). He is a direct descendant of Aaron through Zadok, founder of the line of priests established by David and Solomon (1 Chronicles 6:3, 8–15). His father, Jehozadak, had gone into Babylonian exile in 586 BC, so by Zechariah's night visions in 519 BC, Jeshua must certainly have been an old man.

In the vision, Jeshua appears in a state of ritual impurity, so much so that he is being condemned for it by Satan in the presence of the Lord (3:1). The accusation is not stated, but it may be inferred from 3:3: He is unfit for the priestly ministry. The accuser and the accused are both standing, the former at the right side of the latter, not unlike in a modern courtroom. The judge is the messenger/angel of the Lord.

Critical Observation

A comprehensive biblical theology deduces that the devil was incarnated in the serpent of the temptation account in Genesis 3. How and why he became the adversary remains a mystery, but it is plain throughout scripture that he is subservient to the sovereignty of God and that his pernicious conduct as the accuser is something permitted to him by an all-wise God. The commonly held position, that primitive Israelite theology regarded Satan as a previously upright being employed by God for high and holy ends and then he departed from that role in historical times to become the adversary of God, finds no support in the Bible. In fact, the New Testament teaching is the opposite: "The devil has been sinning from the beginning" (1 John 3:8 NIV). The doctrine of a personal devil or accuser, known by name as Satan, only gradually emerged in Old Testament revelation. When it originated is not known.

When Satan challenges Jeshua's right to function under these circumstances, the judge speaks up, perhaps even before Satan can open his mouth, and rebukes the accuser to his face (3:2). The rationale for the rebuke is that Satan has overlooked the fact that the Lord, who had chosen Jerusalem, had also declared Jeshua to be a brand snatched from the fire (3:2). When it looked as though all was lost where the covenant community and its worship were concerned, the Lord graciously stepped in and rescued a remnant by which He will reconstitute a believing people.

According to the law, the accusation of Satan is valid; the uncleanness of a priest attempting to minister can lead to his excommunication (Leviticus 22:3). Jeshua (and the entire remnant nation for that matter) may appear impure, but the elective grace of God is still in effect. It is precisely at this point of the priest's need that the Lord speaks, commanding those attending him to remove Jeshua's filthy clothing and replace it with fine garments (Zechariah 3:4). Simultaneously, the Lord verbally absolves Jeshua's iniquity in an act of grace.

Zechariah is also a priest, and he speaks out as he recognizes the need for a proper headdress for Jeshua (3:5; see Exodus 28:36–38). Such interruption of a vision by the one receiving it is not common among other prophets, but it occurs rather frequently in the book of Zechariah.

By investing Jeshua with pure, clean clothes and a spotless turban, the Lord has prepared the priest for a larger role in the covenant community, provided Jeshua responds to God's act of grace by assuming the task to which his reinstatement has called him.

Jeshua must meet two conditions, one having to do with his way of life and the other with his specific vocation as priest. First, he must walk in the ways of the Lord. Second, he must keep the requirements of the particular office to which he has been called (3:7).

Then, with a sharp command, the Lord addresses both Jeshua and his companions who sit before him. It is likely that the seated figures are a sign concerning the coming of the branch and the restoration of Israel as a priestly nation (3:8). Zechariah will later aver that this messianic branch/servant will build the temple of the Lord (6:12–13). It seems likely, then, that the stone placed before Jeshua (3:9) must be taken to be the foundation of the second temple.

It isn't uncommon for a stone to be used as a messianic symbol throughout the Bible (see Isaiah 28:16). But the stone in Zechariah's oracle is unique; it has seven eyes (3:9). In biblical numerology, the number seven signifies fullness or completeness, so the seven eyes suggest omniscience or undimmed vision. In the following vision, Zechariah will identify the seven eyes as the eyes of the Lord that take in everything that is happening on the earth (4:10). And, in addition to the eyes, the stone is about to be inscribed by the Lord.

Demystifying Zechariah

It seems evident that the stone in 3:9 is the cornerstone of a building, most likely the temple of the Lord. In the ancient Near Eastern world, cornerstones frequently bore inscriptions to identify the builder and the purpose of the building. The eyes on the stone are to be the divine signature of the Lord as the architect and builder of the structure. The statement of purpose is a reference to the temple as a place of expiation of sin.

In summary, Zechariah's fourth vision describes a day of redemption in which Jeshua (typical or representative of Israel as a priestly people) will be cleansed of his impurities and reinstalled in his capacity as high priest. This presupposes a temple in which this can take place, so Jeshua will build such a structure. This temple will only be a model for one yet to come, one whose cornerstone is the Lord Himself. That cornerstone contains the glorious promise of the regeneration of the nation, a mighty event of salvation that will be consummated in a single day.

Take It Home

The book of Zechariah is not the simplest portion of scripture to understand and apply. How do you feel about having to work a bit harder to comprehend what is going on? Do you enjoy the challenge of deeper thought and extra study, or do you prefer more clear-cut portions of the Bible? Based on what you've seen in Zechariah so far, how would you describe it to a friend?

ZECHARIAH 4:1–6:15

ZECHARIAH'S NIGHT VISIONS, PART II

Setting Up the Section

This section continues to present the visions of Zechariah. This opening series of visions helps provide a basis for understanding the prophet's writings that follow them.

4:1–14

VISION FIVE: A GOLD LAMPSTAND AND TWO OLIVE TREES

Zechariah's fifth vision forms a matching pair with his fourth, both in juxtaposition and subject matter. Both deal with cultic persons or objects (the high priest and the menorah, respectively), both mention historical persons who were Zechariah's contemporaries (Jeshua and Zerubbabel), both refer to temple building, and both reach their climax on a strong messianic note.

The prophet sees in this vision a golden lampstand (menorah) flanked by two olive trees, the whole of which symbolizes the Spirit of the Lord. The messenger who speaks to Zechariah (4:1), a principal figure in the previous visions (except for the fourth), returns now and awakens the prophet. Since Zechariah continues in a visionary state, he is not waking from sleep, but his sensibilities have been so heightened as to be comparable to a man waking from a slumber.

Zechariah immediately recognizes the golden lampstand, as any priest would. The menorah was traditionally located on the south side of the Holy Place in the temple. Its purpose was to illuminate the interior of the Holy Place (Exodus 25:37), and it also represented the illumination of the presence of the Lord Himself.

However, the lampstand of Zechariah's vision is different from the menorah described in Exodus (4:2–3). First, it appears to have a general vessel for storing the oil located somewhere above its center. The oil for this lampstand is not poured into the lamps by the Levites but comes from the reservoir, a second difference. And finally, its connection to the olive trees is a third difference. The trees directly yield their oil without the need for plucking and crushing olives, and the oil appears to flow from the olive trees to the reservoir and then into the cups with no human hand or effort whatsoever.

Critical Observation

The major source of lamp oil in ancient Palestine was the olive, so it is not surprising that two olive trees appear in Zechariah's vision to provide that fuel. It is important to note that the trees are not to the left and the right of the menorah, but they flank the reservoir. The oil could not go straight to the cups but had to be mediated through the upper container that received it directly from the trees.

Baffled by what he has seen, the prophet proceeds to ask several questions of the interpreting messenger (4:4–6, 11–14). This time the interpretation of the vision is divided by the oracular response section (4:7–10). Zechariah first inquires as to the menorah and then, following the oracle, asks about the two olive trees (4:11). The question from the interpreting messenger (4:5) is not to infer that Zechariah is ignorant, but instead it confirms that the prophet cannot possibly understand what he is seeing without supernatural insight.

Everything Zechariah has seen so far, the messenger explains, is the Word of the Lord to Zerubbabel (4:6). This is the first time that Zerubbabel is mentioned in Zechariah's book, and he is named only three more times, all in the oracle section that immediately follows. In fact, it seems that the reason this vision has its interpretation divided by the oracle is to maintain the emphasis on Zerubbabel.

Critical Observation

Old Testament theology is not clear concerning the person of the Holy Spirit, the third person of the Godhead who is so central to New Testament revelation. Yet we read of the Spirit of God moving over the primordial waters during creation (Genesis 1:2), the tabernacle workers being filled with God's Spirit to do their creative work (Exodus 28:3; 31:3), and the Spirit's power and insight providing for the work of Israel's judges (Judges 3:10; 6:34; 11:29; 13:25; 14:6, 19; 15:14, 19) and prophets (2 Kings 2:15–16; Ezekiel 2:2; 3:12, 14; 8:3; 11:1, 5). Particularly relevant is the reference to the Spirit of the Lord in the commissioning oracle of Isaiah 11:1–5, one recognized by all scholars as messianic and eschatological, or pertaining to end times. The language in that passage is reflected in Zechariah 3–6. The branch in Zechariah 3:8 provides the same messianic allusion as the sprout from the root of Jesse in Isaiah 11:1.

The Spirit of the Lord will empower Zerubbabel, the branch (6:12), to accomplish mighty works, including the completion of the temple (4:7–8), the assumption of rulership (Haggai 2:23; Zechariah 6:13), and the reduction of iniquity and sinful forces (Haggai 2:21–22; Zechariah 3:9).

Zechariah has faithfully described what he has seen, yet he cannot understand its significance (4:11–12). For a second time, the interpreting messenger underlines the prophet's inability to comprehend by asking him if indeed he fails to discern these aspects of the vision (4:13). At this point, the messenger reaches the climax of the dialogue by declaring that the olive trees are the two anointed ones who stand by the Lord of the earth (4:14). It is important to connect these two anointed ones with the trees that symbolize them. They are not just anointed, but they are anointed with the oil of these trees.

Officials who were anointed in Old Testament Israel were the high priest, the king, and, on occasion, prophets. In Zechariah's own time and perspective, the two anointed ones would likely refer to Jeshua and Zerubbabel. Both are direct descendants of the heads of their lines, Aaron and David. Both have already been singled out for their involvement in the restoration of the postexilic community (Haggai 1:1, 12, 14; Zechariah 3; 4:6). And both have been given evidence of having been chosen by God (Haggai 2:23; Zechariah 3:2).

The significance of Zerubbabel is confirmed in the oracle portion of this vision (4:7–10). Zechariah is confident that the mountainous project of rebuilding can be completed with God's help—so much so that he addresses the mountain of obstacles (4:7). He is convinced that Zerubbabel will be able to face the mountain, level it to a plain, and completely achieve the rebuilding committed to his charge (4:9).

As if his message to Zerubbabel is not clear enough so far, Zechariah is most explicit as to what overcoming mountains and raising capstones are all about. He calls to mind that Zerubbabel has already, nearly twenty years earlier, made preparation for the temple foundation. Now the hands that had begun the work will complete it, a promise repeated in 6:12–13 and fulfilled four years later, in 515 BC (Ezra 6:15).

This fifth vision of Zechariah's is seemingly tied to earlier visions. The seven eyes of the Lord that "range throughout the earth" (4:10 NIV) seem connected to the seven eyes on the engraved stone in vision four (3:9). And the reference to running "to and fro" through all the earth conveys a similar image as Zechariah's first vision, where the four horses walk throughout the earth (1:8–11).

5:1–4

VISION SIX: THE FLYING SCROLL

Zechariah's sixth vision has several things in common with his third one. Both have a national focus and highlight the centrality of Judah in the restoration program. In contrast to other visions, a solitary individual is the recipient of these two. Both have an emphasis on length and breadth measurements, be it the city of Jerusalem (2:2) or an unusual scroll (5:1–2). And they both feature movement: The man of vision three is on the move to accomplish his task, and the scroll in this vision is flying.

Critical Observation

Scrolls from this era were typically made of leather or parchment, consisting of single sheets sewn together and rolled around wooden rollers at either end. Writing would ordinarily be on the inside, with only the description of its contents or other brief notations written outside the roll. Usually the length of a scroll would be many times its width, the width being the measurement of a single sheet from top to bottom (seldom exceeding eight to twelve inches). The length of a scroll would rarely be more than twenty-five to thirty feet.

The measurements of the scroll are so different from the norm that one must realize immediately that the dimensions are really not of the scroll itself but of something described within the scroll. Thus the thirty feet by fifteen feet (5:2) either defines an actual area or refers to something or some place whose length is twice its width. Among biblical objects or places that fit such criteria are the Holy Place in the tabernacle (Exodus 26:31–35), the porch of Solomon's temple (1 Kings 6:3), and the great bronze altar of the temple (2 Chronicles 4:2). All three of these options have to do with the sanctuary, the place where the Lord meets with His people.

The connection of the scroll with the dwelling place of the Lord leads to the conclusion that the scroll contains the covenant document that binds God and the nation together. The interpretation of the vision (5:3–4) is filled with covenant terminology and motifs that make it certain that the scroll either is the Jewish Torah or contains covenant texts of the Torah. The unidentified speaker immediately equates the scroll with the *curse*—a technical term referring to the sanctions of covenant documents.

The flying scroll of Zechariah mentions only two of the covenant stipulations (5:3), although those two represent the entire law. One has to do with interpersonal, human relations, and the other deals with the individual's responsibility before God. Someone who steals violates the eighth commandment (Exodus 20:15), a breach, therefore, of the entire second half of the law. He who swears falsely in the name of the Lord violates the third commandment (Exodus 20:7), a statute that is representative of the first part of the law. Whoever breaks either or both parts has sinned grievously, having violated the covenant that the Lord has made.

The purging (banishing) mentioned in 5:3 is explained in 5:4. The scroll, the Lord says, is something He has authored and sent out. It is a message but also a weapon by which He will judge His recalcitrant people. It is His powerful Word that accomplishes the objective for which it is sent, whether that be salvation or condemnation (Isaiah 55:11). Using a verb normally found in situations of hospitality, Zechariah states that the scroll will spend the night in the homes of the thief and of him who swears falsely in the Lord's name. It will remain there until its intended mission is accomplished. The covenant breaker will discover that his sins against God and against others will lead inexorably to utter devastation (Zechariah 5:4).

One more instructive parallel should be drawn between this vision and Zechariah's third one. In the third vision, the surveyor is about the business of building, the result of which is a city with no wall of protection other than the Lord Himself, the "wall of fire" (2:5). Here the scroll does not build but, to the contrary, destroys—leaving no wall, roof, or foundation. In the first case, the remnant people who trust confidently in the Lord will find adequate shelter in His presence among them. In the present case, the thief and blasphemer will know nothing of this protective grace but only the wrath of a holy God whose covenant mercies have been spurned (see Habakkuk 2:9–11).

5:5–11

VISION SEVEN: THE EPHAH

This is one of the most perplexing of the night visions of Zechariah, not only because of the bizarre nature of what is being presented, but also due to conundrums of grammar and syntax. An *ephah* (5:6) was a familiar unit of solid or liquid measure approximately equal to five gallons. But due to the description in the vision, several translations refer instead to the *container* for the measurement ("basket," "vessel," "measuring basket," etc.).

In this vision, as in the fifth one (4:1), the interpreting angel takes the initiative to introduce the scene (5:5). Zechariah sees "the lead cover of the basket" (5:7 CEV). In the context, this can only mean a cover for the ephah (5:8). He then sees one woman within the ephah (to be differentiated from two others mentioned later) (5:9). It is when the cover is raised that the woman therein becomes visible to the prophet.

Because these are visions, Zechariah is not seeing objects necessarily to scale. For a woman to be contained in a five-gallon vessel is, in actual life, impossible. Similarly, the dimensions of the scroll in the previous vision are disproportionate and exaggerated, but they clearly communicate a message.

At last the woman is identified—she is called *Wickedness* (5:8). The woman's danger is most apparent, for no sooner has the interpreting messenger pronounced her name than he slams the heavy cover down upon the ephah to be certain that she cannot escape (5:8). In the original Hebrew, the urgency is magnified: The messenger *threw* the woman into the ephah and *threw* the lead weight upon its top. The ephah has become not only a means of conveyance but also a cage.

Once the woman is secure, the ephah takes flight, supported by two women with stork-like wings (5:9). The fact that the bearers are also women is consistent with the feminine flavor of the entire vision. The reference to the wind in their wings is no doubt intended as a double entendre. The same word translated *wind* also means "spirit." So the same spirit that empowers Zerubbabel in temple building (4:6) is now at work transporting Wickedness to her destination.

Critical Observation

The stork was among the list of unclean birds for the Israelites, one that could not be eaten because it was an abomination (Leviticus 11:13, 19). Yet even people in ancient times recognized its affectionate care for its young and its appropriate name (in the original language, "loving, faithful, constant"). So Zechariah's paradoxical picture of an unclean bird is appropriate considering the cargo and mission of the women with stork-like wings—providing tender care of their charge as they fulfilled the mandate of the Lord.

Wanting to understand the destination of the flying ephah, Zechariah learns that the location is Shinar (Babylonia), where the stork-like women will build Wickedness a house and settle her there (5:10–11). Reference to Shinar is tantamount to Babylon. It was at Babylon, in the land of Shinar, that the rebel human race erected a great ziggurat, or tower, the purpose of which was to frustrate God's mandate to fill the earth (Genesis 11:4; see 1:28; 9:1). From that time, Babylon became synonymous with arrogant human independence.

According to various biblical writers, Babylon—whether past, present, or future—is the paradigm of wickedness and of hostility to the gracious purposes of God. From Zechariah's perspective, Babylon's role must have been exclusively future. By 520 BC, Babylon had been swallowed up by the irrepressible Persian Empire.

Transporting Wickedness to Shinar/Babylon is returning her to where she belongs. She had come from Babylon and had dogged the steps of God's people for centuries, leading at last to their destruction and captivity. But in the day of restoration, she will submit meekly to the Lord of all the earth and settle into the house built especially for her until the day of her final disposition, something Zechariah does not explicitly address.

6:1–8

VISION EIGHT: THE CHARIOTS

Of all Zechariah's visions that appear to complement one another, the first and the last are most similar, effectively serving as bookends that envelop the whole series. Each concerns four principle objects (horses/horsemen in the first, chariots in this one). The objects in both are sent to do the bidding of the Lord. The interpreting messenger is key in both to disclose the vision and explain its meaning. A valley/ravine is present in both (presumed in the final vision, which is set between two mountains). And both visions share a cosmic, universalistic interest.

Various forms of the verb meaning "come forth," or "go forth" (6:1), appear fifteen times in seventy-seven verses, and with increasing frequency. Its first usage is in the third vision, again in the fifth, twice in the sixth, four times in the seventh, and seven times in this final vision. The pattern suggests an intensely heightened sense of activity. This flurry of action throughout the visions, occasioned by the Lord's work of renewal and redemption, comes to a peaceful end at last when His sovereignty is established.

This time what Zechariah sees going forth are four chariots that emerge from between two mountains (6:1–3). In the Old Testament, a chariot was not just a mode of transportation; its primary use was as a war machine. The four chariots in the vision reflect the worldwide extent of their travels. They are sent forth to reclaim all the earth for the Lord, a result that follows the splitting of the mountain in the Day of the Lord (6:1; 14:10). Zechariah witnesses the arrival of the four chariots between the two mountains, having come there from heaven. Once they are sent forth, there will be peace in Jerusalem (14:11) and throughout the whole earth (6:7–8).

Demystifying Zechariah

The chariots are to go throughout the earth, though it doesn't appear that they are dispatched north, south, east, and west. Due to the geography of Palestine, one must go north even to go to the northwest or northeast. Assyria, Babylon, and even Persia were all considered "north" of Palestine, even though they don't appear quite that way on a map.

There can be little doubt that Zechariah's vision pertains to the nations and circumstances of his own times, but it cannot be limited to that era because of the presence of its eschatological and apocalyptic characters. The picture here is one of final and universal dominion of the Lord over His creation. How that will take place is a major part of the message of the oracles of Zechariah in the chapters that follow (7–14).

6:9–15

A CONCLUDING ORACLE

Zechariah records an oracle that appears to serve as a comment on, and climax to, the night visions as a whole. It does not belong with the series that commences with chapter 7, because that collection is dated more than a year later (7:1). The central portion of Zechariah's writing so far, the content of the fourth and fifth visions, focuses on the elevation of Jeshua and Zerubbabel to positions of honor and influence. Not surprisingly, then, those same two persons are the central concern of this final, summarizing oracle.

The identities of the men listed in 6:10 are not clear. There is at least some chance that, in terms of their names, they are priests who were given their assignment here. They are to take silver and gold to fashion a crown for Jeshua the high priest. The word used for *crown* denotes a regal crown rather than the expected headdress for a priest (turban, mitre, diadem, etc.), so this particular crowning of the priest must have had regal implications.

The Word of the Lord through Zechariah is directed specifically to Jeshua (6:12), thus distinguishing him from another man called the branch (6:12). There is no doubt as to the identity of the branch. Converging lines of identification within Zechariah (4:7–10) and elsewhere (Isaiah 11:1; 53:2; Jeremiah 33:15; Haggai 2:23) make it certain that Zerubbabel is in view. As a direct offspring of the line of David, he is well-qualified to sit on the royal throne of Judah, a responsibility clearly stated in 6:13.

Demystifying Zechariah

Translations of Zechariah vary as to whether the presumed priests are instructed to fashion a *crown* (singular) or *crowns* (plural). The plural form seems to be appropriate. Jeshua wears one as priest, and Zerubbabel (the branch) wears another as king.

Priest and king come together in 6:13. The harmony between the two figures clarifies that two separate persons are in view. Jeshua and the branch (Zerubbabel) are both the center of attention. Both are crowned and enthroned, charged with administering, under the Lord, the affairs of their respective civil and religious realms. The two complement each other. The quality of office is anticipated in the fifth vision, where Zerubbabel and Jeshua appear as olive trees and anointed ones of the Lord (4:11–14).

In addition to being important leaders in their own time, Jeshua and Zerubbabel are also symbolic, anointed ones whose messianic significance is unmistakable (Haggai 2:23; Zechariah 3:2–5, 8; 4:14; 6:11–13). They point toward something far more remarkable and transcendent than anyone could have anticipated. Beginning with David is the undeniable presumption that royal and priestly rule will someday merge in one individual. This anointed one of the Lord will reign from Zion and be heir of all the nations (Psalm 2:2, 6–8). As universal ruler, he will also be a priest after the line of Melchizedek (Psalm 110:4).

Apart from Psalm 110, no Old Testament passage comes as close as this one to uniting the royal and priestly offices. With this in mind, the harmony between the two takes on a greatly enhanced meaning. Jeshua and Zerubbabel are messianic forerunners whose persons and functions prototypically portray the One to come who dies as servant, intercedes as priest, and will return as king.

Take It Home

It can be a struggle to make sense of Zechariah's visions. Part of the difficulty lies in the fact that the visions contain a number of objects that may have had a great significance for his original audience but are quite foreign to modern readers. How might this awareness influence you the next time you are discussing your faith with someone else? For example, could it be that you find yourself using words or phrases that are meaningful to you but unfamiliar to your listener, causing him or her to struggle more than necessary in attempting to comprehend?

ZECHARIAH 7:1–14:21

ZECHARIAH'S ORACLES

Setting Up the Section

A clear break exists between the content of Zechariah 7 and the material that precedes it. Based on the dates Zechariah provides (1:7; 7:1), the oracles of this section begin about twenty-two months later. Unfortunately, the biblical record is silent about the impact of Zechariah's previous visions. Apart from the tantalizingly brief historical references here, there is very little that can be known at all about that period of time. Still, Zechariah has much more relevant information to record.

7:1–8:23

ORACLES CONCERNING HYPOCRITICAL FASTING

This portion of Zechariah lies between the night visions of chapters 1–6 and the self-designated oracles of chapters 9–14. The prophet's topic is fasting, a theme elaborated in both negative and positive manners. Zechariah does not specifically designate this section as an oracle, as he does in following passages, but its formal character defines it as such.

It is evident that progress is well under way on the temple by the date of this oracle (7:3). The priesthood is active there with some degree of formality and legitimacy, although it is also clear that the temple is not completely finished (8:9).

A group of travelers arrives to inquire about a religious matter (7:2–3). For a number of years, the travelers' community had fasted and wept in the fifth month (in observance of the destruction of Solomon's temple, a disaster that had occurred almost exactly seventy years earlier). The next anniversary is just a few months away, and they are asking if it is appropriate to create holy days to observe occasions that had arisen in the post-Mosaic period.

Yet what may have appeared to be an innocent query about the propriety of fasting is instead a question fraught with hypocrisy. In fact, God's response is a sharp rebuke. Their fasting and mourning, not only on the fifth but also during the seventh month, had for seventy long years been an empty exercise designed to enhance not the Lord but rather those who engaged in it in a hypocritical manner. Their religion had become one of outward show with no inner content. God points out that just as they eat and drink for their own satisfaction, so, too, do they fast (7:6). Their religious activity is centered on themselves, not their holy and loving God.

Demystifying Zechariah

The unspecified observance of the seventh month (7:5) evidently dates back to the murder of Gedaliah, the Jewish governor appointed by Nebuchadnezzar after the fall of Jerusalem (Jeremiah 40:5). He had come from an honored family, one that enjoyed the confidence of good King Josiah. However, some anti-Babylonian survivors of Jerusalem's destruction and exile formed a conspiracy to assassinate him (Jeremiah 41:1–2). Gedaliah's death was an extremely traumatic event for the community already crushed nearly to annihilation by the loss of the temple, the ruin of the holy city, and the deportation of most of its leadership.

In 7:7, Zechariah is not asking about the authenticity and accuracy of the earlier prophetic writings but rather if his own contemporaries are willing to obey those words. The Negev was in the south of Judah and consisted largely of desert. For the Negev to be populated, times of unusually suitable climatic conditions and freedom from hostility were necessary. This is even truer of the Shephelah (lowlands, or foothills) between Judah and the western plains. Zechariah's point is very apparent: If mighty and prosperous Jerusalem and Judah had been overthrown for failing to heed the warnings of earlier prophets, it is essential for his own audience to pay strict attention to those words, as their community is struggling for its survival. This is no time for hypocritical self-indulgence.

The Lord then reviews the basis for true worship, including fasting, by appealing to earlier canonical principles that provide its moral and spiritual framework (7:8–10). Such appeals to justice, mercy, compassion, and proper treatment of one another were abundant throughout the texts available to the people of that time, especially in the writings of Moses.

Past generations had responded to the word of witness from the prophets by "giving a shoulder of stubbornness" and "making their ears heavy"—the literal translations of the phrases in 7:11. The result was predictable: The Lord sent great wrath against them (7:12–14). The land had become desolate as a result, so much so that it appeared to be virtually uninhabited (Ezekiel 36:32–36). What had once been a place flowing with milk and honey had become a desert devoid of life and pleasure. Unless Zechariah's audience understands the abhorrence with which the Lord views superficial and self-serving religious observance, they can expect the same calamitous results as those experienced by their forefathers.

Critical Observation

Note the number of times Zechariah uses the name *Lord Almighty* (or *Lord of hosts*) as the name for God in his writing, and particularly throughout this section. As he describes things that appear humanly impossible, each usage of this name is an affirmation that such things can indeed come to pass by the resources of the Almighty One

But the future appears more positive for Judah. When the Lord makes His abode in Jerusalem, the city will be radically transformed (8:1–3), including a repopulation to fill the city (8:4–5). In anticipation of the skepticism that Zechariah's message will surely elicit, the Lord makes it clear that He is speaking and that nothing is too difficult for Him (8:6).

References to the east and west (8:7) indicate the rising and setting of the sun, suggesting that future immigrants to Jerusalem will come from places throughout the world, not just the nearby surrounding areas. After the Lord has verified that He will dwell in the midst of Jerusalem (8:3), He promises to bring His people back to do the same (8:8).

Therefore it is important for the people to shoulder the responsibilities requisite to the fulfillment of God's promise. Their deliverance and return will depend wholly on God's grace (8:7–8), but present and future prosperity in the land will be directly related to their obedience and hard work. So the section in 8:9–13 is bracketed with the Lord's repeated challenge to "let your hands be strong" (NIV).

The reference here is to the rebuilding that commenced during the second year of Darius and not to the initial attempts at construction in 536 BC (8:10–12). Zechariah alludes to the days of social and economic distress in Judah (unemployment, no payment of wages, social unrest, etc.) before the people rearranged their priorities and began to put the Lord and His temple at the center of their community life. But apparently the preaching of the prophets had been effective (8:11), so the latest generations do not suffer the same consequences that their ancestors faced. The remaining remnant of the nation will possess the land during a peaceful, productive time (8:12).

Israel had been a curse (8:13) to other nations in the sense that the people had failed to engagingly attract those nations to the one true God. But now, the Lord says, they will be a blessing. There is no need to look any further than to the Jewish Messiah, Jesus Christ, to see what untold blessing Israel has been to the world.

The painful experience the Lord had previously brought on Judah had been a disciplinary action to produce consciousness of sin and a desire for repentance, and it had accomplished its intent. The Lord was then able to do good again to Judah, and the people could live where truth and justice were restored and valued (8:14–17).

In yet another example of the careful craftsmanship with which Zechariah arranges his material, the final portion of this oracle (chapters 7–8) comes full circle to the theme with which it began: the concern for fasting. At the beginning, only one city sent its representatives (7:2); but at the end, all the languages of the nations will be represented (8:23). And fasting in sorrow will be turned into feasting for joy (7:3; 8:19).

To begin with, there will be a mass pilgrimage of the people of the earth to seek the Lord at Jerusalem (8:20–22), to beseech His leniency and mercy when He might be inclined otherwise. It is impossible to know what prompts the desire, but the wording indicates a great urgency. Zechariah pictures movement on a universal scale—many peoples and strong nations (8:22).

Critical Observation

The idea of the nations converging at Jerusalem to worship the Lord at His temple is a major eschatological theme. Zechariah has already affirmed this explicitly in the oracle following his third vision (2:11). He will have more to say about the matter in chapter 14. No prophet excels Zechariah in his presentation of the universal pilgrimage of nations and their confession of the Lord's kingship.

At a ten-to-one ratio, other people will outnumber the Jews who return to seek the face of the Lord (8:23). The number *ten* is not to be taken literally but rather is symbolic in the Bible of totality or comprehensiveness. So urgent will be their desire, that they will hold onto the people of God (literally, "clutch at the sleeve" NLT) with no intention of letting go.

It is particularly interesting that the reason the nations will want to join themselves to the Jews is that they will have heard that God is with Israel. As the field of interest becomes much broader than Israel, a different name for God is used. *Yahweh* (the Lord Almighty), which has been used so frequently by Zechariah, is here changed to the generic *Elohim*. It suddenly becomes obvious to all the nations that their god is Israel's God. What they have been seeking through the millennia of human history has at last been found (Philippians 2:11; see Isaiah 45:23).

9:1–11:17

AN ORACLE CONCERNING THE LORD'S SOVEREIGNTY

After Zechariah's night visions (1–6) and his oracles on fasting (7–8), the final chapters (9–14) comprise a final main division. This last section consists of two parts: an oracle concerning the nations (9–11) and an oracle concerning Israel (12–14). Chapter 9 begins with his anticipation of the coming of the true King.

Demystifying Zechariah

Many scholars accept the unity of chapters 9–14, but many disagree that this section originated with Zechariah the prophet, attributing it instead to a "Zecharianic school," or a later addition by someone with no original connection to Zechariah. While true that a careful study reveals a change of mood, outlook, style, and composition compared with the first eight chapters, it is not unreasonable to presume that as Zechariah matures, he chooses a different literary form in which to express the grand and glorious ideas that permeate his thinking.

For the first time in the book (with the possible exception of 5:5–11), the prophet directs a message about or against pagan nations. But he does so to provide a backdrop to the coming of the messianic King who will take His royal throne as a result of conquest.

The Word of the Lord against Israel's enemies is described as a march through those nations that will terminate at the temple in Jerusalem (9:8). No sooner has this march of the Lord commenced than it commands the attention of all the surrounding peoples, including Israel (9:1–2). It is uncertain how Hadrach (the point of origin) is related to Damascus, but Damascus is clearly to the south. Third in line is Hamath, a territory to the west and north of Damascus, roughly the territory of modern-day Lebanon. Tyre and Sidon lay west and northwest of Damascus on the Mediterranean coast, and they may be more familiar than some of the other locations because their names are often symbolic of human pride. Zechariah notes that Tyre has amassed and hoarded great revenues of silver and gold but will soon see its power and possessions taken away (9:3–4).

Next on the list are a series of Philistine city-states: Ashkelon, Gaza, Ekron, and Ashdod (9:5–6). The once-proud Philistia will be shamed and embarrassed. The blood and abominable things (9:7) are references to their religious perversions, which no doubt include slaughtering animals considered by Israelites as unclean and eating meat that has not been properly drained of its blood. However, too little is known of the Philistines to determine precisely what practices are in mind here.

Yet Zechariah declares that Philistia will be thoroughly chastened and purified, becoming a remnant for God, like a clan in Judah (9:7–8). By Zechariah's time, the Jebusites have been totally assimilated into Judah. One day Ekron (perhaps representing all of Philistia) will have the same privilege. The Philistines (and by extension the preceding nations as well) will feel the awesome wrath of the Lord, but those who are left—a small remnant—will then be included within the covenant of God.

The march ends at Jerusalem with the Lord, triumphant in His procession, standing guard over His house (the temple). Then He surrounds it with His presence so that no hostile force can ever again oppress His people (9:8). It is a sure thing. What God sees in advance must surely come to pass.

Demystifying Zechariah

This portion of scripture is eschatological literature. Although it is grounded in the present time of the prophet (and uses well-known place names), Zechariah views the future in very stylized and conventional patterns. His point is that the Lord will manifest Himself in the last days as a vanquishing hero. One should not, therefore, look to precise historical events of which this is an account, nor should one anticipate a future scenario in which God will literally march from Hadrach to Jerusalem, establishing His dominion over all opposition.

The following passage of scripture (9:9–13) is one of the most messianically significant passages in the Bible, in both the Jewish and Christian traditions. Judaism sees in it a basis for a royal messianic expectation, while Christianity sees a prophecy of the triumphal entry of Jesus Christ into Jerusalem on the Sunday before His crucifixion (Matthew 21:5; John 12:15). Both agree that a descendant of David is depicted here, one who, though humble, rides as a victor into his capital city of Jerusalem.

On first reading, it appears that the Christian interpretation does not square exactly with Zechariah's prophecy. Although Jesus is described as entering Jerusalem in precisely the manner envisioned by Zechariah in 9:9, He dies within days of the event, never having made any active claim to the throne of David. The New Testament account shows that the servant who will someday be exalted as King must first suffer and die on behalf of those who will make up His kingdom in the ages to come.

After seeing that Jesus' triumphal entry is a historical prototype of an eschatological event that must yet take place, that distinction can be detected in the Zechariah passage. Zechariah provides a clear difference in tone and emphasis between 9:9 and 9:10. The coming One is first described as humble or lowly (9:9), a most inappropriate way to speak of One whose triumph is complete in every respect. Only in 9:10 is that triumph translated into universal dominion. This is precisely why any devotee of Bible study must consider the backdrop of the entire revelation of God, Old Testament and New Testament alike.

Using the metaphor of imprisonment, the Lord says He will release Zion's prisoners from the waterless pit (9:11). This is a backward reference to the release and restoration of the Babylonian exiles. God had released them because of the covenant He had made with His people long ago, sealed with blood, the sign of the covenant. He had promised to do so in the great blessings sections of the covenant texts of Leviticus 26:40–45 and Deuteronomy 30:1–10.

To return "twice as much" (9:12 NIV) suggests a double portion of blessing. A specific manifestation of that blessing, one much in line with the militaristic theme of the whole oracle, is the use the Lord will make of Judah, Ephraim (Israel), and Zion (9:13). He will bend Judah as one draws a bow, using Ephraim as an arrow. Zion will be stirred up against Yawan (Greece), used as a sword in the Lord's hand. Defended by the Lord of hosts, His chosen ones will both devour and subdue their enemies. Such bold imagery suggests that the death of the Lord's foes is in some sense an offering to Him (9:14–15).

The eschatological character of the oracle is underlined again in 9:16 by the use of the classic phrase *in that day*. Thus, the references to Hadrach, Damascus, and even Greece must be viewed as having end-times significance. At the end of this section of his oracle, the prophet bursts out in an expostulation of praise (9:17).

The focus then shifts to the elect people of the King. In a second exodus, they will come from all the nations to the promised land, where they will share His dominion with Him. Things had been bleak, indeed, as the whole history of Israel and Judah can attest, but there is now hope in light of the restoration from exile and particularly in light of God's gracious promises concerning the age to come.

All the Lord's people need to do is ask for rain, the showers of His blessing (10:1), and it is certain to come. God previously withheld the autumn and spring ("latter") rains, but Judah had adamantly remained in rebellion against Him. The result was the exile, a time of drought and despair, "a waterless dungeon" (9:11 NLT). But it is the Lord who makes thunderstorms, so Zechariah offers hope that the latter rain of prosperity will indeed arrive.

Zechariah is still looking to the future, because in his own day, Judah had suffered a devastating crisis of leadership in both her spiritual and political life. Throughout their history, Israel and Judah had turned to illicit religious channels such as teraphim, augurers, and dreamers (10:2), all of whom delivered nothing but falsehood and emptiness.

Demystifying Zechariah

Teraphim were small household images thought to represent supernatural powers and to be a means of eliciting information from the spirit world (Genesis 31:19, 34–35; 1 Samuel 19:13, 16; Hosea 3:4). Many times, *teraphim* is translated simply as "idols." *Augurers* may also be called "diviners"—people who sought supernatural disclosure by examining animal livers, shaking (casting lots with) arrows, or other methods (Ezekiel 21:21).

Zechariah condemns all forms of divination. The result of such an abysmal search for guidance had been the aimless wandering of the people like sheep (10:2–3). The allusion to sheep afforded the prophet a shift from consideration of *spiritual* leadership to that of the kings in the *political* realm. Kings of the time were commonly described as shepherds, and the Old Testament record is replete with references to the kings of Israel, beginning with Saul (1 Samuel 28:3–7), who seek after illicit channels of revelation and end up leading the people to ruin and dispersion. Because of this history of wicked leadership, the Lord is angry (Zechariah 10:3).

Yet in the middle of 10:3, the focus shifts from past and present to future, and from a negative assessment of Judah's leadership to a positive one. Judah is the Lord's flock, and He will care for it. Then, far from being the meek and easily bullied sheep of the past, they will become a charger on which the Lord can ride to battle.

God foresees Judah as the source of four elements: the cornerstone, the peg, the bow, and the ruler (10:4). These should be interpreted in the context of the warfare that prevails here rather than in terms of construction, architecture, or anything else.

Cornerstone (or *corner tower*) occurs as a metaphor for a leader such as a king or governor. It seems that Zechariah is alluding to a future human figure who will provide the very foundation for a revived kingdom structure. Paul understands this One to be Christ, the chief cornerstone (Ephesians 2:20).

Peg can refer to a tent peg. More likely in this instance, it can also indicate a peg in the wall from which items are hung. A person who bears the weight of responsibility might be said to be a peg (Isaiah 22:20–24). Zechariah is writing of someone to serve as a stout hook on which all of Judah's hopes for the future can be suspended.

Battle bow as a personal epithet is otherwise unknown in the Bible. But a helpful reference is that of 9:13, where the Lord says He will bend Judah as a warrior bends a bow. Since Judah is the *source* (10:3–5), the actual bow must be someone who comes out of Judah—an idea that is consistent with Old Testament messianic theology.

As for the *ruler* to come from Judah, it is somewhat surprising that Zechariah doesn't use the expected word that means king or prince. Instead he uses a term usually reserved for oppressive, tyrannical rule. From the perspective of God's foes, His total and violent domination will cast Him as someone to whom they must submit against their will. This impression gains support in 10:5, where the aforementioned rulers (and perhaps the cornerstone, peg, and battle bow as well) will be like warriors treading down in the mud of the streets. They will prevail over their foes because the Lord will be with them (10:5).

Ephraim (Israel) had previously appeared in a metaphor as an arrow projected by the Lord from the bow of Judah (9:13), and the result had been a lavish celebration of victory. Here again, Ephraim's heart will rejoice as with wine, as will that of Israel's offspring, celebrating God's glorious triumph over all opposition (10:6–7).

Zechariah shares a well-established tradition when he looks at the eschatological deliverance of Israel in terms of exodus (see Isaiah 43:1–7; Haggai 2:4–5). In this case, the process of regathering will begin when the Lord signals (sometimes translated *whistles*) for His people to return (Zechariah 10:8). Once they gather, they will multiply as they did in the days of Moses, and the pitiful postexilic remnant will once more become the mighty and innumerable host of God (2:4; 8:4–5).

The people are compared to a bag of seed sowed among the nations. Alive once more, they will return to the Lord and to the land (10:9). The reference to Egypt and Assyria (10:10) represents the universal distribution of the exiles of all ages. Gilead and Lebanon were both nearby, but they are never designated as falling within the land of promise. They merely accommodate the overflow of refugees that will fill the land of Palestine.

Like the original Exodus, this returning influx of people passes safely through the "sea of distress" (10:11). *Nile* is a name for Egypt. Both Egypt and Assyria will cease to be threats to the people of God.

Demystifying Zechariah

Zechariah 11 is one of the most difficult passages in the entire book. The protagonists are not always identified, the speakers and roles are confusing, and the whole temporal orientation is uncertain. The section opens with a poem filled with symbolism.

As Zechariah continues, it soon becomes apparent that the objects he mentions under the guise of trees and animals are the same as the ones he calls shepherds. The poem in 11:1–3, then, turns out to be a lament for the destruction of the evil shepherds who, as already noted, represent kings (11:8, 17). So the cedar tree of Lebanon, the oak of Bashan, and the fir (pine) tree are symbols of powerful rulers. The fact that three trees are mentioned leads one to suspect that the three shepherds of 11:8 are relevant to the total interpretation.

In a most unusual development, God commands Zechariah to undertake a series of actions, doing so in the place of the Lord Himself (11:4–16). First he is to shepherd the flock of slaughter (11:4). The flock had been bought and sold by strangers (probably foreign kings), and the sheep were unprotected by their own shepherds. In what appears to be an incredibly harsh statement, it seems that even the Lord has withdrawn His compassion (11:6). This, of course, is precisely what had taken place in the last decades of Israel's and Judah's history leading up to their respective captivities by the Assyrians and Babylonians.

Critical Observation

The fact that the Lord completes the chastisement begun by foreign oppressors does not exonerate His people from responsibility for their evil ways. God acts out of a spirit of correction, but they act out of spiteful selfishness and depravity. The Lord, then, can condemn foreign nations for their hostility toward His people even though He may have allowed their aggression as part of a greater purpose.

Shepherding the flock may have meant that Zechariah was reliving the Lord's dealings with His people in allegory (if only in his own mind) so he could report in a fresh way what Israel's history was really all about. An indispensable instrument for the job is the shepherd's staff, so Zechariah takes two of them, one named *Pleasantness* (or *Favor*) and the other *Binders* (or *Union*) (11:7). The former name speaks of the relationship between the Lord and His people (11:10) and the latter of that between Israel and Judah (11:14).

Zechariah also eradicates the three shepherds—another clue that he is reliving the Lord's own experience in Israel's history and that his removal of the leaders is symbolic. *One month* (11:8) is best viewed as meaning a short time rather than a specific point in history when three key leaders all fell within a literal period of thirty days.

The dying, perishing, and cannibalism mentioned in 11:8–9 had been a somber part of history. When God withdrew His compassion, surrounding aggressive nations had shown little mercy to Israel and Judah. Jeremiah had predicted Judah's gruesome resorting to cannibalism (Jeremiah 19:9) and later reflected on its fulfillment (Lamentations 2:20).

To dramatize that the fall of Jerusalem and exile of Judah were tantamount to the breaking of the Lord's covenant, Zechariah takes the staff named Pleasantness and breaks it in two (11:10–11). Yet for God to break His covenant with His people is not to suggest an irreparable breach, for the Old Testament witness pervasively attests to the inviolability of that fundamental relationship. What is meant is that the benefits of the covenant—in this case, the benefit of protection from conquest and deportation—have been withheld.

Zechariah, standing in for the Lord, had been a good shepherd to the flock of Israel and Judah when no one else had. Yet when the time comes for him to be compensated for his services, he is offered thirty pieces of silver (11:12)—the pittance paid for a slave who had been gored to death (Exodus 21:32). This is actually the Lord being appraised, and only His service is considered, not His intrinsic value. Therefore, the silver is like refuse because of the insulting attitude it represents (11:13).

Critical Observation

Potters' shops were usually located near refuse pits, where the shards and other unusable or broken materials were cast (Jeremiah 18:2; 19:1–2). The place of the potter, then, was not only a place of creation and beauty but also one of rejection and ruin. It became a metaphor for a scrap heap.

Thirty pieces of silver being cast down in the house of the Lord brings to mind the incident with Judas recorded in Matthew 27:3–5. Just as the Lord is priced at only thirty silver shekels as far as His service to Israel is concerned, so Jesus is later viewed by Judas and his generation as having no more value than a slave. In this sense, the rejection of the Lord in Zechariah 11:13 is a prophecy fulfilled in Matthew 27:9.

Having accomplished this part of his commission, Zechariah takes the second staff (Binders) and cuts it in two (11:14), signifying the unbinding of the brotherhood of Israel and Judah. Indeed, Israel had ceased to exist as a separate entity at the Babylonian deportation and was not reestablished as a nation until the twentieth century.

Once again the Lord commands Zechariah to dramatize his message by taking up the implements of an unwise shepherd (11:15). Although Zechariah was previously reliving the *history* of his people, at this point his orientation is exclusively *future* in both historical and eschatological terms. It is fruitless to try to identify the foolish shepherd. It is best, perhaps, to see the figure as the whole collective leadership of Israel from Zechariah's time forward, culminating at last in the epitome of godless despotism, the individual identified in the New Testament as the Antichrist (Matthew 24:5, 24; 2 Thessalonians 2:3–4; 1 John 2:18, 22).

Fundamental to the work of a shepherd should be his concern for any sheep that might have separated from the flock and gone their own way (Isaiah 53:6; Matthew 18:12–14). Yet the foolish shepherd will not seek the scattered ones nor heal the broken ones. He will even stop nourishing the healthy sheep. So thorough and cruel will be his disposition of these defenseless ones that he will rip their very hoofs from them (Zechariah 11:15–16).

The Lord is not oblivious to the shepherd who so abuses and exploits his people, however. The woe-judgment that comes upon him will be a sword that wounds his arm and his right eye (11:17). Without the arm to carry the sheep and the eye with which to search and find, the shepherd truly is worthless—not only in a moral sense but in a practical, functional sense as well. Why the shepherd is not killed is unclear, but he is so severely incapacitated that he can no longer function.

Although this particular oracle ends on a pessimistic note, Zechariah's message as a whole has not ended. In the following, final oracle, he offers glorious hope of a triumphant shepherd yet to come.

12:1–14:21

AN ORACLE CONCERNING ISRAEL

The final great oracle of Zechariah, embracing all of chapters 12–14, stands in sharp contrast with what has immediately preceded in chapter 11 as it picks up the eschatological themes of chapters 9–10. This section introduces a cosmic, universalistic motif and focuses on the messianic aspect of the end-times redemption, going so far as to identify the Lord Himself as the messianic figure (12:10–14; 13:7–9). One of the clues that the oracle's thrust is eschatological is the focus on *Israel* rather than *Judah*. Israel, from Zechariah's standpoint, is a thing of the past.

The opening description of the Lord is one of Creator (12:1). His grand actions underline His creative and redemptive role. Here at the brink of a new age, it is important to realize that the same God who brought everything into existence is well able to usher in the new creation of a restored people in a renewed and universal kingdom.

The mighty Lord will use His chosen people Judah as an instrument by which He does battle with the nations and brings them under His dominion. This is what is meant in describing Jerusalem as an "intoxicating drink" (12:2 NLT). The nations will drink of Jerusalem—partake of her in hostility and conquest—but they will end up inebriated.

Jerusalem is also a stone of burden (12:3). God's people are likened to pillage being carried off by victors, but they will be heavier than the looters bargained for, so heavy and jagged that they will lacerate the shoulders of those who try to spirit them away. Drunken and scarred, the nations come in for further judgment. The Lord will confuse their horses and cavalrymen. Their horses will be blinded, but God will open His own eyes on behalf of the house of Judah (12:4).

When all this comes to pass, Judah's rulers will realize that the people of Jerusalem have been their greatest strength. The Lord of hosts used them as a discomfit to their enemies and has guaranteed that the nation will survive. The rulers will themselves become a "firepot among pieces of wood" and a "flaming torch among sheaves" (12:5–6 NASB), incinerating all the surrounding woods that threaten Israel.

In addition to Jerusalem, even tents and humble habitations throughout Judah will enjoy pride of place among God's people (12:7). In that day, the Lord will defend the residents of Jerusalem in such a powerful way that even the weakest among them is comparable to the great warrior King David. And in an even more startling hyperbole, the dynasty of David is compared to God (12:8).

Demystifying Zechariah

One must not allow any literary device such as hyperbole (great exaggeration) to determine one's understanding of the theological content in a passage such as 12:8. All that is intended is an argument to magnify the Lord's glorious redemption of His people. The weak become strong and the strong become stronger—as powerful as God Himself if the syllogism requires it to be so.

Once the Lord has accomplished His work of judgment on the nations and secured Judah and Jerusalem from them (12:9), He will begin a work of grace among the redeemed. The spirit of grace will pour out on God's people, though they little deserve it. In fact, the Lord must extend His grace to enable His people to seek it in the first place.

Grace, however, is an abstraction. It must take shape from some occasion or action that produces an awareness of the need for divine favor. Zechariah cites one such action: "They will look on [the Lord], the one they have pierced" (12:10 NIV). But the prophet's references to the Lord shift immediately from *me* to *Him*. This is an extremely difficult text within the confines of its Old Testament setting. The most satisfying resolution is to accept a change in pronoun as a grammatical, stylistic feature without a change of the subject. From the Lord's viewpoint, it is *me* that is the focus; from the standpoint of the people, it is *Him*.

Yet that raises another question, this one a theological concern. The people of the Old Testament know nothing of a mortal God, One who can be fatally wounded as in this passage. Zechariah's audience likely presumes that the Lord has been pierced in a figurative way, in the sense that they have wounded His holiness and violated His righteousness.

By New Testament times, however, Zechariah 12:10 was considered clearly messianic in both Jewish tradition and Christian theology. The verse anticipates the day when the royal house of David and all Jerusalem will receive from the Lord a spirit of grace, enabling people to seek His forgiveness for millennia of waywardness. They will look to the Lord, the One they have mortally wounded by their heartbreaking behavior, a look that produces in them a sense of great sorrow. The only sorrow comparable is that of the loss of a firstborn son in death (Genesis 22:2), and such sorrow is a sign of genuine repentance.

Critical Observation

The great weeping of Hadad-rimmon (12:11) is believed to be the expression of sorrow that took place after the violent and premature death of King Josiah, when he foolishly interposed his tiny army between the Egyptians and the Assyrians (2 Kings 23:29–30). The tragic event was commemorated from that time on (2 Chronicles 35:25). Nathan (12:12) was the third son of David. Though the kings of Judah after Solomon until the exile were all descendants of Solomon (1 Chronicles 3:10–16), a change occurred at that point, and royal descent began to be traced through Nathan.

Usually community or corporate repentance is standard, but in this case it appears that each member and entity of the community feels individually culpable and must individually give account before God (12:11–14). Judah's lamentation of repentance will result in their forgiveness, followed by purification and cleansing (13:1) described with the metaphor of an artesian well that gushes forth. The cleansing is widespread and removes sin and iniquity, idols in the land, false prophets, and the underlying spirit of impurity that has been so pervasive (13:1–2).

The charlatan prophets will attempt to downplay any involvement in false prophesying. They will deny having had visions, change their apparel, and lie about their participation. But even after removing the traditional hairy cloak of a prophet (13:4), the false prophets will be exposed by the marks on their chests—incisions made by many Canaanite religious practitioners to impress various deities by their acts of wholesale devotion (13:5–6). Their feeble lies will not be convincing.

Problems in the priesthood (13:1–2) and among the so-called prophets (13:2–6) are followed by Zechariah's attention to the monarchy (13:7–9). Again he refers to Israel's kings as *shepherds*. After a bold assertion by the Lord that the shepherd-king is an associate comes a poignant command to strike the leader so that the flock will become scattered. This action will cause not only the leaders of the community to suffer the blow of the Lord's righteous indignation but also the flock (described as insignificant or "little").

The scattering of the sheep, far from being an accidental consequence of the striking of the shepherd, is for the purpose of ridding the flock of the elements that must be purged (13:7). Afterward, only one-third remain. That remnant will pass through a refining process designed to equip them to have minds and hearts that are open and responsive to the sovereign claims of the Lord (13:8–9).

Demystifying Zechariah

Zechariah's original hearers perhaps considered these statements an eschatological repetition of their exile: The shepherd-kings of Israel will suffer the wrath of God, the flock-people will endure pestilence and sword, and the surviving community will be scattered. Then, from the dispersed population will emerge a purified remnant that knows the Lord. But clearly the New Testament evangelists, and Jesus Himself, regarded the Zechariah text as a messianic testimonial (Matthew 26:31; Mark 14:27). It may be that New Testament usage is intended as a maxim to indicate simply that when shepherds are struck down, sheep invariably scatter. After all, Jesus never says directly that He is fulfilling this prophecy; He simply affirms the aphorism of the cause and effect established by the removal of a shepherd from His flock. More likely, however, this is an instance where messianic truth, communicated by a text, may never have been so intended by the original prophet-author.

This oracle, as well as the entire prophecy of Zechariah, ends on the grand and glorious note of the sovereignty of the Lord and the establishment of His universal and eternal kingdom. Triumph comes through tribulation, so the prophet speaks of the Day of the Lord in the context of struggle and conflict (14:1–2). Restoration and dominion cannot come until all the forces of evil that seek to subvert it are put down once and for all. So the nations of the whole earth come against Jerusalem, defeat her, and divide their spoils of war in her very midst.

It is important to note that it is the Lord who gathers the nations (14:2), not only to purify His people in tribulation, but also to provide an occasion for the destruction of their enemies. Zechariah has already described a scene in which Jerusalem is attacked but suffers no loss (12:1–9). But in chapter 14, the deliverance of Jerusalem will be coincident with the triumphant coming of the Lord. The effect of His coming is not only victory for His people (14:3) but also the establishment of His earthly kingdom (14:9–11). Zechariah thus distinguishes between the kingdom of the Lord's universal, unchallenged dominion and a preliminary one in which His lordship prevails and His people are secure only as He exercises direct and forcible predominance.

Shortly after the defeat and pillaging of Jerusalem, the Lord will go forth to do battle, which will bring about cataclysmic changes in the terrain itself, as well as in the patterns of light and darkness and in the seasons (14:3–7). When all seems lost, the Lord leads His people forth and parts the Mount of Olives by the very act of treading on it (14:4), not unlike the way Moses parted the Red Sea to deliver the Israelites. The splitting of the mountain creates a new valley through which the people will flee (14:5). This is no mere earthquake, however, but a shaking of the whole universe as the Lord comes in judgment. This will occur on a day known only to God (14:7).

One result will be life-giving waters that flow from Jerusalem, half to the Dead Sea and half to the Mediterranean Sea (14:8). The meaning of the Hebrew indicates that these are not waters that give life but waters that are alive—moving, fast-flowing, and sparkling.

The Jewish Shema (Deuteronomy 6:4–5) is the very heart of Israel's covenant faith—a confession of the Lord's self-consistency as well as His uniqueness and exclusivity. Zechariah makes unmistakable reference to the Shema in 14:9. The original statement of monotheism, however, breaks out of an exclusively Jewish viewpoint and speaks of the oneness of God on a universal scale. There is no reference to *our* God because the Lord will be the one and only God of *all* the nations.

However, Jerusalem will continue to be the center from which the grace of God will radiate to all the earth. To express the continued centrality of Israel, Zechariah visualizes the leveling of the remainder of the Holy Land and the elevation of Jerusalem so that the city stands high above in a position of eminence and security (14:10).

Demystifying Zechariah

Geba was in the northernmost extent of Judah, and Rimmon was in the far south (14:10). So the whole land, from northern hill to southern height, would become as level as the Arabah—the southern extension of the Great Rift depression south of the Dead Sea, an area unexcelled for flatness.

The prophet isn't trying to provide precise delineations of the eschatological city, but he does want his generation to understand that the idealism of the future is rooted and grounded in the present, in actual history and geography. People will once more occupy Jerusalem, and the city will never again be destroyed (14:11).

All those who have persecuted and tormented God's people, however, will be inflicted with a horrible plague or pestilence of some kind that attacks both humans and animals (14:12–15). In addition to the plague's grotesque physical consequences, it will trigger a panic among the people, causing them to lash out and destroy one another. It appears that the plague and its related events best fit chronologically with the conflict described in 14:3–8, prior to the elevation of Jerusalem (14:9–11).

After the great fire that marks the beginning of the Lord's reign, the survivors among the nations acknowledge Him as King (14:9) and come regularly to offer Him homage (14:16). This is not to suggest, however, that they have undergone conversion in the religious sense (14:17–19). The word used for *worship* in verse 16 can mean only to bow down or do obeisance.

The particular occasion of pilgrimage is the Feast of Tabernacles, one of the three annual events in Israel's calendar when the Lord's able-bodied people are to appear before Him at the central sanctuary. Immediately after the celebration, the Levites will lead the assembly in a great ceremony of covenant renewal (Nehemiah 9:1–38) that culminates in a solemn commitment by the people to reaffirm their covenant allegiance to the Lord (Nehemiah 9:38; 10:29). It is evident that the Zechariah passage should also be viewed against a covenant background (Zechariah 14:17).

In the Bible, Egypt is frequently a symbol of the world at large (Isaiah 27:13; Revelation 11:8). Therefore, it is not distinguished here from the nations just mentioned but appears as a synonym for them (Zechariah 14:18–19).

In closing, Zechariah describes a number of transformations to take place "in that day" (14:20–21). The horse is considered an unclean animal, yet in the Day of the Lord, horses will wear bells bearing the inscription "HOLY TO THE LORD." Lowly pots used formerly as receptacles for ashes (Exodus 27:3) will be elevated to function as the holy bowls before the altar used for sacrifice. These examples point to the fact that "there will no longer be a Canaanite in the house of the LORD Almighty" (14:21 NIV).

The Canaanite, of course, symbolizes what is most reprehensible to God. The Canaanites are a cursed people (Genesis 9:25) and are to be annihilated by the conquest of Israel (Joshua 3:10). To think of their participation in the worship of God at all is scandalous, and to envision their doing so within the holy precincts of the temple is incomprehensible. Yet in the Day of the Lord, all are welcome because they all will be the people of God.

It is impossible to improve on Paul's assessment of the transformation that will characterize that glorious day: "There is neither Jew nor Greek, there is neither slave nor free man, there is neither male nor female; for you are all one in Christ Jesus" (Galatians 3:28 NASB).

Take It Home

Zechariah makes any number of noteworthy points in his final oracles, but perhaps one of the most relevant to today is the ease with which hypocrisy can infiltrate worship habits. Until such hypocrisy was removed, God would not respond. According to Zechariah, earlier generations had ignored the problem and suffered for it; later generations would repent and receive God's blessings. Do you think hypocrisy is a problem in today's church? Do you detect any instances where people in church settings seem more focused on themselves than on God's presence? What do you think is the best way for individuals and congregations to prevent hypocrisy from becoming a problem?

MALACHI

INTRODUCTION TO MALACHI

The book of Malachi is a summons to repentance and revival. In six disputations, the prophet summons the people to forsake their spiritual doldrums and halfhearted commitment to the Lord and return to an active faith and the practice of devotion to God.

AUTHOR

Some have wondered if Malachi's name, which means "my messenger," could be a title rather than a name. But there is no reason to believe that Malachi is written by anyone other than Malachi himself.

PURPOSE

Malachi addresses his people—the small group of exiled Jews who return from Babylonia. He confronts his people for keeping the best for themselves and leaving their leftovers for God. He calls his people back to their commitment and faith, particularly in light of the future judgment awaiting those who do not repent.

OCCASION

The concerns raised by Ezra and Nehemiah in their work of reformation are some of the same that Malachi mentions: spiritually mixed marriages, the neglect of tithing, disregard for keeping the Sabbath, the corruption of the priesthood, and social injustice. Some scholars suggest that it is likely Malachi preached before the reforms of Ezra and Nehemiah, preparing the way for them.

THEMES

Malachi uses the disputation form: Certain people raise a point, which is then contradicted by the prophet or, better, by the Lord speaking through the prophet. Malachi is not the only prophet to use this device. We find it in one form or another in Amos, Micah, and Ezekiel, as well as in Isaiah and Jeremiah. But only Malachi raises it to the organizing principle of his prophecy.

The covenant that God made with His people in the Pentateuch is fundamental to the message of Malachi. Malachi presumes this covenant is to establish a living relationship between the Lord and His people. Beginning in 1:1, Malachi uses the name *Israel* for the people of God. The covenant name has been applied to what remains of the people of God. The northern tribes, who were specifically referred to as Israel during the days of the divided kingdom, are no more, but Israel lives on in the remnant of the entire nation that returns from exile, primarily the descendants of the tribes of Judah and Benjamin.

HISTORICAL CONTEXT

A small company of Jews returns to Jerusalem from Babylon after the exile. The city is still largely in ruins from its destruction fifty years before. By Malachi's time, any enthusiasm and hopefulness has faded. The people are past believing that God is going to do anything grand on their behalf. It is now a time of spiritual discouragement, complaining, and a growing indifference to God's law of perfunctory worship.

So the situation Malachi faces is the same situation faced by Ezra when he came to Jerusalem in 458 BC, eighty years after the first return of exiles from Babylon, and by Nehemiah when he came to Jerusalem in 445 BC.

OUTLINE

ISRAEL AND THE PRIESTS 1:1–2:9

God's Call on Israel 1:1–5
The Contemptuous Priests 1:6–2:9

THE SINS OF THE PEOPLE 2:10–3:5

Rebellion 2:10–16
Self-Deceit 2:17–3:5

THE FUTILITY OF THE PEOPLE 3:6–4:6

Selfishness 3:6–12
Self-Sufficiency 3:13–4:3
Restoration Ahead 4:4–6

MALACHI 1:1–2:9

ISRAEL AND THE PRIESTS

Setting Up the Section

Malachi opens with a statement about nations rather than individuals. The Israelites, descendants of Jacob, are God's people, as opposed to the Edomites, descendants of Jacob's brother, Esau.

1:1–5

GOD'S CALL ON ISRAEL

Verse 1 identifies this writing as an oracle, one given through Malachi, a name that is Hebrew for "my messenger." The oracle is addressed to the nation of Israel. In this writing, the people who make up that nation are also referred to as *Judah* (2:11; 3:4) and *Jacob* (1:2; 2:12; 3:6).

In the first few verses, the term *hate* probably refers to a rejection. God selected Israel and rejected Edom as His chosen people.

Demystifying Malachi

Edom, though a little country, was often used as an emblem for all the enemies of Israel. At no point in Israel's history is Edom an ally, as are (at one time or another) most of the other nearby nations. Prophets such as Ezekiel and Obadiah speak against Edom (Ezekiel 25:12–14; Obadiah 1:1–7). The region is gradually overrun and by the middle/late fifth century has become a non-nation, but verse 5 indicates that in Malachi's time, the Edomites have not yet been thoroughly destroyed.

1:6–2:9

THE CONTEMPTUOUS PRIESTS

This section, containing Malachi's second disputation, concerns Israel's priests' neglect of their duties. The people are complicit in this neglect, as Malachi will say, but the priests are more responsible. This disputation, the longest in the book, takes up twenty-three of a total fifty-five verses.

Critical Observation

As a demonstration that Malachi is not calling Israel to a new set of standards but calling her back to the ancient covenant, three texts from Numbers and Deuteronomy are woven through this disputation: Numbers 6:23–27 (the Aaronic benediction); Numbers 25:12–13 (the Levitical covenant of peace); and Deuteronomy 33:8–11 (Moses' blessing of the tribe of Levi and his enumeration of the priests' responsibilities). Malachi's people would have immediately recognized the ironic comparison that is being made.

Malachi 1:6 credits God with the message. The phrase "says the LORD Almighty" (or "says the LORD of hosts") is used often in this disputation. Malachi is attacking the priests, after all. They would be almost certain to react badly to Malachi's criticism, so it is important for him to emphasize that his message is from the Lord.

According to verse 8, the priests are violating the law that requires the best and the first of all the people's property be given to God. The firstborn, the firstfruits, and the most excellent of one's property belongs to God. This is a test of faith because the best animals are, of course, the best breeding stock, and in order to give that stock away to God, one has to believe it is better to honor the Lord than to seek material prosperity.

Malachi doesn't give a detailed reason the priests consent to let the people bring less than their best. It is to the priests' benefit that the people bring in the appropriate offerings. After all, part of these offerings provides sustenance for the priests, who are forbidden to own land. Ignorance is not the problem. The law is specific and emphatic on this point. The priests and the people would have never considered making these kinds of offerings to a dignitary, yet they are skimping on worship.

The doors mentioned in verse 10 are those to the temple courtyard. The sacrifices are offered outside.

Take It Home

We tend to think that lukewarm is better than cold, and something is better than nothing. But when it comes to worship, this is not God's perspective. He holds His people to a high standard. This is a common theme in the Old Testament Prophets. God doesn't want our worship if we are giving it begrudgingly, halfheartedly, and only out of a sense of duty. He doesn't want our worship if it is not an act of true faith.

Verse 11 describes a time when the whole world will worship the Lord. Malachi is interested in the future fulfillment of the plan of salvation. In contrast, according to verses 13–14, the priests are guilty of doing their jobs in a spirit of boredom, and the people seem to prefer it that way.

The moniker "great king" is a common title in some ancient texts and refers to the king over all the other lesser kings—the emperor (1:14). The Lord is the great King who will enforce the penalties of His covenant upon those who betray its requirements.

Demystifying Malachi

The requirement of giving a male animal—while it certainly foreshadows the greater sacrifice of Christ, who is a male, and is made necessary by the representative role of the male in society—is a kindness on the Lord's part. The females are needed to give milk and bear young, but only a few males are needed for breeding. So in this sense, less is lost to the flock when males are sacrificed.

Verse 1 of chapter 2 begins the curses threatened upon the priests for their unbelief and disobedience. According to verse 2, a primary role of the priests—pronouncing blessing—will become futile. The priests will pronounce blessing, as with the Aaronic benediction (Numbers 6:23–27), but the people will get curses instead.

The first curse is particularly heavy for the priest because a man became a priest by family line only (2:2). If descendants are cut off, the family will lose the right to the sacred office. The second curse is one of degradation and dishonor. Priests had to be cleaner than anyone else, and here God Himself is throwing dung in their faces (2:3).

The text of the covenant in verse 4 is found in Numbers 25:11–13, and its language is spread throughout Malachi 2:1–8, as is the blessing of Levi found in Deuteronomy 33:8–11 (Malachi 2:7). No Israelite would have missed the connection.

We read what kind of preacher and teacher a minister ought to be in 2:6–7—Malachi says that a faithful minister turns many from sin and communicates the knowledge and the instruction of the Lord. He does this, Malachi says, because he himself walks with the Lord. Contrarily, verses 8–9 reveal the hearts of the priests in this day. They teach without power, even tailor their messages to certain people's advantage and to others' disadvantage. These verses make it clear that the people have stumbled and the law is up for sale. Israel is sinking into spiritual doldrums and, from there, might eventually sink into spiritual death.

MALACHI 2:10–3:5

THE SINS OF THE PEOPLE

Rebellion	2:10–16
Self-Deceit	2:17–3:5

Setting Up the Section

Malachi's third disputation returns to the sins of the people, specifically the marital unfaithfulness among the people of God. The same format is followed as in the previous disputations: The Lord asserts through His prophet that His people have violated the covenant (2:10–13). This is followed by the people's questioning reply, the Lord's response (2:14), and the implication (2:15–16).

2:10–16

REBELLION

In verse 10, Malachi reminds the people of their special relationship to God, their Father. Israel must live in obedience to God and in union with one another as brothers and sisters, at least in God's family. In this, the Israelites are breaking faith.

Verse 11 reveals the sin of Malachi's people to be spiritual intermarriage. Jews are marrying outside the faith. The fact that Judah is blamed for the sin suggests that it is a national sin, widespread and generally countenanced. The problem with these marriages is religious, not racial or ethnic. Members of other peoples are welcomed into Israelite life and society and into marriage with Israelites so long as they accept the faith of Israel.

Malachi looks to the Lord to enforce the curses of the covenant upon the violator (2:12). The people may have thought that as long as they continue to offer their sacrifices it didn't matter if they also took part in pagan rituals. But God doesn't need their offerings, and He doesn't want them unless they are symbols of faith and trust.

The tears mentioned in verse 13 probably refer to loud displays of emotion during sacrifices. Many religions of the day believed that these protestations of earnestness would influence God to act. What is scorned here is emotion intended to manipulate God.

In verse 14, the same word is used of two kinds of marital sins—improper intermarriage and improper divorce. Marriage is regarded as a covenant. It takes on features like that of God's covenant with His people; it requires fidelity on the part of the covenant partners.

The wife of one's youth probably reflects the fact that many, if not most, marriages in these days are arranged before the children grow to be adults (2:14). Notice the egalitarian language at the end of verse 14: The wife is referred to as a *partner*, not an underling.

Critical Observation

What is specifically being forbidden in verse 16 is divorce because a husband has lost interest in his wife. Old Testament law permits divorce for indecency on the part of the spouse (such as sexual infidelity), but it does not permit divorce for a lack of affection or romantic attraction.

2:17–3:5

SELF-DECEIT

The failure of the people identified in this sixth disputation is doubt of the Lord's justice. The Lord's reply is a promise of a divine messenger to cleanse His people, to restore true worship, and to enact justice. Malachi again addresses the need for the reform of the priesthood and the purification of Israel's worship.

In verse 17, the statement that those who do evil are good in the eyes of God is a statement of irony. It is not likely that anyone is actually saying or even thinking this. The point is that it doesn't seem that God is doing anything about this evil. Does it matter to Him?

The opening verse of chapter 3 answers the concern of 2:17. God will respond, and His response will be in the form of a messenger. The word translated *messenger* here is the same used in 1:1.

The ministry of the messenger described in 3:2–5 is clearly the ministry of a divine figure. He does the things that only the Lord has the power and the authority to do.

The day of the Lord's coming, mentioned in 3:2, is a concept found frequently in the Old Testament Prophets. It refers broadly to a time when the Lord will appear as a conquering judge to punish the wicked and vindicate the righteous, ushering in a new era of blessing. But here, as elsewhere in the Prophets, there is a surprising reversal. The assumption of the people is that the Day of the Lord will be a great day for them. They will be delivered from their enemies and granted prosperity. But here Malachi asks who will be able to endure this day. For those who have kept the covenant, the Day of the Lord will be welcome deliverance. For those who have broken it, it will be a time of judgment and curses.

Demystifying Malachi

A refiner's fire functions to purify metal. Malachi draws this image from the everyday life of Israel. The prophets often use this image to describe either the Lord's elimination of the impurities from His people or His purifying of them. The launderer's soap was a form of lye used to soak the dirt out of clothes. Both fire and lye are agents by which what deserves to remain is separated from what does not.

Verses 4–5 conclude this disputation with a description of renewed worship and reformed justice—right worship *and* right living. Verse 5 catalogs some of the sins that are commonplace in Malachi's time. Seven violations of the covenant law are mentioned, a sampling of the way in which the people show contempt for God.

MALACHI 3:6–4:6

THE FUTILITY OF THE PEOPLE

Setting Up the Section

This section contains Malachi's final two disputations. The first one addresses the people's failure to give ample offerings to God. The second one involves the promise of vindication for those who have put their faith in God.

3:6–12

SELFISHNESS

Verses 6–12 contain the fifth of Malachi's six disputations. As in the second disputation, we find two questions put by the people instead of just one. The subject in both disputations is broadly the same—Israel's begrudging offerings—though in the second disputation the emphasis falls on the priests' failure, and here it falls on the people's failure.

Verses 6–7 focus on God's immutability. It is God's immutability that explains why Israel, though she has violated God's covenant with her generation after generation, has not been destroyed. The Lord is a merciful God, faithful to His covenant and to the promises He made to be Israel's God.

Verse 8 addresses tithes and offerings. The tithe is the requirement to give a tenth of one's income to the Lord. The offerings are gifts above the tithe. Giving of these things is a symbol of recognition that all one has belongs to God.

Verses 9–11 reveal other failures of the people. Either they are holding back part of what they owe by law or not everyone is giving a tithe. Since the tithes are the allotment of the priests and Levites, the people's disobedience causes them hardship.

The floodgates mentioned in verse 10 are a reference to rain, the lack of which has blighted Israel's crops. But verse 11 reveals another layer of meaning. Rain is a symbol of all manner of blessing. Agricultural abundance is an image frequently employed by the prophets to describe the blessing of the new age.

Take It Home

To some, verses 10–12 sound like promises that if we live righteous lives, we will be rich. The fact is, it is plainly understood by faithful people in the Old Testament that God is not promising riches to the pious, at least not in this world. They struggle, as we do today, with the obvious fact that often we find wicked people richer than godly people.

As Christians, we worship a God who is faithful to His promises. It is our responsibility to trust and obey, no matter how we might calculate the costs and likely benefits. God often makes us trust Him before He will show us His blessing.

3:13–4:3

SELF-SUFFICIENCY

In the sixth and final disputation, the people complain that God is not vindicating them by rewarding the righteous or punishing the wicked. The Lord's reply, through Malachi, is that He will most definitely vindicate His people. That day will come, and any doubts about the importance of trusting the Lord and obeying Him will be forever put to rest.

Given that Malachi has confronted his people about their disobedience, verse 14 seems ironic. The people complain about carrying out requirements, but in light of Malachi's charges against the people, what are all the requirements they have carried out?

The mourning they mention was probably the same kind of ritual mourning mentioned in 2:13. Malachi condemns the people for a show of mourning and penitence before the Lord that is nothing but an attempt to manipulate Him.

In verse 15, the idea of challenging or testing God refers to those who openly do what God forbids. Their actions test to see if God will respond. The people here called *evildoers*, or *wicked*, are simply those who are doing other kinds of evil than the insolent and complaining Israelites are doing.

Verse 16 contains the only narrative in the book of Malachi. The people described here (obviously a distinct minority among Israel as a whole) are pious, faithful, and devout. They stir one another up to love and good deeds, and the Lord takes special notice of their spiritual conversation.

The *scroll* (or *book*) *of remembrance* mentioned in verse 16 is probably a document that contains the names of all those who ascribe to some written commitment to the Lord. Another possibility is that it is a scroll akin to "the books," in which are written the record of the lives of men and women, or even to "the book of life," in which are found the names of those whom God has saved.

Fire, mentioned in the first verse of chapter 4, is an image often used to describe the effects of the Lord's judgment. Malachi has already referred to a refiner's fire in 3:2. This is a metaphor.

The fire renders the wicked stubble (4:1). *Stubble*, used here as a term of agriculture, is what is left when everything valuable has been taken away—the leftovers after the field has been cut down with a scythe.

Verse 2 contains a complex figure of speech in the "sun of righteousness" that "will rise with healing in its wings."

There is the image of reversal of fortune in 4:3. The wicked, who generally ride in triumph over the righteous in this world, will be trampled under the feet of the righteous in the Day of the Lord. This, too, is a frequently employed image of divine judgment. The prosperity of the wicked is overtaken in a moment.

4:4–6

RESTORATION AHEAD

Verse 4 mentions the Law of Moses, which summarizes the focal point of the first three disputations. Verses 5–6 mention the Day of the Lord, which is a focus of the last three.

Demystifying Malachi

Verse 5 contains a promise of the coming of Elijah, the quintessential prophet. Does this mean he will return in person? In Matthew 11:7–10 and 17:10–13, we read Jesus' interpretation of this text. In both cases, Jesus mentions John the Baptist as the "Elijah" of whom Malachi speaks.

The sense of verse 6 is not merely that when the Messiah and the Day of the Lord come they will usher in a new harmony in family relationships. The mention of parents and children is a way of saying that when the Day of the Lord comes, He will turn everyone back to faithfulness to the covenant. This is a promise of great revival.

Take It Home

If God is for us, who can be against us? This is Malachi's point from the beginning. Our enemies cannot prevail, and our Edoms can do us no harm with the Lord on our side. Let us then live for Him and walk with Him in the covenant He has so graciously made with us; let us rest in His love. If we have blessings, they have come from His hand.

CONTRIBUTING EDITORS

Stan Campbell has an MA from Wheaton College and has been a freelance writer for over 25 years, overlapping with ten years in Christian publishing and 18 years on staff as a church youth director. Among his almost three dozen books are *The Complete Idiot's Guide to the Bible* and *Bible to Go: Genesis to Revelation in One Hour.*

Dr. Ralph Davis is the Minister-in-Residence at First Christian Presbyterian Church in Columbia, South Carolina. He is well known for his excellent Old Testament commentaries, and his book *The Word Became Fresh: How to Preach from Old Testament Narrative Texts.* He is formerly the professor of Old Testament at Reformed Theological Seminary in Jackson, Mississippi.

Robert L. Deffinbaugh, Th.M., graduated from Dallas Theological Seminary with his Th.M. in 1971. Bob served for over 35 years as a teaching elder at Community Bible Chapel in Richardson, Texas. Since his retirement from full-time preaching, Bob continues serving as an elder and works for Bible.org as a ministry facilitator. Many of Bob's sermons are posted on Bible.org. He also serves on the staff of Biblicaleldership.com.

Pastor Joe Guglielmo is the Senior Pastor at Calvary Chapel of Manitowoc, in Manitowoc, Wisconsin. His passion is to teach God's Word and to equip the saints to grow in their relationship with the Lord, through a verse-by-verse study of God's Word. Over the past nineteen years he has completed a verse-by-verse study through the Bible and is starting his second time through. Pastor Joe has been married to his wife Julie for thirty-five years and they have two sons, Joe and Tony and their wives, Ashely and Kara. Tony and Kara have two sons, Liam and Kaine. Joe and Ashely have two children, Talan and Aspen. You can check out Pastor Joe's Bible studies, the written notes and audio files for free at www.ccmanitowoc.org as well as listen to their radio station with sound Biblical teaching, The Sustaining Word, at 96.3 FM and live stream from their web page.

David Guzik is the director of Calvary Chapel Bible College Germany, near Siegen, Germany. David took this position in January of 2003, after serving for 14 years as the founding and Senior Pastor of Calvary Chapel of Simi Valley. He has been in pastoral ministry since 1982.

Pastor John Hanneman is a preaching pastor at Peninsula Bible Church Cupertino. He was a software engineer for 10 years and has now been in the ministry for over 30 years, working with young singles for most of that time. He is passionate about discipling men and leading people in contemplative practices. John and his wife, Liz, have three children and five grandchildren.

David Hatcher has been in the ministry for over 25 years and has been the pastor of Trinity Church in Kirkland, WA, for the last 15 years. David and his wife, Kim, have six faithful children and one new grandson. David completed his pastoral studies at Greyfriars' Hall in Moscow, Idaho.

The late **J. Hampton Keathley III, Th.M.** was a 1966 graduate of Dallas Theological Seminary and a former pastor of 28 years. Hampton wrote many articles and on occasion taught New Testament Greek at Moody Bible Institute, Northwest Extension for External Studies in Spokane, Washington. In August 2002 he succumbed to lung cancer and went home to be with the Lord.

Keith Krell, M.Div. is the senior pastor of Fourth Memorial Church in Spokane, WA, and associate professor of biblical exposition at Moody Bible Institute–Spokane. He is a graduate of Multnomah University and Multnomah Biblical Seminary (BATh; M.Div.), Talbot School of Theology (D.Min), and the University of Bristol (Ph.D). Keith has been married since 1993 to his wife, Lori, who is also a graduate of Multnomah University. They have three children.

Dr. Stephen Leston is pastor of Kishwaukee Bible Church in DeKalb, Illinois. He is passionate about training people for ministry and has served as a pastor at Grace Church of DuPage (Warrenville, Illinois) and Petersburg Bible Church (Petersburg, Alaska). He is the author of several commentaries as well as the author of *The Bible and World History: Putting Scripture in a Global Context* and *The Illustrated Guide to Bible Battles.* He is married and has four children. Stephen holds a Bachelor of Ministry (emphasis in New Testament Greek), Master of Theology and Doctor of Bible Studies Degree (emphasis in Philosophy and Apologetics).

Rev. Stephen C. Magee, MBA, M.Div., is pastor of Exeter Presbyterian Church in Exeter, New Hampshire. He has preached through every chapter of the Bible as part of daily worship at the Exeter Church. He also writes an online devotional series at www.epcblog.blogspot.com.

Pastor Doug McIntosh has served Cornerstone Bible Church of Lilburn, Georgia since its beginnings in 1971. Doug is a graduate of Dallas Theological Seminary and served for nine years as a member of the Board of Directors of Wycliffe Bible Translators USA. He has a degree from Trinity Evangelical Divinity School. Doug has also published a number of books through Moody Press and Broadman & Holman.

Jeff Miller holds a Th.M. degree from Dallas Theological Seminary and is completing his doctorate at Duke University Divinity School. Jeff is coauthor of the *Zondervan Dictionary of Bible and Theology Words* and *A New Reader's Lexicon of the Greek New Testament* (Kregel Publications). He has also written nearly fifty articles. He is best known for his ministry to men, along with his book *Hazards of Being a Man* (Baker Books). Jeff is Senior Pastor of Trinity Bible Church in Richardson, Texas where he lives with his wife, Jenny, and two daughters. Visit Jeff at www.jeffreyemiller.com.

Dr. Robert Rayburn holds a Master of Divinity degree from Covenant Theological Seminary and a doctorate in New Testament from the University of Aberdeen, Scotland. His commentary on Hebrews was published in the *Evangelical Commentary of the Bible.* He is pastor of Faith Presbyterian Church (PCA) in Tacoma, WA.

Dr. Derek W. H. Thomas is professor of practical and systematic theology at Reformed Theological Seminary. After pastoring for 17 years in Belfast, Northern Ireland, Dr. Thomas returned to the US in 1996 where, in addition to his work at the seminary, he serves as the *Minister of Teaching* at First Presbyterian Church in Jackson, Mississippi. He has been married to his wife, Rosemary, for almost 30 years. They have two adult children.

CONSULTING EDITOR

Dr. Tremper Longman is the Robert H. Gundry Professor of Biblical Studies at Westmont University. He has taught at Westmont since 1998 and taught before that for 18 years at the Westminster Theological Seminary in Philadelphia. Dr. Longman has degrees from Ohio Wesleyan University (B.A.), Westminster Theological Seminary (M.Div.), and Yale University (M.Phil.; Ph.D.). He has also been active in the area of Bible translation, in particular he serves on the central committee that produced and now monitors the New Living Translation.

WITH SPECIAL THANKS TO BIBLE.ORG:

Bible.org is a nonprofit 501(c)(3) Christian ministry headquartered in Dallas, Texas. In the last decade, Bible.org has grown to serve millions of individuals around the world and provides thousands of trustworthy resources for Bible study including the new NET BIBLE® translation.

Bible.org offers thousands of free resources for:

- Spiritual formation and discipleship
- Men's ministry
- Women's ministry
- Pastoral helps
- Small group curriculum and much more. . .

Bible.org can be accessed through www.bible.org.

NOTES

NOTES

NOTES

NOTES

NOTES

NOTES